LET'S GO

■ PAGES PACKED WITH ESSENTIAL INFORMATION

"Value-packed, unbeatable, accurate, and comprehensive."

—The Los Angeles Times

"The guides are aimed not only at young budget travelers but at the independent traveler; a sort of streetwise cookbook for traveling alone."

—The New York Times

"Unbeatable; good sight-seeing advice; up-to-date info on restaurants, hotels, and inns; a commitment to money-saving travel; and a wry style that brightens nearly every page."

—The Washington Post

■ THE BEST TRAVEL BARGAINS IN YOUR BUDGET

"All the dirt, dirt cheap."

—People

"Let's Go follows the creed that you don't have to toss your life's savings to the wind to travel—unless you want to."

—The Salt Lake Tribune

■ REAL ADVICE FOR REAL EXPERIENCES

"The writers seem to have experienced every rooster-packed bus and lunar-surfaced mattress about which they write."

—The New York Times

"[Let's Go's] devoted updaters really walk the walk (and thumb the ride, and trek the trail). Learn how to fish, haggle, find work—anywhere."

—Food & Wine

"A world-wise traveling companion—always ready with friendly advice and helpful hints, all sprinkled with a bit of wit."

—The Philadelphia Inquirer

■ A GUIDE WITH A SPIRIT AND A SOCIAL CONSCIENCE

"Lighthearted and sophisticated, informative and fun to read. [Let's Go] helps the novice traveler navigate like a knowledgeable old hand."

—Atlanta Journal-Constitution

"The serious mission at the book's core reveals itself in exhortations to respect the culture and the environment—and, if possible, to visit as a volunteer, a student, or a teacher rather than a tourist."

—San Francisco Chronicle

LET'S GO PUBLICATIONS

TRAVEL GUIDES

Australia 9th edition
Austria & Switzerland 12th edition
Brazil 1st edition
Britain 2007
California 10th edition
Central America 9th edition
Chile 2nd edition
China 5th edition
Costa Rica 3rd edition
Eastern Europe 12th edition
Ecuador 1st edition
Egypt 2nd edition
Europe 2007
France 2007
Germany 13th edition
Greece 8th edition
Hawaii 4th edition
India & Nepal 8th edition
Ireland 12th edition
Israel 4th edition
Italy 2007
Japan 1st edition
Mexico 21st edition
Middle East 4th edition
New Zealand 7th edition
Peru 1st edition
Puerto Rico 2nd edition
South Africa 5th edition
Southeast Asia 9th edition
Spain & Portugal 2007
Thailand 3rd edition
Turkey 5th edition
USA 23rd edition
Vietnam 2nd edition
Western Europe 2007

ROADTRIP GUIDE

Roadtripping USA 2nd edition

ADVENTURE GUIDES

Alaska 1st edition
Pacific Northwest 1st edition
Southwest USA 3rd edition

CITY GUIDES

Amsterdam 4th edition
Barcelona 3rd edition
Boston 4th edition
London 15th edition
New York City 16th edition
Paris 14th edition
Rome 12th edition
San Francisco 4th edition
Washington, D.C. 13th edition

POCKET CITY GUIDES

Amsterdam
Berlin
Boston
Chicago
London
New York City
Paris
San Francisco
Venice
Washington, D.C.

LET'S GO AUSTRALIA

Anne S. Day Editor
Beverly K. Chu Associate Editor
Matthew R. Conroy Associate Editor

Researcher-Writers
Andrew Brunner **Seth Greenberg**
Bryce Haac **Nazir Khan**
Elsa Ò Riain **David Paltiel**
Brandon Presser **Megan Smith**
Jeremy Todd

Mariah Evarts Map Editor
Samantha Gelfand Managing Editor

St. Martin's Press New York

HELPING LET'S GO. If you want to share your discoveries, suggestions, or corrections, please drop us a line. We read every piece of correspondence, whether a postcard, a 10-page email, or a coconut. **Address mail to:**

Let's Go: Australia
67 Mount Auburn St.
Cambridge, MA 02138
USA

Visit Let's Go at **http://www.letsgo.com,** or send email to:

feedback@letsgo.com
Subject: "Let's Go: Australia"

In addition to the invaluable travel advice our readers share with us, many are kind enough to offer their services as researchers or editors. Unfortunately, our charter enables us to employ only currently enrolled Harvard students.

Distributed outside the USA and Canada by Macmillan.

ISBN-13: 978-0-312-36086-3
ISBN-10: 0-312-36086-X
Ninth edition
10 9 8 7 6 5 4 3 2 1

Let's Go: Australia is written by Let's Go Publications, 67 Mount Auburn St., Cambridge, MA 02138, USA.

ABOUT LET'S GO

NOT YOUR PARENTS' TRAVEL GUIDE

At Let's Go, we see every trip as the chance of a lifetime. If your dream is to grab a machete and forge through the jungles of Brazil, we can take you there. If you'd rather bask in the Riviera sun at a beachside cafe, we'll set you a table. We write for readers who know that there's more to travel than sharing double deckers with tourists and who believe that travel can change both themselves and the world—whether they plan to spend six days in London or six months in Latin America. We'll show you just how far your money can go, and prove that the greatest limitation on your adventures is not your wallet, but your imagination.

BEYOND THE TOURIST EXPERIENCE

To help you gain a deeper connection with the places you travel, our fearless researchers scour the globe to give you the heads-up on both world-renowned and off-the-beaten-track attractions, sights, and destinations. They engage with the local culture, only to emerge with the freshest insights on everything from local festivals to regional cuisine. We've also opened our pages to respected writers and scholars to hear their takes on the countries and regions we cover, and asked travelers who have worked, studied, or volunteered abroad to contribute first-person accounts of their experiences. In addition, we've increased our coverage of responsible travel and expanded each guide's Beyond Tourism chapter to share more ideas about how to give back while on the road.

FORTY-SEVEN YEARS OF WISDOM

Let's Go got its start in 1960, when a group of creative and well-traveled students compiled their experience and advice into a 20-page mimeographed pamphlet, which they gave to travelers on charter flights to Europe. Four and a half decades later, we've expanded to cover six continents and all kinds of travel—while retaining our founders' adventurous attitude toward the world. Laced with witty prose and total candor, our guides are still researched and written entirely by students on shoestring budgets, experienced travelers who know that train strikes, stolen luggage, food poisoning, and marriage proposals are all part of a day's work.

THE LET'S GO COMMUNITY

More than just a travel guide company, Let's Go is a community. Our small staff comes together because of our shared passion for travel and our desire to help other travelers see the world the way it was meant to be seen. We love it when our readers become part of the Let's Go community as well—when you travel, drop us a postcard (67 Mt. Auburn St., Cambridge, MA 02138, USA), send us an e-mail (feedback@letsgo.com), or post on our forum (http://www.letsgo.com/connect/forum) to tell us about your adventures and discoveries.

For more information, visit us online: www.letsgo.com.

CONTENTS

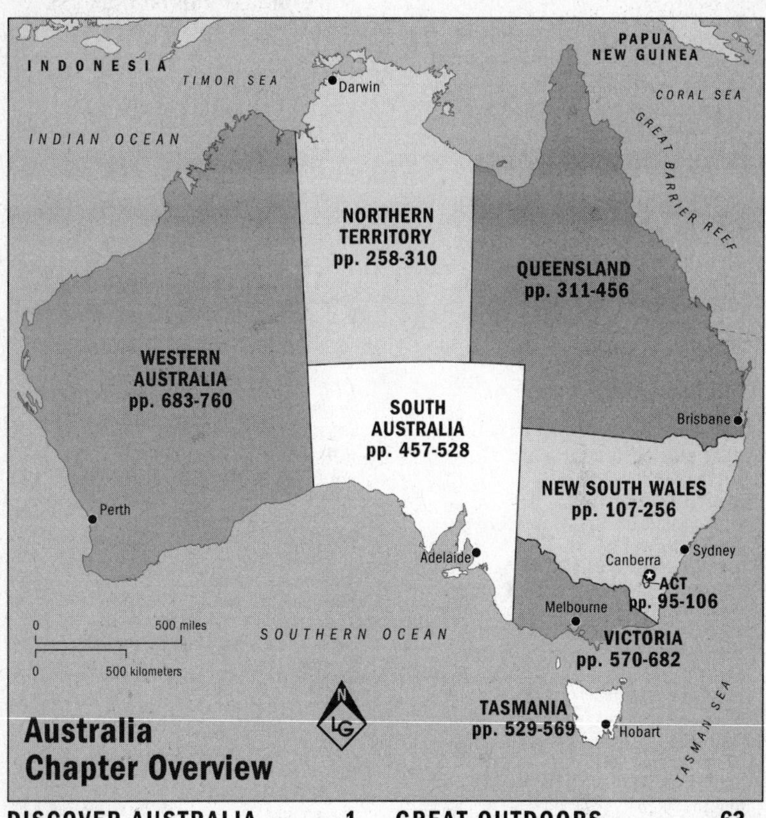

INDONESIA
TIMOR SEA
Darwin
PAPUA NEW GUINEA
CORAL SEA
INDIAN OCEAN
GREAT BARRIER REEF
NORTHERN TERRITORY pp. 258-310
QUEENSLAND pp. 311-456
WESTERN AUSTRALIA pp. 683-760
SOUTH AUSTRALIA pp. 457-528
Brisbane
NEW SOUTH WALES pp. 107-256
Perth
Adelaide
Sydney
Canberra
ACT pp. 95-106
Melbourne
0 500 miles
0 500 kilometers
SOUTHERN OCEAN
VICTORIA pp. 570-682
TASMANIA pp. 529-569
Hobart
TASMAN SEA
Australia Chapter Overview

RESEARCHER-WRITERS

Andrew Brunner *Western Australia*

As he drove the coast of Western Australia, Andy meticulously covered the great cities and sights in an often underrated region of the continent. He survived long drives and a hectic schedule, returning home with more stories than there are pages in our book. He learned to surf, swam with giant manta rays, and developed an unhealthy addiction to tea and scones, which he will be taking with him to medical school. We wish him the best of luck.

Seth Greenberg *Southern Queensland*

From skydiving to swimming with sharks, Seth's sense of adventure set the standard for intrepid researching. He slid down sand dunes on Fraser Island, chatted with fruit-pickers in Bundaberg, dodged oncoming 'roos in his 4WD, and brought his experienced traveler's eye to each new locale. His enthusiastic, adrenaline-infused coverage of the Gold Coast is be an inspiration to backpackers everywhere, and his pictures will plaster our walls for years to come.

Bryce Haac *Northern Territory and the Kimberley*

The average researcher often has trouble with the more rugged sections of the Outback, but Bryce is not the average researcher. Facing her route's challenges with inspiring enthusiasm, she braved the Gibb River Road, battled throngs of tourists at Uluru, and celebrated Northern Territory Day like a local. Freezing nights and scorching days could not deter Bryce from her work, nor from her recent mastery of the didgeridoo.

Nazir Khan *Northern Queensland*

A Seamus Heany-quoting English major disguised as a wild-bearded backpacker, this New York native tackled each challenge with steely determination. He arm-wrestled salties, kick-boxed with kangaroos, and managed a 4WD across treacherous riverbeds, beating a path to a place where no Let's Go researcher had gone before: the Tip of Cape York. He likes his steak rare, his journeys epic, and his writing lyrical; his excellent work bears testament to both his grit and grace.

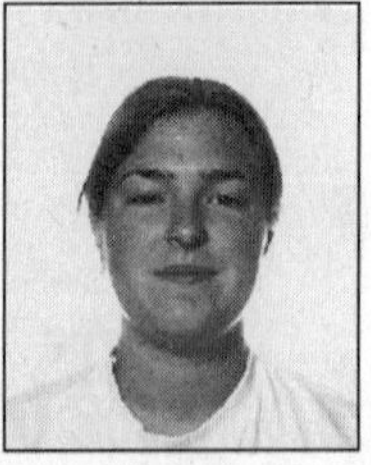

Elsa Ò Riain *Sydney and Surrounds*

From the restaurants and nightclubs of Sydney to the wineries of the Hunter Valley, Elsa saw it all in New South Wales. In her first week on the job she expanded our coverage of Sydney, fitting right in among the Aussies. She even had the opportunity to celebrate the Socceroos World Cup performance in the streets, and to do a little skiing when her work was done. Perhaps next time this nationally ranked tennis player heads to Oz, it will be for the Australian Open.

David Paltiel *ACT and New South Wales*

A former Let's Go map editor extraordinaire, Dave moved out of the office and onto the road this summer, where his fine attention to detail carried over brilliantly to thorough, quality research-writing. Unfazed by encounters with outback creatures and the occasional sand dune, Dave successfully overcame his fear of left-side driving and returned from the land of national parks and fish 'n' chips with a great summer story and a didgeridoo.

Brandon Presser *Victoria and southwestern New South Wales*

Spelunking his way through rural Victoria with the same ease with which he partied his way through Melbourne, Brandon eagerly approached Australian life and all it has to offer. Going out of his way to research places he wasn't even assigned, his fun-loving spirit permeates our pages from Cairns to Ballarat. This adventurer and Let's Go veteran is the man behind the Melbourne pub crawl, the Tim Tam Index, and nearly every inappropriate pun in the book.

Megan Smith *South Australia and the Great Ocean Road*

This Let's Go vet has traveled the world with us from Boston to Hawaii to the Nullarbor Plain of South Australia. She faced dust storms, enjoyed rowdy concerts, and celebrated life in the Barossa Valley. Through it all, her irreverent wit and unparalleled stories made her adventures as much fun to read as they were to experience. The Aussies must have really made her feel at home—she fell in love with the country, and now resides in Perth.

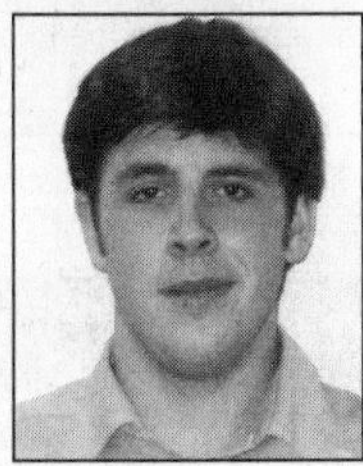

Jeremy Todd *Tasmania and southeastern Victoria*

Researching Tasmania requires one tough dude, so we sent JTodd. Now an expert in all things Down Under—and a lover of echidnas and Tasmanian Devils—Jeremy kept us entertained with hilarious anecdotes and commentary from the road. He managed to escape injury from a jellyfish and a surly proprietress, and impressed us (though not surprisingly) with excellent coverage.

CONTRIBUTING WRITERS

Tim Rowse works in the History Program, Research School of Social Sciences at the Australian National University. His publications on Australian history include studies of colonial policy in Central Australia and a biography of H.C. Coombs; his most recent book is *Indigenous Futures: Choice and Development in Aboriginal and Islander Australia.*

Julie Stephens is a graduate of Harvard University with a degree in Social Studies. A former Publishing Director for *Let's Go*, Julie took a year off from college to attend culinary school in Sydney, study Indian art in Rajasthan, and work on her thesis in London.

PRICE RANGES>>AUSTRALIA

Our researchers list establishments in order of value from best to worst; our favorites are denoted by the Let's Go thumbs-up (☒). Since the best value is not always the cheapest price, however, we have also incorporated a system of price ranges, based on a rough expectation of what you'll spend. For **accommodations,** we base our range on the cheapest price for which a single traveler can stay for one night. For **restaurants** and other dining establishments, we estimate the average amount a traveler will spend. The table tells you what you'll *typically* find in Australia in the corresponding price range; keep in mind that no system can allow for every individual establishment's quirks, and you'll typically get more for your money in larger cities. In other words: expect anything. Prices are in AUS$.

ACCOMMODATIONS	RANGE	WHAT YOU'RE *LIKELY* TO FIND
❶	under $16	Camping and dorm rooms or dorm-style rooms. Expect bunk beds and a communal bath; you may have to provide or rent towels and sheets.
❷	$16-25	Upper-end hostels or small hotels. You may have a private bathroom, or there may be a sink in your room and communal shower in the hall.
❸	$26-40	A small room with a private bath. Should have decent amenities, such as phone and TV. Breakfast may be included in the price of the room.
❹	$41-60	Similar to 3, but may have more amenities or be in a more touristed area.
❺	over $60	Large hotels or upscale chains. If it's a 5 and it doesn't have the perks you want, you've paid too much.
FOOD	**RANGE**	**WHAT YOU'RE *LIKELY* TO FIND**
❶	under $11	Mostly street-corner stands, pizza places, or fast-food joints. Rarely ever a sit-down meal.
❷	$11-15	Some sandwiches and take-out options, but also quite a few sit-down restaurants.
❸	$16-20	Entrees are more expensive, but chances are, you're paying for decor and ambience.
❹	$21-25	As in 3, the higher prices are probably related to better service, but in these restaurants, the food will tend to be a little fancier or more elaborate.
❺	over $25	If you're not getting delicious food with great service in a well-appointed space, you're paying for nothing more than hype.

ACKNOWLEDGMENTS

TEAM AUS THANKS: Sam, for her patience, devotion, and smiles; our intrepid RWs for handling it all, from killer pigeons to errant cows; our surly map editor, Mariah, for her dry wit, attention to detail, and beach days; LM for Essentials and more; K-fed and Vendetta for bringing sexy back; and the fine staff of TD's for their "support." *No goannas were harmed in the making of this guide.*

ANNIE THANKS: Matt and Bev for being simply the best; SG for her guidance and grins; AMD for introducing me to LG; K&V for being AUSITA's better half; M&D for the support, weekends away, and laundry; A, W, & R for understanding me and loving me anyway; Ry for love and patience; my blockmates for everything; the CABs—for summer fun.

MATT THANKS: Annie and Bev for their hard work and incredible devotion; Sam for her patience and great friendship; Kathleen and Victoria for great memories and many laughs; the whole office crew for making all the work worth it; Elana of the Sox for dealing with my crazy schedule; friends like CV, ML, JM, ES, TG for being there; Mom and Dad for their continued support.

BEV THANKS: Annie and Matt for being such an AUSome team; Sam "Le Hôt Pocket" for being an incredible ME and friend; KFed and V for ITA love; MnD, Leslie, and J for support and understanding; Nick for patience and love; Julie "The Best" for encouraging me to apply; Cliff's blanket; Anne, Helen, and Julie for making the apartment "home"; and everyone at the 'Go for an amazing summer.

MARIAH THANKS: Annie, Matt, and Bev for all their careful attention to the maps; the wonderful times spent with OZITA; Cliff, Tom, Kevin, Shiyang, Richard, and Chase for a summer filled with laughter and fun; and youtube.com for the talking cats and dogs.

INDONESIA
TIMOR SEA
Melville Island
Bathurst Island
Darwin
Jabiru
Katherine
INDIAN OCEAN
Wyndham
Kununurra
THE KIMBERLEY
Dunmara
Derby
Broome
Halls Creek
Fitzroy Crossing
NORTH
TERR
GREAT SANDY DESERT
Port Hedland
Karratha
PILBARA
Lake Mackay
Onslow
HAMERSLEY RANGE
Alice Springs
Ningaloo Reef
Exmouth
Tom Price
Newman
MACDONNELL
GIBSON DESERT
Coral Bay
Kata Tjuta
Uluru (Ayers Rock)
WESTERN AUSTRALIA
Carnarvon
Shark Bay
Denham
GREAT VICTORIA DESERT
SOUTH
Mt. Magnet
Kalbarri
Geraldton
Kalgoorlie-Boulder
NULLARBOR PLAIN
The Pinnacles
Ceduna
Lancelin
Norseman
Perth
Fremantle
GREAT AUSTRALIAN BIGHT
Bunbury
Esperance
Margaret River
Augusta
Pemberton
Albany
SOUTHERN OCEAN
N
LG
Australia
0
200 miles
0
200 kilometers

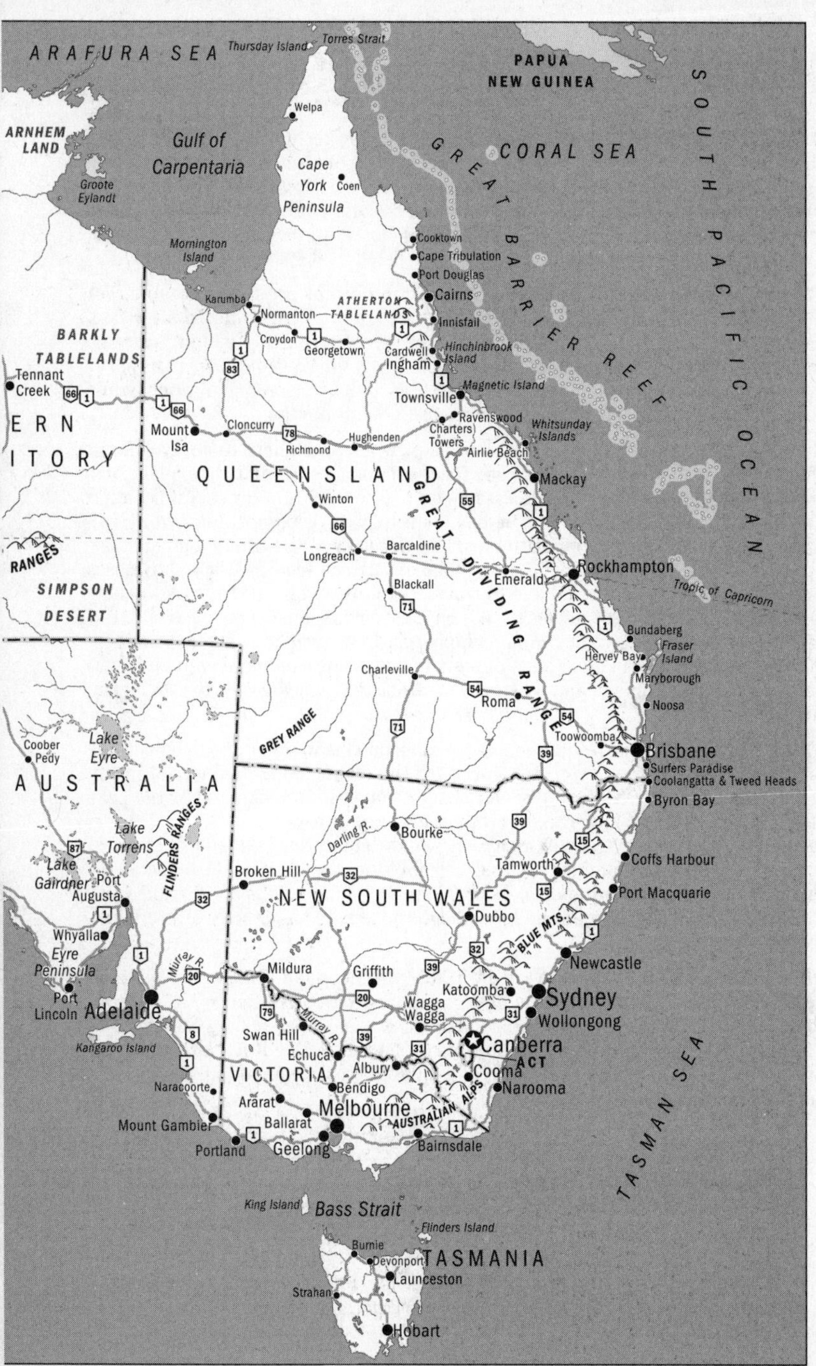
ARAFURA SEA
Thursday Island
Torres Strait
PAPUA
NEW GUINEA
SOUTH PACIFIC OCEAN
Welpa
ARNHEM LAND
Gulf of Carpentaria
Cape York Peninsula
Coen
CORAL SEA
GREAT BARRIER REEF
Groote Eylandt
Mornington Island
Cooktown
Cape Tribulation
Port Douglas
Cairns
ATHERTON TABLELANDS
Karumba
Normanton
Innisfail
Croydon
Georgetown
Cardwell
Ingham
Hinchinbrook Island
BARKLY TABLELANDS
Tennant Creek
Magnetic Island
Townsville
Ravenswood
Charters Towers
Whitsunday Islands
Airlie Beach
Mount Isa
Cloncurry
Richmond
Hughenden
ERN
ITORY
QUEENSLAND
Mackay
GREAT DIVIDING RANGE
Winton
Barcaldine
Longreach
Emerald
Rockhampton
Tropic of Capricorn
RANGES
SIMPSON DESERT
Blackall
Bundaberg
Hervey Bay
Fraser Island
Maryborough
Charleville
Roma
Noosa
GREY RANGE
Toowoomba
Brisbane
Surfers Paradise
Coolangatta & Tweed Heads
Byron Bay
Coober Pedy
Lake Eyre
AUSTRALIA
Lake Torrens
FLINDERS RANGES
Darling R.
Bourke
Coffs Harbour
Tamworth
Lake Gairdner
Port Augusta
Broken Hill
NEW SOUTH WALES
Port Macquarie
Dubbo
BLUE MTS.
Whyalla
Eyre Peninsula
Newcastle
Murray R.
Mildura
Griffith
Katoomba
Sydney
Port Lincoln
Adelaide
Wagga Wagga
Wollongong
Kangaroo Island
Swan Hill
Murray R.
Canberra
ACT
Echuca
Albury
Cooma
Narooma
TASMAN SEA
VICTORIA
Naracoorte
Bendigo
Ararat
Melbourne
AUSTRALIAN ALPS
Ballarat
Mount Gambier
Portland
Geelong
Bairnsdale
King Island
Bass Strait
Flinders Island
Burnie
Devonport
TASMANIA
Launceston
Strahan
Hobart

HOW TO USE THIS BOOK

COVERAGE LAYOUT. Australia has six states and two territories. Each chapter of this book corresponds to a state or territory, and begins with information on that region's capital city. The remaining towns and cities are organized by the "center-out" principle: they are listed in a clockwise, circular pattern, radiating outward from the capital city. The town or city located closest to the capital is listed first, and we continue from there. The chapters are listed in alphabetical order.

TRANSPORTATION INFO. Public transportation options are listed in tables for major hubs; for all other cities and towns, "(duration, price)" is noted after each destination listing. Due to the sheer distances involved in travel within Australia, most travelers find that a car is indispensible for getting around. **Essentials** (p. 9) has information on renting and buying cars, as well as insurance options, while **Great Outdoors** (p. 63) has important driving safety information.

COVERING THE BASICS. For a rough idea of when and where to go, check out the **Discover** section (p. 1). Our **Life and Times** section (p. 49) will help explain Australian history and culture, while **Essentials** (p. 9) contains practical information and tips for traveling in Australia. **Beyond Tourism** (p. 81) lists short-term work, volunteer, and study abroad opportunities. Our **Scholarly Article** offers a unique perspective on the Australian experience, while our **Beyond Tourism Article** showcases one of the many options available to travelers interested in studying or working Down Under. The **Great Outdoors** (p. 63) chapter covers important practical information to help you stay safe while camping and bushwalking. The **Appendix** (p. 761) has climate information, a list of bank holidays, measurement conversions, a basic map of government, and a **Glossary of 'Strine** to teach you how to talk like an Aussie.

PRICE DIVERSITY. Our researchers list establishments in order of value, with the best values listed first. Keep an eye out for the establishments covered in Big Splurge and Hidden Deal features. Our absolute favorites are denoted by the Let's Go thumb pick (☒). Since the best value does not always mean the best price, we've incorporated a system of price ranges in the guide, represented from least to most expensive by the numbers ❶ to ❺. Symbols are based on the lowest cost for one person, excluding any special deals. Many accommodations in Australia offer different types of lodging in one locale, and those listed as ❶ may offer higher-priced options as well.

PHONE CODES AND TELEPHONE NUMBERS. Area codes for each city or town appear opposite the name of the city or town and are denoted by the ☎ icon. Phone numbers in text are also preceded by the ☎ icon. When dialing from outside of Australia, don't dial the first digit of an area or city code if it's a zero. Phone numbers that are six digits in length, and numbers that begin with 0500 or 1800, can only be dialed within Australia.

A NOTE TO OUR READERS. The information for this book was gathered by *Let's Go* researchers from May through August of 2006. Each listing is based on one researcher's opinion, formed during his or her visit at a particular time. Those traveling at other times may have different experiences since prices, dates, hours, and conditions are always subject to change. You are urged to check the facts presented in this book beforehand to avoid inconvenience and surprises.

DISCOVER

DISCOVER AUSTRALIA

For over 40,000 years, people have been arriving awestruck on this far-flung island at the edge of the earth. Australia's diverse population testifies to the fact that, time after time, the strange and fantastic land made the long journey there worthwhile. Even for today's visitors, the continent retains a magical, dream-like quality unlike anywhere else. Because of its isolation, Australia is home to thousands of unique plant and animal species; it also contains 15 World Heritage Sites. Shimmering cosmopolitan oases are populated by denizens entirely genuine in their mantra of "no worries, mate." Where else can you enjoy world-class wine tasting, get dangerously close to a saltwater croc, learn to play the didgeridoo, snorkel in expanses of ancient coral reef, and dance the night away at the largest club in the Southern Hemisphere? What other continent offers a bustling metropolis like Sydney on the same platter as the vast Outback, the rainforests of Cape York, and the colored sands of Fraser Island? The locals have discovered this ancient continent's secret, and so will you: it's not a dream, it's Australia.

FACTS AND FIGURES

CAPITAL: Canberra

WEST-TO-EAST DIAMETER: 4000km

NUMBER OF ABORIGINAL LANGUAGES: Over 500

HUMAN POPULATION: 20.6 million

KANGAROO POPULATION: 58.6 million

AUSTRALIANS WHO FOLLOW THE JEDI FAITH: 70,509 (2001 Census)

NUMBER OF BEACHES: Over 10,000

CLAIM TO LOCOMOTIVE FAME: World's longest stretch of straight railway (478km), across the Nullarbor plain

MOST VALIANT ATTEMPT TO SAVE SHEEP: World's longest fence (5531km) keeps Queensland's dingoes in the north away from sheep in the south

NUMBER OF PLANT SPECIES: 25,000 (Europe supports only 17,000)

AMOUNT OF FOLIAGE KOALAS MUST EAT DAILY: 9kg (about 20 lb.)

ANNUAL BEER CONSUMPTION, PER AUSTRALIAN: 94.5L

JARS OF VEGEMITE CONSUMED PER YEAR: 22 million

WHEN TO GO

Since Australia is huge and climate can vary greatly between regions, the best time to visit should be determined by the things you'd like to do rather than by the calendar or season. Crowds and prices of everything from flights to hostel bunks tend to be directly proportional to the quality of the weather.

In southern Australia, the **seasons** of the temperate climate zone are reversed from those in the Northern Hemisphere. Summer lasts from December to February, autumn from March to May, winter from June to August, and spring from September to November. In general, Australian winters are mild, comparable to the southern US or southern Europe. While snow is infrequent, except in the mountains, in winter it's generally too cold to have much fun at the beach. In the south, high season falls roughly between November and April.

Northern Australia, however, is an entirely different story—many people forget that over one-third of the country is in the sweltering tropics. Seasons here are defined by wildly varying precipitation rather than temperatures. During **the Wet** (November to April), heavy downpours and violent storms plague the land, especially on the north coast. During **the Dry** (May to October), sections of Australia away from the temperate zone endure drought. Traveling during the Wet is not recommended for the faint of heart; the heavy rains wash out unsealed roads, making driving a challenge in rural areas.

Diving on the Great Barrier Reef is seasonal as well. January and February are rainy months; the water is clearest between April and October. The toxic **box jellyfish** (p. 66) is most common around the northeast coast between October and April.

Ski season in New South Wales, Victoria, and Tasmania runs from late June to September, and the famous wildflowers of Western Australia bloom from September to December. For help deciding when and where to go, read below, and see the chart of **temperature and rainfall** (p. 764) and the list of major **holidays and festivals** (p. 765).

WHAT TO DO

THE OUTBACK

Geographically contained by the continent's more developed coasts, Australia's Outback seems like the most infinite, empty place on earth. Every year, travelers and Aussies take on the *Never-Never*, looking for adventure or serious solitude. During the Dry, the **Kimberley** (p. 746) opens to those brave souls who dare to rumble along the rough but stunning **Gibb River Road** (p. 753). In the Northern Territory, **Kakadu National Park** (p. 269) is the gateway to a world of thundering waterfalls, snapping crocs, and mystical beauty. The Aboriginal homeland of **Arnhem Land** (p. 287) may be the most well known outback attraction. In Australia's Red Centre, imposing **Uluru (Ayers Rock)** (p. 307) and its cousin **Kata Tjuta** (p. 307) keep watch over the rest of the Outback. Down in South Australia, **Coober Pedy** (p. 512), the "Opal Capital of the World," brings out the tough Down Under mentality—scorching temperatures force residents to carve their homes underground. The **Nullarbor** (p. 526), as its name suggests, is a vast stretch of empty plain. For travelers who don't make it out of the east, Queensland's outback mining towns and New South Wales's **Broken Hill** (p. 251) represent the limits of Australia's most-developed regions, offering just a taste of what lies beyond.

THE OUTDOORS

Australia has a national park around every corner, preserving all types of landscapes—from rainforest to desert, mountain to coast. The **Macdonnell Ranges** (p. 301) have some of the continent's best hiking, and just next door is the spectacular **Kings Canyon** (p. 306). Up the track, the write-home-to-mum lookouts of **Nitmiluk (Katherine Gorge;** p. 284) are equaled by the spectacular waterfalls of **Litchfield** (p. 279). In Queensland, lush rainforest complements the nearby reef from the tip of **Cape York** (p. 444) all the way down to **Eungella** (p. 391). Further south, visitors flock to the watersports at **Surfers Paradise** (p. 342), and the world's best surfers catch a break off the Gold Coast's **Coolangatta and Tweed Heads** (p. 338). To see more pros in action, head to **Bells Beach** (p. 618) in Torquay, Victoria, every Easter for the Rip Curl Pro Classic. The **Blue Mountains** of New South Wales (p. 155) attract avid abseilers, and in winter, **Kosciuszko** (p. 233) becomes a haven for skiers. There are also a number of beautiful North Coast hinterland parks, such as **Mount Warning** (p. 211), which offer bushwalks for all skill levels. **Wilsons Promontory** (p. 671) is a gorgeous stretch of southern coast and part of a UNESCO Biosphere Reserve. Tasmania is Australia's hiking mecca, and the **Overland Track** (p. 550) is one of the best bushwalks in the world. South Australia's **Flinders Ranges** (p. 500) cater to the truly hardcore, while Western Australia showcases marine life, including the whales and dolphins that call **Bunbury** (p. 704) and **Monkey Mia** (p. 735) home. Travelers to the region can also pursue the off-the-beaten-track paradise of **Kangaroo Island** (p. 480) off the coast of South Australia.

DIVING

Whether you're a seasoned scuba diver or a determined beginner, you probably have "see the Great Barrier Reef" on your list of things to do in your lifetime. And for good reason—off the coast of Queensland, the 2000km reef system encompasses hundreds of islands, cays, and thousands of smaller coral reefs, all of which amount to a quintessential collection of Australian wildlife and natural beauty. Most choose to venture out from **Cairns** (p. 416), the main gateway to the reef. Farther south near **Townsville** (p. 402), the sunken *S.S. Yongala* is among the best wreck dives in the world. **Airlie Beach** (p. 393), considered the "heart of the Great Barrier Reef" by many visitors, draws backpackers ready to leave the bars for the thrill of the spectacular sights off-shore. Most of Australia's other coasts have good diving spots as well. In New South Wales, the diving in **Batemans Bay** (p. 227) and **Coffs Harbour** (p. 191) is spectacular and highly accessible. In South Australia, **Innes National Park** (p. 500) provides access to the Southern Ocean's depths. In Western Australia, giant whale sharks patrol **Ningaloo Reef** in Exmouth (p. 738), making for an exhilarating dive among the largest fish in the world. The cheapest diving certification courses can be found in Queensland at **Hervey Bay** (p. 367), **Bundaberg** (p. 377), and **Magnetic Island** (p. 407). For additional diving information, see **The Great Barrier Reef** (p. 314).

ABORIGINAL CULTURE

Aboriginal cultures traditionally believe in a strong connection between the earth and its inhabitants. During the "Dreaming," spirits are believed to have

TOP TEN LIST

TOP 10 ESCAPES FROM THE TOURIST TRAP

1. Perth's West Coast Eagles vs Freo's Dockers, WT (p. 711) Melbourne and Sydney have nothing on this Aussie Rules rivalry.

2. The unnamed road leading from Bamaga to the Cape York Tip, QLD (p. 449). Travel the rough and tumble track to the top of the world and the tip of the continent.

3. The breaks at Cooly and Tweed Heads, QLD (p. 338). Ditch Surfers Paradise and head south for renowned waves surfed by the sport's biggest names.

4. North Stradbroke Island, QLD (p. 333). Experience the pristine beaches and world-class diving on this spectacular sand island.

5. The Overland Track, TAS (p. 548). A stunning six-day bushwalk over mountains, past waterfalls and through unique ecosystems.

6. Cape Conran Coastal Park VIC (p. 681). Stand on isolated beaches, or try your hand at windsurfing or rock pooling.

7. The Torres Strait Islands (p. 444). Approximately 274 naturally and culturally rich island form the link between Australia and its Asian neighbors.

8. Abseiling and rock climbing at Grampians National Park, VIC (p. 636). Rock out at the 60m abseil over "The Ledge," or on an of the multi-pitch climbs.

9. Camel Safaris, NT (p. 306) Traverse the red center between two humps.

10. Panthers Ironman Australia Triathlon, NSW (p. 711). Test yourself against the best in this 226km race.

carved the canyons and gorges that contribute to Australia's amazing landscape, and come to life as animals and trees. In New South Wales, **Mungo National Park** (p. 256) records the earliest Aboriginal presence. Sacred regions and timeless rock art sites can be found everywhere from **Tasmania** (p. 529) to **Kakadu National Park** (p. 269) in the Northern Territory's Top End. **Tjapukai** (p. 426) near Cairns, **The Brambuk Centre** (p. 638) in Grampians National Park, and **Warradjan Aboriginal Cultural Centre** (p. 273) in Kakadu National Park attempt to present accurate representations of "Dreaming" stories and European interaction with Aborigines. Modern Aboriginal art can be found in small galleries in many larger cities, but the **National Gallery of Australia** in Canberra (p. 102) has the continent's best collection; it will definitely please any visitor with an interest in art or the history of a captivating culture.

CITY SIGHTS

Australia's cosmopolitan meccas are enticing enough to lure travelers away from the rugged beauty of the Outback. Multicultural **Sydney** (p. 110) enjoys a relaxed lifestyle while maintaining the excitement of a global center. **Melbourne** (p. 572) offers style and genteel grandeur—incredible nightlife, a thriving social cafe scene, incredible budget food options, and a sports-loving culture unmatched anywhere else in the world. Meticulously planned **Canberra** (p. 95) offers visitors insight into the heart of Australian government. Charming and historic **Hobart** (p. 531) is Tasmania's vibrant capital at the foot of Mt. Wellington. **Adelaide** (p. 458), though it moves at a slower pace, enjoys a monopoly on the tourist attractions of some of South Australia's most breathtaking coastline. **Perth** (p. 685) and **Darwin** (p. 260) have relaxed coastal stretches and hopping nightlife on the Western and Northern edges of the country.

LET'S GO PICKS

BEST VIEW: Magnificent **Sydney Harbour,** NSW (p. 142), from the top of the Harbour Bridge, or the pristine **Franklin River,** TAS (p. 552) in a white-water raft.

BEST PLACE TO SHOUT YOURSELF SILLY: An Aussie Rules Football game at the **Melborne Cricket Ground,** VIC (p. 590), or by testing the astounding acoustics of **Jenolan Caves,** NSW (p. 169).

BEST PLACE TO GET A BITE: The land of wine and honey in **Mudgee,** NSW (p. 243), or with a shark at Scuba World, in **Maroochy Shire,** QLD (p. 355).

BEST UNDERGROUND SCENE: Subterranean town **Coober Pedy,** SA (p. 512), or the artsy highlights of the **Adelaide Fringe Festival,** SA (p. 765).

BEST PLACE FOR DREAMING: Under the stars along the **Gibb River Road,** WA (p. 753), or in the Aboriginal art galleries of **Kakadu National Park,** NT (p. 269).

MOST UNDERRATED: South Coast, NSW (p. 220), **Perth,** WA (p. 685), or **Tasmania** (p. 529).

BEST PLACE TO PONDER YOUR INSIGNIFICANCE: The surreal emptiness of the **Nullarbor Plain,** SA (p. 526), or the bustling **Great Barrier Reef,** QLD (p. 314).

BEST PLACE TO GET WRECKED: At one of the top 10 wreck dives in the world, the *S.S. Yongala,* off **Townsville,** QLD (p. 402), or for free in the wine vineyards of the **Hunter Valley,** NSW (p. 169).

BEST PLACE TO ROCK OUT: The amazing formations of **Devil's Marbles,** NT (p. 294), or Sydney's annual **Telstra Country Music Festival,** NSW (p. 765).

BEST PLACE TO GET FRIED: On the sun-baked shores of Sydney's **Manly Beach,** NSW (p. 136), or enjoying the famous fish 'n' chips at Port Stephens' **John Dory's Seafoods,** NSW (p. 180).

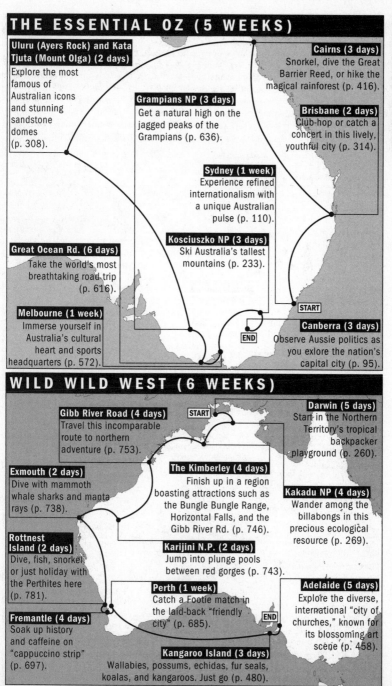

THE ESSENTIAL OZ (5 WEEKS)

Uluru (Ayers Rock) and Kata Tjuta (Mount Olga) (2 days)
Explore the most famous of Australian icons and stunning sandstone domes (p. 308).

Cairns (3 days)
Snorkel, dive the Great Barrier Reed, or hike the magical rainforest (p. 416).

Grampians NP (3 days)
Get a natural high on the jagged peaks of the Grampians (p. 636).

Brisbane (2 days)
Club-hop or catch a concert in this lively, youthful city (p. 314).

Sydney (1 week)
Experience refined internationalism with a unique Australian pulse (p. 110).

Kosciuszko NP (3 days)
Ski Australia's tallest mountains (p. 233).

Great Ocean Rd. (6 days)
Take the world's most breathtaking road trip (p. 616).

START

Melbourne (1 week)
Immerse yourself in Australia's cultural heart and sports headquarters (p. 572).

END

Canberra (3 days)
Observe Aussie politics as you exlore the nation's capital city (p. 95).

WILD WILD WEST (6 WEEKS)

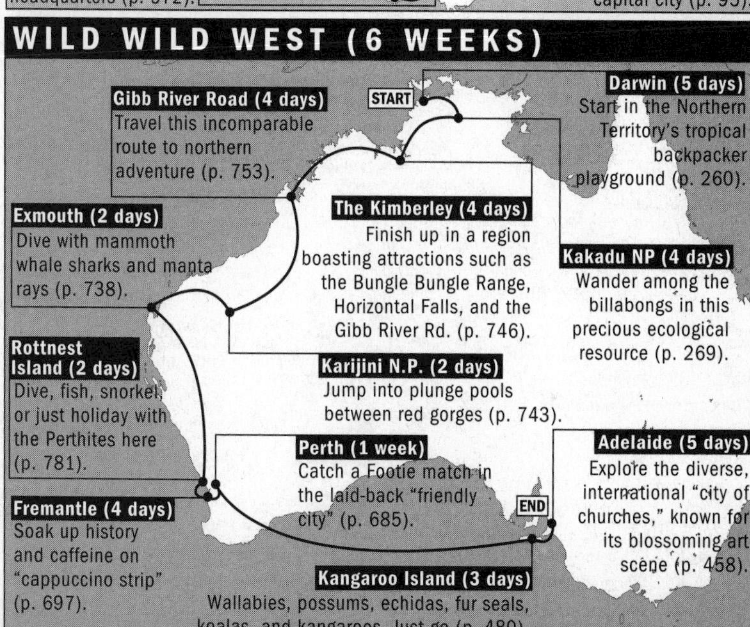
START
Darwin (5 days)
Start in the Northern Territory's tropical backpacker playground (p. 260).
Gibb River Road (4 days)
Travel this incomparable route to northern adventure (p. 753).
Exmouth (2 days)
Dive with mammoth whale sharks and manta rays (p. 738).
The Kimberley (4 days)
Finish up in a region boasting attractions such as the Bungle Bungle Range, Horizontal Falls, and the Gibb River Rd. (p. 746).
Kakadu NP (4 days)
Wander among the billabongs in this precious ecological resource (p. 269).
Rottnest Island (2 days)
Dive, fish, snorkel, or just holiday with the Perthites here (p. 781).
Karijini N.P. (2 days)
Jump into plunge pools between red gorges (p. 743).
Perth (1 week)
Catch a Footie match in the laid-back "friendly city" (p. 685).
Adelaide (5 days)
Explore the diverse, international "city of churches," known for its blossoming art scene (p. 458).
END
Fremantle (4 days)
Soak up history and caffeine on "cappuccino strip" (p. 697).
Kangaroo Island (3 days)
Wallabies, possums, echidas, fur seals, koalas, and kangaroos. Just go (p. 480).

AUSTRALIA UNABRIDGED (UP TO A LIFETIME)

Perth
Get back in touch with city life in the middle of the wild wild West (p. 685).

Kakadu
Don't miss the postcard-perfect waterfalls and landscapes (p. 269).

Cooktown
Take a tour of the town named for the famous Captain Cook (p. 441).

North Stradbroke Island
Step off the beaten path to this beachcomber's paradise, one half of an island split by fierce weather and explosives (p. 371).

Broome
Explore the gateway to the wilderness (p. 746).

The Whitsunday Islands
Island hop or just relax on a pristine stretch of sand (p. 398).

Darwin
Learn about Aboriginal culture in this tropical city named for the renowned naturalist (p. 260).

Cairns
Stop here to skydive, parasail, or scuba dive at the "gateway to the Great Barrier Reef" (p. 416).

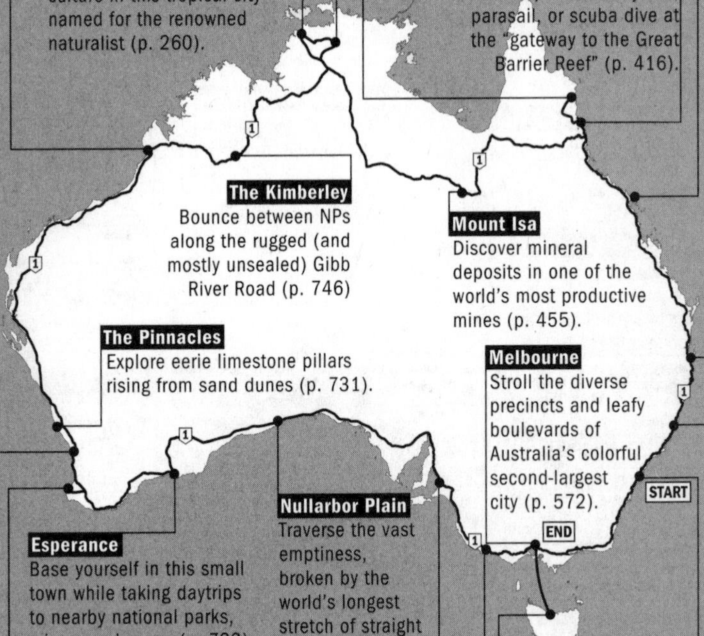

The Kimberley
Bounce between NPs along the rugged (and mostly unsealed) Gibb River Road (p. 746)

Mount Isa
Discover mineral deposits in one of the world's most productive mines (p. 455).

The Pinnacles
Explore eerie limestone pillars rising from sand dunes (p. 731).

Melbourne
Stroll the diverse precincts and leafy boulevards of Australia's colorful second-largest city (p. 572).

START

END

Nullarbor Plain
Traverse the vast emptiness, broken by the world's longest stretch of straight railway (p. 730).

Esperance
Base yourself in this small town while taking daytrips to nearby national parks, mines, and oases (p. 723).

Tasmania
Walk the world-famous Overland Track or raft the stunning Franklin River (p. 529).

Adelaide
Let the culinary capital put some meat on your well-traveled bones (p. 458).

Great Ocean Road
Pause for photo-ops along the amazing coastal thoroughfare (p. 606).

Sydney
Begin your journey by exploring the cool urbanity of Australia's most iconic city (p. 110).

Margaret River
Sample the wines and surf off this vacation mecca (p. 705).

Port Macquerie
The world's largest urban koala population calls this pristine port town home. Don't pass it by (p. 185).

EAST COAST ODYSSEY (7 WEEKS)

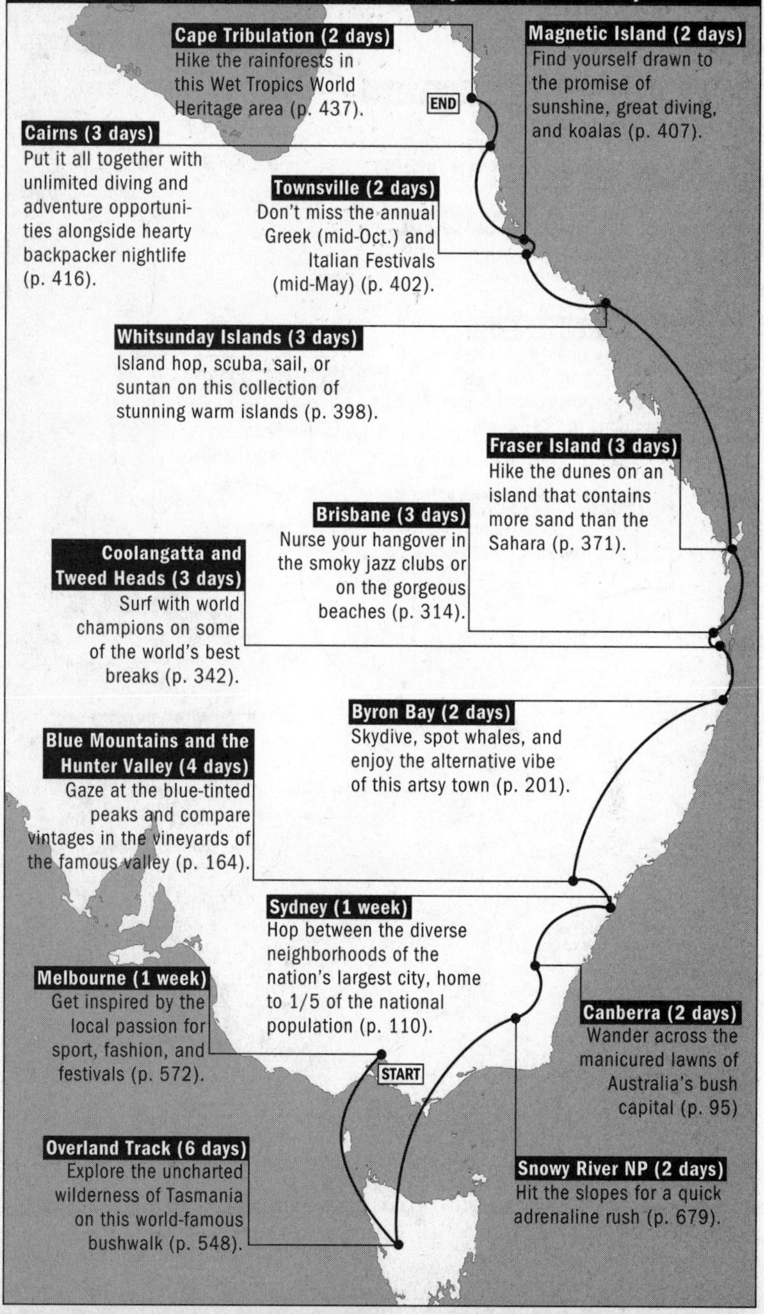

Cape Tribulation (2 days)
Hike the rainforests in this Wet Tropics World Heritage area (p. 437).

END

Magnetic Island (2 days)
Find yourself drawn to the promise of sunshine, great diving, and koalas (p. 407).

Cairns (3 days)
Put it all together with unlimited diving and adventure opportunities alongside hearty backpacker nightlife (p. 416).

Townsville (2 days)
Don't miss the annual Greek (mid-Oct.) and Italian Festivals (mid-May) (p. 402).

Whitsunday Islands (3 days)
Island hop, scuba, sail, or suntan on this collection of stunning warm islands (p. 398).

Fraser Island (3 days)
Hike the dunes on an island that contains more sand than the Sahara (p. 371).

Brisbane (3 days)
Nurse your hangover in the smoky jazz clubs or on the gorgeous beaches (p. 314).

Coolangatta and Tweed Heads (3 days)
Surf with world champions on some of the world's best breaks (p. 342).

Byron Bay (2 days)
Skydive, spot whales, and enjoy the alternative vibe of this artsy town (p. 201).

Blue Mountains and the Hunter Valley (4 days)
Gaze at the blue-tinted peaks and compare vintages in the vineyards of the famous valley (p. 164).

Sydney (1 week)
Hop between the diverse neighborhoods of the nation's largest city, home to 1/5 of the national population (p. 110).

Melbourne (1 week)
Get inspired by the local passion for sport, fashion, and festivals (p. 572).

START

Canberra (2 days)
Wander across the manicured lawns of Australia's bush capital (p. 95)

Overland Track (6 days)
Explore the uncharted wilderness of Tasmania on this world-famous bushwalk (p. 548).

Snowy River NP (2 days)
Hit the slopes for a quick adrenaline rush (p. 679).

A 3000-MILE PUB CRAWL (4-5 WEEKS)

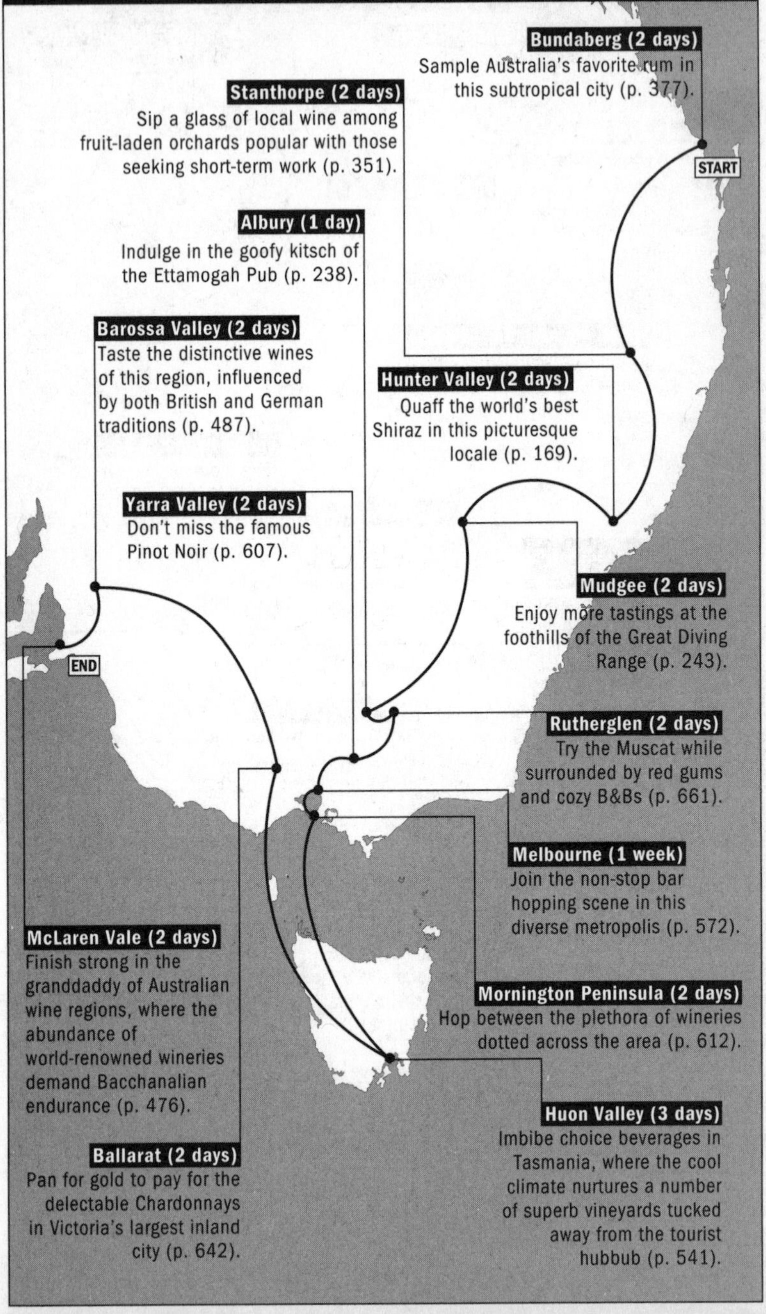

Bundaberg (2 days)
Sample Australia's favorite rum in this subtropical city (p. 377).

START

Stanthorpe (2 days)
Sip a glass of local wine among fruit-laden orchards popular with those seeking short-term work (p. 351).

Hunter Valley (2 days)
Quaff the world's best Shiraz in this picturesque locale (p. 169).

Mudgee (2 days)
Enjoy more tastings at the foothills of the Great Diving Range (p. 243).

Albury (1 day)
Indulge in the goofy kitsch of the Ettamogah Pub (p. 238).

Rutherglen (2 days)
Try the Muscat while surrounded by red gums and cozy B&Bs (p. 661).

Yarra Valley (2 days)
Don't miss the famous Pinot Noir (p. 607).

Melbourne (1 week)
Join the non-stop bar hopping scene in this diverse metropolis (p. 572).

Mornington Peninsula (2 days)
Hop between the plethora of wineries dotted across the area (p. 612).

Huon Valley (3 days)
Imbibe choice beverages in Tasmania, where the cool climate nurtures a number of superb vineyards tucked away from the tourist hubbub (p. 541).

Ballarat (2 days)
Pan for gold to pay for the delectable Chardonnays in Victoria's largest inland city (p. 642).

Barossa Valley (2 days)
Taste the distinctive wines of this region, influenced by both British and German traditions (p. 487).

McLaren Vale (2 days)
Finish strong in the granddaddy of Australian wine regions, where the abundance of world-renowned wineries demand Bacchanalian endurance (p. 476).

END

ESSENTIALS

PLANNING YOUR TRIP

ENTRANCE REQUIREMENTS

Passport (p. 10). Required of all visitors.

Visa (p. 11). Required of all visitors except holders of Australian and New Zealand passports. Eligible short-term visitors may alternatively purchase an **ETA** (p. 11) or apply for a **Sponsored Family Visitor Visa.**

Working Visa (p. 11). Required of all foreigners planning to work in Australia.

Student Visa (p. 11). Required of all foreigners planning to study in Australia.

Recommended Inoculations (p. 19). Hepatitis B, Japanese Encephalitis (for Northern Australia and the Torres Strait Islands), Rabies, and boosters for Tetanus and Measles.

EMBASSIES AND CONSULATES

AUSTRALIAN CONSULAR SERVICES ABROAD

The Australian consulate in each of the following countries provides information to foreign nationals on obtaining visas or applying for citizenship.

Canada: High Commission, 50 O'Connor St. #710, Ottawa, ON K1P 6L2 (☎613-236-0841; www.ahc-ottawa.org).

Ireland: Fitzwilton House, 7th fl., Wilton Terr., Dublin (☎01 664 5300; www.australianembassy.ie).

New Zealand: High Commission, 72-78 Hobson St., P.O. Box 4036, Wellington (☎04 473 6411; www.australia.org.nz). **Consulate:** Level 7, Price Waterhouse Coopers Tower, 186-194 Quay St., Private Bag 92023, Auckland (☎09 921 8800).

UK: High Commission, Australia House, The Strand, London WC2B 4LA (☎20 7379 4334; www.australia.org.uk). **Consulate:** Melrose House, 93 George St., Edinburgh EH2 2JG (☎131 624 3333).

US: 1601 Massachusetts Ave. NW, Washington, D.C. 20036-2273 (☎202-797-3000; www.austemb.org/DIMA). For general visa information, call the Australian visa service at 1-888-990-8888. Visa requests must go through the Washington, D.C. embassy. **Consulates:** 150 E. 42nd St., 34th fl., New York, NY 10017-5612 (☎212-351-6500) and 2049 Century Park E, 19th fl., Los Angeles, CA 90067-3121 (☎310-229-4800).

CONSULAR SERVICES IN AUSTRALIA

In Australia, each foreign consulate can help its citizens obtain, renew, or replace a passport (though regulations since September 11th have in some cases restricted this), or provide temporary travel papers to citizens who have lost their passport. Other services include information on money transfers, tax obligations when abroad, citizenship, travel cautions, and general information on legal matters.

Canada: High Commission, Commonwealth Ave., **Canberra** ACT 2600 (☎02 6270 4000;). **Consulates:** 267 St. George's Terr., **Perth** WA 6000 (☎08 9322 7930); Level 5, Quay West Building, 111 Harrington St., **Sydney** NSW 2000 (☎02 9364 3000).

Ireland: Embassy, 20 Arkana St., Yarralumla, **Canberra** ACT 2600 (☎02 6273 3022). **Consulates:** P.O. Box 250, Floreat Forum, **Perth** WA 6014 (☎/fax 08 9385 8247); Level 30, 400 George St., **Sydney** NSW 2000 (☎02 9231 6999).

New Zealand: High Commission, Commonwealth Ave., **Canberra** ACT 2600 (☎02 6270 4211). **Consulate:** Level 10, 55 Hunter St., GPO Box 365, **Sydney** NSW 2001 (passport ☎02 9223 0222, visa 9223 0144).

UK: High Commission, Commonwealth Ave., Yarralumla, **Canberra** ACT 2600 (☎02 6270 6666). **Consulates:** 17th fl., 90 Collins St., **Melbourne** VIC 3000 (☎03 9652 1670); Level 26, Allendale Sq., 77 St. George's Terr., **Perth** WA 6000 (☎08 9224 4700); Level 16, The Gateway, 1 Macquarie Pl., **Sydney** NSW 2000 (☎02 9247 7521).

US: Embassy, Moonah Pl., Yarralumla, **Canberra** ACT 2600 (☎02 6214 5600; http://canberra.usembassy.gov). **Consulates:** Level 59, MLC Ctr., 19-29 Martin Pl., **Sydney** NSW 2000 (☎02 9373 9200); 553 St. Kilda Rd., **Melbourne** VIC 3004 (☎03 9526 5900); 13th fl., 16 St. George's Terr., **Perth** WA 6000 (☎08 9202 1224).

TOURIST OFFICES

The government-sponsored **Australian Tourist Commission (ATC)** promotes tourism internationally, distributes literature, and sponsors help lines. The ATC carries books, magazines, and fact sheets for backpackers, younger people, disabled travelers, and others with special concerns. More information is available at www.australia.com and www.atc.net.au, or these office affiliates:

Australia (Head Office): Level 4, 80 William St., Wolloomooloo NSW 2011. **Branch:** GPO Box 2721, Sydney NSW 1006 (☎02 9360 1111).

New Zealand: Level 3, 125 The Strand, Parnell, Auckland 1 (☎09 915 2826).

United Kingdom: Gemini House, 10-18 Putney Hill, London SW15 6AA (☎20 8780 2229).

US and Canada: 2049 Century Park E, Ste. 1920, Los Angeles, CA 90067 (☎310-229-4870).

DOCUMENTS AND FORMALITIES

PASSPORTS

REQUIREMENTS

Travelers need valid passports to enter Australia and to re-enter their home countries. Entrance is not allowed if the holder's passport expires within six months of entry; returning home with an expired passport is illegal, and may result in a fine.

NEW PASSPORTS

Citizens of Australia, Canada, Ireland, New Zealand, the UK, and the US can apply for a passport at any passport office or at selected post offices and courts of law. Citizens of these countries may also download passport applications from the website of their country's government or passport office. New passport or renewal applications must be filed well in advance (at least 6 weeks) of departure, though most passport offices offer rush services for a steep fee (US$60 plus delivery costs). Note, however, that "rushed" passports still take up to two weeks to arrive.

PASSPORT MAINTENANCE

Photocopy the page of your passport with your photo, as well as your visas, traveler's check numbers, IDs, credit cards, and other important documents. Carry one set of copies in a safe place, apart from the originals, and leave another set at home; they will be extremely helpful in case of loss or theft of the originals. Consulates recommend that you also carry an expired passport or an official copy of your birth certificate in your baggage, separate from your other documents.

If you lose your passport, immediately notify the local police and the nearest embassy or consulate of your home government. To expedite its replacement, you will need to know all information previously recorded and show ID and proof of citizenship. In some cases, a replacement may take weeks to process, and it may only be valid for a limited time. Any visas stamped in your old passport will be irretrievably lost. In an emergency, ask for immediate temporary traveling papers that will permit you to re-enter your home country.

VISAS, INVITATIONS, AND WORK PERMITS

VISAS

Do not purchase your plane ticket before you have acquired a visa or an ETA. Australia requires all visitors except Australian citizens and New Zealand passport holders to have a visa. If you are a citizen of one of 32 approved countries (see www.immi.gov.au/eta/countries.htm for the full list), including the US, the UK, Canada, and Ireland, you can obtain an **Electronic Travel Authority** (**ETA;** AUS$20) while purchasing your ticket at a travel agency, airport ticket counter, or online (www.eta.immi.gov.au). Quick and simple, the electronic **ETA replaces a standard visa,** allowing multiple visits within a one-year period provided that no trip lasts longer than three months. An ETA is for tourist purposes; it doesn't replace a work visa. Travelers are encouraged to plan ahead rather than attempt to obtain a new or extended ETA when in Australia. To extend a visit over three months, or to obtain a work visa, contact the Department of Immigration and Multicultural and Indigenous Affairs in Australia before the end of your three-month stay.

Standard visa cost varies; the Department of Immigration requests that travelers consult form 990i (www.immi.gov.au/allforms/990i.htm) for a fee schedule. North Americans can also call the Australian embassy in the US (☎888-990-8888) with visa queries. Visa processing times average three weeks (when arranged by mail and in person), but can be highly variable.

Standard **short-stay visas** (under 3 months) and **long-stay visas** (between 3 and 6 months, extendable to a year) may be obtained from the nearest Australian high commission, embassy, or consulate. Visa extensions are not always possible. When they are, they come with a fee which varies depending on length of stay and type of visa. Contact the nearest Department of Immigration and Multicultural and Indigenous Affairs office before your stay period expires (go to www.immi.gov.au, and click on the "Information and Contact Details" link at the bottom of the left hand column). Otherwise, contact an Australian consulate or embassy (p. 9).

US citizens can take advantage of the **Center for International Business and Travel** (**CIBT;** ☎800-929-2428; www.cibt.com), which secures visas for travel to most countries for a variable service charge.

Be sure to double-check on entrance requirements at the nearest Australian embassy or consulate for up-to-date info before departure. US citizens can also consult http://travel.state.gov.

WORK PERMITS

Admission as a visitor does not include the right to work, which is authorized only by a work permit. Work permits can be obtained from the Australian embassy. For more information, see **Beyond Tourism** (p. 81).

IDENTIFICATION

When you travel, always carry at least two forms of identification on your person, including at least one photo ID, such as a passport, driver's license, or birth certificate. Never carry all of your IDs together; split them up in case of theft or loss, and keep photocopies of all of them in your luggage and at home.

STUDENT, TEACHER, AND YOUTH IDENTIFICATION

The **International Student Identity Card (ISIC),** the most widely accepted form of student ID, provides discounts at some Australian sights, accommodations, restaurants, and transport; access to a 24hr. emergency help line; and insurance benefits for US cardholders (see **Insurance,** p. 20). Applicants must be full-time secondary or post-secondary school students at least 12 years of age.

The **International Teacher Identity Card (ITIC)** offers teachers the same insurance coverage as the ISIC and similar but limited discounts. For travelers who are 25 years old or under but are not students, the **International Youth Travel Card (IYTC)** also offers many of the same benefits as the ISIC.

Each of these cards costs US$22 (if you provide your own photo) or equivalent. ISICs, ITICS, and IYTCs are valid for one year from the date of issue. To learn more about the cards, try www.myisic.com. Many student travel agencies (p. 26) issue ISICs, ITICS, and IYTCs; for a list of issuing agencies or more information, see the **International Student Travel Confederation (ISTC)** website (www.istc.org).

The **International Student Exchange Card (ISE Card)** is a similar identification card available to students, faculty, and youth age 12 to 26. The card provides discounts, medical benefits, access to a 24hr. emergency help line, and the ability to purchase student airfares. The card costs US$25; call ☎800-255-8000 (US) or ☎480-951-1177 (International) for more info, or visit www.isecard.com.

CUSTOMS

Upon entering Australia, you must declare certain items from abroad and pay a duty on the value of those articles if they exceed the allowance established by Australia's customs service. Note that goods and gifts purchased at **duty-free** shops abroad are not exempt from duty or sales tax; "duty-free" merely means that you need not pay a tax in the country of purchase. Upon returning home, you must likewise declare all articles acquired abroad and pay a duty on the value of articles in excess of your home country's allowance. In order to expedite your return, make a list of any valuables brought from home and register them with customs before traveling abroad, and be sure to keep receipts for all goods acquired abroad.

Articles not automatically forbidden but subject to a **quarantine inspection** upon arrival may include: camping equipment, live animals, food, animal and plant products, plants, and protected wildlife. Don't risk large fines or hassles when entering Australia—throw questionable items in the customs bins as you leave the plane, and declare anything about which you have any suspicion (including airplane food). The beagles in orange smocks know their stuff, and they *will* find you out.

If you must bring your pets with you, contact the **Australian Quarantine and Inspections Service** (☎02 6272 3933; animalimp@aqis.gov.au) to obtain a permit. Pick up *Customs Information for Travellers* at an Australian consulate or any travel agency for more information. Australia expressly forbids the entry of drugs, steroids, and weapons.

Visitors over 18 may bring into Australia up to 2.25L of alcohol and 250 cigarettes (or 250g tobacco) **duty-free.** For other goods the allowance is AUS$900 (for visitors over 18) or AUS$450 (under 18). Upon returning home, you must declare articles acquired abroad and pay a **duty** on the value of articles that exceeds the allowance established by your country's customs service. Australia recently implemented a **Tourist Refund Scheme (TRS)** that refunds the **Goods and Services Tax** (GST) on items bought in Australia (see **Taxes,** p. 15). For more information on customs requirements, contact the **Australian Customs Service** (in Australia ☎1300 363 263, elsewhere 61 2 6275 6666; www.customs.gov.au).

MONEY

CURRENCY AND EXCHANGE

Australia's currency is **Australian dollars** ($) and **cents** (¢). Notes come in $5, $10, $20, $50, and $100 bills, and coins in 5¢, 10¢, 20¢, 50¢, $1, and $2 denominations (for exchange rates see **Appendix,** p. 761). Credit cards are widely accepted in cities; in rural areas it's a good idea to carry cash. Personal checks are rarely accepted, and even traveler's checks may not be accepted in some locations.

As a general rule, it's cheaper to convert money in Australia than at home. While currency exchange will probably be available in your arrival airport, it's wise to bring enough foreign currency to last for the first 24-72 hours of your trip.

When changing money abroad, try to go only to banks or bureaux de change that have at most a 5% margin between their buy and sell prices. Since you lose money with every transaction, **convert large sums** (unless the currency is depreciating rapidly), **but no more than you'll need.**

If you use traveler's checks or bills, carry some in small denominations (the equivalent of US$50 or less) for times when you have to exchange money at disadvantageous rates, but bring a range of denominations since charges may be levied per check cashed. Store your money in a variety of forms; ideally, at any given time you will be carrying cash, some traveler's checks, and an ATM and/or credit card.

TRAVELER'S CHECKS

Traveler's checks are one of the safest means of carrying funds, and are generally accepted in metropolitan areas of Australia. **American Express** and **Visa** are the most recognized brands. Many banks and agencies sell them for a small commission. Check issuers provide refunds if the checks are lost or stolen, and many provide additional services, such as toll-free refund hotlines abroad, emergency message services, and stolen credit card assistance. Ask about refund hotlines and the location of refund centers when purchasing checks, and always carry emergency cash.

American Express: Checks available with commission at select banks, at all AmEx offices, and online (www.americanexpress.com; US residents only). American Express cardholders can also purchase checks by phone (☎800-721-9768). Available in a wide range of currencies. Also offers the Travelers Cheque Card, a prepaid reloadable card. For purchase locations or more information, contact AmEx's service centers: in Australia ☎800 688 022, in New Zealand 423 74 409, in the UK 0800 587 6023, in the US and Canada 800-221-7282; elsewhere, call the US collect at 801-964-6665.

Travelex: Thomas Cook MasterCard and Interpayment Visa traveler's checks available. For information about Thomas Cook MasterCard in Canada and the US call ☎800-223-7373, in the UK 0800 622 101; elsewhere call the UK collect at +44 1733 318 950. For information about Interpayment Visa in the US and Canada call ☎800-732-1322, in the UK 0800 515 884; elsewhere call the UK collect at +44 1733 318 949. For more information, visit www.travelex.com.

Visa: Checks available (generally with commission) at banks worldwide. For the location of the nearest office, call the Visa Travelers Cheque Global Refund and Assistance Center: in the UK ☎0800 515 884, in the US 800-227-6811, elsewhere, call the UK collect at +44 2079 378 091. Visa also offers TravelMoney, a prepaid debit card that can be reloaded online or by phone. For more information on Visa travel services, see http://usa.visa.com/personal/using_visa/travel_with_visa.html.

CREDIT, DEBIT, AND ATM CARDS

Credit cards are accepted at most locations in Australia, though particularly small or rural accommodations, restaurants, and businesses are still often cash only. Credit cards should be used as often possible, as they offer superior exchange rates—up to 5% better than the retail rate used by banks and other currency exchange establishments. Credit cards may also offer services such as insurance or emergency help, and are sometimes necessary to reserve hotel rooms or rental cars. **Mastercard** and **Visa** are most often welcomed; **American Express** cards work at some ATMs and at AmEx offices in large Australian cities and airports. **Bank of America** cards are accepted, with no fees, by Westpac ATMs in Australia.

The use of ATM cards are widespread in Australia. Depending on the system that your home bank uses, you can most likely access your personal bank account from abroad. ATMs get the same wholesale exchange rate as credit cards, but there is often a limit on the amount of money you can withdraw per day (around US$500). Most importantly, computerized withdrawal networks sometimes fail. There is typically a surcharge of US$1-5 per withdrawal, unless explicitly stated otherwise.

Most ATMs charge a transaction fee paid to the bank that owns the ATM. **Cirrus** (US ☎800-424-7787; www.mastercard.com) is the most widespread ATM network in Australia; **PLUS** (US ☎800-843-7587; www.visa.com) is almost as frequent, and **Visa,** though probably third best, is still fairly common. **MasterCard** and **American Express** are found less often and **NYCE** not at all. Though ATMs are increasingly prevalent in smaller towns and rural areas, they are scarce in Northwestern Australia and more remote interior areas.

PINS AND ATMS. To use a cash or credit card to withdraw money from a cash machine (ATM) in Europe, you must have a four-digit **Personal Identification Number (PIN).** If your PIN is longer than four digits, ask your bank whether you can just use the first four, or if you'll need a new one. **Credit cards** don't usually come with PINs; if you intend to use credit cards at ATMs to get cash advances, request a PIN from your credit card company before leaving.

Travelers with alphabetic, rather than numerical, PINs may also be thrown off by the lack of letters on European cash machines. Note that if you mistakenly punch the wrong code into the machine three times, it will swallow your card for good.

Debit cards are as convenient as credit cards but have a more immediate impact on your funds. A debit card can be used wherever its associated credit card company (usually MasterCard or Visa) is accepted, yet the money is withdrawn directly from the holder's checking account. Debit cards often also function as ATM cards and can be used to withdraw cash from associated banks and ATMs throughout Australia. Check with your credit card company to see if your credit card can also function as an ATM card. While in Australia you might see references to **Electronic Funds Transfer at Point Of Sale (EFTPOS),** which is a common way for Australians to pay for goods, and works like a debit card.

WIRING MONEY

It is possible to arrange a **bank money transfer,** which means asking a bank back home to wire money to a bank in Australia. This is the cheapest way to transfer cash, but it's also the slowest, usually taking several days, if not more. Note that some banks may only release your funds in local currency, potentially sticking you with a poor exchange rate; inquire about this in advance. Money transfer services like **Western Union** are faster and more convenient than bank transfers—but much more expensive. Western Union has many locations worldwide. To find one, visit www.westernunion.com, or call, in Australia ☎800 173 833, in Canada 800-235-0000, in the UK 0800 83 38 33, or in the US 800-325-6000. Money transfer services are also available at **American Express** and **Thomas Cook** offices.

US STATE DEPARTMENT (US CITIZENS ONLY)

In serious emergencies only, the US State Department will forward money within hours to the nearest consular office, which will then disburse it according to instructions for a US$30 fee. Contact the Overseas Citizens Service division of the US State Department (☎202-624-4750 or toll-free 888-407-4747) to use this service.

COSTS

The cost of your trip will vary considerably, depending on where you go, how you travel, and where you stay. The most significant expenses will probably be your round-trip (return) **airfare** to Australia (see **Getting to Australia,** p. 25). Before you go, spend some time calculating a reasonable daily **budget.**

STAYING ON A BUDGET

A bare-bones day in Australia (camping or sleeping in hostels or guesthouses, buying food at supermarkets) costs about AUS$40; a slightly more comfortable day (sleeping in hostels, guesthouses, or the occasional budget hotel, eating one meal per day at a restaurant, sightseeing, going out at night) costs about AUS$60; and for a luxurious day, the sky's the limit. Don't forget to factor in emergency reserve funds (at least AUS$300) when planning how much money you'll need.

TIPS FOR SAVING MONEY

Some simple ways include searching out opportunities for free entertainment, splitting accommodation and food costs with travelers, and buying food in supermarkets to cook in the hostel. Bring a **sleepsack** to save on hostel sheet charges, and do your **laundry** in the sink (unless you're explicitly prohibited from doing so). Museums often have days when admission is free; plan accordingly. If you are eligible, consider getting an ISIC or an IYTC; many sights, transportation, and museums offer reduced admission to students and youths. For fast travel, bikes are an economical option. Renting a bike is cheaper than renting a moped or scooter. Don't forget about walking, though; you can learn a lot about a city by seeing it on foot. That said, don't go overboard; staying within your budget is important, but don't do so at the expense of your health or a great travel experience.

TIPPING

In Australia, tipping is not expected at restaurants, bars, taxis, or hotels—service workers do not rely on tips for income. Tips are occasionally left at fancy restaurants, when the service is exceptional. In this case, 10% is more than enough. Taxes are always included in the bill, so pay only the price that is advertised.

TAXES

The New Tax System of 2000 provides for a **10% Goods and Services Tax (GST).** Some goods such as basic foods and medicines are not subject to this tax. However,

TOP TEN LIST

TOP 10 WAYS TO SAVE IN AUSTRALIA

Australia is a backpacker paradise, and with some planning—and a touch of innovation—it's not hard to live within a budget. You won't even have to sacrifice food, fun, or fantastic experiences; go wild without burning a hole in your pocket.

1. Buy food at markets and grocery stores instead of restaurants; try the Fremantle markets for Aussie oddities and groceries at rock-bottom prices.

2. Design your own bus pass, tailored to your itinerary, with Greyhound Australia.

3. Score a seasonal fruit-picking job to offset travel costs.

4. Inquire at restaurants about backpacker specials or discounts affiliated with your hostel.

5. Take public transportation or walk as much as possible.

6. Find free Internet access in libraries and tourist offices.

7. Avoid the ensuite double and opt for free bushcamping instead.

8. Build more outdoors experiences into your itinerary. (Brisbane, for example, is particularly stunning when viewed at the summit of Mount Coot-tha.)

9. Head to the show early and snap up student rush tickets at the Sydney Opera House

10. Work at your hostel part-time in exchange for accommodation.

the System also implemented a **Tourist Refund Scheme (TRS)** whereby tourists may be entitled to a refund of the GST and of the **Wine Equalisation Tax (WET)** on purchases of goods bought from Australian retailers. The refund is only good for GST or WET paid on purchases of $300 or more. Travelers can claim the refund at TRS booths in international terminals by presenting tax receipts from retailers, valid passport, proof of travel, and the items themselves. More restrictions apply, see the Australian Customs Service website for details (www.customs.gov.au).

PACKING

Pack lightly: Lay out only what you need, then take half the clothes and twice the money. Save extra space for souvenirs or other items that you might collect along the way. The Travelite FAQ (www.travelite.org) is a good resource for tips on traveling light. The online **Universal Packing List** (http://upl.codeq.info) will generate a customized list of suggested items based on your trip length, the expected climate, your planned activities, and other factors. If you plan to do a lot of outdoor activities, consult **Great Outdoors,** p. 63 and **Camping and the Outdoors,** p. 69.

Luggage: If you plan to travel mostly by foot, a sturdy **frame backpack** is unbeatable. Toting a **suitcase** or **trunk** is fine if you plan to stay in one place, but not a great idea if you want to move around frequently. A small backpack or courier bag which can be used as a "daypack" is recommended for all travelers.

Clothing: No matter when you're traveling, it's always a good idea to bring a **warm jacket** or **sweater,** a **rain jacket** (Gore-Tex® is both waterproof and breathable), **sturdy shoes** or **hiking boots,** and **thick socks. Flip-flops** or **waterproof sandals** are crucial for hostel showers, and extra socks are always a good idea. If you plan to go to bars and clubs in major cities, pack at least **one nice outfit and pair of shoes** – many city bars don't allow sneakers or flip flops at night (no matter how chic they are) and many clubs have dress codes. If you plan to visit religious or cultural sites, remember that you will need modest and respectful dress.

Sleepsack: Some hostels require that you either provide your own linen or rent sheets from them. Save cash by making your own sleepsack: fold a full-size sheet in half the long way, then sew it closed along the long side and one of the short sides. Keep in mind that some of the bigger hostels in large cities prohibit sleeping bags.

Converters and Adapters: In Australia, electricity is **230-240V AC, 50Hz,** enough to fry North American appliances calibrated for 120V. Hardware stores sell **adapters** (to change the shape of the plug) and **converters** (to change the voltage). Don't make the mistake of using only an adapter without a converter unless instructions state otherwise.

Toiletries: Condoms, deodorant, razors, tampons, and toothbrushes are often available, but it may be difficult to find your preferred brand; bring extras. Bring enough pairs of contact lenses and solution for your entire trip. Also bring your glasses and a copy of your prescription in case you need emergency replacements.

First-Aid Kit: For a basic first-aid kit, pack bandages, pain relievers, antibiotic cream, a thermometer, a pocket knife (Swiss Army or Leatherman), tweezers, moleskin, decongestant, motion-sickness remedy, diarrhea or upset-stomach medication (Pepto Bismol® or Imodium®), an antihistamine, insect repellent, sunscreen, and burn ointment.

Film: Film and photo developing facilities are available, although digital photography has overtaken the market. Less serious photographers may want to bring disposable cameras. For film-users: beware, airport security X-rays can fog film; pack film in your carry-on luggage, since higher-intensity X-rays are used on checked luggage.

Other Useful Items: For safety purposes, you should bring a **money belt** and small **padlock.** Basic **outdoors equipment** (plastic water bottle, compass, waterproof matches, pocketknife, sunglasses, hat) may also prove useful. **Sunscreen is essential.** Quick repairs of torn garments can be done on the road with a **needle and thread; electrical tape** patches luggage tears. If you want to do laundry by hand, bring **detergent,** a small rubber ball to stop up the sink, and string for a makeshift clothes line. Other things you may forget: a **rain poncho** (check region-specific weather trends), an **alarm clock, rubber bands, garbage bags, safety pins, long pants** and **hiking boots** that cover your ankles (if hiking in the bush), a **flashlight,** and **earplugs.** Also bring sturdy, resealable **plastic bags** for damp clothes, soap, food, shampoo, and other spillables, and for electronic items (laptops, cell phones, CD players) to protect against dust damage on Outback roads. A cell phone can be a lifesaver (literally) on the road; see p. 36 for info on acquiring one that will work in Australia.

Important Documents: Don't forget your **passport, traveler's checks, ATM** and/or **credit cards, government-issued ID, proof of ETA** or **visa** purchase, **driver's license** (if you plan to drive less than three months) or **international driving permit** (if you plan to drive in the same state for more than three months), and **photocopies** of all of the aforementioned documents in case they are lost or stolen.

SAFETY AND HEALTH

GENERAL ADVICE

In any type of crisis situation, the most important thing to do is **stay calm.** Your country's embassy abroad (p. 9) is usually your best resource when things go wrong; registering with that embassy upon arrival in the country is often a good idea. The government offices listed in the **Travel Advisories** box (p. 18) can provide information on the services they offer their citizens in case of emergencies abroad.

EMERGENCY	Throughout Australia, dial ☎**000,** or **112** from cell phones.

LOCAL LAWS AND POLICE

Ignorance is not an excuse with regard to Australian laws: most strict laws deal with drugs and alcohol (see below). Other types of law enforcement you may encounter besides local police include park rangers.

DRUGS, ALCOHOL, AND TOBACCO

Australia has strict drug laws which distinguish between users and traffickers. There is currently a debate over whether or not to legalize marijuana, but for now it is illegal. Australia doesn't differentiate between illicit substances; all are illegal in any quantity. Drivers may be asked to perform random saliva tests to detect drugs. If you carry **prescription drugs,** take a copy of the prescription with you.

There are very strict **drunk-driving** (or "drink-driving," as Aussies say) laws in effect all over the country. Random breath-testing is common. The maximum legal blood-alcohol limit for "experienced drivers" (over 18, have had license for 3 years) is 0.05%. For drivers under 25 who have had their license for less than three years, the maximum blood-alcohol limit is 0%. Drunk-driving offenses may result in the cancellation of your license. *You must be 18 or older to purchase alcohol or consume it in public.* It is illegal for anyone to sell or give alcohol to a minor. Some public areas prohibit alcohol possession and consumption; obey any signs and postings.

Smoking is prohibited in all public places in Australia; this includes outdoor facilities providing food and drink, beaches, playgrounds, sports arenas, and domestic and international flights. Violation of this law results in fines and penalties.

SPECIFIC CONCERNS

BUSHFIRES. The threat of bushfire is a serious problem, especially in Western Australia, between May and September. Though Western Australia is particularly susceptible, most other areas are historically also affected. Fire-prime conditions include low relative humidity, high wind, and low rainfall. Check out http://australiasevereweather.com/fires/index.html for more information.

CYCLONES. Most Australian cyclones form off the northeast and northwest coasts. The two most commonly affected states are Queensland and Western Australia. The destructive cyclones can even close roads and highways, so always check road conditions before starting a long drive, especially during February and March, cyclone peak season. Find more info online at www.bom.gov.au/weather, the Australian Government Bureau of Meteorology.

TRAVEL ADVISORIES. The following government offices provide travel information and advisories by telephone, by fax, or via the web:

Australian Department of Foreign Affairs and Trade: ☎61 2 6261 1111; www.dfat.gov.au.

Canadian Department of Foreign Affairs and International Trade (DFAIT): ☎800-267-8376; www.dfait-maeci.gc.ca. Call for their free booklet, *Bon Voyage...But.*

New Zealand Ministry of Foreign Affairs: ☎64 4 439 8000; www.mfat.govt.nz/

United Kingdom Foreign and Commonwealth Office: ☎020 7008 1500; www.fco.gov.uk.

US Department of State: ☎202-501-4444; http://travel.state.gov. Visit the website to print the document *A Safe Trip Abroad.*

PERSONAL SAFETY

EXPLORING AND TRAVELING

Familiarize yourself with your surroundings before setting out and carry yourself with confidence. Stop into shops and restaurants to check your map instead of standing on the street. If you are traveling by yourself, be sure someone at home knows your itinerary. Never admit to strangers that you're traveling alone. At night, stick to busy, well-lit streets and avoid dark alleyways. If you feel uncomfortable in a situation, leave as quickly and directly as you can. Find out about unsafe areas from police, tourist offices, the manager of your hotel or hostel, or a local whom you trust. You may want to carry a **whistle** to scare off attackers or attract attention. For emergency medical help, police, or fire, dial ☎**000** anywhere in Australia, or ☎**112** from cell phones.

There is no surefire way to avoid all the threatening situations, but a good **self-defense course** will give you concrete ways to react to unwanted advances. **Impact** (www.impactsafety.org), **Prepare** (☎800-345-5425, www.prepareinc.com), and **Model Mugging** (www.modelmugging.org) can refer you to local self-defense courses in the US and internationally. Workshops (2-4hr.) start at US$50; full courses (20hr.) run US$350-500.

If you are using a **car,** familiarize yourself with Australian driving signals and road signs. Always wear a seatbelt. Children under 40 lb. should ride only in specially designed carseats, available for a small fee from most car rental agencies. Study route maps before you hit the road, and **if you plan on spending a lot of time on the road, or are driving in the Outback, always bring spare parts, food, and plenty of water.** If your car breaks down, stay near it, and wait for the police to assist you. For long drives in remote areas, invest in a RFDS-compatible radio, a cell phone (not guaranteed to work in remote areas), and a roadside assistance program (p. 33). In urban areas, park your vehicle in a garage or well-traveled area, and use a steering wheel locking device. See **Driving in the Outback** (p. 74) for more info. **Sleeping in your car** is the most dangerous way to get your rest, and it's also **illegal** in many countries. For info on the perils of **hitchhiking,** see p. 34.

POSSESSIONS AND VALUABLES

Never leave your belongings unattended; crime occurs in even the most safe-looking hostel or hotel. Bring your own padlock for hostel lockers, and don't ever store valuables in a locker. Be particularly careful on **buses** and **trains;** horror stories abound about determined thieves who wait for travelers to fall asleep. Carry your bag or purse in front of you, where you can see it. When traveling with others, sleep in alternate shifts. When alone, use good judgment in selecting a train compartment: never stay in an empty one, and use a lock to secure your pack to the luggage rack. Use extra caution if traveling at night or on overnight trains. Try to sleep on top bunks with your luggage stored above you (if not in bed with you), and keep important documents and other valuables on you at all times.

There are a few steps you can take to minimize the financial risk associated with traveling. First, **bring as little with you as possible.** Second, buy a few combination **padlocks** to secure your belongings either in your pack or in a locker at a hostel or train station. Third, **carry as little cash as possible.** Keep your traveler's checks and ATM and/or credit cards in a **money belt**—not a "fanny pack"—along with your passport and ID cards. Fourth, **keep a small cash reserve separate from your primary stash.** This should be about US$50 sewn into or stored in the depths of your pack, along with your traveler's check numbers and photocopies of your passport, your birth certificate, and other important documents.

In large cities **con artists** often work in groups and may involve children. Beware of certain classics: sob stories that require money, rolls of bills "found" on the street, mustard spilled (or saliva spit) onto your shoulder to distract you while they snatch your bag. **Never let your passport and your bags out of your sight.** Beware of **pickpockets** in city crowds, especially on public transportation. Also, be alert in public telephone booths: if you must say your calling card number, do so very quietly; if you punch it in, make sure no one can look over your shoulder.

PRE-DEPARTURE HEALTH

In your **passport,** write the names of any people you wish to be contacted in case of a medical emergency, and list any allergies or medical conditions. Remember that matching a prescription to an Australian equivalent is not always easy; if you take prescription drugs, carry up-to-date, legible prescriptions or a statement from your doctor stating the medication's trade name, manufacturer, chemical name, and dosage. Be sure to keep all medication with you in your carry-on luggage. For tips on packing a basic **first-aid kit** and other essentials, see p. 16.

IMMUNIZATIONS AND PRECAUTIONS

The Australian government recommends that travelers over two years of age have the following vaccines up to date: MMR (for measles, mumps, and rubella); DTaP or Td (for diphtheria, tetanus, and pertussis); IPV (for polio); Hib (for *haemophilus* influenza B); and HepB (for Hepatitis B). Vaccinations are not required unless you have visited a yellow fever-infected country or zone within six days prior to arrival. (See www.health.gov.au/pubhlth/strateg/communic/factsheets/yellow.htm for information.) For recommendations on immunizations and prophylaxis, consult the Centers for Disease Control and Prevention (CDC; p. 20) in the US or the equivalent in your home country. Also check with a doctor for guidance.

INSURANCE

Travel insurance covers four basic areas: medical/health problems, property loss, trip cancellation/interruption, and emergency evacuation. Though regular insurance policies sometimes extend to travel-related accidents, you may consider purchasing separate travel insurance if the cost of potential trip cancellation, interruption, or emergency medical evacuation is greater than you can absorb. Prices for travel insurance purchased separately generally run about US$50 per week for full coverage, while trip cancellation/interruption may be purchased separately at a rate of US$3-5 per day depending on length of stay.

Medical insurance (especially university policies) often covers costs incurred abroad; check with your provider. **US Medicare** does not cover foreign travel. **Canadian** provincial health insurance plans increasingly do not cover foreign travel; check with the provincial Ministry of Health or Health Plan Headquarters for details. Australia provides limited Medicare service in cases of "immediately necessary treatment" for nationals of the following countries (within certain time limits, and not applicable to visitors on student visas): Finland, Ireland, Italy, Malta, Netherlands, New Zealand, Norway, UK, and Sweden (see www.medicareaustralia.gov.au for details). **Homeowners' insurance** (or your family's coverage) often covers theft during travel and loss of travel documents (passport, plane ticket, railpass, etc.) up to US$500.

ISIC and **ITIC** (p. 12) provide basic insurance benefits to US cardholders, including US$100 per day of in-hospital sickness for up to 100 days and US$10,000 of accident-related medical insurance including $500 Emergency Dental Coverage (see www.myisic.com for details). Cardholders have access to a toll-free 24hr. help line for medical, legal, and financial emergencies. **American Express** (☎800-338-1670) grants most cardholders automatic collision and theft car rental insurance on rentals made with the card.

INSURANCE PROVIDERS

STA (p. 26) offers a range of plans to supplement your basic coverage. Other private insurance providers in the US and Canada include: **Access America** (☎800-729-6021; www.accessamerica.com); **Berkely Group** (☎800-797-4514; www.berkely.com); and **CSA Travel Protection** (☎800-873-9855; www.csatravelprotection.com). **Columbus Direct** (☎0870 033 9988; www.columbusdirect.co.uk) operates in the UK.

USEFUL ORGANIZATIONS AND PUBLICATIONS

The US **Centers for Disease Control and Prevention** (☎877-349-8747; www.cdc.gov/travel) maintains an international travelers' hotline and an informative website. Consult the appropriate government agency of your home country for consular information sheets on health, entry requirements, and other issues. For quick information on health and other travel warnings, call the **Overseas Citizens Services** (M-F 8am-8pm from US ☎888-407-4747, from overseas 202-501-4444), or contact a passport agency, embassy, or consulate abroad. For information on medical evacuation services and travel insurance firms, see the US government's website at http://travel.state.gov/travel/abroad_health.html or the British Foreign and Commonwealth Office (www.fco.gov.uk). For general health info, contact the American Red Cross (☎202-303-4498; www.redcross.org).

STAYING HEALTHY

Common sense is the simplest prescription for good health while traveling in Australia. Drink plenty of fluids to prevent dehydration and constipation in the bright Australian sun, and always wear sturdy, broken-in shoes with clean socks. Be aware of special safety concerns associated with the Australian environment and wildlife. In the event of a serious illness or emergency, call **☎000 from any land line** or **☎112 from a cell phone** to connect to police, an ambulance, or the fire department.

ENVIRONMENTAL HAZARDS

Heat exhaustion and dehydration: Heat exhaustion can be a serious concern in Australia, particularly in the Outback. Symptoms include nausea, excessive thirst, headaches, and dizziness. Avoid it by drinking plenty of fluids, eating salty foods (e.g., crackers), staying away from dehydrating beverages (e.g., alcohol and caffeinated beverages), and always wearing sunscreen. Also remember to always carry extra water in your car and, when hiking, on your person. Continuous heat stress can eventually lead to heatstroke, characterized by rising body temperature, severe headache, delirium, and failure to sweat. Victims should be cooled off with wet towels and taken to a doctor.

Sunburn: Australia has the highest rate of skin cancer in the world, with more than 8800 people diagnosed each year. Always wear sunscreen (SPF 30 or higher) when spending a significant amount of time outdoors. If you are planning on spending time near water, in the desert, or on long hikes, you are at a higher risk of getting burned, even through clouds. If you get sunburned, drink more fluids than usual and apply an aloe-based lotion. Severe sunburns can lead to sun poisoning, a condition that affects the entire body, causing fever, chills, nausea, and vomiting; it should be treated by a doctor.

Hypothermia and frostbite: A rapid drop in body temperature is the clearest sign of overexposure to cold. Victims may also shiver, feel exhausted, have poor coordination or slurred speech, hallucinate, or suffer amnesia. Do not let hypothermia victims fall asleep. To avoid hypothermia, keep dry, wear layers, and stay out of the wind. When the temperature is below freezing, watch out for frostbite. If skin turns white or blue, waxy, and cold, do not rub the area. Drink warm beverages, stay dry, and slowly warm the area with dry fabric or steady body contact until a doctor can be found.

High Altitude: Allow your body a couple of days to adjust to less oxygen before exerting yourself. Note that alcohol is more potent and UV rays are stronger at high elevations.

INSECT-BORNE DISEASES

Many diseases are transmitted by insects—mainly mosquitoes, fleas, ticks, and lice. Be aware of insects in wet or forested areas, especially while hiking and camping; wear long pants and long sleeves, tuck your pants into your socks, and use a mosquito net. Use insect repellents such as DEET and soak or spray your gear with permethrin (licensed in the US only for use on clothing). **Mosquitoes**—responsible for malaria, dengue fever, and yellow fever—can be particularly abundant in wet, swampy, or wooded areas like those found in national parks. **Ticks**—which can carry Lyme and other diseases—can be particularly dangerous in rural and forested regions. Outbreaks of insect-borne diseases do sometimes occur in Australia; consult the **Infectious Diseases** section of the **Australian Health Website** (www.healthinsite.gov.au/topics/Infectious_Diseases) for a complete list.

Lyme disease: A bacterial infection carried by ticks and marked by a circular bull's-eye rash of 2 in. or more. Later symptoms include fever, headache, fatigue, and aches and pains. Antibiotics are effective if administered early. Left untreated, Lyme can cause problems in joints, the heart, and the nervous system. If you find a tick attached to your skin, grasp the head with tweezers as close to your skin as possible and apply slow, steady traction. Removing a tick within 24 hours greatly reduces the risk of infection. Do not try to remove ticks with petroleum jelly, nail polish remover, or a hot match. Ticks usually inhabit moist, shaded environments and heavily wooded areas. If you are going to be hiking in these areas, wear long clothes and DEET.

FOOD- AND WATER-BORNE DISEASES

Prevention is the best cure: be sure that your food is properly cooked and the water you drink is clean. If the region's tap water is known to be unsanitary, peel fruits and vegetables before eating them and avoid tap water (including ice cubes and anything washed in tap water, like salad). Watch out for food from markets or street vendors that may have been cooked in unhygienic conditions. Other culprits are raw shellfish, unpasteurized milk, and sauces containing raw eggs. Buy bottled water, or purify your own water by bringing it to a rolling boil or treating it with **iodine tablets;** note, however, that some parasites such as *giardia* have exteriors that resist iodine treatment, so boiling is more reliable. Always wash your hands before eating or bring a quick-drying purifying liquid hand cleaner.

Traveler's diarrhea: Results from drinking fecally contaminated water or eating uncooked and contaminated foods. Symptoms include nausea, bloating, and urgency. Try quick-energy, non-sugary foods with protein and carbohydrates to keep your strength up. Over-the-counter anti-diarrheals (e.g., Imodium) may counteract the problem. The most dangerous side effect is dehydration; drink 8 oz. of water with ½ tsp. of sugar or honey and a pinch of salt, try decaffeinated soft drinks, or eat salted crackers. If you develop a fever or your symptoms don't go away after 4-5 days, consult a doctor. Consult a doctor immediately for treatment of diarrhea in children.

Dysentery: Results from an intestinal infection caused by bacteria in contaminated food or water. Symptoms include bloody diarrhea, fever, and abdominal pain and tenderness. The most common type of dysentery generally only lasts a week, but it is highly contagious. Seek medical help immediately. Dysentery can be treated with the drugs norfloxacin or ciprofloxacin (commonly known as Cipro).

Cholera: An intestinal disease caused by bacteria in contaminated food. Symptoms include diarrhea, dehydration, vomiting, and muscle cramps. See a doctor immediately; if left untreated, cholera can be lethal within hours. Antibiotics are available, but the most important treatment is rehydration. No vaccine is available in the US.

Hepatitis A: A viral infection of the liver acquired through contaminated water or shellfish from contaminated water. Symptoms include fatigue, fever, loss of appetite, nausea, dark urine, jaundice, vomiting, aches and pains, and light stools. The risk is highest in rural areas and the countryside, but it is also present in urban areas. Ask your doctor about the Hepatitis A vaccine or an injection of immune globulin.

Giardiasis: Transmitted through parasites and acquired by drinking untreated water from streams or lakes. Symptoms include diarrhea, cramps, bloating, fatigue, weight loss, and nausea. If untreated it can lead to severe dehydration. Giardiasis occurs worldwide.

Leptospirosis: A bacterial disease caused by exposure to fresh water or soil contaminated by the urine of infected animals. Able to enter the human body through cut skin, mucus membranes, and through ingestion, it is most common in tropical climates. Symptoms include a high fever, chills, nausea, and vomiting. If not treated it can lead to liver failure and meningitis. There is no vaccine; consult a doctor for treatment.

OTHER INFECTIOUS DISEASES

The following diseases exist in every part of the world. Travelers should know how to recognize them and what to do if they suspect they have been infected.

Rabies: Transmitted through the saliva of infected animals; fatal if untreated. By the time symptoms (thirst and muscle spasms) appear, the disease is in its terminal stage. If you are bitten, wash the wound, seek immediate medical care, and try to have the animal located. A rabies vaccine, which consists of 3 shots given over a 21-day period, is available and recommended for travel in the developing world, but is only semi-effective.

Hepatitis B: A viral infection of the liver transmitted via blood or other bodily fluids. Symptoms, which may not surface until years after infection, include jaundice, appetite loss, fever, and joint pain. It is transmitted through unprotected sex and unclean needles. A 3-

shot vaccination sequence is recommended for sexually-active travelers and anyone planning to seek medical treatment abroad; it must begin 6 months before traveling.

Hepatitis C: Like Hepatitis B, but the mode of transmission differs. IV drug users, those with occupational exposure to blood, hemodialysis patients, and recipients of blood transfusions are at the highest risk, but the disease can also be spread through sexual contact or sharing items like razors and toothbrushes that may have traces of blood on them. No symptoms are usually exhibited. If untreated, it can lead to liver failure.

AIDS and HIV: For detailed information on Acquired Immune Deficiency Syndrome (AIDS) in Australia, call the US Centers for Disease Control's 24hr. hotline at ☎800-342-2437. Note that Australia screens incoming travelers for AIDS, primarily those planning extended visits for work or study, and could deny entrance to those who test HIV-positive. Contact the consulate of Australia for information.

Sexually transmitted diseases (STDs): Gonorrhea, chlamydia, genital warts, syphilis, herpes, and other STDs are easier to catch than HIV and can be just as serious. Though condoms may protect you from some STDs, oral or even tactile contact can lead to transmission. If you think you may have contracted an STD, see a doctor immediately.

OTHER HEALTH CONCERNS

MEDICAL CARE ON THE ROAD

Most of Australia is covered by state emergency ambulance and hospital services; emergency medical care in rural Australia is provided by the RFDS (Royal Flying Doctor Service; www.flyingdoctor.net). If you plan on traveling in a remote area of Australia, please see our special Outback safety coverage on p. 71 for general safety advice as well as specific information on remote communication devices. If your regular **insurance** policy does not cover travel in Australia, you may wish to purchase additional coverage (p. 20).

If you are concerned about obtaining medical assistance while traveling, you may wish to employ special support services. The *MedPass* from **GlobalCare, Inc.,** 6875 Shiloh Rd. East, Alpharetta, GA 30005, USA (☎800-860-1111; www.globalcare.net), provides 24hr. international medical assistance, support, and medical evacuation resources. The **International Association for Medical Assistance to Travelers** (**IAMAT;** US ☎716-754-4883, Canada 519-836-0102; www.iamat.org) has free membership, lists English-speaking doctors worldwide, and offers detailed info on immunization requirements and sanitation. If your regular **insurance** policy does not cover travel abroad, you may wish to purchase additional coverage (p. 20).

Those with medical conditions (such as diabetes, allergies to antibiotics, epilepsy, or heart conditions) may want to obtain a **MedicAlert** membership (first year US$35, annually thereafter US$20), which includes among other things a stainless steel ID tag and a 24hr. collect-call number. Contact the MedicAlert Foundation, 2323 Colorado Ave., Turlock, CA 95382, USA (☎888-633-4298, outside US ☎209-668-3333; www.medicalert.org).

WOMEN'S HEALTH

Women traveling in unsanitary conditions are vulnerable to **urinary tract (including bladder and kidney) infections.** Over-the-counter medicines can sometimes alleviate symptoms, but if they persist, see a doctor. **Vaginal yeast infections** may flare up in hot and humid climates. Wearing loosely fitting trousers or a skirt and cotton underwear will help, as will over-the-counter remedies like Monistat or Gynelotrimin. Bring supplies from home if you are prone to infection, as they may be difficult to find on the road. And, since **tampons, pads,** and reliable **contraceptive devices** are sometimes hard to find when traveling, bring supplies with you. **Abortion** is legal in Australia. Check out www.whv.org.au/packages/abortion.htm for more info.

GETTING TO AUSTRALIA

BY PLANE

When it comes to airfare, a little effort can save you a bundle. If your plans are flexible enough to deal with the restrictions, courier fares are the cheapest. Tickets bought from consolidators and standby seating are also good deals, but last-minute specials and airfare wars often beat these prices. The key is to hunt around, be flexible, and ask persistently about discounts. Students, seniors, and those under 26 should never pay full price for a ticket.

AIRFARES

Airfares to Australia peak between December and February; holidays are also expensive. The cheapest time to travel to Australia is between September and November. Midweek (M-Th morning) round-trip (return) flights run US$40-50 cheaper than weekend flights, but they are generally more crowded and less likely to permit frequent-flier upgrades. Traveling with an "open return" ticket can be more expensive than fixing a return date when buying the ticket, but are obviously more flexible for those planning longer trips. Round-trip flights are by far the cheapest; "open-jaw" (arriving in and departing from different cities, e.g. Los Angeles-Sydney and Melbourne-Los Angeles) tickets tend to be pricier. Patching one-way flights together is the most expensive way to travel. Flights between Australia's regional hubs—Sydney, Brisbane, Melbourne, and increasingly, Darwin—will tend to be less expensive.

If Australia is only one stop on a more extensive globe trotting trip, consider a round-the-world (RTW) ticket. Tickets usually include at least five stops and are valid for a year; prices range US$1200-5000. Try **Northwest Airlines/KLM** (US ☎800-225-2525; www.nwa.com) or **Star Alliance,** a consortium of 22 airlines including United Airlines and U.S. Airways (www.staralliance.com).

FLIGHT PLANNING ON THE INTERNET. The Internet may be a budget traveler's dream when it comes to finding and booking bargain fares, but the array of options can be overwhelming. **STA** (www.sta-travel.com) and **StudentUniverse** (www.studentuniverse.com) provide quotes on student tickets, while **Orbitz** (www.orbitz.com), **Expedia** (www.expedia.com), **Travelocity** (www.travelocity.com), and **Zuji** (www.zuji.com) offer full travel services. **Priceline** (www.priceline.com) lets you specify a price, and obligates you to buy any ticket that meets or beats it; **Hotwire** (www.hotwire.com) offers bargain fares, but won't reveal the airline or flight times until you buy. Other sites that compile deals include www.bestfares.com, www.flights.com, www.lowestfare.com, www.onetravel.com, and www.travelzoo.com. Increasingly, there are online tools available to sift through multiple offers; **SideStep** (www.sidestep.com) and **Booking Buddy** (www.bookingbuddy.com) let you enter trip information once and search multiple sites. An indispensable resource on the Internet is the **Air Traveler's Handbook** (www.faqs.org/faqs/travel/air/handbook), a comprehensive listing of links to everything you need to know before you board a plane.

The privilege of spending 24 hours or more on a plane doesn't come cheap. Full-price round-trip **fares** to Australia from the US or Canada (depending upon which coast of each continent you are heading to and from) can be US$1000-2000 and up; from the UK, £600-1200 and up; from New Zealand, NZ$500-800 and up.

BUDGET AND STUDENT TRAVEL AGENCIES

While knowledgeable agents specializing in flights to Australia can make your life easier and help you save some money, they may not spend the time to find you the lowest possible fare—they get paid on commission. Travelers holding **ISICs** and **IYTCs** (p. 12) qualify for big discounts from student travel agencies. Most flights from budget agencies are on major airlines, but in high season some may sell seats on less reliable chartered aircraft.

CTS Travel, 30 Rathbone Pl., London W1T 1GQ, UK (☎0207 209 0630; www.ctstravel.co.uk). A British student travel agency with offices in 39 countries including the US, Empire State Building, 350 5th Ave., Ste. 7813, New York, NY 10118 (☎877-287-6665; www.ctstravelusa.com).

STA Travel, 5900 Wilshire Blvd., Ste. 900, Los Angeles, CA 90036, USA (24hr. reservations and info ☎800-781-4040; www.statravel.com). A student and youth travel organization with over 150 offices worldwide (check their website for a listing of all their offices), including US offices in Boston, Chicago, L.A., New York, Seattle, San Francisco, and Washington, D.C. Ticket booking, travel insurance, railpasses, and more. Walk-in offices are located throughout Australia (☎03 9207 5900), New Zealand (☎09 309 9723), and the UK (☎08701 630 026).

Travel CUTS (Canadian Universities Travel Services Limited), 187 College St., **Toronto,** ON M5T 1P7 (toll free ☎1-888-592-2887; www.travelcuts.com). Offices across Canada and the US including L.A., New York, and Seattle.

USIT, 19-21 Aston Quay, Dublin 2 (☎01 602 1904; www.usit.ie), Ireland's leading budget travel agency. 20 offices throughout Northern Ireland and the Republic of Ireland.

Flight Centre (Australia ☎133 133; www.flightcentre.com.au). Offices throughout Australia, New Zealand (☎0800 24 35 44), the UK (☎0870 499 0040), Canada (☎1877 967 5302), and other anglophone countries, plus a user-friendly website. Books flights, tour packages, cruises, railpasses, and has information about various destinations.

COMMERCIAL AIRLINES

Commercial airlines' lowest regular offer is the **APEX** (Advance Purchase Excursion) fare, which provides confirmed reservations and allows "open-jaw" tickets. Reservations should be made seven to 21 days ahead of departure, with seven- to 14-day minimum-stay and up to 90-day maximum-stay restrictions. These fares carry hefty cancellation and change penalties (fees rise in summer). Book peak-season APEX fares early. Use **Expedia** (www.expedia.com), **Travelocity** (www.travelocity.com), or **Travel.com** (www.travel.com.au) to get an idea of the lowest published fares, then use the resources outlined here to try to beat them. Low-season fares should be cheaper than the high-season (Nov.-Apr.) ones listed here.

Popular carriers to Australia include **Air New Zealand** (www.airnewzealand.co.nz), **British Airways** (www.britishairways.com), **Cathay Pacific** (www.cathaypacific.com), and **United Airways** (www.united.com), most of which have daily nonstop flights from Los Angeles to Sydney. **Qantas** (www.qantas.com.au) is Australia's main airline and has the most international connections. Basic round-trip fares to Australia start around $2000.

AIR COURIER FLIGHTS

Those who travel light should consider courier flights. Couriers help transport cargo on international flights by using their checked luggage space for freight. Generally, couriers must travel with carry-ons only and deal with complex flight restrictions. Most flights are round-trip only, with short fixed-length stays (usually 1 week) and a limit of one ticket per issue. Round-trip courier fares from the US to Australia are about 45-75% less than the current, standard airfares. Most flights arrive in Sydney, and depart from Los Angeles, Miami, New York, or San Francisco in the US; London in England; and Montreal, Toronto, or Vancouver in Canada. Generally, US couriers must be over 21, and UK couriers over 18. In summer, the most popular destinations usually require an advance reservation of about two weeks (you can usually book up to 2 months ahead). Super-discounted fares are common for "last-minute" flights (3-14 days ahead). The organizations below provide members with lists of opportunities and courier brokers for an annual fee.

Air Courier Association, P.O. Box 2036, Cherry Hill, NJ 08034 (☎800-461-8856; www.aircourier.org). One-year membership US$39.

International Association of Air Travel Couriers (IAATC), P.O. Box 847, Scottsbluff, NE 69363 (☎308-632-3273; www.courier.org). One-year membership US$45.

STANDBY FLIGHTS

Traveling standby requires flexibility in arrival and departure dates and cities. Companies dealing in standby flights sell vouchers rather than tickets, along with the promise to get you to your destination (or nearby) within a certain window of time (typically 1-5 days). You call in before your specific window of time to hear your flight options and the probability that you will be able to board each flight. You can then decide which flights you want to try to make, show up at the appropriate airport at the appropriate time, present your voucher, and board if space is available. Vouchers can usually be bought for both one-way and round-trip travel. You may receive a monetary refund only if every available flight within your date range is full; if you opt not to take an available (but perhaps less convenient) flight, you can only get credit toward future travel. Carefully read agreements with any company offering standby flights as tricky fine print can leave you in the lurch. To check on a company's service record in the US, call the Better Business Bureau (☎703-276-0100; www.bbb.org). It is difficult to receive refunds, and clients' vouchers will not be honored when an airline fails to receive payment in time.

TICKET CONSOLIDATORS

Ticket consolidators, or **"bucket shops,"** buy unsold tickets in bulk from commercial airlines and sell them at discounted rates. The best place to look is in the Sunday travel section of any major newspaper (such as *The New York Times*), where many bucket shops place tiny ads. Call quickly, as availability is typically extremely limited. Not all bucket shops are reliable, so insist on a receipt that gives full details of restrictions, refunds, and tickets, and pay by credit card (in spite of the 2-5% fee) so you can stop payment if you never receive your tickets. For more info, see www.travel-library.com/air-travel/consolidators.html.

TRAVELING FROM THE US AND CANADA

Some consolidators worth trying are **Rebel** (☎800-732-3588; www.rebeltours.com), **Cheap Tickets** (www.cheaptickets.com), **Flights.com** (www.flights.com), and **TravelHUB** (www.travelhub.com). But these are just suggestions to get you started in your research. Let's Go does not endorse any of these agencies. As always, be cautious, and research companies before you hand over your credit card number.

CHARTER FLIGHTS

Tour operators contract charter flights with airlines in order to fly extra loads of passengers during peak season. These flights are far from hassle free. They occur less frequently than major airlines, make refunds particularly difficult, and are almost always fully booked. Their scheduled times may change and they may be cancelled at the last moment (as late as 48 hours before the trip, and without a full refund).

And check-in, boarding, and baggage claim for them are often much slower. They can be, however, much cheaper.

Discount clubs and fare brokers offer members savings on last-minute charter and tour deals. Study contracts closely; you don't want to end up with an unwanted overnight layover.

GETTING AROUND AUSTRALIA

BY PLANE

Because Australia is so large, many travelers, even those on a budget, take a domestic flight at some point while touring the country. Oz Experience (p. 29) and Qantas offer an **Air-Bus Pass** with which travelers can fly one-way and bus back (or vice versa) around Australia. Passes are valid for six months with unlimited stops; all dates can be changed.

Jetstar: Reservations ☎13 15 38; www.jetstar.com. Qantas's low-cost carrier services the east coast with frequent rock-bottom deals.

Qantas: Reservations ☎13 13 13 in Australia, 888-256-1775 in Canada and the US, 800 0014 0014 in the UK; www.qantas.com.au. Qantas "boomerang passes" allow travelers to change flight dates for free on domestic flights; cities can be changed for AUS$50. For international travelers, a boomerang pass may be the best domestic flight option (2-flight min., max. 10). 1-way passes within zones from AUS$160, between zones from AUS$300. First 2 segments must be purchased before arriving in Australia.

Regional Express (Rex): Reservations ☎13 17 13; www.regionalexpress.com.au. Offers service to much of South Australia, New South Wales, Victoria, and Tasmania. Earn frequent flier miles and rewards by enrolling in Rex Flier (one-time fee AUS$27.50).

VirginBlue: Reservations ☎13 67 89 in Australia, 7 3295 2296 outside Australia; www.virginblue.com.au. Service between many coastal cities, Cooks Islands, Fiji, New Zealand, Tasmania, and Vanuatu.

BY TRAIN

Australia does not have a comprehensive rail system, and with current airfare competition, train travel is not necessarily cheaper than flying. Nonetheless, trains can provide easy and comfortable travel on certain routes. **Rail Australia** offers a **Backpacker Rail Pass** (www.railaustralia.com.au/rail_passes.htm) that allows unlimited travel on all CountryLink trains and coaches (predominately in New South Wales) over consecutive days within a given period (14 days AUS$218, 30 days $251). The **Austrail Flexipass** allows you to purchase eight (AUS$600), 15 ($862), or 22 ($1210) traveling days to be used over a more extensive train network in a six-month period. The **East Coast Discovery Pass** allows unlimited stops in one direction on the Eastern Seaboard within six months (Sydney-Cairns AUS$341, Melbourne-Cairns $429). Agents can be contacted in the US (☎800-423-2880), Canada (☎416-322-7086), New Zealand (☎0800 801 060), and the UK (☎870 751 5000).

Each state runs its own rail service, and transfers between services may require a bus trip to the next station. Wheelchair access on interstate trains can be poor, as the corridors are often too narrow. Some (but not all) larger stations provide collapsible wheelchairs. The main rail companies are:

Countrylink (☎13 22 32; www.countrylink.nsw.gov.au), based in New South Wales. Ages 4-15 and ISIC card holders 50% discount.

Great Southern Railways (☎13 21 47; www.gsr.com.au) in South Australia and the Northern Territory via Alice Springs. Consists of the *Indian Pacific*, the *Overland*, and *The Ghan*. 50% discount for students, backpackers, pensioners, and children age 4-16.

Queensland Rail (☎13 16 17; www.qr.com.au) in Queensland. The cheapest and fastest way to travel Queensland's coast. Children and ISIC card holders 50% discount.

Transwa (☎13 10 53; www.transwa.wa.gov.au) in Western Australia. Pensioners, seniors, and children 50% discount.

V/Line (☎13 61 96; www.vline.com.au) in Victoria. Children, concessions 50% discount on interstate travel. Group discounts available. YHA/VIP Backpackers discount 10%.

BY BUS

Buses cover more of the rural landscape of Australia than trains, but journeys off the beaten track may require a few days' wait. It may be more cost effective to buy a kilometer or multi-day pass if you're planning on a large amount of bus travel.

GREYHOUND AUSTRALIA

Greyhound Australia (in Australia ☎13 14 99, elsewhere ☎7 4690 9950; www.greyhound.com.au) is the nation's premier bus service, with travel options in every state. Formerly McCafferty's/Greyhound, Greyhound Australia offers a standard 10% concessions discount. Fares booked over the phone include an additional fee; fares booked on the internet are least expensive (no additional fee) and may include discounts. The company sells a number of passes that allow you to save if you plan to spend more than six nonconsecutive days traveling by bus. Through their website, you can enter which cities and towns you plan to visit and you will receive instant suggestions about passes and special deals that are applicable to your intended route. The most popular passes are the **All Australian Pass**, which allows you to hop on and off anywhere in Australia on Greyhound's network, hitting all the highlights over the course of 2-12 months, and the **Aussie Highlights Pass**, which lets you see the most popular spots, including everything from Kakadu NP to the Great Barrier Reef. Other options include the **Aussie Kilometre Pass**, which allows travelers to purchase a set amount of kilometers (from 2,000 to 20,000) and use them to explore Australia on any of Greyhound's bus lines until their pre-purchased kilometer package runs out. All in all, Greyhound Australia offers a plan for any traveler looking to see any or all of the Land Down Under.

OZ EXPERIENCE

This popular bus company (☎1300 654 604; www.ozexperience.com) offers flexible backpacker packages and charismatic drivers who double as tour guides. The packages must be purchased for predetermined routes (cheaper if bought outside of Australia), and travelers can usually take up to six months to complete their route, often with unlimited stopovers. Oz Experience also offers a number of different passes to suit any travel plan, including the **Cobber**, which starts in Cairns and ends in Sydney or Melbourne, and the **Whipper Snapper**, which runs between Darwin and Sydney or Melbourne. Be prepared for a younger, party-ready crowd.

BY CAR

The public highways in Australia are well-maintained and follow the circumference of the country. Despite this, public transportation options are often inadequate in sparsely populated areas, and certain locations are reachable by car only. However, be aware that off the highway, the road system can be basic and poorly maintained. To travel on most outback roads and in national parks, you will need a **four-wheel-drive (4WD)**, which can double the cost of renting or buying. Shop ahead of time and be advised that some trips may be prohibitively expensive.

RENTING

Although the cost of renting a car can be too great for an individual traveler, rentals can become cost-efficient when traveling with a group.

RENTAL AGENCIES

You can generally make reservations with large rental agencies before you leave by calling their offices in your home country. However, occasionally the price and availability information they give doesn't jive with what the local offices in Australia will tell you. In fact, even Australian national and local offices may even give you different responses on issues like car availability and driver eligibility. Try checking with both local and national numbers to get the best price and most accurate information. Local desk numbers are included in town listings; for home-country numbers, check your local directory.

To rent a car from most establishments in Australia, you need to be at least 21 years old. While most companies charge an underage surcharge for drivers aged 21-24 (roughly AUS$15-25 per day), some agencies do not rent to drivers under 25. **Delta Europcar** (nationwide ☎1300 13 13 90; www.europcar.com.au) is a great place to start for drivers under 25, offering low daily surcharges for young drivers ($13.20 per day), cheap upgrades to automatic transmission (from $6 per day), significant long-term rental discounts, and excellent customer service. **Britz** (☎03 8379 8890, nationwide ☎1800 331 454; www.britz.com.au) often has competitive rates. Britz rents 4WDs to drivers under 25 and does not levy an age surcharge. Small local operations occasionally rent to people under 21, but be sure to ask about the insurance coverage and deductible, and always read the fine print.

Larger international companies offer reasonable rates to drivers **over 25,** and their Australian contact information is listed below:

Avis (☎612 9353 9000, nationwide ☎13 63 33; www.avis.com.au).

Budget (☎02 9353 9399, nationwide ☎1300 794 344; www.budget.com.au).

Hertz (☎03 9698 2555, nationwide ☎13 30 39; www.hertz.com.au).

Thrifty (head office ☎02 8337 2700, reservations ☎02 8337 2790, nationwide ☎1300 36 72 27; www.thrifty.com.au).

COSTS AND INSURANCE

Rental car prices in Australia start at around AUS$50 a day from national companies and AUS$35 from local agencies. Expect to pay more for larger cars and for 4WD vehicles. Cars with automatic transmission cost up to AUS$5-20 a day more than manual (stick shift) cars.

Many rental packages allow unlimited kilometers, while others offer 100-600km per day with a surcharge of approximately AUS$0.30 per kilometer after that. Returning the car with a full tank of petrol will eliminate high fuel charges at the end, but prepaid fuel packages can sometimes be a good deal; it's wise to compare these packages with the per liter petrol charges in the area. Before renting, be sure to ask whether the price includes **insurance** against theft and collision. Remember that if you are driving a conventional rental vehicle on an **unsealed (unpaved) road,** you are almost never covered by insurance; ask rental agencies about coverage. Most 4WDs have different restrictions than 2WDs.

Check with your credit card company to see if cars rented on an **American Express** or **Visa/MasterCard Gold** or **Platinum** credit card in Australia still carry the automatic insurance that they do in other countries. Insurance plans almost always come with an **excess** (or deductible) of around AUS$1000 for conventional vehicles. Younger drivers and those renting 4WD should be prepared to assume an excess up to around AUS$2500 (with younger drivers sometimes responsible for up to AUS$5500 for 4WDs). This means you pay for all damages up to that sum, unless they are the fault of another vehicle. The excess you will be quoted applies to collisions with other vehicles. Collisions with non-vehicles, such as trees or kangaroos ("single-vehicle collisions"), will cost you even more. If you decide to pay for an **excess reduction** package for between AUS$10-40 per day (available when you pick up the car), the excess can be reduced to a more reasonable amount or waived entirely. These packages are often a good idea, road hazards in Australia are much more prevalent than in the US or UK; windshield damage from loose pebbles could carry a large penalty.

CAR INSURANCE AT A GLANCE. Here is a run-down of the basic options you have for insuring your car:

Third-party personal injury insurance (a.k.a. green slip): automatically included with every registered vehicle. Covers any person who may be injured except the driver at fault; does not cover damage or repairs to cars or property.

Third-party property damage insurance: covers cost of repair to other people's cars or property if you're responsible for an accident.

Full comprehensive insurance: covers damage to all vehicles.

International Insurance Certificate: provided by the rental company or car dealer on all rented, leased, and borrowed cars; basic collision insurance.

National chains often allow travelers to arrange **one-way rentals,** where the vehicle is picked up in one city and dropped off in another. There is usually a minimum rental period, and sometimes there is a drop-off charge of several hundred dollars. Inquire at individual agencies about their one-way rental policy. Most rental agencies also charge an additional standardized fee for one-way and round-trip rentals originating and/or ending in certain **remote locations,** as the cars need to be brought back by the employees of the rental agency when there is no local fleet.

BUYING AND SELLING USED CARS

Buying used cars and then reselling them is popular among long-term travelers or those too young to rent. Automotive independence can cost under AUS$5000. However, used car dealers have been known to rip off foreigners, especially backpackers. Research prices, or ask a trustworthy Aussie about reasonable prices; some people recommend bringing a local along when purchasing the car. Buying from a private owner or fellow traveler is often a cheaper alternative. In many cities, hundreds of private sellers rent space at used car lots; buyers stroll around and haggle. Hostel or university bulletin boards are another good bet. In Sydney, check the weekly **Trading Post** on Thursdays (or online at www.tradingpost.com.au) for used car advertisements and the **Daily Telegraph Mirror** and **Sydney Morning Herald** on Saturdays. Also check out **Craig's List** (http://geo.craigslist.org/iso/au) which recently branched out to Australia. When selling a car back, consider the high tourist season for the region you're in. Vehicles are also easier to sell if they are registered in the state where they are being sold—new owners need to register the car, and some states don't allow registration transfer by mail. If you buy a car privately, check the registration papers against the license of the person who is selling the car. Australia's national consumer website also has good information about buying used cars (www.consumersonline.gov.au).

WHAT TO LOOK FOR

Before buying a used car, check with the local branch of the AAA, as states have varying requirements for a transfer of ownership, and local organizations can advise you on how to get your money's worth. The NRMA in New South Wales publishes *International Tourists Car Buying Advice.* In Victoria, all cars are required to carry a Road Worthiness Certificate. Local auto clubs also offer inspections (NRMA inspections ☎ 13 11 22 or 02 8741 6000).

BEFORE YOU BUY

When buying a car, call the **Register of Encumbered Vehicles** (nationwide ☎ 13 32 20) or check online at www.revs.nsw.gov.au to confirm that a vehicle is unencumbered—that it has not been reported as stolen and has no outstanding financial obligations or traffic warrants. You'll need to provide the registration-, engine-, and VIN/chassis-numbers of the vehicle. In New South Wales, a car must have a pink inspection certificate to guarantee that it is roadworthy. It is valid for 28 days and available at most service stations.

REGISTRATION

Within two weeks of purchase, you'll need to **register** the car in your name at the Motor Vehicle Registry. Although requirements vary between states, re-registration costs about $20. The local automobile organization can always help. Further information on vehicle registration in Australia can be found through the Department of Motor Vehicle's US website at www.onlinedmv.com.

DRIVING PERMITS AND CAR INSURANCE

INTERNATIONAL DRIVING PERMIT (IDP)

If you plan to drive a car for less than three months in Australia, your home country's driver's license will suffice. If your home country's driver's license is not printed in English, you must have an English translation with you. If you plan to drive in the same state for more than three months, you must obtain an International Driving Permit (IDP). Your IDP, valid for one year, must be issued in your own country before you depart; AAA affiliates cannot issue IDPs valid in their own country. You must be over 18 to receive the IDP. A valid driver's license from your home country must always accompany the IDP. An application for an IDP usually needs to include one or two photos, a current local license, an additional form of identification, and a fee. To apply, contact your home country's Automobile Association. Be careful when purchasing an IDP online or anywhere other than your home automobile association. Many vendors sell permits of questionable legitimacy for higher prices.

Canada: www.caa.ca. Permits CDN$15.

Ireland: www.aaireland.ie/travel/idp.asp. Permits €5.08.

New Zealand: www.aa.co.nz. Permits NZ$20.

UK: www.theaa.com/getaway/idp. Permits UK£4.

US: www.aaa.com/Vacation/idpf.html. Permits US$10.

CAR INSURANCE

Most credit cards cover standard insurance. If you rent, lease, or borrow a car, you will need a Green Card, or International Insurance Certificate, to certify that you have liability insurance and that it applies abroad. Green cards can be obtained at car rental agencies, car dealers (for those leasing cars), some travel agents, and some border crossings. Rental agencies may require you to purchase theft insurance in countries that they consider to have a high risk of auto theft.

ON THE ROAD

Australians drive on the **left side** of the road. In unmarked intersections, a driver must yield to vehicles entering the intersection from the right. In some big cities, right turns often must take place from the farthest left lane, after the light has turned red—keep your eyes peeled for signs to that effect. By law, **seat belts** must be worn at all times by all persons riding in the vehicle. Children under 40 lb. should ride only in a carseat, available for a small fee at most car rental agencies. The speed limit in most cities is 60kph and 100 or 110kph on highways. Radar guns are often used to patrol well-traveled roads; sly speed cameras nab offenders on less populated paths. Straight roads in rural areas occasionally have no speed limit, as indicated by a black circle with a slash through it. **Petrol (gasoline)** prices vary by state. Learn about Australian driving laws, signs, and signals before hitting the road (www.rta.nsw.gov.au/rulesregulations).

PRECAUTIONS

When traveling in the summer or in the Outback, bring substantial amounts of **water** (no less than 5L of water per person per day) for drinking and for the radiator. For long outback drives, travelers should check in with police before beginning the trek and again upon arrival at the destination. Check with the local automobile club for details. In the north, **four-wheel-drive (4WD)** is essential for seeing the parks, particularly in the wet season, when dirt roads turn to mud. If you have a breakdown, **stay with your car;** if you wander off, it's less likely that trackers will find you. See **Driving in the Outback** (p. 74) for more information.

Blood alcohol limits in Australia have recently become more stringent, with 0.05% being the standard in most states. (In New South Wales, renters should take note that the legal limit for rental cars is 0.02%.) These low-tolerance policies have caused a bit of a stir; products with an alcoholic base such as mouthwash and fruitcake have been shown to send drivers over the legal limit. The Australian government advises drivers to "check labels and avoid driving if they have eaten something with an alcoholic base."

CAR ASSISTANCE

The **Australian Automobile Association (AAA)** is the national umbrella organization for all of the local automobile organizations. You won't often see it called the AAA, though; in most states, the local organization is called the **Royal Automobile Club**

(RAC). In New South Wales and the ACT, it's the **National Royal Motorist Association (NRMA).** In the Northern Territory, it's the **Automobile Association of the Northern Territory (AANT).** Services—from breakdown assistance to map provision—are similar to those offered by automobile associations in other countries. Most overseas organizations have reciprocal membership with AAA (including AAA in the US; AA and RAC in the UK; NZAA in New Zealand). Bring proof of your membership to Australia, and you'll be able to use AAA facilities free of charge. If, for some reason, your membership is not honored, your AAA at home with reimburse you for fees incurred. **AAA New South Wales** can be reached at ☎02 9292 9222. It's possible to join AAA through any state's automobile organization. This book lists the location of the state organization in the introduction to each state.

BY BICYCLE

Australia has many **bike paths** to attract cyclists. Much of the country is flat, and road bikers can travel long distances without too much strain. In theory, bicycles can go on **buses and trains,** but most major bus companies require you to disassemble your bike and pay a flat fee of at least AUS$25. You may not be allowed to bring your bike into train compartments. Helmets are required by law in Australia. A quality **helmet** costs about AUS$45—much cheaper than brain surgery or the costs of any injury out on the road. Travel with good **maps** from the state Automobile Associations, and obey all traffic laws and signals.

The **Bicycle Federation of Australia (BFA),** P.O. Box 499, Civic Sq., Canberra, ACT 2608 (☎02 6249 6761; www.bfa.asn.au), is a nonprofit bicycle advocacy group. The BFA publishes *Australian Cyclist* magazine (www.australiancyclist.com.au) and has a list of regional bicycling organizations on its web page.

BY THUMB

LET'S GO STRONGLY DISCOURAGES HITCHHIKING. Let's Go does not recommend hitching as a safe means of transportation, and none of the information printed here is intended to do so.

Let's Go strongly urges you to consider the risks before you choose to hitchhike. Hitching means entrusting your life to a stranger and risking assault, sexual harassment, theft, and unsafe driving. For women traveling alone (or even in pairs), hitching is just too dangerous. A man and a woman are a less dangerous combination; two men will have a harder time getting a lift, while three men will go nowhere. Given the infrequency of public transportation to several popular destinations, travelers sometimes need to find other ways to get where they're going. Hostels frequently have message boards where those seeking rides and those seeking to share the cost of gas can meet up. On the east coast, hitchhiking traffic moves from Sydney to Brisbane and possibly as far north as Cairns.

KEEPING IN TOUCH

BY EMAIL AND INTERNET

Internet cafes are commonplace in almost every decent-sized city in Australia. In most major cities, Internet shops will have booths offering discounted international calling as well. Access to the Internet ranges from as low as **free** at some libraries and accommodations, to as high as $10 per hour. Coin-operated Internet kiosks are an expensive (usually $2 per 10min.) and common option in cities and hostels. Many public libraries offer free access to the web, though sometimes you are restricted from checking email or must make a reservation with the library beforehand. This guide lists Internet access options in the **Practical Information** section of towns and cities. Other Internet access points in Australia can be found at www.gnomon.com.au/publications/netaccess.

Increasingly, travelers find that taking their **laptop computers** on the road with them can be a convenient way to stay connected. Laptop users can call an Internet service provider via a modem using long-distance phone cards specifically intended for such calls. They may also find Internet cafes that allow them to connect their laptops to the Internet. For information on insuring your laptop while traveling, see p. 20.

BY TELEPHONE

CALLING HOME FROM AUSTRALIA

A **calling card** is probably your cheapest bet. You can frequently call collect without even possessing a company's calling card, just by calling their access number and following the instructions. Prepaid calling cards from Australian phone companies are often sold at newsstands and grocery stores.

COMPANY	TO OBTAIN A CARD:	TO CALL ABROAD:
AT&T (US)	800-364-9292 or www.att.com	1800 551 155 (O) or 1800 881 011 (T)
Canada Direct	800-561-8868 or www.infocanadadirect.com	1800 551 177 or 1800 881 150 (Tasmania)
MCI (US)	800-777-5000 or www.minutepass.com	1800 551 111 (O) or 1800 881 100 (T)
Telecom New Zealand Direct	www.telecom.co.nz	1800 551 164 (O) or 1800 881 640 (T)

You can usually make **direct international calls** from pay phones in Australia. Prepaid phone cards and occasionally major credit cards can be used for direct international calls as well, but they tend to be less cost effective. In-room hotel calls invariably include an arbitrary and sky-high surcharge. The expensive alternative to dialing direct or using a calling card is using an international operator to place a **collect call.**

CALLING WITHIN AUSTRALIA

Public phones are easy to find nearly everywhere you go in Australia. Some phone booths in Australia are coin-operated, some are phone-card operated, and some accept either coins or phone cards. Local calls made from phone booths cost $0.50 and are untimed. Note that you will not get change if you insert more than a call costs. Public phones (often small blue- or orange-colored boxes) can also sometimes be found in select bars and hotels; be aware that local calls placed on these are often more expensive than those made from phone booths. **Long-distance calls** within Australia use STD (Subscriber Trunk Dialing) services. You must dial an **area code** (listed next to town names in this guide) before the eight-digit number.

Australia has two main telecommunications companies: **Optus** and **Telstra.** Prepaid phone cards that you can insert into phone-card operated public phones carry a certain amount of phone time. Another kind of prepaid phone card has a toll-free access number and a personal identification number (PIN). Instead of inserting the card into the phone, you call the access number and follow the directions on the card. These cards can be used to make international as well as domestic calls and usually have better rates than those offered by Optus and Telstra. Some public phones in Australia (mostly located at airports, in and around city centers, and at major hotels) will allow you to charge a call to your **credit card.**

For local and national **directory assistance** in Australia, you can call toll-free ☎ 1223 from any phone; for international assistance dial ☎ 1225 instead. Six-digit phone numbers beginning with **13** are information numbers that can be dialed from anywhere in Australia for the same price as a local call. Numbers beginning with **1300** operate similarly. Numbers beginning **1800 or 0800** are **toll-free** and can be dialed as such from public phones.

CELLULAR PHONES

Cellular phones are common in urban Australia. Cell phone numbers are nine or 10 digits long and always begin with one of two codes; nine-digit cell phone numbers always begin with 01, while all 10-digit cellular numbers begin with 04. Incoming calls are usually free; charges for the caller run about AUS$0.25 per minute.

The international standard for cell phones is **Global System for Mobile Communication (GSM).** To make and receive calls in Australia you will need a **GSM-compatible phone** and a **SIM (Subscriber Identity Module) card,** a country-specific, thumbnail-sized chip that gives you a local phone number and plugs you into the network. Australia's **GSM** network is compatible with most phones used in Europe, but only with some phones from the US. Contact Telstra (www.telstra.com) or Vodafone (www.vodafone.com) for more information. Many SIM cards are **prepaid,** meaning that they come with calling time included and you don't need to sign up for a monthly service plan. When you use up the prepaid time, you can buy additional cards or vouchers (usually available at convenience stores) to get more. For more information on GSM phones, check out www.telestial.com, www.orange.co.uk, www.roadpost.com, or www.planetomni.com. Companies like **Cellular Abroad** (www.cellularabroad.com) rent cell phones that work in a variety of destinations around the world, providing a simpler option than picking up a phone in-country.

TIME DIFFERENCES

TIME ZONES	GMT	WA	NT	SA*	QLD	ACT, NSW, TAS, VIC*
Greenwich Mean Time (GMT)		+8	+9.5	+9.5	+10	+10
Western Australia (WA)	-8		+1.5	+1.5	+2	+2
Northern Territory (NT)	-9.5	-1.5		0	+0.5	+0.5
Southern Australia* (SA)	-9.5	-1.5	0		+0.5	+0.5
Queensland (QLD)	-10	-2	-0.5	-0.5		0
ACT, NSW, Tasmania, Victoria*	-10	-2	-0.5	-0.5	0	

Although there are formally only three time zones in Australia, they can be a bit confusing for travelers due to inconsistent observance of **Daylight Saving Time (DST),** which happens every year from late October to late March or early April. Five of the seven states observe DST, meaning that Australia's time zones end up following state borders both vertically and horizontally (for time zones, see **inside back cover**). Greenwich Mean Time (GMT), also known as Universal Standard Time (UST), is not affected by DST, so it provides a standard to calculate differences in time zones. In the table above, the column on the left represents where you are. The values indicate the time in other regions relative to the time in your region. To calculate the time in a different zone, simply add or subtract the difference in hours between the two places. For example, if it is noon in GMT, then it is 10pm in Victoria. Remember that the date is affected in some cases—Australia is ahead of the Western Hemisphere, so Monday evening in New York is Tuesday morning in Sydney. All regions that observe DST have an asterisk. Therefore, during DST, if you start in a row with an asterisk, you must subtract 1hr. If you end in a column with an asterisk, you must add one hour. For example, if it is noon in GMT during DST, then it is 11pm in Victoria. South Australia, Victoria, New South Wales, and the Australia Capital Territory start DST on the last Sunday in October, while Tasmania begins its observation on the first Sunday. of October. All states end DST on the last Sunday in March or the first Sunday in April

BY MAIL

SENDING MAIL HOME FROM AUSTRALIA

Airmail is the best way to send mail home from Australia. **Aerogrammes,** printed sheets that fold into envelopes and travel via airmail, are available at all post offices. Write *"par avion"* or "air mail" on the front. Most post offices will charge exorbitant fees or simply refuse to send aerogrammes with enclosures. **Surface mail** is by far the cheapest and slowest way to send mail. It takes one to two months to cross the Atlantic and one to three months to cross the Pacific—perfect for items you don't need to see for a while. The **Australia Post** website (www.auspost.com) has a postage calculator for international deliveries. These are standard rates for mail from Australia to:

Canada: Allow 5-7 days for regular airmail. Postcards and aerogrammes cost AUS$1. Letters up to 50g cost $1.85; packages up to 0.5kg $13.50, up to 2kg $45.

New Zealand: Allow 3-4 days for regular airmail. Postcards and aerogrammes cost AUS$1. Letters up to 50g cost $1.25; packages up to 0.5kg $9.50, up to 2kg $29.

UK and Ireland: Allow 4-5 days for regular airmail. Postcards and aerogrammes cost AUS$1. Letters up to 50g cost $1.85; packages up to 0.5kg $16.50, up to 2kg $57.

US: Allow 4-6 days for regular airmail. Postcards and aerogrammes cost AUS$1. Letters up to 50g cost $1.85; packages up to 0.5kg $13.50, up to 2kg $45.

SENDING MAIL TO AUSTRALIA

To ensure timely delivery, mark envelopes "airmail" or *"par avion."* In addition to the standard postage system whose rates are listed below, **Federal Express** (Australia ☎ 13 26 10, Canada and US ☎ 800-247-4747, Ireland ☎ 800 535 800, New Zealand ☎ 0800 733 339, UK ☎ 08456 07 08 09; www.fedex.com) handles express mail services from the above countries to Australia. Declare the contents of all packages, or risk week-long delivery delays. Sending a postcard within Australia costs AUS$0.45, while a letter (up to 250g) costs AUS$0.50.

There are several ways to arrange pickup of letters sent to you by loved ones while you are abroad in Australia. Mail can be sent fairly reliably via **Poste Restante** (known as General Delivery in the US) to almost any city or town in Australia with a general post office. Address *Poste Restante* letters with the recipient's name and the city, state, and postal code of the post office. For example:

The Right Honorable Samantha GELFAND
C/- Poste Restante
Sydney, NSW 2000

The mail will be held in the central post office of the town indicated, unless the writer specifies a post office by exact street address (listed in the **Practical Information** section of most towns in this guide). It's best to use the largest post office, since mail may be sent there regardless. Bring a passport for pickup.

American Express's travel offices throughout the world offer a free **Client Letter Service** (mail held up to 30 days and forwarded upon request) for cardholders who contact them in advance. Some offices will offer these services to non-cardholders (especially AmEx Traveler's Cheque holders), but call ahead to make sure. This book lists AmEx office locations for most large cities in **Practical Information** sections; for a complete, free list, call ☎800-528-4800, or visit www.americanexpress.com/travel.

ACCOMMODATIONS

2007 AUSTRALIAN SCHOOL HOLIDAYS BY STATE

State	Easter	Winter	Spring	Christmas/Summer
ACT	Apr. 14 - Apr. 29	July 7 - July 22	Sept. 29 - Oct. 14	Dec. 22 - Jan. 29
New South Wales	Apr. 6 - Apr. 22	June 30 - July 15	Sept. 29 - Oct. 14	Dec. 22 - Jan. 29
Northern Territory	Apr. 6 - Apr. 15	June 23 - July 22	Sept. 29 - Oct. 7	Dec. 15 - Jan. 29
Queensland	Apr. 6 - Apr. 16	June 23 - July 9	Sept. 22 - Oct. 7	Dec. 15 - Jan. 29
South Australia	Apr. 14 - Apr. 29	July 7 - July 22	Sept. 29 - Oct. 14	Dec. 15 - Jan. 29
Tasmania	Apr. 6 - Apr. 13	June 2 - June 17	Sept. 8 - Sept. 23	Dec. 21 - Jan. 29
Victoria	Mar. 31 - Apr. 15	June 30 - July 15	Sept. 22 - Oct. 7	Dec. 22 - Jan. 29
Western Australia	Apr. 5 - Apr. 22	July 7 - July 23	Sept. 29 - Oct. 15	Dec. 14 - Feb. 3

While it is generally easy to find accommodations when traveling in Australia, travelers should be aware that bookings (reservations) must often be made months in advance for holidays, particularly school holidays. It is also not uncommon for accommodations to raise, even double, their rates during these times.

HOSTELS

Hostels are generally dorm-style accommodations, often with single-sex rooms and bunk beds, though many hostels also offer private rooms for families and couples. Some have bike rentals, storage areas, transportation to airports and train stations, breakfast and other meals, kitchens and utensils, organized tours, and laundry facilities. There can be drawbacks: hostels may close during certain daytime "lockout" hours, have a curfew, do not accept reservations, impose a maximum stay, or, less frequently, require that you do chores. Bring your own **padlock** for your storage locker. Many hostels allow guests to leave valuables in a safe at the front desk. In Australia, a bed in a hostel will average around AUS$15-20 and a private room around AUS$25-30. A **VIP** membership card offered by **VIP Backpackers** (www.backpackers.com.au) gets discounts at many hostels. *Let's Go* designates these hostels with a VIP at the end of the listing. The two most common hostel chains in Australia are YHA and NOMADS (see below). A list of many hostels, regardless of affiliation, can be found at www.hostels.com.

A HOSTELER'S BILL OF RIGHTS. There are certain standard features that we do not include in our hostel listings. Unless we state otherwise, you can expect that every hostel has no lockout, no curfew, a kitchen, free hot showers, and no key deposit.

HOSTELLING INTERNATIONAL

Joining the youth hostel association in your own country (listed below) automatically grants you membership privileges in **Hostelling International (HI),** a federation of national hostelling associations. Non-HI members may be allowed to stay in some hostels, but will have to pay extra to do so. The Australian branch of HI, **YHA**

Australia (☎02 9565 1699), has hostels and agencies throughout Australia that are typically less expensive than private hostels. HI's umbrella organization's web page (www.hihostels.com) lists the websites and phone numbers of hostel associations and can be a great place to research regional hostelling.

Most HI hostels also honor **guest memberships**—you'll get a blank card with space for six validation stamps, one for each visit. Each night you'll pay a non-member supplement (one-sixth the membership fee) and earn one guest stamp; get six stamps, and you're a member. This system works well in most places, but you may need to remind the hostel reception. A new membership benefit is the FreeNites program, which allows hostelers to gain points toward free rooms. Most student travel agencies sell HI cards (p. 26), as do all of the national hostelling organizations listed below. All prices listed are valid for **one-year memberships** unless otherwise noted.

Australian Youth Hostels Association (AYHA), 422 Kent St., Sydney, NSW 200 (☎02 9261 1111; www.yha.com.au). AUS$52, under 18 AUS$19.

Hostelling International-Canada (HI-C), 205 Catherine St. #400, Ottawa, ON K2P 1C3 (☎613-237-7884; www.hihostels.ca). CDN$35, under 18 free.

Youth Hostels Association of New Zealand (YHANZ), Level 1, 166 Moorhouse Ave., P.O. Box 436, Christchurch (☎0800 278 299 (NZ only) or 03 379 9970; www.yha.org.nz). NZ$40, under 18 free.

Youth Hostels Association (England and Wales), Trevelyan House, Dimple Rd., Matlock, Derbyshire DE4 3YH, UK (☎0870 770 8868 or 44 1629 5927 00; www.yha.org.uk). UK£16, under 26 UK£10.

Hostelling International-USA, 8401 Colesville Rd., Ste. 600, Silver Spring, MD 20910 (☎301-495-1240; www.hiayh.org). US$28, under 18 free.

NOMADS

Another large hostelling chain in Australia is NOMADS Backpackers (www.nomadsworld.com). NOMADS has approximately 60 hostels nationwide, and you don't have to be a member to stay in one. The NOMADS Travel Guide and Adventure Card is a complete guide for backpacker discounts in Australia. Priced at AUS$34, it offers $1 off per night or seventh night free, discount international calling and Internet access, and hundreds of other adventure travel, touring, shopping and transport discounts.

NOMADS also offers bargain and adventure packages into all Australian gateways; these packages organize accommodations and activities for the first few days of a trip. For those who like to plan ahead, NOMADS also offers "Bed Hopper" accommodation vouchers that can be pre-purchased for 5, 10, 20, or 30 nights. Book online (www.nomadsworld.com) or with youth travel agencies worldwide.

BOOKING HOSTELS ONLINE. One of the easiest ways to ensure you've got a bed for the night is by reserving online. Click to the **Hostelworld** booking engine through **www.letsgo.com,** and you'll have access to bargain accommodations from Argentina to Zimbabwe with no added commission.

OTHER TYPES OF ACCOMMODATIONS

HOTELS

While **hotels** in large cities are similar to those in the rest of the world, "hotels" in rural Australia, particularly in Victoria and New South Wales, are often simple furnished rooms above local pubs. Some resemble fancy Victorian-era lodging with grand staircases, high ceilings, and wrap-around verandas. Others have been converted to long-term worker housing, and are thus less conducive to brief overnight stays. Singles in these hotels usually cost AUS$20-35. This generally includes a towel, a shared bathroom, and a private room. The pubs downstairs can be noisy. **Motels** in Australia are mid-range accommodations. Quality and price varies, but most motel rooms will include private bathroom (ensuite), TV, and fridge. If you make reservations in writing, indicate your night of arrival and the number of nights you plan to stay. The hotel will send you a confirmation and may request payment for the first night.

BED AND BREAKFASTS (B&BS)

A much more personal alternative to hotel rooms, Australian B&Bs (private homes with rooms available to travelers) range from acceptable to sublime. Hosts will sometimes go out of their way to be accommodating by giving personalized tours or offering home-cooked meals. On the other hand, many B&Bs do not provide phones, TVs, or private bathrooms. Rooms in B&Bs generally cost AUS$45-90 for a single and AUS$65-120 for a double but are more expensive in heavily touristed areas. Check out **BABS** (www.babs.com.au) for a list of Australian B&Bs.

UNIVERSITY DORMS

Many colleges and universities open their residence halls to travelers when school is not in session; some do so even during term-time. Getting a room may take a couple of phone calls and require advanced planning, but rates tend to be low and many offer free local calls and Internet access.

University of New South Wales, Level 16 Mathews Building, UNSW Kensington, Sydney NSW (☎02 9385 1000; www.housing.unsw.edu.au/extaccom.htm).

University of Sydney, Services Building G12, The University of Sydney, NSW 2006 (☎02 9351 5865; www.usyd.edu.au/su/properties).

University of Melbourne, International Centre, University of Melbourne, VIC 3010 (☎03 8344 6550; www.services.unimelb.edu.au/housing).

Australian National University, International Education Office, Australian National University, Canberra ACT 0200 (☎02 6125 5111; http://accom.anu.edu.au/Accomm/Renting/db.php).

HOME EXCHANGES AND HOSPITALITY CLUBS

Home exchange offers the traveler various types of homes (generally houses, apartments, or condominiums), plus the opportunity to live like a native and to cut down on accommodation fees. For more information, contact HomeExchange.com, P.O. Box 787, Hermosa Beach, CA 90254 USA (☎800-877-8723; www.homeexchange.com), or Intervac International Home Exchange (☎02 9969 3169; www.intervac.com).

Hospitality clubs link their members with individuals or families abroad who are willing to host travelers for free or for a small fee to promote cultural exchange and general good karma. In exchange, members usually must be willing to host travelers in their own homes; a small membership fee may also be required. **GlobalFreeloaders.com** (www.globalfreeloaders.com) and **The Hospitality Club** (www.hospitalityclub.org) are good places to start. **Servas** (www.servas.org) is an established, more formal, peace-based organization, and it requires a fee and an interview to join. An Internet search will find many similar organizations, some of which cater to special interests (e.g., women, gay and lesbian travelers, or members of certain professions). As always, use common sense when planning to stay with or host someone you do not know.

LONG-TERM ACCOMMODATIONS

Travelers planning to stay in Australia for extended periods of time may find it most cost-effective to rent an **apartment.** A basic one-bedroom (or studio) apartment in Sydney will start at around AUS$1500 per month. Besides the rent itself, prospective tenants usually are also required to front a security deposit (frequently one month's rent) and the last month's rent. Check apartment listings at www.realestate.com.au or http://www.rent-a-home.com.au.

CAMPING

Camping is by far the cheapest way to spend the night. The ubiquitous caravan parks found throughout the country offer basic camping sites, with or without power, for campers; in addition, some hostels have basic camping facilities or at the least allow guests to pitch their tents in the front or back yard. Unpowered campsites can vary in price, from free to $25 per night for a prime spot during Christmas holidays; most powered sites go for about $4-6 more. The Great Outdoor Recreation Pages (www.gorp.com) provides general information for travelers planning on camping or spending time in the outdoors.

Caravanning is popular in Australia, where many campgrounds double as caravan parks, consisting of both tent sites and powered sites for caravans. On-site caravans (also called on-site vans) are a frequent feature at caravan parks and are anchored permanently to the site and rented out. "Cabins" at caravan parks are often analogous to an on-site van, with a toilet inside.

In Australia there is a distinction drawn between **caravans** and **campervans (RVs).** The former is pulled as a trailer, while the latter has its own cab. Renting a caravan or campervan is expensive, but cheaper than renting a car and staying in hotels. The convenience of bringing along your own bedroom, bathroom, and kitchen makes caravanning an attractive option, especially for older travelers and families traveling with children.

It's not difficult to arrange a campervan rental for your trip to Australia, although you should definitely start gathering information several months before your departure. Rates vary widely by region, season (Dec.-Feb. is the most expensive), and type of van. It pays to contact several different companies to compare vehicles and prices. **Maui Rentals** (☎03 8379 8891; www.maui-rentals.com) and **Britz Campervan Rentals and Tours** (☎03 8379 8890; www.britz.com) rent RVs in Australia. Check out **Family Parks of Australia** (www.familyparks.com.au) for a list of caravan and cabin parks across Australia belonging to their chain. For in-depth information on outdoor activities, wildlife, safety and camping in the Australian Outback, see **Great Outdoors,** p. 63.

SPECIFIC CONCERNS

SUSTAINABLE TRAVEL

As the number of travelers on the road continues to rise, the detrimental effect they can have on natural environments becomes an increasing concern. With this in mind, *Let's Go* promotes the philosophy of **sustainable travel.** Through a sensitivity to issues of ecology and sustainability, today's travelers can be a powerful force in preserving as well as restoring the places they visit.

Ecotourism, a rising trend in sustainable travel, focuses on the conservation of natural habitats and how to use them to build up the economy without exploitation or overdevelopment. In a country such as Australia, home to a wide variety of different environmental zones, from coral reefs to deserts, responsible tourism is extremely important. Travelers can make a difference by doing research in advance and by supporting organizations and establishments that pay attention to their impact on their natural surroundings and that strive to be environmentally friendly (see **Volunteering,** in **Beyond Tourism,** p. 82). Check out www.ecotourism.org.au for more information on how you can get involved.

ECOTOURISM RESOURCES. For more information on environmentally responsible tourism, contact one of the organizations below:

Conservation International, 1919 M St. NW, Ste. 600, Washington, D.C. 20036, USA (☎800-406-2306 or 202-912-1000; www.conservation.org).

Green Globe 21 (☎61 2 6257 9102; www.greenglobe.com).

International Ecotourism Society, 733 15th St. NW, Ste. 1000, Washington, D.C. 20005, USA (☎202-347-9203; www.ecotourism.org).

United Nations Environment Program (UNEP), 39-43 Quai André Citroën, 75739 Paris Cedex 15, France (☎33 1 44 37 14 50; www.uneptie.org/pc/tourism).

RESPONSIBLE TRAVEL

The impact of tourist dollars on the destinations you visit should not be underestimated. The choices you make during your trip can have powerful effects on local communities—for better or for worse. Travelers who care about the destinations and environments they explore should make themselves aware of the social and cultural implications of the choices they make when they travel. Simple decisions such as buying local products instead of globally available ones, paying fair prices for products or services, and attempting to say a few words in the local language can have a strong, positive effect on the community.

Community-based tourism aims to channel tourist dollars into the local economy by emphasizing tours and cultural programs that are run by members of the host community and that often benefit disadvantaged groups. This type of tourism also benefits the tourists themselves, as it often takes them beyond the traditional tours of the region. World Heritage sites protected by the United Nations Educational, Scientific and Cultural Organization (UNESCO) that are also hot tourist spots include the Great Barrier Reef, Kakadu National Park, the Tasmanian Wilderness, Shark Bay, and Fraser Island, among others. See http://whc.unesco.org for more information. Excellent resources for general information on community-based travel include *The Good Alternative Travel Guide* (US$25) and *The Ethical Travel Guide* (US$22.50), projects of **Tourism Concern** (www.tourismconcern.org.uk) published by **Earthscan** (http://www.earthscan.co.uk).

In general, remember always to be careful when visiting national parks; leave trails, campsites, and all other locations you visit exactly as you found them. Do not feed animals, or they will become dependent on humans feeding them.

TRAVELING ALONE

There are many benefits to traveling alone, including independence and greater interaction with local Australians and their culture. On the other hand, any solo traveler is a more vulnerable target of harassment and street theft. As a lone traveler, try not to stand out as a tourist, look confident, and be especially careful in deserted or very crowded areas. If questioned, never admit that you are traveling alone. Maintain regular contact with someone at home who knows your itinerary and make yourself aware of emergency resources in the specific area in which you're traveling. For more tips, pick up *Traveling Solo* by Eleanor Berman (Globe Pequot Press, US$13), visit www.travelaloneandloveit.com, or subscribe to **Connecting: Solo Travel Network,** 689 Park Rd., Unit 6, Gibsons, BC V0N 1V7, Canada (☎604-886-9099; www.cstn.org; membership US$30-48).

WOMEN TRAVELERS

Women venturing out on their own inevitably face some additional safety concerns while traveling, but it's easy to be adventurous without taking unnecessary risks. It is generally safe for women to travel alone in Australia. If you are concerned about traveling on your own, consider staying in either hostels that offer single rooms that can be locked from the inside or in organizations that have rooms set aside for women only. Communal showers in some hostels are safer than others; always be sure to check the facilities before settling in. Stick to centrally located accommodations and avoid solitary late-night treks or bus rides.

Always remember to carry extra money with you for a phone call, bus, or taxi, preferably kept somewhere secure and separate from your regular stash of funds. **Hitchhiking** is never safe for women traveling alone, or even for two women traveling together. Let's Go does not recommend hitchhiking as a safe way to travel.

Your best answer to verbal harassment is no answer at all; non-responsiveness, sitting motionless, and staring straight ahead at nothing in particular will do a world of good that reactions usually don't achieve. Generally, the less you look like a tourist, the better off you'll be. Wearing a conspicuous **wedding band** sometimes helps to prevent unwanted overtures. Don't hesitate to seek out a police officer or a passerby if you are being harassed. Memorize the Australian emergency services numbers (☎000 and ☎112 on cell phones), and consider carrying a whistle on your key chain. A self-defense course will both prepare you for a potential attack and raise your level of awareness of your surroundings (see **Personal Safety,** p. 18). For general information, contact Australia's **Women's Electoral Lobby**, P.O. Box 191, Civic Square ACT 2608; (☎02 6247 6679; www.wel.org.au).

Unlike in the US, the morning-after pill has been available over-the-counter in Australia since January 2004.

GLBT TRAVELERS

The profile of the gay, lesbian, bisexual, and transgendered (GLBT) community in Australia has risen in recent years, most notably in the popularity of the **Gay and Lesbian Mardi Gras** in Sydney, now the largest gay and lesbian gathering in the world (p. 149). Though pockets of discrimination exist everywhere, the east coast is especially gay-friendly—Sydney ranks among the most diverse and accepting cities on earth. The farther into the interior you get, the more homophobia you are likely to encounter, even though homosexual acts are now legal in every Australian state and territory.

Gay and Lesbian Tourism Australia (GALTA) is a nonprofit nationwide network of tourism industry professionals who are dedicated to the welfare and satisfaction of gay and lesbian travelers to, from, and within Australia (general inquiries, 08 8267 4634; www.galta.com.au). Listed below are contact organizations, mail-order catalogs, and publishers that offer materials addressing some specific concerns. Although not specific to Australia, **Planet Out** (www.planetout.com) offers

a weekly newsletter and a comprehensive website addressing gay travel concerns. The online newspaper **365gay.com** also has a travel section (www.365gay.com/travel/travelchannel.htm). The **International Lesbian and Gay Association (ILGA)** provides political information, such as homosexuality laws of individual countries. (☎32 2 502 2471; www.ilga.org)

ADDITIONAL RESOURCES: GLBT.

Gay's the Word, 66 Marchmont St., London WC1N 1AB, UK (☎44 020 7278 7654; http://freespace.virgin.net/gays.theword/). The largest gay and lesbian bookshop in the UK, with both fiction and non-fiction titles. Mail-order service available.

Giovanni's Room, 345 South 12th St., Philadelphia, PA 19107, USA (☎215-923-2960; www.queerbooks.com). An international lesbian and gay bookstore with mail-order service (carries many of the publications listed below).

Spartacus 2005-2006: International Gay Guide. Bruno Gmunder Verlag (US$33). A best-selling gay guide and travel planner.

TRAVELERS WITH DISABILITIES

Travelers with disabilities should inform airlines and accommodations of their needs when making arrangements for travel; some time may be needed to prepare special accommodations. Call ahead to restaurants, hotels, parks, and other facilities to find out about the existence of ramps, the widths of doors, the dimensions of elevators, etc. **Guide dog owners** should inquire as to the quarantine policies of each destination country. At the very least, they will need to provide a certificate of immunization against rabies. After the 2000 Sydney Olympics and Paralympics, many locations in Australia (particularly the east) became wheelchair accessible, and budget options for the disabled are increasingly available.

USEFUL ORGANIZATIONS

Accessibility.com.au, provides information about disability-accessible opportunities in all the major cities with links to the disability sections of Australia's tourism websites.

Accessible Journeys, 35 West Sellers Ave., Ridley Park, PA 19078, USA (☎800-846-4537). Offers travel planning and group vacations for the physically-challenged throughout the world.

Flying Wheels, 143 W. Bridge St., P.O. Box 382, Owatonna, MN 55060, USA (☎507-451-5005; www.flyingwheelstravel.com). Specializes in escorted trips to Europe for people with physical disabilities; plans custom trips worldwide.

National Information Communication Network (NICAN), P.O. Box 407, Curtin ACT 2605 (☎02 6285 3713; www.nican.com.au). National database of accommodations, recreation, tourism, sports, and arts for the disabled.

Wheelabout Van Rental, 86 Mallawa Dr., Palm Beach QLD 4221 (☎1300 301 903 or 0439 963 563; www.wheelabout.com). Rents and sells wheelchair-accessible vans.

MINORITY TRAVELERS

Some would classify many Caucasian Australians as racist in their attitudes toward **Aborigines,** and this assessment may not be unfounded. Black travelers and some travelers of color may get a few stares or encounter some hostility in more remote Outback areas. As is the case in most parts of the world, cities tend to be more diverse and tolerant than far-flung, less populated destinations. Yet even Sydney has had recent troubles, most notably during the 2005 Cronulla Riots, which garnered international attention when caucasian youths clashed with youths perceived to be Middle Eastern. This was the most recent manifestation of the protests aimed at Muslim Australians which has brought issues of race relations back to the big cities. That being said, Australia, like many nations, continues to deal with the advantages and disadvantages of a very diverse populace.

DIETARY CONCERNS

The travel section of the The Vegetarian Resource Group's website, at www.vrg.org/travel, has a comprehensive list of organizations and websites that are geared toward helping vegetarians and vegans traveling abroad. For more information, visit your local bookstore or health food store, and consult *The Vegetarian Traveler: Where to Stay if You're Vegetarian, Vegan, Environmentally Sensitive*, by Jed and Susan Civic (Larson Publications; US$16). Vegetarians will also find numerous resources on the web; try www.vegdining.com, www.happycow.net, and www.vegetariansabroad.com, for starters.

Travelers who keep kosher should contact synagogues in larger cities for information on kosher restaurants. Your own synagogue or college Hillel should have access to lists of Jewish institutions across the nation. If you are strict in your observance, you may have to prepare your own food on the road. A good resource is the *Jewish Travel Guide*, edited by Michael Zaidner (Vallentine Mitchell; US$18). Travelers looking for halal restaurants may find www.zabihah.com useful.

OTHER RESOURCES

Let's Go tries to cover all aspects of budget travel, but if we put *everything* in our guides you wouldn't be able to carry them. Listed below are resources that can serve as starting points for your own research.

USEFUL PUBLICATIONS

Besides the printed travel resources listed so far, there are a number of general publications that may be good to peruse before heading down under. Try *Culture Shock! Australia*, by Ilsa Sharp (Graphic Arts Center Publishing; US$13.95), to get you started. History buffs should pick up *Australia: A New History of the Great Southern Land*, by Frank Welsh (Overlook Hardcover; US$37.50). Before you leave, get a taste of what's to come by reading about past travelers' experiences in *Australia: True Stories of Life Down Under*, by Larry Habegger (Travelers' Tales Guides; US$11.50).

WORLD WIDE WEB

Almost every aspect of budget travel is accessible via the web. In 10min. at the keyboard, you can make a hostel reservation, get advice on travel hot spots from other travelers, or find out how much a train from Perth to Sydney costs. Listed here are some regional and travel-related sites to start your surfing; other relevant websites are listed throughout the book. Because website turnover is rapid, use search engines (such as www.google.com) to strike out on your own.

WWW.LETSGO.COM. Let's Go's website features a wealth of information and valuable advice at your fingertips. It offers excerpts from all our guides as well as monthly features on new hot spots in the most popular destinations. In addition to our online bookstore, we have great deals on everything from airfares to cell phones. Our resources section is full of information you'll need before you hit the road, and our forums are buzzing with advice from other travelers. Check back often to see constant updates, exciting new tips, and prize giveaways. See you soon!

THE ART OF TRAVEL

Backpacker's Ultimate Guide: www.bugaustralia.com. Tips on packing, transportation, and where to go. Also tons of country-specific travel information.

BootsnAll.com: www.bootsnall.com. Numerous resources for independent travelers, from planning your trip to reporting on it when you get back.

How to See the World: www.artoftravel.com. A compendium of great travel tips, from cheap flights to self defense to interacting with local culture.

Travel Intelligence: www.travelintelligence.net. A large collection of travel writing by distinguished travel writers with an accompanying searchable archive of accommodations in major cities.

Travel Library: www.travel-library.com. A fantastic set of links for general information and trip-planning as well as personal travelogues.

World Hum: www.worldhum.com. An independently produced collection of "travel dispatches from a shrinking planet."

INFORMATION ON AUSTRALIA

Australian Tourist Commission: www.australia.com. Information about Australia and travel including climate, economy, health, and safety concerns.

Australian Whitepages: www.whitepages.com.au. The place to go if you ever need a phone number or address in Australia.

CitySearch Sydney: www.sydney.citysearch.com.au. Enough rated bars, restaurants, museums, and events to make you feel like a local.

Travel Australia: www.travelaustralia.com.au. A comprehensive, searchable source for accommodations, activities, attractions, and tours in every region of Australia.

Embassy of Australia: www.austemb.org. Facts about Australia and travel information related to Australian law and politics.

World Travel Guide: www.travel-guides.com/region/aus.asp. Helpful practical info about Australia, including the major national attractions.

LIFE AND TIMES

Often overlooked in the past by travelers who confined themselves to the Northern Hemisphere, Australia is becoming a wildly popular tourist destination. More and more travelers are making the trek, finding out for themselves that not all Australians are like Crocodile Dundee, and that kangaroos really do inhabit the land as unremarkably as squirrels do up north. A continent, an island, *and* a country, the Land Down Under is home to rich history and a fascinating culture. For tourists, this means that this "jewel" of the Southern Hemisphere has even more to offer than its beautiful beaches, sparkling waters, spectacular national parks, and impressive wildlife. Australia is a must for anyone seeking a destination that so deftly combines natural beauty and cultural dynamism.

HISTORY

ABORIGINAL AUSTRALIA

THE PEOPLE. Although the actual amount of time is subject to debate, the Aboriginal community boasts a long tradition in Australia with the earliest population dating back at least 60,000 years. Archaeologists have unveiled evidence of ancient art, complex burial practices, and even Stone Age boomerangs. Estimates of the Aboriginal population of Australia just prior to European colonization vary widely, from 300,000 to over one million. Aborigines were hunter-gatherers, migrating in search of food and increasing the land's fertility by setting controlled fires. Aborigines have had a crucial role in defining Australian history and culture.

60,000 BC
The first inhabitants are thought to have arrived in Australia.

35,000 BC
Aborigines are thought to have reached Tasmania.

2000 BC
The dingo is the first domesticated animal in Australia.

AD 5
The didgeridoo is invented.

COMMUNITY LIFE. The Aborigines have formed groups largely based on territorial claims. While language did not determine boundaries for these groups, it has been estimated that more than 200 languages, with up to 600 dialects, have defined these groups. Within their tribes, Aborigines divide into smaller groups made up of two or three different families. In place of a system of private land ownership, unwritten charters tie the groups to the territory they cover in their travels. Along with strong ties to the land, there is a significant cultural emphasis on personal relationships, namely those bonds formed through kinship, marriage, and ceremony. The Aboriginal community experienced its perhaps greatest recent achievement in the performance of track star Cathy Freeman in the 2000 Summer Olympics in Sydney. In a triumphant victory, Freeman won the Gold Medal in the 400m and had the honor of igniting the olympic torch during the Opening Ceremonies. She was the first female Aborigine to win a medal for Australia at a worldwide event.

BELIEF SYSTEMS. Although Aboriginal people across Australia have historically belonged to separate groups, each with their own legends, customs, and ceremonies, most of these groups share similar religious beliefs. Aborigines believe the world was created during **The Dreaming,** or Creation Time, a mythological period when powerful ancestral beings shaped the land and populated it with humans, animals, and plants. The **spirit ancestors** provided the people with laws and customs and are the source of the songs, dances, and rituals that are the basis of Aboriginal religious expression. There are three types of sacred land in Aboriginal culture: ceremonial sites, *djang*, and *djang andjamun*. Ceremonial sites are now used for burials, rites of passage, and other events. At *djang* sites, a creator passed through, took shape, and entered or exited the Earth, leaving the site safe to visit. At *djang andjamun* sites, however, the ancestor still lingers, and *djang andjamun* are considered spiritual hazard zones for which there are laws that forbid entry. Since these areas are linked to the ancestors, they are considered sacred sites rather than inheritable territories.

EUROPEAN SETTLEMENT

COLONIZATION

1606
Willem Jansz makes the first recorded European landfall, on Cape York.

EXPLORATION. Chinese explorers were among the first to arrive, but **Dutch** explorers made the first recorded European landfall in 1606, laying claim to "New Holland." In 1616 the Dutch left a memorial at **Shark Bay** (p. 735). In 1642, Dutch explorer **Abel Tasman** sailed south to chart the rest of Australia and discovered a "new" southern island which came to be known as Tasmania. Though he explored Australia's coast, a settlement was never established. In 1770, the English captain **James Cook** explored the eastern coast of the continent aboard the ship *Endeavor*. Cook and his crew of astronomers and scientists discovered and named **Botany Bay** (p. 152), and returned to England with stories of strange plants and animals.

1788
The English First Fleet arrives and founds the first European penal colony under Captain Arthur Phillip.

1806
English naval captain Matthew Flinders becomes the first to circumnavigate the continent.

THE FIRST FLEET. The motives for the British colonization of Australia have been a matter of debate. The traditional explanation is that Britain needed to solve its prison-overcrowding problem, while another explanation suggests that the English hoped to establish a global-navy base with plentiful natural resources and an available work force, particularly prisoners. In any case, the prisons in London were full, and on May 13, 1787, the 11-ship **First Fleet** left from England. Led by **Arthur Phillip,** whom British Home Secretary **Lord Sydney** had appointed to command, the fleet arrived with over 700 convicts in Botany Bay after a grueling eight-month voyage. After local resources were deemed insufficient, Phillip headed north to Port Jackson, raising the British flag in what stands as present-day **Sydney** (p. 110). Commemorating the event, January 26 eventually became **Australia Day,** a major national holiday.

THE CONVICT ERA

BEGINNINGS. Upon arrival in Australia, the convicts and their guards faced a strange and inhospitable land. The colony saw little success: half of the workforce spent the whole time guarding the other half, livestock escaped into the bush, relations with Aborigines deteriorated, and most supply ships were wrecked. The convicts themselves were mainly petty criminals from the slums of London with no agricultural experience. The seeds and cuttings that the fleet had carefully carried across the sea failed in the local climate. Phillip's grand plans for 200-foot-wide streets had to be scrapped; no mill or team of cattle would be available for years.

ABORIGINAL INTERACTION. When the British landed in Australia and claimed the land for the Crown, they did so under a doctrine of ***terra nullius*** (empty land), which meant either that there were no people on the continent, or that inhabitants were mere occupants rather than landowners. Under common law, this conveniently gave the British free reign to take whatever land they wished without the hassle of treaties or agreements. Many Aborigines were relocated, others simply killed; European settlement destroyed watering holes, displaced communities, and introduced numerous diseases. Many Aboriginal children were kidnapped and forced into assimilation programs, a practice continued until relatively late in the 20th century. The history of Aboriginal and white interaction in Tasmania, where the Aborigines had remained isolated for thousands of years, is particularly atrocious; genocide of the Aboriginal population caused their near-complete disappearance within 70 years of contact.

EXPANSION

FREE SETTLERS. After the appointment of Governor Macquarie in 1809, convicts who had served for seven years were allowed to start their lives again as free citizens. England also encouraged free settler emigration with land grants and inexpensive passage for young, single women. Since upkeep of the convicts was an increasingly onerous economic burden, the Crown began to heed protests of free settlers against continued deportation of convicts to Australia. The last criminal-packed ship arrived in 1868, after approximately 165,000 convicts had been sent to Australia.

PROSPERITY. Wool was Australia's major export and by 1845, sheep farming was the most profitable business in the country. The discovery of gold in 1851 triggered a **gold rush,** leading to mass immigration and growing national wealth, ultimately increasing the population two-fold to over 1.1 million in the decade following. Competition for gold inevitably led to conflict, and the 1854 **Eureka Stockade Rebellion** marked Australia's closest brush with civil war. Miners in **Ballarat** (p. 642) formed a collective and built a stockade in protest of the government's licensing fees for miners. Government forces crushed the uprising in a 15-minute clash that cost about two dozen miners their lives.

1817
Australia's first bank, the Bank of New South Wales, opens.

1829
The British Empire claims all of Australia.

1850
The University of Sydney, the country's first university, is founded.

1858
Electric Telegraph links Sydney and Melbourne.

1868
The last convict settlers arrive in Australia.

1880
Bushranger Ned Kelly is hanged.

TWENTIETH CENTURY

UNIFICATION

FEDERATION. Before the formation of a central government, each of Australia's six individual colonies had very little to do

1883
The Sydney-Melbourne rail opens.

1900
The Australian constitution is passed by British Parliament.

1901
Australia becomes a federation on January 1.

1902
Women gain federal suffrage.

1904
Dalgety becomes the new capital.

1907
Photocopying is developed at the University of Sydney.

1909
The nation's first airplane takes off.

1911
Canberra becomes the nation's capital.

1914
Australia enters WWI.

1915
Duke Kahanamoku, famous Hawaiian swimmer, first introduces surfing in Australia.

1920
QANTAS airline is founded.

1923
Vegemite spreads its way across the nation.

with one another, communicating directly with London instead. The **Commonwealth of Australia** was founded on January 1, 1901. Federation had been a difficult process for Australia; the new constitution was only ratified after a decade of debate among the colonies. The constitution united the colonies into six states, all of which are still in place: New South Wales, Queensland, South Australia, Tasmania, Victoria, and Western Australia. The Northern Territory and the Australian Capital Territory are self-governing regions that do not have state status.

SUFFRAGE. In 1902, Australia became the second country in the world (after New Zealand) to grant federal **suffrage to women.** In 1921, Western Australia's **Edith Dircksey Cowan** became the first female in an Australian state parliament.

RACE. When convicts stopped arriving, Europeans encouraged the immigration of Chinese laborers. However, race-based immigration restrictions were soon adopted, especially when **Chinese immigrants** started working the gold fields. By 1888 the "Chinese question" was center stage, and a Queensland journal coined the racist rallying cry, **"White Australia!"** In 1896, immigration restrictions were extended to include all non-whites. The **Immigration Restriction Act of 1901** required immigrants to pass a 50-word dictation test in any European language—chosen at the discretion of the immigration officers. Not surprisingly, most Chinese immigrants failed this highly dubious test.

WORLD WARS

THE GREAT WAR. At the outset of **World War I,** Australia's prime minister declared support for the mother country, saying: "Our duty is quite clear—to gird up our loins and remember that we are Britons." About 330,000 Australians were sent into battle and 60,000 lost their lives. One hundred sixty-five thousand more soldiers were wounded—a shocking percentage of the country's relatively small population. The single worst day of battle was April 25, 1915, when 2000 members of the **Australian and New Zealand Army Corps** (ANZAC) were killed at **Gallipoli,** Turkey, while initiating a campaign that eventually took 8500 Australian lives and forced evacuation of the troops. Australia celebrates **Anzac Day** on April 25 each year to remember their heroism and loss.

WORLD WAR II. A generation later, The Royal Australian Air Force reaffirmed its commitment to Great Britain and its allies in **World War II,** and Australian troops enjoyed victories at Tobruk and El-Alamein in North Africa. After the Japanese attack on Pearl Harbor (Dec. 7, 1941) and the fall of British-protected Singapore (Feb. 15, 1942), Australian citizens became increasingly concerned about safety on their own shores. On February 19, 1942, **Darwin,** the capital of the Northern Territory, suffered the first of many bombings by the Japanese. The US, engaged in the Pacific Theater, became a closer Australian ally. About 30,000 Australian soldiers died during the war.

AFTER 1945

POST-WAR BOOM. The 50s were a time of relative peace and prosperity for Australians, and the era was marked by rapid immigration. In fact, the population nearly doubled in the 30 years following the end of the war, growing from seven million in 1945 to 13.5 million by 1975. Immigrants came first from southern Europe, and later from Asia after the abolition of the "White Australia" policy in 1965.

POWERFUL FRIENDS. Australia has gradually moved its foreign policy allegiances away from the "Mother Country" of Britain to the United States. Australian-American relations were formalized in 1951 with the **Australia-New Zealand-United States** (ANZUS) pact. Consequently, when the United States became embroiled in the **Vietnam** conflict, Australians were drafted, touching off a slowly gathering storm of anti-war protest. These protests led Australian policy makers to steadily refocus their attention eastward as successive governments in the 90s promoted Australian interests in Asia. Their efforts resulted in increasingly important economic ties between the continents, which has also contributed to Asian emigration to Australia.

TODAY

Australia may not hit international headline news with great frequency, but no traveler should arrive in the country without brushing up on recent history and current events.

TERRORISM. The bombing of a nightclub in Bali's heavily touristed beach district in October 2002—the largest terrorist attack since September 11, 2001—carried grim significance for Australia. Bali is a popular destination for Australian tourists; approximately half of the 200 victims of the attack were Australian. The bombing was widely seen as a proxy attack on Australia, an active member of the US-led coalition to depose Saddam Hussein's regime. Fifteen hundred Australian troops were committed to the **war in Iraq.** The issue divided the nation, and massive peace rallies were held in all capital cities.

IN THE PRIME. In 2004 John Howard won his fourth term as Australia's prime minister, making him the most electorally successful prime minister in nearly 20 years. The country has since seen industrial relation reforms, full privatization of the telecommunications conglomerate Telstra, and the outlawing of same-sex civil unions.

FLAMING BUSH. January 2005 brought sweeping fires across the Eyre Peninsula bush, the most destructive fires seen by Australia in more than two decades. The subsequent deaths of nine citizens called for significant reform in bushfire-fighting protocol by the Country Fire Service.

1926
First Miss Australia contest is held.

1929
The Great Depression hits.

1939
Oz enters WWII.

1942
Daylight Savings Time introduced as wartime measure.

1943
Damien Parer, a wartime cinematographer, wins Australia's first Oscar.

1945
Australia becomes a founding member of the UN.

1946
Australia's Norman Makin is voted first President of the UN Security Council.

1951
Australia signs the ANZUS treaty with the US and NZ.

1956
Melbourne hosts Summer Olympics.

1958
Australian researchers invent the Black Box Flight Recorder.

1964
The Beatles tour Oz.

1970
Anti-Vietnam War protests lead to largest demonstrations in Australian history.

1973
The world-famous Sydney Opera House opens.

1973
The federal voting age drops from 21 to 18.

1977
"Advance Australia Fair" becomes the national anthem.

1995
The Northern Territory legalizes voluntary euthanasia.

2000
Sydney hosts the Summer Olympics.

2004
Prime Minister John Howard is elected to his fourth term in office.

2005
Sixteen people are charged with planning terrorist attacks in Sydney and Melbourne.

PEOPLE

The Commonwealth of Australia is home to 20.3 million people, 1% of whom are indigenous Australians. Immigration has defined the Australian narrative, with almost a quarter of the population born overseas. A formal immigration policy began after WWII out of the need to fill the sparsely populated landmass. This first wave of immigrants came primarily from Europe, the US, Turkey, and the former USSR. In recent years, increasing numbers of migrants have arrived from Asia. Asians now account for about 7% of the Australian population.

DIVERSITY. Multiculturalism as a planned government project of cultural diversity is today regarded as a cornerstone of the Australian national identity. Yet as much as immigration and cultural integration have defined Australia's history from the beginning, deep-seated racial tensions have become a reality of widespread concern. From the beaches of Sydney to its inner-city neighborhoods, demonstrations against Muslim Australians, particularly those 300,000 of Lebanese descent, as well as widespread discrimination against Aboriginal groups, have received international attention and caused a severe crisis of conscience for such a diverse nation.

DEMOGRAPHICS. Australia's population density is 2.6 people per square kilometer. In comparison, the US averages 28.2 people per square kilometer, and the UK a whopping 250.8. Almost 90% of Australians live in urban areas, and the suburbs are still growing. The vast majority live on or relatively near the coasts, particularly the east coast—the massive, inhospitable desert in the center of the country is perhaps the main reason for this coastal population concentration.

English (see **'Strine,** p. 762, for some quirks of Australian English) is Australia's only national language, spoken in 85% of Australian homes. According to the most recent census in 2001, about 68% of Australians declare themselves **Christians; non-Christian** religions comprise more than 5%. The rest (about 27%) either identified with no religion or chose not to respond.

CULTURE

FOOD AND DRINK

Though Australian cuisine has traditionally been regarded as uninspiring and reminiscent of English "pub food," each new wave of immigrants has introduced a new spectrum of flavors to the Australian palate. European and Middle Eastern arrivals spiced up the Australian menu in the post-WWII boom. Japanese, Thai, Malay, Vietnamese, and Chinese restaurants are also now abundant, particularly in cosmopolitan urban centers.

ON THE MENU. An emerging Modern Australian cuisine involves the use of high-quality fare indigenous to Australia prepared in a fusion of Asian styles. French, German, and Italian immigrants have influenced development of Australian vineyards, which are gaining more and more renown worldwide.

Breakfast, or **"brekkie,"** is usually not eaten out, and most restaurants don't open until noon except in the larger cities. **Vegemite,** an infamous yeast by-product of the beer-brewing process, spread thinly on toast is the quintessential Aussie breakfast. The evening meal of **"tea"** is the largest meal of the day. Beware of ordering only an **"entree"**; it's an appetizer in Australia. **Tipping** in Australian restaurants or pubs is rare and never expected. Despite Australia's carnivorous reputation, **vegetarians** won't go hungry as the sheer variety of culinary influences from abroad have ushered in tasty salads, pasta dishes, and other varieties of ethnic cuisine to menus throughout Australia.

AUSTRALIAN CUISINE

FRUIT, MEAT, AND SEAFOOD. The Australian continent boasts a cornucopia of fruit. Tropical north Queensland produces the most exotic offerings, including custard apples, lychees, passion fruit, star fruit, coconuts, quandong, and pineapples. Meat and seafood are generally cheap and high quality. Though Australian beef is world-class fare, contents of the **meat-pie** may be of more dubious origin. Its doughy shell is often doused with a ketchup-like tomato sauce to disguise the taste. Veal and lamb are popular and available at uncommonly low prices. Seafood is an Australian favorite, with regional specialities including king prawns (shrimp), Balmain Bugs (a type of lobster), and Barramundi (a freshwater fish).

BUSH TUCKER. Coastal Aborigines have eaten crayfish, **yabbies** (freshwater shrimp), and fish for centuries. Neophytes to the cuisine may find **witchetty grubs** (ghost moth larvae) and **wild magpie goose eggs** less appetizing. Australia has recently discovered a taste for its "exotic" indigenous food, and with "bush tucker" (indigenous bush foods) as the new urban catch phrase, menus are increasingly inclined to incorporate Aboriginal wild foods like bunya nuts, Kakadu plums, and wild rosella flowers with specialty meats such as the exotic yet frequent kangaroo filet, crocodile meat, and Northern Territory buffalo.

CHEAP EATS. Australia offers plenty of ways to eat well on a budget. Self-catering is easy, as most budget accommodations offer kitchen facilities. Public BBQs are usually available at parks, beaches, and campsites. Your best bet for an inexpensive midday meal out is a pub **counter lunch,** which usually entails generous portions of "meat and two veg." **Fish 'n' chips** is another Aussie institution and is available at any **takeaway** (takeout restaurant). Basic Australian fish 'n' chips is often made from flake, a type of shark. The fish is battered, fried, and served with British-style chips (thick french fries). Finally, take advantage of Australian-style bakeries, which offer breads baked with cheese, onion, or other savory additions, sandwich-ready **rolls** (like hamburger buns), and true-blue treats like the **lamington** (coconut-covered chunk of pound cake dipped in chocolate) or **pavlova** (giant meringue).

BEVERAGES

COFFEE AND TEA. Ordering "just coffee" is nearly impossible in Australia, particularly in the cappuccino culture of the major cities. If you need help ordering, see **Cool Beans,** p. 761. Tea, often affectionately referred to as a **cuppa,** is also very popular. Sweet-toothed fans of cafe culture may opt instead for **iced chocolate,** a frothy and creamy concoction of ice cream, cream, and chocolate syrup.

BEER. Australia produces some delicious brews, and Australians consume them readily. The best place to "share a coldie with your mates" is at one of the omnipresent Aussie **pubs.** Traditional payment etiquette is the **shout,** in which drinking mates alternate rounds. If the beach is more your style, throw a **slab**

(24-pack) in the **Esky** (ice chest) and head to the shore. Although Foster's was marketed worldwide with the slogan, "Foster's: Australian for Beer," other locals brews are gaining in popularity and are definitely worth a try. For more beer terminology and information on the types of beer available, consult **Terms of Enbeerment,** p. 761.

WINE. Australian **wines** are now among the best in the world. Overseas export started soon after the first vineyards began to produce wine in the early 1800s, and the industry gained renown after a post-WWII influx of European talent. The **Hunter Valley** (p. 169), the **Barossa** and **Clare Valleys** (p. 487), the **Swan** and **Margaret Rivers** (p. 705), and the **Derwent** and **Tamar Valleys** (p. 544) possess some of the best Aussie vineyards. Many cafes and restaurants advertise that they are **BYO,** or "bring your own," meaning patrons should bring their own bottle of wine.

CUSTOMS AND ETIQUETTE

PUBLIC BEHAVIOR AND TABOOS. Australians are known for their friendly informality. Most people initiate a first-name basis immediately with a refreshing lack of pretension. There's no need to **tip;** once regarded as offensive due to the Australians' disregard for rank, tipping is now acceptable but not expected. While it's generally difficult to offend an Aussie, it's best to avoid public pronouncements on **sensitive topics,** such as race relations, refugees, or involvement in the Middle East. Extending your **middle finger** at someone (also known as "giving the finger") is considered very rude and might get you into trouble. Finally, **littering** in this environmentally conscious society is not taken lightly.

WHAT TO WEAR. For women, almost anything is acceptable as long as it covers the essential parts—tube tops, halters, and tank tops are all common. For men, pants or shorts are the norm. **Cossies/swimmers/togs** (affectionate terms for Australia's favorite garment, the swimsuit) are usually appropriate only at the beach.

SPORTS AND RECREATION

Sport is an essential part of Australian national identity all year round. In winter, Western Australia, South Australia, and Victoria catch **footy fever** for **Australian Rules Football,** while New South Wales and Queensland traditionally follow **rugby league** and **rugby union.** In summer, **cricket** is the spectator sport of choice across the nation. Tune in to H. G. Nelson and Roy Slaven's Sunday afternoon Triple-J radio show *This Sporting Life* for a comedic taste of Aussie sport culture, or check out the hugely popular *Footy Show*, on television's Channel 9.

CRICKET. The uninitiated may have trouble making sense of a sport in which players can "bowl a maiden or a googly to the stumps," but visitors won't be able to avoid the enthusiasm for these contests that can last anywhere from an afternoon to five days. Each summer, cricket captures the headlines as international teams arrive for a **full tour,** consisting of five matches, one each in Melbourne, Sydney, Perth, Adelaide, and Brisbane in December and January. Toward the end of the summer, the country turns its attention to national cricket matches and the **Sheffield Shield** (now known as the **Pura Cup**) finals in March.

AUSTRALIAN RULES FOOTBALL. In Victoria, South Australia, and Western Australia, the **Australian Football League (AFL)** teams fill the winter void that the end of the cricket season leaves. Played on large cricket ovals between teams of 18 players, the game was originally designed to keep cricket players in shape in the off-season. The **AFL Grand Final,** in September, is a stunning spectacle at the home of Australian sport, the **Melbourne Cricket Ground** (p. 590).

RUGBY. According to legend, **rugby** was born one glorious day in 1823 when an inspired (or perhaps frustrated) student in Rugby, England, picked up a soccer ball and ran it into the goal. Since then, rugby has evolved into an intricately punishing game with two main variants: 15-player **rugby union,** and 13-player **rugby league.** On the international level, Australia has had a long history of dominance in the sport, winning the World Cup in 1999 and reaching the finals in 2003. Major tournaments such as the **Tri-nation Series** (Australia, South Africa, and New Zealand) pack stadiums and pubs and grab the attention of devoted fans around the world. At home, the National Rugby league attracts a large following, especially in New South Wales and Queensland. The national league competition culminates in September's **National Rugby League (NRL) final.** The only match that comes close to matching the intensity or popularity of the NRL final is June's **State of Origin** series, when Queensland takes on New South Wales. Both games promise a mix of blood, mud, and beer.

SURFING. Australia is famous for its surfing, which is for some a competitive sport and for others a great way to spend a weekend. Big waves and challenging surf are the norm all over the coast, particularly on the famous **Gold Coast** (p. 337). Local surf shops are generally the best sources of information on competitions and conditions, though the internet can also be useful. Visit **www.surfingaustralia.com.au** for comprehensive coverage of competitions, camps, lessons, and conditions. Web surfers can also find information on the **Association of Surfing Professionals (ASP) Australasia,** the premier pro circuit in the region.

MORE SPORTS. Since the Australian national team's recent 2006 World Cup appearance (the first since 1974) in Germany, **soccer** has become a point of national interest and pride with the entire continent backing the "Socceroos." Their performance, the best in the nation's history, instantly vaulted Australian soccer to a level of international prominence. Melbourne hosts one of the premier Grand Slam events in **tennis,** the **Australian Open,** each January, attracting the world's best players to the nation's hard courts. Most towns also have a horse racing track, and on the first Tuesday in November, the entire country stops to watch the prestigious **Melbourne Cup** horse race, where fashionable and outlandish attire sometimes seems more important than the competition. Melbourne is also home to Formula One racing's **Australian Grand Prix** in early March, during which Australians satisfy their need for speed. On Boxing Day (the day after Christmas), half of Australia's amateur sailing community fills Sydney Harbour with billowing white sails to begin the **Sydney-to-Hobart yacht race,** the highlight of the already full calendar of water sports. The sport of **triathlon** has also become immensely popular, and Australia hosts two of the biggest endurance competitions in the world: Ironman Australia in Port Macquarie, NSW, and Ironman Western Australia in Busselton, WA. Attracting athletes from around the world, these grueling races force competitors to swim, bike, and run over 140 miles.

THE ARTS

Australia is a young nation still seeking a balance between distinctively Australian and more universal themes in its national arts. Historically, European influences shaped the work of non-Aboriginal Australian artists and writers. Today, Australian artists and writers work in a variety of styles and genres, reflecting the nation's diffuse identity and evolving national consciousness.

LITERATURE

THE DREAMING. The literature of indigenous Australians is comprised of over 50,000 years of **oral tradition** and is intertwined with Aboriginal conceptions of spirituality. The Dreaming involves legends of creation set in a mythological time where the landscape is endowed with mythic and symbolic status. Narratives of the Dreaming represent a complex network of beliefs, practices, and customs that define Aboriginal spiritual beliefs and unique connection with the land.

BUSH BALLADS. Possibly the first true Australian literature was the bush ballad, a form of poetry that celebrated the working man and the superiority of bush life to urban life. The most famous of these ballads is AB Banjo Paterson's **Waltzing Matilda,** often considered the unofficial Australian national anthem. Henry Lawson celebrated bush life through both poetry and short story, with works like **The Drover's Wife** providing a popular mythology for this heavily urbanized society.

EARLY NOVELISTS. Early colonial novels tended to focus on the convict experience, seen both in the first Australian novel, **Henry Savory's** *Quintus Servinton,* as well as perhaps the first real Australian classic, **Marcus Clarke's** *For the Term of His Natural Life.* In the early 20th century, two female writers highlighted the changing face of the newly independent nation. Early feminist **Miles Franklin's** *My Brilliant Career* is a portrait of an independent and strong-willed woman seeking emancipation, while another female writer, **Henry Handel Richardson,** documented an immigrant family's history in *The Fortunes of Richard Mahoney.*

TRAVEL WRITING WITH A TWIST

In a Sunburned Country, by Bill Bryson (2001). With an eye for detail and historical accuracy, along with the insatiable sense of humor to back it all up, Bryson takes on the road less-traveled and heads to the Outback for an unforgettable journey. From the Nullarbor Plain to the cities of the coast, this accomplished traveler and prolific writer lends his dry, observational wit to an exploration of the Land Down Under.

CONTEMPORARY FICTION. Since WWII, Australian literature has adopted a more outward-looking and cosmopolitan voice. *Voss,* by Nobel Prize winner **Patrick White,** is Australian in its depiction of the bleak emptiness of the center and universal in its treatment of individual isolation. **Thomas Keneally** writes with a strong social conscience; his *The Chant of Jimmie Blacksmith* is a gut-wrenching portrayal of domestic, turn-of-the-century race relations, while his Holocaust epic *Schindler's Ark* was later made into the film *Schindler's List.* Two-time Booker Prize winner **Peter Carey** is best known for his dark satire, *Oscar and Lucinda,* and more recently, *The True History of the Kelly Gang,* an imaginative account of outlaw and Australian folk hero Ned Kelly. **David Malouf's** work explores the relation between cultural centers and peripheries in the immigrant experience, with his background as a poet emerging in novels like *Remembering Babylon.* Australia's unofficial poet laureate, **Les Murray,** celebrates the anti-authoritarian with his "larrakin" characters and brought much-deserved attention to Australian poetry from every era, while the late **Judith Wright** maintains a niche for a female poetic voice.

POPULAR MUSIC

ROCK 'N' ROLL. Popular music in Australia developed in the late 50s, epitomized by rocker **Johnny O'Keefe** (hit single "Shout"), whose sound took the country by storm. The British explosion in the 60s also caused an Australian ripple effect, with **The Easybeats** scoring big internationally with their infectious tune, "Friday on My Mind." The wholesome acoustic sounds of **The Seekers** led the folk bandwagon.

PUB ROCK. In the late 70s, **AC/DC** hit the charts with blues-influenced heavy metal grown out of pub culture. **The Skyhooks, Cold Chisel,** and **Australian Crawl** gained local fame and influence with Aussie-themed hits that refused to emulate sounds from across the seas. In the 80s, politically aware pub-rock bands like **Midnight Oil** became famous for their energetic and enthusiastic live shows. **Men at Work** broke into the American music scene and paved the way for superbands like **INXS** in the late 80s and thereafter.

THE 90S: INDIGENOUS AND INDIE. After the success of Arnhem Land group **Yothu Yindi** in the 90s, who blended dance music and rock in politically conscious hits like "Treaty," indigenous music was seen as commercially viable. Other similarly politicized Aboriginal "bush rock" artists are the **Coloured Stones,** the **Warrumpi Band,** and **Archie Roach.** Indigenous pop artists in the charts recently include **Shakaya** and **Christine Anu.** At the same time, indie rock was made popular by such artists as **Silverchair, Severed Heads,** and **Savage Garden.**

RECENT HITS. International purveyors of pop include **Delta Goodrem** and the pint-sized Aussie icon **Kylie Minogue,** while rock is represented with such bands as **The Vines, Jet,** and the increasingly world-popular **John Butler Trio. Nick Cave and the Bad Seeds** carry a fair-sized European following, while country artist **Kasey Chambers** is popular in the US. Australia's nation-wide radio station, **Triple J** (www.triplej.net.au), plays contemporary local music and actively promotes new acts.

VISUAL ARTS

ABORIGINAL ART. Aboriginal art is not exclusively aesthetic; it also serves educational and spiritual functions. Australia's most well-known Aboriginal artist, **Albert Namatjira,** is famous for his Western-style depictions of Outback landscapes. His work made him a pioneer for the Aboriginal community, and he received full Australian citizenship in 1957. While traditionally limited in the public consciousness to "bark paintings," artists like Namatjira have pushed the limits of Aboriginal art, which is now celebrated in its many forms, including mural art, body painting, and rock painting.

AUSTRALIAN IMPRESSIONISTS. The **Heidelberg School** of Australian impressionists, led by **Arthur Streeton,** depicted distinctively Australian landscapes, usually on plein-air canvases. **Tom Roberts** found inspiration in the red land of the cattle station, while **Frederick McCubbin** drew on the thin forests of smoky green gum trees. These three, along with **Charles Conder,** ushered in a tremendously productive period in the history of Australian art during the late 19th century.

CONTEMPORARY ARTISTS. Possibly the most famous Australian work is **Sidney Nolan's** Ned Kelly series, which tells the story of the folk hero's exploits, final capture, and execution through a series of vibrantly colored paintings. Other artists in the last half-century who have found a distinctively Australian idiom include the acclaimed but controversial **Brett Whitely, Russell Drysdale, Arthur Boyd,** and abstract artist **John Colburn.** First awarded in 1921, the Archibald Prize represents the pinnacle of Australian art and is awarded for special achievement in portraiture.

FILM

SILENT ERA. Given the national love of a good yarn, it's little wonder that Australia also boasts one of the world's most prolific and innovative film industries. The world's first feature film, Charles Tait's *The Story of the Kelly Gang* (1906), was an Australian production. Australian directors during this period pioneered the field with classic productions such as Raymond Langford's *The Sentimental Bloke* and Norman Dawn's *For the Term of His Natural Life*.

POST-WAR AND NEW-WAVE. Despite auspicious beginnings, Aussie films suffered budget woes until foreign financing picked up in the post-WWII economic boom. Films like Leslie Norman's *The Shiralee*, a joint British-Australian production about a fancy-free wanderer, spurred questions about whether local productions should aspire to a national perspective or a more universal one. Australian film didn't emerge from this crisis of confidence until the 70s, when generous government support ushered in the "New Wave" of films like Peter Weir's eerie *Picnic at Hanging Rock* and Bruce Beresford's Boer War epic *Breaker Morant*.

AUSSIE STARS. Australian movie stars with recent international success include: **Geoffrey Rush** (*Shine, Shakespeare in Love, Pirates of the Caribbean, Munich*), **Cate Blanchett** (*Elizabeth*, the *Lord of the Rings* series, *The Aviator*), **Nicole Kidman** (*Moulin Rouge!, The Hours, Cold Mountain*), **Russell Crowe,** born a Kiwi but raised an Aussie (*Gladiator, A Beautiful Mind, Master and Commander, Cinderella Man*), **Guy Pearce** (*Memento*), **Heath Ledger** (*10 Things I Hate About You, A Knight's Tale, Brokeback Mountain*), **Hugh Jackman** (*X-Men* series, *Kate and Leopold*), **Toni Collette** (*About a Boy, The Sixth Sense*), **Hugo Weaving,** born in Nigeria but relocated Down Under (*The Matrix, Lord of the Rings* series, *V for Vendetta*), and **Mel Gibson** (*Conspiracy Theory, Braveheart, The Patriot*, dir. *The Passion of the Christ*).

BOX-OFFICE BLITZ. After the critical successes of the 70s, the 80s brought Australian films into commercial favor at the box office, both at home and abroad, with hits like *Mad Max* (dir. George Miller) and *Crocodile Dundee* (dir. Peter Faiman). Films of the 90s were personal, Australia-specific, and often quirky—especially in intriguing character studies like *Muriel's Wedding* and *Shine*. Recent productions, such as New South Wales-native Baz Luhrmann's *Moulin Rouge!* and Phillip Noyce's *Rabbit-Proof Fence*, demonstrate the multiplicity of themes and styles present in contemporary Australian film.

ADDITIONAL RESOURCES

GENERAL HISTORY

The Fatal Shore: The Epic of Australia's Founding, by Robert Hughes (1988). A vast and entertaining tableau of Australia's early history that looks at the effects of the convict transportation system on colonists and Aborigines.

A Short History of Australia, by Manning Clark (1987). A considerably condensed version of Clark's six-volume history; voted the most influential work of Australian nonfiction in a recent poll.

Damned Whores and God's Police: the Colonization of Women in Australia, by Anne Summers (1975). A landmark work that details the treatment of women in Australian society from the colonial era to contemporary times.

Prehistory of Australia, by John Mulvaney and Johan Kamminga (1999). Offers a detailed account of the development of Aboriginal culture over the course of the last 40,000 years, from the continent's initial colonization to current issues of Aboriginal control over archaeological fieldwork.

The Rush that Never Ended: A History of Australian Mining, by Geoffrey Blainey (2003). A chronicle of an industry that has shaped Australian history and culture from the beginning as well as defined much of the continent's geography in the process.

TRAVEL BOOKS

The Songlines, by Bruce Chatwin (1987). Outback travel story based on the "dreaming-tracks" or "songlines" of Aboriginal Australia. Combines history, science, and thought.

Sydney, by Jan Morris (1992). An impressionistic, elegant account of Australia's greatest city that provides a portrait of modern Sydney illuminated through historical details.

Tracks: A Woman's Solo Trek Across 1,700 Miles of Australian Outback, by Robyn Davidson (1995). Armed with four camels and accompanied by a National Geographic photographer, Robyn Davidson crosses the desert and lives to tell the tale.

The Confessions of a Beachcomber, by E.J. Banfield (2001). Following Thoreau's example, Banfield ditches a stressful life and heads for the sun and sand of Dunk Island.

From Oppression to Reconciliation

In acquiring the Australian landmass in 1788, the British acted upon two assumptions that had served their interests well in North America. First, though the native peoples (dubbed "Australian Aborigines") evidently had "customs," these did not amount to a system of law and government, which would entitle them to indigenous sovereignty. Second, they roamed the land, hunting and gathering, and did not cultivate crops; therefore, the land was not their "property." Aborigines, who had previously occupied the continent for 50,000 years, suffered greatly under the British colonists. Investors in the wool industry rapidly dispersed flocks over their hunting grounds. When Aborigines killed these animals, the colonists responded with force ranging from imprisonment to summary execution. When Aborigines attempted trade (including men offering the sexual hospitality of their women), colonists did not honor reciprocity. Australia's pastoral and mining frontiers were very often marked by greed, racism, misunderstanding and suspicion. Lacking firearms, horses, and fortifications, Aborigines were at a military disadvantage. These "frontier" conditions could be found in Australia as recently as the eve of WWII. The last known (unpunished) mass killing of Aborigines was in 1928, near Alice Springs. Twenty thousand slain is a reasonable estimate of the Aboriginal toll over the 140-year war of invasion, about ten times the known toll on colonists. Disease has probably been an even greater killer. There were three waves of smallpox—around 1789, 1830, and the late 1860s—against which Aborigines had neither immunity nor systems of care. Influenza, measles, and venereal diseases brought further devestation.

Aborigines lucky enough to survive the violence and diseases faced colonial authorities unsure of what to do about them. The first wave of Christian missionaries had found them difficult to convert. Rangers began cautiously to employ them. "Half-castes"—children of (usually) white men and Aboriginal women—were trained in what were considered useful occupations so that they could be absorbed into the wider population.

Through it all Aborigines tried to maintain and adapt their communal life. They sought land security, requesting to learn the colonists' agriculture, as well as education and health services. However, Aborigines' efforts to become members of their communities were hindered by both popular prejudice and restrictive laws. Aborigines found that their extended kinship networks were often their only source of emotional and material security. Where land security and services were granted, it was usually poorly funded and badly supervised. One form of "help" is now recalled with particular shame by most Australians. From 1897, state after state removed children from Aboriginal parents, reasoning that it was the state's duty to "rescue" younger Aboriginals from their cultural milieu. The emotional pain of these "Stolen Generations" got a respectful public hearing in Australia in 1997; the practice of racially-motivated removal had ceased by the 1970s.

Despite this ill treatment, some Aborigines developed sufficient loyalty to "King and Country" to enlist for the first and second World Wars. After WWII, the Australian government began to dismantle discriminatory legal and institutional devices. Aborigines who had "risen" to white standards were now rewarded with assimilation. This policy's most important benefit was admission to the social security system at a time when economic change was destroying the rural job market. However, assimilation required Aborigines to renounce their claims to land and to comply with prejudicial views of their heritage. Remote Aborigines, as well as those with longer exposure to colonial authority, refused assimilation, instead proposing the alternative policy of self-determination.

Since the 1970s, Australian governments have acknowledged Aboriginal title to about one fifth of the continent. Some land-based industries enable Aboriginal pride and modest prosperity, but most Aborigines must find their opportunities in towns and cities. There, old prejudices compete with new understandings, sincere regrets about the past, and more or less helpful affirmations of the worth of "Aboriginality." Disproportionately unemployed, imprisoned, and afflicted by physical and emotional disorders, Aboriginal Australians still find that the colonial past weighs heavily. But a communal sense of being a "surviving" people remains strong.

Tim Rowse *works in the History Program, Research School of Social Sciences at the Australian National University. His publications on Australian history include studies of colonial policy in Central Australia and a biography of H.C. Coombs.*

GREAT OUTDOORS

Australia's myriad ecosystems provide unparalleled opportunities for hiking, water sports, and off-roading—often hundreds of kilometers from another living human being. Nature lovers are rarely disappointed; the country's 50-million-year isolation from the rest of the planet has allowed many species to evolve, making it home to some of the most extraordinary plants and animals on earth.

Australia's relatively recent contact with the outside world, however, has upset its delicate ecology, presenting an enormous challenge: it is believed that at least 13 species have become extinct since European settlement. The government has recently started working to safeguard Australia's biodiversity.

This section provides travelers with useful information about Australian wildlife, plants, natural wonders, outdoor and adventure activities, and camping essentials. It also includes important advice for navigating Australia's rougher roads and avoiding tour scams, as well as a glossary of Australian outdoors terminology.

THE AUSTRALIAN GREAT OUTDOORS AT A GLANCE

- The **duck-billed platypus** is a venomous mammal. Males have spurs on the heel of each hind leg that they use to inject poison into adversaries.
- The bite of the **Tasmanian Devil** is roughly equal in power to the chomp of a crocodile.
- The venom of the **Taipan snake,** found in Queensland and the Northern Territory, is the most deadly in the world. Venom from one snake is enough to kill millions of mice.
- Over **800 species of birds** are found in Australia.
- The **Golden Orb Spider** comes the closest of any animal to spinning gold: the golden silk with which they spin the world's largest webs is almost as strong as Kevlar.
- All of the world's 10 **deadliest snakes** are found in Australia.
- The **Great Barrier Reef** is the largest living organism in the world; the reef covers an area larger than Italy and is visible from outer space.
- Australia's largest **cattle station,** Strangeray Springs Station in South Australia, is only slightly smaller than Belgium.
- The town of Tully, Queensland, holds the average annual **rainfall** record for the continent, averaging almost 12 ft. per year.

PLANTS

FLOWERS. Wildflowers are abundant in fertile areas of Australia. Western Australia in particular stands out for its variety; the landscape is painted annually with **swamp bottlebrush, kangaroo paw, Ashby's banksia,** and nearly 10,000 others. Yellow and pink **everlastings** cover fields across the country, while rare **spider orchids,** hidden in the forest, are only found by the most persistent botany-buffs.

TREES AND OTHER FLORA. Dominating forests from coast to coast, the **eucalyptus** (or **gum tree**) amazes biologists with its successful adaptation to diverse environments. The majestic **karri** soars to over 50m along well-watered valleys, while the **mallee** gum tends to grow in stunted copses across scrubland. The characteristically bulging trunk and splayed branches of the **boab** mark the horizon, particularly in The Kimberley (p. 746), Western Australia's arid region to the north.

In the drier areas of the southeast, a common species of the **acacia** tree known as the **golden wattle** is distinguished by its fragrant blossom, which happens to be Australia's national flower. Perhaps the most rare and unusual tree in Australia is the **Wollemi Pine,** discovered only a few years ago by scientists who previously thought that the species was extinct (see Wollemi National Park, p. 167). Other trees common to the bush and coastal thickets include **banksias, tea trees,** and **grevillias.** Feathery and almost pine-like in appearance, **casuarinas** also exist in multiple habitats. In temperate, rain-fed stretches of Victoria and Tasmania, valleys of tall, dinosaur-era **tree ferns** loom overhead. The **mangrove,** found along parts of Australia's tropical coasts, has adapted readily to its unfavorable environment, its stilt-like trunks clinging tenaciously to the briny mud of alluvial swamps. Australia also has wide expanses of land with few, if any, trees. The arid Outback is dominated instead by dense tufts of **spinifex** grasses. Another common plant is the **saltbush,** a hearty shrub pivotal in converting harsh habitats to livestock pastures.

Most of Australia's large tree species have trunks that are lighter in color than their leaves, which usually grow high above the ground. The overall effect is quite different than that of European or North American forests. Here **bushwalkers** find themselves surrounded by white and gray rather than brown and green.

DANGEROUS ANIMALS

While Australia is home to some of the world's most deadly creatures, travelers who take adequate safety precautions have little reason to worry. Remember that some of the most dangerous animals are also some of the most harmless looking. When exploring, keep a respectful distance from the wildlife.

Much of the danger associated with smaller land animals can be decreased by minimizing exposed skin, so wear boots, long pants, and long sleeves while hiking. If bitten or stung, it is best to take the offending creature to the hospital with you (if you are not in danger of being bitten or stung again) so that doctors can administer the correct treatment. The following list enumerates potentially harmful Australian creatures, as well as information about appropriate safety precautions.

IF YOU GIVE A CROC A COOKIE, HE'LL BITE YOUR ARM OFF. While some animals may be safer to approach than others, creating domestic habits in wildlife is never a good idea. In addition to provoking attacks, feeding or interacting with wild animals can throw off the delicate balances of ecosystems and decrease the appropriate fear of humans that keeps them out of cities and your campsite. Feeding wild animals can also make them dependent on food from humans and therefore unable to fend for themselves.

Ticks and mites: Sure, snakes are scary, but small animals can be harmful too. Mites and ticks vary in size, from barely visible to a centimeter across. They are found all over Australia, particularly in eastern coastal areas, and can carry **scrub typhus.** Female **scrub ticks** can also inject a toxin that can cause paralysis. Be particularly vigilant if camping or hiking in the bush. Symptoms of a tick bite vary, but can include headache, nausea, swelling, and itchiness. **Safety information:** Wearing light-colored clothing makes it easier to spot ticks. Spray yourself with a repellent that contains DEET. Don't touch dead or rotting wood, and avoid sitting directly on the ground or on logs. Check your skin for lumps or swelling when hiking or camping. Seek medical attention if you develop symptoms of tick paralysis (weakness, swollen lymph nodes, fever, flu-like symptoms, partial paralysis) or scrub typhus (headache, muscle pain, fever, gastrointestinal discomfort). **Potential Antidote:** If infested with small larval-stage ticks (grass ticks), take a 45min. bath with 1 cup of baking soda.

Snakes: Australia is home to the world's most poisonous snakes, but the majority of species are scared enough of humans that they will slither away at the sound of footsteps. If cornered, however, some will attack in self-defense. Snakes are of greatest concern in the Wet (see When to Go, p. 272). **Safety information:** Avoid walking through brush or grass too tall or dense to allow you to clearly see where you are walking. Step on (rather than over) logs, as snakes often bask next to them. If bitten, tightly wrap the wounded area, working the bandage down to the tip of the limb and back up to the next joint to help slow the spread of venom. Seek medical attention immediately, and keep the affected area immobile. Do not try to suck out the venom or clean the bite, and don't panic—most snake bites can be treated effectively if dealt with quickly. Bites from unidentified snakes should *always* be treated as potentially dangerous.

Spiders: The famous **Golden Orb Spider** can grow to be as big as a child's head but poses little threat to humans. The **funnel-web** and **redback** are among the most dangerous. The funnel-web is oval-shaped with brown or gray markings, favors cool, wet, sheltered places in eastern Australia (including Tasmania), and can cause serious illness and death. The redback (common throughout Australia, especially in urban areas) is so-called because of its red-striped back (sometimes brown or orange-striped). **Safety information:** Funnel-web bite symptoms include pain, sweating, excessive salivation, abdominal discomfort, vomiting, and mouth numbness. Redback bites can be treated with an antivenom. If bitten, apply an ice pack and seek immediate medical attention. Symptoms include pain, swelling, sweating, fever, headache, and nausea. Any spider bite should be examined by a doctor.

Crocodiles: Saltwater crocodiles, a.k.a. **estuarine crocodiles** or **salties** (some Aussies refer to them as "snapping handbags"), actually live in both salt and freshwater, and can grow to lengths of over 7m. Freshwater crocodiles **(freshies)** are found only in freshwater; though they will bite if provoked, they generally present little danger to adults. Crocodiles are found almost exclusively in the tropical north of Australia, although they range farther inland than you might expect (hundreds of kilometers, especially during the Wet). **Safety information:** Salties are difficult to see and will attack without provocation. When in croc territory, always camp, prepare food, and wash dishes more than 50m from water, and at least 2m above the high water mark. Do not swim in croc territory unless the state parks service has posted signs indicating that it is safe. Be particularly careful during the **breeding season** (Sept.-Apr.), and at night, when crocs are most active. A good way to identify dangerous areas is to look for mud slides where crocs have entered and exited the water. When **crossing a stream** in a 4WD, stay inside your vehicle—even if stuck, you're better off waiting for another car to provide assistance than attempting to dislodge your vehicle amid snapping crocs (if you're stuck in a stream in a remote area, well, good luck, mate).

Sharks: While sharks generally do not bother humans unless provoked or attracted by blood, several shark attacks occur each year in Australia. **Safety information:** Lifeguards at popular beaches generally keep good watch, but never swim outside the flagged areas. Exit the water immediately if you are cut or bleeding, or if you see a fin.

Dingoes: Believed to be descendants of wild Asian dogs, dingoes probably found their way to the continent 5000 years ago as the result of trade between Aboriginal and Indonesian peoples. Only 4975 years later, they found their way into pop culture when defendants in a notorious murder case claimed that a dingo had eaten their baby. Dingoes pose little threat to adults but can injure or even kill small children. **Safety information:** When in dingo country, pack away all food and keep fishing bait off the ground.

Blue-Ringed Octopus: At rest, the blue-ringed octopus is normally yellow or brown; the bright blue rings appear only when the animal is about to attack. Though small (from the size of a pea to 10 in. across) and often pretty, they carry enough poison to kill 25 adults (or one marine biology class) at any given time. Their painless bite can penetrate a wetsuit and is followed by paralysis, respiratory arrest, and death. **Safety information:** Blue-ringed octopi can vary in color and size. Be careful when walking on the beach. Do not walk through tidal rock or coral pools, and avoid darkened areas. If stung, seek immediate medical attention.

Box Jellyfish: Box jellyfish are both attractive and lethal. These *femmes fatale* of the ocean are large, translucent white, and have tentacles up to 2m in length. They are hard to spot, and inhabit the waters of the Top End Oct.-Apr., and the northern shores on the west and east coasts Nov.-Apr. **Safety information:** Warnings to stay out of the water should be strictly observed. Box jellyfish that have washed up on shore are still dangerous. Stings can be fatal; the pain alone causes immediate shock. Do not attempt to remove jellyfish tentacles, as this can increase the amount of toxin absorbed and can also sting a second party. Vinegar should be poured over affected areas as quickly as possible to prevent further discharge of toxins, and immediate medical care is crucial.

Irukandji jellyfish: The Irukandji sting is not necessarily painful, but can be lethal. The Irukandji is tiny (2cm) and swimmers sometimes don't realize they've been stung, even though stings are often characterized by a rash. Symptoms can develop any time from an hour to a few days after the sting. As always, seek medical attention if you have any doubts. Many **other jellyfish stings** can be treated by dousing the stings with vinegar. Calamine lotion and antihistamines help to relieve pain.

Cassowaries: Imagine, if you will, a gigantic, brightly colored turkey on stilts. Now imagine it has huge, velociraptor-like claws. At this point, you have a good mental image of a cassowary. These large, flightless birds found mainly in Queensland can grow up to 2m in height and run 50kph. When threatened, they strike out with both sets of claws (which can slice through wood). **Safety information:** Cassowaries are most likely to attack during mating season (winter). Do not approach a cassowary; rather, watch it quietly, then back away slowly. If threatened, try to put something big between you and the cassowary, like a tree, a car, or your least favorite travel companion.

Cone shell snails: Killer *snails?* Proof that the universe has a twisted sense of humor. These sea snails, often beautiful with plain, spotted, or striped cone-shaped shells, can cause serious injury or even death in humans. The Cone variety is most often found in reef waters, sand flats, tidal pools, and mud. **Safety information:** Wear water shoes or sandals when exploring any of the aforementioned areas. Be careful about picking up shells, and keep a close eye on children. If you experience pain, blurry vision, disturbed speech or hearing, swelling, numbness, or nausea, seek immediate medical attention.

Stonefish: The stonefish is the most deadly fish in the world, with venomous spines lining its back. They are found on the seabed and in tidal inlets. True to their name, stonefish are virtually indistinguishable from rocks. **Safety information:** Wear water shoes, watch where you step, and tread lightly. Contact with stonefish spines causes intense pain and muscle weakness and requires, say it with us, immediate medical attention.

OTHER ANIMALS

BIRDS. Australia is home to over 800 species of birds from the large emu to the tiny fairy penguin. Australia's flying birds include noisy flocks of **galahs, budgies (parakeets),** and colorful **rainbow lorikeets.** Songs and poems have immortalized the unmistakable laugh of the **kookaburra.** All of these native Australian animals can be seen, and many can be handled, at open-air zoos such as the **Healesville Sanctuary** (p. 608) in Victoria and the **Western Plains Zoo** (p. 246) in New South Wales.

INTRODUCED AND INVASIVE SPECIES. Humans have been responsible for the introduction of animals to Australia since prehistoric times, and many of these introduced species are now considered pests. The **dingo** (see Dangerous Animals, p. 64), crossed the Timor Sea during Aboriginal trade several thousand years ago. Accidental introductions such as European **rats** and **cane toads** present serious threats to native fauna. The overpopulation of **rabbits,** purportedly introduced to

Australia as targets for marksmen, has become one of Australia's most serious wildlife problems. **Foxes** also upset delicate ecosystems, particularly in Tasmania.

Domesticated **cattle** and **sheep** have been of tremendous economic importance in Australia since European settlement; stations (ranches) can be found throughout the country. Vast tracts of land have been converted to pasture to support the meat industry, resulting in a dramatic impact on ecological balance. The farming of non-native **honeybees** has also become a growing part of the economy.

MAMMALS. Marsupials, or mammals that nurse their young in a pouch, historically had few competitors on the Australian continent and consequently flourished, filling various ecological niches. Perhaps the best known marsupial, the **kangaroo** can grow up to 10 ft. long, nose to tail, and is capable of propelling itself nearly 30 ft. in a single bound. The kangaroo's smaller look-alike cousin, the **wallaby,** is also a common sight in the Outback. Australia's other well-known marsupial, the **koala,** sleeps 18hr. a day and lives among the leaves of eucalyptus trees. Other native marsupials include **wombats** (a rare, rotund, and profoundly cuddly-looking burrowing creature), **possums, bandicoots,** and **quolls.**

Giant marsupials once roamed the prehistoric Australian landscape. These megafauna, which included towering relatives of kangaroos called diprotodons, disappeared soon after the arrival of humans. One infamous marsupial carnivore has survived, however. Fierce **Tasmanian devils** are nocturnal scavengers who hunt small prey and kill livestock with their powerful jaws.

Two families of monotremes, or egg-laying mammals, also call Australia home. **Echidnas** are small porcupine-like ant-eaters with protruding snouts. The **platypus** sports an odd combination of zoological features: the bill of a duck, the fur of an otter, the tail of a beaver, and webbed claws unique to its own species. So outrageous did this anatomy seem to colonists that early British naturalists believed the stuffed specimens to be frauds.

MARINE LIFE. Fur seals, elephant seals, and **sea lions** populate Australia's southern shores during summer breeding seasons. Kangaroo Island, South Australia (p. 480), is a particularly good place to see sea lions in their natural habitat. **Dolphins** are another common sight on Australia's coasts, particularly in Bunbury, Western Australia (p. 704); Monkey Mia, Western Australia (p. 735); and Sorrento, Victoria (p. 612). **Humpback Whales** also frequent the eastern waters in Hervey Bay (p. 367) and near the Great Barrier Reef (p. 314) between July and November.

REPTILES. In addition to **crocodiles,** Australia's reptiles include **goannas** (large lizards growing up to 3 or 4m long—its likeness made an appearance in the kids' movie *The Rescuers Down Under*) and a wide array of **snakes,** many of them poisonous (see Dangerous Animals, p. 64).

CORAL. Hard corals range in hue, from purple to emerald to red, and are mostly categorized as branched, boulder, or plate coral. The reefs that make up the Great Barrier Reef take a number of different forms. Closest to the shore are **patch reefs,** comprised of stretches of hard and soft coral. Farther out from shore are **fringe reefs.** Their arrangement in circular patterns deeply entrenched in the sea floor means that they frequently fill with silt, clouding visibility for divers. The far outer reef is made up of 710km of **ribbon reef.**

FISH. Australia's waters, and the Great Barrier Reef in particular, houses a spectacular variety of fish, from the enormous **potato cod** to the **fusaleres,** a family of fish that change color at night. Many shops sell **fish identification cards** that you can take to the water with you. A few names to know: the **wrasse** is a long, slender, cigar-like fish; the **angel** and **surgeon fish** have similar oblong shapes, but the surgeon has a razor-sharp barb close to its tail; the **butterfly** and **bat fish** are round, but the latter is larger and has a black stripe across the eye; the **parrotfish** eats bits of coral by cracking it in its beak-like mouth and at night envelops itself in a protective mucus sac. Despite Australia's reputation for **sharks,** only gray **reef sharks** (and the very rare **tiger shark**) are seen around the Great Barrier Reef, and are typically harmless if unprovoked. Besides fish, the Reef houses **turtles, giant clams, dolphins,** and **whales,** as well as **echinoderms:** sea cucumbers, sea stars, feather stars, and brittle stars.

NATIONAL PARKS

Australia's variety of protected space is a major source of national pride. From the scrub plains of the Red Centre to the great sandy beaches of the east coast and the mountains of the southwest, Australia offers a dramatic landscape, much of which is accessible to campers, climbers, and bushwalkers of all levels.

GREAT BARRIER REEF MARINE PARK

The Great Barrier Reef (p. 314) is one of Australia's most popular attractions and a scuba diving wonderland. The longest coral formation in the world, it is actually a series of many reefs that stretches more than 2000km along the eastern coast of Queensland from the Tropic of Capricorn to Papua New Guinea. Although adult **polyps** are sedentary, corals belong to the animal kingdom. Thus, the Great Barrier Reef is the only community of animals visible from space. There are strict national marine park rules against removing living creatures from the sea; fines exceed $500 for removing any piece of a coral reef.

NATIONAL PARKS ON LAND

Most national parks require visitor fees; day passes are normally $6-12 per vehicle (more for week passes), while Parks Passes allow you to make unlimited visits to selected parks within a given period. Some parks require camping permits (usually around $5-10) which can be obtained from the local ranger station. The list below contains contact information for each state's parks service, most of whom provide free publications on state and national protected areas. For direct links to individual parks across Australia, visit www.ea.gov.au/pa/contacts.html.

Conservation and Land Management (CALM), Western Australia, Locked Bag 104, Bentley Delivery Ctr. WA 6983 (head office ☎08 9442 0300, general inquiries 9334 0333; www.calm.wa.gov.au).

Nature Foundation South Australia, The Manse, 32 Holden St., Hindmarsh SA 5007 (☎08 8340 2880; www.naturefoundation.org.au).

Natural Resources, Environment and the Arts, Goyder Centre, 25 Chung Wah Terr., Palmerston NT 0830 (☎08 8999 4555; www.nt.gov.au/nreta/parks).

New South Wales National Parks and Wildlife Service, P.O. Box 1967, 43 Bridge St., Hurstville NSW 2220 (☎02 9585 6444; www.nationalparks.nsw.gov.au).

Parks Victoria, Level 10, 535 Bourke St., Melbourne VIC 3000 (☎03 8627 4699; www.parkweb.vic.gov.au).

Queensland Parks and Wildlife Service, P.O. Box 15155, City East QLD 4002 (☎07 3227 8185; www.epa.qld.gov.au).

Tasmania Parks & Wildlife Service, P.O. Box 1751, Hobart TAS 7001 (☎1300 135 513; www.parks.tas.gov.au).

CAMPING AND BUSHWALKING

Camping, hiking and bushwalking (hiking off marked trails) are the best ways to experience Australia's wilderness. Camping outside designated campsites is usually not permitted near campgrounds, trailheads, or picnic areas. **Bush camping** is often free, but lacks all amenities; in some cases, permits may be required and can cost up to $10. Bush camping is allowed in specific sections of parks—check with a parks office or ranger before setting up camp. As tempting as it may be, avoid camping on sandy creek beds, as rains can turn your convenient camping spot into a raging torrent without warning.

Campers should be careful to leave no trace of human presence. A portable stove is a safer (and more efficient) way to cook than using vegetation to build a campfire. If you must make a fire, keep it small and use only dead branches or brush rather than cutting live plants. If there are no toilet facilities, bury human waste at least 15cm deep and 50m from any water source or campsite (paper should be carried out or burned with a lighter). Always pack and carry your garbage in a plastic bag until you reach a trash receptacle.

Two excellent general resources for travelers planning camping or hiking trips in Australia are www.camping.com.au and the **Great Outdoor Recreation Pages** (www.gorp.com). **The Mountaineers Books** (☎206 223 6303; www.mountaineersbooks.org) is another good resource, with over 600 titles on hiking, biking, mountaineering, natural history, and conservation. **Hiking Tropical Australia,** by Lewis P. Hinchman and John N. Serio (Grass Tree Press; US$16) provides planning tips, directions, and trail descriptions. For **topographical maps of Australia,** contact Geoscience Australia (☎02 6249 9111 or 1800 800 173; www.ga.gov.au), or write to GPO Box 378, Canberra ACT 2601. Local visitor centers provide information on park-specific camping and wildlife, and have maps and brochures.

Australia has its share of long treks for the adventurous. The 220km **Larapinta Trail** (p. 301) winds from Alice Springs into the West MacDonnell ranges. The **Overland Track** (p. 550), perhaps Australia's most famous trail, connects Cradle Mountain and Lake St. Clair through 80km of World Heritage wilderness in Tasmania. For highlights of Australia's bushwalks, see **Discover Australia,** p. 1.

LEAVE NO TRACE. Let's Go encourages travelers to adopt the "Leave No Trace" ethic, minimizing their impact on natural environments and protecting them for future generations. Set up camp on durable surfaces, use cook stoves instead of campfires, and respect wildlife and natural objects. For more information, contact the **Leave No Trace Center for Outdoor Ethics,** P.O. Box 997, Boulder, CO 80306, USA (☎800-332-4100 or 303-442-8222; www.lnt.org).

OUTDOORS ESSENTIALS

EQUIPMENT

WHAT TO BUY. Good camping equipment is sturdy and light, and generally more expensive in Australia than in North America.

Swags and Sleeping Bags: Swags are miniature tents made of tough, water-resistant canvas, with built-in sleeping bags that usually contain foam mattresses. They are a popular, uniquely Australian option, and start at AUS$90-300. Travelers who don't want to drop cash on a swag in Australia will usually bring a sleeping bag from home. Most **sleeping bags** are rated by season ("summer" means 30-40°F at night; "four-season" or "winter" often means below 0°F). Prices range from US$80-210 for a summer synthetic to US$250-300 for a good down winter bag. **Sleeping bag pads** include foam pads (US$10-30), air mattresses (US$15-50), and self-inflating pads (US$30-120). Bring a **stuff sack** lined with a plastic bag to store your sleeping bag and keep it dry.

Tent: The best tents are free-standing (with their own frames and suspension systems), set up quickly, and only require staking in high winds. Low-profile dome tents are the best for variable conditions. Good 2-person tents start at US$100, 4-person at US$160. Make sure your tent has a fly and waterproof seams. Other useful accessories include a **battery-operated lantern,** a plastic **groundcloth,** and a nylon **tarp.**

Backpack: Internal-frame packs mould better to your back, keep a lower center of gravity, and flex adequately to adapt to difficult conditions. **External-frame packs** are more comfortable for long hikes over even terrain, as they keep weight higher and distribute it more evenly. Make sure your pack has a strong, padded hip-belt to transfer weight to your core. Any serious backpacking requires a pack of at least 4000 cubic inches (16,000cc), plus 500 cubic inches to fit sleeping bags. Sturdy backpacks cost anywhere from US$125-420, and are an item for which it doesn't pay to economize. Before buying, fill the pack with something heavy and walk around the store to get a sense of how it distributes weight. Either buy a **rain cover** (US$10-20) or store all of your belongings in **plastic bags** inside your pack.

Boots: Be sure to wear hiking boots with good **ankle support.** They should fit snugly over 1-2 pairs of wool socks and thin liner socks. Break in boots over several weeks before you leave in order to spare yourself painful blisters. Waterproof your boots with **waterproofing treatment** before leaving on a hike. Boots also provide protection against snake bites, mites, and ticks, and are absolutely necessary for outback bushwalks.

Water Purification and Transport: On long hikes, you will need to carry water or purify any that you might find along the trail. **Boiling** water for 3-5min. is the most effective, though not the most convenient, method of purification. Though iodine and chlorine tablets are the cheapest alternative method, they will not rid dirty water of its muck or its characteristic taste. Moreover, it can be unhealthy to consume iodine tablets over a long period of time, and neither chlorine nor iodine reliably kill all bacteria. Portable **water filters** pump out a crystal clear product but often require careful maintenance and extra filters. Do not pump dirty water unless you want to repeatedly clean or replace clogged filter cartridges. For transport, plastic **canteens** or water bottles keep water cooler than metal ones do, and are virtually shatter- and leak-proof. Large plastic **water bags** (**bladders**) can hold up to several gallons and are perfect for long-haul travel. When empty, bladders occupy virtually no space and weigh next to nothing.

Other Necessities: Synthetic layers, like those made of polypropylene, and a **pile** (**fleece**) **jacket** will keep you warm even when wet. A **space blanket** will help you to retain your body heat and doubles as a groundcloth (US$5-15). In Australia, fires are only permitted in designated fireplaces; to cook elsewhere you'll need a **camp stove** (the classic Coleman starts at US$50) and a propane-filled **fuel bottle** to operate it. Also, don't forget a **first-aid kit, flashlight, pocketknife, insect repellent, calamine lotion,** and **waterproof matches** or a **lighter.**

WHERE TO BUY IT. The mail-order and online companies listed below offer lower prices than many retail outlets, but visit local camping or outdoors stores to get a good sense of the look and feel of necessary items.

Recreational Equipment, Inc. (REI), Sumner, WA 98352, USA (US and Canada ☎800-426-4840, elsewhere 253-891-2500; www.rei.com).

Campmor, 28 Parkway, P.O. Box 700, Upper Saddle River, NJ 07458, USA (☎800-525-4784 or 201-825-8300; www.campmor.com).

Discount Camping, 880 Main North Rd., Pooraka, South Australia 5095, Australia (☎08 8262 3399; www.discountcamping.com.au).

Mountain Designs, 443a Nudgee Rd., Hendra, Queensland 4011, Australia (☎07 3856 2344; www.mountaindesigns.com).

Eastern Mountain Sports (EMS), 1 Vose Farm Rd., Peterborough, NH 03458, USA (☎888-463-6367; www.ems.com).

WILDERNESS SAFETY

Stay warm, dry, and hydrated. The vast majority of life-threatening wilderness situations can be avoided by following this simple advice. Take enough **water** with you when exploring outdoors; the average person requires at least 2 liters per day. Avoid alcohol and coffee, which accelerate dehydration. Prepare yourself for an emergency, by always packing **raingear,** a **hat** and **mittens** (in season), a **first-aid kit,** a **reflector,** a **whistle, high energy food,** and **extra water.** On a longer trip, you should carry a **compass** and a detailed **topographical map** of the area where you are hiking. During cold months, or when camping, bring clothing with warm layers of **synthetic materials** designed for the outdoors, such as pile (fleece) jackets, Gore-Tex® raingear, or **wool.** Never rely on **cotton** for warmth; it is useless when wet. Make sure to check all equipment for defects before setting out. Look at **weather forecasts** and pay attention to the skies when hiking, since weather patterns can change suddenly. Always let someone know when and where you are hiking—it could be a friend, hostel, park ranger, or local hiking organization. **National Parks and Wildlife Service (NPWS)** offices at the entrance to many larger parks often offer registration services.

Sunglasses, sunscreen, and a **hat** are essential sun protection. **Light-colored clothing** also helps reflect the sun's rays. Total **fire bans** are common in many parts of the country. Make sure you check on this before going hiking, as walks are sometimes closed due to fire dangers.

If you plan on **bushwalking,** it's an excellent idea to rent an **Electronic Position Indicator Radio Beacon (EPIRB),** also known as a **Personal Locating Beacon (PLB).** EPIRBs use satellite tracking to pinpoint your location and send a distress signal to emergency workers. EPIRB rentals cost AUS$50-100. If you need to be rescued, simply turn on (and leave on) the EPIRB; a helicopter will be sent to find you. A more expensive option is a satellite phone. Many car rental companies provide EPIRB or satellite phone rental options.

WATER ACTIVITIES

Australia offers unparalleled **surfing, scuba diving, kayaking** and **whitewater rafting** conditions. **Waterskiing** is also common in the southeast, while **windsurfing** and **sailing** are particularly popular in the **Whitsunday Islands** (p. 397). Rental equipment is available from most resorts and some hostels. Put on waterproof, high SPF sunblock before undertaking any water activities. Australia has the highest rate of skin cancer in the world, a testament to the strength of the Australian sun and the outdoor lifestyle popular with Aussies.

SWIMMING. Many of Australia's **beaches** are patrolled by lifeguards, especially during the summer months. Patrolled beaches will be clearly marked with yellow and red striped flags that designate areas safe for swimming; make sure you swim only between these flags. **Rips (undertows)** are very common. If you get caught in a

1 **Sydney Harbour:** Island-hop in the urban jungle.

2 **Blue Mountains National Park:** Ride the world's steepest railway or bushwalk through 140km of trails.

3 **Kanangra-Boyd National Park:** Join experienced bushwalkers in the remote solitude of the rugged wilderness.

4 **Kosciuszko National Park:** Ski, hike, or just enjoy Australia's tallest mountains.

5 **Croajingolong National Park:** Trek through 100km of temperate rainforest in this UNESCO World Biosphere reserve.

6 **Wilson's Promontory National Park:** Take dayhikes and overnight trails in this wildly popular, unspoiled marine park.

7 **Mount William National Park:** Lounge on some of the best beaches in Tasmania, or bushwalk among marsupials.

8 **Freycinet National Park:** Enjoy prime swimming or snorkeling in this picturesque park.

9 **Mt. Field National Park:** Walk from rainforest to alpine plateau (and every biome in between) in just a matter of hours.

10 **Southwest National Park:** Take in non-stop kilometers of gorgeous mountains and lakes.

11 **Mole Creek Karst National Park:** Explore two caves open to the public out of over 300.

12 **Narawntapu National Park:** Try popular tracks and enjoy abundant wallaby company.

13 **Royal National Park:** Tour the world's second-oldest national park and its 16,000 hectares of diverse ecosystems.

14 **Grampians National Park:** Learn about Aboriginal culture while surrounded by rugged beauty.

15 **Flinders Chase National Park:** Hang out at the Remarkable Rocks in the company of New Zealand Fur Seals on the western coast of Kangaroo Island.

16 **Cape Leeuwin:** The southwesternmost point of mainland Australia boasts magnificent ocean vistas.

17 **Leeuwin-Naturaliste National Park:** From great whale-watching spots to fossil-filled caves, anyone can find adventure here.

18 **Ningaloo Marine Park:** Swim with whale sharks as you dive the reef.

19 **Karijini National Park:** Hike through Dale's Gorge and swim the rock pools near Fortescue Falls.

Purnululu (Bungle Bungle) National Park: Hike by the Bungle Bungle Range or through the narrow Echidna Chasm.

21 **Litchfield National Park:** Marvel at the Magnetic Termite mounds, some approaching 7m high, which are dominated only by the area's waterfalls.

22 **Nitmiluk National Park:** Canoe through 13 gorges on the beautiful Katherine River.

23 **Kakadu National Park:** Observe the massive 150m waterfalls set against Aboriginal rock art galleries.

24 **Arnhem Land:** Experience some of the roughest outback excursions that Australia can offer in this Aboriginal homeland in the Top End.

25 **Uluru and Kata Tjutu National Park:** Visit the iconic symbol of the Australian Outback.

26 **Iron Range National Park:** Explore the dense rainforest at the tip of the continent.

27 **Cape Tribulation National Park:** Witness the collision of two World Heritage Parks as the rainforest meets the reef.

28 **Great Barrier Reef:** Snorkel or scuba dive in and around the largest living organism in the world.

29 **Eungella National Park:** Walk the misty slopes and valleys in the "land where clouds lie low over the mountains."

30 **Fraser Island:** Roam the pristine dunes on the world's largest sand island.

31 **Lamington National Park:** Waterfalls, rainforests, and an ancient volcanic crater provide a scenic backdrop to this bushwalker's paradise.

32 **Border Ranges National Park:** Enjoy prime picnic areas and views that rival those of more touristed, neighboring parks.

33 **Mount Warning National Park:** Visit the largest caldera in the Southern Hemisphere, formed by an ominous ancient volcano.

34 **Dorrigo National Park:** Hike through lush rainforest filled with wildlife.

35 **Booti Booti National Park:** Climb the 20m tower for spectacular views of coastal wetlands.

36 **Oxley Wild Rivers National Park:** Gaze at gorgeous gorges, endangered wildlife, and waterfalls in over 140,000 hectares of national park.

37 **Warrumbungle:** Enjoy long walks and excellent wildlife sightings among craggy volcanic peaks.

38 **Wollemi National Park:** Encounter pockets of undiscovered land in the second largest park in NSW.

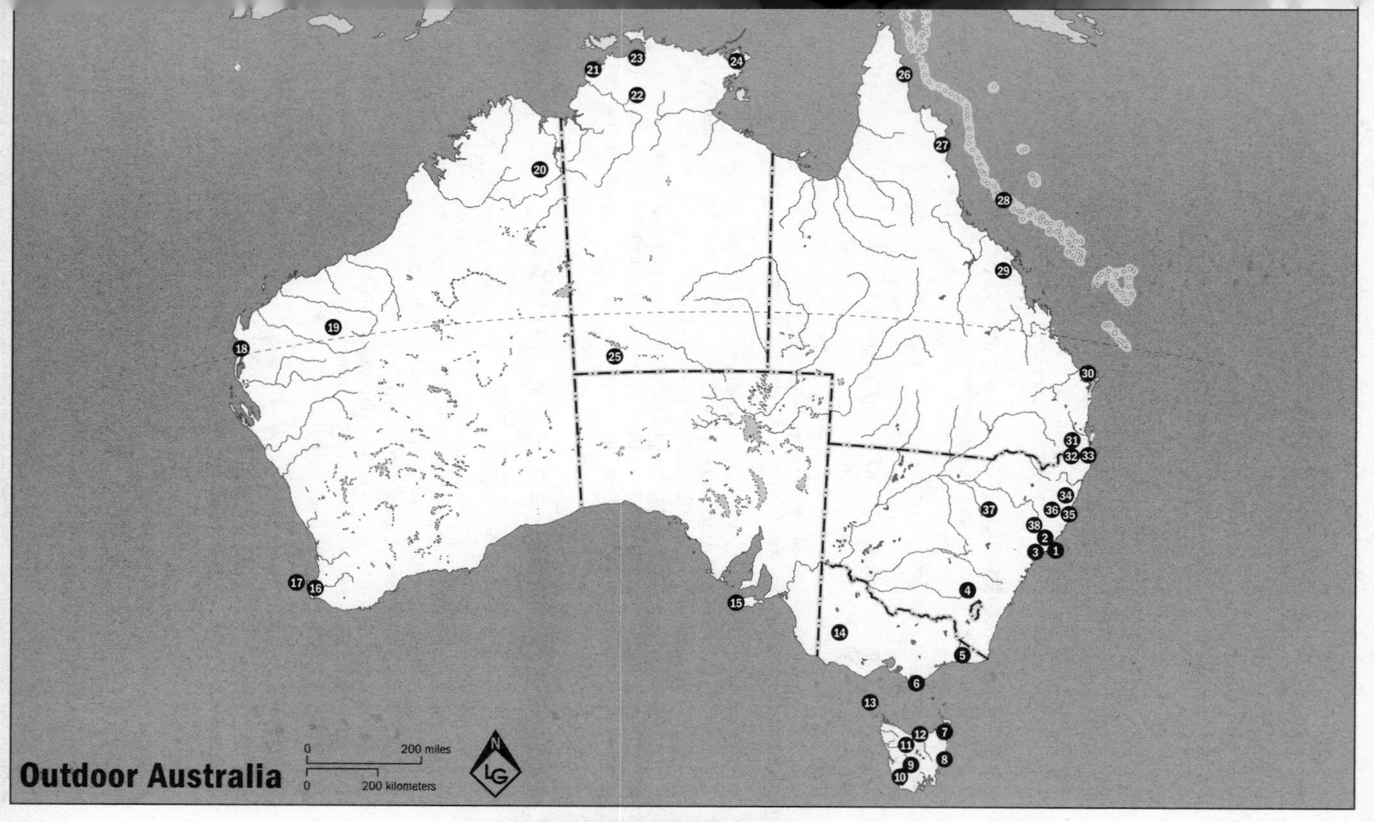
Outdoor Australia
0
200 miles
0
200 kilometers
N
LG
1
2
3
4
5
6
7
8
9
10
11
12
13
14
15
16
17
18
19
20
21
22
23
24
25
26
27
28
29
30
31
32
33
34
35
36
37
38

rip, don't try to swim against it, instead swim parallel to the shore until out of the rip and only then swim back to shore. Make sure you **check with locals** about conditions if you are going to swim at an unpatrolled beach.

SURFING. Australia's beaches offer excellent conditions for surfers of all levels. Beginners should look for sandy beaches, where waves break on sand bars rather than reefs. A 2hr. lesson should be enough to get you upright on a longboard, though practice is required to ride the more maneuverable shortboard. Sunburn is a serious concern when laying on a board all day—consider wearing a **rash guard** (a tight-fitting, lightweight shirt of swimsuit-like material) to protect yourself. As with swimming, watch out for **rips** and check conditions at unpatrolled beaches. For **surf conditions** and live surfcams, visit www.coastalwatch.com. *Surfing Australia*, by Mark Thornley, Peter Wilson, and Veda Dante (Tuttle Publishing; US$25) is a comprehensive guide to hitting the waves in Australia.

SCUBA DIVING AND SNORKELING. Australia offers some of the best scuba diving opportunities in the world. For beginners, most dive operators offer **introductory dives** with a trained guide. For those who want to take it to the next level, the most common certification course is with the Professional Association of Diving Instructors (PADI). The cheapest courses in Queensland can be found at **Hervey Bay** (p. 367), **Bundaberg** (p. 377), and **Magnetic Island** (p. 407); however, courses are generally even cheaper in less-touristed areas. A **diving medical exam** is required for certified dives and certification courses, usually cheapest in diving hotspots like **Cairns** and **Airlie Beach** ($60). **Snorkeling** is also popular: all you need is a **mask, snorkel,** and **fins,** available at most hostels and resorts for a small fee.

KAYAKING AND RAFTING. Whitewater enthusiasts can tackle rapids on Australia's rivers while passing through spectacular wilderness areas. The **Franklin River** (p. 552) in Tasmania is a hotspot for whitewater kayaking and rafting. **Sea-kayaking** is an increasingly popular activity, with more stable boats and calmer waters than its river equivalent. Sea-kayakers have the freedom to explore remote coastal wilderness, often inaccessible by car or foot. Opportunities are widespread, particularly in the **Whitsunday Islands** (p. 397) in Queensland.

ADVENTURE TRIPS AND TOURS

Organized adventure tours offer another way to explore the wilderness. Activities may include hiking, biking, horseback riding, skiing, canoeing, kayaking, rafting, and climbing. Tourism bureaus can often suggest trails and outfitters; camping and outdoor equipment companies are also good sources of information. Companies such as **Adventure Tours Australia** (☎08 8309 2277 or 1300 654 604; www.adventuretours.com.au) and **Adventure Company Australia** (☎07 4051 4777; www.adventures.com.au) provide educational programs on ecology and Aboriginal culture in addition to adventure activities.

DRIVING IN THE OUTBACK

Driving is the easiest way to get around outback Australia. Public transport is limited outside major urban areas, and a car may be the only way to visit many sights. But be prepared for some very long roadtrips. Certain roads and national parks are inaccessible without a **4WD** vehicle. If renting, be aware that rental companies have complicated policies. Be sure you fully understand where you are allowed to drive (many do not allow you to drive 2WD vehicles on roads not maintained by the government, making some parks difficult to access) and what your insurance does and does not cover (windshield dings, scratches, underbody damage from sharp rocks, flat tires, and kangaroo collision damage are all common problems that can result in hefty fines). See Costs and Insurance (p. 30) for more info.

IF IT SOUNDS TOO GOOD TO BE TRUE, IT PROBABLY IS. Backpackers thrive on being able to move about on a whim, heading in a new direction simply because. Australia, perhaps more than any other destination, caters to this lifestyle with its well-developed transportation system, tourism industry, and a seemingly endless supply of unique destinations.

Recently, however, the traditional backpacking philosophy has been abandoned by some in the name of cost-cutting and convenience, often with disastrous consequences. Budget travelers are now bombarded with pre-packaged "deals" upon arrival in regional hubs. These packages promise to cover everything from accommodations to food to adventure, sometimes at prices so outrageously low that it's no surprise that operators can't deliver.

Popular east coast travel routes, especially those in Queensland, have been particularly hard hit by this kind of pre-packaging. Some operators promise the whole Queensland coast for under $300, including 4WD tours on Fraser Island, sailing around the Whitsundays, and diving the Great Barrier Reef. But once travelers arrive at each destination, extra charges start to add up.

Travelers find themselves in over-crowded hostels, on sailboats with more passengers than beds, and saddled with unexpected fees for things like linens, fuel, insurance, food, and park entrance fees. One scam has travelers arriving at their departure point, only to be told that their packaged sailboat tour has a three week wait—but they can jump to the front of the line by paying an extra fee. Other backpackers have found themselves on dilapidated boats that suffer breakdowns mid-tour, leaving them stranded at sea and forced to use buckets due to toilet failure.

Of course, not all tour companies are out to fleece you; many reputable ones offer decent savings. A little investigation will fend off disappointment. If a tour package sounds suspicious, look up the companies involved, ask around, and determine whether their descriptions match your expectations. Be sure to ask about the length of time spent in each place, as some companies promise three-day tours but deliver less. Ask other travelers and locals if they have been on a certain tour. Ask about hidden charges associated with food, fuel, accommodation, insurance, upgrades, and park entrance fees (some tour companies will double "park fees," keeping half for themselves), and ask to get it all in writing.

If you're spending a significant amount of time on the road you might want to consider an automobile club membership, which can provide **roadside assistance.** The **Australian Automobile Association (AAA)** provides roadside assistance and has reciprocal relationships with automobile associations in other countries (see **Essentials,** p. 9). Roadside assistance is generally limited to sealed (bitumen) roads and is restricted to electrical and mechanical breakdown. An excess fee applies to most other problems (such as damage caused by rocks, trees, or animals); extra charges also apply to assistance outside coverage zones. Talk to the state AAA office about coverage details before embarking on your trip.

BEFORE YOU GO

If you're using a 4WD and you've never driven one before, it may be worth taking a short introductory lesson; many rental companies offer half- and full-day classes.

Make sure you have **up-to-date, accurate maps;** regional topographic maps are particularly useful. Also, always inquire locally about road conditions.

VEHICLE SUPPLIES. Australia's vast expanses mean that help on the road is often hundreds of kilometers away, making it important to carry your own emergency vehicle supplies. Rental companies should supply a **breakdown kit,** and may also offer a **survival pack,** which you will only be charged for if opened (around AUS$90). You'll probably have to pick up additional supplies on your own. The most important of these is **extra fuel.** If your vehicle doesn't have 1 long-range or 2 regular fuel tanks, secure at least a tank of fuel in a metal safety can in your trunk (so it does not slosh around). Plastic cans are cheaper, but they are also more apt to spill, creating noxious fumes and a fire hazard. Other essentials include: **2 spare tires** and a **jack** (as well as a **jack plate** if you'll be driving on unsealed roads); **jumper cables;** a **wrench;** Phillips and flat-head **screwdrivers** (both small and large, and long enough to reach concealed engine spaces); **pliers** (a bigger pair for gripping larger items and a needle-nosed pair for reaching into tight spots); a **knife;** a **flashlight;** and extra **oil, coolant, clean water,** and **hose sealant.** Also important are a **new battery** (if your current one is old or corroded) in static-resistant, absorbent packaging; **road flares;** a **tire iron** and **pressure gauge;** extra **fan belts, rope,** and **sheeting;** a **compass, blankets,** and **food.** Useful but nonessential items include **duct tape,** extra **windshield washer fluid** (for especially dusty treks), an **ice scraper,** a **funnel, tow rope,** a **spray bottle filled with glass cleaner, rags,** and **matches.**

One of the simplest ways to get yourself stalled in the middle of nowhere is to overlook your **battery;** if it is old or corroded get a new one before heading out. Some travelers carry a charged battery in the trunk of their car in case of emergency, but remember that battery acid is highly corrosive; a spare should be stored very carefully in static-resistant, absorbent packaging.

Roadside supply stops are rare, so self-sufficiency is a must. Water is most important; carry at least 5L of water per person per day. Also bring ample food. You'll need light clothing for the day, sturdy boots for hiking, and warm clothes for nights (the temperature in some parts of the country can fall below freezing). In case of emergency, bring a first-aid kit and a fire extinguisher. Cell phones do not work in remote areas of the Outback; bushwalkers swear by the Electronic Position Indicator Radio Beacon (EPIRB). For more info, see Wilderness Safety, p. 71.

ON THE ROAD

If your vehicle breaks down, it is generally best to stay with it; it is likely that you will eventually be discovered by a passerby. Putting up your car bonnet (hood) is a universal signal of distress. If you decide to stop for other reasons, give passing cars a thumbs-up to let them know you're okay; if you pass a stopped car, slow down and look for the thumbs-up sign before continuing.

Don't drive at night, while tired, or after drinking (Australia has strict drunk-driving laws; see **Essentials,** p. 9). Road conditions change quickly, often without warning, especially on 4WD-only tracks. For your safety and the safety of others, it is best to use your **headlights** at all times while driving.

TIRES

Australia has a surprising number of unsealed (unpaved) roads, often covered with gravel and fallen branches. This characteristic virtually guarantees that you'll have at least one blown tire. As petrol stations are often hundreds of miles apart, learning how to change a tire *before* setting out is essential.

MAINTENANCE. The best defense against tire problems is good maintenance. Look on the tires, on the inside of your driver's side door, or in your vehicle's owner's manual for the appropriate pressure to which your tires should be inflated. You can use a **tire pressure gauge** to determine the actual pressure of your tires. Overinflation and underinflation are both dangerous and can contribute to tire failure; you should check the pressure periodically throughout your trip. Since hot temperatures will give you inaccurate readings, check the pressure after your tires have cooled down after driving.

RUPTURES. The first sign of a tire rupture will probably involve a change in the way the vehicle feels while you are driving. You might notice that the car doesn't turn as easily, or it might feel a bit more wobbly than usual. Pull over to a safe place at the first sign of trouble; make sure that you stop somewhere off the road, away from blind corners, and on level ground. You will feel a **tire blowout** (or tread separation) right away. The car will suddenly become much more difficult to steer, especially on turns, and you may be tugged forcefully in a particular direction.

To handle a tire blowout, *do not slam on the brakes*, even though this may be your first instinct. A blown tire (especially a blown front tire) will reduce your braking capability, and slamming on the brakes will just send you into an uncontrollable skid. Grip the wheel firmly while you take your foot off of the gas pedal, steering only enough to keep the vehicle in a straight line or away from obstructions. Let the vehicle gradually come to a complete stop.

OVERHEATING

PRECAUTIONS. Take several liters of **clean water** with you. It is possible to use impure stream or lake water to top off your radiator, though you'll need to have the radiator flushed afterwards. You should also carry additional **coolant.** It needs to be mixed with water after being poured into the radiator. On a hot day, you can help prevent overheating by turning off your air conditioning system. If your vehicle has a temperature gauge, check it frequently. If not, stop periodically and check for signs of overheating—any sort of boiling noise under your hood is a strong indicator that you need to let the vehicle cool.

SOLUTIONS. If your car overheats, pull off the road and turn the heater on full force to cool the engine. If the radiator fluid is steaming or bubbling, turn off the car for at least 30min. If not, run the car in neutral at about 1500 rpm for a few minutes, allowing the coolant to circulate. *Never pour water over the engine, and never try to lift a hot car bonnet (hood).* If you need to open your radiator cap, always wait at least 45min. until the coolant loses its heat—otherwise, you may be splashed with boiling coolant. Even after waiting, you may still be spattered with warm coolant, so stand to the side. Remember that "topping off" your radiator does not mean filling it completely. Pour in a small amount of water and coolant (equal amounts) and wait for it to work its way into the system, and then add more. Continue to do so until the radiator is filled to the level indicated by the reservoir or your vehicle's manual. Coolant leaks are sometimes just the product of overheating pressure, which forces coolant out of the gaps between the hoses and their connections to the radiator. If this happens to you, allowing the vehicle and coolant to cool down may be enough. If not, or if there are other holes in the hose, it helps to have **hose sealant** on hand. Treat sealant only as a short-term solution; get the vehicle to a service station as soon as possible.

OIL

Dust loves Australia. This means you will need to **change your oil** and your **filter** more frequently than in other places. Most service stations offer oil changes, though prices may rise in remote areas. Check your oil level every few days by taking your vehicle's dipstick and sliding it into the engine's oil level test tube. To get an accurate measurement, wipe it off first and then plunge it in and out of the tube, checking the actual level against the level recommended on the dipstick or in your vehicle's manual. Test the level only after your vehicle has been at rest for several minutes. If your level is low, add more oil. The owner's manual will list appropriate grades of motor oil for your particular vehicle. Check these against the oil you pour into your engine—the grade is usually indicated on its packaging.

HOSES AND BELTS

Hoses and **belts** are important to monitor for wear and tear. Even small problems with vacuum hoses, for instance, will prevent your vehicle from starting. **Fan belts** are notorious for snapping in the worst locations. It is worthwhile to carry a few extra fan belts, but it is even better to get failing belts replaced before setting out. Replace the fan belt if it looks loose, cracked, glazed or shiny (signs that it is at risk of cracking). In an emergency, **pantyhose** can serve as a very temporary substitute, allowing you to hobble back to a garage at low speed.

AUSTRALIAN ROAD HAZARDS

The signs along the road come in all shapes and sizes, but they all mean one thing: *slow down*. All signs refer to possible driving or visibility obstructions.

GETTING BOGGED. Getting stuck in soft ground (or "bogged," as Australians say) is a common occurrence when off-roading or exploring unsealed roads. More often than not, the best way to extract your vehicle is to winch your car to a tree or rock. Unfortunately, some rental cars don't have winches, and travelers are left hoping that someone with a winch will stop to help. Most rental companies will provide a **snatch strap** and **D-shackles** (used in tandem to de-bog vehicles) for a fee. If driving in particularly remote areas, be sure to bring a shovel and some boards. Use the shovel to dig the mud or sand away from the tires. Place boards under each tire; this should give you enough traction to extract your car. If boards fail, you may want to try the "kanga-jack" method: with a large enough jack, you can get one end of your car far off the ground, then push it forward so it lands a bit closer to where you want to be. Repeat the hopping motion until you are unstuck.

A last resort method is to let almost all the air out of your tires (get down to 15-50psi), then take advantage of the added traction flat tires provide to drive out of the sand. Do not attempt to drive far on a set of flat tires.

KANGAROOS. Kangaroos are a common hazard on Australian roads. Signs alerting you to their presence are common along highways, but less frequent on small roads. Dusk and dawn are particularly dangerous times. **Kangaroos are a serious danger** and may jump in front of or into the side of cars, causing significant damage. **Never assume that an animal will get out of your way.** Many Australian drivers outfit their cars with metal bull bars or 'roo bars, which attach to bumpers and protect cars from seemingly inevitable collisions with Australia's big marsupials.

UNSEALED ROADS. **Unsealed roads** are common in rural Australia, and conditions range from smooth, hard-packed sand to an eroded mixture of mud, sand, and stones. Locals are a good source of information on the roads in the immediate vicinity. When driving on unsealed roads, **call regional tourist boards ahead of time for road conditions,** especially in the north, as the Wet sometimes makes roads impassible even after the rains stop. When driving on unsealed roads, you should allow at least twice as much time as you would for travel on paved roads. Remember that it is extremely easy to skid on gravel. Loose gravel may feel comfortable at high speeds if you are traveling in a straight line, but as soon as you attempt to turn or brake, you will realize why it is unwise to take things too quickly.

GREAT OUTDOORS GLOSSARY

ABSEILING. The Aussie word for rappelling; to climb down a mountain or cliff with rope and harness.

BITUMEN ROAD. A paved road.

BUSH CAMPING. The cheapest way to get a night's sleep, implies total self-sufficiency—generally no toilets, no fire pits, and no reliable sources of water. Bring your own supplies. Typically allowed only in specified sections of parks; check with a ranger or visitors center before setting up camp.

BUSHWALKING. Often used interchangeably with hiking, the term refers more specifically to exploring the wilderness without a trail to follow.

CALM. **C**onservation **a**nd **L**and **M**anagement, an organization that oversees Western Australia's national and regional parks, and provides visitors with maps and info.

EPIRB. **E**lectronic **P**osition **I**ndicator **R**adio **B**eacon, a safety device to call for emergency rescue. (see Wilderness Safety, p. 71.)

FRESHIES. The crocodiles that (probably) won't eat you. Freshwater crocodiles have long, thin snouts and are less aggressive than their saltwater kin; still quite dangerous and harder to spot.

JACK PLATE. Usually made of plywood or metal, used with jacks when replacing tires on unsealed roads and soft terrain. The plate distributes the weight of the car over a larger surface so that your jack doesn't get buried in the ground.

MIDGIES. Sandflies (gnats).

MOZZIES. Mosquitoes, commonly found in the Top End and Northern Queensland; kept at bay by using insect repellant.

NEVER NEVER. A slang term for particularly harsh, remote regions of the Outback.

RIPS. Strong currents that can pull a swimmer or surfer out to sea. If caught in one, don't panic—swim across (not against) it until out, or signal if help is nearby.

'ROO BAR. Also known as kangaroo or bull bars, these metal bars attach to bumpers, protecting cars from collisions with Australia's pocket-laden wildlife.

ROYAL FLYING DOCTORS SERVICE (RFDS). Provides medical and emergency care to residents and travelers in remote regions of Australia.

SALTIES. Big, powerful, and hungry. Saltwater crocodiles have a shorter, wider snout than freshwater crocs, and often lurk just below the water's surface.

SNORKELS (VEHICLE). Essential for river and creek crossings, snorkels help keep water out of your 4WD's engine by raising the point of air intake.

SWAG. A piece of heavy canvas, somewhat like a sleeping bag, with a foam mattress inside. Swags often replace tents, and keep you warm and dry (AUS $90-300).

TORCH. A flashlight.

UNSEALED. Unpaved. Many roads through parks and remote areas are gravel, dirt, packed sand, or some combination thereof. Corrugated roads (unpacked gravel) are the bumpiest.

ROAD TRAINS. "Road train" refers to any truck with three or more trailers; some are over 150 ft. long and have nearly 100 wheels. Keep a distance at least as long as the road train between you and the last trailer; they can kick up an enormous amount of debris which often damages cars or causes drivers to swerve. It's a good idea to roll up your window if one is headed toward you (even on sealed roads) so that your vehicle's cabin is not flooded by a cloud of dust.

STREAM CROSSINGS. On some northern roads, **stream crossings** are not bridged, meaning you will need to **ford** them. Before attempting this, scout the area as extensively as you can. Wade into the water and **check the conditions of the bottom,** removing any logs. Do not wade in if there is a risk of crocodiles in the area; storms during the Wet season bring salties far inland to even the most innocuous looking streams. If crocs aren't a concern, feel for silt that could catch your wheels. Look for sharp, protruding rocks and entangling weeds. Choose your exit point on the other side of the stream and inspect the area. Take a stick and find out how deep the deepest part of the crossing is. Compare this to your vehicle; if it rises above the undercarriage, or if the water is especially violent, you may want to turn around. Be especially cautious during or after rain.

If you decide to ford the stream, do it relatively quickly to avoid becoming stuck in the streambed. Start driving toward the stream from a few dozen meters down the road and enter it in full motion, not stopping until you're across. If you are stuck in the middle of a stream during or after rain, remember that the water levels may rise very quickly, and that it doesn't take much depth to lift your vehicle and send it down river. If you experience a punctured tire while fording a stream, your best option is to keep on driving until you can get to flat, level ground on the other side. Throwing it into reverse might be all right if you've just entered the stream, but under most circumstances, it will just bog you down for good.

BEYOND TOURISM

A PHILOSOPHY FOR TRAVELERS

HIGHLIGHTS OF BEYOND TOURISM IN AUSTRALIA

STUDY at the University of New South Wales, and learn about Australian history in the classroom with Sydney as a backdrop. (p. 41)

RESCUE endangered species off the coastline in Queensland or volunteer with the Australian Koala Foundation. (p. 85)

TRAIN at Leconfield Jackaroo and Jillaroo School to experience life and work in the Outback. (p. 89)

HARVEST fruit all year long in the various temperate zones of Australia while you travel around the country. (p. 88)

As a tourist, you are always a foreigner. While hostel-hopping and sightseeing can be great fun, you may want to consider going *beyond* tourism. Connecting with a foreign place through studying, volunteering, or working can help reduce that stranger-in-a-strange-land feeling. Moreover, travelers can make a positive impact on the natural and cultural environments they visit. With this Beyond Tourism chapter, *Let's Go* hopes to promote a better understanding of Australia and to provide suggestions for those who want more than a photo album out of their travels.

Australia's vast national park system and impressively diverse ecosystems make opportunities to contribute through **volunteer** work relatively easy to find. Additionally, the warm climate, laid-back lifestyle, unique outback culture, and world-class universities make it a popular destination for study, work, and work-holidays. See **Working** (p. 88) for information about job opportunities and important legal requirements.

As a **volunteer** in Australia, you can participate in projects from protecting endangered **coral reef** species to aiding the **Australian Koala Foundation** to restore the natural habitat of one of the country's most beloved creatures, either on a short-term basis or as the main component of your trip. Later in this chapter, we recommend organizations that can help you find the opportunities that best suit your interests, whether you're looking to pitch in for a day or a year.

Studying at a college or university is another option in Australia. Many students come from around the world to study at some of the nation's finest universities such as the **University of New South Wales** in Sydney or the **Australian National University** in Canberra. These schools offer the opportunity to learn more about any number of subjects, including many specific to Australia, alongside local students.

Many travelers also structure their trips by the **work** that they can do along the way—either odd jobs as they go, or full-time stints in cities where they plan to stay for some time. From fruit-picking to farming to manning a ski lift, there are plenty of short-term employment options to keep any traveler busy. Australia provides several types of special visas (p. 11) for those wishing to work during their stay.

Start your search at www.beyondtourism.com, Let's Go's new searchable database of alternatives to tourism, where you can find exciting feature articles and helpful program listings divided by country, continent, and program type.

VOLUNTEERING

In Australia, travelers looking to do their part will find an enormous range of projects, from rainforest preservation, to wildlife rescue, to Aboriginal community initiatives. Keep in mind, however, that most volunteer organizations require a minimum time commitment. Read below for general volunteering suggestions as well as specific organization listings.

Depth of involvement varies depending on the individual program and your interest level; be sure to acquire the appropriate **tourist visa** for your plans before committing to an organization. (Oddly enough, the Australian government classifies volunteer work under the same designation as paid work; thus, individuals may theoretically only volunteer full time on a tourist visa for up to 45% of the length of their stay, or part time for the entire duration of the visa. See p. 11 for more work and study visa information.) Don't sign up for the first volunteer program you come across; research a variety of opportunities and weigh your options. Also keep in mind that volunteer work, particularly with wildlife or in environmental rehabilitation and protection, is not as glamorous as it might seem; plan on a fair amount of repetitive, strenuous labor rather than days full of swimming with dolphins, comforting baby koalas, and swinging through the rainforest canopy. Cleaning and maintenance work are a significant part of many volunteer positions.

WHY PAY MONEY TO VOLUNTEER? Many volunteers are surprised to learn that some organizations require large fees or "donations." While this may seem ridiculous at first glance, such fees often keep the organization afloat, in addition to covering room, board, and administrative expenses for the volunteers. (Other organizations must rely on private donations and government subsidies.) If you're concerned about how a program spends its fees, request an annual report or finance account. A reputable organization won't refuse to inform you of how volunteer money is spent.

Most volunteer groups that charge a fee will provide for a support system and processing of logistical details. These fees can be surprisingly hefty, though they sometimes cover airfare, living expenses, and basic insurance. Volunteers should always purchase their own travel insurance in addition to anything provided by a program. Research a program thoroughly before committing–talk to people who have previously participated and find out exactly what you're getting into, as living and working conditions can vary greatly.

Pay-to-volunteer programs might be a good idea for young travelers who are looking for more support and structure (such as pre-arranged transportation and housing), or anyone who'd rather not deal with the uncertainty implicit in creating a volunteer experience from scratch.

Those looking for longer, more intensive volunteer opportunities usually choose to go through a parent organization that takes care of logistical details and often provides a group environment and support system—for a fee. There are two main types of organizations—religious and non-sectarian—although there are rarely restrictions on participation for either. The best way to find opportunities that match your interests is to check local or national volunteer centers before you depart. Australian state government websites often list volunteer opportunities. State parks services in particular are almost always in need of volunteers for wildlife and parks preservation projects; although these positions are usually geared toward locals, they are often open to travelers willing to make a minimum time commitment. Volunteer listings can be found on Parks Department webpages for New South Wales (☎02 9585 6444; www.nationalparks.nsw.gov.au), Northern Territory (☎08 8999 4555; www.nt.gov.au/ipe/pwcnt/), Queensland (☎07 3227 8185; www.epa.qld.gov.au), and Victoria (☎03 8627 4699; www.parkweb.vic.gov.au). Regional parks offices are also good places to inquire about local volunteer opportunities within Australian national parks. For general Australian Parks links, visit www.deh.gov.au/parks/links.

Go Volunteer (www.govolunteer.com.au) and Volunteer Western Australia (www.volunteer.org.au) are good web resources. For detailed, though not Australia-specific, information on volunteering abroad, check out *How to Live your Dream of Volunteering Overseas* (Penguin Books, by Joseph Collins et al.).

VOLUNTEER OPPORTUNITIES

Unless otherwise specified, assume that the volunteer listings in this section expect volunteers to be responsible for their own food, transportation, insurance, accommodation, and incidentals.

LAND CONSERVATION

In the coming century, nearly 3000 natural habitats are predicted to disappear from Australia forever, taking more than 1500 species with them. Much of this can be attributed to the destruction of native bushlands, forests, savannah woodlands and native grasslands, as well as the draining of wetlands. Several organizations have mobilized to combat these threats. Environmental conservation is by far the most popular choice for volunteers. Check out www.afconline.org.au for general information from the Australian Conservation Foundation.

Bunya Mountains National Park, MS 501, Dalby QLD 4405 (☎07 4668 3127). Volunteer opportunities are arranged on a case-by-case basis. Generally, volunteers can expect to help with station upkeep (cleaning), track maintenance, and information center staffing, while also learning about local flora and fauna. Limited accommodation sometimes available.

Bushcare Australia, Contact Annie Keys, Australian Government NRM, Bushcare, QLD (☎07 3214 2650; www.deh.gov.au). With only 20% of native Australian bush habitat remaining, Bushcare's goal is to reverse the long-term decline of native vegetation.

Conservation Volunteers Australia, P.O. Box 423, Ballarat VIC 3353 (☎03 5333 1483 or nationwide ☎1800 032 501; www.conservationvolunteers.com.au). Offers travel volunteer packages (AUS$30 per day, members and concessions $20) that include service opportunities (wildlife and environmental work) as well as accommodation, meals, and project-related transport.

Earthwatch, 3 Clocktower Pl., Maynard MA 01754-0075, USA (☎800-776-0188 or 978-461-0081; www.earthwatch.org). Melbourne office 126 Bank St. South, Melbourne VIC 3205, (☎03 9682 6828; www.earthwatch.org/australia). Arranges 1 to 3wk. programs promoting conservation of natural resources, wildlife ecology, and other environmental studies. Costs vary based on program location and duration, but average US$3000. Total cost covers room, board, transportation (excluding airfare), insurance, and program costs. Some financial aid available for high school students.

International Volunteers for Peace (IVP), see **Community-based Projects,** p. 85.

Landcare Australia, P.O. Box 5666, West Chatswood NSW 1515 (☎02 9412 1040; www.landcareaustralia.com.au). Landcare Australia works to raise funds for, and awareness of, environmental issues. It also acts as an umbrella organization for Bushcare and Coastcare Australia. Contact regional headquarters to learn how you can help.

Volunteers for Peace, see **Community-based Projects,** p. 85.

Wet Tropics Volunteers, P.O. Box 2050, Cairns QLD 4870 (☎07 4052 0555; www.wettropics.gov.au). Volunteers work in programs for park visitors and schools, as well as environment rehabilitation, at the Wet Tropics World Heritage Area.

COASTAL PRESERVATION

With 25,760km of coastline, Australian beaches are second to none. Unfortunately, these national treasures are feeling the strain of increased development. In a country where 70% of the population lives within 100km of the coast, there is much to be done to protect coastal regions.

Coastcare Australia, Marine and Water Division, Environment Australia, P.O. Box 787, Canberra, ACT 2601 (☎1800 803 772). Volunteers build access paths, remove weeds, fence dunes, and educate visitors about the fragility of coastal ecosystems. Join one of the 2000 groups in Australia.

Order of Underwater Coral Heroes (OUCH), P.O. Box 180, Airlie Beach, QLD 4802 (☎07 4946 7435; www.ouchvolunteers.org). OUCH volunteers work on a part-time basis, monitoring endangered stretches of coral reef.

Shell Coastal Volunteers, Conservation Volunteers Australia, 41 Tribune St., South Brisbane, QLD 4101 (☎03 5333 1483; www.conservationvolunteers.com.au/shell). In a joint effort with Conservation Volunteers Australia, Shell Coastal Volunteers addresses problems like pollution, threats to marine biodiversity, and habitat degradation. The organization undertakes about 100 urban and regional projects every year along Australia's coastline.

Before handing your money over to any volunteer or study program, make sure you know exactly what you're getting into. Get the names of previous participants and ask them about their experiences, as some programs sound much better on paper than in reality. The questions below are a good place to start:

- What will your responsibilities be? What is a typical day like?
- Will you be the only person in the program? If not, what are other participants like? How old are they? How much interaction will you have with them?
- Are room and board included? If so, what is the arrangement? Will you be expected to share a room? A bathroom? What are the meals like?
- Is transportation included? Are there any additional expenses?
- How much free time will you have? Will you be able to travel around?
- What kind of safety net is set up? Will you still be covered by your home insurance? Does the program have an emergency plan?

WILDLIFE PROTECTION AND RESCUE

The Australian continent is well-known throughout the world for its exotic wildlife. Unfortunately, Australia also has the worst mammalian extinction rate on the planet due to development and the encroachment of non-native, or "feral," species. Hundreds of animals currently reside on the government's list of endangered or vulnerable species (including emu, bat, petrel, frog, turtle, bandicoot, wallaby, parrot, and kangaroo species). Numerous organizations seek volunteers for protection efforts.

Australian Koala Foundation, GPO Box 2659, 1/40 Charlotte St., Brisbane QLD 4000 (☎07 3229 7233; www.savethekoala.com). With an estimated 80% of their original habitat destroyed, Australia's koalas are seriously threatened. The AKF works to save their natural habitat. Volunteers can participate in a 2-week trip, working with researchers and staff in the field. The field trip cost of AUS$2500 includes food, accommodation, domestic transportation, and basic insurance.

Birds Australia, 415 Riversdale Rd., Hawthorn East VIC 3123 (☎03 9882 2622). Volunteer with the Threatened Bird Network to protect native Australian avians.

Cape Tribulation Tropical Research Station, PMB 5, Cape Tribulation QLD 4873 (☎07 4098 0063; www.austrop.org.au). Volunteers, students, interns, and researchers work to conserve threatened lowland tropical ecosystems and coastal environments. The station also works to save the Spectacled Flying Fox. Min. 2wk. commitment. All station members are expected assist with station cleaning duties in addition to conservation work. Inquire about fees. Cost includes 3 meals per day and accommodation. Transportation and insurance are not provided.

Dolphin Discovery Centre, P.O. Box 1178, Bunbury WA 6231 (☎08 9791 3088; www.dolphindiscovery.com.au). Volunteer duties include public education, keeping the beach clean, and supervising the interaction zone where visitors meet the dolphins. The center selects 30-40 temporary staff each year, most of whom are non-Australians. Short-term and long-term volunteer options available. Lunch provided. Formal training in marine biology not required.

Earthwatch, see **Land Conservation,** p. 83.

Involvement Volunteers, see **Community Based Projects,** p. 85.

Mon Repos Conservation Park, P.O. Box 1735, Bundaberg QLD 4670 (☎07 4131 1600). The MRCP serves as a contact point for the Queensland Turtle Research Program. The program seeks volunteers who can dedicate at least 2wk. to assist with measuring turtles, recording tag numbers, and relocating eggs during turtle season (Nov.-Mar.).

COMMUNITY-BASED PROJECTS

Though Australia is one of the most developed countries in the world, not all communities have benefitted equally, particularly in economically depressed Aboriginal regions. Volunteers in these communities typically work to promote economic self-sufficiency through education and facilities construction.

Amizade, Ltd., P.O. Box 110107, Pittsburgh, PA 15232, USA (☎888-973-4443; www.amizade.org). Volunteers spend 2½ weeks in an Aboriginal community in Hervey Bay, QLD, working to promote Aboriginal culture and provide opportunities for economic self-sufficiency. Volunteers must be 12 or older (ages 12-17 need to be accompanied by a parent or guardian). The US$2060 program fee includes room, board, program materials, and cultural, educational, and recreational experiences. Does not include insurance or airfare. US$250 deposit required.

Cape York Partnerships, P.O. Box 2528, Cairns QLD 4870 (☎07 4048 1422; www.capeyorkpartnerships.com). Facilitates placement of volunteers in Aboriginal communities in Cairns as well as remote towns and stations. Volunteers work on projects in education, business, land management, preservation, and other projects. Offers variety of programs from 4 weeks to 12 months of service. Provides basic accommodation only; volunteers are responsible for transportation, food, insurance, and other expenses.

International Volunteers for Peace (IVP), 499 Elizabeth St., Surry Hills NSW 2010 (☎02 9699 1129; www.ivp.org.au). Arranges placement in Australian community work camps for members age 18 and up. Membership AUS$35. AUS$350 work camp fee includes room, board, and basic insurance. Outside Australia, contact **Service Civil International (SCI),** IVP's affiliate, in your home country (www.sciint.org).

Volunteers for Peace, 1034 Tiffany Rd., Belmont, VT 05730, USA (☎802-259-2759; www.vfp.org). Partnered, but not synonymous, with IVP (above). Arranges placement in work camps in Australia. Camp projects vary each year, but usually include environmental and social work and arts projects. Membership required for registration. Programs average US$200-500 for 2-3 weeks; the program fee includes room and board, as well as work materials.

Involvement Volunteers, P.O. Box 218, Port Melbourne VIC 3207 (☎03 9646 5504; www.volunteering.org.au). Offers volunteering options in Australia including social service, research, education, wildlife conservation, and farmwork. Structure and support varies. Registration fee AUS$275.

Habitat for Humanity Australia, P.O. Box 1154, Parramatta NSW 2124 (info@habitat.org.au; www.habitat.org.au). Offers volunteer opportunities in Australia to live and build houses in a host community. Short-term program costs range from AUS$1700-5500 and include all in-country expenses except airfare.

STUDYING

Study abroad programs in Australia range from informal cultural courses to college-level classes, often for credit. Unless you plan to complete your full degree in Australia, *most undergraduate programs require current enrollment in a university.* In order to choose the program that best fits you, be sure to research costs, duration, and type of accommodation available, as well as what kind of students participate in the program, before making your decision. A good resource for finding programs that cater to your particular interests is www.studyabroad.com, which has links to different semester abroad programs based on a variety of criteria, including desired location and focus of study. Although this section deals primarily with university-level study abroad, International Student Exchange Australia (www.i-s-e.com.au) features programs for high school students, and Elderhostel, Inc. (☎800 454 5768; www.elderhostel.org) has two- to five-week educational opportunities for seniors ages 55 and over.

STUDENT VISA INFORMATION See the Department of Immigration and Multicultural and Indigenous Affairs website (www.immi.gov.au) to apply for visas. The following visa is required for temporary study in Australia:

Student Visa. All students planning to study in Australia need student visas. Obtaining one requires an application and AUS$420 fee, a valid passport, and Electronic Confirmation of Enrollment (eCoE)/Acceptance Advice Form from Australian institution. Students enrolling for over 12 months need a signed medical report. Citizens of the US, Sweden, and Norway visiting for a year or less can get a visa online at www.immi.gov.au/e_visa/students.htm.

Students of conservation and natural resource management may be particularly drawn to Australia, where they can conduct practical placements or work for credit in the country's many national parks. Contact Parks Victoria (☎03 8627 4699; www.parkweb.vic.gov.au) for more information.

While the easiest way to arrange to study abroad in Australia is through your own university, the following list of organizations can help place you in programs if your school's options are limited.

AMERICAN PROGRAMS

Arcadia University for Education Abroad, 450 S. Easton Rd., Glenside, PA 19038, USA (☎866-927-2234; www.arcadia.edu/cea). Offers undergraduate and graduate programs all over Australia. Costs range from US$9000-15,000 (semester) to US$16,000-32,000 (full-year) and include room and board.

Council on International Educational Exchange (CIEE), 7 Custom House St., 3rd fl., Portland, ME 04101, USA (☎800-407-8839; www.ciee.org/study). Sponsors university study in Melbourne, Perth, Sydney, and Wollongong. Costs range from US$12,000-16,000 (semester) to US$19,000-25,000 (full-year) and include housing.

Institute for the International Education of Students (IES), 33 N. LaSalle St., 15th fl., Chicago, IL 60602, USA (☎800-995-2300; www.IESabroad.org). Offers year-long, semester, and summer programs for university study in Adelaide and Melbourne. Costs differ by location: Adelaide US$13,000/25,000 (semester/year), Melbourne US$16,000/30,000, Sydney US$13,000/29,000. Room and board included. Scholarships available.

American Institute for Foreign Study, College Division, River Plaza, 9 West Broad St., Stamford, CT 06902, USA (☎800-727-2437, ext. 5163; www.aifsabroad.com). Runs a program with Macquarie University in Sydney. Costs range from US$15,000 (semester) to US$28,000 (full-year), and include room and board. Scholarships available.

School for International Training, College Semester Abroad, Admissions, Kipling Rd., P.O. Box 676, Brattleboro, VT 05302, USA (☎802-258-3212; www.sit.edu). Offers programs with environmental or multicultural focuses. Semester-long programs cost around US$17,000 and include housing, meals, and flights. Also runs the **Experiment in International Living** (☎802 257 7751; www.usexperiment.org), with a 5wk. summer program that offers high-school students cross-cultural homestays, community service, ecological adventures, and costs US$5950.

AUSTRALIAN UNIVERSITIES

Applying directly to Australian universities can be much cheaper than using an outside program, though it is generally more difficult to receive academic credit (and often housing). A fairly comprehensive list of schools and services is available at www.studyabroadlinks.com/search/Australia. The Australian government's website, www.studyinaustralia.gov.au, is another good tool, with information on institutions, requirements, the application process, visas, and living costs. IDP Education Australia (☎02 6285 8222; www.idp.com) is a non-profit organization that can help guide you through the process, with info on institutions, access to IDP counselors, and a free application and enrollment processing service.

Listed below are several Australian universities that run their own international study programs. Costs vary widely by program and field of study.

University of New South Wales, Level 16 Mathews Building, UNSW Kensington, Sydney NSW (☎02 9385 3179; www.studyabroad.unsw.edu.au). UNSW has both semester offerings (AUS$9250), and 6-week study programs during the Northern Hemisphere summer for undergraduates and graduate students looking for a shorter study experience in Australia. Subjects include Australian history, media and environmentalism, biogeography, and conservation, among others.

University of Sydney, Services Building G12, The University of Sydney, NSW 2006 (☎02 9351 3699; www.usyd.edu.au/fstudent/studyabroad). The university's study abroad offers an opportunity to study in Australia's most famous city. Applicants should have a GPA of 3.0 or higher.

University of Melbourne, International Centre, University of Melbourne, VIC 3010 (☎03 8344 6593; www.futurestudents.unimelb.edu.au/int/saex/index.html). Students choose from a variety of courses while experiencing the sophistication of Melbourne.

Australian National University, International Education Office, Australian National University, Canberra ACT 0200 (☎02 6125 5111; www.anu.edu.au/ieo/ivsp/index_int.html). Situated in the national capital, ANU boasts a multicultural community of over 1000 international students. Applicants should have a GPA of 3.0 or higher.

WORKING

Many visitors to Australia find that short-term work is a great way to experience Aussie culture while funding further travels. As with volunteering, work opportunities tend to fall into two categories: long-term jobs that allow travelers to get to know another part of the world as a member of the community, and short-term jobs to finance the next leg of travel. Australia's various climates mean that there is always something to be harvested somewhere, and many travelers pay their way around the continent by picking fruit. Compared to fruit pickers who enjoy a more nomadic lifestyle, those seeking long-term work can stay in one place, immersed in local life. Before signing on to either, be sure you can get a work permit. US citizens can currently only acquire a four-month work visa for Australia (called a **Special Program Visa**) by going through a placement agency, such as those listed below under Long-Term Work, while Canadians and most Europeans have greater flexibility under the 12-month **Working Holiday Visa**. See the box on p. 11 for specific **visa requirements** to work in Australia.

If you plan to work in Australia, you should apply for a **tax file number (TFN)** from the Australian Taxation Office (www.ato.gov.au). Without a TFN, you may be taxed at a much higher rate than necessary. You also may consider opening a **bank account,** which is easier to do in Australia than from overseas. An excellent resource for those considering working in Australia is *Live & Work in Australia & New Zealand* (Vacation Work Publications, by Dan Boothby and Susan Kelly).

The following towns and cities are known to be particularly good places for travelers to find work. (Most short-term work is seasonal, see **Short-Term Work,** p. 91 for more information. Fruit-picking is generally the most reliable bet.)

WORK OPPORTUNITIES BY CITY AND TOWN

STATE	CITY OR TOWN	PAGE	TYPE OF WORK
ACT	**Canberra**	p. 95	Restaurants and hospitality, wineries.
New South Wales	**Katoomba**	p. 158	Hospitality and fruit-picking.
	Jindabyne	p. 231	Hospitality and ski work.
	Riverina	p. 238	Farm work and fruit-picking.
	Sydney	p. 110	Variable.
	Tamworth	p. 218	Ranches.
Northern Territory	**Alice Springs**	p. 295	Office and computer work.
	Katherine	p. 282	Farming.
Queensland	**Bowen**	p. 401	Fruit-picking. Considered by some to be QLD's best stop for short-term employment.
	Brisbane	p. 314	Restaurants, childcare, promotions.
	Bundaberg	p. 377	Harvesting vegetables.

WORK OPPORTUNITIES BY CITY AND TOWN			
STATE	**CITY OR TOWN**	**PAGE**	**TYPE OF WORK**
Queensland, continued	**Innisfail**	p. 416	Fruit-picking.
	Maroochy Shire	p. 355	Fruit-picking.
	Stanthrope	p. 351	Fruit-picking.
South Australia	**Barossa Valley**	p. 487	Wineries and vineyards.
Tasmania	**Cygnet and Huon Valley**	p. 541	Fruit-picking.
Victoria	**Gelantipy**	p. 679	Cattle farming.
	Mildura	p. 655	Variable.
Western Australia	**Broome**	p. 746	Hospitality and food service.
	Carnarvon	p. 736	Fruit-picking.
	Kalgoorlie	p. 727	Mining.
	Margaret River	p. 705	Wineries and vineyards.
	Perth	p. 685	Hospitality, restaurant work, and ranch and roadhouse work.

VISA INFORMATION

See the Department of Immigration and Multicultural and Indigenous Affairs website (www.immi.gov.au) to apply for visas. The following visas are required for temporary work in Australia.

Working Holiday Visa. For 18- to 30-year-old citizens of Canada, China, Denmark, Finland, France, Germany, Hong Kong, Ireland, Italy, Japan, Korea, Malta, the Netherlands, Norway, Sweden, and the UK. Valid for 12 months, but does not allow work for any one employer for more than 3 months. Requirements include application and AUS$165 fee, valid passport, and proof of adequate funds for a flight home.

Special Program Visa. For 18- to 30-year-old US citizens. Allows up to 4 months of temporary work with an approved exchange program. Requirements include application and AUS$165 fee, valid passport, flight itinerary, proof of funds, and letter from employment program (see p. 89 for eligible programs).

LONG-TERM WORK

If you're planning on spending more than two months working in Oz, search for a job well in advance and be aware of visa restrictions (see p. 11). Some traditional Australian jobs may be easier to obtain with proper training. **Leconfield Jackaroo and Jillaroo School** offers 11-day training packages on traditional bush methods necessary for work on outback cattle stations, but does not offer placement. (☎02 6769 4230; www.leconfieldjackaroo.com. AUS$950, AUS$150 deposit required.)

International **placement agencies** are often the easiest way to find employment abroad, and they are *the only option for US citizens due to visa requirements.* Be wary of advertisements or companies that claim the ability to get you a job abroad for a fee—oftentimes the listings are out of date, or the same info is available online or in newspapers. If searching on your own, try **CareerOne** (www.careerone.com.au), Australia's largest job network; or **Monster Work Abroad**

(☎800-MONSTER; www.workabroad.monster.com), which lists openings by citizenship and desired work location. A few placement agencies are listed below; when going through an organization be sure to use one that's reputable.

BUNAC, 16 Bowling Green Ln., London, EC1R 0QH (☎02 7251 3472 or 203-264-0901 in US; www.bunac.com). Helps organize working holidays; arranges visas, bank accounts, and tax file numbers; forwards mail; provides Internet access and prepaid phone cards; and helps find jobs and accommodations. Program cost does not include visa fees. US$595 plus mandatory travel insurance.

International Cooperative Education, 15 Spiros Way, Menlo Park, CA, 94025, USA (☎650-323-4944; www.icemenlo.com). Finds summer jobs (2-3 months) for students in Australia. Specific programs include Aboriginal community work in Western Australia. Costs include a US$250 application fee and a US$700 placement fee.

Travellers Contact Point, Level 7, 428 George St., Sydney NSW (☎9221 8744; info@travellers.com.au). Employment board and recruiting officers for travelers with work visas, specifically during holidays. Open M-F 9am-6pm, Sa 10am-4pm.

Visitoz, Springbrook Farm, Goomeri QLD 4601 (☎07 4168 6106; www.visitoz.org). Arranges jobs in rural Australia, as well as English-language instruction, farm holidays, and agricultural training. Job options range from work in pubs and hostels to teaching in the Outback. Farm and station work requires introductory agricultural courses at a Visitoz training farm. Program fee approximately AUS$1790.

Work Experience Down Under, 2330 Marinship Way, Suite 250, Sausalito, CA 94965, USA (☎888-449-3872; www.ccusa.com). Work for up to 12 months (US Citizens 4 months). The program costs US$360, plus an additional US$35 application fee and US$45 per month for insurance. Services include visa processing, pre- and post-arrival aid, use of Job Search Centres in Sydney, and two nights accommodation.

AU PAIR WORK

Au pairs are typically women (although sometimes men), aged 18-27, who work as live-in nannies, caring for children and doing light housework in exchange for room, board, and a small spending allowance or stipend. Most former au pairs speak favorably of their experience. One perk of the job is that it allows you to really get to know the country without the high expenses of traveling. Drawbacks, however, often include mediocre pay and long hours. The average weekly stipend ranges from AUS$190-220/US$140-165. Much of the au pair experience depends on the family with whom you're placed. The agencies below are a good starting point for looking for employment as an au pair.

Au-Pair Australia, PO Box 1164, Glebe NSW 2037 (☎61 2 9571 6121; www.aupair-australia.com.au).

Childcare International, Ltd., Trafalgar House, Grenville Pl., London NW7 3SA (☎44 020 8906-3116; www.childint.co.uk).

InterExchange, 161 Sixth Ave., New York, NY 10013, USA (☎212-924-0446; fax 924-0575; www.interexchange.org).

INTERNSHIPS AND WORK EXPERIENCES

For the career-minded traveler, professional experience in Australia is a great way to get ahead while getting away. Internships in Australia can most often be found in the media industry, but can also be found in a variety of other professional fields. Although the terms "internship" and "work experience" are often used interchangeably, work experience tends to be more laid-back and unstructured. The most economical way to plan an experience is to organize a placement on your own; however, this can be difficult for someone without connections. Listed below are several internship and work experience placement programs that will take care of the leg-work.

Australian National Internships Program (ANIP), Building 3, 1 Block, Old Administration Area, Tennis Court Ln., Australian National University, Canberra ACT 0200. (☎02 6125 5111; www.anu.edu.au/anip). Arranges internships in public policy for college and graduate students from Australia or abroad. In addition to on-the-job experience, interns learn interview techniques and hone their computer skills. Cost falls between AUS$5400-8100.

Australearn, 12050 N. Pecos St., #320, Westminster, CO 80234, USA (☎800-980-0033; www.australearn.org/Programs/Internship/intern.htm). A US-based company that coordinates with Global Internship Services. Opportunities exist to work in a variety of fields. Expect to pay US$3400-4900 for 8- to 12-week programs. Scholarship applications available online.

Australia Internships, Ste. 1, Savoir Faire Park Rd. Milton, Brisbane QLD 4064. (☎07 3305 8408; www.interships.com.au). Organizes internships lasting from a month to a year in fields ranging from accounting to forestry. Fee of AUS$1900-4300 includes custom-designed internship placement, assistance with the visa process, and counseling support services.

International Association for the Exchange of Students for Technical Experience (IAESTE), 10400 Little Patuxent Pkwy. Ste. 250, Columbia, MD 21044-3519, USA (☎410-997-3069; www.aipt.org/subpages/iaeste_us/index.php). Offers 8- to 12-week paid work programs in Australia for college students. US$500 program fee plus US$50 registration fee and US$100 refundable deposit.

SHORT-TERM WORK

Traveling for long periods of time is expensive; many backpackers try their hand at odd jobs for a few weeks to support their travel habit. Climatic diversity across the continent ensures that picking jobs are available year-round, and the popularity of the work has created a sort of fruit-picking subculture. Pickers are paid by the piece-rate wage and can expect to earn about AUS$300 per week after taxes once they get the hang of it. Many hostels in picking areas cater specifically to workers, offering transportation to worksites and other such amenities.

FRUIT-PICKING OPPORTUNITIES BY REGION

STATE	LOCATION	AUSTRALIAN SEASON	WORK AVAILABLE
New South Wales	Bathurst, Dubbo, Orange	Summer	Orchard, stone, and other fruits, onions, asparagus
	North Coast	Summer Winter	Bananas Citrus, grapes
Queensland	Inland on NSW border; Warwick	Summer	Stone and orchard fruits; grapes
	Central Coast	May-December	Fruit and vegetables
	Northern Coast	May-November	Sugar cane, bananas, tobacco
	Bundaberg, Childers	Year-round	Fruit and vegetables
South Australia	Barossa Valley	February-April	Grapes
	The Riverland	Year-round	Citrus, peaches, tomatoes
Tasmania	Anywhere	Summer	Orchard and soft fruits, grapes

FRUIT-PICKING OPPORTUNITIES BY REGION			
STATE	LOCATION	AUSTRALIAN SEASON	WORK AVAILABLE
Victoria	Central Northern areas	Summer	Orchard and soft fruits, berries, tobacco, and grapes
Western Australia	Southwest	February-June	Grapes and orchard fruits, prawn
	West Coast	March-October	Crayfish, prawn, and scallop fishing and processing
	Northeast	May-October	Fruit and vegetables

In cities and highly touristed areas, hostels often contain employment boards and sometimes offer employment services to help lodgers find temporary work. One popular option is to work several hours a day at a hostel in exchange for free or discounted room and/or board. Most often, these short-term jobs are found by word of mouth or simply by asking owners of hostels or restaurants. Due to high turnover in the tourism industry there are always establishments eager for help, even if only temporary.

Some tour companies allow travelers to work in exchange for a trip or adventure experience. Those who can't afford the expense of a Whitsunday sailing safari, for example, may be able to see the islands by volunteering on a boat. **"Vollies,"** as they are affectionately called, do much of the cooking and cleaning, with a little time left over for the beach. These positions are very competitive, however. Some companies have wait lists for volunteers, while others may have positions on an informal basis. The best way to find a *vollie* spot is to ask around.

While word of mouth is generally an effective method of finding work, many employers join networks that connect workers to jobs nationwide. These services sometimes charge a membership fee, but often their (free) websites alone can be helpful. The following resources provide information and access to job networks.

Australian Job Search (www.jobsearch.gov.au). A government agency with tens of thousands of employment listings. The website features a 'Harvest Trail' that backpackers can use to find harvesting work by location and date.

Go Harvest (Harvest Hotline ☎1300 720 126; www.goharvest.com). Features a placement service that connects experienced and beginner pickers to harvesting openings. Numerous positions available include pickers, truck drivers, and machinery operators.

Harvest Hotline Australia (☎07 4922 6033; www.harvesthotlineaustralia.com.au). Recruits seasonal backpackers for picking work (10-12hr. shifts), and provides members with assistance in filing taxes, setting up medical insurance and bank accounts, discount travel packages, and phone cards. Membership AUS$60 for 3 months, AUS$160 for a year.

Willing Workers on Organic Farms (WWOOF) (☎03 5155 0218; www.wwoof.com.au). Exchange your labor for food, accommodation, and local culture. Work is generally at organic farms or cooperatives, and average expectations are 4-6hr. of service per day. Membership (AUS$55 or AUS$65 for 2 people) includes a guide to hosts in Australia and can be purchased from outlets throughout the country.

Workabout Australia (☎02 6884 7777; www.workaboutaustralia.com.au). Joining the club costs AUS$55/US$40. The website sells *Workabout Australia,* a book containing seasonal and casual employment info by state; website also offers a free preview list of short-term employment vacancies by state, including employers' contact information.

Workstay (☎9226 0970; www.workstay.com.au). Workstay arranges live-in work at country pubs, roadhouses, and cattle stations in WA. Minimum time ranges from 6 to 12 weeks, generally paying AUS$14-16 per hr. Open M-F 9:30am-5:30pm.

SHORT-TERM HOUSING

The short-term nature of most experiences abroad in Australia, combined with the desire for mobility, mean that the majority of visitors who come on working holiday or student visas live in hostels or dorms. Throughout *Let's Go: Australia*, hostels that cater to working travelers with job transportation help and low weekly rates are noted. Some hostels even provide free room and board to travelers willing to work for them a few hours a day. (Many hostels don't advertise these opportunities; it's always worth it to ask.) Similarly, those volunteering in a national park may find that the park is able to provide reasonably priced housing in a cabin or caravan. Another option sometimes utilized by students and volunteers is a **homestay** with an Australian family. In living with a family, there is potential to build lifelong friendships with native Aussies and to experience day-to-day life as a local, but conditions can vary greatly from one household to the next. **Study Abroad Links** (www.studyabroadlinks.com/search/Australia/Homestay_Programs/) lists websites of homestay programs throughout Australia, catering to students and non-students alike.

Australians have a strong preference for owning rather than **renting** homes. As a result, availability is low. On the bright side, renting in Australia is surprisingly inexpensive, with a three-bedroom house in cosmopolitan Melbourne going for an average of AUS$200-500 per week. Apartments are generally referred to as **'units,'** and are advertised for rent under the **'To Let'** heading in the classified section of newspapers and weekly community guides. Additionally, universities, cafes, and hostels often have notice boards advertising rentals, sublets, and shares. Finally, **Craigslist** (www.craigslist.org) has expanded recently into Australia and is typically a great resource for rentals, shares, and furnishings.

SHARE YOUR EXPERIENCE. Have you had a particularly enjoyable volunteer, study, or work experience in Australia that you'd like to share with other travelers? Email feedback@letsgo.com and let us know about it!

SYDNEY CULINARY SCHOOL

When I told people that I was heading to Sydney for ten weeks to attend French culinary school, I got more than a few strange looks. Many asked why I wasn't heading to Paris to bake souffles and croissants; others wanted to know why I would spend my time in Australia in a hot kitchen rather than surfing at Bondi Beach. I myself can't fully explain how I ended up at the Cordon Bleu in Sydney, but my experience there speaks for itself.

The Cordon Bleu, founded in 1895, is one of the most famous culinary schools in the world. It has 22 institutes across the globe, including locations in France, Korea, Mexico, Japan, and, of course, Australia. Though the flagship school is in Paris, the Sydney site offers several attractive advantages. Courses are taught in English rather than in French with translation, as in Paris. Aspiring chefs can find true inspiration in Australia's world famous restaurants, where chefs are known for their innovative Mod Oz fusion cuisine. And Sydney offers an amazing variety of quality raw materials, from local seafood, to produce, to wine.

Best of all, Sydney is one of the Cordon Bleu's less expensive locations, though it is by no means cheap. Tuition runs AUS$7500, as compared to €7000 in Paris, a difference of over US$3000. Additionally, the cost of living in Australia is far lower than in France. And to offset their tuition bills, Sydney students can work in Australia. Unlike normal tourists, they can apply for student visas, which allow foreign students to work 20 hours a week during the school term and unlimited hours during during vacations.

The Cordon Bleu in Sydney offers six courses: basic, intermediate, and superior levels of both cuisine and pastry. Each course consists of three six-hour lessons per week and lasts ten weeks. While the school is designed to provide professional training, many of the students in the basic class are there just to become better home cooks, not five-star chefs. In each class, the chef instructor cooks the day's menu in a special kitchen equipped with lecture seating and cameras. After the demonstration, students individually prepare the same dishes. In the basic class we learned how to use different types of knives, make stocks, and handle pastry dough, among other things. In addition to traditional French cuisine, we prepared dishes that highlighted native Australian ingredients, including kangaroo meat and wild limes.

Although the classes were wonderful, it was the other students that made the experience memorable. We each had our own workstation, but professional kitchens rely on teamwork, and the classroom experience was no different. Students in my courses helped each other out, whether showing a classmate how to trim a rack of lamb or saving someone's unattended sauce from burning. After class, we explored Sydney together, particularly the city's restaurants and markets. I've never had a more interesting meal than the one I shared with fellow students at Bécasse, one of Sydney's top restaurants. We ordered a tasting menu, took pictures of the presentation of each dish, and carefully critiqued everything as we ate.

Though I spent more than a few afternoons at Manly soaking up the sun, being enrolled at the Cordon Bleu introduced me to a different side of Sydney. From my field trip to the auction room of the Sydney Fish Market to stories from the kitchens of Australia's best restaurants, I was given a unique glimpse into the Australian culinary world. And though I have no intention of pursuing a culinary career, I hope to return to Sydney someday to wine and dine at the restaurants where my old schoolmates are working as the next generation of Australian chefs.

The Cordon Bleu (☎08 8346 3700; www.cordonbleu.net) offers ten-week culinary courses in Sydney (beginning in January, April, July, and October) and advanced programs in Adelaide. Those wanting to learn more about Sydney's culinary scene without spending ten weeks slaving over a hot stove can attend any number of one-day cooking classes at the Sydney Fish Market.

Julie Stephens *is a graduate of Harvard University with a degree in Social Studies. A former Publishing Director for Let's Go, she spent a year off from college attending cooking school in Sydney, studying Indian art in Rajasthan, and working on her honors thesis at the British Library in London.*

AUSTRALIAN CAPITAL TERRITORY

Carved out of New South Wales in 1908, the Australian Capital Territory (ACT), was a geographic and political compromise between Sydney and Melbourne in the competition to serve as capital of the newly-federated Australia. Although ACT is not a fully qualified state, Canberra is the center and capital of the territory, not to mention the political heart of the country. The quiet metropolitan region is filled with neatly designed commuter towns, creeping outward from Canberra toward the bush. The ACT's fusion of cosmopolitanism and outback flavor promises visitors a truly capital look at high culture and government.

CANBERRA ☎02

For a city that is home to 310,000 people and the government of an entire continent, Canberra's streets are remarkably quiet. Wide avenues, huge green spaces, and sleek modern architecture offer a utopian vision of a metropolis; yet the city feels empty. Still, Canberra contains a number of beautifully planned, state-of-the-art tourist attractions—everything from space centers to dinosaur museums—even though it has few tourists to appreciate them. This emptiness can be traced to Canberra's reputation for dullness as a tourist spot.

Despite slow tourist traffic, there are few other places on the east coast with so many worthwhile **free sights.** The city itself is a unique attraction: designed by Walter Burley Griffin, student of famed architect Frank Lloyd Wright, Canberra is an entirely planned urban space, built from raw farmland. Its subsequent precision comes off as somehow eerie, but inspiring; from certain spots in the city, it is apparent that you're standing in the middle of a geometric plan.

HIGHLIGHTS OF THE AUSTRALIAN CAPITAL TERRITORY

DON'T MISS the **political antics** that ensue when Parliament floor debates. (p. 102)

LEARN about the history of the nation through the **National Museum of Australia's** state-of-the-art exhibits that are at turns affecting and fanciful. (p. 103)

PERUSE the massive **National Gallery of Australia's** Australian and International art, contemporary and ancient, for free. (p. 102)

WALK by monuments lining Anzac Pde. to reach the **Australian War Memorial.** (p. 103)

INTERCITY TRANSPORTATION

BY PLANE

Located in Pialligo, 7km east of the Central Business District (CBD), the **Canberra International Airport** is easy to get to by car. From Commonwealth Ave., take Parkes Way east past the roundabout at Kings Ave., which becomes Morshead Dr., then Pialligo Ave. On weekdays, **Deane's Buslines** (☎6299 3722; http://deanesbuslines.com.au) operates the **Air Liner,** a shuttle service that transports passengers between the airport and the City Interchange (20min.; M-F 26 per day; $7, $12 round-trip). For weekend transit, a **taxi** (☎13 22 27) is your best bet. ($18-20 from the CBD.) The airport offers domestic flights to only five cities; all international travel requires a stop in Sydney.

All flights listed are one-way, unless otherwise specified: **Virgin Blue Airlines,** (☎13 67 89; www.virginblue.com.au) offers low fares to: Adelaide (1¼hr., 4 per day, from $115); Brisbane (2hr., 3 per day, from $129); Melbourne (1hr., 5 per day, from $99). **Qantas** (☎13 13 13; www.qantas.com.au) connects to: Adelaide (1¼hr., 2-4 per day, from $138); Brisbane (1¼hr., 5 per day, from $150); Melbourne (1hr., 12 per day, from $114); Perth (3hr., 1 per day, from $297); Sydney (50min., 25 per day, from $105).

BY TRAIN

The **Canberra Railway Station,** on the corner of Wentworth Ave. and Mildura St. in Kingston, 6km from CBD, is on ACTION bus routes #39 (bus to Civic 25min., at least 1 per hr.), 80, 83, and 84. **Countrylink** has an office located inside the railway station. (☎13 22 32; www.countrylink.info. Open M-F 6am-5:30pm, Su 10:30am-5:30pm. Seasonal discounts for in-person or credit card bookings. Student discount 50%.) Buses go to Melbourne (9hr., 1 per day, $81), and Brisbane (24hr., 1 per day, $117) via Sydney (4hr., 2 per day, $43).

BY BUS

Intercity **buses** meet at **Jolimont Tourist Centre,** 65-67 Northbourne Ave., north of Alinga St. in Civic. (Open daily in summer 6am-10:30pm; in winter 5am-10:30pm.) Lockers cost $7-12 per day. Bus companies and **Qantas** have desks in the building.

Greyhound Australia, (☎13 14 99 or 13 20 30; www.greyhound.com.au). To: **Adelaide** (18hr., 1 per day, $154); **Albury-Wodonga** (4-6hr., 3 per day, $55); **Goulburn** (1hr., 3-4 per day, $16); **Griffith** (6hr., 1 per day, $57); **Gundagai** (2hr., 3 per day, $34); **Melbourne** (8hr., 3 per day, $77); **Parramatta** (3½hr., 3 per day, $36); **Sydney** (3-4hr., 9 per day, $36); and **Wagga Wagga** (2½-3hr., 2 per day, $43). June-Oct. buses run to: **Cooma** (1½hr., 2 per day, $38); **Perisher Blue** via the **Skitube** (3hr., 2 per day; 1-way $25, same-day return $38, open return $52; families $81/92/131); and **Thredbo** (3¼hr., 2 per day, $62). Open M-F 8am-6pm, Sa 8am-12:30pm, Su 11:30am-6pm.

Murrays, (☎13 22 51; www.murrays.com.au). To: **Batemans Bay** (3hr., 1-2 per day, $24); **Goulburn** (1¼hr., 1 per day, $10); **Narooma** (4¼hr., 1-2 per day, $36); **Sydney** (3-4hr., 3-5 per day, $36); **Wollongong** (3½hr., 1 per day, $31). **Ski-season service** to: **Cooma** (1¼hr., 1 per day, $42); **Jindabyne** (2hr., 1 per day, $42); **Perisher Blue** (2¼hr., 1 per day, $42); and **Thredbo** (3hr., 1 per day, $48). Offers **ski packages,** which include round-trip transport, lift tickets, ski rental, and park entrance from $139.

Countrylink, (☎13 22 32; www.countrylink.info). To: **Cooma** (1¼hr., 1 per day, $15); **Goulburn** (1¼hr., 2 per day, $12). Discounts available for advance bookings online.

BY CAR

The **NRMA automobile club,** 92 Northbourne Ave., is the place to turn with car problems. (☎13 21 32. Open M-F 9:30am-5pm.) For 24hr. **emergency road service,** call ☎13 11 11. All rental companies (except Value) have offices in Braddon and the airport.

Avis, 17 Lonsdale St. (☎6249 6088; www.avis.com.au). Open M-F 8am-6pm, Sa-Sun 8am-noon.

Budget (☎6257 2200; www.budget.com.au), in the Rydges Lakeside Hotel on London Circuit. Open M-F 8am-5pm, Sa 8am-noon.

Europcar, 74 Northbourne Ave. (☎13 13 90; www.europcar.com.au). Open M-F 8am-6pm, Sa-Su 8am-4pm.

Hertz, 32 Mort St. (☎13 30 39 or 6257 4877; www.hertz.com.au.). Open M-F 8am-6pm, Sa 8am-3pm, Su 9am-3pm.

Value Rent-a-Car, (☎1800 629 561.) in the Rydges Capital Hill Hotel on the corner of National Circuit and Canberra Ave. Often has cheaper rates than the larger companies. Open M-F 8am-5pm, Sa-Su 8am-noon.

ORIENTATION

Lake Burley Griffin, formed by the damming of the Molonglo River, splits Canberra in two; on each side is a central hill with concentric roads leading outward. **Commonwealth Avenue** spans the lake and connects the hills. To the north of the lake is **Vernon Circle,** marking the center of Canberra and the southern edge of the area known as **Civic.** Civic serves as the city's social center and bus interchange. Restaurants, shops, and nightclubs crowd the pedestrian mall known as **City Walk** in the area between Northbourne Ave., Akuna St., Bunda St., and London Circuit. Immediately north of Vernon Circle, Commonwealth Ave. becomes Northbourne Ave. To the south of the lake is **State Circle** and the governmental part of the capital. Within State Circle, **Capital Hill's** huge four-pronged flagpole reaches up from the new Parliament House. **Parliamentary Triangle** encloses most of the city's museums and government-related establishments.

If you drive, a good map is essential. Signs often refer to districts rather than streets. The railway station and an assortment of budget lodgings are found in **Kingston,** southeast of Capital Hill, which, along with neighboring **Manuka** (MAHN-ah-ka), is home to trendy restaurants and nightspots. Embassies fill **Yarralumla,** west of Capital Hill. **Dickson,** northeast of Civic via Northbourne Ave. and Antill St., has moderately priced restaurants and markets.

LOCAL TRANSPORTATION

The primary hub for Canberra's public transit system centers on the city bus interchange, located at the junction of East Row, Alinga, and Mort St. Full maps and timetables for all routes are available, free of charge, at the ACTION **information office,** next to the Civic Library on East Row, between Alinga St. and London Circuit. Route maps are also clearly posted near the passenger shelters at the city bus interchange. Timetables are posted at bus stops. Buses generally run M-Sa 6am-midnight and Su 8am-7:30pm, though some routes have more limited hours.

Public Transportation: ACTION bus service (☎13 17 10; www.action.act.gov.au) has converted to a "1 fare, anywhere" policy: $3 will buy 1 trip; ask for a **transfer ticket** from the bus driver, which is good for 1½hr. A **full-day ticket** is $6.60, but get more for your money with a **Shopper's Off-Peak Daily ticket** ($4), valid weekdays 9am-4:30pm and after 6pm, and all-day weekends and public holidays. **Fare-saver tickets** ($22) are available for 10 rides. Tickets can be purchased onboard or at most news agencies.

Taxis: Canberra Cabs (☎13 22 27) covers the city and suburbs 24hr.

Bike Rental: A superb system of **bicycle paths,** allows coverage of the capital by a bike. A ride along the shores of Lake Burley Griffin is an excellent way to take in Parliamentary Triangle. Many hostels rent bikes ($15 per day). **Row 'n' Ride** (☎6228 1264) offers mountain bikes (½ day $30, full day $39), with free delivery and pickup.

PRACTICAL INFORMATION

TOURIST AND FINANCIAL SERVICES

Tourist Offices: Canberra and Region Visitors Centre, 330 Northbourne Ave. (☎6205 0044, accommodations booking ☎1800 100 660; www.visitcanberra.com.au), about

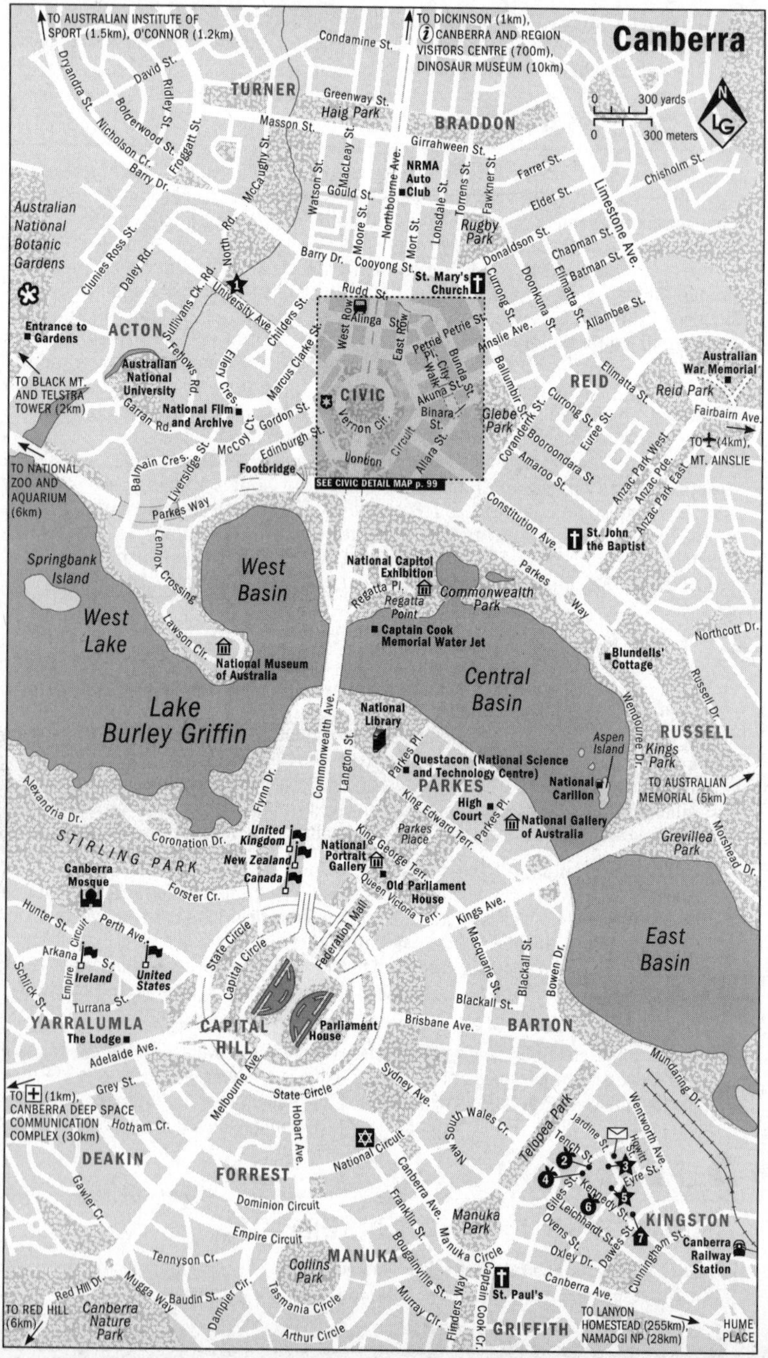

Canberra

TO AUSTRALIAN INSTITUTE OF SPORT (1.5km), O'CONNOR (1.2km)

TO DICKINSON (1km), CANBERRA AND REGION VISITORS CENTRE (700m), DINOSAUR MUSEUM (10km)

0 300 yards
0 300 meters

TURNER
Haig Park
BRADDON
NRMA Auto Club
Rugby Park
Australian National Botanic Gardens
Entrance to Gardens
ACTON
Australian National University
National Film and Archive
TO BLACK MT. AND TELSTRA TOWER (2km)
St. Mary's Church
CIVIC
Footbridge
SEE CIVIC DETAIL MAP p. 99
REID
Reid Park
Australian War Memorial
Glebe Park
TO (4km), MT. AINSLIE
TO NATIONAL ZOO AND AQUARIUM (6km)
St. John the Baptist
Springbank Island
West Lake
West Basin
National Capitol Exhibition
Commonwealth Park
Regatta Point
Captain Cook Memorial Water Jet
National Museum of Australia
Blundells' Cottage
Central Basin
Lake Burley Griffin
National Library
Questacon (National Science and Technology Centre)
PARKES
Aspen Island
National Carillon
RUSSELL
Kings Park
TO AUSTRALIAN MEMORIAL (5km)
High Court
National Gallery of Australia
Grevillea Park
STIRLING PARK
United Kingdom
New Zealand
Canada
National Portrait Gallery
Old Parliament House
Parkes Place
Canberra Mosque
East Basin
Ireland
United States
YARRALUMLA
The Lodge
CAPITAL HILL
Parliament House
BARTON
TO (1km), CANBERRA DEEP SPACE COMMUNICATION COMPLEX (30km)
DEAKIN
FORREST
Telopea Park
Manuka Park
KINGSTON
Canberra Railway Station
MANUKA
Collins Park
St. Paul's
TO RED HILL (6km)
Canberra Nature Park
GRIFFITH
TO LANYON HOMESTEAD (255km), NAMADGI NP (28km)
HUME PLACE

Streets: Condamine St., David St., Ridley St., Dryandra St., Bolderwood St., Froggatt St., Nicholson Cr., Barry Dr., Greenway St., Masson St., McCaughey St., Watson St., MacLeay St., Northbourne Ave., Girrahween St., Lonsdale St., Torrens St., Fawkner St., Farrer St., Elder St., Limestone Ave., Chisholm St., Gould St., Moore St., Mort St., Donaldson St., Chapman St., Batman St., Clunies Ross St., Daley Rd., North Rd., Barry Dr., Cooyong St., Rudd St., Currong St., Doonkuna St., Elimatta St., Allambee St., Sullivans Ck. Rd., University Ave., Childers St., Alinga St., West Row, East Row, Petrie Pl., Petrie St., Ainslie Ave., Fellows Rd., Ellery Cres., Marcus Clarke St., City Walk, Bunda St., Akuna St., Ballumbir St., Elimatta St., Garran Rd., Gordon St., Vernon Cir., Binara St., Currong St., Euree St., Fairbairn Ave., McCoy Ct., Edinburgh St., London Circuit, Allara St., Coranderrk St., Booroondara St., Amaroo St., Anzac Park West, Anzac Pde., Anzac Park East, Balmain Cres., Liversidge St., Parkes Way, Constitution Ave., Lennox Crossing, Regatta Pl., Parkes Way, Lawson Cir., Northcott Dr., Russell Dr., Wendouree Dr., Commonwealth Ave., Langton St., Parkes Pl., Flynn Dr., King Edward Terr., Alexandria Dr., Coronation Dr., King George Terr., Parkes Pl., Morshead Dr., Queen Victoria Terr., Forster Cr., Kings Ave., Hunter St., Perth Ave., Circuit, State Circle, Capital Circle, Federation Mall, Macquarie St., Blackall St., Bowen Dr., Arkana St., Empire Circuit, Schlick St., Turrana St., Blackall St., Brisbane Ave., Adelaide Ave., Melbourne Ave., Sydney Ave., Mundaring Dr., Grey St., Hotham Cr., State Circle, Hobart Ave., New South Wales Cr., Jardine St., Tench St., Wentworth Ave., Howitt St., Eyre St., National Circuit, Canberra Ave., Giles St., Kennedy St., Gawler Cr., Dominion Circuit, Franklin St., Leichhardt St., Ovens St., Empire Circuit, Manuka Circle, Oxley Dr., Dawes St., Cunningham St., Tennyson Cr., Bougainville St., Captain Cook Cr., Canberra Ave., Mugga Way, Red Hill Dr., Baudin St., Dampier Cr., Tasmania Circle, Murray Cr., Flinders Way, Arthur Circle

ACT

3km north of Vernon Circle, answers all your questions about Canberra and current happenings. Take bus #51, 52, 56, or 80. Open M-F 9am-5:30pm, Sa-Su 9am-4pm. Wheelchair accessible. **Canberra Tourism Booth** is inside **Jolimont Tourist Centre,** 2 blocks from the city bus interchange. Open M-F 9am-5pm, Sa-Su 10am-2pm.

Budget Travel: STA Travel, 13 Garema Pl. (☎6247 8633; www.statravel.com.au), on the corner of City Walk. Open M-Th 9am-5pm, F 9am-6pm, Sa 10am-4pm.

Embassies: Unless specified, all locations listed below are located in Yarralumla. Getting there can involve a complicated transport network, but bus route #31 or 32 will take you there. **Canada** (☎6270 4000), on Commonwealth Ave. south of the lake. Open M-F 8:30am-12:30pm and 1-4:30pm. **Ireland,** 20 Arkana St. (☎6273 3022). Open M-F 9:30am-12:45pm and 2-4pm. **New Zealand** (☎6270 4211), on Commonwealth Ave. south of the lake. Open M-F 8:45am-5pm. **UK** (☎6270 6666), on Commonwealth Ave. Open M-F 9am-5pm. Consular services also located at 39 Brindlebellah Circuit at the Canberra Airport. Open M-F 8:45am-3pm. **US,** 21 Moonah Pl. (☎6214 5600, emergency ☎6214 5900). Open M-F 8am-5pm. For routine consular services, contact the US consulate in Sydney at 19-29 Martin Pl. (☎9373 9200).

Currency Exchange: Travelex (☎6247 9984), inside Harvey World Travel in the Canberra Centre shopping mall, off Petrie St., offers a flat fee of $8 or 2% on currency exchange and 1% on checks. Open M-F 9am-5pm, Sa 9:30am-12:30pm.

LOCAL SERVICES

Library: Civic Library (☎6205 9000; www.library.act.gov.au), on East Row between Alinga St. and London Circuit. 1 of 9 ACT branches. Open M-Th 10am-5:30pm, F 10am-7pm, Sa 9:30am-5pm. See also **National Library of Australia,** p. 103.

Ticket Agencies: Ticketek, 11 Akuna St., Civic (☎6219 6666; www.ticketek.com). Tickets to sports and music events and **Royal Theatre.** Open M-F 9am-5pm, Sa 9am-noon. **Canberra Ticketing** (☎6275 2700 or 1800 802 025; www.canberraticketing.com.au), in Civic Square London Circuit, covers the **Canberra Theatre, Playhouse,** and **Courtyard Studio.** Open M-F 9am-5pm, Sa 10am-2pm, later on show nights.

Travel Books and Maps: Map World (☎6230 4097), inside the Jolimont Tourist Centre. Open M-F 9am-5:30pm, Sa 9am-3pm.

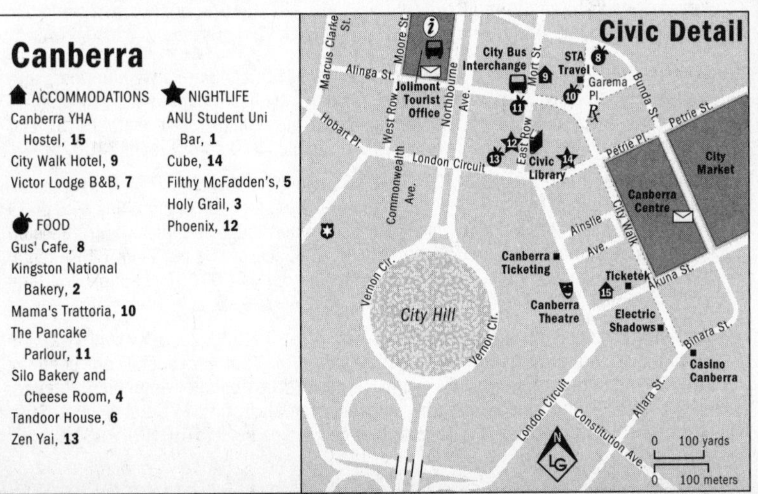

Public Markets: Gorman House Markets (☎6249 7377; www.gormanhouse.com.au), on Ainslie Ave. between Currong and Doonkuma St., vend crafts, clothing, and miscellany. Open daily 9am-5pm. The **Old Bus Depot Markets,** 21 Wentworth Ave., Kingston (☎6292 8391; www.obdm.com.au), feature food and arts-and-crafts stalls, as well as live entertainment. Open Jan.-Nov. Su 10am-4pm; Dec. Sa 10am-4pm.

MEDIA AND PUBLICATIONS

Newspapers: The main newspaper is the *Canberra Times* ($1.20), but also look out for *The Chronicle*, a local suburban newspaper.

Entertainment: *bma* is Canberra's free, alternative entertainment bimonthly. *Times Out*, in the Thursday *Canberra Times*, also lists entertainment options.

Radio: Easy listening, 106.3FM; Rock, Triple J 101.5FM; News, ABC 666AM.

EMERGENCY AND COMMUNICATIONS

Police: ☎13 14 44. On London Circuit opposite University Ave., Civic.

Drug and Alcohol Crisis Line: ☎6207 9977. 24hr.

Gay/Lesbian Counseling Service: ☎9207 2800. Open daily 4pm-midnight.

Women's Info and Referral Centre: ☎6205 1075; M-F 9am-5pm.

Pharmacy: 9 Sargood St. (☎6248 7050), in shopping center. Open daily 9am-11pm.

Hospital/Medical Services: Canberra Hospital on Yama Dr., Garren. ☎6244 2222, emergency ☎6244 2222. Follow signs to Woden southwest from Capital Hill.

Internet Access: Not many Internet cafes, but cheap access is available. The **ACT Library Service** offers free sessions in 15min. blocks; book ahead. **The National Library of Australia** (p. 103) also offers free Internet access.

Post Office: General Post Office (GPO), 53-73 Alinga St. by Jolimont Tourist Centre. (☎13 13 18). Open M-F 8:30am-5:30pm. **Branch** outside Canberra Centre Mall, on Bunda St. between Petrie Pl. and Akuna St. Open M-F 8:45am-5:15pm. **Postal Code:** 2600.

ACCOMMODATIONS

Canberra doesn't have many affordable options, but the few hostels available are comfortable and conveniently located in downtown Civic or swanky Kingston.

Canberra YHA Hostel, 7 Akuna St., Civic (☎6248 9155; canberracity@yhansw.org.au). Near cafes and clubs, this family-friendly, clean hostel has a helpful staff. Kitchen, TV room, pool, BBQ, and movies. Internet access ($2 per 20min.), bike rental ($15), and laundry ($3). Reception 24hr. Dorms $24-27; doubles $70; family room $100. ❷

Victor Lodge Bed and Breakfast, 29 Dawes St., Kingston (☎6295 7777; www.victorlodge.com.au), 6km south of the CBD, 5min. walk from the train station. Bus #38 or 39 from Civic stops 2 blocks away on Eyre St. This quiet lodge is 1 block from Kingston shops and restaurants. Kitchen, TV, laundry, Internet access ($1 per 7min.), bike rental ($15), and breakfast (7:30-9am) included. Key deposit $20. Reception 7:30am-9:30pm. Dorms $27; singles $59; twins and doubles $76. ❸

City Walk Hotel, 2 Mort St. (☎6257 0124 or 1800 600 124; www.citywalkhotel.com.au), in the center of Civic, just off City Walk. Not very social, but centrally located and comfortable. Private rooms come with basic motel amenities. Kitchen, lounge with TV and videos, laundry, and bike rental. Dorms $26-28; singles $50, ensuite $80; doubles $65-90/90; ensuite family rooms from $105. NOMADS. ❸

FOOD

Cheap food isn't easy to find in Canberra. However, inexpensive cafes can be found near the city bus interchange in Civic. Another good bet is the food court at **Canberra Centre** (☎6247 5611), a three-story mall with main entrances off either City Walk or Bunda St. Opposite the Canberra Centre, the **City Market** complex packs in fruit stands, butcher shops, and prepared food stalls. You'll also find a huge **Supabarn** supermarket. (☎6257 4055. Open M-F 7am-10pm, Sa-Su 7am-9pm.) Kingston has over 30 restaurants of all varieties around its main commercial block, and nearby Manuka is another dining hotspot with lots of posh options. Dickson, north of the CBD, is a miniature Chinatown.

CIVIC

Food courts, coffee shops, and bar-and-grill restaurants dominate Civic's eating scene. For something different, try one of the restaurants listed below.

Gus' Cafe, (☎6248 8118) corner of Bunda and Genge St. Trendy locals meet in this open-air cafe to chat over a cuppa or quick bite. Sample focaccia fingers with chili and garlic ($6.90), or sip a pineapple frappe ($5.50). Try a steaming bowl of porridge ($7) or poached eggs with spinach and mushrooms ($15) from the all-day breakfast menu. 10% surcharge on public holidays. Open daily 7:30am-latenight. AmEx/DC/MC/V. ❷

Zen Yai, 111 London Circuit (☎6262 7594). Sizzling stir-fries, noodle dishes, and spicy salads keep locals coming back to this fine Thai restaurant. Lean cuts of meat and fresh vegetables separate it from most area Asian eateries. BYO. Takeaway and delivery (min. $30) available. Open M-Sa 11:30am-3pm and 5-10pm, Su 5-10pm. AmEx/MC/V. ❸

Mama's Trattoria, 7 Garema Pl. (☎6248 0936). Mama's dishes up huge portions of home-style Italian favorites. Dig into a hot bowl of mushroom *risotto* while being serenaded by Sinatra. The friendly servers make Mama's a welcomed retreat from the pub scene. Lunch $7-14, dinner $12-18. Open daily 10am-latenight. AmEx/D/MC/V. ❷

The Pancake Parlour, 122 Alinga St. (☎6247 2982), 2 doors away from Tasuke. A great place to satisfy late-night munchies and early-morning cravings, whether you opt for fruit pancakes ($13.50), creative crepes ($18-20), or more standard steak and fish fare ($20-24). Free wireless Internet access. 10% off with YHA. Early bird specials 7-9am and 5-7pm. Open M-Th and Su 7am-10:30pm, F-Sa 7am-1am. AmEx/DC/MC/V. ❸

KINGSTON

As in Civic, it's difficult to find a cheap meal in Kingston; trendy cafes and expensive multicultural restaurants stretch as far as the eye can see. If you've got the cash, take your pick of any of the superb multicultural restaurants that line Giles and Kennedy St. However, if you want your money to last as long as the walk, try one of these quality—and wallet-friendly—establishments.

Kingston National Bakery, 56 Giles St., (☎6295 9646). Takeaway meat pies ($2-4) and fruit pastries ($1-3) can be enjoyed at tables in front of this classic Aussie pie- and sweet-shop. Indulge in a rich apple turnover ($2). Open daily 8am-7pm. Cash only. ❶

Silo Bakery and Cheese Room, 36 Giles St., (☎6260 6060). Known by locals as the best bakery in Canberra. Though it offers only a few dishes each day, Silo creates delicate, intense appetizers and main dishes ($13-20) that feature imported cheeses and freshly baked breads. Open Tu-Sa for breakfast and lunch. AmEx/DC/MC/V. ❸

Tandoor House, 39 Kennedy St., (☎6295 7318). There's nothing too special about this little Indian restaurant except that it offers one of the few affordable finer dining experiences in Kingston. Sit back and savor subtly spiced curries, vindaloos, and masalas ($13-15). Open daily M-F noon-2:30pm, Sa-Su 5:30-10pm. AmEx/DC/MC/V. ❷

SIGHTS

PARLIAMENTARY TRIANGLE

A showpiece of grand architecture and cultural attractions, Canberra's Parliamentary Triangle is the center of the capital. The triangle is bordered by Commonwealth Ave., Kings Ave., and Parkes Way across the lake.

PARLIAMENT HOUSE. The building is actually built into Capital Hill so that two sides jut out of the earth, leaving the grassy hilltop on its roof open to the public via an internal lift. The design intentionally places the people above Parliament. Balanced on top of this landmark is a four-pronged stainless steel flagpole visible from nearly every part of Canberra. Inside, **free guided tours** give an overview of the building's unique features and the workings of the government housed inside. **Self-guided audio tours** are available in multiple languages. Visitors can observe houses in action from viewing galleries. The **House of Representatives** allows advance bookings. The televised **Question Time** provides entertaining acrimony. When the House and Senate are sitting, the floor is opened up at 2pm for on-the-spot questioning of the Prime Minister and other officials. *(Take Bus #34 from Civic. Wheelchair accessible. ☎6277 5399. To reserve tickets for* Question Time *call ☎6277 4889; www.aph.gov.au. Open daily 9am-5pm, as late as 11pm when in session. Consult info desk for free tour times. Audio tours $2. House and Senate sit M-Th in approx. 2wk. blocks, total 20wk. per yr.; recess Jan. and July.)*

NATIONAL GALLERY OF AUSTRALIA. On the southeastern end of Parkes Pl., near the intersection of King Edward Tce. and Kings Ave., the National Gallery displays an impressive collection of Australian, Aboriginal, and Torres Strait Islander art. The gallery opens with an Aboriginal installation of painted hollow tubes that creates a winding river that visitors can walk through. Their contemporary paintings alone, including a captivating work by Jackson Pollock, are well worth the visit. Keep your eyes open for a few big-name French Impressionists/post-Impressionists like Cezanne, Monet, and Matisse. After exploring the airy galleries on the first and second floors, take a stroll through the sculpture garden. *(On King Edward Terr. Take Bus #34 from Civic. ☎6240 6502, info 6240 65011; www.nga.gov.au. Open daily 10am-5pm. 1hr. guided tours daily 11am and 2pm. Aboriginal art tour Th and Su 11am. Wheelchair accessible. Free. Separate fees for special exhibits $15-18.)*

ACT

QUESTACON (NATIONAL SCIENCE AND TECHNOLOGY CENTRE). Despite being a children's museum, Questacon's interactive, state-of-the-art exhibits will captivate minds of any age. Interact with tribal elders on video screens, experience a faux earthquake, or come face-to-face with some of the world's largest (animatronic) predators. *(Take Bus #34 from Civic. ☎1800 020 603; www.questacon.edu.au. $14, concessions $9.50, children $8, families $42. Open daily 9am-5pm.)*

OLD PARLIAMENT HOUSE AND NATIONAL PORTRAIT GALLERY. This classic building is aligned with the front of its more modern counterpart, the Parliament House, and was Australia's seat of government from 1927 until 1988, when the current Parliament House was completed. The sitting rooms around the house and senate chambers have been turned into galleries, complete with stories of the behind-the-scenes political maneuvering that used to take place there. The building also houses the impressive **National Portrait Gallery,** which features portraits of famous Australians as well as circulating exhibits. *(On King George Terr. Take Bus #34 from Civic. ☎6270 8222, gallery 6270 8236; www.oph.gov.au. Wheelchair accessible. Daily tours of Old Parliament House every 45min. 9:30am-3:15pm. Tours of the Portrait Gallery daily 11:30am and 2:30pm. Open daily 9am-5pm. $2, concessions $1.)*

NATIONAL LIBRARY OF AUSTRALIA. The nation's largest library (5.7 million volumes) is the final stop on Parkes Way. Open for research and visitation, it houses copies of Australian publications on over 200km of shelving. The library also features rotating exhibits on Australian topics. Free **Internet** access available. *(Take Bus #34 from Civic. Wheelchair accessible. ☎6262 1111; www.nla.gov.au. Free tours Th 12:30pm. Open M-Th 9am-9pm, F-Sa 9am-5pm, Su 1:30-5pm.)*

LAKE BURLEY GRIFFIN. The last two attractions in the Parliamentary Triangle are actually located in the middle of the lake. The **Captain Cook Memorial Jet** blows a six-ton column of water to heights of up to 147m to commemorate Captain James Cook's arrival at the east coast of Australia. The bell tower of the **National Carillon** is located on Aspen Island at the other end of the lake's central basin. A gift from Britain on Canberra's 50th birthday in 1970, the Carillon, one of the largest musical instruments in the world, is rung several times a week and can be heard from anywhere in the Parliamentary Triangle. Small tours can also be arranged and are particularly recommended for the musically inclined. *(For info on the Jet or the Carillon, contact the National Capital Authority ☎6271 2888; concert schedule www.nationalcapital.gov.au/experience/attractions/national_carillon.)*

PARLIAMENTARY TRIANGLE SURROUNDS

NATIONAL MUSEUM OF AUSTRALIA. A short trip from the CBD, this architectural wonder recounts the history of the nation and the stories of its people in profoundly moving fashion. Five permanent exhibits range from an exploration of Australian history through the nation's expressions and symbols to a glimpse into the lives of ordinary and extraordinary Australians alike. State-of-the-art multimedia components include **Circa,** a futuristic rotating theater that poignantly introduces visitors to the museum's themes of "Land, Nation, and People." *(Take bus #34 from Civic. On Acton Peninsula off Lawson Cresc. ☎6208 5000 or 1800 026 132. www.nma.gov.au. Open daily 9am-5pm. Free; fees for special exhibitions. Tours M-F 10 and 11:30am, Sa-Su 10:30am, noon, 1:30pm. $7.50, students $5.50, children $5, families $20.)*

AUSTRALIAN WAR MEMORIAL. The stories of Australia's heroes in combat overseas and helping the war effort at home are retold with artifacts, photos, and depictions of wartime life by Australian artists. The expansive tribute and attached museum merit an full day of exploration. The **Hall of Memory** holds the tomb of an unknown Australian soldier beneath a mosaic dome. Lining the ANZAC (Australian New Zealand Army Corps) Parade on the way up to the memorial are sculptures commemorating Australians and New Zealanders who served in major military conflicts. Exhibits include **"Sport and War,"** a look at the relationship between Australian athletics and the reality of armed conflict. *(Anzac Pde., on bus route #33 from Civic. ☎6243 4211. Tours daily; call for times. Open daily 10am-5pm. Free.)*

GOVERNMENT BUILDINGS. West of Capital Hill, on the south side of the lake, Yarralumla is peppered with the embassies of over 70 nations, displaying 70 different styles of international architecture (take bus route #31, 32, or 84). **The Lodge,** home to the Australian Prime Minister, is on the corner of Adelaide Ave. and National Circuit, but hecklers be warned: it's closed to the public (take bus route #34 or 39). At the **Royal Australian Mint,** on Denison St. in Deakin, you can watch coins being minted. Push a button to "press your own" dollar coin—for $2.50. *(Take bus #30, 31, or 32. ☎6202 6819; www.ramint.gov.au. Open M-F 9am-4pm, Sa-Su 10am-4pm; coin production M-F 9am-noon and 1-4pm. Wheelchair accessible. Free.)*

NATIONAL FILM AND SOUND ARCHIVE. Formerly known as **Screensound,** this archive is one of Canberra's least-known but most enjoyable attractions. The bonanza of sight-and-sound relics of Australian radio, film, and television ranges from the 19th century to today. Watch snippets from old-time Australian movies and listen to early 20th-century sports broadcasts. *(On McCoy Circuit in Acton. Take bus #34 to Liversidge St. ☎6248 2000. www.nfsa.afc.gov.au. Wheelchair accessible. Open M-F 9am-5pm, Sa-Su 10am-5pm. Free for permanent exhibit; changing gallery has various fees.)*

AUSTRALIAN NATIONAL BOTANIC GARDENS. Designed in the 1950s and opened to the public in 1970, the park is a living monument to the nation's unique biodiversity. Planting groups such as the **Eucalyptus Lawn** and **Rainforest Gully** highlight the variety of Australia's native species. A 30min. walk will take you through the gardens. Take a breather in the **Rock Garden,** an open, grassy space. The athletically inclined can take the **Black Mountain Summit Walk,** a 2.7km, steep path to Telstra Tower accessible from the garden path. *(Take bus #34 to Daley Rd.; walk 20min. toward the lake along Clunies Ross Rd. ☎6250 9540. www.anbg.gov.au/anbg. Ask at the visitors center for guided walk times. Open daily 8:30am-5pm. Visitors center open 9am-4:30pm. Free.)*

AUSTRALIAN INSTITUTE OF SPORT (AIS). Tours led by resident athletes take you to see competitors in training. Stop at the hands-on **Sportex exhibit** where you can try your hand at rowing, golfing, wheelchair basketball, simulated ski runs, and rock climbing. Bring a bathing suit to take part in one of the many underwater activities. *(On Leverrier Cresc. just northwest of O'Connor. Take bus #80 from Civic. ☎6214 1010. Open M-F 8:30am-5pm, Sa-Su 10am-4pm. Tours daily at 10, 11:30am, 1, 2:30pm. Pool $4.50, concessions $3; swim cap mandatory. $13, students $10, children $7, families $36.)*

NATIONAL ZOO AND AQUARIUM. Unless you're a kid (or have one), you may have trouble justifying the long trip out; there is no direct public transport. The seven-hectare sanctuary for native animals does have some redeeming features, though these unique up-close animal opportunities are a bit of a splurge. Special tours include a 2hr. hand-feed **Zooventure Tour** (from $95, children from $45). The King Cheetah, loved for its large size and impressive mane, is one of only 20 such big cats in the world and can be visited on a **Meet the King Tour** for $195. *(About 3½km from the city. From Parkes Way, heading out of the city to the west, Lady Denman Dr. branches south toward the zoo at Scrivener Dam. ☎6287 8400. www.nationalzoo.com.au. Open daily 9am-5pm. $23.50, students $18.50, children $12.50, families from $69.50.)*

ACT

LOOKOUTS. A stop at one of the city's lookouts can give you a general idea of what's in store on a sightseeing tour. On a hill in Commonwealth Park at Regatta Point, on the north shore of Lake Burley Griffin, the **National Capital Exhibition** is a great place to start your explorations and learn the fascinating story of the city. It provides a panorama of Canberra with a 5min. interactive display about its planning and growth. Brochures are available for self-guided walking tours of the city. *(☎6257 1068; www.nationalcapital.gov.au. Wheelchair accessible. Open daily 9am-5pm. Free.)* Farther back from the CBD, Mt. Ainslie and Black Mountain offer broader views of the city and are within walking distance. North of Lake Burley Griffin and east of the CBD, **Mount Ainslie** rises 846m above the lake, the Parliamentary Triangle, and the Australian War Memorial, providing the classic postcard view down Anzac Pde. To reach the summit by car, turn right on Fairbairn Ave. from the Memorial end of Anzac Pde., to Mt. Ainslie Dr. Hiking trails lead to the top from directly behind the War Memorial. Two lookout points above the city on **Black Mountain** (812m) are a vigorous walk away. From the peak of Black Mountain, **Telstra Tower** climbs 195m to ensure viewers an unobstructed gaze in every direction. Exhibits in the tower catalogue the history of Australian telecommunications. *(☎6248 1991 or 1800 806 718. Open daily 9am-10pm. $4.40, children $1.90.)* To the south of the city, **Red Hill** is harder to get to, but offers an equally stunning view. By car, take Melbourne Ave. from Capital Hill to Red Hill Dr. Another option for those hoping to get a bird's eye view of Canberra's geometric symmetry is in a sunrise **hot-air bal-**

loon flight with **Balloon Aloft.** *(☎6285 1540, www.balloon.canberra.net.au. Weekday flight $230, children under 12 ½-price; weekend deluxe flight $290; winter flight $200.)*

ENTERTAINMENT AND FESTIVALS

In addition to the usual first-run cinemas, Canberra is home to several funky art-house alternatives, including **Electric Shadows,** on Akuna St. near City Walk. (☎6247 5060; www.electricshadows.com.au. $15, students $9; before 5pm $9/8. W $8 all day.) Housing venues in varying shapes and sizes, the **Canberra Theatre** on London Circuit is the best place for live entertainment. Register for the free "Under 27 Club" and receive savings on tickets. (☎6275 2700; www.canberratheatre.org.au. $30-100; ages 18-27 available for most performances $30-60.) Canberra's calendar is packed with small **festivals,** but a few annual events temporarily transform the city. For 10 days in March, the **Celebrate Canberra Festival** (www.celebratecanberra.com) is filled with artistic displays, food showcases, hot-air balloon rides, and **Canberra Day** festivities. **Floriade** (mid-Sept. to mid-Oct.) paints Lake Burley Griffin's shores in Commonwealth Park with thousands of blooms and fills accommodations; book ahead. (☎6205 0666; www.floriadeaustralia.com.)

NIGHTLIFE

Canberra's after-hours scene is surprisingly vibrant. The city's student population supports a solid range of bars and clubs. Most places close "latenight," meaning midnight on slow nights and at "the end of the party" on busier nights.

CIVIC

Phoenix, 21 East Row (☎6247 1606). This bohemian bar attracts a motley crew of artists, intellectuals, and all kinds of folk. The mix of people matches the odd assortment of tables and seats. Frequent live music. Open M-Sa noon-latenight, Su 1pm-latenight.

Cube, 33 Petrie Plaza., Civic (☎6257 1110; www.cubenightclub.com.au). A gay-friendly, groovin' club. Particularly hot F-Sa. Open Th-F 8pm-5am, Sa 10pm-5am, Su 8pm-5am.

ANU Student Uni Bar (☎6125 3660; www.anuunion.com.au), in the student union, near the corner of North Rd. and University Ave. This popular uni hangout is the cheapest pub in town and hosts big names in music. Check *bma* (p. 100) or the website for gig listing. Open M-F noon-latenight, Sa 4pm-latenight.

KINGSTON

Filthy McFadden's (☎6239 5303), intersection of Jardine and Eyre St. Possibly the best-named pub ever, Filthy's boasts the largest whiskey collection in the southern hemisphere. Frequented by backpackers and regulars, this place epitomizes the Irish country pub. Pint of Guinness $6.50. Open daily noon-latenight. AmEx/MC/V.

Holy Grail (☎6295 6071), in Green Square at the intersection of Jardine and Eyre St. This colorful, trendy bistro and bar turns into a packed nightclub F-Sa nights, with live cover bands and DJs. Cover $5. Open daily 9am-latenight. AmEx/MC/V.

DAYTRIPS FROM CANBERRA

LANYON HOMESTEAD. Built in the 1800s, the buildings at Lanyon Homestead survey Canberra's European architectural history from the days of convict labor through Federation. An Aboriginal canoe tree, viewable by reservation only, is evidence of earlier habitation. Lanyon's greatest draw may be the **Nolan Gallery,** which has many of Sidney Nolan's whimsical paintings of bushranger Ned Kelly. *(Tharwa Dr., 30km south of Canberra. Homestead ☎6235 5677, gallery ☎6235 5688. Open Tu-Su 10am-4pm. Both buildings $8, concessions $6, families $18.)*

CANBERRA DEEP SPACE COMMUNICATION COMPLEX. One of the most powerful antenna centers in the world, the Complex awes novices and space cadets alike. The 70m **dish** is the largest in the Southern Hemisphere. The Space Centre has displays on the history of space exploration. *(Take Adelaide Ave., which becomes Cotter Rd., to Paddy's River Rd. Off Paddy's River Rd., 35km southwest of Civic. ☎6201 7880; www.cdscc.nasa.gov. Open daily in summer 9am-5pm, in winter 9am-6pm. Free.)*

NAMADGI NATIONAL PARK. The expansive Namadgi National Park fills almost all of southern ACT with alpine wilderness traversed by only one major paved route: the Naas/Boboyan Rd. The park has walking tracks for all experience levels, but it is most famous for the untrammeled recesses accessible only to serious hikers. Birdwatchers and fishermen are also drawn to this wildlife haven. **Campsites** ❶ at Orroral River, Honeysuckle and Mt. Clear, with parking nearby, have firewood, untreated water, and toilets. The **Namadgi Visitors Centre,** on the Naas/Boboyan Rd. 3km south of Tharwa, has maps and info on Aboriginal paintings and camping options. *(☎6207 2900; namadginationalpark@act.gov.au. Register at visitors center. 33km south of Civic. Sites $5 per person per night. Open M-F 9am-4pm, Sa-Su 9am-4:30pm.)*

NATIONAL DINOSAUR MUSEUM. This private museum has over 300 fossils, full-sized dinosaur skeletons, and reconstructions. *(Corner of Barton Hwy. and Gold Creek Rd. Take bus #51 or 52. ☎6230 2655; www.nationaldinosaurmuseum.com.au. Open daily 10am-5pm. $9.50, concessions $7.50, children $6.50, families $30.)*

NEW SOUTH WALES

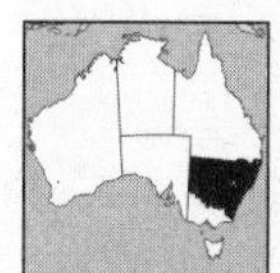

From a historical perspective, there's no disputing that New South Wales has been the site of many of Australia's seminal experiences. It was here that British convicts survived the first bitter years of colonization, dreaming of what might lie beyond the impassable Blue Mountains; it was here that explorers first broke through the Great Dividing Range, opening the country's interior for settlement and ensuring the stability of the colony. In the central plains and the rich land of the Riverina, merino wool and agricultural success provided the state with its first glimpses of prosperity. Then, in 1851, prospectors struck gold just west of the mountains, and Australia's history changed forever. New South Wales shook off its prison colony mantle overnight, transforming into a place that promised a new life and an inflated bank account. Though the gold rush days are long gone, New South Wales has continued to grow. Today, it's the most populous state and—thanks largely to Sydney—the diverse and sophisticated center of modern Australia.

Sydney, the nation's biggest and flashiest city, sits midway along the state's coastline. Sandy beaches fan out from it in an almost unbroken succession. During the summer, a trip up the coast is the ultimate backpacker party, with epicenters in the large coastal towns of Port Macquarie and Byron Bay. The south coast is colder, but less crowded and just as beautiful. Some of the state's best getaways are found in the Blue Mountains, west of Sydney's suburban reaches. The New England Plateau, along the Great Dividing Range north of the Hunter Valley wineries, creates a lush setting for a cozy collection of small towns and stunning national parks. Just below the carved-out enclave of the Australian Capital Territory, the Snowy Mountains offer enticing winter skiing and superb summer hiking.

Attractions of New South Wales are as varied as the terrain. From the cosmopolitan buzz of Sydney to the ski community of Thredbo, or the laid-back surf culture of Byron to the post-apocalyptic Outback, visitors find plenty to write home about.

HIGHLIGHTS OF NEW SOUTH WALES

LOSE YOURSELF in one of the world's most fascinating cities, **Sydney.** (p. 110)

ESCAPE from urban life to Sydney's great outdoors, the **Blue Mountains.** (p. 155)

TOUR some of the most respected **vineyards** in the world and taste the fine red and white wines of the **Hunter Valley.** (p. 169)

SKI down the **black diamond** slopes of **Thredbo.** (p. 236)

INHALE the **counterculture** of **Nimbin.** (p. 207)

TRANSPORTATION

The cities and towns of New South Wales are connected by the state's excellent **public transportation** system, as well as by numerous reliable private transportation companies. Route information for all bus, rail, and ferry systems in the Sydney-metro area is available from the **Sydney Transit Authority** (☎13 15 00; www.sta.nsw.gov.au). For info on more extensive travel throughout NSW and beyond, call **Rail Australia** (☎08 8213 4592; www.railaustralia.com) or **Greyhound Australia** (☎13 14 99 or 13 20 30; www.greyhound.com.au).

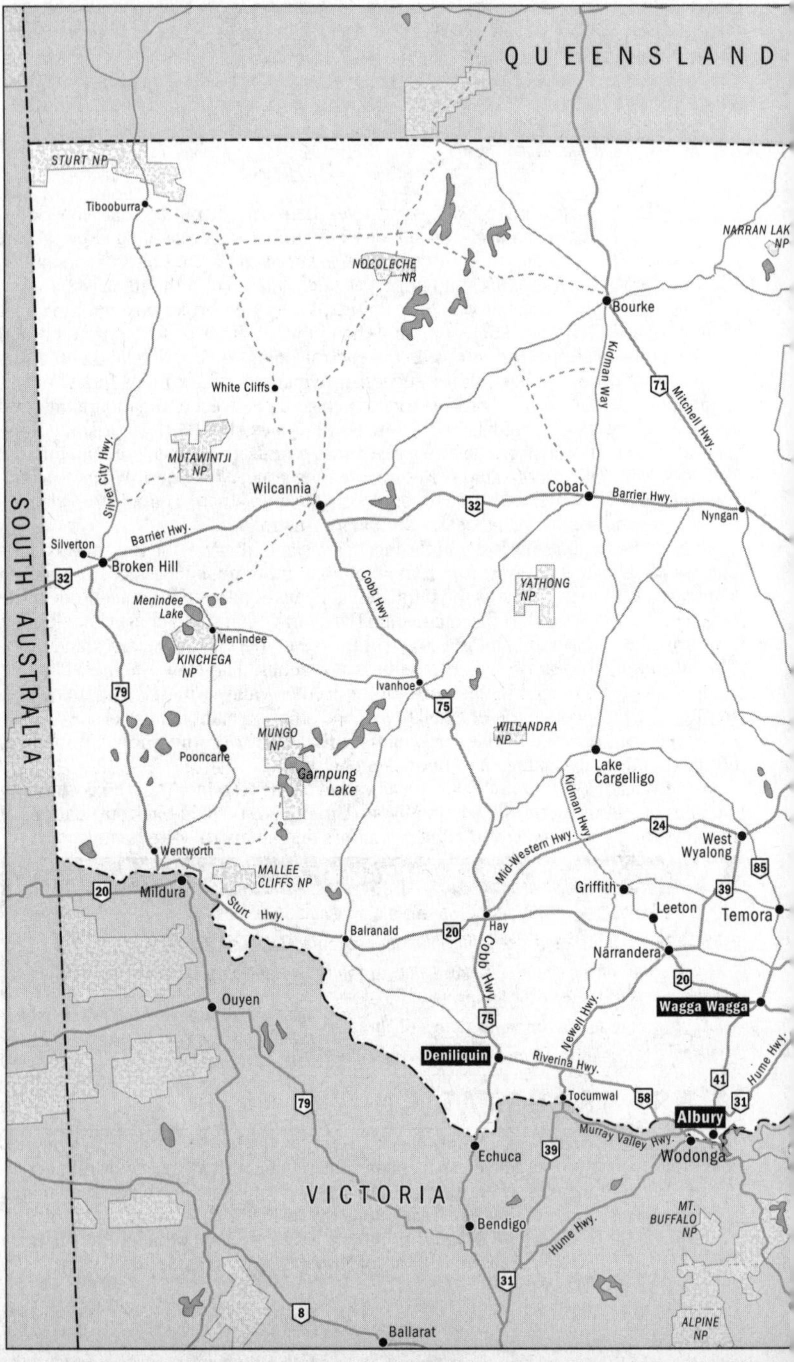

QUEENSLAND
SOUTH AUSTRALIA
VICTORIA
STURT NP
Tibooburra
NOCOLECHE NR
NARRAN LAK NP
Bourke
Kidman Way
71
Mitchell Hwy.
White Cliffs
MUTAWINTJI NP
Silver City Hwy.
Wilcannia
Cobar
Barrier Hwy.
32
Nyngan
Barrier Hwy.
Silverton
Broken Hill
32
Menindee Lake
Menindee
KINCHEGA NP
Cobb Hwy.
YATHONG NP
Ivanhoe
75
79
WILLANDRA NP
MUNGO NP
Garnpung Lake
Pooncarie
Lake Cargelligo
Kidman Hwy.
24
Mid-Western Hwy.
West Wyalong
85
Wentworth
MALLEE CLIFFS NP
20
Mildura
Sturt Hwy.
Balranald
20
Hay
Griffith
39
Leeton
Temora
Narrandera
Cobb Hwy.
20
Wagga Wagga
Ouyen
75
Newell Hwy.
Deniliquin
Riverina Hwy.
Hume Hwy.
41
79
Tocumwal
58
31
Albury
Murray Valley Hwy.
Echuca
39
Wodonga
Bendigo
Hume Hwy.
MT. BUFFALO NP
31
8
Ballarat
ALPINE NP

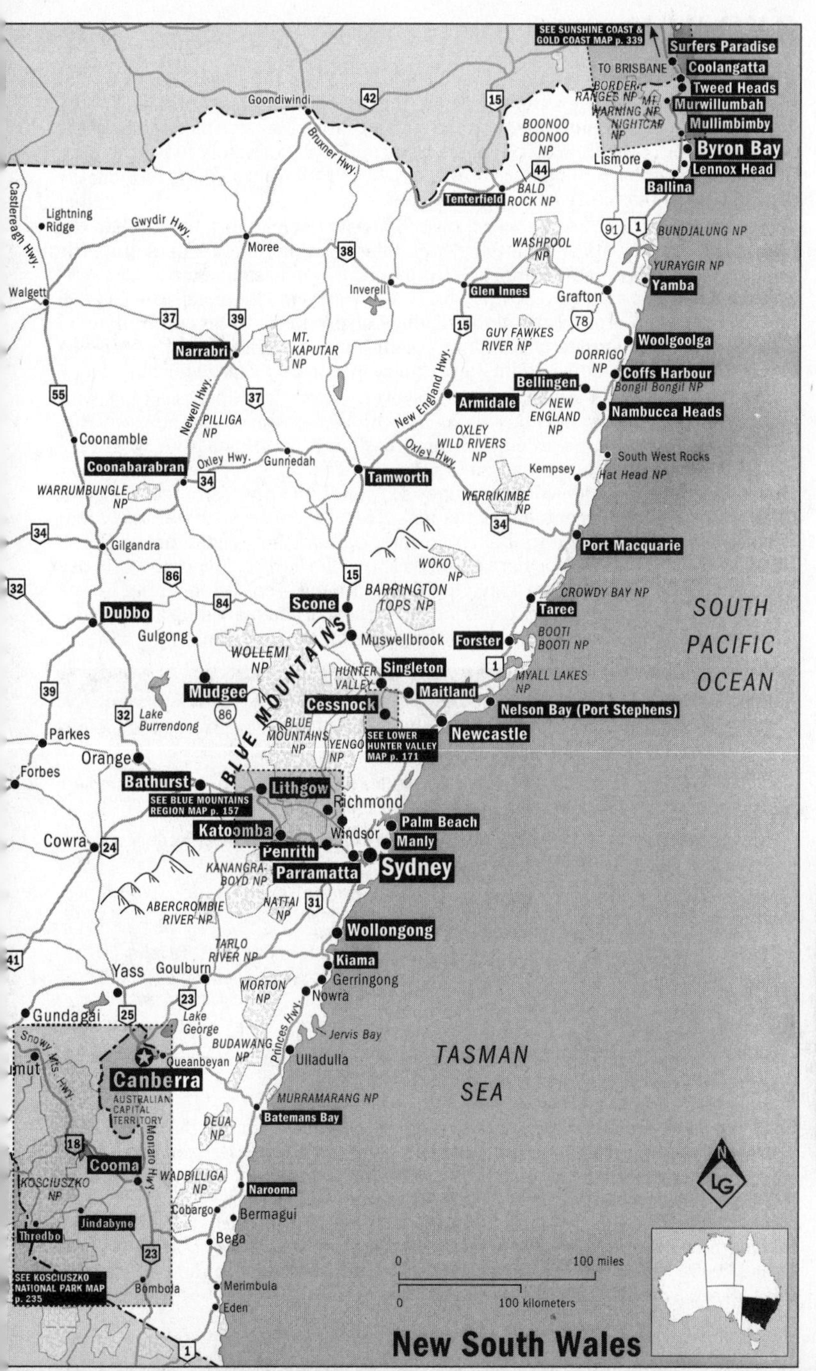

NEW SOUTH WALES

SYDNEY ☎02

Australia's unofficial capital, Sydney blends liveliness and loveliness as one of the world's greatest cities. Home to more than one-fifth of the continent's population, Sydney is undoubtedly Australia's major urban center. Since the building boom brought on by the 2000 Olympic Games, the city certainly looks the part, from the new athletic complexes down to the elevated train snaking through the skyscrapers of the futuristic financial center.

Like many major cities the world over, Sydney is much more liberal than the rest of the country. Its substantial gay population is out and about, setting the tone for "what's hot" in nightlife, and the annual Gay & Lesbian Mardi Gras celebration, deemed by many to be the world's best, attracts enormous crowds of all persuasions from around the globe. Sydney also refuses to be culturally contained, as the wide range of available cuisines makes clear. The city houses a diverse Asian population, and bustling Chinatown district is growing quickly.

For all of Sydney's urban bustle, however, it is refreshingly in tune with nature. Its beautiful architecture is famous throughout the world, most notably the astounding structures found in Sydney harbor. It was this harbor where the First Fleet of colonists and convicts landed in 1788. Today, the iconic Opera House and Harbour Bridge define Sydney's skyline and draw visitors to the boat-filled water's edge for gorgeous ferry rides. The city's obsession with the water is also displayed through its beach culture, epitomized by glamorous Bondi Beach and the secluded Northern Beaches above the harbor. Many travelers use Sydney as a springboard for traveling the continent—but after dining by the waterfront, raging in the clubs, relaxing on the beach, and marveling at this peerless city, you'll be ready to relocate Sydney-side for the long haul.

HIGHLIGHTS OF SYDNEY

TOUR the stunning Concert Hall at **SYDNEY OPERA HOUSE,** the defining structure of Sydney's skyline and a masterpiece recognized the world over (p. 142).

RIDE THE FERRY to the friendly surfing suburb **MANLY** for grand coastal walks and a glimpse of the utopia that is the Northern Beaches (p. 136).

VISIT Sydney's Eden at the **ROYAL BOTANIC GARDENS,** which offers spectacular views of Sydney Harbour at Mrs. Macquarie's Point (p. 138).

EXPERIENCE the 24hr. neon den of sin in **KINGS CROSS,** Sydney's neighborhood of active nightlife and seedy streets (p. 127).

CHEER at **MOORE PARK,** for the Sydney Swans and Sydney City Roosters, the city's Aussie Rules Football and Rugby teams that call this mecca of sports home (p. 141).

INTERCITY TRANSPORTATION

BY PLANE

Kingsford-Smith Airport, 10km southwest of the Central Business District (CBD), serves most major international carriers. **Qantas** (☎13 13 13) and **Virgin Blue** (☎13 67 89) cover most domestic destinations. Though locker storage is not available, **Smarte Carte** (☎9667 0926) holds bags. (up to 6hr. $6-12 per bag, 6-24hr. $8-20.) The **Sydney Airport Visitor Centre** kiosk, on the arrivals level in the international terminal, offers booking service and free calls to area hostels. (☎9667 6050. Open daily 5:00am-last flight.) Transportation to the city is available directly outside the terminal. **Airport Link** (☎13 15 00; www.airportlink.com.au) is part of the underground CityRail network, which runs trains M-F 5am-12:30am, Sa-Su 5am-12:40am along the green East Hills line to the City Circle, including Circular Quay (15min., every 10min.; $12.80, same day round-trip $16.50-19). **Kingsford-Smith Transport (KST),** one of several airport shuttle companies, runs buses to city and inner suburb accommodations. (☎9666 9988; www.kst.com.au. Daily every 20min. 5am-10pm. $10, round-trip $15.) Many hostels offer free pickup. A **taxi** to the city center costs about $30 from domestic terminals, $35 from international.

BY TRAIN

Countrylink trains (☎13 22 32; www.countrylink.info) depart from the **Central Railway Station** above Eddy Ave. Tickets are sold in three classes: economy, first-class, and first-class sleeper. ISIC members receive an automatic 50% discount. Combining the **Countrylink** and **Queensland Rail** options, the **Backtracker Rail Pass** enables passengers to travel the East Coast at their own pace with unlimited stops along the way (passes available from **Countrylink** centers and selected travel agents; $110-376). For travel throughout the South, **Great Southern** (☎13 21 47; www.gsr.com.au) tickets come in three classes that vary greatly in price: Red Kangaroo seat, Red Kangaroo sleeper, and Gold Kangaroo sleeper. Round-trip fares are all double the price of one-way fares. **Great Southern** also offers international backpackers a six-month unlimited travel card on all their services for $590. Please note that train times can and do change frequently, so call ahead.

The table below lists information and **adult fares** for trains running from Sydney:

DESTINATION	COMPANY	DURATION	DAYS	PRICE
Adelaide	Great Southern	25hr.	Sa, W	$245
Alice Springs	Great Southern	45hr.	Sa, W	$480
Brisbane	Countrylink	14½-15hr.	2 per day	$125
Byron Bay	Countrylink	12½hr.	2 per day	$110
Canberra	Countrylink	4hr.	3 per day	$54
Coffs Harbour	Countrylink	8hr.	3 per day	$91
Melbourne	Countrylink	10½hr.	2 per day	$125
Surfers Paradise	Countrylink	14-15hr.	2 per day	$119
Perth	Great Southern	3 days	Sa, W	$560

BY BUS

Fifteen bus companies operate from the **Sydney Coach Terminal,** Central Station, on the corner of Eddy Ave. at Pitt St. (☎9281 9366. Open M-F 6am-7.30pm, Sa-Su 8am-6pm.) **Luggage storage** is also available ($5-15). The major national bus company, **Greyhound Australia** (☎13 14 99; www.greyhound.com.au) generally offers more frequent trips to major destinations than the smaller, regional carriers, but their rates are often higher. Greyhound Australia tickets can be purchased online, by phone, at the bus station, or at any Australian post office. Check online for special deals. Their Aussie Explorer Pass allows travelers to make unlimited stops in one direction along a pre-set route; the Mini Travelers route, which runs along the east coast, is especially popular (☎13 20 30. Mini Travelers $327 from Sydney, ISIC/YHA/VIP/NOMADS $294). The **Oz Experience** offers a similar service by also providing driver guides and travel agents to help along the way. Their main office is at 804 George St. in the city center. (☎9213 1766; www.ozexperience.com).

The table on the next page refers to the Greyhound Australia service and lists information and **adult fares** for buses running from Sydney:

DESTINATION	DURATION	TIMES	PRICE
Adelaide (via Canberra)	24hr.	3 per day	$161
Alice Springs (via Adelaide)	40hr.	3 per day	$402
Brisbane	17hr.	9 per day	$113
Byron Bay	13hr.	2 per day	$104
Cairns (via Brisbane)	2½ days	3 per day	$340
Canberra	4¾hr.	10 per day	$37
Coffs Harbour	9hr.	4 per day	$74
Darwin (via Alice Springs)	3½ days	1 per day	$610
Melbourne	12hr.	7 per day	$72
Mount Isa (via Brisbane)	3½ days	7 per day	$307
Surfers Paradise	15hr.	4 per day	$109

ORIENTATION

The Sydney metropolitan area is immense. The city seems to be contained only by the forces of nature, with **Ku-Ring-Gai Chase National Park** to the north, the **Blue Mountains** to the west, **Royal National Park** to the south, and the **Pacific Ocean,** the **Tasman Sea,** and **Sydney Harbour** to the east. Much of this area consists of quiet, residential outer suburbs. Unlike its metropolitan area, Sydney's actual center is of manageable size. The walk to Circular Quay along Pitt St. takes only 30min. from Central Station and only 20min. from Kings Cross. Outside the city center, are the inner suburbs—large neighborhoods such as Glebe and Surry Hills, each with a distinctive feel. For a bird's eye view of it all, ascend **Centrepoint Tower** (p. 125).

NEIGHBORHOODS AT A GLANCE

NEIGHBORHOOD	FEATURES	LOCAL BUS ROUTES
Bondi Beach	Home to most of Sydney's celebrities.	380, L82
CBD	Martin Place, Chinatown, Paddy's Market.	380, 394
Circular Quay	Sydney Opera House and all ferry wharves.	380, 394
Coogee Beach	Bondi's rival; youthful energy and vibrant nightlife.	372, 373, 374
Darling Harbour	Sydney Aquarium and Powerhouse Museum. Touristy, with a swanky nightlife scene.	Short walk from Town Hall or monorail
Darlinghurst and Paddington	Young, fashionable, creative types.	378, 380, L82, 389
Glebe	Bohemian cafes, pubs, and bookstores; neighboring student population.	431, 432, 433
Kings Cross	Seedy center of Sydney backpacker culture, with hostels, cafes, strip shows, and crazy nightlife.	324, 325, 326, 327, 311
Manly	Friendly resort area with great beaches and surfing.	175, 178, 180, L80, 185, L85
Mosman	Taronga Park Zoo, other parks and gardens.	247, 244
Newtown	Vintage clothing, used books, and great eateries.	423, 422, 426, 428
North Sydney	Tree-lined financial district, upmarket cafes.	202, 207, 208, 263, 273, 252, 253, 254, 261
The Rocks	Historic neighborhood, upscale boutiques; perfect for an afternoon pint.	Short Walk from Circular Quay.
Surry Hills	Artsy cafes and clothing stores.	301, 302, 303, 374, 376, 339, 372, 393, 395, 391
Vaucluse/Rose Bay	Historic, upscale homes and Euro-style shopping.	325, 324

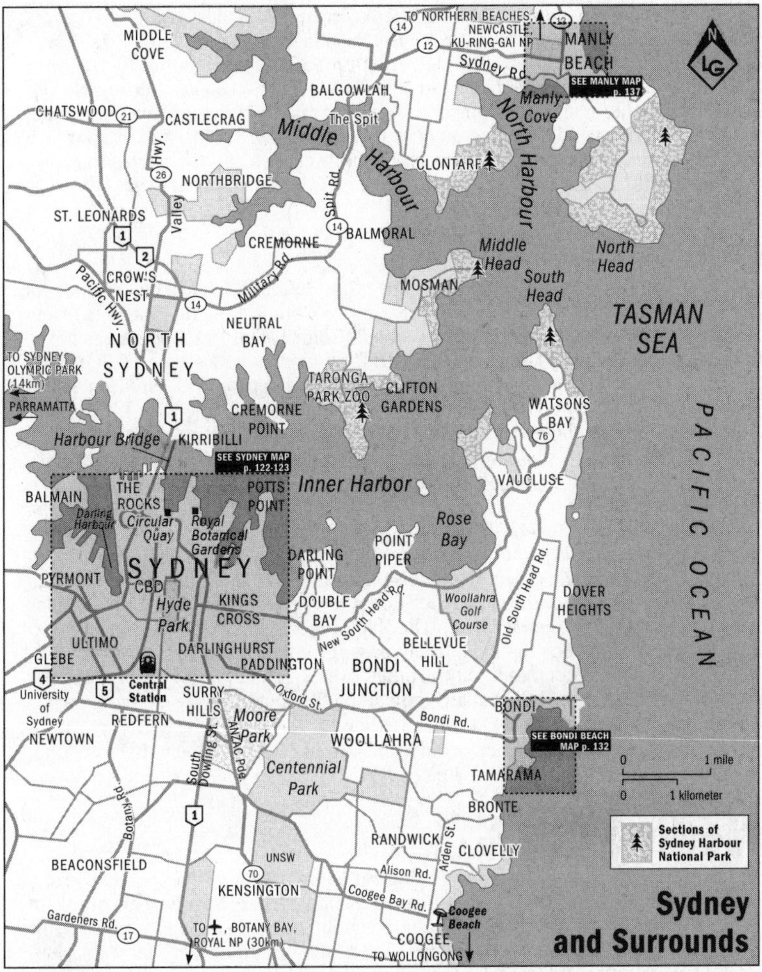

Sydney and Surrounds

OUR COVERAGE OF SYDNEY. Much of Sydney's great diversity of features and character is due to its many different neighborhoods. With this in mind, we have grouped together each neighborhood's accommodations, food, sights, and nightlife. Information on entertainment, local activities, area festivals, and daytrips from Sydney can be found at the end of the section.

LOCAL TRANSPORTATION

Sydney's well-oiled public transportation system makes it easy to travel within the city limits. The **Sydney Transit Authority (STA)** controls city **buses, CityRail trains,** and **ferries;** the network stops nearly everywhere. For information on any part of the STA system, call ☎ 13 15 00. Check prices for various passes, as they are frequently cheaper than paying individual fares. The **DayTripper** ($15, ages 4-15 $7.50) grants unlimited use of Sydney ferries, local buses, and central CityRail lines. The **TravelPass** (Red $32, ages 4-15 $16; Purple (premiere) $54/27) covers the four central zones and includes unlimited seven-day access to buses, trains, and ferries. The **Sydney Pass** includes unlimited bus, train, and ferry use within the TravelPass zone, round-trip Airport Link service, access to the Sydney, Bondi, and Parramatta Explorer buses, and passage on Sydney Harbour cruises and the ferries to Manly and Parramatta. (3-day pass $110, ages 4-15 $50, families $275; 5-day pass $145/70/360; 7-day pass $150/75/375.)

BY BUS

Buses do not automatically stop at all bus stops; hail them from the sidewalk as you would a taxi. Pay as you board; fares range from $1.80-5 (ages 4-15 ½-price, seniors $1.10-3; ask for student concessions). Color-coded **TravelTen** passes cover 10 trips at a discount and can be purchased from most news agencies. (Blue TravelTen for 10 trips from $13.60, children $6.) The **Bus Tripper** ($11, children $5.60) covers one full day of bus travel. Most buses run between 5am and 11:30pm, but there is 24hr. service between the city center and central locales.

In addition to the local commuter bus service, the Sydney Transport Authority operates two sightseeing buses, the **Sydney Explorer** and the **Bondi Explorer,** which allow passengers to get on and off at major attractions along designated routes. The Sydney Explorer covers sights between Sydney Harbour and Central Station, moving as far east as Woolloomooloo Bay and as far west as Darling Harbour, originating in Circular Quay (every 20min. 8:40am-5:20pm). The Bondi Explorer visits the eastern bays and southern beaches down to Coogee, departing from Circular Quay (every 30min. 8:45am-4:15pm). The Explorer services are expensive but also an excellent way to tour the city. (1-day pass for either route $39, ages 4-15 $18, families $97; tickets combining both routes over 2 non-consecutive days $62/31/155. Purchase tickets on a bus at any stop along the route.)

A **bus information kiosk,** labeled "Transit Shop," is located on the corner of Alfred and Loftus St. between the McDonald's and Circular Quay. (Open M-F 7am-7pm, Sa-Su 8:30am-5pm.) The STA info line (☎13 15 00; www.sydneypass.info) also has schedule details.

BY SUBWAY AND TRAIN

Sydney's **CityRail** train system (M-Th and Su 5am-12:35am, F-Sa 5am-2am) runs from Bondi Junction in the east to the most distant corners of suburban sprawl in the north, west, and south. Service is fast, frequent, and easy to navigate. CityRail's lowest one-way fare is $2.20; most trips cost a bit more. Round-trip fares are double the one-way price when purchased on weekdays before 9am. At all other times the purchase of a round-trip "off-peak" ticket gets you up to a 40% reduction of the one-way fare. The combined **TravelPass** is a bargain for regular train users. (Good for 1wk. beginning on day of validation; Red Pass for city center and beaches $32; Green Pass, which includes Manly Beach, $40.) **Train information offices** are at Circular Quay (open daily 9am-4:30pm) and at Central Station (☎8202 2000; open daily 6:30am-9:30pm).

Monorail and **Light Rail** (☎9285 5600; www.monorail.com.au or www.metrolightrail.com.au), operated by the same company, provide transportation above the city bustle, which is a nice change if you are traveling directly and don't mind the slightly heftier fee. The Monorail links the City Center with Darling Harbour and Chinatown. (Every 3-5min. M-Th 7am-10pm, F-Sa 7am-midnight, Su 8am-10pm. $4.50, seniors $2.20, under 5 free, families $22; day passes with unlimited transport $9.) The more practical Light Rail connects Chinatown, Darling Harbour, Glebe, Star City, and

Ultimo. (Daily every 10-15min. 6am-midnight; every 30min. midnight-6am. $3-5.50, seniors and ages 4-15 $1.80-4, families $20; unlimited day pass $8.50.)

BY FERRY

STA green and gold ferries (www.sydneyferries.nsw.gov.au) offer a magnificent view of the harbor. Ferries leave from the **Circular Quay** wharves between the Opera House and the Harbour Bridge (daily 6am-midnight; check the timetables for schedules). Short one-way trips in the harbor cost $5; a FerryTen pass for the same area costs $32.50 and works much like the TravelTen bus pass (p. 114). The fare for the **JetCat** to Manly is $7.90 (FerryTen pass $65.70). STA's fastest commuter ferry services its most distant port: take the RiverCat to Parramatta ($7.50, FerryTen $52.60, ages 4-15 ½-price).

STA has several **Sydney Ferries Harbour Cruises:** the Morning Cruise (1hr.; daily 10:30am; $18, ages 4-16 $9, families $45); the Afternoon Cruise (2½hr.; M-F 1pm, Sa-Su and public holidays 12:30pm; $24/12/60); and the after-dark Evening Harbour Cruise (1½hr., M-Sa 8pm, $22/11/55). Posher private ships, such as Captain Cook and Majestic Cruises, have slightly more comprehensive harbor cruises. Browse along East Circular Quay for the lowest fare; fares range from $24-45, with some ships offering dinner cruises from $59-159. Ships depart from mid-morning to evening. The **ferry information office** is located in East Circular Quay. (☎9207 3170. Open M-F 7am-6pm, Sa-Su 8am-6pm.)

BY CAR

All major **car rental** companies have desks in Kingsford-Smith Airport, and most appear again on William St. near Kings Cross. The big names include: **Avis,** 200 William St. (☎13 63 33 or 9357 2000); **Budget,** 93 William St. (☎13 27 27 or 8255 9600); **Hertz** (☎13 30 39 or 9360 6621, ext. 3), corner of William and Riley St.; **Thrifty,** 75 William St. (☎8374 6172 or 1300 367 227). All rental cars start around $45 per day, with surcharges of up to $25 per day for 21- to 25-year-olds. In general, local and regional outfits offer much better prices than the big companies, but fewer locations translates to more difficult interstate travel and drop-off. **Bayswater Car Rental,** 180 William St., at corner of Dowling, Kings Cross, charges $15 per day for a week or longer, adding $6 per day for drivers 21-25. (☎9360 3622; www.bayswatercarrental.com.au. Open M-F 8am-6pm, Sa 8am-noon, Su 9am-11:30am.) All companies offer reduced long-term rates, and most offer free pickup from the airport or Central Station.

Hostel notice boards overflow with fliers for privately owned cars, campers, and motorcycles selling for as little as several hundred dollars. When purchasing a car this way, it's a good idea to make sure it's registered to the seller so the registration can be transferred. For more information on car sales, see **Buying and Selling Used Cars,** p. 32. **Kings Cross Backpackers Car Market,** Level 2, Kings Cross Carpark, on the corner of Ward Ave. and Elizabeth Bay Rd., brings buyers and sellers together. They offer third-party insurance for travelers (see **Insurance,** p. 20), and their knowledgeable staff has valuable information on registration and other matters for car-buyers. (☎9358 5000 or 1800 808 188; www.carmarket.com.au. Open daily 9am-5pm. Weekly charge for sellers from $60. Required vehicle inspection from $28.) **Travellers Auto Barn,** 177 William St. (☎9360 1500 or 1800 674 374), rents cars and offers guaranteed buyback agreements on cars they sell for over $3000. Minimum buyback rates are 30-50% of purchase price, depending on how long you have the car. Cheaper cars are available but do not come with warranties or buyback guarantees, whereas purchases over $3000 include 5000km engine and gearbox warranties and free NRMA Roadside Service membership. There are six branches around the country, meaning that one-way rentals and buybacks are also offered. (Open M-Sa 9am-6pm, Su 10:30am-3pm.)

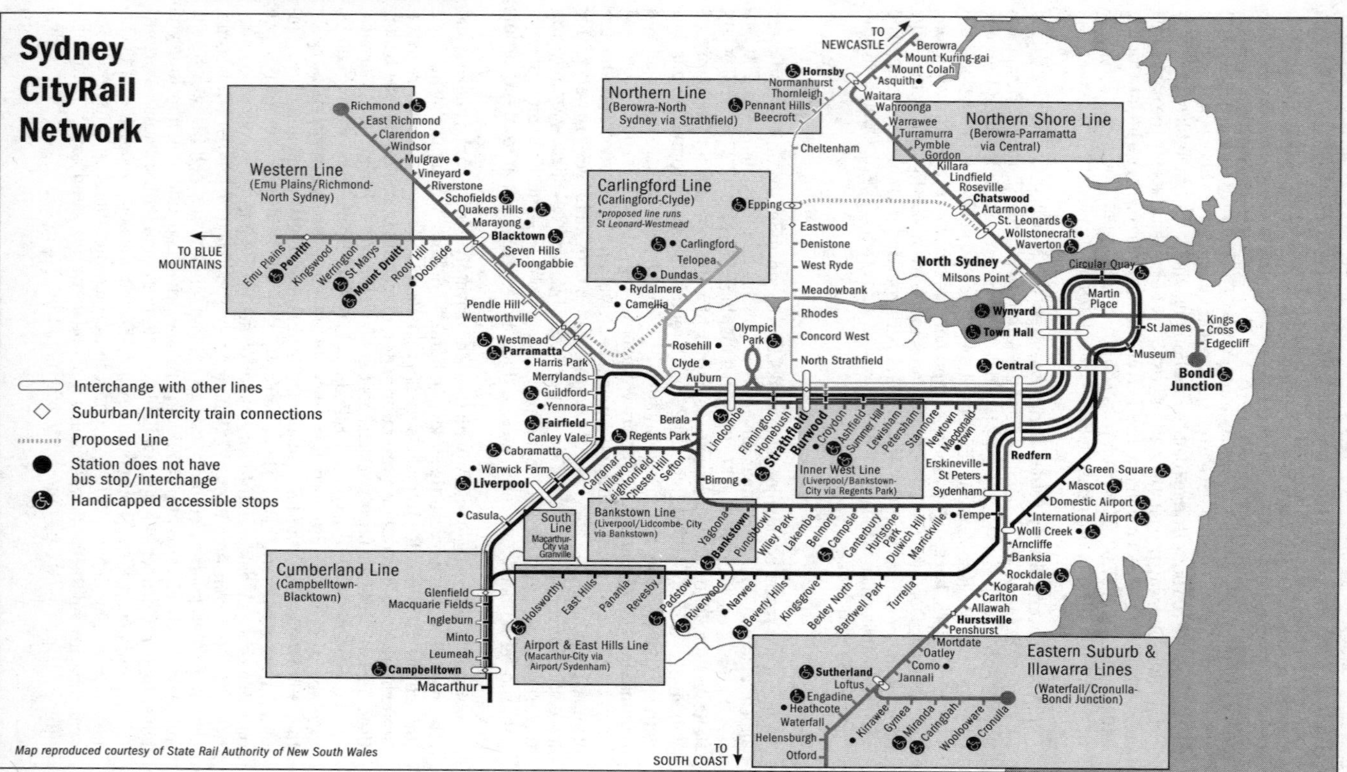

Map reproduced courtesy of State Rail Authority of New South Wales

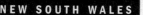

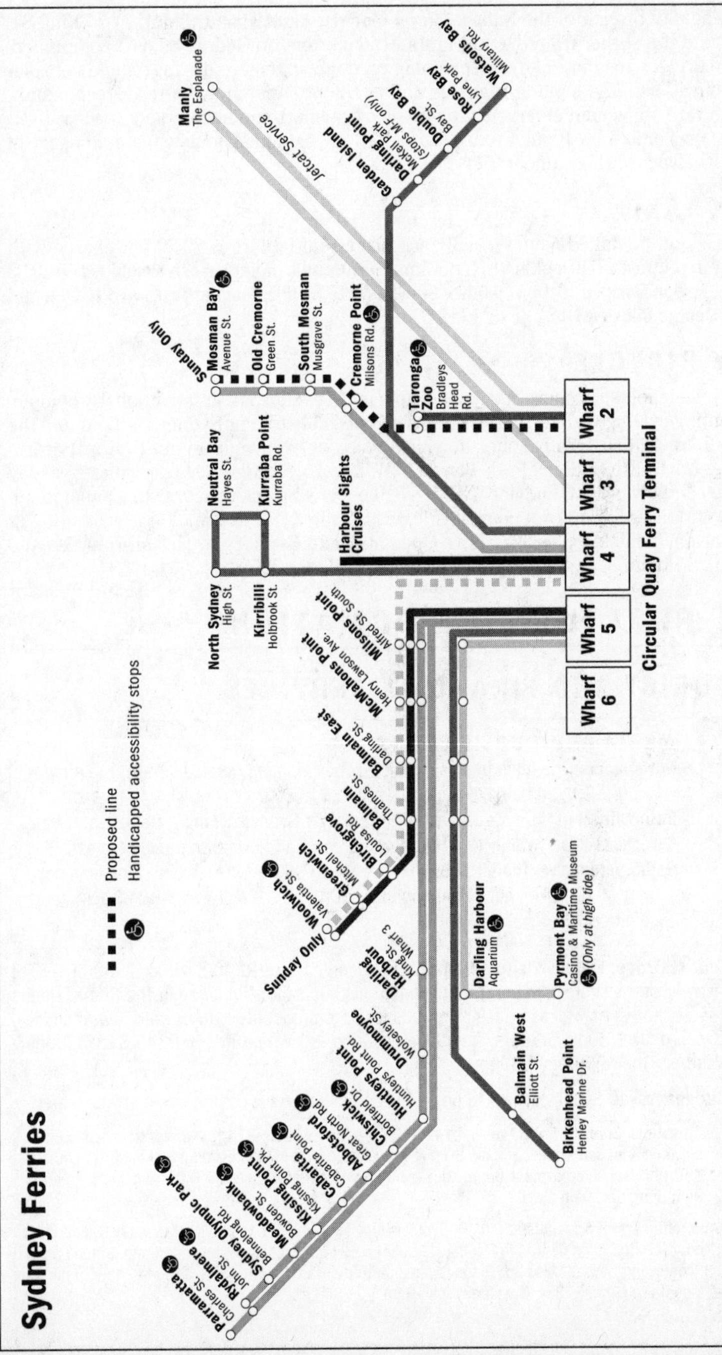

Sydney Ferries

■■■■■ Proposed line
♿ Handicapped accessibility stops

Parramatta
Charles St.
Rydalmere
John St.
Sydney Olympic Park
Bennelong Rd.
Meadowbank
Bowden St.
Kissing Point
Kissing Point Pk.
Cabarita
Cabarita Point
Abbotsford
Great North Rd.
Chiswick
Bortfield Dr.
Huntleys Point
Huntleys Point Rd.
Drummoyne
Wolseley St.
Darling Harbour
King St.
Wharf 3
Sunday Only
Woolwich
Valentia St.
Greenwich
Mitchell St.
Birchgrove
Louisa Rd.
Balmain
Thames St.
Balmain East
Darling St.
McMahons Point
Henry Lawson Ave.
Milsons Point
Alfred St. South
Balmain West
Elliott St.
Birkenhead Point
Henley Marine Dr.
Darling Harbour
Aquarium
Pyrmont Bay
Casino & Maritime Museum
(Only at high tide)
North Sydney
High St.
Kirribilli
Holbrook St.
Neutral Bay
Hayes St.
Kurraba Point
Kurraba Rd.
Harbour Sights Cruises
Sunday Only
Mosman Bay
Avenue St.
Old Cremorne
Green St.
South Mosman
Musgrave St.
Cremorne Point
Milsons Rd.
Taronga Zoo
Bradleys Head Rd.
Manly
The Esplanade
Jetcat Service
Garden Island
Darling Point
McKell Park
(stops M-F only)
Double Bay
Bay St.
Rose Bay
Lyne Park
Watsons Bay
Military Rd.
Wharf 6
Wharf 5
Wharf 4
Wharf 3
Wharf 2
Circular Quay Ferry Terminal

Map reproduced courtesy of The State Transit Authority of New South Wales

The city branch of the **National Royal Motorist Association (NRMA),** 74-76 King St., around the corner from the corporate headquarters on George St., is a comprehensive driver's resource. Anyone planning on doing extensive driving should consider joining—benefits include roadside and accident assistance, knowledgeable staff, accurate maps, and emergency passenger transport and accommodation. (☎13 21 32. Open daily 7am-10pm. From $71-148 for 1 yr., excluding joining fee. Joining fee of $52 waived for those under 25.)

BY TAXI

Taxis can be hailed from virtually any street. Initial fare is $2.80 (surcharge with call-in request $1.40), plus $1.62 per km. Companies include: **Taxis Combined** (☎13 33 00); **Legion Cabs** (☎13 14 51); **Silver Service** (☎13 31 00); **Premier Taxi** (☎13 10 17); and **St. George Cabs** (☎13 21 66 or 13 21 77).

BY BICYCLE

To take in lots of scenery at a manageable pace, cycling is a great option. By complementing cycling with ferries and trains, it's possible to tour Sydney Harbour and the northern and eastern beaches in a single day, or even venture out to Royal or Ku-Ring-Gai Chase National Park. **Bicycle NSW,** Level 5, 822 George St., organizes weekly rides and gives rental advice. (☎9218 5400; www.bicyclensw.org.au. Annual membership dues $85.) For a coastal ride, visit **Manly Cycle Centre,** 36 Pittwater Rd., at Denison St. in Manly. (☎9977 1189. Open M-W and F 9am-6pm, Th 9am-7pm, Sa 9am-6pm, Su 10am-5pm. $15 per hr., $25 per 2hr., full day $55.)

PRACTICAL INFORMATION

TOURIST AND FINANCIAL SERVICES

MEDIA AND PUBLICATIONS

Newspapers: The main papers are the *Sydney Morning Herald* ($2.20), *The Australian* ($2.20), and tabloid *Daily Telegraph* ($1.50).

Entertainment: The Metro section of Friday's Sydney Morning Herald, and free weeklies *Beat, Sydney City Hub, Streetpress,* and *Revolver* (in music stores).

Radio: Alternative, Triple J 105.7FM; pop, Nova 969 96.9FM; mainly American pop, Triple M 104.9FM; adult contemporary, 2DAY 104.1FM; News, ABC 630AM; tourist info, 88FM.

Tourist Office: Sydney Visitors Centre, 106 George St. (☎9240 8788 or 1800 067 676; www.sydneyvisitorcentre.com), in the white historic sailors' building in The Rocks. Heaps of brochures, as well as booking services for accommodations, tours, and harbor cruises. Open daily 9:30am-5:30pm. Additional location, 33 Wheat Rd. (☎9240 8788), Darling Harbor. Open 9:30am-5:30pm..

Budget Travel: Sydney seems to post travel offices at every corner, some of which are:

Travellers Contact Point, Level 7, 428 George St. (☎9221 8744; sydney@travellers.com.au), between King and Market St. Free 30min. **Internet** access. Mail forwarding and holding in Australia $50 per year. Employment board with recruiting officers for travelers with work visas. Open M-F 9am-6pm, Sa 10am-4pm.

Australian Travel Specialists, Jetty 6, Circular Quay (☎9247 5151; www.castaway.com), and in Harbourside Shopping Centre, in Darling Harbour (☎9211 3192). Comprehensive info on trips around Sydney and beyond. Also books tours, ranging from a Harbour tour (1hr., $22) to a tour of the Blue Mountains (9hr., $135). Open daily 9am-9pm

YHA Travel Center, 422 Kent St. (☎9261 1111; www.yha.com.au), behind town hall. Also at 11 Rawson Pl. (☎9281 9444), next to Sydney Central YHA. Caters to backpackers' needs in particular. Open M-W and F 9am-5pm, Th 9am-6pm, Sa 10am-2pm

Consulates: Canada, Level 5, 111 Harrington St. (☎9364 3000). Open M-F 8:30am-4:30pm. **New Zealand,** Level 10, 55 Hunter St. (passport ☎9225 2300, visa 9223 0144). Open M-F 9am-5pm, W 9.30am-4pm. **UK,** Level 16, 1 Macquarie Pl. (☎9247 7521). Open M-F 10am-4:30pm. **US,** Level 10, 19-29 Martin Pl., MLC Centre (☎9373 9200). Open M-F 8am-11.30am; phones answered 8am-5pm. **Ireland,** 50th fl., 400 George St. (☎9231 6999). Open M-F 10:30am-1pm and 2-4pm.

FINANCIAL SERVICES

Banks: Commonwealth and National pack the CBD. ATMs, located in convenience stores, usually accept MasterCard and Visa. Open M-Th 9am-4pm, F 9am-5pm.

American Express: (☎1300 139 060). Dozens of locations around the city, including 296 George St., CBD. $8 charge on traveler's checks and currency exchanges. Min. $13.20 or 1.1% commission to buy checks. Open M-F 9am-5pm.

Travelex (☎1800 801 002). Several locations in the international terminal (☎9317 2100) of the airport. $4-8 charge on traveler's checks and currency exchanges. Open daily 5:15am-9:30pm. There are dozens of other offices, including on the ground fl. of the QVB. Open M-F 9am-6pm, Sa 10am-3pm, Su 11am-3pm.

LOCAL SERVICES

State Library of New South Wales (☎9273 1414), next to the Parliament House on Macquarie St., houses galleries and research facilities, but does not lend books. Open M-Th 9am-9pm, F 9am-6pm, Sa-Su 11am-5pm.

Ticket Agencies: Ticketek (☎13 28 49; www.ticketek.com.au), has offices in retail stores and an information kiosk at 195 Elizabeth St. Full-price advance booking for music, theater, sports, and select museums. Phone lines open for purchases by credit card M-Sa 9am-9pm, Su 9am-8pm. **Ticketmaster** (☎13 61 00; www.ticketmaster7.com). Information kiosk at 13 Cambell St. Open M-F 9am-5pm. Phones answered M-Sa 9am-9pm, Su 9am-5pm.

EMERGENCY AND COMMUNICATIONS

CYBER-SYDNEY

www.cityofsydney.nsw.gov.au The Sydney homepage. Visitor guide and information on services provided by the local government.

http://sydney.citysearch.com.au A comprehensive business directory, entertainment listings, shopping, restaurants, and gay/lesbian info.

www.sydney.com.au Sydney's sights, accommodations, and transportation.

Police: 570 George St. (☎9265 6595). Kings Cross police station, 1-15 Elizabeth Bay Rd. (☎8356 0099), in Fitzroy Gardens.

Crisis Lines: Rape Crisis, Mental Health, STD Clinic, Darlinghurst Community Healthcare, (☎8382 1911) 301 Forbes St. **HIV/AIDS Information Line** (☎9332 4000. Open M-F 8am-7pm, Sa 10am-6pm). **Suicide prevention** (☎9331 2000). **Gay & Lesbian Counseling Service** (☎8594 9596 or 1800 184 527; open daily 5:30-10:30pm). **Sex Workers Outreach Program** (☎9319 4866)

Late-Night Pharmacy: Crest Hotel Pharmacy, (☎9358 1822) 91-93 Darlinghurst Rd., Kings Cross, 4 doors left of the rail station. Open 8am-midnight. **Wu's Pharmacy,** (☎9211 1805) 629 George St., Chinatown. Open M-Sa 9am-9pm, Su 9am-7pm.

Medical Services: Sydney Hospital (☎9382 7111 or 9382 7009), on Macquarie St. opposite the Martin Pl. station. **St. Vincent's Hospital** (8382 1111), corner of Victoria and Burton St. **Sydney Medical Centre,** 580 George St. (☎9261 9261), in the Pavilion Plaza. Consultation fee $60. Open daily 7am-9pm. **Contraceptive Services,** Level 1, 195 Macquarie St. (☎9221 1933). Consultation fee $45. Open M-F 8:30am-1pm. Pregnancy consultations and abortions available M-F by appointment only.

Telephones: Public pay phones are common in Sydney; local calls cost $0.40. For international calls, invest in a cheap **calling card,** which can be easily found in Chinatown and at convenience stores in the CBD. **Apple** brand calling cards have particularly good rates. Calls to the US and UK cost $0.39 per min. all day, and there is no connection fee. **Global Gossip** offers super-cheap rates ($0.04 per min. to the US and UK from noon-6pm with pre-paid phone card, plus a $0.59 connection fee). Another good option is investing in a **pre-paid mobile phone,** which often allows you to accept calls for free (see **Essentials,** p. 9). **Directory Assistance:** ☎1223.

Internet Access: Internet cafes abound, especially on George St. near Chinatown and the Sydney YHA, and in Kings Cross. Common charges in the CBD are $2-4 per hr., but rates fluctuate. **Global Gossip** (☎9212 4444; www.globalgossip.com) charges $3 per hr., and their shops are franchised across the city. Hours vary by location. Their main store is at 790 George St., near Sydney Central YHA. Open daily 9am-midnight.

Post Office: Sydney General Post Office (GPO), 1 Martin Pl. (☎9244 3710). Open M-F 8:15am-5:30pm, Sa 10am-1pm. *Poste Restante* available at 310 George St., inside Hunter Connection across from Wynyard Station; holds mail for up to 1 month. Enter up the ramp marked by the "Hunter Connection" sign. Open M-F 8:15am-5:30pm. Many hostels will also hold mail for up to 1 month. **Postal Code:** 2000.

ACCOMMODATIONS

The city center is an obvious choice for accommodation because of its convenient location and the sheer abundance of options. The huge hostels near Central Station are more like hotels with dorm rooms, which usually means their facilities are excellent and noise levels are usually high. More tight-knit backpacker communities exist in hostels on Pitt St., but as you go farther downtown, there's a trade-off in quality of facilities. Well-located, traveler-friendly, and party-ready, Kings Cross is another established backpacker mecca, and the high concentration of steadily improving hostels ensures that beds are almost always available. However, the number of alleys and strip clubs makes many travelers uncomfortable. If you do opt to stay in the Cross, be sure you feel satisfied with your hostel's security measures before letting your valuables out of sight. Good suburban bets include Coogee Beach and Glebe, which both offer many relaxed backpacker accommodations in close proximity to cafes and student nightlife.

Unless stated otherwise, hostels accept major credit cards. Most dorm beds increase in price by a few dollars ($2-5) during high season (Nov.-Feb.) and school holidays (p. 38). The most expensive time to travel is late December and April.

FOOD

Sydney's multicultural makeup shines through in its food. **Asian** options, most notably small sushi and Thai shops, are abundant all over the city. The CBD is packed with many cheap options. Slightly south, a Spanish quarter provides classier, pricier meals, while Chinatown's numerous restaurants are always packed.

Just east of the city center, the Oxford St. social artery that runs from Surry Hills in the south, is lined with ethnic restaurants. A (very) **Little Italy** is located on Stanley St., between Crown and Riley St., in Darlinghurst. For a larger selection of authentic Italian food, head out to **Norton Street** in the suburb of Leichardt. Continuing east through Darlinghurst, the strip of restaurants on Oxford St. near St. Vincent's Hospital are a mix of cafes and Asian restaurants. Victoria St. runs north from Oxford St. at the hospital into the land of **cappuccino chic** before depositing the last of its cafe class amid the hostels of Kings Cross. In the Cross, Darlinghurst Rd. and Bayswater Rd. offer **late-night cheap bites** and fast-food chains.

As usual, a large student population means good, **cheap cafes** and restaurants on both Glebe Point Rd. in Glebe and King St. in Newtown. Blues Point Rd. on McMahons Point, Fitzroy St. in Kirribilli, and Military Rd. through Neutral Bay and Mosman lead the North Shore's stylish and affordable offerings, with well-loved local cafes as well as a plethora of ethnic-inspired, family-focused eateries. At most **coastal cafes** in Manly and Balmoral in the north and Bondi and Coogee in the south, $6-7 buys a large cooked breakfast and an excuse to appreciate the view over the morning paper. Though the neighborhoods vary in their offerings, none disappoint. The CBD is rife with quick lunch stops for the professional masses working in the skyscrapers; sandwiches, meat pies, and focaccia run $2.50-6 at the district's diners. Slightly south, away from Circular Quay, the feeding frenzy of **Chinatown** lurks west of Central Station, and the best Chinese takeaways ($7.50) can be found lining **Goulburn Street.** Unless otherwise noted, major credit cards are accepted everywhere in the many malls of the city center.

SIGHTS

The main sights of Sydney are the two **harbors** (Sydney Harbour and Darling Harbour) and the **green spaces** of the Royal Botanic Gardens, Hyde Park, and the Domain. Each of these merits a day of strolling and exploration. Find adrenaline-fixes in **Activities** (p. 150) and the top spots for retail therapy in **Shopping** (p. 148).

NIGHTLIFE

Whether they're out on the town dancing or huddling around a pub TV for the latest sports telecast, many locals hit the pub and club scene as many as five times per week. Different neighborhoods have distinct scenes, which vary from night to night. The dress code tends to be "smart casual" in the clubs, meaning no shorts or sandals, and trendy sneakers only.

Sydney's city center is a bit more upscale, particularly in the **suit-filled** CBD and the **trendy** Darling Harbour. The Rocks is more laid-back though still expensive with numerous **English-style pubs.** Bars in Kings Cross attract a sizeable straight male contingent that quickly spills over from the strip joints into the pubs and dance clubs. Backpackers round out the mix in this neighborhood, giving several spots an international feel. **Gay and lesbian** Sydney struts its stuff on Oxford St., in Darlinghurst and Paddington, and also in Newtown. Some establishments are specifically gay or lesbian and many others are mixed. Because the gay clubs provide much of the city's **best dance music,** flocks of young, beautiful clubbers of all persuasions fill any extra space on the vibrant, vampy dance floors. Taylor Sq., at the intersection of Oxford, Flinders, and Bourke St., is the heart of this district. For more casual pub crawling, wander on Bourke and Flinders St. in Surry Hills. Large **student populations** in Glebe and Newtown make for a younger crowd and cheaper drinks on special nights at local pubs. Manly holds up the North Shore's end of the nightlife equation, with options for the more chill partygoer.

The Sydney clubber's bible is *3-D World* (www.threedworld.com.au), a free weekly publication that can be found in hostels, music stores, and clothing boutiques. Look for the free *Streetpress* or *The Revolver*, which highlight weekly dance hotspots; *Drum Media* covers music. *Sx News* (www.sxnews.com.au) and *Sydney Star Observer* (www.ssonet.com.au) focus on the gay community.

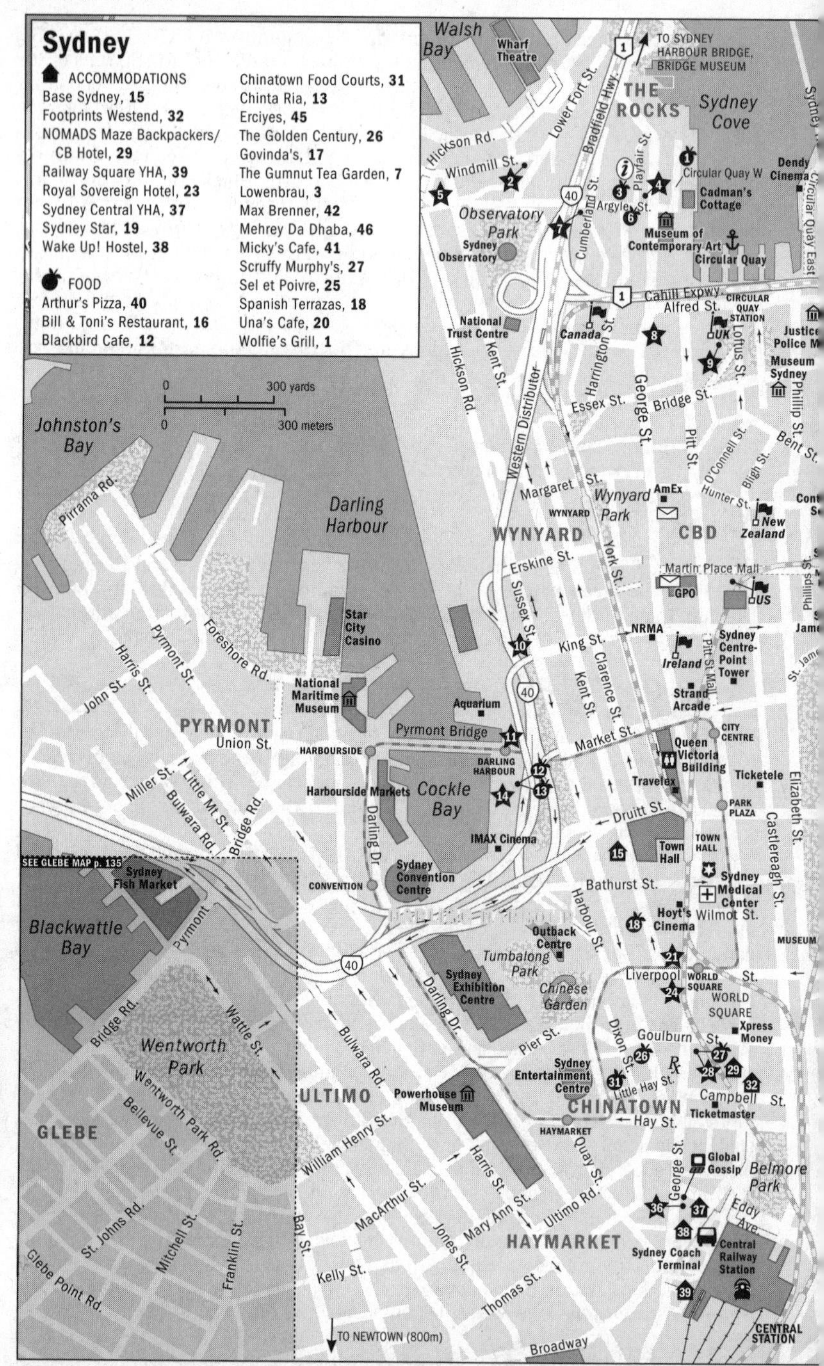

NEW SOUTH WALES

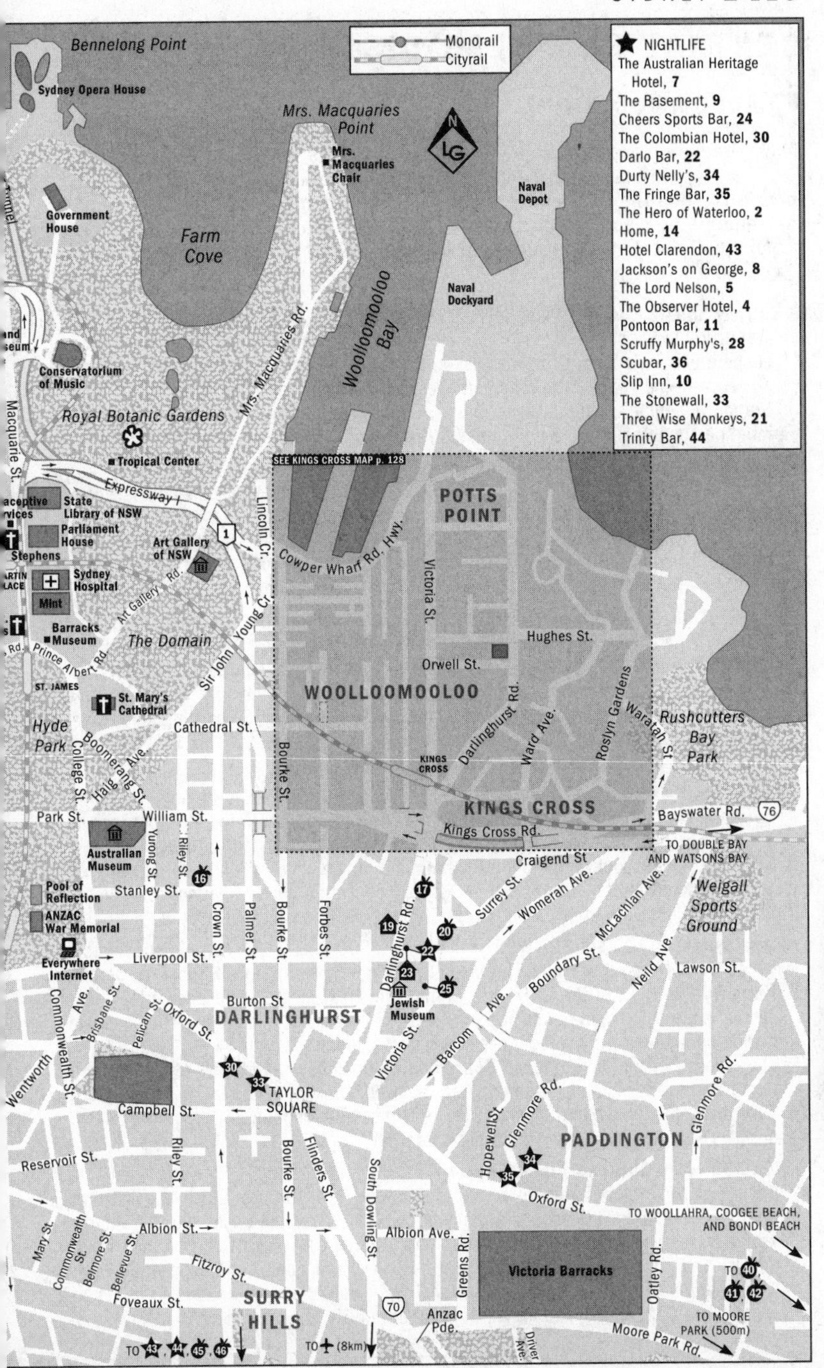
Monorail
Cityrail
NIGHTLIFE
The Australian Heritage Hotel, 7
The Basement, 9
Cheers Sports Bar, 24
The Colombian Hotel, 30
Darlo Bar, 22
Durty Nelly's, 34
The Fringe Bar, 35
The Hero of Waterloo, 2
Home, 14
Hotel Clarendon, 43
Jackson's on George, 8
The Lord Nelson, 5
The Observer Hotel, 4
Pontoon Bar, 11
Scruffy Murphy's, 28
Scubar, 36
Slip Inn, 10
The Stonewall, 33
Three Wise Monkeys, 21
Trinity Bar, 44
Bennelong Point
Sydney Opera House
Mrs. Macquaries Point
Mrs. Macquaries Chair
Naval Depot
Government House
Farm Cove
Woolloomooloo Bay
Naval Dockyard
Conservatorium of Music
Royal Botanic Gardens
Tropical Center
Mrs. Macquaries Rd.
Macquarie St.
Expressway
State Library of NSW
Parliament House
Art Gallery of NSW
Sydney Hospital
Mint
Barracks Museum
The Domain
St. Mary's Cathedral
Hyde Park
SEE KINGS CROSS MAP p. 128
POTTS POINT
Cowper Wharf Rd. Hwy.
Lincoln Cr.
Victoria St.
Hughes St.
Orwell St.
WOOLLOOMOOLOO
Darlinghurst Rd.
Ward Ave.
Roslyn Gardens
Waratah St.
Rushcutters Bay Park
KINGS CROSS
Kings Cross Rd.
Bayswater Rd.
TO DOUBLE BAY AND WATSONS BAY
Craigend St.
Art Gallery Rd.
Prince Albert Rd.
Sir John Young Cr.
Cathedral St.
College St.
Boomerang St.
Haig Ave.
Bourke St.
Park St.
William St.
Australian Museum
Yurong St.
Riley St.
Stanley St.
Pool of Reflection
ANZAC War Memorial
Crown St.
Palmer St.
Forbes St.
Surrey St.
Womerah Ave.
McLachlan Ave.
Weigall Sports Ground
Everywhere Internet
Liverpool St.
Boundary St.
Neild Ave.
Lawson St.
Jewish Museum
Burton St
DARLINGHURST
Oxford St.
Commonwealth St.
Brisbane St.
Pelican St.
Wentworth Ave.
Victoria St.
Barcom Ave.
TAYLOR SQUARE
Campbell St.
Glenmore Rd.
Hopewell St.
PADDINGTON
Reservoir St.
Flinders St.
South Dowling St.
TO WOOLLAHRA, COOGEE BEACH, AND BONDI BEACH
Albion St.
Albion Ave.
Mary St.
Belmore St.
Bellevue St.
Fitzroy St.
Greens Rd.
Victoria Barracks
Oatley Rd.
Foveaux St.
SURRY HILLS
Anzac Pde.
Driver Ave.
Moore Park Rd.
TO MOORE PARK (500m)
TO (8km)
TO 43, 44, 45, 46
TO 40, 41, 42

CENTRAL BUSINESS DISTRICT

ACCOMMODATIONS

These backpacker-friendly accommodations, located primarily in the CBD close to Central Station and other main transportation lines, can't be beat for location. While the CBD is not Sydney's most charming area, it is terrifically convenient; most accommodations are only steps from the food of Chinatown, the shopping of the CBD, and about a 10min. walk from the sights of Circular Quay and The Rocks.

Railway Square YHA, 8-10 Lee St. (☎9281 9688), next to Central Station. Newest 5-star hostel in Sydney, this former parcels shed is now a modern facility with spa pool, kitchen, and TV lounge. Day tour desk and Internet access ($3 per hr.). Some rooms are even in the shape of railway carriages. Lots of light and little noise from Central Station. Amenities comparable to Sydney Central though overall size is smaller with a more personal feel. 4- to 8-bed dorms $29-35; doubles $84; ensuite $94. ❸

Sydney Central YHA, 11 Rawson Pl. (☎9218 9000; sydneycentral@yhansw.org.au), near the corner of Pitt St. and Rawson Pl. Top-of-the-line hostel with incredible facilities: pool, sauna, game room, travel desks, TV rooms, Internet access ($2 per 30min., $3 per hr.), parking ($14 per night), multiple kitchens, bar, and cafe. No sleeping bags allowed. Lockers $2-6. Laundry $6. Max. 2wk. stay. Reception 24hr. Check-in from noon. Check-out 10am. Dorms $29-34; twins $86; ensuite doubles $98. YHA. ❸

Wake up! Hostel, 509 Pitt St. (☎9288 7888; www.wakeup.com.au), opposite Central Station. Voted Best Large Hostel in the World 2005 and Best Hostel in Oceania in both 2004 and 2005 by HostelWorld; this spot lives up to its reputation. Just 4yr. old, it has a sleek, modern feel and rooms with high ceilings. Brightly painted floors have different themes and colors. Cafe and bar boasts big screen TV and nightly events. Internet access ($4 per hr.), travel desk, and TV lounge area. Laundry $7. Reception 24hr. Dorms $25-35; doubles $79; ensuite $88. ❸

Footprints Westend, 412 Pitt St. (☎9211 4588 or 1800 013 186; www.footprintswestend.com.au), opposite NOMADS Maze Backpackers/CB Hotel. Makes up for its simple, small rooms—all ensuite—with the liveliest staff around and daily planned activities, like discount trips to the Blue Mountains, beach trips, and pub crawls. Free airport pickup with 3-night stay. Breakfast $2. Lockers $5 per day. Laundry $8. Reception 24hr. Check-out 10am. Dorms $24-30; twins $70; ensuite $80-85. ❷

NEW SOUTH WALES

Base Sydney, 477 Kent St. (☎9267 7718 or 1800 242 273; www.basebackpackers.com), between Druitt and Bathurst St., a block from Town Hall. Close to Darling Harbour, the heart of the CBD, and Chinatown. Best located and one of the most secure in the city. Clean rooms and 340 beds, friendly staff, and many facilities: basic TV and pool rooms, employment and travel desks, tanning booth ($4 per 3min.), Internet access ($4 per hr.) Attached **Scary Canary Bar** has cheap meals ($4.50-8) and numerous Happy hours. No sleeping bags allowed. Lockers $2-8 per day. Laundry $6. Max. 4wk. stay. Free airport shuttle with 3-night stay. Reception 24hr. Dorms $24-34; doubles $89. VIP $1 discount. 7th night free. ❷

NOMADS Maze Backpackers/CB Hotel, 417 Pitt St. (☎9211 5115; www.mazebackpackers.com), 3 blocks from Central Station toward Circular Quay. Close to Chinatown and good nightlife. 500 beds and dimly lit common areas are basic, but the friendly staff creates welcoming social atmosphere. Events like free BBQ, free wine, pub crawls, and yoga sessions. Employment desk, TV, and pool rooms. Lockers $3 per day. Laundry $6. Free airport pickup for 3-night stay. Reception 24hr. 4- to 6-bed dorms from $22; singles from $49; doubles from $65. ❷

 FOOD

City Center is packed with opportunities to eat a delicious meal overlooking the water, take in a live music performance, or watch a chef cook the day's menu right before your eyes. For a quick, inexpensive bite, try one of the hundreds of food courts scattered throughout the city—you won't be disappointed.

Blackbird Cafe (☎9283 7385), Cockle Bay Wharf, in Darling Harbour. Trendy eatery with photo-op fountain, spiral staircase, lounging atmosphere, and delightful view of the harbor. F-Sa nights DJs provide great music. Diverse selection of pizza ($7-17), as well as breakfast ($4-13) and delicious desserts ($6-8). Open daily 9:30am-latenight. ❷

Spanish Terrazas, 541 Kent St. (☎9283 3046; www.spanishterrazas.com.au). Affordable tapas ($9-13.50) and mixed grill paella ($29-42 for 2) in the pricey Spanish Quarter. Wash it all down with a mixed drink ($12) or a pitcher of sangria ($20)–the smoothest you'll ever taste–while enjoying live Latin music F-Sa. Open for lunch M-F noon-3pm, for dinner M-Th 5:30-10pm, F-Sa 5:30pm-11pm. ❹

Chinta Ria: Temple of Love (☎9264 3211), Roof Terr. Level 2, Cockle Bay Wharf, in Darling Harbour. A fantastic spot for soaking in the trendy wharf neighborhood amid stunning Malaysian decor. Big Buddha statue greets you at the door. Authentic Malaysian fare ($13-26.50). Full bar and BYOB option. Open M-Sa noon-2:30pm and 6-11pm, Su 6-pm-10:30pm. No reservations. ❸

Scruffy Murphy's, 43 Goulburn St. (☎9211 2002; www.scruffymurphys.com.au). There's no better place in the city to get a hearty meal without overspending. Big Australian breakfast (eggs, sausage, bacon, mushrooms, chips, toast, and tomato; $5). Steak, pasta, and chicken ($5) served all day. Restaurant is relatively quiet until the bar crowd moves in around 9:30pm. Open 8am-latenight with 24hr. license. ❶

Chinatown food courts, along Dixon St., all serve cheap meals ($5-9): **Dixon House Food Court,** 80 Dixon St., downstairs, at Little Hay St. (open daily 10:30am-8:30pm); **Sussex House Food Court,** 60 Dixon St. (open daily 10:30am-9:30pm); and **Harbour Plaza Eating World,** on Dixon at Goulburn St. (open daily 10am-10pm; cash only). ❶

The Golden Century, 393-399 Sussex St. (☎9212 3901). This massive, 2-level Chinese restaurant is best known for its fresh seafood and long lines. Savvy customers, however, know the fine food and unique atmosphere to be well worth the wait. Pass the time by choosing your own entree from the huge tanks of crab, lobster, and fresh fish that line the walls. Open daily noon-4am. ❷

SIGHTS

SYDNEY CENTREPOINT TOWER. Rising 325m above sea level (and containing four floors of shopping malls), the tower affords a stunning panoramic view of the city and its surroundings. The 40 second ride to the top of Australia's highest building is steep in grade and price, so don't waste the trip on a cloudy day. When the sky is clear, views extend as far as the Blue Mountains to the west, the central coast to the north, and Wollongong to the south. Night rides offer a romantic view of Sydney's city lights. **Sydney Tower Restaurant** ❺, the city's revolving restaurant, spins on the second-highest floor. *(100 Market St. ☎9333 9222; www.sydneytoweroztrek.com.au. Open M-F and Su 9am-10:30pm, Sa 9am-11:30pm. $24, ages 4-15 $14, families $42-70. Restaurant reservations ☎8223 3800. Buffet lunch $45, dinner $58. Fixed-price menu also available.)*

ART GALLERY OF NEW SOUTH WALES. Sydney's major art museum is not to be missed, particularly since it's free. Take a break from your walk through the

Botanic Gardens to view this fresh display of modern and old European art. Its strength lies in contemporary Australian works, such as its extensive Aboriginal and Torres Strait Islander gallery, and its new Asian wing. Bonnard, Picasso, and other big names are also represented. *(Northeast corner of the Domain, on Art Gallery Rd. ☎9225 1744; www.artgallery.nsw.gov.au. Open daily 10am-5pm. Free.)*

QUEEN VICTORIA BUILDING. An imposing statue of Queen Victoria guards the main entrance to this lavish building. The Romanesque edifice was constructed in 1898 as a home for the plebeian city markets, but recent renovations have brought in four floors of ritzy shopping venues. Fortunately, a stroll through the beautifully tiled and carpeted interior still doesn't cost a cent. Sports shops and designer stores are featured side-by-side in this great shopping destination. *(455 George St. ☎9265 6855; www.qvb.com.au. Open M-W and F-Sa 9am-6pm, Th 9am-9pm, Su 11am-5pm. Guided tours on the history and architecture of the building daily 2:30pm; $10.)*

TOWN HALL. Sydney's age ensures that architecture in the city center is far from uniformly modern. The Italian Renaissance-style Town Hall was built in the prosperity of the late 1800s. The building is frequently used today as a performance venue. *(483 George St. ☎9265 9007. Open daily 9am-5pm. Free.)*

HYDE PARK. Between Elizabeth and College St. at the eastern edge of the city center, Hyde Park was set aside in 1810 by Governor Lachlan Macquarie and is still Sydney's most structured public park, complete with fountains and stately trees. A buzzing urban oasis during the day, the park warrants caution at night. In the southern half, below Park St., the Art Deco-style **ANZAC Memorial** commemorates the service of the Australian and New Zealand Army Corps in WWI, as well as all Australians who have fought in war. *(☎9267 7668. Open daily 9am-5pm.)* To the park's east sits the Neo-Gothic **St. Mary's Cathedral.** The structure was first erected in 1833 to appease the growing population of Catholic convicts, burned to the ground in 1865, and rebuilt in 1928. Construction on the two Gothic towers at the southern end was finally completed in 2000. An exhibit placed awkwardly in the crypt gives an informative account of the cathedral's role in a modern city. *(☎9220 0400. Crypt open daily 10am-4pm. Admission $5. Tours Su noon after mass or by arrangement.)*

AUSTRALIAN MUSEUM. This museum houses a unique mix of natural and indigenous cultural history. Stuffed recreations of prehistoric Australian megafauna cast shadows over popular Aussie animals such as the koala and kangaroo. Though the science exhibits are fun for kids, the museum is fascinating for all ages. The size of the sperm whale skeleton, which beached itself in Sydney over 100 years ago, must be seen to be believed. *(6 College St., on the east side of Hyde Park. ☎9320 6000; www.amonline.net.au. Open daily 9:30am-5pm. $10, ages 5-15 $5, under 5 free, families $17.50-25. Special and temporary exhibits cost up to $8 extra.)*

HYDE PARK BARRACKS MUSEUM. A small, unusual display of artifacts from the days of convict immigration is housed in this eerie building, once a barracks, women's immigration depot, and asylum. Visitors can lie in convicts' hammocks and search for convict ancestors in a database. *(In Queens Sq., on Macquarie St. ☎8239 2311; www.hht.net.au. Open daily 9:30am-5pm. $7, students with ID $3, families $17.)*

SYDNEY HOSPITAL AND NSW PARLIAMENT HOUSE. The three-building complex of the Parliament House, Hospital, and Royal Mint was once the Rum Hospital, so-called because of the Rum monopoly offered to the developers of the hospital in exchange for building it. The 1814 hospital building is a landmark of colonial architecture; the central section is still the main medical center. Visitors are welcome in the **NSW Parliament House,** the Rum Hospital's former north wing. During parliamentary sessions, visitors can access public viewing galleries or take a free tour. *(Parliament faces Macquarie St. between Martin Pl. and Hunter St. ☎9230 3444. Open M-F 9:30am-4pm. Free tour 1pm 1st Th of every month. Book ahead for tours.)*

NIGHTLIFE

Three Wise Monkeys, 555 George St. (☎9283 5855), corner of George and Liverpool St. Trendy yet unpretentious. Twenty-somethings pack 3 intimate, red-swathed levels of bars. Top-40 hits play for a dancing crowd on the top level. F-Sa live music 10pm. Schooners $4.30. You will leave this place hoping everyone will hear-no-evil and speak-no-evil of you. Open M-Th and Su 10am-2am, F-Sa 10am-3am.

The Basement, 29 Reiby Pl. (☎9251 2797). Arguably the hottest live music venue in the CBD. With acts ranging from jazz to rock, this landmark institution has been a music mecca since the 1970s. Bottles from $6. Cover $10, up to $50 for the most exclusive acts. Open M-F noon-3pm for lunch and 7:30pm-late, Sa-Su 7pm-latenight.

Scruffy Murphy's, 43 Goulburn St. (☎9211 2002). Offering live entertainment almost every night—from musical performances to trivia games to talent shows—it's no wonder that this Irish pub attracts such a large, rowdy crowd. Schooners $4. Open daily 11am-latenight with 24hr. license.

Jackson's on George, 176 George St. (☎9247 2727), near Circular Quay. City-center hotspot with 4 levels holds 6 bars, dance club, and restaurant. Slot machines abound in the basement for those who are feeling flush with cash. Happy hour daily 5-7pm. Schooners $4. Drink specials Sa-Su 4:30-6:30pm. Cover F-Sa $10 after 10pm. Dress nicely—no sandals allowed. Open M-Th 9am-latenight, F 9am-6am, Sa-Su 10am-6am.

Cheers Sports Bar, 561 George St. (☎9261 8313), corner of George and Liverpool St., near Three Wise Monkeys. When a game's on, this chill sports bar gets raucous. Mixture of backpackers and locals hits the relaxed dance club downstairs. The drinks and atmosphere are worthy of recommendation, the food not as much. Schooners $4.10. Open M-Th and Su 10am-5:30am, Sa-Su 10am-6am.

Scubar, 4 Rawson Pl. (☎9212 4244; www.scubar.com.au), next to the YHA, 1min. from Central Station walking toward George St. Billiard competitions, big screen TV, and the ever-popular M night hermit crab racing. $7 jugs and $3 wine and champers bring backpackers over from next door in droves. Not really a place to meet locals, but a hot spot for international travelers. Open M-F noon-latenight, Sa-Su 3pm-latenight.

KINGS CROSS

ACCOMMODATIONS

If you decide to take up residence in the Cross, you can expect good nightlife, lots of backpacking company, and seedy streets—here, "ladies of the night" are morning people too. Some accommodations can be pretty run-down, but plenty of clean, well-maintained rooms exist. **CityRail** runs from Martin Pl. in the city to Kings Cross Station. **Buses** also run from Circular Quay (#324, 325, or 326) and Chatswood (#200) to the Cross. The walk from City Center takes about 20min.

Original Backpackers, 160-162 Victoria St. (☎9356 3232; www.originalbackpackers.com.au). Kitchen, TV lounge, dining area, and courtyard with plants and fountains. Many planned activities and enthusiastic staff. Constant cleaning keeps old building well maintained. Internet access $5 per 50min. Cable TV, safe, and laundry ($6). Luggage storage free. Every room has TV and fridge; some ensuite, with kitchen and balcony at no extra cost. Key deposit $20. Reception 24hr. Check-out 10am. Dorms $22-25; singles $55; doubles $65. Weekly $149/350/420. ❷

Eva's Backpackers, 6-8 Orwell St. (☎9358 2185). Guests rave about clean and spacious family-run hostel. Large, brightly colored rooms and rooftop garden with spectacular views of the city. Free Internet access, rooftop BBQ (Tu and F), and fax.

Laundry $3. TV area. Free safe at reception. Breakfast, linen, and towels included. Reception 7:30am-7pm. Dorms $24; doubles $60. Weekly $140/350. ❷

The Pink House, 6-8 Barncleuth Sq. (☎9358 1689 or 1800 806 385; www.pinkhouse.com.au), off Ward Ave. Feels like a house—a big, fun, light-pink Victorian mansion. Group activities (daytrips, pub outings, skydiving, soccer) promote family atmosphere. Brick kitchen next to BBQ terrace. All rooms have TV and wooden bed; most have decorative fireplace. Free Internet access (max. 20min.). Luggage storage free. Laundry $5. Reception 8:30am-9pm. Breakfast included. Dorms $22; twins and doubles $55; triples $69. Discounts for long-term stays. Book ahead. VIP/YHA. ❷

O'Malley's Hotel, 228 William St. (☎9357 2211), above the popular pub. Entrance is to the left of the pub. 15 furnished rooms with TV, bathroom, and fridge are quieter than you would expect from the location; each room is soundproofed. Pub downstairs features live music nightly. Breakfast included. Check-out 10am. Reception M-F 8am-5pm, Sa-Su 9am-midnight. Singles and doubles $71.50; triples $104.50. ❺

Sydney Central Backpackers, 16 Orwell St. (☎9358 6600 or 1800 440 202; www.sydneybackpackers.com.au), next to Eva's. Safe atmosphere with clean bedrooms. Rooftop patio has great eating area and views of the opera house. Weekly entertainment. Free pickup from airport or Central Station. Free wireless Internet access. Lockers in rooms. Laundry $3. Breakfast included. Key deposit $20, blanket deposit $10. Reception 7am-9pm. Dorms $20; twins and doubles $50-55. Weekly $126/330-370. VIP. ❷

Jolly Swagman Backpackers, 27 Orwell St. (☎9358 6400 or 1800 805 870). TV room and courtyard help you meet new friends, as do the free drinks and BBQ. Free airport pickup (min. 3 night stay). Breakfast included, reception 24hr., Internet access, and travel desk. Dorms $24; twins and doubles with TV $70. Weekly rates $144/420. ❷

Blue Parrot Backpackers, 87 Macleay St. (☎9356 4888 or 1800 252 299). Darlinghurst Rd. turns into Macleay St. past Fitzroy Gardens. Recent addition to the Kings Cross scene. Small and very blue hostel has the feel of a bungalow. Great outdoor terrace, TV lounge with fireplace, and bright kitchen. Spacious lockers in rooms. Free Internet access. Dorms $25-29; twins and doubles $79. ❸

KINGS CROSS. Make sure to stick to the well-lit streets at night. Darlinghurst, Victoria, and Bayswater Rd. are all well populated and relatively safe. Avoid narrow, dark lanes where unsavory characters might hide.

FOOD

Though locals might look at you funny if you say you're going to Kings Cross for a meal, there are a few restaurants in the area that rival those in the City Center—and they're much less expensive.

Govinda's, 112 Darlinghurst Rd. (☎9380 5155; www.govindas.com.au). A unique restaurant and cinema where $21.90 covers a mostly Indian, wholly vegetarian, all-you-can-eat buffet, and a current arthouse movie in the intimate, upstairs theater with cushy couch-like chairs. Reservations strongly recommended. Open daily 5:45-10:30pm. ❷

Thaipower, 146 Victoria St. (☎8354 0434). Design your own noodle dish ($9.50-14.50) or stick to Thai favorites like garlic and pepper beef ($11) or basil vegetables and tofu ($9.50). Lunch specials, offered noon-4pm, bring everything on the menu down to $7.50. BYO. Open daily noon-10:30pm. ❶

Roy's, 176 Victoria St. (☎9357 3579). Huge portions and terrace seating make this a popular place for a sandwich ($8-9.50) or hearty meal ($10-21). W pasta night with wine $15.50 after 6pm. Su roast dinner. Full bar. Open M-F and Su 7am-10pm, Sa 7am-midnight. ❷

Macleay Pizza Bar, 101a Macleay St. (☎9356 4262). The best pizza spot in the Cross and the long lines every night prove it. The smells of freshly made dough that emanate from Macleays make it hard to pass by without eating there. All ingredients and pizzas are freshly made on the premises. Pizzas range from traditional to more original choices ($7-15). Open M-Th and Su noon-2:30am, F-Sa noon-4:30am. ❷

Little Penang, 38 Llankelly Pl. (☎9356 2224). Cozy eatery is just the place for a bite before hitting the nightspots in the Cross. Options range from noodles ($7-11.50) to vegetarian bites ($8.50-12.50). Try the beef-fried ho fun ($9.50) for something really flavorful and tasty. Open M-Sa 11am-3pm and 5-10:30pm, Su 5-10:30pm. ❶

Dov Delectica, 130 Victoria St. (☎9368 0600). Original menu complemented by a funky decor. Friendly staff and relaxed atmosphere add to the charm. Entrees include duck *pâté* ($12.50), braised lamb shanks ($23), and the Dov beef burger ($11). Open M-Tu 7am-4pm, W-F 7am-10:30pm, Sa 7:30am-10:30pm, Su 8:30am-3pm. ❸

NIGHTLIFE

Kings Cross is a 24hr. buzz of activity, and nightlife is its specialty. The bars are crammed with backpackers and locals alike. Be sure to use caution late at night.

Old Fitzroy Hotel, 129 Dowling St. (☎9356 3848), corner of Cathedral St. From William St., walk down McElhone St. (not Dowling St.), take the 1st left at Reid Ave. and you'll see it. Neighborhood pub set apart from the more hectic Cross. Cozy downstairs bar has fireplace, while the upstairs level hosts a younger crowd. Pool $3 per game. Also connected to a Malaysian **restaurant ❶**, serving their famous *laksa* (under $10) alongside more traditional pub grub, and a theater ($30 for dinner, beer, and play). Frequent discounts through local hostels. Happy hour M 5:30-7:30pm and Th 6-9pm. Tu free pool. Schooners $4.20. Open M-F 11am-midnight, Sa noon-midnight, Su 3-10pm.

The World, 24 Bayswater Rd. (☎9357 7700). Former brothel celebrates its roots with red mood lighting. Happy hour daily 6-7pm make the World go 'round and 'round (schooners $2.50), as do the teapots full of shots ($15). Live DJs daily. W free pool; F classic house; Sa house. No sandals after 9pm. Open M-Th 1pm-latenight, F-Su noon-6am.

Bourbon, 26 Darlinghurst Rd. (☎9358 1144). With its simple design, this bar, bistro, and nightclub stands out in the Cross. Alcohol is served 'round the clock as DJs play lounge music on weekdays and rev it up with house music on the weekend. Schooners $5. Mixed drinks $12. Open M-Th and Su 10am-4am, F-Sa 10am-6am.

Kings X Hotel, 248 William St. (☎9358 3377), opposite the Coca-Cola sign. What it lacks in atmosphere, the Kings X makes up for with its central location—at the heart of all the action and a good place for an alcoholic refueling. Happy hour daily 6-7pm and 11pm-midnight schooners $3, mixed drinks $8, spirits $5. Open daily 11am-4am.

O'Malley's Hotel, 228 William St. (☎9357 2211; www.omalleyshotel.com.au). If the walk up William St. becomes a little steep, then this is the perfect place to stop and recharge the batteries. Live music daily from 9:30pm drawing a mixed crowd. Locals and tourists alike flock to this 'home away from home.' Open daily 10am-latenight.

Iguana Bar, 15 Kellett St. (☎9357 2609). Well hidden bar has been the watering hole of many celebrities over the years; the walls lined with signed pictures prove it. Young and trendy converge here F Retro night and Sa Funky House. Also has **restaurant ❷** at the front; specialty is kangaroo fillet ($14.90). Great place to spend an evening, and who knows, your dance moves might land you a part in the next Kylie music video. Mixed drinks $12.50. Beer $6.50. Open M-Th and Su 9pm-4am, F-Sa 9pm-6am. Restaurant open daily 6:30pm-1am.

DARLINGHURST

ACCOMMODATIONS

Many of the old-school Aussie pubs in and around the greater Darlinghurst area double as reasonably priced hotels for travelers.

Sydney Star Accommodation, 275 Darlinghurst Rd. (☎1800 134 455), opposite Darlo Bar corner of Liverpool St. Quiet hotel ideal for longer stays. Each room comes equipped with a TV, fridge, and microwave; there is also a common kitchen downstairs. Free wireless Internet access. Reception noon-5pm. Singles $50-55; twins and doubles $55-65; deluxe suite (sleeps 4) $80-85. Weekly $200-250/280-340/450-480. ❹

Royal Sovereign Hotel (☎9331 3672; www.royalsov.com.au), above Darlo Bar on the corner of Liverpool St. All 19 pea-green rooms with TV and fridge are doubles. Shared bathrooms are modern and well kept. Reception at Darlo Bar. Level 1 rooms directly above the bar $66; Level 2 rooms with A/C $77. ❺

FOOD

The suburbs of East Sydney have some of the city's best dining, particularly along Oxford and Stanley St. Oxford St. addresses start at the street's origin on Hyde Park, but confusingly begin again at the intersection with Victoria and South Dowling St., the dividing line between Darlinghurst and Paddington.

Una's Cafe and Restaurant, 340 Victoria St. (☎9360 6885). Austrian food in a delightful wood and brick enclave, complete with outdoor seating. Locals have been coming here for more than 35yr.; you can (and will) wait for your table in the bar upstairs, giving you ample time to sample the great selection of imported beer and Schnapps. Great place for a big breakfast ($9) or Vienna *schnitzel* lunch ($15.90). Daily dinner specials $15-18. Open daily 7:30am-10:30pm. Licensed. Cash only. ❷

Sel et Poivre, 263 Victoria St. (☎9361 6530). Fancy French cuisine served in light, airy dining room or on the patio. Extensive wine list accompanies impressive menu. Duck *pâté* on a baguette ($8.90). *Steak au Poivre* ($29.90) and braised beef cheek ($23.90) top the dinner menu. Open M-F 7am-11pm, Sa-Su 8am-11pm. ❹

Bill & Toni's Restaurant, 74 Stanley St. (☎9360 4702), between Riley and Crown St. Huge pasta dishes $8.50. Meatier entrees include steak and casseroles, with delicious takeaway sandwiches ($3-8) at the cafe. Tuna melt on Turkish bread ($7.80) can't be beat. Open daily noon-2:30pm and 6-10:30pm. BYO. Cash only. ❷

SIGHTS

SYDNEY JEWISH MUSEUM. Designed around a staircase in the shape of the star of David, this museum is a modest but moving exhibition of Australia's Jewish heritage and the horrors of the Holocaust. It's run entirely by volunteers—many of whom are Holocaust survivors—who work as guides to the museum's seven levels. *(148 Darlinghurst Rd., of Burton St. ☎9360 7999; www.sydneyjewishmuseum.com.au. Open M-Th and Su 10am-4pm, F 10am-2pm. $10, student $7, children $6, families $22.)*

NIGHTLIFE

Darlinghurst's night scene matches its day scene—here is where the gay, lesbian, bisexual, and fun-loving straight people come to play. The artsy and alternative outnumber the preppy and jockish two to one. The nightclubs in this area will provide the perfect amount of mixed drinks and mixed crowds.

The Stonewall, 175 Oxford St. (☎9360 1963). A very happening gay bar with buff bartenders and lots of live entertainment (Tu karaoke, Th go-go dancers, F-Sa drag shows). DJs spin funky dance music, while patrons mingle on couches upstairs, and lip-sync and shake their booty to cookie-cutter pop downstairs. Happy hour schooners $3 daily until 7pm. Open M-Th and Su 11am-5am, F-Sa 11am-6am.

The Colombian Hotel, 117-123 Oxford St. (☎9360 2151), corner of Crown St. The casual but trendy upstairs level, which features DJs W-Su, boasts numerous chandeliers, giving the cocktail lounge a classy vibe. Mixed drinks $12. Schooners before 10pm $3.50-4, after 10pm $5-7. Open M-Th and Su 10am-4am, F-Sa 9am-6am.

Darlo Bar, 306 Liverpool St. (☎9331 3672), corner of Darlinghurst Rd. Chill retro lounge attracts mixed crowd. Schooners $4.30. Rooms available. Open M-Sa 10am-midnight, Su noon-midnight.

BONDI AND COOGEE BEACH

ACCOMMODATIONS

Take bus #380, 382, or L82 from Circular Quay via Oxford St., or drive east along Oxford St.; it's stop 12 on Bondi Explorer. **CityRail** runs to Bondi Jct., where buses #380 and 381 run to the waterfront. To reach Coogee Beach, take bus #373 or 374 from Circular Quay, #372 from Central Station, or #314 from Bondi Junction.

GETTING TO BONDI. For those who are traveling from the city center to Bondi Beach: the train will deposit you at Bondi Junction, a good bus ride away from the beach, whereas the bus will drop you right on the waterfront; taking the bus will also enable you to avoid paying two fares in one trip.

Noah's Bondi Beach, 2 Campbell Pde. (☎9365 7100, reservations 1800 226 662), at the top of the beach's southern end. Bondi's biggest and best hostel. Great rooftop views and BBQ. Free boogie board use. Pool table. TV. Dinner in connected bar and restaurant $5-12. Female-only ensuite dorm available. Laundry $3. Key deposit $20. Reception 24hr. Internet $5 per 90min. Lockers in rooms. Dorms $20-25; twins and doubles $55; beachside doubles $60. Weekly $150/330/360. NOMADS. ❷

Bondi Beachouse YHA (☎9365 2088), corner of Fletcher and Dellview St. Immaculate hostel where guests actually know how to have fun. Perks include: movie room, game room, large kitchen, rooftop balcony, BBQ, weekly activities, and great view of the ocean. Surfboard, bodyboard, and snorkeling gear rentals included. Internet $4 per hr. Laundry $6. Reception 8am-9pm. Dorms $29; twins and doubles $70, ensuite $80; family rooms $110-130. YHA. ❷

Bondi Backpackers, 110 Campbell Pde. (☎9130 4660). Cosy little hostel that's in a prime spot just across the street from the ocean. Free boogie board use and TV. Breakfast and linen included. Laundry $5. Reception open 8am-10:30pm. Dorms $19-31; singles $35 (in winter); doubles $47-75. Discounts for ISIC, VIP, and YHA. ❷

Surfside Backpackers Bondi Beach, 35A Hall St. (☎8300 8802 or 1800 150 971; www.surfsidebackpackers.com.au), 1½ blocks inland from Campbell Pde. Surfboard exchange program. TV, video games, and video library. Free use of bikes, in-line skates, wetsuits, and boards. Breakfast included. Internet access $2 per 30min. Laundry $4. Key deposit $30. Reception 8am-10pm. Large dorms $21-23; doubles at 252 Campbell Pde. $50. Weekly $140/305. VIP. ❷

Coogee Beach Wizard of Oz, 172 Coogee Bay Rd. (☎9315 7876 or 1800 013 460; www.wizardofoz.com.au.) Hardwood floors and spacious dorms make this a great place for relaxation and socializing. Th summer BBQs. Free pickup in summer. No smoking. Laundry $6. Key deposit $20. Reception 8am-noon and 5-7pm. Check-out 9:30am. Dorms $22-44; doubles $55-110; families from $90. ❷

Bondi Beach

ACCOMMODATIONS
Bondi Backpackers, 6
Bondi Beachouse YHA, 9
Noah's Bondi Beach, 8
Surfside Backpackers Bondi Beach, 3

FOOD
Bondi Tratt, 4
Gelato Bar Restaurant, 2
Mojo's Cafe, 5

NIGHTLIFE
Beach Road Hotel, 1
Bondi Icebergs Club, 7

FOOD

Campbell Parade is lined with takeaway joints and fast food restaurants. Listed below are a few trendy cafes facing the beach, while perpendicular **Hall Street** has cheaper sitdown restaurants. Check out Coogee Bay Rd. for its active cafe social scene in Coogee Beach.

Bondi Tratt, 34b Campbell Pde. (☎9365 4303), in Bondi Beach. Its outdoor terrace high on Campbell Pde. provides excellent beach views. This restaurant will wow you with authentic Italian entrees $9.50-18.50, pasta and pizza $12-18.50, and main dishes $12-30. BYO and licensed. Open M-F 7am-10pm, Sa-Su 8am-10pm. ❸

Mojo's Cafe, 32 Campbell Pde. (☎9130 1322), in Bondi Beach. Don't be deterred by the dark interior of this trendy tapas bar. Fruity Sangria ($7 per glass) and delicious meat, seafood, and vegetable tapas ($5-17) are some of the best you'll get without breaking the bank. Attentive and knowledgeable staff makes stellar suggestions. Packed in the evening. Open M-Th 6pm-latenight, F-Su 4pm-latenight. ❸

Gelato Bar Restaurant, 140 Campbell Pde. (☎9130 4033 or 9130 3211), in Bondi Beach. You won't be able to resist the delectable display of cakes and tortes ($5-6.50). Serves a variety of chicken and steak dishes ($22.50-24), as well as basic sandwiches ($9.20-16). Takeaway available. Open M-F and Su 8am-11pm, Sa 8am-midnight. ❸

Coogee Plate Cafe, 209B Coogee Bay Rd. (☎9665 5588), in Coogee Beach. A refreshing and more reasonably priced dining experience than the many others on this street. The friendly staff and nice location add to the charm of this little eatery. Breakfast $10-15, salads $8.90-15.90, and gourmet sandwiches $9.90-10.90. The house speciality is seafood ($9-18). Open M-Sa 9:30am-9pm, Su 9:30am-6pm. ❷

Coogee Cafe, 221 Coogee Bay Rd. (☎9665 5779), in Coogee Beach. Modern cafe that's just the place for a quick lunch. Nicely located close to the beach. Stands out from the crowd thanks to its decor and friendly staff. Try their special fish 'n' chips ($14) before heading to the beach to catch some fish of your own. Open daily 7am-5pm. ❷

NIGHTLIFE

Bondi's nightlife, like its beach, is more glamorous than its southern rival. But Coogee Beach—with its younger, less pretentious, and more energetic options—ultimately knows how to party harder.

Coogee Bay Hotel (☎9665 0000; www.coogeebayhotel.com.au), corner of Coogee Bay Rd. and Arden St., in Coogee Beach. Backpackers, locals, and uni students alike mingle in this well-known spot, and it's easy to see why with multiple bars, beer garden, nightly live music, and a nightclub with a modest cover of $5 on weekends. **Selina's Entertainment Centre,** in the hotel, is a top concert venue and gets international acts. Happy hour M-Sa 5-7pm. Schooners $4. Open M-Th and Su 9am-3am, F-Sa 9am-5am or later.

The Palace, 169 Dolphin St. (☎9664 2900), corner of Dolphin and Arden St. in Coogee Beach. The Palace features 3 levels of nighttime craziness: the ground-floor Beach Bar is your standard sports bar (open M-Th 11am-1am, F-Sa 11am-3am, Su 11am-midnight). The Mid-Palace dance club, popular with a well-dressed younger crowd, blasts R&B and dance music (open W-Th 8pm-1am, F-Sa 9pm-3am; Sa cover $5). The top-level Aquarium Bar features a much more casual, diverse crowd and live entertainment (open M-F 5pm-midnight, Sa-Su noon-midnight).

Beach Road Hotel, 71 Beach Rd. (☎9130 7247), in Bondi Beach. A staple of Bondi nightlife; this place fills up fast on weekends. The ground-level sports bar is frequented by a slightly older crowd, while upstairs draws uni students and young travelers to its theme nights, live bands, dance floor, and pool tables. Two new restaurants serving both Italian and modern Australian fare are also good reasons to pay this place a visit. Lower level open M-Tu 10am-11:30pm, W-F 10am-1:30am, Sa 9am-1:30am, Su 10am-9:30pm. Upper level open M-W 2pm-midnight, Th-Sa until 1am, Su until 10pm. Restaurants open daily noon-3pm and 6-10pm.

Bondi Icebergs Club, 1 Notts Ave. (☎9130 3120), in Bondi Beach. This world-famous club plays host not only to a great bar and cafe, but also to one of the best outdoor swimming pools in Sydney. Just off southern Bondi Beach, the views are amazing. If surfing isn't your thing, then sit back with a pint and enjoy the sun balcony. Live music F-Su 8pm. Open M-Th and Su 10am-11pm, F-Sa 10am-midnight.

GLEBE

ACCOMMODATIONS

To get to Glebe Point Rd., the main strip in this bohemian town, take bus #431, 432, 433, or 434. Or, from Central Station, follow George St., then Broadway west 15min. to Victoria Park and turn right onto Glebe Point Rd.

Wattle House, 44 Hereford St. (☎9552 4997; www.wattlehouse.com.au), a 5min. walk from Glebe Point Rd. This is one of Sydney's smallest–and nicest–guest houses. Restored Victorian decor includes brick kitchen and manicured garden. Plush bean-bags fill the small TV room, where guests actually get to know each other. Breakfast included. Laundry $6. Reception 8:30am-1pm; reservations 8am-8pm. Max. 2wk. stay. Book way ahead. Singles $60-75; doubles, twins, and triples $75-95. ❺

Alishan International Guest House, 100 Glebe Point Rd. (☎9566 4048; www.alishan.com.au). Classy, 3-star Victorian house with an open common area surrounded by a terrace. Private rooms have TV, fridge, and bath; dorms have wooden beds. Parking available. Internet access $3.33 per hr. Key deposit $10. Laundry $7. Reception 8am-10:30pm. Wheelchair accessible. Dorms $27-33; singles $88-99; doubles $99-115; 4-person family room $154. Extra person $16. ❸

Glebe Point YHA, 262-264 Glebe Point Rd. (☎9692 8418; glebe@yhansw.org.au). Guests hang out in basement common spaces or on the large roof for BBQs, which are provided every F night ($5). For something a little more exotic try rooftop salsa dancing W fortnightly ($5). Spacious kitchen and dining area. In-room sinks. Internet access $1 per 15min. Bus service to the airport $11. No sleeping bags allowed. Luggage storage free for returning guests. Laundry $6. Key deposit $10. Reception 7am-10:45pm. Dorms $28.50-32.50, weekly $161; twins and doubles $77. $7 off twins with YHA. ❸

FOOD

Glebe Point Rd. is packed with small cafes, second hand shops, bakeries, and supermarkets. It's one-stop shopping for all meals cheap, tasty, Thai, Indian, Italian, or some interesting combination thereof.

Badde Manors, 37 Glebe Point Rd. (☎9660 3797), corner of Francis St. Look for the plastic angels on the roof. An artsy vegetarian and vegan cafe with super-friendly staff, gourmet coffee, fresh sorbet, and smoothies. Tofu or lentil burger $9. Delicious daily soup specials $7.50. Dessert cakes $6.50 (try the sticky date pudding). Open M-Th 7:30am-midnight, F-Sa 7:30am-1am, Su 9am-midnight. Cash only. ❶

Cafe Otto, 79 Glebe Point Rd. (☎9552 1519). High ceilings, old-fashioned furnace, and heated outdoor courtyard where sophisticated-looking people gather for meals. Everything from bacon and eggs ($8.50), pastas ($12.50-29.50), and pizzas ($14.50-22) to meat dishes like shepherd's pie ($23). Schooners $4.70. BYO wine only. Open M-Tu noon-10:30pm, W-Th 9am-11pm, F-Sa 9am-midnight, Su 9am-10pm. ❸

E Lounge, 92 Glebe Point Rd. (☎9518 6002). A trendy little wood-fired pizza place that specializes in unusual combinations, such as lamb fillets with spinach ($13.90-18.90). With something for everyone, it also features a large selection of vegan, vegetarian, and halal dishes. Open M-F and Su 5-10:30pm, Sa noon-10:30pm. ❷

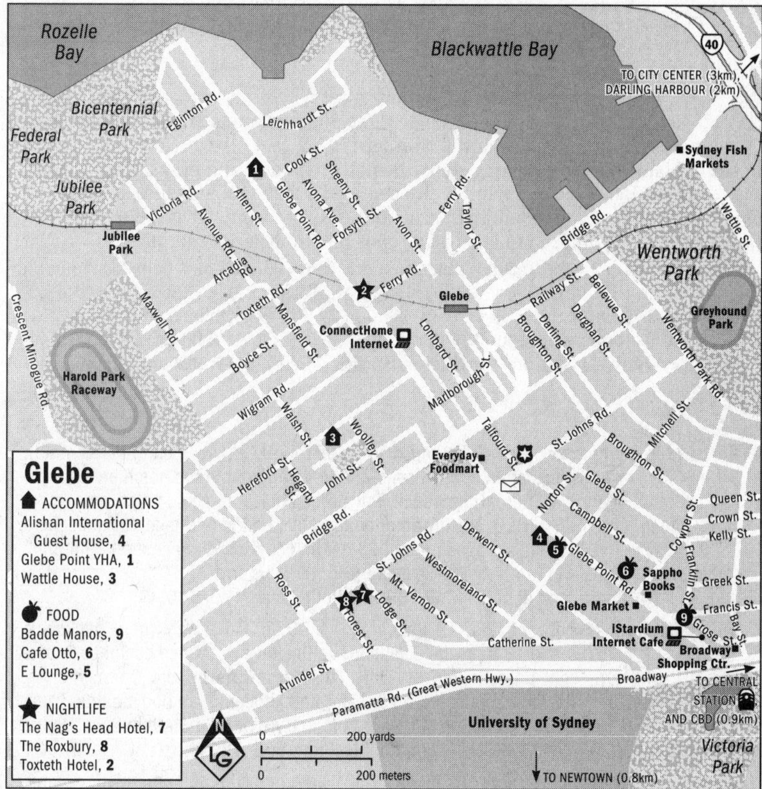

NIGHTLIFE

Glebe nightlife can be hit or miss depending on whether school is in session for University of Sydney students. The bars listed below tend to attract a steady crowd year-round.

The Nag's Head Hotel, 162 St. Johns Rd. (☎9660 1591), corner of Lodge St. Relaxed Irish pub with a rooftop terrace and lots of rugby pride. Patrons sing along to live performances of "Sweet Caroline," "Piano Man," and other crowd favorites. Beer tasting 1st F of every month. F-Sa live music 8pm. Su free pool. Schooners $4. Open M-Sa 9am-midnight, Su 10am-midnight.

The Roxbury, 182 St. Johns Rd. (☎9692 0822). A stylish yet unpretentious lounge bar with upbeat live music and a dance floor. Special nights include $5 meals on M-Tu and Su, W trivia, F-Sa 2-for-1 Happy hour 7:30-8:30pm, and Su live music. No cover, except for special events. Schooners $4.20, cocktails $13. Open daily 11am-midnight.

Toxteth Hotel, 345 Glebe Point Rd. (☎9660 2370). Welcomes locals, students, and travelers alike. Slightly away from the main Glebe pulse. Tu Trivia, W pool comp, Su free pool. Beer garden for warm days with bistro and big screen TV for sporting events make this a stop for all seasons. Schooners $4. Open M-Sa 11am-1am, Su 11am-midnight.

MANLY AND THE NORTHERN BEACHES

ACCOMMODATIONS

Lively, surfside Manly has a good range of accommodations and is the best base for travelers exploring the beautiful Northern Beaches. Collaroy (located just 8km north of Manly) features a truly stellar hostel, great surf, and easy access to both the Northern Beaches and Manly's city center. Though you may feel far from the action in Collaroy, you're still right around the corner from Sylvia's Pie Shop, restaurants featuring international cuisine, and some rollicking nightlife.

To get to Manly from Circular Quay, take the **ferry** (30min.; M-F 6am-11:45pm, Sa 8am-11:45pm, Su 8am-11pm; $6.20) or **Jetcat** (15min.; M-F 6-9:25am and 4:20-8:30pm, Sa 6:10am-3:35pm, Su 7:10am-3:35pm; $7.90). For Collaroy, take the #151, 155, or 156 from anywhere along Pittwater St., or take bus #L90 or L88 from Railway Sq. or Wynyard Station (Carrington St. side). See **Local Transportation,** p. 113.

MANLY

Boardrider Backpacker, Rear 63, The Corso (☎9977 6077; www.boardrider.com.au). Manly's newest hostel is often booked solid due to its affordable top-notch atmosphere and central location 80m from the beach. Private balconies, large common area, modern kitchen, and rooftop BBQ. Nightly entertainment also adds to the great atmosphere of the place. Free luggage storage. Internet $3 per hr. Laundry $6. Reception 8am-8pm. Dorms $24; twins and doubles $60, ensuite $65; motel rooms $75/85. Weekly rates: dorms $144; twins and doubles $360/390; motel rooms $450/510. ❷

Manly Backpackers Beachside, 28 Raglan St. (☎9977 3411; www.manlybackpackers.com.au). From the ferry, cross the Esplanade to Belgrave St., which becomes Pittwater St., and turn right onto Raglan St. Only 100m from the beach. Open, friendly atmosphere. Large TV room, courtyard area, safe, and kitchen. Free bodyboards. Laundry $6. Key deposit $30. Reception M-F 9am-1pm and 4-7pm, Sa-Su 9am-2pm. Dorms from $22, weekly from $133; twins and doubles from $55. VIP. ❷

Manly Lodge, 22 Victoria Pde. (☎9977 8655; www.manlylodge.com.au). Luxurious ensuite rooms with A/C, TV, and kitchenettes. Sauna and spa. Laundry $6. Continental breakfast included. Reception 7am-10pm. Budget rooms $98-120; doubles $120-160, deluxe with hot tub $160-210. Extra person $35, ages 9 and under $20. ❺

COLLAROY

Sydney Beachouse/Northern Beaches YHA, 4 Collaroy St. (☎9981 1177; www.sydneybeachouse.com.au). Spectacular hostel located across the street from the beach. Modern, social hostel with TV lounge, large common space, kitchen, cafe, pool table and arcade, free surfboards, snorkeling gear, bikes. Heated outdoor pool. Free luggage storage. Internet $4 per hr. Laundry $4. Key and cutlery deposit $20. Reception summer 8am-8pm; winter 8:30am-7pm. Wheelchair accessible. Dorms $26; doubles $64, ensuite $84; ensuite family rooms for 5 $104. Cheaper rates for longer stays. ❸

FOOD

In and around Manly, fashionable open-terraced cafes line the beachfront on **South Steyne.** Cheaper options, including several fast-food chains, can be found on **The Corso.** This buzzing pedestrian mall connects the beachfront to the harbor, and also splits Steyne St. into North and South. Of the beaches farther north, **Palm Beach** has the most eating options, with plenty of trendy oceanfront cafes. The listings below are all in Manly. **Coles** supermarket is near the intersection of The Corso and Whistler St. (☎9977 3811. Open daily 6am-midnight.)

Sylvia's Uppercrust Pie Shop, 1003 Pittwater Rd., Collaroy (☎9971 5182) The best pies in New South Wales; winner of the 2001 and 2002 Great Aussie Pie Competitions, 2005 Northern Beaches Business Award honoree. Baking begins at 2am each day and produces delicious pies with multicultural twists (from $3.80). Open daily 7am-5pm.

Green's Eatery, 1-3 Sydney Rd. (☎9977 1904), on the pedestrian stretch of Sydney Rd. near the ocean. Sunny, mostly vegetarian cafe serves hearty meals, with rice and interesting vegetable combos ($5.50-8.50). Roll-ups $5.50-6, salads $5.50-7. Fancy, affordable chicken dishes $6. Open daily 8am-5pm. Cash only. ❶

Wood and Stone, Manly Wharf (☎9977 1000), located across from the ferry drop-off. The allure of this wood-fire pizza restaurant is enough to draw Sydneysiders to Manly just to eat. Great food and people-watching opportunities. Friendly service, streetside seating, and specials like Battered Crocodile ($19.90) and Camembert Chicken ($18.50). Good for singles and lovebirds alike. BYO wine. Open daily noon-10pm. ❷

Blue Water Cafe, 28 South Steyne (☎9976 2051), just below The Corso. One of many trendy oceanfront cafes lining the South Steyne waterfront, Blue Water serves dependable dishes at a decent price, from bacon and eggs to Thai salmon. Main courses $15-28.90. 10% surcharge on Su. Open daily 7:30am-10:30pm. ❸

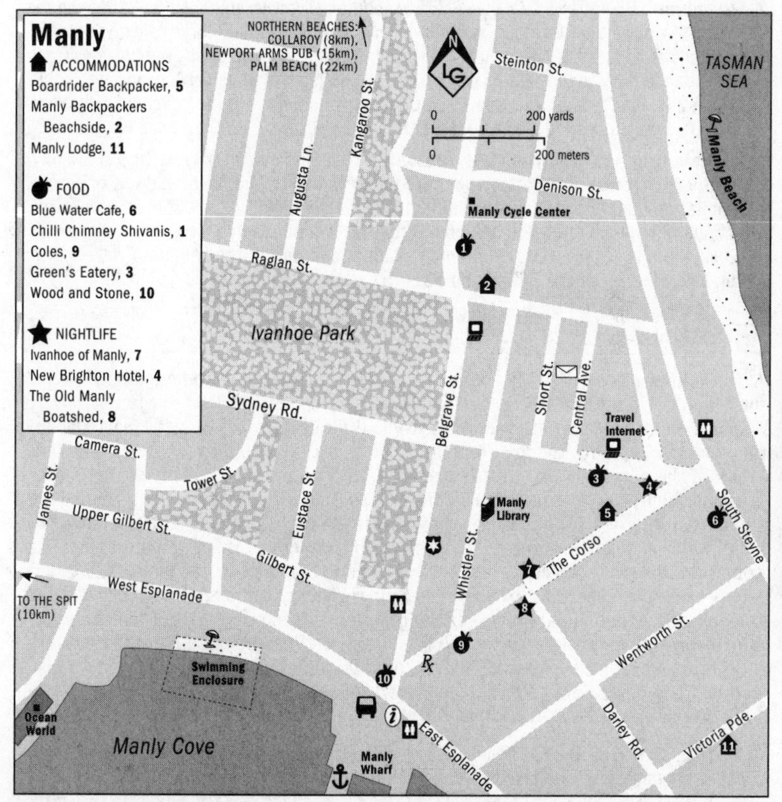

Chilli Chimney Shivanis, 26-28 Pittwater Rd. (☎9977 2890), located north of the town center, near the intersection with Denison St. Mouth-watering curry and tandoori dishes including chicken, lamb, and beef ($13-14). The chef's speciality is a tropical-flavored Goan fish curry ($15.50). 10% off with takeaway. Free delivery. BYO wine only. F-Sa live music. Open Tu-Su 5:30-latenight. ❸

THE ROCKS

FOOD

The Rocks has some of Sydney's most tourist-targeted eating, and you can pay dearly for an evening dining at the harbor's edge. However, plenty of cheap food can still be found, and many restaurants have breathtaking views of The Rocks and Sydney Harbour.

The Gumnut Tea Garden, 28 Harrington St. (☎9247 9591). Tucked away on the corner of Harrington and Argyle St., the Gumnut charms customers with assorted cakes and puddings all day ($3-8), as well as breakfast ($10-15, until 11:30am) and lunch ($12-16). The front room is lit by a fireplace, and the leafy garden terrace has live music F 6-9pm and Su noon-3pm. Open M, Th, F 8am-10pm, Tu-W and Sa-Su 8am-5pm. ❷

Lowenbrau, 12 Argyle St. (☎9247 7785), corner of Argyle and Playfair St. Known for being Sydney's best Bavarian restaurant, this diamond in The Rocks takes you out of Australia and into the Swiss Alps. Waitstaff dressed in traditional German and Swiss garb dance daily to the sounds of the Oom Pah Pah Band while serving chicken *schnitzel* ($24), Klau's Goulash Soup ($12.50) and, of course, a wide variety of Schnapps ($7-8). Outside seating available. Open daily 9am-11pm, F-Sa 9am-2am. ❸

Wolfie's Grill and **Waterfront Restaurant,** 17-21 Circular Quay West (☎9241 5577 and 9247 3666). Both restaurants are under the same management and offer very similar menus. At Wolfie's you will find 2 levels of elegant candlelit dining for lovers of Australian beef and fresh seafood. At the Waterfront, expect more of the same with 3 levels of excellent views. Supremely good eating and priceless harbor views make up for the steep prices (grill items $32-45). Both open daily noon-10pm. ❺

SIGHTS

At the southern base of the Harbour Bridge, The Rocks is the commercialized site of the original Sydney Town settlement, where living spaces were, at one time, literally chiseled out of the face of the shoreline rock. Built up slowly during the lean years of the colony's founding, the area remained rough-and-tumble into the 1900s. The outbreak of the plague in the early 1900s led to the destruction of many of the poorer areas of The Rocks in an effort to halt its spread. In the 1970s, when plans to raze the slums that had developed in the area were revealed, a movement to preserve the neighborhood began in earnest. Today, popular bars, quaint restaurants, and historic homes dot the stone streets. Street performers and bands liven up The Rocks Market (every Sa-Su; see **Shopping,** p. 148). The **Sydney Visitors Centre** and the **Rocks Walking Company** share the white, three-story Sailors' Home at 106 George St. The former has information on local attractions, and the latter conducts informative walking tours of The Rocks. *(Tourist office ☎9240 8788 or 1800 067 676. Open daily 9:30am-5.30pm. Walking Co. ☎9247 6678. 90min. tours depart M-F 10:30am, 12:30, and 2:30pm; Sa-Su 11:30am and 2pm. $20, ages 10-16 and seniors $10.50, backpackers $16, under 10 free.)*

ROYAL BOTANIC GARDENS. The city center's greenery is concentrated in landscaped plants, flowers, and trees filling 30 Eden-like hectares around Farm Cove. Daily guided walks begin at the visitors center, in the southeast corner of the park near Art Gallery Rd. Within the gardens, attractions such as the Aboriginal plant trail, formal rose garden, and cockatoo and fruit bat sightings are free, but the **Tropical Centre** greenhouses charge for admission. *(Open daily 10am-4pm. $4.40, ISIC $2.20, families $8.80.)* **Government House,** in the northwest corner of the Gardens, continues to serve as the home of the governor of New South Wales. *(☎9931 5222. Grounds open daily 10am-4pm; free house tours every 30min. F-Su 10:30am-3pm.)* On the eastern headland of Farm Cove, the Botanic Gardens end at **Mrs. Macquaries Chair.** The chair, which looks like a simple bench carved in the stone, is now a classic Sydney photo-op—though turning the camera around so that it faces the gorgeous view of the harbor makes more sense. *(☎9231 8111; www.rbgsyd.nsw.gov.au. Open daily 9:30am-5pm. Gardens open 7am-sunset. Free. 1½hr. guided walks daily 10:30am; 1hr. lunchtime walks Mar.-Nov. M-F 1pm.)*

JUSTICE AND POLICE MUSEUM. A small but well-designed museum dedicated to the history of Sydney crime over the last 150 years, including gruesome murders such as the "Pajama Girl" and "Shark Arm" cases. Rotating exhibits include a history of drug use Down Under. Visitors can view an old courtroom and prisoner holding cells. *(Corner of Albert and Phillip St. ☎9252 1144; www.hht.nsw.gov.au. Open Sa-Su 10am-5pm. $8, ISIC $4, families $17.)*

MUSEUM OF CONTEMPORARY ART (MCA). The main entrance is on Circular Quay West; entering on George St. puts you on Level 2. Enjoy three floors of contemporary artwork along with exciting temporary exhibits. *(140 George St. ☎9245 2400. Open daily 10am-5pm. Free.)*

MUSEUM OF SYDNEY. You'll have to love history to appreciate the meticulous attention paid to Sydney's social past through artifacts and stylish high-tech multimedia. The tourism exhibit is particularly interesting. *(37 Phillip St., corner of Bridge St. ☎9251 5988; www.hht.net.au. Open daily 9:30am-5pm. $7, ISIC $3, families $17.)*

NIGHTLIFE

With relatively early closing times, bars in The Rocks tend to be standing-room-only by 9:30pm on weekend nights. Though they attract an older, more sophisticated crowd, more than a few rough-and-tumble backpackers have been known to grab a pint—or two or three—in this historic district.

The Observer Hotel, 69 George St. (☎9252 4169). A mixed crowd packs this popular pub in the heart of The

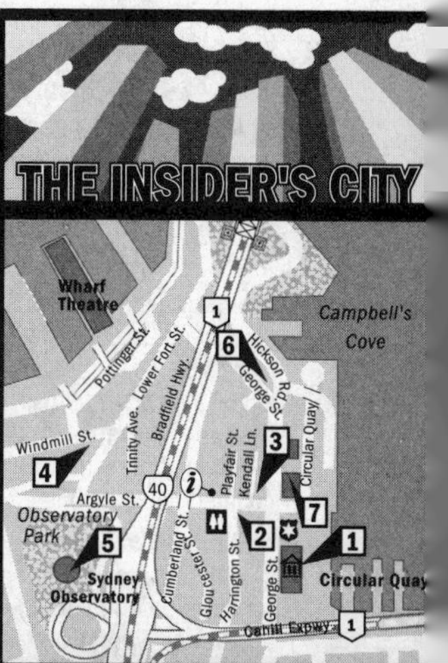

THE ROCKS

In Sydney's historic tourist center, it's all about the eclectic.

1. The **Museum of Contemporary Art** has an excellent Aboriginal art collection (☎9245 2400).
2. Enjoy free live music with your scones at the **Gumnut Tea Garden** (☎9247 9591).
3. Indulge your inner child at **The Rocks Discovery Museum** (☎1800 067 676).
4. Enjoy live Irish music at **The Hero of Waterloo Pub**, a local favorite since 1845 (☎9252 4553).
5. Enjoy little gardens and big views at the **Sydney Observatory** (☎9241 3767).
6. Satisfy all your local arts-and-crafts, homeware, and collectible needs at the **Rocks Market,** which often features live music shows.
7. Visit the site of Sydney's oldest surviving building at **Cadman's Cottage,** just off Circular Quay.

Rocks. Live music daily 8pm and even earlier on weekends. New bistro and courtyard. Schooners M-Th $3.90, F-Sa $4.90. Open M-W and F 10am-11:30pm, Th 10am-midnight, F-Sa 10am-2:30am; Apr.-Aug. open from 11am.

The Lord Nelson, 19 Kent St. (☎9251 4044), at Argyle St. Nautical flags drape from sturdy wooden beams in this colonial building. Sydney's oldest hotel and pub attracts a young crowd. Very chill place for an after-work pint from one of Sydney's only micro-breweries. Tours of the brewery available upon request. Try the award-winning Three Sheets, Nelsons Blood, or Old Admiral (pints $7). Open daily 11am-11pm.

The Australian Heritage Hotel, 100 Cumberland St. (☎9247 2229; www.australianheritagehotel.com). High-quality Australian beer flows like water in this popular pub, and the Australian pizzas (with meats like kangaroo, crocodile, and emu; $13.50-19) are the best in the city. Outdoor seating sets the perfect stage for a relaxed evening. Arrive early to ensure a seat on weekends. For those who can't tear themselves away, there are also a number of beautifully furnished bedrooms upstairs with rates from $125, including breakfast. Discounted rates are offered for extended stays. Open M-Sa 11am-midnight, Su 11am-10pm.

The Hero of Waterloo, 81 Lower Fort St. (☎9252 4553). Since 1843, this pub has been a local favorite; its underground tunnels were once used for rum smuggling. A great place for an afternoon pint. Live Irish and folk music played by musicians of all ages daily starting around 7pm. Open M-Sa 10am-11pm, Su 10am-10pm.

PADDINGTON

FOOD

Fortunately, the cost of food in Paddington is far less than the cost of clothes sold in its fancy boutiques. That said, if shopping is your forte, then the Paddington section of Oxford St. is a must.

Max Brenner, 437 Oxford St. (☎9357 5055). Creator Max Brenner thinks chocolate brings out the best, and even the sexiest, in people. If you agree, or simply want to find out for yourself, stop by this one-of-a-kind chocolate "bar." Try a chocolate cocktail ($6.50) with a pastry or fudge ($6-10). Popular strawberry fondue plate $15.50. Mobbed on weekends. Open M-F 11:30am-6pm, Sa-Su 10am-6pm. ❶

Arthur's Pizza, 260 Oxford St. (☎9332 2220). Hits the spot with Italian fare, including gourmet pizza options like lamb sausage and double-smoked ham. Be prepared for lots of noise and 1hr. waits during peak hours. Pizzas from $10-20, family size $25. Open M-F 5pm-midnight, Sa-Su noon-midnight. ❷

Micky's Cafe, 268 Oxford St. (☎9361 5157). This dimly lit cafe offers every combination under the sun: stir-fry, burgers, burritos, cheesecakes, pasta, and chicken satay. Meals from $14.50-29; burgers $15-17.50. Splurge on the Mars bar cheesecake ($9.50). Open M-F 11am-midnight, Sa 9am-1am, Su 9am-midnight. ❷

NIGHTLIFE

Though it's next to the boisterous nightlife of Darlinghurst, Paddington is much tamer. If you make it this far down Oxford St. before sunrise, hit these nightspots.

Durty Nelly's, 9-11 Glenmore Rd. (☎9360 4467; www.durtynellyssydney.com.au), off Oxford St. at Gipps St. Though wedged in on a street of frou-frou shops, Nelly takes her Guinness very seriously (schooners $4.40). Even on weekends when it's standing room only and impossible to hear the person next to you, the dark wood decor and jovial staff create a relaxing refuge from the nearby Oxford St. melee. Come for just 1, or stay for 99 more to join the 100-pint Guiness club. Open M-Sa 11am-midnight, Su noon-10pm.

The Fringe Bar, 106 Oxford St. (☎9360 5443), around the corner from Durty Nelly's. Always hopping on a weekend night, this dark bar with neon lights attracts a good-looking 20-something crowd for drinking, dancing, pool, and comedy shows (M only). 2-for-1 creative mixed drinks Th night are sure to please adventurous drinkers. Open M-W noon-1am, Th-Sa noon-3am, Su noon-midnight.

The Paddington Inn, 338 Oxford St. (☎9380 5913). The newest addition to Paddington nightlife boasts not only great mixed drinks ($11-15) but also great food as well. Happy hour M-Th 4-7pm. Relax by playing pool, or watch shoppers pass by. The Paddo Mixed Plate ($16) is a must. Open M-W and Su noon-midnight, Th-Sa noon-1am.

SURRY HILLS

FOOD

Tucked beneath Oxford St. east of Central Station, the former industrial wasteland of Surry Hills is now a pleasant residential area. It's home to student-artist types, working-class old-timers, and recent immigrants—a diversity well-reflected by the range of multicultural restaurants that line Crown St. At night, reach Surry Hills by walking down Crown St. from Oxford St. instead of coming from Central Station.

Mehrey Da Dhaba Indian Street Restaurant, 466 Cleveland St. (☎9319 6260). Mehrey Da, the oldest *dhaba* in Sydney, has a storied tradition of serving up inexpensive and filling East Indian food. Whole Tandoori chicken $12.90. Vegetarian meals $6.90-10.90; meat dishes $12.90-14.90. *Naan* or *roti* $2. Open M-Tu and Su 5:30-10:30pm, W-F noon-3pm and 5:30-11pm, F-Sa noon-3am. BYO. Cash only. ❷

Erciyes, 409 Cleveland St. (☎9319 1309). This unsuspecting Turkish delight serves a wonderful array of gourmet pizza (lamb, cheese, spinach, and egg on folded Turkish bread; $12) and traditional Turkish dishes such as chicken kebab with tabbouleh ($13). The welcoming and attentive staff is a sign that the food is made with care. Takeaway dishes are also on offer as well as their tasty mixed dips ($6-12). F-Sa evenings live entertainment. Open daily 10am-midnight. ❷

SIGHTS

MOORE PARK. Southeast of Surry Hills, Moore Park contains the **Sydney Football Stadium** and the city's major **cricket oval** (see **Sports and Recreation,** p. 56). For a tour of the stadium and a museum of Aussie sports history (given by an actor who plays Australia's most energetic sports fan), call **Sportspace.** *(☎9380 0398. Tours M-F 10am and 1pm on non-game days only. $23.50, concessions $15.50, families $62.50.)*

NIGHTLIFE

Crown St., the main drag of Surry Hills, is wide-awake at night and easily accessible from Oxford St., which it intersects in Darlinghurst.

Trinity Bar, 505 Crown St. (☎9319 6802), corner of Devonshire St. A 10min. walk from Oxford St., the Trinity Bar is a hopping sports bar with a terrace and, oddly enough, jam-packed bookshelves. The mixed, mostly local crowd, however, is too busy socializing to read. Great place to watch a big game or grab some delicious pub grub ($11-22). Schooners $4.20. M-Th 11am-midnight, F-Sa 11am-2am, Su noon-midnight.

Hotel Clarendon, 156 Devonshire St. (☎9319 6881; www.hotelclarendon.com.au). The motto is "The place to be seen, the heart of Surry Hills," and it certainly holds true. Laid-back lounge upstairs for sexy young things. The courtyard and balcony areas offer quality sun exposure. Enjoy the fresh air with one of their famous pizzas ($10). Open M-W and Su 10am-midnight, Th-Sa 10am-3am.

NEWTOWN

FOOD

King St. bisects Newtown and provides cheap eats, from Indian and Thai takeaways to filling espresso-shop breakfast deals. In this young and bohemian neighborhood, cheap and tasty options are endless, and include plenty of organic, vegan, and other health food choices.

The Peasant's Feast, 121a King St. (☎9516 5998). The restaurant that reforms skeptics of organic food. Delicious, affordable gourmet dishes like potato gnocchi with chorizo ($12.50) and grilled oak farm chicken breast ($22.50). BYO. Open Tu-Th 6-9:30pm, F-Sa 6-10pm. ❹

Green Gourmet, 115-117 King St. (☎9519 5330; www.greengourmet.com.au). A great mix of Asian-inspired vegan cuisine awaits inside. Try a pair of delicious Kumera Ginger Purses (a hearty sweet-potato pastry with ginger and vegetable filling; $3) or the Lion King's Clay Pot ($14.80). Open M-Th and Su noon-3pm and 6-10pm, F-Sa noon-3pm and 6-11pm. While you're in the area, be sure to check out the neighboring **Vegan's Choice Grocery,** 113 King St. (☎9519 7646). ❷

Taste, 235 King St. (☎9519 7944; www.tastenewtown.com). What this place does with chemical free chicken is truly amazing, from Lap Gai Yang chicken salad to chicken lasagna and even roast chicken and pumpkin pasta ($5.50-9.90). Roast beef with roasted potatoes ($7.50-13.50) and steak burgers ($6). Vegetable pad thai ($5-9). In winter, hot soup ($5) and the friendly and helpful staff will warm you up. Takeaway available. Limited seating. Open daily 10am-8:30pm. ❶

NIGHTLIFE

After enjoying a vegan pizza or kangaroo burger from one of the unusual restaurants in Newtown, join bar-goers of all types for a night out on King St.

Kuletos Cocktail Bar, 157 King St. (☎9519 6369). Deliciously fruity liqueurs go down smooth during Kuletos' Happy hour (M-W and F-Su 6-7:30pm, Th 9:30-10:30pm), with 2-for-1 mixed drinks ($10-14.50). The Toblerone, everyone's favorite pointy chocolate, and the Red Corvette are by far the best. Schooners $4. Long Island Iced Tea $14.50 on Su. Open M-W 4pm-latenight, Th-Su 4pm-3am.

Marlborough Hotel, 145 King St. (☎9519 1222). The Marly is the place to be after Kuletos Happy hour for pokies, casual boozin', dancin', and some decent local musical talent. Large venue that sets the stage for a big party. Th-F DJ; Sa band night. Schooners $3.70. Open M-Sa 10am-3am, Su noon-midnight.

SYDNEY HARBOUR

SIGHTS

SYDNEY OPERA HOUSE. Built to look like a fleet of sails, the Opera House defines all harbor views of Sydney. Designed by Danish architect Jørn Utzon, Sydney's pride and joy took 14 years and more than $100 million to construct—a decade and 90 million dollars more than originally planned. A saga of bureaucracy and broken budgets characterized the construction, eventually leading the architect to abandon the project. Finally opened in 1973, the Opera House has recovered from a rocky start by starring in thousands of tourist photographs daily and hosting operas, ballets, classical concerts, plays, and films. The **Concert Hall,**

which holds a massive pipe organ that took a decade to build, is stunning. *(On Bennelong Point, opposite the base of the Harbour Bridge. ☎9250 7250; www.sydneyoperahouse.com. For box office info, see Entertainment, (p. 146). 1hr. tours every 30min. M-Sa 9am-5pm. $23, ages 4-15 and ISIC $16, families $63.)*

SYDNEY HARBOUR BRIDGE. Spanning the harbor, the arching steel latticework of the massive Harbour Bridge has been a visual symbol of the city and the best place to get a look at the Harbour and the cityscape since its opening in 1932. The stone tunnels at either end were added later in response to complaints that the simplicity of the steel beam construction made people too afraid to drive on it. Pedestrians can enter the bridge walkway from a set of stairs on Cumberland St. above Argyle St. in The Rocks. At the bridge's southern pylon, there is an entry on the walkway which leads up to solid photo-ops. The **Harbour Bridge Exhibition** inside the pylon tells the fascinating story of the bridge's construction. *(☎9247 7833. Open daily 10am-5pm. Lookout and museum $8.50, children $3, families $12.)* For high adventure, **Bridgeclimb** will take you up to the summit for a view of the city and harbor. Only mildly strenuous and very safe, this offers maximum bragging rights with minimum stress, though it will noticeably lighten your wallet. All climbers must first take a Breathalyzer test, so don't hit the pubs beforehand. *(5 Cumberland St. From Argyle St., go all the way up the Argyle Stairs before the bridge at the "bel mundo" sign; turn right on Cumberland St. ☎8274 7777; www.bridgeclimb.com. Open daily 7am-4:30pm. 3hr. climbs every 10min. Day climbs M-F $169, ages 10-16 $100; Sa-Su $189/125. Twilight climbs daily $249/185. Night climbs M-F $169/100 and Sa-Su $189/125. Dawn climbs on the 1st Sa of each month $295/195).*

CIRCULAR QUAY. Between Dawes Point and Bennelong Point is the departure site for both the city ferry system and numerous private cruise companies. The Quay (KEY) is always a lively hub of tourist activity, with street performers, souvenir shops, and easy access to many major sights. It's also a prime location for sun-worshippers who find that the concrete jungle of the CBD blocks their rays.

SYDNEY HARBOUR CRUISES. **Ferry cruises** are a great way to take in the harbor. In addition to Sydney Ferries (p. 115), **Australian Travel Specialists** books 1-3hr. harbor cruises from Circular Quay and Darling Harbour. *(Jetty 6, Circular Quay. ☎9247 5151 or 1800 355 537. Departs 9:30am-8pm. From $22.)*

SYDNEY HARBOUR ISLANDS. The **Sydney Harbour National Park** is comprised of four Harbour islands, several south shore beaches, a few green patches on the northern headlands, and North and South Head. Guided visits to the islands must be booked ahead through the park's information center. *(Info center in Cadman's Cottage, 110 George St., The Rocks. ☎9247 5033. Open M-F 11:45am-3pm, Sa-Su 11:30am-3pm.)* The two most popular tours are the **Fort Denison Heritage Tour,** which explores the history of the island off Mrs. Macquaries Point *(M-F 11:30am, Sa-Su also 2:30pm; $22, children and concessions $18, families $72)* and the creepy Quarantine Station **Ghost Tour,** which takes visitors by lantern light to a hospital, cemetery, isolation ward, and mortuary *(W and F-Su 7:30pm; $22-27.50, under 12 not allowed.)* On **Fort Denison Island,** once known as Pinchgut Island and accessible by guided tour only, the early colony's most troublesome convicts were isolated on the exposed rock with a diet consisting of only bread and water. Though the island houses a cafe, save money by taking a picnic and bottle of wine to enjoy on the grassy shores. **Shark Island** (named for its shape), near Rose Bay, and **Clark Island** near Darling Point, are lovely picnic areas. **Rodd Island,** in Iron Cove near Birkenhead Point, has a colonial-style hall. *(All 3 islands open daily 9am-5pm.)*

DARLING HARBOUR

SIGHTS

The site of several events of the 2000 Summer Olympics, Darling Harbour, on the west side of city center, is a popular tourist stop for movies, music, bars, clubs, restaurants, shopping, museums, and magnificent views of the city's skyline. The concentration of attractions in this small area makes it perfect for an afternoon of sightseeing, just as the waterfalls, carousels, and jungle gyms make it ideal for families with small children. Check harborside bulletins for schedules of free concerts. On foot, Darling Harbour is 5min. from Town Hall Station. Follow George St. toward Circular Quay, then turn left on Market St. to Pyrmont Bridge. Bus #888 approaches Darling Harbour from Circular Quay by way of Town Hall, and ferries run from Circular Quay to the Aquarium steps. For transport as tourist-oriented as the destination, hop on the **monorail** from Pitt St., at Park or Market St. in the CBD.

POWERHOUSE MUSEUM. Give yourself plenty of time for this gigantic museum, which explores the vague, potentially boundless topic of human ingenuity. Exhibits and interactive displays focus on technology and applied science. Unusual traveling exhibits often visit; The History of Australian Television is one recent example. *(500 Harris St., just south of Darling Harbour between Ultimo and Haymarket St. ☎9217 0444; www.powerhousemuseum.com. Open daily 10am-5pm. $10, students $6, ages 5-15 $5, under 5 free, families $25.)*

OUTBACK CENTRE. Don't pass up a visit to this colorful arts and crafts museum, gallery, and gift shop, particularly when live didgeridoo performances accompanied by a slide show of images from the Outback take place in the air-conditioned theater. *(28 Darling Walk, 1-25 Harbour St. ☎9283 7477. 30min. performances daily 1, 3, and 5pm. Open daily 10am-6pm. Free.)*

SYDNEY AQUARIUM. Over 11,000 Australian marine animals inhabit the tanks on the pier at Darling Harbour's eastern shore. Seal, crocodile, and penguin exhibits are interspersed between the colorful fish tanks. The three underground and underwater oceanariums, featuring huge enclosures of fish, sharks, and stingrays, help justify the hefty admission. *(On Aquarium Pier. ☎9262 2300; www.sydneyaquarium.com.au. Open daily 9am-10pm; last entry 9pm. Seal sanctuary closes at sunset. $27, ages 3-15 $14, under 3 free, families of 5 $65. Discounted tickets available online.)*

CHINESE GARDEN. This serene garden was a bicentennial gift to New South Wales from her sister province of Guangdong, China. The delicately manicured plot in traditional southern Chinese style provides a sheltered break from the hubbub of the city. You can dress up as an emperor or empress for free at the **Chinese Royalty Costume Shop,** though permission to take photos costs $10. *(Corner of Harbour and Pier St. ☎9281 6863. Open daily 9.30am-5pm; teahouse open 10am-4:30pm. $6, ages 4-15 $3, families $15.)*

NIGHTLIFE

If you thought Darling Harbour was just a tourist playground, come back at night. When the sun goes down, Darling Harbour gets ready to party.

Slip Inn, 111 Sussex St. (☎8295 9999). A refreshing break from the pretentiousness of other venues. Bar area includes a ground-level bar and pool area, chill courtyard, and downstairs sandbar. Schooners $4.60, mixed drinks $14. Its underground streetwear-only nightclub, **Chinese Laundry,** hosts F Break Inn and Sa The Laundry. Cover F $10 before 10pm, $15 after; Sa $10 before 10pm, $20 after. Open M-Th noon-midnight, F noon-2am, Sa noon-4am.

Home, 101 Cockle Bay Wharf (☎9266 0600; www.homesydney.com). This UK-inspired nightclub hit Sydney with a vengeance. Scene is trendy and happening–be prepared for huge lines. Steep cover charge, but the crowds keep coming. On F 4 dance floors and 15 DJs have the place grinding with everything from disco to breakbeat 11pm-7am. Sa live bands keep the place jumping. Cover $25. Open F-Sa 11pm-latenight.

Pontoon Bar, 201 Sussex St., The Promenade, Cockle Bay Wharf (☎9267 7099), right at the bridge. Sleek and stylish, the entire bar is an open terrace right on the harbor. Slightly more casual than Cargo, with a younger, rowdier crowd. Schmitties $4.50, Mixed drinks $13-14. Open M-Th and Su noon-1am, F-Sa noon-4am.

NORTH SHORE

SIGHTS

The Lower North Shore, between Sydney Harbour and Middle Harbour, is primarily home to wealthy Sydneysiders. Its residential neighborhoods and upscale boutiques are lovely but don't draw many travelers—with the exception of Mosman, which holds the Taronga Park Zoo. The popular Northern Beaches start in the lively suburb of Manly after the Spit Bridge and run up the coast to Palm Beach.

MOSMAN AND MIDDLE HARBOUR. Mosman is best known for the **Taronga Park Zoo,** at the end of Bradley's Head Rd. The impressive collection has animals from all over Australia and the world, complete with views of Sydney Harbour thanks to the zoo's hilltop position. Photo opportunities with the koalas and giraffes are especially popular. Admission includes an enclosed chair-lift safari ride, often considered the best part of any visit. To reach the zoo, take a 12min. ferry ride from Circular Quay. *(☎9969 2777; www.zoo.nsw.gov.au. Ticket discounts available online. Parking $10. Open daily 9am-5pm. $30, students $21, families $79. A Zoopass, purchased at Circular Quay, covers admission, ferry, and bus. $37, students $27, children $20.)* Near Mosman, the boat-filled Middle Harbour is particularly beautiful around the **Spit Bridge,** which has several seafood restaurants and kayak rental stores. The picturesque **Balmoral Beach** is popular with North Shore families.

TARONGA ZOO. If you're spending your birthday in Sydney, then a trip to Taronga Zoo is worthwhile. Until June 30th, 2007, you can access to the Zoo for only 90 cents, an offer which coincides with the Zoo's own 90th birthday.

MANLY. It seems fitting that there's no train access to Manly, since the gorgeous **ferry ride** from Circular Quay sets the tone perfectly for the oceanside suburb, whose major sights and activities are all water-related. The 30min. ride passes by the Opera House and Kirribilli House, the Prime Minister's Sydney residence, ending at Manly Wharf. The **visitors center** (☎9976 1430; www.manlyweb.com.au. Open M-F 9am-5pm, Sa-Su 10am-4pm) is in front of the wharf near the enclosed **Manly Cove** swimming area. (☎9976 1430; www.manlyweb.com.au. Open M-F 9am-5pm, Sa-Su 10am-4pm.) The cove is the starting point of the famous **Manly to Spit Walk.** The 9.5km walk (3hr.) offers harbor coastline, sandy beaches, national parklands, and bayside homes. From the Spit Bridge, buses #144 and 143 run back to Manly or onward to Sydney.

Oceanworld, on the West Esplanade at Manly Cove, is very modest compared to the Sydney Aquarium, but it has a shark tunnel where you can dive, as well as a show about Australia's dangerous animals (see **Great Outdoors,** p. 63). (☎8251 7877. Open daily 10am-5:30pm. $17.95, concessions $12.95, children $9.50, families $29.95-43.95. Admission reduced 15% after 3:30pm. Xtreme shark dive 2½hr.; $245 for uncertified divers, $180 certified; includes admission.) **The Corso,** a pedestrian street lined with cheap cafes and fast food joints, can take you from the cove and wharf area to the popular surfing area of **Manly Beach.** Off The Corso is the pedestrian part of **Sydney Road,** which turns into an arts and crafts marketplace on weekends.

NORTHERN BEACHES. A string of popular surfing beaches lines the Pacific Ocean above Manly. Most are also suitable for families because they have beach pools or areas with calm water. **Dee Why Beach** is about 4km north of Manly, just below surf-friendly **Collaroy Beach** and **Narrabean Beach.** Crowds flock to **Newport Beach,** as well as stunning **Avalon Beach,** chosen as the set for "Baywatch" until locals balked at the idea. **Palm Beach,** the gem of the northern beaches, hosts the popular Aussie soapie "Home and Away." There is no train access to the Northern Beaches. *(Take the Northern Beach express bus L88 or L90 from Sydney; change at Warringah Mall for Manly services. Buses #183, 187, 188, 189, 190, and 151 originate at Wynyard Station—Carrington St. side—and will also get you there. Or, take a ferry to Manly, and catch bus #151 and 155. www.sydneybeaches.com.au has tips on what to see and do in the northern beaches.)*

NIGHTLIFE

The North Shore is somewhat quieter than the city center, but it still knows how to party. Manly keeps it lively at night with fashionable bars and clubs.

New Brighton Hotel, 71 The Corso (☎9977 3305). This unassuming pub is well worth a visit if Manly is your destination for a night out. Each night brings something new. Tu student nights with schooners $3, spirits $4, and mixed drinks $6. Th live music. Tasty bar food ($7-15). Open daily 10am-5am.

The Old Manly Boatshed, 40 The Corso (☎9977 4443). A cozy, subterranean pub with a reputation for being a good "meeting place" with live music most weeknights. Serves bottled beverages only. M comedy. Open daily 6pm-3am.

Oaks Hotel, 118 Military Rd. (☎9953 5515), at the intersection of Ben Boyd Rd., in Neutral Bay. A huge old oak tree dominates the immensely popular outdoor beer garden, providing shade in the day and a lit-up centerpiece for yuppie gatherings at night. Attracts a diverse but uniformly cool clientele, with a younger crowd in the public bar, and sports fans in the Garden Palace Bar. Grill your own steak ($22-25) at dinner. Gourmet pizzas also available ($17-22). Schooners $4.50. Open daily 10am-1am.

Ivanhoe of Manly, 27 The Corso (☎9976 3955), opposite the fountain. A popular nightspot with 4 different levels. The ground-level lobby bar has live bands W-Sa (open M, Tu, and Su 9am-midnight, W-Th 9am-1am, F-Sa 9am-3am). Downstairs, Base Nightclub spins techno, trance, and R&B (open daily noon-3am; Sa cover $2), while the dressier Arriba Cocktail Lounge upstairs plays house music. The top floor lounge welcomes a semi-trendy crowd. Open F-Sa 5pm-5am.

ENTERTAINMENT

THEATER

The iconic **Sydney Opera House** is the lynchpin of Sydney's creative culture. With five stages, the Opera House serves as the main venue for a variety of the city's artistic endeavors. (Box office for all venues ☎9250 7777; www.sydneyoperahouse.com.au. Open M-Sa 9am-8:30pm, Su 2hr. prior to show only for ticket pickup. Doors close at showtime. Student rush ticket policy differs from company to company; contact each one for information.)

Concert Hall: The 2679-seat Concert Hall, the most majestic of the Opera House's stages, is the primary venue for symphony, chamber, and orchestral music performances. **Sydney Symphony Orchestra** (☎9334 4644) and the innovative **Australian Chamber Orchestra** (☎8274 3800; www.aco.com.au) perform here throughout the year.

Opera Theatre: The excellent **Opera Australia** (☎9699 1099, tickets 9318 8200; www.opera-australia.org.au) performs here. Reserved seats range from $96-220 and sell out fast, even though there are 1547 of them. Partial-view seats start at $50. Standing room and listening-only tickets are available over-the-counter after 9am on the morning of the performance, depending on availability; limit 2 per person. Leftover tickets are sometimes sold 1hr. before showtime as rush tickets (Prices vary from show to show). Doors close promptly at showtime—be sure to arrive on time. The **Australian Ballet Company** (☎1300 369 741; www.australianballet.com.au) and the **Sydney Dance Company** (☎9221 4811; www.sydneydance.com.au) share the same theater space.

Drama Theatre: This 544-seat theater frequently stars the **Sydney Theatre Company** (☎9250 1777; www.sydneytheatre.com.au). Advance seating from $69; standing room tickets from $24, 1hr. prior to show, depending on availability; student rush tickets from $20, 30min. prior to show, also depending on availability.

Playhouse Theatre: A traditional round-stage forum with 398 seats. Contact the **Bell Shakespeare Company** (☎9241 2722; bellshakespeare@orangemail.com.au) for information on which of Will's classics they'll be presenting.

Studio Stage: This catch-all, transformable stage exhibits less traditional Opera House offerings, including cabaret shows and contemporary performances. Seats 318.

MUSIC

Sydney's daily **live music** scene consists largely of local cover bands casting their pearls for free before pub crowds. The *Metro* section of the Friday *Sydney Morning Herald* and free weeklies such as *Beat* and *Sydney City Hub* contain listings for upcoming shows, along with information on art showings, movies, theater, and DJ appearances city-wide. Major concerts are held in the **Sydney Entertainment Centre,** on Harbour St., Haymarket (☎9320 4200; www.sydentcent.com.au; box office open M-F 9am-5pm, Sa 10am-1pm) and in the **Enmore Theatre,** 130 Enmore Rd., Newtown (☎9550 3666). The **Capitol Theater,** 13 Cambell St., Haymarket, has hosted Broadway shows and other top-notch acts for over 100 years. (☎9320 5000. Newly renovated, with tickets running from $40. Box office open M-Sa 9am-5pm.)

SPECTATOR SPORTS

Like Australians everywhere, Sydneysiders are sports mega-fans. All events below sell tickets through **Ticketek** (☎13 28 49; www.ticketek.com.au) and are played in stadiums in Moore Park, accessible by buses #373, 391, 393, and 395. The main number for all the stadiums is for the Cricket Ground. (☎9360 6601; www.sydneycricketground.com.au.) See **Sports and Recreation,** p. 56.

Cricket: To some, cricketers are men wearing white straw hats and sweater vests; to others, they're gods. Decide for yourself at the **Sydney Cricket Ground,** on Moore Park Rd. Tickets $25-119, depending upon the game.

Rugby League: The **Sydney Football Stadium,** on the corner of Driver Ave. and Moore Park Rd., is home to the **Sydney City Roosters.** It draws rowdy, fiercely loyal fans throughout the winter season and in Sept. for the Telstra Premiership. Tickets $20-35. **Rugby Union** (www.rfu.com) is the other popular "footy" league in NSW, though it does not field a Sydney team. The main difference between the 2 leagues is that **RU** has 15 players on the field whereas **RL** has 13.

Australian Rules Football: This head-crushing, uniquely Aussie game engages cross-state competition and is held at the Sydney Football Stadium. What separates ARF from other leagues is that the clock stops during the game. Root for the not-so-swan-like **Sydney Swans.** Tickets cost more and are harder to get than rugby tickets ($29-106).

CINEMAS

Sydney's film scene contains a variety of independent movie houses, as well as mainstream cinemas showing American blockbusters. Tuesdays are often **bargain day,** with half-price tickets. The rest of the week, prices hover around $12-15 and $10-11 for children. For info on the **Sydney Film Festival,** see p. 149.

Dendy Cinemas, 2 East Circular Quay, CBD (☎9247 3800; www.dendy.com.au) and 261-263 King St., Newtown (☎9550 5699). All locations show quality arthouse films while the adjacent cafes serve delicious and affordable meals. Open daily noon-9pm; bar closes at midnight.

Govinda's, 112 Darlinghurst Rd. (☎9380 5155), Darlinghurst. Shows 2-3 acclaimed contemporary films per day in a cushion-filled lounge, and throws in an all-you-can eat vegetarian buffet.

LG IMAX Cinema (☎9281 3300), Southern Pde., Darling Harbour. The 8-story-high movie screen is the largest in the world. A different film is shown every hr. Open daily 10am-10pm.

Greater Union, 505-525 George St. (☎9273 7431). The largest mainstream cinema, located halfway between Chinatown and the CBD.

SHOPPING

Sydneysiders love to shop, and the city's numerous department stores, designer boutiques, factory outlets, and vintage stores make it easy for them. Fittingly, Sydney's commercial heart, the **CBD,** is also its shopping epicenter. Designer names like Chanel, Versace, and Louis Vuitton line **Castlereagh Street,** while department stores like **David Jones,** on Market and Castlereagh St., and **Grace Bros,** 436 George St., link to the **Pitt Street Mall** (see **Malls**). **The Rocks** holds small, upscale boutiques on Argyle and George St. geared toward tourists, as well as a weekend market (see **Markets,** below). **Paddington** has pricey boutiques on Oxford St., while mellow **Newtown** has the best selection of secondhand clothing stores along King St. **Leichhardt,** Sydney's Little Italy, has fine Italian shoes and clothing on Norton St. Shopaholics should pick up a free copy of *Sydney Shopping: The Official Guide* from The Rocks' visitors center.

MALLS. You haven't been to a real mall until you've been to Sydney's multi-mall multiplex **Pitt Street Mall,** comprised of several pedestrian-only blocks on Pitt St. and lined with shopping complexes like **Mid City Centre, Westfield Centrepoint, Skygarden,** and **Sydney Central Plaza.** For high-end shopping in elegant, old-world style, head to the ornate **Strand Arcade** and **Queen Victoria Building** (p. 126). Both of these shopping arcades feature upmarket Australian designer boutiques, ranging from the hypercolored Ken Done in the QVB to high fashion labels like Bettina Liano, Alannah Hill, and Third Millennium in the Strand. In Darling Harbour, **Harbourside** has Australian homewares; in Haymarket, **Market City** holds factory outlets and the famous Paddy's Market (see **Markets**).

MARKETS. Sydney's year-round weekend markets tend to specialize in arts, crafts, and souvenirs. With so many markets to choose from, it's helpful to know what you're looking for and what you'll find at each of the different shopping grounds. Some vendors fly all the way from Melbourne to showcase their goods at **The Rocks Market,** on Oxford St. in The Rocks, a quaint arts and crafts fair tucked away in the hills. Homemade preserves and handmade crafts (like stationery and boomerangs) are among the one-of-a-kind souvenirs available for purchase here. (Open Sa-Su 10am-5pm.) **Glebe Market,** on Glebe Point Rd. in Glebe, features a variety of clothing and housewares, sold for half the price of what you'll pay in most Sydney stores. Deliciously unusual food stands contribute to the overall bohemian theme. (Open Sa 9:30am-4:30pm.) With its elegant clothing and stunning jewelry, **Paddington Market,** on Oxford St. in Paddington, feels more like a jaunt down Park Ave. than a stroll through a residential street. If you've got the funds, there's no better place to find an overpriced outfit—with an opal necklace to match—that is sure to turn heads. (Open Sa 10am-4pm.) **Paddy's Market,** in Haymarket, Chinatown, is perhaps the most famous of all of Sydney markets. This massive indoor display of wholesale goods is best used as a one-stop gourmet grocer. What the wholesale goods lack in quality, the fresh meat, fish, fruit and vegetable stands make up for in taste, presentation, and unbeatable prices. (Open Th-Su 9am-5pm.) The **Sydney Opera House Markets,** at Bennelong Point at Circular Quay, are known for their arts and crafts. They are more spread-out but just as touristy as The Rocks. (Open Su 9am-5pm.) The hip **Bondi Beach Market** (☎9315 8988; www.bondimarkets.com.au), at Bondi Beach Public School on Campbell Pde., features local arts and crafts. (Open Su 10am-5pm, weather permitting.)

FESTIVALS

Sydney Festival, throughout Jan. (☎8248 6500; www.sydneyfestival.org.au). Features arts and entertainment events. Check the *Daily Telegraph* for details on free concerts in The Domain, street theater in The Rocks, and fireworks in Darling Harbour.

Tropfest, last Su in Feb. (☎9368 0434; www.tropfest.com.au). World's largest short film festival has screens in The Domain and Royal Botanic Gardens.

Gay and Lesbian Mardi Gras, Mar. (☎9568 8600; www.mardigras.org.au). This huge international event is always a rip-roaring good time. Climaxes on its final day with a parade attended by over 500,000 people and a gala party at the RAS Show Ground in Moore Park. Though the party is restricted and the guest list fills up far in advance, travelers can get on the list by becoming "International Members of Mardi Gras" for $29.

Royal Agricultural Society's Easter Show, mid-Apr. (☎9704 1111; www.eastershow.com.au). Held at Sydney Olympic Park. The carnival atmosphere and rides make it fun even for those with no interest in farming.

Sydney Film Festival, mid-June (☎9280 0511; www.sydneyfilmfestival.org). The ornate State Theatre, 49 Market St., between George and Pitt St., and Dendy Opera Quays showcase documentaries, retrospectives, and art films from around the world. The festival tours Australia throughout the year.

City to Surf Run, Aug. (☎9282 3606). Draws 60,000 contestants for a semi-serious 14km trot from Park St. to Bondi Beach. Some are world-class runners; others treat the race as a lengthy pub crawl. Entries ($35) are accepted up to race day.

Manly Jazz Festival, early Oct. (☎9976 1430). Australia's biggest jazz festival, featuring all types of national and international artists.

Bondi Beach Party, Dec. 25. Bondi sets the pace for debauchery all along the coast as people from around the world gather for a foot-stomping Christmas party.

Sydney-to-Hobart Yacht Race, Dec. 26. Brings the city's hungover attention back to civilized entertainment.

ACTIVITIES

BEACHES

Sydney is home to many world-class beaches. Most are packed during the summer, but the Northern Beaches are more secluded and offer great surfing.

BEACH	FEATURES	TAKE BUS
SOUTH		
Bondi	"A-list" beach. Surfing makes the postcards.	380, 382, L82
Bronte	Quiet, family beach with strong undertow.	378
Coogee	Bondi's young rival, often just as packed. Good ocean pools.	372, 373, 374
Maroubra	Locals' beach gaining in popularity. Great surf.	376, 377, 395, 396
Tamarama	"Glamarama" is just beneath Bondi. Strong undertow.	380, 382, L82
NORTH		
Avalon	Beautiful spot, almost chosen as set of "Baywatch."	L88, L90
Balmoral	Quiet, elegant harbor beach. Good for kids.	238, 257, 258
Collaroy	Attracts families and surfers, with sand running to Narrabeen.	L85, L88, L90, 185
Manly	Popular beach with fantastic surfing and people-watching.	151 or Manly ferry
Newport	Home to stunning waters, cliffs, and an ocean peak, surfable off both sides.	L88, L90
Palm Beach	Glam set of TV soap "Home and Away" with easy access to great views from the Barenjoey Lighthouse.	L90

WATER SPORTS

SURFING. While **Bondi** is Sydney's famous surfing beach, **Manly** and the more secluded **Northern Beaches** (including Freshwater, Curl Curl, Dee Why, Collaroy, Narrabeen, Newport, and Avalon) are even better options. The **Manly Surf School,** at the North Steyne Surf Club and at the Lifeguard Pavilion in Palm Beach, gives lessons to surfers of all skill levels. (☎9977 6977; www.manlysurfschool.com. Open for lessons year-round. 1 lesson $50; 5-day $170; 10-day $280. Private lessons $80 per hr.; prices include gear. Booking required.) In Manly, **Aloha Surf,** 44 Pittwater Rd., rents boards and wetsuits. (☎9977 3777. Open daily 9am-6pm. Short and long boards ½ day $30, full day $40.) **Bondi Surf Co.,** 72-76 Campbell Pde., rents surfboards and bodyboards with wetsuits. (☎9365 0870. Open daily 10am-5pm. Credit card or passport deposit required. $15 per hr., $25 per 2hr., $50 per full day.)

NEW SOUTH WALES

JETBOATING. Several jetboat companies take poncho-clad passengers on adventure rides in Darling and Sydney Harbours. Go for the exhilarating ride but don't expect gorgeous harbor views; the boat will be spinning, turning, and braking too fast for you to see much. **Sydney Jet,** located in Cockle Bay Wharf, Darling Harbour, is one of the cheapest options. (☎9930 2000. 40min. "Jet Thrill" ride departs M-F every hr. from 10am, Sa-Su every hr. from noon. $60, children $40. 55min. "Adventure Thrill" ride departs M-F 10am, Sa-Su 10 and 11am. $75/55.) For a more leisurely ride, see **Harbour Cruises** (p. 143).

DIVING. **ProDive** has excellent advice on local diving spots, gear, and certification courses. (CBD: Shop 8, 35 Harrington St. The Rocks: ☎1800 820 820. Manly: 169 Pittwater Rd. ☎9977 5966. Coogee: 27 Alfreda St. ☎9665 6333. Open M-W and F-Su 9am-5:30pm, Th 9am-6pm. 4-day courses from $287; trips and courses for other Australian locations can be arranged.)

SAILING. On any sunny day, white sails can be seen gliding across the water. **East Sail Sailing School,** at d'Albora Marina on Rushcutters Bay, caters to all levels and offers small courses and trips. (☎9327 1166; www.eastsail.com.au. 2½hr. "Coffee Cruise" yacht trips depart daily 10am; 2-12 passengers. $95. Introductory sailing course from $475.) **Sydney by Sail** runs intro lessons from the National Maritime Museum. (☎9280 1110; www.sydneybysail.com. Max. 8-12 person. 3hr. harbor sail to Port Jackson $130. Introductory course $425. Book ahead.)

WHALE WATCHING AND FISHING. Whale watching season runs from June-July and Sept.-Oct. **Halicat,** 410 Elizabeth St., Surry Hills., has both fishing and whale watching tours for up to 23 people running from Rose Bay and Cremorne. (☎9280 3043. Trips depart 6:30am and return mid-afternoon. Reef fishing $110. Sport fishing trips $200; these go farther out and find bigger fish. 5hr. whale watching weekend trips $75, seniors and students $65, children $45, families $200.) A number of charter boats run guided deep-sea **fishing** trips; groups get cheaper rates. Acclaimed **Broadbill** runs a smaller operation (boat holds six) at competitive prices from Sans Souci Wharf. (☎9534 2378; www.gamefishingcharters.com.au. Trips depart 7am and return 5-6pm. Sport fishing $240.)

AIR ADVENTURES

SKYDIVING. Skydiving in Australia is cheaper than anywhere else. **Sydney Skydivers,** 77 Wentworth Ave., runs ½-day tandem dives—Sydney's highest diving option. (☎8307 3834; www.sydneyskydivers.com.au. From $275.) **Simply Skydive Australia** offers similar services, diving up to 14,000 ft. (☎1800 759 348; www.simplyskydive.com.au. From $325.)

SCENIC FLIGHTS. For aerial views of Sydney without a parachute, several places offer scenic flights around the Sydney area. **Sydney Air Scenic Flights** runs from the Bankstown Airport. (☎9790 0628. Sydney Harbour: 1hr. $500, or Blue Mountains: 1½hr. $750 for 5 people.)

OLYMPIC PARK

The golden era of the 2000 Olympic Games in Sydney may be a thing of the past, but visitors are still welcome to visit the impressive Homebush Bay Olympic Site. From the 80,000 seat **Telstra Stadium** to the stellar **Aquatic Centre,** the facilities are still a hive of activity and make for a fun trip. Follow up your tour of the facilities with a hike and a picnic in the adjacent 100-hectare Bicentennial Park. *(Take CityRail to Olympic Park Station, 14km west of the city center along the Parramatta River. ☎9714 7888; www.sydneyolympicpark.com.au. Swimming $6.20, students $5. Tours $15-27.50.)*

TOURS OF SYDNEY

WALKING TOURS. The recently revamped walking tours of The Rocks depart from the visitors center at 106 George St. (☎9247 6678; p. 118.) Themed walks include ghost tours, historical tours, and pub crawls. The visitors center also provides information on self-guided walking tours and the best routes to take for getting the most out of your time in Sydney.

SYDNEY BY DIVA. Grab your falsies and get on board this 3hr. comedy bus tour of Sydney, hosted by the most fabulous drag queens in town. As queens-in-training, guests are given wigs and drag names before heading off to the Opera House, Bondi Beach, and to Erskineville's Imperial Hotel (used in *Priscilla, Queen of the Desert*) for a final performance. First class tickets garner less teasing and finer champagne than coach, but it's all in good fun, honey. Tours leave from the Oxford

Hotel in Darlinghurst. (☎9360 5557; www.sydneybydiva.com. Refreshments and mandatory dance lessons included. Tours every Su 5-8pm. First class $85, economy $65. Book at least 2 wk. ahead.)

SYDNEY'S BEST CITY AND COASTAL WALKS

Opera House to Mrs. Macquaries Point. This 20min. stroll along the edge of the lush Royal Botanic Gardens has one of the best views of the Opera House and the boat-filled harbor at Farm Cove.

Across the Harbour Bridge. You can cross the Harbour Bridge for free by foot, beginning in The Rocks near Argyle St. Once across the bridge in Kirribilli, walk downhill on Broughton St. for a spectacular harbor view.

Hyde Park to Darling Harbour. A 15min. walk down Market St. from either end leads you through the heart of the city and right by the Centrepoint Tower, Pitt Street Mall, Strand Arcade, Queen Victoria Building, and designer shops.

Bondi to Coogee. This 1hr. coastal hike will take you along cliffs and through a cemetery for good views of Sydney's southern beaches.

Manly to Spit. A slightly strenuous 3hr. coastal walk that will give you a taste of bushland and the northern beaches.

Mosman to Cremorne Wharf. A picturesque 40min. walk along the harbor foreshore between 2 ferry wharves. Bring your swimsuit–the world's prettiest harborside pool is en route and open to the public year-round.

DAYTRIPS FROM SYDNEY

Sydney's attractions are not limited to the city proper. The national parklands that encompass the surrounding hills and valleys are representative of the natural beauty for which the continent is known. If your stay in Oz is confined to Sydney, these daytrips offer a taste of the rest of the country.

ROYAL NATIONAL PARK. Just 32km south of Sydney's city center, Royal National Park is an easy escape from city life, with deserted beaches, quiet marshlands, and secluded rainforests. It's the world's second-oldest national park (after Yellowstone in the United States), and consists of more than 16,000 hectares of beach, heath, rainforest, and woodland, which contain 43 species of mammals and nearly 240 species of birds. Across the Princes Hwy. on the west side of the park, the smaller, often forgotten **Heathcote National Park** offers 2000 additional hectares of wildlife. **Escape Sydney Ecotours** (☎9664 3047; www.escapecotours.com.au) takes travelers from several pickup locations in Sydney to the highlights of the park. Tours range from a half-day whale-watching trek (May-Aug. only; $40, includes transport and park entry) to a two-day coast walk tour ($240, includes transport, park entry, and accommodation). To get there by car, turn off the Princes Hwy. at Farnell Ave., south of Loftus, or at McKell Ave. at Waterfall ($11 park fee for cars). CityRail trains (☎13 15 00) run from Sydney to both Engadine and Heathcote stations ($4.40). A ferry from Cronulla will get you to the park at Bundeena (☎9523 2990; $5).

BOTANY BAY NATIONAL PARK. Captain Cook and his crew first made contact with Aboriginal people on these lands in 1770. The Banks-Solander Track (1km), which takes you past stunning sandstone cliffs, is one of the most beautiful walks in the park; some of the same kinds of vegetation that Cook's botanist first studied still grow here. The Cape Baily Coast walk (8km) takes you along heath-covered coast past many Cook-related sites. The La Perouse Museum documents the park's other role in history as the place where French explorer Le Comte de La Perouse established France as a key player in Europe's conquest of Australia. The NPWS-run Bare Island Fort Tour digs through the history of the fort, built in 1885 when British colonists feared a Russian invasion. (☎9247 5033. 1hr.; meets at the fort entrance. Su 1:30 and 2:30pm. $7.70, children $5.50, families $22.) By car, drive to the end of Anzac Pde. to reach La Perouse in the northern section of the park. To get to the park's southern end, take Rocky Point Rd. off the Princes Hwy., then Captain Cook Dr. ($7 park fee for cars.) Bus #394 from Circular Quay also runs to La Perouse, and bus #987 arrives at Captain Cook Dr. from Cronulla Station.

PARRAMATTA ☎02

Australia's second oldest settlement, the bustling city of Parramatta is a mecca for lovers of Australian history. Its homes and upscale dining also attract Sydneysiders and tourists alike.

Parramatta has several buildings from the early days of colonization, including the **Old Government House,** in Parramatta Park at the town's west end. The house, the oldest public building in Australia, is perfectly preserved and portrays how the governor's household ran. (☎9635 8149. Open M-F 10am-4pm, Sa-Su 10:30am-4pm. $8, concessions $5, families $18; with farm $10/7/25.) Of course, old buildings are full of intrigue, and some are even reportedly haunted. A nighttime ghost tour of the house is offered once every month ($25; www.friendsofogh.com). On the opposite side of town along the Harris Park Heritage Walk, **Elizabeth Farm,** 70 Alice St., in Rosehill, was home to John and Elizabeth Macarthur, founders of the Australian merino wool industry. (☎9635 9488. Open daily 10am-5pm. $8, concessions $4, families $17.) Locally, **Church Street** is known as "Eat Street" for its many fine dining options. **Encore at Riverside ❸,** 353 Church St., opposite the tourist office, serves inventive salads and more traditional main dishes for $14-25. (☎9630 0511. Open M-Sa 8:30am-10:30pm, Su 8:30am-4:30pm.)

Paramatta is best reached from Sydney by way of a scenic 50min. ferry ride on the **RiverCat** pontoon (departs Wharf 2, 1 per hr., $7). Otherwise the city is a 20min. drive along Parramatta Rd., which becomes the M4 Tollway at Strathfield, the most direct route to the Blue Mountains. **CityRail** also runs to: Blackheath ($10.40); Katoomba ($10); Lithgow ($13.20); Penrith ($4.40); and Sydney ($4). The **Parramatta Visitors Center,** 346 Church St., is within the Heritage Center. (☎8839 3311; www.parracity.nsw.gov.au. Open daily 9am-5pm.)

PENRITH ☎02

Though the beauty of Penrith's outdoor offerings pales in comparison to those of the southern coast, the town is only 45min. from Sydney and is a good base for an introduction to the Blue Mountains. The urban center of Penrith sits at the foot of the Blue Mountains, 35km west of Parramatta along the Great Western Hwy. (Hwy. 44) or the M4 Motorway, on the edge of Sydney's sphere of suburban influence. Though small compared to Sydney, Penrith has the urban feel of a city. With a professional football team, a large shopping plaza, and commercial **High Street,** Penrith makes up for its lack of size. Running through the western half of town, the placid **Nepean River** is a touch of beauty in an otherwise plain landscape.

In **Blue Mountains National Park,** you can rent a canoe and paddle your way through Nepean Gorge or take a ride on the **Nepean Belle,** an old-time paddlewheel riverboat. (☎4733 1274; www.nepeanbelle.com.au. Departs Tench Reserve Park, off Tench Ave., with morning, afternoon, and dinner cruises. Shortest cruise 1½hr. $15.) For an aerial view of the Nepean River, follow Mulgoa Rd. south toward Wallacia and stop at **Rock Lookout.** Just across the river in Emu Plains, the **Penrith**

Regional Gallery & The Lewers Bequest, 86 River Rd., showcases contemporary Australian sculptures in tidy gardens. (☎4735 1100. Open daily 10am-5pm. Free.)

Explorers Lodge ❸, 111 Station St., is Penrith's premier backpacker accommodation, with spacious rooms. (☎4731 3616; www.explorerslodge.com. Reception 9am-9pm. Check-out 11am. 6-bed dorms $27.50, weekly $165; singles $44/264; doubles $66/330.) **Nepean River Caravan Park ❷,** on MacKellar St., in Emu Plains, is a short drive over the river (or a 500m walk from the rail station). It has campsites and cabins, and provides a kitchen, pool, game room, and TV lounge. (☎4735 4425; www.nepeanriver-hv.com.au. Linen $10. Reception M-F 8am-7pm, Sa-Su 8-11am and 4-6pm. Tent sites for 2 $20, powered $28; dorms $25; cabins from $75.)

CityRail trains (ticket office at railway; open M-F 5am-9pm, Sa 5:45am-8:30pm, Su 6:45am-8:30pm) run to: Blackheath (1½hr., 15-21 per day, $8.20); Katoomba (1hr., 15-21 per day, $6.20); Lithgow (2hr., 12-14 per day, $10.40); Parramatta (30min., 23-34 per day, $4.40); Sydney (1hr., 23-33 per day, $6.80). The **Penrith Valley Visitors Center,** on Mulgoa Rd., in the Panthers World of Entertainment Complex carpark, provides useful info on Penrith. (☎4732 7671 or 1300 736 836; www.penrithvalley.com.au. Open daily 9am-4:30pm.)

KU-RING-GAI CHASE NATIONAL PARK

Founded in 1894, Ku-Ring-Gai Chase National Park is the second oldest national park in New South Wales (after the Royal National Park). Ku-Ring-Gai Chase covers some 15,000 hectares of land traditionally occupied by the Guringai Aboriginal people. Today, visitors to the rugged park come for the numerous Aboriginal rock engravings, the bright wildflowers that bloom in early August, and the peace and quiet found beside hidden creeks and in the depths of the forest.

It's much easier to access the park with a car, as public transportation will only get you to the park's entrances. Ku-Ring-Gai Chase is split in two by access roads. **Ku-Ring-Gai Chase Road** from the Pacific Hwy. and **Bobbin Head Road** from Turramurra provide access to the southwest area of the park, while **West Head Road** runs through the eastern section. From Sydney, you can reach the Bobbin Head Rd. entrance by taking the **train** to Turramurra (40min., $4) and then catching bus #577 of **Shorelink Bus Company** from North Turramurra Station to the park gates. (☎9457 8888 or 13 15 00; www.shorelink.com.au. 15min.; M-F every 30min., Sa every hr., Su every 2hr.; $5.40.) A 3hr. hike then brings you to the Kalkari Visitors Centre. Another option is to take **bus** L90 or L85, which runs from Circular Quay in Sydney (1½hr.) to Church Point, where it's possible to catch a **ferry** (☎9999 3492 or 04 0829 6997; $5, round-trip $10) or **water taxi** with Pink Water Taxi across Broken Bay to Halls Wharf, with free and direct hiking access to the park. (☎9979 9750, urgent 04 2823 8190; www.pinkwatertaxi.au.com. Max. 6 people. Available 24hr. $16 one-way.) **Palm Beach Ferry Service** (☎9974 2411; www.palmbeachferry.com.au) departs from Palm Beach (accessible from Sydney by bus L90) and stops at The Basin, the park's camping area (every hr., $11.80 round-trip). **Palm Cruises** runs scenic cruises from Palm Beach to Bobbin Head. (☎9997 4815. Rates vary.)

The Bobbin Head area in the southwest is home to the **Kalkari Visitors Centre,** on Ku-Ring-Gai Chase Rd., 3km inside the park gates. The center distributes free hiking maps and offers educational information on the park's wildlife. (☎9472 9300. Open daily 9am-5pm.) One kilometer farther, the **Bobbin Head Information Centre,** inside the Wildlife Shop at the bottom of the hill, also distributes info about the park. (☎9472 8949. Open daily 10am-4pm.) Both centers run guided tours—call for schedule and details. Additionally, general inquiries can be made at **The Rocks Visitors Centre** (☎1300 361 967 or 9253 4600; www.npws.nsw.gov.au) in Sydney.

The only place you can **camp** in Ku-Ring-Gai Chase National Park is at **The Basin ❶.** You can get there on foot along The Basin Track, by car on West Head Rd., or by the hourly ferry from Palm Beach ($11.80 round-trip). Campsites have cold showers, toilets, gas BBQ, and a public phone; all supplies other than bait and drinks must be carried in. Vehicles staying overnight require a special pass ($11). Booking is required and must be arranged through the NPWS 24hr. automated reservation service; your call will be returned within three days. (☎9974 1011. Max. 8 per site. Sites Sept.-Apr. $10, $5 per child.)

Certainly the most refreshing and remote hostel in the greater Sydney area, the **Pittwater YHA Hostel ❷** is set among greenery in a lofty, terraced perch over Pittwater. The open, outdoorsy hostel provides a secluded retreat without TV or radio. You'll need to bring your own food (the only grocery store is a ferry ride away), as well as a flashlight. To get there, follow the confusing path 15min. uphill from Halls Wharf, accessible by ferry from Church Point ($5, round-trip $10). To reach Church Point, drive along Pittwater Rd., or take bus #156 from Manly (1hr.), bus E86 from Wynyard (1¼hr.), or bus L85 or L90 from Sydney. (☎9999 5748. Kayak rental $15 per hr., $25 per 3hr. Reception 8-11am and 5-8pm. Dorms $24; twins $62. Booking required.)

Ku-Ring-Gai Chase has **bushwalks** for any level of expertise. The **Discovery Walk** (20min.; wheelchair accessible), just outside the Kalkari Visitors Centre, is a quick and easy way to spot a few kangaroos, emus, and some native plant life. A moderately difficult bushwalk (10km) begins at the Bobbin Head Rd. entrance to the park and follows the **Sphinx-Warrimoo Track** (6.5km) to Bobbin Head. The hike can be made into a circuit by taking the Bobbin Head Track (3.5km) back to the park entrance. The bushwalk passes through mangroves, along a creek, and near an Aboriginal engraving site. The **Basin Bay Track** and **Mackerel Track** at West Head are both moderately difficult hikes that feature stunning Aboriginal engraving sites accessible by West Head Rd. Rock engravings, up to 8m long, depict mythical beings and whales. For the best views of the Hawkesbury River as it feeds into Broken Bay, head north along West Head Rd. until you reach the **West Head Lookout.** For an outstanding view of Sydney, head to the recently restored **Barrenjoey Lighthouse** to tackle the 10min. climb to the top. (Su every 30min. 11am-3pm. $3.)

BLUE MOUNTAINS

The gorgeous Blue Mountains region is Sydney's favorite escape, a tourist wonderland just outside the city, yet very much away from it all. Although a variety of adventure activities, such as abseiling and canyon rafting, have become popular in recent years, the primary draw of the Blue Mountains remains its excellent hiking. The remarkable blue color of the hazy valleys and ridges in this area is the result of sunlight filtering through the eucalyptus oil in the air. From lookout points along canyon edges, the earth falls away to endless blue foliage speckled with white bark and bordered by distant sandstone cliffs. Travelers who want to take a dip in a plunge pool, hike through serene rainforest, view Aboriginal ceremonial grounds, abseil into a deep canyon, or enjoy jaw-dropping panoramic views will find all their desires fulfilled here.

TRANSPORTATION

The Blue Mountains are an easy 1½hr. drive west of Sydney. The **M4 Motorway** runs to Penrith ($3.80 toll) and meets the **Great Western Highway,** the main route through the mountains. All service centers and attractions lie on or near this road. Alternatively, the northern route, **Bells Line of Road** (p. 167), meanders west from Windsor, northeast of Parramatta, providing a more scenic passage.

CityRail trains stop throughout the Blue Mountains at most of the towns along the Great Western Hwy., offering the least expensive option for travelers who are willing to walk sizable distances from rail stations and bus stops to trailheads. Within the towns, most distances are walkable, and local bus companies cover those that aren't (for bus info, see **Katoomba,** p. 158). There is **no public transportation** to Kanangra-Boyd or Wollemi National Park.

There are three above-average companies that run **small bus tours** into the Blue Mountains from Sydney. The advantage to using one of these companies is that the groups are usually smaller, which translates to a more personalized, less touristy experience. **Wonderbus** offers a tour of the Blue Mountains that covers highlights of the mountains, Olympic sights, and the Featherdales Wildlife Park. For a more leisurely pace, opt for an overnight stay in the mountains. (☎1300 556 357. Departs daily at 7:15am, returns 7pm. Blue Mountains tour $109, ISIC/NOMADS/VIP/YHA $89.) The **OzTrails** tour takes you and 13 others to regional highlights and provides tea and lunch. (☎9387 8390; www.oztrails.com.au. Departs 8am, returns 6pm; $83.) **Wildframe Ecotours** provides similar services and offers a trip into Grand Canyon, a tremendous rainforest-filled gorge in Blackheath. (☎9440 9915. Daytrip $76, concessions $68; with 1 night at the Katoomba YHA $123, 2 nights $145.) Several companies run **large-bus tours** to the mountains from Sydney. **AAT Kings,** Jetty 6, on Circular Quay, offers a basic tour of the mountains and Jenolan Caves. (☎9700 0133. Basic tour departs 8:45am, returns 6pm; $108. Jenolan Caves tour departs 8:40am, returns 6:45pm; $129.)

ORIENTATION

Three national parks divide the wild stretches of the region. **Blue Mountains National Park** (p. 164), the largest and most accessible of the three, spans most of the Jamison Valley (south of the Great Western Hwy. between Glenbrook and Katoomba), the Megalong Valley (south of the Great Western Hwy., west of Katoomba), and the Grose Valley (north of the Great Western Hwy. and east of Blackheath). The Grose and Jamison Valleys appeal primarily to hikers, while horseback riders favor the Megalong Valley (for more information on horseback riding, see **Blackheath,** p. 162). **Kanangra-Boyd National Park** (p. 168), tucked between two sections of the Blue Mountains in the southwest reaches of the park, is reserved for skilled bushwalkers. The park is accessible by partially paved roads from Oberon and from Jenolan Caves. **Wollemi National Park** (p. 167) contains the state's largest preserved wilderness area. It's so unspoiled and untrafficked that a species of pine tree thought to be long extinct was found here in 1994. Access to Wollemi, which abuts the north side of **Bells Line of Road,** is available at Bilpin and at several points north of the central Blue Mountains.

The national parks of the Blue Mountains region are administered by different branches of the **National Parks and Wildlife Services (NPWS).** If you are planning to bushcamp or drive into these parks, contact the appropriate NPWS branch a few days in advance to ensure that no bushfire bans are in place and the roads are drivable (this is important as roads are closed more often than you might think). For a great all-in-one resource on the Blue Mountain region, including up-to-the-minute weather reports and detailed advice on all outdoor activities, go to www.bluemts.com.au. It is also highly recommended that you leave a bushwalk plan filed with the appropriate NPWS office before you go.

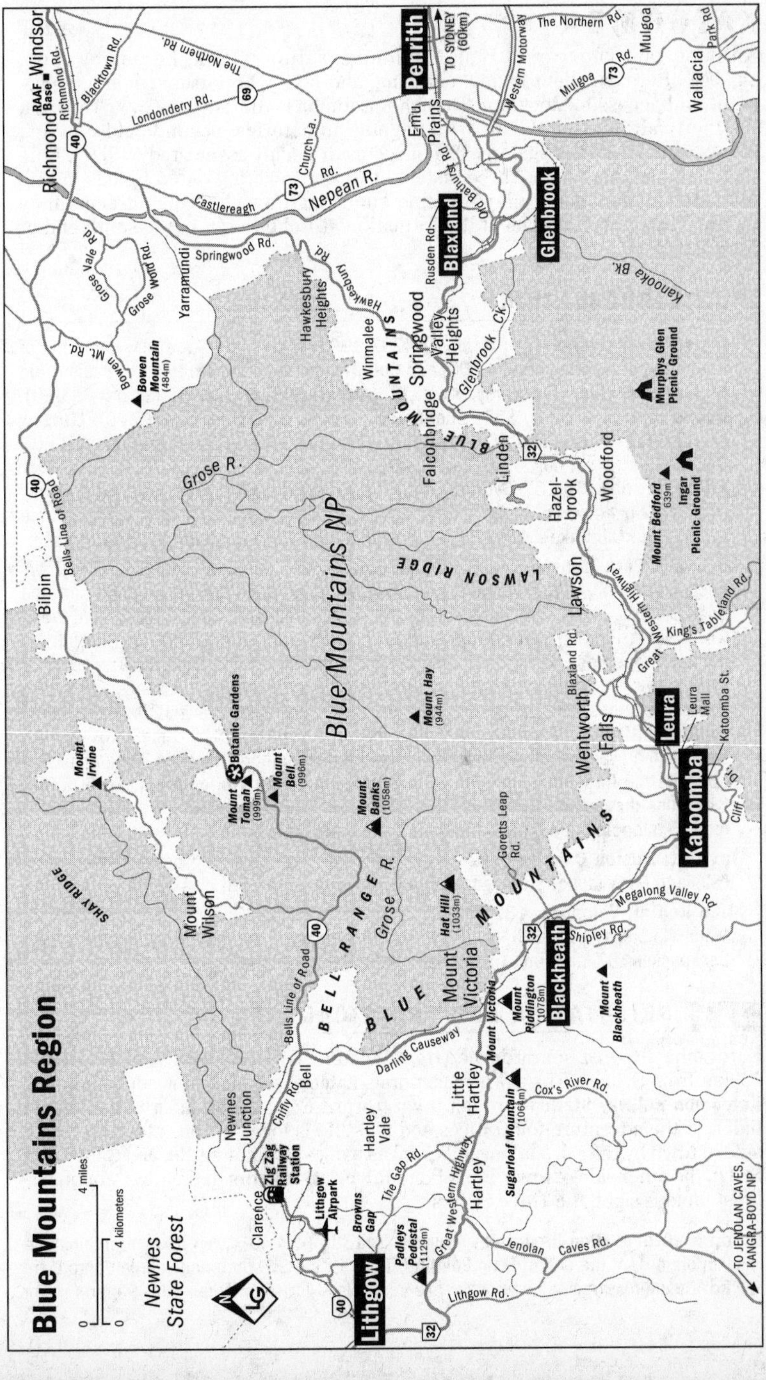

Blue Mountains Region

0 4 miles
0 4 kilometers

Newnes State Forest
Lithgow
Padleys Pedestal (1129m)
Browns Gap
Lithgow Airpark
Clarence
Zig Zag Railway Station
Newnes Junction
Hartley Vale
Hartley
Little Hartley
Sugarloaf Mountain (1064m)
Mount Victoria
Mount Piddington (1078m)
Blackheath
Mount Blackheath
Bell
Chifley Rd.
Bells Line of Road
Darling Causeway
The Gap Rd.
Great Western Highway
Jenolan Caves Rd.
Lithgow Rd.
Cox's River Rd.
TO JENOLAN CAVES, KANGRA-BOYD NP
Shipley Rd.
Megalong Valley Rd.
Goretts Leap Rd.
Hat Hill (1033m)
Grose R.
BELL RANGE
BLUE MOUNTAINS
Mount Wilson
SHAY RIDGE
Mount Irvine
Mount Tomah (999m)
Botanic Gardens
Mount Bell (996m)
Mount Banks (1058m)
Mount Hay (944m)
Blue Mountains NP
Katoomba
Katoomba St.
Cliff Dr.
Leura
Leura Mall
Wentworth Falls
Blaxland Rd.
Great Western Highway
King's Tableland Rd.
Lawson
LAWSON RIDGE
Hazelbrook
Woodford
Mount Bedford 639m
Ingar Picnic Ground
Murphys Glen Picnic Ground
Linden
Falconbridge
Valley Heights
Springwood
Glenbrook Ck.
Winmalee
Hawkesbury Heights
Hawkesbury Rd.
Blaxland
Rusden Rd.
Old Bathurst Rd.
Glenbrook
Kanooka Bk.
Bilpin
Bells Line of Road
Grose R.
Bowen Mountain (484m)
Bowen Mt. Rd.
Grose Vale Rd.
Grose Wold Rd.
Yarramundi
Springwood Rd.
Castlereagh Rd.
Nepean R.
Church La.
Emu Plains
Penrith
TO SYDNEY (60km)
Londonderry Rd.
Blacktown Rd.
The Northern Rd.
Richmond
RAAF Base
Richmond Rd.
Windsor
Western Motorway
Mulgoa Rd.
Mulgoa
Wallacia
Park Rd.

NEW SOUTH WALES

KATOOMBA ☎02

An important gateway to Blue Mountains National Park, Katoomba (pop. 14,000) offers excellent hiking, climbing, and biking opportunities in a convenient, rail-accessible location. Though Katoomba is touristy, the town retains a distinctly alternative flavor, with vegetarian eateries, secondhand clothing stores, and dreadlocks galore. The image most widely associated with the Blue Mountains is that of the Three Sisters, a trio of towering outcroppings jutting out into the Jamison Valley, holding silent vigil over the blue-green valley below. Visitors can marvel at the formation at Echo Point, in the south end of Katoomba.

TRANSPORTATION

Trains: Katoomba Railway Station (☎4782 1902) is on Main St., at the north end of Katoomba St. **CityRail** (☎13 15 00) and **Countrylink** (☎13 22 32) trains and buses run to: **Bathurst** (2hr., 7 per day, $13); **Blackheath** (13min., 17-23 per day, $3.20); **Dubbo** (5hr., 1 per day, $52); **Glenbrook** (50min., 18-28 per day, $5.20); **Lithgow** (45min., 12-15 per day, $6.20); **Mount Victoria** (20min., 12-15 per day, $3.60); **Orange** (3hr., 1 per day, $29); **Parramatta** (1½hr., 20-29 per day, $10); **Penrith** (1hr., 19-26 per day, $6.20); **Sydney** (2hr., 20-29 per day, $11.60); **Zig Zag Railway** (45min., 2 per day, $5.20; be sure to request this stop with the guard at the rear of the train). **Mountainlink** (☎4782 3333) runs to **Leura** ($3) and **Mount Victoria** ($5.30).

Local and Park Transportation: Blue Mountains Bus Company (☎4782 4213) connects Katoomba to Wentworth Station, with stops at Woodford, near Echo Point, the Edge Cinema, Leura Mall, the Valley of the Waters trailhead, Scenic World, and Wentworth Falls. Regular service M-F approx. 7:30am-6pm, Sa-Su 7:30am-3pm. $1-6; unlimited day pass $12. The double decker **Blue Mountains Explorer Bus** (☎4782 1866; www.explorerbus.com.au) runs a 27-stop circuit allowing passengers to get on and off as often as they choose. Buses run daily every hr. (and every 30min. along the clifftop) 9:30am-5:15pm. Day pass $32, children $16, ISIC $26. Timetables for both services are available at the Blue Mountains Tourism Authority on Echo Point. All pickup opposite the Carrington Hotel on Main St. **Mountainlink Trolley Tours** (☎1800 801 877) runs the cheapest bus tours in the area, with all-day access and unlimited stops for $15, stopping throughout the Leura and Katoomba areas.

Taxis: Katoomba Cabs (☎4782 1311) picks up 24hr. anywhere between Wentworth Falls and Mt. Victoria. Starting fare $2.80, booking fee $1.50, plus $1.62 per km.

Bike Rental: Velonova, 182 Katoomba St. (☎4782 2800; www.velonova.com.au). Mountain bikes ½ day $25, full day $40. Helmets, locks, and repair kits included. YHA/backpacker 10% discount. Open M and W-Su 9am-5:30pm.

ORIENTATION AND PRACTICAL INFORMATION

Katoomba sits just south of the Great Western Hwy., 2km west of Leura and 109km from Sydney. The town's main drag, **Katoomba Street,** runs south from the **Katoomba Railway Station** through town toward Echo Point. **Main Street,** where much of the adventure tour offices and nightlife is located, runs along the north side of town by the rail station, and changes names to Bathurst Rd. and Gang Gang St. On the other side of town, Echo Point Rd. brings visitors to the Blue Mountains' most famous sight, the Three Sisters.

Tourist Office: Blue Mountains Tourism (☎1300 653 408; www.bluemountainstourism.org.au), at the end of Echo Point Rd. Take Lurline St. south and veer left onto Echo Rd. Brochures are sparse; most of this center is a gift shop. Open daily 9am-5pm. For

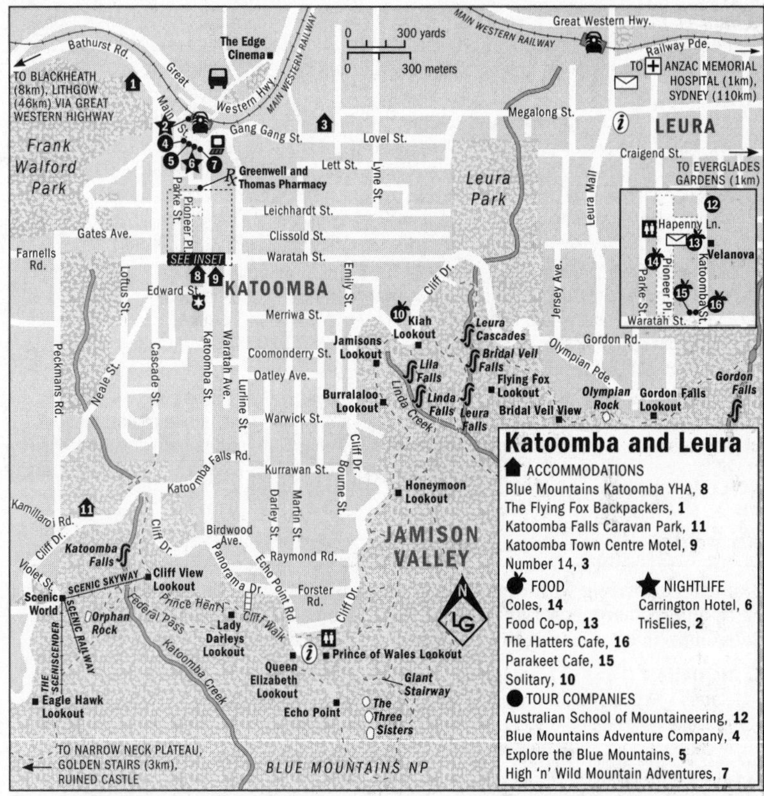

friendly hiking advice, talk to park rangers; try the **NPWS Blue Mountain Heritage Center** in Blackheath (p. 162).

Hospital: Blue Mountains District Anzac Memorial Hospital (☎4784 6500), on the Great Western Hwy., 1km east of the railway station.

Internet Access: Katoomba Book Exchange, 34 Katoomba St. (☎4782 9997), offers 15min. free Internet access with purchase. Otherwise $2.60 per 15min., $8 per hr. Open daily 10am-6pm.

Post Office: (☎13 13 18), on Pioneer Pl. Open M-F 9am-5pm. **Postal Code:** 2780.

ACCOMMODATIONS

Katoomba is especially backpacker-friendly. Although beds here are plentiful, so are the vacationers that swamp the town from November to April and on winter weekends. Book ahead during these times.

Blue Mountains Katoomba YHA, 207 Katoomba St. (☎4782 1416; bluemountains@yhansw.org.au), 10min. walk downhill from the train station. Spacious kitchen. Dining and common areas with fireplace, pool table, TV and video lounge, terrace, laundry, lockers, and parking. Helpful staff provides heaps of info. Internet access $2 per 30min. Linen included. Reception 7am-10pm. Dorms $24-26; doubles $73; ensuite $82; families $116. Non-YHA members add $3.50 per person. ❷

Number 14, 14 Lovel St. (☎4782 7104; www.bluemts.com.au/no14), small yellow house 5min. from train station. Quiet, friendly atmosphere. Outstanding kitchen and comfortable furnishings. Offers a fully self-sufficient house for 10. Reception 9-11am, 5-8:30pm. Dorms $22; doubles $59; ensuite $65; triples $66; house $250. ❷

The Flying Fox Backpackers, 190 Bathurst Rd. (☎4782 4226 or 1800 624 226; www.theflyingfox.com.au), 5min. walk west of the station. Fun, friendly, mellow, and aimed at young crowd. Small kitchen, dining area with TV, common room with log fire, outdoor chill-out hut with BBQ. Free luggage storage. Internet access $1 per 15min. Laundry $6. Key deposit $10. Reception 9am-9pm. Sites $12; dorms $22; twins and doubles $60. Weekly discounts. VIP/YHA. ❷

Katoomba Falls Caravan Park (☎4782 1835), on Katoomba Falls Rd., south of town via Katoomba St. Great location for bushwalks and Scenic World. Toilets, hot showers, indoor BBQ, laundry, and children's playground. No linen. Key deposit $20. Reception 8am-7pm. Sites for 2 $25, powered $31.70; families $26.10/34; ensuite cabins for 2 $81.55. Extra adult $13.60, extra child $6.80. ❷

Katoomba Town Centre Motel, 218-224 Katoomba St. (☎4782 1266; www.katoombamotel.com). This friendly motel is just a short stroll from the bustle of Katoomba St. and a short drive to Echo Point. Garden BBQ, game room, and laundry facilities available. Wireless Internet $4 per hr. Breakfast included. M-Th and Su standard room $104, F $124, Sa $144; superior room $118/138/158. ❺

FOOD

You can't go wrong with food on Katoomba St., which is packed with delicious cafes and restaurants serving a variety of cuisines and many vegetarian options. **Coles** supermarket is next to K-Mart on Parke St. (Open daily 6am-midnight.)

The Hatters Cafe, 197 Katoomba St. (☎4782 4212). Attached to the Hattery store. Caters to special diets including wheat-free, dairy-free, vegetarian, and vegan. Try the hotcakes with rhubarb ($11.50) or the pumpkin-macadamia nut soup ($8.50). Open M-Sa 8am-5pm, Su 8am-4pm. ❷

Food Co-Op (☎4782 5890), on Hapenny Ln. off Katoomba St. behind the post office. Sells incredibly inexpensive organic foods–fruits, nuts, wheats, and other ingredients that make the best trail mix. Open M-W and F 9am-5:30pm, Th 9am-6:30pm, Sa 8:30am-6pm, Su 10am-4:30pm. YHA 10% discount. ❶

Solitary, 90 Cliff Dr. (☎4782 1164), set on clifftop border between Katoomba and Leura. Serves great meals like mussels ($21.50) and Black Angus beef ($33.50). Outdoor seating available. Open W-F 6:30-9pm, Sa-Su noon-3pm and 6:30-9pm. ❹

Parakeet Cafe, 195b Katoomba St. (☎4782 1815), next door to The Hatters Cafe. Prepares delicious sandwiches ($5.50-6) along with more substantial meals from schnitzel ($18) to nachos ($13). Takeaway is also available. Open daily 8:30am-latenight. ❶

ENTERTAINMENT AND NIGHTLIFE

The **Edge Maxvision Cinema,** 225 Great Western Hwy., a 5min. walk from the rail station, projects *The Edge,* a 38min. IMAX/3D film on the Blue Mountains, onto a six-story screen. It's definitely a worthwhile expense. The movie, which focuses on the fragile ecosystem of the Blue Mountains, shows viewers several places inaccessible to visitors, including the secret grove where the Wollemi Pine species was recently discovered. The cinema also shows other giant-format and recent feature films. Movies play daily at 10:20, 11:05am, 12:10, 1:30, 2:15, and 5:30pm. (☎4782 8900. The Edge: $14.50; concessions $12.50; children, seniors, and YHA $9.50. Other films: M and W-Su $12.50/11.50/9.50, Tu $8.50.) Outdoor **markets**—where used clothing, flea market-type finds, and mountain-area products and produce are sold—run year-round in the Blue Mountains region. The markets tend to be hit or miss, but they can be a good place to find mountain goods in particular. In Katoomba, they are held on the 1st and 4th Saturday of each month at the Civic Centre; the 1st Sunday of each month at the Leura public school on the Great Western Hwy. in Leura; the 2nd Sunday of each month at Imperial Park in Mt. Victoria; the 3rd Sunday of each month at the community hall on the Great Western in Blackheath; and on the 2nd Saturday of each month on Macquarie Rd. in Springwood.

Katoomba's nightlife revolves around the area by the rail station. The historic **Carrington Hotel,** 15-47 Katoomba St., runs two bars: a small, mellow piano bar with live music Th-Su next to the Carrington Place on Katoomba St. (open M-Th noon-10pm, F-Sa noon-midnight, Su noon-8:30pm), and a large pub with an upstairs nightclub at 86 Main St. (☎4782 1111. Pub open M-Sa 9:30am-2am, Su 10am-11pm. Nightclub open Sa until 5am. Cover $5.) **TrisElies,** 287 Bathurst Rd., next to the rail station—not to be confused with the Greek restaurant by the same name on Main St.—is Katoomba's coolest nightclub, and draws a younger crowd with big-name DJs Friday night. By day, it's a Mexican restaurant decorated with artwork. (☎4782 1217. Nightclub open Th-Sa 9pm-3am, Su until midnight. Cover F up to $20, Sa $7.)

LOOKOUTS, WALKS, AND ACTIVITIES

ECHO POINT. Nearly everyone who visits the Blue Mountains ventures out to Echo Point, at the southernmost tip of Katoomba, to take in the geological grandeur of the **Three Sisters.** According to Aboriginal legend, the Three Sisters are beautiful maidens trapped since The Dreaming (Aboriginal creation period) in stone pillars. After sunset, strategically placed floodlights lend a surreal brilliance to these three golden dames (dusk-11pm). There are numerous short trails and dramatic overlooks in the Echo Point area, but if you're up for a longer, more demanding circuit, descend the steep and taxing 860-step **Giant Stairway Walk** (2½hr.) down the back of the Three Sisters and connect up with the **Federal Pass Trail.** At the trail junction, turn right and follow Federal Pass as it snakes its way through the Jamison Valley and past the base of **Katoomba Falls,** and the beautiful, free-standing pillar known as **Orphan Rock.** Just beyond the base of Orphan Rock are two ways out of the valley. You can hike the seemingly endless **Furber Steps** and ascend through sandstone and clay rock formations, past the spray of waterfalls and through rainforest foliage; or you can buy a ticket for the adrenaline rush of the mechanized **Scenic Railway** (see below) or walk ten minutes along the boardwalk to the sleek, steady **Scenic Cableway** (see below). From the top of the canyon, it's also possible to return to Echo Point via the uneventful **Prince Henry Cliff Walk.**

SCENIC WORLD. At the corner of Violet St. and Cliff Dr., this touristy transportation hub offers three unique perspectives on the Blue Mountains region. The **Scenic Railway** (1½hr. one-way), the world's steepest-inclined passenger-railway, is an attraction in its own right. Originally designed to haul unappreciative chunks of coal, its 52° pitch now thrills tourists and hikers during its very short trip in or out of the depths of the Jamison Valley ($8 one-way). The large, transparent **Scenic Cableway** cable car coasts from clifftop to valley floor and vice versa, offering passengers a more relaxing view of the Jamison Valley ($8 one-way). The Scenic Railway links up with popular hikes around Echo Point (see above). The **Scenic Skyway** is a cable gondola suspended high over the Katoomba Falls Gorge. Along the way, a door on the floor slides open to reveal a glass bottom, giving the impression that you are floating atop the world—the views looking down are tremendous ($8 one-way). (☎4782 2699; www.scenicworld.com.au. Open daily 9am-5pm. Trips depart approx. every 10min.)

NARROW NECK PLATEAU. Jutting out and separating the Jamison Valley and the Megalong Valley, the Narrow Neck Plateau offers short and long **walks,** excellent **mountain biking,** panoramic views, and spectacular sunsets. To reach the plateau by car, follow Cliff Dr. west out of Katoomba. Just past the Landslide Lookout, turn right onto the gravel **Glen Raphael Drive.** You can drive about 1.5km along Narrow Neck up to a locked gate, but the next 7km is for walkers or cyclists only. One kilometer after the Cliff Dr. turn-off is the trailhead for the **Golden Stairs.** This track runs down the cliff face and intersects the Federal Pass track. To get to the Scenic Railway turn left at the bottom of the stairs. **Ruined Castle** (5-6hr. round-trip), a distinctive rock formation reminiscent of crumbling turrets, can be reached by turning right at the bottom and following the path to the Ruined Castle turn-off on the right. At the Ruined Castle, a short climb to the top yields views straight across the valley to distant parts of the Blue Mountains and Kanangra-Boyd National Parks. On the return from Ruined Castle, some walkers avoid going back up the Golden Stairs and continue east instead to the Scenic Railway (see above). If you do this, add another hour to your itinerary.

TOURS. Several companies in Katoomba organize adventure trips throughout the Blue Mountains. Most are clustered at the top of Katoomba St. across from the rail station. Prices are similar across companies.

High 'n' Wild Mountain Adventures, 3/5 Katoomba St. (☎4782 6224; www.high-n-wild.com.au). Abseiling courses ½ day $95, full day $135; rock climbing $119/169; mountain bike tours $109/149; canyoning courses from $145. Winter ice-climbing courses by demand. Student/backpacker discount $10. Open daily 8:30am-5:30pm.

Explore the Blue Mountains, 1 Katoomba St. (☎4780 0000). Offers standard packages for abseiling, rock climbing, horseback riding, and canyoning. 3-Day Experience Pass includes all of the above. Prices vary, call for rates. Open daily 9am-6pm.

Blue Mountains Adventure Company, 84a Bathurst Rd. (☎4782 1271; www.bmac.com.au), opposite the rail station. Offers abseiling (full day $135), canyoning ($175), rock climbing ($165), and mountain biking on both Anderson's and Oaks Fire Trails ($185). Open daily 9am-5pm.

Australian School of Mountaineering, 166 Katoomba St. (☎4782 2014; www.asmguides.com.au), inside the Paddy Pallin outdoor shop. Offers introductory and advanced technical courses 1-10 days in length. All-day abseiling trip with lunch $125, YHA $120. Open daily 9am-5:30pm.

Blue Mountains Walkabout (☎04 0844 3822; www.bluemountainswalkabout.com). Evan, who is part Darug, takes groups on a challenging 8hr. bushwalk to Aboriginal ceremonial and living spaces, with ochre body painting, sample bush tucker, and boomerang lessons along the way. Begins at Faulconbridge rail station, ends at Springwood rail station. Tours leave daily; call for times. 16+. $95.

Tread Lightly Eco-Tours (☎4788 1229; www.treadlightly.com.au). One of few tour operators with National Advanced Ecotourism accreditation. Focuses on ecology, flora and fauna, history, and Aboriginal culture of Blue Mountains. Wilderness walks from $35; Grand Canyon walk from $85; "Rocks to Rainforest" 4WD from $95. YHA 10% discount.

BLACKHEATH ☎02

Blackheath's location makes it a natural choice as a Blue Mountains gateway, though its services are more limited than Katoomba's. To the northeast, the beautiful Grose Valley offers many of the area's best lookouts and most challenging walks. To the south, Megalong Valley is a popular spot for horseback riding. If

Blackheath is too big for you, head 7km west on the Great Western Hwy. to Mount Victoria, a quiet village that serves as an alternate Blue Mountains base.

TRANSPORTATION AND PRACTICAL INFORMATION. The Great Western Hwy. snakes 11km west and north from Katoomba to the town of Blackheath en route to Mt. Victoria and Lithgow. **Mountainlink** runs buses from Katoomba to Mt. Victoria via Blackheath and comes as close as possible to the town's major trailheads. (☎4782 3333. M-F 7:30am-6pm, Sa 6:30am-4:30pm; from $5.20.) **CityRail** train service connects Blackheath to: Glenbrook (1hr., 15-22 per day, $6.20); Katoomba (11min., 15-23 per day, $3.20); Lithgow (30min., 12 per day, $5.20); Parramatta (2hr., 15-20 per day, $10.40); Penrith (1¼hr., 15-20 per day, $8.20); Sydney (2½hr., 15-20 per day, $13). Blackheath Station is 3km from the trailhead at Govetts Leap.

Travelers can access regional tourist information with **Blue Mountains Tourism,** at Echo Point, Katoomba (☎1300 653 408). Questions about Blue Mountains National Park, Wollemi National Park, and Kanangra-Boyd National Park are best handled by the NPWS-run **Blue Mountains Heritage Centre,** at the roundabout near the end of Govetts Leap Rd. The center also has exhibits, detailed trail guides ($2-4), and refreshments. (☎4787 8877. Open daily 9am-4:30pm.)

ACCOMMODATIONS AND FOOD. The **New Ivanhoe Hotel ❸,** at the corner of the Great Western Hwy. and Govetts Leap Rd., has clean, tasteful rooms. The bistro downstairs also offers delectable meals. (☎4787 8158. Light breakfast included. Reception at bar M-Th and Su 6am-midnight, F-Sa 6am-2am. Dorms $33; ensuite $44; twins and doubles $66; ensuite family rooms $88.) **Blackheath Caravan Park ❶,** on Prince Edward St. off Govetts Leap Rd., opposite Memorial Park, has toilets, showers, and BBQ. It is also the only toilet dump point in the Blackheath area. (☎4787 8101. Key deposit $10. Reception 8am-7pm. Sites $11.35, powered $14.75; cabins for 2 $45.35, extra adult $6.80; ensuite $61.20/13.60). There are two **NPWS camping areas ❶** accessible from Blackheath: **Perrys Lookdown,** 8km from the Great Western Hwy. at the end of the mostly unpaved Hat Hill Rd. (5 walk-in sites; max. 1-night stay), and **Acacia Flat,** on the Grose Valley floor, a 4hr. hike from Govetts Leap and a 2-3hr. hike from Perrys Lookdown. Both sites are free and lack facilities beyond pit toilets. Campfires are not permitted. Water from Govetts Creek is available at Acacia Flat, but it must be treated. There is no reliable water source at Perrys Lookdown. The **Victoria and Albert Guesthouse ❺,** 19 Station St., is a beautifully restored B&B home with a pool, spa, and sauna. (☎4787 1241; victoria.albert@ourguest.com.au. Reception 8am-9pm. Doubles $120; ensuite $140, with spa $160.) Down the street from New Ivanhoe Hotel, **Vulcan's ❷,** 33 Govetts Leap Rd., is the local favorite with juicy burgers ($9-11.50), tasty pasta dishes ($8.50-13), and fresh salads ($8-12) in an informal setting. (☎4787 6899. Open F-Su noon-2:30pm and 6-9pm.)

HIKES AND LOOKOUTS. Walks in the Blackheath area vary widely in length and level of difficulty. The **Fairfax Heritage Track** (1hr. round-trip) is wheelchair accessible and leads to **Govetts Leap,** one of the most magnificent lookouts in Blue Mountains National Park. From Govetts Leap, the moderate **Pulpit Rock Track** (3hr. round-trip) follows the cliff line north for spectacular views along the way of Horseshoe Falls and a fantastic view of the Grose Valley from the Pulpit Rock lookout. The **Cliff Top Walk** travels the other direction to **Evans Lookout** (1½hr. round-trip) past the wispy **Govetts Leap Falls,** a thin stream that takes nearly ten seconds to tumble all the way into the valley below. The moderate **Grand Canyon Walking Track** (5km; 3-4hr. round-trip) is undoubtedly one of the most popular hikes in all the Blue Mountains. You can start at either **Neates Glen** or **Evans Lookout,** but if you need to park a car, leave it at the Grand Canyon Loop Carpark along the Evans Lookout Rd. The circuit passes through sandstone cliffs, wet rainforest, and exposed heathland. Anthropologists speculate that the Grand Canyon was probably a route used by Aboriginal people to gain access to the deposits of chert (a quartzite rock used in cutting tools) at the base of **Beauchamp Falls.** Archaeological evidence suggests that Aborigines occupied the Grand Canyon at least 12,000 years ago. Six kilometers north of Blackheath along the Great Western Hwy. is **Hat Hill Road,** a mostly dirt route that bumps and bounces to an excellent lookout and a popular trailhead for the **Blue Gum Forest.** Near the end of the road, the turn-off leading to the parking area for **Anvil Rock** and the magical features of the misnamed **Wind Eroded Cave** (water, actually) is well worth the side trip.

The scenic drive into the **Megalong Valley** begins on Shipley Rd., across the Great Western Hwy. from Govett's Leap Rd. Cross the railroad tracks from the highway and take an immediate left onto Station St., following it until it turns right onto Shipley Rd. Megalong Rd. is a left turn from Shipley Rd., leading down to a picturesque farmland area that contrasts nicely with the surrounding wilderness. In the valley, outfitters supply horses and conduct guided trail rides. **Werriberri Trail Rides** is 10km along Megalong Rd. near Werriberri Lodge. (☎4787 9171. Open daily 9am-3:30pm; reservations 7:30am-4pm. $48 per hr.; $63 per 1½hr.; $78 per 2hr. 2-9 day rides by request.) The **Megalong Australian Heritage Centre,** a bit farther south on Megalong Rd., is an aspiring cowboy's dream. The sprawling country-western ranch features upscale accommodations, an affordable restaurant that serves modern Australian cuisine, a friendly staff, livestock-lassoing shows, guided horseback riding tours, and guided 4WD bush trips. It also rents horses and 4WD vehicles for self-guided tours on more than 2000 acres of land. Inquire about job offerings. (☎4787 8188; www.megalong.com. Open daily 8am-5:30pm. Rides daily 9, 11am, 1, 3pm. 2hr. ride $85, full day $165; self-guided $60 per hr. 4WD 2hr. $50.)

BLUE MOUNTAINS NATIONAL PARK

The largest and most touristed of the Blue Mountain parks, the Blue Mountains National Park is one of eight protected areas making up the World Heritage site collectively known as the Greater Blue Mountains Area.

BLUE MOUNTAINS AT A GLANCE

AREA: 208,756 hectares.

FEATURES: Govetts Leap (Blackheath), Three Sisters (Katoomba), Wentworth Falls.

HIGHLIGHTS: Over 140km bushwalking trails, horseback riding, canyoning, and riding the world's steepest railway.

GATEWAYS: Glenbrook (p. 165), Katoomba (p. 158), Blackheath (p. 162).

CAMPING: Minimum-impact camping allowed; see individual regions.

FEES: Vehicles $7 (Glenbrook only).

ORIENTATION AND PRACTICAL INFORMATION

Blue Mountains National Park lies between Kanangra-Boyd National Park to the south and Wollemi National Park to the north. Two east-west highways partition the park into three sections: the section north of the **Bells Line of Road,** the section south of the **Great Western Highway,** and the small section between the two.

Blue Mountains Tourism operates offices in Glenbrook and Katoomba. (☎1300 653 408; www.australiabluemountains.com.au. Glenbrook open M-F 9am-5pm, Sa-Su 8:30am-4:30pm. Katoomba open daily 9am-5pm.) The NPWS-run **Blue Mountains Heritage Centre,** at the roundabout near the end of Govetts Leap Rd. in Blackheath, handles questions regarding the parks. (☎4787 8877. Open daily 9am-4:30pm.)

BLUE MOUNTAINS: A TOWN-BY-TOWN GUIDE

ALONG THE GREAT WESTERN HIGHWAY

Leaving Sydney, the Great Western Hwy. passes Penrith just before the entrance to the Blue Mountains National Park. It extends to Lithgow, passing Katoomba and Blackheath on its way through the park.

GLENBROOK. Glenbrook is a gateway town just north of the easternmost entrance to the park. From the highway, take Ross St. until it ends, turn left on Burfitt Pde. (later named Bruce Rd.), and follow it to the park. The walking track to **Red Hands Cave** starts at the national park's entrance station and runs an easy 8km circuit that follows a creek through patches of open forest, leading ultimately to a gallery of **hand stencils** attributed to the Darug Aborigines. Along the way to the cave, the trail passes the turn-off for **Jellybean Pool,** a popular swimming hole near the park's entrance. You can reduce the length of the hike to a mere 300m stroll if you drive to the Red Hands carpark and begin there.

The **Tourist Information Centre,** off the Great Western Hwy., is a convenient place to pick up maps and information about the Blue Mountains before heading further into the region. (☎4739 6266. Open daily 9am-5pm.) Four kilometers beyond the Bruce Rd. entrance, over mostly paved roads, is the **Euroka Campground ❶.** The site has pit toilets and BBQ, but no water. Kangaroos congregate in the area at dawn and dusk. The park entrance is locked in the evenings (in summer 7pm-8:30am; in winter 6pm-8:30am); campers are advised to bring ample firewood, food, and drinking water. Call the **NPWS** in Richmond to book ahead. (☎4588 5247. Open M-F 9am-5pm. Sites $5, children $3. Vehicles $7 per day.) Bush camping is free.

BLAXLAND. At Blaxland, roughly 4km west of Glenbrook, Layton Ave. turns off onto a pleasant 2km detour toward **Lennox Bridge,** the **oldest bridge** on the Australian mainland. West of Blaxland (and the towns of Warrimoo, Valley Heights, and Springwood) lies **Faulconbridge,** site of the National Trust-owned **Norman Lindsay Gallery,** at 14 Norman Lindsay Cres. The gallery displays a large collection of sculptures, oil paintings, etchings, marionettes, and ship models by the multitalented artist who once inhabited the house. To get to the gallery from Sydney, turn right off the Great Western Hwy. onto Grose Rd., in Falconbridge, and follow the well-posted signs. (☎4751 1067. Open daily 10am-4pm. $9, ISIC $6.) Public transportation to the site is limited to **taxis** from the Springwood Railway Station.

LOCAL LEGEND

THE THREE SISTERS

The Blue Mountains, spanning over 200,000 hectares, are a beauty to behold. Their name comes from a distinctive blue haze produced by a combination of tiny droplets of eucalyptus oil, dust particles, and water vapour, which scatter rays of light predominantly blue in color.

The unusual mist lends an eerie glow to the area, made more otherworldly by the myriad Aboriginal tales which explain the park's unusual formations.

Among the most famous of these stories is the legend of the Three Sisters, one of the mountains' main attractions. It tells the tragic story of "Meehni," "Wimlah" and "Gunnedoo," members of the Aboringinal Katoomba tribe. Legend has it that the sisters had fallen in love with brothers from another tribe, and tribal law forbade them to marry. A battle ensued when the brothers tried to fight for their loves. Sensing the danger, a witchdoctor cast a spell over the sisters to protect them. He turned them into stone and set them high above the mountain valley, intending to return them to human form after the battle.

But it was not to be. The witchdoctor was killed in the battle, and the sisters are for all eternity cast in stone. They still preside over the valley today; their plight a symbol of the ancient battle, and a sad reminder of the love they never had.

WOODFORD. Woodford, about 15km east of Katoomba on the Great Western Hwy., is the start of a popular **mountain biking** trail. The **Woodford Oaks Fire Trail** is a 27km, mostly downhill track that leads to Glenbrook. Woodford also serves as a turn-off to a few popular campgrounds. A left off the highway onto Park Rd., a left onto Railway Pde., and a right onto Bedford Rd., leads to the **Murphys Glen Campground,** 10km south of Woodford. Located within a eucalyptus and angophoras forest, the campground is free and has pit toilets but lacks drinking water. Contact the **Blackheath Office** (☎4787 8877).

WENTWORTH FALLS. The town of **Wentworth Falls,** 14km beyond Woodford, is renowned for its picturesque waterfall walks and plant diversity—more varieties of plants are found in the Blue Mountains than in all of Europe. To find the trailhead at the **Wentworth Falls Picnic Area,** turn off the Great Western Hwy. onto Falls Rd. and continue to the end of the road. From this area, several viewpoints are within easy reach. The 15min. walk to **Princes Rock** offers the best views for the least effort. It ends at a lookout with views of Wentworth Falls, Kings Tableland, and Mt. Solitary. The 45min. walk to **Rocket Point Lookout** wanders through open heathland and has views of the Jamison Valley. To find the trailhead at the **Conservation Hut,** turn off the highway at either Falls Rd. or Valley Rd., turn right onto Fletcher St., and continue straight to the carpark.

For an ambitious and stunning loop hike, begin at the hut off Fletcher St. and follow the **Valley of the Waters Track** to **Empress Lookout,** head down the metal stairs, then follow the trail along the Valley of Waters Creek. Take the **Wentworth Pass** (6km, 5hr.)—a strenuous trail with major payoffs, including spectacular falls, rainforests, and views—through the valley to Slacks Stairs, where the steep steps take you up to **Wentworth Falls** and the **Wentworth Falls Picnic Area.** From the carpark, you can head back to the hut via the **Shortcut Track** (5hr.) or the **Undercliff-Overcliff Track** (4km, 2hr.). Spectacular scenery and lush hanging swamps will reward the extra effort. **National Pass** (5.4km, 4hr.), an alternate route through the valley between Empress Lookout and Slacks Stairs, is another good option. On starry nights, visit the **Kings Tableland Observatory,** 55 Hordern Rd. A local astronomer shows you constellations, globular clusters, and planets. (☎4757 2954. Open F-Su from 7pm; Daylight Saving Time from 8pm, Sa-Su 10am-4pm for solar observing. $9.90, families $28.) To reach the **Ingar Campground ❶,** drive west past Woodford (and the towns of Hazelbrook, Lawson, and Bullburra), turn left off the highway onto Tableland Rd., travel 1.6km, turn left at Queen Elizabeth Dr., and proceed 9.5km along an unpaved road to Ingar. Set amid a grove of Scribbly Gum Trees with trunks "scribbled on" by burrowing insects, the free campground has pit toilets and BBQs but lacks drinking water and cooking facilities. Nearby, a small pond and creek make the spot popular for picnics and camping.

LEURA. The pleasant and affluent summertime town of Leura, 5km west of Wentworth Falls and adjacent to Katoomba, offers shops, cafes, and galleries along its central street, Leura Mall. **Everglades Gardens,** 37 Everglades St., is a lush example of the floral cultivation for which the town is known. Designed by Dutch master gardener Paul Sorensen, this five-hectare estate in the Jamison Valley is a great example of classical Australian landscaping, and is now owned by the National Trust. (☎4784 1938. Open daily Sept.-Feb. 10am-5pm; Mar.-Aug. 10am-4pm. $7, children $3, YHA $5.) Near the gardens, Fitzroy St. intersects Everglades Rd. and leads east to Watkins Rd., which turns into Sublime Point Rd. before ending at the breathtaking overlook at **Sublime Point.** For travelers continuing toward Katoomba, the 8km **Cliff Drive,** beginning at Gordon Rd. near the south end of Leura Mall, provides a scenic escape from the road, passing many lookouts and trailheads. In Katoomba, Cliff Dr. turns into Echo Point Rd. The staff at the **Blue Mountains Accommodation Centre,** 208 The Mall, books lodging and guided tours. (☎4784 2222. Open Tu-Sa 10am-5pm.)

ALONG THE BELLS LINE OF ROAD

This 87km drive runs north of the Great Western Hwy. through the Blue Mountains and just below Wollemi National Park. It connects with the Great Western Hwy. in the town of Lithgow in the west, and runs east to Windsor.

MOUNT TOMAH BOTANIC GARDEN. Twelve kilometers west of Bilpin, Mt. Tomah Botanic Garden is the cool-climate and high-altitude plant collection of Sydney's Royal Botanic Garden. With the exception of the formal terrace garden, the plants (including 13 Wollemi pines) thrive on the rich volcanic soil and grow in natural conditions. In spring (Sept.-Oct.), the large collection of rhododendrons and other flowers bloom, and in autumn (Apr.-May), the deciduous forests change their colors. Free tours depart from the visitors center. (☎4567 2154. Open daily Oct.-Feb. 10am-5pm; Mar.-Sept. 10am-4pm. $4.40, children $2.20, families $8.80.)

MOUNT WILSON. People come from far and wide to see the formal gardens and unspoiled rainforest of Mt. Wilson, 8km north of Bells Line of Road, between Mt. Tomah and Bell. For a sample of the fern-laden rainforest, turn right onto Queens Ave. off the main road through town and proceed about 500m until you reach a park area on the left. From there, follow signs to the moderate 45min. **Waterfall Trek** (with steep steps) that leads to the base of two small waterfalls. The gardens stay open throughout the year, including **Sefton Cottage,** on Church Ln. (☎4756 2034; open daily 9am-6pm; $3) and **Merry Garth,** on Davies Ln., 500m from Mt. Irvine Rd. (☎4756 2121. Open daily 9am-6pm. $3.)

ZIG ZAG RAILWAY. The Zig Zag Railway, 10km east of Lithgow at Clarence, is a functional train operating on a piece of the 1869 track that first made regular travel possible across the Blue Mountains and down into the Lithgow Valley. The classic views combined with the historical value of the trip justifies the hefty ticket price. (☎6355 2955. 1½hr. tours depart daily at 11am, 1, and 3pm. Round-trip $20, concessions $16, ages 18 and under $10, families $50.) By request, **CityRail** trains from Sydney's Central Station stop near the bottom of the track ($15.20).

LITHGOW. The Great Western Hwy. and Bells Line of Road meet on the west side of the Blue Mountains at Lithgow, a medium-sized, semi-industrial town at the end of Sydney's CityRail line. The town provides a good base from which to explore nearby wilderness areas such as Wollemi National Park (p. 167) and the Jenolan Caves and Kanangra-Boyd National Park (p. 168). The highest lookout in the region (1130m) is well worth the 5min. detour along the **Hassans Walls Link** drive. **Blackfellows Hands Reserve,** 24km north of Lithgow, off Wolgen Rd. to Newnes, was a meeting place for Aboriginal tribes; paintings still adorn the walls of the cave. The 4WD-accessible **Gardens of Stone National Park,** 30km north of Lithgow, features pagoda-like formations created by millions of years of erosion. The spectacular granite formations of **Evans Crown Nature Reserve** (☎6354 8155), 32km west of Lithgow, make for a climbers' paradise.

Several hotels line Main St., but the **Grand Central Hotel ❷**, 69 Main St., is the pick of the litter. Take a left out of the train station and walk two blocks. (☎6351 3050. Bistro open M-F noon-2pm and 6-9pm. Key deposit $20. Breakfast included. Singles $25.) The **Blue Bird Cafe ❶**, 118 Main St., serves sandwiches ($3-7), fried dishes, and tasty milkshakes. (☎6352 4211. Open daily 6:30am-7pm.) The **visitors center,** 1 Cooerwull Rd. off the Great Western Hwy., just past the intersection with Main St., books accommodations and provides maps and information on Wollemi National Park. (☎1300 760 276; www.tourism.lithgow.com. Open daily 9am-5pm.)

WOLLEMI NATIONAL PARK

Covering 4875 sq. km, Wollemi (WOOL-em-eye) National Park is the largest wilderness area and second largest park in New South Wales. It extends north of Blue Mountains

National Park all the way to the Hunter and Goulburn River valleys (see **Mudgee,** p. 243). Because 2WD access is limited, the park still has many pockets of undiscovered land. One such area yielded an amazing find in 1994, when scientists found a species of pine tree known previously only through fossils. Fewer than 50 adult **Wollemi Pine** trees have been found in three remote locations in the region, but these few trees provide a link to the past that has helped researchers retrace evolutionary steps back to the era of dinosaurs. The grove location is a well-kept secret, and scientists studying the trees must sterilize instruments and clothing to avoid bringing disease to the grove.

The southernmost entrance to the park is at **Bilpin** on Bells Line of Road. In this corner of the park, also accessible from Putty Rd. north of Windsor, the **Colo River** slices the landscape along the 30km Colo Gorge. The picturesque, car-accessible **camping area** at **Wheeny Creek ❶** lies near good walking tracks and swimming holes. Entrance and campgrounds are free. Additional info is available at the **NPWS** office, 370 Windsor Rd., in Richmond. (☎4588 5247. Open M-F 9:30am-12:30pm and 1:30-5pm.) The NPWS office in Mudgee (☎6372 7199; mudgee@npws.nsw.gov.au; open M-Th 9am-4pm) services the northwest section of the park and can give info about camping in **Dunns Swamp ❶**, 25km east of Rylstone. (Compost toilets, no water. $3, children $2.) Farther west, a 37km unsealed road from Lithgow takes observers within 1.5km of **Glow Worm Tunnel,** an abandoned railway tunnel housing hundreds of tiny bioluminescent worms. There are no marked trails in the northern section of Wollemi National Park.

KANANGRA-BOYD NATIONAL PARK

Southwest of the Blue Mountains National Park, Kanangra-Boyd National Park stuns visitors with stark wilderness punctuated by rivers, creeks, caves, and the dramatic sandstone cliffs that mark the edges of the Boyd Plateau. The park's remote location and rugged terrain attract experienced bushwalkers.

The park is nonetheless worthwhile for casual visitors who follow its only 2WD access road, the unpaved Kanangra Walls Rd., across the **Boyd Plateau** to the famous lookouts at **Kanangra Walls.** Use caution when driving; accidents from speeding are common as the roads are often unsealed and frequently crossed by wildlife. From the east past Mt. Victoria, drive to Jenolan Caves off the Great Western Hwy. From there, a 5km dirt road will lead to the park and the junction with Kanangra Walls Rd. Turn left at the intersection and drive another 26km to the Kanangra Walls carpark. From the west, drive to the town of **Oberon** and follow the unpaved Jenolan Caves Rd. south to the junction with Kanangra Walls Rd. Turn right to reach the lookouts. The **NPWS** office, 38 Ross St., Oberon (northeast of the park), has details on the park's longer tracks. Be sure to call before visiting, or you may find the branch unattended. Cave permits must be obtained from NPWS at least four weeks in advance. (☎6336 1972. Open M-F 9am-4:30pm.)

The **Boyd River Campground ❶,** on Kanangra Walls Rd. 6km before Kanangra Walls, has the park's only car-accessible camping. There are pit toilets and fireplaces. Bring your own wood or a camp stove. Water is available from the Boyd River but it should be treated before consumption. Camping is free, but park fees apply ($7 per vehicle per day). Most bushwalks in the park are not signposted, with the exception of three **scenic walks,** which begin at the Kanangra Walls carpark. **Lookout Walk** (20min. round-trip) is a wheelchair-accessible path leading to two viewpoints. The first gazes out across the Kanangra Creek gorge toward **Mount Cloudmaker,** and the other peers into the ravines at the head of the eight-tiered, 400m **Kanangra Falls.** The **Waterfall Walk** (20min. one-way with steep return) leads from the second lookout on a sparkling pool at the bottom of **Kalang Falls.** The moderate **Plateau Walk** (2-3hr.) branches off from the Lookout Walk between the carpark and the lookout on Mount Cloudmaker, descending briefly from the plateau before ascending to Kanangra Tops for views of Kanangra Walls. Along the way to the Tops, **Dance Floor Cave** contains indented floors and other signs of old-time recreation in the park. A water container placed in the cave in 1940 catches pure, drinkable water that drips down from the cave ceiling. Longer walks are available in the park as well, including the three- to four-day **hike** from Kanangra Walls to Katoomba via Mt. Stormbreaker, Mt. Cloudmaker, the Wild Dog Mountains, and the Narrow Neck Plateau. These longer, more intensive walks must always be planned in advance with help from the NPWS.

JENOLAN CAVES

The amazing limestone and crystal formations of the Jenolan Caves have intrigued visitors since they opened to the public in 1838. All of the caves are stunning just to look at, and several adventure tours (see below) offer visitors the chance to explore further. The caves, which are 46km south of the Great Western Hwy. from Hartley, on the northwestern edge of Kanangra-Boyd National park, can be reached by bus from Katoomba (p. 158). The **Jenolan Caves Reserve Trust,** located at the Jenolan Caves turn-off, runs **guided tours** to nine different areas within the massive cave system. (☎6359 3911; www.jenolancaves.org.au. Ticket office open daily 9am-4:45pm. M-F 14 tours per day, Sa 24, Su 21. $17-32. YHA 10% discount.)

If you only have time to explore one cave, head to Lucas Cave, Imperial Cave, or Chiefly Cave. **Lucas Cave** (1½hr., $17) displays a broad range of features including a 54m high cathedral, though the large crowds detract from the experience. Cello concerts are given once a month in the cathedral; call ahead for dates. ($45, children $25; includes cave admission.) **Imperial Cave** (1½hr., $17) has a more tolerable flow of visitors as well as fascinating stalactites and stalagmites. Kids—and even adults—marvel at the artificial colored lights reflected in **Chifley Cave** (1hr., $17). The **Temple of Baal** (1½hr., $25) and the **River Cave** (2hr., $32) are also exciting options for spelunkers hoping to escape tourist mobs. **Orient Cave** and **Chifley Cave** (1½hr., $17) are partially wheelchair accessible.

Adventure tours, run by the National Trust, takes small groups of people who want to get down and dirty in some of the cave system's less accessible areas. These trips involve moderate to strenuous climbing, some crawling, and a healthy dose of darkness. The most popular adventure tour runs to the **Plughole** (2hr., $58; departs daily 1:15pm). Spelunkers heading to the Plughole must be at least 10 years old; those venturing into **Aladdin Cave** (3hr., $60.50; departs 9am last Su every month) must be at least 12 years old, and those exploring **Mammoth Cave** (6hr., $155; 1st Sa every month) must be at least 16. Check out the **Themes, Mysteries, Legends and Ghosts Tour** to add entertainment to your cave exploration. (2hr., $32.) For those who prefer to stay above ground, many pathways amble along the surface and lead to **Carlotta Arch, Devils Coachhouse, McKeown's Valley,** and the **Blue Lake.**

Free overnight **camping** ❶ is available at Jenolan Caves. Each site has a fire pit, and the campground has shared amenities with drinking water. Serious outdoor enthusiasts might want to head off for two to three days of hiking along the original dirt roadway that once connected Katoomba and Jenolan Caves back in the late 1800s. Today there is the **Six Foot Track,** a 42km trail that runs from the Jenolan Caves to Nellies Glen Rd. off the Great Western Hwy., at the western end of Katoomba. The trail takes three days and is quite steep in places; hikers must bring their own water. Overnight camping is also available at four primitive sites along the way. One-way transfers with **Fantastic Aussie Tours** (☎4782 1866) to Katoomba are available from Jenolan Caves. ($35, children $25.)

HUNTER VALLEY

Located within a few hours' drive of Sydney and known for its famous wine exports, the Hunter Valley is a popular holiday destination for international travelers and Sydneysiders alike. Over 120 wineries take advantage of the region's warm, dry climate, and sandy loam creek soils. Guesthouses and B&Bs dot the landscape, catering to the weekend tourist crowd. Though only 8-10% of all Australian wines are made from Hunter Valley fruit, local vintages claim more than their share of national wine trophies and medals. Chief among the varieties produced in the area are the peppery red Shiraz and the citrusy white Semillon. The region can be explored on a budget via free wine and cheese tastings, a rental car, and a designated driver. Most of the vineyards are clustered around Pokolbin in the lower Hunter Valley, just outside Cessnock's town center at the base of the Brokenback Mountains, but several notable labels are situated in the upper Hunter, centered around the small town of Denman.

TRANSPORTATION AND TOURS

The best time to visit the Hunter Valley is mid-week, when there are fewer people and tours and accommodations are less expensive. **Countrylink** (☎13 22 32) departs daily from Sydney to Scone (4½hr., $43) via Muswellbrook (3½hr., $38). **Rover Coaches,** 231 Vincent St., in Cessnock, runs a bus from Sydney Central Station to Cessnock and the Cessnock Visitor Information Centre. (☎4990 1699; www.rovercoaches.com.au. Departs 8:30am. $35, round-trip $60. ISIC $25/40.) A bus also directly connects Cessnock and Newcastle (1¼hr.; M-F 5 per day, Sa 2 per day; $12). Try taking the bus to Maitland (35min.; M-F 14 per day, Sa-Su 3-6per day; $8) and then catch the **CityRail** train to Newcastle (50min., every 30min, $4.40). **Bicycle rental** is available from **Hunter Valley Cycling,** in the Hunter Valley Garden complex (☎04 1828 1480; www.huntervalleycycling.com.au; full day $30, 2 days $45), as well as **Grapemobile Bicycle Hire** in Pokolbin, at the corner of McDonalds Rd. and Palmers Ln. (☎04 1840 4039. ½ day $22, full day $30.) A general guideline for drivers is that five tastings (20mL each) equals one standard drink. If your revelries get the best of you, **Cessnock Radio Cabs** (☎4990 1111) can get you home safely.

Starting in Newcastle or Maitland, the standard 10- to 20-person tour generally lasts from 9am to 5pm (10am-4pm from Cessnock) and visits four or five wineries. The **Vineyard Shuttle Service** lets passengers request stops instead of following a strict itinerary. (☎4991 3655; www.vineyardshuttle.com.au. M-F $42, Sa-Su $45. Add $10 for evening restaurant, airport, and golf transfers.) **Shadows** visits boutiques and large, commercial wineries. Book ahead to arrange door-to-door transfers for Newcastle and surrounding addresses. (☎4990 7002; $45.) **Hunter Vineyard Tours** (☎4991 1659; www.huntervineyardtours.com.au) picks up from Cessnock ($50, with lunch $75), Newcastle, and Maitland (both $55/80). **Trekabout** creates a more intimate setting by limiting tours to 12. (☎4990 8277. ½ day $35, full day $45.) **Horse-drawn carriage tours** generally start at $45 and are available through **Paxton Brown** (☎4998 7362), on Deasys Rd., and **Pokolbin Horse Coaches** (☎4998 7305), on McDonald's Rd. **Wonderbus** runs 20-person groups straight to the Hunter Valley from Sydney. Wonderbus also offers a combo trip to the Blue Mountains in the morning followed by a wine tour in the Hunter Valley, a trip to a wildlife park, and a cruise on Sydney Harbour. (☎9630 0529 or 1300 556 357; www.wonderbus.com.au. Departs 7am, returns 7:15pm. $109, ISIC and backpackers $89.)

WINERIES

Most wineries are open for free tastings and occasional tours daily 10am-5pm (some 9:30am-4:30pm), although some of the smaller ones are only open on weekends. Of the over 100 wineries, the largest are **Drayton's, Lindemans, McGuigan's, McWilliams-Mount Pleasant Estate, Rothbury Estate, Tyrrell's,** and **Wyndham Estate.** Smaller boutiques, such as **Ivanhoe, Pokolbin Estate, Rothvale,** and **Sobel's,** only sell their wines on the premises. While not as glitzy, they are generally more intimate and relaxed. Check with Hunter Valley Wine Country Tourism about free tours of individual wineries. Wine prices vary widely, but bottles typically start around $15.

LOWER HUNTER VALLEY ☎02

Most visitors to the Hunter stay in the very accessible lower valley, where wineries are concentrated in the Pokolbin and Rothbury shires, just north of the town of **Cessnock** (pop. 45,000). Travelers who use Cessnock as a base to explore the wineries can save money by staying at one of the town's budget motels or pub stays, but Cessnock lacks the charm that impels many to visit the valley in the first place.

ORIENTATION AND PRACTICAL INFORMATION. Those traveling by car should follow signs on the **F3 Freeway** (Sydney-Newcastle) to Cessnock, which is approximately 2hr. from Sydney and 20min. from Newcastle. The **Hunter Valley Wine Country Tourism Inc. and Visitors Centre** (☎4990 0900; www.winecountry.com.au), 455 Wine Country Dr., 6km north of Cessnock toward Branxton, will book vineyard tours and accommodations, and has a daily specials board with cheaper standby rates at guesthouses and B&Bs. The free *Hunter Valley Wine Country Visitors*

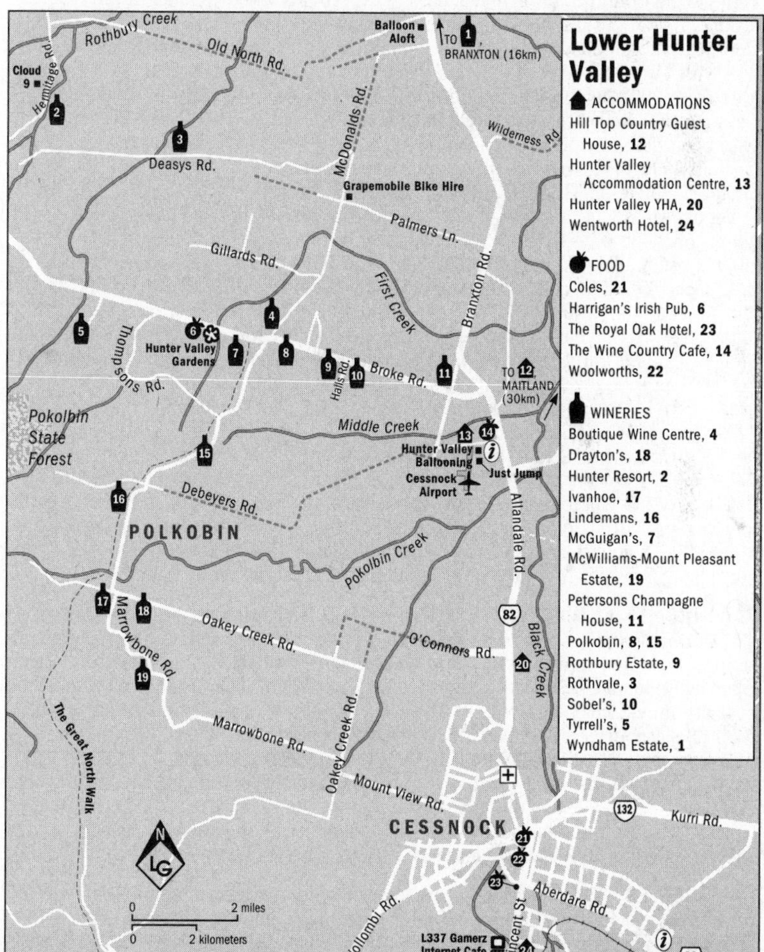

NEW SOUTH WALES

Guide has an indispensable map, as well as information on wineries, cellars, attractions, restaurants, and accommodations. (☎4990 0900; www.winecountry.com.au. Open M-F 9am-5.30pm, Sa 9am-5pm, Su 9am-4pm.)

ACCOMMODATIONS AND FOOD. The **Hunter Valley YHA ❷,** 100 Country Dr., offers very affordable backpacker accommodations close to the wineries. Facilities include a pool, sauna, BBQ area, and library. (☎4991 3278. Internet $8 per 2hr. Laundry $7. Free bike rental. Organized tours $35. Dorms $25-28; doubles $79, ensuite $90.) The **Hill Top Country Guest House ❹,** 81 Talga Rd., in Rothbury, is a 15min. drive from the visitors center via Lovedale Rd.; it offers horseback riding, a pool, billiards, and a gorgeous view of the countryside. (☎4930 7111; www.hilltopguesthouse.com.au. Breakfast included. Twins and kings with shared bath M-Th and Su $90-180, F-Sa $290-480 for 2 nights.) The **Hunter Valley Accommodation Centre ❸,** 453 Wine Country Dr., about a 10min. drive north of Cessnock, next to Hunter Valley Wine Country Tourism, has basic, clean rooms and the cheapest motel rates around. Ask about discounts on skydiving next door. (☎4991 4222. Pool and BBQ. Continental breakfast included. Wheelchair accessible. Heated ensuite motel doubles with TV M-Th and Su $70, F-Sa $100; family rooms that sleep up to 13 also available from $90. Discounts available.) Less expensive pub stays are available in Cessnock's town center. **Wentworth Hotel ❸,** on Vincent St., is one of the nicer ones, with beautifully decorated, spacious rooms and a staff that takes pride in its business. (☎4990 1364; www.wentworthhotelcessnock.com.au. Continental breakfast included. Singles M-Th $50, F-Su $75; doubles $70/95.)

Though Cessnock has few, if any, noteworthy restaurants and cafes, there are a couple of cheap ways to eat well in the Lower Hunter. **The Wine Country Cafe ❶,** at the Hunter Valley Wine Country Visitors Centre on Wine Country Dr., serves big breakfast meals ($5-14.50), delicious gourmet sandwiches ($10.50-13.50), hot drinks ($3-5), and sweet treats. (☎4990 9208; www.winecountrycafe.com.au. Open daily 9am-5pm.) Many vineyards have restaurants and cafes. Both **Woolworths** and **Coles** supermarkets lie near Cooper and Darwin St. in Cessnock. **Harrigans Irish Pub** is the center of Lower Hunter Valley nightlife. Friday and Saturday nights are packed with a mixed crowd partying to popular funk, while Tuesday night from 7pm is poker night. (☎4998 4000. Open M-W and Su 7:30am-11:30pm, Th-Sa 7:30am-2am.) For pub-going in Cessnock's town center, head to one of the local favorites that line Vincent St. **The Royal Oak Hotel,** 221 Vincent St., which is a popular scene for many locals, plays host to the **Oak Brasserie ❸** where seafood is the speciality of the house. Honey and sesame chili king prawns ($16) and fresh ocean trout ($17) are two of the favorites. Set menus for lunch ($7-13) and dinner ($10-15) are also available. (☎4990 2366. Open noon-2pm and 6-8pm. Bar open M-F 11am-midnight, Sa 10am-1am, Su noon-10.30pm.)

SIGHTS AND ACTIVITIES. The **Hunter Valley Gardens,** on the corner of Broke and McDonalds Rd., is a touristy shopping complex that also contains 25 hectares of stunning sculpted gardens with 12 different themes. (☎4998 4000; www.hvg.com.au. Open daily 9am-5pm. $19.50, children $10, families $49.) The views are well worth the cost at the **Just Jump Skydive,** 210 Allandale Rd. (☎4322 9884. Tandem dives from $320.) **Balloon Aloft** (☎1800 028 568; www.balloonaloft.com), **Cloud Nine** (☎1300 555 711; www.cloud9balloonflights.com), and **Hunter Valley Ballooning** (☎1800 818 191; www.balloonsafaris.com.au) all have sunrise hot air balloon flights lasting roughly one hour. ($250-295, usually includes a champagne breakfast.) Hill Top Country Guest House (see **Accommodations,** p. 172) conducts 1½hr. **horseback rides** ($50) as well as nighttime **4WD wildlife tours** ($30, children $15) to observe nocturnal animals.

WINERIES. The vineyards of the lower Hunter are situated along a tangle of rural roads; the free **map** from the Hunter Valley Wine Country Visitors Centre is the best way to navigate them. Even so, the entire area is well-signposted with large billboard maps at major intersections. A good place to start is the Hunter Resort, where the **Hunter Valley Wine School** gives wine tasting lessons. The tour of their Hermitage Road Cellar ($5, daily 11am and 2pm) finishes with an evaluation of three whites and three reds. (☎4998 7777. Daily 9-11am; $25. Book ahead.) In addition to free tastings, **Tyrrell's** (☎4993 7000), on Broke Rd., gives free 1hr. tours (M-Sa 1:30pm) at this 145-year-old, family-run business. **McGuigan's** (☎4998 7402; www.mcguigan-wines.com.au), on McDonalds Rd., is the valley's busiest winery. Daily tours ($3) depart at noon. Also in the McGuigan complex, the **Hunter Valley Cheese Factory** (☎4998 7744) offers free tastings. **Wyndham Estate** (☎4938 3444; www.wyndhamestate.com), on Dalwood Rd., is the oldest winery in Australia, having first planted vines in 1828. Today, it has a huge tasting room and gives free tours at 11am. **Petersons Champagne House** (☎4998 7881; www.petersonhouse.com.au), at the corner of Broke and Branxton Rd., is the only place in New South Wales strictly devoted to the bubbly, and also has an interesting selection of sparkling red wines. Of the smaller boutique wineries in the lower valley, **Rothvale** (☎4998 7290), on Deasys Rd., consistently receives high praise. Groups can arrange for a free 1½hr. wine education session. Also notable, **Ivanhoe** (☎4998 7325; www.ivanhoewines.com.au), on Marrowbone Rd., is owned and operated by a member of the distinguished Drayton wine-making family. The vineyard produces gutsy reds and a deliciously fruity dessert wine. The **Boutique Wine Centre** (☎4998 7474), on Broke Rd., centers its extensive collection on the "rising stars" of the Hunter Valley.

UPPER HUNTER VALLEY ☎02

A few towns northeast of Cessnock are popular bases for exploring Upper Hunter; budget accommodations and cheap food can be found in all of them.

SINGLETON. This sleepy town (pop. 21,000) is in between Lower and Upper Hunter on the New England Hwy. Most notable for its massive sundial—the Southern Hemisphere's largest—Singleton is less upscale than Scone and less lively than Muswellbrook. Nevertheless, Singleton attracts visitors with its central location and numerous pub stays, specialty shops, and takeaway counters, most of which line the town's main drag, **George Street.** If pub stays aren't for you, clean, affordable rooms can be found at **Benjamin Singleton Motel ❺**, 24 New England Hwy. (☎6572 2922. At the start of George St., just as you exit the New England Hwy. Singles $69-72; doubles $79-84. Extra person $12.) The **Visitors Information Centre,** 39 George St., on the New England Hwy., provides heaps of info about the Hunter. (☎6571 5888. Open daily 9am-5pm.)

MUSWELLBROOK. Farther northwest on the New England Hwy., Muswellbrook (MUSCLE-brook; pop. 16,000) is closest to Upper Hunter Valley attractions. The town has a large shopping center, and many historic buildings line the 4.5km **Muswellbrook Heritage walk,** beginning at the Old Tea House on Bridge St. (New England Hwy.). The highway is also the site of a living **Vietnam Memorial;** a grove of 519 trees represents each Australian casualty. **Eatons Hotel ❸,** 188 Bridge St., has basic rooms in an 1830s building. (☎6543 2403. Reception and pub open M-Th 7am-midnight, F-Sa 7am-1:30am, Su 7am-10pm. Singles $35; doubles $50; triples $75.) **Pinaroo Leisure Park ❶** is 3km south on the New England Hwy. (☎6543 3905. Pool, laundry, BBQ, and social room. Powered sites for 2 $20; cabins $55.) The **tourist office,** 87 Hill St., just off Bridge St., shares a building with the Upper Hunter Wine Centre, which gives free regional wine tastings. (☎6541 4050; www.muswellbrook.org.au. Open daily 9am-5pm.)

SCONE. Scone, 26km north on the New England Hwy., is a more charming option than Singleton and Muswellbrook for Upper Hunter Valley accommodations. Scone is a small, pretty town that prides itself on being the horse capital of Australia. Each year the two-week-long **Scone Horse Festival** (www.sconehorsefestival.com) in mid-May culminates in two days of thoroughbred racing for the Scone Cup. The race course is five minutes from the town center. The **Highway Caravan Park ❶**, 248 New England Hwy., is a serviceable place to pitch a tent, albeit next to the humming of road noise. The two-bedroom ensuite cabins and cottages are a nicer option than most of the pub stays. (☎/fax 6545 1078. Sites for 2 $13.20, powered $18; cabins and cottages from $66.) The **Scone Visitor Information Centre** is at the corner of Kelly St. (New England Hwy.) and Susan St., in front of the train station. (☎6545 1526; www.horsecapital.com.au. Internet access $2.50 per 30min. Open daily 9am-5pm.)

WINERIES OF THE UPPER HUNTER VALLEY. The Upper Hunter Valley has fewer wineries and tourists than the Lower Hunter, but its wines are fabulous, and the countryside is beautiful. Pick up the *Vineyards of the Upper Hunter Valley* brochure with listings and a map from any area visitors center. The vineyards are all off the New England Hwy., beginning a few kilometers north of Muswellbrook. Unfortunately, no tour groups operate in Upper Hunter, so you need your own car. That said, one advantage to Upper Hunter is that you can easily visit all the wineries in a single day. **Rosemount Estate** (☎6549 6450), on Rosemount Rd., in Denman, is the largest Upper Hunter vineyard. Exporting much of its stock throughout the world, Rosemount has an extraordinary variety of wines, ranging from a light Sauvignon Blanc to a peppery Cabernet Sauvignon. **Arrowfield** (☎6576 4041), on the Golden Hwy. in Jerrys Plains, sits on the Hunter River and prides itself on producing respected, affordable wines. **Cruickshank Callatoota Estate,** 2656 Wybong Rd. (☎6547 8149; www.cruickshank.com.au), specializes in Cabernet Sauvignon, Shiraz, and Cabernet Franc. **James Estate,** 951 Bylong Valley Way (☎6547 5168; www.jamesestatewines.com.au), in Sandy Hollow, produces a delicious White Sylvander and sells in bulk at a discount.

CENTRAL COAST

Known widely as the Holiday Coast, mid-New South Wales beaches are too often passed over by international tourists eager to reach the bright lights and holiday hot spots farther north. The region's slightly slower pace of life lies somewhere between the metropolitan rat race and the permanent vacation attitude of the north coast. Thriving coastal cities like Newcastle and Port Macquarie draw locals with ample opportunities to sunbathe, water-ski, or hang ten, as well as easy access to nearby national parks.

NEWCASTLE ☎02

Newcastle, dubbed "Sydney's Siberia" because of its reputation as the original colony reserved for the most troublesome convicts, is now a growing city. As the world's largest coal exporter, Newcastle ships out over one and a half million tons each week, giving it a reputation as a smokestack-ridden industrial metropolis. Today, Newcastle works hard to change its industrial image. High-adrenaline surfing, spectacular Pacific views, and easy access to the nearby Hunter Valley wineries and wetland reserves put Newcastle in sync with its vibrant, international uni student crowd and flourishing live music scene.

TRANSPORTATION

Trains: Newcastle Railway Station (☎13 15 00), corner of Scott and Watt St. **CityRail trains** to Sydney (2¾hr., at least 1 per hr. 2:35am-9:06pm, $17). The main transfer station for **CountryLink** (☎13 22 32) and access to the northern coast is **Broadmeadow,** a 5min. train ride on CityRail. From Broadmeadow, Countrylink runs to: **Brisbane** (12hr., 2 per day, $66); **Coffs Harbour** (6-7hr., 3 per day, $60); and **Surfers Paradise** (12hr., 1 per day, $88). Broadmeadow station open daily 6am-7:15pm; ticket machines available

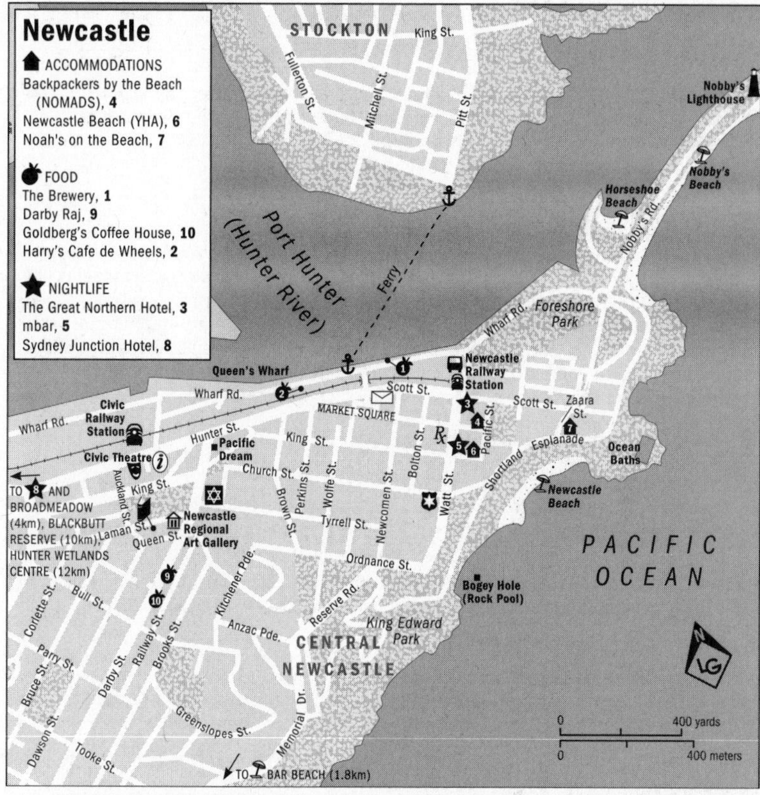

24hr. Broadmeadow CountryLink office open M-F 8am-5:30pm, Sa-Su 8am-3:30pm; Newcastle office open 9am-5pm. Discounts for booking 1 or 2 wk. in advance. ISIC holders get a 50% discount on CountryLink.

Buses: The bus depot abuts the wharf side of the railway station. Several bus lines including **Greyhound Australia** (☎13 14 99 or 13 20 30; www.greyhound.com.au) zip to: **Brisbane** (14hr., 3 per day, $90); **Byron Bay** (11hr., 2 per day, $83); **Coffs Harbour** (7hr., 3 per day, $63); **Port Macquarie** (4hr., 3 per day, $51); **Surfers Paradise** (12hr., 3 per day, $90); **Sydney** (2½hr., at least 3 per day, $39); **Taree** (3½hr., 1 per day, $34). **Rover Coaches** (☎4990 1699; www.rovercoaches.com.au) goes to Cessnock, which is a gateway for the Hunter Valley vineyards (1¼hr.; M-F 2-4 per day; $12, children $6.30). **Port Stephens Coaches** (☎4982 2940; www.pscoaches.com.au) shuttles to **Port Stephens** (about 1½hr.; M-F 11 per day, Sa-Su 5 per day; up to $11, backpackers and students $5.50; the Bay Rover Pack includes round-trip ticket and travel between Port Stephens' townships, $22/11). Purchase tickets ahead from a Newcastle travel agency, online, on the bus.

Ferries: Passenger ferries (☎13 15 00) depart from the wharf near the train station and cross the river north to **Stockton.** The ferry leaves every 30min. M-Sa 5:15am-midnight, Su and holidays 8:30am-10:00pm. Tickets $2, concessions $1; purchase onboard.

Public Transportation: City **buses** (☎13 15 00; www.131500.com) run along Hunter St. every few minutes during the day, less frequently at night, some as late as 3:30am. Tickets allow travel within a certain time limit and are for sale onboard (1hr. $2.60, 4hr. $5, all day

$8). Some routes within the CBD are free. Check at the tourist office for more information and a map.

Taxis: Newcastle Taxis (☎4979 3000).

Car Rental: All have locations in the city and at the airport: **Europcar,** 66 Hannell St., Wickham (☎4965 1328; www.europcar.com.au), **Thrifty,** 113 Parry St., Hamilton (☎4942 2266; www.thrifty.com.au), and **Budget,** 107 Tudor St. (☎4927 6375; www.budget.com.au). Check websites for online specials.

ORIENTATION

Hunter Street, at the heart of the city, is Newcastle's commercial district and runs parallel to the wharf. On the eastern end of the main drag and atop a peninsular hill lies Fort Scratchley, a number of hostels and seaside bars, and the emerald-green **Foreshore Park.** North-south **Darby Street** to has Newcastle's hip happenings. For another dose of chic, a significant trek farther west will take you to **Beaumont Street** in Hamilton; the bus might be a better option. The New England Hwy. heads west toward the **Hunter Valley** wineries.

PRACTICAL INFORMATION

Tourist Office: 361 Hunter St. (☎4974 2999 or 1800 654 558; www.visitnewcastle.com.au). From rail station, take a right on Scott St. and continue as it merges with Hunter St. Office is on left, couple of blocks past Darby St. Free maps of Newcastle and Macquarie; accommodation and tour bookings. Open M-F 9am-5pm, Sa-Su 9:30am-4:30pm.

Library: (☎4974 5324), in the Newcastle War Memorial Cultural Centre on Laman St., next to the art gallery. **Internet** access $3 per 30min. Book ahead. Open M-F 9:30am-8pm, Sa 9:30am-2pm.

Surf Shop: Pacific Dreams, 7 Darby St. (☎4926 3355; www.pacificdreams.com.au), rents boogie boards $20 per day; short boards $50; long $60. Open M-W 9am-5:30pm, Th 9am-8pm, F 9am-5:30pm, Sa 9am-4pm, Su 10am-3pm. Credit card and contact number required.

Police: (☎4929 0999), corner of Church and Watt St.

Post Office: (☎13 13 18), corner of Scott and Market St. Open M-F 8:30am-5pm. **Postal Code:** 2300.

ACCOMMODATIONS

With tourism on the rise, budget accommodations have become few and far between in Newcastle. Pub rooms abound (in summer from $40; in winter from $30), but the listings below are better bets. Book ahead in peak periods.

Newcastle Beach (YHA), 30 Pacific St. (☎4925 3544). Around the corner from the beach and train station. Breezy, retro-flavored building. Spacious rooms and common area reminiscent of a country club with TV, pool table, and fireplace, kitchen. Free dinner at Finnegan's for YHA M-Tu and Su and at the Brewery Th. Internet $2 per 30min. Winery tour $45. Laundry $6. Free surf and boogie boards available. Reception 7am-10:30pm. Book ahead in summer. Dorms $26, YHA $20-22; singles and doubles $42. MC/V. ❷

Backpackers by the Beach (NOMADS), 34-36 Hunter St. (☎1800 008 972; www.backpackersbythebeach.com.au). 4min. walk north of train station, this hostel is on the corner of Hunter and Pacific St. Small rooms feel bigger than they are due to bright lights and high ceilings. Single-sex dorms. Surfboard rentals $8 per hr., bodyboards $2 per hr., bikes $3 per hr., snorkels $2 per hr. Th free BBQ, F free pizza. Internet access $4 per hr. Key deposit $15. Reception 7am-11pm. Book ahead for weekends. Dorms $25, weekly $123; doubles $55/336. ISIC/NOMADS/VIP/YHA. MC/V. ❷

Noah's on the Beach (☎4929 5181; www.noahsonthebeach.com.au), corner of The Esplanade and Zaara St. A big, standard hotel with beachy feel and stunning views of the

Pacific. All rooms come with A/C and heat, TV, data port, mini-fridge, bar, coffee, and tea. Free parking and laundry services. Reception 24hr. Standard singles, doubles, and twins from $165; oceanview singles, doubles, and twins from $175; family rooms from $195. Discounts for 3 nights or more. AmEx/DC/MC/V. ❺

FOOD

Darby Street is the best place in town to hunt for eateries. **Hunter Street** has $5-6 lunch specials, but stick to the Pacific St. end if you want atmosphere. Though it's a 25-30min. walk southwest of the city center, Hamilton's **Beaumont Street** is lined with over 80 restaurants. Cheap food-court options can also be found at **Market Square,** in the center of a pedestrian mall on Hunter St., running from Newcomen to Perkins St. The huge 24hr. **Bi-Lo** supermarket (☎4926 4494) is in the Marketown shopping center at the corner of National Park and King St.

Goldberg's Coffee House, 137 Darby St. (☎4929 3122). Many meet here early in the evening for dinner or drinks before heading out for the night. Dark hardwood interior with a classy soundtrack and garden patio out back. Swing in for a late cup of coffee ($2.75-3.50) or a glass of wine ($4.40). Varied and reasonably priced menu; lunch and dinner dishes $7-20. Open daily 7am-midnight. AmEx/DC/MC/V. ❷

The Brewery, 150 Wharf Rd. (☎4929 6333; www.qwb.com.au). Fine dining hops at this popular wharf-side restaurant and multi-level bar. Attracting steak and seafood lovers for meals (lunch $10-20, dinner $16-30) and a mixed crowd for evening drinks, there's something for everyone to enjoy here. Live entertainment, trivia, and daily drink specials. Open M-Tu, Th, and Su 10am-midnight; W, F, Sa 10am-3am. AmEx/DC/MC/V. ❹

Darby Raj, 115 Darby St. (☎4926 2443). With delicious North Indian curries to devour at one of the tables outside, Darby Raj is a treasured find. Choose 1-3 curries on rice for $8.90, or for a light lunch grab a couple of *samosas* ($2 each) and cool your palate with a *Lassi* ($2.50). Vegetarian-friendly. Takeaway available. Open M 4-10pm; Tu-W and Su 11am-10pm; Th-Sa 11am-10:30pm. AmEx/MC/V. ❶

Harry's Cafe de Wheels (☎4926 2165), on Wharf Rd. on the waterfront. What better place to sample a famous Australian meat pie than the longest running takeaway joint in the nation? The "Tiger" is a hearty pie smothered in peas, mashed potatoes, and steaming gravy ($5). Open M-Tu 8:30am-10pm, W and F 8:30am-3:30am, Th 8:30am-11pm, Sa 10am-4:30am, and Su 10am-11pm. Cash only. ❶

SIGHTS AND ACTIVITIES

Though the ornate, convict-built **heritage buildings** and the towering **cathedral** in the CBD are impressive, visitors don't flock to Newcastle for Victorian balconies. They come instead to enjoy the laid-back Australian coastal lifestyle, with all the creature comforts of a major urban center. Newcastle's a place to chill, with plenty of oceanfront parks, good surf, and the ever-present sound of crashing waves.

BEACHES. Newcastle's shore is lined with white sand beaches, tidal pools, and landscaped parks. At the tip of Nobby's Head peninsula is a walkable seawall and **Nobby's Lighthouse,** in the middle of **Nobby's Beach,** a popular surfing spot. A walk down the coastline from Nobby's leads to a surf pavilion, then to the **Ocean Baths,** a public saltwater pool. Keep walking to find its predecessor, **Bogey Hole,** a convict-built ocean bath at the edge of the manicured **King Edward Park.** Farther along, you'll see the large **Bar Beach,** terrific for surfing. To tackle all the beaches, follow the **Bather's Way** coastal walk from Nobby's to Merewether.

NEWCASTLE REGION ART GALLERY. On a rainy day, stroll through this small museum's collection of contemporary paintings and multimedia presentations. *(☎4974 5100. Corner of Laman and Darby St. Open Tu-Su 10am-5pm. Free.)*

BLACKBUTT RESERVE. A 182-hectare tree sanctuary with over 20km of walking trails and many animals along the way. Bring your own picnic to **Black Duck Picnic Area** where there's BBQ equipment, a jungle gym, a pioneer cottage that replicates domestic life for 19th-century Newcastle settlers, a koala enclosure, and kangaroo, peacock, and emu reserves. If you're lucky, you can even pet a koala on weekends at 2:30pm. *(Take bus #224 or 225 from the city center for 30min. to the corner of Carnley Ave. and Orchardtown Rd. Walk up Carnley Ave. to the entrance on the right. By car, turn left on Stewart Ave., the Pacific Highway, from Hunter St. After about 20min., hang a right on Northcott, and at the roundabout turn right on Carnley Ave. ☎4957 6436; www.ncc.nsw.gov.au. Open daily in summer 7am-5pm; wildlife exhibits 9am-5pm. Free.)*

HUNTER WETLANDS CENTRE. Founded in 1985 to provide sanctuary to birds and reptiles, these "rehabilitated wetlands" also offer respite to city-weary humans with walking paths and a creek for canoeing. Swans, egrets, ibis, blue herons, and parrots are just a few of the feathered fliers who frequent this place. Monthly events include breakfast with the birds, twilight treks, and canoe safaris. Check website in advance for details. *(Take CityRail to Sandgate, in the suburb of Shortland, and then walk 10min. on Sandgate Rd. By car, take the Pacific Highway to Sandgate Rd. ☎4951 6466; www.wetlands.org.au. Canoe rental: 2hr. 2-person $7.50; 3-person $10. Open daily 9am-5pm. $5, concessions $3, children $2.50, families $9.)*

NEWCASTLE'S TRAM. The famous tram offers an informative city overview. The ride is a great way to get a quick feel for the city's sights, from historical architecture to whales breaching off the coastline. *(☎4932 4022. 45min. Departs from Newcastle Railway Station M-F at 10am and 1pm. $12, children $6.)*

FESTIVALS. Surfest *(www.surfest.com)* rides into town in late February and early March for a two-week international surfing extravaganza. The **Newcastle Jazz Festival** *(☎4973 2160; www.newcastlejazz.com.au)* plays out in late August at City Hall. The **King Street Fair** *(☎4974 2859)* is a city-wide carnival in late November and early December. **Newcastle Maritime Festival's** *(☎4927 0470)* boat races and water sports are in October. The **This is Not Art Festival** *(☎4927 0470; www.thisisnotart.org.au)* brings together Newcastle's young musicians, artists, writers, media-makers, and troublemakers for five days of creative energy at the end of September and early October. *(For more info, visit www.newcastletourism.com.)*

ENTERTAINMENT AND NIGHTLIFE

Newcastle is fast becoming one of Australia's major musical hubs. *The Post,* a free newspaper, publishes a weekly guide to live music around the area, or peruse the free guide *TE (That's Entertainment)* at the tourist office. Wednesday night is "Uni Night" all around town; keep your eyes open for special events and offers, as well as late closing times.

The Great Northern Hotel (☎4927 5728), on the southeast corner of Watt and Scott St., is the latest uni party spot. Chill atmosphere. Open M noon-10pm, Tu and Sa noon-midnight, W and F noon-4am, Th noon-2am. V.

Sydney Junction Hotel, 8 Beaumont St. (☎4961 2537; www.sjh.com.au), is a super-slick establishment with a packed line-up: an all-in-one cocktail lounge, dance club, and sports bar. Rock bands Th-Su. F and Sa live music in back room and DJ up front. W Karaoke night. Free pool all day Su. Open daily 7am-latenight. AmEx/DC/MC/V.

mbar, 23 Watt St. (☎4927 1694), is the most convincingly trendy dance club in town. The high-energy scene attracts crowds, especially when DJs from Sydney and overseas are shipped in. $5 cover for high-profile DJs. Open W and F-Sa 9pm-5am.

PORT STEPHENS BAY ☎02

North of Newcastle, **Port Stephens** is a region comprised of a placid, secluded bay, sleepy townships, beautiful blue-green water, and tons of outdoor activities in and around **Tomaree National Park.** Most of the region's attractions, restaurants, and facilities are in Nelson Bay. Anna Bay and Shoal Bay offer beautiful and somewhat isolated beaches. During the summer, surfing beaches and luxury resorts draw backpackers and families alike, clogging central shopping areas with traffic. Dolphins are visible year-round in the harbor and are quite cheeky—they'll come right up and tag along with the daily dolphin cruises. The whale watching season runs from June-Oct., when about 5000 giants head north to warmer waters to breed.

TRANSPORTATION

Port Stephens Coaches (☎4982 2940; www.pscoaches.com.au) shuttles to and around Port Stephens; Newcastle (1½hr.; M-F 11 per day, Sa-Su 5 per day; up to $11. Backpackers and students $5.50. The Bay Rover Pack includes round-trip ticket and travel within and between Port Stephens' townships $22/11.) The main stop in Nelson Bay is at the Bi-Lo supermarket on Stockton St. **Local buses** run all week. (M-F hourly, Sa and Su every 2hr. $3; 1-day unlimited travel $11.) It may be more convenient to rent a car from Newcastle to avoid being stranded in one township for hours. The **Port Stephens Ferry Service** (☎04 1268 2117) makes trips to Tea Garden, a fishing village across the water from Nelson Bay. (8:30am, noon, and 3:30pm. Round-trip $20, children $10, concessions $18, families $50. Book ahead.) Call a **taxi** (☎4984 6699) for service around town. **Shoal Bay Bike Hire,** 63 Shoal Bay Rd., near the Shoal Bay Motel, is a cheap rental option. (☎4981 4121. From $9 per hr., $58 per wk. Open daily 8am-7pm in summer, 9am-5pm in winter.)

ORIENTATION AND PRACTICAL INFORMATION

Nelson Bay Road leads from Newcastle to Port Stephens's four residential townships. The road forks onto **Gan Gan Road,** which leads to the seaside **Anna Bay,** home to **Stockton Beach,** the largest sand dune area in the Southern Hemisphere. It's also close to the popular surfing destination, **One Mile Beach,** known as "The Big Beach" by locals. Gan Gan and Nelson Bay Rd. rejoin and lead to three other townships: **Nelson Bay** (the largest), **Shoal Bay,** and the rural **Fingal Bay.** The marina, shopping complex, and cafes are on **Victoria Parade** and **Stockton Street** in Nelson Bay. The **tourist office** (☎4981 1579 or 1800 808 900; www.portstephens.org.au.), on Victoria Pde. by the wharf, arranges bookings for local attractions. (Open daily 9am-5pm.) The **Tomaree Public Library,** in the Salamander Shopping Centre (☎4982 0670), has free **Internet** access. (Open M, W, F 9:30am-6pm; Tu and Th 9:30am-8pm; Sa 9:30am-2pm.) Additional access is available at **Shop 2** on Magnus St. in Nelson Bay. ($10 per hr. Open M-F 9:30am-7pm, Sa-Su 10am-5pm.)

ACCOMMODATIONS AND CAMPING

Budget accommodation abounds in Port Stephens Bay. **Samurai Beach Bungalows Backpackers/Port Stephens YHA ❷,** is on Robert Connell Cir. Reached by Frost Rd. off Nelson Bay Rd., the hostel is located amid dense bushland, making for a romantic stay. Guests enjoy simple yet stylish rooms, a volleyball court, an outdoor kitchen, an alternative rec room with TV, a pool table, free boogie boards, and a nightly campfire. Sand boards, bikes, and surf boards are also available for rent. (☎4982 1921; www.portstephens.org.au/samurai. Laundry $3. Reception 8:30am-10:30pm. 5-bunk dorms with fridge $23; doubles with TV, bar, and fridge from $62-79; family room with all amenities $70. Rates higher in the summer; book ahead. ISIC/VIP/YHA.) **Shoal Bay Holiday Park ❷,**

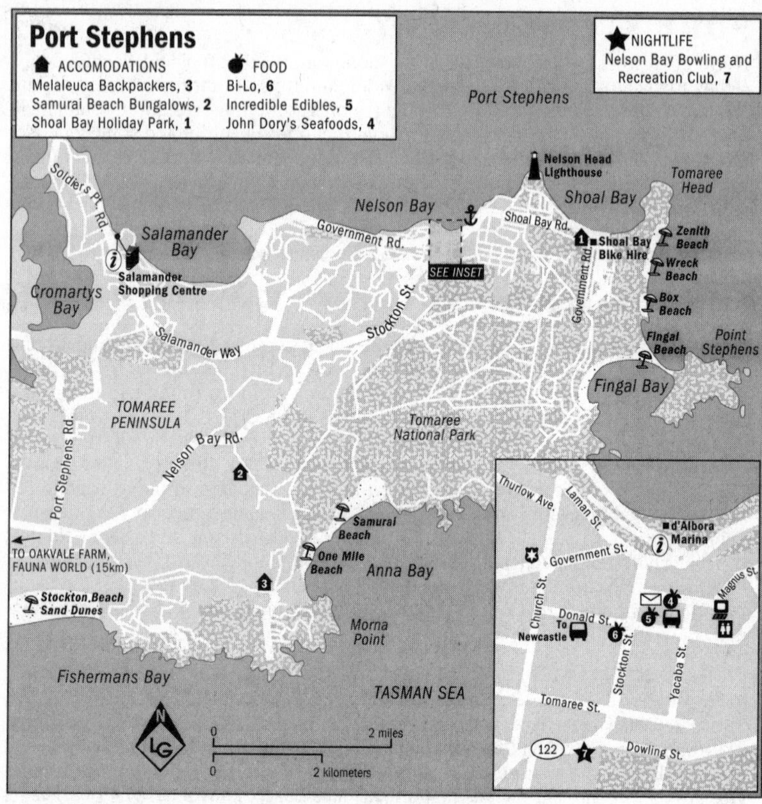

on Shoal Bay Rd., near the turnoff for Fingal Bay, has a new kitchen, two common TV areas, a rec room with ping-pong tables, and a tennis court. (☎4981 1427 or 1800 600 200; shoalbay@beachsideholidays.com.au. Laundry $3. Reception 8:15am-6pm. Powered sites for 2 $27-49, weekly $150-315, additional adult $15, children $6; ensuite caravan sites $40-65, weekly $239-420; ensuite bungalows with kitchen and TV for 5 $59-169, weekly $379-975. Extra adult $15.) **Malaleuca Backpackers ❷**, 33 Koala Pl., offers comfortable cabins and camping. Head down Gan Gan Rd. and turn left on Koala Pl., formerly Eucalyptus Dr. (☎4981 9422 or 04 2720 0950. Laundry $2. Sites $12-14; dorm beds $25; cabins $30. Book 2-3 months ahead for summer and holidays. VIP.)

FOOD

Nelson Bay—the Port Stephens hub—is the best place to find cheap food, particularly on Magnus and Donald St., parallel to Victoria Pde. **John Dory's Seafoods ❶**, 138 Magnus St. has unbeatable fish 'n' chips ($7). Be prepared for a generous platter. (☎4981 3881. Takeaways available. Open daily 11am-8pm. Cash only.) **Incredible Edibles ❶**, Shop 6 on Donald St. serves scrumptious sandwiches ($5-6.20) made with the freshest ingredients. (☎4981 4511. Open in summer daily 8am-4pm, in winter M-Sa 8am-4pm. Cash only.) Trusty supermarket **Bi-Lo** has locations on the corner of Stockton and Donald St. (☎4981 1666) and in the Salamander Shopping Centre (☎4982 7888), which also offers a **Woolworths** and a number of fast-food joints.

Though Port Stephens is not known for its party scene, locals and backpackers alike enjoy good times and cheap drinks at **Nelson Bay Bowling and Recreation Club,** Stockon St., just up from the village center. (☎4981 1272. Live music F-Sa. Open M-F 10am-10pm, Sa-Su 10am-midnight.)

SIGHTS AND ACTIVITIES

You've probably seen sport-utility vehicle ads on TV and wondered if anyone really drives off-road like that. Now's your chance to find out. The fun-loving folks at Port Stephens Visitors Centre (☎4981 1579) will let you buy a $5 day pass so you and your 4WD can go play on **Stockton Beach,** the biggest sand dune in the Southern Hemisphere (about 26km long and 1km wide, the ancient dunes are said to move inland every year). Passes are also available at the Mobil station in Anna Bay. Follow signs to Anna Bay from Nelson Bay Rd.; the Mobil is past the beach access sign. To get to the dunes, take Gan Gan Rd. to James Patterson St. For renting or participating in more organized group-duning, try a 1½hr. or 2½hr. trip with **6-Wheeler Bushmobile Dune Adventure** and conquer the deserts for just $15-20 per person. (☎0500 55 00 66 or 04 1811 6142; www.bushmobile.com.au. Departs from the James Paterson St. carpark. Includes sandboarding excursion.) **Sand Safaris** offers an incredible two hours on your very own ATV and an award-winning guided trip at 40kph over dunes nearly 60m high. (☎4965 0215 or 04 1820 9747; www.sandsafaris.com.au. No children. 4-5 trips daily; pickup near Williamtown. $129 per person.) For a more tame sand activity, join **Sahara Trails** on spectacular 2hr. dune and beach horse rides or a 1hr. beginner's bush ride starting at $40 per hr. (☎4981 9077; www.saharatrails.com. Open daily. Book ahead.)

Whale watching and **dolphin cruise boats** depart five times per day in the summer (winter trips are weather-permitting). The cheapest is the large **Tamboi Queen,** which cruises the harbor for sightings of some of the 150 dolphins that live there year-round. (☎4981 1959; www.tamboiqueencruises.com. Trips daily at 10:30am, 12:30, and 2pm depart from Wharf 1 in Nelson Bay. 1½hr. dolphin cruise $17, concessions $14, children $9.) On the ocean side, try **Moonshadow Cruises** (☎4984 9388; www.moonshadow.com.au) for whale watching trips, departing from d'Albora Marina. (Cruises May-Oct. depart 10am and 1:30pm. Adults $55, students $50, children $21.50.) **Blue Water Sea Kayaking** (☎4981 5177 or 04 0940 8618; www.seakayaking.com.au) offers trips starting at $25 but does not operate June-August. For less action and more cuddling, stop off at **Oakvale Farm and Fauna World,** 2828 Nelson Bay Rd., to pet or feed a koala or kangaroo. (☎4982 6222; www.oakvalefarm.com.au. Open daily 10am-5pm; feeding times 11am and 2pm. Wheelchair accessible. Adults $13, children $8.50.) For unparalleled views of Port Stephens Bay's rippling blue-green water and stark headlands, take the 20-40min. walk to the summit of **Tomaree Head** at the end of Shoal Bay. The Anna Bay shore offers opportunities for **surfing** and **nude bathing;** inquire at the Port Stephens tourist office in Nelson Bay for information.

GREAT LAKES

This underrated region is home to some of the most spectacular coastal scenery. The beautiful waters invite scuba exploration, and a host of little-known national parks provide opportunities for solitude and unusual wildlife sightings.

FORSTER ☎02

The small towns of Forster (FOS-ter) and Tuncurry are the most urban locales in the popular Great Lakes region. Although Forster's beaches pale in comparison to those just south, the town is a pleasant stop near Sydney or Byron Bay. It is also the most comfortable stopover for exploring the Great Lakes region.

TRANSPORTATION AND PRACTICAL INFORMATION. Approaching the **Pacific Hwy.** from the south, exit at **The Lakes Way.** The turn-off heads east after Buladelah, and Forster is 1hr. up the road. From the north on the Pacific Hwy., turn east onto The Lakes Way in Rainbow Flat; Forster is a 15min. drive. **Tuncurry** is on the north side of The Lakes Way bridge, before you cross into Forster. **Busways** (☎1800 043 263) runs to Bluey's Beach (30min.; M-F 3 per day, Sa-Su 2 per day; $10.50, concessions $5.20); Newcastle (2½hr.; 3 per day M-F, 2 per day Sa-Su; $31/15.50); Sydney (5½hr.; 1 per day 7:15am; $49/33.50). **Eggins Comfort Coaches** (☎6552 2700) goes to Taree (1hr.; M-Sa 2-4 per day; $12.40/6.20).

The **Forster Visitors Centre,** 2 Little St. by the wharf, is the **bus terminal** and a booking agency. Tickets can also be bought onboard. As the main visitors center for the Great Lakes region, this is the place to gather info on nearby beaches and national parks. Be sure to pick up a **map** of the area, since much of its charm lies in the many secluded beaches off main roads. (☎6554 8799 or 1800 802 692; www.greatlakes.org.au. Open daily 9am-5pm.) The **police station** (☎6555 1299) is on Lake and West St., and the **post office** is on the corner of Wallis Ln. and Beach St. in the center of Forster. **Postal Code:** 2428.

ACCOMMODATIONS AND FOOD. The owners of the **Dolphin Lodge (YHA)** ❷, 43 Head St., treat their guests to a TV lounge with cable and videos, all just a block from the beach and four blocks from town. They also offer bike rentals and pre-arranged pickup at bus stops in Nabiac, off the Pacific Hwy. (☎6555 8155; dolphin_lodge@hotmail.com. Internet access $2 per 20min. Key deposit $10. Dorms $24; singles $45; ensuite doubles $60.) **Smugglers' Cove Holiday Village** ❷, 45 The Lakes Way, has top-notch (and loosely pirate-themed) facilities, including a kitchen, pool, and minigolf. (☎6554 6666. Canoe rental $5 per hr. Sites $20, in peak season $30, powered $25/35; economy cabins $60/75, ensuite $75/115.) The tourist office can provide a list of budget motels in the area.

Chilli Jam ❷, 58 Wharf St., serves veggie-packed salads and stir-fry noodle bowls ($10-13), as well as a traditional breakfast. (☎6557 6000. Open daily 8am-5:30pm. AmEx/MC/V.) For a bit of a splurge, try the cosmopolitan **Casa del Mundo** ❸, 8 Little St., off the town center, a tapas bar and restaurant that carries off the fusion of Spanish and world cuisine with considerable aplomb. (☎6554 5906. Lunch special $5. Tapas $3.50-17, main courses $24-28. Open Sept.-Apr. M-Sa 5pm-latenight.) **The Wharf Bar and Grill** ❶, 32 Wharf St., has gourmet grill meals and a great view of the river. (☎6555 7200. Open daily 11:30am-2pm and 5:30pm-10pm. AmEx/MC/V.) Wharf St., in the town center, has food **markets** and restaurants serving burgers and fresh seafood. Many establishments close or run shorter hours in winter.

NEW SOUTH WALES

SIGHTS AND ACTIVITIES. **Tobwabba** (taw-WAB-buh), 10 Breckenridge St., is an Aboriginal studio and art gallery. The beautiful prints and canvasses are good alternatives to the ubiquitous stuffed kangaroos and koala souvenirs. (☎6554 5755; www.tobwabba.com.au. Open M-F 9am-5pm.) At the south end of **Forster Beach,** three blocks north of town on West St., are toilets, a BBQ, and a saltwater swimming pool. The **Bicentennial Walk** runs from Forster Beach to Pebbly Beach, with rock pools and dolphin-spotting along the way. For better beaches, head south 20km on The Lake Way or to Booti Booti National Park (p. 183).

Clarendon Forest Retreat, near Forster, offers **horseback riding.** (☎6554 3162; www.cfr.com.au. From $55, children from $50.) Boat and tackle rental sheds line the shore. **Forster's Dive School,** at Fisherman's Wharf opposite the post office, runs a variety of trips, including a swim with dolphins cruise ($60, non-swimmers $30) and a dive with gray nurse sharks near Seal Rock. (☎6554 7478; www.diveforster.com.au. 2 dives with equipment approx. $140.) Consult the visitors center for more fishing and diving options. **Cross Shore Kiteboarding,** 50-56 Manning St. in Tuncurry, offers kite surfing lessons for adventure-seekers. (☎6557 5133; www.xshore.com.au. Group lessons $70 per hr.)

MYALL LAKES NATIONAL PARK

Over 10,000 hectares of lakes, 40km of beaches, and walking tracks traversing coastal rainforest, heath, and paperbark swamp await ecotourists at Myall Lakes National Park. There are only two major vehicular access points (with honesty boxes to pay the $7 vehicle entry fee) to the area: one from the south through **Tea Gardens** and the other from the north at **Bulahdelah.** Coming from the south, turn off Pacific Hwy. at Tea Garden Rd. and continue through Hawks Nest to Mungo Brush Road. The northern entrance is the more popular option and is accessible through Bulahdelah, 83km north of Newcastle. The **Bulahdelah Visitors Centre,** at the corner of Pacific Hwy. and Crawford St., serves as the park's only "interpretive center." (☎4997 4981. Open M-F 10am-4pm, Sa-Su 9am-2pm.) Pick up the free *Great Lakes National Parks Visitors Guide,* with a **map** and info of campsites.

From Bulahdelah, take Bombah Point Rd., semi-paved road with no speed limit. Beware of cars, caravans, and boat tugs on the road. Lakes Rd. finishes at **Bombah Point,** a center of activity for both Myall Lakes and Bombah Broadwater. Here, the office of the **Ecopoint Myall Shores Resort ❷,** right before the ferry crossing, rents canoes ($15 per hr.), bikes ($10 per hr.) and outboards ($45 per 2hr.), and sells petrol. Facilities include BBQs, laundry, store, pool, and restaurant. (☎4997 4495; www.myallshores.com.au. Sites $11-26, powered $13-30; cabins $68-211. MC/V.)

The **Mungo Brush** area of the park is accessible by vehicle **ferry** (5min., every 30min. 8am-6pm, $3). The paved **Mungo Brush Road** runs 25km along the coast to the park's south edge passing eight campgrounds, including **Mungo Brush ❶,** with toilets, BBQ, and lake access, but no drinking water. (NPWS office ☎6591 0300. Sites $5 per day plus $7 per day vehicle fee. Pay a ranger or use the honesty box.)

The northern tip of the park is accessible from Bungwahl on the The Lakes Way, 30km east of Bulahdelah and 34km south of Forster. Seal Rocks Rd. leads to the secluded **Yagon Campsite ❶,** on the headland. Travel down Seal Rocks Rd. for a lighthouse and great views. Facing the beach at Seal Rocks is **Seal Rocks Camping Reserve ❷,** with easy access to the powerful surf. (☎1800 112 234; www.sealrockscampingreserve.com.au. Sites $22, powered $25; cabins $55-120. MC/V.)

BOOTI BOOTI NATIONAL PARK

Booti Booti, one of the largest areas of coastal rainforest in New South Wales, features extensive coastal wetlands and heath communities, as well as palm forest along the edge of Wallis Lake. Follow The Lakes Way south of Forster along the coastline of Elizabeth Beach to reach the park. **Biking** from Forster to the park's beaches is the best way to go (allow at least 1hr. each way). Bike rental is available from the Dolphin Lodge YHA ($10 per 4hr.; $16 per day, guests and members $8/12). Booti Booti's highlight is the spectacular view from **Cape Hawke lookout,** just a few kilometers from Forster (follow Cape Hawke Dr. off of The Lakes Way until the carpark). A 420m climb up a wooded path leads to a 20m tower, from which the beautiful beaches and forests encompassing Forster can be seen. The park **info center** is at **The Ruins Camping Area ❶,** by the soft white sand of **Seven-Mile Beach** and a mangrove forest. (☎6591 0300. Info center open M-F 8:30am-4:30pm. BBQ, toilets, and showers. Pay fees in slots at the entrance to camping area. Sites $8, vehicle fee $7.) **Sundowner Tiona Tourist Park ❷,** 15min. south of Forster and 500m north of The Ruins, rents sites on both the lake and beach sides of the road. (☎6554 0291; www.sundownerholidays.com. Sites $19-28, powered $22-32; cabins $55-400. MC/V.) A walk around the lake through cabbage tree palms and eucalyptus trees leads to the ocean and **Elizabeth Beach** (p. 184).

PACIFIC PALMS AND NEARBY BEACHES

Approximately 20min. along The Lakes Way, south of Forster, a sign appears for Lakeside Dr., which passes several beaches on its way through the small town of Pacific Palms. It becomes Boomerang Dr. before rejoining The Lakes Way a few kilometers south. **Elizabeth Beach** is the first turn-off on the left. Patrolled by lifeguards and pelicans, the waves usually die down in summer, making the surf ideal for swimmers. Right next door is **Shelly's Beach,** a secluded stretch that is unofficially clothing-optional, reached by a short walk through the wooded area next to Elizabeth Beach. A sewage pipe running into the ocean at Shelly's makes the beach a better bet for sunbathing than swimming. **Boomerang Beach,** home to many avid surfers, is just minutes farther down. From here, the road passes Boomerang Point and the turn off to the long, pristine **Bluey's Beach.** Boomerang Dr. then loops through **Pacific Palms,** which has a small strip of shops selling sundries and surf gear. At the strip's end is a **visitors center.** (☎6554 0123. Open daily 9am-3pm.)

Just a few hundred meters farther you can camp in style at the **Oasis Caravan Park ❷**, with petrol, a market, and a pool on premises. (☎6554 0488. Reception 8am-8pm; in summer open later. Sites $16-20, powered $20-30; cabins $85-130. MC/V.) About 4km south of the southern end of Boomerang Dr., along The Lakes Way, is the turn-off for a dirt road that runs to the **Sandbar and Bushland Park.** Travel to its end to reach the **Sandbar and Bushland Caravan Park ❷**, on **Smith's Lake.** (☎6554 4095. Sites $9-30; cabins $45-95, ensuite $55-110; prices vary seasonally.) Take a left off the main dirt road to reach **Celito Beach,** accessible only by 4WD or bike.

NORTH COAST

The north coast of New South Wales may be a well-trodden route, but it remains in top form with a seemingly endless stretch of bush, beach, and impressive tourist amenities. Inexpensive accommodations and a thriving adventure sports industry draw budget travelers to the lively beachside cities, while smaller oceanside villages offer first-rate surf and pristine rainforests.

TAREE ☎02

Taree (pop. 20,000), off the Pacific Hwy., on the Manning River, is a small but convenient base for exploring nearby beaches and parks. Taree and nearby Wingham's growing "country retreat" industry provides relaxing getaways.

The **beaches** near Taree are gorgeous and inviting but have unexpected currents, so swim only where patrolled. The closest is **Old Bar Beach,** a 15min. drive southeast from the town center on Old Bar Rd. **Wallabi Point,** to the south, offers great **surfing,** and **Saltwater** has a swimming lagoon. Farther south, **Hallidays Point** includes the well-known **Diamond Beach** and **Black Head Beach. Crowdy Head,** the site of a lighthouse lookout, is a 40min. drive to the north.

Accommodations are plentiful but not cheap; most hotels offer backpacker rates. **Namaste Beach House ❷**, 31 David St., is a great alternative to staying in Taree. It has modern leather furniture, a meditation room, TV nook, and BBQ, and is only a block from the beach. (☎6557 4224; www.namastebeachhouse.com. Dorms $30; singles $40; doubles and twins $60. VIP/YHA discount $5. MC/V.) **Exchange Hotel ❷**, on the corner of Victoria and Manning St., has basic, well-kept rooms. (☎6552 1160. Reception at bar 10am-late. Singles $35; doubles $50; twins $55. Cash only.) **Fotheringham Hotel ❷**, on Victoria St., has basic rooms. (☎6552 1153. Singles $45; doubles $55. Cash only.) **Twilight Caravan Park ❷**, 3km south of the town center on Manning River Dr., has laundry ($3), BBQ, a small pool, and a kitchen. (☎05 0085 4448; twilight@tsn.cc. Linen $5 per person. Powered sites for 2 $24; caravans for 2 $42; cabins from $50, ensuite from $55.) Catch a bite to eat at **Taste Buds,** 36 Manning St., which serves cheap sandwiches ($4-

8) and other lunch fare. (☎6552 4647. Open daily 8:30am-5pm.) Manning St. also has a **Woolworths** (☎6551 7067; open M-Sa 7am-10pm, Su 8am-8pm) inside a shopping center.

Taree's main road, **Victoria Street,** feeds directly into the Pacific Hwy. Most establishments are on Victoria St. or the streets between Pulteney and Macquarie St. **Busways** (☎1800 043 263), **Countrylink** (☎13 22 32), **Eggins Comfort Coaches** (☎6552 2700), **Greyhound Australia** (☎13 14 99 or 13 20 30), and **Premier** (☎13 34 10) run **buses** to: Brisbane (9-10½hr., 5 per day, $59-80); Byron Bay (4-7¾hr., 7 per day, $51-74); Coffs Harbour (4hr., 4 per day, $40-53); Forster (45min., 2-4 per day, $5-10); Port Macquarie (1-1¼hr., 4 per day, $9-45); Sydney (5-6hr., 8 per day, $38-68).

The **Manning Valley Visitors Information Centre** on Manning River Dr., 4km north of town, is past the Big Oyster car dealership. (☎6592 5444; www.manningvalley.info. Open daily 9am-5pm, public holidays and winter weekends 9am-4pm.) The **library,** 2 Pulteney St., offers free **Internet** access. (☎6592 5290. Open M-W and F 9:30am-5pm, Th 9:30am-6pm, Sa 9:30am-12:30pm.) The **post office** is on Albert St., near the intersection with Manning St. (Open daily 8:30am-5pm.) **Postal Code:** 2430.

FROM TAREE TO PORT MACQUARIE

There are two routes from Taree to Port Macquarie, each with its own charm. Beach bums are advised to stick to the Pacific Hwy., with a stopover in Crowdy Bay. Joyriding daytrippers can take the scenic 132km Tourist Drive 8, which curves inland before meeting up again with the Pacific Hwy.

CROWDY BAY NATIONAL PARK. Crowdy Bay, 22km north of Taree off the Pacific Hwy., is home to some of the area's most popular **beaches,** bushwalks, and picnic areas, as well as an abundance of kangaroos. Coralville Rd., at Moorland on the Pacific Hwy., leads into the park's southern entrance. Wild eastern grey kangaroos live at the three **campsites: Diamond Head, Indian Head,** and **Kylie's Rest Area.** There are flush toilets and cold showers at Diamond Head; all other sites have composting toilets. (Campsites $5, children $3.) Groups of **kangaroos** hop within feet of astounded visitors and **whales** can be seen off the headlands, but it often takes an expert to spot more elusive **koalas** at Indian Head and Kylie's Hut. There are three reasonably tame **bushwalks** in the park that pass through habitats stunted by exposure to wind and harsh salt sprays. The shortest **walk** is along the base of the headland cliff, accessible from Diamond Head at low tide. The longer **Diamond Head Loop Track** (4.8km) links Diamond Head and Indian Head, while a third track goes from Kylie's to the Crowdy Bay beach (1.2km return). Bring your own water into the park. The roads are 2WD-accessible dirt tracks. (Daily vehicle fee $7.)

TOURIST DRIVE 8. A 132km bumpy road linking Taree to Wauchope and Port Macquarie, Tourist Drive 8 passes through Wingham and Elands, before continuing through the lush Emerald Heartland. It then continues on to Oxley Hwy. and Port Macquarie or back onto the Pacific Hwy. A quarter of the road is unsealed and rough, but 2WD-accessible if driven cautiously. The most spectacular sight is **Ellenborough Falls** in Elands. Created by a fault line 30 million years ago, Ellenborough has one of the largest drops in the southern hemisphere (200m). There are multiple walking tracks, the most difficult of which leads to the bottom of the gorge.

PORT MACQUARIE ☎02

Travelers often make the sad mistake of bypassing the pristine port town of Port Macquarie (ma-KWAR-ee; pop. 45,000), once a lock-up for Sydney's worst offenders. Today, killers have been replaced by koalas—Port Macquarie houses the world's largest urban population of the cuddly marsupial. Adrenaline junkies are also at home here, as the meeting of the Hastings River and the Pacific Ocean provides a variety of adventure activities at bargain prices year-round.

TRANSPORTATION

Major bus lines, including **Greyhound Australia** (☎13 14 99 or 13 20 30) and **Premier** (☎13 34 10), pass through town three times a day on their Sydney-Brisbane routes. Check to make sure your bus stops at Hayward St. rather than out on the highway. Car rental outfits include: **Budget** (☎6583 3761 or 13 27 27), at the corner of Gordon and Hollingsworth St.; **Hertz,** 102 Gordon St. (☎6583 6599); and **Thrifty** (☎6584 2122), on the corner of Horton and Hayward St.

ORIENTATION AND PRACTICAL INFORMATION

The Central Business District (CBD) is bordered to the north by the **Hastings River** and to the west by a bridged section of **Kooloonbung Creek. Horton Street** is the main commercial drag. Perpendicular to Horton St. and running along the river to the Marina is **Clarence Street,** along which you'll find numerous restaurants and cafes, as well as the **Port Central Mall.** The brand-new **Visitors Information Centre** is at the corner of Gordon and Gore St. (☎1300 303 155; www.portmacquarieinfo.com.au. Open M-F 8:30am-5pm, Sa-Su 9am-4pm.) **Banks** with **ATMs** line Horton St. between Clarence and William St. The **library,** on the corner of Grant and Gordon St., has **Internet** access (☎6581 8755; $2 per 30min.; open M-F 9:30am-6pm, Sa 9am-noon), as does **Port Surf Hub,** 57 Clarence St. (☎6584 4744. Open M-W and Su 9am-6pm, Th-Sa 9am-7pm. $2.50 initial access fee, plus $0.07 per min.) The **police** station (☎6584 3714) is on the corner of Hay St. and Sunset Pde. A **post office** is on the corner of William and Short St. (☎6588 3100. Open M-F 9am-5pm.) **Postal Code:** 2444.

ACCOMMODATIONS

Port Macquarie has a range of good budget options, most of which offer weekly discounts. Book ahead during peak season, when motels and caravan parks sometimes double their prices.

Ozzie Pozzie Backpackers, 36 Waugh St. (☎6583 8133; www.ozziepozzie.com), off Gore St. between Buller and Bridge St. Friendly owners offer activities board and personalized recommendations. Freebies include breakfast, bikes, boogie boards, and video collection (with deposits). Kitchen, Internet access ($1 per 15min), and TV lounge. Free pickup from bus stop. Lockers $10 deposit. Dorms from $23; doubles from $58, ensuite from $65. MC/V. Credit card fee $2. ❷

Beachside Backpackers (YHA), 40 Church St. (☎6583 5512 or 1800 880 008). Close to the beaches and 5min. walk from CBD. Clean and friendly. Free boogie boards and fishing rods. Internet access $2 per 20min. Bike rental $5 per day. Summer F night feast $5. Arranges cheap PADI certification. Free pickup from bus stop. Reception 8am-10pm. Dorms from $24, YHA $22; doubles from $60; twins from $65. AmEx/MC/V. ❷

Port Macquarie Hotel (☎6580 7888; www.macquariehotel.com.au), at the corner of Horton and Clarence St. Location can't be beat: in the middle of the CBD and above some great bars, ½ block from the water. The old-style Port Macquarie Hotel is outfitted in Art Deco design. Basic singles from $40; doubles $50, ensuite $60. AmEx/MC/V. ❹

Sundowner Breakwall Tourist Park, 1 Munster St. (☎6583 2755 or 1800 636 452; www.sundownerholidays.com). A huge waterfront park adjacent to the Town Beach and the Hastings River. Pool, BBQ, and 1hr. free Internet access. Book ahead in summer. Sites $25-47, powered $31-60; cabins and cottages for 2 $65-335. MC/V. ❷

FOOD

Clarence St. is lined with a number of affordable cafes and takeaways. The **Port Central Mall,** on Claren St., has a food court, deli, and **supermarket.** There is also a **Food for**

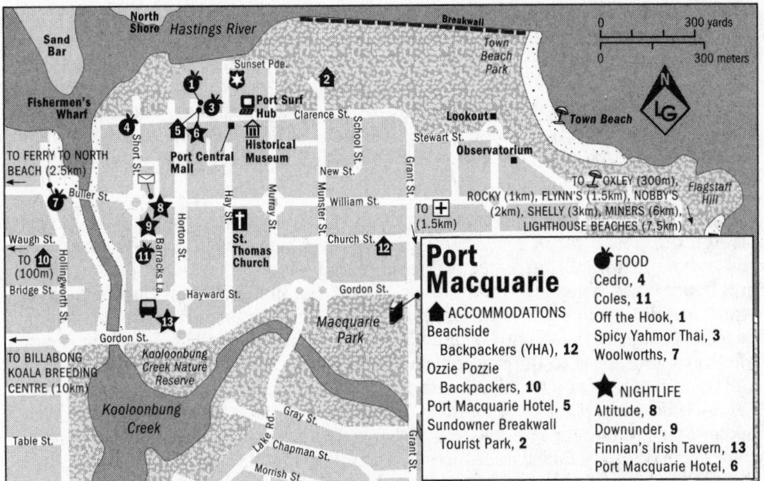

Less on Short and Buller St. (☎6583 2364; open M-Sa 8am-9pm, Su 8am-8pm) and a 24hr. **Coles** one block up (☎6583 2544).

Off the Hook (☎6584 1146), on Horton St., off the town green. The best bet for fresh seafood takeaway. Your choice of fish is cooked while you wait. Fish 'n' chips or fish-burgers from $4.50. Open daily 10:30am-7pm. Cash only. ❶

Cedro, 72 Clarence St. (☎6583 5529). Scrumptious breakfasts and healthful salads and soups. Try banana bread with lemon ricotta ($6.50) or a salad with roast pumpkin ($14.50). Open M-F 7:30am-2:30pm, Sa-Su 8am-2:30pm. MC/V. ❷

Spicy Yahmor Thai (☎6583 9043) on Clarence St., in the middle of town, has spicy curries ($14-17) and noodles ($13-17). Open daily 5:30-10pm. AmEx/MC/V. ❷

SIGHTS

KOALAS. Port Macquarie is home to two of the best koala facilities in the state. The **Billabong Koala Breeding Centre,** 10km west of Port Macquarie at 61 Billabong Dr., offers unparalleled opportunities to interact with Australia's most adorable marsupials; visitors can pet and feed koalas, wallabies, and kangaroos. The center also has dozens of exotic birds, monkeys, and cassowaries. By car, take the Gordon St. west towards Wauchope; those without cars can reach the center by taking bus #335, which runs 2-6 times per day. (☎6585 1060. Presentations 10:30am, 1:30, and 3:30pm. $12, children $8.) The volunteer-led **Koala Hospital,** has four permanent residents and a varying number of sick koalas receiving care. Visitors can see the treatment center or walk around the grounds. (☎6584 1522; www.koalahospital.org.au. Feedings daily at 8am and 3pm. Donation requested.)

BEACHES. The closest sand is at **Town Beach,** where the 8km-long **beach and headland walk** starts. From the headlands overlooking Town Beach, you can see **North Beach** and **Hasting River,** across the inlet. Heading southeast along the coast, you'll find **Oxley Beach, Rocky Beach,** and **Flynn's Beach** (popular with families). From there, follow **Nobby's Beach** to **Nobby's Hill,** where an obelisk stands in memory of those who died swimming in the dangerous blowhole—don't even think about trying it. Next in line is **Shelly Beach,** home to huge goannas and powerful surf. It's a perfect picnic spot, complete with BBQ area. The last part of the track leads to

Miners Beach (an unofficial nude beach) and the **Tacking Point Lighthouse,** a popular lookout over **Lighthouse Beach,** a great surf spot. Hostels are usually willing to drop off guests at the lighthouse if they want to take the walk back. To reach the beaches by car, drive along William St. to Pacific Dr., which hugs the coast. Turn left on Lighthouse Rd. to reach Miners Beach, the lighthouse, and Lighthouse Beach. Lighthouse, Flynn's, and Town Beach are patrolled during summer. Public toilets are located at Town, Flynn's, Shelly, Nobby's Hill, and the carpark just before the lighthouse.

PARKS. The **Sea Acres Rainforest Centre,** at Shelly Beach, preserves the largest stretch of coastal rainforest in the country. A 1.3km raised boardwalk circles through a portion of the 72-hectare reserve and allows glimpses of bush turkeys and flying foxes. You can explore on your own, but illuminating, volunteer-guided walks are also available. The **visitors center** has a 20min. film and ecological display. (☎6582 3355. Open daily 9am-4:30pm. $6, children $3.) At the end of Horton St. is one of several entrances to the **Kooloonbung Creek Nature Reserve,** a 52-hectare conservation area of peaceful bushland with footpaths through mangroves and wetlands. On the other side of the Hasting River, North Beach leads to **Point Plomer** and **Limeburner Creek Nature Reserve,** the site of Aboriginal artifacts and the **Big Hill walking track** (2km). Ferries take cars from Settlement Point, at the end of Settlement Point Rd. (called Park St. at the intersection with Hastings River Dr.), to North Shore Dr. From there, turn right onto the 16km coastal Point Plommer Rd., which is unsealed but bikeable. Those in 2WDs should take Maria River Rd. instead. **Campsites** ❶ are available at Melaleuca near Big Hill, and at Barries Bay at Point Plomer. The campgrounds have toilets and cold showers, but no drinking water. (☎6583 8805. Check-in at campground kiosk daily 8am-4pm. $5 per site, $3 per child.)

ACTIVITIES

ON LAND. Aussie adventurer Greg leads **Port Macquarie Camel Safaris.** Caravan along Lighthouse Beach and perhaps spot a wild koala. Pickup in the camel car can be arranged. (☎6585 5996 or 04 1256 6333. 30min. Operates Tu, W, F, Sa, and Su 9:30am-1pm. $23, children $17.) **Bikes** can be rented from **Graham Seers Cyclery,** at Shop 1 Port Marina on Park St. (☎6583 2333. $40 per day, $70 per wk. Open M-F 9am-5pm, Sa 9am-1:30pm.) Most hostels also loan bikes. For mountain biking or abseiling, try **EdgeExperience,** with tours for cyclists and climbers for all levels. (☎04 2732 4009; www.edgeexperience.com. ½-day mountain biking or introductory abseiling $50, full day $85; twilight bike ride $35. Free pickup.)

IN WATER. Hang ten with **Port Macquarie Surf School,** which offers classes for newbies and intermediate surfers. (☎6585 5433; www.portmacquariesurfschool.com.au. 2hr. group lessons $40.) Great deals on diving are available through the Beachside Backpackers YHA (p. 186), which will set up travelers with a three-day **PADI course** for only $170. **Port Venture** runs 2hr. dolphin watching cruises in a large ship (☎6583 3058; $25). For whale-watching, try **Aquatic Blue,** which offers 2hr. cruises with tea. (☎6583 8811; www.aquaticbluecharters.com.au. $55, students and backpackers $45, children $35.)

IN AIR. Coastal Skydivers offers tandem jumps from 10,000 ft. (☎04 2847 1227; $310). **High Adventure Air Park** offers a variety of tandem flights. (☎6559 8665. 30min. coastal paragliding $130, mountains $150; 30min. flight in a microlite plane $150.) To see the sky with your feet planted on the ground, visit the **Observatorium,** situated in Rotary Park on the corner of Stewart and Lord St., where a large telescope offers good views of the Southern Hemisphere's constellations. (☎6584 9164. Apr.-Oct. W and Su beginning 7:30pm; end of Oct. to early Apr. 8:15pm. $5.)

NIGHTLIFE

The **Port Macquarie Hotel,** on the corner of Clarence and Horton St., is the most popular nightspot in town, with several bars and a dance floor. (☎6583 1011. W and Su karaoke. F-Sa live music. Open M-Tu and Su 10am-midnight, W-Th 10am-1:30am, F-Sa 10am-3am.) **Downunder,** on Short St. next to Coles, has W karaoke and live music on weekends. (☎6583 4018. F-Sa cover $5. Open daily 9pm-4am with last entrance at 2:30am.) **Finnian's Irish Tavern,** on the corner of Gordon and Horton St., attracts a slightly older, relaxed crowd. (☎6583 4646. F-Sa live music, Th trivia. Open M-Th and Su until midnight, F-Sa until 2am.)

NAMBUCCA HEADS ☎02

For the traveler in need of a break from tourist attractions and constant activities, Nambucca Heads (pop. 10,000) provides a convenient stopover and welcome respite. Though it lacks hostels, Nambucca Heads has plenty of accommodations within walking distance of the charming river and the area's well-kept beaches.

Nambucca is full of whimsical artwork; it's one of the few places where graffiti artists are welcomed and even provided with an outdoor gallery. A 3-D mosaic made from old teapots, colorful mugs, and broken pieces of glass forms a Gaudí-esque bench along Fraser St. There are **walks** of varying difficulty throughout the beach and bush areas of Nambucca, some of which pass by the gorgeous **Rotary, Captain Cook,** and **Lions Lookouts.** For more structured exploration, **Kyeewa Bushwalkers,** a volunteer-based group, organizes a variety of free walks. Visit the info center or check online (www.here.com.au/kyeewa) for an updated schedule.

Nambucca and the surrounding townships of Bowraville, Scotts Head, and Valla Beach are overflowing with caravan parks situated near the beaches or along the Pacific Hwy. near the tourist office. **White Albatross Holiday Centre ❷,** at the ocean end of Wellington Dr., next to the V-Wall Tavern, is a sprawling caravan park with a gorgeous setting near a swimming lagoon and the Nambucca River. Amenities include picnic and BBQ areas, kitchen, laundry, game room, and a small store. (☎6569 4698; www.whitealbatross.com.au. Linens $5.50. Sites from $26; vans from $35; cabins from $65. Book ahead in summer. MC/V.) **Aukaka Caravan Park ❷,** 2 Pacific Hwy., is fine for overnight stopovers, but the facilities are a bit run down. (☎6568 6647. Sites from $17, powered from $20; cabins from $30. MC/V.)

Bowra St. has an assortment of quick, cheap food possibilities. **The Bookshop and Internet Cafe ❷,** on the corner of Bowra and Ridge St., is the perfect place to trade in old books or have a delicious lunch. The cafe serves mouth-watering sandwiches ($5-12), soups ($9), and smoothies ($5.50). (☎6568 5855. Internet access $8.80 per hr. Open daily in summer 9am-5pm, in winter 8:30am-4:30pm. Cash only.) The **V-Wall Tavern ❶,** at the mouth of the Nambucca River on Wellington Dr., has river views, televised sports, and an active nightlife scene that includes discos and karaoke. (☎6568 6344. Meals from $7.50. Open daily 10am-midnight. MC/V.) **Nambucca Tasty Tucka ❶,** at 40 Bowra St., serves fish 'n' chips (from $5) and burgers. (☎6568 7800. Open M-Th and Su 11am-7:30pm, F-Sa 11am-8pm. Cash only.)

The **railway station** is 3km out of town. From Mann St., bear right at the roundabout to Railway Rd. **Countrylink** (☎13 22 32) goes to Coffs Harbour (40min., 3 per day, $4). The bus stop is at the visitors center, just outside town at the Pacific Hwy. and Riverside Dr. **Busways** (☎1300 555 611) runs to Bellingen (45min., 3 per day, $6.60) and Coffs Harbour (1hr., 5 per day, $6.30). **Greyhound** (☎13 14 99 or 13 20 30) and **Premier** (☎13 34 10) stop a few times daily on Sydney-Brisbane routes.

The main road in Nambucca Heads is **Riverside Drive,** which becomes Fraser St. and then Bowra St. as it passes through the town center. It then becomes Mann St., then Old Coast Road, where it reconnects with the highway. Follow

Ridge Street to Liston St. which heads toward the town's beaches. The **Nambucca Valley Visitor Information Centre** is at the intersection of the Pacific Hwy. and Riverside Dr. (☎6568 6954; www.nambuccatourism.com. Open daily 9am-5pm.) A **Woolworths** is in town off Bowra St., up the hill from the RSL Club. (☎6569 4505. Open M-Sa 7:30am-10pm, Su 7:30am-8pm.) For cheap **Internet** access ($3 per hr.), head to the **public library** on Ridge St. (☎6568 6906. Open M-Th 9:30am-12:30pm and 2-5:30pm, F 9:30am-5:30pm.) The **post office** is on the corner of Bowra and Ridge St. (☎6598 7320. Open M-F 9am-5pm.) **Postal Code:** 2448.

BELLINGEN ☎02

Bellingen (pop. 3000) sits on the banks of the Bellinger River, 30min. from World Heritage-listed Dorrigo National Park (p. 191), and is halfway between Coffs Harbour and Nambucca Heads. "Bello," as locals call it, has reinvented itself as a laid-back country town which reputedly has the most artists per capita in Australia.

TRANSPORTATION. **Buses** stop at Hyde and Church St. **Busways** (☎1300 555 611) services Coffs Harbour (1hr.; M-F 3 per day, Sa 2 per day; $6.60) and Nambucca Heads (45min., 3 per day, $6.60). **Keans** (☎1800 043 339) travels to Port Macquarie (3hr.; M, W, F 1 per day; $35) via Coffs Harbour (35min., $21) and Nambucca Heads (1¼hr., $25); and Tamworth (4¾hr.; T, Th, Su 1 per day; $61) via Dorrigo (35min., $15) and Armidale (3hr., $35). **Bellingen World Travel,** 42 Hyde St. (☎6655 2055; open M-F 9am-5pm), books seats on various bus services.

ORIENTATION AND PRACTICAL INFORMATION. **Hyde Street** runs parallel to the Bellinger River and cuts through the center of town. The **Bellingen Shire Tourist Information Centre** is located on the Pacific Hwy., in the small town of Urunga. (☎6655 5711; www.bellingermagic.com. Open M-Sa 9am-5pm, Su 10am-2pm.) The smaller **Bellingen Visitor Centre** has friendly volunteers and is on the east end of Hyde St. in the Old Butter Factory, which is now an art gallery. (☎6655 1522. Open daily in summer 9am-5pm; in winter 9:30am-4:30pm.) The **library,** in the park in the center of town, has **Internet** access. (☎6655 1744. $3 per hr. Open Tu-W 10:30am-5:30pm, Th-F 10:30am-12:30pm and 1:30-5:30pm, Sa 9:30am-noon.) A well-stocked **IGA** supermarket is at 62 Hyde St. (☎6655 1042. Open daily 7am-8pm.) The **police station** is at 47 Hyde St. (☎6655 1444) and the **post office** is next door on the corner of Bridge St. (☎6655 1020. Open M-F 9am-5pm). **Postal Code:** 2454

ACCOMMODATIONS. **Bellingen Backpackers (YHA) ❶,** 2 Short St., impresses with its huge verandas overlooking the Bellinger River. Turn off Hyde St. at the driveway for the Lodge 241 Gallery Cafe in the north end of town. The lounge has floor pillows, didgeridoos, and a TV. The friendly staff arranges daytrips to Dorrigo National Park ($15) and will pick up guests from Urunga train or bus stations. Bike rental ($5), laundry ($4), and Internet access ($5 per hr.) are available. (☎6655 1116. Sites for 2 $20; dorms $26; doubles or twins $60. YHA discount $2.) The **Federal Hotel ❶,** 77 Hyde St., is a tidy pubstay with small fridges and brick fireplaces in every room. The bar and bistro downstairs often bring live music, featuring Sunday afternoon jazz. (☎6655 9345; www.federalhotel.com.au. 10-bed dorms $25; twins $45; triples $60. MC/V.)

FOOD. Scrumptious **Riverstone ❷,** 105-109 Hyde St., serves big breakfasts and lunches in a modern yet cozy atmosphere. (☎6655 9099; www.riverstone.com. Open daily 8am-4pm. MC/V.) Halfway to Dorrigo in Thora, 15km west of Bellingen, **Lombok on Waterfall ❷,** 2479 Waterfall Way, serves gourmet breakfasts and Asian-inspired dishes for lunch. Have satays ($16), a steak sandwich ($12), or a veggie pizza with pumpkin, spinach, and eggplant ($12). The stilted deck overlooks a farm valley. (☎6655 8855; low.cafe@bigpond.net.au. Open W-Su 8am-5pm. MC/V.) The **Lodge 241**

Gallery Cafe ❷, 117-121 Hyde St., on the western edge of town, combines panoramic views, local art displays, and generous portions of freshly prepared dishes. Try the chicken curry ($15), risotto cake with pumpkin and spinach ($15), or scrumptious options from burgers to soup. (☎6655 2470; www.bellingen.com/thelodge. Breakfast and lunch $6-14. Open daily 8am-5pm. AmEx/MC/V.)

SIGHTS AND ACTIVITIES. Even if you're not necessarily in the market for a "didge" or have no idea how to circular breathe, **Heartland Didgeridoos,** 25 Hyde St., opposite the Shell Service Station, has an outstanding collection of homemade instruments and offers lessons and a didge-making course. (☎6655 9881; www.heartdidg.com. Open M-F 9am-5pm, Sa 10am-4pm. Didgeridoos from $100 to $1000. Make your own from $150. 30min. lessons $15, 1hr. $20. Make your own from $150.) Just across the Bellinger River on Hammond St. is the entrance to **Bellingen Island,** home to an active colony of "flying foxes," or **fruit bats,** which have a 3 ft. wingspan. A forest trail loops through the open understory for excellent views. Turning right off Hammond St. onto Black St. leads to the showground, where an **organic market** is held the 2nd and 4th Saturday of every month. A larger produce, crafts, and antiques **community market** with 250 stalls and live music takes place every 3rd Saturday of the month. The three-day **Bellingen Jazz and Blues Festival** (☎6655 9345; www.bellingenjazzfestival.com.au) falls the 3rd weekend of August and brings more than a dozen performers to many town venues.

DORRIGO NATIONAL PARK

Dorrigo National Park, part of the World Heritage "Central Eastern Rainforest Reserves of Australia," is just 29km west of Belligen and 64km west of Coffs Harbour. The easiest way to visit is by car, but **Keans** offers bus service to Dorrigo. (☎1800 043 339. 1½hr. Leaves for Dorrigo Tu, Th, Sa, and returns M, W, F. $17.)

Begin your exploration of Dorrigo at the **Rainforest Centre,** 2km east of Dorrigo, which has a cafe and educational displays. Watch for red-necked **pademelons** and brush turkeys in the picnic area. (☎6657 2309. Open daily 9am-5pm.) Dorrigo is pure rainforest, with sections of multi-layered canopy and wet eucalyptus forest. When the rain makes things sloppy (not usually a problem on fully sealed trails), the **leeches** have a field day. Pick them off, or buy some insect repellent from the center. The spectacular, 75m-long **Skywalk** extends out and over the steep slope behind the Rainforest Centre and through the tree canopy, 21m above the forest floor.FFor a less vertigo-inducing stroll, descend to the forest floor via the **Lyrebird Link** (800m, 20min. round-trip), which connects to the **Wonga Walk,** (6.6km, 2½hr. loop). You'll soak your shoes as you walk behind the **Crystal Shower Falls** (1.6km, 30min. from the Lyrebird-Wonga junction). The **Walk with Birds** is a boardwalk that rises mid-level in the forest (700m, 15min. from the Lyrebird-Wonga junction).

Dome Road connects the Rainforest Centre to the **Never Never Picnic Area** (10km, 5km sealed, 5km unsealed maintained for 2WD) for several hiking tracks. **Glade Picnic Area** is 1km up the road from the center. From the park, follow Megan Rd. through the town of Dorrigo to visit the spectacular **Dangar Falls** lookout. A sealed pathway leads from the viewpoint to the base of the falls, a good swimming spot. Numerous picnic areas, walks, and attractions make this a good day excursion. If you do decide to stay the night, **Gracemere Grange ❷,** 325 Dome Road, just 2km from the park, offers beautiful, B&B-style accommodations. (☎6657 2630; www.dorrigo.com/gracemere. Singles $35; doubles $60-70.)

COFFS HARBOUR ☎02

Situated along the coast, backed by the hills of the Great Dividing Range, and covered in lush banana plantations, Coffs Harbour (pop. 70,000) is a popular spot for party-goers, scuba divers, and adrenaline junkies. The town is also known for its proximity to Solitary Islands National Marine Park. Coffs's continuing expansion has come at the expense of its coastal charm, but the town's tight-knit community and its scenic harbor make it a worthwhile stop.

TRANSPORTATION

Trains: Railway station is at end of Angus McLeod Pl. by the jetty. From Harbour Dr., turn onto Camperdown St. and take first left. **Countrylink** (☎13 22 32) goes to: **Brisbane** (6½-8hr., 5 per day, $65); **Byron Bay** (4½-5½hr., 4 per day, $38); **Nambucca Heads** (40min., 3 per day, $5); **Sydney** (9hr., 3 per day, $72). Student discounts.

Buses: The bus stop is off the Pacific Hwy., on the corner of Elizabeth and McLean St.

Busways (☎6652 2744 or 1300 555 611): **Bellingen** (1-1¼hr.; M-F 3 per day, Sa 2 per day; $6.60) and **Nambucca Heads** (1hr.; M-F 5 per day, Sa 2 per day; $7.20).

Greyhound Australia (☎13 14 99 or 13 20 30): **Ballina** (2½-3½hr., 5 per day, $45); **Brisbane** (6½-8hr., 5 per day, $65); **Byron Bay** (4-5hr., 5 per day, $53); **Newcastle** (6¾-8hr., 4 per day, $56); **Port Macquarie** (3hr., 3 per day, $45); **Sydney** (9-10hr., 4 per day, $74). ISIC/VIP/YHA 10% discount.

Keans (☎1800 043 339) Tu, Th, and Su 1 per day to: **Armidale** (3½hr., $35); **Bellingen** (35min., $15); **Dorrigo** (1½hr., $19); **Tamworth** (5hr., $60). Return trips M, W, and F.

Premier (☎13 34 10): **Brisbane** (7½hr., 2 per day, $54); **Byron Bay** (4¼hr., 3 per day, $46); **Nambucca Heads** (35min., 3 per day, $30); **Newcastle** (6½hr., 2 per day, $53); **Port Macquarie** (2½hr., 2 per day, $43); **Taree** (2¾hr., 2 per day, $46); **Sydney** (8½hr., 3 per day, $61). ISIC/VIP/YHA discount 15%.

TAKE A LOAD OFF. Coffs Harbour is nearly impossible to navigate on foot. Take advantage of free shuttles offered by hostels, or consider renting a bike.

Car Rental: Coffs Harbour Rent-A-Car (☎6652 5022), at the Shell Service Station, is on the corner of Pacific Hwy. and Marcia St. National firms such as **Budget** (☎6651 4994 or 13 27 27) and **Delta Europcar** (☎6651 8558 or 13 13 90) are also at the airport.

Taxi: Coffs District Taxi Network (☎13 10 08).

ORIENTATION AND PRACTICAL INFORMATION

As it passes through the city of Coffs Harbour, the Pacific Hwy. takes on three new names: **Grafton Street, Woolgoolga Road,** and **Bellingen Road.** Coffs is divided into two main clusters: the **Palms Centre** on Vernon St. is the Central Business District (CBD), while the **Jetty Village Shopping Centre** on Harbour Dr. has a smaller strip of shops by the harbor. The NPWS **Muttonbird Island Nature Reserve** is accessible by walking along the breakwater boardwalk at the end of Marina Dr. The city can be difficult to maneuver without a car, but hostels will often provide rides to attractions that are more than a 15min. walk away.

Tourist Office: Coffs Coast Visitor Information Center (☎6652 1522; www.coffscoast.com.au), on the corner of the Pacific Hwy. and McLean St. Open daily 9am-5pm.

Police: 20 Moonee St. (☎6652 0299).

Hospital: 345 Pacific Hwy. (☎6656 7000).

Internet Access: Coffs Harbour City Library (☎6648 4900), on the corner of Coffs and Duke St. Free 30min. sessions. Open M-F 9:30am-6pm, Sa 9:30am-3pm.

Post Office: (☎6648 7290) in Palms Centre; (☎6652 7499) in the Park Beach Plaza; and (☎6652 3200) across from the Jetty Village Shopping Centre. All open M-F 9am-5pm, Sa 9am-noon. **Postal Code:** 2450.

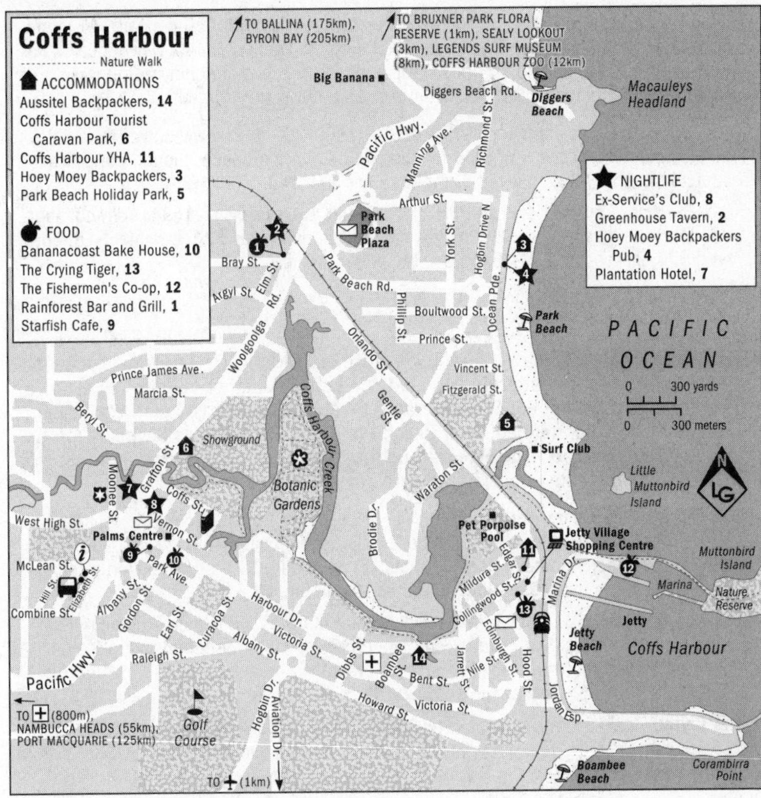

ACCOMMODATIONS AND CAMPING

Many motels are clustered along the Pacific Hwy. and Park Beach Rd. Caravan parks and hostels often offer weekly discounts in the low season. For longer stays and larger groups, you can book apartments at the visitors center. There are also several urban camping options.

Coffs Harbour YHA, 51 Collingwood St. (☎6652 6462). New hostel near jetty has spacious rooms, kitchen, snack shop, lounge area, TV, Internet access ($5 per hr.), laundry ($6), and pool. Bikes, boogie boards, and surfboards for $5-10 (with $50 deposit). Free pickup and drop-off. Reception May-Sept. 8am-10pm; Oct.-Apr. 7am-11pm. 6-bed dorms $23-25, 4-bed $25-27; doubles and twins $70-80. AmEx/MC/V. ❷

Aussitel Backpackers, 312 Harbour Dr. (☎6651 1871 or 1800 330 335; www.aussitel.com), 20min. walk from CBD and 10min. walk from the beach. Social and clean. Internet access, TV, pool, BBQ, foosball, luggage storage, and laundry ($5.20), free boogie boards and bikes for rent ($5 per day). Tie-ins with tour groups and dive centers give guests great deals. Free pickup and drop-off. Events nightly, Tu punch night ($6). Dorms $26, in winter $20-24; twins and doubles $50. NOMADS/VIP/YHA. MC/V. ❷

Hoey Moey Backpackers (☎6651 7966 or 1800 683 322; hoey@hoeymoey.com.au), on Ocean Pde., at end of Park Beach Rd. 1min. from beach and 10min. to Park Beach Plaza. Hoey Moey, slang for "Hotel Motel," is a backpackers, motel, and pub all rolled into one. Free surf and boogie boards. Bikes ($5 per day with $20 deposit). All rooms have bath, TV, small fridge. Free pickup and drop-off. Laundry $5.40. Key deposit $10. Reception 6-11:30am and 1:30pm-7:30pm; check in at pub after hours. Dorms $24, in winter $20; motel rooms $35. Discounts for 1wk. stays. VIP/YHA. MC/V. ❷

Park Beach Holiday Park (☎6648 4888 or 1800 200 111; www.parkbeachholiday-park.com.au), near the Surf Club on Ocean Pde. On the beach, though not the best stretch. Sites $23-32, powered $26-40; cabins $57-144. MC/V. ❷

Coffs Harbour Tourist Caravan Park, 123 Pacific Hwy. (☎6652 1694; www.coffsharbourtouristpark.com) is another nearby camping option. Sites $22, in winter $18; powered $25/21; cabins $70-95/58-84. ❷

FOOD

Across from the Jetty Village Shopping Centre on Harbour Dr. is a row of popular but expensive restaurants serving up Thai, Vietnamese, Indian, Chinese, Mod Oz (a new twist on Australian cuisine generated by popular Sydney chefs), and Italian meals. The **Palms Centre Mall, Park Beach Plaza,** and **Jetty Village Shopping Centre** each have **supermarkets.** The Plantation Hotel has cheap pub meals, including a generous steak or pasta dinner for $6 with any alcohol purchase.

The Fisherman's Co-op, 69 Marina Dr. (☎6652 2811), by the breakwater boardwalk. Serves fresh seafood straight off the boat, with fish 'n' chip meals ($7.50) and cajun-grilled hoki or herb-crumbed dory ($6). Market open daily 9am-6pm; takeaway counter open daily in summer 10am-9pm, in winter 10am-6pm. ❶

Starfish Cafe (☎6651 5005), in the City Square plaza by the Palms Shopping Centre, serves enormous burgers, salads, and smoothies. Try their butternut pumpkin, basil, and sundried tomato burger ($9) or cool off with a banana shake ($3). Open M-F 7:45am-3:30pm, Sa 7:45am-noon. MC/V. ❶

The Crying Tiger, 384a Harbour Dr. (☎6650 0195), in the Jetty Village shopping area. Serves contemporary Thai dishes amid colorful cushions under tall ceilings. Stir-fry and curries from $17-22. Open M-F 7:30am-5pm, Sa 7:30am-2pm. Cash only. ❶

Bananacoast Bake House, 22a Gordon St. (☎6652 2032). Traditional, no-frills bakery with cheap scones ($0.45), pies ($3), and sandwiches ($3). Open M-F 7:30am-5pm, Sa 7:30am-2pm. Cash only. ❶

Rainforest Bar and Grill (☎6651 5488), in the spacious, tropical Greenhouse Tavern at the corner of Bray St. and the Pacific Hwy. An extensive menu including hamburgers from $9 and steaks from $20. Open daily for lunch noon-2pm, dinner 6-8:30pm. ❷

SIGHTS

The Coffs Harbour Jetty, once part of a busy maritime industry, was built in 1892 and is now a nexus of recreation with some commercial fishing. The jetty has BBQ facilities and is an easy walk from **Jetty Beach.** The breakwater boardwalk, near the marina, connects the mainland to **Muttonbird Island** (named after the wedge-tailed shearwaters that nest there), a terrific lookout for spotting **whales.** The island was sacred to the region's Gumbayngirr Aborigines; according to a dreamtime story, a giant moon-man guarded the island and the muttonbirds. The occasionally patrolled **Park Beach** and the beach immediately north of the marina are also popular hangouts but have dangerous currents. The **Botanic Gardens,** on Hardacre St., one block north of Harbour Dr., is definitely worth the walk for the beautiful birds that flock to its exotic plants. (☎6648 4188. Open daily 9am-5pm. Donation requested.) The 4km-long **Coffs Creek Walk** connects Rotary Park, at the intersection of Gordon and Coffs St. in the

CBD, and the Coffs Creek inlet, near Orlando St.; it also has a detour to the gardens. Make the hike a 10km circuit by continuing on the **Coffs Creek Habitat Walk** (6km) which follows the northern bank of the creek. Pick up a map from the visitors center.

The Big Banana, 4km north of town on the Pacific Hwy., embodies quintessential kitsch. Take an interactive tour to learn more than you need to know about banana cultivation ($15, students $13.50, children $10), go tobogganing ($5, 5 rides $15), hike up through the plantation for a view over the city, or just gape at the giant banana out front. A cafe sells outstanding treats, including frozen, chocolate-covered bananas ($2.60) and banana splits ($7). A candy-maker, puzzle shop, and trike rental are on the grounds. (☎6652 4355; www.bigbanana.com. Open daily 9am-4pm. Admission free.) For more banana-y goodness, drive another kilometer up the road, and turn left at Bruxner Park Road. A 7km scenic road winds through banana plantations up to **Sealy Lookout** and **Bruxner Park Flora Reserve.** Farmers sell bags of bananas and avocados ($1-2) in wooden stands along the way; leave the money in metal courtesy boxes.

The **Coffs Harbour Zoo,** 1530 Pacific Hwy., 10km north of Coffs and past Moonee Beach, offers daily presentations on koalas at 11am and 3pm, wombats at 10:30am, and echidnas at 10:45am. To make the trip and entry costs worthwhile, be sure to catch the animal shows. (☎6656 1330. Open daily 9am-4pm, later during holidays. $16, students $12, children $8, families $40.) Advertisements all over town point to the **Pet Porpoise Pool (Oceanarium),** on Orlando St. by Coffs Creek. Catch the dolphin shows at 10am and 1pm. Come 30min. early and a dolphin will give you a peck on the cheek. (☎6652 2164; www.petporpoisepool.com. Open daily in summer 9am-4pm; in winter 9am-3pm. $25, backpackers $20, students $18, children $12.50, families $70.)

ACTIVITIES

There's no shortage of activities in Coffs. Hostels generally offer good rates, but don't hesitate to call tour agencies to find commission-free fun. Nearly all companies operate year-round, and some offer discounts during the winter.

DIVING. **Jetty Dive Centre,** 398 Harbour Dr., offers a 4-day PADI course ($195 for backpackers staying at any Coffs hostel). The course is run off Muttonbird Island, not in the Solitary Islands, making for better prices but less exotic visuals. For $245 the half-and-half course offers two dives at Muttonbird Island and two in the Solitary Islands. An extra $95 required for medical check-up and textbook. (☎6651 1611; www.jettydive.com.au. Single intro-dive $125; double intro-dive $155; double boat-dive with gear from $130; snorkeling $55. Open daily 9am-5:30pm.) **Solitary Islands Marine Reserve** stretches 70km from Coffs Harbour to the Sandon River and encompasses nearly 100,000 hectares of protected beaches, headlands, creeks, and rocky islands. Due to the unique mix of warm, tropical waters from the north and cool, temperate waters from the south, the area has some of the most diverse marine life on the coast. Species common to the Great Barrier Reef mingle with those typically found near Tasmania. Visibility is usually best during the winter, when the water is chilly. Swim with harmless gray **nurse sharks** year-round. Contact the **NSW Fisheries and Marine Parks Office,** 32 Marina Dr., for more info. (☎6652 3977; www.mpa.nsw.gov.au. Open M-F 8:30am-5pm.)

FISHING AND WHALE WATCHING. Fishing boats **Adriatic III** (☎04 1252 2002) and **Cougar Cat 12** (☎6651 6715 or 04 1866 6715; www.cougarcat12.com.au) will set you up with bait, line, and tackle. (½-day reef fishing $80-90; game fishing by appointment.) Whales swim past Coffs June-July and again Sept.-Nov.; spot them during the winter months with **Spirit Cruises.** (☎6650 0155; www.spiritofcoffs.com.au. 2½hr. Leaves daily at 9:30am and also 1pm on weekends. $35-49.) The **Pacific Explorer** catamaran also runs whale-watching cruises. (☎6652 7225. 2-2½hr. trips depart 9am. $20-30 per person.)

WHITEWATER RAFTING AND JET SKIING. The **Nymboida River,** 2hr. west of Coffs, is the most popular place to raft. The rapids, mostly Class I-V sections, pass through dense rainforest. Award-winning **Wildwater Adventures,** 754 Pacific Hwy. (☎6654 1114), 7km south of Coffs leads trips down the Nymboida, complete with BBQ dinner. (Full day $155, 2-day with camping $325.) The **Goolang River,** a man-made kayaking course is usually Class III, but flow depends on seasonal conditions. **Liquid Assets Adventure Tours,** the pioneers of surf-rafting, run unbeatable whitewater rafting on the Goolang and Nymboida, as well as slightly tamer but still adrenaline-charged sea-kayak and rafting tours. (☎6658 0850; www.surfrafting.com. Meals included with full-day tours. Goolang ½ day $80; full day on the Nymboida $150. 3hr. sea kayaking $35; 3hr. surf-rafting $40; combo kayak and surf-rafting $50; "Big Day Out" combo of kayaking, surf-rafting, and whitewater rafting $135.)

SURFING. East Coast Surf School has a remarkable success rate with novices. Classes for advanced surfers are also available. Call to arrange pickup from hostels. (☎6651 5515 or 04 1225 7233; www.eastcoastsurfschool.com.au. 2hr. group lesson $50, 5 lessons $200; 1hr. private lesson $60.) Liquid Assets also offers "learn to surf" classes (3hr. class $40). Most hostels provide surfboards and boogie boards for rental. The best **surfing** is at **Diggers Beach** (patrolled during school holidays), north of Macauleys Headland, accessible off the Pacific Hwy. From the Big Banana (p. 195), turn onto Diggers Beach Rd. and follow it to the end. **The Gallows Beach,** down at the Jetty, also offers good breaks. To learn about surfing without getting your feet wet, visit former surfing champ Scott Dillon's **Legends Surf Museum,** at 3/18 Gaudron's Rd. in Korora, about 2km north of Coffs Harbour on the Pacific Hwy. (☎6653 6536; dafin@key.net.au. Open daily 10am-4pm. $5, children $2.)

ENTERTAINMENT AND NIGHTLIFE

Coffs nightlife, focused around Grafton St., isn't quite as pumping as the daytime scene, but finding the party crowd isn't too difficult in the summertime. Hostels sometimes organize nights out for their guests. Most pubs have cover bands or DJs on weekends. The **Plantation Hotel,** on Grafton St., is the hippest nightspot in town, with a sports bar, lounge rooms, dance floor, and frequent big-name bands. (☎6652 3855; www.plantationhotel.com.au. Cover F-Sa $5 Open M-Th and Su until 2am, F-Sa until 4am.) The somewhat bland **Ex-Service's Club** (☎6652 3888), on the corner of Grafton and Vernon St., has cheap drinks. Non-members must arrive before 11pm. The 20min. walk from town to the **Greenhouse Tavern** (☎6651 5488), on the Pacific Hwy. by the Park Beach Plaza, is rewarded with a tropical setting plus multiple bars and live music offerings.

COFFS HARBOUR TO BALLINA ☎02

As the Pacific Hwy. winds from Coffs Harbour north to Ballina, the small coastal towns of the Clarence Valley may make for relaxing stopping points or peaceful extended stays.

WOOLGOOLGA. Twenty-five kilometers north of Coffs Harbour lies Woolgoolga, a small coastal town with an intriguing blend of cultures. To the south, the strikingly white Indian temple, **Guru Nanak Sikh Gurdwara,** heralds Woolgoolga's thriving Punjabi Sikh community. If you leave the Pacific Hwy. and continue to the tiny town center, however, Indian influence fades and the beautiful coastline takes center-stage. There are fantastic views from the **Woolgoolga Headland** of the **Solitary Islands Marine Reserve**, an aquatic sanctuary with marine biodiversity approaching that of the Great Barrier Reef. A number of motels line the road to town, and there are a handful of caravan parks just a short walk from the beach. Try the **Lakeside Caravan Park ❶,** with direct access to the beach and a lake. (☎6654 1210. Reception

8am-5:30pm. Sites for 2 $19-26, powered $20-30; cabins $52-115. Can for off-peak weekly rates. MC/V.) **Grafton** and **Maclean,** both west of the Pacific Hwy., are the largest nearby towns in the Clarence Valley. Both have **visitors centers,** motels, **libraries,** and **ATMs.**

YAMBA. The coastal town of Yamba (pop. 6750), halfway to Ballina and 15km from the Pacific Hwy., is a charming village with lookouts for whale-watching and bays for fishing. The town marks the northern tip of **Yuraygir National Park,** once home to Yaegl and Gumbaingirr Aboriginals. The park has four **campsites ❶** and strong surf at the Angourie Bay picnic area. A block from the lighthouse, the **Pacific Hotel ❷,** at 18 Pilot St. sits on a cliff over the sea. (☎6646 2466; pacifichotelyamba.com.au. 4-bed dorms $25, ocean-view $30; doubles $55; ocean-view motel rooms $100. AmEx/MC/V.) Campers and caravans can head to **Calypso Holiday Park ❷,** on Harbour St. (☎6646 8477; www.calypsoyamba.com.au. Sites $21-23, powered $24-28; ensuite cabins with A/C and TV $60-70. Weekly rates available. MC/V.)

ILUKA. A ferry connects Yamba to Iluka (pop. 2700) across the bay four times per day. (☎04 0866 4556. $5.70, children $2.85.) Cars can get there from the Pacific Hwy. by taking the Iluka Rd. turnoff. The World Heritage-listed **Iluka Nature Reserve** is the largest littoral rainforest in New South Wales, with over 140 species of birds. Seashells blanket every square inch of the beach by the **Iluka Bluff** picnic area. The **Bundjalung National Park** stretches along the shoreline from Iluka to just outside Evans Head. The preserve is renowned for its crescent-shaped inlets, white sand beaches, and surrounding rainforest. It also has picnic facilities, pristine beaches, and two **camping ❶** areas at Black Rocks and Woody Head. Contact the Grafton NPWS office (☎6641 1500) for more info.

BALLINA ☎02

Technically an island, Ballina (pop. 19,000) is a peaceful port and beach town 2½hr. north of Coffs Harbour and 30min. south of Byron Bay. Getting around is surprisingly easy if you utilize the extensive network of **bike paths** linking Ballina and Lennox Head; pick up a map from the visitors center. **Lighthouse Beach** is a great vantage point for whale watching. The 68-hectare reserve at **Angels Beach,** in East Ballina, sometimes has playful dolphins. In addition to being a fantastic surfing destination, **Flat Rock** possesses an incredible array of marine life including octopi, sea anemones, and sea stars.

Learn to surf or perfect your technique at **Surf School,** great for families. (☎6682 4393. In Ballina: private 2hr. lessons $100, small group lessons $45. In Evans Head: private 2hr. lessons $75, small group lessons $40. Ask about accommodation and lesson packages.) Swing by the **Ballina Naval and Maritime Museum,** on the corner of North St. and Regatta Ave., just down from the visitors center, to see one of the three original rafts that crossed the Pacific from Ecuador to Australia on the 1973 Las Balsas Trans Pacific Expedition. (☎6681 1002. Open daily 9am-4pm. Donations encouraged.) For a leisurely afternoon, try **Richmond River Cruises.** (☎6687 5688 or 04 0732 9851. W and Su 2hr. tours. $22-24, includes coffee or Devonshire tea.) For self-guided exploring, **Jack Ransom Cycles,** 16 Cherry St., just off River St., rents bikes. (☎6686 3485. Open M-F 8am-5pm, Sa 8am-noon. ½ day $10, full day $16.50, week $50. Deposit $50.)

The **Ballina Travelers Lodge (YHA) ❷,** 36 Tamar St., is a motel and hostel in one. Go one block up Norton St. from the tourist office, then turn left. The friendly owners keep the lodge quiet and meticulously clean. The YHA part of the complex has four basic rooms, a sparkling clean kitchen and TV area, BBQ, and laundry. The larger motel rooms have individual TVs and lots of amenities. There's a small saltwater pool, bikes ($5 per stay), limited fishing gear, and free boogie boards. (☎6686 6737. Courtesy pickup from the transit center by arrangement. Dorms from $23; motel rooms $72-86.) The **Ballina Central Caravan Park ❷,** 1 River St., is just north of the info center. (☎6686 2220; www.bscp.com.au/central. Open daily 7am-7pm. Sites $21-25, powered $24-30; cabins $50-116. Weekly rates available. MC/V.) Delicious deli food awaits at **Sasha's Gourmet Eatery ❶,** in the Wigmore Arcade, off River St. Takeaway selections like pasta salad, quiche, and gourmet sandwiches ($4-7) make perfect picnic fare. (☎6681 1118. Open M-F 8am-5pm, Sa 8am-1pm. MC/V.) **Pelican 181 ❷,** on the water across from the Wigmore Arcade, is an upscale restaurant with a takeaway breakfast and lunch counter. Try fishcakes ($7) or a barramundi fillet ($10). (☎6686 9181. Open daily 8am-5pm. Cash only.) **Paddy McGinty's ❷,** 56 River St., is the local Irish pub and serves counter lunches and dinners. (☎6686 2135. Burgers from $9.50, main courses from $11. Open daily 11:30am-2:30pm and 6-9pm, bar until 10pm.)

Greyhound Australia (☎13 14 99) and **Premier** (☎13 34 10) stop in Ballina on their Sydney-Brisbane runs. Greyhound departs from the **Transit Centre,** 4km from the town center in a large complex known as **The Big Prawn** because of the enormous pink fiberglass prawn nailed to its roof; tickets can be purchased inside the restaurant. Premier leaves from the Ampol petrol station on the corner of Bangalow Rd. and Kerr St. Regional bus companies stop in town at the Tamar St. bus zone. **Blanch's Bus Company** (☎6686 2144) travels daily to Byron Bay (50min.; M-F 7 per day, Sa 6 per day, Su 3 per day; $9) with a stop in Lennox Head (20min.; $5.60). **Ballina Taxi Cabs** (☎6686 9999 or 1800 065 870) will take you into town for $10-12.

The **Visitor Information Centre,** on the eastern edge of town at the corner of Las Balsa Plaza and **River Street** (the main street in town), has info on regional activities. (☎1800 777 666; www.discoverballina.com. Open daily 9am-5pm.) Hop on the **Internet** at the public **library,** next to the visitors center. (☎6686 1277. Open M-Tu and F 9:30am-6pm, W-Th 9:30am-8pm, Sa 9am-noon. $2.20 per 30min.) **Woolworths** supermarket is at 72 River St. (☎6686 3189. M-F 8am-9pm, Sa-Su 8am-6pm.) Another is located in the Ballina Fair Shopping Centre on Kerr Rd. (☎6686 4825; open M-F 8am-9pm, Sa-Su 8am-8pm), and a **Coles** is directly across the street. (☎6686 9377. Open M-F 6am-midnight, Sa 6am-10pm, Su 8am-8pm.) The **post office** is at 85 Tamar St. on the corner with Moon St. (☎6626 8810. Open M-F 9am-5pm.) **Postal Code:** 2478.

LENNOX HEAD ☎02

Lennox Head (pop. 28,000), between Ballina and Byron Bay (15min. from both), is a serene and tranquil alternative to its neighbors. It may not appear on the average traveler's itinerary except as a lodging point, but it's a relaxing break from the hype of Byron and beyond.

Lennox is renowned for its excellent **surf. Lennox Point,** 2km south of town, has one of the longest right hand surf breaks in the world; from June to August it is among the top 10 international surfing areas. Tamer surf spots are found along Seven Mile Beach. **All Above Board,** 68 Ballina St. (☎6687 7522), rents surfboards (½ day $20, full day $25, week $140), and body boards ($5/20/80). An age-old **Aboriginal Bora Ring** is only two blocks from the hostel and caravan park at the end of Ross St. The indented area 40m in circumference was a spiritual spot for ancient Aboriginal coming-of-age ceremonies.

Off the Pacific Hwy., Lennox Head is connected to Ballina by **The Coast Road,** which continues north to Byron Bay as **Byron Bay Rd.** The town center is accessible by taking the roundabout to coastal Ballina St., which becomes Pacific Pde. and runs along **Seven Mile Beach,** prime dolphin-spotting territory. **Lennox Point (Head),** 2km south, is an excellent but crowded surf area. To check out the pros and maybe a migrating whale or two, head to **Pat Morton Lookout** at the top of Lennox Head. Only a 100m walk from the carpark off The Coast Rd. **Blanch's Coaches** (☎6686 2144) go through Lennox Head daily to Ballina ($5.60/2.80) and Byron Bay ($7, children and concessions $3.50); bus stop is on Ballina St. near town center, but you can also flag buses down along Pacific Pde.

The recently renovated **Backpackers Beach ❶**, 49 Ballina St., is one of the least expensive hostels around and is the closest you can get to the breaks at Lennox Point. Located only 100m from the beach, guests returning from the surf can snooze in one of the provided hammocks. Free shuttles to and from Byron Bay. (☎6687 6600; www.backpackers-beach.com. 8-bed dorms $20-25, 1 motel room $80. Cash only.) The intimate **Lennox Head Beach House YHA ❷**, 3 Ross St., is north of the town center just off Pacific Pde., and is a short walk from Lake Ainsworth. The hostel offers boogie boards, tennis racquets, bikes, and fishing rods for $5 (plus $20 deposit), surfboards for $20, and free windsurfing lessons. Aspiring gourmands can help themselves to the herb garden and dine in the courtyard. On Thursdays, enjoy a free 10min. massage. Bedrooms are small but tidy, with solid wood beds. (☎6687 7636. Internet $2 per 20min. 4-bed dorms $25-26; doubles $60-62. Ask about weekly rates. YHA. MC/V.) The **Lake Ainsworth Caravan Park ❷** is across Ross St., next to the lake. (☎6687 7249. Office open 7am-7pm. Sites $21-25, powered $24-30; cabins $50-95. Linen $5. MC/V.) **Fishy Fishy ❶**, 80 Ballina St. dishes up tasty seafood in heaping portions. (☎6687 5599. Fish or calamari with chips $7. Open daily 11am-8pm. DC/MC/V.) The **Ocean View Cafe ❶**, on Pacific Pde. one block past Ross St. at the surf club, is true to its name, with a spectacular view of the beach all the way down to Lennox Point, and remarkably cheap food. (☎6687 7380. Open M-F 8:30am-4pm, Sa-Su 8am-3pm. Breakfast from $2, burgers from $5. Cash only.) At **Cafe de Mer ❷**, 1/70 Ballina St., you can sit back and watch the town go by while sipping delicious fresh-squeezed juices for less than $5. (☎6687 7132. Breakfast or lunch $5-14. Open daily 8:30am-5pm. Cash only.)

ATMs, eateries, and the local pub can all be found on Ballina St. There's also an **IGA** supermarket at 80-84 Ballina St. (☎6687 7594. Open in summer daily 6am-9m; in winter M-Sa 6am-8:30pm, Su 6am-8pm.) The **post office** is at 74 Ballina St. (☎6687 7240. Open M-F 8:30am-5pm.) **Postal Code:** 2478.

LISMORE ☎02

Forty-five kilometers inland from Byron Bay, Lismore (pop. 44,000) has soaked up nearby Nimbin's hippie vibe, offering visitors a laid-back atmosphere in a more urban environment. Bare feet and dreadlocks are common sights on Lismore's wide boulevards. Students at Southern Cross University help to promote Lismore's first-rate art scene. Outside the town center,

GOT SURF?

Though the crashing waves may look daunting to beginners, the surf off **Lennox Head** is candy to top-notch surfers. The talented few who can hang ten on Lennox's world-renowned breaks are rewarded with a wide, uncrowded beach and great waves. There is action available for bold intermediate surfers as well.

Lennox Head's main surf spot, **Seven Mile Beach,** is filled with swimmers who glide over the surf and relax on the beautiful white sand. Seven Mile is also popular with fishermen who wade out onto sandbars just before sunset to toss their lines.

Besides being a popular area for casual beachgoers, Lennox Head is home to several annual competitions as well. Each June, the normally uncrowded beaches at Lennox Head become packed for one of Australia's most exciting surfing contest, the **All Girls Surf Showdown.** More than 200 girls take to the waves to strut their stuff in an all-out surfing extravaganza. The annual event takes place over the long weekend in June; the fifteenth showdown will be June 9-11, 2007.

The **Rusty Gromfest,** another popular Lennox Head surf-off, is the largest junior surf competition in Australia, with hundreds of eight- to 16-year-old competitors from all around the world. It takes place in mid-July, and the twelfth annual Gromfest will be held July 6-10, 2007.

three World Heritage rainforests and the volcanic remains at Mt. Warning National Park beckon backpackers and nature-lovers. The disproportionately high number of rainbows (due to the position of local valleys) earn the area the nickname "Rainbow Region."

TRANSPORTATION. The **railway station** is on Union St., across the river. **Countrylink** (☎13 22 32) connects from Casino to Sydney (12½hr., 2 per day, $121) and Brisbane (3hr., 1 per day, $31). The new **Transit Centre** (☎6621 8620) is on the corner of Molesworth and Magellan St. **Kirkland's** (☎6622 1499 or 1300 367 077) runs buses to: Brisbane (3½hr.; 2-3 per day; $35, students $18) via Byron Bay (1hr., $11/6) and Surfers Paradise (2½hr., 2 per day, $33/25); Murwillumbah (2hr., 1 per day, $20); Tenterfield (3hr., M-F 1 per day, $27). **Premier** (☎9281 2233; www.premierms.com.au) sends buses once per day to Brisbane (5½hr., $39) and Sydney (11½hr., $81-92). The best way to get around is to rent a **car.** Options include **Hertz,** 49 Dawson St. (☎6621 8855 or 13 30 39), and **Thrifty,** 2/31 Dawson St. (☎6622 2266 or 1300 367 227). For a **taxi,** call ☎13 10 08.

ORIENTATION AND PRACTICAL INFORMATION. In the hinterlands west of Ballina, Lismore lies off the Bruxner Hwy. (called **Ballina Street** in town) just east of **Wilson's River.** Approaching the river from the east, Ballina St. crosses **Dawson, Keen,** and **Molesworth Street,** the busiest part of town. Perpendicular to these streets in the town center are small **Conway** and **Magellan Street.** One block past Magellan St., **Woodlark Street** crosses the river to **Bridge Street,** leading to the north side of town and Nimbin.

At the corner of Molesworth and Ballina St., the **Lismore Visitor Information Centre** has a small indoor tropical rainforest and social history exhibit. (☎6622 0100 or 1300 369 795; www.visitlismore.com.au. Open M-F 9:30am-4pm, Sa-Su 10am-3pm.) **ATMs** can be found anywhere in the town center. **Internet** access is available at the visitors center ($5 per hr.) and at the **library** at 110 Magellan St. (☎6622 2721. Open M-W 9:30am-5pm, Th-F 9:30am-7:30pm, Sa 9am-1pm.) **Police** (☎6621 9699) are on Molesworth St. and the **Lismore Base Hospital** is at 60 Uralba St. (☎6621 8000). A **post office** is on Conway St. between Molesworth and Keen St. (☎6627 7316. Open M-F 8:30am-5pm.) **Postal Code:** 2480.

ACCOMMODATIONS AND FOOD. Budget accommodations are nearly impossible to find in Lismore. For a motel room, try **Lismore City Motor Inn ❹,** 129 Magellan St. (☎6621 4455), on the corner of Dawson St., which features spacious ensuite rooms with TV, fridge, and A/C. (Pool and laundry available. Reception daily 7:30am-9pm. Singles $50-62; twins and doubles $69-95; extra person $10. AmEx/MC/V.) **Lismore Palms Caravan Park ❶,** 42 Brunswick St. (☎6621 7067), offers basic rooms with an on-site kitchen and pool. Follow Dawson St. north and turn right onto Brunswick St. (Laundry $6. Linen $5. Sites $16-18, powered $22-25; ensuite cabins $57-67. Weekly rates available. MC/V.)

The uni-student demand for cheap vegetarian eats has resulted in some terrifically funky cafes. No cows are served at the vegan **20,000 Cows ❸,** 58 Bridge St. Surrounded by wild tablecloths, tall candlesticks, and comfy sofas, diners wolf down fresh pasta, and Indian and Middle Eastern food. (☎6622 2517. Open W-Su from 6pm.) Another student haunt, **Dr. Juice Bar ❶,** 142 Keen St., serves tasty vegetarian/vegan dishes. The Doctor prescribes marvelous, fresh smoothies, veggie burgers, and wildly popular tofu cheesecake, all for less than $7. (☎6622 4440. Open M-F 9:30am-4pm, Sa 10am-2pm. Cash only.) **Caddies Coffee ❷,** 20 Carrington St., serves excellent coffee, sandwiches ($7-10), and salads ($9-13), as well as an all-day breakfast ($6-13). The outdoor patio and art-adorned indoor deck make this cafe a sure shot. (☎6621 7709. Open M-F 8am-6pm, Sa 8am-1:30pm. Cash only.) For a meaty meal in an otherwise veggie town, try **Mary Gilhooley's ❸,** on the corner of Keen and Woodlark St. Mary's serves traditional Irish fare, including Guinness pie ($20) and steak $20-24, often with live music in the background. (☎6622 2924. Open M-W 10am-11pm, Th-F 10am-2am, Sa 10am-4am, Su 10am-10pm. AmEx/DC/MC/V.) For groceries, head to **Woolworths** on Keen St., with a back entrance on Carrington St. (Open M-Sa 7am-10pm, Su 9am-6pm.)

SIGHTS. The fabulous **Richmond River Historical Society,** 165 Molesworth St., in the Municipal Building, houses a natural-history room with preserved baby crocs and mummified tropical birds, as well as a hallway of Aboriginal boomerangs. (☎6621 9993. Open M-Th 10am-4pm. $2.) The **Boatharbour Nature Reserve,** 7km northeast of Lismore on Bangalow Rd., boasts 17 hectares of rainforest trees, the remnants of the "Big Scrub Forest." The original 75,000 hectares of lowland forest throughout northern New South Wales has been almost completely decimated. **Tucki Tucki Nature Reserve,** which doubles as a koala sanctuary, is 15min. from Lismore on Wyrallah Rd. Lismore's water supply comes from the **Rocky Creek Dam,** home to a waterfront boardwalk and platypus lagoon. From the north side of town, take Tweed St. for about 30km. To protect the endangered Fleay's Barred Frog, don't go swimming..

KOALA TRACKS. When trying to spy a napping koala, check the base of the trunks for a scratch marks. The furry bears are most likely clinging to marked trees, nestled in the fork between two branches.

BYRON BAY ☎02

A 1½hr. drive south from the hipsters of Surfers Paradise and east from the hippies of Nimbin, Byron Bay (pop. 12,000) combines the best of both worlds. Though smaller than Surfers and less out-there than Nimbin, Byron draws 1.7 million visitors of all types with its family- and surfer-friendly beaches, massage spas, palm readers, kebab shops, and bistros.

TRANSPORTATION

Buses: Buses depart from the **bus depot** outside the visitors center on Jonson St. Purchase tickets at **Peterpan Adventures** (see below).

Blanch's (☎6686 2144; www.blanchs.com.au): **Ballina** (50min., 2-8 per day, $9); **Lennox Head** (30min., 2-8 per day, $5.60); **Mullumbimby** (30min., 2-4 per day, $5.60).

Countrylink (☎13 22 32; www.countrylink.com.au): **Ballina** (40min., 1 per day, $6); **Grafton** (3¾hr., 1 per day, $27); **Lennox Head** (35min., 1 per day, $6); **Lismore** (1½hr., 3 per day, $7); **Mullumbimby** (20min., 1 per day, $6); **Murwillumbah** (1hr., 2 per day, $6); **Surfers Paradise** (1¾hr., 1 per day, $14); **Sydney** (14hr., 4 per day, $88). Prices vary by season.

Greyhound Australia (☎13 14 10; www.greyhound.com.au): **Brisbane** (3-4hr., 7 per day, $37); **Coffs Harbour** (4hr., 4 per day, $53); **Lismore** (2hr., 1 per day, $43); **Murwillumbah** (50min., 2 per day, $16); **Port Macquarie** (7hr., 3 per day, $74); **Surfers Paradise** (1½-2hr., 8 per day, $29); **Sydney** (13-14hr., 4 per day, $105). Backpacker discount 10%.

Premier (☎13 34 10; www.premierms.com.au): **Brisbane** ($32) and **Sydney** ($86) with multiple stops in both directions.

Taxis: Byron Bay Taxis (☎6685 5008). 24hr. Wheelchair-accessible taxis available.

Car Rental: Earth Car Rentals, 18 Fletcher St. (☎6685 7472; www.earthcar.com.au). Cars from $34 per day. $550 deposit. **Jetset Travel** (☎6685 6554), on Marvell just off Jonson St., rents manual cars from $49 per day.

Tours: Grasshoppers Eco-Explorer Tour (☎0500 881 881; www.grasshoppers.com.au) offers an all-day trip to subtropical rainforest, waterfalls, koala- and platypus-sighting spots, and **Nimbin.** Daily tours 10am-6pm. $35, includes BBQ lunch. Adventure tours (mountain biking, caving, abseiling, trekking) range $55-129. **Jim's Alternative Tours** (☎6685 7720; www.jimsalternativetours.com) offers a great 8hr. trip with synchronized CD soundtrack through **Minyan Falls, Nimbin,** and **Nightcap National Park.** Includes a stop at **Paul Recher's Fruit Spirit Botanical Gardens,** reforested with 350 different varieties of exotic fruit from around the world. $35.

ORIENTATION AND PRACTICAL INFORMATION

Byron is not on the Pacific Hwy., but is accessible from it via nearby Bangalow (15km south) or Ewingsdale (6km north) Rd. **Bangalow Road** enters Byron Bay from the south. Turn off a roundabout on **Browning Street,** which leads to **Jonson Street,** the southern boundary of the Central Business District (CBD). **Lawson Street,** to the north of town, runs along **Main Beach.** To the east, Lawson St. becomes **Lighthouse Road,** running past **Clarkes Beach,** the **Pass** surfing spot, **Wategos Beach,** the lighthouse, and the Cape Byron lookout. To the west, Lawson becomes **Shirley Street** and curves off to **Belongil Beach.** Farther west it becomes **Ewingsdale Road** and passes the **Arts and Industrial Estate** before reaching the Pacific Hwy.

Tourist Office: Byron Visitors Centre, 80 Jonson St. (☎6680 8558; www.visitbyronbay.com), at the bus station. Friendly staff books local adventure activities and hotel rooms. Open daily 9am-5pm.

Budget Travel: Backpacker travel centers cluster around the bus station, and most hostels have travel desks that book trips and local activities. The friendly staff at **Peterpan Adventures,** 87 Jonson St. (☎1800 252 459; www.peterpanstravel.com), does the same, and will book most local activities for free. Open daily in summer 9am-9pm; in winter 9:30am-8pm. **Wicked Travel,** 89 Jonson St. (☎1800 555 339; www.wickedtravel.com.au) offers similar services and **Internet** access for $1 per hr. Open daily 9am-7pm.

Currency Exchange: Banks on Jonson St. are open M-Th 9:30am-4pm, F 9:30am-5pm. **ATMs** are across the street from the visitors center. The **Byron Foreign Exchange Shop,** 4 Central Arcade, Byron St. (☎6685 7787), advertises the lowest fees and best rates. Open M-Sa 9am-5pm, Su 10am-4pm.

Police: (☎6685 9499), on the corner of Butler and Shirley St.

Hospital: Byron Bay Hospital (☎6685 6200), corner of Shirley and Wordsworth St.

Internet Access: Internet cafes are everywhere in Byron; some pass out vouchers on the street for free or discounted access. Most activity-booking offices also offer free Internet access with bookings. Even without a booking, **Peterpan Adventures** (p. 202) may give you free 30min. sessions, and charges just $1 per hr. thereafter with ISIC/VIP/YHA. **Global Gossip,** 84 Jonson St. (☎6680 9140), at the bus stop, has Internet for $4.50 per hr. Open daily in summer 9am-midnight, in winter 9am-10pm. The cafe also offers locker rental (large enough for 2 full backpacks) for $6 per day.

Post Office: 61 Jonson St. (☎13 13 18). Open M-F 9am-5pm, Sa 9am-2pm. **Postal Code:** 2481.

ACCOMMODATIONS AND CAMPING

In summer, especially around Christmas, Byron is saturated with thousands of tourists; some accommodation prices double accordingly. The best advice is to book early, but demand is so high that some hostels don't even accept reservations during the summer season. Many would-be Byron visitors are forced to stay in Lennox Head (p. 198) or Ballina (p. 197), 10 and 20min. south, respectively. Sleeping in cars or on the beach is prohibited. Unless specified, all hostels offer free pickup in town.

Aquarius Backpackers, 16 Lawson St. (☎6685 7663 or 1800 028 909; www.aquariusbackpackers.com.au), corner of Middleton St. Formerly 4-star motel, many of the spacious rooms have 2 levels, porch, and fridge. Poolside bar with Happy hour, nightly meals ($8), travel desk, parking, kitchen, and cafe. Internet access $4 per hr. Free boogie

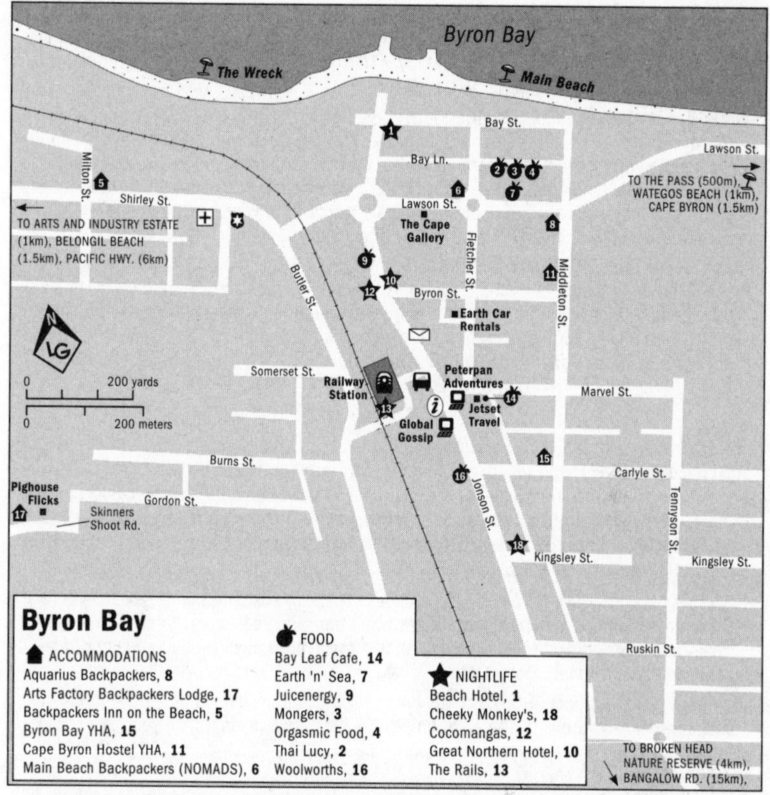

boards. Linen $1, blanket deposit $10. Laundry $4. Key deposit $10. Free nightclub entry. Reception 7am-10pm. Ensuite dorms $23-27; doubles $60-75; motel units $130-260, 2 with spa $150-300. 3- and 7-day discounts. VIP/YHA $1 off. MC/V. ❷

Arts Factory Backpackers Lodge (☎6685 7709; www.artsfactory.com.au), on Skinners Shoot Rd. Sprawling 5-acre grounds with teepees and island bungalows. Bring bug repellent. Free didgeridoo workshops. Pool and ping-pong tournaments. Yoga classes $5-10. Internet access $1 per 10min. Learn bush survival on free "tucker walks" M-W at 4pm. Heated pool (lit for nighttime pool parties), sauna, and cafe. Shuttles to town. Laundry $6. Lockers $2 per 12hr.; keyed wallet lockers $1. Reception 7am-1pm and 4-9pm. Sites $15; teepees $22-28; dorms $30; twins and doubles $85; bungalows $75. Discounts for longer stays. VIP. MC/V. ❷

Backpackers Inn on the Beach, 29 Shirley St. (☎6685 8231; www.byron-bay.com/backpackersinn). Large and social with direct beach access. Loft kitchen, volleyball, heated pool, BBQ, billiards, cable TV, and games. Internet access $4 per hr. Blanket fee $1. Free luggage storage, bikes ($20 deposit), and boogie boards. Surfboard rentals $15 per 3hr. and $25 per day. W and Sa BBQ $5. W Sangria night $4. Wheelchair accessible. Secure parking. Laundry $5. Reception M-F 8am-8pm, Sa-Su 8am-2pm and 4pm-8pm. Dorms $20-25; doubles $62-68. Book ahead. ISIC/VIP/YHA. MC/V. ❷

Byron Bay YHA, 7 Carlyle St. (☎6685 8853 or 1800 678 195); 300m from beach, 200m from bus stop. Clean, colorful, and cozy, the hostel has one of the best all-you-can-eat-and-drink BBQ deals in town during summer. Billiards and picnic tables in an upstairs covered pavilion, large kitchen, heated pool, and secure parking. Family-friendly. Free bikes ($50 deposit) and boogie boards. Surf boards $10 per day ($100 deposit). Laundry $6. Lockers $2-7 per day. Internet $3 per hr. Towel $1. Reception 8am-9pm. Dorms $25-32, YHA $22-29; twins and doubles $70-80, ensuite $80-95; family rooms from $90. Book at least 1wk. ahead. MC/V. ❷

Main Beach Backpackers (NOMADS) (☎6685 8695 or 1800 150 233), corner of Lawson and Fletcher St. High ceilings, fireplace, rooftop deck with billiards, patio, pool, secured parking, lockers, and common room with TV. BBQ twice per wk. in summer. Free boogie boards. Laundry $5. Key deposit $20. Wheelchair accessible. Reception 8am-9:30pm. Dorms start at $25; doubles at $55, ensuite $60. Winter and multiple night discounts. Book ahead. ISIC/NOMADS/VIP/YHA discount $3. AmEx/MC/V. ❷

Cape Byron Hostel (YHA) (☎6685 8788 or 1800 652 627), on the corner of Middleton and Byron St. Pinball, pool table, TV, and VCR. Upstairs deck and eating area overlook a solar-heated pool bordered by lush palm trees. Internet $4 per hr. Th BBQ in summer ($10). Free bikes ($50 deposit) and boogie boards ($20 deposit). Free parking. Laundry $5. Lockers $4 per day. Reception 6:45am-10pm. Dorms $25-27; twins and doubles $70-100, ensuite $90-120. MC/V. ❷

FOOD

You can't take two steps in downtown Byron without stumbling into an outdoor cafe, takeaway eatery, or upscale restaurant. A **Woolworths** supermarket is on Dawson St. (open M-F 8am-9pm, Sa-Su 8am-8pm), and the **Byron Farmers' Market** is held every Thursday 8-11am on Butler St. across the train tracks.

Mongers (☎6680 8080), on Bay Ln., in the alley opposite Hog's Breath Cafe on Jonson St. This back-alley fish 'n' chips joint reels in hordes of customers with delicious grilled calamari, marinated octopus, tempura prawns, and hand-cut chips. Reasonable prices (main courses $9-15) and non-greasy fish will keep your wallet padded and your fingers dry. Open daily noon-9:30pm. Cash only. ❷

Bay Leaf Cafe (☎6685 8900), on Marvel St., ½ block from Jonson St. Scrumptious salads, sandwiches, and coffee in an open-air cafe ideal for lounging. Take your pick of tamarind and tofu or chickpea and eggplant salads (small $8, large $12). Open daily 7:30am-5pm. Cash only. ❶

Earth 'n' Sea, 11 Lawson St. (☎6685 6029 or 6685 5011), specializes in odd pizzas. "Beethoven" pizza consists of delicious combination of prawns, banana, and pineapple. Surfer decor. Great place to unwind. Pastas from $11, 20 different pizzas from $16-32. Delivery available. Open daily 5:30-9pm; extended hr. in summer. AmEx/DC/MC/V. ❸

Thai Lucy, 2/4 Bay Ln. (☎6680 8083). Every savory bite is worth the price (main courses $15-21), and the wait to get in. Indoor and outdoor seating. Open daily noon-3pm and 5:30-10pm. Cash only. ❷

Juicenergy, 20 Jonson St. (☎6680 7780), fixes up fresh juices ($4-6), smoothies ($5-6), wheatgrass, and herbal shots ($2-5). Open daily 8am-6pm. Cash only. ❶

Orgasmic Food (☎6680 7778), on Bay Ln. behind the Beach Hotel. Serves fantastic Middle Eastern food (from $6.50) that will keep you coming. Outdoor seating. Open daily 10am-latenight. Cash only. ❶

SIGHTS

Crowds assemble daily in the pre-dawn darkness to wait for sunrise along the paths leading to Cape Byron's crowning glory, the **Byron Bay Lighthouse,** at the end of Lighthouse Rd. Resting on cliffs above the easternmost point of the mainland and visible 50km out to sea, the lighthouse is one of the brightest in Australia. The last keeper left in 1989, long after the landmark became fully automated. His cottage is now an info center and shop, and assistant keeper cottages are available for private holiday rental. Parking at the lighthouse is $6, but there is a free carpark 150m away off Lighthouse Rd. The walk to the lighthouse is 2km from Main Beach. (Contact Cape Byron Trust ☎6685 5955, or Professionals Real Estate at ☎6685 6552 for rental info. Grounds open daily sunrise-sunset. Tours Tu and Th 11am, 12:30, and 2pm and during school holidays Sa-Su 10, 11am, 12:30, 2, and 3:30pm; $8, children and concessions $6, families $25.) A boardwalk follows Lighthouse Rd. and continues past the lighthouse to the **Headland Lookout,** an excellent place for spotting dolphins and whales. From there, a walking circuit descends into the **Headland Reserve,** passing through **Wategos Beach, The Pass,** and **Clarkes Beach,** returning back to Lighthouse Rd. at the **Captain Cook Lookout. Byron Bay Sunrise Tour** leads a popular 2hr. early-morning trip to see the first rays (☎6685 7721 or 04 1204 8333. Breakfast included. $15).

Byron's artistic community is flourishing; the best example is **The Cape Gallery,** 2 Lawson St., which exhibits local art and a fine pottery collection. (☎6685 7659; www.capegallery.com.au. Open daily in summer 10am-6pm; in winter M-Sa 10am-5pm, Su 11am-4pm.) **Didgeri-U-doo,** above Peter Pan Travel on Jonson St., has Aboriginal art and free daily didgeridoo lessons at 3pm. (☎04 0133 5694. Open daily 11am-6pm.) West of town, the **Arts and Industry Estate,** off Ewingsdale Rd. (called Shirley Rd. in town), is a compound full of stores where local craftsmen sell industrial glass and metal, paintings, sculptures, crafts, and, oddly enough, shoes. Colin Heaney **blows glass** at 6 Acacia St., and the gallery is filled with an impressive collection of his work. (☎6685 7044; www.colinheaney.com. Gallery open M-F 9am-5pm, Sa-Su 10am-4pm; glass-blowing M-Th 9am-4pm, F 9am-2:30pm.)

ACTIVITIES

For travelers seeking constant stimulation, Byron provides it on land (massages for body and meditation for mind), in the water (boards and boats of every shape and size), and in the air (sky diving, ultralights, and hang gliders). Many packages include free pickup and drop-off. The Byron Bay Visitors Centre books activities, as do Peterpan Adventures (p. 202), Wicked Travel (p. 202), and many hostels.

SURFING

Herds of bleached-blonde surfers with boards slung over their shoulders trudge dutifully to Byron's beaches every morning at sunrise. Surf schools entice novices by providing all equipment; most guarantee you'll be standing on the board by the end of your lessons. Byron has excellent surfing spots all around the bay, so regardless of wind conditions there are always good waves somewhere. **The Wreck,** just off Main Beach, is known for waves that break close to shore. Down the shore toward the lighthouse, **The Pass** promises long, challenging rides, but can be dangerous because of overcrowding, sharp rocks, and boats. The water off **Wategos Beach,** close to The Pass, is best for longboards since the waves are slow and rolling. **Tallows,** on the other side of the headland from Wategos, has great northern-wind surfing, but watch for heavy rips. **Belongil Beach,** to the north of Main Beach, is long and sandy with clothing-optional sections. **Broken Head Nature Reserve,** 4km south of Byron on the Coast Rd., has verdant rainforest growing right down to its magnificent beaches. Take the track from Broken Head Caravan Park along the clifftop to **King's Beach,** or try **Broken Head** or **Whites Beaches** for serious surf.

Black Dog Surfing (☎6680 9828; www.blackdogsurfing.com), in Shop 8 next to Woolworths, Jonson St. 3hr. lesson $50-60, includes food and drink upon return; 2-day course $105, 3-day $135, 5-day $200. Private or female-only lessons available. Surfboard rental full day $20, weekly $120. Wetsuits $5-10.

Surfing Byron Bay (☎6685 7099; www.gosurfingbyronbay.com), behind Global Gossip (p. 202) on Jonson St. 3½hr. lesson $60, backpackers $55; 2-day course $106; 3-day course $134. Free board rentals the day after lessons.

Byron Bay Surf School, 127 Jonson St. (☎1800 707 274; www.byronbaysurfschool.com). 3½hr. group lesson $65, private lesson $90 per hr., 3-day course $165, 5-day $235. Softboard and wetsuit rental $35 per day.

Byron Bay Kiteboarding (☎1300 888 938; www.byronbaykiteboarding.com). Try the newest craze in water sports. Summer only. Private 3hr. lesson $300.

MULTI-DAY SURF TRIPS

A Real Surf Journey (☎1800 828 888; www.arealsurfjourney.com.au), takes a 3-day trip from Byron north to Noosa every M and F and hits the best surf breaks along the coast. All experience levels. Camping or cabin accommodations. All food (including vegetarian) provided. $330.

Surfaris (☎1800 634 951; www.surfaris.com), offers 5-day surf trips between Sydney and Byron (850km of coast). Departs M from Sydney, Su from Byron. All meals and camping included. $549.

DIVING

Most diving is done at **Julian Rocks Marine Park,** 2.5km off Main Beach, widely considered one of Australia's best dive sites. It has both warm and cold currents, and is home to 500 species of fish and the occasional grey nurse shark. Required medical clearances cost $60. Dive certification courses can go up by $70-100 or more during the summer.

Sundive (☎6685 7755 or 1800 008 755; www.sundive.com.au), on Middleton St. behind Aquarius Backpackers. On-site pool. Courses usually start Tu or F, but 2-weekend certification courses are sometimes offered. 4-day PADI certification $350. Snorkeling $45; intro dives $150, day dives $70-80, additional trips $60-70.

Byron Bay Dive Centre, 9 Marvel St. (☎6685 8333 or 1800 243 483; www.byronbaydivecentre.com.au), between Middleton and Fletcher St. 4-day SSI certification courses start M and Th $350; 4½hr. intro dives $150, day dives $80, additional trips $70; snorkeling $50. Seasonal 2½hr. whale watching trips $70.

KAYAKING AND RAFTING

Cape Byron Kayaks (☎6685 4161). 3½hr. trips around the Cape with afternoon tea. Trips in summer 8:30am and 12:30pm; in winter 12:30pm. Book 1 day ahead. $60.

Dolphin Kayaking (☎6685 8044; www.dolphinkayaking.com.au). ½-day guided tour of Byron's marine life; takes guests right up to local dolphins or whales. Trips in summer 9am and 2pm; in winter 11am. $60.

IN THE SKY

Soaring Adventures (☎6684 7572 or 04 1455 8794; www.byronbaygliding.com). Learn to fly ultralight glider. Flights to lighthouse, Cape Byron, or Mt. Warning. $95-270.

Flightzone Hang Gliding School (☎6685 8768 or 04 0844 1742; www.flightzone.com.au). 30min. flights $135. 10-day certification course $1500. Cash only.

Skydive Cape Byron (☎6685 5990 or 1800 666 770; www.skydive-cape-byron.com). Tandem skydiving with instructors directly over Cape Byron from $239. Book ahead.

Byron Bay Skydiving Centre (☎6684 1323; www.skydivebyronbay.com). 8000-14,000 ft. dives over Cape Byron $239-344, with video or photo packages ranging from $99-159. Discounts for groups of 5 or 10.

OTHER ACTIVITIES

Byron Bay Bicycles, 93 Jonson St. (☎6685 6067), in the Woolworths shopping plaza. ½ day $15, full day $22, weekly $95. $50 security deposit includes helmet and lock.

Pegasus Park Equestrian Centre (☎6687 1446), 10min. west of Byron. Pickup available. Leads horseback rides along Byron Creek ($40 per hr.) and the beach ($70 per hr., $90 per 2hr.). Cash only.

Seahorse Riding Centre (☎6680 8155), 20min. west of Byron. Offers ½- and full-day packages with rainforest rides and ponies for children. $50-100.

NIGHTLIFE

Cheeky Monkey's (☎6685 5886), on the corner of Jonson and Kingsley St. The tables are basically the only place to dance at what promises to be a rocking party any night of the week. Theme nights and frequent backpacker specials. The Cheeky Monkey Party Van scans the streets and swings past hostels to whisk you away. Dinner from $5 (F $2). Happy hour 10:30pm. Open in summer M-Sa noon-3am, Su noon-midnight; in winter M-Sa 7pm-3am. Cover $5 after 10:30pm.

Cocomangas, 32 Jonson St. (☎6685 8493), features a smaller, calmer dance floor and affordable mixed drinks. Try the Jam Jar (juice, gin, Malibu rum, and Triple Sec; $3.50). Check for freebies in hostels. Happy hour 9-11:30pm. M retro, Tu global music, Th R&B. Cover $3-5 in summer after 10pm; in winter after 10:30pm. Open M-Sa until 3am.

The Rails, (☎6685 7662), behind the visitors center on the train tracks, draws large crowds to its outdoor bar and restaurant. Live bands playing anything from jazz to country hit the stage before chatty locals at picnic tables. Nightly live music 7pm-midnight.

Beach Hotel (☎6685 6402), on Jonson St., overlooking the beach. Local favorite with garden bar and huge patio. Large indoor stage hosts local and nationally recognized bands. Aquariums hang over one of the indoor bars and surf videos play in an adjoining room. Th-Su live music. Su live DJs. Open until midnight.

Great Northern Hotel, (☎6685 6454), on the corner of Jonson and Byron St. An incredible venue for live music, daily around 10pm. Everything from contemporary folk to rock and punk. Cover varies. Frequent freebies. Open M-Sa until 3am, Su until midnight.

ENTERTAINMENT AND FESTIVALS

Check out the weekly entertainment magazine *Echo* for gig information (found on the streets or online at www.echo.net.au every Tu morning). Byron also offers a number of alternative entertainment options including a thriving music scene. The town is packed every year for two major music festivals, which pull in well-known international acts as well as Australia-based performers. **Pighouse Flicks,** at the Lounge Cinema in the Arts Factory, screens classic, arthouse, foreign, and mainstream films in a funky theater upholstered in cowprint. (☎6685 5828. Opens 30min. before showtime. $10, concessions $9, daily specials $8.) Music festival **Splendour in the Grass** (www.splendourinthegrass.com) is the 3rd weekend in July and the **Blues and Roots Music Festival** (☎6685 8310; www.bluesfest.com.au) takes place five nights every Easter weekend. Buy tickets and book accommodation far in advance. **A Taste of Byron** (☎04 1917 0407) is a popular food festival that falls on the 3rd week in September. The **Byron Bay Writers Festival** (☎6685 6262) is a popular four-day literary event that falls on the 1st weekend in August.

NIMBIN ☎02

Once a small dairy farming town, Nimbin (pop. 800) is now Australia's cannabis capital. The town is a popular daytrip from Byron among backpackers looking for a taste (and smell) of the nation's alternative culture. Though marijuana is illegal in Australia, visitors will find themselves solicited for "bush," "cookies," "dope," "pot," or any of a dozen other euphemisms for marijuana as they walk up Cullen St., the town's only avenue. The street is lined with eateries and markets specializing in organic and bulk foods, as well as half a dozen shops offering every imaginable piece of paraphernalia with pot-related puns. Guitars and bong(o) drums lie invitingly in cafes and accommodations, available for impromptu jam sessions.

In 1973, thousands of university students descended on Nimbin Village for the **Aquarius Festival,** the antipodean answer to America's Woodstock, and the community has ever since retained its image as Australia's alternative/hippie hub. Some local residents resent the town's reputation and a surprising percentage don't partake, emphasizing instead Nimbin's earth-conscious agriculture ("permaculture") and alternative energy. The town is one of hundreds of shared communities, some open to the public, which lie in the fruitful volcanic valley of Mt. Warning. WWOOF (see **Volunteering,** p. 82) has a strong presence here, with many area farms accepting travelers for farmstays and organic farming opportunities. Residents' lives are closely intertwined with the land and its fruits, most of which are legal.

NIMBIN TIME. Hours listed for Nimbin businesses are flexible. The town runs on "Nimbin Time"—establishments open and close on their own schedules, which may not depend on customer demand or advertised hours of operation.

TRANSPORTATION AND PRACTICAL INFORMATION. The **Nimbin Shuttle Bus** (☎6680 9189; www.nimbintours.com) and **The Happy Coach** (☎6685 3996; www.happycoach.com.au) are the only direct public transportation to the village from Byron. The shuttle departs daily from Byron Bay at 11am (1½hr.), and leaves Nimbin at 3pm ($14, round-trip $25), and the coach leaves daily at 10am (3hr.) and returns at 2pm ($18, round-trip $25. For visitors seeking just a glimpse of the place, **Grasshoppers Eco-Explorer Tours** stops in town for an hour or two as part of a day-long trip that includes the area's national parks (☎0500 881 881; www.grasshoppers.com.au; $35 with lunch), as does Byron-based **Jim's Alternative Tours** (☎6685 7720; www.jimsalternativetours.com; trips daily 10am-6pm; $35).

Nimbin's town center is on **Cullen Street,** between the police station and the hotel on the corner—you can't miss the vivid murals, wild storefront displays, and thin wisps of smoke. **The Nimbin Connexion,** 2/80 Cullen St., at the north end of town, has info on local activities and regional WWOOFing opportunities and membership; it also serves as a transportation booking agency, a gift shop, currency exchange, and the cheapest **Internet** access in town. (☎6689 1388; www.nimbinconnexion.com. $1.50 per 15min. Open daily 9am-5pm.) Find **police** (☎6689 1244) at the south end of Cullen St., and the **hospital** (☎6689 1400) at 35 Cullen St. The **post office** is at 43 Cullen St. (☎6689 1301. Open M-F 7am-5pm.) **Postal Code:** 2480.

ACCOMMODATIONS AND FOOD. Although many visitors come for just an afternoon, staying a few days at any one of the town's unique hostels provides the best chance to see through the town's smoky haze. **Nimbin Rox YHA ❷,** 74 Thorburn St., is worth the 20min. walk from town for its breathtaking views and intimate, family-guest-house feel. Take a left onto Thorburn from Cullen St., just across the green creek; the hostel is up an unpaved driveway through a horse pasture. (☎6689 0022; www.nimbinrox.com. Internet access $1.50 per 15min. Dorms $22; doubles $56; 2-person cabins $54; 6-person teepee $22 per person. AmEx/MC/V.) For the best idea of what the town was like in the 1970s, spend the night in a mushroom bungalow or a gypsy wagon at the **Rainbow Retreat ❶,** 75 Thorburn St., where horses wander the grounds. Amenities include a kitchen, open-air cafe, and common rooms with an impressive collection of musical instruments (including didgeridoos and a full drum set) alongside a large TV. (☎6689 1262. Sites $10; teepee $12; dorms $15; doubles

$40. Cash only.) If mushroom living isn't your style, spend the night in the converted railway car at **Nimbin Backpackers at Granny's Farm ❶**, a 10min. walk north on Cullen St. from the town center; turn left before the bridge. The 10-acre creekside lodge has two pools (one chlorine, one saltwater), a large kitchen and TV room, BBQ, nightly outdoor fires, free-roaming horses, and platypi wading in the creek. (☎6689 1333; www.nimbinbackpackers.com. Laundry $4. Sites $10 per person; dorms $22; doubles $48. VIP.)

Nimbin cafes, pubs, and streets are home to a vibrant music scene. The **Rainbow Cafe ❶**, 64A Cullen St., has sandwiches ($7.50), fresh juices ($4.50), vegetarian options, and a sunny garden patio out back. (☎6689 1997. Open daily 8:30am-5pm. Cash only.) Late at night, share a pot of Chai tea ($5) on the patio outside **Nimbin's Oasis ❶**, 80 Cullen (☎6689 1205). A nearby grocery store, the **Nimbin Emporium**, 58 Cullen St., sells health and bulk foods and rents videos. (☎6689 1205. M-Sa 7:30am-7:15pm, Su 9:45am-7pm.)

SIGHTS. The odd **Nimbin Museum**, 62 Cullen St., redefines creativity and historical interpretation. Its strangeness is ingenious and oddly beautiful. The rooms relate the founders' version of regional history through myriad murals, chaotic collages, stimulating quotes, and trinkets. The museum has extensive, proportionate coverage of all three major historical periods: the first room is about Aborigines, the second about European settlers, and the next six about hippies. (☎6689 1123. Open 10am-dark. $2.) The **Bush Theatre/Picture Factory ❷**, across the bridge north of the town center on Cullen St. plays movies for $5 and serves reasonably priced dinners. The venue also has frequent live music events and dance parties; check the sidewalks in town for announcements written in chalk. (☎6689 1111. Open Tu-W and F-Su. Old and new art-house movies $7.50. Cash only.) The building, a former butter factory, also houses a number of local businesses, including the **Nimbin Candle Factory**, where artists craft colorful handmade candles. The **HEMP (Help End Marijuana Prohibition) Party** bases itself at the **Hemp Embassy**, 51 Cullen St. (☎6689 1842; www.nimbinaustralia.com/hemp. Open daily 9am-6pm.) The attached **Hemp Bar** offers refreshments. (☎6689 1842; www.nimbinhempbar.com.) To see a bit beyond Nimbin's drug culture, swing by the **Nimbin Artists Gallery**, 49 Cullen St., which displays the work of local artists. (☎6689 1444. Open daily 10am-4pm.) Nimbin is also known for its earth-friendly lifestyle. The **Rainbow Power Company**, on your right after a 10min. walk from the town center down Cullen St. to Alternative Way, is a remarkable achievement in solar and wind energy production; it sells its

LET'S GROW

Though walking the center of Nimbin any time of the year gives new meaning to the phrase "main drag," reefer-induced revelry reaches its peak the 1st weekend in May, when Nimbin hosts its annual Mardi Grass Cannabis Law Reform Rally. In 1988, public protest for marijuana legalization coincided with the Aquarius Festival, a celebration of counter-culture on a broader level. The 1993 rally ended with chanting pot smokers brandishing a massive joint with "Let It Grow" inscribed in 4 ft. tall letters outside the Nimbin Hemp Embassy.

The following year, Mardi Grass became an official event. Activities include the Hemp Olympics, in which contestants compete in everything from bong-throwing to joint-rolling contests. Judges score growers' products for aroma, size, and effect. It may seem like a party, but protesters say the real fun will begin only once political change is effected.

Local police have begun to weed out Mardi Grass participants who flaunt the law. In 2006, increased vigilance meant roadblocks and vehicle checks. The press reported that a major crackdown had occurred, but the 50 arrests didn't extinguish Nimbin's party spirit. Despite concerns over tighter law enforcement, plans for a revamped 2007 festival are well under way.

excess generated power to the electricity grid for general consumption. (☎6689 1430; www.rpc.com.au. Open M-F 9am-5pm, Sa 9am-noon. 1hr. group tours by arrangement in advance. $2.20 per person, min. 15 people. AmEx/MC/V.) For a hands-on look at earth-conscious living, trek to **Djanbung Gardens Permaculture Centre,** 74 Cecil St. Take a left onto Cecil St. at the southern end of Cullen; the Djanbung Gardens are just after Neem Rd. A resource center offers workshops on organic gardening, design, and community development. Ask about accommodation for workshop and class stays. (☎6689 1755; www.earthwise.org.au. Open Tu-Sa 10am-3:30pm. Guided garden tours Tu and Th 10:30am, $10. In-depth farm tour Sa 11am or by appointment $15. Rooms $15 per day, $75 including lessons in "earthwise living.") Beyond Djanbung lies Jarlanbah, a community that lives by a permaculture (closed to outsiders) code.

MURWILLUMBAH ☎02

Located in a mountain valley halfway between Byron Bay and Tweed Heads, Murwillumbah (mur-WUH-lum-bah) is a charming country town. The town serves as a base for exploring several nearby national parks, including Border Ranges, Mebbin, Mooball, Mount Jerusalem, Mount Warning, Nightcap, and Wollumbin.

The **Mount Warning/Murwillumbah YHA ❷,** 1 Tumbulgum Rd., is a well-kept, colorful lodge 18km from the base of the mountain. From the tourist center, cross the Alma St. bridge, turn right on Commercial Rd., and follow the river around the bend about 150m. The lodge sits on the riverbank, with a wrap-around deck facing Mt. Warning, and offers free use of inner tubes, a canoe, and comfy hammocks. Enjoy the nightly free ice cream at 9pm. (☎6672 3763. Laundry $7-9. Bike rental $10 per day, $50 deposit. Free transportation to Mt. Warning for guests staying min. 2 nights. Dorms $25; doubles $54. Key deposit $10.) The **Hotel Murwillumbah ❷,** 17 Wharf St., offers cheap pubstays on the backpacker-friendly second floor. (☎6672 1139. Dorms $20, weekly $100; doubles $40-50/120. Cash only.)

Most eateries are cafes and fish 'n' chips shops on Main St., with a handful of multicultural restaurants on Wollumbin St. and Commercial Rd. Try **Riverside Pizza Cafe ❷,** 6 Commercial Rd., which has a handful of Thai offerings ($13-18) alongside pizza ($11-19) and other Italian basics. (☎6672 1935. Open daily 5-9:30pm. Cash only.) For lunch, locals love **Austral Cafe ❶,** 86 Main St., with delicious pies ($3), milkshakes ($4), and sandwiches ($3-5), all served in large dinner booths. (☎6672 2624. M-Sa 7:30am-5:30pm. Cash only.) A **Coles** supermarket is in the Sunnyside Shopping Center on the corner of Brisbane and Wollumbin St. (☎6672 4213. Open M-F 6am-midnight, Sa 6am-10pm, Su 8am-8pm.)

To get to Murwillumbah by car, turn off the Pacific Hwy. onto Tweed Valley Way. **Countrylink** (☎1300 367 077) offers bus service to Casino, where riders can connect by rail to Sydney. Southbound buses stop at the **railway station** on the Pacific Hwy.; northbound buses stop outside the tourist info center. **Kirkland's** buses (☎1300 367 077) run to: Brisbane (2¼hr.; M-F 2 per day, Sa-Su 1 per day; $23); Byron Bay (1hr., 1 per day, $15); and Surfers Paradise (1hr., 1 per day, $17). **Greyhound Australia** (☎13 14 99 or 13 20 30) services Brisbane (2¼-3¼hr., 2 per day, $29) and Byron Bay (1hr., 2 per day, $16). Local **Surfside Buslines** (☎13 12 30) heads to Tweed Heads (1hr.; 2-7 per day). Additionally, **Premier** (☎13 34 10) stops in Murwillumbah on its Sydney/Brisbane route.

Though most of the town lies west of the Tweed River, you'll find **Tweed Valley Way,** the visitors center, and the **railway station** on its east bank. To reach the town center, cross the Tweed River on the **Alma Street** bridge. Alma St. crosses Commercial Rd. and becomes **Wollumbin Street.** The **Tourist Information Centre,** in **Budd Park,** at the corner of Tweed Valley Way and Alma St., is located inside the **World Heritage Rainforest Centre,** which has displays about area natural wonders. (☎6672 1340 or 1800 674 414; www.tweedcoolangatta.com.au. Open M-Sa 9am-4:30pm, Su

9:30am-4pm.) **Internet** access ($5 per hr.) can be found at **Precise PCs,** 13 Commercial Rd. (☎6672 8300; open M-F 9am-5pm, Sa 9am-noon) and at the **library** (☎6670 2427. $2.20 per 30min.; open M-W and F 9:30am-5pm, Th 9:30am-7:30pm, Sa 9am-noon). Find **police** at 81 Murwillumbah St. (☎6672 8300), and a **post office** (☎6670 2030) on the corner of Brisbane and Murwillumbah St. **Postal Code:** 2484.

MOUNT WARNING AND BORDER RANGES ☎02

The stony spire of Mt. Warning resembles a gigantic **thumbs-up** from the south, and an elephant's head from the north. Captain Cook named the promontory in 1770 to warn European travelers that they were approaching Australia's rocky shoals at Point Danger. Formerly a shield volcano, most of the ancient lava flows have eroded away, leaving behind an enormous bowl-shaped landform known as a caldera—the largest in the Southern Hemisphere. The prominent spire in the middle of the caldera represents the volcano's erosion-resistant central chamber, which serves as a plug over the volcano's core.

Many hikers tackle the **Summit Track** (8.8km, 4-5hr. round-trip) on Mt. Warning in early-morning darkness in order to be the first on the continent to greet the dawn. The climb to the peak is moderate to strenuous—the last segment is a vertical rock scramble with a chain handrail—but the spectacular sunrise and fantastic 360° view make it more than worthwhile. The Dry (June-Nov.) offers the best chance for clear skies. You'll need a flashlight for the climb; there are often glow-bugs, but don't count on them to light the way. A good jacket or sweater and change of shirt and socks are advisable—you'll work up a sweat on the climb, but the summit can be chilly even when the sun is up. Bring your own water and keep in mind that the only toilets are at the start of the walk. To reach the Summit Track from Murwillumbah, take Kyogle Rd. 12km west, turn on Mt. Warning Rd., and go about 6km to Breakfast Creek. Camping on Mt. Warning is not allowed.

The nearest hostel is the **Murwillumbah YHA** (p. 210). The **Mount Warning Caravan Park ❶**, on Mt. Warning Rd., 2km from the junction with Kyogle Rd., also makes a great base for exploring the mountain. (☎6679 5120; www.mtwarningholiday-park.com. TV room, pool, camp kitchen, BBQ, and a few friendly wallabies. Linen $5. Reception 8am-5pm. Sites $18, powered $20; caravans $45; cabins $55, ensuite $85. Extra person $7. Weekly rates available. MC/V.)

If you find Mt. Warning too overrun, the 32,000 gorgeous hectares of **Border Ranges National Park** offer extravagant views that rival those of its more touristed neighbor. (Call the NPWS office in Kyogle office at ☎6632 0000 for more info.) Though farther than some other parks, Border Ranges rewards intrepid travelers with the shade of a lush canopy and great vantage points for viewing the volcano region. To get to Border Ranges, take the Kyogle Rd. west from Murwillumbah for 44km; 5.2km past the turn-off to Nimbin marks the start of the signposted **Tweed Range Scenic Drive** (60km, 4-5hr.). The Barker Vale turn-off leads 15km along gravel road to the park entrance. The drive exits the park at **Wiangaree,** 13km from Kyogle and 66km from Murwillumbah. The first picnic area in the park is **Bar Mountain,** with a lovely beech glade. Less than 1km farther is the even more remarkable **Blackbutts picnic area,** with striking views of Mt. Warning and the basin. Another 8km north, **Pinnacle Lookout** offers a similarly spectacular view. To reach the **Forest Tops ❶** camping area, travel 4km past the lookout, turn left at the junction, go another 4km, and turn left again ($3, children $2). If you turn right instead of left at this last junction, you'll wind up at the **Brindle Creek picnic area,** the departure point for the **Brindle Creek Walk** (10km round-trip; 3-4hr.), a track that winds among rainforests and waterfalls and ends at the **Antarctic Beech** picnic area, home to 2000-year-old trees. For a shorter scenic trip, turn off Kyogle Rd. at Doon Doon Rd., 1km past Uki Village, and head to **Cram's Farm picnic area,** a delightful spot on the lake. Travel farther down Doon Doon Rd., turn right at Doon Doon Hall, and follow the path down to its dead-end to catch a glimpse of **Doughboy,** a smaller, but nevertheless impressive, volcanic plug.

NEW ENGLAND

The **New England Highway** begins just northwest of Brisbane, swinging south through Queensland's wine country before entering the New England region via Tenterfield. On its way south to Tamworth, the highway branches off to **Waterfall Way** and later on to the **Oxley Highway,** leading to waterfall-filled national parks.

TENTERFIELD AND NEARBY PARKS ☎02

It was in 1889 Tenterfield (pop. 3500) that Sir Henry Parkes cried out, "One people, one destiny," in a speech that foresaw Australia's federation. Although it clings to its history with preserved buildings and the Sir Henry Parkes Festival—a celebration of nationhood and community achievement—travelers today know Tenterfield, the "Birthplace of Australia," as a base for exploring nearby national parks.

To explore the town's history on foot, pick up a **heritage walk** brochure from the visitors center. Tenterfield lies near three national parks ($7 NPWS entry fee applies), all of which can be reached by Mt. Lindsay Rd. Take Rouse St. north, turn right on Nass St., then quickly bear left onto Mt. Lindsay Rd. Before reaching the parks, history buffs might want to take a look at the remains of Tenterfield's **WWII tank traps,** about 11km from town. These traps constituted part of the Brisbane Line, Australia's second line of defense in case the northern part of the country fell into enemy hands. Tenterfield was a major strategic center; during the war, up to 10,000 troops were camped in the area. About 3km farther, a narrow, sandy lane leads to **Basket Swamp National Park,** a preserved woodland area with picnic and bushcamping sites.

The entrance to **Boonoo Boonoo** (BUN-na buh-NOO) **National Park** is 24km north of Tenterfield, with another 14km of gravel leading to the stunning, carved-granite **Boonoo Boonoo Gorge and Falls.** From the carpark, one path leads to a lookout over the mammoth falls (300m) and another accesses a swimming hole above the cascade (200m). Camping is available at **Cypress Pine Camping Area ❶,** and includes water, toilets, picnic tables, and BBQ ($5, children $3; vehicle entry fee $7). For a less-touristed look at a giant monolith, skip Uluru and head to **Bald Rock National Park,** home to the largest exposed granite rock in the Southern Hemisphere. To reach it, head down Mt. Lindesay Rd. for 29km to a sealed road that runs 5km to the park's camping and picnic areas. Two paths lead to the 1277m summit, with amazing views of the McPherson Ranges. The **Burgoona Walk** (2.5km) is a scenic hiking path and the **Summit Direct Path** (1.2km) is a steep scramble up the rock face (follow the white dotted trail). You can also take the gradual ascent and clamber down in 3hr. round-trip. **Girraween National Park** (p. 354) is just west of Bald Rock, across the Queensland border. Take the New England Hwy to Wyberba and follow Pyramids Rd. for 9km.

For cheap accommodation, you can try the **Tenterfield Lodge Caravan Park ❷,** 2 Manners St., which houses a hostel with a friendly host who helps travelers find seasonal work. Call in advance for free pickup from the bus station. (☎6736 1477. Sites for 2 $15, powered $18.50; cabins $55, ensuite $60. Extra adult $4. Dorms $22.50; singles $30; doubles $45, ensuite $60. VIP.) A couple of hotels exist in town; try the **Royal Hotel ❷,** 130 High St., for basic rooms. (☎6736 1833; tenterfieldhotel@bigpond.net. Hotel rooms $25; motel $50. MC/V.) Three unsealed kilometers north of Bald Rock National Park on Mt. Lindsay Rd. is the wonderful **Bald Rock Bush Retreat ❷,** which includes a backpacker guest house and luxurious waterfront cabin. (☎4686 1227; www.baldrockbushretreat.com. Groups only; bring sleeping bags. 8-person bunk house for min. 4 people from $120, extra adult $30; doubles $60-150; ensuite cabin for $150. AmEx/MC/V.) Once every other January or so, the retreat hosts the **Exodus Festival** (www.grooven.org/exodus), a week-long summer trance party and music extravaganza that pulls in international DJs and combines Aboriginal stylings with typical rave fare. The festival may or may not happen any given year, but in off-years it's still a safe bet they'll host a series of smaller, but still rocking, summer weekend parties.

The Willow Tree ❷, 274 Rouse St., serves delicious gourmet sandwiches on thick toasted breads ($11). Warm up by the crackling fire or sun on the patio out back. (☎6736 2135. Open M-F 8:30am-4pm, Sa-Su 8:30am-3pm. DC/MC/V.)

Tenterfield is 150km from Lismore and 95km from Glen Innes. Because it is the northern point of entry to the region, the town is known as the "Gateway to New England." **Greyhound Australia** (☎13 14 99 or 13 20 30) runs to Brisbane (5½hr.; daily 1:35am and 12:40pm; $73, students $65) and Sydney (12hr., daily at midnight, $104/93). Tickets can be purchased at the Seven Knights (BP) Service Station on the New England Hwy. south of town. **Kirkland's** (☎6622 1499) runs to Lismore (3hr., M-F 2pm, $27) and from there to Byron Bay (1hr., $14). **Crisp's Coaches** (☎07 4661 8333) runs to Brisbane daily (4¼hr.; M-F 11:15am, Su 3:15pm; $66, students $57). Book Kirkland's or Crisp's at Sullivan's Newsagency, 232 Rouse St. (☎6736 1252). Buses stop at various points on Rouse St.; call for details. **Countrylink** runs buses to Armidale (2¾hr., daily 5:50am, $27), from which travelers can take the train to Sydney (11¼hr. total, $82). Book at Tenterfield Insurance Agencies, 279 Rouse St. (☎6736 2426. Bookings 9am-4:30pm.)

The **Tenterfield Visitors Centre,** 157 Rouse St. (New England Hwy.), has info on all New England destinations. (☎6736 1082; www.tenterfield.com. Open M-F 9:30am-5pm, Sa-Su 9:30am-4pm.) **Rouse Street** is lined with shops, restaurants, pubs, **ATMs,** motels to the south, and the **public library** (☎6736 1454; open M-F from 10am-8pm, Sa 9am-noon). The **police station** is at 94 Molesworth St. (☎6736 1144), and the **NPWS office** is at 10 Miles St. (☎6736 4298; open M-F 8am-4pm). The **hospital** (☎6739 5200) is at 1-5 Naas St. The **post office** is at 225 Rouse St. **Postal Code:** 2372.

GLEN INNES ☎02

Glen Innes (pop. 10,000) celebrates its Celtic heritage every spring with a three-day festival. (May 3-7, 2007. Call the visitors center for more info.) Many of the festivities are set in the shadow of the **Standing Stones,** a series of massive granite blocks in the tradition of an ancient Celtic form of timekeeping, erected on **Martins Lookout,** 1km east of the visitors center on Meade St. (Gwydir Highway). Every conceivable piece of pioneer equipment, from 150 types of barbed wire to an entire 19th-century slab cottage, can be found at the **"Land of the Beardies" History House Museum** (☎6732 1035) in the historic hospital building on the corner of West Ave. and Ferguson St. (Open M-F 10am-noon and 1-4pm, Sa-Su 1-4pm. $6, students and children $1, seniors $4.) **Fossicking** and **fishing** are both very popular; there are many opportunities to do both in and around Glen Innes.

Cheap rooms are available at the **pubs ❷** on Grey St. (singles $30-40; doubles $45-55), and motels line the New England Hwy. Your best bet may be the **Club Hotel ❷** on the corner of Grey and Wentworth St., which has rooms with sinks and electric blankets. (☎6732 3043. Breakfast $10. Singles $38; doubles $48. MC/V.) More charming stays are found a bit west of town. **Bullock Mountain Homestead ❺,** on Bullock Mountain Rd., is a horse ranch with B&B-style accommodations and meals. (☎6732 1599; www.bullockmountainhomestead.com. Arrange for free pickup from bus stop in town or call for directions. Free laundry. $85 per person.) The Homestead also runs a variety of splurge-worthy **horseback rides,** including the popular pub crawl on horseback. (Weekend $375, 5-day trip $1850; meals and accommodation included. Book ahead. AmEx/MC/V.) For a different sort of experience, head to **Three Waters Au Naturel Rural Retreat ❶,** 15km northwest of Glen Innes, also on Bullock Mountain. Undress and unwind on 420 hectares of secluded countryside. Unpowered campsites line the river, and access to homestead showers, toilets, laundry, and gas BBQ is available. Free accommodation and meals are also possible for backpackers willing to do a bit of work around the property. Au Naturel offers the same activities as Bullock Mountain Homestead, except, well, sans apparel. (☎6732 4863; www.gleninnes.com/3waters. Fossicking $6, horseback riding $25 per hr. Sites $12 for 1, $20 for 2; cabins $60. Cash only.)

For good eats, try **Crofters Cottage ❷,** at Centennial Parklands next to the Standing Stones. Crofters serves gourmet main dishes ($9-12) and terrific toasted sandwiches. (☎6732 5668. Open M-W and F-Su 10am-5pm, Th 10am-4pm. MC/V.)

Countrylink (☎13 22 32) has bus service to Sydney (9½hr., 1 per day, $91), as well as direct service to nearby towns. **Greyhound Australia** (☎13 14 99 or 13 20 30) sends buses to: Brisbane (6½hr.; 2 per day; $76, students $69); Sydney (11hr., 1 per day, $100/90); Tamworth (3½hr., 1 per day, $54/48), and other small regional centers. Contact individual companies for details about local service. Call **taxis** at ☎6732 1300. All transportation can be booked at the visitors center for a $5 fee.

The main commercial street in town is **Grey Street,** parallel to and one block west of the **New England Highway** (called Church Street in town), which runs north 93km to Tenterfield and south 95km to Armidale. The **Gwydir Highway,** known in town as **Meade Street** and **Ferguson Street,** runs east-west. The **Glen Innes Visitors Centre,** 152 Church St., is near the intersection of the New England and Gwydir Hwy. (☎6730 2400; www.gleninnestourism.com.au. Open M-F 9am-5pm, Sa-Su and public holidays 9am-3pm.) Grey St. is home to several **banks** with **ATMs, supermarkets,** pubstays, basic eateries, and a **library** with free **Internet** access. (☎6732 2302. Open M-F 10am-5pm, Sa 9:30am-noon.)

ARMIDALE ☎02

The highest city in Australia at 980m above sea level, Armidale (pop. 25,000) is conveniently located at the beginning of **Waterfall Way** (p. 215), making it a great base for exploration of the magnificent countryside. A healthy pub scene is kept lively by students from the University of New England.

The visitors center provides a free 2hr. **heritage tour** of Armidale daily; call to book. Following Marsh St. south uphill to the corner of Kentucky St. leads you to the **New England Regional Art Museum,** which features works from classic Australian painters in its $45 million collection. (☎6772 5255. Open Tu-Sa and Su 10:30am-5pm. Free.) Next door at 128 Kentucky St. is the **Aboriginal Cultural Centre and Keeping Place** with permanent and rotating art galleries of boomerangs, carved kangaroos, dot paintings, message sticks, and more. (☎6771 3606; www.acckp.com.au. Open M-F 9:30am-4pm, Sa-Su 9am-3pm. Donations appreciated.)

The **Pembroke Caravan Park ❶,** 39 Waterfall Way (also known as Grafton Rd. and Barney St. in town), is 1.5km east of town and has an adjoining **YHA hostel ❷** with a recreation room and TV lounge area. Tennis courts, a solar heated pool, kitchen, and laundry facilities are among the hostel's offerings. (☎6772 6470 or 1800 355 578; www.pembroke.com.au. Reception 7:30am-6pm. Sites $20, powered sites $25; dorms $26.50, with YHA discount $23; vans $37-43; cabins $58-86. AmEx/MC/V.) **Tattersall's Hotel,** 174 Beardy St., is a central pubstay with small and quiet rooms. (☎6772 7781. Singles $27.50; doubles $44, extra person $11. MC/V.)

Rumours on the Mall ❶, at 190 Beardy St., serves breakfast ($3-8) and lunch ($5-16). (☎6772 3084. Open M-F 8am-5pm, Sa-Su 8am-2pm. Cash only.) Grab some traditional pub grub at **Newie's ❸,** on the corner of Beardy and Dangar St. Main dishes range from $14-25. To sample the uni pub scene, stop by the nightclub upstairs at

Newie's later in the evening. (☎6772 7622. Open M-Sa noon-2pm and 6-9pm. AmEx/DC/MC/V.) A **Coles** supermarket is on Marsh St. between Beardy and Dumaresq St. (Open M-Sa 6am-midnight, Su 8am-8pm.)

The **visitors center,** 82 Marsh St., is attached to the bus terminal. (☎6772 4655 or 1800 627 736; www.armidaletourism.com.au. Open M-F 9am-5pm, Sa 9am-4pm, Su 10am-4pm.) **Greyhound Australia** (☎13 20 30) runs to Brisbane (5½-6¾hr., 2 per day, $88/79); Newcastle (7¼hr.; 1 per day at 3:25am; $76/69); and Sydney (10hr.; 1 per day at 3:25am; $99, students $89). **Keans Travel Express** (☎1800 043 339) runs to Port Macquarie (6hr.; M, W, F 1 per day; $53, students $43), via Coffs Harbour (3½hr., $27/22). Book ahead. **Countrylink** (☎13 22 32) connects by coach to Tenterfield (2½hr., daily 6:30pm, $27) via Glen Innes (1¼hr., $12), and by train to Sydney (8¼hr., daily 8:50am, $72). One block south of the visitors center on Marsh St. is the beginning of the **Beardy Street Mall,** an outdoor cluster of shops and cafes. **New England Travel Centre,** 188 Beardy Mall, is helpful for booking buses and trains. (☎6772 1722. Open M-F 9am-5pm, Sa 9am-noon.) The Armidale **NPWS office** (☎6776 0000), in the W. J. McCarthy Building at 85-87 Faulkner St., has info on area parks. (Open M-F 8:30am-4:30pm.) For a **taxi,** call **Armidale Radio Taxis** at ☎13 10 08 or 6771 1455. The **library** on the corner of Faulkner St. and Cinders Ln. has free **Internet** terminals for booking. (☎6772 4711. Open M-F 10am-6pm, Sa 10am-1pm.) The **police station** (☎6771 0699) is at 1 Moore St. Internet access is also available at **Armidale Computers,** 100 Jessie St. (☎6771 2712. $1.10 per 15min. Open M-F 9am-5pm, Sa 9am-12:30pm.) **ATMs** are available on Beardy St. between Marsh and Dangar St.; and the **post office** is at 158 Beardy St. **Postal Code:** 2350.

NATIONAL PARKS IN THE NEW ENGLAND TABLELANDS

Tucked between the red dirt roads of Big Sky country and the crashing surf along the coast, the New England Tablelands' bevy of national parks offer travelers an easy wilderness escape. Mountain bike the subtropical wilderness or gaze at cascading waterfalls. Waterfall Way (Rte. 78) stretches from Armidale to the Pacific Highway just south of Coffs Harbour. Straddling the southern side of the parks, Oxley Highway connects Walcha to Port Macquarie. These roads link to more than a dozen forests and reserves, providing a range of rugged terrain.

WATERFALL WAY. Waterfall Way runs east-west between Armidale and the north coast of New South Wales. Along the way, the tourist route passes four excellent national parks with campgrounds, several tiny hamlets, and the charming town of Bellingen (p. 190). In addition to the parks below, the Ebor Falls (approximately 4km east of Cathedral Rock, 42km west of Dorrigo, and 600m off the highway) provide an excellent photo-op. A 600m walk from the carpark leads to a breathtaking lookout.

OXLEY WILD RIVERS NATIONAL PARK. This World Heritage site is full of waterfalls tumbling into expansive gorges and is home to a variety of endangered species like the brush-tailed rock-wallaby. Pamphlets can help you choose a camp or picnic site; contact the Armidale **NPWS** (☎6776 0000) or **Armidale Visitors Centre** (☎1800 627 736) for more info. The **Port Macquarie** (☎6584 2203), **Dorrigo** (☎6657 2309), and **Walcha** (☎6777 4700) **NPWS offices** have info as well. To find out more on **Apsley** and **Tia Gorges** at the more remote western end of the park, see p. 217.

Two of Oxley's best vistas are not far from Armidale: less than 20km south of the city, platforms offer views of the 120m Dangar Falls. Take Kentucky St. east to Dangarsleigh Rd. and drive 8km south; 10km of gravel road leads to the gorge. The rest area is the trailhead for a series of walks ranging in length from the Gorge Lookout path (100m) to half-day treks; it is also equipped with BBQ, firewood, and pit toilets. After passing the grid, make your first left into the park for **campgrounds**

❶ ($3). **Gara Gorge,** also a popular daytrip from Armidale, is the site of Australia's first public hydro-electric scheme, built in 1894. East from Armidale, Waterfall Way leads to Castledoyle Rd.; it's only an 18km trip, with about 3km of gravel as you approach the gorge. The **Threlfall Walk** (an easy 5.5km) circles the edge of the gorge, surveying leftover sites from the historic engineering scheme.

OXLEY WILD RIVERS NATIONAL PARK AT A GLANCE

AREA: 142,223 hectares.

LOCATION: Between Armidale and the coast of NSW, south of Hwy. 78.

FEATURES: Apsley Tia, and Gara Gorges, Dangar Falls, Wollomombi Falls (2nd highest in Southern Hemisphere).

GATEWAYS: Armidale, Walcha.

CAMPING: Wollomombi Falls, Dangar Gorge, Long Point (bush camping).

FEES: Camping $5 or less. On-site self-registration.

Long Point is a secluded wilderness area in an open eucalyptus forest adjacent to a rare dry rainforest. The turn-off for Long Point appears 40km east of Armidale along Waterfall Way. A 7km stretch of sealed track passes through Hillgrove, where a left turn leads onto a dirt track which reaches the park 20km below. The attached **campsite** ❶ has pit toilets, picnic tables, and fresh water. It also serves as the trailhead for the excellent **Chandler Walk** (5km, 2-2½hr.), which leads through a grove of mosses, vines, and yellow-spotted Hillgrove Gums, unique to the area. Tremendous lookouts along the walk survey the valley and Chandler River.

The **Wollomombi Falls** gorge, located 40km east of Armidale, is the easiest part of Oxley to access from the east—75km west of Dorrigo, the Falls are just 2km south of Waterfall Way. **Wollomombi Lookout** (150m), **Checks Lookout** (500m), and **Chandler Lookout** (1.5km) all provide stunning views. The moderately strenuous **Wollomombi Walk** (2km round-trip) takes you around the rim of the gorge, and a series of lookouts. There is a **camping** ❶ site with gas BBQ near the entrance to the gorge area.

NEW ENGLAND NATIONAL PARK. New England National Park, also World Heritage-listed (for its range of cool-temperate to warm-subtropical rainforest), offers some fabulous bushwalking. Its densely vegetated basalt cliffs were formed 18 million years ago by the Ebor volcano.

Near the entrance, 85km from Armidale and 75km from Dorrigo, is the **Thungutti Campground** ❶ ($3). Nearby the **Lookout Walk** (2½hr.) and the **Cascades Walk** (2hr.) begin. Most people skip these outskirts, instead taking Point Lookout Rd. (11km gravel; 2.5km sealed) to the **Point Lookout Picnic Area,** the park's hub, with toilets, fire pits, and ample parking. Point Lookout marks the start of nine walks ranging from 5min. to 3½hr., all of which can be linked for nearly a full day of walking. **The Point Lookout,** an escarpment rising 1564m above sea level, surveys dense forest often shrouded in mist. Follow the **Eagles Nest Track** (2.5km, 2hr. round-trip) along the steep cliffside and through dry eucalyptus, which give way to extraordinary Antarctic beeches shortly after the lookout. At the end of the track, icicles hang like frozen tears from **Weeping Rock;** the shattered remnants of which litter the walkway. From here, a 10min. walk leads back to the road (about 1km from the Point), while continuing on the difficult **Lyrebird Walk** makes for a full-day hike.

The NPWS also rents three cabins in the park, each with a 2-night minimum and 7-night maximum stay. **The Residence** ❶ ($70-90; sleeps 10) and **The Chalet** ❶ ($50-60; sleeps 6) are both fully self-contained (all you need to bring are blankets, pillows, and linens); **Tom's Cabin** ❶ ($35-40; sleeps 8), on the other hand, is an unadorned, unpowered camper's cabin. Contact the Dorrigo **NPWS** office (☎6657 2309) for bookings, which can be made up to six months ahead.

CATHEDRAL ROCK NATIONAL PARK. Though drier than most of its peers along Waterfall Way, Cathedral Rock National Park has some great walks leading through stacks of improbably balanced granite boulders and eucalyptus forest. About 3km past the New England NP turn-off is the entrance for the park, where 8km of gravel road will lead you to the Barokee Rest Area. The **Warrigal Track** (1km, 30min. round-trip) is an easy stroll with a few boulders and, in the spring and summer, native orchids. The **Cathedral Rock Track** (5.8km, 2½hr. round-trip) intersects with a short walking route (400m) to the top of Cathedral Rock, which has deep crevasses and can be slippery. Your agility will be rewarded with expansive views. **Camping ❶** is available at the Barokee Rest Area ($3, children $2).

OXLEY HIGHWAY NATIONAL PARKS

APSLEY AND TIA GORGES. The must-see highlights of the southwestern end of **Oxley Wild Rivers National Park** (p. 215) are the waterfalls in the Apsley and Tia Gorges, which are most easily accessed from the Oxley Hwy. The larger part of the park is usually accessed from Waterfall Way, closer to Armidale (p. 214). About 83km south from Armidale and 20km east of Walcha is the turn-off for the **Apsley Gorge,** 1km off the highway. The waterfall is not only one of the most spectacular in the park, but also one of the easiest to view—a staircase leading down into the gorge provides an outstanding, unobstructed lookout. The **Oxley Walk** (2.7km, 2hr. round-trip) takes you around the rim of the gorge and across a bridge over the Apsley River. Campsites and fresh water are available at **Lions Lookout ❶,** one of the area's most scenic camping spots. Nineteen kilometers south of the Apsley Falls entrance is a 5.5km unsealed road leading to the small picnic and camping area of **Tia Falls ❶. Tia Gorge** is a short 650m walk and the Tiara Walk (5km return) crosses the river by footbridge and follows the gorge's western bluff. (Both sites $3 per person plus $6 entrance fee.)

Small and charming, **Walcha** (pop. 1800) is still a useful starting point for Apsley and Tia Gorges and the rest of Oxley Wild Rivers National Park, though the town lacks excitement. You'll find info on the local parks at the **Visitor Information Centre,** on the corner of Fitzroy and South St. (☎6774 2460; open M-F 9am-4:30pm, Sa-Su 10-4), and the **NPWS outpost** at 188 W. North St. From the only roundabout in Walcha, turn north onto Darby St., then left at the showground onto North St. (☎6777 4700. Open M-F 8:30am-4:30pm.) The **Commercial Hotel ❸,** on Meridian St. off the highway, has food and rooms. (☎6777 2551. Singles $45; doubles $65; twins $75.)

WERRIKIMBE NATIONAL PARK. More rugged than its neighbors, Werrikimbe is home to temperate and subtropical rainforest, eucalyptus forest, and snow gum woodlands. District managers in Walcha (☎6777 4700) or Port Macquarie (☎6586 8300) offer extensive information. The first 15km of this track isn't too bad, but the twisting, climbing, and loose gravel path may be difficult for conventional vehicles, especially after rain. Inside the park, the tracks to the campground and visitor facilities are maintained to a 2WD standard (any further travel into the park will require a 4WD). Upon entering, travelers may choose to turn left into the **Mooraback Rest Area** or right to **Cobcroft's Rest Area;** both trailhead facilities have parking, picnic tables, and toilets; Mooraback also has campsites. Mooraback is set amid snow gum woodlands by the Mooraback Creek, where the Hastings River begins its descent to the coast at Port Macquarie. The **Platypus Pools** track (2hr. round-trip) meanders past a series of pools where, if your timing is right, you might catch a glimpse of a monotreme or two. The rest area is the starting point for the 15min. Mooraback Track and the popular 3- to 4-day **Werrikimbe Trail.**

The rest area at Cobcroft is set in an open eucalyptus forest sprinkled with tree ferns. The Carrabeen Walk (1hr. round-trip) passes through an adjacent temperate rainforest. Longer walks into the Werrikimbe Wilderness Area, including the 8hr. Mesa Trail, are possible, but you should consult the NPWS office first.

Three spots are accessible from the Oxley Hwy. on the eastern side of the park, along **Forbes River Road** or **Hastings Forest Way** (note that these are more conveniently reached from Port Macquarie): **Grass Tree Rest Area, Brushy Mountain Camping Area,** and **Plateau Beech Camping Area.** All three are trailheads for walks of varying lengths. Of particular note, the vivid passage from the Plateau Beech Camping Area crosses through gullies of Antarctic beeches, with gnarled, web-like bases that take on outstanding shapes, before the trailheads on to King Fern Falls and Filmy Ferns Cascades (1½hr. round-trip). The eastern and western sides of the park are linked by the 4WD-only **Racecourse Trail.**

Ten kilometers farther down the Oxley Hwy. from Werrikimbe (65km east of Walcha) is a beautiful drive through the towering canopies of **Cottan-Bimbang National Park.** The park's main feature is the 15km **Myrtle Scrub Scenic Drive,** a looping, 2WD, dry-weather track that stops at a picnic ground, adjacent to a magnificent timber bridge over Cells River.

TAMWORTH ☎02

Every January Tamworth (pop. 37,500) hosts the **Country Music Festival** (Jan. 19-28, 2007 and Jan. 18-27, 2008; www.country.com.au), drawing famous crooners and hordes of fans. A more recent tradition, the **Hats Off to Country Festival** brings smaller crowds every July but promises a full slate of live music for the four-day weekend. The country spirit is otherwise maintained by gallon-hatted city slickers and tie-in tourist attractions, like the giant golden guitar and a concrete slab with handprints of country artists. The town is a destination for country-music lovers and is a pleasant stopover for those headed to nearby national parks or Brisbane. It is also close to several of the popular Jackaroo and Jillaroo schools.

TRANSPORTATION. The **train station,** on Marius St. between Brisbane and Bourke St., has a travel center that books tickets. (☎6766 2357. Open M-F 8:30am-5:30pm, Sa 8:30am-noon.) **Countrylink** (☎13 22 32) runs express trains to Sydney (6¼hr.; 1 per day; $64, concessions $32). All buses run from the **coach terminal** outside the visitors center. **Greyhound Australia** (☎13 14 99 or 13 20 30) travels to: Brisbane (9¼hr.; daily 9am and 9:50pm; $93, concessions $84); and Sydney (7½hr., daily 5:45am, $88/79) via Newcastle (5hr., $65/59). **Keans Travel Express** (☎6543 1322) goes to Port Macquarie (8¼hr.; M, W 9am, F 1:30pm; $74) via Coffs Harbour (6hr.; $60). For **car rental, Budget** (☎13 27 27) and **Thrifty** (☎6765 3699) have branches in town. Call **Tamworth Radio Cabs** (☎13 10 08) for a **taxi.**

ORIENTATION AND PRACTICAL INFORMATION. Tamworth is 412km north of Sydney on the New England Hwy. (which, from Armidale, enters town from the east and departs south) and is a convenient rest stop for those journeying to Brisbane (578km). The town's Central Business District (CBD) lies along **Peel Street.** The main intersection is with **Brisbane Street** (New England Hwy.), which crosses the Peel River, becoming **Bridge Street** in West Tamworth. The **visitors center** is at the corner of Peel and Murray St. (☎6755 4300; www.tamworth.nsw.gov.au. Open daily 9am-5pm.) The **library,** 466 Peel St., has free **Internet** access. (☎6755 4460. Open M-Th 10am-7pm, F 10am-6pm, Sa 9am-2pm.) **Banks** and **ATMs** are all along Peel St. **Police** (☎6768 2999) are located at 40 Fitzroy St. The **post office,** 406 Peel St. (☎6755 5988), is on the corner with Fitzroy St. **Postal Code:** 2340.

ACCOMMODATIONS AND FOOD. Beds are generally plentiful, except during January's Country Music Festival (book a year ahead). Several hotels offer pubstays for $25-35 a night. The **Tamworth YHA ❷,** 169 Marius St., offers cheap beds just two blocks from the CBD. Breakfast is included, and a well-stocked kitchen is available. (☎6761 2600. Internet $1 per 15min. Laundry $6. Dorms $23-26; doubles $48. 3-day dorm stays for $55. Cash only.) **Paradise Caravan Park ❶,** next to the visitors center along the creek on Peel St., has electric grills, a pool, and a playground. (☎6766 3120. Linen $5 for singles, $8 for doubles. Laundry $5. Key deposit $5. Reception daily 7am-7pm. Sites for 2 $20, powered $24; cabins $50-90, in off-peak season 7th night free. Extra adult $9-12, child $6-8. MC/V.)

The Vault ❸, 429 Peel St., has gourmet pizzas pulled from the mouth of a gargoyle-shaped wood-fire oven ($14-18). Live music in summer Thursday and Saturday nights, in winter Friday night and Sunday afternoon, fills the high ceilings of this refurbished 1892 former bank. (☎6766 6975. M 8am-5pm, Tu-F 8am-latenight, Sa 8:30am-latenight, Su 8am-4pm. AmEx/DC/MC/V.) The **Old Vic Cafe ❷,** 261 Peel St., is frequented by a laid-back local clientele and fixes gourmet main courses ($13-16), as well as Turkish bread sandwiches ($9-10), freshly squeezed juices ($3.20-4), and homemade sauces and vinaigrettes. All-day breakfast is available. (☎6766 3435. Open M-F 8am-5pm, Sa 8:30am-3pm. MC/V.) **Coles** supermarket is at 436-444 Peel St., in the City Plaza shopping mall. (Open M-Sa 6am-midnight, Su 8am-8pm.)

SIGHTS AND ACTIVITIES. You don't have to be a country music fan to enjoy Tamworth; you just need a high tolerance for kitsch. **The Golden Guitar Complex** is worth the 10min. trip south on the New England Hwy., as much for the gift shop as for the 12m guitar itself. A realistic "Gallery of Stars" **wax museum** dresses 24 replicas in clothes donated by the stars themselves, including Slim Dusty, "The Man Who is Australia." In odd juxtaposition, an impressive gem and mineral display shares the complex. (☎6765 2688; www.biggoldenguitar.com.au. Open daily 9am-5pm. $8, children $4, families $18.) The popular **Hands of Fame Cornerstone,** on Brisbane St. at Kable Ave., bears the handprints of country music celebrities. The **Walk a Country Mile Interpretive Centre** at the visitors center takes you through an interactive history of country music in Australia. ($6, children $2, families $15.) Bring out your inner cowboy or cowgirl at one of the **Jackaroo and Jillaroo schools** in the Tamworth area, with crash courses on how to ride horses, train dogs, milk cows, lasso, operate farm equipment, and muster cattle from the saddle. Certificates and job searches are given upon completion. **Leconfield** runs an excellent school an hour out of Tamworth. (☎6769 4328; www.leconfield.com. Free pickup at Tamworth YHA. 5-day course begins every Monday. $490 includes food and accommodation; book a month ahead. Cash only, $200 advance deposit required.)

ENTERTAINMENT AND NIGHTLIFE. Tamworth is a country town, and its nightlife definitely has a local flavor. Most establishments close after 2am, but the standard 1 or 1:30am curfew means you must be in the establishment door by that hour. The **West Diggers Club** (☎6766 4661), on Kable Ave., off Brisbane St., has good country music lineups on the weekend. The **Imperial Hotel,** on the corner of Marius and Brisbane St., draws a younger crowd uninterested in its country music heritage. (☎6766 2613. Live music Th-Sa. Curfew 1:30am.) The **Central Hotel,** on the corner of Brisbane and Peel St., features rock and country live music Th-Sa. Check out a free copy of *The Gig Guide* in Thursday's *Leader*, Tamworth's local paper, for details and other venues.

SOUTH COAST

While the path from Sydney up the North Coast has been well-worn by hordes of backpackers, the South Coast has only recently been discovered. Local residents proudly proclaim that it's one of Australia's best-kept secrets, and city-weary visitors will be inclined to agree. The region's beaches are only minutes from lush rainforests and far less crowded than those in the north. Princes Hwy., south of Sydney, links South Coast destinations like Bateman's Bay, Jervis Bay, and Kiama.

DON'T FEED THE ANIMALS! While you might be tempted to give the remarkably tame kangaroos some of your sandwich, feeding wildlife ruins their ability to fend for themselves, making them dependent on human food instead. For the love of the 'roos, don't do it.

WOLLONGONG ☎02

About 80km south of Sydney, Wollongong (pop. 250,000) is the coastal gateway to scenic Shoalhaven and is not a bad place to stop for water sports or a night of big-time partying (W-Sa). As the third-largest metropolitan area in New South Wales, Wollongong is anxious to push its cosmopolitan city appeal, but it's still essentially a small, friendly, beachside university town with boisterous nightlife and great surf beaches. While its foundations lie in industry, the 'Gong, which is bordered by steep mountains and miles of coastline, can't help but support outdoor activities. In addition to world-class surfing, there are adrenaline-pumping activities in nearby Stanwell Park, and great views of Illawarra Escarpment.

TRANSPORTATION AND PRACTICAL INFORMATION. **CityRail trains** (☎13 15 00) stop at Wollongong City Station on Station St. and run to: Bomaderry, near Nowra (1½hr., 4-10 per day, $8.20); Kiama (45min., 11-16 per day, $5.20); Sydney (1½hr., 12-28 per day, $9). **Premier Motor Service** (☎13 34 10) buses run to: Batemans Bay (3-3¾hr., 2 per day, $39); Bermagui (6hr., 1 per day, $51); Melbourne (15hr., 1 per day, $77); Narooma (4½-5¼hr., 2 per day, $48); Sydney (1½-2hr., 2 per day, $16); Ulladulla (2¾hr., 2-3 per day, $28). **Murrays** (☎13 22 51) runs to Canberra (3½hr., 1 per day, $30.80). The Princes Hwy. runs into Wollongong, becoming **Flinders Street** north of the city and merging into **Keira Street** in the CBD. The pedestrian **Crown Street Mall** is between Keira and Kembla St. **ATMs** are abundant here. **Tourism Wollongong,** 93 Crown St., is on the corner of Crown and Kembla St. (☎4227 5545 or 1800 240 737; www.tourismwollongong.com.au. Open M-F 9am-5pm, Sa 9am-4pm, Su 10am-4pm.) **Network Cafe,** 157 Crown St., has **Internet** access. (☎4228 8686. $3.50 per hr. Open M-W 10am-6pm, Th 10am-9pm, F-Sa 10am-midnight, Su 10am-5pm.) The **post office** is at 110-116 Crown St., in the pedestrian mall. (☎13 13 18. Open M-F 9am-5pm.) **Postal Code:** 2500.

ACCOMMODATIONS. **YHA Wollongong ❷** (also known as Keiraview Accommodation), 75-79 Keira St., is Wollongong's most impressive place to stay. The spacious, airy rooms all contain fridges, and guests have BBQ equipment and a TV lounge at their disposal. (☎4229 1132 or 4229 9700; www.keiraviewaccommodation.com.au. Internet access $4 per hr. Laundry $2. Wheelchair accessible. Reception 8am-8.30pm. Dorms from $25; twins from $36; ensuite singles $55; doubles $99; 4- to 8-bed family rooms from $77.) **Wollongong Surf Leisure Resort ❷,** on Pioneer Rd. in Fairy Meadow, is the nearest campground, 4.5km north of the CBD and a 20min. walk from Fairy Meadow CityRail station. By car from Wollongong, go north on Corrimal St. to Stuart Park, then to George Hanley Dr. at the roundabout. Turn right when it ends, then right onto Pioneer Rd. (☎4283 6999; www.wslr.com.au. Laundry, pool, spa,

minigolf, and indoor tennis courts. Bike rental $5 per hr. Reception M-Sa 8am-9pm, Su 8am-6pm. Sites for 2 from $20, powered from $25; family-style cabins from $85.)

FOOD AND NIGHTLIFE. The restaurants lining Keira, Corrimal, and lower Crown St. offer a variety of Asian cuisines, with entrees starting at around $10. Wollongong also has many Indian and Italian restaurants. **Trang ❶**, 165 Keira St., serves delicious Vietnamese food at affordable prices, including vermicelli spring rolls ($5), grilled pork, lemongrass beef, and prawns with salad (all $11). The recently redone dining space creates a stylish yet relaxed atmosphere. (☎4229 6883. Open daily 11am-11pm.) At North Beach, trendy **Café La Mer ❷**, 1-5 Bourke St., opposite the Novotel at the corner of Cliffe St., overlooks the ocean and serves dishes, like reef and beef ($26.90) and beef and prawn pizza ($12.90) with exotic twists. (☎4225 7701. Open M-F 11am-8:30pm, Sa-Su 7:30am-8:30pm.) The **Woolworths** supermarket is on the corner of Kembla and Burelli St. (☎4228 8066. Open M-Sa 7:30am-10pm, Su 8am-10pm.)

The **Glasshouse Tavern,** 90 Crown St., between Kembla and Corrimal St., attracts a young crowd eager to impress, especially on the extremely popular Wednesday Uni Night and on weekends, when its back room transforms into a dance club. (☎4226 4305. Open M-Tu 10am-9pm, W 10am-1am, Th 10am-1am, F 10am-5am, Sa 10am-5am. Nightclub open W-F 7pm-5am, Sa 8pm-5am.) After the Glasshouse closes, those in the know head to **Rustys Nightclub,** 5 Victoria St., on Th nights to enjoy a hot dance and singles scene. (☎4227 2058. Open W-Th 8pm-3am.) The **Bour-**

bon Street Night Club, 150 Keira St., often has party-goers lined up as early as 8pm, eager to join the in-crowd at this triple-decker dance club. DJs spin techno, R&B, and Top-40. (☎4226 1215. Open Sa 8pm-3am.)

SIGHTS AND ACTIVITIES. Like most of the South Coast, Wollongong's best features are found outdoors. **Wollongong Harbour** is the city's most scenic spot. The small, convict-built cove shelters sailboats and the local fishing fleet. The two **lighthouses,** both visible from the beach, add an air of vintage charm. Visitors and residents alike enjoy the beautiful walking and cycling path along the harbor's edge to **North Beach,** a popular surf spot. Wollongong's other surfing beach is **City Beach,** a few blocks from the tourist office. For more info on bikes, boards, and extreme sports, contact the **Tourism Wollongong** activities hotline (☎1800 240 737; www.tourismwollongong.com). Near Wollongong, **Stanwell Park** offers even more adventure sports. Back indoors, the **Wollongong City Gallery,** on the corner of Kembla and Burelli St., creatively displays regional, Aboriginal, and contemporary art. (☎4228 7500. Open Tu-F 10am-5pm, Sa-Su and holidays noon-4pm. Free.)

DAYTRIPS FROM WOLLONGONG

NORTHERN SCENIC DRIVE. The winding Bulli Pass track twists and turns inland to the Southern Fwy., 12km north of Wollongong, and leads to Bulli Tops, a magnificent panoramic view of the coastline and bordering beach towns. Stopping points along the way, like **Bulli Lookout,** offer fantastic views of the mountains, sea, sand, and white-capped waves. Down at sea level, Wollongong's biggest attractions await at **Bulli Point** (also known as Sandon Point Headland), **Thirroul Beach** to the south, and, farther north, **Austinmer Beach.** The daring flock to Bulli or Thirroul for some of the area's best surfing, whereas more family-oriented beachgoers head to Austinmer. For those without a car, CityRail runs from Wollongong to Thirroul ($3.20). For several months in 1922, English writer D.H. Lawrence resided in Thirroul and described the area in his novel *Kangaroo.* His home is privately owned and inaccessible to the public, but the beach is open for strolling. North of Bulli Pass, Lawrence Hargrave Dr. winds along the coast, providing tantalizing glimpses of the shore below before reaching the lookout at Bald Hill, north of Stanwell Park, considered by many to be the best view on this stretch of coast. You can get a bird's-eye view of Stanwell Park up in the air; both **HanggIideOz** (☎04 1793 9200; www.hangglideoz.com.au) and **Sydney Hang Gliding Center** (☎4294 4294; www.hanggliding.com.au) have tandem hang gliding trips starting at $180.

ILLAWARRA ESCARPMENT. The Illawarra Escarpment defines Wollongong's inland border. Panoramic views of Lake Illawara make traversing the inclines worthwhile. The nearest peak, Mt. Keira, is a short drive from town on Mt. Keira Rd. Take bus #39 to get within 8km of Mt. Keira's peak. Several hiking trails lead to fantastic views at the top. The Cockatoo Run, a scenic mountain railway, stops at Wollongong City Station and offers day-long excursions in restored 1930s train carriages. (☎1300 653 801; www.3801limited.com.au. Operates W and Su 1 per day most of the year; departs Wollongong 11am, returns 4:35pm. Booking required in summer. $40, seniors $35, children $30, families $110.)

KIAMA ☎02

Lovely Kiama (KAI-amma) is well worth a stop for its craggy cliffs, turbulent surf, and friendly, small-town feel. Kiama, whose name appropriately means "sound of the sea," is a B&B-filled town known for its geyser-like **Blowhole.** Under the right conditions, when the wind is high and the waves surge from the southeast, water washing into a sea cave is forced noisily upward through a hole in the rocks to heights of 20-

35m. At **Marsden Head,** at the end of Tingira Cres., near the Endeavour Lookout, the **Little Blowhole** erupts when the ocean swell comes from the opposite direction. It's worth the extra trip if its big brother proves to be a disappointment. For swimming, check out the **natural rock pool** on the north side of Blowhole Point or the deeper rock pool, north of Kiama Harbour at Pheasant Point. To the north of Pheasant Point, experienced **surfers** brave the riptides at **Bombo Beach.** Slightly north of Bombo Beach, just around the next headland, sightseers will discover the striking rock formation known as **Cathedral Rock.** Surfers refer to this same area as the **Boneyard;** despite the menacing nickname, it's a popular spot for catching waves. Less experienced surfers and swimmers should head south to popular **Surf Beach,** where the waters are patrolled. For those who get tired of gazing idly out across the ocean, **Kiama Charter Service** (☎4237 8496), **Kiama Harbour Game and Reef Fishing Charter** (☎4232 1725), and **MV Signa** can send you out to the deep sea for some sportfishing. (☎04 2325 1603; www.mvsigna.com.au). Their fishing expeditions generally last 7-8hr. and cost $70-100, including bait and gear. Lastly, if you're in Kiama and are a surfing fan (or just a beach-lover), you'd be wise to make the 10km trip south to South Australia's largest and most famous surf shop, **Natural Necessity Surf Shop,** opposite Town Hall in neighboring **Gerringong** (☎4234 1636. Open daily 9am-9pm). From there, continue 4km to exquisite **Seven Mile Beach** in the small town of **Geroa.** A local craft market is hosted on the 3rd Sunday of every month at Black Beach (☎4237 6111).

Thanks to Kiama's popularity, particularly its reputation as an ideal spot for romantic getaways in upscale accommodations, it's difficult to find an affordable room in town. The small **Kiama Backpackers Hostel ❷,** 31 Bong Bong St., next to the train station, feels like an old university dormitory. (☎/fax 4233 1881. TV, kitchen. Internet access $4 per hr. Key deposit $10. Dorms $20; singles $25; doubles $49.) The **Kiama Harbour Cabins ❺** has picturesque harbor views. (☎4232 2707. Cabins $190-250.) Locals recommend the fish 'n' chips ($10) at **Barnacle's Takeaway ❶,** right on the harbor below the Blowhole Point Holiday Park. (☎4232 1138. Open daily 10:30am-7:30pm, later during summer.) Meanwhile, fine—and healthy—dining takes place at **Saltwater ❷,** 104 Terralong St., where the outdoor seating offers a nice view of the bay. The sea chest (fresh fish, calamari, scallops, and salad; $18.50) is a great choice. (☎4232 1104. Open daily 11am-7pm.) In addition to selling books, the intimate **Coffee Table Bookshop ❶,** 2/3 Railway Pde., at the corner of Terralong St., serves sandwiches and salads for $7-10. Internet access also available for $5.50 per 30min. (☎4233 1060. Open M-Sa 9am-5pm, Su 10am-4pm.)

From the **CityRail** station, on Bong Bong St., just west of Blowhole Pt., trains (☎13 15 00) run to: Bomaderry/Nowra (30min., 10-15 per day, $4.40); Sydney (2hr., 12-16 per day, $13); and Wollongong (45min., 13-17 per day, $5.20). From the Bombo Railway Station, **Premier Motor Service** (☎13 34 10) buses run to: Batemans Bay (2½-3¼hr., 2 per day, $39); Bermagui (5¼hr., 1 per day, $49); Melbourne (15hr., 1 per day, $77); Narooma (4-4¼hr., 2 per day, $50); Nowra (40min., 2 per day, $16); Sydney (2½hr., 2 per day, $22); Ulladulla (2¼hr., 2 per day, $28); Wollongong (35min., 2 per day, $16). The **visitors center** is on Blowhole Pt. (☎4232 3322 or 1300 654 262; www.kiama.com.au. Open daily 9am-5pm.) **Internet** access is available in the **Kiama Library,** 7 Railway Pde. (☎4233 1133. Email $5 per hr. Open M and W-F 9:30am-5:30pm, Tu 9:30am-8pm, Sa 9:30am-2pm.) The **post office** is at 24 Terralong St. (☎13 13 13. Open M-F 9am-5pm.) **Postal Code:** 2533.

NOWRA AND BOMADERRY ☎02

Every sign along the Princes Hwy. directs you to Nowra—falsely implying that there's something to see there. Truth be told, Nowra is best used as a base for exploring more scenic areas like Kangaroo Valley and Jervis Bay. Smaller sibling Bomaderry lies north and is the end of the rail line at the Nowra-Bomaderry stop.

Due to its proximity to Kangaroo Valley and Jervis Bay, many choose to stay in Nowra when exploring the area. The cozy, bungalow-style **M&M's Guesthouse ❸**, 1A Scenic Dr., on the right off Bridge Rd. just across the bridge into Nowra, has a backpackers' building and adjacent motel. (☎4421 2044; www.mmguesthouse.com. Laundry, TV, fireplace, and kitchen. Reception 8am-6pm. Dorms $30; motel singles $65; doubles $75.) For camping sites next to a wildlife park, head for **Shoalhaven Ski Park ❶.** From Bomaderry, take a right on Illaroo Rd., just before the gray metal bridge to Nowra; follow McMahon's Rd. left from the roundabout, and take a left at the first stop sign onto Rock Hill Rd. The owner also directs travelers to local climbing sites. (☎4423 2488. Toilets and hot showers. Reception 7am-7pm. Sites $13, powered $17.) Campers get discounts at the nearby **Nowra wildlife park,** which has wombats, koalas, and kangaroos. (☎4421 3949. Open daily 9am-5pm. $14, campers $10; children $8; families $40.) Area climbers recommend **Thompson's Point,** on the southern shore of the Shoalhaven river and find PC, Grotto, and South Central to be challenging. Climbers must supply their own gear. **The Gym** (☎4421 0587), at the corner of McMahons and Illaroo Rd., takes climbers to locations in North Nowra. **Skydive Nowra** (☎04 1944 6904) offers tandem skydives ($395 with video) and freefall courses ($450 with video). Be sure to book ahead.

CityRail's (☎13 15 00) last stop is in Bomaderry on Railway St. **Trains** run to: Kiama (30min., 12-15 per day, $4.40); Sydney (2¾hr., 12-15 per day, $15.20); Wollongong (1½-2hr., 9 per day, $8.20). **Premier** (☎13 34 10; www.premierms.com.au) buses run to: Batemans Bay (1¾hr., 2 per day, $20); Bega (4¼hr., 2 per day, $35); Bermagui (4hr., 1 per day, $31); Kiama (40min., 2 per day, $12); Melbourne (13½hr., 1 per day, $55); Narooma (2¾hr., 2 per day, $29); Sydney (3-3¼hr., 2 per day, $18); Ulladulla (1hr., 2 per day, $13); Wollongong (1¼hr., 2 per day, $12). **Kennedy's Coaches** (☎4421 7596 or 04 1123 2101) services Fitzroy Falls (1hr., 1 per day, $15.40) and Kangaroo Valley (½hr., 2 per day, $7). The **Shoalhaven Visitors Centre** lies on the corner of Princes Hwy. and Pleasant Way, south of the bridge to Nowra. (☎4421 0778 or 1300 662 808; www.shoalhaven.nsw.gov.au. Open daily 9am-5pm.) For ideas about what to do in Nowra and throughout the South Coast, visit www.nowrabackpackers.com. The **National Parks and Wildlife Service,** 55 Graham St., Nowra, has park info. (☎4423 2170. Open M-F 8:30am-5pm.) The **Nowra Public Library,** on Berry St., has **Internet** access. (☎4429 3705. $2.20 per hr.) The **police station** (☎4421 9699) is on Kinghorn St. The **post office** is at 59 Junction St. (☎4429 4140. Open M-F 9am-5pm.) **Postal Code:** 2541.

KANGAROO VALLEY ☎02

More than just a place to spot kangaroos, tiny Kangaroo Valley (pop. 350) is a good launching point for canoe trips down the Kangaroo and Shoalhaven Rivers. It has the pleasant feel of a rural area, which makes it popular for camping retreats, and its main street, Moss Vale Rd., is dotted with arts-and-crafts shops, restaurants, and cafes. At the northwest end of town, the **Hampden Bridge** spans the Kangaroo River. Built in 1898, it is Australia's oldest suspension bridge. With two locations on the north side of the bridge, **Kangaroo Valley Safaris,** 2210 Moss Vale Rd., organizes beginner-intermediate canoe camping trips to Kangaroo and Shoalhaven, including a 25km overnight canoe trip. A shuttle picks boaters up from the rail station. (☎4465 1502; www.kangaroovalleycanoes.com.au. Open daily 7am-7pm. Canoes $50 per day, kayaks $30 per day, overnight sea kayaks $65, tents $40 per day.) **Fitzroy Falls** greets visitors at the northern entrance of **Morton National Park,** 20km from Kangaroo Valley on Moss Vale Rd. The **Bendeela Campground ❶,** 7km outside town, provides free **camping** with toilets, BBQ, and water. Reach it by driving north of town and turning left on Bendeela Rd., following signs to the entrance. **Prior's Bus Service** (☎1800 816 234) runs M-F and Su to: Batemans Bay (2¼hr., $30); Narooma (4hr., M-Sa $35); Parramatta (3hr., $27); and Ulladulla (1½hr., $20). Run by the NPWS, the **Fitzroy Falls**

Visitors Centre has bushwalking trail maps. (☎4887 7270. Open daily 9am-5:30pm.) By car, avoid the steep, winding Kangaroo Valley Rd. leading west from Berry and opt for Moss Vale Rd., which leads northwest from Bombaderry, off the Princes Hwy. Caution should be used on the narrow, winding Moss Vale Rd.; check road conditions ahead of time for both routes. Tourist info is available at **News Agents,** next to the post office. (☎4465 1150; www.kangaroovalley.net. Open daily 6am-6pm.)

JERVIS BAY ☎02

The jewel of the South Coast, **Jervis Bay** is a serene body of water surrounded by striking white beaches and magnificent national parks. Full of marine life and underwater rock formations, the bay offers some of the best diving in Australia outside of the Great Barrier Reef.

Divers rave about the massive archways and rock shelves (Cathedral Cave and Smuggler's Cave are popular for **cave diving**), bushwalkers hunt for hidden creeks and waterfalls, fishermen boast about their catches, and animal lovers marvel at dolphins, kangaroos, penguins, and a large variety of colorful birds. Barry Moore, owner of **Barry's Bush Tucker Tours,** 14 Bottom St. (☎4442 1168), and a Wadi Wadi tribe member, leads fascinating Aboriginal history tours through the bush. Back in the water, the Arch, Stoney Creek Reef, and the Ten Fathom Dropoff are known for deep diving. **Steamers Beach Seal Colony** is great for open-water dives and snorkeling. Visibility is best from April to early August. **Deep 6 Diving,** 64 Owen St. (☎4441 5255; www.deep6divingjervisbay.com.au), takes certified divers on two dives for a day ($144, including gear). They also offer a four-day PADI course ($445). **Jervis Bay Sea Sports,** 47 Owen St. (☎4441 5012; www.jbseasports.com.au), offers slightly more expensive services. For those content to enjoy marine life from a drier vantage point, **Dolphin Watch Cruises,** 50 Owen St. (☎1800 246 010; www.dolphinwatch.com.au), and **Dolphin Explorer Cruises,** 62 Owen St. (☎4441 5455 or 1800 444 330; www.dolphincruises.com.au), offer 2½hr. dolphin cruises with views of the cliffs daily at 12:30 and 1pm ($27-28, ISIC $22, family $76-77). Each company also offers 3hr. whale watching trips ($50-55, ISIC $42, family $130) during peak whale migrations daily 9 and 9:30am (June-Nov.). If you just want to paddle around, **Jervis Bay Kayak Company,** Shop 7b in Campbell Ct., off the Wool Rd. in Vincentia, leads kayak tours. The price includes transport, snack, and park entry fees. (☎4441 7157; www.jervisbaykayaks.com.au. Rentals $60-90 per day; ½-day guided tours $96. Open M and W-F 9:30am-5pm, Sa-Su 9:30am-3pm.)

HUSKISSON ☎02

Twenty-four kilometers southeast of Nowra along the coast of Jervis Bay lies the tiny town of Huskisson (nicknamed "Husky"; pop. 1500). Husky is only slightly off the beaten track and is the perfect place to stop for fish 'n' chips overlooking the bay. **Leisure Haven Caravan Park ❷,** 1.5km outside town along Currambene Creek on Woollamia Rd., provides sites with free hot showers, laundry, BBQ, TV, and a kitchen. (☎4441 5046; www.leisurehaven.com.au. Key deposit $20. Reception 8am-6pm. 7th night free. Sites for 2 from $20, powered from $25; cabins for 2 from $55; ensuite from $80.) **The Husky Pub ❸,** on Owen St. overlooking the Bay, has a menu of fish, burgers, and fries ($10.50-17.50), and is the town's **pub stay ❹.** The rooms are basic, have shared toilets, and are right above the Jervis Bay latenight hotspot. (☎4441 5001; www.thehuskypub.com.au. Bar and reception 11am-midnight. Singles $50; doubles $70.) **The Kiosk ❸,** 66 Owen St., is the best place in town for a mouth-watering meal— whether you're in the mood for a pancake breakfast, light lunch, or gourmet dinner. (☎4441 5464. Open M-Tu, Th, and Su 8am-4pm, F-Sa 8am-10pm.) On the way out of Huskisson, heading toward Booderee National Park through **Vincentia,** many beautiful beaches lie hidden down side streets just off the main road. Almost any street will lead to a scenic bit of coast. Especially beautiful are **Greenfields Beach** and **Hyams Beach,** said to have the world's whitest sand. For tourist info, visit the antique-filled **Huskisson Trading Post** on the corner of Tomerong and Dent St. (☎4441 5241. Open daily 9am-5pm.)

BOODEREE NATIONAL PARK

On the southern end of the bay, **Booderee National Park,** which is under joint Aboriginal management, covers over 6000 hectares of land with gorgeous beaches accessible by way of short hikes through wildlife-filled forest. The **Botanic Gardens** have numerous walks, a rainforest gully, and many native plants and birds. (☎4442 1006. Open daily 8am-5pm. Free.) You have to enter the park to reach many of Jervis Bay's most beautiful beaches. Locals rave about the beach at **Green Patch,** a popular snorkeling spot and a good place to see rainbow lorikeets and eastern gray kangaroos. **Murrays Beach** is staggeringly beautiful and a great place to swim. At **Steamers Beach,** you can snorkel amid a seal colony.

The **visitors center,** just beyond the park entry gates, accepts campsite bookings and can provide maps to hiking tracks. (☎4443 0977. Park use fee $10, included in camping fee. Open daily 9am-4pm.) The park also has three small group **camping** areas: **Green Patch ❷,** on Jervis Bay (hot showers, toilets, and water; sites $10-45); **Bristol Point ❷** (hot showers, toilets, and water; sites $10-52); **Cave Beach ❶,** near Wreck Bay to the south (cold showers, no electricity; max. 5 people; sites $7-11). All camping sites also charge per person fees of $5-10.

BE TIDY! One of the main threats to the National Parks in Australia is tourists. Some campers and day trippers leave their mark by littering and crushing plants underfoot. Visitors are encouraged to tread lightly and minimize damage by leaving their campsites as they found them.

ULLADULLA ☎02

Moving south through the Shoalhaven, the next major town is Ulladulla (uh-luh-DUH-luh; pop. 17,000). Outdoorsy, beautiful Ulladulla has plenty of diving, surfing, and fishing. Off the coast between Jervis Bay and Ulladulla Harbour lie shipwrecks for divers to explore, including the famous 1870 wreck of the *Walter Hood.* Still, the most beautiful draw is the Pigeon House bushwalk.

Bushwalkers generally stop in Ulladulla for the **Pigeon House Walk,** a 5km hike with steep climbing and knock-out views at the top. (Allow 3-4hr. Turn off the Princes Hwy. onto Wheelbarrow Rd. 3km south of Burrill Lake. The trailhead is 27km farther on unsealed road at a picnic area.) **One Track for All** is a gentle 2km trail dotted with hand-carved stumps, statues, and logs depicting Aboriginal and post-settlement history. The trail, which winds about the North Head cliffs near Ulladulla Harbour, affords several staggering ocean views. (Turn off Princes Hwy. onto North St., across from the police station. Take a left onto Burrill St., then a right onto Dolphin St.; the trailhead is at the end and is wheelchair accessible.) The **Ulladulla Dive Shop,** 150 Princes Hwy., at the corner of Deering St., operates dive charters and offers expert advice on **reef diving** in the area. (☎4455 5303. Open Nov.-Apr. daily 8am-6pm; May-Oct. M-F 9am-5pm, Sa-Su 8am-5pm. Gear $70 per day; intro dives $95.) The **Ulladulla Dive and Adventure Centre,** 211 Princes Hwy., at the southern end of Ulladulla near Dolphin Point, offers diving, snorkeling, canoe, and kayak lessons. PADI diving courses are also available. (☎4455 3029. Open M-Tu and Th-Sa 8:30am-5:30pm, Su 8:30am-5pm.) Nearby **Lakes Burrill** and **Conjola** have nice **swimming** beaches, and **Mollymook Beach,** just north of town, is good for **surfing** and dolphin-spotting.

Cheap motels line Princes Hwy. The local guest house, **Travellers Rest Guest House ❷**, 63 Princes Hwy., between Narrawallee and North St., is a small, impeccably tidy operation with beautiful hardwood floors, brightly colored walls, and a great sundeck and hammock area. (☎4454 0500. Key deposit $10. Dorms $20-25; doubles $45-55.) At the end of South St., **Holiday Haven Tourist Park ❶** has camping space, though the site slopes slightly. (☎4455 2457 or 1300 733 021. Showers, toilets, laundry, BBQ, minigolf, and pool. Sites $10, powered $15; cabins $100-165, low season $45-90.)

Premier (☎13 34 10; www.premierms.com.au) buses stop at the Marlin Hotel (southbound) and the Traveland Travel Agency (northbound) en route to: Batemans Bay (45min., 2 per day, $13); Bermagui (3hr., 1 per day, $27); Kiama (2¼hr., 2 per day, $28); Melbourne (13hr., 1 per day, $74); Narooma (1¾hr., 2 per day, $22); Nowra (1½hr., 2 per day, $16); Sydney (5hr., 2 per day, $30); Wollongong (3hr., 2 per day, $27). The **Visitors Centre** is on the Princes Hwy. (☎4455 1269. Open M-F 10am-6pm, Sa-Su 9am-5pm.) **Internet** access is available at the center, as well as the adjacent **library.** ($1.25 per 30min. Open M-F 10am-6pm, Sa 9am-2pm.) The **police** station (☎4454 2542) is on the corner of Princes Hwy. and North St. The **post office** is at the corner of Princes Hwy. and Green St. **Postal Code:** 2539.

MURRAMARANG NATIONAL PARK

With expansive views of the Pacific, the coastline of the Murramarang National Park makes a great detour. It is also a superb spot to check out the surprisingly tame kangaroos and parrots that play on the grass at **Pebbly Beach.** A number of campgrounds and caravan parks are speckled throughout the park, but tent **camping ❶** sites are cheapest at the Pebbly Beach camping area, which boasts even more kangaroos than the beach. (☎4478 6023; www.pebblybeach.com.au. Sites $5 per person plus $7 per vehicle; cabins for 2 from $85.) At the southernmost point in the Shoalhaven half of Murramarang National Park, **Durras North** looks onto Durras Lake and a windswept ocean beach. Pick up a brochure on self-guided bushwalks from the tourist office in Batemans Bay. The **Murramarang Beach Resort ❷**, on Durras Rd. off the Princes Hwy., is a luxurious campsite with "Ocean Front Luxury" cabin suites. (☎4478 6355 or 1300 767 255; www.murramarangresort.com. Reception Sept.-Mar. M-Th and Su 8am-midnight, F-Sa 8am-1am; Apr.-Aug. M-Th and Su 8am-10pm, F-Sa 8am-midnight. Sites $15-49, powered $23-65; ensuite $49-86; 4- to 6-person garden villas from $92; cabin suites from $272.)

BATEMANS BAY ☎02

Situated south of the junction at the mouth of Clyde River, Batemans Bay—and its picturesque harbor—begins where the Kings Hwy. from Canberra meets the Princes Hwy. at the coast. Though you won't see any fins from shore, dozens of gray nurse sharks, one of Australia's largest colonies, circle the islands offshore, making Batemans Bay a popular dive spot. If you're not impressed by zombie-eyed fish, join the backpackers and celebrities alike who come to this relaxed village for its proximity to the 'roos and parrots at Murramarang National Park.

TRANSPORTATION AND PRACTICAL INFORMATION. **Buses** leave from outside the Promenade Plaza on Orient St. **Premier Motor Service** (☎13 34 10; www.premierms.com.au) goes to: Bega (3hr., 2 per day, $25); Bermagui (2½hr., 1 per day, $18); Kiama (3hr., 2 per day, $39); Melbourne (12hr., 1 per day, $65); Narooma (1¾hr., 2 per day, $17); Nowra (2hr., 2 per day, $24); Sydney (5½hr., 2 per day, $41); Ulladulla (45min., 2 per day, $13); Wollongong (3½hr., 2 per day, $39). **Murrays** (☎13 22 51) offers a 10% YHA discount and goes to Canberra (2½hr.,

1-2 per day, $24). The staff at **Batemans Bay Tourist Information Centre,** on Princes Hwy. at Beach Rd., will book your accommodation in town at no charge and supply you with stacks of brochures and suggestions. (☎4472 6900 or 1800 802 528. Open daily 9am-5pm.) **Internet** access is available at **Total Computer Care,** Shop 10 Citi Centre Arcade, for $5 per hr. (☎4472 2745. Open M-F 9am-5pm, Sa-Su 9am-2pm.) The **police station** is at 28 Orient St. (☎4472 0099). The **post office** is also on Orient St., adjacent to the bus stop. (Open M-F 9am-5pm.) **Postal Code:** 2536.

ACCOMMODATIONS AND FOOD. Plenty of motels reside on Orient St. and Beach Rd.; rooms usually start at $60-70 in winter. The **Batemans Bay Backpackers (YHA) ❷,** inside a caravan park on the corner of Old Princes Hwy. and South St., offers tidy facilities as well as trips to Pebbly Beach ($20) and Mogo ($5) when there is enough guest interest. (☎4472 4972; www.shadywillows.com.au. Laundry, kitchen, TV, pool, and boogie boards. Call to arrange pickup from the bus stop in town. Dorms $25, YHA $22; doubles $54/48.) The **Clyde River Motor Inn ❺,** 3 Clyde St., offers basic rooms at reasonable rates in the heart of the town. Amenities include A/C, TV, and pool. (☎4472 6444; www.clydemotel.com.au. Singles from $75; doubles from $79; family rooms from $119.) Fish 'n' chips seems to be the town's favorite meal; try **The Boat Shed ❶,** opposite the Clyde River Motor Inn on Clyde St., where basic fish 'n' chips runs $11. (☎4472 4052. Open daily in summer 9am-8pm; in winter 9am-7pm.) The Boat Shed also offers cruises on the Clyde River. (☎4472 4052. 3hr., daily 11:30am, $25.)

SIGHTS AND ACTIVITIES. The 1880 wreck of the *Lady Darling* is a fantastic dive and is suitable for all skill levels. Other dives include the Burrawarra Wall, the Maze, and, for scoping out the nurse sharks, Montague Island. The **Dive Shop,** 33 Orient St., can be your link to the water world. (☎4472 9930. Single boat dive $50; double $90; full equipment rental from $48.) The compact **Opal and Shell Museum,** 142 Beach Rd., owned and operated by a veteran miner, showcases an extensive display of opals and shells from Australia and around the world; for those interested in buying a souvenir opal, prices are much more affordable here than in larger cities. (☎4472 7284. $1.50, families $3. Open M and W-Su 10am-6pm. Closed Aug.) To bushwalk, join the locals from **Batemans Bay Bushwalkers** ($5). Contact Bronwyn (☎4472 6608; www.bushwalking.org.au/~batemansbay) or ask the tourist office for a schedule. Traveling south on the coastal road, Malua Bay and Broulee have good surf. **Broulee Surf School,** 77 Coronation Dr., offers private and group lessons. (☎4471 7370; www.brouleesurfschool.com.au. Lessons range from $40-160.)

NAROOMA AND MONTAGUE ISLAND ☎02

With several parks and one stunning island nearby, the town of Narooma is a good base for outdoor exploration. Only 7km offshore, fur seals, crested terns, and fairy penguins inhabit the **Montague Island Nature Reserve.** The island was inhabited by Aborigines for over 4500 years. In 1770, Captain Cook was the first European to sight the island, but he mistakenly thought it was a point on the headland, naming it Point Dromedary. It wasn't recognized as an island until 1790, when the passing convict ship *Surprise* named it after the ship's sponsor, George Montagu Dunk, Earl of Halifax (the "e" was added later). Settlers introduced goats and rabbits to Montague to feed shipwreck victims; horses and cows continued the destruction of the island's original habitat.

Today, National Parks and Wildlife Service (NPWS) is working hard to preserve the island's amazing range of wildlife by restoring the natural habitat and managing the *kykuyu* grass that has choked much of the original vegetation, making it difficult for fairy penguins and other birds to nest. The reserve is only accessible through **NPWS-sanctioned tours;** a percentage of the fee for the tour goes to the island's preservation. Be sure to ask about the Marx Brothers-esque story of the **lighthouse's** construction. In spring, watch for whales on the ferry trip to the island. (4hr.; 1-2 per day. $99, families $330. 90 visitors per day, tours must have 8 to depart.) Book through the visitors center.

The popular, 2WD-accessible **Eurobodalla National Park** (☎4476 2888) protects a 30km stretch of coastline, from Moruya Head in the north to Tilba Tilba Lake in the south, and features, among other things, lush spotted gum forest. The park has a **campground ❶** at Congo, near the town of **Moruya** ($5 per person). On Wagonga Head, off Bar Rock Rd., ocean waves, coastal winds, and a bit of chiseling have left one rock, known as **Australia Rock,** with a hole the shape of Australia (minus a bit of the Cape York peninsula). Depending on the winds, **surfers** head out to Bar, Carters, Dalmeny, or Handkerchief Beach.

Lynch's Hotel ❸, 135 Wagonga St. (Princes Hwy.), offers cozy pub accommodations upstairs with expansive views of the bay from wood balconies. Good pub grub is available downstairs. (☎4476 2001. Kitchen, TV, lounge, tea, and coffee. Singles $40; doubles $60; triples $70.) **Narooma Golf Club and Surfbeach Resort ❷,** on Ballingala St., has fine views of the water and good facilities. (☎4476 2522. Reception 8:30am-5:30pm. Sites for 2 $18-30, powered $22-35; cabins from $50-275.)

Premier Motor Service (☎13 34 10; www.premierms.com.au) stops in Narooma and goes to: Batemans Bay (13-14hr., 2 per day, $16); Kiama (5hr., 2 per day, $48); Melbourne (11hr., 1 per day, $57); Nowra (3½hr., 2 per day, $36); Sydney (7hr., 2 per day, $50); Ulladulla (2½hr., 2 per day, $22); Wollongong (5hr., 2 per day, $48). **Murrays** (☎13 22 51; www.murrays.com.au) runs from Narooma Plaza to Canberra (4½hr., 1-2 per day, $36.25). The **Narooma Visitors Centre,** on Princes Hwy., handles tour bookings and assists in finding accommodations. (☎4476 2881 or 1800 240 003. Open daily 9am-5pm.) The **NPWS** office is on the corner of Princes Hwy. and Field St. (☎4476 2888. Open M-F 8:30am-4:30pm.) The **post office** is just up the hill on Princes Hwy. (☎13 13 18. Open M-F 9am-5pm.) **Postal Code:** 2546.

SNOWY MOUNTAINS

While skiers and snowboarders make the Snowies their winter playground, the warmer months attract swarms of hikers to the nation's highest mountains. Kosciuszko National Park, home of **Mt. Kosciuszko** (2228m), Australia's tallest peak, covers most of this area. The Snowy Mountains Hwy. and the Alpine Way ramble past boulder-strewn countryside where the skiing industry is king, though compared to other mountain ranges around the world, the runs are shorter and less challenging. Conditions vary wildly by mountain: **Thredbo** is a black diamond paradise with challenging advanced slopes; **Perisher,** despite its ominous-sounding name, is a favorite of hikers; and **Mount Selwyn** offers great deals and family-friendly slopes. Naturally, the price of accommodations in the Snowy Mountains jumps in the winter, so be sure to check rates before deciding where to stay.

COOMA ☎02

The self-proclaimed "Capital of the Snowy Mountains" links Canberra and the coast with the mountains. Because of its peripheral location on the eastern edge of the Snowy Mountains, Cooma is far enough from the price-inflated snowfields to permit reasonable ski-season rates for those willing to make the commute. Cooma is also a base for traveling to Mt. Selwyn and Perisher/Thredbo.

TRANSPORTATION AND PRACTICAL INFORMATION. Cooma's main drag is **Sharp Street,** flanked on either side by Massie and Commissioner St. **Buses** come through frequently during ski season, but service is severely curtailed the rest of the year. **Countrylink** (☎13 22 32) runs to Canberra (1¾-2¼hr., 1-2 per day, $19), where you can connect with a train to Sydney ($45 total from Cooma). **Transborder Alpinexpress** (☎6241 0033; www.transborder.com.au) offers year-round service from Centennial Park next to the visitors center on Bombala St. to Canberra (1½hr., 1 per day, $37); Jindabyne (50min., 1 per day, $20); Thredbo (1½hr., 1 per day, $35). Reserve tickets in advance, or purchase on the bus. **Greyhound Australia** (☎13 20 30) Ski Express buses run to: Canberra (1½-1¾hr., 1-2 per day, $38); Sydney (6hr., 1-2 per day, $66); Jindabyne (55min., 1-2 per day, $22); and Thredbo (1¾hr., 1-2 per day, $51) from June to October. **Murray's** (☎13 22 51) services the mountains once a day during ski season as well. **Snowliner Coaches,** 120 Sharp St. (☎6452 1584; www.snowliner.com.au), services Jindabyne (1hr.; M-F 2 per day; $15, correct change required). **Europcar** (☎6452 5465 or 1300 13 13 90; www.europcar.com.au) and **Thrifty** (☎6452 5300 or 1800 552 008; www.thrifty.com.au) have locations in Cooma at Snowy Mountains Airport. Call when your flight lands to ensure available service.

Cooma Visitors Centre, 119 Sharp St., is in the center of town. (☎6450 1742; www.visitcooma.com.au. Open daily mid-Oct. to May 9am-5pm, June to mid-Oct. 7am-5pm.) The visitors center provides **Internet** access ($1 per 10min.) and will book accommodations, though some hotel owners charge extra if you use this service. **Internet** access is also available at the self-service coin-operated **Internet Access,** 63 Sharp St., at $1 per 10min. (open M-F 10am-7pm, Sa 10am-5pm) and **Percy's News Agency,** 158 Sharp St. (☎6452 2880. $3 per 30min. Open M-F 6am-6pm, Sa 6am-2pm, Su 6am-1pm.) The **police station** is on Massie St., just up the street from the **post office,** on the corner of Massie and Vale St. across from Dawson St. (☎6452 0099. Open M-F 9am-5pm.) **Postal Code:** 2630.

ACCOMMODATIONS AND FOOD. The **Cooma Bunkhouse Motel ❸,** 28-30 Soho St., on the corner of Commissioner St., has great year-round hostel accommodations. Every room at this former maternity ward is equipped with a private bathroom, kitchen, and TV. (☎6452 2983; www.bunkhousemotel.com.au. Breakfast $10. Reception 24hr. Heated dorms $25-30; singles $35-45; doubles $50-55; family units from $65. VIP. MC/V.) The pricier **White Manor Motel ❹,** 252 Sharp St., has 12 rooms with satellite TV, A/C, heat, and electric blankets. (☎6452 1152; www.whitemanor.com. Reception 7am-10:30pm. Ensuite singles $95-110; doubles $105-120; family units from $92. AmEx/D/MC/V.) On Sharp St., 1.1km west of the town center, **Snowtels Caravan Park ❶** provides a kitchen and laundry. (☎6452 1828. www.snowtels.com.au. Reception 8am-8:30pm. Sites $18, powered $22; basic cabins from $65; ensuite cabins for 5 $70-100. MC/V.)

Grumpy's Diner ❶, across from the visitors center at 112 Sharp St., has traveler-friendly staff (despite its name), delicious meals, and some of the best coffee in town. Open-faced melts, sandwiches, and filling veggie options run $6-12. (☎6452 1002. Open M-F 7am-5pm, Sa-Su 7am-3pm. MC/V.) For something a little more exotic, head to **Rose's ❷,** 69 Massie St., for a juicy, authentic Lebanese kebab ($8). The full banquet ($25) is a bit of a splurge, but it offers a taste of all things Middle Eastern, and for those arriving famished from the slopes, it's a big meal well earned. Dine in or takeaway. (☎6452 4512. Open M-Sa 11:30am-2:30pm and 6-10pm. AmEx/MC/V.) Get groceries at **Woolworths,** on the corner of Vale and Massie St. (Open daily 7am-10pm.)

SKIING. Because the ski resorts of Thredbo, Perisher, and Mt. Selwyn lie within 100km of Cooma, **rental shops** clutter the town's street, with flashing signs advertising "around-the-clock" rentals with cheaper rates than you'll find closer to the mountains. Skis, poles, and boot rentals run about $40 the first day and $10-15 per day thereafter; snowboard and boot rental cost about $45 for the first day and $10-20 for every day after; clothing rental $27; snowchains $20. The visitors center (p. 230) has brochures with 10-15% discount coupons.

JINDABYNE ☎02

On the scenic shores of **Lake Jindabyne,** "Jindy" acts as a satellite ski town in-season, with corresponding services and high prices. After the ski season, prices and visitor numbers drop significantly, and bushwalkers stop through while exploring vast Kosciuszko National Park.

TRANSPORTATION. During the busy ski season, **Jindabyne Motors Alpine Express** (☎6456 7340 or 0414 400 378) runs shuttles daily to the Skitube by reservation ($15 round-trip). From there, it's possible to catch a train to **Perisher Blue** (round-trip $38, families $92). Transport into Jindabyne from the northeast passes through Cooma (p. 229). **Transborder Alpinexpress** (☎6241 0033; www.transborder.com.au) offers daily year-round service from Canberra to Jindabyne and Thredbo via Cooma. **Greyhound Australia** (☎13 20 30) operates limited service in the winter and summer, as does **Countrylink** (☎13 22 32). Snow and ski packages are a popular option. **Oz Snow Adventures** (☎1800 851 101; www.ozsnowadventures.com.au) offers trips from Sydney and Canberra starting at $225, including accommodation, transportation, meals, and national park fees.

To get to Perisher by car, follow Kosciuszko Rd. (2WD vehicles must carry **snowchains** by law). Alternatively, follow the **Alpine Way** to the Skitube station at Bullocks Flat (21km from town), which services the Perisher Blue resorts. The Alpine Way then continues 15km farther on to Thredbo (chains might be required in extreme weather). From Thredbo, the Alpine Way extends through the mountains to **Khancoban,** a full-service town on the western edge of Kosciuszko National Park. The **Shell station** at the Perisher-Thredbo junction, outside Jindabyne, rents snow chains for $30 per day and has a drop-off program with the Khancoban Shell station. Other service stations offer similar programs.

PRACTICAL INFORMATION. The **Snowy Region Visitors Centre,** on Kosciuszko Rd. in the center of town, is a NPWS office and a tourist center. They have tons of info and also sell entry passes for the national park. (☎6450 5600, road conditions 6450 5551, snow reports 6450 5553, weather 6450 5550. Open daily in summer 8:30am-5pm, in winter 8am-5pm.) **ATMs** can be found in Nuggets Crossing Shopping Centre. The **police station** (☎6456 2244) is on Thredbo Terr. **Snowy Mountain Backpackers** (see below) has **Internet** access. ($3 per 20min.) The **post office** (☎6456 2394) is on the corner of Gippsland St. and Snow River Ave. **Postal Code**: 2627.

Job opportunities are everywhere in Jindabyne (mainly hospitality and ski-related work); many of the skiers and snowboarders who love Thredbo and Perisher find work in Jindabyne through postings and word of mouth. Three great places to look for postings include outside the **IGA** supermarket in Nuggets Crossing Shopping Centre, on the bulletin board of Snowy Mountain Backpackers (see below), and at the Snowy Region Visitors Centre.

ACCOMMODATIONS. Affordable accommodations in Jindabyne exist even in the height of ski madness, but availability may be a problem. Be sure to book well in advance. **Snowy Mountain Backpackers ❸,** 7-8 Gippsland St., behind the Nuggets Crossing Shopping Centre, combines an unbeatable location with new facilities, laundry, Internet access, TV room, and a kitchen. Cafe SuSu and a massage center are also on the premises. (☎6456 1500 or 1800 333 468; www.snowybackpackers.com.au. Key deposit $10. Wheelchair accessible. Reception June-Oct. 8am-8pm. Bunks $30; doubles $90. VIP. MC/V.) The **Jindy Inn ❹,** 18 Clyde St., has private ensuite rooms with TV and fridge. There's a kitchen downstairs and an adjoining restaurant (winter only). During ski season the inn functions more like a B&B. Bookings are required and single-night stays are rare, especially on weekends. (☎6456 1957; www.jindyinn.com. Breakfast included in winter. Discounts for 3-day stays or longer. Twin-shares from $66.) **Jindabyne Holiday Park ❶** is in the center of town on a choice stretch of Lake Jindabyne shoreline. (☎6456 2249; www.jindabyneholidaypark.com.au. Laundry, kitchen, ski and snowboard rentals. Sites for 2 $22-25, powered $35-40. Extra person $10. On-site caravans June, Sept.-Oct. from $75, July-Aug. from $85. D/DC/MC/V.)

FOOD. Cheap food is hard to come by. Preparing a flavorful range of traditional grub and some multicultural dishes, **Cafe SuSu ❷,** 8 Gippsland St., part of the Snowy Mountain Backpackers, has decent prices (most meals $8-12) and a relaxed, funky interior. (☎6456 1503. Open M-F 9am-5pm, Sa-Su 8am-9pm.) **Wrap-A-Go-Go ❷,** in Lakeview Plaza behind the Westpac at 2 Snowy River Ave., features spicy Mexican meals and tasty wraps. (☎6457 1887. Open daily noon-9pm; closed M in summer. Main dishes around $12-15.) **Mountain Munchies ❶,** 10a in Nuggets Crossing, serves up cheap comfort food, with all-day breakfast averaging $4-13 and sandwiches from $4-7. (☎6457 2255. Open daily 6am-4pm. Cash only.) An **IGA** supermarket is also in Nuggets Crossing.

ACTIVITIES. The experts at **Wilderness Sports,** 4 Nuggets Crossing, rent equipment—including snowshoes, telemark and cross-country skis, and snow-camping gear—and organize cross-country skiing, snowboarding, snowshoe, and alpine touring adventures from $99 for 3hr. (☎6456 2966; www.wildernesssports.com.au. Open June-Oct. daily 8am-5pm, Nov.-May M-Tu and Th-Sa 9am-5pm. Prices generally depend upon group size.) Their **Snowsport Adventure Centre** in Perisher Valley also offers myriad rentals, as well as activity courses like snowcamping and rock climbing. (☎6457 5966. Open daily 9am-4pm. Snowshoe rental $25-35 per day; full-day abseiling $169; full-day Mt. Kosciuszko tour $149, includes lunch for min. 4 people.) **Rebel Sport** offers package deals with skis, boots, parka, and pants from $68 per day or a snowboarding package for $70. (☎6457 2166. www.rebelsport.com.au. Open daily 7am-7pm and all night F.) **Paddy Pallin,** next to the Shell station at the Perisher-Thredbo junction, offers similar services as well as mountaineering courses and **mountain bike rental.** (☎6456 2922 or 1800 623 459; www.mountainadventurecentre.com.au. Open daily in summer 9am-5pm, in winter M-Th 8am-6pm, F 7:30am-noon, Sa-Su 7:30am-7pm. Full-day intro to mountaineering course July-Aug. $159; full-day Mt. Kosciuszko champagne ride $99. 4-person min. for bookings. Mountain bike and helmet $16 per hr., $36 ½ day, $50 full day.)

Rapid Descents Whitewater Rafting, based in Canberra, runs rafting on the Murray River in spring and summer. (☎6228 1264; www.rapiddescents.com.au. Book ahead.) **Snowline Caravan Park,** at the Kosciuszko-Thredbo Road Junction, offers **boat hire.** (☎6456 2099 or 1800 248 148; www.bestonparks.com.au. Fishing boats for 5-6 adults $40 for 1st 2hr., $18 per hr. thereafter, $116 per day, $100 deposit; paddle boats and aqua bikes $15 per 30min.; canoes $20 for 1st hr., $8 per additional hr., $50 deposit.)

NIGHTLIFE. Nightlife roars in Jindy throughout most of the snow season, fueled mainly by those who work on the mountains. As Wednesday is payday at all ski-related spots in the area, things go off that night with the same intensity as the weekend, if not greater. Crowds of locals swarm to the **Banjo Paterson Inn,** 1 Kosciuszko Rd. (☎6458 2372; banjopatersoninn.com), which houses three full bars and casino tables and features DJs and live bands many nights of the week. The place reaches capacity quickly, go early. (Bars open daily until latenight. Nightclub W and F-Sa until 2am. No cover.) **Lake Jindabyne Hotel,** on Kosciuszko Rd. across from Nuggets Crossing, offers a quieter scene, a handful of pool tables, and live cover bands Sa nights. (☎6456 2203. Open daily 10am-latenight.) The **Station Resort** throws the biggest parties and pulls in the biggest DJs throughout the season; you won't be able to miss the brochures and posters around town.

KOSCIUSZKO NATIONAL PARK

KOSCIUSZKO NATIONAL PARK AT A GLANCE	
AREA: 6494 sq. km, about 700,000 hectares—the largest park in New South Wales. **HEIGHTS:** Mount Kosciuszko: 2228m, Australia's highest peak. **FEATURES:** Australia's tallest mountain, for which the park is named; the Snowy River; Yarrongobilly Caves; almost two dozen scenic camping sites. **HIGHLIGHTS:** Skiing some of Australia's best slopes; camping and hiking during the warmer months.	**GATEWAYS:** Cooma and Jindabyne (JIN-duh-bine) in the east, Khancoban (kin-KOH-bin) in the west. **CAMPING:** Free, except for one site just west of Lake Jindabyne that is privately owned and charges fees. **FEES:** $27 per day vehicle fee during ski season, $16 in summer. Year-long pass $190. Motorists passing through non-stop on Alpine Way are exempt. Fees are strictly enforced by rangers. **SKI SEASON:** June to mid-October.

Named after the revered Polish nationalist, Tadiusz Kosciuszko (incorrectly pronounced by Australians as KOZ-ee-OSS-koh), Kosciuszko National Park contains Australia's **highest mountains,** the alluring **Yarrangobilly Caves,** several stunning **wilderness hikes,** and NSW's premier **ski fields.**

There are numerous tourist bureaus surrounding the park including the **Snowy Region Visitors Centre** on Kosciuszko Rd. in Jindabyne (☎6450 5600; open daily 8:30am-5pm), which can assist visitors in booking accommodations. **Tumut** (TOO-mit) has a visitors center in the Old Butter Factory on Adelong Rd. (☎6947 7025. Open daily 9am-5pm.) **Khancoban Information Centre** at the corner of Scott and Mitchell St. at the west entrance of the park is available to visitors as well. (☎6076 9373. Open daily 9am-noon and 1-4pm.) There are also information centers within the park at Perisher Blue and the Yarrangobilly Caves. For **weather information** call ☎6450 5550, **road conditions** 6450 5551, and **fishing report** 6450 5553.

Numerous **hiking tracks** and **camping** areas are available throughout the park, and a network of over 80 regularly maintained huts connects trails for long-term hikers. Bush camping is free in Kosciuszko National Park with the exception of one privately run camping locale just west of Lake Jindabyne. The many camping areas are popular and clearly delineated throughout the park. A map of campsites is available at all tourist offices. Visitors entering with their own vehicles are required to pay an entry fee ($27, in summer $16) valid for 24hr. upon purchase. Motorists who pass through the park without stopping along Alpine Way are exempt. If you enter the park after the ticketing stations have closed, you must purchase your pass in the morning at the nearest news agency. **Fees are strictly enforced** by park rangers who check automobiles daily. During ski season, 2WD vehicles must carry snow chains. The Shell stations along Alpine Way and in Khancoban and Jindabyne allow one-way chain rental and drop-off ($35). Cars without snow chains will receive immediate fines starting at $135.

SKI SLOPE OVERVIEW

Cross-country skiing is always free on the following slopes:

SKI SLOPE	THE LOWDOWN	FEATURES	PRICES
PERISHER BLUE	Australia's premier resort, with Perisher Valley, Blue Cow, Smiggins, and Guthega alpine villages.	7 peaks, 51 lifts, and over 95 trails.	$93 per day, under 14 $52; night skiing (Tu, Sa) $17/11. Lift pass and lesson $108/72. First-timer $61.
SELWYN SNOWFIELDS	Lacks the difficulty of other mountains in the park, and experiences a shorter ski season due to lack of snow, but has 45 hectares of marked trails and beats the rest for value.	Beginner runs as well as a few expert runs; draws families and budget skiers.	$63 per day, under 15 $32. Lift pass and lesson $81/54.
THREDBO	Perisher's toughest and most worthy competitor. Home to Australia's longest slopes. Outdoor activities abound year-round.	13 lifts of mostly intermediate runs.	$125 per 2 days, under 15 $45; night skiing (Tu and Sa) free with valid lift pass. Lift pass and lesson $110/75. First-timer $85/61.

PERISHER BLUE

New South Wales' premier ski resort, Perisher Blue (☎1300 655 822; www.perisherblue.com.au) is actually four resorts in one. One lift ticket buys entry to the interconnected slopes of all the resorts, leading down to the **Perisher Valley, Blue Cow, Smiggins,** and **Guthega** alpine villages. Transfer between the seven peaks is relatively easy. Situated above the natural snow line, with a slightly higher elevation than its competitors, Perisher offers some of the best snow around. All **lift tickets** include unlimited use of the Perisher-Blue Cow segment of the Skitube. Purchase tickets at Bullocks Flat or at the **Perisher Blue Jindabyne Ticket Office** in the Nuggets Crossing shopping center. (☎6456 1659. Open daily in winter 7am-7pm.) **Mojo Snow Transport** (☎1800 111 103) offers transport from Jindabyne, Canberra, or Sydney and helps manage all logistical nightmares including equipment rentals, lessons, passes, and accommodations.

Perisher is not a full-service budget travel village; it has neither budget accommodations nor overnight parking. To get there by car, follow Kosciuszko Rd. (2WD are required to have snow chains on this road). The Perisher Valley day lot fills up quickly on busy days, and is often entirely inaccessible due to road conditions, but the **Skitube** (☎6456 2010) is an all-weather train that makes the 8km journey into the Perisher Valley Alpine Village from **Bullocks Flat,** located along the Alpine Way (round-trip $31, children $18). You can either start your adventures in the village or keep riding the Skitube all the way up to the Blue Cow terminal. There, chairlifts take skiers and boarders of all levels to runs atop **Guthega Peak** and **Mount Blue Cow.** To get to the Skitube station at Bullocks Flat, take **Jindabyne Coaches** (☎6457 2117), which runs shuttles from **Jindabyne** (4 per day, round-trip $15). **Summit Coaches** also runs to the Skitube twice a day (☎1800 608 008; round-trip $35). By **car,** drive along the Alpine Way from Jindabyne until you reach the station; there's plenty of parking. Once at the Perisher Station, follow your nose to the Bullocks Flat platform, on the lower level, to **Lil' Orbits Donuts** ❶ (☎6457 5655). If donuts aren't enough, **Gingers** ❶ (☎6457 5558), on the main floor, serves up inexpensive toasted sandwiches.

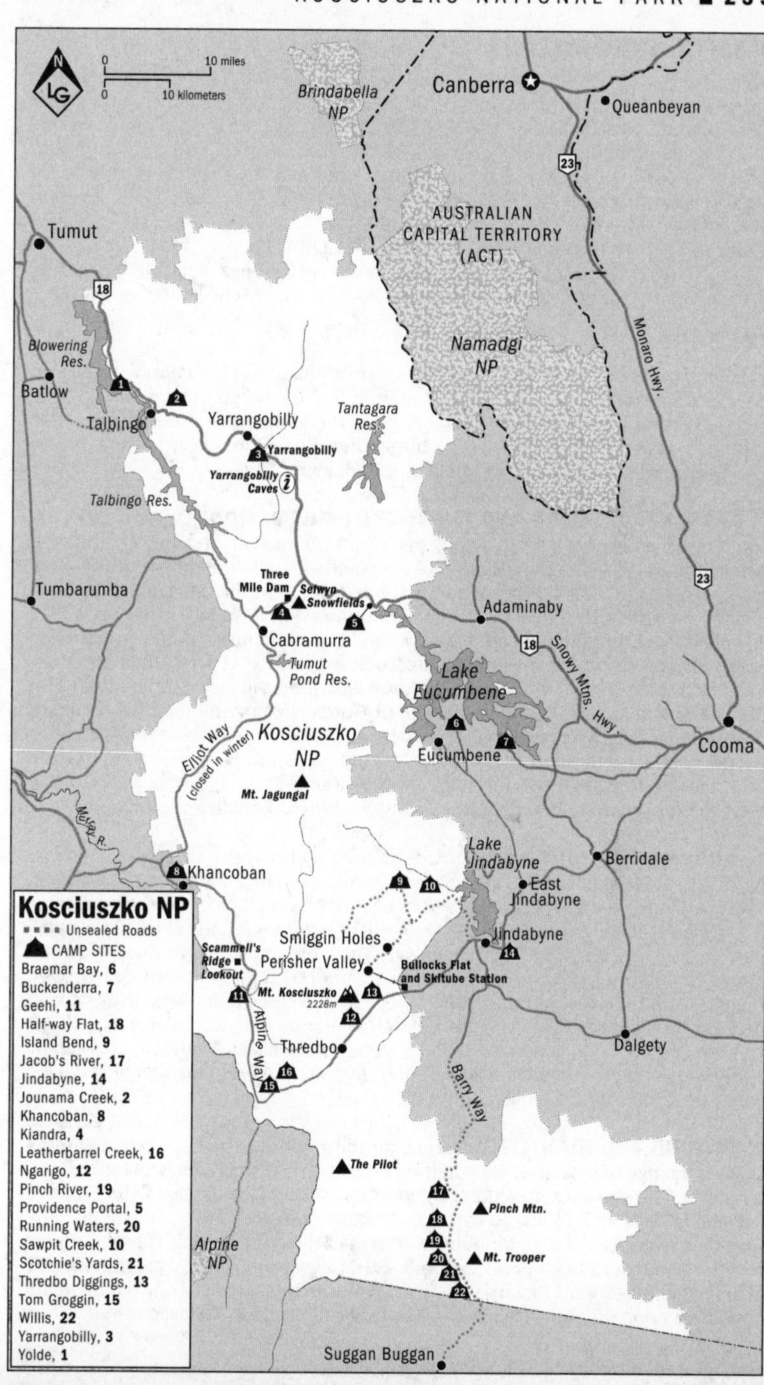
0 10 miles
0 10 kilometers
LG
Brindabella NP
Canberra
Queanbeyan
23
AUSTRALIAN CAPITAL TERRITORY (ACT)
Namadgi NP
Monaro Hwy.
Tumut
18
Blowering Res.
Batlow
Talbingo
Yarrangobilly
Yarrangobilly
Yarrangobilly Caves
Tantagara Res.
Talbingo Res.
Tumbarumba
Three Mile Dam
Selwyn Snowfields
Adaminaby
Cabramurra
Tumut Pond Res.
Snowy Mtns. Hwy.
Lake Eucumbene
Eucumbene
Cooma
Elliot Way (closed in winter)
Kosciuszko NP
Mt. Jagungal
Murray R.
Khancoban
Lake Jindabyne
Berridale
East Jindabyne
Jindabyne
Smiggin Holes
Perisher Valley
Scammell's Ridge Lookout
Bullocks Flat and Skitube Station
Mt. Kosciuszko 2228m
Alpine Way
Thredbo
Dalgety
Barry Way
The Pilot
Pinch Mtn.
Mt. Trooper
Alpine NP
Suggan Buggan
Kosciuszko NP
Unsealed Roads
CAMP SITES
Braemar Bay, 6
Buckenderra, 7
Geehi, 11
Half-way Flat, 18
Island Bend, 9
Jacob's River, 17
Jindabyne, 14
Jounama Creek, 2
Khancoban, 8
Kiandra, 4
Leatherbarrel Creek, 16
Ngarigo, 12
Pinch River, 19
Providence Portal, 5
Running Waters, 20
Sawpit Creek, 10
Scotchie's Yards, 21
Thredbo Diggings, 13
Tom Groggin, 15
Willis, 22
Yarrangobilly, 3
Yolde, 1

SELWYN SNOWFIELDS

Along the Snowy Mountains Hwy., halfway between Cooma and Tumut, **Selwyn Snowfields** offers beginner and budget skiing, snowboarding, and other snow recreation options. (☎6454 9488; www.selwynsnow.com.au.) Primarily a family resort, Selwyn has a small number of trails, minimal amenities, and only a couple advanced runs. Elevation at the base is 1492m, and the summit is only 122m higher. Selwyn bolsters its light natural snowfall with man-made snow used on over 80% of its terrain. On the bright side, **lift tickets** are inexpensive. ($70 per day, under 15 $36. Lift pass and 1½hr. lesson $81/54. Lift value pack for 1 day $36/19.) Forty-five hectares of marked trails make **cross-country skiing** an attractive option. (Cross-country skiing is free on all mountains with the Kosciuzko Park entry fee.)

THREDBO

In 2000, Thredbo was named the **NSW Tourist Destination of the Decade.** Though it does not have as many runs as Perisher, it sports the longest slope (5.9km), the biggest vertical drop, and doesn't shut down in the summer. Thredbo's main resort is renowned for its nightlife, but it's a big splurge; budget-minded travelers tend to eat, sleep, and party in nearby Cooma and Jindabyne.

TRANSPORTATION AND PRACTICAL INFORMATION. During ski season, **Greyhound Australia** (☎13 20 30) runs from Cooma via Jindabyne (1½hr., 1-2 per day, $45). Thredbo-bound hitchhikers stand at the roundabout outside Jindabyne—Let's Go does not recommend hitchhiking. **Thredbo Information Centre** is located on Friday Dr. (Resort, accommodation booking, and snow report ☎1800 020 589; www.thredbo.com.au. Open daily in winter 8am-6pm, in summer 9am-5pm.) Ski and snowboard rentals at **Thredbo Sports** (☎6459 4119), at the base of the Kosciuszko Express chairlift, and at the east end of the village near the Friday Flat lift, are $10-20 higher than in Jindabyne or Cooma. Many find it worth the extra cost to rent near the slopes in case anything goes wrong. Check out www.transborder.com.au and www.mountainpass.com.au for additional transportation information. Regularly scheduled flights to Cooma from Sydney cost $90 each way; JetStar provides complimentary shuttle buses to Thredbo.

ACCOMMODATIONS. With nearby competition charging hundreds of dollars per night, the **Thredbo YHA Lodge ❸**, 8 Jack Adams Path, is by far the best deal in town. Although the rooms are encased in cinderblocks, the common areas exude a cozy chalet feeling. A large kitchen and Internet access ($2 per 15min.) are available to guests. (☎6457 6376; thredbo@yhansw.org.au. YHA parking is located along the highway before the entrance to Thredbo; guests must trek down two flights of stairs to reach the entrance. Reception 8-10am and 3-8pm. Nov.-May 4-bed dorms $25; twins $58, ensuite $66. Rates increase significantly during June-Oct. ski season; book accommodation several weeks ahead.) Other lodges can be booked through the **Thredbo Resort Centre.** (☎1800 020 589. Open daily May-Oct. 9am-6pm; Sept.-Apr. 9am-5pm; hours vary.)

FOOD AND NIGHTLIFE. Eating on the mountain is expensive, though there is a range of options from takeaway to high-end restaurants with million-dollar views. The cheapest breakfast and lunch is at **Snowflakes Bakery ❶,** in Thredbo Village. (☎6457 7157. Pies, pastries, and sandwiches $3-7. Open daily May-Sept. 6am-6pm; Oct.-Apr. 7am-5pm.) **Alfresco Pizzeria ❸,** just below the Thredbo Alpine Hotel, serves pastas and pizza that will satisfy even the biggest appetite. (☎6457 6327. Small pies from $12, large pies from $15. Open in winter M-Th and Su noon-9pm, F-Sa noon-9:30pm; in summer W-Su 5:30-8:30pm.) A small **supermarket** is hidden in Mowamba Pl. in the village. (Open in winter daily 8am-8pm; in summer M-Sa 9:30am-5:30pm, Su 9:30am-1:30pm.) After a tiring day on the slopes, collapse at the **Schuss Barn,** in the Thredbo Alpine Hotel, for an evening of live entertainment. The **Keller Bar Nightclub,** also in the hotel, provides riproaring nightlife.

SUMMER ACTIVITIES. A few chairlifts operate year-round for hikers. (One-way $19, round-trip $25. Daily 9am-4:30pm, service ends at 4:30pm sharp.) Several excellent walks depart from the top of the chairlift, leading to panoramic perspectives of Kosciuszko National Park. The **Mount Kosciuszko Walk** (13km round-trip) leads to the highest point on the entire continent and promises endless alpine views in all directions. One of the acclaimed "Seven Summits" of the world, the climb is significantly easier than the other continental peaks and offers a collection of unique flora indigenous only to the mountain. Hikers must bring warm clothes, water, a snack, lots of sunblock, and Bug spray. The summit has notoriously fickle weather. For those interested in a shorter trek, visit the rather unimpressive **Kosciuszko Lookout,** which lacks sweeping vistas but has a picture-perfect view of the summit. Another option is the **Dead Horse Gap and Thredbo River Track** (10km), which ends in the village. Hardier hikers should branch off the Mt. Kosciuszko Walk 800m before the summit and take the narrow **Main Range Track** (32km round-trip) along the ridgeline for varied and spectacular views of rocky plains, verdant nooks, and mountaintops rolling to the horizon. Short of completing the massive 8-10hr. hike, a 7km round-trip detour from Rawson Pass will get you as far as picturesque **Lake Albina,** one of the five glacial lakes in the region. Nestled icily in the mountainside, Lake Albina is well worth the extra effort. Free maps of all trails with descriptions are available throughout Thredbo.

The Thredbo Activities Booking Desk (☎6459 4119) arranges adventure activities through various other companies during the summer, including horseback riding, abseiling, and rafting. Raw NRG, just next door to Thredbo Sports at the base of the lift, handles mountain biking excursions and offers initiation courses down the infamous 4.2km Cannonball Run. (☎6457 6282. Open daily 9am-4:30pm.)

YARRANGOBILLY CAVES

Hidden on the valley floor in the beautiful northern scrub wilderness of the Kosciuszko National Park, the Yarrangobilly Caves attract curious visitors and hardcore spelunkers alike. The caves are well marked and located 6.5km off the highway on a winding, unsealed road. Visitors coming from outside the park must contribute a small fee which changes regularly.

Over the last two million years, the churning waters of the Yarrangobilly River have been chewing their way through the dense limestone of the valley, creating some of the most breathtaking subterranean formations in the world. The region is ever-changing as speleologists are uncovering newly formed caverns every year. Of the dozens of navigable caves, only six are open to visitors; the rest have been marked for preservation. The **Jersey Cave** is rather unremarkable upon entry, but visitors are soon treated to amazing collection of colorful spires or "straws," which dangle incredibly close overhead. The **North Glory Cave** contains similarly breathtaking sights. The **South Glory Cave** is about 100,000 years old and is the only cave open for a self-guided tour (45min.), but you'll need a token from the tourist office to explore beyond the unusual "glory arch" entrance. (Open daily 9am-4pm. $11, children $6.50, families $29.) Other caves foster a significantly different ethereal atmosphere than the South Glory Cave. These caves are open to **guided tours** (1½hr. tour daily 11am, 1, and 3pm; $13, children $8.50, families $38). Handicapped individuals can access **Jillabenan Cave** with a special wheelchair provided by the visitors center. After wandering underground, head to the surface and try a short bushwalk on a maintained trail, or take a load off in the 27°C (81°F) **thermal pools** near the river, a 700m steep downhill walk from the carpark (free). The **NPWS Visitors Centre** at the site should be your first stop. (☎6454 9597. Open daily 9am-5pm. $3 site fee.) There is **no camping** at the caves; camping is available at Yarrangobilly Village, 15km north of the caves off the Snowy Mountains Hwy.

RIVERINA

A collection of sunburnt towns linked by a rich Aboriginal history and meandering waterways, the Riverina is a worthwhile sojourn on the trek from Melbourne to Sydney. The two main rivers are the Murrumbidgee, which starts as a trickle in the Snowy Mountains, and the Murray, which becomes significant at Albury-Wodonga and flows all the way to Adelaide. Although it lacks traditional tourist bait (like sweeping ocean views), the Riverina is still a popular spot for backpackers, with a plethora of farming and picking opportunities (see **Beyond Tourism,** p. 81).

ALBURY-WODONGA ☎02

At the foothills of Mount Murramarrumbong, west of Talangatta, and not too far from Wondillagong and Mullandandrah, the metropolitan area of Albury-Wodonga (pop. 100,000) spans both sides of the Murray River, the natural border between Victoria and New South Wales. The Hume Hwy. rumbles through the center of town, making Albury-Wodonga an obvious pitstop for weary travelers. Many plan an extended stay because of the proximity to world-renowned wineries, excellent ski slopes, and work in nearby farms.

TRANSPORTATION

Trains: Countrylink Travel Centre, in the railway station, books Countrylink and V/Line transport. (☎6041 9555. Open M-F 9am-5pm.) **Countrylink** (☎13 22 32; open 6am-10pm) trains run to: **Goulburn** (5hr., 2 per day, $75); **Melbourne** (3hr., 2 per day, $60); **Sydney** (7½hr., 2 per day, $100); **Wagga Wagga** (1¼hr., 2 per day, $25); **Wangaratta** (45min., 2 per day, $15); **Yass** (4hr., 2 per day, $50).

Buses: V/Line (☎13 61 96) services destinations in Victoria frequently and cheaply. To: **Echuca** (3-4hr., 1-2 per day, $27); **Melbourne** (3½hr., 4-6 per day, $50); **Mildura** (10hr.; M, W, Th, Sa mornings; $70); **Rutherglen** (40min.; M, W, Th, Sa mornings; $8); **Swan Hill** (6-7hr., 1-2 per day, $45); **Wangaratta** (45min., 4-6 per day, $15). **Greyhound Australia** (☎13 20 30) runs from next to the railway station to: **Adelaide** (16½hr., 3 per day, $100); **Brisbane** (26½hr., 5 per day, $150); **Canberra** (5hr., 4 per day, $35); **Melbourne** (4½hr., 5 per day, $40); **Sydney** (9½hr., 5 per day, $50); **Wangaratta** (45min., 2 per day, $50). Several companies, including **Wayward Busline** and **Firefly** tours, offer service from Albury-Wodonga to **Melbourne** and **Sydney** while stopping in various scenic locations along each route. Contact Firefly at www.fireflyexpress.com.au or ☎1800 631 164 for further information.

ORIENTATION AND PRACTICAL INFORMATION

The **Hume Highway** (Hwy. M31) from Sydney enters Albury-Wodonga from the northeast and winds through the center of town before resuming its southward course into Wodonga. The **Murray Valley Highway** (Hwy. 16) runs along the Victoria side and enters Wodonga from the southeast, running through town before uniting with the Hume Hwy. Along the river on the New South Wales side, the **Riverina Highway**

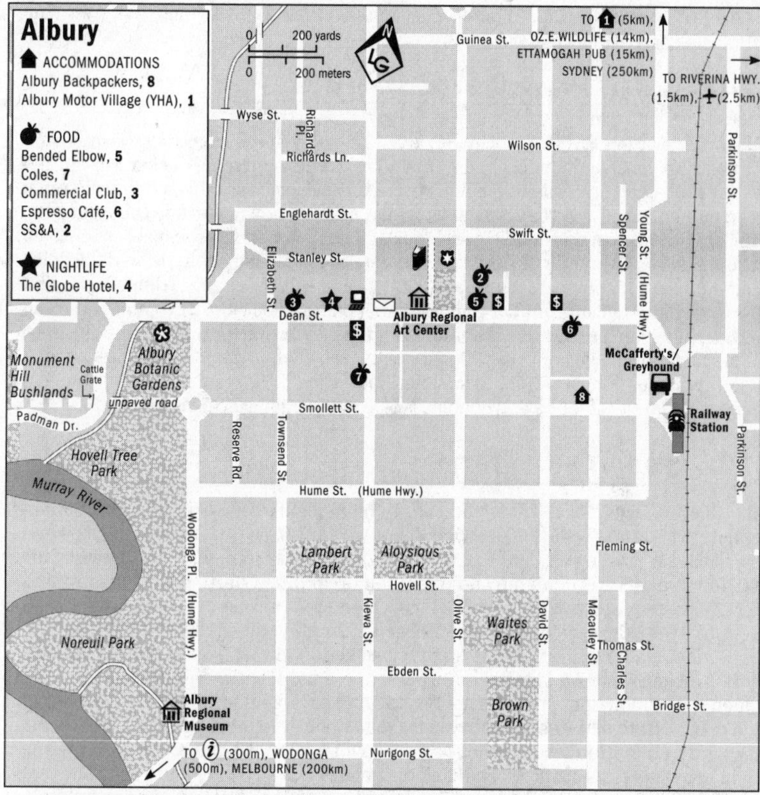

(Hwy. 58) runs west to Corowa. The heart of Albury-Wodonga can be found in the half-dozen blocks radiating from **Dean Street.** Because the area is quite urban relative to neighboring regions, temporary farming is scarce; look to the abundance of cafes and restaurants to provide hospitality work. The centrally located city can also be a useful place to base yourself while searching for fruit-picking jobs.

Tourist Office: Gateway Visitors Information Centre (☎1300 796 222) is located in the Gateway Village between Albury and Wodonga, just south of the Murray on the Hume Hwy. A bus runs between Albury and Wodonga and can be hailed as it passes the info center every 30min. Open daily 9am-5pm. 24hr. tourist information touchscreen.

Currency Exchange: Several banks and 24hr. **ATMs** line Dean St. Open M-Th 9:30am-4pm and F 9:30am-5pm.

Police: 539-543 Olive St. (☎6023 9299), near Swift St.

Internet Access: Albury City Library (☎6051 3470), in the city block behind the Regional Art Centre, has 2 terminals. Free for research. Email $2.75 per 30min. Book ahead. Open M-F 9am-7pm, Sa 9am-2pm. **The Lan Mine,** 501 David St. (☎6021 2076; www.lanmine.net) near the corner with Dean St., offers Internet facilities as well as extensive network gaming for $5.50 per hr. Open daily noon-midnight. **Oz-Chat,** 1/171 Lawrence St. (☎6056 0888), offers Internet access and online gaming in Wodonga for $6 per hr. Open daily 9am-latenight.

Post Office: (☎6051 3633), at the corner of Dean and Kiewa St. Open M-F 9am-5pm. *Poste Restante.* **Postal Code:** 2640.

ACCOMMODATIONS

Albury Backpackers ❷, 430 Smollett St., is one of the most easygoing hostels in Australia. With expansive common space (including a vintage double-decker bus stuffed with beanbag chairs), guests quickly become friends and have been known to organize pub crawls. Dave, the hospitable owner, offers renowned canoe trips along the Murray River for an unbeatable price. (☎6041 1822; www.alburybackpackers.com.au. Internet access $4 per hr. Wheelchair accessible. Check-out 11am. Dorms $23; twins and doubles $46.) **Albury Motor Village (YHA) ❷** is at 372 Wagga Rd., Hume Hwy. 5km north of the city center in Lavington just beyond Kaylock Rd. The calm and clean motor village mostly attracts families with their own transportation. (☎6040 2999; albury@motorvillage.com.au. A/C and heat. Pool, TV lounge, kitchen, parking, and laundry. Reception 8am-8pm. In summer book ahead. Dorms $21.50, non-members $25; powered sites for two $22; doubles $45-50; self-contained cabins for two $65-130.)

FOOD AND NIGHTLIFE

The Bended Elbow ❷, 480 Dean St., offers high-quality pub grub in a clean atmosphere with a lovely dark hardwood decor. (☎6023 6266. Tu steak with chips and salad $10. W "Parm and Pint" $12.50. Open daily 11am-latenight.) **The Espresso Cafe ❷**, 449c Dean St., is quite hip and offers full breakfasts (starting at $10) as well as focaccias and sandwiches. (☎6023 4730. Open M-W and Su 9am-4pm, Th-Sa 9am-10pm.) At the **Commercial Club ❷**, 618 Dean St., stuff yourself silly with all-you-can-eat lunch and dinner buffets with a large selection of meats, vegetables, and desserts for only $13. All visitors must present a valid ID at the door. (☎6021 1133. Open daily noon-2pm and 6-9pm.) **The SS&A Club ❶** behind Dean St., just west of Olive St., offers dinner specials every night. All visitors must present a valid ID at the door. (W bottomless bowl of pasta $7. Open noon-2:30pm and 6-9pm.) A student crowd parties at **The Globe Hotel,** on Dean St., where they lounge in shiny red chairs and soak up the frequent live music. (☎6021 2622. Pot of beer from $3. Schooner $4.40. Open M-Tu 10am-midnight, W-Sa 10am-4am.)

SIGHTS AND ACTIVITIES

The **Murray River** is by far the most popular sight in Albury-Wodonga, and on hot summer afternoons, most of the town takes to the water. The river has a fairly strong current that carries swimmers westward through forests of gnarled red gum trees. Though it technically belongs to New South Wales, the mighty Murray rolls for well over 2000km until it empties out into the ocean in Adelaide. A good place for a dip can be found just south of the botanic gardens in **Noreuil Park,** though this spot is popular among families with young (and often loud) children. Dave, the owner of the Albury Backpackers (see **Accommodations**) runs not-to-be-missed **canoe and kayak trips** (½-day Murray trip $25, full-day $30, 2-day $65).

On Wodonga Pl. between Smollett and Dean St., the **Albury Botanic Gardens** (☎6023 8111) have diverse arboreal displays and plenty of grassy picnic space. To take in a sweeping view of the region (or just to get some exercise), climb to the top of the **Monument Hill Bushlands** and gaze out onto Albury-Wodonga from the base of the Art Deco obelisk that is the Albury War Memorial. To find out more about the extensive trail and park system in Albury-Wodonga, visit the **Parklands Albury-Wodonga** office behind the Gateway Visitors Information Centre. (☎6023 6714.

Open M-F 8:30am-4:30pm.) The visitors center also recommends **The Albury Region Heritage Trail,** a free self-guided tour around historical Albury-Wodonga. Alternatively, try the **Burraja** indigenous culture "journey," which can also be booked at the visitors center. Visit www.wongawetlands.nsw.gov.au or call ☎0418 267 805 before heading out to the **Wonga Wetlands** to enjoy a day bouncing amid billabongs and learning about conservation and the regions ecosystem.

Just 15km north of Albury-Wodonga along the Hume Hwy., the goofy humor of the **Ettamogah Pub** caters to gawking tourists by satirizing and stereotyping all things Aussie. The late cartoonist Ken Maynard had been drawing a place like it for the *Australia Post* for years before someone decided to actually construct it. The tourist complex is composed of eye-popping buildings decorated with a running stream of off-color witticisms and cartoons. The centerpiece is the hilariously constructed and fully operational Ettamogah Pub itself, capped with a vintage Fosters beer truck on the roof and a crashed airplane next door. (☎6026 2366. Pub open M-F 10am-9pm, Sa-Su 10:30am-10pm. Bistro open F-Sa 6-9pm.)

Don't forget to make a stop at the nearby **OZ.e.wildlife.** It's a small, laid-back preserve filled with audacious kangaroos that will get up close and personal on their insatiable quest for food. Visitors can also feed wallabies and see penguins and koalas. Be sure to maintain a safe distance from the dingoes. (☎6040 3677. Open daily 9am-5pm. $10, concessions $8, children $5, families $25.)

WAGGA WAGGA ☎02

The largest inland city in New South Wales is known to most Australian simply as "Wagga" (WOH-guh; pop. 57,000). It derives its name from the local Aboriginal tribe for whom repetition implied plurality. *Wagga* means crow; hence, *wagga wagga* is the place of many crows. Locals proudly proclaim that their town is so good, they named it twice. Largely populated by students, Wagga is a surprisingly lively stop on the trek from Sydney to Melbourne; the pubs cater to the uni population with city-wide discounts on Wednesday evenings.

TRANSPORTATION AND PRACTICAL INFORMATION. The Stuart Hwy. (Hammond Ave. or Edward St. in town) intersects with **Baylis Street,** the town's main drag, and Baylis St. becomes **Fitzmaurice Street** once it crosses the bridge over Wollundry Lagoon. The bus stop and railway station are at Station Pl., the southern terminus of Baylis St. **Countrylink** (☎13 22 32) and **Fearnes Coaches** (☎1800 029 918 or 6921 2316) operate **bus** service to Canberra (3½hr., 2 per day, $32/41 respectively) and Sydney (6½-8hr., 2 per day, $53). **Greyhound Australia** offers similar service ($43 to Canberra, $60 to Sydney), plus a route to Melbourne (7hr., 1 per day, $62). The **visitors center** at 183 Tarcutta St. provides maps and brochures about local accommodations, restaurants, and sights. (☎6926 9621; www.tourism-waggawagga.com.au or www.discoverwagga.com.au. Open daily 9am-5pm. 24hr. touch-screen information kiosk.) There is a **post office** in the Wagga Wagga Marketplace, on Baylis St. (Open M-F 8:30am-5pm, Sa 9am-noon.) **Postal Code:** 2650.

ACCOMMODATIONS AND FOOD. The **Victoria Hotel ❷,** 55 Baylis St., is just a 5min. walk from the train station down Baylis St. Perched above the bustling pub and restaurant, the "Vic" has clean carpeted rooms and antique armoires. (☎6921 5233. Singles $25; doubles or twins $40.) **Romano's ❸** is another pub with reasonable accommodations located over the bridge where Baylis turns into Fitzmaurice St. (☎6921 2031. Singles $38; doubles $50, with shower $59; ensuite $78. Extra bed $13). **Wagga Wagga Beach Caravan Park ❶,** at the end of Johnston St., has sites and ensuite units with TV, A/C, and kitchen. Laundry and BBQ facilities are available. (☎6931 0603. Sites for 2 $15-18, powered $17-21; standard units $55-65.)

There are two large supermarkets along Baylis St. in the center of town. A **Coles** is in the Sturt Mall and a **Woolworths** is in the Wagga Wagga Marketplace, both near the intersection of Forsyth St. The **Baylis St. Bistro ❷** is on the ground floor of the Victoria Hotel and serves heaping lunch and dinner portions (from $8) at reasonable prices. The **Bridge Tavern ❶**, 188 Fitzmaurice St., is a popular horse racing pub and bistro attached to a plush steakhouse by the same name. Tavern bar fare is significantly less expensive than steakhouse grub. Try the delicious grilled chicken sandwich ($9.90) with fixings. (☎6921 2222. Main courses $8-13. Open M-Sa 10am-latenight, Su 10am-10pm.)

SIGHTS AND ENTERTAINMENT. The **Wiradjuri Walking Track** features most of the Wagga's major landmarks, meandering through the city in a 30km loop starting at the visitors center (where you can pick up the detailed brochure). The Civic Centre at the north end of Baylis St. houses several galleries, including the **National Art Glass Gallery** and the **Wagga Wagga Art Gallery.** (Free. Open Tu-Sa 10am-5pm, Su noon-4pm.) The city library is also located in this complex and offers free research Internet access. (Email $2.40 per 30min.) Rest at the **Botanic Gardens** and absorb the quaint atmosphere. (☎6925 4065. Open daily dawn-dusk. Free.) In summer, **Wagga Beach,** at Cabriata Park, is a popular spot. **The Capital** is the only large nightclub venue in Wagga, catering primarily to the local university crowd. City officials have imposed a lock-down system at night; at 1:30am, all establishments lock their doors. If you're already inside, stay until the wee hours of the morning; you're just not allowed to switch pubs. (F dance club. Open W-Sa 9pm-3am.)

BIG SKY

The cities and towns in Big Sky country lie between the rugged plateaus of the Blue Mountains and the arid expanses of outback New South Wales. Surrounded by miles of placidly rolling hills, most are regarded as stopovers between grander destinations, but even short stays will be rewarded by brilliant sunsets.

BATHURST ☎02

Bathurst (pop. 37,000) features wide avenues and large, ornate lampposts which suggest that it was once headed for greatness. However, it is the motorway in the southwest corner of town that has put the city on the map. Originally built in 1938 as a scenic drive, the 6km loop up and down Mt. Panorama doubles as a public road and the track for the **V-8 Supercars** and the **24-hour Race,** held in early October and mid-November, respectively. During these events, over 150,000 people descend on the usually low-profile town.

TRANSPORTATION AND PRACTICAL INFORMATION. Bathurst is 98km west of Katoomba on the Great Western Hwy. **Trains** and **buses** leave the **Railway Station** at the corner of Keppel and Havannah St. **Countrylink** (☎6332 4844 or 13 22 32) goes to: Cowra (1½hr., 1 per day, $15); Dubbo (3hr., 2 per day, $31); Forbes and Parkes (3-3½hr., 1 per day, $26); Katoomba (2hr., 1 per day, $17); Lithgow (1-1¼hr., 3-7 per day, $11); Parramatta and Penrith (3hr., 2 per day, $26-27); Sydney (3½hr., 1 per day, $34). For a **taxi,** call ☎13 10 08. The stellar **Bathurst Visitor Information Centre,** 1 Kendall Ave., has brochures and maps. (☎6332 1444 or 1800 681 000. Open daily 9am-5pm.) **ATMs** abound on William and Howick St. Free **Internet** access can be found at the **library** at 70-78 Keppel St. (☎6332 2130. Open M-F 10am-6pm, Sa 10am-5pm, Su 11am-2pm.) The **police station** (☎6332 8699), 139 Rankin St., lies between Russell and Howick St. The **post office,** 230 Howick St., is between George and William St. (☎6332 4553. Open M-F 9am-5pm.) **Postal Code:** 2795.

ACCOMMODATIONS AND FOOD. During the races, rates for all accommodations skyrocket faster than the cars themselves. Bathurst has a few pubstays downtown; the nicest affordable option is the backpacker-friendly **Commercial Hotel ❶,** 135 George St., which also serves up cheap traditional pub food ($5-12) in its **restaurant ❶** downstairs. (☎6331 2712; www.commercialhotel.com.au. Dorms $20; singles $29; doubles $49.) The **Bathurst Motor Inn ❺,** 87 Durham St., on the corner of George St., offers rooms with TV, fridge, heat and A/C, and coffee maker. Movie rentals $5. (☎6331 2222. Reception 7am-10:30pm, Su 7am-9pm. Singles from $65; twins and doubles $75, extra person $10.)

A great departure from the town's greasy spoons, **Ziegler's Cafe ❷,** 52 Keppel St., serves a wide range of healthy salads, grilled veggie dishes, and gourmet burgers on focaccia. (☎6332 1565. Lunches $11-20, dinners $12-22. Open M-Sa 9am-9pm, Su 9am-3pm. AmEx/DC/MC/V.) A **Woolworths** supermarket is in the Stockland Mall off William St. (☎6331 9144. Open daily 7am-10pm.)

SIGHTS. No trip to Bathurst would be complete without a spin round the **Mount Panorama circuit head,** southwest on William St. where it becomes Panorama Ave. As you twist your way up and down the steep hills, you'll gain an appreciation for the pros who do it in excess of 200kph during officially sanctioned races. Don't let the banner ads and tire piles seduce you; local police patrol the area frequently, looking for drivers who edge above the 60kph speed limit. The recently expanded **National Motor Racing Museum,** near the starting line, keeps the thrill of the race alive year-round. (☎6332 1872. Open daily 9am-4:30pm. $7, concessions $5, children $2.20.) The **Bathurst Historical Museum** in the court's eastern wing gives a more historical account of the town. Chock full of treasured objects like shoe hooks, a concertina, and a ship's spar, the museum tells the story of the town's gold rush days. (Open Tu-W and Sa-Su 10am-4pm.) The **Chifley Home,** 10 Busby St. (☎6332 1444), abode of Ben Chifley, prime minister from 1945-49, is so simple and unpretentious that it serves as a symbol of hope for political humility. (Open M and Sa-Su 11am-3pm. $5, children $3.)

Don't miss the **Abercrombie Caves,** part of the Jenolan Caves Trust, 70km south of Bathurst via Trunkey Creek. The majestic Grand Arch is the largest limestone archway in the southern hemisphere. (☎6368 8603; www.jenolancaves.org.au. Open daily 9am-4pm. Self-guided archway tour $13, children $8.) **Fossicking**—amateur mining, in this case for gold—is popular in the area and its surrounds. **Bathurst Goldfields,** 428 Conrod Straight on Mt. Panorama, is a reconstructed mining area that allows you to try your hand panning for gold as the company pans for the tourist dollar. (☎6332 2022. 2hr. tours on select dates start at 2pm. $10.)

MUDGEE ☎02

A land of wine and honey cradled in the foothills of the Great Dividing Range, Mudgee (Aboriginal for "nest in the hills"; pop. 23,000) has over 35 vineyards and plenty of small town charm. Locals proudly proclaim that Mudgee is "tasting better each year," a claim confirmed by even a tipsy visit to nearby cellar doors.

Pubstay accommodations are readily available in town. **The Woolpack Hotel ❷,** 67 Market St., is down the street from the visitors center, near the corner of Church St. A friendly, colorful cast of characters frequents the downstairs pub and TV lounge. Rooms include fridge, coffee maker, and A/C. (☎6372 1908. Reception noon-midnight at bar. Backpacker rooms $20; singles from $25; doubles $40. MC/V.) Another good option is **The Lawson Hotel ❸,** 1 Church St. Spacious, comfortable rooms for three come with electric blankets and beds. There's a TV room with a kitchen at the end of the hall. (☎6372 2183. Continental breakfast included. Singles, doubles, and triples from $40. AmEx/DC/MC/V.) The **Mudgee Riverside Caravan and Tourist Park ❶**, 22 Short St., behind the visitors center, has showers and laundry. (☎6372 2531; www.mudgeeriverside.com.au. Linen $11. Laundry $2. Reception 8am-8pm. Sites for 2 $17, powered $20; ensuite cabins with A/C, kitchen, and TV from $60. MC/V.) A number of motels are scattered through town, the cheapest of which is **Central Motel ❸**, 120 Church St. (☎1800 457 222. Reception 8am-10pm. Singles $40-120; doubles $60-120. AmEx/DC/MC/V.)

The Lawson Park Grill and Carvery ❸, 1 Church St., inside the Lawson Park Hotel, is a great spot for live entertainment and good grub—grill your own steak ($17-20) and enjoy it with a bottle of local wine (from $10). Main dishes ($15-18) come with salad bar or vegetables. (☎6372 2183. Open daily noon-2:30pm and 6-9pm. AmEx/V/MC.) Stop in at **Melon Tree ❶**, 75 Church St. (☎6372 4005), to grab a gourmet sandwich ($6-9) or pick up a picnic pack for a day at the wineries. Breakfast for under $10 might also help pad your stomach before you set out. (Open M-Sa 8am-6pm, Su 9am-6pm. Cash only.) A **Bi-Lo** supermarket (☎6372 7155) is on Church St., in the Town Centre shopping plaza. (Open M-Sa 7am-10pm, Su 8am-8pm).

Mudgee's selling points are its viticultural offerings, ranging from small, communal vineyards to large, self-sufficient **wineries;** consult the tourist office for extensive information on which will most suit your palate. During the **Mudgee Wine Festival** in September, travelers passing through will watch the streets come alive, but you can fill your glass with Mudgee's renowned reds year round. If you want to do the wine-tasting circuit but also wish to avoid running afoul of stringent drunk-driving laws, try **On the Bus Tours.** (☎1767 8619; www.onthebus.com.au.) **Biking** is also an option, and **Countryfit,** at 36-42 Short St., rents. ($15 per hr., $25 per ½ day, $30 per full day. Tandems available.) With transportation covered, choosing among the 35 area vineyards will be your big challenge.

EXCUSE ME, THERE'S A PLUM IN MY GLASS. When people describe wine's overtones or tinges, they don't mean that sweet plums, limes, toffee, or tobacco are actually in the wine. Rather, the texture, taste, and aroma merely remind connoisseurs of those flavors.

Not far from the center of town, **Frog's Rock** has an impressive range of earthy wines ready to be sampled. From town, take Cassilis Rd. to Edgell Ln. (☎6372 2408; www.frogrockwines.com. Open daily 10am-5pm.) **Botobolar,** 89 Botobolar Rd., 16km northeast of town, is Australia's oldest organic vineyard and offers daily tastings. (☎6373 3840. Open M-Sa 10am-5pm, Su 10am-3pm.) **Huntington Estate Wines,** 8km from town past the airport on Cassilis Rd., has an array of reds to taste on the free self-guided tour. (☎6373 3825; www.huntington-estate.com.au. Open M-F 9am-5pm, Sa 10am-5pm, Su 10am-3pm.)

Mudgee is a 3½hr. drive from Sydney on Hwy. 86 (Castlereagh Hwy.), between Lithgow (126km) and Dubbo (133km). **Countrylink** (☎13 22 32) connects by **coach** to Mudgee and runs one to two times per day to: Coonabarabran (3hr., $27); Lithgow (2½hr., $20); and Sydney (5½hr., $40). Book at **Harvey World Travel,** 68 Church St. (☎6372 6077. Open M-F 8:30am-5:30pm, Sa 9am-noon.) Because trains no longer pass through Mudgee, the old railway station on the corner of Church and Inglis St. is now home to a cafe and gallery of local art. Countrylink coaches stop there and at the visitors center. For **taxis,** call ☎13 10

08. The **Mudgee Visitors Centre,** 84 Market St., is armed with maps. (☎6372 1020 or 1800 816 304. Open M-F 9am-5pm, Sa 9am-3:30pm, Su 9:30am-2pm.) The **NPWS office,** 160 Church St., across from the train station, administers the northwest section of Wollemi National Park. (☎6372 7199; mudgee@npws.nsw.gov.au. Open M-F 9am-4pm, but rangers may be out on patrol on F or during brushfire season.) Free **Internet** access is available at the **library** at 64 Market St. (☎6378 2740. Open M-F 10am-6pm, Sa 9:30am-12:30pm.) **Banks** and **ATMs** are on Church St. **Police** (☎6372 8599) are located at 94 Market St. In an emergency call an **ambulance** at ☎000. A **post office** (☎6378 2021) is at 80 Market St., on the corner with Perry St. **Postal Code:** 2850.

DUBBO ☎02

The hub of the Big Sky region, Dubbo (DUH-boh; pop. 39,000) is a bustling, blue-collar service city and a common stop on journeys between Sydney and Brisbane. In the middle of the town's buzzing Central Business District (CBD), it's possible to forget how close you are to the Outback, but a drive after dark in any direction (not recommended) will reveal how isolated you are. Dubbo has a smattering of attractions, but the city's headliner is the Western Plains Zoo; no visit to the Big Sky region would be complete without a stop at the amazing menagerie.

TRANSPORTATION. **Countrylink** (☎13 22 32) **trains** and **buses** depart from the **railway station** on Talbragar St. to: Albury (7hr.; Tu, Th, Su 1 per day; $72); Broken Hill (8½hr., 1 per day, $78); Forbes (2hr.; Tu, Th, Su 1 per day; $17); Melbourne (10½hr.; Tu, Th, Su 1 per day; $88); Sydney (7-11hr., 1 per day, $60); Wagga Wagga (5½hr.; Tu, Th, Su 1 per day; $43). The Shell Station at the intersection of the Newell and Mitchell Hwy. is the drop-off point for coaches. **Greyhound Australia** (☎13 14 99 or 13 20 30) services: Adelaide (15hr., 2 per day, $166); Brisbane (12½hr., 1 per day, $133); Coonabarabran (2hr., 1 per day, $40); and Melbourne (12½hr., 1 per day, $123). All tickets can be booked online, over the phone, or at the railway station. (Open M-F 8am-5pm, Sa-Su 8-9:30am and 10:30am-2pm.) Taxis run 24hr. (☎6882 1911 or 13 10 08). **Darrell Wheeler Cycles,** 25 Bultje St., rents bikes for $15 per day. (☎6882 9899. Open M-F 8:30am-5:30pm, Sa 8:30am-1pm. Call ahead for Su rental.) Bike trails cross town, run alongside the Macquarie River, and head out toward the zoo.

ORIENTATION AND PRACTICAL INFORMATION. Dubbo sits at the intersection of the **Newell Highway,** which runs between Melbourne (856km) and Brisbane (895km), and the **Mitchell Highway,** which connects Sydney (414km) to western cities. The town's sprawling layout could make life difficult for the carless, though major sights are clustered around the zoo and CBD, which is marked by the intersection of Talbragar and Macquarie St. **Talbragar Street** runs east-west, parallel to the two major highways that sandwich the town. **Macquarie Street** is lined with banks, ATMs, pharmacies, and supermarkets.

The **Dubbo Visitors Centre,** on the corner of Erskine and Macquarie St. (Newell Hwy.) in the northwest corner of the small downtown area, is stocked with **maps** of biking trails and driving routes. (☎6801 4450; www.dubbotourism.com.au. Open daily 9am-5pm.) The **police station** (☎6881 3222) is at 143 Brisbane St., across from the Grape Vine Cafe. Find **Internet** access at the **Dubbo Regional Library,** on the southwest corner of Macquarie and Talbragar St. (☎6801 4510. $1.35 per 15min. Open M-F 10am-6pm, Sa 10am-3pm, Su noon-4pm.) The **post office** is at 65-69 Talbragar St. between Brisbane and Macquarie St. (☎6841 3210. Open daily 9am-5pm.) **Postal Code:** 2830.

ACCOMMODATIONS AND FOOD. Plenty of hotels are clustered near Talbragar St. in the CBD, with singles from $35-50; motels in the area generally run $70-100 for a double. The cheapest beds are at the **Dubbo YHA Hostel ❸**, 87 Brisbane St., near the corner of the Newell Hwy. The verandas off each room add character to the otherwise simple hostel, as do nightly fire-side gatherings, a talking cockatoo, and organized morning zoo walks. With no heat and only three bathrooms, this YHA is more basic than most, though the friendliness of the managing couple is unparalleled. (☎6882 0922. Internet access $3 per hr. Washer $3, no dryer. Bikes $7 per day. Linen but no towels provided. Reception 8am-10:30pm. Dorms from $26, YHA $23; twins and doubles from $38; family rooms from $50.) Swankier digs can be found at **Amaroo Hotel ❺,** 83 Macquarie St., in the middle of town. Amaroo features modern ensuite rooms with TV, fridge, electric blankets, heat, and A/C. (☎6882 3533. Singles $59; doubles $80. Extra person $30.) The **Dubbo City Caravan Park ❷,** on Whylandra St. just before it becomes the Newell Hwy., has beautiful shaded sites overlooking the Macquarie River. (☎6882 4820; dccp@dubbo.nsw.gov.au. Linen $15 per bed. Laundry $3. Curfew 10pm. Reception 7:30am-7:30pm. Check-in 1pm. Sites for 2 from $16, powered $21, ensuite $28; caravans from $30; cabins with A/C, TV, and toilet from $46, with shower $53; motel-style family units with linen and kitchen from $70. $10 surcharge on cabins during school holidays. Extra adult $7-10; extra child $4-8. AmEx/MC/V.)

Sandwich shops and bakeries are plentiful in the CBD, but cheap restaurants are few and far between. For the best coffee concoctions, pastries, and light meals, try the chic **Grape Vine Cafe ❷,** 144 Brisbane St. When the weather's nice, regulars enjoy iced coffee on the patio out back; during colder months, sip hot chocolate at modern tables with cushioned banquettes. (☎6884 7354. Breakfast and lunch $8-15. Open M-F 8am-5pm, Sa-Su 9am-4pm.) There are **local markets** offering crafts, produce, and bric-a-brac at the showground on Wingewarra St. every 2nd Sunday of the month. (Open 8am-1pm.) A **Woolworths** supermarket is in the **Riverdale Shopping Centre** on Macquarie St. (☎6882 1633. Open M-Sa 7am-10pm, Su 8am-8pm.)

SIGHTS. Dubbo's premier tourist attraction is the **Western Plains Zoo,** on Obley Rd., 4km south of the city center off the Newell Hwy. It's an awesome place to visit if you're in the area, but not worth a special trip from Sydney. In addition to Australian native species, the zoo houses Bengal tigers, lions, black rhinoceroses, and Australia's only resident African elephants, all wandering through loose enclosures. Don't miss the **children's zoo,** where you can stroke the fur of an albino kangaroo or look eye-to-eye with a portly wombat. Exhibits are arranged by continent around a paved track suitable for driving or biking; BBQ and picnic areas abound along the way. Signs posted throughout the zoo announce feeding times and recent births. On weekends, and Wednesdays and Fridays during school holidays, 6:45am zoo walks provide a behind-the-scenes look at the animals ($10, children $5). For a real adventure, try the **Lion Encounter,** offered every day at noon for $50. The **Tiger Encounter,** at the same price, happens daily at 11:30am. Two-hour zoo tours ($25, children $14.50) depart daily at 10:45am. (☎6882 5888; www.zoo.nsw.gov.au. Open daily 9am-5pm; last entry 3:30pm. 2-day pass $30, students $21, children $16.50. 4hr. bike rental $15 plus license or credit card deposit.)Learn about aerodynamics, Aboriginal history, and woodcraft at **Jedda Boomerangs,** on Minore Rd, White Pines. As you head southwest to the zoo, turn right onto Minore. and follow it for 4km. Watch the entertaining and knowledgeable staff craft a boomerang from wood, then take a throwing lesson ($5.50) or design your own boomerang ($8-16). For the musically inclined, didgeridoo lessons ($20 per hr.) can be made by appointment.

(☎6882 3110; www.jeddaboomerangs.com.au. Open daily 10am-5pm.) The **Tracker Riley Cycleway** offers an easy path along the banks of the Macquarie River for bikers and walkers alike. **Dundullimal Homestead,** on Obley Rd., 2min. past the zoo, is the oldest timber slab house in Australia. Built in the early 1840s, the house offers a glimpse of Dubbo's roots as a frontier town. The property is part of Australia's National Trust and features period furniture and costumed story-telling characters from Dubbo's past. (☎6884 9984. Open daily 10am-5pm. $8, children $4, families $20.)

DON'T GAZE AND GRAZE. Bring a sack lunch, but don't eat while observing the animals—it gets them all riled up.

COONABARABRAN ☎02

Find answers to universal questions in the "Astronomy Capital of Australia," Coonabarabran (coon-a-BAR-a-bran; pop. 3000). Home to several observatories and the country's two largest telescopes, the small town is halfway between Melbourne and Brisbane, making it a great place to appreciate skies free of light at night.

TRANSPORTATION AND PRACTICAL INFORMATION. Coonabarabran lies 159km northeast of Dubbo, 120km south of Narrabri and 182km west of Tamworth on the Newell Hwy. It's accessible from the northeast through Gunnedah, 105km away on the Oxley Hwy., which joins Newell. **Countrylink** (☎13 22 32) runs **buses** from the visitors center to Lithgow, where they connect with the train to Sydney (8hr., M-F and Su 1 per day, $68). **Greyhound Australia** (☎13 14 99 or 13 20 30) buses leave from the Caltex Service Station outside of town once a day to Brisbane (10hr., $120) and Melbourne (11½hr., $141). **Teed Up Travel,** 79 John St., will book transport for a $5.50 fee. (☎6842 1566. Open M-F 9am-5pm, Sa 9am-noon.) For **taxi** service, try **Satellite Taxis** (☎1800 421 113).

The clock tower marks the intersection of **John Street** (Newell Hwy.) and **Dalgarno Street,** which leads west to the observatories and Warrumbungle National Park. The **Visitor Information Centre,** at the south end of town on the Newell Hwy., has a display on Australian megafauna, including the skeleton of a 33,500-year-old giant diprotodon, the largest marsupial that has ever roamed the earth. (☎6849 2144 or 1800 242 881; www.coonabarabran.com. Open daily 9am-5pm.) Other services include: 24hr. **ATMs** and a **library** (☎6842 1093) on John St. (Free **Internet** access; email and chat $2.75 per 30min.; open M 10am-1pm, Tu-F 10am-5:30pm, Sa 9:30am-noon); **Internet** access can also be found across the street at the **Community Technology Center** at 71 John St. (☎6842 2920; $5.50 per hr.; student discount; open M-F 9am-5pm); and the **police** station (☎6842 7299), on the southeast corner of John and Dalgarno St. The **post office** is right in the center of town at 71a John St. (☎6842 1197. Open M-F 9am-5pm.) **Postal Code:** 2357.

ACCOMMODATIONS AND FOOD. A number of B&Bs and farmstays are also available in Coonabarabran and the Warrumbungle area, with singles from $40; inquire at the visitors center. Book ahead during school holidays. The **Imperial Hotel ❷**, a pubstay at the corner of John and Dalgarno St., has cheap rooms with heated blankets. (☎6842 1023. Reception 7am-midnight. Check-out 10am. Singles $25, ensuite $35; doubles $35/45; twins $44/50. Extra adult $15.) More expensive motel options line John St. Halfway between town and the entrance to Warrumbungle National Park, the new **Warrumbungles Holiday Camp ❶** is 12km west of the clock tower on Timor Rd. (☎6842 3400. Reception 8am-dusk. On-site volleyball net, pool, kitchen, and BBQ. Bunkhouse beds $16; cabins $50.) At **John Oxley Cara-**

van Park ❶, 1km north of town on Oxley Hwy., the affable owners run a shop and BBQ. (☎6842 1635. Linen $8 per person, $10 for 2. Reception 8am-noon and 2-7pm. Sites for 2 $15, powered $19, extra person $6; ensuite cabins $48, $49 for 2, extra person $8. AmEx/MC/V.)

The **Woop Woop Cafe,** at 38a John St., offers healthy breakfasts ($6-12) and gourmet lunches ($6-15) in a high-ceilinged room flooded with light. (☎6842 4755. Open Tu-Sa 8am-6pm, and Su 10am-4pm. AmEx/MC/V.) The **Golden Sea Dragon Restaurant ❷,** next to the visitors center, features a golden Buddha and an impressive gold-inlay interior. (☎6842 2388. 2-course Traveler's Special $12. Open M-F 5-10pm, Sa-Su 5-11pm. Lunch daily noon-2:30pm. AmEx/DC/MC/V.) Supermarkets are found on Dalgarno St. on either side of the clock tower: **IGA** is at 35 Dalgarno St. (☎6842 1179. Open M-W and F 8:15am-6:30pm, Th 8:15am-7pm, Sa 8:15am-4:30pm, Su 8:45am-1:30pm.) **Bi-Lo** is at 64 Dalgarno St. (☎6842 1911. Open M-F 9am-7pm, Sa 9am-5pm, Su 10am-4pm).

SIGHTS. The highlight of Coonabarabran is the **Skywatch Day and Night Observatory,** 2km down the road to Warrumbungle National Park. The effusive staff guides nightly viewings, giving visitors the opportunity to observe planets, constellations, and galaxies. During the day, use a lens with a solar filter to view the sun's surface. (☎6842 3303; www.skywatchobservatory.com. Open daily 10:30am-late. Sessions nightly Nov.-Jan. at 9 and 10pm; Feb. 9pm; Mar. 8:30 and 9:30pm; Apr.-Sept. 7 and 8pm; and Oct. 7:30 and 8:30pm. Display $4, students $3, children $2; display and nightshow $15/11/9. Solar viewing $5. Book ahead during school holidays.) While Skywatch is entertaining, the real work is done at **Siding Spring Observatory,** a complex of white domes resting high in the hills that is credited with many recent breakthroughs, including the discovery of several extrasolar planets. For a small fee, the observatory visitors center offers an exhibit about the work of resident astronomers. A short walk from the visitors center leads to a colorful photo collection featuring shots of distant galaxies taken by the on-site telescope.

DARK SIDE OF THE MOON. The best time of the month to see the stars is during a crescent moon. When the moon is full, its glow brightens the night sky, making it difficult to see distant nebulae.

Impressive **sandstone caves,** hollowed out by wind and water erosion, can be found in the **Pilliga Nature Reserve.** They are tricky to locate and are a sacred site for local Aboriginal groups, so check with the tourist office for more info.

WARRUMBUNGLE NATIONAL PARK ☎02

The jagged spires and rambling peaks of the Warrumbungle Mountains are the result of ancient volcanic activity. Softer sandstone worn away under hardened lava rock has left unusual shapes slicing into the sky above the forested hills. Resident kangaroos, koalas, and wedge-tailed eagles make frequent appearances on the park's excellent trails.

Warrumbungle offers a range of short walks and challenging multi-day hikes. The **Whitegum Lookout,** 7km before the park office, offers a spectacular view of the spiky skyline along an easy 500m walk through the shade of eucalyptus trees. The most popular long walk is the **Breadknife/Grand High Tops Circuit** (12.5km, 4-5hr., steep grade), which passes the 90m-high dyke known as the Breadknife, a narrow rock formation whose peaks seem to form the serrated edge of a bread slicer. **Gould's Circuit** is a less strenuous hike (8km, 3hr., medium grade) that offers a view of the Grand High Tops and a turn-off to the summit of Macha Tor.

A 75km **scenic drive** (3km unsealed) branches off from the Newell Hwy. 39km north of Gilgandra and runs through the park, circling back to the highway at Coonabarabran. The park entry fee ($7 per car) can be paid at the **Warrumbungle National Park Visitors Centre,** on the park road 33km west of Coonabarabran. They also have free bush camping and rock climbing permits for most peaks, but not Breadknife. (☎6825 4364. Open daily 9am-4pm.) On school holidays or by prior arrangement, the visitors center also offers **Discovery Walks, Talks, and Tours** with Aboriginal guides. Tours include a Tara Cave Walk, Breakfast with the Birds, and a trip to the **Sandstone Caves** (p. 248). Book with the visitors center.

The park has four **camping ❶** areas (most without showers) open to independent travelers. **Camp Blackman** is car-accessible and has toilets, rainwater, hot showers, laundry tubs, and a pay phone ($5, children $3; powered sites $8/4). **Camp Wambelong** and **Guneemooroo** are both car-accessible and have unpowered sites and toilets ($5/3). **Wambelong** is on the edge of the main park road, and **Guneemooroo** ("place of snakes") can be reached by an unsealed road from **Tooraweenah. Camp Pincham,** the starting point for the Breadknife hike, lies a short walk from the nearest carpark and has toilets and unpowered sites ($3, children $2). Bring your own firewood or pack a fuel stove. Contact the visitors center for information on free bush sites and accommodations for large groups.

NARRABRI ☎02

The roads to Narrabri (NEHR-uh-BRYE, meaning "forked waters"; pop. 7200) are lined with tufts of cotton, the region's "white gold." The town, equidistant from Sydney and Brisbane (560km) and 120km north of Coonabarabran on the Newell Hwy., has a new museum with exhibits about high-tech cotton production. If you don't think fiber facts are fun, Narrabri is also conveniently close to the Southern Hemisphere's largest radio telescope array and the rugged beauty of Mt. Kaputar National Park. This is Australia's Big Sky country: watch the sunset with streaks of pink and orange as the sky fades from blue and lavender to pitch black.

TRANSPORTATION AND PRACTICAL INFORMATION. **Countrylink** (☎13 22 32) trains run to Sydney (8hr., 1 per day 9:25am, $84) from the station at the east end of Bowen St., four blocks from Maitland St. **Greyhound Australia** (☎13 14 99 or 13 20 30) buses depart from the visitors center. They leave for Brisbane (8½hr., 1 per day 10:20am, $99) and Melbourne (17hr., 1 per day 2:50pm, $168) via Coonabarabran (2hr., 1 per day, $29) and Dubbo (3hr., 1 per day, $48). Tickets can be booked through **Harvey World Travel,** 60 Maitland St., for a $5.50 service fee. (☎6792 2555. Open M-F 8am-5:30pm, Sa 8:30-11:30am.) On the east side of town is **Maitland Street,** which runs parallel to Tibbereena St. (Newell Hwy.), and traces the Narrabri Creek. The **Narrabri Visitors Centre** is opposite Lloyd St. on Tibbereena St., which veers north along the Creek. (☎6799 6760 or 1800 659 931. Open M-F 9am-5pm, Sa-Su 9am-2pm.) The **NPWS** office, 100 Maitland St., Level 1, offers info about outdoor activities. Enter around the corner on Dewhurst St. and go up the stairs. (☎6792 7300. Open M-F 8:30am-4:30pm.) The **post office** is at 140 Maitland St. (☎6799 5999. Open M-F 9am-5pm.) **Postal Code:** 2390.

ACCOMMODATIONS AND FOOD. Many of the pubs along the central stretch of Maitland St. offer inexpensive accommodation, and there are a number of motels on the highway leading into town. Your cheapest, clean but no-frills option may be the **Club House Hotel ❷** at 97 Maitland St., in the middle of town. (☎6792 2027. Singles $22; doubles $35; families $45. MC/V.) **Narrabri Backpackers B&B ❷,** on the west side of town at 30 Mooloobar St., was recently refurbished, complete with a coat of bright pink paint and a garden. (☎6792 6473;

NEW SOUTH WALES

dshweiki67@hotmail.com. Free laundry. Continental breakfast included. Dorms $20; triples $40. AmEx/MC/V.) The **Dulcinea Holiday Retreat** ❺ on Mt. Kaputar Rd., has two cabins just 20km from the top of the mountain. Peacocks roam the property's gardens. (☎6793 5246; dulcineacabins@hotmail.com. Twin cottages $70. Extra person $10. Cash only.) **BigSky Caravan Park** ❶, on Tibbereena St. just up the road from the visitors center, is next door to a community pool available for guest use ($2) in the summer. (☎6792 5799. Reception daily 8am-7pm. Tent sites for 2 $17, powered $20; ensuite cabins $55. Extra person $6. MC/V.) Several B&Bs and farmstays are also available. **Dawsons Spring Camping Area** ❶ is 21km inside, near the Mt. Kaputar summit; and has hot showers, toilets, and BBQ ($3, children $2); bring your own firewood. The **cabins** ❹ each have four beds, a kitchen, and shower: a great deal for families or groups. (Book ahead at the NPWS office ☎6792 7300. $55; min. 2 night stay.)

The aroma of freshly baked bread at **Watson's Kitchen** ❶, 151 Maitland St., can be smelled halfway down the street. Stop in for a sandwich ($3-7), or a pastry. (☎6792 1366. Open M-F 6am-6pm, Sa 6am-1pm, Su 7am-noon.) **Woolworths,** at 173 Maitland St., sells groceries. (Open M-F 7am-10pm, Sa 7am-9pm, Su 8am-8pm.)

ACTIVITIES. Narrabri's newest attraction is the **Australian Cotton Centre,** located next to the visitors center on the Newell Hwy. The center has fascinating interactive exhibits including a 3-D theater and a giant cotton-picking machine. A self-guided tour takes you "from field to fabric" and explains the crop's varied uses, anywhere from textiles to explosives. (☎6792 6443 or 1300 663 853; www.australiancottoncentre.com.au. Open daily 8:30am-4:30pm. $8, concession $7, children $5.50, families $19.) Signs on the Newell Hwy. heading toward Coonabarabran lead to the **Australia Telescope,** 24km west of Narrabri. This set of six large dishes comprises the largest, most powerful array of radio telescopes in the Southern Hemisphere. Interactive displays show how radio waves can be used to make visible images and explain how radio telescopes can "see" objects that normal optical telescopes cannot. The 22m diameter dishes are fenced off, but you can pick up radio waves emitted by the sun using a hand-operated telescope. (☎6790 4070. Open daily 8am-4pm. Free.) East of Narrabri, the peaks of the **Nandewar Range** beckon travelers to leave the paved road and scale the summit of **Mount Kaputar,** from which one-tenth of the entire state of New South Wales can be seen. The entrance to the central section of **Mount Kaputar National Park** lies 31km east of Narrabri; head south on Maitland St. and Old Gunnedah Rd. and continue for 20km. The park's most famous attraction is **Sawn Rocks,** a basalt rock formation that looks like a pipe organ. The natural art form is in the northern section, accessible from the Newell Hwy. north of Narrabri (30min. drive northeast 10min. on an unsealed road, 15min. walk from the carpark; not accessible from the rest of the park). Try the NPWS office in Narrabri for pamphlets on walking tracks and hiking info. The roads to and within the park are mostly unsealed and unstable after rain; call the NPWS office (☎6792 7300) for conditions.

OUTBACK NEW SOUTH WALES

The empty stretches of northwest New South Wales are sparsely populated, difficult to reach, and largely untouched. The vast expanses lure truly intrepid travelers, and the emptiness is so far-reaching that the curvature of the earth is often visible. Those who venture into these arid lands are rewarded with bragging rights and can tell fellow travelers that they've been "Back o' Bourke," a small town which lies on the Mitchell Hwy. (Hwy. 71), 367km northwest of Dubbo and 142km south of the Queensland-NSW border.

MUTAWINTJI NATIONAL PARK

For tens of thousands of years, both humans and animals having been congregating among the shady trees of Mutawintji. The name is an Aboriginal term meaning "meeting place," and this oasis is a ceremonial base where different tribes exchange goods and ideas. The park is dominated by red cliffs, boulder-filled gorges, shady trees, and has the only freshwater sources for miles. With a dependable water supply, the banks of the gushing ravines are home to a wealth of flora and fauna endemic to the Outback. Aboriginal societies (including the Malyankapa and Pandjikali people to whom these lands traditionally belong) have lived here continuously for over 8000 years, a fact that becomes apparent on any of the several trails that wind past rock art sites, ancient fireplaces, and tool remnants. Whether appreciated over the course of a day or an extended trip, Mutawintji's undisturbed beauty will not disappoint those willing to make the journey.

Mutawintji is 130km northeast of Broken Hill. **Mutawintji Heritage Tours** (☎08 8088 7000) runs guided trips through the **Mutawintji Historic Site** Apr.-Nov. (the park can be extremely hot Dec.-Mar.). The tour includes explanations of Aboriginal mythology and visits to rock engravings near a site where initiation and rainmaking ceremonies have been held for thousands of years by Aboriginal tribes. (Tours depart W and Sa at 11am.) Extensive information on the park is available at the **National Parks and Wildlife Service** office in Broken Hill, 183 Argent St. (☎08 8080 3200. Open M-F 8:30am-4:30pm.) The tourist center in Broken Hill has additional information as well.

No fuel or food is available at Mutawintji, and wet weather can strand cars easily: visitors should bring plenty of provisions, regardless of how briefly they plan on staying. Be sure to bring lots of water on any hiking expeditions. **Camping** is available at the **Homestead Creek Camping Ground ❶**, about 1.5km past the visitors center on the right. ($5, children $3; max. 8 people.) Most **hiking trails** begin from the **Homestead Creek Day Area,** about 2km past the visitors center (bearing left at the first fork) and off the main road to the right shortly after the campground. Although most terrain in Mutawintji is fairly rugged, there is one wheelchair-accessible trail, **Thaaklatjika Mingkana Walk** (500m; 30min. round-trip; easy), which provides glimpses of the gorges and red cliffs, and winds past a rock-art site with examples of both Aboriginal and European engraving: look for the Burke and Wills expedition's blue triangle stenciled over an Aboriginal work. For more serious hikers, the **Bynguano Range Walk** (6km; 4-5hr. round-trip; difficult) offers a strenuous but rewarding trip through a large portion of the park. The trail twists through narrow gullies (including one permanently installed 2m rope-abseil), scrambles over rock faces, and passes several isolated pools of water. The high altitude points along the way offer stunning views over the range, down through the gorges, and beyond to the seemingly endless flatlands of the Outback.

BROKEN HILL ☎08

Set at the edge of nowhere, Broken Hill represents the limit of the infinite Outback and the perfect jumping-off point for the road less traveled. Located 1167km west of Sydney, the remote town came into being in 1883 when young Charles Rasp, along with six other surveyors, realized that an odd-looking craggy butte was in fact the biggest lode of silver-lead ore in the entire world. Broken Hill was erected around the misshapen mount almost overnight, and mining promptly began. Today significant resources have been exhausted, and there has been a shift toward the mining of zinc, which is also abundant in the area. The town has also attracted a considerable number of local artists who find inspiration in the ethereal topography. This curious fusion of gritty labor, innovative art, and geographical isolation has made for a truly unusual town.

TRANSPORTATION

Over the last several years, transportation has been reduced in the region. While transcontinental trains chug through on a regular basis, buses and planes are limited. For any additional transportation queries, contact the **visitors center** or visit the helpful **Jetset Broken Hill** at 380 Argent St. (☎8087 8175).

Air: Rex Airlines offers frequent flights from **Adelaide** (1¼hr.; M-F 3 per day, Sa-Su 1 per day; $160) and **Sydney** (2½hr., daily, $221).

Trains: The train station (☎8087 1400; desk open M-F 8am-5pm) is on Crystal St. near the intersection with Chloride St. **Great Southern** (☎13 21 47) runs the famous **Indian-Pacific** train across the nation. Trains to **Sydney** depart every Tu and F at 6:30pm and arrive at 10:15am the next day (1-way $110, students $100). Trains from Sydney arrive in Broken Hill on W and Sa at 2:55pm. Trains heading west to **Perth** and **Adelaide** depart every Th and Su at 8:20am and arrive at 3:05pm in Adelaide ($75, students $40; arrives in Perth approximately 2 days later $360, students $200). **Countrylink's Outback Explorer** (☎13 22 32) trains run daily to **Sydney,** leaving at 3:45am with a 1hr. stop in **Dubbo** where passengers switch to a coach ($133, students $72). On Tu, a direct route departs at 7:45am for the same price. Trains arrive from Sydney daily 10:45pm, Tu 7:10pm.

Buses: The bus depot (☎8087 2735; open M-F 9am-4pm) is just outside the visitors center (where tickets are sold), at the corner of Blende and Bromide St. **Tom Evans Junction Tours** (☎03 5027 4309 or 04 0859 6438) runs coaches between **Broken Hill** and **Mildura** (3½hr.; M, W, F departing at 3:45pm; $60, students $50). **Buses R Us** (☎8262 6900; www.busesrus.com.au) offers service to and from **Adelaide** (7hr.; 1-way $74, round-trip $130, students $57/104). Adelaide to Broken Hill Tu, F, Su; Broken Hill to Adelaide M, W, Sa.

Local Buses: Murton's Citybus runs 4 routes through greater Broken Hill. M-F 8:30am-5pm, Sa only the Southern and Hillside routes. Timetables at the visitors center.

Taxis: Yellow Radio Cabs (☎13 10 08). **Independent Taxis** (☎8087 7744 or 04 1285 8293).

Car Rental: Expect to pay more than $50 per day. Try **Thrifty,** 190 Argent St. (☎8088 1928), **Avis,** 195 Argent St. (☎8087 7532 or 0409 877 021), or **Hertz** (☎8087 2719), at the visitors center.

Bike Rental: The **YHA Tourist Lodge** (☎8088 2086) rents bikes for $15 per day.

PRACTICAL INFORMATION

TIME WARP. Broken Hill uses the **phone code** of South Australia (☎08), and its **time zone,** Central Standard Time (CST), 30min. behind the rest of NSW.

Tourist Office: Broken Hill Visitors Information Centre (☎8087 6077; www.visitbrokenhill.com.au), corner of Blende and Bromide St. From the railway station, turn left onto Crystal St. and walk 2 blocks west, then turn right onto Bromide St.; the office is 2 blocks down on the left. The extremely helpful staff can answer any inquiries and assist with booking a multitude of outback activities. Be sure to pick up Broken Hill's comprehensive visitor's guide as well as the invaluable *Wide Canvas Country* brochure which beautifully depicts the oddities of the region. Open daily 8:30am-5pm.

Tours: A wide variety of tours are available from several tour operators venturing to Silverton, the Living Desert Sculptures, nearby national parks, outback safaris, other mining towns, and stations a bit farther afield. Book through the tourist office.

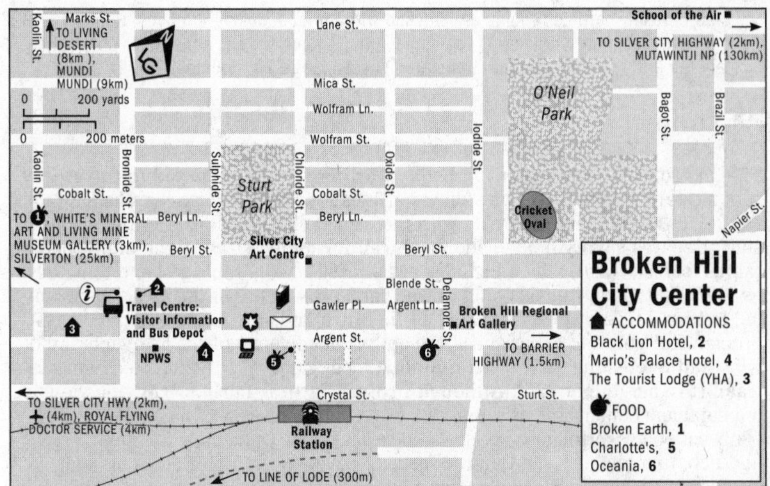

National Parks Information: New South Wales National Parks and Wildlife Service (NPWS), 183 Argent St. (☎8080 3200). Open M-F 8:30am-4:30pm. The visitors center (see above) has considerable information as well.

Banks: ANZ, 357 Argent St. (☎13 13 14), is right next to **Commonwealth,** 338-340 Argent St. (☎13 22 21). Both open M-Th 9:30am-4pm, F 9:30am-5pm. 24hr. **ATMs.**

Police: 252 Argent St. (☎8087 0299).

Internet Access: Free 1hr. access is available at the **Broken Hill Library** (☎8088 3317), on Blende St. Book ahead to avoid waiting for a terminal. Open M-W 10am-8pm, Th-F 10am-6pm, Sa 10am-1pm, Su 1-5pm. **Fully Loaded Computers,** 195 Argent St. (☎8088 4255), has a monopoly on Internet outlets scattered throughout the town including at the visitors center, Centro Westside Shopping Center on Galena St., and the Musician's club on Crystal St. $1 per 10min.

Post Office: 260 Argent St. (☎8087 7071). Open M-F 9am-5pm. *Poste Restante* available; pickup at the window around the side of the building. **Postal Code:** 2880.

ACCOMMODATIONS

NEW SOUTH WALES

Mario's Palace Hotel, 227 Argent St. (☎8088 1699). Even if you decide to stay elsewhere, check out this wildly decorated hotel, covered in imaginative frescoes created by a local Aboriginal artist. The 6-person "Room E" was featured in *Priscilla, Queen of the Desert,* as was the dining room. Free visits to Room E are available if the room is unoccupied. Reception 9am-9pm. Dorms $23; singles $37; ensuite $60; doubles $55/80; Room E $170 ($120 for a couple). ❷

The Tourist Lodge (YHA), 100 Argent St. (☎8088 2086; bhlodge@bigpond.net.au), conveniently located by the bus depot and visitors center. The older facility has a clean kidney-shaped swimming pool, which is a lifesaver in desert summers. Although the cooking facilities are limited, ample common space with TV and a ping-pong table will satisfy backpackers. All rooms have A/C and heat. Dorms $26; singles $34; twins and doubles $50 per person. $4 YHA discount. ❸

Black Lion Inn Hotel, corner of Blende and Bromide St. (☎8087 4801; theblack@westnet.com.au), located across the street from the visitors center and coach terminal.

Clean, freshly carpeted rooms are stocked with antique-looking armoires. Request 1 of the newly renovated rooms. All rooms have A/C, some with TV and fridge. Complimentary tea and coffee. Reception 9am-latenight. Singles $24; doubles $36. ❷

FOOD

The gastronomic assortment in Broken Hill is generally limited to the greasy spoons along Argent St. serving filling portions for reasonable prices. **Charlotte's at the Grand** ❶ is an endearing cafe with the backpacker in mind. The friendly local staff prepares savory homemade meals, all for under $10. Try the unfinishable "Miner's Meal," ($10) which includes eggs, toast, bacon, sausages, and tomatoes. (☎8087 2230. Open 7am-5:30pm.) **Broken Earth** ❹ is on top of the area's main mining lode and offers sweeping views of the town and surrounding terrain. A self-proclaimed "gourmet experience," the aptly named venue offers its own brand of wine and interesting dishes incorporating local game. Try the smoked emu pastrami ($15.50, dinner $27). Although Broken Earth is fairly pricey, the view is unbeatable. (Lunch 11:30am-2pm, dinner 6-10pm.) **Oceania** ❷ has a hot-food bar ($10) with an assortment of Asian fare. (☎8088 4539. Open daily 5-9:30pm, closed mid-Feb. to mid-Mar.) The Centro Westside Plaza, located on Galena St. near the corner of Galena and Blende St., has a huge **Woolworths** supermarket and a **BIG W,** as well. (☎8088 3833. Open daily M-Sa 7am-10pm, Su 10am-4pm.)

SIGHTS

A trip to the visitors center is imperative, as it is an excellent resource for activities within the town and throughout the region. Several self-guided walking tours are available for purchase at the bureau, and most activities can be booked through the center as well. Pick up Broken Hill's comprehensive visitor's guide as well as the excellent *Wide Canvas Country* guide (both free).

DELPRAT'S MINE TOUR. Gain insight into the city's rugged history with a tour of the original Broken Hill Proprietary Mine. The fascinating 2hr. trip is conducted 400m underground. It features demonstrations and an insightful comparison of the mining labor system through time, with former miners as tour guides who candidly recollect past experiences. Closed-toed shoes are strongly recommended. *(The BHP mine site is on Broken Hill. Follow the sealed road off Iodide St. just past the train tracks. ☎8088 1604. Tours M-F 10:30am, Sa 2pm. $40, concessions $36, children $30, families from $105. Book ahead during school holidays and cool-weather months.)*

LIVING DESERT RESERVE. In 1993, the Broken Hill Sculpture Symposium commissioned a group of local and international sculptors to create sandstone works atop a hill. The masterful pieces combine Aboriginal, modern, and international influences, each one blending seamlessly into the surrounding landscape without losing its thematic particularities. They are all best viewed at sunrise and **sunset,** when the light plays on the colors. A 1½hr. walking trail loops from the sculpture site past gullies, ledges, and outback animals. *(From Argent St., turn left onto Bromide, left onto Williams, then right onto Kaolin. Head north 8km along the northern segment of Kaolin St. You can drive all the way up the hill by obtaining a gate key from the tourist office for $6 with a $10 deposit, but the 15min. hike from a nearby carpark is free and more fun.)*

MUNDI MUNDI LOOKOUT. The über-flat terrain viewed from the west-facing lookout offers one of the only places on the planet where you can see the curvature of the earth. Visits at sunset are particularly impressive. Head west towards Silverton and you will pass the lookout about 9km on route.

WHITE'S MINERAL ART AND LIVING MINE MUSEUM. Former miner Bushy White and his wife Betty teach the history of Broken Hill mining through creative dioramas and demonstrations. Over 250 of White's delicate mineral art works use locally mined minerals to depict mining equipment and techniques as well as landscapes and assorted Australiana. Oddly intermixed with the mine exhibits are religious portraits and a collection of over 1000 dolls and teddy bears, making for a whole so deliciously weird it's mesmerizing. The Whites are proud to announce that there is "truly something for everyone" at this museum of sundry knickknacks. *(1 Allendale St., off Brookfield Ave., about 2km west of the CBD. ☎8087 2878. Tours upon request. Open daily 9am-5pm. Wheelchair accessible. $4, families $10.)*

MINER'S MEMORIAL. This rust-colored form sits atop the main lode overlooking the entire town, paying homage to the hundreds of miners who have died from the 1850s to the present. The Miner's Memorial also contains a touchscreen database of fallen miners, and an expensive cafe with panoramic views of the city. The same views are available for free from atop the giant red bench next to the building. *(Miner's Memorial $2.50, concessions $2, under 16 free. Open daily 8:30am-sunset.)*

ROYAL FLYING DOCTOR SERVICE. A museum and inspirational 20min. film detail the history of this noble institution, which provides health care to outback residents living across 90% of the Australian continent. The display is as genuine a display of day-to-day heroism as you'll find in the world of tourism. Guided tours of the facilities, including a peek inside the airplane hangar, are worth the extra time. *(At the Broken Hill Airport. ☎8080 1714 or 8080 1777. Open M-F 9am-5pm, Sa-Su 11am-4pm. 1hr. tour $5.50, concessions $4.40, children $2.20, families $15.)*

SCHOOL OF THE AIR. The School of the Air provides education for schoolchildren in remote regions. Visitors can observe lessons conducted via Internet and satellite from M-F, but must book at the visitors center (p. 252) the day before and be seated by 8:30am—demerits for tardiness. The proceedings give authentic insight into the quirks of bush and outback life. *(On Lane St., 2 blocks east of Iodide St. ☎8087 6077 for booking, or book at the visitors center; www.schoolair-p.schools.nsw.edu.au. 1hr. school sessions $4.40.)*

GALLERIES

With close to 40 art galleries, Broken Hill's reputation is gradually shifting from mining town to artists' enclave. The galleries vary greatly in size and theme; some are privately run workshops, others are larger gatherings of indigenous work from around the country. Don't miss out on the several public buildings throughout the town which feature beautiful murals and are definitely worth a peek.

BROKEN HILL REGIONAL ART GALLERY. This collection's seven galleries constitute the oldest regional gallery in the state, showcasing local and 20th-century Australian painting, sculpture, and photography. The gallery's signature piece, *Silver Tree*, is a delicate arboreal sculpture commissioned for the 1882 Royal Melbourne Colonial Exhibition. *(At Sully's Emporium on Argent St., across from Hungry Jack's. ☎8088 5491. Open M-Sa 10am-5pm, Su 10am-4pm. Donations greatly appreciated.)*

SILVER CITY ART CENTRE. The gimmick here is *The Big Picture*, the largest canvas painting in the Southern Hemisphere. Created by local artist Peter Andrew Anderson, it took over two years to paint. At 100m long and 12m high, the wraparound work depicts the greater Broken Hill Outback. The gallery also includes an active silver workshop. *(☎8088 6166. Gallery free; admission to The Big Picture $4.95.)*

PRO HART GALLERY. A local legend, Pro has been a popular local painter for as long as anyone can remember. *(108 Wyman St. ☎8088 2992. Open M-Sa 10am-5pm.)*

DEIRDRE EDWARDS ART STUDIO. This innovative artist specializes in creations made from galvanized iron. *(34 Williams St. ☎8088 3913. Open M-Sa 10am-5pm.)*

BUSH 'N' BEYOND. Artists Wendy Martin and Ian Lewis share a studio but create different types of pieces using oil, pastel, and watercolor. Their themes include Australian landscape, still life, and wildlife. *(4 Argent St. off of Gossan St. ☎8087 8807. Open M-Sa 10am-5pm, Su 10am-4pm. Donations greatly appreciated.)*

DAYTRIP FROM BROKEN HILL

SILVERTON. Located 25km west of Broken Hill, the eerie and desolate Silverton is less of a ghost town than a cluster of dilapidated cottages. When silver, zinc, and lead ore were discovered nearby in 1876, Silverton burst into existence. After only nine years of mining, the supply was gone. Nearby Broken Hill was just beginning to boom, and many miners picked up their homes and rolled them down the road to the new lode. Today, Silverton is home to a handful of artists, and over a dozen movies have been shot on the bizarre terrain. The **Daydream Mine,** located 13km off the road connecting Silverton with Broken Hill, offers regular 1hr. tours through this antiquated mine. Sturdy footwear is recommended. (☎8088 9700. $15, concessions $14, children $8, families from $38.) Grab a beer at the **Silverton Hotel ❸** and check out a replica of the futuristic car from *Mad Max II*, which was shot in Silverton. The car is parked out front. For those who decide that one afternoon of meandering through rubble is not enough, the hotel offers "Grave Yard" accommodation in four small ensuite cabins each with A/C, fridge, and tea and coffee. Note that the water at the hotel bar is not potable. (☎8088 5313. Linens $5.50. Singles $33; doubles $44. Extra adult $7.70.) The **Silverton Camel Farm,** on the road from Broken Hill, offers rides on the temperamental humped beasts. (☎8088 5316. $15 per 30min., $25 per hr.; 2hr. sunset safari $80.)

MUNGO NATIONAL PARK

From Mildura, 110km of rugged unsealed road terminates at Mungo National Park, where the oldest evidence of human life ever recorded was found between the windy crags of the preserve. Ages before the pyramids at Giza were a twinkle in a pharaoh's eye, hunter-gatherer communities flourished on the banks of Lake Mungo, in the extreme southwest corner of present-day New South Wales. Today, the lake is dry (and has been for 15,000 years) and Mungo has undergone spectacular weathering. Sand dunes around the lake bed have eroded into strange, ethereal landforms, accelerated over the past hundred years by settlers' introduction of grazing sheep and foraging rabbits. From a distance, the grand **Walls of China** look like the crumbling fortifications of an ancient empire. Even today, the white-washed dunes continue to reveal fossils and artifacts, including the oldest male and female bones in the world, dubbed Adam and Eve by locals. They are believed to be over 40,000 years old and recent findings suggest they could be as old as 60,000 years. The archaeological information uncovered here has earned the **Willandra Lakes** area status as a **World Heritage Site.**

Roads to and within Mungo National Park are unsealed and subject to weather conditions; call ahead to the NPWS (☎5021 8900). Warnings should be taken very seriously as wet weather instantly turns the sand tracks into thick gooey mud; visitors are advised to carry their own food, drinking water, and petrol.

The park's infrequently staffed visitors center has pamphlets with info on the park's history, visitor regulations, and the incredible 70km **self-guided drive tour** that allows visitors to see the diverse wonders of the park at their own pace. This is also the place to pay camping and vehicle fees. (Camping $3 per person, children $2. Vehicles $7 per day.) No one is staffed to monitor payment, so please consider the fee a donation to keep up park maintenance. The small museum display in the **visitors center** is worth checking out before rolling on to the self-guided tour. Fossils from Lake Mungo, artifacts and explanations relating to regional Aboriginal culture, a few mock-ups of extinct fauna, and ecological projections give an evocative impression of the life in Mungo over the course of its eons of human habitation.

Camping facilities are available at **Main Camp ❶,** near the park entrance, and at **Belah Camp ❶,** farther into the park on the drive tour. Both sites have toilets and tables, but wood fires are only allowed at Main Camp. Between November and March, however, fires may be banned entirely; check at the visitors center before lighting up. (Both sites $3, children $2.) The **Mungo Lodge ❺,** on the park road just before the park entrance, is the only available accommodation that doesn't require "roughing it." Clean ensuite cabins with heat and A/C are available. (☎5029 7297; www.mungolodge.com.au. Reception 7:30am-8pm. Book ahead. Singles $98; doubles $128-138. Extra person $35.)

NORTHERN TERRITORY

Against the backdrop of a fiery sunset, silver eucalyptus trees contort their limbs into ghost-like curves. Cockatoos squawk noisily from their branches. Sparse foliage and palm trees punctuate the otherwise dry woodland. The thick smoke of bush fires bruises the horizon. A well-worn 4WD rumbles down an endless road, billowing orange-colored dust behind its growling motor. The mud-caked license plate reads "Northern Territory: Outback Australia." Welcome to the Never Never.

From the lush and tropical Top End, where cyclones and floods are of constant concern, to the Red Center's dusty desert expanses, where a drop of rain has everyone talking, the Northern Territory (NT) stretches into the country's most extreme regions. Still, the weather is not nearly as dramatic as the landscapes over which it looms. It is no surprise that people often say the land rules the people in these parts; according to Aboriginal legend, the Earth was sculpted by rainbow serpents, monsters, and blue-tongued lizards.

Only 200,000 people inhabit the Territory's 1.3 million square kilometers, and nearly half live in the city of Darwin. The rest reside in towns like Alice Springs and Katherine. Cattle stations and Aboriginal homelands also comprise small outposts of human life in the immense outback expanses. Traveling through the NT is becoming easier as the infrastructure improves. Kakadu and Litchfield National Park in the Top End, and Uluru and Watarrka in the Red Centre, are accessible once the vast distances between them are overcome. Exploring the NT is certainly more adventurous than participating in the overcrowded beach culture of the east coast, but the far-flung sights require a greater investment of time from those who seek their thrilling rewards.

HIGHLIGHTS OF THE NORTHERN TERRITORY

BOAT past 150m-high Jim Jim Falls, through croc territory, to a white sand beach, complete with emerald plunge pool in Kakadu National Park (p. 269).

VISIT ULURU, a symbol of Oz's natural beauty to which all else is compared (p. 307).

Experience Darwin's creative side at **Mindil Beach Market;** crafts, culture, and delicious food emerge in festive form to greet the Top End twilight (p. 266).

ROCK OUT at the 7m in diameter granite Devil's Marbles, one of nature's most unusual rock formations (p. 294).

TRANSPORTATION

The Northern Territory's vast expanses make transportation a big concern. Darwin, Alice Springs, and Yulara are most commonly reached by air. *The Ghan* (☎13 21 47; www.trainways.com.au) connects Darwin to Adelaide and Melbourne through Katherine and Alice Springs once a week (W 10am). Fares in the Daynighter Class range from $290 to Alice Springs (students $250) up to $525 to Adelaide (students $400). **Greyhound Australia** (☎13 14 99 or 13 20 30) buses service most major tourist centers, but not the farther reaches of the national parks. Rent-

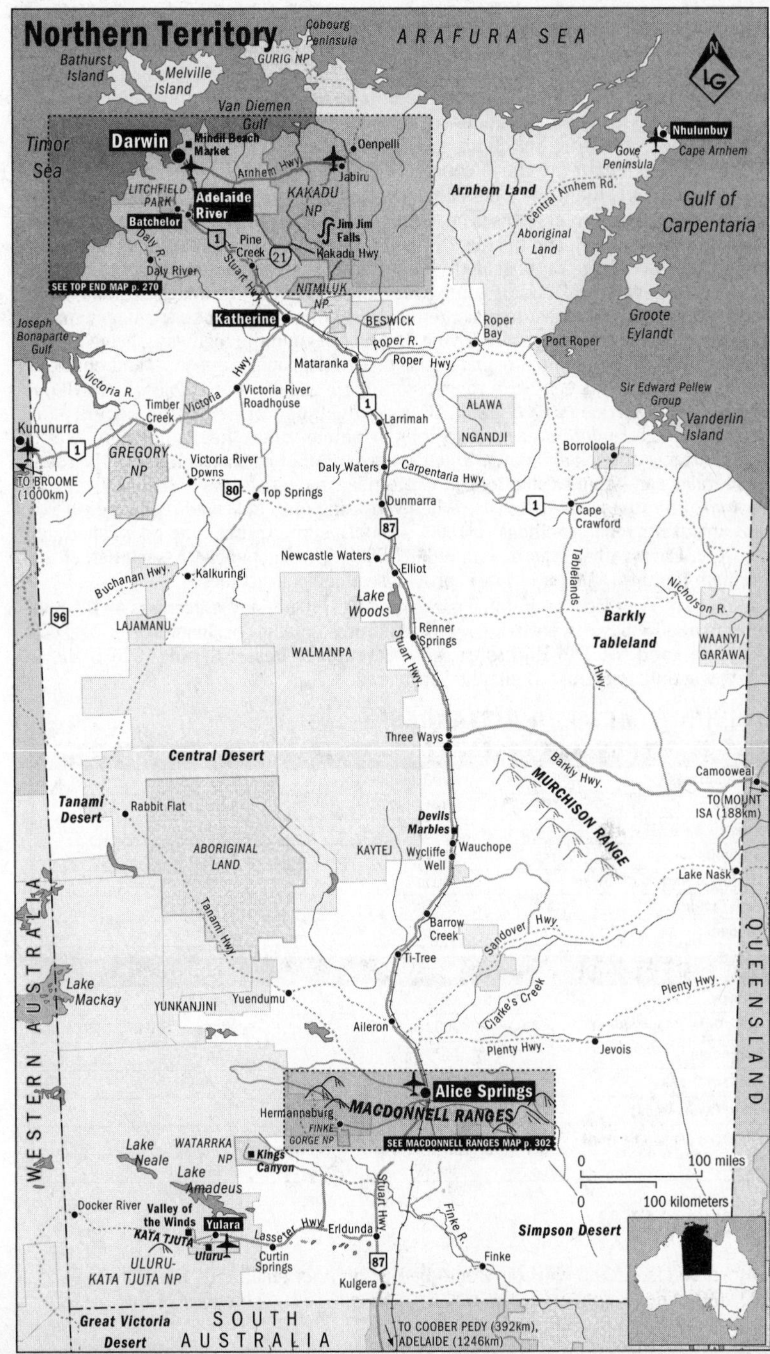
Northern Territory
Cobourg Peninsula
ARAFURA SEA
GURIG NP
Bathurst Island
Melville Island
Van Diemen Gulf
Timor Sea
Darwin
Mindil Beach Market
Oenpelli
Arnhem Hwy.
Jabiru
Nhulunbuy
Gove Peninsula
Cape Arnhem
LITCHFIELD PARK
Adelaide River
KAKADU NP
Arnhem Land
Central Arnhem Rd.
Gulf of Carpentaria
Batchelor
Jim Jim Falls
Aboriginal Land
Daly R.
Pine Creek
Kakadu Hwy.
Stuart Hwy.
Daly River
SEE TOP END MAP p. 270
NITMILUK NP
Katherine
BESWICK
Roper Bay
Port Roper
Groote Eylandt
Joseph Bonaparte Gulf
Roper R.
Mataranka
Roper Hwy.
Victoria R.
Victoria Hwy.
Victoria River Roadhouse
Sir Edward Pellew Group
ALAWA
Timber Creek
Larrimah
NGANDJI
Vanderlin Island
Kununurra
GREGORY NP
Borroloola
Victoria River Downs
Daly Waters
Carpentaria Hwy.
TO BROOME (1000km)
Top Springs
Dunmarra
Cape Crawford
Newcastle Waters
Tablelands
Elliot
Buchanan Hwy.
Kalkuringi
Lake Woods
Nicholson R.
LAJAMANU
Barkly Tableland
Renner Springs
WALMANPA
WAANYI/ GARAWA
Hwy.
Three Ways
Central Desert
Barkly Hwy.
Camooweal
MURCHISON RANGE
TO MOUNT ISA (188km)
Tanami Desert
Rabbit Flat
Devils Marbles
ABORIGINAL LAND
KAYTEJ
Wauchope
Wycliffe Well
Lake Nask
Tanami Hwy.
Barrow Creek
Sandover Hwy.
Ti-Tree
Clarke's Creek
Plenty Hwy.
Lake Mackay
YUNKANJINI
Yuendumu
Aileron
Jevois
Alice Springs
Hermannsburg
MACDONNELL RANGES
FINKE GORGE NP
SEE MACDONNELL RANGES MAP p. 302
Lake Neale
WATARRKA NP
Kings Canyon
0
100 miles
Lake Amadeus
0
100 kilometers
Docker River
Valley of the Winds
Yulara
Lasseter Hwy.
Erldunda
Finke R.
Simpson Desert
KATA TJUTA
Uluru
Curtin Springs
Finke
ULURU-KATA TJUTA NP
Kulgera
WESTERN AUSTRALIA
QUEENSLAND
SOUTH AUSTRALIA
Great Victoria Desert
TO COOBER PEDY (392km), ADELAIDE (1246km)
1
21
80
87
96
LG

ing a car is the best way to see these areas, but it's also the most expensive. Many national chains have offices all over the NT; **Territory-Thrifty Car Rental** (☎1800 891 125) and **Budget** (☎13 27 27) are the cheapest but limit km (100-200km per day, each additional km $0.25-0.32), whereas **Britz** (☎1800 331 454) offers unlimited km and rents 4WD to customers under 25. **Europcar** (☎13 13 90) offers sedans from $58 per day, not including km charges. Each company does one-way rentals, but charges a high fee for the convenience.

Major tourist centers are accessible by sealed or gravel roads. You'll need a 4WD to venture onto dirt tracks; this is necessary to see many of the spectacular sights of Kakadu National Park and the MacDonnell Ranges. Furthermore, rentals are rarely insured for accidents on unsealed roads. Rental companies determine their own restrictions, even for 4WDs. If going to remote areas, ask for a **high-clearance 4WD** with **two petrol tanks.** Also, make sure the 4WD you rent is not so top-heavy that it could flip over in rough terrain driving. If going beyond the highways, bring lots of extra water, food, emergency materials (tire, tools, rope, jack, etc.), and check in with a friend, visitors center, or ranger station. HF radios, compatible with the **Royal Flying Doctor Service** (☎02 8238 3333; www.flyingdoctor.net), offer security for drives through remote areas where cellular phones and other radios don't work. Avoid driving at dusk and dawn, when **kangaroos** and **wild camels** loiter in the road. **Road trains** can be up to 50m long, and often leave dust storms in their wake. *It is dangerous to pass road trains.* When venturing onto unsealed roads, be sure to call ahead for **road conditions** (☎1800 246 199); some tracks may be washed out entirely. For **weather reports,** call ☎8982 3826. The **Automobile Association of the Northern Territory** (**AANT;** ☎13 11 11) provides valuable assistance.

Many 4WD tours cover national parks for $100-140 per day. **Wilderness 4WD Adventures** (☎1800 808 288; www.wildernessadventures.com.au) or **Gondwana** (☎1800 658 378) are good for Top End tours, and **Wayoutback Desert Safaris** (☎8952 4324; www.wayoutback.com.au) hits the Uluru area.

DRIVING TIMES AND DISTANCES

FROM DARWIN TO:	DISTANCE	APPROXIMATE TIME
Alice Springs	1490km	15hr.
Batchelor	98km	1¼hr.
Kakadu National Park	260km	3hr.
Katherine	315km	3½hr.
Litchfield National Park	130km	1½hr.
Pine Creek	226km	2½hr.
Tennant Creek	986km	10hr.

FROM ALICE SPRINGS TO:	DISTANCE	APPROXIMATE TIME
Darwin	1490km	15hr.
Kata Tjuta (Mount Olga)	500km	5¼hr.
Katherine	1177km	12hr.
Tennant Creek	504km	5hr.
Uluru (Ayers Rock)	460km	4¾hr.
Watarrka (King's Canyon)	330km	4hr.
Yulara	444km	4½hr.

DARWIN ☎08

Anywhere else in the world it would be just another small city, but Darwin (pop. 100,000) is not anywhere else—it is the gateway to the splendor of the Top End.

From its incessant sunshine and azure beaches to its thumping nightlife, Darwin offers an escape from the limitless expanse of Outback that surrounds it. Seasons here are divided only into the wet season ("the Wet"; Nov.-Apr.) and the desert-like dry season ("the Dry"; May-Oct.). Tourist traffic peaks in the Dry, when central Darwin is awash in beer, noise, and backpackers. Travelers ensnared by the city's charm (or who spend all of their money on Bundy rum) stick around for the Wet.

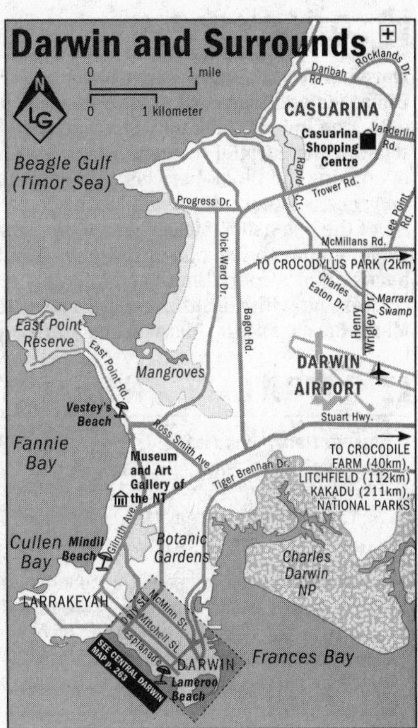

Darwin has not always been the party capital it is today. Two years of intense Japanese bombing reduced the city to rubble during WWII. The city was rebuilt, only to be cruelly decimated a second time by Cyclone Tracey on Christmas Eve, 1974. With true Territorian grit, Darwin started from scratch once again, creating the convenient Central Business District (CBD), manicured parks, and breezy outdoor malls you see today. Modern Darwin can provide whatever you've been missing in the Outback, be it museums, refined cuisine, or a rip-roaring party.

INTERCITY TRANSPORTATION

BY PLANE. **Darwin International Airport** (☎8920 1850) is about 10km northeast of the CBD on McMillans Rd.; from the CBD, take a left on Bagot Rd. off the Stuart Hwy. **Qantas,** 16 Bennett St. (☎13 13 13), **Virgin Blue** (☎13 67 89), and **Jetstar** (☎13 15 38) fly to destinations within Australia. Various airlines offer service to Southeast Asia. Other airline offices include **Royal Brunei Airlines,** 22 Cavenagh St. (☎8941 0966); **Merpati Nusantara,** off Cavenagh St. (☎1800 624 932); and the regional carrier **Airnorth** (☎8945 2866). For transport between the city and the airport, the **Darwin Airport Shuttle** is your best bet. (☎8981 5066 or 1800 358 945. $8, round-trip $16.) Most accommodations will reimburse patrons for the ride. **Taxis** (☎8981 3777) run to the airport for $30.

BY TRAIN. **The Ghan** (☎13 21 47; www.trainways.com.au) runs once a week, departing W at 10am for **Adelaide, Alice Springs, Katherine, Melbourne,** and **Sydney.** One-way "Daynighter" fares range from $69-400 for students and from $80-525 for adults. Sleeper cabins can cost thousands of dollars. Book ahead.

BY BUS. The **Transit Centre** is at 67-69 Mitchell St., between Peel and Nuttall St. (☎8941 0911. Open M-F 6-9am and 10am-1:15pm, Su 6-11am.) **Greyhound Australia** (☎13 14 99 or 13 20 30) runs to: **Adelaide** (39hr., 1 per day, $526); **Alice Springs** (20hr., 1 per day, $278); **Broome** (24hr., 1 per day, $353); **Katherine** (4hr., 2 per day, $76); **Tennant Creek** (12hr., 1 per day, $201). For **Cairns** (41hr., 1 per day), **Melbourne** (51hr., 1 per day) or **Sydney** via **Alice Springs** and **Adelaide** (67hr., 1 per day) it is cheapest to buy a Greyhound pass based on distance that allows for stopovers.

ORIENTATION

Darwin is on a peninsula, with the CBD in the southeast corner. The tree-lined **Esplanade** and the rocky **Lameroo Beach** run along the western edge of the peninsula. The hub of the backpacker district is the Transit Centre on **Mitchell Street,** which runs parallel to the Esplanade. The **Smith Street Mall,** a pedestrian zone occupying the block between Knuckey and Bennett St., is home to many shops and services, and runs parallel to Mitchell St. at the southern end of the city. At the tip of the peninsula, **Stokes Hill** and the **Wharf** area hold several sights.

Moving northeast out of the city, **Daly Street** becomes the **Stuart Highway** and heads to the airport. Smith and Mitchell St. both continue north of the CBD before converging with Gilruth Ave. at **Lambell Terrace,** which leads to the **MGM Casino, Mindil Beach,** and the **Museum and Art Gallery of the Northern Territory.**

LOCAL TRANSPORTATION

Buses: Darwinbus (☎8924 7666) runs to suburbs and beaches along the major thoroughfares. The terminal is between Harry Chan Ave. and Bennett St. just south of the Smith St. Mall. Stops along Mitchell and Cavenagh St. $1.40-2.40. **Tourcards** allow unlimited travel for a day ($5, concessions $2.50) or a week ($25, concessions $13).

Taxis: Darwin Radio Taxis (☎13 10 08). $1.26 per km.

Car Rental: Rental companies abound but demand can outstrip availability in the Dry, so book several weeks ahead. Be sure to ask what roads are prohibited by your agency before setting out; even a 4WD can be banned from specific routes if road conditions are poor. Sedans from $60 per day and small 4WDs from $160 per day, including 100km per day and $0.27 per extra km. Damage liability can usually be reduced for an additional $17-25 per day. Large agencies include: **Avis,** 145 Stuart Hwy. (☎8981 9922); **Budget,** 3 Daly St. (☎8981 9800), at the corner of Doctors Gully Rd.; **Hertz** (☎8941 0944), at the corner of Smith and Daly St.; **Territory Rent-a-Car,** 64 Stuart Hwy. (☎8981 4796). For short distances, **Port** (☎8981 8441), at Fisherman's Wharf, and **Delta Europcar,** 77 Cavenagh St. (☎8941 0300) offer good base rates (from $39 per day) and charge per km, while unlimited km is available at **Britz,** 44-66 Stuart Hwy. (☎8981 2081), and **Advance/Nifty,** 86 Mitchell St. (☎8981 2999 or 1800 811 541). Europcar rents sedans to those over 21, but you must be 25 for a 4WD. The minimum age for rental is 21 at Britz and **Apollo** (☎8981 4796 or 1800 777 779), 75 McMinn St.; the rest usually require renters to be at least 25. Most major chains offer 4WD options, and Britz rents 4WDs with sleeper compartments ideal for long treks into the bush.

Buying and Selling Used Cars: The **Travelers Car Market** (☎0418 600 830), at Peel and Mitchell St., caters to backpackers. Sellers pay $40 per wk. to cram into the lot, but buyers browse for free. Cars sell fastest May-Oct. Open daily 8am-4pm. Also check bulletin boards at hostels and Internet cafes. Registration requirements vary for each state. See **Buying and Selling Used Cars,** p. 32.

Automobile Club: The **Auto Association of the Northern Territory (AANT),** 79-81 Smith St. (☎8981 3837). Open M-F 9am-5pm.

Bike Rental: Available through most hostels ($5 per hr., $20 per day).

PRACTICAL INFORMATION

TOURIST AND FINANCIAL SERVICES

Tourist Office: Tourism Top End (☎8936 2499), at the corner of Mitchell and Knuckey St. Open M-F 8:30am-5pm, Sa-Su 9am-3pm. The main office of the **Parks & Wildlife Com-**

Darwin

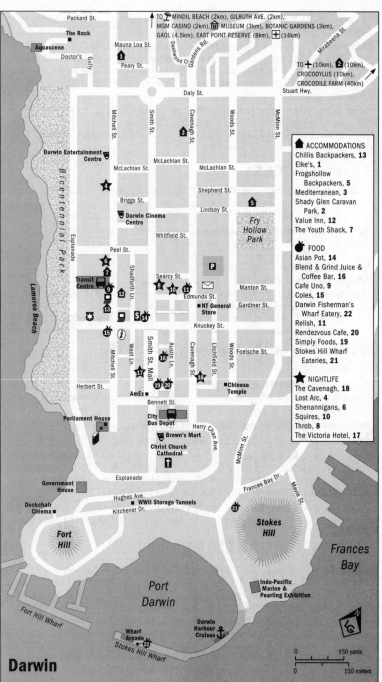

TO MINDIL BEACH (2km), GILRUTH AVE. (2km), MGM CASINO (2km), MUSEUM (3km), BOTANIC GARDENS (3km), GAOL (4.5km), EAST POINT RESERVE (8km), (14km)

TO (10km), 2 (10km), CROCODYLUS (10km), CROCODILE FARM (40km)

Packard St.
The Rock
Aquascene
Doctor's Gully
Mauna Loa St.
Peary St.
Dashwood Cr.
Gardens Rd.
Mirabeena St.
Daly St.
Stuart Hwy.
Mitchell St.
Smith St.
Cavenagh St.
Woods St.
McMinn St.
Darwin Entertainment Centre
McLachlan St.
Bicentennial Park
Shepherd St.
Briggs St.
Lindsay St.
Darwin Cinema Centre
Fry Hollow Park
Whitfield St.
Esplanade
Peel St.
Shadforth Ln.
Searcy St.
Transit Centre
Lameroo Beach
Manton St.
Edmunds St.
NT General Store
Gardiner St.
Knuckey St.
West Ln.
Smith St. Mall
Austin Ln.
Litchfield St.
Foelsche St.
Herbert St.
Chinese Temple
AmEx
Bennett St.
Parliament House
City Bus Depot
Harry Chan Ave.
Brown's Mart
Christ Church Cathedral
McMinn St.
Esplanade
Government House
Hughes Ave.
WWII Storage Tunnels
Frances Bay Dr.
Mavie St.
Deckchair Cinema
Kitchener Dr.
Fort Hill
Stokes Hill
Frances Bay
Port Darwin
Indo-Pacific Marine & Pearling Exhibition
Fort Hill Wharf
Darwin Harbour Cruises
Wharf Arcade
Stokes Hill Wharf

0 150 yards
0 150 meters

ACCOMMODATIONS
Chillis Backpackers, **13**
Elke's, **1**
Frogshollow Backpackers, **5**
Mediterranean, **3**
Shady Glen Caravan Park, **2**
Value Inn, **12**
The Youth Shack, **7**

FOOD
Asian Pot, **14**
Blend & Grind Juice & Coffee Bar, **16**
Cafe Uno, **9**
Coles, **15**
Darwin Fisherman's Wharf Eatery, **22**
Relish, **11**
Rendezvous Cafe, **20**
Simply Foods, **19**
Stokes Hill Wharf Eateries, **21**

NIGHTLIFE
The Cavenagh, **18**
Lost Arc, **4**
Shenannigans, **6**
Squires, **10**
Throb, **8**
The Victoria Hotel, **17**

mission of the Northern Territory (☎8999 4555; www.nt.gov.au/nreta/parks) is in Palmerston, but info can also be found at the tourist office.

Budget Travel: Tours can be booked from many locations on Mitchell St. or the Smith St. Mall. **STA** (☎8941 2955), in the Casuarina shopping center, sells ISIC ($18) and VIP ($34) cards. Open M-Th 9am-5pm, F 9am-6pm, Sa 10am-4pm. **Flight Centre,** 24 Cavenagh St. (☎13 16 00), guarantees to beat any quoted airfare price. Open M-F 8:30am-5pm, Sa 9am-2pm.

Currency Exchange: Bank South Australia, 13 Knuckey St. (☎13 13 76). Open M-Th 9:30am-4pm, F 9:30am-5pm. **Westpac Bank,** at 24 Smith St. in the Smith Street Mall, has an **American Express** agency inside (☎8981 9522 or AmEx ☎1300 139 060). Open M-Th 9:30am-4pm, F 9:30am-5pm.

LOCAL SERVICES

Backpacking Supplies: NT General Store, 42 Cavenagh St. (☎8981 8242), at Edmunds St., has everything you need for the outdoors. Open M-W 8:30am-5:30pm, Th-F 8:30am-6pm, Sa 8:30am-1pm.

Book Exchange: Read Back Book Exchange (☎8981 8885), Star Village off Smith St. Mall. Open M-F 9am-6pm, Sa 9am-4pm, Su 10am-3pm.

MEDIA AND PUBLICATIONS

Newspapers: *NT News* (daily; $1.10); *Darwin Sun* (W).

Entertainment: *The Top End Visitors' Guide* monthly; *Arts Darwin* monthly; Entertainment section of *NT News* (W and F).

Radio: Rock, Triple J 103.3 FM and HOT-100 101.1 FM; News, ABC 105.7 FM.

EMERGENCY AND COMMUNICATIONS

Emergency: ☎000.

Hospital: Darwin Private Hospital (☎8920 6011, after hours 8920 6055) and **Royal Doctors Hospital** (☎8922 8887) are near each other, north of Darwin near Casuarina on Rocklands St.

Police: (☎8922 1503), Mitchell Centre, corner of Mitchell and Knuckey St. 24hr.

Crisis Lines: General ☎1800 019 116; **Sexual Assault** ☎8922 7156.

Internet Access: Northern Territory Library (☎8946 1434), in the Parliament building at the corner of Mitchell and Bennett St. Open M-F 10am-6pm, Sa-Su 1-5pm. Free Internet access, though not intended for long email sessions. Mitchell St. has many Internet cafes. Hostels also offer Internet at competitive rates (from $4 per hr.)

Post Office: General Post Office Darwin, 48 Cavenagh St. (☎13 13 18), at Edmunds St. *Poste Restante* held 30 days. Open M-F 9am-5pm, Sa 9am-12:30pm. **Postal Code:** 0800.

ACCOMMODATIONS

Many of Darwin's hostels and budget accommodations are clumped around the Transit Centre on Mitchell St.; their offerings are pretty standard. High-end, generally overpriced accommodations sit along the Esplanade. For better prices (and nicer facilities), try the spots along Smith and Cavenagh St. Book several days ahead in the Dry; try to bargain in the Wet.

Camping options in central Darwin are limited. Camping or sleeping in cars is strictly forbidden around the Mindil Beach area. The **Shady Glen Caravan Park** ❶ is closest to the city, about 10km from central Darwin at the intersection of the Stuart Hwy. and Farrell Cres. Patrons here are treated to a pool, kitchen, BBQ, and laundry. (☎8984 3330. Sites $12.50 per person, powered for 2 $27.)

The Youth Shack, 69 Mitchell St. (☎1300 792 302), next to the Transit Centre. Sparkling clean and efficient–the most liveable of Darwin's downtown hostels. Independent, international crowd and competent staff. Internet access ($4 per hr.), A/C, pool, kitchen, dining area, sun deck, TV rooms, large lockers, and luggage storage. Key, linen, and cutlery deposit $30. Laundry $3. Reception 24hr. Dorms $24; doubles $56. YHA $2 discount. VIP/YHA/ISIC. ❷

Chillis Backpackers, 69a Mitchell St. (☎9841 9722 or 1800 351 313; www.chillis.com.au). Chill with hip, friendly backpackers in the two jacuzzis. Internet access. Youth Shack pool available. Key, linen, and cutlery deposit $30. Breakfast included. Clean and comfortable 4- and 8-bed dorms $24; doubles $56. VIP/YHA/ISIC. ❷

Elke's, 112 Mitchell St. (☎8981 8399), a 7min. walk from downtown. Caring staff lends a relaxed feel to this beautiful hostel with large outdoor spaces and a pool surrounded by lush greenery. 4-bed dorms $24; twins and doubles $65. YHA. ❷

Frogshollow Backpackers, 27 Lindsay St. (☎8941 2600 or 1800 068 686; www.frogshollow.com.au), 10min. from the Transit Centre. A good walk from the CBD. Exceptional facilities amid palm trees. Internet access $7 per hr. Key, linen, and cutlery deposit $20. Most rooms have A/C. Lockers, luggage storage and safe, pool, spa, laundry, spacious kitchen, and TV room. Breakfast included. Reception 6am-9pm. Dorms $22-26; twins and doubles $54; ensuite $70. VIP/YHA/ISIC $1 discount. ❷

Value Inn, 50 Mitchell St. (☎8981 4733), across from the Transit Centre. The most centrally located motel in Darwin features modest, clean ensuite rooms, all equipped with TV and A/C. Pool. Wheelchair accessible. Book ahead. Reception 10am-9pm. 1- to 3-person rooms in the Dry $99; in the Wet $59. ❺

Mediterranean, 81 Cavenagh St. (☎8981 7771 or 1800 357 760; www.valueinn.com.au). Though not much to look at from the outside, on the inside it offers spacious ensuite rooms with huge sitting area, full kitchen, A/C, and satellite TV. Parking, swimming pool. Wheelchair accessible. Rooms in the Dry $210; in the Wet $110. ❺

FOOD

Darwin has no shortage of places to eat, though good, low-cost options are hard to find. The food stalls inside the **Transit Centre** serve decent food at reasonable prices. The eateries at **Stokes Hill Wharf** serve heaping portions for low prices. You can get anything from pan-Asian food and fish 'n' chips (from $6.50) to crocodile and kangaroo burgers ($6-8.50) and steaks ($10-15). Choose your eatery and take your food out to the picnic tables that overlook the water. **Mindil Beach Market** (see **Sights**) overflows with delicious pan-Asian food ($6-10). The **Parap Market** is smaller, more mellow, and popular with locals. Take bus #4 to Parap Shopping Plaza. (Open Sa 8am-2pm.) The **Victoria Hotel** (see **Nightlife,** p. 268) lures backpackers with heaping plates of food for around $6. Groceries are available at **Coles,** on the corner of Mitchell and Knuckey St. (Open 24hr.) All restaurants listed below accept credit cards.

Asian Pot (☎8941 9833), corner of Smith and Knuckey St., Shop 6 in Arcade. Scrumptious pan-Asian fare. Noodle and rice dishes ($7-11). Open M-Sa 10am-2:30pm. ❶

Rendezvous Cafe, Star Village (☎8981 9231), Smith St. Mall. Tucked into an arcade at the south end of Smith St. One of the city's better Malaysian restaurants. Main courses $10-13. Open M-F 10:30am-2:30pm and Sa 9am-2pm; Th-Sa 5:30-9pm. ❷

Relish, 35 Cavenagh St. (☎8941 1900), across from the general store. The best sandwich joint in town. Devour one of their wild creations or invent your own for $7. Try it toasted on one of their melt-in-your-mouth rolls, on focaccia, or wrapped and ready to go as a snack. Lots of vegetarian options. Open M-F 7:30am-2:30pm. ❶

Cafe Uno, 69 Mitchell St. (☎8942 2500), next to the Transit Centre. Though it serves everything from gourmet pizzas ($15-22) to huge burgers ($10-14), Cafe Uno's specialty is breakfast. Try any of the eggs served with thick-cut toast ($10) while people-watching from the outdoor seating. Open daily 8am-latenight. ❷

Simply Foods (☎8981 4765), Star Village at Smith St. Mall. Perfect for a light salad or sandwich packed with fresh, healthy ingredients ($4-7). Open M-F 9:30am-2:30pm. ❶

Blend and Grind, Shop 4, Anthony Plaza (☎8981 1561), at Smith St. Mall. Fresh squeezed juices (from $4.40) and tempting pies ($3.20), pastries, and other sinful delights baked fresh daily. Open M-Sa 7am-5pm, Su 9am-3pm. ❶

Darwin Fisherman's Wharf Eatery, Frances Bay Dr. (☎8981 1113). On the wharf with all the wholesale seafood vendors, this unassuming eatery serves scrumptiously fresh fish and seafood. Fish 'n' chips (from $7.50). Open M-Tu 8:30am-8pm, W-Sa 8:30am-8:30pm, Su 10:30am-8:30pm. ❶

SIGHTS

For many visitors, Darwin is merely a pit stop for a pint and a party before heading out to the vast natural wonderland beyond. However, the city has some interesting sights of its own. Many are a long walk or moderate bike ride from the CBD. The underutilized bus system (see **Local Transportation,** p. 262) is also an option. The **Tour Tub** rounds up passengers at major accommodations and the corner of Smith and Knuckey St., and takes them to ten popular sights from Stokes Hill Wharf to East Point Reserve, offering discount admissions to many sites. (☎8985 6322. Operates daily 9am-4pm. ½-day pass valid 1-4pm $15; full-day pass $25.)

MINDIL BEACH SUNSET MARKET. This collection of arts, crafts, and food stalls showcases the creativity of Darwin's cosmopolitan populace, too often buried by backpacker-wooing travel agencies and bars downtown. As the sun sets over the waves, musicians entertain the mingling, munching crowds while booths hawk crocodile skulls, saris, and laksa. *(Heading away from the CBD, take Smith St. past Daly St. and turn right onto Gilruth Ave. at the traffic circle. Take the 30min. walk, or catch bus #4 or 6. Open Th 4-10pm and Su 4-9pm.)*

MUSEUM AND ART GALLERY OF THE NORTHERN TERRITORY. An extensive gallery traces the development of Aboriginal art, from some of the earliest known rock paintings in the world to its current kaleidoscope of styles. Pictures and a short film reveal the devastation wreaked on the city by Cyclone Tracey. Neon-lit exhibits investigate the history of natural life in Darwin, from ancestral megafauna to today. Nearby, but less thrilling, is the **Fannie Bay Gaol,** with self-guided tours through the facility that served as Darwin's jail from 1883-1979. *(Museum is along the shore toward Vestey's Beach; turn left on Conacher St. off East Point Rd. Gaol is 1km farther on the right. Wheelchair accessible. ☎8999 8201. Open M-F 9am-5pm, Sa-Su 10am-5pm. Free.)*

MINDIL BEACH AND VESTEY'S BEACH. These prime locales for soaking up rays are north of the city, just off Gilruth Ave. Mindil Beach is on the left behind the casino, and Vestey's Beach is just north of the museum. Box jellyfish warnings (see **Dangerous Animals,** p. 64) apply from October to March, but stings have been recorded all months of the year. Saltwater crocs are also a year-round concern. *(Bus #4 or 6.)*

AQUASCENE. True, $8 may seem a bit steep to feed bread to fish. But the crowds of tourists that line up are seldom disappointed by the throngs of fish that arrive with each high tide. Wade into the teeming waters or watch from the concrete bleachers. *(28 Doctors Gully Rd. North off Daly St. ☎8981 7837; www.aquascene.com.au. Call ahead for the feeding schedule. $8, under 15 $5.)*

PARKS. The area around Darwin is full of tranquil parks. Just north of Daly St., the shaded paths of the **Botanic Gardens** wind through a series of Australian ecosystems: rainforest, mangroves, and dunes. The hearty gardens survived cyclones in 1897, 1937, and 1974. *(Entrances on Geranium St. off the Stuart Hwy. and just past Mindil Beach on the opposite side of Gilruth Ave. Wheelchair accessible. Gates open 7am-7pm.)* The **East Point Reserve,** on the peninsula to the north of Mindil and Vestey's Beach, beckons with picnic areas, plus croc-and-jelly-free swimming in Lake Alexander. Wallabies are often spotted, especially in the evening. *(Access from East Point Rd. 45min. bike ride from city. No bus service.)* Walking trails, picnic areas, and views of Darwin Harbour lie in wait at **Charles Darwin National Park.** *(Bennett St. eastbound becomes Tiger Brennan Dr. Follow for 5km to the park entrance. ☎8947 2305. Open daily 7am-7pm.)*

CROCODYLUS PARK. This research and education center holds lions, rheas, iguanas, and other assorted critters in addition to the featured reptiles. Sure, you might encounter crocs in the wild, but they probably won't let you hold them and pose for a picture. Come during the feedings for real action. *(Take local bus #5, then walk 10min. ☎8922 4500. Open daily 9am-5pm. Feedings and tours 10am, noon, and 2pm. $25, seniors $20, ages 3-15 $12.50. YHA 15% discount.)*

CROCODILE FARM. Somewhat less spectacular than Crocodylus but cheaper, The Crocodile Farm welcomes visitors to the daily 2pm crocodile feeding and Bert, a 5.2m salty who starred in Crocodile Dundee. Be forewarned: admission is cheap because the farm makes most of its money by turning their crocs into boots and purses. *(40km from Darwin on the Stuart Hwy. ☎8988 1491. Open daily 9am-4pm. $10, concessions $8, children $5.50.)*

OTHER MUSEUMS AND EXHIBITS. At the **East Point Military Museum,** photos and a video show the decimation caused by the Japanese bombing of Darwin Harbour in 1942. *(East Point Rd. at East Point Reserve. It's a 7min. drive or 45min. bike ride from the CBD. ☎8981 9702. Open daily 9:30am-5pm. $10, seniors $9, children $5, families $28.)* The **Australian Aviation Heritage Centre's** collection of old aircraft is crowned by an old American B-52 bomber. *(10km from Darwin on the Stuart Hwy., served by bus #8. ☎8947 2145. Open daily 9:30am-5pm. $12, students $7.50, children $7, families $30.)* **Indo-Pacific Marine** features one of three self-sustaining, man-made coral reef systems in the world, with no feeding and no filters. All that has been added in 14 years is rainwater. *(On Stokes Hill Wharf. ☎8999 5573. Open daily 10am-5pm. $16, concessions $14, under 14 $6, families $38. Free talks every 30min.)*

ACTIVITIES. Darwin also offers a selection of gravity-defying adventures. At **The Rock,** on Doctors Gully Rd. next to Aquascene, climbing connoisseurs can tackle a variety of **wall climbs** in the old tanker. (☎8941 0747. Bouldering sessions $11; climbing $25; includes boot and harness rentals.) Go **skydiving** from 10,000 ft. with **Top End Tandem.** (☎04 1719 0140. Tandem $290.) **Parasailing** with **Odyssey Adventures** provides breathtaking aerial views. Sunset flights run from June to September; book ahead. (☎04 1889 1998. Single $65; tandem $60 per person.) **Biking** is a convenient way to explore Darwin. A 45min. bike path extends from Darwin City to East Point Reserve.

ENTERTAINMENT AND FESTIVALS

The **Deckchair Cinema,** on a beautiful spot overlooking the ocean, has a mixed program, ranging from blockbusters to lesser-known arthouse films. Enjoy a beer while sitting on canvas benches under the stars. (In Wharf Precinct below Parliament House, near Fort Hill. ☎8981 0700; www.deckchaircinema.com. Open in the Dry only. Daily 7pm, occasional shows F-Sa 9:30pm. $13, concessions $10.) The **Darwin Entertainment Centre,** 93 Mitchell St., puts on a variety of theatrical productions. Call the box office for same-day 50% discounts and free shows. (☎8981 1222. Open M-F 10am-5:30pm.) **Brown's Mart,** 12 Smith St. (☎8981 5522), near Bennett St., hosts shows in one of Darwin's oldest buildings. The **Botanic Gardens Amphitheatre** has open-air performances in the midst of lush gardens. Risk-lovers can take their chances at the 24hr. **MGM Grand Casino** (☎1800 891 118).

Darwin celebrates the Dry with a number of **festivals.** The **Darwin Beer Can Regatta,** held off Mindil Beach in early August, is about more than just sailing. Teams of devout beer-chuggers use their empties to make vessels and race them across the harbor. Featuring partying and horse races, the **Darwin Cup Carnival,** begins in July and ends with Cup Day in August (around the same time as the Territory's Picnic Day). On the second Sunday in June, the Greek population of Darwin stages the **Glenti Festival.** Held on the Esplanade, it is a musical and culinary celebration of heritage. Late June also brings the annual Gay Pride Week (www.darwinpride.com). **Australian Football League** games occur every weekend in the Dry. Ask the tourist office for a schedule. As the dry season dwindles, Darwin goes for broke with the seventeen-day **Festival of Darwin** in mid-August.

NIGHTLIFE

Central Darwin is alive every night, pulsating with party-starved backpacking refugees from the surrounding Outback. Gender ratios can be rather off, as males flock to Darwin in far greater numbers than females, but everyone seems to have fun. Pubs and clubs advertise aggressively and might even accost you by the hostel pool. Darwin city law requires latenight clubs to charge a cover, but it's generally only a modest sum. Some don't start charging until midnight, making it possible to dodge fees entirely with some planning.

The Victoria Hotel, 27 Smith St. Mall (☎8981 4011). Only place in town guaranteed to see huge parties every night. Sexually charged backpacker bar with inexpensive liquors, brews (beers from $4), and 2 dance floors. Trivia nights provide opportunities to think your way to drunkenness. Cover $10 after 11pm on weekends. Open daily 10am-4am.

Shenannigans, 69 Mitchell St. (☎8981 2100). Loud Irish pub always packed with boisterous patrons. Live music draws locals into a mostly backpacker crowd. M karaoke. Tu trivia night. Happy hour F 4:30-6:30pm. Open M-Sa 10am-2am, Su noon-2am.

Throb, 64 Smith St. (☎8942 3435). Escape Top-20 blues and break it down at one of Darwin's hippest venues. Gay- and lesbian-friendly club not as raunchy as its name suggests; stylish and chill crowd. Pool tables, friendly staff, and by far the best music in town. Drag shows daily at midnight. Cover $5. Open Th-Sa 10pm-4am.

The Cavenagh, 12-16 Cavenagh St. Fewer peanuts and beers, more oysters and wine. This swanky lounge with outdoor bar attracts fashionable locals and tourists. Things get wilder at "the Cav" on Su, with a pool party from 2pm-latenight. Open 24hr.

Lost Arc, 89 Mitchell St. (☎8942 3300). Chill in the packed, but not overcrowded, interior. Open M-Th and Su 4pm-4am, F-Sa 4pm-2am. Next door, the deservedly-hyped **Discovery** showcases talented local DJs and the occasional international superstar. Cover $10. Open F-Sa 9pm-4am.

Squires, 3 Edmund St. (☎8981 9761), off Smith St. Away from the backpacking hordes, locals know the place to go for a no-frills beer and a game of pool. $8 jugs. Happy hour M-F 4-6pm. Open M-Sa 11am-latenight, Su 4pm-latenight.

TOP END

A lush tropical crown atop the vast, arid interior, the winterless Top End enjoys perpetually warm weather. In the Dry, backpack-toting pilgrims descend on Darwin and use this island of civilization as a base to explore the region's prime natural wonders—Kakadu, Litchfield, and Nitmiluk National Parks. The trickle of travelers who brave the Top End during the Wet are rewarded by the region at its most dramatic. Biblical rains flatten the red landscape, followed by outbursts of velvet green vegetation. Eternal summer has its drawbacks, however; be prepared for broiling heat and plagues of mosquitoes.

ARNHEM HIGHWAY: TOP END WETLANDS

Intersecting the Stuart Hwy. 33km southeast of Darwin, the **Arnhem Highway** glides for 120km through the **Adelaide** and **Mary River Wetlands** before hitting **Kakadu National Park.** During the Dry, these wetlands are a lush sanctuary for birds and crocs; during the Wet, much of the area floods. A wide variety of birds frequent the **Fogg Dam Conservation Reserve,** 25km east of the junction of the Stuart and Arnhem Hwy. and 10km north on an access road.

KAKADU NATIONAL PARK

Kakadu is one of Australia's most famous national parks, and with good reason—the density of the natural wonders packed within its borders is awe-inspiring. Its biological diversity alone is astounding: within Kakadu are six distinct ecosystems with 64 mammal, 100 reptile, 200 ant, and 1000 fly species, as well as one-third of all bird species found in Australia. Alongside this natural heterogeneity stands the world's most extensive (and perhaps oldest) rock art galleries, some of which date back tens of thousands of years. Geologically, Kakadu incorporates the four Alligator river systems, the low-lying floodplains of the west, and the proud stone escarpments of the east with their panoramic views and pounding waterfalls. In the Wet, lush greenery covers the park, the sky fills with lightning, and rain soaks the landscape. In the dry season, rainfall ceases almost entirely and what were once lush fields become flat, cracked, cinnamon-colored expanses..

KAKADU AT A GLANCE	
AREA: 19,804 sq. km **FEATURES:** Stone country, floodplains of the Alligator River System, the township of Jabiru. **HIGHLIGHTS:** Jim Jim and Twin Falls, galleries of Aboriginal rock art, sunset lookout points, riverboat cruises, 4WD treks to waterfalls and plunge pools.	**GATEWAYS:** Darwin (p. 260) and Pine Creek (p. 282). **CAMPING:** From free bushcamping to commercial campgrounds. **FEES:** Free entrance. Additional fees are required for river cruises, Jim Jim tours, and Twin Falls tours.

Intertwined with this awe-inspiring landscape is the living legacy of the Aboriginal community that resides in Kakadu. Aboriginal people have inhabited this land for approximately 50,000 years, but today the population has dwindled from the original European estimate of 2000 to a mere 400. The number of clans has likewise decreased from 20 to 12, and of the dozen languages once spoken here, only three remain active. The language of *Gagudju*, no longer spoken in Kakadu, lives on in the park's name. Aboriginal people are active in the management and conservation of the park, and about 40% of the park's employees are of Aboriginal descent. Half of Kakadu is still owned by its traditional Aboriginal owners, who leased their land to the National

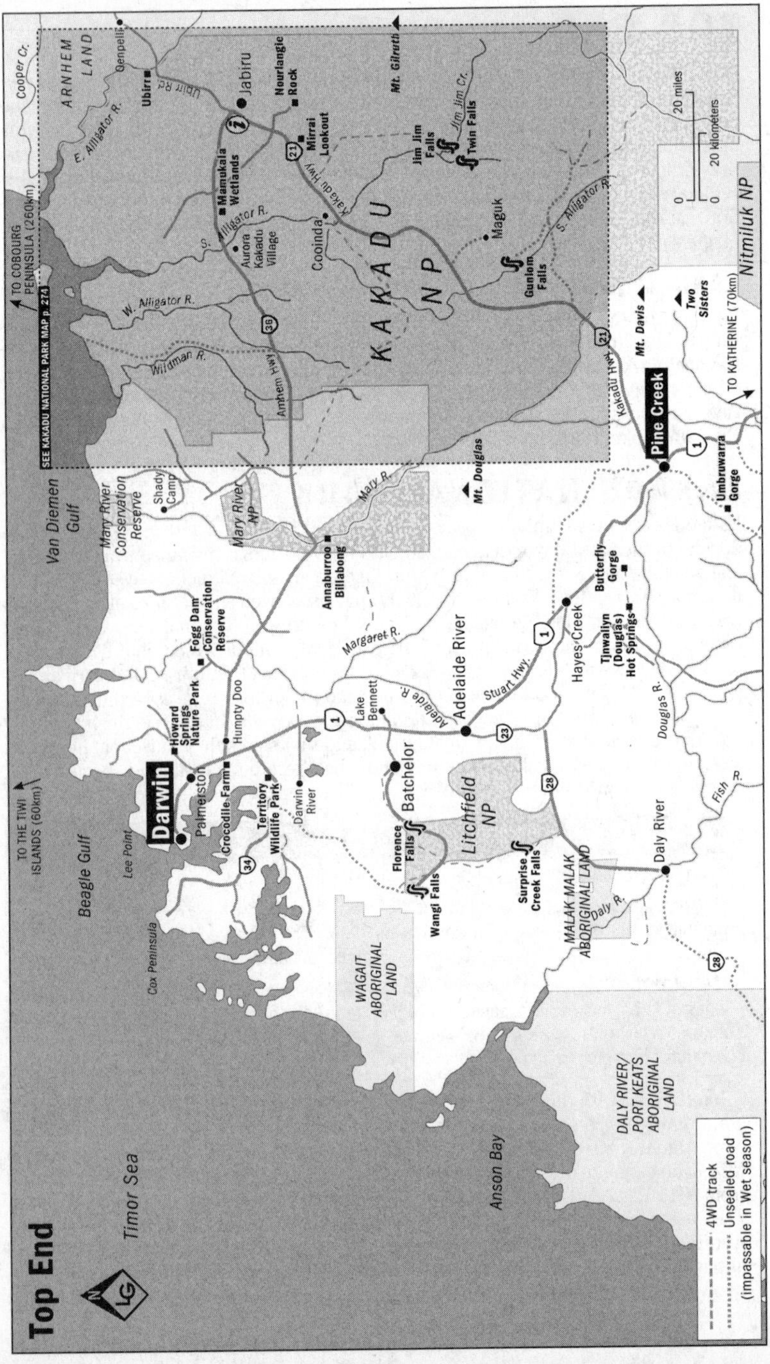

Top End

4WD track
Unsealed road (impassable in Wet season)

0 20 miles
0 20 kilometers

Timor Sea
Anson Bay
Beagle Gulf
Van Diemen Gulf
Cox Peninsula
Lee Point
TO THE TIWI ISLANDS (60km)
Darwin
Palmerston
Howard Springs Nature Park
Humpty Doo
Crocodile Farm
Territory Wildlife Park
Darwin River
Fogg Dam Conservation Reserve
Mary River Conservation Reserve
Shady Camp
Mary River NP
Mary R.
Annaburroo Billabong
Margaret R.
Lake Bennett
Adelaide R.
Adelaide River
Batchelor
Florence Falls
Wangi Falls
Litchfield NP
Surprise Creek Falls
WAGAIT ABORIGINAL LAND
MALAK MALAK ABORIGINAL LAND
Daly R.
Daly River
DALY RIVER/ PORT KEATS ABORIGINAL LAND
Stuart Hwy.
Hayes Creek
Tjuwaliyn (Douglas) Hot Springs
Douglas R.
Fish R.
Butterfly Gorge
Pine Creek
Umbruwarra Gorge
TO KATHERINE (70km)
Mt. Douglas
Mt. Davis
Two Sisters
Nitmiluk NP
SEE KAKADU NATIONAL PARK MAP p. 274
TO COBOURG PENINSULA (260km)
Wildman R.
W. Alligator R.
S. Alligator R.
E. Alligator R.
Arnhem Hwy
Kakadu Hwy
KAKADU NP
Aurora Kakadu Village
Cooinda
Mamukala Wetlands
Jabiru
Nourlangie Rock
Mirrai Lookout
Ubirr
Ubirr Rd
Oenpelli
ARNHEM LAND
Cooper Cr.
Mt. Gilruth
Jim Jim Falls
Jim Jim Cr.
Twin Falls
Maguk
Gunlom Falls

Parks and Wildlife Service in 1978. Cultural sensitivity is a primary goal throughout the park, and the most sacred Aboriginal Dreaming sights remain off-limits to visitors.

Visitors returning to Kakadu may be disappointed to learn that many of its rough edges have been forcibly smoothed, and the formerly untamed wilderness is now firmly in the control of man. Where visitors were once able to perform Crocodile Dundee-esque stunts—scaling gorges, navigating underwater caves, swimming through croc-infested rivers to remote falls, etc.—tours and restricted paths now reign supreme. For this reason, many locals joke that Kakadu is becoming Kakadon't. However, this shouldn't stop you from visiting—the park may not be as wild as it was, but the area is still spectacular

TRANSPORTATION

Armed with *Kakadu National Park Visitor Guide and Map*, you can best see Kakadu in your own car. A 4WD is ideal, as it allows for a more personal, off-the-beaten-path experience. Renting a 4WD, however, is expensive, and rental companies might not allow access to certain sights even if the roads are open; check with them before you book. While ignoring rental rules may be tempting, companies have been known to have people report license numbers of rental cars seen on forbidden roads, so don't do it unless you're willing to risk a huge fine. A 2WD will get you to the top tourist destinations in the dry season, except Jim Jim and Twin Falls, which are prohibited even for 4WD rental vehicles. The only way to see Jim Jim and Twin Falls is on a tour or in a hardcore, non-rental 4WD.

Day tours from Darwin with **Greyhound Australia** can be expanded to three or more days. Conductors double as knowledgeable, witty tour guides, although the visit compresses the sights without exploring the park's more rugged, remote gems. You have the option of connecting with independent tours of the rivers and Jim Jim and Twin Falls. (☎13 14 99. $70 one-way.) Plenty of **tour companies** offer packages, and almost all operate out of Darwin. **Wilderness 4WD Adventures** specializes in tours geared toward fit nature-lovers with biology-savvy guides. (☎1800 808 288. 3- to 5-day tours $450-745.) **Kakadu Dreams** also offers 4WD safaris. (☎1800 813 266. 2- to 5-day safaris $330-680.)

Flights: Jabiru Airport (☎8979 2411), 6.5km east of Jabiru on the Arnhem Hwy., is the base for aerial tours of Kakadu. **Kakadu Air** offers bird's-eye **scenic flights** of Kakadu ($110 per 30min., $185 per hr.). **The Scenic Flight Company** also offers flights at comparable prices ($100 per 30min., $175 per hr.). Flights during the Wet are popular since many roads close. Courtesy shuttles run between the airport and Jabiru.

Car Rental: Rent out of Darwin if you can; options there are considerably cheaper. In Jabiru, **Territory Rent-a-Car** (☎04 1885 8601) has a desk in the Gagudja Croc Hotel on Flinders St. Small sedans from $90 per day with 100km limit.

ORIENTATION

Kakadu National Park is roughly rectangular. The two entries into the park are the **Arnhem Highway** in the north, which runs east-west, and the **Kakadu Highway** in the south, which runs northeast-southwest. These two paved roads converge in the park's northeastern interior near **Jabiru** (JAB-ber-roo; pop. 1100). The roads remain open year-round, except during the most severe floods in the Wet. The park is divided into seven regions. Kakadu's north gate enters into the **South Alligator Region,** which includes the Aurora Kakadu Resort. From here, the Arnhem Hwy. enters the **East Alligator Region** and arrives at **Ubirr Road** leading to Ubirr Rock. The Kakadu Hostel and Border Store are near Ubirr. The **Bowali Visitors Centre** is 5km from Jabiru on the Kakadu Hwy. Running between Jabiru and Kakadu's south entrance, Kakadu Hwy.

provides access to the remaining four regions: **Nourlangie, Yellow Water, Jim Jim and Twin Falls** (4WD accessible only), and **Mary River.** A copy of the invaluable *Kakadu National Park Visitor Guide and Map* is available at the Bowali Visitors Centre and at several stops within and around the park.

WHEN TO GO. Locals say they have a hard time describing wet-season Kakadu to dry-season visitors, and vice versa.

Dry season, from April to October, is the most convenient and comfortable season to visit. Dry season temperatures are moderate (30°C/86°F highs and 17°C/59°F lows), and the humidity is low. It can get cold at night; travelers should carry an extra layer and repellent to ward off mosquitoes. Almost all roads are open except for a few unpaved ones early in the season. Check at the Bowali Visitors Centre for road openings. Most camping, accommodations, and attractions operate during the dry season.

Wet season dramatically alters the landscape of Kakadu with its monsoon rains and floods. Locals insist that the Wet is the most beautiful time of the year as the land teems with foliage and flowers. Still, the humidity, heat (35°C/95°F highs and 25°C/77°F lows), and bugs make the park harder to enjoy. The famous falls, particularly Jim Jim and Twin, are at their most powerful but can only be seen from the air. One bonus is that boat cruises run when Ubirr Rd. becomes a river (see **Sights and Hikes,** p. 276).

PRACTICAL INFORMATION

Tourist Office: The **Bowali Visitors Centre** (☎8938 1120; www.deh.gov.au/parks/kakadu), 2km south of Jabiru on the Kakadu Hwy. A great first stop for all visitors, Bowali provides a thorough overview of the park, multi-day itineraries, maps, free permits for certain walks, and camping and cultural information. Bowali is also the only place in the park with cellular phone reception. During the Dry, rangers give free daily talks and guided walks. Wheelchair accessible. Open daily 8am-5pm.

Tours: See Kakadu (☎8979 3432) on Lakeside Dr. behind the Mobil, and **Kakadu Tours and Travel** (☎8979 2548) at Jabiru Plaza can both book scenic flights, water cruises, and Arnhem Land and Kakadu 4WD tours.

Police and Park Rangers: Jabiru Police, 10 Tasman Cres. (**Emergency** ☎000 or 8979 2122), across the street from Jabiru Plaza at the end of Flinders St. Ranger stations can relay information to the police and clinic from remote areas, but the stations are only open to the public sporadically (daily 8am-4pm, but rangers are often away from the office). Phone numbers are listed under the Parks Australia North entry in the phone book. A better bet is to find the nearest **emergency call box** marked by an ECD pictogram on the free Kakadu Visitor Map. You will be immediately connected with emergency personnel who will be able to help. Boxes are located at the information bay on Arnhem Hwy., 17km from the western boundary of the park; they can also be found at various campgrounds (Waldak Irmbal, Gunlom, and Jarrangbarnmi), and at many of the more remote carparks (Jim Jim Falls, Twin Falls, and Maguk).

Auto Services: Fuel stations are at the Aurora Kakadu Village, Jabiru, Cooinda, the Border Store near Ubirr, and the Mary River Roadhouse at the south entrance. **Jabiru's Mobil Station** (☎8979 2001) has **auto repair.** Open daily 6:30am-8:30pm.

Swimming: The safest places to swim in Kakadu are the lodge pools and the Olympic-size **Jabiru Pool.** (☎8979 2127. Open M, W, F 10am-6pm; Tu, Th, Su noon-6pm; Sa 10am-4pm. $3.) The park watches swimming holes for crocs. Signs at the holes will indicate if the water is safe for swimming.

Banks: Westpac Bank (☎8979 2432), at Jabiru Plaza, has currency exchange and a 24hr. **ATM.** Open M-Th 9:30am-4pm, F 9:30am-5pm.

Internet Access: Library (☎8979 2097), at Jabiru Plaza. $3 per 20min. Open Tu 10:30am-5:30pm, W-F 10:30am-4:30pm, Sa 10:30am-1:30pm. **Gagudju Lodge Cooinda** (p. 273). $2 per 10min. Open 24hr., but sometimes unreliable.

Post Office: (☎8979 2020), at Jabiru Plaza. Open M-F 9am-5pm, Sa 9am-1pm, Su 9am-noon. **Postal Code:** 0886.

KAKADU REGIONS OVERVIEW

REGION	MAJOR SIGHTS	ACCOMMODATION	SERVICES
East Alligator	Ubirr, Guluyambi River Cruise	East Alligator Kakadu Hostel	Food and fuel at the Border Store
Jabiru	Bowali Visitors Centre	Kakadu Lodge and Caravan Park, Lakeview Park	Food and fuel in Jabiru
Jim Jim/Twin Falls	Jim Jim/Twin Falls	Camping	None
Mary River	Gunlom, Barramundi Gorge	Mary River Road House	Food and fuel at Mary River Road House
Nourlangie	Nourlangie rock paintings	Camping	None
South Alligator	Mamukala Wetlands	Aurora Kakadu Resort	Food and fuel at Aurora Kakadu Resort
Yellow River	Gunlom Warradjan Aboriginal Cultural Centre, Yellow Water Cruise	Gagudju Lodge Cooinda (YHA)	Food and fuel at Cooinda

ACCOMMODATIONS AND FOOD

Aside from camping, Kakadu is sorely lacking in budget accommodations. Budget dorms generally leave much to be desired and motel rooms are expensive, though prices generally drop in the Wet. Campsites tend to be situated in attractive spots with well-maintained, convenient facilities. However, sites with facilities are usually crowded in the Dry, and their close proximity to water means they are rife with mosquitoes. Simple camping areas with pit toilets are numerous and less crowded (Jim Jim and Twin Falls are exceptions). Throughout the park, bring your own food and plenty of water.

DRINKING WATER. Clean, safe drinking water is available at Bowali, Jabiru, Cooinda, and Aurora Kakadu Resort. Rangers recommend boiling water from any other source, including the campgrounds listed below.

JABIRU, NOURLANGIE, AND YELLOW WATER REGIONS

The Jabiru, Nourlangie, and Yellow Water regions are just a short drive from each other. **Lakeview Park ❺**, in Jabiru off Lakeside Dr., has rustic "bush bungalows" with canvas roofs, as well as two-bedroom cabins. (☎8979 3144; www.lakeviewkakadu.com.au. Bungalows $85, wet season $70; doubles $110/90; cabins $180/150.) Also in Jabiru, **Kakadu Lodge and Caravan Park ❶** is friendly, well kept, and brimming with comforts such as a pool, A/C, linen, laundry, and a bistro. Occasional slide shows by park rangers are a popular draw. (On the right on Jabiru Dr. before town. ☎8979 2422. Reception 7:30am-7:30pm in the Dry. Sites for 2 $22.50, powered $27.50; dorms $34; lodge rooms for up to 4 $134; ensuite cabins with kitchen for 5 $200.) **Gagudju Lodge Cooinda (YHA) ❷**, down a 5km turn-off in the Yellow Water region, has expensive motel rooms, a campground, and budget rooms. (☎8979 0145. Internet

access $2 per 10min. Sites for 2 $15, powered $35; dorms $34, YHA $27; budget doubles $70/60; motel doubles $250.)

The two standard-fee campsites ($5.40 per person) in the area have good facilities but are plagued by mosquitoes after dark. **Muirella Park Campground ❶,** down a 6km gravel track from the Kakadu Hwy. 30km from Jabiru, is in Nourlangie. **Mardugal Campground ❶** is 2km south of the turn-off for Yellow Water. Here you get shower and toilet facilities, plus some of the best star-gazing in the park. **Free bush camping** is available at **Sandy Billabong ❶,** just 5km of unsealed road past Muirella; **Jim Jim Billabong ❶,** on a 6km 4WD turn-off across from the Yellow Water turn-off; and **Malabanjbanjdju ❶** and **Burdulba ❶,** both around 16km south of the junction of the Arnhem and Kakadu Hwy. The latter two give lovely views of Burdulba Billabong, but flies and mosquitoes can be unbearable at times.

Supplies are available in Jabiru at the Jabiru Plaza. Take a left on Castenzoon St. from Jabiru Dr. The **supermarket** is well stocked but expensive. (Open M-F 9am-5:30pm, Sa 9am-3pm, Su 10am-1pm.) The **Jabiru Cafe ❶,** also in the plaza, has hot dishes for $7.50-22. (☎8979 2570. Open M-F 7am-8pm, Sa 8am-8pm, Su 8:30am-latenight.) Farther south, **Gagudju Lodge Cooinda ❷** has petrol, basic groceries, and filling buffet meals three times a day. (Meals $20. Open daily 6:30am-9pm.) Fuel is also available at Cooinda and various places in Jabiru.

SOUTH ALLIGATOR REGION

The impressive and well-run **Aurora Kakadu Resort ❶,** 40km west of Jabiru and 73km from the Northern Entry Station, has good mattresses, A/C, laundry, and a swimming pool. (☎8979 1666; www.aurora-resorts.com.au. Sites $7.50; dorms $26; budget twins $50; motel singles $80; doubles $198.) Just past the Northern Entry Station, a 4WD track extends north into the park. For 80km it bumps its way to **Van Diemen's Gulf.** Along this road are two free, secluded campsites with refreshingly few campers. **Two Mile Hole ❶** and **Four Mile Hole ❶** are 8km and 38km from the Arnhem Hwy., respectively. They lack facilities but offer peaceful camping along the Wildman River. Be prepared, however, for swarms of mosquitoes. **Food, fuel,** and **beer** can all be found at the Aurora Kakadu Resort.

EAST ALLIGATOR REGION

There are two places to stay in East Alligator, both near Ubirr. The **East Alligator Kakadu Hostel ❷,** run out of the **Border Store,** 3km south of Ubirr and 36km north of Jabiru, is the only hostel in Kakadu, and is a decent option currently undergoing a major face-lift. (☎8979 2474. Call ahead for prices and to check for re-opening.) **Merl Campground** is 4km before Ubirr and has shaded sites. Swarms of mosquitoes, however, make it inhospitable in the Dry. Alternatively, the more varied and cushy accommodations of Jabiru are a short half-hour drive away.

The Border Store has groceries and fuel, although it's only a short drive to Jabiru where there are more supplies and lower prices. Buffalo, beef, or croc burgers ($12) at the store are a good way to inject some protein into your diet.

JIM JIM/TWIN FALLS REGION

Accommodations in this region are limited to a few campsites with well-kept facilities. **Garnamarr campground ❶** is perhaps the best camping spot in the park, with few mosquitoes, a toilet, and views of the looming escarpment. It is located two-thirds of the way on the 4WD track to Jim Jim Falls. **Jim Jim Creek Campground ❶,** at the falls, is brilliantly located but often crowded. There are no services available along the 4WD track to the falls.

MARY RIVER REGION

The only non-camping option in the Mary River region is just outside the park border. The **Wirnwirnmila Mary River Road House ❶** is on the Kakadu Hwy., 11km from the Southern Entry Station. It is fairly priced, uncrowded, and has a pool, bar, and basic grocery store. (☎8975 4564. Reception 7:30am-latenight. Call ahead if arriving late and a staff member will wait for you. Sites $6.50 per person, children free; powered for 2 $17; bunks $17; budget singles $30; twins $40; hotel doubles $90.) For bedding options further afield, **Pine Creek** (p. 282) is 59km south of the park entrance. Along the Kakadu Hwy. lie a few free campsites. **Maguk ❶** and **Gungural ❶** are roughly halfway from the southern entrance to Yellow Water. **Gunlom ❶** is next to the major attraction of the same name. **Yurmikmik ❶,** perhaps the best of the bunch due to its slightly greater distance from water (and hence fewer mosquitoes), is halfway down the track to Gunlom, 24km north of the park's southern entrance. **Fuel, meals,** and **groceries** are available at the roadhouse.

SIGHTS AND HIKES

Don't let Kakadu's subdivisions fool you: the most striking attractions (with the exception of Jim Jim and Twin Falls) are actually relatively close to each other. A route starting at Mamukala in the west and reaching Ubirr, the Bowali Visitors Centre, Nourlangie, and Yellow Water, traverses only 170km, all on sealed roads.

Walks and hikes range in difficulty levels. The main sights can be viewed from short, easy walking trails; a few are wheelchair accessible. The climbs to the lookout points at Ubirr and Nourlangie are steeper. A number of excellent, longer walks reward the fit and adventurous who choose to venture farther into the bush. Recent park restrictions, however, have limited hiking and swimming opportunities, frustrating those who remember the days before permits. Be sure to check with the Bowali Visitors Centre for new closures.

The visitors centers provide detailed information for each walk. For experienced hikers, unmarked **overnight bushwalks** are a great way to see Kakadu without the crowds. These routes generally follow the creek lines and gorges along the escarpment. Routes and campsites on unmarked walks must be approved. For camping permits and route plan approval, contact the Bowali Visitors Centre (p. 272). Permits are free and take five business days to process.

HIKING SAFETY TIPS. Self-sufficiency is the key to a safe adventure in Kakadu, as help and supplies are often hours away.

Bring: Lots of **water** (at least 1L per hr. of walking), insect repellent, sunscreen, and sturdy shoes.

Beware: These areas are full of **snakes** and **spiders;** long trousers and thick socks help protect against bites. **Crocs,** including salties, are also common; keep a generous distance from the edges of bodies of water and don't swim. For more information on dangerous Aussie animals, see p. 64.

Call: Cell phones do not get reception in most of Kakadu. There are **emergency call boxes** at the carparks of some of the more remote hikes, such as Jim Jim. On tours, ask if guides carry emergency equipment like a satellite phone.

SOUTH ALLIGATOR REGION

The squawks and whistles of hundreds of bird species greet you as you walk the 100m **wheelchair-accessible path** to the viewing platform at **Mamukala Wetlands,** on Arnhem Hwy., 29km west of Jabiru. In the Dry, the horizons of the floodplains surrounding Mamukala are thickly clustered with birds, from darting rainbow bee-eaters to plodding Jabiru storks. A 3km walk branches off from the path to wind along the edge of the wetlands.

EAST ALLIGATOR REGION

Although it may be underwhelming to those who have visited Uluru, **Ubirr Rock** is a popular substitute. Here, in the stone country of northeastern Kakadu, hundreds of generations of Aboriginal artists created some of the world's most intricate and extensive rock paintings in one of the Top End's most striking geological regions. A short **wheelchair-accessible circuit** (1km, 30min.) passes the major galleries. Paintings in the natural rock shelters around the sandstone monolith document successful hunts, age-old ceremonies, and creation stories. They include depictions of long-extinct animals as well as more recent images, such as two silhouettes of early bushmen smoking pipes. A short **climb** (250m; 15min.) leads to the top of Ubirr, with a spectacular view of the distant stone escarpment and the emerald floodplains. **Sunsets** on top of Ubirr are magical, but be prepared to share the experience with a crowd of tourists. (Open daily Apr.-Nov. 8:30am-sunset, Dec.-Mar. 2pm-sunset.) Free art site talks are given during the Dry. Consult the *What's On* activity guide from the Bowali Visitors Centre for up-to-date schedules.

The **Guluyambi River Cruise** concentrates on educating guests about Aboriginal life. While drifting by the salties on the banks of the East Alligator River, Aboriginal guides explain local practices and demonstrate the use of traditional tools and preparation of Aboriginal foods. (☎1800 089 113. 1¾hr. Departs daily Apr.-Nov. 9, 11am, 1, and 3pm. Call for schedules Dec.-May. $40, children $20.) The **Bardedjilidji Sandstone Walk** (2.5km, 40min.) highlights the intriguing weathered sandstone pillars, arches, and caves of the stone country. The trailhead is near the upstream boat ramp on a turn-off 1km south of the Border Store. The flat **Manngarre Monsoon Rainforest Walk** (1.5km, 30min.) ambles through a lush rainforest on a flat and easy trail to a viewing platform. The beautiful, tropical walk features occasional croc sightings along the East Alligator River.

JABIRU REGION

Jabiru's most useful site is the **Bowali Visitors Centre** (p. 272), which provides an overview of the biology, geology, and cultural traditions of the park. A 25min. nature film follows the region's wildlife through its annual cycle (every hr. on the ½hr.). A nine-screen slide show with soundtrack shows hundreds of colorful photographs of the park, progressing from the Wet through the dry (every hr. on the hr.). The **Iligadjarr Walk** (3.8km, 2hr.) leaves from the Burdulba or Malabanjbanjdju campsites, crosses floodplains, and skirts the edge of Burdulba Billabong.

NOURLANGIE REGION

The principal draw of this part of the park is **Nourlangie** itself, a huge rock outcropping used as a shelter and art studio by early Aborigines. A winding **wheelchair-accessible track** (1.5km, 1hr.) connects the major art sites. Among the most engaging are the **Main Gallery,** with an extensive collection of layered work, and the **Anbangbang Rock Shelter,** a shady overhang beneath a large boulder that has been frequented by indigenous people since at least the last ice age. On the walls are the images of many spirits, including that of *Nalbulwinj-bulwinj,* who eats females after striking them with a yam. The farthest point on the loop is **Gunwarrdehwarrde Lookout,** a craggy climb to a view of the escarpment, where Lightning Man *Namarrgon* is said to live. Free talks are given during the Dry. Consult the *What's On* guide from the Bowali Visitors Centre for schedule information.

The stunning **Barrk Sandstone Bushwalk** (12km, 4-5hr.), one of the longest and most dramatic established trails in the park, branches off from the walk around Nourlangie. Strictly for the fit and sure-footed, it heads straight up Nourlangie's steep sides to spine-tingling vistas of the surrounding region. Along the way back you'll pass the **Nanguluwur Art Gallery.** Some of the shorter walks in the region offer views of Nourlangie from afar. The **Nawurlandja Lookout** (600m, 20min.) and **Mirrai Lookout** (1.8km, 30min.) are short, steep climbs with stunning views. The **Anbangbang Billabong** track (2.5km, 30min.; accessible only in the Dry) is easy and popular, circling lily-filled waters alongside jagged cliffs. The **Gubara Pools** are a good place to spend your time during the hottest hours of the day. One of the most accessible swimming-safe areas in the park, these cool pools can revitalize even the weariest hiker. Don't miss the second pool and small waterfall that lie around the corner from the first. (6km round-trip walk off a 9km unsealed road.)

JIM JIM/TWIN FALLS REGION

The opening day of the 4WD-only access road (usually in early June) is eagerly awaited by tourists and tour guides, but is frustratingly uncertain. **Jim Jim** and Twin Falls are far and away the most breathtaking attractions in Kakadu. Located at the

OF NO FIXED ABODE

When I found out that I would be researching one of the roughest areas of the Outback I was thrilled and nervous. Everyone told me that I was headed to a place ruled by the deadliest snakes, spiders, and salties. I was a little unsure of my abilities to survive in such extreme conditions, but after a few days on the road, I met some Aussies who assuaged my fears.

A few days into my route, I rolled up to a serene spot and met some local couples. Seeing that I looked exhausted, they invited me over to the fire and offered me a glass of wine. We spent the night sharing stories and gawking at the spectacular scenery, and the next morning, one of them handed me their card. On it was written their VKS Radio Network callsign and address: Of no fixed abode. Explorers of the Outback.

As I read the card, it hit me. Things are different out here: isolated yes, but lonely no. In the Outback, a car may only pass once every hour, but the driver always waves and smiles. If you are ever in trouble, the first person to see you (and the next ten after that) is sure to smile and offer help. We are all in it together and without each other, we would never discover the most isolated features (or survive them for that matter). The only rule: smile, wave, and make sure you share your good fortune.

—Bryce Haac

top of a tough 60km road, Jim Jim Falls cascades 150m down into a deep, clear green pool. In the Wet, the falls rush with roaring intensity, yet the same rain that causes the awesome spectacle also prevents road access to it; the only way to see the falls during this time is by air. There is a **lookout** 200m from the carpark. To get to the falls, first take a brief boat ride (every 15min., free) up the croc-filled river to a walking path. A boulder-laden **walk** (1km, 30min.) leads to the deep plunge pool, which remains quite cold for much of the Dry due to a lack of direct sunlight. Next to the plunge pool is a spectacular beach. The stunning **Barrk Marlam walk** (3km, 4hr.) branches off the path at the lookout, allowing experienced hikers to climb the escarpment and enjoy expansive views of the gorge.

The long journey to **Twin Falls** begins at the Jim Jim Campground. The first challenge is a formidable river crossing, for which a good 4WD with a snorkel system is needed. A 10km rumble through the woods ends at the trailhead; an easy 400m stretch leads to a sandy beach. The double falls cascade over sandstone steps to a plunge pool. Although the water is clean, swimming is prohibited. For the 4WD-less, a few tour companies depart daily from both Jabiru and Cooinda. Try **Top End Explorer Tours** (☎8979 3615; $149, children $119; YHA discount) or **Kakadu Gorge and Waterfall Tours** (☎8979 0145; $145, children $120).

YELLOW WATER REGION

Yellow Water, part of Jim Jim Creek, teems with bird life salties. There are two ways to view the area. A **wheelchair-accessible path,** leaving from the Yellow Water carpark, leads to a platform with wetland views. The area is difficult to access on foot but is easily seen by boat. Try **Yellow Water Cruises.** (☎8979 0145. Book at the Gagudju Lodge Cooinda. 1½hr. cruises leave 11:30am, 1:15, 2:45pm in the Dry; 8:30, 11:45am, 1:30, 3:30pm in the Wet; $33. 2hr. cruises leave 6:45, 9am, 4:30pm in the Dry; $40.)

The **Warrandjan Aboriginal Cultural Centre,** 1km from the Gagudju Lodge Cooinda, is also a worthwhile stopover. The exhibits show the complexity of Aboriginal culture and do a good job of placing into context the otherwise disjointed bits of information found throughout the park. Built in the shape of a *warradjan* (turtle), the center contains wonderful displays on hunting techniques, Aboriginal arts, and the struggle to keep the culture alive. (☎8979 0051. Open daily 9am-5pm. Free.)

A pair of easy walks depart the Mardugal campground. The **Gun-garden walk** is a 2km circuit through woodlands, while the **Mardugal Billabong walk** is a 1km stroll past the billabong with good bird-watching.

MARY RIVER REGION

Mary River, the region most recently incorporated into Kakadu National Park, lies in the far southwest corner of Kakadu, just inside the Southern Entry Station. Mary River boasts a collection of enjoyable walks as well as peaceful Gunlom, the only 2WD-accessible escarpment waterfall in the entire park. For those with a limited amount of time in the park, Mary River often gets short shrift—it is far from the major sights of the north and its attractions take a bit more effort to access.

Popular **Gunlom Falls** is the biggest draw in the Mary River region. A short **wheel-chair-accessible path** leads to a plunge pool surrounded by rocky walls situated just beneath the falls. A steep **trail** (1km, 30min.) travels to the top of the falls and has beautiful views of the surrounding area.

The secondary sights in the region provide greater challenges for cars and legs alike. **Maguk,** or **Barramundi Falls,** is a smaller cascade; the 4WD turn-off is 32km north of the Gunlom turn-off on the Kakadu Hwy. The falls are reached via 12km road and then a rocky **hike** (2km, 1hr.) through monsoon forest. Some hike to the top of the falls and swim in the beautiful waters there. The **Yurmikmik Walking Tracks** pass wet-season waterfalls. The trailhead is 21km down Gunlom Rd. off the Kakadu Hwy. There are three different circular tracks (2km, 45min.; 5km, 2hr.; 7.5km, 4hr.) and two longer tracks that require overnight permits; the 11km walk features a series of waterfalls, and the 13.5km walk has plunge pools during the Wet. Both of these longer walks are difficult, unmarked, and require good navigation and preparation. Near the Yurmikmik walks is **Jarrangbarnmi,** one of the *djang andjamun* areas that represent sacred spiritual sites to Aboriginal groups. The series of pools on **Koolpin Creek** is home to *Bula* and *Bolung*, two creation ancestors. Visitor numbers are restricted, and no one can enter the area without a permit and entry key organized by the Southern Entry Station (☎8975 4859).

LITCHFIELD NATIONAL PARK

At Litchfield National Park, dusty roads wind through lush forests and massive termite mounds. A series of generally tame walks yields stunning vistas en route to inviting pools tucked into the bases of tumbling, roaring waterfalls. While its proximity to Darwin makes solitude hard to find at the major sights, visiting Litchfield with a 4WD and staying for more than a day allow you to escape the crowds and explore the park's wonders on your own. Even without a 4WD, many of the park's highlights are accessible, making Litchfield a rewarding daytrip from Darwin.

LITCHFIELD NATIONAL PARK AT A GLANCE

AREA: 1460 sq. km

CLIMATE: Monsoonal, with distinct wet (Nov.-Apr.) and dry (May-Oct.) seasons.

HIGHLIGHTS: Spectacular waterfalls, tranquil walks, 4WD tracks, and towering termite mounds.

GATEWAYS: Batchelor, Darwin (p. 260).

CAMPING: Buley Rockhole, Florence Falls, Surprise Creek Falls, Tjaynera (Sandy Creek) Falls (4WD only), Wangi Falls, and Walker Creek.

FEES: None.

ORIENTATION AND PRACTICAL INFORMATION

The park, 118km southwest of Darwin, is accessed by two routes. About 90km down the Stuart Hwy., **Litchfield Park Road** juts west, passing through Batchelor on its way to the eastern border of the park. On the other side of the park, it connects to an unsealed road that leads back to Darwin (115km). Most sights lie along Litchfield Park Rd. **Tjaynera Falls** and **Surprise Creek** are on a 4WD track just west of

Greenant Creek. Litchfield Park Rd. is generally open to all vehicles in all seasons, while the 4WD tracks close in the Wet.

There is no ranger station, but information is available through the **Parks and Wildlife Commission of the Northern Territory** (☎8999 5511) in Darwin, and detailed maps are available for free at the **Batchelor Store** (☎8976 0045), 20km from the park, and at the **information hut** across the street. Park entry is **free.** Tours from Darwin to the park abound. Run by **Greyhound Australia,** the cheapest is a bus daytrip to the major sites accessible by sealed roads. (☎8941 5872. $75.) **Darwin Day Tours** runs similar tours. (☎8924 1124. $149, children $87; lunch included.) Most companies charge $80-150 for day tours. Call ☎8976 0282 for **road conditions,** especially during the Wet. **Petrol** is available at the Batchelor Store. The nearest **post office** is in Batchelor. (☎8976 0020. Open M-F 9am-5pm, Sa 9am-1:30pm.)

ACCOMMODATIONS AND CAMPING

Spending a night in Litchfield is highly recommended, if only for the superb stargazing. Try the **Butterfly Farm ❷** with Balinese decor and a relaxing atmosphere. (☎8976 0199; www.butterflyfarm.net. Dorms $25; 3-person rooms $75; 4-person king room $85.) **Camping ❶** in the park generally costs $6.60 for unpowered sites with showers and toilets. Payment is made at drop boxes upon entering the campsites. The **Wangi Falls** campground fills up early in the day and can be uncomfortably crowded; more serene options lie near **Florence Falls** and **Buley Rockhole.** Visitors with a 4WD have more choices at Florence Falls and **Tjaynera (Sandy Creek) Falls. Surprise Creek Falls** and **Walker Creek** have toilets and are half the cost. Be prepared for ravenous swarms of mosquitoes. Caravan camping is allowed only at Wangi Falls and Surprise Creek, and generators are not permitted anywhere.

Litchfield Tourist & Van Park ❶ is 4km from the park border, on the way from Litchfield to fishing spots on the Finnis River. (☎8976 0070. Sites for 2 $16, powered $22; families $22/29; 2-person cabins $60.) Just down the road is the family-run **Banyan Tree Caravan Park ❶,** with phones and power. (☎8976 0330; www.banyantree.com.au. Sites $8.50, powered sites for 2 $22.) The well-manicured **Rum Jungle Bungalows ❺,** next door to the Butterfly Farm in Batchelor (☎8976 0555; bungalows for 2 $120, extra person $10) is a more upscale option.

FOOD

There is a food kiosk at **Wangi Falls.** (Open daily 9am-5pm.) In Batchelor, the **Butterfly Cafe Restaurant ❶** has hearty home-cooked meals; check out the **Bird and Butterfly Sanctuary** on the premises. (☎8976 0199. Cafe open daily 7am-8:30pm. Sanctuary open daily 9am-4:30pm. $8, children $3.50.) Basic **groceries** and liquid propane fuel for stoves are available at the **Batchelor Store.** (☎8976 0045. Open M-F 7am-6pm, Sa-Su 7am-5pm.)

SIGHTS AND ACTIVITIES

FLORENCE FALLS. The most impressive falls in the park are reached by a 15min. walk along the creek. Even in the Dry, copious amounts of water tumble 100m into a clear, calm pool. Nearby **Buley Rockhole** is a series of small but deep pools perfect for quick dips. A 3km drive or walk through verdant monsoon forest connects the two sights.

SURPRISE CREEK FALLS. Twenty kilometers farther along the Tjaynera track from the Sandy Creek Falls, a series of pools connected by attractive falls create a refreshing oasis. A pond and two small bowl-shaped pools make for peaceful swimming; thrill-seekers often jump from the top pool into the bottom. The typically deserted falls are one of the best secrets in the Top End.

WANGI FALLS. Converging streams cascade into a pool of clear water at the bottom of Wangi (WONG-gye) Falls. Come early to avoid the throng of tourists. Snorkeling and swimming are relatively safe, but heed the warning and closure signs—salties sometimes like to swim here too. A walking trail (1.6km loop, 45min.) passes through the forest atop Wangi, but affords no view of the falls themselves.

TOLMER FALLS. Only a short distance southwest from Florence Falls on the main road, a mild 1.5km walking loop winds past a natural stone arch and a lookout deck with a view of the falls and a peaceful creek. Swimming is prohibited to protect the fragile ecosystem, home to several species of bats.

MAGNETIC TERMITE MOUNDS. Throughout Litchfield, majestic termite mounds approaching 7m in height dominate the flat, open landscape. They are the handywork of two species of termites; cathedral termites build towering conical mounds, while magnetic termites construct flat, gravestone-like homes. The magnetic mounds are all aligned with their broad faces pointing east and west for temperature regulation—they soak up the softer light of morning and evening while escaping the harsh midday glare. Information boards explaining termite life can be found at the Magnetic Termite Mounds site near the eastern edge of the park. Several mounds can also be viewed on the 4WD track to Surprise Creek.

LOST CITY. A 10km 4WD track leads to this collection of eroded rock outcroppings. A maze of short trails winds among the twists and turns, arches, and turrets of the formations, allowing for endless exploration. In the early morning, a shroud of hazy mist heightens the towers' veil of mystery.

TJAYNERA FALLS (SANDY CREEK FALLS). About 7km off Litchfield Park Rd. on a 4WD track, a mild 1.7km path leads to tranquil falls. The falls and surrounding area are beautiful, and offer welcome solitude after the crowds of Wangi Falls.

STUART HIGHWAY: DARWIN TO KATHERINE

The lonely Stuart Hwy. connects Darwin to Adelaide, slicing the continent down the middle. The first stretch runs 314km from Darwin to Katherine with several diversions along the way. About 35km south of Darwin, **Cox Peninsula Road** runs 11km west to **Territory Wildlife Park.** A nocturnal wildlife house, reptile pavilion, and a number of pens feature a wide range of native fauna. The Birds of Prey presentation and enclosed tunnel aquarium are highlights. (☎8988 7200. Open daily 8:30am-6pm, last entry 4pm. $20, students and concessions $14, families $35.) **Darwin Day Tours** runs a half-day tour to the park. (☎8924 1124. Daily 7:30am-1:30pm. $64, children $32; includes entrance fee.) **Berry Springs,** next to the Wildlife Park, makes for a great stop. Watch the steam rise from these dolomite hot springs as you get a massage from the small waterfall in the first pool. (Open 9am-6pm. Free.)

Eighty kilometers south of Darwin, and 7km down an access road, lies **Lake Bennett Resort ❶**, an upscale lodge with budget accommodations next to a tranquil lake. Swim, canoe ($13.20 per hr., $44 per day), fish, or play golf before watching the sunset. Guest rooms include fridge, A/C, and TV, with shared bath and kitchen facilities. The staff will meet bus travelers at the Stuart Hwy. (☎8976 0960; www.lakebennettwildernessresort.com.au. Sites $10 per person, powered $25; dorms $25; twins $170; triples $195.) The turn-off for **Batchelor** and **Litchfield National Park** (p. 279) is 6km south of the resort.

Adelaide River is the next town where you can re-fuel, and it boasts more than a small BP station. The **Adelaide River Inn Pub** behind the BP serves heaping plates of "the original and the best" Barri 'n' Chips in all of Australia. (☎8976 7047. Battered or breaded $16.50, grilled $19.50.) Between the fuel stations at Adelaide River and Hayes Creek, and 200km from Darwin, **Tjuwaliyn (Douglas) Hot Springs** is a worthwhile stop. The last 7km of the access road is gravel, but is tame enough for all cars in the Dry. At some places, the springs are extremely hot; head downstream for cooler currents. **Camping ❶** is available ($4.50, children $2, families $10). **Pine Creek** is the final stop on the route, 50km north of Katherine.

PINE CREEK ☎08

Tiny, friendly Pine Creek (pop. 650) slumbers at the junction of the Stuart and Kakadu Hwy., offering a few places to stay and a decent pub. Next to the pub is **Ah Toys,** the general store that doubles as a **bus depot.** (☎8976 1202. Open M-F 9am-5pm, Sa 9am-12:30pm.) **Greyhound Australia** runs to Darwin (3hr., 2 per day, $62) and Katherine (1hr., 2 per day, $40). Around the corner, **Mayse's Cafe ❶** serves good meals for $6-10 and pizzas for $12-18. (☎8976 1241. Open daily 7am-3pm.) Next door, the **Pine Creek Hotel ❺,** 40 Moule St. has nice motel-style rooms. Their **restaurant ❷** serves counter meals for $12-38. (☎8976 1288. Singles $71.50; doubles $88.) The **Pine Creek Service Station ❶** across the street has very basic, but cheap accommodations. They also occasionally cook up value meals for guests. (☎8976 1217. Sites for 2 $10, powered $16; singles $25; doubles $40. Extra person $5.) The casual and congenial **Kakadu Gateway Caravan Park ❶** has a range of accommodations, as well as a BBQ, kitchen, TV room, and laundry. (☎8976 1166. Book sites at Ah Toys. Sites $8 per person; ensuite powered sites $15 per person; singles $25; budget doubles $44; doubles and twins $55; family rooms $75.) About 20km south of town on the Stuart Hwy., a turn-off leads to **Umbrawarra Gorge.** A fairly easy walk (1km, 30min.) leads to the river at the foot of the gorge. From here, it's possible to explore the length of the riverside track. Around the corner from the bus depot on Moule St., the **post office** doubles as a **bank.** (☎8976 1220. Open M-F 9am-1pm.)

KATHERINE ☎08

The only stoplight along the 1500km of the Stuart Hwy. between Darwin and Alice Springs is in the rough-and-tumble town of Katherine (pop. 9000), gateway to Nitmiluk National Park (p. 284). The town is rowdy; noisy, drunken conflict along the main streets is not unusual. However, groceries in town are just as cheap as in Darwin, and Katherine might just boast the last reasonably priced pharmacy, travel agent, book store, or cinema you'll find for a long while.

TRANSPORTATION

The **Transit Centre** is on the southern end of Katherine Terr. near **Lindsay Street. Woolworth's** Plaza is on the corner of Lindsay St. and Katherine Terr. and includes a **pharmacy. Greyhound Australia buses** (☎1800 089 103) stop at the Transit Centre on Katherine Terr. and run to: Alice Springs (15hr., 1 per day, $214), Broome (19hr., 1 per day, $276), Darwin (4hr., 2 per day, $73), and Townsville (30hr., 1 per day, $390). Local car rental agencies include **Thrifty,** 6 Katherine Terr. (☎1800 891 125), in the Transit Centre, and **Hertz,** 392 Katherine Terr. (☎8971 1111), which has 4WDs.

ORIENTATION AND PRACTICAL INFORMATION

Katherine marks the intersection of three main roads. The **Stuart Highway** becomes **Katherine Terrace** in town; most shops and services are found here. The **Victoria Highway** leaves from the northern side of town, passing the hot springs and heading toward the Kimberley region. Finally, **Giles Street** heads east from the middle of town toward **Nitmiluk National Park** (29km).

Tourist Office: Katherine Region Tourist Association (☎8972 2650), on the corner of Lindsay St. and Katherine Terr., across from the Transit Centre. Open Apr.-Oct. M-F 8:30am-5pm, Sa-Su 8:30am-4pm; Nov.-Mar. M-F 8:30am-5pm.

Bank: Several **banks** and 24hr. **ATMs** on Katherine Terr. All open M-Th 9:30am-4pm, F 9:30am-5pm.

Work Opportunities: Working at a hostel in exchange for accommodation is a popular option in Katherine; call ahead for availability. **Grunt Labour Services** (☎1300 881 988), produces the *Harvest Workers Guide* and can connect you with local mango farms during picking season (Sept.-Nov.).

Police: (☎8972 0111) 2.5km south of town on the Stuart Hwy.

Internet Access: Katherine Library, on Katherine Terr. across the street from Woolworths, has the best connection. $4 per 30min. CD burning. Open Tu 8:30am-5pm, W-F 10am-5pm, Sa 10am-1pm. **The Didj Shop Internet Cafe** (☎8972 2485), on Giles St. a block west of Katherine Terr., has Internet access ($8 per hr.) and Aboriginal art.

Post Office: corner of Katherine Terr. and Giles St. Open M-F 9am-5pm. **Postal Code:** 0850.

ACCOMMODATIONS AND CAMPING

Accommodations in Katherine are full of travelers planning trips to Kakadu. While all hostels are happy to book canoe trips, cruises, or other tours for you, the prices generally run $5-15 more than what you would pay if you were to book through the Nitmiluk National Park Visitors Center or through Nitmiluk tour operators directly. **Camping** is also an option along the Victoria Hwy.

Palm Court Backpackers YHA (☎8972 2722 or 1800 626 722; www.travelnorth.com.au), on the corner of 3rd and Giles St. Make-your-own pancakes in the morning encourages a friendly atmosphere in this converted motel. Pool and BBQ. All rooms ensuite. Free pickup and drop-off from transit center. Internet access $2 per 20min. Laundry $3. Key deposit $10. Bikes $10 per day. Reception 7am-7pm. Dorms $19; twins and doubles $49. NOMADS/VIP/YHA $2 discount. ❷

Coco's Backpackers, 21 1st St. (☎8971 2889). Behind the didgeridoo shop, a ragtag mixture of Aboriginal artists, musicians, and international travelers mill about in the cluttered yard. The rooms are simple and bare, but for those tired of the typical party-hostel, it just might be a perfect fit. Call ahead. Sites $10 per person; dorms $17-18. ❷

Red Gum Caravan Park (☎8972 2239). Just 1km from town along Victoria Hwy. Laundry, pool, and BBQ. Sites $9; for 2 $18, powered $23; cabins $65, for more than 2 $80. ❶

Riverview Caravan Park and Motel, at the hot springs along the Victoria Hwy. (☎8972 1011). Pool, laundry, and BBQ. Sites for 2 $19, powered $24; singles $55; doubles $70; budget cabins for 2 $65. ❷

FOOD

There is a limited number of food options in Katherine, but a few good meals can still be rustled up at two local joints. At Shop 1 on Katherine Terr., **Bucking Bull Burger Bar ❶,** serves up mouth-watering burgers and mango smoothies from $5. Breakfast specials from $8.50 are also available. (☎8972 1734. Open daily 6:30am-4pm.) Just down the street, **Starvin's Pizza and Cafe ❷,** 32 Katherine Terr., offers a laid-back cafe with some of the best food in Katherine, including gourmet pizzas from $12.50-16.50. (☎8972 3633. Open M-Sa 3:30-10pm.) A giant **Woolworths** supermarket is across from the transit center on Katherine Terr. (☎8972 3055. Open daily 6:30am-10pm.)

ACTIVITIES

Two kilometers along the Victoria Hwy. from Katherine Terr., **hot springs** bubble along the Katherine River. Though the springs are popular, travelers in a rush won't miss anything special. The area is free and open to swimmers. There are toilets nearby, and the springs are wheelchair accessible along Croker St. **Coco's Place,** by Coco's Backpackers (see **Accommodations,** p. 283) is a didgeridoo shop run by experts, making it a far better place to learn about the instrument than the backpacker-targeted shops in Darwin. **Travel North** runs a **crocodile night tour** along the Johnstone River that includes wine and stew. (☎1800 089 103; www.travelnorth.com.au. Nightly 6:30pm. $49.50, children $24.50. Pickup $13/7 extra.)

NITMILUK NATIONAL PARK (KATHERINE GORGE)

NITMILUK AT A GLANCE	
AREA: 292,008 hectares. **FEATURES:** Katherine River, 13 gorges, Edith Falls, 17 Mile Creek. **HIGHLIGHTS:** Canoeing, hiking up cliffs and through gorges.	**GATEWAYS:** Katherine (p. 282). **CAMPING:** Permanent campgrounds near the visitors center and at Edith Falls; registered overnight bush camping. **FEES:** Camping $9.50-12; bush camping requires additional $50 deposit.

A broad, majestic river runs through the chiseled walls and sandy embankments of the highly touristed Katherine Gorge, drawing visitors by canoe, car, double decker tourist boat, and even helicopter. The 450 rock art galleries dotting the park, which include a series of paintings in the gorges themselves, are reminders that shutter-snapping tourists are not the area's first visitors. Since 1989, the park has been owned by its traditional residents, the Jawoyn people, who have leased it to the government of the Northern Territory for 99 years. The history of the Jawoyn people are displayed throughout the park, from the Dreamtime stories relayed in the paintings to the sometimes sober meditations on the future of Aboriginal culture found in the visitors center's exhibits.

TRANSPORTATION AND PRACTICAL INFORMATION

The 13 gorges on the Katherine River form the centerpiece of Nitmiluk. The easiest and most popular way to access the park is by car, though hostels in Katherine also arrange park tours. The gorges and all water sports can be accessed by boat or foot on the Southern Walks from the **Nitmiluk Visitor Centre,** at the end of the sealed Gorge Rd. 30km east of Katherine. A second entrance to the park lies 40km north of Katherine on the Stuart Hwy., where a 20km access road leads to Edith Falls. The 66km **Jatbula Trail** connects the two.

WHEN TO GO. The climate is most comfortable May-Sept., after the seasonal storms but before the unbearable humidity. Though greenery is most vivid during the Wet, floods limit activities in the park.

Buses: The Jawoyn Association (☎1300 146 743) runs buses from accommodations in Katherine to the visitors center. Book ahead. (25min., 2-3 per day, $23 round-trip.)

Tourist Office: Nitmiluk Visitors Centre provides hiking information and camping permits. Tourist desk in the gift shop books canoe, helicopter, and boat tours, along with campsites. Free exhibits present a broad introduction to the park, from natural history to local Jawoyn culture. Licensed **bistro** ❶ serves $7.50-11 burgers and sandwiches. (Centre ☎8972 1253. Open daily 7am-6:30pm. Bistro ☎8972 3150. Open daily 8am-8:30pm.) Contact the **Parks and Wildlife Commission,** which has a desk in the visitors center, for more information on Katherine Gorge. (☎8972 1886.)

Tours: Nitmiluk Tours offers **helicopter flights** and a number of other creative ways to see the area. Three-gorge tour $70, 8-gorge $105, 13-gorge $160. Min. 2 person. Book at the visitors center (☎8972 1253). **Helimasters** (☎8972 2402), just outside of the park entrance, offers similarly priced packages, as well as a more extensive gorge tour including Edith Falls $320. Book 1-2 days ahead.

CAMPING

The shady, popular **caravan park** ❶ near the visitors center has toilets, showers, laundry, phones, and BBQ facilities. Be sure to clean up your campsite before bedding down for the night or scavenging wallabies will do the job for you. Register at the visitors center. (Sites $9.50 per person, powered $12.) Sites are also available at a **campground** ❶ (Sites $9.50 per person, powered $12) next to Edith Falls, with showers, BBQ, food kiosk, and picnic area. The falls are a pleasant, cool spot to relax. Beneath the waterfall, a **lower pool** is a short walk from the carpark.

Bush camping ❶ is permitted, but campers must register at the visitors center. ($3.30 with $50 deposit.) Campsites with toilets and (usually) a water source are found along the Jatbula Trail and at the 4th, 5th, and 8th gorges in the Southern Walks area. Fires are permitted along the Jatbula but not in the Southern Walks.

NITMILUK BY WATER

Getting out on the Katherine River has many advantages; you can see much more of the gorges than you can along the trails, and it is often considerably cooler on the water than on shore. From May to September, quiet waters allow for canoeing and boat tours, but you must book several days in advance. **Nitmiluk Tours** (☎8972 1253; see **Tours,** above) is the only option for canoe rental and cruises, which can be booked at most accommodations in Katherine or at the visitors center. Canoeing affords some solitude despite the throngs of fellow paddlers and passing boat tours that limit the relaxing atmosphere.

CANOEING. Nitmiluk Tours rents Canadian-style canoes, which are a cross between a canoe and a kayak. This design was chosen for safety, not speed, yet it can be awkward to operate. Consider taking a full-day trip, which allows you to get away from the stream of fellow paddlers at the 3rd gorge, where you can climb from a sandy side beach to the pristine Lily Pond Falls. No more than 75 canoes are permitted in the gorge at once, so book several days in advance. (☎8972 1253. Single canoe ½ day $35, full day $47, overnight $95; double canoe $63/71/143. $20 cash deposit. Overnight canoes require a $3.30 camping permit.)

CRUISES. Glide along the gorges in flat, shaded motor vessels. Be warned: the crowded arrangement makes it sometimes difficult to enjoy the natural tranquility of the area, and the hustling tours hurt any chance of moving at one's own pace. (Departs from the boat jetty. 2hr.; 4 per day in the Dry; $43.50, children $17.) Daily "adventure" and "safari" tours combine boating and hiking. Book in advance. (Departs 9am. 4hr. $63; 8hr. $104.50.)

SWIMMING. The scorching sun makes taking a dip a popular activity, but be careful because you may be sharing the bath with freshwater crocs and power boats. Many people like to swim near the boathouse, at the plunge pools, or at gorge access points toward the end of some hikes.

NITMILUK BY LAND

Although the walking trails are not as easy to access as the boating and canoeing trips, they tend to be less crowded, and the views of the gorge are truly phenomenal. However, unrelenting sun can make the trails (10°C hotter than areas near the water) uncomfortably hot. **Walking tracks** in the park run the spectrum from strolls to struggles and range from 2.5km to 66km. The Southern Walks are usually open year-round; the Jatbula Trail is open only in the Dry. For all overnight walks, register with the rangers station before setting out. Semi-detailed aerial maps are $6.55 at the visitors center. Smaller trail maps are available for free.

SOUTHERN WALKS

The main trail of the area starts at the visitors center and runs parallel to the rim of the gorge. Each side trail meanders diagonally toward the gorge. The main trail follows a riverbed past large boulders and eucalyptus saplings, providing photo-worthy vistas. Trails are listed below, starting with those closest to the visitors center.

Lookout Loop (3.7km, 2hr. round-trip, moderate). Steep, well-maintained climb up the side of the gorge offers excellent views of the river and **Seventeen Mile Valley.** After the climb, the trail widens to an easy walk. Signs along the way detail the park's mythological and geological history.

Windolf Walk (8.4km, 3½hr., moderate). Side trail of the Windolf Walk follows a riverbed almost to the edge of the gorge where it forks. The right trail leads to **Pat's Lookout** on the gorge rim, while the left descends to the **Southern Rock Hole.** Pat's Lookout overlooks a bend in the gorge with a sandy beach at the foot of a menacing cliff. The trail to the left passes a wet-season waterfall and plunge pool, before reaching an inlet. A very steep, narrow trail leads to the right beyond Pat's Lookout to the base of the gorge. From here, bold hikers may swim across to the sandy beach, and then walk along the right-hand canyon wall to reach an **Aboriginal rock art gallery.** The sure-footed can follow the bank up the river to the end of the first gorge; if the water is low enough, you can cross the natural rock bridge. With slippery rocks and raging water underneath, it is a harrowing experience. If you do cross, follow the footpaths to the galleries.

Butterfly Gorge Walk (12km, 4½hr., difficult). A good overview of the region, with woodlands and rock formations giving way to a dense, tranquil monsoon forest in a side gorge. The last few hundred meters take you through clouds of butterflies. After a short but strenuous scramble down the cliff face, the walk ends at a deep swimming hole.

Lily Ponds Trail (20km, 6½hr., difficult). A challenging scramble in sections; leads to a sheltered pool in the third gorge. Few tourists.

Eighth Gorge and Jawoyn Valley (30-40km, overnight, very difficult). The longest of the Southern Walks takes a night in the bush with a return by midday. The terrain is fierce. Carry extra supplies. The Jawoyn loop passes a rock art gallery. All overnight treks require a $3.30 camping permit and a $50 deposit.

JATBULA TRAIL AND OTHER TRAILS

The popular Jatbula Trail winds 66km over the 5-day journey from the visitors center to Edith Falls. Split into eight segments, the trail threads through pockets of rainforest and skirts waterfalls. The first section (8km, 4hr., moderate) is the only plausible day walk; it departs from the visitors center and winds through a valley before reaching the **Northern Rockhole** and adjacent rock face. The trail continues past **Biddlecombe Cascades** (day 1-2, 11.5km mark), beautiful **Crystal Falls** (day 2,

20.5km), an interesting **Aboriginal amphitheater** (day 2-3, 31km), **Seventeen Mile Falls** (day 2-3, 34.5km), the **Edith River Crossing** (day 3-4, 45.5km), **Sandy Camp Pool** (day 3-4, 51km), **Edith River South** (day 4, 56.6km), **Sweetwater Pool** (day 4, 61.5km), and finally into **Leliyn** (day 4-5, 66km). Two short walks leave from the Edith Falls carpark at the end of the Jatbula Trail. The **Sweetwater Pool** walk (8.6km return, 4hr., moderate) leads to a waterhole and good camping. The **Leliyn Trail** (2.6km loop, 2hr., easy) heads to the smaller upper pools.

ABORIGINAL ART

The first gorge harbors a series of impressive rock art galleries, some of which are over 10,000 years old. Each gallery has layered images, with more recent paintings superimposed on older work. Little is known about the paintings of the **West Gallery,** now faded to a faint red shadow. Depicting what they found in each area of the gorge on the closest walls, the aboriginal art gives clues to the use and contents of different parts of the area. The mysterious **Central Gallery** depicts a hunt or ritual. Curiously, the figures are upside down, signifying sleep, a ceremonial preparation, initiation, or death. The oldest and most layered **East Gallery** depicts a non-human male figure, a woman in a headdress, and a black wallaroo with joey.

ARNHEM LAND

Take the expansive wilderness, serenity, and culture of Kakadu, multiply it by ten, and you still won't do justice to Arnhem Land. Sprawling across the entire northeastern region of the Top End, this Aboriginal homeland was established in 1931 and is isolated from the rest of the continent by geography and local law. Though most of Arnhem Land is uninhabited, it has two modest towns (Oenpelli and Nhulunbuy), several smaller settlements, and around 150 Aboriginal outposts. Visitors should know that while many Aborigines welcome tourism and its revenues, there are also those who would prefer to see their land free from swarms of outsiders.

Venturing into Arnhem Land is a serious matter. There are very few roads (those that do exist are navigable only in the Dry), and virtually no signs or services. Moreover, Arnhem Land is off-limits to non-Aborigines, so a destination-specific **permit** is required to enter. The **Northern Land Council** in the Jabiru Shopping Centre, next to the library, can issue permits for three locations close to Kakadu. (☎8979 2410. Open M-F 8am-4pm.) A permit for **Injalak** (IN-yaluk; $14 per day) and for **Sandy Creek** and **Wunyu Beach** (5 days, $88 per vehicle) takes 10 days to process. To venture to the secluded beaches and wildlife of **Gurig National Park** on the Cooburg Peninsula, contact the **Parks and Wildlife Commission of the Northern Territory.** (☎8979 0244. 7 nights, $211 per vehicle.) If you're venturing to Nhulunbuy on the Central Arnhem Hwy., permits are available through the **Northern Land Council** in Katherine (see **Central Arnhem Highway,** p. 288). For permits to other sections of Arnhem Land, contact Darwin's Northern Land Council (☎8920 5100).

For those seeking experienced guides and drivers, tours of Arnhem Land are available. Multi-day tours with flights from Darwin can run several thousands of dollars; 4WD daytrips from Kakadu are cheaper. **Lord's Kakadu and Arnhemland Safaris** departs from Jabiru. (☎8948 2200. $189, children $149.)

OENPELLI ☎08

Oenpelli (a.k.a. Gunbalanya) is a short 16km drive on unsealed road from Ubirr; the road crosses the tidal **East Alligator River** at **Cahills Crossing.** Before setting out, check with the Northern Land Council about tidal information to avoid capsizing your car.

The community is home to the **Injalak Arts & Crafts Centre,** where artists make baskets, limited-edition bark and paper paintings, screen-printed textiles, and *yirdaki*. The works are distributed to art galleries around the world, but visitors can purchase pieces on-site at discounted rates. (☎8979 0190. Open M-F 8am-5pm, Sa 8:30am-1:30pm.) Injalak also sponsors **Aboriginal-guided tours** through a local rock art gallery, the breadth and isolation of which put Ubirr and Nourlangie to shame—there are no crowds or roped-off sections here. (Tours leave 8:30-9:30am. 2½hr. $150 for 1-6 people. Book ahead.)

NORTHERN COAST

The highlights of the Northern Coast are the beautiful, remote beaches. **Wunyu Beach** is long, windy, virtually untouched, and ideal for relaxing and strolling. **Sandy Creek,** on Arnhem's north shore, offers excellent barramundi, salmon, and tuna fishing. Sunbathers and would-be swimmers beware—both Wunyu and Sandy Creek teem with **saltwater crocs.** The drive to Sandy Creek (3hr.) is 4WD only. The drive to Wunyu takes at least 2½hr. on a 4WD track. Neither Sandy Creek nor Wunyu Beach have facilities; camp at your own risk. Campers must bring their own water, food, and shelter. Camping on the roads to Sandy Creek and Wunyu is prohibited.

CENTRAL ARNHEM HIGHWAY

The Central Arnhem Hwy. begins south of Katherine and passes through central and east Arnhem Land to the Gove Peninsula. The road is difficult, but the reward is well worth the effort. Let's Go recommends using a 4WD vehicle for the 706km journey from Katherine, though a high-clearance 2WD is adequate. Locals (and insane travelers) have been known to attempt the drive in low-clearance 2WD vehicles, but the risk of serious damage from rocks or engine flooding is high. If you do decide to tempt fate, consider plugging your engine's air intake with a cloth and waiting for a 4WD to tow you through the deeper stream crossings; better yet, find some locals planning to make the drive and ask to follow them. The trickiest parts are the **Wilton** and **Goyder** rivers. When crossing streams in this area, walk through before driving through to test for depth and bottom conditions—better you five ft. under than your car. It is also a good idea to leave your engine running on the other side for as long as possible, since a flooded engine may not start again for quite some time. If you plan to visit Gove by road, your first phone call should be to the **Northern Territory Road Conditions Hotline** (☎1800 246 199).

There are no services and only one reliable source of fuel along the Central Arnhem Hwy. The first turn-off on the left, 16km from the Stuart Hwy., is a **police** station. The next two landmarks are the Barunga and Beswick communities; stopping at either one is prohibited. Refuel at the **Mainoru Store** (☎8975 4390), about 200km from the Stuart Hwy. Mainoru also sells food and basic supplies. The store is open daily 10am-4pm during the Dry; hours vary during the Wet. The **Bulman Store** (☎8975 4887), 57km past Mainoru just before the Wilton River crossing, also sells fuel but has unpredictable hours and is often closed. Bulman may have more up-to-date information about the river crossings than the NT roads hotline, so consider giving them a ring before setting out.

Though the highway is not busy, there is some traffic; stay alert for road-weary oncoming drivers at crests or around turns, and take frequent breaks. Travel time from Katherine to Nhulunbuy is at least 10 hours; exercise caution and plan ahead.

Because the road passes through Aboriginal lands, you must have a permit from the **Northern Land Council** in Katherine (☎8972 2799) before you start the drive. The permit is free, but can take several days to process. You must be visiting a resident or have a booking at an accommodation in Nhulunbuy before you apply.

NHULUNBUY AND GOVE ☎08

Nhulunbuy, a rugged bauxite mining town (pop. 4000), is an outpost of civilization in the vast frontier that is far northeastern Arnhem Land. Nhulunbuy is the sort of place where the speedway and motorcross track are the most visible icons on the way into town, and nearly every house sports a rough-and-tumble 4WD and a boat. The town is a popular base for exploring the stunning beaches, dunes, and pristine bushlands of the Gove Peninsula. Nhulunbuy is also a good place to learn about the culture of the Yolngu people, who have lived in this part of the world for many generations (perhaps as long as 60,000 years) and remained generally undisturbed by European influence. The didgeridoo (called *yirdaki* in local languages) is originally from northeastern Arnhem Land, and the Yolngu are its traditional custodians. They possess ancient knowledge about making and playing the instrument.

TRANSPORTATION. The best way to visit Nhulunbuy and the Gove Peninsula is by air, and flights can be affordable with some advance planning. **Qantas** (☎13 13 13) flies to Nhulunbuy from **Cairns** and **Darwin. Airnorth** (☎8920 4000) flies from Darwin and often has fares under $300, though flights are in a small turbo-prop aircraft. Permits from the Northern Land Council are required to fly to Nhulunbuy.

Once here, the best way to see Gove is in your own 4WD. Failing that, a high-clearance 2WD is adequate for exploring the beaches closer to town. Most rentals in Gove are booked solid three or four months in advance, so plan ahead or rent from Darwin. **Manny's** (☎8987 2300) rents 4WDs and 2WD utes (utility vehicles). **Gove Rentals** has 4WD vehicles, 2WD utes, and standard cars, but only rents to drivers over 25. (☎8987 1700. 4WD $147-158 per day, utes $75, cars $86.) **Kansas Pty. Ltd.** (☎8987 2872) rents 2WD twincab utes (from $87 per day) and 4WDs (from $148.50). For **taxis** call **Radio Taxis** (☎13 10 08) or **Gove Bus Service** (☎04 1737 1450).

ORIENTATION. Heading toward town, the **Central Arnhem Highway** and the road from the airport converge to become **Melville Bay Road,** which runs past the large Aboriginal community of **Yirrkala** and **Matthew Flinders Way** in the direction of the harbor. On the drive into town along Matthew Flinders Way, the first left is Arnhem Rd., the location of the **Captain Cook Shopping Centre.** In town, **Westall Street,** off Matthew Flinders Way, borders **Endeavor Square,** the center of town.

PRACTICAL INFORMATION. The **East Arnhem Land Tourist Association,** in Endeavour House off the Woolworths carpark, is a good source of information and brochures about local services, food, and accommodations. They also have a free town map. (☎8987 2255. Open M-F 9am-5pm.) **Dhimurru Land Management,** in the Captain Cook Shopping Centre, is the Gove Peninsula's unofficial tourist office. An incorporated Aboriginal organization, it was established by Yolngu landowners to manage outside access to Yolngu land. (☎8987 3992. Open M-F 8:30am-noon and 1-4pm.) To leave town legally, a two-month general visitor's recreation **permit** ($45) is required. Some areas, such as Cape Arnhem, Caves Beach, Oyster Beach, Wonga Creek, and Memorial Park, require advance booking and special permits. An invaluable resource for any visitor to Gove is *A Visitor's Guide to Recreation Areas*, available at Dhimurru for $10. The booklet, which has detailed information about every beach, creek, and campsite in the area (including photographs), is well worth the price. It also explains Yolngu history and has a fascinating description of the intricate social system. The **Northern Land Council,** in Endeavour Sq. off the Woolworths carpark, processes permit applications for driving along the Central Arnhem Hwy. and for anywhere not covered by Dhimurru permits. (☎8987 2602. Open M-F 8am-5:30pm.)

The **library,** 73 Matthew Flinders Way, has free **Internet** access. (☎8987 0860. Open M-W and F 10am-5pm, Th 10am-7pm, Sa 10am-1pm.) **Nambara Arts & Crafts,** in the YBE complex between town and the harbor, sells high-quality paintings and *yirdaki.* (☎8987 2233. Open M-F 8am-4:30pm.) **YBE** is the largest Aboriginal-owned company in Australia, providing civil engineering and mine-site rehabilitation services. The **police** (☎000 or 13 14 44) and a **hospital** (☎8987 0211) are both on Matthew Flinders Way, and a **post office** can be found on Westall St. across from the taxi stand. (☎8987 1333. Open M-F 9am-5pm.) **Postal Code:** 0881.

ACCOMMODATIONS AND FOOD. Everything in Nhulunbuy is expensive, and there are no dorm beds in town. For most budget travelers, **camping** ❶ is the best option. Failing that, the least expensive place to stay is the **Gove Peninsula Motel** ❺ on Matthew Flinders Way at Melville Bay Rd. All rooms are ensuite and have kitchenettes. (☎8987 0700. Singles $125; doubles $135.) If you prefer rooms with an ocean view, try the **Walkabout Lodge** ❺, 12 Westall St. (☎8987 1777. Singles $160; doubles $185; triples $220.)

The least expensive place to buy food is **Woolworths** (☎8987 1714) in Endeavour Sq. (Open daily 8am-8pm.) There's also an **IGA** supermarket and **Mitre 10 Hardware** at the Captain Cook Shopping Ctr. For some good eats, the best value in Arnhem Land is at **Coco's Cafe** ❶ in the shopping center. Delicious plates of curry, Italian food, and noodles are $12, and homemade pies and muffins are $4. (☎8987 2406. Open M-F 8am-3pm.) The best takeaway option is **Fred's Food and Fun** ❷ in Endeavor Sq., which serves up pizzas for $17. (☎8987 2455. Open daily 9am-9pm.)

BEACHES. Gove's beaches, prime examples of the rugged beauty of Arnhem Land, make any trip to the region worthwhile. Gove also has some of the world's best **fishing,** especially among the hundreds of small islands that dot the Arafura Sea. For boats, call **Arnhem Boat Hire** (☎8987 3181). Many beaches have reefs teeming with life, and snorkeling is popular. Be aware that **saltwater crocodiles** are known to frequent all waters in the area, but are much less of a danger than in Darwin or Kakadu. Never enter the water near an estuary, keep a watchful eye out for croc landings (muddy slides at the water's edge), and use common sense.

Gove is so isolated that it has yet to be discovered by most tourists; as a result, it is possible to have a world-class beach all to yourself. The *Dhimurru Visitor's Guide* has photographs and descriptions of all the beaches, as well as driving directions and detailed information about permits and camping. In general, most beaches between the airport and the harbor are accessible in a high-clearance 2WD vehicle, though you may have to park and walk part of the way. The **Rainbow Cliffs** area between Nhulunbuy and Yirrkala is usually the most accessible and has good campsites. The cliffs themselves are a sacred site, so don't walk on them. Nearer to town and accessible in any vehicle, **East Woody Beach,** off East Woody Rd. past the BMX track, has a large estuary and a peninsula with a rocky face.

The best beaches accessible on the general recreation permit are past the airport on the way out of town; follow the turn-off for Daliwuy Bay, an unsealed road that is barely manageable in a 2WD. The first beach is **Daliwuy Bay,** which has a shaded campsite with a boat ramp. The next beach is 4WD-only **Macassans,** noteworthy primarily because of a rock painting of age-old Yolngu trade relations with the Macassan people from present-day Indonesia. The road becomes impassable to 2WDs just before **Turtle Beach,** but you can get close enough to walk if you veer off to the right into the bush just before the main road turns sharply to the left. Turtle Beach is small but breathtaking, with good surf on windy days. It is also a superb place to camp. Only 1.5km farther up the road is one of Gove's jewels, **Little Bondi Beach.** The bay is a near-perfect semicircle; the small rip running straight up the middle takes you quickly to the symmetrical breaks on the left and right, making Little Bondi the best surf beach in Gove.

There are also several excellent freshwater **campsites** ❶ on various creeks, rockholes, and billabongs in the area. **Giddy River, Wonga Creek,** and **Memorial Park** are among the better known, but the latter two require special permits from Dhimurru. There are **no facilities** at any campsites in Gove, so bring all your own supplies (including water). Camping fees are included in the price of your permit.

SIGHTS. The free **Mine Tour** (☎8987 5345) is thorough and engaging, offering a thoughtful, well-balanced view of the mine's impact on the land. The construction of the mine sparked outrage among local Yolngu people, and the legal battle over land rights went all the way to the Supreme Court. Though the mine won the case, the controversy led to the formation of the Northern Land Council, the entity responsible for reclaiming Aboriginal land and giving legal force to the traditional ownership system. The Mine Tour departs from the taxi stand on Westall St. every Friday at 8:30am. Book at least one day ahead, and wear sturdy closed-toe shoes. The **Roy Marika Lookout** on Mt. Saunders off Wuyal Rd. has a decent view of the town and the surrounding coastline. Take Matthew Flinders Way to Arnhem Rd. and then Arnhem to Wuyal Rd.

FESTIVALS. The famous **Garma Festival** (www.garma.telstra.com), organized by the Yothu Yindi Foundation, takes place annually during the second week of August at a site near the Cape Arnhem turn-off. Yothu Yindi are largely responsible for the international popularization of the *yirdaki*, and the festival involves lots of *yirdaki* playing, making, and teaching. *Balanda* (non-Aboriginals) must pay a hefty fee to participate in the week-long event. All meals, camping fees, and permits for the drive from Katherine are included.

YIRRKALA COMMUNITY ☎08

Yirrkala is a large Aboriginal community with a gorgeous, oceanfront setting. Visitors should head straight to the **Buku-Larrngay Mulka Arts and Crafts Centre and Museum.** Buku-Larrngay, a non-profit community cooperative, houses an excellent collection of Aboriginal artwork, burial poles, and bark painting, as well as two renowned church panels depicting the Yolngu creation legend. Each of the sixteen clans in the region is responsible for painting one section of the panels, each in a different style. Buku-Larrngay is also perhaps the best place in Australia to find a traditionally crafted instrument-quality *yirdaki* made by local Yolngu artists; prices start at $200. (☎8987 1701; www.yirrkala.com. Open M-F 8am-4:30pm, Sa 9am-noon. $2.) Visiting Yirrkala requires a free permit from the **Dhanbul Community Association.** (☎8987 3433. Open M-F 9am-4pm.) Yirrkala's secluded **Shady Beach** is breathtaking, but camping is not permitted. To get there, face the water, follow the trail up the hill on the left and through the bush. Be advised that though **kava,** a very popular herb used during cultural ceremonies in this area, is legal in Yirrkala, hefty fines await anyone who attempts to transport it outside town.

CAPE ARNHEM

If you have time, apply for an $11 special permit to visit **Cape Arnhem,** a wonderland of marine life with a divine coastline ideal for camping. Sea turtles and manta rays abound in its waters. Access is limited to ten vehicles at a time, so book ahead with Dhimurru Land Management (p. 289). To visit Cape Arnhem, drive out of town, past the airport and past the Daliwuy turn-off, and turn left at the Dhimurru sign. The track traces the top of a large escarpment; collect firewood before you begin the descent to the coast. At the bottom, be sure to deflate your tires to 20psi before the track becomes sandy. You'll eventually exit the track onto the long, wide **Malupinu Beach,** with a view of **Moon Island** directly in front of you. Keep the water on your right as you drive up along. You'll pass two large rock formations called the **Twin Eagles;** they are sacred sites, so don't camp near them. About halfway to the end of the beach, you'll drive up onto a sand dune; from here the track meanders its way past pandanus trees, through bush that looks more like the Sahara than the tropics, and eventually onto a beach with a huge expanse of rock pools. The track ends at a fence. This area is one of the few places on the Cape with shaded **campsites.** Beyond the fence is a bauxite shelf, and on moonless nights **crayfish** (tropical rock lobster) sit in the pools almost begging to become dinner. There's some decent **snorkeling** beyond the rock pools and along the bauxite shelf, but be cautious of rough currents and rip tides. The entire trip is around 40km and requires a 4WD plus the know-how to maneuver a vehicle on sand.

DOWN THE TRACK

Heading south on the Stuart Hwy. away from the city of Darwin, the lush vegetation and cinnamon-colored earth give way to stretches of land dotted with grasses and shrubs. A barren red expanse stretches for miles in every direction, broken only by the occasional rock outcropping.

VICTORIA HIGHWAY: KATHERINE TO KUNUNURRA

From downtown Katherine, the "Vic" careens westward 512km to Kununurra, Western Australia (p. 757). There's precious little between the two places to distract you from the startling escarpments and mountain ridges that run parallel to the highway. Located 200km west of Katherine, the **Victoria River Roadhouse ❶** has petrol, a restaurant (burgers $6-8), and quiet campsites with views of the nearby escarpment. (☎8975 0744. Sites for 2 $15, powered $20, extra person $7.50/10; doubles $65; motel rooms from $80.) A few Victoria River **cruises** leave from the Roadhouse. (3hr.; daily 9am; min. 4 people, $45.) The boat can be chartered for fishing groups of up to six people for $65 per hr. Scenic helicopter flights also depart the roadhouse. (10, 20, and 30min. flights; $60 per 10min.)

The highway passes through **Gregory National Park** (Timber Creek Ranger Station ☎8975 0888). The Territory's second-largest national park (after Kakadu) features 2WD accessible bushwalks and lookouts over Victoria River Gorge, as well as rugged 4WD tracks through the isolated surroundings. **Timber Creek,** a rowdy roadside town, is another 90km west of Victoria River. The **Wayside Inn ❶** has a small restaurant (Gregory Tavern) and a large selection of accommodations. (☎8975 0722. Sites $6.50 per person, powered $18.50; budget singles $43, budget with ensuite $110.) River cruises can be booked next door at **Max's Victoria River Boat Tours** (☎8975 0850. $70 per 3½hr.). At the 468km mark, **Keep River National Park** is home to Aboriginal art sites and a few bushwalks. Camping is permitted at two sites (15 and 28km down a gravel road). Finally, about 480km west of Katherine (less than 40km from Kununurra) is the border crossing into Western Australia. There are strict quarantines against fruits, veggies, and plants. Also, be aware that clocks in Western Australia are 1½hr. behind those in the Northern Territory.

STUART HIGHWAY: KATHERINE TO TENNANT CREEK

There are 672 long kilometers between Katherine and Tennant Creek. Twenty-seven kilometers south of Katherine is the 200km turn-off to an unsung gem, **Cutta Cutta Caves Nature Park.** Meaning "starry starry," the name refers to the delicate calcite crystals that grow within the dark, temperate passages. The cave extends 720m through an underground labyrinth of limestone columns and jagged ceilings, although visitors can only venture through the first 250m before the depths get too cold and damp. Access to the cave is limited to **tours,** which are led by fun, knowledgeable guides. (☎8972 3977. 1hr. tours depart daily 9, 10, 11am, 1, 2, and 3pm, except during floods in the Wet. $13.50, children $6.75. Cash only.) "Cultural Adventures" are offered at the Aboriginal owned and operated tours of **Manyallaluk,** 100km southeast of Katherine. (50km on the Stuart Hwy. and 50km on an access road. ☎8972 2224 or 1800 634 319. Operates Mar.-Dec. On-site full-day tours $130, children $75. From Katherine full-day tours $170/85. Book 1 day in advance.)

TENNANT CREEK ☎08

Dusty Tennant Creek (pop. 35,000), the self-proclaimed "Golden Heart" of the Northern Territory, appeals to most travelers as a welcome reprieve from the monotonous stretch of road between Alice Springs and Darwin. A product of Australia's last great gold rush in the 1930s, Tennant has remained small despite a four billion dollar output of gold since the 1960s. The **Devil's Marbles** (p. 294) and the artistic flavor of Warumungu Aborigines make Tennant Creek a worthwhile visit.

TRANSPORTATION. All **buses** in and out of town stop at the **Transit Centre** on Paterson St., near the intersection with Stuart St., at the north end of town. (☎8962 1070. Open M-F 7:30am-5:30pm and 9-11pm, Sa 8am-12:30pm and 2:30-4:30am.) **Greyhound Australia** (☎13 14 99) services: Alice Springs (5-6hr., 1 per day, $135); Darwin (13hr., 1 per day, $191); Katherine (8-9hr., 1 per day, $141); Townsville (20hr., 1 per day, $249). **Bicycle rental** is at **Bridgestone Rental,** 52b Paterson St. (☎8962 2361. ½ day $5, full day $10. Open M-F 8:30am-5pm.)

ORIENTATION AND PRACTICAL INFORMATION. The Stuart Hwy., called **Paterson Street** in town, runs from north to south. Intersecting Paterson are **Stuart Street** (not to be confused with the Stuart Hwy.), **Davidson Street,** and **Peko Road** from the east, which becomes **Windley Street** west of Paterson. **Memorial Drive** comes in from the west. **Tennant Creek Regional Tourist Association,** 1.5km up Peko Rd., will book tours. (☎8962 3388. Open May-Sept. daily 9am-5pm; Oct.-Apr. M-F 9am-5pm, Sa 9am-noon.) There is an **ANZ bank** (☎13 13 14), on Paterson St. between Davidson and Stuart St., and a **Westpac bank,** 64 Peko Rd. (☎8962 2801), at the corner of Paterson St. Both are open M-Th 9:30am-4pm, F 9:30am-5pm, with 24hr. **ATMs.** The **police** (☎8962 4444) are on Paterson St. near Windley

DESERT FISHING

Central Australia, known for its endless expanses of red desert, normally wouldn't rank first on the list of major fishing destinations, especially when visitors have some of the best coastline in the world at their fingertips. But recent developments may mean that travelers to the Outback don't have to leave their fishing gear behind. A central Australian entrepreneur is planning to build an "oasis in the middle of the desert," according to a recent report in the *Sunday Territorian.* His oasis, complete with cabins, campsites, and all the typical amenities, would be more than a mirage. The series of manmade fishing lakes would be built near Alice Springs and initially allow permit-based catch-and-release fishing of stocked barramundi, perch, eel, catfish, trout, bass, and cod.

Several details are yet to be worked out. Success of the project will require the resolution of the extensive technical difficulties involved, such as concerns associated with maintaining water quality and availability, sourcing and sustaining the fish population, and obtaining the legal rights to proceed. But, if all goes as planned for this Northern Territory man, as early as next year natives and tourists alike may be throwing nets and fishing poles in their backseats before heading out to the desert.

St. There is **Internet** access at the **library,** on Peko Rd. (☎8962 2401. $2.20 per 30min. Open M-F 10am-6pm, Sa 10am-noon.) It is also available at **Switch,** on Paterson St., just north of the Transit Centre. (☎8962 3124. $5.50 per hr. Open M-F 8:30am-5pm, Sa 9am-1pm.) The **post office** is at the corner of Paterson St. and Memorial Dr. (☎8962 2196. Open M-F 9am-5pm.) **Postal Code:** 0861.

ACCOMMODATIONS AND FOOD **Outback Caravan Park ❷,** 600m from Paterson St. on Peko Rd., offers shady sites, manicured grass, and a fantastic swimming pool. Amenities include kitchen, BBQ, laundry, and friendly staff. (☎8962 2459. Sites for 2 $18, powered $23; deluxe ensuite cabins $48-85.) Reach **Tourists Rest Hostel ❷,** on Leichardt St., by walking south on Paterson St. and turning right on Windley St. This spacious and friendly hostel also has kitchen, pool, TV, laundry, and an aviary. (☎8962 2719. Reception 24hr. Dorms $20, ISIC $19, VIP/YHA/NOMADS $18; twins and doubles $40/39/38. NOMADS/VIP/YHA. Daytrips to Devil's Marbles $55.) **Safari Backpackers YHA ❷,** 12 Davidson St., west of Paterson St., is small, clean, and comfortable. (☎8962 2207. Reception 8am-8pm across the street. Dorms $17; twins and doubles $40. YHA $3 discount.)

Paterson St. is lined with takeaway snack bars and eateries. **Rocky's ❷,** next door to the Transit Centre, provides takeaway-only pizza in a no-frills setting. (☎8962 1925. Large pizzas $10-18. Open daily 4-11pm.) **Top of Town Cafe ❶,** just north of the Transit Centre, has veggie burgers and a sandwich bar for $3-6. (☎8962 1311. Open M-F 8am-6pm, Sa-Su 8am-2pm.) **Mr. Perry's Ice Cream ❶,** on Paterson St. south of Memorial Dr., has an adjoining cafe that serves good Chinese takeaway. (☎8962 2995. Open M-Sa 8am-5:30pm, Su 10am-3pm.) Adjacent to Mr. Perry's is the **Tennant Food Barn,** which sells cheap groceries. (☎8962 2296. Open M-F 8am-6pm, Sa 8:30am-6pm, Su 9am-6pm.)

STUART HIGHWAY: TENNANT TO ALICE SPRINGS

Geologists suspect water erosion. Aboriginal legend credits the Rainbow Serpent. Whatever the cause, the boulders known as the **Devil's Marbles** are beautiful and baffling. Eighty kilometers from Tennant Creek, just off the Stuart Hwy., the nearly spherical (7m in diameter) granite rocks balance precariously on one another. Two tours originate in Tennant Creek and include a BBQ back in town. **Devil's Marbles Tours,** led by witty and well-informed guides, emphasize geological and cultural appreciation. (☎04 1889 1711. Depart daily from Tourists Rest Hostel at noon; $55. Sunrise tours depart M and F 5am; $65.) **Garyo's** occasionally runs more action-packed tours with numerous photo-ops. (☎8962 2024; $55.) **Camping ❶** at the Marbles is basic with pit toilets, BBQ, but no water. ($3.30, children $1.65.) The closest town to Devil's Marbles is **Wauchope,** 9km south, which has petrol, food, and **accommodations ❶.** (☎8964 1963. Sites $7 per person, powered $12; motel singles without bath $30; ensuite doubles $70.) Small towns farther along the highway have roadhouses that also provide basic services such as petrol, food, and accommodations, among the best of which are **Wycliffe Well** (☎8964 1966), rumored to receive frequent UFO visits and have the largest beer selection in all of Australia; **Barrow Creek** (☎8956 9753); **Ti Tree** (☎8956 9741); and **Aileron** (☎8956 9703).

RED CENTRE

Though home to less than 0.5% of Australia's population, for many foreigners, the Red Centre is the essence of the continent. Everything in the Centre seems to have a mythical, larger-than-life quality. The landscapes here are nothing if not arresting, from the red moonscapes of the Centre's vast expanses to the plunging depths of **Watarrka** (Kings Canyon) and the proud monolith of **Uluru** (Ayers Rock). In the endless skies, panoramic watercolor sunsets give way to millions of stars every night.

Alice Springs, cradled in the bluffs of the MacDonnell Ranges, is the only sizeable town in any direction, serving as the region's unofficial capital and gateway for many travelers. But, be forewarned—even Alice is a five-hour drive from Watarrka or Uluru, so if your time is limited, consider flying directly.

ALICE SPRINGS ☎08

Proximity to abundant natural wonders and precious little else has rendered dusty Alice Springs an important center for commerce and tourism. With 30,000 residents, it dwarfs every settlement for nearly 1500km in all directions, and is the largest town between Adelaide on the Southern Ocean and tropical Darwin in the Top End. This position endows Alice with a collection of resources surprising for its size: the shopping is as abundant as the throngs of tourists, who rarely stay for more than a few days after their excursions to Uluru are complete.

A lovely setting amid the MacDonnell ranges, beautiful night sky, and the colorful sunsets make Alice an enjoyable destination. However, the city is not without its problems, and race is its most notable issue. There exists a significant divide between white and Aboriginal populations, challenging the development of the city as a diverse, metropolitan area. This divide also carries over into the management of many parks and reserves throughout this part of Australia, particularly in the Northern Territory. In many Aboriginal lands, strict permit requirements and quotas restrict the number of tourists permitted to visit at any given time.

TRANSPORTATION

Planes: Alice Springs Airport (☎8951 1211), 20km south of the city on Stuart Hwy. Provides info, currency exchange, and car rental. **Qantas,** on Todd Mall and Parsons St. (☎13 13 13) flies to: **Adelaide** (2hr., 2 per day); **Brisbane** (4½hr., 1 per day); **Cairns** (3½hr., 1 per day); **Darwin** (2hr., 3 per day); **Melbourne** (3hr., 1 per day); **Perth** (3½hr., 1 per day); **Sydney** (3½hr., 1 per day); **Yulara** (45min., 3 per day).

Trains: Alice Railway Station is a 20min. walk from central Alice. From George St., take a left on Larapinta Dr., which turns into the Stuart Hwy. and runs to Alice. **The Ghan** (www.gsr.com.au) runs to: **Adelaide** (20hr., Tu and Th 12:45pm, $250); **Darwin** (24hr., M 4pm, $305); **Sydney** (46hr., Tu and Th 12:45pm, $395). The tourist office makes reservations, or you can call *The Ghan* direct (☎13 21 47). Several levels of accommodations available. Prices listed are for the least expensive level, **Red Kangaroo Daynighter.**

Buses: Greyhound Australia (☎8952 7888) runs from the station at the corner of Gregory and Railway Terr. Daily service to: **Adelaide** (20hr., 10am, $243); **Darwin** (20hr., 8:15pm, $223) via **Tennant Creek** (6hr., 8:15pm, $114); **Sydney** (45hr., 10am, $374).

Public Transportation: ASBus (☎8950 0500), the public bus system, runs infrequently to the outskirts of town. Service M-F 8 or 9am-6pm, Sa only in the morning. $1.40-2.20.

Taxis: Alice Springs Taxis (☎8952 1877 or 13 10 18) queues up on Gregory Terr. just east of Todd Mall.

Car Rental: You must be 21 to rent a vehicle and 25 to rent a 4WD in Alice Springs. **Delta Europcar** (☎13 13 90 or 8955 5994), 10 Gap Rd., across from the hospital, has some of the best rates in town, with cars from $58 per day with a $13.20 per day under-25 surcharge. Open M-F 8am-5pm, Sa-Su 8am-1pm. **Territory-Thrifty** (☎8952 9999), on the corner of Hartley St. and Stott Terr., has cars from $78 per day with a $16.50 per day under-25 surcharge; 4WD from $145 per day. Open daily 8am-5:30pm. **Britz** (☎8952 8814 or 800 331 454), on the corner of Stuart Hwy. and Power St., has good deals, renting 2WD from $55, and 4WD or campervans with unlimited km from $100 per day. Open daily 8am-5pm. **Maui** (☎8952 8049), corner of Stuart Hwy. and Power St., has 4WD and campervans.

Roadside Assistance: AANT (24hr. ☎8952 1087).

Road Conditions: 24hr. ☎1800 246 199.

Bike Rental: Many hostels and travel agencies rent bikes. Try **Pioneer YHA** (☎8952 8855; p. 297). $8 per hr., $15 per ½-day, $25 per day.

ORIENTATION

The **Stuart Highway** runs through Alice on its way from Darwin (1486km) to Adelaide (1570km). The dry **Todd River** bed provides a Western border to the CBD; the **MacDonnell Ranges** form a natural border at the southern side of the city. The break between the east-west ranges, called **Heavitree Gap,** allows both the Stuart Hwy. and the Todd to pass through. The true commercial center of town is **Todd Mall,** a pedestrian-only stretch of Todd St. between Wills and Gregory Terr.; the two indoor malls are **Alice Plaza** (Todd Mall at Parsons St.) and **Yeperenye Plaza** (Hartley St. north of Gregory Terr.). Most tour agencies and small shops lie on Todd St., just south of the Todd Mall.

PRACTICAL INFORMATION

Tourist Office: Central Australian Tourism Industry Association (☎8952 5800 or 1800 645 199; www.centralaustraliantourism.com), on Gregory Terr. at the end of Todd Mall. Books transportation, tours, and accommodations, sells road and Larapinta Trail maps, and has National Park info. Grab the excellent, free city map. Open M-F 8:30am-5:30pm, Sa-Su 9am-4pm.

Budget Travel: Flight Centre (☎8953 4081), Shop 18A, Yeperenye Center, guarantees the lowest airfares. Open M-F 9am-5:30pm, Sa 9:30am-12:30pm. **Travelworld,** 40 Todd Mall (☎8953 0488), near Parsons St. Open M-F 9am-5:30pm, Sa 9am-2pm.

Tours: Many hostels run tours that include accommodations. Several agencies just off Todd Mall book tour packages. **Backpacker's World Travel** (☎8953 0666), on Todd St. and Gregory Terr. Open M-F 9:30am-6pm, Sa-Su 10am-4:30pm. Day tours from $99; 3-day all-inclusive Uluru tours $200-350.

Currency Exchange: National Australia (☎8952 1611) and **ANZ** (☎8952 1144) are in Todd Mall, along with **ATMs.** Both open M-Th 9:30am-4pm, F 9:30am-5pm.

Work Opportunities: Alice has a year-round labor shortage that borders on crisis. Those with office or computer skills can get placement through **Work Zone** (☎8952 4300; www.workzone.org), on the corner of Gregory Terr. and Bath St., next to Video EZY. Bulletin boards in many hostels list short-term job opportunities.

Library: (☎8950 0555), on Gregory Terr. near Todd Mall next to the tourist office. Open M-Tu and Th 10am-6pm, W and F 10am-5pm, Sa 9am-1pm, Su 1-5pm.

Book Exchange: Helene's Books and Things, 113 Todd St. (☎8953 2465). Open M-F 9am-5pm, Sa and every other Su 10am-5pm. **Boomerang Book Exchange** (☎8952 5843), on Harris Ln. near Parsons St. Open M-F 9:30am-5pm, Sa 9:30am-1pm.

Emergency: ☎000. **Crisis Line** ☎1800 019 116.

Police: (☎8951 8888), on Parsons St., at the corner of Bath St.

Hospital: Alice Springs Clinic (☎8951 7777), on Gap Rd. between Stuart Terr. and Traeger Ave. Dental and health clinic across the street.

Pharmacy: Amcal (☎8953 0089) in Todd Mall. Open daily 8:30am-7:30pm.

Internet Access: Numerous places along Todd St. between Gregory Terr. and Stuart St. Fast connections and services including digital photo. Rates $3-4 per hr., prorated. **Todd Internet,** 82 Todd Mall. Open M, F, Sa 10am-6pm, Tu-Th 9am-6pm, Su 9am-4pm.

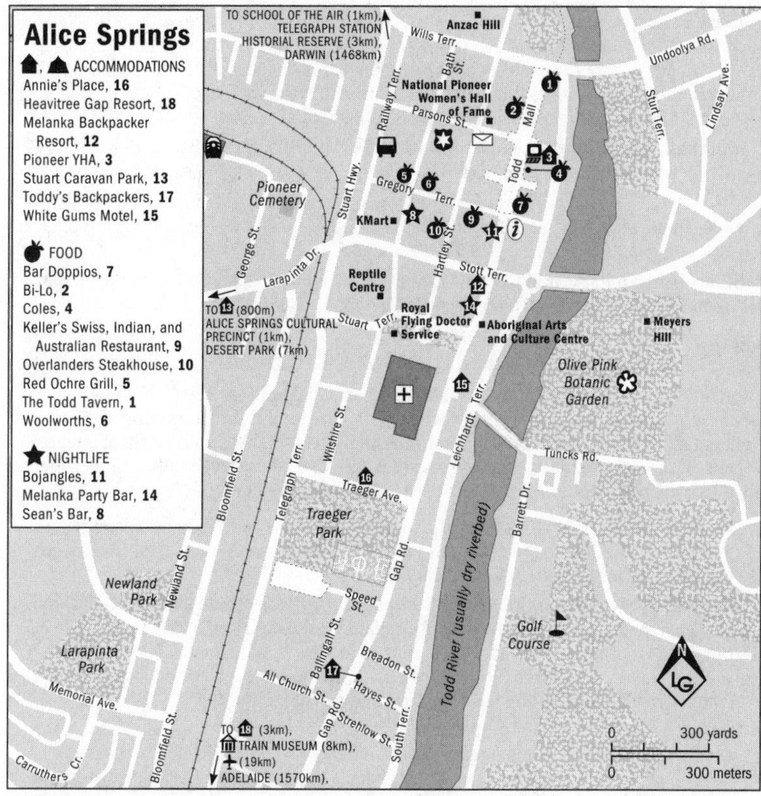

Post Office: GPO (☎8952 1020), on Hartley St. south of Parsons St. Open M-F 8:15am-5pm. **Postal Code:** 0870.

ACCOMMODATIONS AND CAMPING

All of the hostels listed below have A/C and pools; all recommend booking ahead and will be happy to arrange tours; all also accept credit cards. Most have bike rental from $25 per day.

Heavitree Gap Resort, on Palm Circuit. (☎8950 4444; www.aurora-resorts.com.au). Sparkling clean rooms approx. 5km from CBD. Breathtaking location surrounded by bluffs inhabited by blackfooted wallabies. Shuttle bus runs to town; the last shuttle from town is at 4:15pm. Dorms $25; ensuite budget doubles $114; motel doubles (with slightly newer furnishings) from $130. Sites $9 per person, powered for 2 $20. ❷

Annie's Place, 4 Traeger Ave. (☎8952 1545). Clean dorms centered around a palm-lined courtyard. Pool and picnic tables. Bar serves cheap meals (from $5) and drinks. Breakfast included. $5 airport drop-off. Dorms $16; doubles $50, with bath $60.

Pioneer YHA (☎8952 8855), corner of Parsons St. and Leichardt Terr. Excellent facilities include a pool, billiards, and large kitchen. Internet access $5.50 per hr. Key deposit $20. 24hr. free safe and storage. Wheelchair accessible. Reception 7:30am-8:30pm. 6- to 16-bed dorms $22.50-25.50; 4-bed dorms $27.50. YHA discount $3.50. ❷

Toddy's Backpackers, 41 Gap Rd. (☎8952 1322), 10min. walk from the CBD. Many ensuite dorm rooms have their own kitchenette, TV, and balcony. Great all-you-can-eat dinner nightly ($8) and beer ($3). Breakfast included. Reception 6am-8:30pm. Dorms from $12; singles, doubles, and twins with sink and fridge $50; budget motel rooms $65; ensuite motel doubles with TV and fridge $59. Extra person $6. ❶

Melanka Backpacker Resort, 94 Todd St. (☎1800 815 066 or 8952 4744; www.melanka.com.au). Pool, volleyball court, BBQ, and location next door to Melanka Party Bar. 3-person dorms $20; doubles $55. VIP/YHA 10% discount. ❷

White Gums Motel, 17 Gap Rd. (☎8952 5144). Clean, comfortable rooms with kitchenette. Personable service. Singles $80; doubles $90. Extra person $10. ❺

Stuart Caravan Park (☎8952 2547), 2km west of town on Larapinta Dr. Reception 8am-8pm. Sites $1 per person, powered for 2 $27. ❶

FOOD

Food doesn't come cheap in Alice. Todd Mall near Gregory Terr. has a handful of cafes where you can pick up basic sandwiches or snacks without breaking the bank. Cheaper still are the many supermarkets, including a 24hr. **Coles** on Bath St. at Gregory Terr., a **Bi-Lo** with great prices at the end of Todd Mall, and a **Woolworths** in the Yeperenye Plaza. Unless noted, all restaurants accept major credit cards (AmEx/MC/V).

The Todd Tavern, 1 Todd Mall (☎8952 1255), near Wills Terr. Popular among tourists and locals alike, this pub/restaurant includes salad bar with every meal. Hearty specials $9-13. Open daily 10:30am-11pm. ❶

Overlanders Steakhouse, 72 Hartley St. (☎8952 2159). Fantastic entrees of kangaroo, crocodile, and other mouth-watering Australian favorites in a true outback environment. Open fire will warm you up as you eat next to cow skins and beneath horse-saddles. If you're still cold, you can grab a "wobble board" and join into a sing and dance session. Entrees from $15, main courses $20-35. Open daily 6-10pm. ❹

Red Ochre Grill (☎8952 9614), on Todd Mall near Parsons St. Sample what a top-notch chef can do with regional ingredients. Aussie Game Medley ($33) and marinated kangaroo pizza ($12.90) are popular dishes. Check out the $9.90 lunch special or dine early at dinner for 20% off the menu. Open daily 6am-latenight. ❹

Bar Doppios (☎8952 6525), Fan Arcade, at the Gregory Terr. end of Todd Mall. Happening coffee shop serving Mediterranean, Australian, and Middle Eastern fare (main courses $10-16). Don't miss the exceptional breakfasts, served until 11am. Good vegetarian and non-dairy meals. BYO. Open M-Sa 8am-4pm, Su 10am-4pm. Cash only. ❷

Keller's Swiss, Indian, and Australian Restaurant (☎8952 3188), on Gregory Terr. east of Hartley St. Switzerland and India make an odd couple, yet the unlikely pairing works splendidly at Keller's, with hearty and daring vegetarian-friendly fare. Beef vindaloo $21.80. Kangaroo filet stroganoff $24.80. Open M-Sa 5:30pm-latenight. ❸

SIGHTS

The **Alice Wanderer** shuttle service circles past the major sights in the greater Alice Springs area. It's a cheap way to get out to distant attractions. However, the schedule requires that you spend an hour and ten minutes (or multiples thereof) at each sight that you want to see. (☎8952 2111 or 1800 722 111. Runs 9am-4pm, departs from the southern end of Todd Mall. All-day ticket $38.)

CITY CENTER

ANZAC HILL. Though the aerial view of Alice is a trifle drab, Anzac Hill is a great place to see a postcard-perfect sunset with the MacDonnells as a backdrop. *(Walk* *to Wills Terr. between Bath and Hartley St.; a metal arch marks the start of the easy 10min. "Lions Walk" from the base to the obelisk at the top. Vehicle access is around the corner on Stuart Hwy.)*

REPTILE CENTRE. With an impressive collection of local lizards and snakes—some of which you can hold—the Reptile Centre is a fun introduction to cold-blooded Australia. *(9 Stuart Terr., on the corner of Bath St. ☎8952 8900. Open daily 9:30am-5pm. Feedings 11am, 1, and 3:30pm. $9, children $5.)*

ABORIGINAL ARTS AND CULTURE CENTRE. Owned and operated by the Arrernte, the Centre incorporates a small art gallery, a 1hr. "Didgeridoo University" course, and a museum. The museum presents Aboriginal history, including a summary of archaeological evidence for early inhabitation and technical innovation by Aborigines. The focus, however, is strongly on recent history and the struggle for Aboriginal rights. *(125 Todd St. ☎8952 3408; www.aboriginalart.com.au. Open daily 9am-5pm. Didgeridoo course $15. Museum $2 suggested donation.)*

NATIONAL PIONEER WOMEN'S HALL OF FAME. An enthusiastic and enjoyable tribute to over 100 Australian women who broke ground in fields ranging from sports to medicine to politics. *(In the Old Courthouse on Parsons St. at the corner of Hartley St. ☎8952 9006; www.pioneerwomen.com.au. Open daily Feb. to mid-Dec. 10am-5pm. $2.20.)*

OUTSIDE THE CITY CENTER

ALICE SPRINGS CULTURAL PRECINCT. This collection of art galleries and museums is a great way to spend a few hours learning about all aspects of the region. The **Araluen Centre and Galleries** has rotating exhibitions, the largest collection of work by renowned Aboriginal artist Albert Namatjira, and displays of local work. The **Museum of Central Australia** has a wonderful set of exhibits detailing the region's meteorology and biology. The **Central Australian Aviation Museum** tells the story of aviation and the important role it played in the development of this remote region. The nearby cemetery contains Namatjira's grave. *(1km out on Larapinta Dr. ☎8952 5800. Open M-Sa 10am-5pm, Su 11am-3pm. $9, children $6, families $25.)*

DESERT PARK. An impressive collection of local flora and fauna. The nocturnal house is a great place to view such reclusive species as the bilby and dunnart. The **Birds of Prey** show is also popular. *(8km west of town on Larapinta Dr. Desert Park runs a shuttle every 1½hr. 7:30am-6pm from most accommodations to the park. Call for pickup ☎8952 4667. $35, concessions $28; includes admission. Park ☎8951 8788. Open daily 7:30am-6pm. Birds of Prey show 10am and 3:30pm. $20, children $10, families $55.)*

SCHOOL OF THE AIR. Central Australia's answer to the daunting task of educating children living on remote cattle stations, roadhouses, and Aboriginal lands. Using the Royal Flying Doctors' radio network, lessons are broadcast to 140 students over a network covering 1.3 million square kilometers. *(Coming from Alice, before the turn-off to the Reserve, a sign on the Stuart Hwy. points down Head St. ☎8951 6834. Open M-Sa 8:30am-4:30pm, Su 1:30-4:30pm. $6.50, concessions $4.)*

TELEGRAPH STATION HISTORICAL RESERVE. From its early days as a relay station for telegraphs between Darwin and Adelaide, to its 10-year stint as a home for half-white-half-Aboriginal children, to its use as a camp by Aboriginal people banned from Alice Springs after dark, this station has an important history that is brought to life by tours and exhibits. *(Take the turn-off 3km north of the CBD on the Stuart Hwy. ☎8952 3993. 30min. walk from the CBD. $6, children $3.)*

ENTERTAINMENT AND NIGHTLIFE

The *Alice Spring News* ($0.90) has a "Dive Into Live" section listing upcoming events. The 500-seat **Araluen Centre,** on Larapinta Dr., presents indie flicks every Sun-

CAMEL DERBY

'he old adage says that every ;irl's dream is to be swept off her eet by a handsome knight riding ı white horse, but the people of \lice Springs like to do things a ittle differently. Instead of knights hey have cowboys, and instead of horses they have camels. Every 'ear on the second Saturday of uly the town hosts the Camel Cup Carnival, a day dedicated to ood, fun, and camel races.

The tradition began with a bet between two camel farmers who hought it would be fun to see whose humped steed could run aster. Eventually, it expanded to a full-day extravaganza with a series of races and events. The kids race around with a "hobby-camel"—think hobby-horse with some key substitutions—between heir knees, while the cowboys ace some serious competition in he Camel Cup race. The most spectator-friendly event is the Honeymoon Handicap race, in which new husbands stop midway o pick up their brides before con-inuing on to the finish line.

So if you find yourself in Alice around mid-July, grab some grub, find yourself a handsome beast of burden, and join in the excite-ment. Don't forget your wallet, as all the money raised during the event goes to charity.

Races run all day with the opening ceremony at 11:30am and trophy presentations at 4:40pm. Admis-sion paid at the gate ($10).

day and live theater performances. (☎8951 1122. Box office open daily 10am-5pm.) For Hollywood movies, head to **Alice Springs Cinema,** at the North end of Todd Mall. (☎8953 2888. Tickets $14, Tu $10.) For those with more cash, **Red Centre Dreaming** offers a traditional three-course NT dinner with an Aboriginal cultural display that includes an extensive performance by a dance troupe. (☎1800 089 616. Open daily 7-10pm. $98, children $55; includes pickup and drop-off.)

Bojangles, 80 Todd St., has everything you could want in a saloon: a honky-tonk piano in the corner, great food, and a generous helping of outback cowboys. This is the kind of place where throwing peanut shells on the floor is appreciated. Be forewarned that your raucous night will be webcast (seriously, visit www.boslivesaloon.com.au) every night from 9pm-1am. (☎8952 2873. Open daily 11:30am-latenight. DJ daily. Su Blues Jam 3pm-latenight.) A few doors down, **Melanka Party Bar,** 94 Todd St., is extremely popular with the young backpacker crowd. Two big screen TVs share center stage with cheap beers and mixed drinks ($3-8) until midnight, when the dancing really starts. Frequent theme nights include jungle parties and cage dancing. (☎8952 2233. Open 5pm-latenight.) **Sean's Bar,** 51 Bath St., is a local haunt that serves a respectable pint of Guinness for $6.90. (☎8952 1858. Open daily 3:30pm-latenight. Live music F-Sa 8pm, open jam session Su.)

FESTIVALS AND EVENTS

In April, **Heritage Week** features various historical reenactments and displays. Around the same time, Alice plays host to a month-long horse racing festival, the lavish **Alice Springs Cup Carnival,** which takes place at the town's Pioneer Race Park and culminates with the **Bangtail Muster** parade on the first Monday of May. On the Queen's Birthday Weekend in early June, the plucky cars and motorcycles of the **Finke Desert Race** traverse 240km of roadless dusty desert from Alice to Finke. The first Saturday in July hosts the traditional, agriculture-focused **Alice Springs Show.** The not-so-traditional **Camel Cup Carnival** race (www.camelcup.com.au), including a Miss Camel Cup Competition, is held the following weekend. The **Alice Springs Rodeo** and the **Harts Range Annual Races** are both popular events held every August in Alice.

The definitive Alice Springs festival is the **Henley-on-Todd Regatta** (third Saturday in September; www.henleyontodd.com.au). A good-natured mock celebration centered on the dry river; the "regatta" race is done in bottomless "boats" propelled Flintstones-style—by swift feet. The **Corkwood Festival,** on the last Saturday of November, is a traditional folk event featuring daytime craft booths and energetic bush dancing at night.

MACDONNELL RANGES

The MacDonnell Ranges roll east to west across the horizon as far as the eye can see, creating pockets of geological formations and wildlife that break up the flatness of the desert surroundings. From a distance, the green shrubbery that covers the ridges appears to be a soft blanket of grass, but up close, the landscape is identifiably Central Australian, with rusty orange earth, rocky outcroppings, prickly ground-cover, and glowing white ghost gums. The Ranges' myriad pastel colors have inspired painters and photographers throughout the ages, and numerous walking tracks through the area invite visitors to take a closer look.

MACDONNELL RANGES AT A GLANCE

AREA: 460km.

FEATURES: West MacDonnell NP along Namatjira Dr., Finke Gorge NP off Larapinta Dr., and several nature parks to the east.

HIGHLIGHTS: Hiking, swimming, and scenery.

GATEWAYS: Alice Springs (p. 295).

CAMPING: Available but limited. Check with a tour agency in Alice Springs before setting out for any camping trip.

FEES: A small fee is charged only at Standley Chasm (p. 302) and the Hermannsburg Historical Precinct (p. 303).

WEST MACDONNELLS

ORIENTATION

To the north of the Uluru-Kata Tjuta and Watarrka area, immediately outside Alice Springs, lie central Australia's mountains. Larapinta Dr. heads straight out of town, passing turn-offs to **Simpson's Gap** and **Standley Chasm.** After about 25km, the road forks into two branches, with Larapinta Dr. continuing on to Hermannsburg and Finke Gorge, and Namatjira Dr. passing the Ellery Creek Big Hole and Serpentine Gorge en route to the Glen Helen area. The only road that runs between Hermannsburg and Glen Helen is the rough and tumble Tylers Pass loop, a rough 4WD track with extraordinary scenery.

HIKING AND TOURS

The **Larapinta Trail** offers experienced hikers the opportunity to reach remote parts of the range. It stretches 220km from the Telegraph Station in Alice Springs to Mt. Razorback, beyond Glen Helen Gorge. The trail connects the main attractions, making it possible to hike individual two- to four-day chunks from one gorge to another. Before attempting the long hikes, get information from the **Park and Wildlife Commission** in Alice Springs. (☎8951 8250. P.O. Box 2130, Alice Springs NT 0870.) Voluntary registration is a good idea; the $50 deposit is refundable unless the Parks and Wildlife Commission (☎1300 650 730) ends up sending out a search and rescue mission for you. Pick up the flyer *Bushwalks* from the tourist office in Alice for a list of hikes.

The Glen Helen Lodge (p. 304) has the only official accommodations in the West Macdonnells. The best bet for long visits is to take a tour. **AAT Kings Tours** does a day-trip to the range. (☎8952 1700; www.aatkings.com. Departs daily 7:30am. $108, children $54.) **Centre Highlights** makes a 4WD trek to some area highlights, including

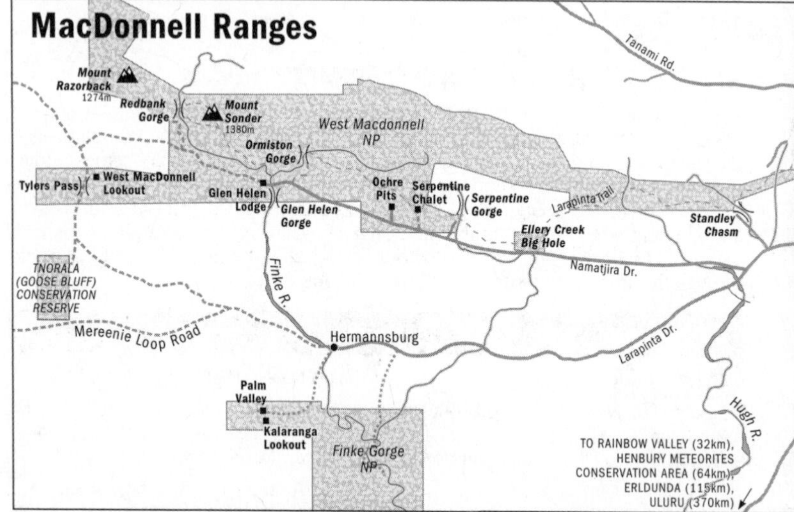

Finke River and Palm Valley. (☎1800 659 574; www.centrehighlights.com.au. Departs M, W, F 8am. $119.) **Centremen Tour** (☎8953 2623) offers daytrips from $95.

SIGHTS

The West MacDonnells' sights lie along two paved roads, Larapinta and Namatjira Dr., heading out from the town of Alice Springs. The westernmost parts of these roads, as well as the Mereenie Loop road, are 4WD only. The distance from Alice is listed in parentheses after the description of each sight.

LARAPINTA DRIVE

JOHN FLYNN MEMORIAL GRAVE. Just off the road is the grave of the minister who created the Royal Flying Doctor Service. Sentiment that his gravestone should be something symbolic of the Outback led to the selection of a massive boulder taken from the Devil's Marbles (p. 294), near Tennant Creek—which led to a twenty-year battle between the caretaker of Flynn's grave and Aborigines, for whom the Devil's Marbles are sacred. The dispute was settled in 1999 with the substitution of a stone from the East MacDonnells and the return of the Devil's Marble to its original location. *(7km.)*

SIMPSON'S GAP. Simpson's Gap, located down a paved 8km turn-off, offers some nice hikes and views of jagged red rocks. The **Gap Walk** is an easy 20min. jaunt from the carpark. The **Cassia Hill Walk** is an equally simple 1.8km (30min.) climb to a lookout. *(18km. Open daily 5am-8pm. Free.)*

STANDLEY CHASM. After traveling down a mostly flat, 30min. path along a creek bed, crowds gather to marvel at the glowing orange walls when the sun shines directly into this 80m fissure at midday. If you venture past a shallow waterhole and up the rocky slide at the far end, you can enjoy a less crowded second chasm and an overhead view of the first. *(46km. ☎8956 7440. Open daily 8am-6pm, last entry 5pm. $7.50, concessions $6.50. Food and drinks available.)*

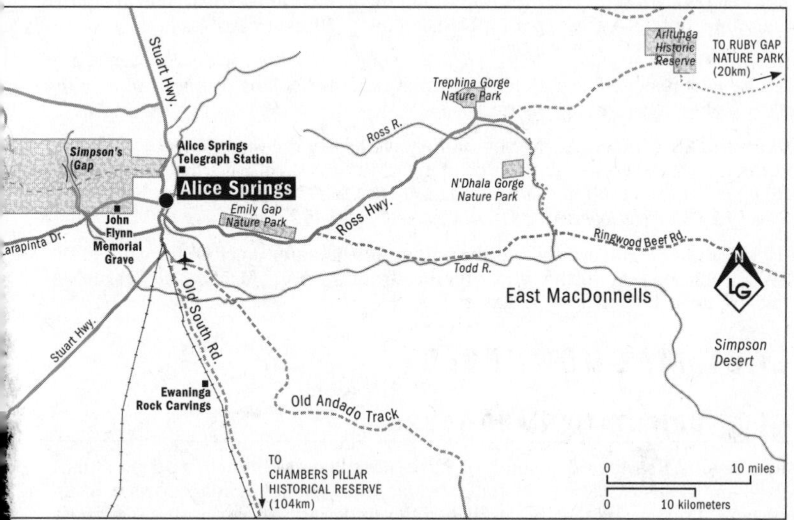

FINKE GORGE NATIONAL PARK. This 46,000 hectare park contains the Finke River, some stretches of which date back 350 million years. The park's main attraction is **Palm Valley,** home to rare Red Cabbage Palms. Two worthwhile walks are the **Mpulungkinya Walk** (5km, 2hr.), which traverses the thickest growth of palms, and the **Arankaia Walk** (2km, 1hr.), which climbs the valley rim. The **Kalaranga Lookout** (1.5km, 45min.) surmounts steep crags to offer 360° views of the park. *(125km. Accessed through the 21km 4WD-only road that follows the path of the mostly dry Finke River, off Larapinta Dr. Sites $6.60 per person, children $3.30, families $15.40.)*

HERMANNSBURG HISTORICAL PRECINCT. Old homes from the early Lutheran mission are here, along with a gallery saluting Aboriginal artist Albert Namatjira. The service station sells the **Mereenie Tour Pass** for the 4WD track to Kings Canyon (p. 306), **petrol,** and **groceries.** *(126km. ☎8956 7402. Open daily Dec.-Feb. 10am-4pm, Mar.-Nov. 9am-4pm. $4, children $3. Gallery $3.)*

NAMATJIRA DRIVE

ORMISTON GORGE. A 10min. walk leads to a few of the gorge's pools (some 14m deep). The wonderful **Ghost Gum Walk** (1hr.) climbs the side of the gorge to an impressive lookout, then drops off further down river, allowing hikers to wander along the creek amid boulders stained silver, blue, and purple. During late afternoon, the orange walls glow in the sinking sun and wallabies come out to play. The **Pound Walk** (7km, 3-4hr.) is more peaceful, offering great views of the surrounding hills before approaching the gorge from the back. *(130km.)*

ELLERY CREEK BIG HOLE. Down a rough 2km access road and a 100m wheelchair-accessible path is this big water hole. In summer, it makes for a very nippy dip; don't even think about it in winter. The nearby **Dolemite Walk** (3km, 1hr.) traverses lush forest and spinifex.

SERPENTINE GORGE. A walk along a service road (1hr.) leads to this serene gorge. The highlight of Serpentine is the **lookout walk,** a short, steep climb starting near the gorge and ending with a great view of the West MacDonnells. *(102km.)*

SERPENTINE CHALET. Down a rough 3km road, the ruins of the Chalet are unremarkable, but it's a great spot for bushcamping. *(105km. No facilities.)*

OCHRE PITS. The exposed cliffs are a key source of ochre used in Aboriginal art. A wheelchair-accessible path leads to a platform overlooking the pits. From there, it's possible to walk along the riverbed and view the banded rock walls. *(108km.)*

GLEN HELEN GORGE. At the end of the paved road, the **Glen Helen Lodge ❷** sits at the foot of the gorge, illuminated at night with spotlights. It's the only place to fill up on gas and food this side of Alice. *(134km. ☎8956 7489. www.glenhelen.com.au. Sites for 2 $25; motel rooms for 2 $160. Helicopter flights $45-295. Book ahead.)*

GOSSE BLUFF. You can see the site of the ancient crater up close from the 11km 4WD track, or take in the whole picture from the **West MacDonnell Lookout,** a turn-off near the north end of Tylers Pass. *(187km.)*

EAST MACDONNELLS

ORIENTATION AND TOURS

Just beyond **Heavitree Gap** south of Alice, **Ross Highway** branches off the Stuart Hwy. and heads eastward into the East MacDonnells. The road narrows to a single lane at times, and the area is filled with wandering **wild camels** that frequently travel down the center of the road. More varied, less crowded, and as fetching as their more lauded western neighbors, the East MacDonnells offer good 4WD tracks and rewarding hikes. The range is accessed primarily through tours; **Discovery Ecotours** (☎1800 803 174) and **Emu Run** (☎8953 7057. 9½hr., departs 8am; $100) run tours of the area if there is enough interest. Campsites are not always open, so check with a tour agency in town before planning your trip.

SIGHTS

The distance from Alice along Ross Hwy. to the turn-off for each listing is given in parentheses after the description of each sight.

EMILY GAP. Bold and unassuming, Emily Gap is an important site in the local Arrernte people's understanding of The Dreaming. The gorge holds a gallery of Aboriginal rock paintings marking the spot where *Intwailuka*, an ancestral hero, cooked and ate caterpillars on his Dreamtime journey. Icy pools often obstruct the path into the gap and the gallery. If the water appears low enough, leave your shoes behind and cross in the center of the pool where it is most shallow. *(7km.)*

TREPHINA GORGE NATURE PARK. A partly paved 8km access road leads to the carpark and the **main campground ❶.** The **Trephina Gorge Walk** (2km, 45min.) follows the gorge rim before descending to the sandy riverbed—pay careful attention: signs become less obvious as the walk wears on. The **Panorama** loop (3km, 1½hr.) climbs to an excellent lookout over the whole park. At the **John Hayes Rockhole,** 4km down a 4WD-only track, there is **more camping ❶.** Here hikers also find the **Chain Ponds Walk** (4km, 1½hr.), a sojourn past a great lookout and through a picture-perfect series of pools. The **Hayes Trephina Bluff Walk** is a 6hr. one-way hike that highlights both regions of the park. All campsites have pit toilets and BBQ. *(72km.)*

ARLTUNGA HISTORIC RESERVE. A left turn off Ross Hwy. leads to the site of Central Australia's first town. Originally a ruby mine, Arltunga seemed doomed when the "fiery gems" were determined to be useless garnets. Gold was discovered the same year but the town was eventually abandoned, as the lack of water for sifting and extraordinary isolation rendered the mining unprofitable. The 33km gravel road leading to the reserve climbs through the hills, a nice break from the surrounding flatness. Bring your flashlight for exploring the old mines. The visitors center is particularly helpful. *(75km.)*

RUBY GAP NATURE PARK. Thirty-nine kilometers along a 4WD track beyond Arltunga lie the stunning gorge and free **bush camping ❶** (no water) of **Ruby Gap Nature Park.** Register with the ranger station at Arltunga before heading out. *(75km.)*

N'DHALA GORGE. An intermittently-marked 11km 4WD track leads through a thigh-deep creek before intersecting a series of dry creek beds on its way to N'Dhala Gorge. An otherwise unspectacular walking track (1.5km, 1hr.) weaves through the gorge, passing a few Aboriginal rock carvings, some of which may be 10,000 years old. **Camping ❶** (without water) is available. *(82km.)*

SIMPSON DESERT

South of Alice, the Stuart Hwy. passes Heavitree Gap and Palm Circuit. The unsealed and isolated **Old South Road,** off the Stuart Hwy., heads right toward the **Simpson Desert.** It's rough country out here. Charles Sturt first explored this part of the Simpson in 1845, and was so bent on conquering the Outback that many of his men died due to the desert's harsh conditions. Stock up on supplies before heading out. Several tours go to the Simpson Desert from Alice Springs. **Emu Run** does an afternoon tour of Rainbow Valley, complete with BBQ dinner. (☎8953 7057; www.emurun.com.au. Offers pickup at most accommodations. $89.)

The first worthwhile spot is the **Ewaninga Rock Carvings,** 39km south of Alice. The weathered petroglyphs are a sacred site for Aborigines. The Aboriginal community of **Maryvale Station,** 62km more along the Old South Rd., marks the 4WD-only turn to **Chambers Pillar Historical Reserve** (4hr. one-way). This sandstone formation was a landmark for early travelers, as demonstrated by their carved initials (a practice now subject to high fines). The trek is more taxing than rewarding, but sunsets at the rock are masterpieces of color. (No water or facilities.)

Rainbow Valley is a jagged, U-shaped ridge of bleached sandstone capped by more iron-rich multi-colored stone. The valley is most famous for its winter sunsets, when the red-orange-yellow formation is illuminated at the ideal angle. A short walk leads to its base. It's a striking sight, but remember that there's 97km of nothing between here and Alice. Another 51km down the Stuart, the unsealed **Ernest Giles Road** heads west toward Watarrka; 11km past the turn-off and 4km north on an access road lie the **Henbury Meteorite Craters.** A 20min. trail leads around the rim of the circular indentation caused 4000 years ago by meteorites.

DRESSING FOR THE DESERT. With scorching days and freezing cold nights it is important to know how to dress to stay comfortable in the desert. Two general rules:

1) Layers, layers, layers: wear multiple layers that you can take on and off to adjust your temperature and stay comfortable.
2) It's harder to get warm than to stay warm, so don't wait until you are cold to put on another layer. Think ahead. If the sun is starting to set, grab a few extra pieces of clothing, and bundle up.

WATARRKA NATIONAL PARK (KINGS CANYON)

The increasingly popular Watarrka National Park centers around Kings Canyon. The views are postcard-quality and the pockets of lush greenery cradled within the canyon's walls are a refreshing change from the region's dusty terrain.

WATARRKA NATIONAL PARK AT A GLANCE

AREA: 720 sq. km

FEATURES: Kings Canyon, with cliffs over 300m high and 1-3hr. walks.

HIGHLIGHTS: Deep canyons, cool reflective streams, and the "Garden of Eden."

GATEWAYS: Alice Springs and Kings Canyon Resort/Kings Creek Station.

CAMPING: Not allowed in NP. Available at Kings Canyon Resort and Kings Creek Station (see Accommodations).

FEES: None

TRANSPORTATION. Watarrka is located on Luritja Rd., 2½hr. north of the junction with Lasseter Hwy. There are three different ways to drive to the park from Alice Springs. First, the fully paved route—the **Stuart Highway**—runs 202km south to the roadhouse settlement of **Erldunda ❶**, where it meets the Lasseter Hwy. Travelers changing buses here may end up spending the night. (☎8956 0984. Sites $10 per person, powered $16; motel singles $82; doubles $100.) From the junction, take the Lasseter Hwy. west 110km and turn right on Luritja Rd., which goes north 167km to the Kings Canyon park entrance. Second, the "short-cut" along **Ernest Giles Road,** a 100km stretch of unpaved road that begins 132km south of Alice off the Stuart Hwy., can cut several hundred kilometers from your trip, but a 4WD is required. Third, Kings Canyon can be reached from Alice Springs via **Hermannsburg** in the West MacDonnells. Take Larapinta Dr. to the scenic but corrugated 4WD-only **Mereenie Loop Road,** which passes through Aboriginal land. There are no accommodations and no camping is allowed on the Mereenie, so plan to do the drive in one day. A $2.20 pass is required and can be obtained in Hermannsburg at the Larapinta Service Station, Glen Helen Lodge (at Kings Canyon Resort), or at the visitors center in Alice. Most **tours** to Kings Canyon are included in Uluru-Kata Tjuta multi-day packages from Alice Springs. **Emu Run** has 12hr. day tours from Alice. (☎8953 7057. $195, children $97.50.)

ACCOMMODATIONS AND FOOD. The **Kings Canyon Resort ❶,** 7km up the road from the canyon turn-off, is clean and pleasant, but expensive. Rooms have A/C, heaters, TV, fridge, shared bath, and kitchen. (☎8956 7442 or 1300 139 889; www.voyages.com.au. Reception 6:30am-10:30pm. Book ahead. Sites $13 per person, powered $14.50; 4-bed dorms $39. Book ahead.) The resort has a cafe (open daily 10am-3pm), small **grocery store** (open 7am-7pm), and **petrol** station. **Outback BBQ ❸** offers pizzas from $17 and steaks from $29 (open daily 6-9pm).

Camping is also available at the well-maintained **Kings Creek Station ❶,** about 30km south of the turn-off to the park. It's a lower-key outpost with a friendly staff and cheap **camel safaris,** which start at $7 for a 5min. ride or $50 for a sunset trek. (☎8956 7474; www.kingscreekstation.com.au. Sites $13 per person, children $7, families $38, powered sites $17/11/42; cabin singles $77; twins $57, includes breakfast.) **No camping** is allowed inside Watarrka National Park.

HIKING. The park has been given a recent facelift, complete with new water facilities, toilets, and dozens of informational signs along all paths. There are three walks to choose from, all of which are best enjoyed with insect repellent at hand. The challenging **Kings Canyon Walk** (6km, 3hr.) is the most visually stunning. The trail begins with a steep climb up the canyon, then winds along the top with panoramic views. Several side tracks are marked along the way. Not to be missed is the **Garden of Eden** (500m round-trip), a 30min. trail mid-way through the hike that runs down to a picturesque stream and reflecting pool where you can take a dip. The easy **Kings Creek Walk** (2.6km, 1hr.) along the bottom of the canyon provides views of the canyon's sheer walls from platforms. The wheelchair-accessible **Kathleen Springs Walk** (2.6km, 1.5hr.) winds through sandstone valleys to a rockhole sacred to local Aborigines. Be sure to bring insect repellent. Those craving a longer hike can try the **Giles Track** (22km) for a relaxed two-day hike. The track winds over the southern rim of the range and connects Kings Canyon with Lilla and Kathleen Springs. Camping is permitted between the 3km and 20km markers.

ULURU-KATA TJUTA NATIONAL PARK

Uluru-Kata Tjuta National Park contains two of Australia's most majestic natural wonders. Mammoth Uluru's brooding colors are transformed with each sunrise and sunset, melting from bright orange to crimson to deep maroon, while sunlight and shadows flicker in the ridges and cave-like pockets of its surface. It is easy to see why this rock has become Australia's most enduring national symbol. The 36 domes of the Kata Tjuta mountain range, with their grainy stone-and-mortar texture, scatter across the landscape, allowing endless exploration of the valleys between each peak. Both natural wonders have been sacred Dreaming sites of the Anangu for over 20,000 years, a history recorded in the artwork around the base of Uluru. Today the park is jointly managed by the National Park Service and Anangu residents in an often uneasy partnership. Most visits to the park consist only of the climb and a few snapshots before sunset. But those who linger, exploring the basewalks at Uluru and the trails around and through Kata Tjuta, are rewarded by a powerful connection with one of the world's most iconic and magnificent areas.

ULURU AND KATA TJUTA AT A GLANCE	
AREA: 1325 sq. km	**GATEWAYS:** Alice Springs and Yulara.
ULURU: 348m high, 9.4km around.	**CAMPING:** No camping within the national park. There is a commercial campground at Yulara.
KATA TJUTA: Mt. Olga peaks at 546m.	**FEES:** 3-day pass $25.
HIGHLIGHTS: Colors of Uluru at sunrise/sunset, Valley of the Winds, Kata Tjuta.	

TRANSPORTATION. Take the Stuart Hwy. to **Erldunda,** 202km south of Alice Springs and 483km north of Coober Pedy, then drive 264km west on **Lasseter Highway** past Yulara into the park. Long before Uluru, you'll see **Mount Connor** in the distance. It is often mistaken for Uluru; it has its own viewing area right off the road.

PRACTICAL INFORMATION. The Uluru-Kata Tjuta National Park **entrance station** (☎8956 2252) lies 5km past the **Yulara** resort village, where all visitors must purchase a three-day pass ($25). The turn-off to Kata Tjuta is 4km ahead and well marked; Uluru is another 10km into the park. (Park open daily 1hr. before sunrise to 1hr. after sunset.) There are toilet facilities at the cultural center, at the main carpark at Uluru, and at the sunset-viewing area at Kata Tjuta. Several water stations are located around the circular Uluru hiking and driving circuits. Picnic tables are at the Cultural Centre and the viewing area. As in the rest of the Red Centre, the **bush flies** can be unbearable from December to April. In case of **emergency,** radio alarms located throughout the park can be used to contact a ranger; otherwise, call direct (☎8956 1128).

The fantastic **Uluru-Kata Tjuta Cultural Centre,** 1km before Uluru, gives the Anangu perspective on the region. (☎8956 1128. Open daily 7am-6pm. Free.) Constructed in shapes representing the park's spiritual ancestors *Kunyia* (a python) and *Liru* (a venomous snake), the center is full of displays relating the Anangu stories of Uluru's origin. A video details the preparation of bush tucker, as thorough a catalog of Aboriginal ingenuity in the face of adversity as is to be found in tourist Australia. There is also an information desk, a snack bar, bathrooms, and several Aboriginal art centers.

ULURU (AYERS ROCK)

Few places could live up to the hype that surrounds Uluru. Towering elegantly over the surrounding arid scrub, Uluru is in fact only the tip of an enormous slab of rock extending underground for some 5-6km. The cracks and dimples of Uluru seen from afar are actually immense gorges and caves when viewed up close.

The two highlights of a visit to the rock are a **walk around the base** and **viewing a sunset.** The seemingly infinite faces and features of Uluru make a walk around the base a constant surprise, as caves, valleys, and gorges are sculpted in a continually changing landscape. At sunset, most flock to a well-marked carpark 5km away for the best show; Uluru displays a series of hues ranging from pastel pink to deep scarlet while the flickering light plays in the caverns. Sunrise is equally stunning and, logically enough, best viewed from the opposite side of the rock.

THE CLIMB UP. The Anangu prefer that people do not climb Uluru because of its spiritual significance. The Cultural Centre will give you a better understanding of the Anangu's wishes. If you decide to neglect the cultural tradition, realize that the hike up Uluru is difficult (a full 2-3hr.), even for the young and able-bodied (notice the plaques at the base that memorialize those who have died in the process—35 deaths in the past 20 years). Visitors should avoid climbing in the middle of the day or if they have medical conditions, and should also leave loose accessories behind; many of the deaths have resulted from chasing after blown hats or cameras. The climb requires at least two to three liters of water and rugged footwear with ankle support. Due to the high level of risk, the climb is closed on excessively warm, rainy, or windy days. A fixed chain helps with the brutal initial uphill, the steepest part of the climb. Past the chain, the path, marked by white blazes, meanders along the top of the rock for over 1km. The trail is rugged and requires the scaling of near vertical sections (at times 2m high). When descending, use extreme care. Sliding down in a sitting position over the coarse rock is not recommended; grasp the chain firmly and take small steps backward, pulling on the chain for support. Despite the hazards, many tourists climb the rock daily.

HIKES AROUND THE BOTTOM. There are several less adventurous, less dangerous, and less intrusive hikes around the base of Uluru. Grab *An Insight into Uluru* ($2), available at the Cultural Centre, for a self-guided tour highlighting the cultural creation features of these walks.

Uluru Base Walk (9.4km, 3-4hr.). Flat and level but long, this walk offers the best opportunity to study the innumerable dimples, grooves, and caverns of the rock. The path, which at times skirts the rock and also follows a road further from the base, is the only real chance to escape the throngs and contemplate the rock in solitude. As it is a circuit, the path can be picked up at many places around the base of Uluru.

Mala Walk (2km, 45min.). Part of the circuit walk, this wheelchair-accessible track leads from main carpark past Aboriginal art sites and a wave-shaped cave on Uluru's wall to **Kantju Gorge,** which holds a sacred Anangu waterhole. Free, engaging, ranger-guided walks along the path present an Aboriginal perspective on Uluru. Meet the ranger at the Mala Walk sign at the base. (1½hr. Daily Oct.-Apr. 8am, May-Sept. 10am. Free.)

Kuniya Walk (1km, 30min.). This flat, wheelchair-accessible track, served by a carpark to the right of the loop entrance, leads to a waterhole that is home to *Wanampi,* an ancestral watersnake. Signs along the way detail the battle between ancestral spirits *Kuniya* and *Liru,* the events of which are recorded in the rock's features.

KATA TJUTA (THE OLGAS)

While Uluru is stunning, many visitors find themselves twiddling their thumbs after staring at the rock for a few minutes. Luckily, the beautiful Kata Tjuta saves the day, providing 36 awe-inspiring domes among which to wander for the remainder of the day. Anangu for "many heads," Kata Tjuta has many faces that adopt new characters and moods as you circle them or walk through their valleys. Rising from the surrounding flatness, the domes are a mysterious and magical site.

The 42km road to Kata Tjuta leaves the main road 4km after the park entrance. The **Dune Viewing Area,** 25km down the road, is at the end of a wheelchair-accessible walk (300m) and allows relaxing, all-encompassing views of Kata Tjuta. The **sunset-viewing area** (toilets available) is near the starting points of the two walks.

Valley of the Winds Walk (7.4km, 2-3hr.). This moderate-grade hike reveals spectacular views of stony countryside and picturesque valleys, viewed between the massive walls of the Olgas. The main circuit passes through the mountains, while a shorter circuit cuts across the beginning section of the main circuit and does not climb between the domes. Midway through the walk is the Karingana Lookout. With a sweeping view into the gorge, this spot is one of the best and least crowded in the entire park.

Walpa Gorge Walk (2.6km, 45min.). An easy path that heads straight between a pair of the most daunting domes. The dome on the right is **Mount Olga,** the highest peak in the range at 546m. The lookout at the end is often crowded, and the view is no more spectacular than the views along the path.

YULARA (AYERS ROCK RESORT) ☎08

Ayers Rock Resort (the municipal name "Yulara" applies only because there is a small employee housing district) is a series of hotels and shops stretched along a side road just outside Uluru-Kata Tjuta NP. The resort is the only game in town, and owns the supermarket, petrol station, hostel, hotel, and apartments. Prices are high, so bring food and supplies from elsewhere if you want to save some money.

TRANSPORTATION AND PRACTICAL INFORMATION. Connellan Airport lies 5km north of town. **Airnorth** and **Qantas** (☎13 13 13) fly to Adelaide, Alice Springs, Brisbane, Cairns, Darwin, Melbourne, Perth, and Sydney. A free airport shuttle run by AAT Kings meets all flights and picks up from all accommodations. **Greyhound Australia** (☎13 14 99 or 13 20 30) **buses** depart for Alice Springs daily from the Outback Pioneer Hotel (6hr., approx. 2pm, $87). Ayers Rock Resort runs a free village shuttle around the resort loop. (Every 20min., daily

10:30am-12:30am.) **Territory Rent-a-Car** (☎8956 2030), **Hertz** (☎8956 2244), and **Avis** (☎8956 2266) have offices at the airport and at the **Tourist Info Centre** in the resort shopping center (☎8957 7324). Prices for cars start around $60-70 per day; you must book ahead, especially in the high season. Most backpackers come to Yulara on camping tours out of Alice Springs, which can be combined with various stops at other sites, such as Watarrka National Park.

Those without cars have several options for traveling to Uluru. **Uluru Express** (☎8956 2152) offers flexible transportation to the rock ($35, children $20) and Kata Tjuta ($50, children $30). For a more comprehensive experience, **Anangu Tours,** owned by the Anangu, gives award-winning cultural tours of Uluru; book at the Cultural Centre. (☎8956 2123. 2hr. tours $58, day tours up to $199.) Another option is to bike the 20km to Uluru (Kata-Tjuta is another 33km); **bike rentals** are available from the Ayers Rock Resort Campground from $20 per day (see below).

The **Tourist Info Centre,** in the shopping center, has general info and tour agencies. (☎8957 7324. Internet kiosks available. Open daily 8am-8pm; service desks maintain shorter hours.) The **Visitors Centre,** with a grand set of stairs rising from the road near the entrance to the village, has a gift shop and museum of desert animals, as well as a detailed history of Uluru. (☎8957 7377. Open daily 9am-5pm.) **Petrol** is available at the Mobil station. (☎8956 2229. Open daily 7am-9pm.) Other services include: **police** (☎8956 2166); **ANZ bank** with 24hr. **ATM** in the shopping center (open M-Th 9:30am-4pm, F 9:30am-5pm); and a **post office.** (☎8956 2288. Open M-F 9am-6pm, Sa-Su 10am-2pm.) **Postal Code:** 0872.

ACCOMMODATIONS AND FOOD. For all lodge bookings, call ☎1300 139 889. The **Outback Pioneer Lodge ❸,** on Yulara Dr., has simple barrack-style digs with a kitchen and large, clean baths. (☎8957 7639. Free storage. Reception 24hr. 20-bed dorms $33, YHA $30; 4-bed $41/37.) The **Ayers Rock Resort Campground ❶** is the only camping option in the area; camping is not permitted in the park. Campers have access to the same facilities as at the Lodge, including a pool, kitchen, laundry, hot showers, and BBQ. (☎8957 7001. Sites $13 per person, children $6.50, families $37; powered $15.50.) Private options consist of "budget" doubles ($157, ensuite $177) at the **Outback Pioneer Hotel ❺.** The only other alternative is 100km away at **Curtain Springs ❶,** which means either missing the sunrise/sunset at Uluru or driving in the dark. (☎8956 2906. Free unpowered sites. Powered $20, showers $2; singles from $50, ensuite $120; doubles from $60, ensuite $120.) Food options are limited; the cheapest choice is to take a shuttle to the supermarket.

QUEENSLAND

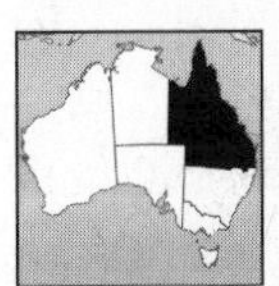

If the continent's natural attractions could be condensed into one state, the result would look something like Queensland, Australia's magnificently layered natural paradise. It encompasses reef islands, sandy shores, hinterland rainforest, and glowing red Outback. In the southeast corner of the state is Brisbane, the youthful, diverse state capital. Queensland's gorgeous coast crawls with backpackers year-round; with the same faces popping up in every town, the journey often feels like a never-ending party. The downside for those on this heavily-touristed route is that real Aussie culture can be masked by the young crowd that floods its shores. Moving from one hotspot to another can be mind-numbing as you wade through a neverending swamp of brochures, billboards, and tourist packages.

Travelers who step off the beaten track find that Queensland is much more than one long beach party. Those willing to trade flip flops for hiking boots can explore the rainforests of the far north and the jewel-bedecked Outback, where history, like tourism, proceeds at a koala's pace. The isolated inland is dotted with charming country towns, pockets of thriving Aboriginal culture, and plenty of history. Across the entire state, opportunities abound for travelers to make money and enjoy camaraderie as part of the flourishing fruit-picking subculture. In Queensland, appreciating the real Oz can be as simple as driving toward Cape Tribulation and watching the dense layers of the forest peel away, the soil at last yielding to sand and ocean, rolling waves cresting to the horizon.

HIGHLIGHTS OF QUEENSLAND

DIVE the Great Barrier Reef and **swim** among shimmering schools of fish. (p. 314)

DRIVE Fraser Island and fulfill your **4WD fantasies** on massive sand dunes. (p. 371)

SURF the legendary **breaks** at Coolangatta and Tweed Heads. (p. 338)

HIKE through lush **rainforest** and misty **valleys** in Eungella National Park. (p. 391)

CAMP on a secluded **rainforest beach** in Cape Tribulation. (p. 437)

TRANSPORTATION

Comprehensive public transportation services the Queensland up through the far north and its interior. Don't underestimate the distances involved; even within the state, many people choose to fly if they want to get from Brisbane to Cairns quickly. If you've got the time for a leisurely trip, taking a bus up the coast allows you to stop at fun spots along the way. The major bus line is **Greyhound Australia** (☎13 20 30 or ☎13 14 99), and the train line is **Queensland Rail** (☎13 22 32). If you have a few friends to chip in for costs or if you're traveling with a family, **renting a car** is an affordable convenience that provides a lot of freedom. All the major car rental agencies have offices in Queensland, as do dozens of cheaper local ones. You'll need a 4WD to tackle the area from Cooktown north through Cape York and some of the desert roads. It can be expensive, and finding an automatic transmission 4WD is tough. Even with a 4WD, roads in the tropics can be harrowing, and often impassible, during and immediately following the **Wet season** (Nov.-Apr.). It's best to call ahead for **road conditions** (☎3361 2406).

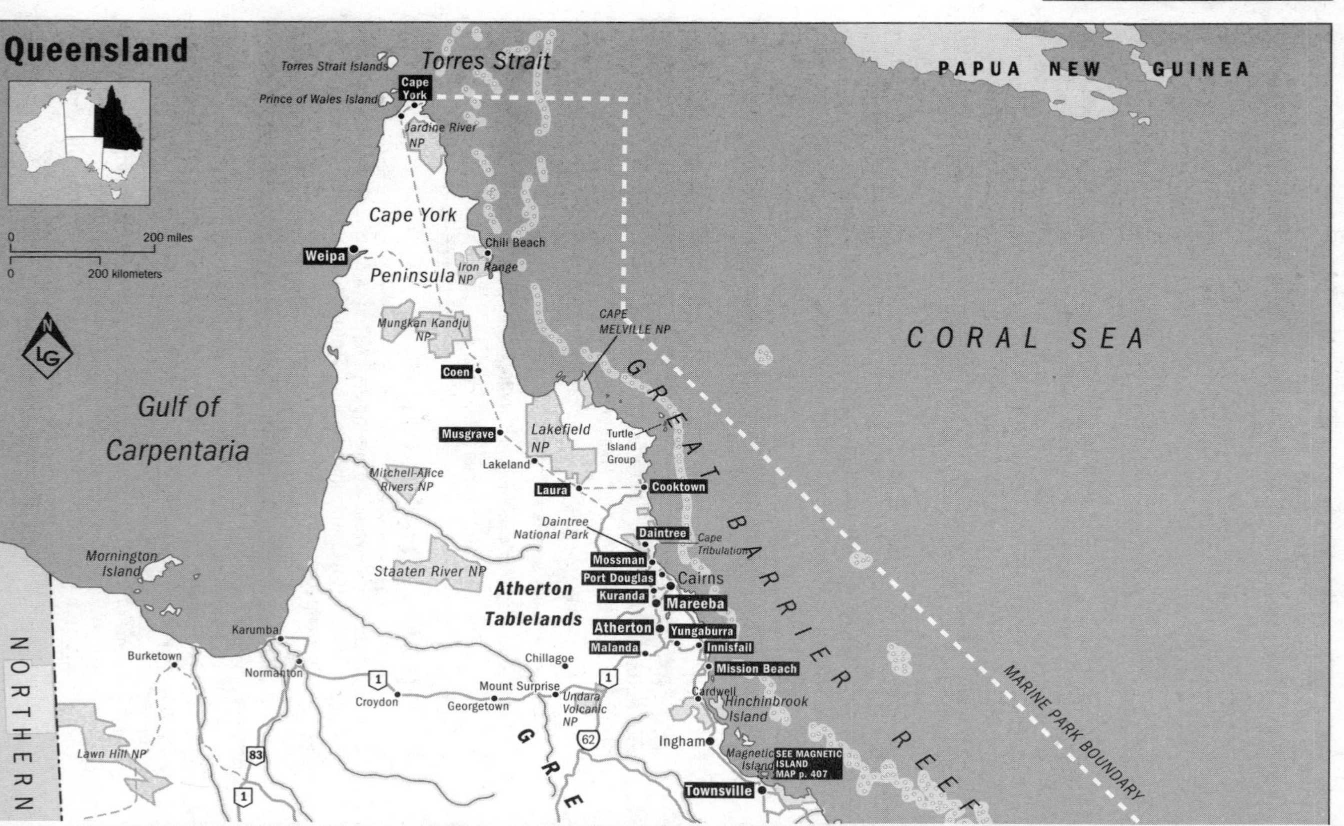
Queensland
0
200 miles
0
200 kilometers
Torres Strait Islands
Torres Strait
Prince of Wales Island
Cape York
Jardine River NP
Cape York Peninsula
Weipa
Chili Beach
Iron Range NP
Mungkan Kandju NP
Coen
Gulf of Carpentaria
Musgrave
Lakefield NP
Turtle Island Group
Lakeland
Mitchell-Alice Rivers NP
Laura
Cooktown
CAPE MELVILLE NP
Daintree National Park
Daintree
Cape Tribulation
Mossman
Port Douglas
Cairns
Kuranda
Mareeba
Atherton Tablelands
Atherton
Yungaburra
Malanda
Innisfail
Mission Beach
Mornington Island
Staaten River NP
Karumba
Burketown
Normanton
Chillagoe
1
Croydon
Mount Surprise
Georgetown
Undara Volcanic NP
62
83
Cardwell
Hinchinbrook Island
Ingham
Magnetic Island
SEE MAGNETIC ISLAND MAP p. 407
Townsville
Lawn Hill NP
NORTHERN
PAPUA NEW GUINEA
CORAL SEA
GREAT BARRIER REEF
MARINE PARK BOUNDARY

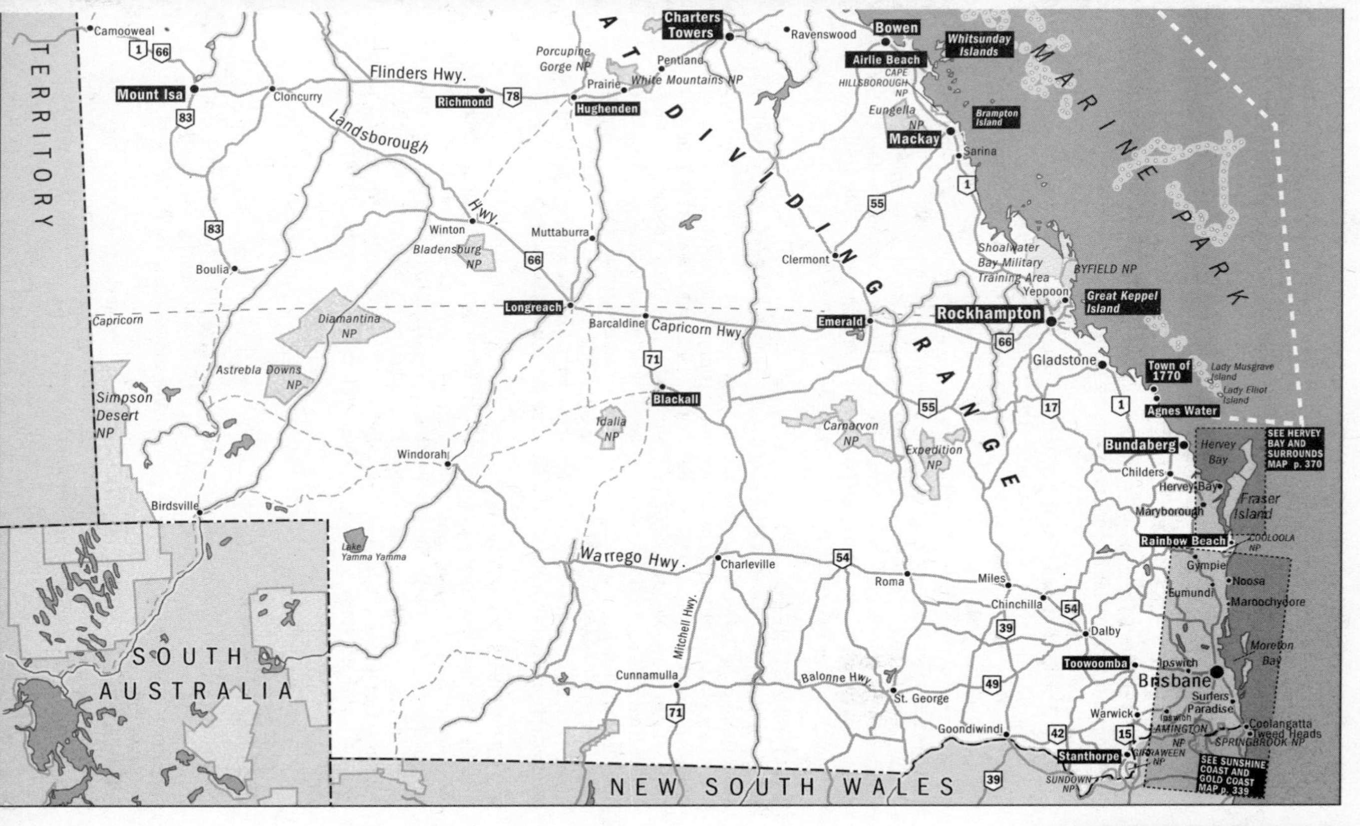
MARINE PARK
GREAT DIVIDING RANGE
TERRITORY
SOUTH AUSTRALIA
NEW SOUTH WALES
SEE HERVEY BAY AND SURROUNDS MAP p. 370
SEE SUNSHINE COAST AND GOLD COAST MAP p. 339
Camooweal
Mount Isa
Cloncurry
Flinders Hwy.
Richmond
Hughenden
Prairie
Pentland
Porcupine Gorge NP
White Mountains NP
Charters Towers
Ravenswood
Bowen
Airlie Beach
Whitsunday Islands
Cape Hillsborough NP
Eungella NP
Brampton Island
Mackay
Sarina
Landsborough Hwy.
Winton
Bladensburg NP
Muttaburra
Boulia
Clermont
Shoalwater Bay Military Training Area
Byfield NP
Yeppoon
Great Keppel Island
Rockhampton
Longreach
Barcaldine
Capricorn Hwy.
Emerald
Capricorn
Diamantina NP
Gladstone
Town of 1770
Lady Musgrave Island
Lady Elliot Island
Agnes Water
Astrebia Downs NP
Simpson Desert NP
Blackall
Idalia NP
Carnarvon NP
Expedition NP
Bundaberg
Hervey Bay
Childers
Windorah
Fraser Island
Maryborough
Birdsville
Rainbow Beach
Cooloola NP
Lake Yamma Yamma
Warrego Hwy.
Charleville
Roma
Miles
Gympie
Noosa
Eumundi
Maroochydore
Chinchilla
Mitchell Hwy.
Dalby
Moreton Bay
Toowoomba
Ipswich
Brisbane
Surfers Paradise
Cunnamulla
Balonne Hwy.
St. George
Warwick
Goondiwindi
Lamington NP
Coolangatta
Tweed Heads
Springbrook NP
Stanthorpe
Girraween NP
Sundown NP
1
15
17
39
42
49
54
55
66
71
78
83

The central office of the **Royal Automobile Club of Queensland (RACQ)** is at 2649 Logan Rd., 8 Mile Plain, Brisbane. With affiliations worldwide, RACQ has excellent maps, car buying and selling tips, and technical services. (☎3361 2444, roadside service ☎13 11 11. Open M-F 8:30am-5:00pm. 1-year membership $62 plus a $33 joining fee.) For more information on driving in Australia, see **Essentials,** p. 9.

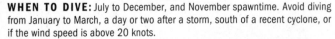

GREAT BARRIER REEF

WHEN TO DIVE: July to December, and November spawntime. Avoid diving from January to March, a day or two after a storm, south of a recent cyclone, or if the wind speed is above 20 knots.

WHERE TO DIVE: Cairns (p. 416), Port Douglas (p. 432), Cape Tribulation (p. 437), Beaver Cay (in Mission Beach; p. 412), Magnetic Island (p. 407), the *S.S. Yongala* wreck (p. 405), and the Whitsundays (p. 397) from Airlie Beach (p. 393).

The Great Barrier Reef stretches 2300km, from just off Bundaberg's shoreline to Papua New Guinea, encompassing hundreds of islands and thousands of reefs. This marine wonderland is easily accessible from the Queensland coast. *Let's Go* describes diving and snorkeling sites and operators throughout the book; get a sense of what you're looking for before you decide on a dive.

WHAT YOU'LL NEED

Queensland requires a **certification card** for all dives. **Hervey Bay** (p. 367) and **Bundaberg** (p. 377) have the cheapest PADI certification courses in the state. Before you begin a course or set out on an extended trip, you might want to try an **introductory dive** with a trained guide to see what it's all about—some people find they have so much trouble stabilizing pressure that a multi-day course would be a waste. If you decide to do a course, try to get boat dives instead of shore dives; the sights are usually better off shore. An open water certification is the minimum qualification to dive without an instructor, but more advanced levels are available for enthusiasts. Medical exams are required for all dive courses and can be arranged with dive centers and area medical specialists for about $60.

ALTERNATIVES TO DIVING

Diving is the best way to get an up-close view of the reef, but it requires significant amounts of time and money. Snorkeling is a convenient alternative for swimmers; renting a mask and fins can be as cheap as $10 per day, though trips on the reef run $50-130 and up. Gear is sometimes free with sailing trips or hostel stays. Good snorkeling is often available just off the shore. When wearing fins, be aware of where you are kicking—you may destroy coral hundreds of years in the making.

BRISBANE ☎07

Often overlooked by those on the coastal pilgrimage, Brisbane (pop. 1.8 million) eschews glitz in favor of staying practical, clean, and lively. Its packed pedestrian malls radiate youthful energy, and the city is a good bet for short-term employment.

The Central Business District (CBD) is full of everything a traveler could need; it's also only a 20min. walk from the each of city's four main neighborhoods. Excellent public transportation connects the CBD with the renowned nightlife

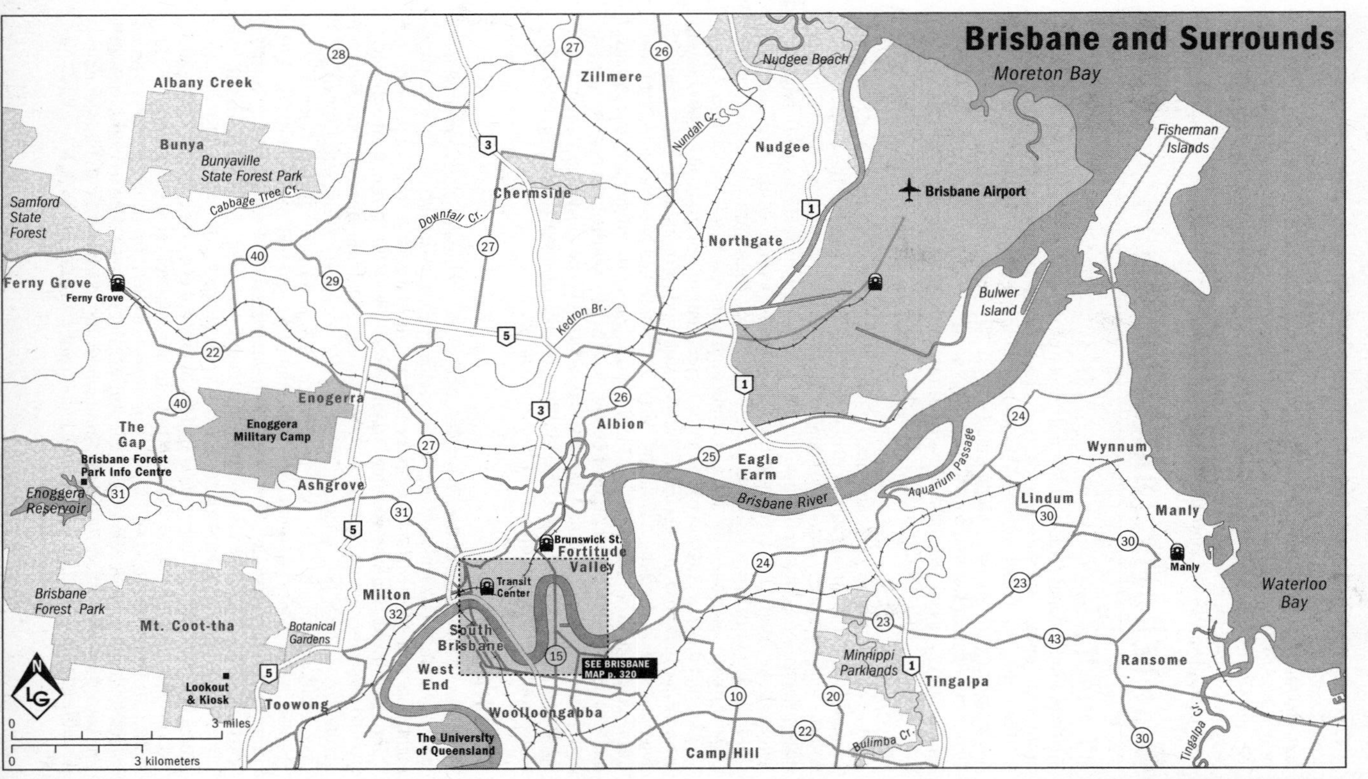

Brisbane and Surrounds
Moreton Bay
Nudgee Beach
Zillmere
Albany Creek
Bunya
Bunyaville State Forest Park
Cabbage Tree Cr.
Samford State Forest
Ferny Grove
Ferny Grove
Nundah Cr.
Nudgee
Chermside
Downfall Cr.
Northgate
Brisbane Airport
Fisherman Islands
Bulwer Island
Kedron Br.
Enogerra
Enoggera Military Camp
The Gap
Brisbane Forest Park Info Centre
Enoggera Reservoir
Ashgrove
Albion
Eagle Farm
Brisbane River
Aquarium Passage
Wynnum
Lindum
Manly
Manly
Waterloo Bay
Brunswick St.
Fortitude Valley
Transit Center
Milton
South Brisbane
West End
SEE BRISBANE MAP p. 320
Woolloongabba
The University of Queensland
Camp Hill
Minnippi Parklands
Tingalpa
Bulimba Cr.
Ransome
Tingalpa Cr.
Brisbane Forest Park
Mt. Coot-tha
Botanical Gardens
Lookout & Kiosk
Toowong
0
3 miles
0
3 kilometers

of Fortitude Valley, the low-key residences in New Farm, the cafe culture of the West End, and the cultural highlights of the South Bank. The pleasant winter climate attracts those eager to shed winter sweaters, and cultural events abound year-round. Visitors enjoy serene waterfront and parklands, cafes, nightclubs, live music, and the opportunity to tour famous Aussie breweries. For a break from the hustle and bustle of city life, the nearby islands of Moreton Bay offer unexploited sand, surf, and seaside hospitality.

INTERCITY TRANSPORTATION

BY PLANE

Brisbane International Airport, 12km northwest of the city, is served by 26 airlines including **Qantas,** 247 Adelaide St. (☎13 13 13; www.qantas.com.au. Open M-F 8:30am-5pm, Sa 9am-1pm), and domestic budget airlines **Jetstar** (☎13 15 38; www.jetstar.com.au.) and **Virgin Blue** (☎13 67 89; www.virginblue.com.au). The **Visitor Information Centre** (☎3406 3190. Open daily 5am-midnight) can be found immediately as you exit customs in the international terminal, 3km from the domestic terminal via the Airtrain ($4, stops running 7:30pm) or the Coachtrans bus ($3) after 7:30pm.

To access the airport by car from the city, make your way to Sir Fred Schonell Dr. and follow the signs (25min. drive from the CBD). A **taxi** to the airport costs about $30-35. Privately owned **Airtrain** (☎3216 3308; www.airtrain.com.au) offers direct service to the airport until 7:30pm, making connections to Brisbane's Queensland Rail and Citytrain in the city (20min., every 30min., $12), and the Gold Coast (1½hr., every 30min., $23). To get to Surfers Paradise, get off at the second to last Airtrain stop, Nerang, and catch Surfside Bus #745 (30min., every 15-20min., $2.60) or Airtrain can arrange a chauffeur to wait for you at the station for a drop-off at your hostel ($37). Many hostels and information centers offer $3 discounted tickets to the airport on Airtrain. Timetables are available from Airtrain, as well as from **Transinfo** (☎13 12 30; www.transinfo.qld.gov.au). **Coachtrans,** on level 3 of the **Roma Street Transit Centre,** runs a daily **shuttle** between the airport and Transit Centre. (☎3238 4700; www.coachtrans.com.au. Every 30min. 5am-9pm; last bus to city 11:10pm. $9, children $6. Direct drop at accommodations $11, round-trip $18; children $7/10. Book ahead.)

BY TRAIN

The **Roma Street Transit Centre,** 500m west of the CBD, is the city's bus and train terminal. (Open M-Th 4am-12:20am, F 4am-1:45am, Sa 5am-1:15am, Su 5:50am-midnight.) Lockers ($6 per day) are on the first and third levels.

For rail travel, **Queensland Rail Travel Centre** (☎13 22 32 or 1800 627 655; www.traveltrain.com.au) can book full packages, including air travel and accommodations. Offices are at Central Station on the corner of Ann and Edward St. (diagonally opposite Palace Backpackers, p. 323) and on the ground floor of the Transit Centre. Only students with ISIC qualify for student prices and YHA/VIP holders get a 10% discount. The sleek **Tilt Train** is the fastest way to travel; it runs north along the coast from Brisbane to Rockhampton (8¾hr.; M-Th 11am, F and Su 11am, 5pm; $110, students $50.60) and Maryborough West (3¾hr.; M-F and Su 11am, 5pm; $55/27.50), with bus transfers to Bundaberg (1hr., $63.80/31.90) and Hervey Bay (1hr., $64.90/33). Transit to Cairns is available twice per week on Tilt (25hr.; M, F 6:25pm; $294.80/147.40) and three times on the cheaper, slower **Sunlander** (32hr.; Tu, Su 8:55am, Th 12:55pm; $201.30/101.20). These trains stop in Mackay (Tilt 13hr., $216.70/108.90; Sunlander 17hr., $147.40/73.70, with an additional train Sa 8:55am), in Whitsunday launch point Proserpine (Tilt 15hr., $227.70/

114.40; Sunlander 18hr., $155.10/78.10), with bus transfer to Airlie Beach (25min., $9.90), and Townsville (Tilt 18½hr., $256.30/128.70; Sunlander 24hr., $174.90/88). Trains also leave for Sydney (14hr.; daily 7:30am, 3:10pm; $74.60-124.30/62.15); the later departure time includes a 12hr. train and a 3hr. bus. Book ahead.

BY BUS

FROM BRISBANE TO:

DESTINATION	COMPANY	DURATION	PER DAY	PRICE
Adelaide	Greyhound	32hr.	1	$275
Airlie Beach	Greyhound	13½-18½hr.	6	$168
	Premier	19½hr.	1	$135
Bundaberg	Greyhound	6½-7hr.	5	$72
	Premier	9¼hr.	1	$47
Byron Bay	Kirklands	3-3½hr.	3 M-F, 2 Sa-Su	$32
	Greyhound	2¾-3hr.	7	$37
	Premier	3½hr.	2	$32
Cairns	Greyhound	29hr.	6	$227
	Premier	29½hr.	1	$193
Coolangatta and Tweed Heads	Kirklands	2hr.	3 M-F, 2 Sa-Su	$16
	Greyhound	2-2¼hr.	6	$26
	Premier	2hr.	2	$15
Hervey Bay	Greyhound	6-7½hr.	7	$55
	Premier	7hr.	1	$36
Mackay	Greyhound	16½hr.	6	$148
	Premier	17½hr.	1	$120
Maroochydore	Greyhound	1½-2¾hr.	9	$25
	Premier	1½hr.	1	$20
Melbourne	Greyhound	25½hr.	1	$217
Mission Beach	Greyhound	27hr.	6	$220
	Premier	27½hr.	1	$184
Mooloolooba	Greyhound	2½hr.	5	$25
	Premier	1½hr.	1	$25
Noosa/Noosa Heads	Greyhound	2½-3½hr.	9	$25
	Premier	2½hr.	1	$20
Rockhampton	Greyhound	11½hr.	4	$103
	Premier	12½hr.	1	$84
Surfers Paradise	Kirklands	1¼hr.	6 M-F, 4 Sa-Su	$16
	Greyhound	1½hr.	7	$23
	Premier	1¼-1½hr.	2	$15
Sydney	Greyhound	16¼-17hr.	4	$113
	Premier	15-17hr.	2	$89

Those with long itineraries should consider purchasing a **Sunshine Rail Pass,** good for a given number of travel days within a six-month period on any Queensland service. Passes are available at the Queensland Rail Travel Centre on the ground floor of the Transit Centre, or from the desk in Central Station. (14-day $335.50, 21-day $388.30, 30-day $487.30; students and children ½-price. Book ahead.) There are many other passes available to overseas travelers (see **Essentials,** p. 9).

Bus coverage along the coast is excellent; **Greyhound Australia** (☎13 14 99; www.greyhound.com.au) and **Premier Motor Service** (☎13 34 10), grant 10% discounts for ISIC/VIP/YHA. Both sell a range of 2- to 6-month travel passes for travelers, though Greyhound offers more options. **Kirklands Coaches** (☎1300 367 077), provides service to the Gold Coast and Byron Bay, offering discounts of 25% to students and backpackers, and 50% for children. Although you may see **Suncoast Pacific** buses, they are now officially owned and operated by Greyhound Australia.

ORIENTATION

The Brisbane River meanders through the city, creating easily identifiable landmarks. The river is traversed by five bridges: the **Merivale Bridge** is the westernmost bridge and is next to the **William Jolly Bridge; Story Bridge** connects Fortitude Valley and Kangaroo Point; the **Captain Cook Bridge** connects the southern edge of the CBD to southbound highways; and the **Victoria Bridge** connects the city to South Bank. The **Transit Centre** is located on Roma St.; a left turn out of the building and a 5min. walk southeast down Roma crosses **Turbot Street** and leads to the corner of **Albert** and **Ann Street** and the grassy **King George Square** (in front of the grand **City Hall**). **Adelaide Street** forms the far side of the square. The **Queen Street Mall** runs parallel to Adelaide; it's a popular pedestrian thoroughfare lined with shops and cafes and is the center of Brisbane proper. Underneath the mall and the adjoining **Myer Centre** shopping complex is the **Queen Street Bus Station.**

Brisbane's neighborhoods radiate out from the CBD. A right turn out of the Transit Centre leads to **Petrie Terrace** and **Paddington,** with accommodations and mellow nightlife. North of Boundary St. is **Spring Hill,** bordered by **Victoria Park** and **Roma Street Parklands,** a 15min. walk from the Queen Street Mall up steep Edward St. A 20min. walk down Ann St., nightclub-heavy **Fortitude Valley** offers a hopping alternative scene and live music. The Valley is also home to a small, authentic **Chinatown.** Turning right down Brunswick St., a 10min. walk brings you to **New Farm,** with its free art galleries, not-so-free cafes, and excellent restaurants. Near the Botanic Gardens at the CBD's southern tip, the Victoria Bridge footpath turns into Melbourne St. and heads into **South Brisbane,** crossing Boundary St. six blocks later as it enters the **West End. South Bank** is to the east of the southern end of the bridge; farther along the riverside, **Kangaroo Point** is the long, narrow peninsula stretching into the River.

BE SAFE. Use caution in the areas around Fortitude Valley and the West End, especially at night. Also be sure to avoid city parks after dark; in particular, stay away from the Botanic Gardens, New Farm Park, and King George Square.

LOCAL TRANSPORTATION

The new **Translink** system coordinates transit on trains, buses, and ferries within Brisbane, extending all the way north to Noosa and south to Coolangatta. For inquiries, contact the helpful operators at **Transinfo** (☎13 12 30; www.transinfo.qld.gov.au). Off-peak (all day Sa-Su and holidays, as well as M-F 9am-3:30pm and after 7pm) travel within one zone costs $2.20 one-way; one zone daily passes are $4.40 for anytime travel on any form of public transit, $3.30 for off-peak. Two-zone travel is $2.60/5.20/3.90. Most travelers will stick to zone one, which incorporates all of central Brisbane, from the West End and Kangaroo Point up through the CBD to New Farm and Fortitude Valley.

Trains: Citytrain, Queensland Rail's intracity train network, has 2 major stations and numerous stops throughout the city. The main station is inside the Roma St. **Transit Centre;** the other is in **Central Station,** on the corner of Ann St. and Edward St. Citytrain also connects to Airtrain, with service to the airport (p. 316). Trains generally run every 30min. Daily 6am-9:30pm. Check schedules for specific line info.

Buses: Buses going to the southern suburbs depart from the **Queen Street Bus Station,** a huge terminal beneath the Myer Centre and the Queen Street Mall. The bus stop for all other destinations is on Adelaide or Elizabeth St. Schedules organized by suburb and bus number are available from the helpful **Queen Street Bus Station Info Centre,** located on Level A of the Myer Centre. (Open M-Th 8:30am-5:30pm, F 8:30am-8pm, Sa 9am-4pm, Su 10am-4pm.) Most bus stops also post times and route maps. **CityXpress** runs from the suburbs to the CBD approximately every 30min. Free red buses operate every 10min. on the **Downtown Loop,** a circular service in the CBD (M-F 7am-7pm). Bus #199 offers convenient routes from West End to New Farm via the Valley.

Ferries: Brisbane's excellent ferry system offers affordable, practical transit with beautiful city views; look for colored signs at ferry stops which indicate service. The sleek **CityCat** runs upstream to the University of Queensland and downstream to Bretts Wharf (every 20-30min. daily 5:50am-10:30pm; blue sign). The CityCat also stops in Riverside, QUT, and North Quay, near the Treasury Casino. The **Inner City Ferry** operates in the CBD and has more stops than the CityCat (every 30min daily 6am-10:30pm; red sign). The **Cross River** runs 4 routes connecting Brisbane's banks, including 2 from Eagle St. to Kangaroo Point (every 10min. daily 6am-10:30pm; green sign). Schedules are posted at every dock and stop.

Taxis: Yellow Cab (☎13 19 24) and **Black and White Cabs** (☎13 10 08) run 24hr.

Car Rental: Network Car and Truck Rentals, 398 St. Paul's Terr. (☎1800 067 414; www.networkrentals.com.au), in Fortitude Valley, rents from $32 a day for 250km. Open M-F 7:30am-5:30pm, weekends 8am-3pm. AmEx/DC/MC/V. **Abel** (☎1800 131 429; www.abel.com.au), on the corner of Wickham and Warren St., rents from $29 per day, with under 25 surcharge of $15 per day. Open daily 7am-7pm. AmEx/DC/MC/V.

PRACTICAL INFORMATION

TOURIST AND FINANCIAL SERVICES

Tourist Office: The very busy **visitors center** (☎3006 6290), in the middle of the Queen Street Mall, provides info only on businesses that pay to advertise there. The center also has a Transinfo rep. Open daily 9am-6pm. Touchscreen available 24hr. The **Brisbane Transit Visitor Information** desk (☎3236 2020), on the 3rd fl. of the Transit Centre, provides information on accommodations and attractions. Open daily 7am-6pm.

Budget Travel Offices: Travel centers are everywhere, but the branches in the **Myer Centre** tend to have the best hours. **Flight Centre** (☎3229 6600 or 13 16 00; www.flightcentre.com.au) has 50 offices in the city and a guarantee to beat any current quote. The Myer Centre branch, on the basement level E, is open M-Th 9am-5:30pm, F 9am-8pm, Sa 9am-4pm, Su 10:30am-4pm. **STA Travel** (☎1300 733 035; www.statravel.com.au) has 3 offices in the CBD, including one at 59 Adelaide St., and one at 243 Edward St. The Myer Centre branch is open M-Th 9am-5:30pm, F 9am-8pm, Sa 9am-4pm. **Student Flights** (☎3006 1744; www.studentflights.com.au) has 3 offices in the city, including 1 on Level A in the Myer Centre, and promises to beat any international fare for students by $10. Open M-Th 9am-5:30pm, F 9am-8pm, Sa 9am-5pm. **YHA Travel,** 450 George St. (☎3236 1680), across from the Transit Centre has budget travel rates. Open M-Tu and Th-F 8:30am-6pm, W 9am-6pm, Sa 9am-3pm.

Consulate: U.K., 1 Eagle St. Level 26 (☎3223 3209). Open M-F 9:30am-3pm.

Banks: Banks are found on Boundary St. in South Brisbane, Brunswick St. in the Valley, and Queen St. in the CBD. Most are open M-Th 9:30am-4pm, F 9:30am-5pm. **ATMs** are located throughout the city.

American Express: 156 Adelaide St. (☎1300 139 060). Open M-F 9am-5pm, Sa 10am-1pm.

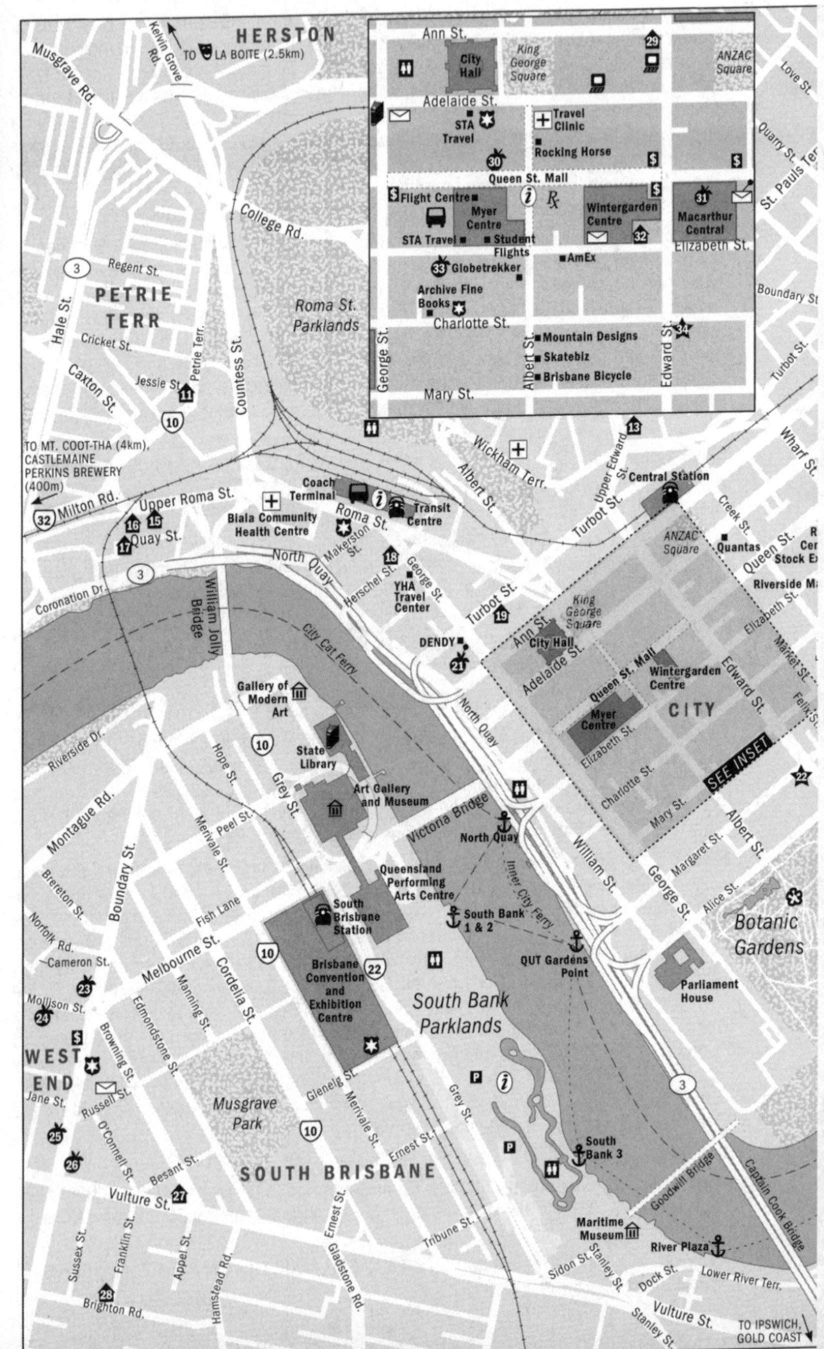
HERSTON
PETRIE TERR
CITY
WEST END
SOUTH BRISBANE
TO LA BOITE (2.5km)
TO MT. COOT-THA (4km), CASTLEMAINE PERKINS BREWERY (400m)
TO IPSWICH, GOLD COAST
Roma St. Parklands
South Bank Parklands
Musgrave Park
Botanic Gardens
Coach Terminal
Transit Centre
Biala Community Health Centre
YHA Travel Center
DENDY
Central Station
Gallery of Modern Art
State Library
Art Gallery and Museum
Queensland Performing Arts Centre
South Brisbane Station
Brisbane Convention and Exhibition Centre
North Quay
South Bank 1 & 2
QUT Gardens Point
South Bank 3
Maritime Museum
River Plaza
Parliament House
Victoria Bridge
William Jolly Bridge
Goodwill Bridge
Captain Cook Bridge
City Cat Ferry
Inner City Ferry
SEE INSET
Ann St.
City Hall
King George Square
ANZAC Square
Adelaide St.
STA Travel
Travel Clinic
Rocking Horse
Queen St. Mall
Flight Centre
Myer Centre
Wintergarden Centre
Macarthur Central
STA Travel
Student Flights
Elizabeth St.
AmEx
Globetrekker
Archive Fine Books
Charlotte St.
Mountain Designs
Skatebiz
Brisbane Bicycle
Mary St.
George St.
Albert St.
Edward St.
Quantas
Musgrave Rd.
Kelvin Grove Rd.
College Rd.
Regent St.
Hale St.
Cricket St.
Petrie Terr.
Caxton St.
Jessie St.
Countess St.
Milton Rd.
Upper Roma St.
Quay St.
Roma St.
Makerston St.
Herschel St.
North Quay
Coronation Dr.
Wickham Terr.
Upper Edward St.
Turbot St.
Wharf St.
Creek St.
Queen St.
Boundary St.
Love St.
Quarry St.
St. Pauls Terr.
Market St.
Felix St.
Margaret St.
Alice St.
William St.
Riverside Dr.
Montague Rd.
Hope St.
Grey St.
Peel St.
Merivale St.
Boundary St.
Brereton St.
Norfolk Rd.
Cameron St.
Fish Lane
Melbourne St.
Cordelia St.
Manning St.
Edmondstone St.
Mollison St.
Browning St.
Jane St.
Russell St.
O'Connell St.
Glenelg St.
Ernest St.
Besant St.
Vulture St.
Tribune St.
Sidon St.
Stanley St.
Dock St.
Lower River Terr.
Sussex St.
Franklin St.
Appel St.
Hamstead Rd.
Gladstone Rd.
Brighton Rd.

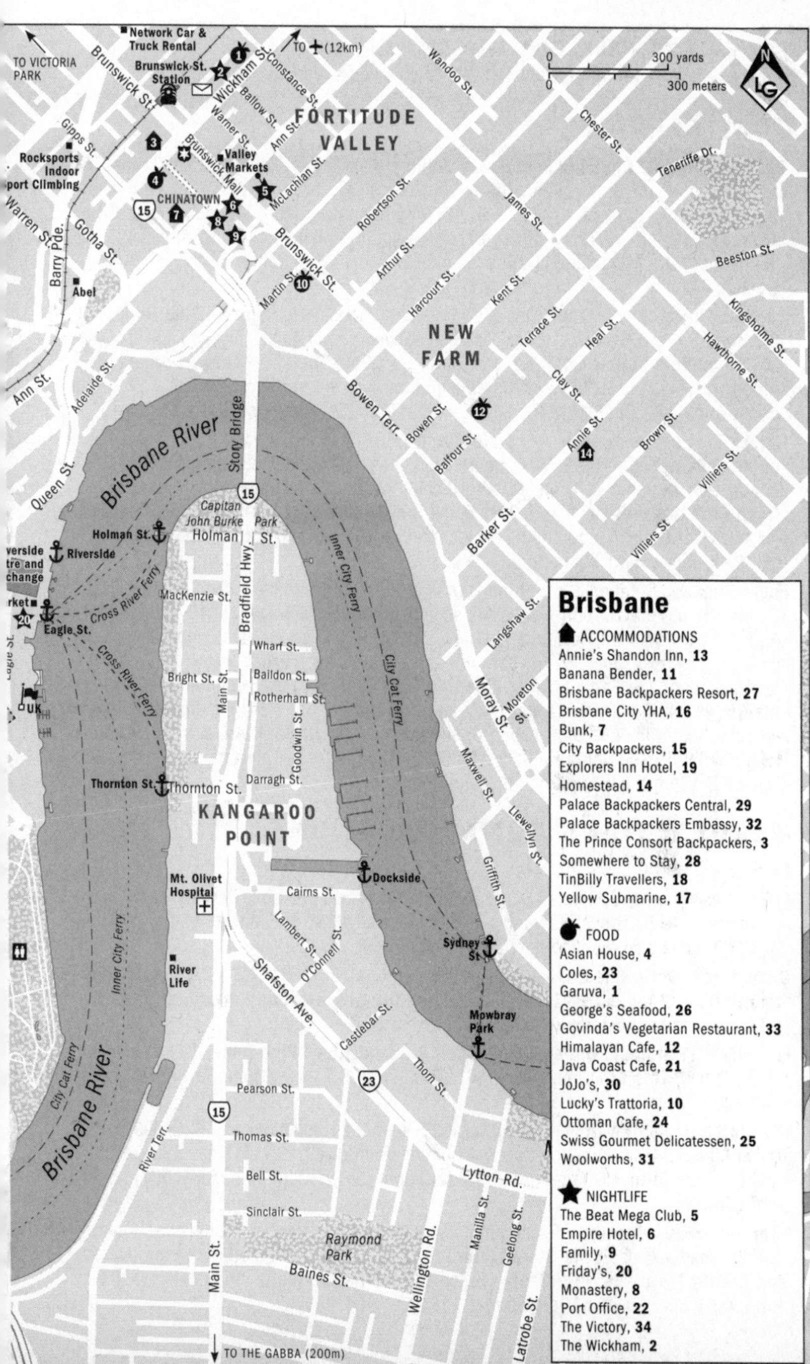
Brisbane
ACCOMMODATIONS
Annie's Shandon Inn, 13
Banana Bender, 11
Brisbane Backpackers Resort, 27
Brisbane City YHA, 16
Bunk, 7
City Backpackers, 15
Explorers Inn Hotel, 19
Homestead, 14
Palace Backpackers Central, 29
Palace Backpackers Embassy, 32
The Prince Consort Backpackers, 3
Somewhere to Stay, 28
TinBilly Travellers, 18
Yellow Submarine, 17
FOOD
Asian House, 4
Coles, 23
Garuva, 1
George's Seafood, 26
Govinda's Vegetarian Restaurant, 33
Himalayan Cafe, 12
Java Coast Cafe, 21
JoJo's, 30
Lucky's Trattoria, 10
Ottoman Cafe, 24
Swiss Gourmet Delicatessen, 25
Woolworths, 31
NIGHTLIFE
The Beat Mega Club, 5
Empire Hotel, 6
Family, 9
Friday's, 20
Monastery, 8
Port Office, 22
The Victory, 34
The Wickham, 2
0 300 yards
0 300 meters
TO VICTORIA PARK
Network Car & Truck Rental
Brunswick St. Station
TO (12km)
FORTITUDE VALLEY
Valley Markets
Rocksports Indoor Sport Climbing
CHINATOWN
Abel
NEW FARM
KANGAROO POINT
Brisbane River
Story Bridge
Capitan John Burke Park
Holman St.
Riverside
Eagle St.
Thornton St.
Dockside
Sydney St.
Mowbray Park
Mt. Olivet Hospital
River Life
Raymond Park
Cross River Ferry
Inner City Ferry
City Cat Ferry
Bradfield Hwy.
Brunswick St.
Wickham St.
Constance St.
Wandoo St.
Ballow St.
Warner St.
Ann St.
Brunswick Mall
McLachlan St.
Gipps St.
Warren St.
Barry Pde.
Gotha St.
Robertson St.
Arthur St.
Martin St.
Harcourt St.
Kent St.
James St.
Chester St.
Teneriffe Dr.
Beeston St.
Kingsholme St.
Hawthorne St.
Terrace St.
Heal St.
Clay St.
Bowen Terr.
Bowen St.
Balfour St.
Annie St.
Brown St.
Villiers St.
Barker St.
Adelaide St.
Queen St.
MacKenzie St.
Wharf St.
Baildon St.
Rotherham St.
Bright St.
Main St.
Goodwin St.
Darragh St.
Langshaw St.
Moray St.
Moreton St.
Maxwell St.
Llewellyn St.
Griffith St.
Cairns St.
Lambert St.
O'Connell St.
Shafston Ave.
Castlebar St.
Thorn St.
Pearson St.
Thomas St.
Bell St.
Sinclair St.
Baines St.
River Terr.
Lytton Rd.
Wellington Rd.
Manilla St.
Geelong St.
Latrobe St.
TO THE GABBA (200m)

WAIT TO WALK. Brisbane police are quick to fine jaywalkers $200 or more for crossing without a signal. In this city, it seems, patience is a virtue.

LOCAL SERVICES

Backpacking and Camping Equipment: There are several equipment stores in the CBD and on Wickham St. between Gotha and Gipps St. in Fortitude Valley. **Mountain Designs,** 109 Albert St. (☎3221 6756; www.mountaindesigns.com.au) and **Globe Trekker,** 142 Albert St. (☎3221 4476; www.globetrekkers.com.au) offer 10% discounts to YHA and students. Both have similar hours: M-Th 9am-5:30pm, F 9am-8pm, Sa 9am-4:30pm, Su 10am-4pm. AmEx/DC/MC/V.

Bookstores: The Queen Street Mall area has many bookstores. **Archive Fine Books,** 40 Charlotte St. (☎3221 0491), has 1 million second-hand books lining its shelves. Open M-Th 9am-6pm, F 9am-9pm, Sa 9am-5pm, Su 10am-5pm. The 3-story **Borders,** 162 Albert St. (☎3210 1220; www.borders.com.au), at the corner of Elizabeth St., sells books and more. Open M-Th 9am-7pm, F 9am-9pm, Sa 9am-6pm, Su 10am-5pm.

Library: The beautifully renovated **State Library** (☎3840 7666; www.slq.qld.gov.au), part of the Cultural Centre (p. 326) in South Bank, has converted itself into a popular destination with exhibitions, galleries, and display centers. Free wireless Internet access. Open M-Th 10am-8pm, F-Su 10am-5pm. The **Central City Library,** 266 George St. (☎3403 4166), is in a beautiful new location. Book borrowing for members only. Open M-F 9am-6pm, Sa-Su 10am-3pm.

Public Markets: Rotating outdoor markets line the streets every weekend. Inquire at the Queen St. information booth for a full schedule. **The Valley Markets** (☎3854 0860), on Brunswick St. Mall, Fortitude Valley, is a retro hippie scene of second-hand items, clothes, and toys. Open Sa-Su 8am-4pm. The **Riverside Market** (☎04 1488 8041), operates along the Eagle St. Pier. Open Su 8am-3pm. For fresh produce, the **Farmers Market** (☎0417 720 943) takes place the 2nd and 4th Sa of every month at the Powerhouse Centre in New Farm. Open 6am-noon. The **South Bank Art & Craft Markets** (☎3355 7999; see **South Bank Parklands,** p. 327) offers a wide array of local talent. Open F 5-10pm, Sa 11am-5pm, Su 9am-5pm.

EMERGENCY AND COMMUNICATIONS

Emergency: ☎000.

Police: Headquarters, 200 Roma St. (☎3364 6464). Branch stations can be found on 46 Charlotte St. (☎3258 2582) and the Brunswick St. Mall in Fortitude Valley (☎3364 6237). There's also a police beat on 67 Adelaide St. (☎3224 4444).

Crisis Lines: Statewide Sexual Assault Helpline (☎1800 010 120). **Suicide Prevention Hotline** (24hr. ☎13 11 14). **Alcohol and Drug Information Service** (☎1800 177 833). **Pregnancy Advisory Centre** (☎1800 672 966).

Late-Night Pharmacy: Queen Street Mall Day and Night Pharmacy, 141 Queen St. (☎3221 4585), on the mall. Open M-Th 7am-9pm, F 7am-9:30pm, Sa 8am-9pm, Su 8:30am-5:30pm.

Hospital: Holy Spirit Northside Hospital, 627 Rode Rd., Chermside (☎3326 3000). **The Travel Clinic,** 245 Albert St., offers vaccinations and dive medicals from $88 (☎3211 3611). Open M-Th 7:30am-7pm, F 7:30am-6pm, Sa 8:30am-5pm, Su 9:30am-5pm. AmEx/MC/V.

Internet Access: Internet cafes abound, especially on Adelaide St. There is free Internet and wireless access at the **State Library** (p. 322). Most hostels offer Internet access, but **TinBilly Travellers,** 462 George St. next to the Transit Centre, has the best rates in town at $1 per hr. Open 10am-5pm.

Post Office: General Post Office, 261 Queen St. (☎13 13 18). ½-block from the end of the mall. Open M-F 7am-6pm. *Poste Restante* available 9am-5pm. For weekend mail, try the branch at Wintergarden Centre Level 2. Open M-F 8:30am-5:30pm, Sa 9am-1pm. **Postal Code:** 4000 (city); 4001 (GPO post boxes).

MEDIA AND PUBLICATIONS

Newspaper: *The Courier-Mail* ($1); *Brisbane News* (every W; free) and *City News* (every Th; free).

Nightlife: *Time Off, Scene,* and *Rave* magazines (free). For info on gay and lesbian nightlife, check out *qp*.

Radio: Rock, Triple M 104.5 FM and Triple J 107.7; Top 40, B105 FM; News, 612 AM (ABC Brisbane), 792 AM (ABC Radio National), and 936 AM (ABC Newsradio); Tourist Info, 88 FM.

ACCOMMODATIONS

Accommodations cluster in four main areas of the city. The CBD is convenient but expensive. Fortitude Valley is a mecca for nightclubs, and its quiet neighbor New Farm caters to long-term stays. The area near the Transit Centre is convenient to both the CBD and clubs in the Valley. The West End and South Brisbane are a little removed from the action. Most of the accommodations listed below offer pickup and drop-off at the Transit Centre; call ahead. Unless otherwise noted, hostels have Internet access, coin-operated laundry, kitchen, BBQ, storage, weekly rate discounts, 10am check-out, lockers, and $10 key deposit. Linens and cutlery are usually free with a deposit.

LOCK IT UP. Many hostels offer lockers free of charge, but leave it to you to supply the lock. Padlocks can be purchased all over Brisbane; buy one in advance to ensure the safety of your valuables.

CBD

Palace Backpackers Embassy (☎1800 676 340; www.palacebackpackers.com.au), at the corner of Edward and Elizabeth St. Because the original Palace Backpackers was so popular, the company opened up shop at a second, smaller location down the street. The newer, cleaner, and more attractive Embassy has outdone its older brother. The atmosphere is less wild, and dorm rooms are just $1 more than at Palace Central. Awesome TV lounge replicates movie theater experience. VIP. MC/V. ❷

Palace Backpackers Central, 308 Edward St. (☎3211 2433 or 1800 676 340; www.palacebackpackers.com.au), on the corner of Ann St. in the heart of the city. 5-level building is a backpacker landmark which fills to 400-person capacity in peak times. Rooms are spacious and clean, but bathrooms aren't always tidy. Its nightly rockin' pub, with cheap dinner specials ($5), makes for one of the best social scenes in the city. Three-story veranda, gas BBQ, and classy cafe with breakfast ($5-10). The $30 job club gives members a guarantee of finding work. Reception 24hr. 3- to 10-bed dorms $23-26; singles $36; doubles $56. VIP. MC/V. ❷

Explorers Inn Hotel, 63 Turbot St. (☎1800 62 32 88; www.explorer.com.au), near the corner of George St., a short walk from the CBD. The best budget hotel around. Affordable restaurant (meals under $12). The compact ensuite rooms have fridge, A/C, and TV. No kitchen. Reception daily 6:30am-10:30pm, latenight check-in with advance notice. Singles from $85; doubles from $89; triples $129. AmEx/DC/MC/V. ❹

Annie's Shandon Inn, 405 Upper Edward St. (☎3831 8684), Spring Hill. The perfect escape from impersonal hostels is just outside the CBD. Like Grandma's house, with family snapshots, cozy beds, and pastels. No kitchen. Continental breakfast included. Reception 7am-8pm. Check-out 9am. Singles $55, doubles with shared facilities $65, ensuite $75. AmEx/MC/V. ❹

FORTITUDE VALLEY AND NEW FARM

Bunk, 11-21 Gipps St. (☎1800 682 865; www.bunkbrisbane.com.au), on the corner of Ann St. This might just be the best hostel in Brisbane. Rooms are well maintained, and staff is friendly and helpful. Just a short walk from nightclubs. If traveling in a group of 4 or 5 and don't mind sharing big beds, ask for an awe-inspiring apartment ($120-140). Attached to the impressively popular **Birdee Num Num** pub and nightclub. Reception 24hr. 4-, 6-, and 8-bed dorms with private bath $18-26; singles $55; ensuite doubles $75. MC/V. ❷

The Prince Consort Backpackers, 230 Wickham St. (☎1800 225 005). This inexpensive hostel has big rooms, shared facilities, and a great location in the heart of Fortitude Valley. Among the less social hostels in Brisbane. On top of **The Elephant & the Wheelbarrow** pub. Free drink on check-in. 4- to 10-bed dorms $19-27; doubles $60. NOMADS/VIP/YHA discount $1. AmEx/DC/MC/V. ❷

Homestead, 57 Annie St. (☎ 3358 3538), New Farm. This hostel, situated on a quiet residential street just a short walk from the action, is quite popular among relaxed, low-key backpackers. 4-bed dorms available in female-only. Beautiful murals. Weekly BBQ and frequent outings. Free transit to airport, Transit Centre, CBD, and F city job fairs. Shared facilities. Free bike use. No lockers. 3- and 4-bed dorms $16-18; doubles $20-38 per person. VIP/YHA. AmEx/DC/MC/V. ❷

WEST END/SOUTH BRISBANE

Somewhere to Stay, 45 Brighton Rd. (☎1800 812 398; www.somewheretostay.com.au), entrance on Franklin St. A homey hostel in a beautiful old Queenslander house with multiple balconies. Large rooms, some with city views. Lush greenery and swimming pool. Far from nightclubs and most nighttime activities. Reception 8am-4am. Check-out 9:30am. Ensuite 4- to 6-bed dorms $19-25; singles $36; doubles $47. ISIC/NOMADS/VIP/YHA discount $1. MC/V. ❷

Brisbane Backpackers Resort, 110 Vulture St. (☎1800 626 452; www.brisbanebackpackers.com.au). A well-maintained hostel with nice amenities, but a hike from most activities. Rooms have bath, TV, and fridge; many have balconies overlooking the courtyard. Free bus to CBD and Transit Centre. Tennis court, swimming pool, bar, and **cafe** ❶ (breakfast $5-7, dinner $8). Reception 24hr. 4- to 8-bed dorms $20-24; singles and doubles $64. VIP/YHA. MC/V. ❷

FOOD

The West End specializes in multicultural cuisine and small sidewalk cafes, particularly along Boundary St. and Hardgrave Rd. Fortitude Valley's Chinatown has cheap Asian fare, while trendier New Farm and the CBD have more expensive eateries. **Woolworths** supermarket is located downstairs at Macarthur Central in the Queen Street Mall (open M-F 8am-9pm, Sa 8am-5:30pm, Su 9am-6pm). For ice cream, try **Cold Rock Ice Creamery** ❶ opposite Little Stanley St., along the river in the Arbour View Cafes in the South Bank Parklands.

CBD

JoJo's (☎3221 2113; www.jojos.com.au), on the corner of Queen St. Mall and Albert St. Sits amid skyscrapers and has a balcony overlooking the center of the mall. The restaurant attracts travelers, students, and yuppie businessmen to its 5 different kitchens which include Thai, Italian, and char-grill. Try the excellent pizzas ($9.95-17.95) or grilled sirloin and chips ($15). Gourmet sandwiches $11.95. Happy hour 4:30pm-6pm. Open daily 11:30am-latenight. AmEx/DC/MC/V. ❷

Govinda's Vegetarian Restaurant, upstairs at 99 Elizabeth St. (☎3210 0255; www.brisbanesgovindas.com). Extremely popular among locals for its $9 buffet (students $8). Recently redecorated, lined with Krishna flags, posters, and books. No meat. Vegan options available. Su feast isn't to be missed. Students $6 from 2-3pm. Open M-Th 11am-3pm, F 11am-8:30pm, Sa 11:30am-2:30pm. Cash only. ❶

Java Coast Cafe, 340 George St. (☎3211 3040), near Ann St. Top pick among Brisbane's hundreds of coffee shops. The jungle-like courtyard dining area in the back is an inner-city sanctuary. Gourmet sandwiches $6.50-8.50. Open M-F 7:30am-4:30pm. ❶

FORTITUDE VALLEY AND NEW FARM

Garuva, 324 Wickham St. (☎3216 0124; www.garuva.com), at the corner with Constance St., Fortitude Valley. Might be the best dining experience in Queensland. The trickling waterfalls, colored lights, and low-arching tropical trees are just the beginning of this intimate eatery. Sit on a cushioned rug while a white curtain is drawn around your table to ensure privacy. Attentive service and international main courses ($17), from cajun blacked chicken to Turkish octopus. Book at least 2 days ahead. Open M-Th and Su 6:30pm-latenight, F-Sa 5:30pm-latenight. AmEx/DC/MC/V. ❸

Himalayan Cafe, 640-642 Brunswick St. (☎3358 4015). Call the number you scribbled on a coaster in the Valley last night, and bring your date to the romantic back room, where patrons sit on cushions and enjoy Tibetan and Nepalese delicacies. Veggie and vegan options abound. Open Tu-Su 5:30pm-latenight. ❸

Lucky's Trattoria, (☎3252 2353) behind the Central Brunswick Complex at the corner of Brunswick and Martin St. in New Farm. Excellent Italian favorites. Try the gnocchi with blue vein cheese sauce ($14-17.20) or the Capriciosa Pizza ($10-16.80). Open daily 6pm-latenight. AmEx/MC/V. ❸

Asian House, 165 Wickham St. (☎3852 1291) in Fortitude Valley. The best of the nondescript Chinatown restaurants. Excellent dishes, friendly service, and casual dining. Try the chicken fillet and sweet ginger ($11.90) or curried Chinese vegetables ($9.90). Open daily 11:30am-3pm and 5-11pm; F open until 11:30. AmEx/DC/MC/V. ❷

WEST END AND SOUTH BANK

George's Seafood, 150 Boundary St. (☎3844 4100). A tiny seafood shop with accommodating and knowledgeable owners who ensure that your meal is exactly as you want it. They will grill, batter, or crumb any fresh fillet for $1 extra. Crumbed cod and chips $5.50. Takeaway only. Open M-F 9:30am-7:30pm, Sa 8:30am-7:30pm, Su 10:30am-7:30pm. Cash only. ❶

Ottoman Cafe, 37 Mollison St. (☎3846 3555), a block west of the Boundary St. corner. The amazing Turkish cuisine, authentic decorations, and genuine service make for one of the best dining experiences in Brisbane. Main courses from $17.50. Open Tu-Sa noon-3pm and 5:30pm-latenight, kitchen closes at 9:30pm. AmEx/MC/V. ❸

Swiss Gourmet Delicatessen, 181 Boundary St. (☎3844 2937). This tiny deli packs a real punch; its prices and taste are hard to beat. Build your own sandwich (from $4) and top it off with a dessert made by the Portuguese owner. Takeaway or dine outside. Open M-F 7:30am-5:30pm, Sa 7:30am-3:30pm. AmEx/DC/MC/V. ❶

SIGHTS

CITY SIGHTS

CITY TOURS. **City Sights** is a 1½hr. bus tour of cultural and historical attractions that allows you to jump on and off as you please. Tickets are purchased on the bus. *(Tours officially leave from Post Office Square, at Queen and Edward St., but you can start at any of the 19 stops. Call Transinfo ☎ 13 12 30 for timetables. Daily every 45min. 9am-3:45pm. $22, concessions $16.)* For a tour of the Brisbane River, the large **Kookaburra River Queen** paddlewheel boat departs twice daily from the Eagle St. Pier. Includes commentary on sights and live accordion music. *(☎ 3221 1300; www.kookaburrariverqueens.com. 2hr. lunch cruise $30-70; 2½hr. dinner cruise $65-85. More expensive on weekends. Departs daily noon and 7:30pm.)* **Tours and Detours**, on the 3rd fl. of the Transit Centre, offers a number of different city and river trips, including a half-day highlight tour *(☎ 1300 300 242; www.daytours.com.au; departs 9:15am, returns 12:30pm. $46, concessions $43, children $28, with river cruise $63/61/43)*, an afternoon float to **Lone Pine Koala Sanctuary** and Mt. Coot-tha *(departs 1:30pm, returns 4:45pm; $52/50/35)*, and a moonlight tour of Brisbane *(departs 6:30pm, returns 9:30pm; $65/60/35)*. Those on foot can pick up a guide to the **Brisbane Heritage Trail.** The 3km path winds its way around the city's historical and cultural sights. *(☎ 3403 8888. Starts in King George Sq. Free maps and guides available at City Hall and the Brisbane City Council.)*

CASTLEMAINE PERKINS BREWERY. XXXX, which proudly proclaims itself "Queensland's beer," is brewed only five minutes from Caxton St. on Milton Rd., adjacent to the Milton train stop. The 1¼hr. walking tour ends with four samples. Meet at the **XXXX Ale House** off Milton Rd. on Paten St. *(☎ 3361 7597; www.xxxx.com.au. Tours M-F every hr. 10am-4pm, also W 6pm. $18, concessions $16.50, non-drinkers $10, children under 10 free. Book ahead. AmEx/DC/MC/V.)*

CARLTON BREWHOUSE. Thirty minutes (41km) south of Brisbane are the brewers of VB, Fosters, and Carlton. The tour through the largest and most modern brewery in Queensland may be slightly dry, but the three beers at the end sure aren't. *(In Yatala. By car, follow the Pacific Hwy. south of the city, and take exit #41. The brewery is inland from the highway. ☎ 3826 5858. Tours M-F 10am, noon, and 2pm; Su noon and 2pm. $18, concessions $12, children $10. Book ahead. AmEx/DC/MC/V.)*

CITY HALL. When it opened in 1932, it earned the nickname "Million Pound Town Hall" for the outrageous cost of construction. The restored **clock tower,** a landmark of the city skyline, is 92m high and has an **observation deck.** The **Museum of Brisbane** hosts three small but well-organized exhibits; at least one display is usually by a local artist. *(Observation deck open M-F 10am-3pm, Sa 10am-2pm. Free. Museum ☎ 3403 6363. Open daily 10am-5pm. Free. Bookings for groups of 10 or more ☎ 3403 4048. Museum admission $5, concessions $3.50, children $2.)*

QUEENSLAND CULTURAL CENTRE. In its numerous buildings on the south side of the Victoria Bridge, the Cultural Centre coordinates many of Brisbane's artistic attractions including the art gallery, museum, performing arts complex (p. 329), state library (p. 322), and brand new museum of modern art. The **Queensland Art Gallery** has over 10,000 works, primarily Australian and contemporary Asian. *(☎ 3840 7303; www.qag.qld.gov.au. Open M-F 10am-5pm, Sa-Su 9am-5pm. Free tours M-F 11am, 1, and 2pm; Sa-Su 11:30am, 1 and 2:30pm. Free admission. Special exhibits $8-15, ask for concession rates.)* The **Queensland Museum** is home to the Sciencentre and a wide range of Australian artifacts of cultural and natural interest. *(☎ 3840 7555; www.southbank.qm.qld.gov.au. Open daily 9:30am-5pm. Free admission. Special exhibitions $10-15; Sciencentre $9.50, concessions and children $7.50.)*

the park the
formances in
the miniature
Train runs M-F

e occasional
ull schedule o
garoo, ogle t
70-acre me
eerwah exit,
follow th
Transit C
ou for a
e at 1
es. A
o:
9.

S

on the former site of the 1988 World Expo, of the river, a cafe-dotted boardwalk, and week- **on** is surrounded by a real sand beach and fills *guard on duty Dec.-Jan. 7am-midnight, Feb.-Mar. and mid- 5pm, early Sept. 9am-6pm.)* The Parklands also con- ecks and models. *(At the old South Brisbane dry dock, 361. Open daily 9:30am-4:30pm; last entry 3:30pm. $6,* kets are on your agenda, the **South Bank Art & Craft** including crafts, jewelry, psychics, clothing, and *m-5pm, Su 9am-5pm.)* The South Bank also organizes ws, fireworks, and weightlifting championships— **a.** A new movie theater shows recent releases at howings on school holidays. Obtain an event calen- center in the center of the park at the Little Stanley *bus to South Bank or Cultural Centre stops, by CityTrain to to terminal stop at South Bank. Info Centre ☎3867 2051; daily 9am-5pm.)*

BO
as mong palm groves, camellia gardens, and lily ponds goa nal birdlife. If you're lucky, you might see a large *☎34 from the CBD on Albert St., at the intersection with Alice St. depar mely dangerous at night and should be avoided. Free tours t St. entrance M-F 11am and 1pm.)*

MOUN section t-tha, about 5km from the CBD, is split into two main from A lens and the summit. Bus #471 services both sections *Sa-Su 10 n. to gardens, 30min. to summit. 1 per hr. M-F 8:45am-3:30pm,* and follo park is also accessible by car: drive down Milton Rd. Japanese nsland's premier subtropical **Botanic Garden** includes a green. *(☎* , tropical dome, bonsai house, and plenty of picnicking *center.)* It a *ns open 8am-5pm. Free tours M-Sa 11am and 1pm from the info* 2578. Open ensland's first planetarium, the **Cosmic Sky Dome.** *(☎3403* *Sa 12:30, 3: m-4:30pm, Sa 10:30am-6:30pm. 45min. programs Tu-F 3:15pm;* *$6.90, familie n; Su 12:30 and 3:15pm. $11.70, concessions $9.70, children* view of the c *k ahead.)* The Mt. Coot-tha Summit offers a spectacular fancier **The Su** The casual **Kuta Cafe** ❷ (most meals under $16) and the **rant** ❺ (main courses $25-35) both have panoramic views. *(www.brisbanelo Kuta Cafe ☎3368 2117. Open M-Th and Su 7am-11pm, F-Sa 7am- midnight. The Su rant ☎3369 9922. Open M-F 11:30am-2:30pm and 5pm-latenight, Sa 11:30am-laten am-10:30am and 11:30am-latenight. AmEx/DC/MC/V.)*

BRISBANE FOR RK. Picnic, camp, bird watch, cycle, ride horses, and hike on over 28,000 h s of eucalyptus forest. The park headquarters offers bush- walking maps for al trails that originate near the office; the HQ also contains the **Walkabout Cre ldlife Centre,** a small sanctuary that houses many of the ani- mals for which So eastern Queensland is famous. Bush camping is permitted in designated areas ($0 per person; book ahead). Camping areas are remote and have no facilities; p sical fitness, as well as navigational and bushwalking skills, is required. *(60 Mt. Neb Rd. ☎13 13 04; www.qld.com.au/camping. Take Musgrave Rd., which turns into Waterworks Rd. and then Mt. Nebo Rd., out of the city. Bus #385 ($3.40) from William St. outside the Treasury Casino (stop 113A) will take you the 14km to park headquarters, depart- ing once per hr. 8:20am-3:20pm. Trails with camping are accessible by private transport only. Info center ☎1300 723 684. Open daily 8:30am-4:15pm. Wildlife Centre $5.30, concessions $3.70, children $2.60, families $13.20.)*

ROMA STREET PARKLANDS. The recent $72 million renovation gav official title of the largest subtropical garden in a CBD. Enjoy free pe the amphitheater, walk through the recreated ecosystems, or ride train. *(☎3006 4545; www.romastreetparkland.com.au. Open dawn to dusk 10am-2pm, Sa-Su 10am-4pm. $5, students $4, children $3.)*

WILDLIFE

AUSTRALIA ZOO. Crocodile Hunter Steve Irwin used to ma appearances at the zoo he owned and operated. The park offers a f feedings and info sessions every day. Cuddle a python, feed a kan world's ten most poisonous snakes, and walk the grounds of this for animal lovers. *(In Beerwah, 75km north of Brisbane. By car, take the B Mountains Tourist Route, off the Pacific Hwy. 60km north of Brisbane, the another 20km. By public transport, catch the Nambour Express from the 8:02am. The train arrives at Beerwah at 9:30am where a free shuttle collects y to the Zoo. Trains run to the Zoo all day, but only the express gets you the shows. Round-trip $16.20, weekends $12.20. Call ☎13 12 30 for timetab also runs to the Zoo from the Sunshine Coast; call Zoo for schedule. Z www.crocodilehunter.com. $43, concessions $35, children $29, families $13 4:30pm.)* **CC's Croc Connections** offers packages that include transi sion. *(☎1300 551 249; www.crocconnections.com. $80, concessions $70*

ALMA PARK ZOO. A hands-on menagerie of koalas, monkeys, a which includes walk-throughs of the kangaroo and deer enclos feeding of some of the friendlier animals. Beautiful tropical ga make it an ideal picnic spot. *(Alma Rd., Dakabin. Alma Park is 28km Bruce Hwy., at the Boundary Rd. exit. By public transportation, take the Ca abin and snag a taxi at the Dakabin station. If you catch the 8:38 or 9:02am you can get a free shuttle to the Zoo from Dakabin station. ☎3204 6 zoo.com.au. Open daily 9am-5pm. Last entry 4pm. Koala petting daily noo $26, ISIC $21, children $17, families $62. MC/V.)*

LONE PINE KOALA SANCTUARY. Lone Pine, the world's larges ...ry, ...ose is home to over 130 of the beloved marsupials with which visito ...ador- and personal. Be sure to check out the mums and babies secti ...more able little ones. If you come at feeding time (usually around ...ame in likely to see the lethargic animals moving around. Check out ...n Pine's the restaurant, where numerous entertainers have been photo ...and follow koalas. *(By car, follow Milton Rd. to the Western Freeway, take the Fig Tre ...#430 from the signs. A taxi should cost around $25 from the city. By public transpo ...opposite City platform B3 in the Myer Centre, 1 per hr.; or bus #445 from stop 45 on A ...Brisbane River: Hall, 1 per hr. You can also take the Mirimar Wildlife Cruise 19km upstrea ...m; free pickup ☎1300 729 742; www.mirimar.com. Departs South Bank 10am, retur ...2, children $26. from city accommodations. Round-trip with park admission $48, concess ...nts $17, children Sanctuary: ☎3378 1366; www.koala.net. Open daily 8:30am-5pm. $19, $14, families $49. NOMADS/VIP/YHA.)*

ACTIVITIES

ROCK CLIMBING AND SKYDIVING

Join **River Life** at the old Naval Stores at Kangaroo Point Cliffs for night kayaking every Th 6:30-8pm and rock climbing every F 6:30-8pm. Don't worry, the area is well lit. ($39, includes equipment). They also have rock climbing, abseiling, in-line skating, and boxing throughout the week. Book ahead. (Lower River Terrace, Kangaroo Point. ☎3891 5766; www.riverlife.com.au.) If you need practice, try indoor climbing with **Rocksports Indoor Sports Climbing** (224 Barry Pde., Fortitude Valley. ☎3216 0462. Open M-F 10am-9:30pm, Sa-Su 10am-5pm. $14 for unlimited climbing. $11 harness, shoes, and chalk rental. Bringing a partner is mandatory. MC/V.) A little higher up, the **Brisbane Skydiving Centre** will show you the city at 200km per hour from 14,000 ft. (☎1800 061 555; www.brisbaneskydive.com.au. 12,000 ft. $265; 14,000 ft. $295. Free pickup. Video $90, with photos $130. MC/V.) **Redcliffe City Skydiving** will drop you on the beach. (☎1300 788 555; skydiveredcliff.com.au. 12,000 ft. $299; 14,000 ft. $329; includes lunch and T-shirt. Video $88, with photos $121. Free pickup.) Enjoy a more leisurely flight on a hot air balloon ride over the Brisbane countryside with **Balloons Above.** (☎1800 648 050; www.balloonsabove.com.au. Daily at sunrise. From $245, children $199; includes champagne breakfast. Book at least 2 days in advance. MC/V.)

WATER ACTIVITIES

Brisbane has many waterways that are perfect for canoeing. Guides to the popular Oxley Creek and Boondall Wetlands are available from libraries or the City Council Customer Services counter, in the City Plaza, on the corner of Ann and George St. For rentals, try **Goodtime Surf and Sail.** (29 Ipswich Rd., Woolloongabba. ☎3391 8588; www.goodtime.com.au. Open M-F 8:30am-5:30pm, Sa 8:30am-4pm, Su 10am-3pm. Canoes from $29.50 per day; kayaks from $24. Deposit $110. Includes paddles and life jackets.) **ProDive** goes to the area's reefs and wrecks. (☎3368 3766; www.prodive.com.au. Open M-W and F 9am-6pm, Th 9am-8pm, Sa-Su 9am-5pm. Daytrip with 2 dives from $139; gear rental $69; includes transit from shop to dive site, morning tea; may include lunch, afternoon tea. Dives Th-Su at 7am.)

ENTERTAINMENT

Brisbane seems to continuously host festivals and an array of theatrical, artistic, and musical performances. Call the **Queensland Cultural Centre** (☎3840 7444) for a current schedule or visit www.ourbrisbane.com. For theater tickets, call **QTIX** (☎13 62 46; www.qtix.com.au). Most places offer discounts to students and backpackers; be sure to ask for concession prices.

FINE ARTS

The Queensland Performing Arts Centre (☎3840 7444; www.qpac.com.au), just across Victoria Bridge in South Bank. Four theaters: the Concert Hall hosts symphony and chamber orchestras as well as contemporary music concerts; the Lyric Theatre sponsors drama, musicals, ballet, and opera; the Playhouse has drama and dance; and the Cremorne Theatre stages more intimate and experimental productions. Ticket office open M-Sa 8:30am-8:30pm and 2hr. before performances. Tour available F 11:30am $7.50, $5 concessions. Book ahead.

The Queensland Conservatorium (☎3735 6241; www.gu.edu.au/concerts), has concerts ranging from classical to pop with national and international acts. Prices free-$20.

Opera Queensland (☎3735 3030; www.operaqueensland.com.au), adjacent to the Conservatorium. Produces three operas annually. Tickets $36-126.

La Boite, 6-8 Musk Ave. (☎3007 8600; www.laboite.com.au), in Kelvin Grove. Contemporary Australian theater; five mainstage productions per yr., typically by local artists.

The Queensland Ballet (☎3013 6666; www.queenslandballet.com.au), presents approx. 100 performances each year; an impressive range of popular classics and full-length story ballets to contemporary works in a variety of dance styles. Tickets $20-65.

The Queensland Theatre Company, 78 Montague Rd. (☎3010 7600; www.qldtheatreco.com.au), offers nine shows annually with a mix of classical and contemporary works. $45-55; under 25 $18.50.

Brisbane Powerhouse Centre for Live Arts, 119 Lamington St. (☎3358 8600; www.brisbanepowerhouse.org.), adjacent to New Farm Park. An alternative arts venue with two separate theaters, as well as art galleries and dining options. Box office open M-F 9am-5pm, Sa-Su noon-4pm, and 2hr. before performances.

MUSIC, MONEY, MOVIES

The enormous **Treasury Casino,** at the top of Queen St., is a Brisbane landmark. It contains five restaurants, seven bars, over 100 gaming tables, and more than 1100 gaming machines. (☎3306 8888; www.treasurycasino.com.au. Open 24hr.) **Birch Carroll & Coyle** shows new releases on level 3 of the Myer Center (☎3229 5949) and at Brisbane Regent, 167 Queen St. (☎3229 5544. $14.80, students $11, children $10.50.) Alternative films play at **DENDY,** 346 George St. (☎3211 3244; www.dendy.com.au. $13, students $10, children $8.50; M all films $8.50.)

SPORTS

Brisbane Entertainment Centre (☎3265 8111; www.brisent.com.au; tickets ☎13 28 49; www.ticketek.com.au), is Brisbane's largest indoor complex for sports, concerts, and events. Citytrain's Shorncliffe line runs to Boondall Station every 30min. The **Gabba,** at Vulture and Stanley St., Woolloongabba, is home to the AFL Brisbane Lions and the Queensland Bulls National Cricket Team. Take the bus to the station on the corner of Main and Stanley St. ($2.60) or the train to Roma St. (☎3008 6166. For AFL tickets, ☎13 28 49; www.ticketek.com.au. For cricket, ☎1300 136 122; www.ticketmaster.com.au.) The new **Suncorp Stadium** (☎3335 1777; www.suncorpstadium.com.au; tickets ☎13 28 49; www.ticketek.com.au), at the intersection of Hale and Milton St., is now home to all football matches, including those played by the rugby league "Brisbane Broncos." The stadium is accessible by foot from the CBD or from Citytrain's Milton and Roma stop.

FESTIVALS

The **Brisbane River Festival** (☎3846 7971; www.riverfestival.com.au) celebrates spring at the end of August or beginning of September with fireworks, concerts, and feasts. The **Brisbane International Film Festival** (☎3007 3007; www.biff.com.au) is held annually in mid-July; the festival features alternative and retrospective film releases. The **Valley Fiesta** (☎3854 0860; www.valleyfiesta.com), sometime between July and September, heats up Fortitude Valley with street festivals, local bands, and dance performances; check website for 2007 details. Most exciting of all, the **Australia Day Cockroach Races** are run every January 26 at the Story Bridge Hotel, 200 Main St., Kangaroo Point (☎3391 2266). This massive social event allows you either to buy your own racing roach or to cheer from the sidelines.

NIGHTLIFE

Brisbane nights roll by in sweaty clubs, noisy pubs, and classy lounges. Fortitude Valley is home to Brisbane's best nightlife scene, with alternative bars, huge dance clubs, live music, and several gay establishments. It was recently granted an exception to the strict noise regulations, allowing it to blast its music like never before. Caxton St. in Petrie Terrace has great atmosphere for watching a rugby game on the telly, while the CBD is a big draw for backpackers with Irish pubs, drink specials, and rocking Thursday nights. Expect long lines on the weekend.

PARKS AND GARDENS

SOUTH BANK PARKLANDS. Built on the former site of the 1988 World Expo, South Bank offers tree-lined views of the river, a cafe-dotted boardwalk, and weekend markets. The man-made **lagoon** is surrounded by a real sand beach and fills with sun-seekers year-round. *(Lifeguard on duty Dec.-Jan. 7am-midnight, Feb.-Mar. and mid-Sept. to Nov. 7am-7pm, Apr.-Aug. 9am-5pm, early Sept. 9am-6pm.)* The Parklands also contain a **Maritime Museum,** with wrecks and models. *(At the old South Brisbane dry dock, south end of the Parklands. ☎3844 5361. Open daily 9:30am-4:30pm; last entry 3:30pm. $6, concessions $5, children $3.)* If markets are on your agenda, the **South Bank Art & Craft Markets** has nearly everything, including crafts, jewelry, psychics, clothing, and massages. *(Open F 5-10pm, Sa 11am-5pm, Su 9am-5pm.)* The South Bank also organizes free events—including car shows, fireworks, and weightlifting championships—often held in the **Suncorp Piazza.** A new movie theater shows recent releases at reduced rates and holds free showings on school holidays. Obtain an event calendar and map from the visitors center in the center of the park at the Little Stanley St. Plaza. *(Accessible by foot, by bus to South Bank or Cultural Centre stops, by CityTrain to South Brisbane station, or by ferry to terminal stop at South Bank. Info Centre ☎3867 2051; www.visitsouthbank.com.au. Open daily 9am-5pm.)*

BOTANIC GARDENS. Stroll among palm groves, camellia gardens, and lily ponds as you take in the exceptional birdlife. If you're lucky, you might see a large goanna lizard. *(A 15min. walk from the CBD on Albert St., at the intersection with Alice St. ☎3403 7067. Open 24hr. Extremely dangerous at night and should be avoided. Free tours depart the rotunda near the Albert St. entrance M-F 11am and 1pm.)*

MOUNT COOT-THA. Mt. Coot-tha, about 5km from the CBD, is split into two main sections: the botanical gardens and the summit. Bus #471 services both sections from Ann St., stop 11. *(25min. to gardens, 30min. to summit. 1 per hr. M-F 8:45am-3:30pm, Sa-Su 10:15am-4:30pm.)* The park is also accessible by car: drive down Milton Rd. and follow the signs. Queensland's premier subtropical **Botanic Garden** includes a Japanese garden, a library, tropical dome, bonsai house, and plenty of picnicking green. *(☎3403 2535. Gardens open 8am-5pm. Free tours M-Sa 11am and 1pm from the info center.)* It also houses Queensland's first planetarium, the **Cosmic Sky Dome.** *(☎3403 2578. Open Tu-F and Su 10am-4:30pm, Sa 10:30am-6:30pm. 45min. programs Tu-F 3:15pm; Sa 12:30, 3:15, and 7:30pm; Su 12:30 and 3:15pm. $11.70, concessions $9.70, children $6.90, families $31.60. Book ahead.)* The Mt. Coot-tha Summit offers a spectacular view of the city at night. The casual **Kuta Cafe** ❷ (most meals under $16) and the fancier **The Summit Restaurant** ❺ (main courses $25-35) both have panoramic views. *(www.brisbanelookout.com. Kuta Cafe ☎3368 2117. Open M-Th and Su 7am-11pm, F-Sa 7am-midnight. The Summit Restaurant ☎3369 9922. Open M-F 11:30am-2:30pm and 5pm-latenight, Sa 11:30am-latenight, Su 8am-10:30am and 11:30am-latenight. AmEx/DC/MC/V.)*

BRISBANE FOREST PARK. Picnic, camp, bird watch, cycle, ride horses, and hike on over 28,000 hectares of eucalyptus forest. The park headquarters offers bushwalking maps for several trails that originate near the office; the HQ also contains the **Walkabout Creek Wildlife Centre,** a small sanctuary that houses many of the animals for which Southeastern Queensland is famous. Bush camping is permitted in designated areas ($4.50 per person; book ahead). Camping areas are remote and have no facilities; physical fitness, as well as navigational and bushwalking skills, is required. *(60 Mt. Nebo Rd. ☎13 13 04; www.qld.com.au/camping. Take Musgrave Rd., which turns into Waterworks Rd., and then Mt. Nebo Rd., out of the city. Bus #385 ($3.40) from William St. outside the Treasury Casino (stop 113A) will take you the 14km to park headquarters, departing once per hr. 8:20am-3:20pm. Trails with camping are accessible by private transport only. Info center ☎1300 723 684. Open daily 8:30am-4:15pm. Wildlife Centre $5.30, concessions $3.70, children $2.60, families $13.20.)*

ROMA STREET PARKLANDS. The recent $72 million renovation gave the park the official title of the largest subtropical garden in a CBD. Enjoy free performances in the amphitheater, walk through the recreated ecosystems, or ride the miniature train. *(☎3006 4545; www.romastreetparkland.com.au. Open dawn to dusk. Train runs M-F 10am-2pm, Sa-Su 10am-4pm. $5, students $4, children $3.)*

WILDLIFE

AUSTRALIA ZOO. Crocodile Hunter Steve Irwin used to make occasional appearances at the zoo he owned and operated. The park offers a full schedule of feedings and info sessions every day. Cuddle a python, feed a kangaroo, ogle the world's ten most poisonous snakes, and walk the grounds of this 70-acre mecca for animal lovers. *(In Beerwah, 75km north of Brisbane. By car, take the Beerwah exit, Glass Mountains Tourist Route, off the Pacific Hwy. 60km north of Brisbane, then follow the signs another 20km. By public transport, catch the Nambour Express from the Transit Centre at 8:02am. The train arrives at Beerwah at 9:30am where a free shuttle collects you for a short drive to the Zoo. Trains run to the Zoo all day, but only the express gets you there at 10am for the shows. Round-trip $16.20, weekends $12.20. Call ☎13 12 30 for timetables. A courtesy bus also runs to the Zoo from the Sunshine Coast; call Zoo for schedule. Zoo: ☎5436 2000; www.crocodilehunter.com. $43, concessions $35, children $29, families $139. Open daily 9am-4:30pm.)* **CC's Croc Connections** offers packages that include transit and Zoo admission. *(☎1300 551 249; www.crocconnections.com. $80, concessions $70, children $50.)*

ALMA PARK ZOO. A hands-on menagerie of koalas, monkeys, and water buffalo which includes walk-throughs of the kangaroo and deer enclosures, and allows feeding of some of the friendlier animals. Beautiful tropical gardens with BBQs make it an ideal picnic spot. *(Alma Rd., Dakabin. Alma Park is 28km north of Brisbane on Bruce Hwy., at the Boundary Rd. exit. By public transportation, take the Caboolture train to Dakabin and snag a taxi at the Dakabin station. If you catch the 8:38 or 9:02am train from Roma St., you can get a free shuttle to the Zoo from Dakabin station. ☎3204 6566; www.almaparkzoo.com.au. Open daily 9am-5pm. Last entry 4pm. Koala petting daily noon and 2:30pm. Adults $26, ISIC $21, children $17, families $62. MC/V.)*

LONE PINE KOALA SANCTUARY. Lone Pine, the world's largest koala sanctuary, is home to over 130 of the beloved marsupials with which visitors can get up close and personal. Be sure to check out the mums and babies section to see the adorable little ones. If you come at feeding time (usually around 2pm), you're more likely to see the lethargic animals moving around. Check out the wall of fame in the restaurant, where numerous entertainers have been photographed with Pine's koalas. *(By car, follow Milton Rd. to the Western Freeway, take the Fig Tree Pocket exit and follow the signs. A taxi should cost around $25 from the city. By public transport, take bus #430 from platform B3 in the Myer Centre, 1 per hr.; or bus #445 from stop 45 on Adelaide St. opposite City Hall, 1 per hr. You can also take the Mirimar Wildlife Cruise 19km upstream on the Brisbane River: ☎1300 729 742; www.mirimar.com. Departs South Bank 10am, returns 2:45pm; free pickup from city accommodations. Round-trip with park admission $48, concessions $42, children $26. Sanctuary: ☎3378 1366; www.koala.net. Open daily 8:30am-5pm. $19, students $17, children $14, families $49. NOMADS/VIP/YHA.)*

ACTIVITIES

ROCK CLIMBING AND SKYDIVING

Join **River Life** at the old Naval Stores at Kangaroo Point Cliffs for night kayaking every Th 6:30-8pm and rock climbing every F 6:30-8pm. Don't worry, the area is well lit. ($39, includes equipment). They also have rock climbing, abseiling, in-line skating, and boxing throughout the week. Book ahead. (Lower River Terrace, Kangaroo Point. ☎3891 5766; www.riverlife.com.au.) If you need practice, try indoor climbing with **Rocksports Indoor Sports Climbing** (224 Barry Pde., Fortitude Valley. ☎3216 0462. Open M-F 10am-9:30pm, Sa-Su 10am-5pm. $14 for unlimited climbing. $11 harness, shoes, and chalk rental. Bringing a partner is mandatory. MC/V.) A little higher up, the **Brisbane Skydiving Centre** will show you the city at 200km per hour from 14,000 ft. (☎1800 061 555; www.brisbaneskydive.com.au. 12,000 ft. $265; 14,000 ft. $295. Free pickup. Video $90, with photos $130. MC/V.) **Redcliffe City Skydiving** will drop you on the beach. (☎1300 788 555; skydiveredcliff.com.au. 12,000 ft. $299; 14,000 ft. $329; includes lunch and T-shirt. Video $88, with photos $121. Free pickup.) Enjoy a more leisurely flight on a hot air balloon ride over the Brisbane countryside with **Balloons Above.** (☎1800 648 050; www.balloonsabove.com.au. Daily at sunrise. From $245, children $199; includes champagne breakfast. Book at least 2 days in advance. MC/V.)

WATER ACTIVITIES

Brisbane has many waterways that are perfect for canoeing. Guides to the popular Oxley Creek and Boondall Wetlands are available from libraries or the City Council Customer Services counter, in the City Plaza, on the corner of Ann and George St. For rentals, try **Goodtime Surf and Sail.** (29 Ipswich Rd., Woolloongabba. ☎3391 8588; www.goodtime.com.au. Open M-F 8:30am-5:30pm, Sa 8:30am-4pm, Su 10am-3pm. Canoes from $29.50 per day; kayaks from $24. Deposit $110. Includes paddles and life jackets.) **ProDive** goes to the area's reefs and wrecks. (☎3368 3766; www.prodive.com.au. Open M-W and F 9am-6pm, Th 9am-8pm, Sa-Su 9am-5pm. Daytrip with 2 dives from $139; gear rental $69; includes transit from shop to dive site, morning tea; may include lunch, afternoon tea. Dives Th-Su at 7am.)

ENTERTAINMENT

Brisbane seems to continuously host festivals and an array of theatrical, artistic, and musical performances. Call the **Queensland Cultural Centre** (☎3840 7444) for a current schedule or visit www.ourbrisbane.com. For theater tickets, call **QTIX** (☎13 62 46; www.qtix.com.au). Most places offer discounts to students and backpackers; be sure to ask for concession prices.

FINE ARTS

The Queensland Performing Arts Centre (☎3840 7444; www.qpac.com.au), just across Victoria Bridge in South Bank. Four theaters: the Concert Hall hosts symphony and chamber orchestras as well as contemporary music concerts; the Lyric Theatre sponsors drama, musicals, ballet, and opera; the Playhouse has drama and dance; and the Cremorne Theatre stages more intimate and experimental productions. Ticket office open M-Sa 8:30am-8:30pm and 2hr. before performances. Tour available F 11:30am $7.50, $5 concessions. Book ahead.

The Queensland Conservatorium (☎3735 6241; www.gu.edu.au/concerts), has concerts ranging from classical to pop with national and international acts. Prices free-$20.

Opera Queensland (☎3735 3030; www.operaqueensland.com.au), adjacent to the Conservatorium. Produces three operas annually. Tickets $36-126.

La Boite, 6-8 Musk Ave. (☎3007 8600; www.laboite.com.au), in Kelvin Grove. Contemporary Australian theater; five mainstage productions per yr., typically by local artists.

The Queensland Ballet (☎3013 6666; www.queenslandballet.com.au), presents approx. 100 performances each year; an impressive range of popular classics and full-length story ballets to contemporary works in a variety of dance styles. Tickets $20-65.

The Queensland Theatre Company, 78 Montague Rd. (☎3010 7600; www.qldtheatreco.com.au), offers nine shows annually with a mix of classical and contemporary works. $45-55; under 25 $18.50.

Brisbane Powerhouse Centre for Live Arts, 119 Lamington St. (☎3358 8600; www.brisbanepowerhouse.org.), adjacent to New Farm Park. An alternative arts venue with two separate theaters, as well as art galleries and dining options. Box office open M-F 9am-5pm, Sa-Su noon-4pm, and 2hr. before performances.

MUSIC, MONEY, MOVIES

The enormous **Treasury Casino,** at the top of Queen St., is a Brisbane landmark. It contains five restaurants, seven bars, over 100 gaming tables, and more than 1100 gaming machines. (☎3306 8888; www.treasurycasino.com.au. Open 24hr.) **Birch Carroll & Coyle** shows new releases on level 3 of the Myer Center (☎3229 5949) and at Brisbane Regent, 167 Queen St. (☎3229 5544. $14.80, students $11, children $10.50.) Alternative films play at **DENDY,** 346 George St. (☎3211 3244; www.dendy.com.au. $13, students $10, children $8.50; M all films $8.50.)

SPORTS

Brisbane Entertainment Centre (☎3265 8111; www.brisent.com.au; tickets ☎13 28 49; www.ticketek.com.au), is Brisbane's largest indoor complex for sports, concerts, and events. Citytrain's Shorncliffe line runs to Boondall Station every 30min. The **Gabba,** at Vulture and Stanley St., Woolloongabba, is home to the AFL Brisbane Lions and the Queensland Bulls National Cricket Team. Take the bus to the station on the corner of Main and Stanley St. ($2.60) or the train to Roma St. (☎3008 6166. For AFL tickets, ☎13 28 49; www.ticketek.com.au. For cricket, ☎1300 136 122; www.ticketmaster.com.au.) The new **Suncorp Stadium** (☎3335 1777; www.suncorpstadium.com.au; tickets ☎13 28 49; www.ticketek.com.au), at the intersection of Hale and Milton St., is now home to all football matches, including those played by the rugby league "Brisbane Broncos." The stadium is accessible by foot from the CBD or from Citytrain's Milton and Roma stop.

FESTIVALS

The **Brisbane River Festival** (☎3846 7971; www.riverfestival.com.au) celebrates spring at the end of August or beginning of September with fireworks, concerts, and feasts. The **Brisbane International Film Festival** (☎3007 3007; www.biff.com.au) is held annually in mid-July; the festival features alternative and retrospective film releases. The **Valley Fiesta** (☎3854 0860; www.valleyfiesta.com), sometime between July and September, heats up Fortitude Valley with street festivals, local bands, and dance performances; check website for 2007 details. Most exciting of all, the **Australia Day Cockroach Races** are run every January 26 at the Story Bridge Hotel, 200 Main St., Kangaroo Point (☎3391 2266). This massive social event allows you either to buy your own racing roach or to cheer from the sidelines.

NIGHTLIFE

Brisbane nights roll by in sweaty clubs, noisy pubs, and classy lounges. Fortitude Valley is home to Brisbane's best nightlife scene, with alternative bars, huge dance clubs, live music, and several gay establishments. It was recently granted an exception to the strict noise regulations, allowing it to blast its music like never before. Caxton St. in Petrie Terrace has great atmosphere for watching a rugby game on the telly, while the CBD is a big draw for backpackers with Irish pubs, drink specials, and rocking Thursday nights. Expect long lines on the weekend.

FORTITUDE VALLEY

Family, 8 Mclachlan St. (☎3852 5000; www.thefamily.com.au). Brilliant neon laser lights fan out across the hip, the young, and the beautiful in *Bartender Magazine*'s recently-named "Best Club in Australia." Faux-industrial decor winds through a 5-story maze of lounges, bars, and dance floors; each new area features a different atmosphere, crowd, and music style. Su Fluffy party is a gay-friendly hospitality night. Cover varies with DJ, usually $8-15. Open F-Su 9pm-5am.

The Beat Mega Club, 677 Ann St. (☎3852 2661; www.thebeatmegaclub.com.au). Perhaps the best dance club in Brisbane, the 15 DJs keep all 5 dance floors and 7 bars packed on F and Sa. Attracts a diverse crowd; extremely popular among the gay population. Cover $10, free before 10:30pm. Open M-Sa 8pm-5am and Su 5pm-5am.

The Wickham, 308 Wickham St. (☎3852 1301; www.thewickham.com.au). Pub which attracts a predominately gay crowd. Morphs into an outrageous dance party on the weekend. Costumes, cabarets—anything goes. Shows Tu-F. Occasional cover charge $5-10. Open M-Tu 9am-1am, W-Th 9am-2am, F-Sa 9am-5am, Su 10am-2am.

Empire Hotel, 339 Brunswick St. (☎3852 1216). Downstairs, the **Corner Bar** and **Press Club** cater to a casual crowd. (Corner Bar M-Th 10am-2pm, F 10am-latenight, Sa-Su noon-latenight. Press Club daily 6pm-latenight.) The upstairs nightclub, consisting of the **Middle Bar** and **Moon Bar,** satisfies a late-nighter of any breed. To the right, comfy couches and alternative tunes; to the left, fresh and funky chemical beats. Cover after 10pm $8-15. Open F-Sa 9pm-5am.

Monastery, 621 Ann St. (☎3257 7081; www.monastery.com.au). Pumps out techno and house music in a not-so-holy atmosphere. Back-lit stained glass and cushy leather couches recall old Europe with an irreverent twist. Rotating DJs and frequent special events. Cover charge varies. Open Th-Su 9pm-5am.

CBD AND RIVERSIDE

The Victory, 127 Edward St. (☎3221 0444), on the corner of Charlotte St. A massive complex which includes a classic Aussie pub, beer garden, nightclub, and karaoke lounge, spread out among 7 bars. Live music, DJ, and karaoke W-Su. Business casual. M-Tu 10am-2am, W-Sa 10am-3am, Su 11am-1am. Nightclub open 8:30pm-3am.

Port Office Hotel, 38 Edward St. (☎3221 0072), on the corner of Edward and Margaret St. A popular combination hotel, bar, and dance joint that makes for a great evening if the journey out to the Valley seems too far. A good mix of music played by in-house DJs will keep your head bobbing.

Friday's, 123 Eagle St. (☎3832 2122; www.fridays.com.au), next to Riverside Centre. A diverse young crowd gets classy at this giant riverfront hangout. The maze of rooms offers a variety of entertainment, from a DJ spinning dance tunes to live performances. Long lines. Live bands F-Sa; W $4 cocktail night 5pm-5am. Th-Sa $8-10 cover after 10pm. Open M-Tu and Su 11:30am-midnight, W-Sa 11:30am-5am.

MORETON BAY AND ISLANDS

Most travelers heading north to Cairns or south towards the Gold Coast bypass the beautiful, relaxed Moreton Bay and its islands; don't let it happen to you. The perpetually laid-back lifestyle in Manly is only a mere 35min. from Brisbane, at the mouth of the Brisbane River. North Stradbroke Island and Moreton Island are idyllic sites, offering diving, hiking, whale and dolphin watching, and swimming. Ferries run to the islands daily; several travel companies and hostels offer package deals that include transportation.

MANLY ☎07

There seem to be more boats than people in the friendly harborside village of Manly. Conveniently located near most ferry services, the town serves as the best base for exploring nearby islands, as well as a quiet place to return to after a day of fishing, sailing, or scuba diving. Lazy Wednesday afternoons bring sailing races, in which visitors can participate at no cost. If you prefer not to stay in a city, Manly is also a perfect base for exploring Brisbane.

Spot wildlife with **Manly Eco Cruises,** which offers family-oriented daytrips around Moreton Bay Marine Park. The trip includes boomnet rides (your chance to sit in a large open net and be dragged behind a boat), tropical lunch, short canoe rides, and commentary on the Bay. (☎3396 9400; www.manlyecocruises.com. Daytrips M-Sa 9am-3pm; $109. Su breakfast cruise 8:30-10:30am; $38. Book ahead.) For free sailing, show up at the **Royal Queensland Yacht Squadron (RQ)** for the friendly **Wednesday Afternoon Gentleman's Sailing (WAGS)** races. Yacht owners are always looking for temporary crew members; if you are a beginner, they may teach you. For many, the race is just an opportunity to share a drink, make new friends, and relax. The winning boat gets a bottle of rum. (☎3396 8666. A 10min. walk down The Esplanade from Cambridge Pde.; W noon to 5pm or later. Don't be late; there are not always enough yacht owners for all aspiring crew. Although it's called Wednesday Afternoon Gentleman's Sailing, women are welcome.)

Moreton Bay Backpackers ❷, 45 Cambridge Pde., is located only 50m from the water. The Backpackers is a warmer, friendlier version of its urban counterparts. Highlights include spacious, theme-painted rooms, large bathrooms, kitchen, nice TV lounge, laundry, lockers, Internet access, and an owner who hosts daily activities. Its prices can't be beat. (☎3396 3020; www.moretonbaylodge.com.au. Free airport and train pickup. Key and linen deposit $10. 6- to 9-bed dorms $10-20; ensuite singles $55; ensuite doubles $70. Extra person $15. Seventh night free. Rates slightly higher Dec.-Jan. Student/backpacker discount 10%. Reception, inside Monkey Bar, open 24hr. in summer; in winter open M-Th and Su 8:30am-8pm and F-Sa 8:30am-10pm. MC/V.) **Manly Hotel ❹,** 54 Cambridge Pde., is a favorite of businessmen, and has several bars and a **restaurant ❸** that serves food all day. (☎3249 5999; www.manlyhotel.com. Th and Su karaoke, F-Su live music, W jam session. Restaurant open daily 7am-9pm; bars open M-Th 10am-midnight, F-Sa 10am-2am, Su 11am-9:30pm. Hotel singles $65-110; doubles $80-125.)

Fish Cafe ❶, 461 The Esplanade, at the intersection with Cambridge Pde., is an excellent choice for quick, cheap seafood. The cod and chips ($7.50) and the fish cake panini burger ($6.50) are both delicious. Takeaway recommended; dine-in is three-times the price. (☎3893 0195; www.fishcafe.com.au. Open daily 8-10:45am and 11am-8:30pm.) Across the stairway from Moreton Bay Backpackers is **Monkey Bar ❷,** offering reasonably priced meals with nightly backpacker specials. The local **IGA** supermarket is in the Manly Harbour Village shopping center. (☎3396 1980. Open daily 6am-10pm.)

From Brisbane, take Citytrain to the Manly stop on the Cleveland line (35-40min. from Roma St., daily at least every 30min., $2.80). With your back to the train station, take the second left turn at the "Boat Harbour" sign to reach **Cambridge Parade,** the main thoroughfare. Cambridge Pde. heads toward the harbor and the **Esplanade,** which runs along the water. The **Tourist Information Centre,** 43A Cambridge Pde., is across from the Manly Hotel. (☎3348 3524. Open M-F 9am-5pm, Sa-Su 10am-3pm.) There is a **Bank of Queensland** with a 24hr. **ATM** located in the Manly Harbour Village shopping center on the corner of Cambridge Pde. and the Esplanade. (Open M-Th 9:30am-4pm, F 9:30am-5pm.) The **post office,** 222 Stratton Terr., also in the shopping center. (☎3396 2735. Open M-F 9am-5pm, Sa 9am-noon.) **Postal Code:** 4179.

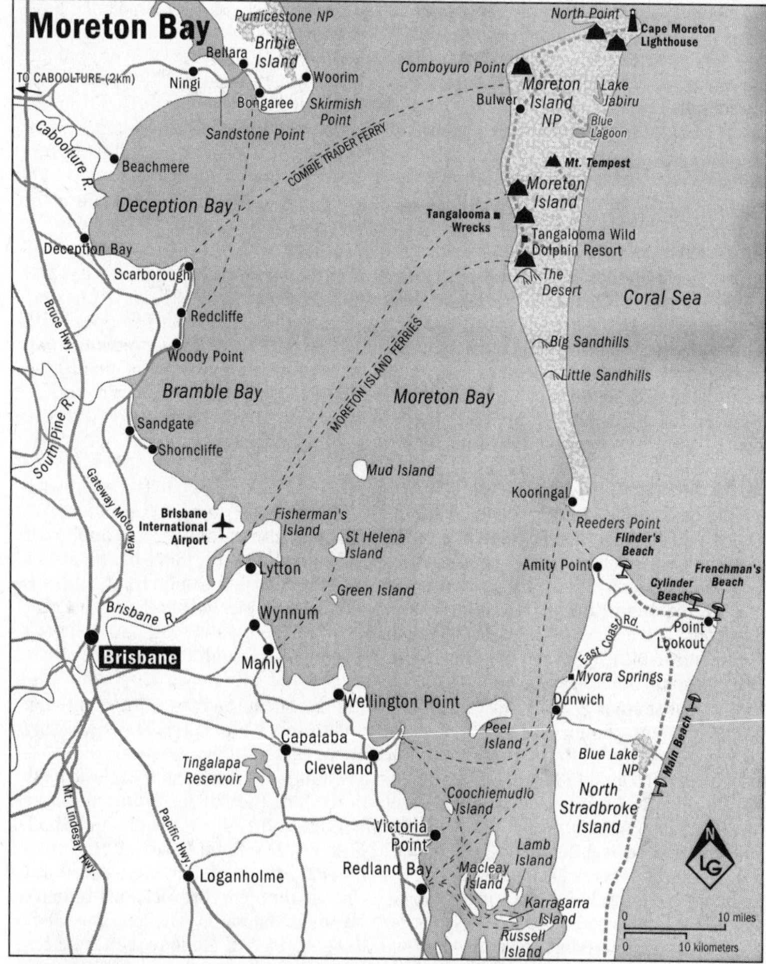

NORTH STRADBROKE ISLAND ☎07

In 1894, a ship carrying explosives was wrecked by fierce storms off what was known as Stradbroke Island. The combination of dynamite and bad weather, helped by the tide, resulted in the clean split of the island into two parts. Since then, the north and south islands have followed different paths; while South Stradbroke (p. 347) has remained relatively uninhabited, its northern counterpart, separated from it by the tiny Jumpinpin Channel, is now home to 3100 people. With miles of sandy white surf beaches, famous blue inland lakes, world-class dive sites, and outdoor activity everywhere you turn, North Stradbroke ("Straddie") is the perfect place to step off the beaten path.

TRANSPORTATION. North Stradbroke is just a few hops on public transportation from Brisbane. Take **Citytrain** to Cleveland (1hr., every 30min., $4.40); from

Cleveland, three different ferry companies service the island. The **Stradbroke Flyer Ferry** is accessible from the train station via courtesy bus. Their "Gold Kat" passenger ferries arrive at One Mile Jetty in Dunwich. (☎3821 3821; www.flyer.com.au. 30min.; every 30-90min. 5am-7:30pm. $16 round-trip, students $12.) Alternatively, **Stradbroke Ferries** runs a passenger **Water Taxi** as well as a vehicular ferry. From the train station, take **Veolia Transport Brisbane** bus #258 (☎3245 3333. 6min., every 30min., $2.20 one-way) to meet the ferry. (☎3286 2666; www.stradbrokeferries.com.au. Passenger ferry 30min.; 10-13 per day 6am-6:15pm; round-trip $17, students $12. Vehicular ferry 45-50min.; 11 per day, 5:30am-6:30pm; round-trip $102 per car.) **Sea Stradbroke** runs a similar service from Cleveland. (☎3488 9777; www.seastradbroke.com. M-F 8-10 per day; $10, cars $102.)

The **North Stradbroke Island Bus Service** runs between Point Lookout, Amity, and Dunwich; timetables make it easy to meet your ferry. (☎3409 7151. 11-12 per day, less frequently to Amity, starting at 6:50am from Point Lookout to 6:45pm from Dunwich. $5.) A **taxi** from Dunwich to Point Lookout costs $30. (**Stradbroke Cab Service** ☎04 0819 3685.) Several companies in Cleveland provide **rental cars** to the island, but **4WD rental** is available only in Brisbane. A permit is necessary if you do plan on driving a 4WD vehicle on the island. These can be purchased from the tourist office or at most campsites. (annual permits only, $32. MC/V.)

ORIENTATION AND PRACTICAL INFORMATION. North Stradbroke Island has three distinct townships: residential **Dunwich,** the ferry drop-off point on the western shore; **Amity Point,** north of Dunwich, with calm beaches and great fishing; and **Point Lookout,** 22km northeast of Dunwich, with most of the area's accommodations and tourist attractions. **East Coast Road** is the main road connecting Dunwich and Point Lookout; its name changes to **Mooloomba Road** in Point Lookout. The middle of the island consists of various lakes, swamps, national park land, and habitat reserves, while sand mines occupy a significant portion of the northern and southern ends of the island.

The **tourist office** is the yellow building on Junner St., at the base of the Dunwich football green, 250 meters from the Stradbroke Ferry Water Taxi. The incredibly helpful staff books tours and accommodations. (☎3409 9555; www.stradbroketourism.com. Open M-F 8:30am-5pm, Sa-Su 8:30am-3pm.) Although there's **no bank** on the island, **ATMs** are located in hotels in each of the towns. Other services include **police** (☎3409 9020), across from the tourist office in Dunwich, and **Stradbroke Island Medical Centre** (☎3409 8660), at Kennedy Dr., Point Lookout. (Open M-F 8:30am-5pm, Sa 9-11am, Su 10-11am.) The **post offices** in Dunwich and Point Lookout also provide some **banking** services for visitors. The **Dunwich Post Office** is located at 3 Welsby St. (☎3409 9010; open M-W and F 8am-5pm, Th 7am-5pm, Sa 8-10:45am) and the **Point Lookout Post** is at Meegera Pl., off Endeavor St. (☎3409 8210. Open M-F 9am-5pm.) **Postal Code:** 4183.

ACCOMMODATIONS AND CAMPING. There are plenty of budget accommodations: two hostels and six campsites—one in Amity, two in Dunwich, and three in Point Lookout. **Manta Lodge and Scuba Centre (YHA) ❷,** on the left side of East Coast Rd., at the entrance to Point Lookout and minutes from Home Beach, has an attached dive center and provides transportation from the Roma St. Transit Centre in Brisbane (in summer M, W, F; in winter M and F; $25 round-trip). The guesthouse rooms are simple and clean with shared facilities. Amenities include Internet access, laundry, kitchen, and a spacious common room. (☎3409 8888; www.mantalodge.com.au. Key deposit $10. Reception in summer 7am-late; in winter 8am-5pm. 4- to 8-bed dorms $27; doubles $60. YHA discount $3. MC/V.) **Point Lookout Backpackers Beach House ❷,** 76 Mooloomba Rd., is in the middle of Pt. Lookout, on the left side when entering from Dunwich, just past Endeavor Rd. and before The Lookout Shopping Village. The large six-bed dorms have their own bath and kitchen. Internet access and laundry are available. The hostel provides free snorkeling equipment and body boards. (☎3409 8679; www.pointlookout-beachhouse.com.au. Reception 9:30am-1:15pm and 3:15-7pm. Dorms $20; doubles $45; weekly discounts. Cash only.) **Camping ❶** is also permitted on all of Flinders Beach (2 people $16) and at least 10km south of the paved causeway on Main Beach ($12.50), both accessible by 4WD only. (Book through the Redlands Shire Council ☎1300 551 253. Sites for 2 $22, powered $27.)

FOOD. Most restaurants are in Point Lookout, along Mooloomba Rd. The dirt-cheap but yummy **Fins 'n' Fish ❶**, next to the post office at Meegera Pl., off Endeavor St., has excellent fish 'n' chips and fish burgers for $5. (☎3409 8080. Open M-Th 11am-2:30pm and 4:30-7:30pm, F-Sa 11am-2:30pm and 4:30-8pm.) **Point Lookout Bowls Club ❷** (☎3409 8182), on the right side of East Coast Road just past Manta Lodge coming from Dunwich, serves up exceptionally large portions for reasonable prices. It is also one of the only places to do any type of evening socializing. **La Focaccia ❸**, at Meegera Pl. off Endeavor St., serves pasta and pizza ($12.50-17) in an open-air setting. (☎3409 8778. Open daily 6-9pm.) The **Stradbroke Island Beach Hotel ❸**, on the left at the top of the hill toward Point Lookout, is being renovated until mid-2007; when re-opened, the restaurant promises to impress. Main courses cost around $16, but the dinner specials are the best value. (☎3409 8188. Open M-Th 7:30am-10pm, F-Sa 7:30am-midnight, Su 7:30am-8:30pm. Food served daily noon-2pm and 6-8pm. Hours will expand when construction is completed.) For groceries, try **Bob's Foodmarket**, Meegera Pl., Point Lookout. (☎3409 8271. Open daily 7am-9pm.)

SIGHTS AND ACTIVITIES. The island is known for world-class **scuba diving** and amazing marine life. The very-professional **Manta Lodge and Scuba Centre** has daily trips to 16 dive sites. (☎3409 8888; www.mantalodge.com.au. Double dive (2 dives) with own gear $110, with gear rental $160; 3-day PADI $420.) **Straddie Kingfisher Tours** will show you island highlights by 4WD. (☎3409 9502 or 04 0912 3586. Half-day $49, children $39, includes tea. Full-day $69/39, tea and BBQ lunch.) **Straddie Adventures** offers popular adventure tours. (☎3409 8414 or 04 1774 1963; www.straddieadventures.com.au. Sandboarding daily 2-4pm $30; sea kayaking and snorkeling 9:30am-12:30pm $60; ½-day 4WD tour $55. Book ahead. Cash only.)

Stradbroke's unspoiled beaches and pristine bush can keep a spirited traveler busy for days. Look for **Frenchman's Beach** as you head toward the end of Point Lookout on Mooloomba Dr., a popular **surf** and **beachwalking** spot. To get there, go past Snapper St. and look for signs before the Lookout Village Shopping Centre. For more exercise, continue past the Shopping Centre on your right; just beyond the public toilets on your left lies the entrance to the circular **Gorge Walk**, a 30-45min. stroll past rocky headlands and gorges, white sand beaches, and blue waters. This walk is famous for **whale watching** June through November; while dolphins, turtles, and manta rays can be glimpsed year-round. The Gorge Walk concludes at Whale rock, which boasts the **Blowhole**, where crashing waves are channeled up a narrow gorge and transformed into fountains of spray. (Check tide tables beforehand.) **Main Beach** stretches 32km down the eastern edge of the island, luring **surfers** with some of Queensland's best waves in the early summer's northerly winds. **Keyholes**, a swimming lagoon 64.5km down Main Beach, is a lovely picnic spot, but can only be reached by 4WD or a vigorous hike. **Cylinder Beach**, which runs in front of the Stradbroke Hotel on the north side of the island, is more swimmer- and family-oriented, but good surfing breaks can be found there most afternoons. **Deadman's Beach**, just past Cylinder

Beach, is a bit secluded and occasionally has good surf and reasonable fishing off the rocks. Though it may not seem appealing, a dip in **Brown Lake,** 3km east of Dunwich, is worth it. The water, dyed a rich amber by the surrounding tea trees and bushlands, leaves skin and hair silky smooth. **Blue Lake National Park,** the only national reserve on the island, can only be reached on foot (6km. round-trip).

MORETON ISLAND ☎07

Remarkably untouristed Moreton is a haven for adventurous souls. While Fraser Island is far more popular, Moreton Island offers similar opportunities in a less developed setting. Just 35km from Brisbane, visitors can snorkel among shipwrecks, hike or toboggan down sand dunes, and spot whales and dolphins. Hiking trails weave among the dunes and to the top of **Mount Tempest,** which at 282m stands as the world's highest compacted sand mountain. **The Desert** and the **Big Sandhills** are popular sandboarding and tobogganing spots. The tea tree tannins that dye the waters of the misnamed **Blue Lagoon** amber will rejuvenate your hair and skin. Around the northern headland is a walking track that leads to the **Cape Moreton Lighthouse,** built in 1857, and a panoramic view of the bay, with great opportunities for whale watching in season. On the eastern coastline, **Ocean Beach** stretches the full 38km length of the island, while the view from the western side is dramatically broken by the **Tangalooma Wrecks.**

The massive **Tangalooma Wild Dolphin Resort ❺** promises that all guests can hand-feed dolphins, but at $230 for singles and $250 for doubles, you can decide whose dinner is more important. (☎1300 652 250. 15min.; pickup from Brisbane accommodations $5. Round-trip $60, children $30. AmEx/DC/MC/V.) Six designated **campsites ❶** with toilets and showers are located on Moreton ($4.50 per person), and free camping is allowed nearly everywhere on the island. Pick up a map and pay camp and 4WD fees ($33.40 per visit) at the ferry site on the mainland. Questions can be answered by the **national park office** (☎3408 2710; www.epa.qld.gov.au), although they rarely answer on the first call. Aside from camping, accommodation on the island is astronomically expensive. While the majority of the island is designated national park land, the resort and three small townships are located on the western side. Fuel, food, and basic supplies are available at the small village of **Bulwer.**

Tours of Moreton Island are the easiest and most economical way to see island highlights. **Moreton Bay Escapes** offers excellent, adventure-oriented trips to the island. Choose from a single day sailing, a one- or two-day 4WD trip, or a sand tobogganing or snorkeling adventure. Travelers can take advantage of the ferry even if they're not on a tour. (☎1300 559 355; www.moretonbayescapes.com.au. Ferry $40; sailing or 4WD $129; 2-day 4WD trip $209. Tours run daily; sailing trips 4 per wk.; 2-day 4WD tour 3 per week. Book ahead. Backpacker and student discount $10. $35 round-trip ferry not included. MC/V.) **Dolphin Wild Island Cruises** also sends a power catamaran from the mainland for an eco-daytrip full of wrecks, dolphins, and snorkeling. (☎3880 4444; www.dolphinwild.com.au. Tours 9:30am-5pm. Depart from Redcliffe, 30min. north of Brisbane. $99, students $90, children $55. Transportation from hotels in Brisbane $18, from Gold Coast $40. MC/V.) **Moreton Island Tourist Service** serves as a taxi service, but also offers full-day tours of the island's highlights. (☎3408 2661; www.moretonisland.net.au. Tours for 4 $120, $15 per extra person. Tours by reservation only; book ahead.) **Tangalooma Dive Shop,** located at the Tangalooma Wild Dolphin Resort, rents out kayaks and fishing rods and offers guided snorkeling and diving. (☎3410 6927. Single kayaks $9 per hr., doubles $12; rods $8 per day; 1½hr. snorkeling at the wrecks $28, children $20; 3hr. intro dives $90, experienced divers $60. MC/V.)

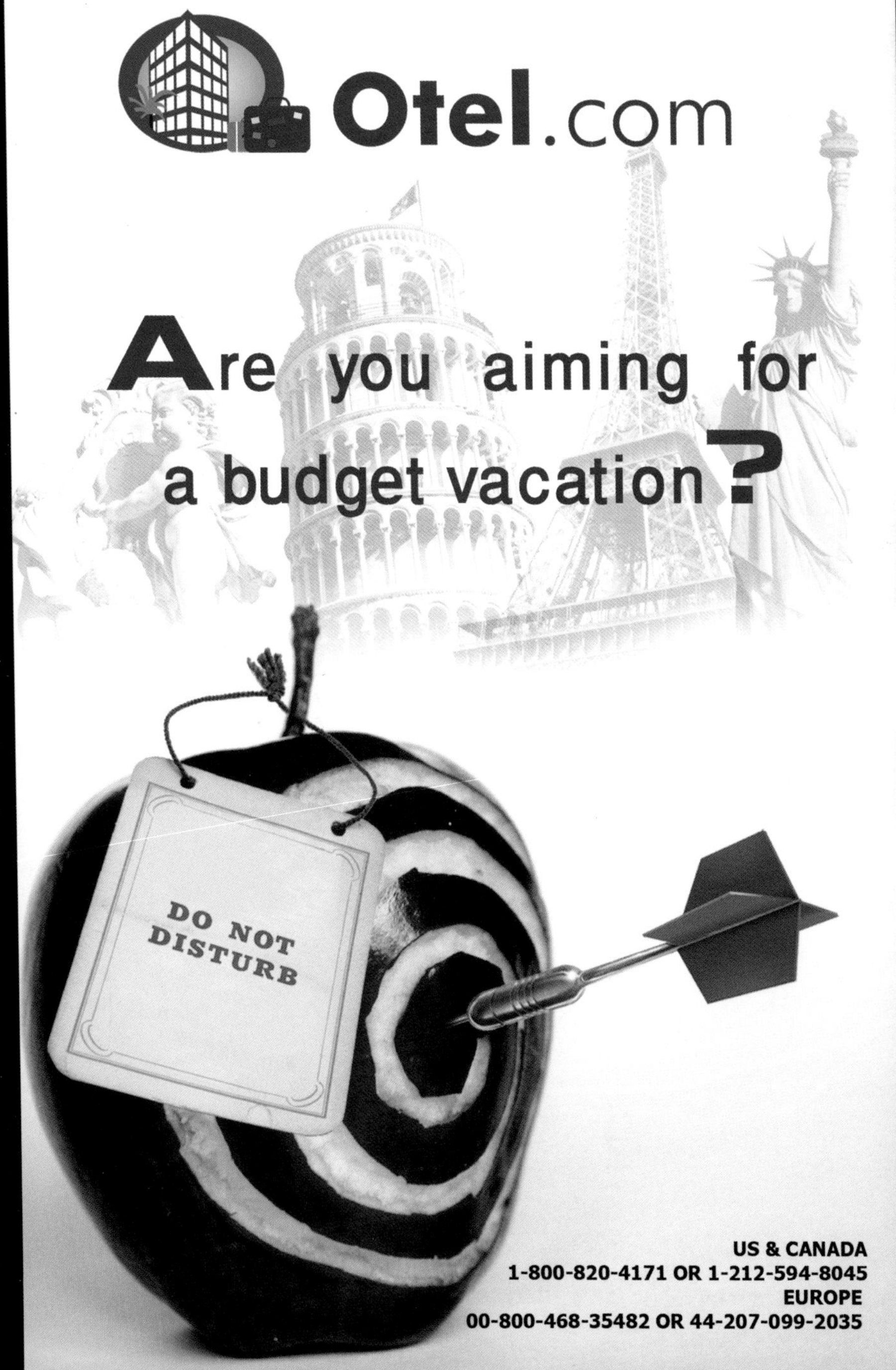
Otel.com
Are you aiming for a budget vacation?
DO NOT DISTURB
US & CANADA
1-800-820-4171 OR 1-212-594-8045
EUROPE
00-800-468-35482 OR 44-207-099-2035

The best way to get around the island is by **4WD;** you either rent one on the mainland or take a 4WD guided tour. There are a number of vehicular ferry options. **Moreton Island Ferries** leave from 14 Howard Smith Dr. in Lytton for the Tangalooma Wrecks on Moreton; take **Citytrain** from Brisbane to Wynnum Central (35min., every 30min., $3.40). On the weekends, you will need to catch a taxi to get there. (☎3909 3333; www.micat.com.au. 15min.; daily 8:30am departure and 3:30pm return, F additional 6:30pm departure, Su additional 2:30pm departure, weekends 1 and 4:30pm return; round-trip $49, children $27, vehicles with 2 adults $150. AmEx/MC/V.) There is also the **Combie Trader Ferry,** which leaves from Thurecht Pde., Scarborough Harbor, and arrives at Bulwer. (☎3203 6399; www.moreton-island.com. 2hr.; in summer M and Sa-Su 2 per day, Tu-Th 4 per day, F 3 per day; in winter M and W-Th 1 per day, F-Su 2 per day. Round-trip $40, concessions $35, children $25. Round-trip vehicles for 2 $175, for 4 $195. Landing fee $4, vehicles $10. AmEx/MC/V.) Guests of the Tangalooma Wild Dolphin Resort can travel by the resort launch transfers.

OTHER ISLANDS IN MORETON BAY

Moreton Bay is dotted with more than 300 islands, many of which make perfect daytrips. Cheap accommodation (other than camping) is sparse, but a day is enough to sample the islands' offerings: pristine beaches, snorkeling, and the occasional whale sighting. Just be sure to start your day early.

COOCHIEMUDLO ISLAND. Coochiemudlo is family-oriented and entices visitors with walkable beaches, restaurants, and occasional craft markets featuring local artists. **Coochiemudlo Island Ferry Service** runs a car and passenger ferry from Victoria Point Jetty; contact Transinfo. (☎3820 7227; www.translink.com.au. 12 vehiculars per day, passenger ferry every 30min. from 5am-11:30pm. Round-trip $35, pedestrians $6, children $3. Cash only.)

BRIBIE ISLAND. At the northern end of Moreton Bay, Bribie is the only island that can be accessed by car. From Brisbane, go 45km north to Caboolture, then 19km east to the Bribie bridge. Or take Citytrain from Brisbane to Caboolture, where Bus #640 runs to Bribie (1¾hr., train leaves every 30min., bus every 1hr., $6.40). The **tourist office** is just over the bridge from the mainland. (☎3408 9026. Open M-F 9am-4pm, Sa 9am-3pm, Su 9:30am-1pm.) Bribie is separated from the mainland by **Pumicestone Passage,** a marine park teeming with dolphins, dugongs, manta rays, turtles, and over 350 species of birds. Bribie is also known for great fishing on the mainland side of the channel and surfing on the eastern side, which has lifeguards year-round.

ST. HELENA ISLAND. From 1867 to 1933, St. Helena was Australia's Alcatraz, with over 300 of the most dangerous criminals on an island where any escape attempt likely meant a feast in the shark-infested waters. Today, St. Helena limits onshore visitors in order to preserve its national parklands. **A B Sea Cruises** runs day and night trips on its **Cat-o'-Nine Tails** vessel where actors role-play St. Helena's colorful past. Cruises run from **Manly.** (☎3396 3994; www.sthelena.com.au. Day tours $69, concessions $59, children $39, families $169. Night tours slightly more expensive. Book ahead. AmEx/DC/MC/V.)

GOLD COAST

Amazing beaches, nightclubs, and theme parks make the Gold Coast Australia's premier holiday destination. The region's population of 409,000 increases to well over a million every summer as tourists flock to the sun, sand, and parties.

COOLANGATTA AND TWEED HEADS ☎07

While Surfers Paradise has the name, Coolangatta, QLD, and Tweed Heads, NSW, provide the goods with some of the best surfing in all of Australia, if not the world. Only a few years ago, "Cooly" and Tweed Heads were sleepy beachside towns popular among retirees from the southern states. But the unbelievable breaks couldn't be kept secret, and they have begun to attract the world's top surfers. Meanwhile tourists have been making Cooly and Tweed Heads a popular alternative to the neon and skyscrapers of the Gold Coast. Development is occurring at a rapid pace though, so expect the area to become more commercialized in the coming years.

TRANSPORTATION

Buses: Greyhound Australia (☎13 14 99; www.greyhound.com.au) has a monopoly on distance travel from the twin towns. While the side of the bus may read **Greyhound, McCafferty's,** or **Suncoast Pacific,** they all fall under the same ownership. Buses leave from the bus shelter on Warren St. behind National Bank, about 100m from Griffith St. To: **Brisbane** (1½-2hr.; 5 per day; $26 online, $30 by phone); **Byron Bay** (1-1½hr., 7 per day, $24 online, $28 by phone); **Noosa** (5½hr.; 7:40am, 3:05pm; $39 online, $47 by phone) via **Maroochy** (4½hr., same time and price as Noosa); **Sydney** (14½hr.; 4 per day; $104 online, $112 by phone). **Surfside Buslines** (☎13 12 30) runs the only **public transportation** in the Gold Coast region. Bus 700 goes to **Southport** (1¼hr., $4.20) via **Surfers Paradise** (1hr., $3.70) and leaves every 30min. from the bus stop in front of the Twin Towers Resort. Bus TX1 will take you to the **theme parks,** and also leaves from the Twin Towers Resort (1¼hr.; 8:10, 8:45am; $5). It returns from **Dreamworld** (4:45, 5:05pm) with stops at **Wet N' Wild** and **Movieworld.** 3-day Ezy Pass offers unlimited rides for $25.

Taxis: Tweed-Coolangatta Taxi Service (24hr. ☎5536 1144).

Car Rental: Economy Rental Cars (☎5536 8104 or 1800 803 874; www.economyrentalcars.com.au), at the Gold Coast Airport. Rentals start at $29 per day, including 75km each day and some insurance. 21+. Gold Coast Tourism Visitor Information Centre can provide free transport to the airport for car pickup.

ORIENTATION AND PRACTICAL INFORMATION

For a stretch of several kilometers, the Pacific Hwy. becomes the Gold Coast Hwy. Ride it into **Musgrave Street,** then bear left onto **Marine Parade** which runs parallel to the beach through **Kirra** and **Coolangatta. Griffith Street,** the main drag in Coolangatta, runs parallel to Marine Pde. At the **Twin Towns Service Club,** turn right from Griffith St. onto **Wharf Street,** the main thoroughfare of **Tweed Heads;** continuing straight from this intersection, Griffith St. turns into **Boundary Street,** which divides the peninsula, terminating at the infamous **Point Danger** and the cliffs responsible for Captain Cook's shipwreck.

Tourist Offices: There are 2 accredited visitor information centers in town. **Gold Coast Tourism Visitor Information Centre** (☎5536 7765 or 1300 309 440; www.VeryGC.com) at Shop 14B, Coolangatta Pl. on the corner of Griffith and Warren St., offers discounts on theme parks and attractions. Free maps also available. Open M-F 8am-5pm, Sa 8am-4pm. The smaller **Tweed and Coolangatta Tourism Inc.** (☎5536 4244 or 1800 674 414; www.tweedcoolangatta.com.au) has a desk inside the Centro Tweed Shopping Centre. Open M-Sa 9am-5pm.

Banks: 24hr. **ATMs** abound on Griffith St., including **National Bank and Bank of Queensland,** 84-88 Griffith St., and **WestPAC,** 4 Griffith St., which accepts Bank of America cards with no extra charge. All banks open M-Th 9:30am-4pm, F 9:30am-5pm.

Backpacking Supplies: Sherry's Camping, 53 Wharf St. (☎5536 3700; www.sherryscamping.com.au), offers a good selection of backpacking and camping gear at reasonable prices. Open summer M-Sa 9am-5:30pm; winter M-Sa 8:30am-5pm. MC/V.

Bookstore: The Bookshop, 26 Griffith St. (☎5536 7715), sells used books. Open M-Sa 8:30am-5:30pm, Su 9am-5pm. **Billabong Bookstore** (☎5536 9986), 114 Griffith St., has a similar selection. Open M-F 9:30am-5pm, Sa 10:30am-4pm, Su 1-4pm).

Pharmacies: Pharmacies line Griffith St., including **Amcal Chemist,** 2 Griffith St. (☎5599 4419), attached to the post office. Open M-F 8am-5:30pm, Sa 9am-5pm.

Internet Access: 3w C@fe, 152 Griffith St. (☎5599 4536), charges $2 per 15min. and a bargain $6 wireless connection per day for laptops. Offers fax service, digital camera photo downloading, and a wide range of phone cards. Open M-F 7am-7pm, Sa-Su 8am-6pm. **Singapore Merlion Restaurant,** 25 McLean St. (☎5536 4678), at the intersection with Griffith St., has Internet access for $2 per 20min. and offers a backpackers' special for $7.50 that includes 30min. of high-speed Internet access, followed by a choice of a chicken, beef, pork, or vegetarian plate. Open daily 10am-10:30pm. Cash only.

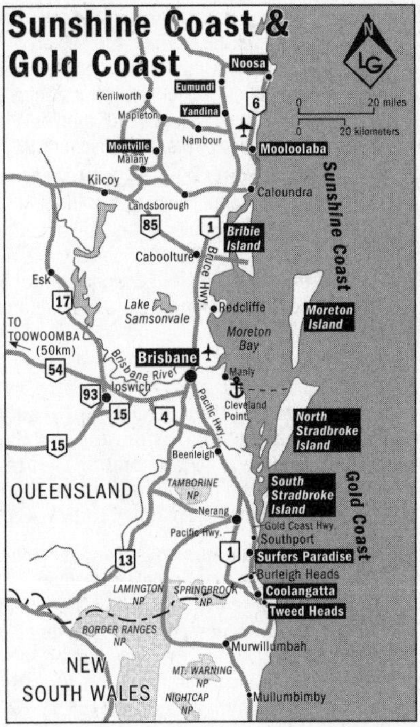

Post Office: 2 Griffith St., at McLean St. Open M-F 9am-5pm. **Postal Code:** 4225.

ACCOMMODATIONS

Finding a place to crash is not a problem, but budget digs are extremely limited, so consider booking ahead, especially in high season.

Coolangatta Ocean View Motel, at the corner of Clark St. and Marine Pde. (☎5536 3722; oceanviewmotel@bigpond.com.au for bookings). Opposite Greenmount Beach, the Ocean View Motel has an excellent location and offers a roof-top deck (open daily 8am-8pm) that provides great views of the entire Gold Coast and a BBQ to rent ($5). Its pink exterior does not impress, but all rooms come with private bath, A/C, refrigerator, TV, and toaster. Free laundry. Reception M-Sa 8am-8pm, Su 9am-7pm. High season singles $70; doubles $80; triples $90. Low season M-Th and Su $60/70/80; F-Sa $70/80/90. Multiple night discounts. AmEx/DC/MC/V. ❸

Sunset Strip, 199 Boundary St. (☎5599 5517; www.sunsetstrip.com.au). Close to town and has the best breaks. Excellent facilities include huge kitchen, pool, and recreation and lounge areas. Shared bathrooms. Key deposit $10. Reception 7am-11pm. Singles $50; doubles $66; triples $99; quads $120. Multiple night discounts. MC/V. ❸

Coolangatta YHA, 230 Coolangatta Rd. (☎5536 7644; www.coolangattayha.com), in Billinga, a 25min. walk north of Cooly; look for the large murals on the outside of the building. Sandwiched between the airport and Coolangatta Rd., the hostel is within a short walking distance of some decent waves. Offers kitchen, laundry, game room, BBQ, TV lounge, pool, bikes, drop-off/pickup at the town center 4 times daily, and Internet access ($2 per 20min.). Courtesy pickup from the Gold Coast Airport or bus stop. Breakfast included. Lockers in the hall, $2-4 depending on size. 6- and 8-bed dorms $25.50; 4-bed dorms $27.50; singles $35.50; doubles $59; family rooms $74-89. Multiple night discounts. YHA discount $3.50 for dorms, $7 for family rooms. ❸

Kirra Beach Tourist Park (☎5581 7744; www.gctp.com.au/kirra), on Charlotte St. in Kirra, near the airport. Great facilities: laundry, pool, TV room, and jungle gym for the kids. Linen $5 per person (free in cabins). Reception 7am-7pm. Unpowered sites for 2 $24-28; powered $26-32. Rooms for 2 with TV and refrigerator, $65 per person, off-peak $45, extra person $10; spacious cabins for 4 with private bathroom and A/C $95-145. Discounts for longer stays. $15 charge for 4pm checkout. MC/V. ❷

FOOD

Whether you want Italian, Mexican, Turkish, or Thai cuisine, your cravings will be satisfied by the many restaurants on Griffith St. **Coles** supermarket is located inside the Centro Tweed Shopping Centre on Wharf St. (M-Sa 6am-10pm, Su 8am-8pm.) **Night Owl** is a useful convenience store in the Showcase Shopping Centre on Marine Pde. (Open M-Tu 5am-11pm, W-Su 24hr.)

Ocean Deck Restaurant, 2 Snapper Rocks Rd. (☎5536 6390), atop the **Rainbow Bay Surf Club,** has a view that rivals those found on postcards. The entire Gold Coast, Brisbane skyline, and all the world-class surfers riding the waves lie right in front of you. Burgers ($12), fish, beef, and chicken ($13). Reservations recommended in summer. Balcony seating. Kitchen open daily 11:30am-2pm and 5:30-8pm. Restaurant open M-Th and Su 10am-10pm, F-Sa 10am-midnight. Restaurant hours vary according to season. MC/V. ❷

Dee and Paul's Rainbow Cafe, 13 Ward St. (☎5536 4999) off Boundary St., provides walls of surf photos and a scrumptious selection of wholesome breakfasts ($6-9), sandwiches ($5-6), and banana smoothies ($4.60). Open daily 7am-6:30pm. Cash only. ❶

Little Malaya Restaurant, 52 Marine Pde. (☎5536 2690), entrance on McLean St. Award plaques hang in the entrance of this fun Chinese-Malaysian restaurant. The chef uses less oil than the norm to better suit the Australian palate. Palm trees, a thatched roof over the entrance, and a wall depicting a Muslim city will make you forget you're even in Australia. The beef rendang ($15.50) and curry lamb ($16) are delicious. Reservations recommended. Open M-Sa noon-2pm and 5:30pm-latenight, Su 5:30pm-latenight. AmEx/DC/MC/V. ❷

SIGHTS AND BEACHES

The area's greatest attractions are the beaches that line its perimeter. **Rainbow Bay, Greenmount Beach, Coolangatta Beach,** and **Kirra** off Marine Pde., have some of the safest swimming on the Gold Coast (lifeguards are on duty every day), but are susceptible to large swells. **Duranbah Beach,** famous among surfers for its reliable waves, lies on the southeast side of the peninsula. The best surfers in town can be found at **Snapper Rocks,** which hosts a professional tour event each summer.

The walkway facing the ocean, which begins to the left of Point Danger, is a beautiful route to Greenmount Beach. You'll trip over kangaroos, koalas, and saltwater crocs at the **Currumbin Wildlife Sanctuary,** 7km (10min. by car) north off the Gold Coast Hwy. on Tomewin St. The sanctuary is also a surfside bus stop (take 700, 760, 765, or TX1 and ask the driver to announce the Currumbin stop). Help feed the wild rainbow lorikeets (daily 8-9:30am and 4-5pm) or take a nocturnal

MIND THE FLAGS. Swimmers should obey all posted warnings; details about up-to-date conditions can be found daily on a chalkboard located on the beach between the red and yellow flags. **Red flags** mean the water is unsafe to enter. **Yellow flags** ask that visitors exercise extreme caution. **Red-and-yellow flags** mean swimming is safe between the flags. **Green flags** are put up when the water is safe for swimmers within indicated areas. Since surfers cannot bring their boards inside the red and yellow flags, **blue flags** indicate where surfing is permitted (although these flags are not always posted).

"wildnight" tour (daily 7-9:45pm; $49, children $27; book ahead). For more information about a daytrip to the sanctuary, call ☎5534 1266 or visit www.currumbin-sanctuary.org.au. (Open daily 8am-5pm. $29.50, children $19.50.) For great views of the ocean, the surrounding communities, and the hinterlands, make your way up to either of two lookouts. **Razorback Lookout** is a small hike from the CBD (30min. on foot): follow Wharf St. inland from the Twin Towns Service Club and take a right on Florence St. At the top of the hill, take a left on Charles St., and follow Razorback Rd. to its end. Continue up the railed footpath for a fabulous panorama of Cooly, Tweed Heads, and Mt. Warning. The less ambitious can head up the hill at the corner of Marine Pde. and McLean St.; the lookout on top provides unparalleled views of the entire Gold Coast. If the idea of walking uphill makes you cringe, walk along the beach, either on the sand or the footpath right above, and take in the magnificent views of the coast. If you want a break, stop at any of the **surf clubs** along the beachside road (Rainbow Bay, North Kirra, Kirra, Coolangatta, or Greenmount) for a bite and a spectacular view.

The twin towns are surfer-friendly, and those who come to ride the waves will be welcomed with plenty of shops aimed to please. **Pipedream,** in the Showcase Shopping Centre on Griffith St., is one of the few surf shops that rents ("hires") surf gear. (☎5599 1164. Boards half-day $20, overnight $30. Bodyboards $15/20. Flippers $5/7. Open daily 9am-5pm.) For a 2hr. group surfing lesson that aims to get you standing in no time, contact **Walkin' on Water.** (☎0418 780 311 or 5534 1886; www.walkinonwater.com. 2hr. group lesson $40, 1½hr. private session $65.)

The annual **Wintersun Festival,** Australia's biggest rock-and-roll event, is held during the 10 days preceding the Queen's Birthday (the 2nd M in June). In 2007, the festival is scheduled for June 1-11 with the party's climax occurring the final weekend. The twin towns will celebrate Elvis and the 1950s with retro cars, dancing, music, artists, and entertainers. (☎5536 9509; www.wintersun.org.au.)

NIGHTLIFE

Though the waves are phenomenal, local nightlife leaves something to be desired. For endless clubs and pubs, head to **Surfers Paradise,** the nightlife hub of the Gold Coast, just a quick bus ride away on Surfside Buslines (see **Transportation,** p. 338).

Calypso Tavern, 91-97 Griffith St. (☎5599 2677). Caters to an upscale crowd, featuring a downstairs bar with a plush club upstairs. Regular promotions and 3 DJs F and Sa night. Open M-Th and Su 10am-midnight, F-Sa 10am-3am. Possible $10 cover upstairs.

Balcony Night Club, on Marine Pde., inside the Coolangatta Hotel (☎5536 9311; www.thecoolyhotel.com.au). A popular spot for young locals to jive to live music (tickets required, available at the hotel) or a DJ ($5 cover). Downstairs, the hotel, has promotional events, billiards, and live music or a DJ Th-Su. Open daily 9am-latenight.

Twin Towns Service Club (☎5536 2277), at Griffith and Wharf St., is like Las Vegas without the glamour. This gigantic spaceship-like club caters to an older crowd, with slot machines, cheap food, 5 eateries, 7 bars, live entertainment, and free movies M 10:30am and 6:30pm.

On weekends, Champions Bar and Images Bar on Level 1 (open until 1:30am and 3:00am, respectively) have gained popularity as a cheap place to drink before heading to the clubs.

SURFERS PARADISE ☎07

If you're looking for great surfing, Surfers Paradise is, ironically, not your best bet. The small breaks off Surfers are good for beginners, but serious surfers should head south to Coolangatta (p. 338). Nevertheless, the town draws thousands of backpackers with its wild nightlife, shopping, and convenient daytrips to nearby theme parks and South Stradbroke Island. When the sun goes down, Surfers comes alive with an unrivaled choice of bars and nightclubs, making it the hottest scene on the Gold Coast. Boasting high-end fashion stores and cafes excellent for people-watching, all within walking distance of gorgeous beaches, it's no wonder that Surfers has become a premier East Coast holiday destination.

TRANSPORTATION

Buses: The **Transit Centre** is on Beach Rd., just off Ferny Ave. (open daily 6:30am-8pm). **Greyhound Australia** (☎13 14 99; www.greyhound.com.au), offers service to: **Brisbane** (1½hr.; 7 per day 4:45am-10pm; $23 online, $27 by phone) and **Sydney** (15-16hr.; 4 per day 8:20am-8:20pm; $107 online, $117 by phone). **Premier Motor Service** (☎13 34 10; www.premierms.com.au) and **Kirklands** (☎1300 367 077; www.kirklands.com.au) offer similar routes. Lockers available at the Transit Centre 6:30am-8pm ($6-10 per day). **J & B Coaches** (☎5592 2655) has a fast, cheap Byron Bay express shuttle (70min.; every 2hr. 8:30am-2:30pm; $28, with student ID $25).

Local Buses: Surfside Buslines (☎13 12 30; www.translink.com.au), the local 24hr. bus company, runs to roadside stops along the **Gold Coast Highway,** as well as the **Pacific Fair Shopping Centre** (buses 704, 706, 745; 45min., walk to the end of Cavill Ave. and turn left; runs every 15min.), the **theme parks** (bus TX2 services **Wet 'N' Wild, Movieworld,** and **Dreamworld,** every 15min., from Appel Park, just north of Cavill Ave. on Ferny Ave.; bus 750 goes to **Sea World,** every 20min., next to the WestPac Bank on the Gold Coast Hwy.) and **Southport** (buses 700, 702, 703, 706, 709; 20min. every 5-10min.; $2.50 one-way). If you are heading to **Brisbane** or the Brisbane airport, bus 745, which picks up directly across from the Transit Centre, will take you to Nerang Train Station where you can transfer. Bus leaves every 30min., and the total journey takes 1½hr. to Brisbane and 2hr. to the airport (Brisbane $9.50, airport $25.50). **Ezy Passes** provide unlimited use of all buses and can be purchased from the drivers (3-, 5-, 7-, 10-, 14-day passes available; $25-60, children $13-30). **Gold Coast Tourist Shuttle** (☎5574 5111) offers transport to all theme parks with pickup and drop-off from local accommodations and, with purchase of 3-, 5-, or 7-day travel, unlimited use of **Surfside Buslines** (3-day Gold pass $42, ages 4-13 $21; 1wk. $78/39).

Taxis: Regent Taxis (☎13 10 08) or **Maxi Taxi** (☎13 62 94), which has vans for up to 8.

Car Rental: There are many options. Conveniently located inside the reception area of the Islander Resort Hotel, **Dave's Car Rental** (☎5504 5955 or 1300 130 242; www.davescarrental.com.au) offers low prices. Cars start at $48 with 150km per day in peak season; $35 off-peak season. Insurance $12. Open daily 8am-5pm.

ORIENTATION AND PRACTICAL INFORMATION

Maps of Surfers are long and thin, reflecting the fact that all the action is squeezed into a strip several kilometers long and just a few blocks wide, sandwiched between the ocean and the **Nerang River.** Three main avenues run parallel to the shore: the **Esplanade,** which skirts the beach; **Surfers Paradise Boulevard** (also known as **Gold Coast Highway**), a block farther inland; and **Ferny Avenue,** one more block inland. The heart of Surfers is **Cavill Mall,** a pedestrian street lined with restaurants, cafes, bars, souvenir shops, and the **Centro Shopping Center.** The Esplanade continues north past **Main Beach** to the **Marina Mirage** and the **Spit at Main Beach,** the end of the peninsula just past Sea World. **Southport** is located along the Gold Coast Hwy., past Main Beach and 3km northwest of the CBD. To the south is **Broadbeach,** home of the enormous **Conrad Hotel Jupiter Casino** and the gigantic **Pacific Fair Shopping Centre.**

Tourist Offices: Gold Coast Tourism (☎5538 4419; www.VeryGC.com), on Cavill Ave., is the only accredited visitor information center in the area. Open M-F 8:30am-5:30pm, Sa 8:30am-5pm, Su 9am-4pm. The **Backpacker's Travel Desk** (☎5592 2911 or 1800 359 830), in the Transit Centre, offers tourist information and arranges transport to most hostels. Open daily 8am-6pm.

Banks: Westpac, on the corner of Cavill Ave. and Gold Coast Hwy., has a 24hr. **ATM,** as does **Commonwealth Bank** next door. Both banks open M-Th 9:30am-4pm, F 9:30am-5pm. ATMs can also be found all over the center of town and in the shopping centers.

Police: 68 Ferny Ave. (☎5570 7888), at Cypress Ave. There's also a substation (☎5583 9733) on the corner of Cavill Mall and the Esplanade.

Medical Services: Gold Coast General Hospital, 108 Nerang St., Southport (☎5571 8211). **Day Night Medical Centre** (☎5592 2299), in the Piazza Mall on the Gold Coast Hwy., is available for basic care. Open daily 7am-11pm.

Internet Access: Peterpan Adventures, a travel agency in the Transit Centre, offers Internet access for $2 per hr. Open daily 10am-5:30pm. **Ozki Photo & Internet,** (☎5538 4937), at the corner of Gold Coast Hwy. and Elkhorn Ave., is popular among backpackers. $3 per hr. Open daily 9am-8pm.

Post Office: The main branch is inside the Centro Shopping Center. Open M-F 9am-5:30pm, Sa 9am-12:30pm. **Postal Code:** 4217.

THE REAL DEAL. If Prada and Louis Vuitton are a little beyond your budget, you can find great bargains at the twice-weekly beachfront markets featuring everything from local arts and crafts to handmade crocodile products. They take place every Wednesday and Friday evening from 5:30-10pm on the Esplanade (☎5584 3700; www.surfersparadise.com). *–Seth Greenberg*

ACCOMMODATIONS

In Surfers, hostel staff assume the role of camp counselors, providing backpackers with endless activities including surfing, kayak outings, and trips to the bush or islands. Most hostels organize nighttime activities as well, and many have bars that are arguably better and more social than the ones you'll find in town. Summer and Easter are peak times—book ahead and expect that listed prices could rise. Unless otherwise specified, hostels have free pickup from the Transit Centre (call before arrival), 10am check-out, and a pool. Internet access and laundry are usually available for a price. Be aware that towels are not provided at many hostels.

Sleeping Inn Surfers, 26 Peninsular Dr. (☎5592 4455 or 1800 817 832; www.sleepinginn.com.au), a 7min. walk from the Transit Centre across Ferny Ave. All 15 units are apartment-style with full kitchens, TV, private baths, and common area. While not as loud as other hostels, Sleeping Inn makes dorm-life a pleasure by offering a mellow, friendly atmosphere and superb comfort at a low price. Free pickup at Transit Centre in a limousine. Key deposit $10. Reception daily 7am-9pm. 4- and 8-person dorms $25;

Surfers Paradise

ACCOMMODATIONS
Backpackers in Paradise, **4**
Islander Resort Hotel (NOMADS), **16**
Sleeping Inn Surfers, **5**
Surfers Paradise Backpackers Resort, **6**
Trekkers, **1**

FOOD
Chiangmai Thai Restaurant, **3**
La Gitara, **8**
Noodle Renaissance, **7**
Papa George's Pizzeria, **13**
Peter's Fish Café, **2**

NIGHTLIFE
The Bedroom Lounge Bar and Nightclub, **9**
Cocktails and Dreams/ The Party, **10**
Melbas, **11**
O'Malley's on the Beach, **15**
Rose & Crown, **14**
Shooters Saloon Bar, **12**

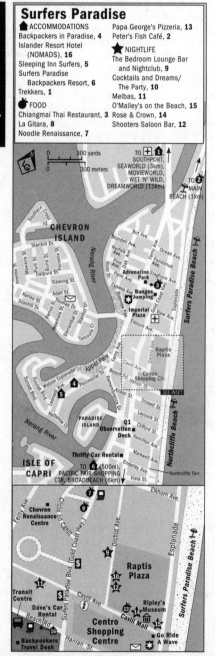

doubles $66. ISIC/VIP/YHA $1 discount. AmEx/MC/V. ❷

Islander Resort Hotel (NOMADS), 6 Beach Rd. (☎5538 8000), immediately adjacent to the Transit Centre. All the amenities of a resort hotel at a hostel price. The closest you'll get to the CBD and just a minute from the beach. The massive complex has rooms with TV, fridge, private bath, and balcony. Hot tub, bar, restaurant, coin-operated arcade, tennis, and squash courts. Not a member of Backpackers Association, but talk to reception about joining the club crawl if interested. Reception 24hr. 8-person dorm $15; 4- and 6-person dorms $26; doubles $75. AmEx/DC/MC/V. ❶

Backpackers In Paradise, 40 Peninsula Dr. (☎1800 268 621; www.backpackersinparadise.com), just a 5min. walk from town; look for the murals. Friendly, fun, relaxed, and close to the beach, with simple dorms, spacious doubles, a bar, and even an on-site convenience store. Rooms have private bath. Organizes nightly trips to nightclubs. 20-person dorm $16; 10-person dorm $20; 4- and 8-person dorms $23; doubles $50; apartments $55. Cheaper rates for longer stays. MC/V. ❷

Trekkers, 22 White St., Southport (☎5591 5616 or 1800 100 004; www.trekkersbackpackers.com.au), 3km north of the CBD. 20min. walk to Main Beach. More friendly, clean, and accommodating than the hostels in Surfers. Courtesy bus goes to town every 2hr. Hostel organizes nightly club outings. Local buses go to Southport every 5-10min. ($2.50). Some dorms have private bath. Boogie board and bike rental available. Saltwater pool on premises. Breakfast included. Free BBQ. Reception daily 7am-10:30pm. 4-, 5-, 6-, and 10-bed dorms $25; doubles $62. VIP/YHA discount. MC/V. ❷

Surfers Paradise Backpackers Resort, 2837 Gold Coast Hwy. (☎5592 4677 or 1800 282 800; www.surfersparadisebackpackers.com.au), a 25min. walk south from the Transit Centre. Upbeat atmosphere and spotless facilities. All rooms ensuite. Kitchen, bar, tennis, basketball, small gym, and free laundry. Free boogie board use. Bikes ½-day $7, full-day $12. Sauna $4 per 45min. Reception daily 7:30am-7pm. 5- and 6-bed dorms $25; doubles $66; triples $87. VIP/YHA discount. MC/V. ❷

FOOD

Of Surfers' outdoor malls and arcades, **Cavill Mall** and **Chevron Renaissance Centre,** lined with mid-range bistros and cafes, are the most popular. For latenight eats, **Papa George's Pizzeria** (at the corner of Cavill and Orchid) is reliably greasy and delicious. For groceries, try **Woolworths,** in the basement of Centro Shopping Center, on Cavill Mall. (Open M-F 8am-9pm, Sa 8am-5:30pm, Su 9am-6pm.)

La Gitara, 3240 Gold Coast Hwy. (☎5592 2355). With a better taste, lower prices, and larger portions than the slew of eateries in the area, La Gitara magically creates Italian cuisine with a Mediterranean flare. The *cevapi* sausages, a Bosnian specialty, served in Turkish bread, are immensely popular (10 for $14.90), as are the garlic prawns ($13.50). The experience is only enhanced by the beautifully painted walls, guitar detailing on the chairs, and upbeat music. Open daily 8am-10pm. ❷

Peter's Fish Cafe, Shop 22, Mariner's Cove, Sea World Dr., Main Beach (☎5531 0077), has the best fish 'n' chips in town (lunch $6, dinner $10; sauces $1-2), and a nice variety of other fresh seafood ($20-24). Open in high season Tu-F noon-3pm and 5-9pm, Sa-Su noon-9pm; in low season Tu-F noon-3pm and 5-8pm, Sa noon-9pm, Su noon-8pm. ❷

Noodle Renaissance, 3240 Gold Coast Hwy. (☎5504 5569), near Elkhorn St. The best cheap lunch food in Surfers. Hong Kong-style Asian food with tasty curries and a large noodle soup menu ($7.70-10). Open M-Sa 11am-7pm, Su 11am-5pm. Cash only. ❶

Chiangmai Thai Restaurant, 5-19 Palm Ave. (☎5526 8891), across from Adrenaline Park. A restaurant with elaborate decor which includes wooden chairs with intricate elephant images, Buddha statues, and gold-plated items just about everywhere. The menu is comprehensive and the food is delicious; chicken and beef dishes ($17), vegetarian plates ($14). Open 5:30-10pm. Reservations recommended. AmEx/DC/MC/V. ❷

BEACHES, SURFING, AND WATER SPORTS

White sand beaches stretch 25km from the quiet **Main Beach** on the Spit to Coolangatta's Snapper Rocks. Surfers Paradise is a bit of a misnomer, however. While the beach breaks are fairly good and the waves uncrowded, the best surfing is to the south of Surfers, near Coolangatta and Tweed Heads (p. 338). Surfing conditions vary considerably, especially as shifting sand alters the breaks; locals sometimes drive up and down the coast looking for the best waves. For more detailed info, go to www.coastalwatch.com or listen to 90.9 Sea FM's surf reports.

The most popular beach among boardless beachgoers is **Surfers Paradise Beach,** which runs a few blocks north and south of Cavill Mall. Farther south is **Broadbeach,** where you'll find **Kurrawa,** near the Pacific Fair Shopping Centre. **Burleigh Heads** offers a world-class break, which means large crowds during peak season. Surfing is also popular at **South Stradbroke Island.** The beaches there are unpatrolled, however, so use common sense and bring a friend who knows the waters.

For equipment, try **Go Ride A Wave,** a kiosk at the corner of Esplanade and Cavill Mall. (☎1300 132 441; www.gorideawave.com.au. Surfboards $25 for 2hr., $35 for 2-4hr., $45 per day. All types of boards and beach equipment available. Bag storage free with rental, otherwise $5.) **Learn 2 Surf,** on the corner of Hanlan St. and Esplanade, has the best deal in town. (☎1800 227 873. Open daily 10am and 2pm. 2hr. group lessons and equipment $35. Book a day ahead.) **Gold Coast Kayaking** runs excellent sea kayaking tours from the Spit to South Stradbroke Island, including tea or breakfast, snorkeling, a bushwalk, and a chance of seeing dolphins on the early morning trip. (☎04 1973 3202; www.goldcoastkayaking.com.au. 6:30-9:30am,

BEACH, BABES, AND BURNING RUBBER

While some countries hold their car races in massive stadiums, Australia brings the speed and fury right to the street. The international **Lexmark Indy 500** (www.indy.com.au) is held in late October along the Surfers Paradise Esplanade. For four days and four nights, much of Surfers is shut down as tires squeal and speeds exceed 270kph. in Australia's largest racecar event. Events include the **Celebrity Cup,** the event in which Angelina Jolie crashed her car a few years ago.

With television cameras everywhere, jet planes performing acrobatic maneuvers in the sky, and over 320,000 spectators lining the streets, the atmosphere is electric. For many, the races are just a good opportunity to party. Nightclubs are packed wall-to-wall, and most even create extensions by setting up tents on the premises. In addition, clubs are permitted to remain open until 7am Sunday morning, catering to those who wish to party until the break of dawn.

Hostels will be sold-out during the weekend. Book at least a month ahead. Tickets for the event can be purchased online at www.ticketek.com, at Golden Casket News Agency, 2 Elkhorn Ave. between the Esplanade and Orchid Ave. in Surfers, or at the gate to the event at Elkhorn Ave. and the Esplanade. Prepurchased tickets are cheaper than those bought at the gate.

$35; 11:30am-1:30pm, $25. Pickup and drop-off included.)

ADVENTURE ACTIVITIES AND THEME PARKS

Surfers Paradise boasts some of the best adventure activities anywhere on the continent. Tickets to all theme parks can be purchased at slightly reduced prices from the tourist info booths at Cavill Mall or in hostels. Surfside Buslines and Gold Coast Tourist Shuttle provide transportation to all parks (see Local Buses, p. 342). Call ahead and check hours as they change with demand.

SKYDIVE BYRON BAY. The friendly and comedic staff at Skydive Byron Bay make the jump unforgettable. They offer free transfers from any hostel in Surfers to Tyagarah Airport, 1¼hr. away. If you ask politely, the driver will drop you off at the Byron Bay lighthouse and town center for a few hours before your return. *(☎6684 1323; www.skydivebyronbay.com. 8000-14,000 ft. $239-329, video $99-159. Book ahead.)*

ADRENALIN PARADISE. This theme park is a haven for those with the need for speed. It offers a Bungy Jump ($99), Sling Shot ($30 per person), the self-explanatory Vomatron ($20 per person), and the terrifying 11-story free-fall Fly Coaster ($39), guaranteed to get your heart racing. *(16 Palm Ave., between Ferny Ave. and Gold Coast Hwy. ☎5570 2700; www.funtime.com.au. Open 10am-10pm. MC/V.)*

EXTREME JETBOATING. Only for those looking for a fun (and nauseating) ride along the Nerang River. The capable handlers will spin you around 360° at 70 kph. *(☎0419 608 978; www.extremejetboating.com. Book ahead.)*

THE Q1 OBSERVATION DECK. The most spectacular view around lies atop one of the world's fastest elevators inside the world's tallest residential building ($16.50, students and backpackers $12, children $9.50). The views from the top are stunning; if you're lucky, you might even see whales and dolphins in the distance. *(3003 Gold Coast Hwy., at the corner of Hamilton Ave. ☎5630 4700; www.Q1observationdeck.com. Open summer M-Th and Su 10am-10pm, F-Sa 10am-midnight; winter M-Th and Su 10am-8pm.)*

DREAMWORLD. Australia's largest theme park will get your blood pumping with the tallest vertical free-fall in the world and the tallest high-speed gravity roller coaster in the Southern Hemisphere. The park also has one of only three interactive tiger exhibits outside the US. *(☎5588 1111 or 1800 073 300; www.dreamworld.com.au. Open daily 10am-5pm. $62, ages 4-13 $40.)*

SEA WORLD. Sea World is home to sea lion and water ski shows. You can also enjoy a small water park, rides, the world's largest man-made shark lagoon, and a polar bear exhibit. View it all from above in a cable car or helicopter ($49-249). *(☎5588 2222; www.seaworld.com.au. Open daily 10am-5pm. $62, ages 4-13 $40.)*

ENTERTAINMENT AND NIGHTLIFE

If you are looking to party, you've come to the right place. The streets of Surfers are more crowded after midnight than during the day. Most of the activity is centered around Orchid Ave., which boasts Surfers' top nightclubs, but be aware that cover charges may rise during peak times. Since many of the clubs have theme nights, the type of people they attract and the music they play may vary. Ask hostel staff about evening events or visit www.surfersparadise.com. Also check out www.goldcoastbackpackers.net to see if your hostel is part of the popular Big Night Out club crawl—it's a good time, and a great deal.

IN DA CLUB. Thinking about club hopping? If so, remember that all foreigners must carry their passports to gain admission, as photocopies and alternative forms of ID are rarely accepted. All bars and clubs are 18+, and this law is strictly enforced. Also, according to Australian law, no one is permitted to enter or re-enter a club after 3am.

Melbas, 46 Cavill Ave. (☎5592 6922). A trendy restaurant downstairs, which turns into a Top 40 music nightclub. Another bumping club upstairs with dance music makes Melbas a popular spot for people of all ages. Happy hour 4-8pm downstairs, 7-10pm upstairs. There is often a long line and cover ($5-10) for entry upstairs. Restaurant open daily 7:30am-5am. Club open daily 7pm-5am. Hours may vary.

The Bedroom Lounge Bar and Nightclub, 26 Orchid Ave. (☎5538 7600; www.thebedroom.net.au). Here's your chance to ask the sweaty person lying next to you to dance. The dance floor is surrounded by beds, providing a unique setup and fun atmosphere. Great DJs and live hip-hop performances. $10 cover may apply. Open daily 9pm-5am.

Shooters Saloon Bar, Level 1, The Mark Building, Orchid Ave. (☎5592 1144). Buffalo heads, cow-horns...and dozens of flat-screen TVs? Country western in decor only. Mainstream dance and R&B music consistently pack the dance floor. Free buffet dinner and drink on Su for backpackers. Cover F-Sa after 10pm $5-10. Open daily 8pm-5am.

Rose & Crown, Level 1, Raptis Plaza on Cavill Ave. (☎5531 5425; www.roseandcrown.com.au). Popular with a younger crowd. Dance and Top-40 play in 1 room, while house music thumps in the swanky lounge. Cover $5-10. Open in summer daily 8pm-5am; in winter Th-Su 8pm-5am.

Cocktails and Dreams, Level 1, Mark Bldg., Orchid Ave. (☎5592 1955). Packed club popular with backpackers. Head downstairs to **The Party,** one of few rock clubs in town. Separate cover (up to $10) for each. Open Th-Su 9pm-5am. Hours vary in summer.

O'Malley's on the Beach (☎5570 4075), at the end of Cavill Mall. Classic Irish pub with balcony views and live pub rock W-Sa. Open 10:30am-latenight.

DAYTRIP FROM SURFERS

SOUTH STRADBROKE ISLAND

Separated from the Spit by a thin channel, South Straddie is one of Surfers' hidden gems. Largely undeveloped and home to friendly, free-roaming wallabies, the long narrow island (22km by 2.5km) is lined by quiet river beaches on the west and gorgeous, empty surf beaches on the east. The patrolled **Surf Beach** is on the ocean side, a 35min. walk from the resort. Check with the resort for current hours.

Ferries, operated by the South Stradbroke Island Resort, run from Gate C of the Runaway Bay Marina, 247 Bayview St., off the Gold Coast Hwy. past Southport. (☎5577 3311; www.ssir.com.au. 25min.; departs daily 10:30am and 4pm; returns M-F 2:30 and 5pm, Sa-Su 3:30 and 5pm; ferry $25 round-trip, with BBQ lunch $45; pickup from Surfers $6 extra.) **Surfside Buslines'** bus 706 (☎13 12 30) connects Surfers Paradise to Runaway Bay (one-way $3.30) and leaves from Appel Park on Ferny Ave. (30min., leaves 20 and 50min. past the hr.)

The **South Stradbroke Island Resort** ❺ is the cheaper of the two resorts on the island. Their extensive offerings include pools, spas, tennis courts, water sports, and restaurants. Individual cabins have TV and fridge. (☎5577 3311 or 1800 074 125. 4- to 6-person rooms from $145. Call resort for specials.) There are four **camping** ❶ areas; all sites have toilets, showers, and cost $16 for two. **Tippler's camping grounds** (☎5577 2849) is just 300m from the resort; the island's other sites are more private and require a water taxi. **Water taxis** (☎04 1875 9789) for up to four leave from Gate C of Runaway Bay to Tippler's (one-way $70), campgrounds at **North** or **South Currigee** (☎5577 3932; one-way $40), and **The Bedrooms** (one-way $100).

GOLD COAST HINTERLAND

Just a little over an hour from the bustling coast, nature-lovers can bushwalk through subtropical rainforest, enjoy spectacular views, and stroll through tiny towns. The Hinterland makes for a wonderful daytrip away from the glitz of the coast. There are limited budget accommodations, but great camping.

Travel by car offers the most flexible and enjoyable means to explore. Head south along the Gold Coast Highway and turn right at Hooker Blvd./Nerang (at Pacific Fair Shopping Centre). You will immediately see signs to **Springbrook National Park** (41km), **Binna Burra** (48km), and **O'Reilly's Plateau/Lamington National Park** (74km). Continue towards Nerang and then follow the signs. Many of the roads inland are not connected, and a fair amount of backtracking is inevitable. However, the parks are close enough to one another that two or more can be combined into a few day trip. Look for kangaroos along the drive. For more info, contact **Queensland Parks and Wildlife Service** (☎13 13 04; www.epa.qld.gov.au).

There are group tours that can transport you to some of the parks. **Scenic Hinterland Tours,** 9 Beach Rd. (☎5531 5536; www.hinterlandtours.com.au.) across from the Surfers Paradise Transit Centre, picks up from Gold Coast resorts and has trips to both Lamington ($51.90) and Springbrook ($64.90) National Parks. While the guided tour is convenient, you will spend most of your time on the bus sitting next to Australian pensioners. Students get a $5 discount. You must book ahead. **All State Scenic Tours** accesses O'Reilly's Park in Lamington from the Transit Centre in Brisbane and will pick up passengers along the Gold Coast. (☎3003 0700; www.brisbanedaytours.com.au. Departs daily 8:30am, returns 5:45pm. $69, children $55. Includes morning tea and wine tasting.)

LAMINGTON NATIONAL PARK

Lamington National Park is split into two accessible sections: **Green Mountains/ O'Reilly's** and **Binna Burra.** The park's 100km of well-trod paths lead to over 300 spectacular waterfalls, clear springs, subtropical rainforests, and the NSW border ridge, with magnificent views of Mt. Warning's ancient volcanic crater. Trails appeal to daytrippers and more serious bushwalkers, ranging in length from short walks and half-day hikes to strenuous full-day treks of 24km. If you're daytripping from Brisbane, **Rob's Rainforest Explorer Day Tours** will take you to Lamington and nearby and Springbrook National Park, but you will spend most of your day on the bus. (☎1300 559 355; www.robsrainforest.com. $99 includes pickup and transport, as well as morning tea, lunch, and afternoon tea. DC/MC/V.)

GREEN MOUNTAINS. Green Mountains (and the privately owned **O'Reilly's Park**) can only be reached via Nerang and Canungra along a switchback road off the Pacific Hwy. After passing through Canungra, the last 25km of road is narrow and winding—there are 405 bends—and unsuitable for caravans. The **information center** is located 5km into the park; leave your car in the carpark below O'Reilly's, walk up the hill, and it will be on your left. The center provides maps, books campsites, and issues bush camping permits. (☎5544 0634. Open M and W-Th 9-11am and 1-3:30pm, Tu and F 1-3:30pm.) The **Tree Top Canopy Walk,** which reaches 15m above the ground and can be accessed via the Booyong Walk, offers visitors a dizzying look at the rainforest from the trees' perspective, with explanatory placards and viewing platforms 24m and 30m high (just climb the ladders). From O'Reilly's Rainforest Retreat (see below), the popular **Toolona Creek circuit** (17.4km, 5-6hr. round-trip) will take you past numerous waterfalls and stands of native beech trees on its way to stunning panoramas. The tracks to **Moran's Falls** (4.4km, 1½hr. round-trip) and **Python Rock** (3.2km, 1hr. round-trip) start about 800m downhill from the info center. The paved Moran's Falls trail descends deep into the rainforest before opening onto views of the waterfall, a gorge, and the Albert River. The Python Rock is a much easier trail that offers views of Moran's Falls, the Albert River Valley, and the impressive Castle Crag. On wet days in late spring and summer, listen for the guttural popping noise of the masked mountain frog.

On-site **camping ❶** includes toilets and hot showers, but campfires are not allowed. (☎13 13 04; www.qld.gov.au/camping. Book ahead. Bush camping permitted Feb.-Nov. $4.50, families $18). **O'Reilly's Rainforest Retreat ❺,** a guesthouse in O'Reilly's Park just minutes from the trails and across from the info center, charges high rates for its excellent location. (☎5544 0511 or 1800 688 722; www.oreillys.com.au. Planned activities 6:45am-9:30pm. Book ahead. Singles from $145; doubles from $250. AmEx/DC/MC/V.)

BINNA BURRA. To get to **Binna Burra,** follow the signs for Beechmont and Binna Burra from Nerang (37km). The **information center** provides bush camping permits ($4.50, families $18) and maps of the different hiking circuits. (☎5533 3584. Open daily 9am-3pm; rangers available M-F 1-3:30pm. Brochures and maps available at all times.) At the time that this guide was published, bush permits were not being issued because of hazardous tree conditions. Call ahead to assess.

The **Caves Circuit** (5km, 1½hr. round-trip) is so popular that it has its own self-guided tour available at the info center, where the hike originates. The short trek provides sweeping views of Coomera Valley and the Darlington Range. Keep your eyes peeled for **koalas,** which are often seen in the open forest areas. **Coomera Circuit** (17.4km, 7hr. round-trip) leaves the Border Track 1.9km from the entrance and is Binna Burra's most popular full-day hike; the path climbs beside the Coomera Gorge and crosses the river several times. These crossings involve rock-hopping, which can be hazardous after heavy rain or if the river is flooded.

On-site camping is available at the **Binna Burra Mountain Campsite ❶,** on your left 1km past the info center and another 500m past the lodge. (☎5533 3622 or 1800 074 260. Book 2 weeks in advance. Reception open M-Th and Su 9am-

5:30pm, F-Sa 9am-7pm. Site $11, students $9; 2-bed safari tent $50; 4-bed safari tent $70.)

SPRINGBROOK NATIONAL PARK

The Springbrook plateau lies on the northern edge of the ridge encircling the spire at the center of Mt. Warning's crater. Covering over 3,300 hectares of land, the park consists of three sections, all separated by a car drive: **Springbrook Plateau,** the **Natural Bridge** to the west, and **Mount Cougal** to the east. Springbrook's highlights are its striking rock formations and waterfalls.

SPRINGBROOK PLATEAU. Follow the signs to Mudgeeraba on the Pacific Hwy., also labeled as M1, and then head toward the mountains on Springbrook Rd. (30km). Follow signs to the unattended **information center** in the old schoolhouse for maps of the park's walks, lookouts, campsites, and picnic areas. (Ranger ☎5533 5147.) **Camping ❶** is available at the Gwongorella picnic area. (Book ahead. $4.50, families $18.) **Rosellas at Canyon Lookout ❸,** 8 Canyon Pde. (☎5533 5120; springbrook.info/canyonguesthouse) is a friendly B&B where each room has private bath, microwave, TV, fridge, DVD player, and electric blankets. (M-Th and Su singles $75; doubles $90. F-Sa singles $90; doubles $110. Follow signs to Canyon Lookout and you will see signs for Rosellas. MC/V.)

On a clear day at the **Best of All Lookout** on the southern end of Springbrook Rd., you'll see Coolangatta, Byron Bay, and a huge shield volcano which dominated the region 23 million years ago. The 700m round-trip walk to the lookout passes by a grove of ancient Antarctic beech trees. The park's best walking tracks are accessible from the **Canyon Lookout,** off Springbrook Rd. Both the impressive **Twin Falls Circuit** (4km, 1½hr. round-trip), which moves in a counterclockwise direction, and the popular day-long **Warrie Circuit** (17km, 5-6hr. round-trip) begin here. Both lead through rock wedge caves and behind, around, and under waterfalls.

NATURAL BRIDGE. The Natural Bridge Circuit (1km round-trip, 30min.) will take you into an arched cave created by a waterfall plunging from above. Go shortly after sunset to beat the evening crowds that flock to see the **glowworms** and bats. Look for signs for the Natural Bridge (30km from Nerang) en route to Springbrook National Park. There aren't any truly rugged routes here, so if you are looking to get off the beaten track, you may want to pass on this one.

MOUNT COUGAL NATIONAL PARK. From the Gold Coast, drive toward Nerang and head south on the Pacific Hwy. Take the Stewarts Rd./Currumbin Valley exit; the park is 21km from the highway. Just 25min. from the road along a paved path, Mt. Cougal offers views of Currumbin Creek as it plummets down a **natural water slide.** Some dive in **Currumbin Rock Pool,** 6km back along Currumbin Rd., but since the creek contains submerged logs, rocks, and eels, you may want to think twice.

DARLING AND SOUTHERN DOWNS

West of the Great Dividing Range lies the **Darling Downs,** with fresh mountain air and breathtaking vistas. Its epicenter is Toowoomba, drawing tourists to its beautiful parks. The **Southern Downs,** the highlight of which is Stanthorpe (p. 351), attracts hordes of backpackers in the fruit-picking season. Nearby Girraween and Sundown National Parks offer with dramatic rock outcroppings, spectacular views, rugged bushwalking, and brilliant wildflowers from September to March.

TOOWOOMBA ☎07

With over 200 parks and gardens, many connected by bike and walking paths, Toowoomba (pop. 116,000) has long outgrown its name, which is (loosely) derived from an Aboriginal word meaning "where the water sits down" or "swamp." The metropolis has since adopted the nickname "the Garden City" for its gorgeous and varied green spaces. Toowoomba is Queensland's largest inland city, yet it continues to possess some rural charm. Just minutes outside the vibrant commercial center are hills which offer breathtaking views of the Great Dividing Range. If you are seeking peace and tranquility, you won't find a better place than **Ju Raku En,** Australia's largest and most traditional Japanese stroll garden, adjacent to the University of Southern Queensland campus. To get there, take a left out of the visitors center carpark onto James St., then a left onto West St. Look for Wuth St. on the right after about 1km, and then turn left a few blocks up on Fleet St. For spectacular views year-round, head up to **Picnic Point,** a city park with short walking paths, a restaurant, and a cafe. From the visitors center carpark, exit right onto James St., and follow the signs. The Garden City is also home to the expansive **Queen's Park Gardens,** on Lindsay St. between Margaret and Campbell St., and **Laurel Bank Park,** on West St. and Herries St. All parks are free and open daily dawn to dusk; they're best visited at full bloom during the spring and summer (Sept.-Mar.). You can also pick up more extensive guides to the numerous parks and gardens at the visitors center. The **Carnival of Flowers** (☎4688 6912; www.thecarnivalofflowers.com.au), held the last full week of September, is Toowoomba's biggest draw. The carnival features a parade, flower shows, and an exhibition of prize-winning private gardens.

Motels abound, but budget accommodation is difficult to find. The **Settlers Inn ❷** at the corner of Ruthven St. and James St., offers a pub stay. Dorms in the back, off the street, are the quietest. (☎4632 3634. Singles $20; doubles $30. Shared facilities. AmEx/DC/MC/V.) **Hotel National ❷,** 59 Russell St., is centrally located, and is the only place that provides 3- and 4-bed dorms (☎4639 2706. Shared facilities. Nice kitchen and common room. Laundry $2. Loud live band plays downstairs at the pub Th-Sa 9pm-1am. $25 per person, $120 per wk. AmEx/MC/V.)

Greyhound Australia, 28-30 Neil St. (☎13 14 99) between Margaret and Russell St., runs to Brisbane (2hr.; nearly every hr. 5am-6pm; $25, students and backpackers $23), Melbourne (23hr., daily 8:50am, $213/192), and Sydney (15hr., daily 8:45pm, $121/109). There is a $8 charge for booking bus tickets over the phone. For northern destinations, connect in Brisbane. Coming from Brisbane, Warrego Hwy. becomes James St.; the **Toowoomba Visitor Information Centre,** 86 James St. (☎4639 3797 or 1800 331 155; www.toowoomba.qld.gov.au), will be on your left. Coming from Warwick, take a right off Ruthven St. onto James St., and you'll see the Centre 1½km on your right. (**Internet** $2 per 10min. Open daily 9am-5pm.) **Internet** can also be found at Ascension, 455 Ruthven St. for $2.25 per 30min. (☎4638 1333. Open daily 10am-9pm.) **Banks** and 24hr. **ATMs** line Ruthven St. **Taxis** are available from Garden City Taxis (☎13 10 08).

STANTHORPE ☎07

If you are itching to leave the bustle of the city, the small town of Stanthorpe, nestled in the Granite Belt, may be just the place. It's location in the heart of Queensland's best wine country makes it a prime vacation spot, and backpackers swarm like locusts to pick fruit and vegetables in the summer months. If wine tasting and work is not enough, the town is also an ideal base for exploring the granite formations and wildflowers of the surrounding national parks: Girraween, Sundown, Boonoo Boonoo, and Bald Rock.

WORK IN STANTHORPE. From September to May each year, the ripened fruit and vegetable fields of the Granite Belt must be harvested, and thousands of backpackers rush to Stanthorpe for short-term work. September marks the start of the stone fruit harvest (plums, cherries, and peaches); December through May is largely tomato and vegetable picking; apples run February through May. Minimum wage is currently $14.90 per hr., but your profit is largely up to you. Jobs either pay by hour or by quantity collected, the latter benefitting experienced pickers. While some hostels arrange jobs, it might be easier to contact the free job-hunting agency **Ready Workforce** (☎4681 6200). Call before you arrive; it can take up to a week to find work. Open M-F 9am-5pm.

TRANSPORTATION AND PRACTICAL INFORMATION

There is no bus station in Stanthorpe; instead the bus stops on the corner of Maryland and Folkestone St. behind the Shell station. General bus information can be found across the street at Barry's Taxi Service. **Crisps Coaches** (☎4681 4577) and **Greyhound Australia** (☎13 14 99; www.greyhound.com.au) both service Stanthorpe. Crisps is by far the faster, cheaper option, with buses to: Brisbane (3½hr.; M-Th 7am, noon; F 7am, noon, 4pm; Sa 10:45am; Su 10:45am, 4pm; $49, children $37) via Warwick (45min., $20/15) and via Toowoomba (2¼hr., M-F, $37/29) and to Tenterfield (45min.; M-Th one per day 7:20pm, F 6:15pm, Su 12:45pm; $20/13). Crisps offers guaranteed seating, and tickets can be purchased on the bus. If you are staying north of town on High St., you can wave down the bus as it passes. Greyhound Australia tickets are more expensive, and can be purchased via phone, online, or at **Harvey World Travel,** 1 Maryland St., across from the post office. If you're driving from the Gold Coast (245km, 3½hr.), follow signs to Nerang, Canungra, Beaudesert, Warwick, then Stanthorpe.

To reach the **tourist information center,** 28 Leslie Pde., follow the information sign that leads you through town and over the bridge at Quart Pot Creek, then turn left immediately. (☎4681 2057. Open daily 8:30am-5pm.) **Banks** and 24hr. **ATMs** can be found in the center of town on Maryland St. **Internet** access is available for $2.50 per 30min. in the **library,** 56 Lock St., next to the park (☎4681 2141). The **post office** is at 14 Maryland St., on the corner of Railway St. (☎4681 2181. Open M-F 9am-5pm.) **Postal Code:** 4380.

RIDIN' DIRTY. If you plan to drive, be aware that some areas are monitored by speed cameras. While the lack of traffic on country roads might make you want to drive fast, you could find out later that you've been ticketed for exceeding the limit. This also applies to rental cars; your credit card will be billed once the ticket arrives at the rental agency. Keep to the posted speed limit, especially since there is heavy wildlife traffic across the roads at all times of day.

ACCOMMODATIONS AND CAMPING

Some accommodations help backpackers find picking jobs and also provide transport to and from work. Although town pubstays do not offer placement services, their central locations, low prices, and private rooms attract workers and travelers alike. If you plan on visiting during the summer, consider making a reservation before the picking season begins—even a few weeks' notice may not be sufficient.

SHUTDOWN. Although the wineries are open year-round, Stanthorpe closes its doors to backpackers in the winter months and most budget accommodations shut down. Camping is possible, but with some evenings reaching below 0°C, be sure to bring a winter-friendly sleeping bag.

Backpackers of Queensland, 80 High St. (☎0429 810 998), on the right about 1½km before you enter town. Backpackers rave about this hostel, which offers seasonal job placement and transportation in addition to excellent facilities and large nightly dinners (from $6). Spacious co-ed ensuite dorms house 5 per room. Lockers and laundry. Free pickup and drop-off. Check-in by 7:30pm or call ahead. No bookings. Call at least 2 days ahead during picking season (Sept.-May) to see if a bed is available. Weekly bookings only, $140. Completely shut down during the winter. MC/V. ❷

Top of Town Accommodation, 10 High St. (☎4681 4888 or 1800 030 123; www.topoftown.com.au), on the right 2½km before town. Houses as many as 120 backpackers on its 20-acre estate during picking season. No job placement or transportation. Pool, ping pong, convenience store, common areas with TVs. Bring linens. 2- and 4-bed dorms (open only during picking season) $25, weekly $125; campsite for 2 $22; on-site caravans $58, weekly $120. Reception daily 8:30am-6:30pm. MC/V. ❷

Country Style Tourist Accommodation Park (☎4683 4358; www.countrystyleaccomodation.com.au), in Glen Aplin, 9km south of Stanthorpe on the New England Hwy. Don't let the distance deter you; Country Style offers free job placement and transportation to and from work or the bus stop. Each dorm includes kitchen, bath, and TV. Internet $5 per hr. Laundry $3 per load. $25 key deposit. Reception 7am-7pm in picking season, 8:30am-5pm off-peak. 4-bed dorms (open only during the picking season) $20, weekly $90; tent sites $55 per wk.; on-site caravans $90 per wk. MC/V. ❷

Country Club Hotel/Motel, 26 Maryland St. (☎4681 1033). The best low season budget accommodation. Travelers can stay in the cheaper hotel rooms with shared toilets above the pub (get one facing away from the street to reduce noise) or in a nicer motel room out back with private bath, TV, fridge, large beds, and 70s decor. No reception, just talk to the bartender. Hotel singles $20, motel $35; doubles $40/50. MC/V. ❷

FOOD

Woolworths supermarket is on the corner of High and Lock St. (Open M-F 8am-9pm, Sa 8am-5pm.)

Applejack's, 130 High St. (☎4681 0356). Popular among locals and travelers alike, Applejack's serves dirt-cheap food in a wonderfully homey atmosphere. The mushroom cheese omelette ($6.20) is a must, and the pizzas ($5.90-17.90) are delicious. Open M-Th 9am-5pm; F 9am-9pm; Sa 10am-2pm and 5:30-9pm. ❶

Cosmo Cafe and Restaurant, 18 Maryland St. (☎4681 3131) across from the post office. The Cosmo (cholesterol) Special of bacon, eggs, sausage, tomato, toast, tea or coffee ($9.90) will leave you full for a week. The 3 daily specials ($7.90) and evening specials ($10.90) are nearly ½-off original price. Open in summer M-W 8am-5pm, Th-Sa 8am-8pm, Su 7am-3pm; in winter M-Sa 8am-5pm, Su 8am-2pm. Cash only. ❶

The Granite Rock Cafe, 161 High St. (☎4681 1365). The 1950s-themed restaurant offers quick, cheap meals for sit-down or takeaway. A variety of focaccias ($5.90), all-day breakfast ($4.90-9.50), and burgers ($4.90-7.50) are great bargains. Open daily 7:30am-latenight. Cash only. ❶

Anna's Restaurant, (☎4681 1265; annas.com.au), on the corner of Wallangarra Rd. and O'Mara Terr. Has some of the best food in town; locals praise the weekend Italian buffets (F $25.90, Sa $32.90). Book ahead. Open daily 6pm-latenight, last seating at 8:30pm. AmEx/DC/MC/V. ❸

WINERIES

More than 50 famous Granite Belt wineries line the New England Hwy. around Stanthorpe, and most offer free tastings. Unfortunately, they cannot be reached by public transportation or on foot. The tourist office has info on local winery tours and provides a detailed local map for those driving. The roads and wineries are well marked. Tours ensure a jolly day and an obligatory late-afternoon nap. The best is **Fillippo's** full-day tour, which imparts an endless stream of amusing local knowledge while covering eight of the best vineyards. Prices include pickup, drop-off, and hot lunch. (☎4681 3130; www.filippostours.com.au. Full-day $65, full-day from Brisbane $110, min. 14 people; ½-day $50, includes lunch.) Several other companies offer similar packages—check with the visitors center. **Ballandean Estate Wines** is Queensland's oldest family-operated winery, though the Catholic Church claims title to the oldest vineyard in the valley. Ballandean sponsors the **Opera in the Vineyard** festival, a black-tie wine-and-dine extravaganza the first weekend in May, and **Jazz in the Vineyard,** a more low-key event, the third weekend in August. (☎4684 1226; www.ballandean-estate.com.au. Open daily 9am-5pm. Free winery tours 11am, 1 and 3pm.)

NATIONAL PARKS OF THE STANTHORPE AREA

In addition to the parks listed below, two New South Wales national parks, **Bald Rock** and **Boonoo Boonoo** (☎02 6376 4298), are accessible from Stanthorpe. None of the parks can be reached by public transportation or by tour bus.

GIRRAWEEN NATIONAL PARK. Girraween is a popular destination for bushwalkers, birdwatchers, campers, and picnickers. In contrast to the Hinterland's dense rainforest, the park consists of open eucalyptus forest populated with massive granite boulders balanced on top of each other. It is also home to Queensland's only common wombat population (though they are very shy and difficult to find). In the spring, wildflowers sprout everywhere, hence the name Girraween, the Aboriginal word meaning "place of flowers." To get to Girraween, drive 26km south on the New England Hwy. from Stanthorpe, turn left at the sign, then drive 9km on a sealed road. The **information center** (☎4684 5157), next to the carpark, is usually open daily; the rangers post the day's hours on a board near the center's entrance. Nearby there are picnic, swimming, and rock climbing areas. **Camping** ❶ is available in two designated areas with hot showers, toilets, and BBQ. (☎13 13 04; www.qld.gov.au/camping. $4.50, families $18. Register over the phone, online, at the information center, or at the park. Book ahead during high season.) Girraween features a number of well-maintained walking tracks. **The Pyramid** (3.4km, 2hr. round-trip), has exhilarating views of immense, artfully stacked granite boulders. At the top, you'll be rewarded with panoramic views of the entire park, the famous **Balancing Rock,** which appears ready to fall any moment, and **Bald Rock,** Australia's largest granite boulder. The last portion of the climb is up a steep granite face; be sure to wear appropriate shoes and do not even consider climbing when wet. A moderate level of fitness is required for the ascent, and the way down can be hazardous, so take it slow. The trail leaves from the picnic area just past the info center. **Castle Rock** (5.2km, 2hr. round-trip) is a moderate climb with a steep final ascent that yields an impressive 360° view. The final section should not be attempted in wet conditions. The trailhead is located in the Castle Rock Campground, just a a short drive up the road to the right of the info center. For a more mellow hike, follow the flat trail out to **Underground Creek** (2.8km, 2hr. round-trip). This track provides spectacular wildflower displays and excellent bird watching opportunities. The trailhead is located 4km down the road from the info center; while some of the road is unsealed, it is suitable for all cars.

SUNDOWN NATIONAL PARK. While Girraween provides well-marked paths, Sundown is less developed and caters almost exclusively to rugged bushwalkers and trailblazers. Those who do make the journey will find chiseled gorges, high peaks, and panoramic views, as well as opportunities for swimming, fishing, and canoeing. Unlike the smooth hills and tenuously balanced granite boulders that characterize neighboring parks, the 16,000 hectares of Sundown are dominated by the sharp ridges and steep gorges of "traprock," dense sedimentary rock molded by faulting, folding, and erosion. The **Severn River** cuts the park in two. To get to Sundown from Stanthorpe, drive west on Texas Rd. and turn left at the signs for **Glenlyon Dam** (75km). Continue until you reach the dirt road marked by a Sundown National Park sign. You'll reach the park entrance after 4km on the rough dirt track; take it slow to avoid bottoming out. At the entrance, look for the left fork of the track and follow it to camp headquarters. From Tenterfield, head north for 5km, then west along the Bruxner Hwy. (52km) to Mingoola. Turn right and travel 12km to the park turnoff. Burrow's camping area is accessible only by 4WD from the east via Sundown Rd. Follow the signs to Ballandean Estate Wines. The 14km gravel road begins just past the winery. The camping area is another 20km inside the park. If taking this approach, call **Camp Headquarters** ❶ (☎02 6737 5235), located at the southwestern edge of the park, to check road conditions. Campsites are available near Headquarters. All sites have pit toilets, fireplaces, and BBQ. (Bookings ☎13 13 04; www.qld.gov.au/camping. $4.50, families $18. Register over the phone, online, at the information center, or at the park.) To explore the park safely, use an official *Queensland Parks and Wildlife Services Map*, available at QPWS offices in Brisbane, Toowoomba, and Girraween, and bring a compass. The park is high, remote, and often cold, and visitors must be self-sufficient. The **Permanent Waterhole** is a pool on a major bend in the river where the occasional platypus has been spotted. To get there, park 400m past the info center. There is a walking track directly ahead which cuts into the hills behind the river (45min. round-trip). The **Split-Rock** and **Double Falls** are well worth the 3- to 4-hr. round-trip hike up **McAllisters Creek.** Cross the river east into the creek; be careful not to get misled by the old 4WD track. The climb up **Ooline Creek** (the first deep gully to the left of the permanent waterhole) also features numerous waterfalls and gorges.

SUNSHINE COAST AND FRASER ISLAND

The Sunshine Coast is a slightly warmer, less crowded, more relaxed alternative to the Gold Coast. Here, the sun shines 300 days a year, quiet beaches and national parks stretch for miles, and resort towns like Noosa Heads rise abruptly from the sand. Fraser Island, the largest sand island in the world, is a beach-and-rainforest playground crisscrossed by 4WD tracks. Its legendary dunes and freshwater lakes make it a mecca for adventurous backpackers.

MAROOCHY SHIRE ☎07

Maroochy Shire (pop. 141,000) refers to the 18km of Sunshine Coast that encompass the towns of **Maroochydore, Headlands,** and **Mooloolaba** (north to south). Diehard surfers fill the beaches, and their chill attitude permeates the region. The area is becoming popular with resort dwellers and wealthy vacationers as well. An urban center located at the mouth of the Maroochy River, Maroochydore has thriving small industries. About 1km southeast, Alexandra Headlands is best known for its great waves. Another 2km south, a cafe-packed esplanade lines Mooloolaba's family beach. The Shire is a popular base for fruit-picking, with ginger, passion fruit, and pineapples in season nearly year-round, strawberries from June-October, and lychee nuts from January-February.

TRANSPORTATION. **Greyhound Australia and Premier** stop at the Maroochydore bus terminal on First Ave. at Scotlyn Fair, off Aerodrome Rd. **Greyhound** (☎13 14 99; phone booking fee $8) runs to: Airlie Beach (17hr.; daily 4pm; $165, students $149); Brisbane (2hr., 7 per day, $25/23); Cairns (28hr., daily 4pm, $229/206); Gold Coast (3½hr., daily 7:45am, $40/36); Hervey Bay (4½-5hr., 3 per day, $37/33); Mackay (15½hr., daily 4pm, $143/129); Rockhampton (10¼hr., daily 4pm, $96/86). **Premier** (☎13 34 10) runs daily to similar destinations at considerably cheaper prices. **Mighty Bus** has the best deals to Brisbane. (☎1300 662 988; www.mightybus.com. 2 per day, $7.95. Phone booking fee $2, online $0.55. Book ahead.) The blue **Sunshine Coast Sunbus** (☎5450 7888) connects the three towns. Bus #600 and #601 run from the Sunshine Plaza in Maroochydore down Cotton Tree Pde. through Alexandra Headlands to Mooloolaba. (M-Sa every 15min., Su every 30min. $2.20.) Bus #620 heads to Noosa from Maroochydore (every 30min., every hr. on weekends, $4.80). Bus #610 departs every hr. passing through Mooloolaba and Sunshine Plaza, Maroochydore, for Nambour ($2.60).

ORIENTATION AND PRACTICAL INFORMATION. **Aerodrome Road** is the main commercial strip in Maroochydore. In Alexandra Headlands, it becomes **Alexandra Parade** as it curves along the ocean. Farther south in Mooloolaba, it becomes the **Mooloolaba Esplanade.** It eventually intersects with **Brisbane Road,** the main thoroughfare in Mooloolaba. **Sunshine Plaza** in Maroochydore is a large, clean pedestrian mall with cafes, shops, and department stores.

The **tourist office** (☎5479 1566) is on Sixth Ave. off Aerodrome Rd. (Open daily 9am-5pm.) A smaller **info kiosk** is in Mooloolaba, at the corner of First Ave. and Brisbane Rd. (☎5478 2233. Open daily 9am-5pm.) There are **banks** and 24hr. **ATMs** on Horton Pde., Maroochydore, and a bank in Mooloolaba on the corner of Hancock St. and Brisbane Rd. Other services include: **taxis** (24hr. ☎13 10 08; about $15 from Maroochydore to Mooloolaba); **police** (☎5475 2444) on Cornmeal Pde., Maroochydore; **7 Day Medical,** 150 Horton Pde. (☎5443 2122; open M-Th 8am-8pm, F-Su 8am-6pm); **Maroochy Day and Night Chemmart pharmacy,** 107-109 Aerodome Rd. (☎5443 6070; open daily 8am-10pm) on the corner of Second Ave.; and **Internet** access at **All Systems Go,** 25 First Ave. Maroochydore. (☎5443 6764. $3.50 per hr. Open M, W, Su 10am-8pm, Th-Sa 10am-10pm.) **Post offices** are at 22 King St., Cotton Tree; on the corner of Walan St. and Brisbane Rd., Mooloolaba; 17 Duporth Ave.; and in the Sunshine Plaza, Maroochydore. (☎13 13 18. All open M-F 9am-5pm, Sunshine Plaza location also open Sa 9am-3:30pm, Su 10:30am-2:30pm.) **Postal Code:** 4557 (Mooloolaba), 4558 (Maroochydore, Cotton Tree).

ACCOMMODATIONS. Most hostels in Maroochy Shire arrange fruit-picking work. **Mooloolaba Beach Backpackers ❸,** 75 Brisbane Rd., in a colorful modern building, is close to the nightlife and the beach. The great pool and common area are perfect for partying, and the bunk dorms have kitchens and TV lounges on every level. Ensuite dorms with TV and spacious doubles are in a separate building. (☎1800 020 120; www.mooloolababackpackers.com. Cafe, Internet access, lockers, laundry. Kayaks and body or surf boards free. Courtesy shuttle to bus station and airport. Reception 8am-10pm. 4-bed dorms $26, ensuite $29; ensuite doubles $70. VIP. MC/V.) **Maroochydore YHA Backpackers ❷,** 24 Schirrmann Dr., is a hike from the center of town, but the friendliness and freebies will blow you away: bikes, kayaks, canoes, body boards, and daily yoga sessions are all on the house, and movie nights are held 3-4 times per week. The YHA also has a large kitchen, common areas, a pool, and

Internet access. (☎1800 302 855; www.yhabackpackers.com. Laundry $3 per machine. Trips to the Hinterland $30. Call for free pickup from the bus station. Reception 8am-7pm. 4- to 8-bed dorms $21-24; singles $48; doubles $58. 7th night free. YHA discount. MC/V.) **Suncoast Backpackers Lodge ❷,** 50 Parker St., off Aerodrome Rd., Maroochydore, is small, family-run, clean, and filled with fruit pickers and surfers. (☎5443 7544. Outdoor common space, kitchen, pool table, and laundry. Reception 8:30am-1pm and 5-8pm. 3- to 6-bed dorms $21; doubles $45. VIP/YHA. MC/V.)

FOOD AND NIGHTLIFE. **Fisheries on the Spit ❶,** along the Wharf at 21-23 Parkyn Pde., sells a spectacular variety of fresh and cooked seafood at shockingly low prices. (☎5444 1165. Open daily in summer 7:30am-8pm; in winter 7:30am-7:30pm. MC/V.) **Buddha Asian Restaurant ❷,** along the Riverwalk in Sunshine Plaza, has pan-Asian offerings in a romantic setting. (☎5479 3382. Main courses $10-14. Open daily 11am-latenight. MC/V.) Maroochy has many good Thai restaurants; the best is **Som Tam Thai ❷,** on the corner of Fifth Ave. and Aerodrome Rd. (☎5479 1700. Main courses $11-21. Open M-Sa noon-2:30pm and 5-9pm, Su 5-9pm. AmEx/DC/MC/V.) **Coles** supermarket (☎5443 4633; open M-F 8am-9pm, Sa 8am-5:30pm, Su 9am-6pm) is on the ground floor of the massive Sunshine Plaza, off Horton Pde., along with a couple hundred shops and a plethora of eateries.

Of the three towns in Maroochy Shire, only Mooloolaba really comes alive after dark. **Zink Bar and Restaurant,** 77 Mooloolaba Esplanade, gets packed on the weekends with hip-hop and house music booming onto the street. Authentic Spanish tapas are served until close. (☎5477 6077; www.zinkbar.com.au. Tu salsa and Latin night. Th and Su live music, F-Sa DJ. Open M-Th and Su noon-latenight, F-Sa noon-2am.) **Motown,** 121 Mooloolaba Esplanade, on the corner of Venning St., is a lounge and nightclub with party beats and a gorgeous second-story deck with ocean views. Come for a sunset dinner (burgers $7, pizza $10), or stay for a long Happy hour (4-8pm; hamburgers $3), then hit the dance floor. (☎5444 5767; www.motownmooloolaba.com.au. Open W-Su 4pm-midnight.) **The Wharf Tavern,** on the Wharf next to UnderWater World, is a modern, laid-back bar downstairs and upstairs, a club with dance and R&B music that attracts young party-goers. (☎5444 8383; www.thewharftavern.com.au. Both open daily 10am-latenight, with W-Sa and Su live music. Nightclub open Tu and F-Su 9pm-3am. Tu basics $2; cover $7.)

ACTIVITIES. Being in Maroochy Shire means spending time near the water. **Maroochydore Beach** has good breaks for short-board riders, while **Alexandra Headlands** has rips, large swells, and big crowds. **Mooloolaba Beach,** near the spit, is the safest beach for swimming. **Bad Company Surf Shop,** 6-8 Aerodrome Rd., Maroochydore, rents out boards across the street from a good strip of beach. (☎5443 2457. Open daily 9am-5pm. Surf boards ½-day $30, full-day $35; body boards $15/20. MC/V.) If you'd rather ride the pavement, **Skate Biz,** 150 Alexandra Pde., Alexandra Headlands, offers in-line skates, bikes, and skateboards. A public skate park is across the street. (☎5443 6111; www.skatebiz.com.au. All rentals $12 per 2hr., $20 per day. Includes basic safety gear. Open M-Sa 9am-5pm, Su 10am-4pm. MC/V.)

UnderWater World, on the Mooloolaba Wharf at Parkyn Pde., has beautiful displays of sea creatures of all kinds; it's the largest tropical oceanarium in the Southern Hemisphere. Glide along a moving walkway underneath a 2.5 million liter aquarium while sharks and giant manta rays swim inches overhead. There are 18 shows daily, including shark and manta ray feedings. Don't miss out on the seals; kiss one, get a behind the scenes tour, or swim with them. (☎5444 8488; www.underwaterworld.com.au. Open daily 9am-6pm; last entry 5pm. Kiss 11am, 1, and 3:30pm.; $6, with photo $15. Tour 11:30am; $30. Swim 2pm; $76 includes photo, admission, 15min. swim. Book ahead for swim. General admission $25.50, students $18, children $15, families $69. Backpacker discounts.) If seals don't give you enough of an adrenaline rush, you can dive with the aquarium's sharks through **Scuba World.** (☎5444 8595; www.scuba-world.com.au. 30min. with sharks. Daily at 1 and 3pm. Dive with own equipment $129 plus $10 for entry; non-divers $165, includes admission, equipment, and lesson. MC/V.)

NOOSA ☎07

Noosa is an eco-friendly spot with beautiful beaches, a relaxed atmosphere, and plenty of wilderness within walking distance. While there are open-air shopping centers, fancy hotels, and chic cafes to keep wealthy couples and pensioners occupied, budget travelers can easily avoid the glitz. The main drag, Hastings St., is perpetually crowded with tourists; given the number of restaurants and shops and the beautiful beach only meters away, it's not hard to understand why. Cooloola National Park, just north of Noosa, is a wilderness area rife with 4WD, hiking, canoeing, and camping opportunities.

TRANSPORTATION

Buses: Noosa has no bus terminal; coaches pickup and drop-off at the **Bus Interchange** on Noosa Pde. near Hastings St. Book ahead. **Greyhound Australia** (☎13 14 99; phone booking fee $8) runs to: **Airlie Beach** (16¼hr.; daily 4:40pm; $155, concessions $139); **Brisbane** (2-2½hr., 7 per day, $25/23); **Cairns** (27¼hr., daily 4:40pm, $228/205); **Gold Coast** (4½hr., daily 6:40am, $40/36); **Hervey Bay** (3½hr., 3 per day, $32/29); **Mackay** (15hr., daily 4:40pm, $138/124); **Rockhampton** (9½hr., daily 4:40pm, $91/82). **Premier** (☎13 34 10) runs 1 service per day to the same destinations at significantly cheaper rates.

Public Transportation: Sunshine Coast Sunbus (☎5450 7888) leaves from the bus interchange and offers frequent hail-and-ride service around Noosa. Bus #620 goes to **Caloundra, Maroochydore,** and **Mooloolaba** (every 30min.; $5.60-8). Bus #627 connects the neighborhoods of Noosa: service starts in **Tewantin,** continues though **Noosa Heads, Noosa Junction, Noosaville,** and terminates in **Sunshine Beach.** Buses run every 15-20min.; $2.20. Bus #630 and #631 head to **Eumundi** every hour or two while Bus #626 heads to **Sunrise Beach** every 30min. All buses run approximately 6:30am-6:30pm, later on weekends.

Taxis: Suncoast Cabs (24hr. ☎13 10 08).

Car Rental: Europcar (☎5447 3777; www.europcar.com.au.), 66 Noosa Dr., rents from $45 per day with unlimited mileage. $14 per day age surcharge for those under 25. Backpacker discount. (Open M-F 8am-5pm, Sa-Su 8am-1pm. AmEx/DC/MC/V.) **Avis** (☎5447 4933; www.avis.com.au), on the corner of Noosa Dr. and Noosa Pde., has cars from $50. $27.50 per day surcharge for those under 25. (Open M-F 8am-5pm, Sa 7:30am-3pm, Su 8:30am-1:30pm. AmEx/DC/MC/V.)

ORIENTATION AND PRACTICAL INFORMATION

Be prepared to say Noosa a lot; nearly everything in the area carries the name. Noosa Heads is the main area; it encompasses **Hastings Street** and the commercial **Noosa Junction.** Noosaville, 3km west, is just off the Noosa River and is a bit quieter. The entrance to **Noosa National Park** is at the eastern end of Hastings St. Head one block away from the beach on Hastings St. to find **Bus Interchange.** A 10-15min. stroll away from the beach on Noosa Dr. leads to the heart of **Noosa Junction,** the area's Central Business District (CBD). **Banks,** the **post office,** and **supermarkets,** are all within 5min. of each other. **Noosaville** is a 1hr. walk (or a quick bus ride) down Noosa Pde. from the intersection with Noosa Dr. Its main street, **Gympie Terrace,** has several international restaurants, motels, and boat rentals. The **Sunshine Beach** area is around the point from Noosa Heads on a beautiful stretch of beach lined with magnificent houses. Both Sunshine Beach

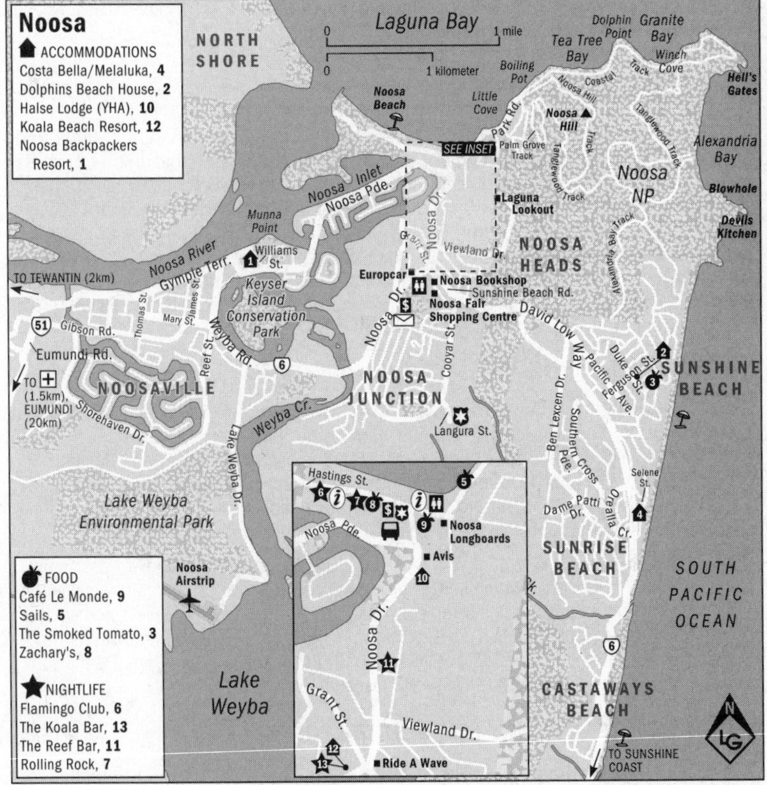

and nearby **Sunrise Beach** are popular spots, but the 40km stretch of sand leaves ample space for sunbathers to spread out.

Tourist Office: Tourism Noosa Information Centre (☎5430 5000; www.tourism-noosa.com.au), at the intersection of Noosa Dr. and Hastings St. Open daily 9am-5pm.

Currency Exchange: Banks and 24hr. **ATMs** are on Hastings St., Noosa Heads; Sunshine Beach Rd., Noosa Junction; and Gympie Terr., Noosaville. All banks open M-Th 9:30am-4pm, F 9:30am-5pm.

Bookstore: Noosa Book Shop (☎5447 3066), in Suntop Plaza, Noosa Junction. Buys, sells, and exchanges used books. Open M-F 9am-5:30pm, Sa-Su 9am-5pm. MC/V.

Police: Main office on Langura St., Noosa Heads (☎5447 5888). Smaller Police Beat on the corner of Hastings St. and Noosa Dr., Noosa Heads.

Medical Services: Noosa Hospital, 111 Goodchap St., Noosaville (☎5455 9200).

Internet Access: Adventure Travel Bugs, 9 Sunshine Beach Rd. (☎1800 666 720; www.oztravelbugs.com). Cheapest in town; you can book tours there as well. $1 per 15min.; backpacker and student discount 50%. Open M-F 8am-8pm, Sa-Su 9am-7pm.

Post Office: 91-93 Noosa Rd., Noosa Junction (☎13 13 18). Open M-F 9am-5pm, Sa 9am-12:30pm. **The Hastings St. Supermarket,** behind the Royal Copenhagen Ice Cream shop, also has postal service. Open daily 6am-8pm. **Postal Code:** 4567 (Noosa Heads, Noosa Junction); 4566 (Noosaville).

ACCOMMODATIONS

Lodging in Noosa falls into one of three general categories: hostels, motels and hotels, and "holiday units," which are usually private homes or apartments. Hostels typically offer cheap meals, courtesy shuttle services, free surfboards, on-site bars, and travel agencies. Because of Noosa's increasing popularity, there aren't always enough budget beds to go around during Christmas and school holidays; be sure to book ahead. The best location is in Noosa Heads, near the beach and all the action on Hastings St. Families may find it more economical to rent units or homes—**Accom Noosa,** 41 Hastings St. can help you find affordable, long-term lodging. (☎1800 072 078; www.accomnoosa.com.au. AmEx/DC/MC/V.)

NOOSA HEADS

Halse Lodge (YHA), 2 Halse Ln. (☎1800 242 567; www.halselodge.com.au), across Noosa Dr. and up the hill from the bus interchange. Picturesque Queenslander home with large verandas and spacious common areas. Close to the beach and Hastings St. Small bar, active until 11:30pm common space lockdown. Free surf and body boards. Laundry, Internet access, lockers, and kitchen. Reception 7am-8pm. 4- to 6-bed dorms $26-28; twins and doubles $68-75. NOMADS/VIP/YHA discounts. MC/V. ❸

Koala Beach Resort, 44 Noosa Dr. (☎1800 357 457; www.koalaadventures.com). 10min. walk from the bus interchange; take a right onto Noosa Dr. and follow it over the hill. If you want to party in this sleepy town, Koala is the place. Spacious 7-bed ensuite dorms, courtesy bus, laundry, pool, volleyball court, basement kitchen, and outdoor eating area. Internet access $3 per hr. Linen $3. Reception 7:30am-8pm. Dorms $25; walk-through twins and doubles $59. VIP discount. MC/V. ❷

SUNSHINE BEACH AND SUNRISE BEACH

Dolphins Beach House, 14 Duke St. (☎1800 454 456; www.dolphinsbeach-house.com). Beautiful apartment-style dorms consist of 2 4-bed rooms that share a common TV area, bathroom, and kitchen. Just step outside your unit to enjoy the mellow hippie appeal of the spacious outdoor area. 3min. walk to Sunshine Beach. Internet access, laundry, courtesy bus, surfboard (½-day $20) and body board (full-day $5) rental. Reception 8am-8pm. Dorms $24; doubles $60. VIP discount. MC/V. ❷

Costa Bella, 7 Selene St. (☎1800 003 663; www.melaluka.com.au). Take the highway to Sunrise Beach; turn left at Vernon St. and make 2 quick rights down the hill. Standard hostel with self-contained units and large common areas. Spacious Costa Bella and **Wistari** units have ocean views, kitchens, dining and TV areas, laundry, and patios or balconies. The less-expensive **Melaluka** building has dorm facilities and apartments. Free bus and Internet access. Reception M-F 9am-5:30pm, Sa-Su 10am-10pm. Costa Bella rooms for 2 $70. Melaluka 2-bed dorms $25; doubles $58. Wistari twins $50; double ensuite $60. MC/V. ❷

NOOSAVILLE

Noosa Backpackers Resort, 9-13 Williams St. (☎1800 626 673; www.noosabackpack-ers.com). Located on a side street 1min. from the river and close to Gympie Rd. 30min. walk to Hastings St. and Main Beach. Location isn't ideal, but the 6-bed ensuite dorms might be the nicest on the East Coast. The Global Cafe is crowded with guests and locals alike, flocking to its tasty food and good prices. Courtesy van, game room, swimming pool, laundry, kitchen, bar, and 24hr. Internet access. Reception 8am-7:30pm. Dorms $26; doubles and twins $58. VIP/YHA discounts. AmEx/MC/V. ❸

FOOD

While there are hundreds of restaurants in Noosa, it's all too easy to hover around the popular Hastings St. area. Cheaper meals can be found around Noosa Junction, and the surf clubs are great places for cheap grub or a sunset beer; try **Noosa Heads Surf Life Saving Club ❶,** 69 Hastings St. (☎5423 3055. Open M-F 11am-midnight, Sa-Su 10am-midnight. MC/V.) Many hostels also offer great meals for $10 or less. **Coles** supermarket is off on Lanyana Way in the Noosa Fair Shopping Centre, Noosa Junction. (☎5447 4000. Open M-F 8am-9pm, Sa 8am-5:30pm, Su 9am-6pm.)

Café Le Monde, 52 Hastings St. (☎5449 2366; www.cafelemonde.com.au), Noosa Heads. A local favorite and gathering place for surfer celebs. Try toasted lunch baguettes (ft. long $9-14 noon-5pm). Pastas $14-23. Main courses $18-32. Live music 4 nights per wk., F-Sa DJ 9pm-midnight. Open daily 6am-latenight. AmEx/MC/V. ❸

The Smoked Tomato, 36 Duke St. (☎5447 3913), Sunshine Beach. Offers terrific lunch specials from pastas ($5) to gourmet pizzas ($10). Lunch noon-3pm. Dine in or take out a few steps to the beach. Open daily 6:30am-latenight. MC/V. ❷

Zachary's, 30 Hastings St. (☎5447 3211; www.zacharys.org), Noosa Heads. Grab a gourmet pizza (from $16.50) and a pint, and watch the Hastings St. action from the balcony. Stay for the hip bar scene. Open daily noon-midnight. AmEx/DC/MC/V. ❸

Sails (☎5447 4235; www.sailsrestaurantnoosa.com), at the corner of Hastings St. and Park Rd., past the info center, on the beach. A great place to splurge. Candlelight, sexy music, and succulent seafood ($30-35) make for a blissful experience. Tables set for two, with the sound of waves in the background. Try the Moreton Bay Bug Tails, a local specialty ($35). Open daily 8am-10pm. AmEx/DC/MC/V. ❹

SIGHTS AND ACTIVITIES

NOOSA NATIONAL PARK. Just 1.4km from the city center, Noosa National Park covers over 400 hectares of rare and threatened vegetation and wildlife. Its highlights can all be observed on the five marked tracks which are ideal for walking or jogging and range from 1-7km in length. With 1.5 million visitors each year, the park is the second most-visited park in Queensland. A short walk east from the Noosa info booth on Hastings St. will land you at the entrance. Koalas are most often spotted on the Coastal Track towards Tea Tree Bay and the foreshore picnic area; daily koala sightings are posted at the ranger station at the entrance to the park, where you can also find maps of the tracks. Rangers urge walkers never to walk alone and to stay on frequented paths. The best walk is the **Coastal Track** (2.7km), which provides elevated views of the ocean and ends at the exhilarating **Hell's Gates.** Rather than return on the same path, jump on the **Tanglewood Track** (4.2km) to return to the park entrance. The **6.9km hike,** which is quite easy, takes 2-3hr. Many places to **surf** are available along the path; **Tea Tree Bay** and **Granite Bay** are popular among surfers and body boarders alike. A beautiful stretch of **beach** on the eastern side of the park at **Alexandria Bay** is accessible primarily from Sunshine Beach. Be aware that there are no lifeguards at Alexandria Bay, and the rip can be extremely strong. Take the **Alexandria Bay Track** from Parkedge Rd. (4.6km round-trip, 1-1½hr.) or from northern Sunshine Beach (2km, 30-40min. round-trip). Water and toilets are available, but camping is strictly prohibited. *(☎5447 3243; www.epa.qld.gov.au. Open daily 9am-3pm.)*

SURFING. Warm water, beautiful surroundings, and an active surfing community make the Sunshine Coast a great place to catch a wave. The most reliable breaks come in cyclone season (Dec.-Mar.). **First Point** is great for longboarders, while the western parts of Main Beach are suitable for beginners. Some of the best waves can be found at **National Park** and **Tea Tree,** where water breaks over granite into long lines and barrel sections. Unfortunately, this is no secret—in good conditions, both spots can be extremely crowded. To avoid the crowds, try **Double Island Point** to the north in Cooloola, but be wary of strong rips and bring a friend. Surfers are also spotted at Sunshine Beach and Alexandria Bay, but conditions are known to be erratic. Beginners should try **Learn to Surf** with world champion Merrick Davis; you're guaranteed to be standing on your board by the end of one lesson. *(☎0418 787 577; www.learntosurf.com.au. 2 classes per day. $55 per 2hr. includes wetsuit, board, and pickup and drop–off. Book ahead.)* **Wavesense Surfing Academy** has twice been voted best surf school in Australia. *(☎04 14 369 076. $55 per 2hr. Book through any hostel, $39.)* Board rentals are available at **Noosa Longboards,** 62 Hastings St., Noosa Heads. *(☎5447 2828; www.noosalongboards.com. Open daily 8am-5:30pm, later in summer. Body boards $15 per 4hr., $20 per day; shortboards $25/40; longboards $35/50. MC/V.)* **Go Ride A Wave,** Shop 3/77 Noosa Dr., also rents boards. *(☎1300 132 441; www.gorideawave.com.au. Open daily 9am-5:30pm. Surf boards $35; full-day $45; body boards $20/25.)*

OTHER ACTIVITIES. Kitesurf Australia will show you what happens when kite meets surfboard in this serious adrenaline sport. *(☎5455 6677; www.kite-surf.com.au. 2hr. lesson $140. MC/V.)* **Clip Clop Horse Treks** takes you on a riding tour through lakes and bush around Lake Weyba. *(☎5449 1254; www.clipcloptreeks.com.au. 2hr. $70, full-day $165. Book ahead. Cash only.)* **Aussie Sea Kayak Company** runs sea kayaking tours in the waterways around the Sunshine Coast, or longer tours up to the Whitsundays. *(☎5477 5335; www.ausseakayak.com.au. Daily 2hr. sunset champagne tour $45, ½-day $65.)* If you want to see the **Everglades** (the name given to the dark tranquil waters of the upper Noosa River), **Beyond Noosa** will take you on a BBQ lunch cruise or combine it with a 4WD tour through Cooloola National Park. *(☎1800 657 666; www.beyond-noosa.com. Tours M-F. Lunch cruise $74, children $45; combined $139/90. MC/V.)* If you *really* want to see the Everglades and appreciate the "river of mirrors," do a 2- or 3-day canoe safari with **Cooloola Canoe Safaris.** *(☎1800 763 077; www.cooloolacanoes.com.au. 2 nights $154, overnight $129; includes park fees.)* If you've always wanted to jump out of a plane, the Sunshine Coast is the place to do it. Several companies offer tandem dives with views of Brisbane and beach landings. With **Sunshine Coast Skydivers,** in Caloundra just south of Mooloolaba, you can jump from 12,000 or 14,000 ft. *(☎5437 0211; www.skydivingaustralia.com.au. 12,000 ft. $305; 14,000 ft. $335. Video $99, with digital photos $145.)* **Ramblers,** based in Coolum Beach, offers a package deal including video, photos, and t-shirt. *(☎1800 999 014; www.ramblers.com.au. 14,000 ft. $350. Video $99, with digital photos $143.)*

NIGHTLIFE

The Koala Bar, 44 Noosa Dr. (☎1800 357 457), located in the hostel. Overflows with drunken, sun-kissed backpackers. Pool tables, Happy hour (5-6pm and 8-9pm), DJs, and nightly specials. Evening ends abruptly at the stroke of midnight. W night live bands are extremely popular; M night pool competition, free beer pot for each ball sunk.

Rolling Rock, Upper Level, Bay Village on Hastings St. (☎5447 2255; www.rollingrock.com.au). The only nightclub serving a drop past midnight. Drinks $4 before 11pm. Cover F-Sa $8, free before 10pm. Open M-Th and Su 9pm-3am, F-Sa 8pm-3am. Closed in winter M-Tu. No entry after 1:30am. Cash only.

Flamingo Club, Bay Village, Hastings St. (☎ 5448 0588). Noosa's most exclusive lounge typically plays house music, but Th is 70s, 80s, 90s Remix, and F Hip-hop. Smoke-free. Dress code. Open W-Su 8pm-latenight.

The Reef Bar, (☎5447 4477; www.thereefhotel.com.au), near the crest of Noosa Dr. A hip, spacious lounge with beautiful ocean views upstairs and thumping dance area downstairs. Featuring W, F, Sa Top 40; Th cover band; and Su hip-hop. Lounge open M-Sa 10am-11pm; downstairs W-Su 9pm-3am.

RAINBOW BEACH ☎07

This small beach community featuring easy access to Cooloola National Park and Fraser Island, is rapidly becoming the coast's worst-kept secret. Known to some as "The Backpackers Shortcut to Fraser Island," Rainbow Beach has more to offer than budget island trips; just check out the slew of outdoor activities, pristine wilderness, and excellent hotels in a relaxed atmosphere.

TRANSPORTATION

There is no proper bus station in Rainbow Beach. **Greyhound Australia** (☎13 14 99; www.greyhound.com.au) and **Premier Motor Service** (☎13 34 10) both stop on Spectrum St., directly in front of the hostels. Greyhound has two buses daily that head north (12:30pm and 3:35pm) and two that go south (9:55am and 12:25pm). They also run to Brisbane (2 per day 10am and 12:25pm; $45, concessions $41). Premier has only one service in each direction (northbound 7pm; southbound 7:40am). Prices vary by distance, but Premier is significantly cheaper. If you are coming **by car** from Noosa, head towards Tewantin and Cooroy, at which point you will see signs to Bruce Hwy. The **Noosa Northshore Ferry** transports 4WD vehicles from Moorindal St. in Tewantin to the north shore of the Noosa River. (☎5447 1321. M-Th and Su 5:30am-10:30pm, F-Sa 5:30am-12:30am. $5 per vehicle each way. Cash only.) From the north shore, 4WD vehicles can cut across to the beach, which serves as the park's main thoroughfare. Check the tide tables to avoid getting stranded on the beach—or worse, swept out to sea.

Polleys Coaches (☎5482 9455; www.polleys.com.au.) travels to Tin Can Bay and Rainbow Beach from Gympie Return Services League (RSL) on Mary St. (M-F 1:20pm; returns from Rainbow Beach 7am; one-way $15, student $7.50; returns from Tin Can 8am, $11.70/5.85.) If you'd rather be your own guide, try **Safari 4WD** at the corner of Carlo and Karoonda Rd., Rainbow Beach (☎5486 8188; www.safari4wdhire.com.au). The company is run by locals who help tailor individual itineraries, do great sand-driving training, and even show you where you can go to camp with Aboriginals on the island. (Open 7am-5pm. 2- to 11-seaters available. Cars range from $90-170 per day.)

LOCAL LEGEND

THE COLOR OF LOVE

With around 70 different shades of colored sands, it may appear that weather patterns and erosion have cast a spell on Rainbow Beach. According to local Aboriginal legend, however, the brilliant hues actually come from a love story with a tragic ending.

The story has it that a beautiful maiden named Murrawar fell in love with the rainbow in the sky that visited her every evening. In a distant place lived an evil man named Burwilla, who possessed a boomerang that was bigger than the tallest tree and was filled with evil spirits. One day, Burwilla stole the young maiden as his slave, often beating her cruelly.

One day, while Burwilla sat admiring his deadly boomerang, Murrawar escaped. As she ran along the beach toward her home, she turned to see Burwilla's boomerang behind her quickly catching up. Terrified, she fell to the ground; too frightened to move, she called for help.

Suddenly, she heard a loud noise in the sky and saw her faithful rainbow racing toward her from across the sea. The wicked boomerang sliced the brave rainbow as they met with a thunderous roar. The rainbow's colors were shattered into the small grains of sand coloring the cliffs and beaches of the area, the remains of the rainbow that gave his life to protect his love.

There are several companies offering transport to Fraser Island by boat. **Fraser Explorer Barges** runs from Inskip Point (6km from Rainbow Beach) to Hook Point, the southern tip of the island. (☎1800 249 122. 10min., operates continuously 7am-5:30pm. No advanced bookings. Vehicles $75; walk-ons $5.) You can also try **Manta Ray Barge,** a privately-run vehicular ferry that also runs from Inskip Point to Hook Point on demand. (☎0418 872 599; www.fraserislandbarge.com.au. 10min.; operates continuously 6:30am-5:30pm. Ferry leaves about every 20min. Advance bookings possible but not required. Vehicles $75; no walk-ons. MC/V.)

PRACTICAL INFORMATION

The **Rainbow Beach Tourist Information Centre,** 8 Rainbow Rd., Rainbow Beach, has **maps** of the tiny town. (☎5486 3227. Open daily 7am-5pm.) There are **no banks** in Rainbow Beach, but look for an **ATM** at the **FoodWorks** supermarket and at the post office. While the town's three hostels all have **Internet** access, you can check your inbox for free at the **Rainbow Beach Library,** 38 Rainbow Rd. (☎5486 3705. Open M 9:30am-12:30pm, W and F 2-5pm, Sa 8:30am-11:30am. Book ahead.) For **camping** equipment, check out **Rainbow Beach Cooloola Hardware,** 38 Rainbow Beach Rd. (☎5486 3444. Open daily 8am-5pm. AmEx/DC/MC/V.) The closest **police** station is Tin Can Bay (☎5486 4125). For medical emergencies, contact the **Gympie Hospital** (☎5489 8444). There is a **Post office** at 6 Rainbow Rd. (☎13 13 18; Open M-F 8:30am-5pm and Sa 8:30am-noon.) **Postal Code:** 4581.

ACCOMMODATIONS

With about 95% of visitors in Rainbow Beach en route to or from Fraser Island, the town's three hostels make it a point to help you on your journey. All are a 5min. walk from the beach and the town center. Each has a deal that includes two nights accommodation, camping equipment ($10 extra for sleeping bag), island permits, ferry passes, maps, and a driving lesson. While prices appear to vary, the initial quotes include differing amounts of insurance, food, and fuel. When all the extras are factored in, each packages costs around $200. Book several days ahead.

The best of the hostels is **Dingo's Backpackers Resort ❷,** 3 Spectrum St., Rainbow Beach. The common room is perpetually crowded, making it a great place to meet fellow adventurers headed for Fraser Island; traveling groups often form at the hostel. The huge ensuite doubles are the same size as the dorm rooms. Internet access, laundry, kitchen, pool, bar, and restaurant available. Excellent free pancake breakfast. Tour agency and 4WD company attached. (☎1800 111 226. 7-bed ensuite dorms 1st night $20, 2nd night $18; doubles $60. VIP discount. MC/V.) **Fraser's on Rainbow Beach Backpackers ❷,** 18 Spectrum St., Rainbow Beach, has spacious ensuite rooms, a huge lounge, outdoor pool, game room, kitchen, laundry, and a bar with restaurant. (☎1800 100 170; www.frasersonrainbow.com. 6- to 8-bed dorms $22; doubles $63. Student and backpacker discount. MC/V.) **Pippies Beachhouse ❶** is on the corner of Spectrum St. and Cypress Ave., Rainbow Beach. Pippies has only seven rooms and is more low key than the other hostels. Amenities include shared facilities, Internet access, laundry, and kitchen. (☎1800 425 356; www.pippiesbeachhouse.com.au. 4- to 6-bed dorms $18; 4-bed family room $75. Student and backpacker discount $1. Cash only.)

Camping ❶ is permitted at a number of sites in Cooloola National Park, as well as along a 15km stretch on Teewah Beach. **Freshwater** campground, at the end of a 16km sand path accessible by 4WD via Rainbow Beach, is the only developed site in the park; it has drinking water, toilets, hot pay showers, and a phone. (☎13 13 04; www.qld.gov.au/camping. $4.50 per person per night. Book ahead.) The **Upper Noosa River** has 11 undeveloped campsites that are accessible by foot or canoe only. **Poverty Point,** accessible by 4WD, is undeveloped and beautiful. The **Cooloola Wilderness Trail**

has four campsites; three are accessible by foot, the other by 4WD. Site information is available at the unattended Kinaba Info Centre near Elanda Point.

FOOD

Restaurant options aren't plentiful in the tiny business center. Dingo's and Fraser's hostels have cheap nightly specials that keep their guests happy. **The Groovy Grape** ❶, 14 Rainbow Rd., (☎5486 3137), is extremely popular for its scrumptious Big Breakfast ($9.50) and delicious filled foccacias and turkish bread sandwiches. (Open daily 5:30am-5pm. Backpacker discount 10%. MC/V.) **Archie's** ❶, 12 Rainbow Rd., (☎5486 3277), offers excellent burgers ($6.60-7.60) and cheap daily specials. (Open daily 7am-8:30pm. MC/V.) There is also a **FoodWorks** supermarket, 4 Rainbow Rd. (☎5486 3629. Open daily 5am-7pm.)

SIGHTS AND ACTIVITIES

COOLOOLA NATIONAL PARK. Extending 50km north of Noosa up to Rainbow Beach is the sandy white coastline of Cooloola National Park. Together with Fraser Island, Cooloola forms the **Great Sandy Region,** the largest sand mass in the world. The rugged terrain and 4WD-accesible tracks make the park a great place to enjoy the pristine wilderness. There are no organized tours, and if you don't have your own 4WD vehicle, you will be limited to the spectacular **Carlo Sandblow** and **Coloured Sands.** Dingo's hostel runs a van to the area, but it is easily walkable. As you head out of town from Rainbow Beach Rd., turn left onto Double Island Dr. Then take a left onto Cooloola Dr. and follow it until the end. An easy 600m walk will bring you to the huge sand bowl of the Carlo Sandblow. Walk toward the ocean for spectacular views of the 200m cliffs and Coloured Sands. For serious bushwalkers, the Cooloola Wilderness Trail offers the ultimate challenge. The 47.9km trail (one-way) connects East Mullen Carpark in the north to Elanda Point in the south. Pick up an information sheet and inform rangers of your itinerary before you set out. Information and maps are available from a number of locations; try the Rainbow Beach Tourist Information Centre or the **Queensland Parks and Wildlife Service** in Rainbow Beach, on the right as you enter town (☎5486 3160; open daily 7am-4pm). For more info, **Cooloola Shire Council** on the corner of Duke and Channon St., Gympie (☎5481 0622; open M-F 8am-5pm) and **Great Sandy Information Centre,** at 240 Moorindil St. in Tewantin can be of assistance. (☎5449 7792. Open daily 7am-4pm.)

SURF, SCUBA, AND SKYDIVE. If bushwalking is not your cup of tea, there are plenty of other things to get excited about in Rainbow Beach. The **Rainbow Beach Surf School** will get you standing by the end of a 3hr. group lesson; you may even get to surf with dolphins. The same company also runs 3-5hr. sea kayaking trips to Double Island Point; they boast a 90% dolphin-sighting rate and good chances of seeing manta rays, turtles, and whales in season. (☎040 873 8192. Surf lesson $55; Sea Kayaking $65.) **Wolf Rock Dive Centre** will plunge you 40m underwater and through vertical gutters, exposing the prolific fish life and grey nurse sharks. (☎5486 8004; www.wolfrockdive.com.au. Introductory dive with gear $170; 2 certified dives with gear $170; 4-day dive certification course $500.) If flying through the air seems more appealing than swimming with sharks, **Skydive Rainbow Beach** (☎041 821 8358; www.skydiverainbowbeach.com) and **Rainbow Paragliding** (☎5486 3048; www.parglidingrainbow.com) both offer spectacular views of Cooloola National Park and Fraser Island. If you want enjoy a 30min. birds-eye view while hang gliding, call James for a tandem jump. (☎0408 863 706.) **Surf & Sand Safaris** offers a tour which includes 4WD on the beach and through the national park, a short boat cruise, a boomnet ride, dolphin and whale watching (in season), and some surfing. (☎5486 3131; www.surfandsandsafaris.com. $80.)

SUNSHINE COAST HINTERLAND

Just inland of the Sunshine Coast lies a smorgasbord of tourist delights: stunning national parks, roadside crafts markets, and kitschy but fun tourist traps. Most of the hinterland is inaccessible by public transportation and is best experienced by car. Several tour operators run trips to the region, but most involve more driving than hiking. **Noosa Hinterland Tours** offers several options, such as a tour of Montville, the Blackall Range, and the Glasshouse Mountains, and an "attractions trip," which includes the ginger factory, the Australia Zoo and UnderWater World, and a morning trip to the Eumundi Markets. (☎5446 3111; www.noosahinterlandtours.com.au. Montville-Glasshouse $62, children $35, seniors $58. Attractions $40/25/38 and discounted entry. Markets $15, children $10. $3 market discounts at select hostels. Cash only.) **Storeyline Tours** covers the same activities as Noosa Hinterland Tours. (☎5474 1500; www.storeylinetours.com.au. Montville-Glasshouse $74, children $39, concessions $70. Attractions not including entry $56/31/54. Markets with pickup and drop-off at Noosa accommodation $15, children $10. AmEx/MC/V.) **Off Beat Rainforest Tours,** 1hr. from Noosa., has exclusive access to Conondale National Park's famously pristine rainforest. (☎5473 5135; www.offbeattours.com.au. Includes gourmet lunch. $135, children $85. MC/V.)

EUMUNDI MARKETS. Every Saturday and Wednesday the sleepy town of Eumundi comes to life, with more than 500 shops offering everything from local desserts to camel rides. Nearly everything is handmade, and the markets are a perfect place to buy presents for those back home. Get there early for the good stuff. The Markets are 20km southwest of Noosa Heads, via Noosaville and Doonan. Blue Sunbus #630 leaves W at 7:25am (25min.), and Bus #631 leaves at 8:45am (25-35min.); Bus #631 leaves Sa at 8 and 8:45am (40min.). Buses leave from the bus interchange on Noosa Pde. For those driving, parking is scarce; try the dirt lots downhill from the market. For more info, contact the Eumundi Historical Association. *(☎5442 7106; www.eumundimarkets.com.au. Open W 8am-1:30pm, Sa 6:30am-2pm.)*

YANDINA. In the town of Yandina, about a 10min. ride south of Eumundi, **The Ginger Factory,** 50 Pioneer Rd., churns out the zest on your sushi and the bite in your ale. It is the largest ginger-processing plant in the Southern Hemisphere. (90min. north of Brisbane on Hwy. 1. Take bus #630. ☎1800 067 686; www.gingerfactory.com.au. Open daily 9am-5pm. Free entry. Walking tour with tasting $10.95, students $9.50, children $7. AmEx/DC/MC/V.) Across the street, **Nutworks** has free samples of its many macadamia nut flavors alongside nut processing displays. (☎5446 3498; www.nutworks.com.au. Open daily 9am-5pm. Free.) On the Nambour Connection Rd., off the Bruce Hwy., it's easy to spot **The Big Pineapple,** a working fruit and macadamia nut plantation. Entry is free but tours are not; among the best is the pineapple train ($11.50, children $9.50, concessions $10.50), which explains the workings of the farm and animal nursery. The cafe makes excellent parfaits ($8.50) big enough for two. (☎5442 1333. From Maroochydore, take bus #610 to Nambour. Open daily 9am-5pm. Free. Access to all tours $26.50, concessions $22.50, children $20.50.)

MONTVILLE AND BLACKALL RANGE. The sheer Blackall Range escarpment rises from the plains, cradling green pastures, rainforests, and the old country villages of Mapleton, Flaxton, Montville, and Maleny. Before you reach Mapleton, take a left at the **Lookout** sign to take in the expansive view. Of the four towns, Montville has the most to offer tourists, with several blocks of antique and crafts shops, galleries, teahouses, and a cuckoo clock shop. From Noosa, follow the Bruce Hwy. south to Nambour and then turn toward the Blackall Range via Mapleton. The **information center** is on Main St., Montville, beyond most of the shops. (☎5478 5544; www.maroochytourism.com. Open daily 10am-4pm.)

GLASS HOUSE MOUNTAINS. Glass House Mountains National Park protects nine of the 16 distinctive peaks which puncture the otherwise flat surrounds. Most of the tracks are recommended for experienced climbers only, although there are a small number of easy- to medium-grade short hikes. Many of the rockier spires, like sharp Mount Coonowrin, are closed to the public. Coonowrin's beauty can be appreciated from an easy hike (20min. round-trip) to **Mountain View Lookout,** located in the Mount Tibrogargan Section just past the designated carpark. A more dramatic view can be seen from the **Glass House Mountain Lookout** off Old Gympie Rd. For those with limited experience but ample physical fitness, the best option is Mount Ngungun. The 1.4km round-trip path is shorter than the others, and the terrain is manageable. Nonetheless, the track shouldn't be attempted in wet weather. Some very good rock climbing can be found on Mt. Tibrogargan and Mt. Ngungun, but it is unsupervised and you must bring your own equipment. In case of emergency, contact the ranger at ☎5494 0150. **Camping** ❶ is permitted only on undeveloped sites in Coochin Creek, 9km east of Beerwah. (☎13 13 04; www.qld.gov.au/camping. $4.50 per person. Book ahead.) Bring your own car or join a tour group; signs on the Glass Mountain Tourist Rd. direct travelers to all sites. From the south, look for signs off the Bruce Hwy. just past Caboolture. From the north, exit the Bruce Hwy. at Landsborough. On your way in, stop by **Big Kart Track,** Australia's largest commercial go-kart track, or the gravity-defying **Bungy Bullet,** which rockets you up 150 ft. in only one second. (☎5494 1613; www.bigkart.com.au. Go-karts $25 per 15min., $40 per 30min., $60 per hr. Bungy Bullet $25.)

HERVEY BAY ☎07

The humpback whale's annual migration through Hervey Bay (pop. 48,000), plus the town's proximity to Fraser Island, have put it firmly on the tourist path. With booking agencies, tour companies, and 4WD rental shops jostling for travelers' attention, Hervey Bay is a jumping-off point for activity.

TRANSPORTATION

Trains: Trainlink bus connects Hervey Bay to **Maryborough West,** the train station off Biggenden Rd. (bus leaves from Hervey Bay Coach Terminal 1hr. before trains depart Maryborough West; $9.90, students $5.50). The **Tilt Train** (☎13 22 32) runs from Maryborough to: **Brisbane** (3½-4hr.; M-F 2 per day, Sa-Su 1 per day; $55, ISIC $27.50); **Bundaberg** (1hr.; M-F and Su 2 per day; $24.20/12.10); **Rockhampton** (5hr.; M-F and Su 2 per day; $66/33).

Buses: Hervey Bay Coach Terminal (☎4124 4000), in Centro shopping center on Boat Harbour Dr., Pialba. Open M-F 6am-5:30pm, Sa 6am-1pm. Lockers $5 per day. **Premier Motor Service** (☎13 34 10) runs 1 northbound bus (8:50pm) and 1 southbound bus (5:55am) per day, while **Greyhound Australia** (☎13 14 99; www.greyhound.com.au) has consistent service at a higher price. **Premier** runs to: **Airlie Beach** (12¼hr.; $100, concessions $90); **Brisbane** (6½hr., $36/32); **Bundaberg** (2¼hr., $14/13); **Cairns** (22½hr., $183/165); **Mackay** (10½hr., $85/77); **Maroochydore** (5hr., $23/21); **Noosa Heads** (4¼hr., $21/19); **Rockhampton** (5¾hr., $47/42). **Wide Bay Transit** (☎4121 3719; www.widebaytransit.com.au) offers limited service. Route #5 connects Hervey Bay to **Maryborough.** Route #14 goes to **Pt. Vernon.** Routes #5, 16, and 18 connect Torquay and the Marina.

Taxis: Hervey Bay Taxi (24hr. ☎13 10 08).

Bike Rental: Bay Bicycle Hire (☎04 1764 4814) offers free delivery and pickup. ½-day $15, full day $20. Tandem bikes $30/40. Open daily 7am-5pm.

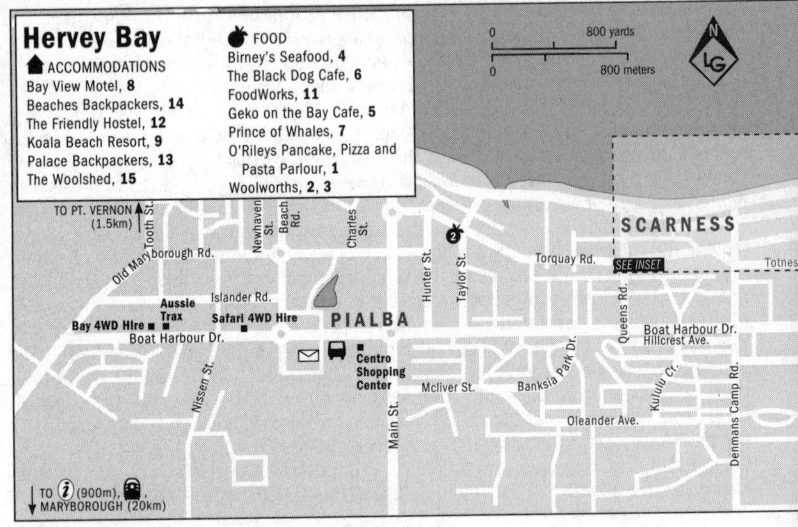

ORIENTATION AND PRACTICAL INFORMATION

Hervey Bay consists of a cluster of suburbs facing north toward the Bay. From west to east, the suburbs are: **Pialba, Port Vernon, Scarness, Torquay,** and **Urangan.** Most action occurs along **The Esplanade** at the water's edge between Scarness and Urangan, which is lined with takeaway shops and tour booking agencies. The harbor and marina are behind Buccaneer Dr. at the eastern end of town.

Tourist Office: The only official tourism bureau is the **Hervey Bay Visitor Information Centre** (☎1800 811 728; www.herveybay.qld.gov.au), located at the corner of Hervey Bay-Maryborough and Urraween Rd., about 5.5km from the Central Business District (CBD). Open daily 9am-5pm. There are also several booking agents on The Esplanade.

Currency Exchange: Banks and 24hr. **ATMs** are located at the Hervey Bay Bus Terminal and on The Esplanade in Torquay. **WestPac** and **National Bank,** 414 and 415 The Esplanade, have **ATMs.** Open M-Th 8:30am-4pm, F 8:30am-5pm.

Police: ☎4123 8111; emergency ☎000. On the corner of Queens and Torquay Rd.

Pharmacy: Beachside Pharmacy, 347 The Esplanade (☎4128 1680), Scarness. Open M-F 8am-6pm, Sa-Su 8:30am-1pm.

Internet Access: At several tourist offices on The Esplanade. Also at **The Adventure Travel Centre,** inside the Koala Beach Resort ($4 per hr., guests $3). Open 7am-10pm.

Post Office: 414 The Esplanade (☎13 13 18), Torquay. Open M-F 8am-5:30pm. There is also an office at **Centro** shopping center in Pialba, across from the bus terminal in Pialba. Open M-F 8:30am-5pm, Sa 8:30-noon. **Postal Code:** 4655.

ACCOMMODATIONS

No matter where you stay in Hervey Bay, you can be fairly confident that the reception will be able to assist you in booking any and all tours. Some hostels have their own 4WD rental company, and nearly all match guests into groups before departing for Fraser Island. In addition, most hostels have a $10 key deposit, laundry facilities, BBQ, courtesy bus, Internet access, and communal kitchens.

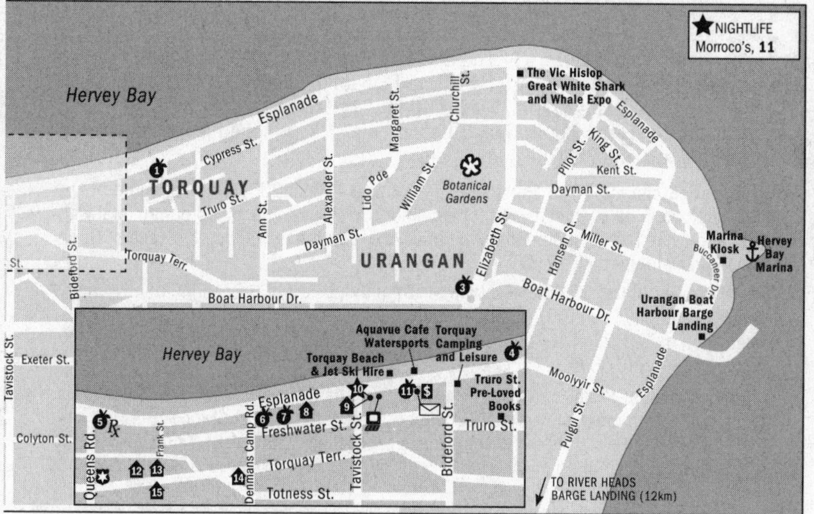

The Friendly Hostel, 182 Torquay Rd., Scarness (☎1800 244 107; www.thefriendly.com.au). Incredibly flexible owners will make sure that this place suits your needs. Apartment-style setup with impressively clean rooms and gorgeous kitchens. Each unit has TV, DVD, games, and books. Free bike rental and Internet access. Reception 6am-8pm. Check-in 24hr. 3-bed dorms $20; doubles and twins $46. MC/V. ❷

Palace Backpackers, 184 Torquay Rd., Scarness. (☎1800 063 168; www.palacebackpackers.com.au). 5min. walk from the beach and The Esplanade. This hostel lives up to its name. With most self-contained units consisting of a common room, kitchen, 2 bathrooms, a double, and 4 small dorms, these social apartments are a great way to make new friends before heading to Fraser in one of their 4WD vehicles. If there's space, they'll allow you to go the morning you arrive. Swimming pool. 3- to 6-bed dorms $19; twins and doubles $44. VIP discount $1. MC/V. ❷

Beaches Backpackers, 195 Torquay Rd., Scarness (☎1800 655 501; www.beaches.com.au). Great 4-bed dorms, a lively bar and bistro, and spectacular packages which include trips to Fraser and the Whitsundays. Exclusive access to base camp at Cathedral Beach, which includes perks like hot showers and sheltered areas. 4- to 14-bed dorms $22; twins and doubles $55; ensuite $60. AmEx/MC/V. ❷

The Woolshed Backpackers, 181 Torquay Rd., Scarness (☎4124 0677; www.woolshedbackpackers.com). 5min. from the beach and The Esplanade. Small, homey hostel surrounded by tropical gardens and mini-waterfalls. Clean co-ed bathrooms. Reception 7am-7pm. 3- to 6-bed dorms $18-20; twins and doubles $44; ensuite $60. MC/V. Credit card fee 4.5%. ❷

Koala Beach Resort, 410 The Esplanade (☎1800 354 535; www.koala-backpackers.com). Party hostel in Hervey Bay. Dorms aren't the best in town but the great location and thumping **Morocco's** nightclub (attached) mean that you spend little time in your room. Swimming pool in jungle-themed atmosphere. In-house 4WD tour agency. Linen $1.50. Reception 7am-10pm. Check-in available at Morocco's until 3am. 4- to 6-bed dorms $22, ensuite $25; doubles and twins $55/67. VIP. AmEx/DC/MC/V. ❷

FOOD AND NIGHTLIFE

For groceries, try **FoodWorks,** 414 The Esplanade (☎4125 2477; open 6am-11pm) or **Woolworths,** on the corner of Torquay Rd. and Taylor St., Pialba. (☎4128 3188. Open M-F 8am-9pm, Sa 8am-5:30pm, Su 9am-6pm.) Hostel bars dominate the backpacker nightlife scene; Koala Beach Resort, with the attached **Morocco's,** is the most legitimate nightclub (open until 3am).

Birney's Seafood, 426 The Esplanade, Torquay (☎4125 2205). Offering some of the best seafood in all of Queensland for incredibly low prices. The grilled barramundi with fries and salad ($8) might be the most pricey item on the menu, but it is superb. Open daily 10:30am-8pm. MC/V. ❶

The Black Dog Cafe, 381 The Esplanade, Torquay (☎4124 3177). This trendy eatery serves sushi rolls ($5-6.50) and outstanding teriyaki burgers ($9.50) in a relaxed setting. Open daily 10am-3pm and 4:30pm-latenight; kitchen closes at 9:30pm. YHA/VIP discount 10%. MC/V. ❷

O'Rileys Pancake, Pizza, and Pasta Parlour, 446 The Esplanade (☎4125 3100). This family-owned restaurant serves some of the best pizza on the coast (2 for $16-22), excellent pastas ($9.50-14), and creative pancake concoctions ($6.50-10). Don't miss the Tu all-you-can-eat pizza and pancake buffet from 5-9pm ($15). Open Tu 5:30pm-latenight,

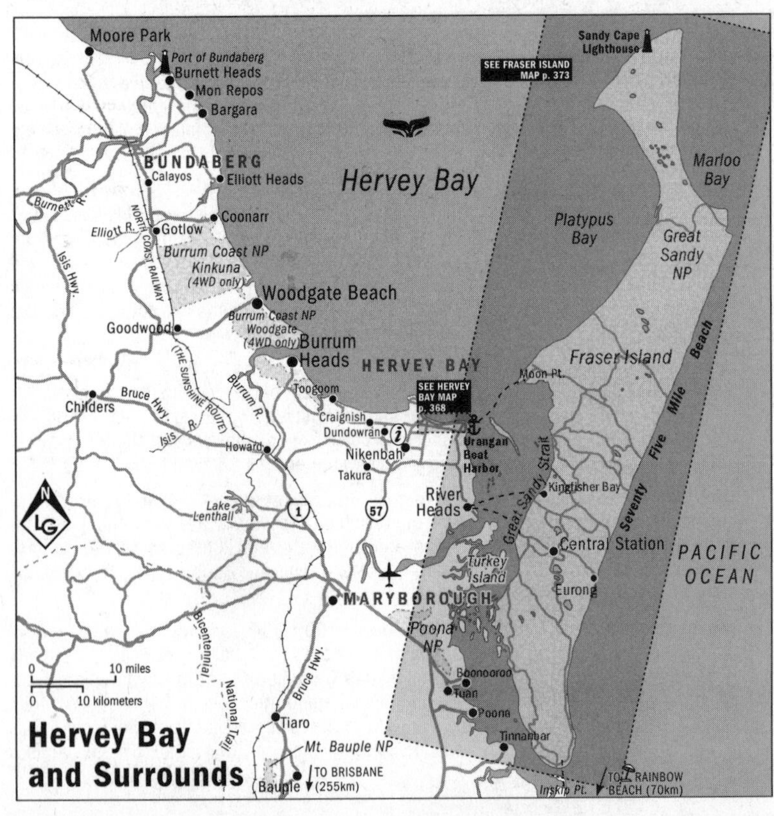

Hervey Bay and Surrounds

W-Sa 11:30am-2pm and 5:30pm-latenight, Su 7:30-11am, 11:30-2pm, and 5:30pm-latenight. AmEx/DC/MC/V. ❷

Geko on the Bay Cafe, 363 The Esplanade, Scarness (☎4128 1338; www.geko-cafe.com.au). Inexpensive, all-day breakfast and gourmet burgers and fries ($10) make this a popular lunch spot. Open W-Su 7:30am-3:30pm. MC/V. ❷

Prince of Whales, 383 The Esplanade, Torquay (☎4124 2466). A traditional English pub covered in British paraphernalia. Serves classics like Ye Olde Steak, Kidney, and Guinness Pie ($15.95). Open daily 4pm-latenight; food served 6-9pm. AmEx/MC/V. ❸

ACTIVITIES

WHALE WATCHING. As Australia's premier whale watching destination, Hervey Bay is filled from late July to early November with whale aficionados. It's the only place in Australia where all boats guarantee sightings during the season (or your next trip is free). Eleven boats operate during high season, all out of the Hervey Bay Marina in Urangan—pick up an info sheet from the **Marina Kiosk** on Buccaneer Dr. (☎4128 9800. Open 7:30am-6pm.) The flagship vessel is the **Spirit of Hervey Bay,** built for whale watching and underwater viewing; it even has a whale-listening hydrophone. (☎1800 642 544. 4hr. cruise departs 8:30am and 1:30pm. $99, concessions $89, children $55. MC/V.) **Quick Catt II** offers a half-day, small-boat experience. (☎1800 671 977; www.herveybaywhalewatchers.com.au. Departs daily 8am and 1pm. $89/85/55.) If the whale season (July-Nov.) has passed, **Whale Song** guarantees dolphin sightings instead. (☎1800 689 610; www.whalesong.com.au. ½-day whale watching daily 7:30am and 1pm. $99/89/55. Dolphin watching during non-whale season daily 9am-2:30pm. $70/45/60. MC/V.) The return of the humpback whales is celebrated annually in early August with the **Hervey Bay Whale Festival,** (☎4125 9855; www.herveybay-whalefestival.com.au) which consists of various events and parades.

OTHER ACTIVITIES. Aquavue Cafe Watersports, across from the post office and National Bank on The Esplanade, rents out equipment for a wide variety of beach activities. (☎4125 5528. Jet ski rental $40 per 15min. 2½hr. guided tour for 1 or 2 to Fraser Island $275. Open daily 7am-5pm. MC/V.) **Hervey Bay Skydivers,** at the Hervey Bay airport, includes a scenic flight over Fraser Island. (☎4183 0119; www.hervey-bayskydivers.com.au. 10,000 ft. $250; 14,000 ft. $270. DVD $99, DVD and photos $120. Beach landing extra $30; $25 levy applied on day of jump.) If 4WD on the island isn't exciting enough, try some acrobatic adventure flights over the island with **Hervey Bay Air Adventures.** (☎4124 9313; www.airadventures.com.au. Stunt planes seat only 1 passenger $130 per 20min. Peaceful scenic flights for 3 $140-440.) **Shayla Sailing Cruises** (☎4125 3727; www.shaylacruises.com.au) will take you on a 4hr. adventure sail ($55) or the 1½hr. romantic champagne sunset cruise ($45). If you want to catch some fish, **Hervey Bay M.V. Daytripper** can help you do so. (☎0401 804 205; www.mvdaytripper.com. 9am-2pm; $59. Min. 5 people. Cash only.). **The Vic Hislop Great White Shark & Whale Expo,** 553 The Esplanade, Urangan, is a small museum with films, articles, and displays about a living shark-hunter, Vic Hislop, who is on a mission to inform the world of the dangers of the Great White. (☎4128 9137. Open daily in summer 8:30am-6pm; in winter until 5:30pm. $15, concessions $12, $7 children. MC/V.)

FRASER ISLAND ☎07

Fraser Island, the world's largest sand island, and is the only place on the planet where rainforest grows directly out of the sand. It is a World Heritage national park that attracts nearly every traveler who passes along the East Coast. With absolutely stunning freshwater lakes dotting the 120km by 15km island, there is good reason for *Forbes Magazine* to name Fraser as one of the 2005 World's Top Five Sexiest

Islands. An ideal destination for bushwalkers, fishing aficionados, and 4WDers, Fraser is fun for the less experienced as well. However, swimming is limited to its beautiful lakes, as tiger sharks and strong currents are commonly found in the waters surrounding the island. The winds perpetually resculpt the topography, but Fraser's unique natural beauty is forever constant.

TRANSPORTATION

BY BOAT

Ferries run to Fraser from several locations and are all owned by the same company. (Round-trip: walk-on $22, vehicles with 4 people $130, extra passenger $9.)

Fraser Dawn Barges (☎1800 072 555) departs Urangan Harbor for Moon Pt. 55min., daily 8:30am and 3:30pm, returns 9:30am and 4:30pm. More services high season.

Fraser Venture Barges (☎1800 072 555) departs from Riverheads (20min. south of Hervey Bay) and arrives at Wanggoolba Creek. Ideal for independent travelers, given proximity to great tracks. 30min.; daily 9, 10:15am, and 3:30pm, Sa also 7am. Returns daily 9:30am, 2:30, and 4pm, Sa also 7:30am.

Kingfisher Barges (☎1800 072 555) leaves from Riverheads. Arrives at the Kingfisher Bay Resort. 45min., daily 7:15, 11am and 2:30pm, returns 8:30am, 1:30, and 4pm.

Kingfisher Fast Cat Passenger Ferry (☎1800 072 555), brings passengers from Urangan Harbor to Kingfisher Bay Resort and best walking tracks. 30min.; daily 6:45, 8:45am, noon, 4, 7, and 10pm. Returns daily 7:40, 10:30am, 2, 5, 8, 11:30pm. $50, children $25.

BY PLANE

Air Fraser Island (☎4125 3600; www.airfraserisland.com.au) sells one-way ($70) and round-trip tickets ($140). Also offer overnight trip (includes flight, 4WD, and camping equipment) $270. Scenic 30min. flights for 2-4 over island $70 per person. MC/V.

BY GUIDED TOUR

Tours provide a structured, safe, and hassle-free way to see the island, though you'll have to forgo some freedom. Some buses seat 40 people, all of whom must shuffle in and out at each stop before continuing on to the next. Be sure to inquire about group size, accommodations, and meals before booking your tour so you know exactly what you're paying for. Tour options are plentiful and varied; two- or three-day tours are the best way to get a feel for the island. Most tour groups are not subjected to the difficulties of serious camping or outdoor cooking, and instead sleep in cabins and eat prepared meals. While taking a tour can cost $100 more per person than an independent visit, once you've factored in food, permits, petrol, and stress for a self-drive tour, there is no significant price difference. All hostels and 4WD companies can also organize guided tours.

Fraser Explorer Tours (☎1800 072 555; www.fraser-is.com). Their daytrips and 2- to 3-day safaris attract a younger set. Accommodation in 4-person rooms at Eurong Beach Resort (p. 374). Day tour $135, children $75; 2-day safari $249-299; 3-day safari $349-399. MC/V.

Sand Island Safaris (☎1800 246 911 or 4124 6911; www.sandislandsafaris.com.au). Runs comprehensive 3 day tours for max. 16 people. Overnight accommodations at Eurong Beach Resort (p. 374). Departure dates vary. Shared rooms for 4 $315; twins and doubles $348. VIP/YHA/ISIC.

Cooldingo Tours (☎1800 072 555; www.cooldingotour.com). Housing at the spacious and beautiful Wilderness Lodge. 4WD bus holds up to 40. Ages 18-35 only. 2-day stay in 4-person rooms $279-329; 3-day $349-399. MC/V.

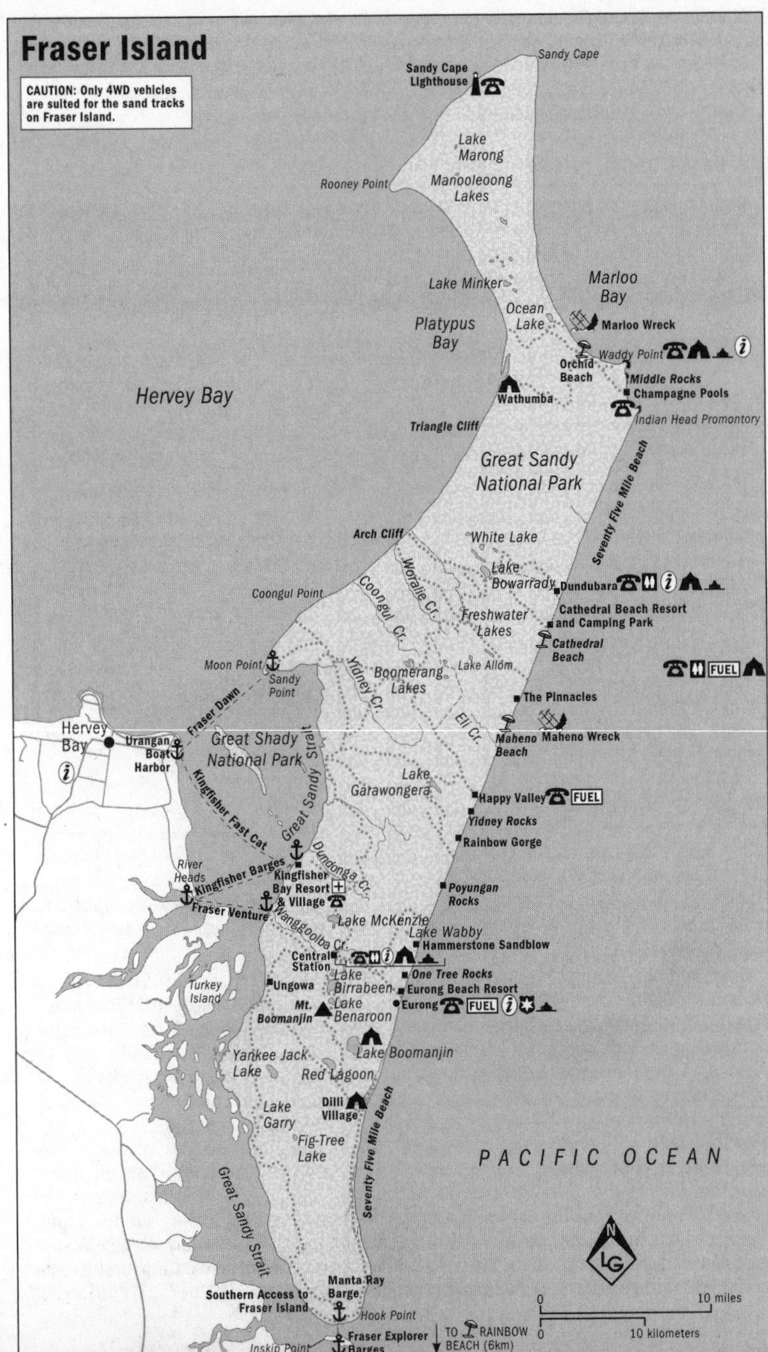
Fraser Island
CAUTION: Only 4WD vehicles are suited for the sand tracks on Fraser Island.
Sandy Cape
Sandy Cape Lighthouse
Lake Marong
Manooleoong Lakes
Rooney Point
Lake Minker
Marloo Bay
Ocean Lake
Platypus Bay
Marloo Wreck
Waddy Point
Orchid Beach
Middle Rocks
Champagne Pools
Hervey Bay
Wathumba
Indian Head Promontory
Triangle Cliff
Great Sandy National Park
Seventy Five Mile Beach
Arch Cliff
White Lake
Lake Bowarrady
Dundubara
Coongul Point
Coongul Cr.
Woralie Cr.
Cathedral Beach Resort and Camping Park
Freshwater Lakes
Cathedral Beach
FUEL
Moon Point
Sandy Point
Boomerang Lakes
Lake Allom
Yidney Cr.
The Pinnacles
Fraser Dawn
Eli Cr.
Hervey Bay
Urangan Boat Harbor
Great Shady National Park
Great Sandy Strait
Maheno Beach
Maheno Wreck
Lake Garawongera
Kingfisher Fast Cat
Happy Valley
FUEL
Yidney Rocks
Rainbow Gorge
Dundonga Cr.
River Heads
Kingfisher Barges
Kingfisher Bay Resort & Village
Poyungan Rocks
Fraser Venture
Wanggoolba Cr.
Lake McKenzie
Lake Wabby
Hammerstone Sandblow
Central Station
One Tree Rocks
Turkey Island
Ungowa
Lake Birrabeen
Eurong Beach Resort
Mt. Boomanjin
Lake Benaroon
Eurong
FUEL
Yankee Jack Lake
Lake Boomanjin
Red Lagoon
Dilli Village
Lake Garry
Fig-Tree Lake
Seventy Five Mile Beach
PACIFIC OCEAN
Great Sandy Strait
N
LG
Manta Ray Barge
Southern Access to Fraser Island
Hook Point
0
10 miles
0
10 kilometers
Fraser Explorer Barges
TO RAINBOW BEACH (6km)
Inskip Point

The Fraser Island Company (☎1800 063 933; www.fraserislandco.com.au). The 1-day safari is well-structured ($135, children $79). Exclusive 1-day tour, with luxury meals and a plush 16-passenger van ($169, children 119). There are 2 different, 2-day safaris ($249/199). The 3-day camping adventure sleeps at incredibly luxurious tents at Cathedral Beach ($399/299). Leaves Tu, F, Su. AmEx/DC/MC/V.

PRACTICAL INFORMATION

Permits: If you're traveling by car, you'll need a **vehicle permit** ($34.40; includes map and island details). Vehicle and camping permits are available from several places, including **Riverheads Information Kiosk,** which is at the carpark at the barge landing, the Queensland Parks and Wildlife Service in Rainbow Beach (☎5486 3160. Open daily 7am-4pm), and the **Marina Kiosk,** on Buccaneer Dr., Urangan, at the harbor. (☎4128 9800. Open daily 7:30am-6pm.)

General Supplies: Stock up at **Eurong Beach Resort** (☎4194 9122; open daily 8am-5:30pm), **Fraser Island Wilderness Retreat** at Happy Valley (☎4125 2343; open daily 8am-6pm), **Kingfisher Bay Resort & Village** (☎1800 072 555; open daily 7:30am-6:30pm), **Frasers at Cathedral Beach Resort** (☎4125 2343; open daily 8am-5pm), or Rainbow Beach's **Fraser Island Bed & Breakfast** (☎4127 9127; open daily 8am-5pm).

Telephones: Central Station, Dundubara, Waddy Point, Indian Head, Yidney Rocks, and all of the above resorts.

Showers: There are cold showers at most campgrounds. Coin-operated hot showers are at Central Station, Waddy Point, and Dundubara. ($1 per 3min.; $1 coins only.)

Emergency: ☎000, cell phones ☎112. Limited medical assistance on the island; stand-by nurse at the Kingfisher Bay Resort & Village (☎1800 072 555).

Taxis: ☎4127 9188 (Eurong)

Tow Truck: ☎4127 9449 (Eurong)

Ranger Stations: Eurong (☎4127 9128), the main station, is generally open 7am-4pm. Branches are found in Central Station (☎4127 9191), Dundubara (☎4127 9138), and Waddy Point (☎4127 9190), but these are only open 8-9am and 3-4pm.

ACCOMMODATIONS AND CAMPING

Eurong Beach Resort ❺ will make sure that you sleep comfortably in their expensive motel units and luxury apartments. (☎4127 9122; www.fraser-is.com. Motel doubles $130; apartments for up to 6 $180, high season $270. MC/V.) **Yidney Rocks ❷** has family holiday units that sleep up to eight. (☎4127 9167; www.yidneyrocks.fi25.com. $180, high season $200.)

Camping ❶ is cheap and convenient and enables visitors to see different parts of the island without returning to the same location each night. There are three main QPWS camping areas, and camping is also allowed on designated beaches, including most of **Eastern Beach.** Pay close attention to the signs that designate camping areas, as camping outside of these areas will result in a fine. **Camping permits** ($4.50 per person) are good for all campgrounds except the privately run Cathedral Beach Resort and Dilli Village, both on the east shore. Some sites require pre-booking (☎13 13 04; www.qld.gov.au/camping), and independent travelers are encouraged to book ahead. Each permit comes with a packet identifying camping areas; all developed campgrounds have 9pm noise curfews. Most campgrounds have taps and toilets and only some have hot showers, BBQs, dingo fences, and picnic tables. Fires are not allowed, except for at Dundabara and Waddy Point. Only milled timber from the mainland can be used to build fires. **Cathedral Beach Resort and Camping Park ❷** has camp sites and cabins. (☎4127 9177. Unpowered sites for 2 $28, low season $20. Powered sites for 2 $38/30. Cabins for up to 6 $150/195. 4-person ensuite cabins $155-189.)

SIGHTS AND HIKING

INLAND. With unbelievably clear waters and white sandy bottoms, Fraser's freshwater lakes are one of its biggest draws. **Lake McKenzie** is the most popular, with two white sand beaches for bathers and water in three shades of gorgeous blue. **Lake Wabby** is at the eastern base of the steep **Hammerstone Sandblow,** which is gradually swallowing the lake and the surrounding forest. Some visitors run down the dune into the lake, but injuries and fatalities have occurred, so be careful. To get to Lake Wabby, follow the 1.4km track from the inland carpark via the massive sand dune (30min. walk one-way), or take the 5.5km round-trip circuit from the eastern beach (45min. one-way). Walking across the dunes is like crossing a desert; in fact, Fraser Island is alleged to contain more sand than the Sahara Desert.

The southernmost lake, **Lake Boomanjin,** is a wonderful place to take a dip in its gleaming white sands and honey-colored water. It also claims that title of "world's largest perched lake." North of Boomanjin is a series of lakes, but **Lake Birabeen** is by far the most impressive—think Lake McKenzie minus the crowds. There are also a number of freshwater creeks good for wading; among them **Eli Creek** and **Wyuna Creek.** Be sure not to miss the crystal-clear waters of **Wanggoolba Creek**. As tempted as you may be, fines are handed down for those wading in the creek.

D-I-N-G-O. Don't confuse the **dingoes** roaming Fraser Island with domesticated dogs; keep your distance, and never feed or pet them. By feeding the dingoes, visitors to Fraser have made them more aggressive and less fearful of humans. Now, dingoes routinely steal food from campsites; attacks on children have occurred in recent years. If you do happen upon a dingo, don't run; pick up some sand or an object and throw it near its front paws while yelling. At the same time, cross your arms over your chest and walk slowly backward, maintaining steady eye contact with the dog.

EASTERN BEACH. There is a lot of beach on Fraser Island, and most of it looks the same, bordered by raging surf and low-lying trees. Eastern Beach is perfect for 4WDing, but be careful (see **Driving on Fraser,** p. 376). The drive from Hook Point north to Indian Head takes a good 2hr. on a registered Queensland highway. Do not even consider swimming in the ocean, as tiger sharks and riptides are real dangers. Heading north from Eurong, patches of rocks decorate the beach, with short bypasses at **Poyungan Rocks, Yidney Rocks,** and a longer route around the **Indian Head** promontory, where one can spot dolphins, sharks, rays, and whales (on calm days, late July to early Nov.). Near the top of passable beachland on **Middle Rocks,** a collection of shallow tide pools called the **Champagne Pools** make good swimming holes at low tide. Be careful at the pools, as the rocks are slippery and incoming waves can cause serious injury. Other attractions along the beach are **Rainbow Gorge,** the **Pinnacles,** and the **Cathedrals**—all impressive demonstrations of colored sand formations—and the **Maheno shipwreck,** the remains of a massive cruise liner that washed ashore in a 1935 winter cyclone. Do not walk on the shipwreck; you are likely get tetanus from the rust, in addition to a hefty fine.

HIKING. Hiking tracks traverse the interior of Fraser, connecting to lakes that are inaccessible by 4WD. Walking is the only safe way to access **Western Beach,** which is filled with mangroves and mud flats. Be sure to wear insect repellent; this strip of sand has high concentrations of sandflies. Do not swim in the ocean; tiger sharks are plentiful. Consider exploring the small corner of the island near Central Station, like **Lake McKenzie** or **Lake Wabby,** before attempting a more ambitious itinerary off the beaten track. **The Great Walk,** which covers over 100km of tracks, contains four sections with several walking-only campsites. It includes short walks, full-day hikes, and overnight treks; it is highly recommended that those attempting the entire walk carry the *Fraser Island Great Walk* topographic map, available from the Naturally Queensland Information Centre in Brisbane. (☎3227 8185; www.epa.qld.gov.au/greatwalk. Open M-F 8:30am-5pm.)

 DRIVING ON FRASER

Driving on Fraser is only possible in a 4WD vehicle. Rental agencies will brief you on island regulations and suggestions for safe travel—it's an insurance precaution for them, but listen up unless you enjoy being fined or pushing trucks through knee-deep sand. Speed limits are established on the island: 80kph on the Eastern Beach and 35kph on inland roads, though 60kph and 20kph, respectively, are recommended. Getting stuck happens often; have shovels handy. Allow at least 30min. to travel 10km on inland roads. The beaches themselves are registered national highways—all normal traffic rules apply, and breathalyzer- and speedgun-wielding police regularly patrol. Larger vehicles—buses in particular—will occasionally stay on the right. If you want to pass, do so with caution. On the beach, keep to hard, wet

> **CRASH COURSE: BEACH DRIVING.** Although beach driving is a lot of fun, reckless driving can lead to disaster. The most serious danger is **creek cuts** in the beach; test the depth of a creek before attempting to cross. Do not cross if the water is higher than your knees; instead, wait for the tide to go down. Hitting washouts at high speed risks the vehicle rolling; it also can break the springs or cause front end damage, leading to expensive repairs. Also, **don't drive at night,** when it is difficult to see and other drivers are more likely to be drunk. Location is important, as well; you're tempting fate by driving north of the Ngkala Rocks, around Hook Point, or on the Western Beach.

sand, and don't try to cross washouts that are more than knee deep. Pay attention to the tides; the best time for beach driving is 3hr. before or after low tide. Rental agencies regularly check trucks for saltwater damage, so don't be overly aggressive or try to push through high tide.

Without a doubt, the most popular trip for backpackers is a self-driven three-day, two-night 4WD expedition. Most go through hostel-organized trips and nearly all come back with crazy stories, dirty clothes, and sand in places they didn't know they had. Unlike those on guided tours, guests camp out at night. Hostel self-drive safaris usually cost around $135, including 4WD rental, ferry passes, camping permits, access fees, camping equipment, and a full preparatory briefing. Petrol, insurance ($40-50), and food ($15-20) are not included. Hostels host either an afternoon meeting or an early morning session before a short 4WD training. You must be over 21 to drive and at least 18 to ride. Bear in mind that the entire group assumes responsibility for vehicle damage regardless of fault, so it's best to keep an eye on whoever is driving.

When choosing a hostel for your Fraser self-drive tour, there are a number of details to consider: first, look at the size of the tour group; most hostels cap group size around 11, although anything more than nine is uncomfortable. Check out the total cost, and be sure to add in the extras including insurance, bonds, and sleeping bag rental. Also, be aware that weather conditions can be harsh on Fraser, particularly in the winter; be prepared for difficult conditions. If hardcore camping is not for you, consider Beaches Backpackers' base camp or a tour group (p. 369).

RENT YOUR OWN 4WD. While hostels will help to create larger groups and develop a social cohesion among several cars, independent travelers will find renting a 4WD a lot less expensive. All rental companies offer similar deals, although their prices appear to vary because of different advertising techniques. Cars seat 2-11 people, and rates range from $120-200 depending on vehicle size, length of rental, and season. While rental companies can assist in obtaining permits and ferry crossings, the price for such services is not included in the overall rental fee; be sure to ask for the grand total (car plus extras) before signing the paperwork. Camping gear is usually $15 per person per night, but competition is intense, so special deals are common and bargaining is possible. Many rental agencies offer discounts to card-holding backpackers. Operators in Hervey Bay include: **Bay 4WD Centre,** 54 Boat Harbour Dr. (☎4128 2981 or 1800 687 178; www.bay4wd.com.au), **Safari 4WD Hire,** 102 Boat Harbour Dr. (☎1800 689 819; www.safari4wdhire.com.au), and **Aussie Trax,** 56 Boat Harbour Dr. (☎1800 062 275; www.fraserisland4wd.com.au). All of these companies pickup locally, help create a personalized itinerary, and hold safety meetings prior to departure. They also offer guided tours. To ensure your safety, ask whether a rental agency belongs to the **Fraser Coast 4WD Hire Association,** the local watchdog agency.

BUNDABERG ☎07

Bundaberg (pop. 46,500) is not an exciting destination; most visitors get coffee at the bus terminal, stretch their legs, and hop back onboard. It is, however, a cheap place to learn to scuba dive, and it is a reliable source of short-term farm work. Many of those who do stay to work, however, complain about worker exploitation since the preponderance of eager laborers ensures fast turnover. Some workers last a day; others, months. Unfortunately, locals and backpackers have a tense relationship, meaning that nearly all social events remain inside the hostels.

TRANSPORTATION

Trains: Bundaberg Railway Station (☎4153 9709) is at the corner of Bourbong and McLean St. Ticket office open M-F 4-5am and 7:45am-5pm, Sa-Su 8:45am-1pm and 2-4:15pm. **Queensland Rail** (☎13 22 32) trains go to: **Brisbane** (M-F 2 per day, Sa-Su 1 per day; $63); **Mackay** (1 per day; M and F $147.70; Tu, Th, Sa-Su $110.10); **Maryborough** (M-F 2 per day, Sa-Su 1 per day; $24.20), with bus connections to **Hervey Bay** ($9.90); **Rockhampton** (1 per day, $57.20). Children and ISIC 50% discount.

Buses: The **Coach Terminal,** 66 Targo St. (☎4152 9700), between Crofton and Electra St. **Premier** (☎13 34 10) runs only 1 service northbound (11:10pm) and 1 southbound (3:30am). More expensive **Greyhound Australia** (☎13 14 99) has 4 buses daily and a 10% student and backpacker discount, but there is an $8 phone booking fee, and trips are generally longer than with Premier. They both run to: **Airlie Beach** (10½-13hr.; Premier $87, concessions $78; Greyhound $124); **Brisbane** (7-10hr.; $47/42, $73); **Cairns** (20¾-23hr.; $156/140, $196); **Hervey Bay** (1¾-2½hr.; $14/13, $16); **Mackay** (8¼-10hr.; $72/65, $105); **Maroochydore** (7-8hr.; $35/32, $58); **Noosa** (6-7¼hr.; $34/31, $58); **Rockhampton** (3¼-4½hr.; $36/32, $57).

Local Transportation: Duffy's City Buses, 28 Barolin St. (☎4151 4226; www.duffysbuses.com.au) run around town, to beaches, and to the Bundaberg Rum Distillery (p. 379). Buses M-Sa 8am-4pm, less frequent on Sa. **Stewart & Sons Coaches,** 66 Targo

St. (☎4153 2646). M-F 3 per day, Sa 2 per day. Depart the **IGA** Supermarket on Woongarra St. for Innes Park, Elliott Heads, and Moore Park ($5.25, concessions $2.70).

Taxis: Bundy Cabs (24hr. ☎13 10 08).

ORIENTATION AND PRACTICAL INFORMATION

Most of Bundy's action takes place on **Bourbong Street,** which runs parallel to and one block south of the **Burnett River.** Crossing Bourbong from west to east are **McLean, Maryborough, Barolin,** and **Targo Street.**

Tourist Office: Bundaberg Region Tourism, 186 Bourbong St. (☎4153 8888; www.bundabergregion.info.) Open M-F 9am-5pm, Sa-Su 9am-noon.

Currency Exchange: ATMs line Bourbong St. between Tantitha and Maryborough St.

Police: 256-258 Bourbong St. (☎4153 9111), just west of the Central Business District (CBD).

Internet Access: The **library,** on Woondooma St. allows 1hr. free access. (☎4153 9253). Open M-Th 9am-6pm, F 9:30am-5pm, Sa 9am-1pm. **The Cosy Corner,** on Barolin St. opposite the post office. $4 per hr.; free 15min. with each hr. Open M-F 8am-7:30pm, Sa 9am-5pm, Su 11am-5pm.

Post Office: 157B Bourbong St. (☎13 13 18). Open M-F 9am-5pm, Sa 8:30am-noon. **Postal Code:** 4670.

ACCOMMODATIONS

Most of the hostels in Bundaberg will help you find work (usually within 24hr. of arrival) and provide transportation. Hostels often host long-term workers, so book ahead. All hostels have laundry, Internet access, and communal kitchens.

Workers & Diving Hostel, 64 Barolin St. (☎4151 6097). From the bus station, call for a ride or walk down Crofton St., and take a left onto Barolin St. (10min.). Despite the name, working is definitely the focus here. Self-contained units with 8 beds and dorm-style accommodations. The apartment beds are worth the additional cost. Social nature among the new and old pickers. Big outdoor common area, pool, and large common room with movies. Reception 8:30am-noon and 3:30-7:30pm. 4- to 6-bed dorms in house $20, weekly $130; in units $21/135; doubles $44/280. NOMADS. MC/V. ❷

Bundaberg Backpackers and Travellers Lodge, 2 Crofton St. (☎4152 2080), across from the bus terminal at the corner of Targo St. A no-nonsense hostel crowded with pickers. While the rooms are nothing to brag about, the A/C is especially nice during the humid summers. Free pickup at train station. Comfortable TV room. Key deposit $20. Reception 8:30-11:30am and 3-7pm. 4- to 8-bed dorms $24, weekly $140. Student and backpacker discount. MC/V. ❷

Kelly's Beach Resort, 6 Trevors Rd., Bargara (☎1800 246 141; www.kellysbeachresort.com.au), on Kelly's beach. The self-contained villas are more expensive and far from Bundy, but the luxurious pool, tennis court, sauna, and trips to see seasonal turtle spawning justify the price. Great for groups. Pickup from Bundaberg $20; Duffy's bus #5 also passes alongside the resort. For 4hr. daily resort work, you get free accommodation and food. Twin share villas $89; 5- or 6-share villa $125. AmEx/DC/MC/V. ❹

FOOD

If you're searching for a healthy bite, try **Jungle Jack's Cafe ❶,** 56 Bourbong St. Lunch options include quiches, salads ($4), seasonal smoothies, and the popular, oven-roasted vegetable stack ($4.40). (☎4152 8513. Open M-F 7am-5pm, Sa 7am-1pm. Cash only.) **Yummy Noodle ❷,** 165 Bourbong St., serves up flavorful noodles and rice dishes

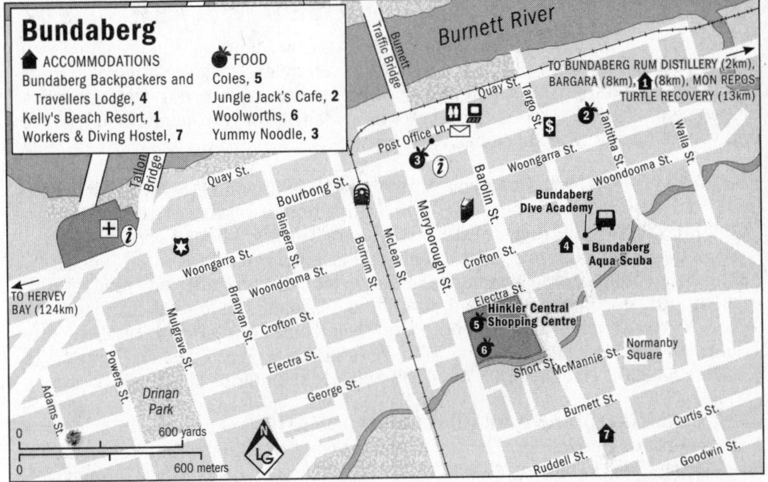

($9.20) and several vegetarian options ($8.50). Large portions and less fat than many Chinese restaurants. Dine-in or takeaway. (☎4152 8868. M-Th and Su 11:30am-9:30pm, F-Sa 11:30am-10pm. Cash only.) Both **Coles** (☎4152 5222; open M-F 8am-9pm, Sa 8am-5pm) and **Woolworths** (☎4153 1055; open M-F 8am-9pm, Sa 8am-5pm) supermarkets are in Hinkler Central Shopping Centre, on the corner of Maryborough and George St.

SIGHTS AND ACTIVITIES

Diving in Bundaberg is quite cheap, but be aware of hidden costs: books and medical exams run about $105 and may not be included in the quoted price. The most popular agency is **Bundaberg Aqua Scuba,** 66 Targo St., next to the bus terminal, which offers two shore dives for $50, two artificial reef dives for $100, and a PADI open-water course that includes four shore dives ($259). (☎4153 5761; www.aquascuba.com. Accommodation $15 per night with course. Open daily 9am-5pm. AmEx/MC/V.) **Bundaberg Dive Academy,** in the Targo St. Transit Centre, will get you a PADI certification for $340. (☎1800 252 668; www.bundabergdiveacademy.com. 4-day class begins weekly M and Th. 2 of 4 open water dives at artificial reef.) If you're already certified, **Dive Musgrave** has incredible three-day overnight cruises with 10 dives around various parts of the southern Great Barrier Reef. (☎1800 552 614; www.divemusgrave.com.au. $595, includes meals, air tanks, and weights. Environmental charge $6 per day.) The less adventurous can head to the **Bundaberg Rum Distillery,** where the tour has a happy two-drink ending. (☎4131 2999; www.bundabergrum.com.au. Duffy's service #4 drops off at the distillery. Tours M-F 10 and 11am and 1, 2, and 3pm, Sa-Su no 3pm tour. 45min.-1hr. tour $9.90, students $7.70, backpackers $4.40.)

Celebrating the start of the turtle nesting season, the week-long **Coral Coast Turtle Festival** in early November features a carnival, markets, and parades. **Mon Repos Turtle Rookery** offers one of the most inspiring wildlife attractions in Australia. This small beach is the nesting ground for loggerhead turtles; night visitors can witness tiny hatchlings scrambling through the sand towards the water. (13km from the CBD; head east on Bargara Beach Rd. and follow signs to the rookery. ☎4159 1652. Open daily Nov.-Mar. 7pm-2am. $8, children $3. Book ahead; pre-paid tickets required. No guarantee of turtle viewing.)

TOWN OF 1770 AND AGNES WATER ☎07

Named for the year of Captain James Cook's second landing, the area's natural beauty remains unmarred by two centuries of sleepy village life. With exceptional outdoor-oriented tours at insanely low prices, the area is known to insiders as the hidden gem of the East Coast. No matter how many days you spend here, you will find yourself wanting to stay longer.

TRANSPORTATION. **Greyhound Australia** (☎13 14 99) and **Premier Motor Service** (☎13 34 10) service the area. Greyhound northbound service arrives at Fingerboard Rd. (30km from Anges Water) at 8:15pm. The southbound service stops in front of Cool Bananas (p. 380) at 6:30am and at Fingerboard Rd. at 8:15am. Greyhound connecting shuttle is included in the ticket price. Premier only reaches Fingerboard Rd.; northbound 12:20am, southbound 2:20am. Hostels will arrange a $10 pickup. If you are continuing on, both Greyhound and Premier go to Brisbane (10-11½hr.; Greyhound $106, Premier $65), Bundaberg (1½hr., $22/18), Hervey Bay (3½-4hr., $44/29), Mackay (7hr., $107/72), and Rockhampton (2¼hr., $60/36).

ORIENTATION AND PRACTICAL INFORMATION. Agnes Water is located 123km north of Bundaberg. The town center lies at the intersection of **Round Hill Road, Springs Road** (which runs south along the ocean), and **Captain Cook Drive** (which runs 6km north to the Town of 1770). Basic supplies and accommodations are available in Agnes Water, and the Marina is in 1770. There is no public transportation between the two towns. **Agnes Water Information Centre,** on Captain Cook Dr. across from Endeavor Plaza, can help book tours and accommodation. (☎4902 1533. Open daily 9am-4:30pm.) The only bank in town is the **Westpac** in Endeavor Plaza, but it does not exchange currency. There are **ATMs** in the Endeavor Plaza IGA supermarket and FoodWorks in Agnes Water Shopping Centre. **Internet** access can be found at the Rural Transaction Centre and Library, across from Endeavor Plaza. (☎4902 1515. $3 per 30min. Open M-F 9am-4:30pm, Sa 9am-noon.) There is a **laundromat** in Endeavor Plaza. (Open daily 7:30am-8pm; wash $3, dry $1 per 10min.) The **police** (☎4974 9708) are in Agnes Water on Springs Rd. near Cool Bananas. The **post office** is in the Agnes Water Shopping Centre. (☎ 13 13 18. Open M-F 9am-5:30pm.) **Postal Code:** 4677.

ACCOMMODATIONS AND FOOD. The two local hostels are both in Agnes Water, so if you want to stay in 1770 you will have to camp or pay resort prices. **Cool Bananas ❷**, 2 Springs Rd., Agnes Water, has a campfire, Internet access, kitchen, and a bar. They also offer a free shuttle tour, free tea and coffee, and free body boards. Guests commonly claim that this one of the best hostels they've ever stayed in, with exceptionally clean, spacious dorms, a pretty patio, hammocks, and funky, jungle-like bathrooms. (☎1800 227 660; www.coolbananas.net.au. Reception daily 7am-midnight. 6- to 8-bed dorms $24. Book ahead.) **1770 Backpackers ❷,** next to Endeavor Plaza on Captain Cook Dr., is a small, friendly, clean hostel only a 3min. walk to a surfing beach. (☎1800 121 700; www.the1770backpackers.com. Reception daily 8am-9:30pm; after-hours arrival permitted. 4- to 12-bed ensuite dorms $24, doubles $50. VIP discount $1. MC/V.) **1770 Camping Grounds ❶,** on Captain Cook Dr. past the Marina, has beachfront camping with campfire and breathtakingly beautiful grounds. Other amenities include hot showers, BBQ, kitchen, and laundry. (☎4974 9268. Sites for 2 $24, powered $27. Extra person $10. Reception and convenience store open daily 7:30am-6:30pm. Book ahead. MC/V.)

Catch the sunset at **Saltwater Cafe ❸,** past the Marina on Captain Cook Dr., with some excellent potato wedges for two ($7.50) and large pizzas from $22.50. (☎4974 9599. Bar open daily 10:30am-latenight; food served daily 11am-2pm and 5-8pm.) **The Tavern ❷,** on Tavern Rd. at the top of the hill as you enter Agnes Water, is newly renovated and has backpacker specials, like a bowl of spaghetti and a pitcher of beer ($10). A shuttle bus with pickup and drop-off from hostels is available for $2 per person. (☎4974 9469. Open M-Th and Su 10am-midnight, F-Sa 10am-2am.) Groceries can be purchased at the **IGA** supermarket, in Endeavor Plaza (☎4974 7991; open daily 6:45am-7pm), or at the **FoodWorks** in the Agnes Water Shopping Centre (☎4974 9911; open daily M-Sa 6:30am-7:30pm, Su 7am-7:30pm).

SIGHTS AND ACTIVITIES. Agnes Water and 1770 have a slew of activities, and, in an effort to increase appeal, charge some of the lowest prices in Australia. The towns are also located only 90min. from the extraordinary Lady Musgrave Island, which offers some of the best snorkeling and diving on the coast. **Scooter-Roo Tours,** a 3½hr., 60km motorbike ride with spectacular views and heaps of wild kangaroos and wallabies, has been called "the best tour on the East Coast" by backpackers. (☎4974 7697; www.scooterrootours.com. Single $35, tandem $45, mini-motorcycle $45. Book through your hostel.) **1770 Great Barrier Reef Cruises,** in Endeavor Plaza, will take you to the pristine and heavenly Lady Musgrave Island. (☎1800 631 770; www.1770reefcruises.com. Glass-bottom boat and snorkel gear included. $150, concessions $140, children $75. MC/V.) **Liquid Adventures** has an extremely popular, 3hr. guided sea-kayak safari through the waterways where you can try your skills at kayak surfing. (☎0428 956 630. $35, includes lunch. Book through your hostel.) **Fitzroy Reef Jet** has exclusive access to Fitzroy Reef Coral Lagoon, the newest destination on the southern reef. The stunning scenery and lack of crowds make it more enjoyable than most other reef excursions. (☎1800 177 011; www.1770holidays.com.au. Full-day cruise $145, concessions $130, children $70; scuba diving from $60.) **Dive 1770** has the luxury of year-round warm water, and it is far less crowded (and cheaper) than Airlie Beach and Cairns. (☎4974 9359; www.dive1770.com. 4-day open water PADI course $250; dive medical check-up required $60. Courses W, Sa, and by demand.) While the waves here in Town of 1770 and Agnes Water aren't as good as in the south, **Reef 2 Beach Surf School,** in the Agnes Water Shopping Centre, offers 1hr. lessons at an unbeatable price. (☎4974 9072; www.reef2beachsurf.com. 3hr. lessons $16.50 per person. Board rental $10 per hr., $30 per day. Cash only.) With beaches bordered by two national parks, **shorts walks** around the rocky headlands lead to spectacular and romantic photo opportunities. Directly behind the museum on Springs Rd. is a split track; the right-hand track leads to the gorgeous **Workman's Beach** (20min. round-trip); to the left are several lookout points (25min. round-trip). **LARCs (Lighter Amphibious Resupply Cargos),** enormous ex-military boats with wheels, rumble through unreachable areas, and traverse Eurimbula Creek into **Eurimbula National Park.** (☎1800 177 011; www.1770larctours.com.au. 1hr. sunset cruise $25; full-day tours M, W, Sa $105.50, students $101.50, children $65.50-75.50. MC/V.) Look to the beautiful Bustard Head Lightstation for **sand tobogganing.**

CAPRICORN COAST

Straddling the Tropic of Capricorn and sandwiched between temperate and coastal zones, the Capricorn Coast is said to have 70% of all flora and fauna found on this massive continent. Sleepy seaside towns and secluded islands beckon travelers to the place known to "capture the true essence of Australia."

ROCKHAMPTON ☎07

The beef capital of Australia counters the backpacker routine of burgers, club beats, and beaches with outstanding steaks, country music, and rodeos. For the most part, Rockhampton (pop. 59,000) is a quiet town, a pleasant place to take a short break from the fast-paced East Coast trek. Most travelers en route to Great Keppel Island stay in Rocky for at least a day.

TRANSPORTATION

Trains: Train Station, 320 Murray St. (☎4932 0453), at the end of the road. From the Central Business District (CBD), head away from the river on any street, then turn left on Murray St. Day lockers available $4-6. **Queensland Rail** (☎13 22 32; www.traveltrain.com.au) goes north and south along the coast, including stops at: **Brisbane** (8½hr., $110); **Cairns** (16-19½hr., $155.10); **Mackay** (4-5hr., $61.60); **Maryborough** (4½hr., $66) with bus connection to **Hervey Bay** (45min., $9.90); **Proserpine** (6-8hr., $116.60) with bus connection to **Airlie Beach** (25min., $9.90); **Townsville** (9½-12¼hr., $116.60). Northbound, expensive but fast **Tilt trains** depart Tu and Sa 3:23am. The cheap but slow **Sunlander T,** departs Th 11:35pm and Sa, Su 8:25pm. Southbound trains depart daily 7:25am. ISIC 50% discount. **Spirit of the Outback** also leaves W 4:35am and Sa 11:20pm for: **Barcaldine** (11hr., $92.40); **Emerald** (5hr., $55); **Longreach** (13½hr., $108.90). ISIC discount 50%; backpackers 10%.

Buses: Greyhound Australia (☎13 14 99) and **Premier** (☎13 34 10) depart from the Mobil station at 91 George St., between Fitzroy and Archer St. Greyhound has 3-4 services per day and Premier has 1 northbound (3:05am), and 1 southbound (12:15am). Both go to: **Airlie Beach** (6½hr.; Greyhound $74, Premier $53); **Brisbane** (11½-13hr., $104/84); **Bundaberg** (3¼-4½hr., $57/36); **Cairns** (16½-17¼hr., $161/130); **Hervey Bay** (5¾-6½hr., $73/47); **Mackay** (4½hr., $55/37); **Noosa** (9¼-10hr., $89/68).

Public Transportation: The blue **Sunbus** (☎4936 2133; www.sunbus.com.au) leaves from Kern Arcade, on Bolsover St. between Denham and William St., and covers most corners of the city. M-F 6:30am-6pm, Sa 8:30am-noon, Su no service. Route maps posted at most stops and available at tourist office. Fares $0.75-2.95.

Taxis: Rocky Cabs (24hr. ☎13 10 08), on the corner of Denham St. and East St. mall.

Car Rental: Thrifty, 43 Fitzroy St. (☎4927 8755; www.thrifty.com.au). Cars with 200km limit from $55. Under 25 surcharge $15 per day. 21+. Open daily 7am-6pm. AmEx/DC/MC/V.

ORIENTATION AND PRACTICAL INFORMATION

The **Fitzroy River,** the second largest river in Australia, is the defining landmark. On its south side, the city has a flawless grid design, with most of the action near the river's edge along **Quay Street.**

Tourist Office: Rockhampton Tourist and Business Information, 208 Quay St. (☎4922 5339; www.rockhamptoninfo.com). Open M-F 8:30am-4:30pm, Sa-Su 9am-4pm.

Currency Exchange: Banks and 24hr. **ATMs** are on the East St. pedestrian mall. Most open M-Th 9:30am-4pm, F 9:30am-5pm. Free cash exchange at **Harvey World Travel,** on Denham and Bolsover St. (☎4922 6111. Open M-F 8:30am-5pm, Sa 9am-noon.)

Backpacking and Camping Equipment: Campco's, on the corner of William and Kent St. An impressive range of gear. (☎4922 2366; www.campco.com.au.) AmEx/MC/V.

Pharmacy: C.Q. Day and Night Chemist (☎4922 1621), on the corner of Denham and Alma St. Open M-Sa 8am-9pm, Su 9am-9pm.

Internet Access: Connect at **Cybernet,** 12 William St. (☎4927 3633; www.cybernet.com.au), for $5 per hr. Open M-F 9am-5:30pm, Su 10am-1pm. The **library,** 69 William St. (☎4936 8265), on the corner of Alma St. offers free access on 2 computers. Book ahead, or be prepared to wait. Open M-Tu and F 9:15am-5:30pm, W 1-8pm, Th 9:15am-8pm, Sa 9:15am-4:30pm.

Post Office: 150 East St. (☎13 13 18), between William and Derby St. Open M-F 8:30am-5:30pm. **Postal Code:** 4700.

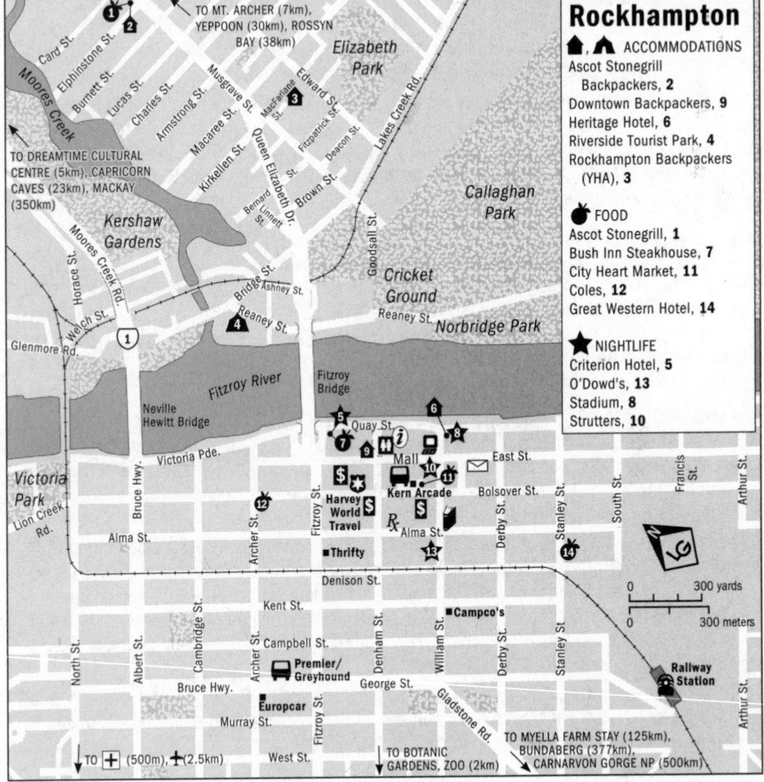

ACCOMMODATIONS AND CAMPING

Ascot Stonegrill Backpackers, 117 Musgrave St. (☎4922 4719) atop Stonegrill. A small common area makes for a good social atmosphere and guests have nothing but positive comments. The restaurant downstairs has the best steaks in Rocky. Laundry, kitchen, and courtesy van to bus and train stations. Reception open 6am-10pm. 3- to 6-bed dorms $20; twins and doubles $40. YHA/VIP discount. AmEx/DC/MC/V. ❷

Heritage Hotel (☎4927 6996), on the corner of William and Quay St. This heritage-listed hotel just got a face-lift, and the new look will blow you away. If you are tired of hostels, this hotel offers terrific budget accommodation. Laundry. Key deposit $20. Check-out 11am. All rooms have A/C, TV, and fridge. 4-bed dorms $20; singles $45; doubles $60. Weekly rates available. AmEx/DC/MC/V. ❷

Downtown Backpackers, (☎4922 1837; www.downtownbackpackers.com.au) on the corner of East and Denham St., atop the Oxford Hotel. While it doesn't feel like a hostel, its central location, 2-bed dorms, and price are difficult to beat. Kitchen, Internet access, and laundry. Key deposit $10. Will leave keys at bus station for late arrivals. Reception is at the bar or at the Sidewalk Cafe next door; open M-Tu 8:30am-6pm, W-Th 8:30am-10pm, F-Sa 8:30am-midnight, Su 9:30am-7pm. 10:30am check-out. 2- and 4-bed dorms $19.50. AmEx/DC/MC/V. ❷

Rockhampton Backpackers (YHA), 60 MacFarlane St. (☎1800 617 194). Clean, spacious hostel with A/C in most rooms. Kitchen, Internet access, laundry, and TV room. Pickup and drop-off at bus or train stations. Reception 7am-9:30pm. Dorms $23; doubles $50; ensuite cabins for 2 $56. Backpacker and student discounts. MC/V. ❷

Riverside Tourist Park, 2 Reaney St. (☎4922 3779; www.islandcabins.com.au/rockhampton), along the Fitzroy River, right off the highway. Offers caravan and tent sites and well-maintained cabins. BBQ and laundry facilities. Reception M-Sa 7am-7pm, Su 8am-7pm. Sites for 2 $16, powered $23, extra person $7; on-site vans $35; self-contained cabins for 2 $60-80, extra person $10. ❷

FOOD

Beef is what's for dinner in Rockhampton. Buy your own at **Coles** supermarket, City Centre Plaza, at Archer and Bolsover St. (open M-F 8am-9pm, Sa 8am-5pm), and cook it on a riverside BBQ. **The City Heart Market,** in the Kern Arcade carpark on Bolsover St., has just about everything, from crafts to fruits and vegetables. (☎4927 1199. Open Su 7:30am-12:30pm.)

Ascot Stonegrill, 117 Musgrave St. (☎4922 4719; www.stonegrill.com), at the Ascot Hotel. Amazingly tender, raw meat is brought out on hot slabs of stone, allowing you to cook it to personal perfection. Try the porterhouse steak with vegetables and excellent dipping sauces, or be more adventurous with kangaroo and crocodile ($26). Open daily noon-2:30pm and 5:30-8:30pm. AmEx/MC/V. ❹

Great Western Hotel, 39 Stanley St. (☎4922 2185; www.greatwesternhotel.com.au). A true display of outback pride, this restaurant offers delicious rump steaks ($16.50-22.50) in a superb atmosphere. The monthly bull-riding event in the 600 person stadium should not be missed; the stadium also hosts concerts. Open M-Th and Su 10am-midnight, F-Sa 10am-3am. Food served daily noon-2pm and 6-9pm. Bull-riding: $15, students $12, backpackers $10. MC/V. ❸

Bush Inn Steakhouse, 150 Quay St. (☎4922 1225), in The Criterion Hotel Motel. A local favorite for its excellent steaks. Main courses $15-27. Food served daily noon-2pm and 6-9pm. Book ahead on weekends. AmEx/DC/MC/V. ❸

SIGHTS AND ACTIVITIES

CAPRICORN COAST ECO-DIVERSITY. Capricorn Dave's Adventures, the most popular excursion for backpackers, is a great introduction to the region. The customized tour may include a tea tree mud bath, plus a chance to hold large spiders, search for snakes, stand on an ant hill, follow kangaroos, and gather 'round a bonfire at sunset. The day-trip is a sufficient glimpse, but longer trips are available. The tour gained fame when Steve-O from MTV's Jackass took part for the TV program Wildboyz. *(☎1800 753 786; www.capricorndave.com.au. Day trip including lunch and tea $99. 3 days/2 nights including camping and Great Keppel Island $215. Book ahead. MC/V.)*

CAVES. The limestone **Capricorn Caves** feature incredible natural acoustics and a natural light spectacle during the summer solstice (early Dec. to mid-Jan. on the 11am tour). The 1hr. Cathedral Tour covers highlights of the cave system. The caverns also hosts the popular **Wild Caving Adventure Tours:** two hours of rock climbing, including sardine-style squeezes through tiny tunnels. *(23km north of Rockhampton. ☎4934 2883; www.capricorncaves.com.au. Book at least 24hr. in advance. Open daily 8:30am-6pm; tours 9am-4pm. Admission and 1hr. tour $18, children $9. Backpacker discount 10%. Transport from Rockhampton M, W, F $40/20; adventure tour $60. AmEx/MC/V.)*

FARM STAY. Myella Farm Stay offers an all-inclusive farm stay with horse- and motorbike-riding, 4WD tours, cow milking, and a relaxed, educational rural experience. *(125km southwest of Rockhampton. ☎4998 1290; www.myella.com. Buffet meals, activities, and transport included. Daytrip $80; 2 days $180; 3 days/2 nights $260. MC/V.)*

CARNARVON GORGE NATIONAL PARK. This rugged national park offers Aboriginal rock art sites, deep pools, and soaring sandstone cliffs. The gorges, however, are the main attraction. The park campsites are only available during school holidays (p. 38). Cool temperatures make March through November the best time to visit, but be aware that night temperatures fall below freezing. *(500km southwest of Rockhampton and Gladstone on Bruce Hwy. For more info, pick up a map in the tourist office or contact the ranger ☎4984 4505.)* **Takarakka Bush Resort ❶**, 4km from the park, has sites and cabins. *(☎4984 4535; www.takarakka.com.au. Linen $10. Sites $12 per person, powered for 2 $30; cabins from $80, extra person $15.)*

HIKING. Looming 603.5m over Rockhampton, **Mount Archer** offers amazing views of the city and surrounding countryside just a short walk from the carpark. Drive 5km from the base to the summit and walk a few different tracks at the top. Hardy hikers can trek back to the base via **Turkey First** (11km, 4-5hr.), but will need a friend for pickup at the bottom, as the walk into town is a long one (7km). Brochures at the tourist office provide more information. *(By car, head northeast toward the summit on Musgrave St. to Moores Creek Rd. Turn right on Norman Rd., and then left on Frenchville Rd., which winds up to the top. Open dawn-dusk. Camping prohibited.)*

DREAMTIME CULTURAL CENTRE. The center provides a modest, elegant portrayal of the indigenous peoples of Central Queensland and the Torres Strait Islands, said to be the oldest living cultures in the world. Learn to throw a boomerang and hear a didgeridoo demonstration at the end of the tour. *(5min. north of Rockhampton by car, on the corner of Yeppoon Rd. and the Bruce Hwy. Sunbus #10 runs from the arcade carpark daily every hr. 8:35am-5:35pm; $2.95. ☎4936 1655; www.dreamtimecentre.com.au. Open M-F 10am-3:30pm. 1-1½hr. tours are best for seeing the center; 10:30am and 1pm. $12.75, concession $10.50, children $6. AmEx/MC/V.)*

BOTANIC GARDENS AND ZOO. The zoo has an enormous walk-through avian dome, chimpanzees, and the usual line-up of Aussie animals. Tours ($3.30) of the garden can be arranged upon request. *(15min. ride from the city on Sunbus #4A; departs from the Kern Arcade carpark M-F 15min. past the hr. 7:15am-5:15pm, Sa 8:15-11:15am; one-way $2.05. ☎4922 1654. Feedings 3-3:15pm. Zoo open daily 8am-4:30pm; gardens open daily 6am-6pm. Both free.)* If you don't like the formal nature of botanic gardens, the **Kershaw Gardens,** stretching 1km along the Bruce Hwy. between Dowling and High St., recreate an Australian bush environment. *(☎4922 1654. Open daily 7am-6pm. Tours can be arranged upon request.)*

NIGHTLIFE AND ENTERTAINMENT

For a pint of Guinness ($6.20), live rock music Friday and Saturday nights, and some excellent $6 meals when you buy a beer, good laddies and lassies hit **O'Dowd's,** 100 Williams St. (☎4927 0344; www.odowds.com.au. Open M-Sa 8am-2am, Su 10am-4pm. Restaurant open M-Sa noon-2pm and 6-9pm.) If you're looking for a more traditional nightclub, **Stadium Nightclub,** 228 Quay St. next to the Heritage Hotel, is the best in town. On the weekend, head upstairs to the glass bar to watch the heads bobbing down below. (☎4927 9988. F-Sa cover after 11pm $5. Open W-Sa 8pm-5am. Glass bar F-Sa 10pm-4am.) **Strutters,** on the corner of East St. and William St., is a little less classy but equally fun. (☎4922 2882. W and F-Sa $5 cover. Open W-Th 8pm-3am, F-Sa 8pm-5am.) **The Criterion Hotel Motel,** 150 Quay St., has two bars and a restaurant that converts to a bar at night. It always attracts a crowd of regulars. (☎4922 1225. Open daily 11am-3am.)

GREAT KEPPEL ISLAND

☎07

The most developed of the largely untouched Keppel Island Group is Great Keppel, which boasts 17 beaches, clear waters, and good snorkeling right off-shore. Great hiking tracks lead to spectacular, elevated views and pristine beaches. Whether you hope to break a sweat, lounge around in the sand, or check out the marine life, don't bypass this rugged paradise on the road less traveled.

TRANSPORTATION. From Rockhampton, it only takes a bus transfer (50min.) and a ferry ride (30min.) to reach the island. Check with your accommodations to see if they can arrange these for you: otherwise, call the companies directly. **Young's Bus Service** (Route #20) runs to the ferry from Kern Arcade, on Bolsover St., Rockhampton. (☎4922 3813; www.youngsbusservice.com.au. M-F 13 per day, Sa 6 per day, Su 5 per day. $8.10 one-way.) **Rothery's Coaches** will pickup and drop-off at your Rocky accommodation. (☎4922 4320. Round-trip $16.50, children $8.25. Pay the driver; cash only.)

Freedom Fast Cats leaves from Keppel Bay Marina, Rosslyn Bay. (☎1800 336 244; www.keppelbaymarina.com.au. Departs daily 9, 11:30am, 3:30pm. Returns 10am, 2:15 and 4:15pm. Round-trip $37, students $32, children $19.) They also run day cruises from $58/48/32, including the ferry ride. Book ahead for tours. All rides have $2 fuel charge. Those driving should follow the signs from Yeppon for the Rosslyn Bay Marina. Free parking is available at the ferry terminal. There is also the **Great Keppel Island Security Carpark** on the Scenic Hwy., just before the turn-off for Rosslyn Bay; it has a secured lot and courtesy bus to the marina. (☎4933 6670. $8 per day, covered $10). The ferry lets passengers out on Fisherman's Beach, the island's main stretch of sand. Parallel to the beach is the island's only real path, the red-tinted **Yellow Brick Road,** leading to the island's few shops.

ACCOMMODATIONS. Packages that include bus and ferry transfers and rooms on the mainland don't save you much money, but will spare you the hassle of arranging everything yourself. Camping is not allowed on Great Keppel but is available on the nearby Keppel Island Group. The **Great Keppel Island Holiday Village (YHA) ❸** is friendly and relaxed, with one 6-bed dorm, several powered tents, and more expensive cabins. Free snorkel gear is available for all guests. The energetic managers run 3hr. sea-kayak adventures ($40) and motorized canoe trips ($25) for excellent snorkeling opportunities. (☎1800 180 235; www.gkiholidayvillage.com.au. Kitchen, BBQ, and laundry. Reception and mini-grocery store 9am-1pm and 3:30-5pm. 11am checkout. Dorms $33; tents with hard floors and reed beds $76; cabins for 2 with shower $120. Extra person $20. YHA discount. Book ahead. MC/V.) **Keppel Haven ❸** is spread out over 11 acres and, even when filled to capacity, feels uncrowded and tranquil. There are basic twin-bed dorms in powered tents, or groups can request more comfortable cabins; the ones along the beach are the best. The **on-site bar** offers reasonably-priced fare. (☎4933 6744. Kitchen, laundry, BBQ, and free Internet access for guests, $3 per 30min. for non-guests. Reception 7am-5pm. Tents $28 per person; singles $35; doubles $84; self-contained cabins with A/C for 2 $120, up to 4 extra people $10 each. MC/V.)

FOOD AND NIGHTLIFE. Food on the island is expensive, so stock up prior to departure at **FoodWorks,** 18 James St., Yeppoon. (☎4939 2200. Open daily 6am-9pm.) Once on Great Keppel, all commerce is oriented around the Yellow Brick Road. **Island Pizza ❸** serves tasty but pricey pizzas from $16.90. (☎4939 4699. Open in summer Tu-Sa 6-9pm and Sa-Su 12:30-2pm; in winter W-Su 6-9pm. MC/V.) **Reef ❷,** part of the main resort, serves delicious potato wedges ($6.50) and good burgers ($10.50-11). Steer clear of the rainbow lorikeets, which will swoop down and try to eat your meal. (☎4939 5044. Open daily 11:30am-3pm, F-Sa also 5:30-9pm. Cash only.) Nightlife on the island is virtually non-existent, as there are only two bars. **The Wreck Bar,** part of the main resort, offers theme nights (like bingo or trivia night) during the week and livens up on the weekends. (☎4939 5044. ATM outside. Open M-Th and Su 11am-latenight, F-Sa 10am-latenight.) The other bar is inside **Keppel Haven,** and while the latenight scene leaves something to be desired, it has some of the cheapest food and drinks around. Massive burger and chips ($10.90) and dinners ($14-22.50). (Happy hour 5:30-7pm. Open daily 10am-latenight.)

ACTIVITIES. Keppel's calm beaches are perfect for swimming and snorkeling. **Shelving Beach,** a mere 30min. jaunt from the resort, has the best easily accessible snorkeling. **Monkey Beach,** 20min. farther, also has great snorkeling opportunities. **Clam Bay,** on the island's south side, has the most vibrant coral and the best snorkeling, reachable via the **Homestead Path** (3½hr. round-trip). **Long Beach,** a 40min. walk past the airstrip, is splendidly isolated (3.6km round-trip). The hiking on the island is spectacular, but signs are sparse, so go with a friend and bring a map. Buy souvenir charts of Great Keppel Island ($0.50 at the Keppel Tourist Services ferry terminal on the mainland; $2 on the island). Walks begin on the main track, which leaves from the water sports hut at the ferry drop-off. The uphill hike to **Mount Wyndham** offers spectacular views of the heavily forested island (2½hr., 7km round-trip). Other walks go to the **Homestead** (1½hr., 5.6km round-trip) and across the entire island to the **lighthouse** (4½hr., 15.4km round-trip).

The **Keppel Island Dive Centre,** on Putney Beach, offers dive and snorkel trips. (☎4939 5022; www.keppeldive.com. Introductory dive $120; certified dive $75, without gear rental $55. Snorkeling $43, without gear rental $33.) The resort offers plenty to do if diving isn't your cup of tea. To ride out to the smaller islands, visit the friendly fellas at the **water sports hut,** on Fisherman's Beach in front of the ferry drop-off. (☎4939 5044. Open daily 9am-4pm.) They offer catamaran rentals ($20 per hr.), parasailing ($75), and waterskiing and wakeboarding ($30 per 10min.). The catamaran *Grace* runs a sailing expedition into the surrounding waters. (M, W, F 11:30am and 4pm. $125, children $65. F romantic 2hr. sunset cruise $55.) There is also a romantic 2hr. sunset cruise every F ($55). For a slower pace, go **camel riding** on the beach ($40 per 30min., 1hr. sunset ride $60). Book at the resort's activity center, next to The Wreck Bar.

KEPPEL GROUP

The isolated, largely deserted islands in the Keppel Group are open for independent exploration, but getting there is difficult and expensive. The privately-owned, coconut-covered **Pumpkin Island,** 16km from Yeppon's coastline, has beautiful vegetation, coral, and white sand beaches. There are **tents** ❶ and five **cabins** ❺ available for rent; each cabin holds up to six people. Bring your own food and drink. (☎4939 4413; www.pumpkinisland.com.au. Toilets, showers, BBQ, and drinking water. Linens $10. Unpowered tent sites $15; cabins from $240.) The island's owners can provide transportation for groups of up to five ($65 per person). To reach surrounding islands, take a water taxi (☎4933 6133); be warned that they are pricey so renting a kayak or tinny from Great Keppel might be your best bet. **Humpy Island, Middle Island,** and **North Keppel** offer camping; permits are available at the QPWS in Rosslyn Bay, adjacent to the **Tourist Services office.**

WHITSUNDAY COAST

Stretching from Mackay to the small town of Bowen, the coast's moniker aptly highlights its greatest assets: the Whitsunday Islands. This archipelago, accessible from Airlie Beach, draws a crowd but still offers ample opportunities to enjoy the solitude that is characteristic of northern Queensland. The sun, sand, diving, and tropical waters are a must for anyone exploring the region.

MACKAY ☎07

Rising from a sea of sugar cane, the town of Mackay (mick-EYE; pop. 70,000) is a convenient gateway to inland rainforests, or last stop before venturing to the isolated islands offshore. A small, quiet city, eclipsed on the backpacker circuit by nearby Airlie Beach, most shops and services close here after dusk. Numerous outdoor attractions—hiking, swimming, and an abundance of wildlife—are within an hour's drive at Eungella and Cape Hillsborough National Parks.

TRANSPORTATION

Trains: The **train station** (☎4952 7418) is about 5km south of town on Connors Rd. There is no public transport from the station, and a taxi costs about $10. Purchase tickets at the station (open M-F 9am-4:30pm) or in town. Trains run less frequently and take longer than buses. Lockers $2.

Buses: Prices may vary depending on season and weather conditions. **Mackay Bus Terminal** (☎4944 2144) is on the corner of Macalister and Victoria St. **Premier** and **Greyhound Australia** (www.greyhound.com.au) run to: **Airlie Beach** (1¾-2hr., 2-6 per day, $30); **Brisbane** (14hr., 1-7 per day, $150); **Bundaberg** (8¼-9¾hr., 1-3 per day, $104); **Cairns** (9½-12hr., 1-7 per day, $125); **Hervey Bay** (10¾hr., 1-6 per day, $110); **Maroochydore** via **Noosa** (12hr., 1-3 per day, $140); **Rockhampton** (4¼hr., 1-7 per day, $55). Ticket office open M-F 7am-6pm, Sa-Su 7am-2pm. Infrequent local bus service runs from Caneland Shopping Center; schedules are available at the visitors center or at your accommodation.

BOOK ONLINE. Save money by booking buses online, as many travel agents charge as much as a 30% commission.

Taxis: Mackay Taxi (24hr. ☎13 10 08).

Car Rental: Rental companies are spread throughout the city; ask the visitors center or your accommodation for directions to the closest one. **Europcar,** 174 Boundary Rd. (☎1300 131 390) offers cars from $59 per day with courtesy pickup. **Avis** (☎13 63 33 or 4951 1266) is located at the airport. **Thrifty** (☎4942 8755 or 1800 818 050), at the corner of Bruce Hwy. and Sands Rd., also offers courtesy pickup.

Bike Rental: Rock 'n' Road Cycles, 164 Victoria St. (☎4957 4484; www.rocknroad.com.au). As cheap as $10 per day.

ORIENTATION AND PRACTICAL INFORMATION

Mackay's Central Business District (CBD) runs along on the southern bank of the Pioneer River. **River Street** hugs the waterfront, and the town's main drag, **Victoria Street,** runs parallel to it one block away. Nightlife and restaurants line **Sydney Street** and **Wood Street,** which run perpendicular to Victoria St. The **Bruce Highway** comes into the west side of town and exits to **Gordon Street,** the third street from the river, parallel to Victoria St. As the Bruce Hwy. curves south, it changes to **Nebo Road** and hits the town's major accommodations and the tourist office. The rest of the city is geared toward those with vehicles. The marina is 7km from the CBD (north along Sydney St. past the bridge over the Pioneer River), and there are beaches spread throughout the region—the closest is 4km from the CBD at the eastern end of Gordon St.

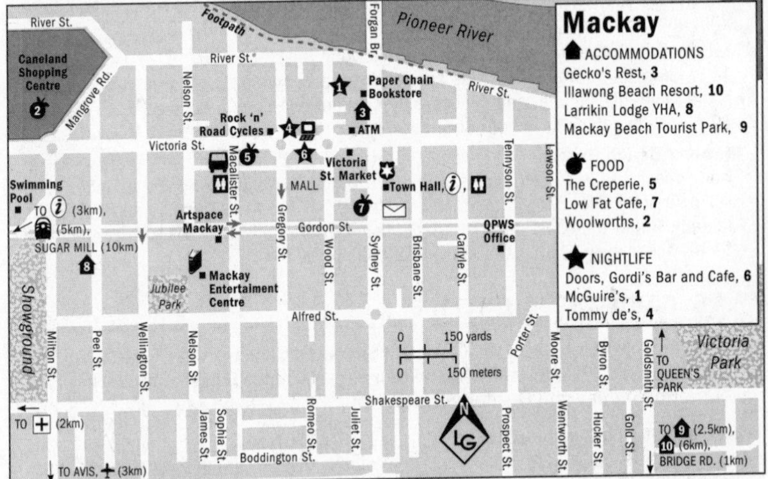

Tourist Office: Mackay Tourism Office, 320 Nebo Rd. (☎4952 2677; www.mackayregion.com), 3km southwest of the CBD. Open M-F 8:30am-5pm, Sa-Su 9am-4pm. A small **Information Booth** (☎4951 4803) is located in the Old Town Hall on Sydney St. Open M-F 8:30am-5pm.

Parks Office: Queensland Parks and Wildlife Service (☎4944 7800; www.epa.qld.gov.au), at Tennyson and Gordon St. National park info and camping permits for the Cumberland Islands (permits $4.50 per person). Open M-F 8:30am-5pm.

Currency Exchange: Banks and 24hr. **ATMs** line Victoria St. between Gregory and Brisbane St. All offer traveler's check and currency exchange for a $5-7 fee and are open M-Th 9:30am-4pm, F 9:30am-5pm.

Internet Access: Hong Kong Importers, 128 Victoria St. (☎4953 3188), has the most terminals in town for $5 per hr. Open M-F 8:45am-5:15pm, Sa-Su 9am-1pm. Or try the **library** (☎4957 1787), behind the Civic Centre on Gordon St. Internet $5 per hr. for non-members. Open M, W, F 9am-5pm, Tu 10am-6pm, Th 10am-8pm, Sa 9am-3pm.

Market: Victoria Street Markets feature arts and crafts. Open Su 8:30am-12:30pm.

Police: 57-59 Sydney St. (☎4968 3444), between Victoria and Gordon St. Open 24hr.

Post Office: 69 Sydney St. (☎13 13 18), between Victoria and Gordon St. Open M-F 8am-5:30pm. **Postal Code:** 4740.

ACCOMMODATIONS

Because Mackay is not a popular tourist destination, hostels are scarce. Budget motels line the streets of the CBD and are also found along Nebo Rd. Additionally, several caravan parks lie on the outskirts of town.

Gecko's Rest, 34 Sydney St. (☎4944 1230; www.geckosrest.com.au). Smack dab in the CBD, this well-maintained hostel offers a comfortable night's rest in spacious 4-bed dorms. Laundry, A/C, and Internet access $5 per hr. Key deposit $20. Reception 7am-10pm. Dorms $21; singles $32; twins and doubles $48. AmEx/DC/MC/V. ❷

Larrikin Lodge YHA, 32 Peel St. (☎4951 3728; larrikin@mackay.net.au), a 10min. walk from the CBD. This small 32-bed hostel has a friendly atmosphere. The affable owners offer day tours to local National Parks and will outfit you with complete camping gear

($20 plus deposit). Internet access $4 per hr. Laundry $2. Lockers $1. Reception 7am-2pm and 5-8:30pm. Dorms $23, YHA $20; twins $54. AmEx/DC/MC/V. ❷

Mackay Beach Tourist Park, 8 Petrie St., Illawong Beach (☎4957 4021 or 1800 645 111), 3km south of the CBD. Has the beach for a backyard. Pool, kitchen, small gym, game room, playground, and peacocks. Reception 7am-7pm. Sites for 2 $18, powered $24; ensuite cabins for 2 from $65; basic motel rooms $54. AmEx/DC/MC/V. ❷

Illawong Beach Resort, 77 Illawong Dr. (☎4957 8427 or 1800 656 944; www.illawong-beach.com.au), 6km south of the CBD on the beachfront. Spacious, motel-style self-contained villas with 2 bedrooms, A/C, and TV. Pool, lake, tennis courts, and restaurant. Buffet breakfast included. Reception 7am-5:30pm. Doubles with garden view $140, ocean view $150. Extra person $20. AmEx/DC/MC/V. ❺

FOOD AND NIGHTLIFE

Woolworths supermarket is in the Caneland Shopping Centre, located inland on Victoria St. (☎4951 2288. Open M-F 8am-9pm, Sa 8am-5pm.) **Coles** supermarket is at the corner of Sydney and Gordon St. (Open M-F 8am-9pm, Sa 8am-5pm.)

Low Fat Cafe: Pure and Natural Mackay (☎4957 6136), on Sydney St. across from the police station. Earns both parts of its name with its tasty low-fat and vegetarian options for breakfast and lunch. Try a baguette sandwich or refreshing tropical fruit smoothie. Open M-F 7:30am-3:30pm, Sa 8am-1pm. ❶

The Creperie (☎4951 1226), at the corner of Gregory and Victoria St. Serves up the delightful French dishes in meal and snack sizes. Meal crepes ($10-13) include meat, seafood, and vegetarian options, while dessert crepes ($6-9) feature fruits, liqueurs, and other sweets. Open M-F 11am-2pm, Tu-Sa 6pm-latenight, Su 6-9pm. ❷

McGuire's, 17 Wood St. (☎4957 7464). Attracts a young crowd, cheap jugs of Toohey's New ($8) in hand. Live entertainment W-Su. Contests for free beer and eternal fame in the McGuire's Liars Club. Open M-W 9am-1am, Th-Sa 9am-2am, Su 10am-midnight.

Doors, 85 Victoria St. (☎4951 2611). Drink specials, big screen with not-so-subliminal messages like "take home someone ugly tonite," and great dance pit make for a sweaty night of drunken fun. Downstairs, the more casual set at **Gordi's Bar and Cafe** spills out onto the street for drinks and cheap counter meals. Doors open Tu-Sa 8:30pm-3am. Cover F-Sa $5. Gordi's open daily 10am-3am.

Tommy de's, 148 Victoria St. (☎4957 7737). One of the most popular Mackay nightspots. DJ-hosted party madness rages around pool tables and two bars. Spirits $4 10pm-midnight. Open W-Su 10pm-3am. F-Sa cover $5.

SIGHTS

While most of Mackay's draw can be attributed to its surroundings, the town does offer a few interesting sights. Pick up the tourist center's free guide, *A Heritage Walk in Mackay*, which will direct you to historical and cultural attractions. Don't miss **Queen's Park,** on Goldsmith St. just north of Victoria Park, where the lovely **Orchid Gardens** overflow with flowers. The **Mackay Entertainment Centre,** next door to the library on Gordon St., is your one-stop destination for drama, comedy, and concerts. (☎4957 1777 or 1800 646 574. Open M-F 9am-5pm, Sa 10am-1pm; also 1½hr. before shows.) The center also hosts the **Mackay Festival of Arts** (www.festivalmackay.org.au) in July, a two-week celebration with concerts, fashion parades, food fairs, and comedy shows. Next to the Centre, **Artspace Mackay** displays traveling exhibitions by famous artists for free. (☎4057 1775. Open Tu-Su 10am-5pm.) Outside of town, the **Farleigh Sugar Mill** offers 2hr. tours of their working mill during the sugar-crushing season (late June-Nov.). There is no public transport available; take the Bruce Hwy. 9km north toward Proserpine, then turn right at Childlow St. (☎4963 2700. Tours M-F 1pm. $15, children $8, families $35.) At sunset, in front of the **board-walk** along the Pioneer River on River St., hundreds of starlings suddenly fly together over the golden water back and forth under the bridge.

BRAMPTON AND CARLISLE ISLANDS

While both islands are national parks, Brampton Island is dominated by a resort, making it generally inaccessible to anyone unwilling to shell out $320 for luxury accommodation. The island resort's guest ferry (☎4951 4499) sometimes takes non-guests. Inquire at the National Parks Office on Tennyson St. **Jungle Johno's Bush, Beach, and Beyond Tours** (see Eungella National Park, p. 391) also does daytours to Brampton Island, leaving from the Mackay Marina. (Sa 8:30am, Su 8:00am.) At low tide, beautiful Carlisle is accessible from Brampton via a sand bridge. Those who make the trek are rewarded with secluded island camping. (Pit toilet, BBQ, and rain water tank. Be sure to boil water before using it. $4.50.) While Carlisle has no hiking, Brampton Island offers 11km of **walking tracks** over dunes, past rocky headlands, and through eucalyptus forests. Pick up a trail map and arrange camping permits through the Parks office in Mackay.

MACKAY TO EUNGELLA

To reach Eungella ("yun-gla"), follow the Bruce Hwy. (Nebo Rd.) south. Turn right onto Peak Downs Hwy. (Archibald Rd.) just past the visitors center and follow it until you reach a junction with Pioneer Valley Rd., where you'll find signs for Eungella State Park. The road stretches through endless acres of sugar cane fields before steeply winding up and over the Clarke Range to Eungella.

After passing the town of Marian on Eungella Rd., the **Illawong Sanctuary** is 4km past **Mirani,** 44km from Mackay. In this unique wildlife sanctuary, run by a very friendly couple, you can feed the 'roos, talk to a cockatoo, and wonder at the peculiar ice cream-eating emu. (☎4959 1777. Open daily 9:30am-5pm. $12, children $6. **Accommodation ❹** at the sanctuary $65, includes dinner and breakfast. Cash only.) Farther along the Pioneer Valley Rd. is **The Pinnacle Hotel ❶,** an eatery where you can grab one of Wendy's famous homemade pies ($3.50) and a beer. (☎4958 5207. Open daily 10am-latenight.)

EUNGELLA NATIONAL PARK

Eighty kilometers west of Mackay on Pioneer Valley Rd. is the 52,000 hectare **Eungella National Park,** a range of steep rainforest-covered slopes and deep misty valleys. At Eungella, the "land where clouds lie low over the mountains," 10 walking trails lead to spectacular hilltop and creekside views. Red cedars, palms, and giant ferns coat the slopes; platypi are common in waterways.

Walking tracks are in two sections of the park: the **Finch Hatton Gorge** area and **Eungella/Broken River.** Trail maps are available at the QPWS office in Mackay or the ranger station at Broken River (☎4958 4552). Although no public transportation runs to Eungella, the park is easily reached via car and is only a 1hr. drive from Mackay. Ambitious day hikers can walk from the township to Broken River and beyond by stringing smaller hikes together; however, be prepared to hike the same trails back as there are no long circuit hikes. Behind the Eungella Chalet, the **Pine Grove Circuit** (1.5km) forks at 700m into the excellent **Cedar Grove Track** (3km, 30min.), which winds past stately red cedars to a roadside picnic area and lookout track. Two hundred meters down the road from the picnic area is the Palm Grove trailhead (1.8km), which gives you the option of continuing on to Broken River via **Clarke Range Track** (6.5km, 1¾hr.). Five kilometers on Eungella Rd. from the Chalet, you'll cross **Broken River,** with an excellent **platypus-viewing platform** (see **Ather-**

ton Tablelands, p. 428), picnic area, **campground** ❶ with toilets and hot showers ($4.50), and ranger station. (☎4958 4552. Open M-F 8:30am-5pm.) Several trails lead from Broken River, including the **Credition Creek Trail** (8.5km one-way), which follows the river's course, meandering in and out of the forest before reaching granite cascades and a scenic pool.

For an organized tour of the park, **Jungle Johno's Bush, Beach, and Beyond Tours** is led by farmer-turned-tour-guide Wayne, who is deeply knowledgeable in topics from horticulture to folklore. He'll take you to Finch Hatton Gorge and Broken River. (☎4951 3728. ½-day $59, full-day $75.) Jungle Johno also does day tours to Brampton Island from Mackay (p. 388). Col Adamson's **Reeforest Adventure Tours** takes daytrips to Eungella and Cape Hillsborough. (☎4953 1000; www.reeforest.com. $95; seniors, VIP, and YHA $85; children $53.)

FINCH HATTON GORGE. After the Pinnacle Hotel is a well-marked turn-off to beautiful **Finch Hatton Gorge** (10km from Pioneer Valley Rd.). Nestled deep in a canyon where brilliant waterfalls meet undisturbed rainforest, this section of park sees few visitors. Contact the Finch Hatton Gorge Ranger (☎4958 4552) or check with locals for the latest area road conditions, as the narrow track dips through several creeks that are sometimes too deep to cross after heavy rains.

On the dirt road to Finch Hatton Gorge is the rustic **Platypus Bush Camp** ❶, where open-air huts, abundant wildlife, and the adjacent creek (ideal for an afternoon dip) afford an authentic Aussie experience that you won't find at cookie-cutter resorts. There's also an outdoor kitchen, creekside hot tubs forged from river rocks, and a snug enclosure surrounding a woodburning stove—the perfect venue for campsongs and traveler's tales. For those weary of sleeping outdoors, an old touring bus has been converted into sleeping quarters. (☎4958 3204; www.bushcamp.net. Campsites $7.50 per person; dorms $25; huts/doubles $75.) Just past the bush camp, the **Finch Hatton Gorge Cabins** ❶ have two small 4-bed dorms and two ensuite luxury cabins. Hot showers and a kitchen are also available. Just honk your horn for reception. (☎4958 3281. Campsites $7.30; dorms $16.50; double cabins $88.) Across from the cabins, the **Finch Hatton Gorge Kiosk** ❶ sells homemade pies ($4) for lunch and mango ice cream for dessert. They also have **Internet** access for $5 per hr. (☎4958 3321. Open M and W-Su 10am-5pm.)

Finch Hatton's one hiking track leaves from the picnic area at the end of the Gorge Rd. The trail to **Wheel of Fire Cascades** (4.2km, 1hr.) follows rapids as they cascade down the rocky riverbed; the last kilometer is a steep stair-climb. To see the rainforest from above, book a trip with **Forest Flying,** which suspends visitors on two treetop zip lines and sends them whizzing through the canopy. (☎4958 3359; www.forestflying.com. Pickup from Gorge cabins or Kiosk. 2-3hr. depending on group size. Bookings required. $45, children $30.)

EUNGELLA. Twenty kilometers past the turn-off for Finch Hatton Gorge on Pioneer Valley Rd. is the **Eungella township.** The road is steep and curvy, climbing 800m in just 3km. At the top of the hill is the historic **Eungella Chalet** ❸. Overlooking the vast Pioneer Valley, this mountaintop resort has a large restaurant, swimming pool, extensive gardens, and a soaring view of the valley below. The nearby skytop restaurant serves counter meals, including hearty dinners. (☎4958 4509. Chalmer St. Guest house singles $38; doubles $50, ensuites $72. AmEx/DC/MC/V.) Just past the Chalet on the right is **Suzanna's Hideaway Cafe** ❶, where friendly owner Suzanna invites guests to sit on her porch and enjoy fresh-baked treats from her oven. Famous for her apple strudel ($3.50) and coffee, she also cooks more filling meals, like chicken *schnitzel* ($8) and vegetarian options. The German immigrant has also found time between baking and conversation to construct a very curious jewel and rock garden in her backyard. (☎4958 4533. Open daily 8am-4pm.)

CAPE HILLSBOROUGH NATIONAL PARK

A peninsula north of Mackay, Cape Hillsborough is a remarkable study in contrasts: sandy beaches abut rugged pine- and eucalyptus-covered hills. Rocky outcrops protrude from the tropical rainforest where kangaroos, lizards, and scrub turkeys roam. At dusk and dawn, kangaroos make their way out of the rocky headlands and hop around the beach. With sandy stretches and scenic hiking, the park makes a great daytrip from Mackay. Take the Bruce Hwy. 20km northwest from the city to the turn-off for Seaforth Rd.; turn right after another 20km on Seaforth Rd. to reach the Cape. The road to the Cape ends at the **Cape Hillsborough Tourist Resort ❶**, with beachfront access, a pool, BBQ, store, and restaurant. (☎4959 0152; www.capehillsboroughresort.com.au. Reception 8am-8pm. Sites $13, powered $18; rooms $39-79. AmEx/DC/MC/V.) Adjacent to Cape Hillsborough is tiny **Smalley's Beach** on a short, unsealed road to Bali Bay. The beach's **campsite ❶** has toilets, water, and the beach as its yard. ($4.50; self-register at the campsite.)

Five short walking trails are concentrated on the eastern tip of the Cape. For more information on tracks, pick up a map at the parks office in Mackay, or peruse maps posted at the resort or the seldom-staffed ranger station (☎4959 0410) located in the picnic area at the end of the cape. The **Diversity Boardwalk** (1.2km), at the park's entrance, is an aptly-named jaunt through mangroves of many varieties and an area of open woodland. After an initial steep ascent, the **Andrews Point Track** (2.6km, 45min. one-way) follows the ridge around the point, offering five spectacular lookouts and sea breezes. Return via the same track or along the beach, provided the tide is out. At low tide, the rocky beaches of **Wedge Island** become accessible, despite the absence of an official track. The **Junipera Plant Trail** (1.2km, 1hr. round-trip) is a self-guided walk that highlights plants foods used by the Junipera Aboriginal people for tucker. The trail also passes an Aboriginal midden heap (massive pile of shells). The **Beachcomber Cove Track** (1.6km) provides good views from the ridge before ending at the cove.

AIRLIE BEACH ☎07

Airlie serves those seeking a gateway to the Whitsundays or looking for a nonstop party. It was nothing but mudflats until an enterprising developer's proposal to make a beach was turned down by the nearby shire of Bowen, and he was redirected to

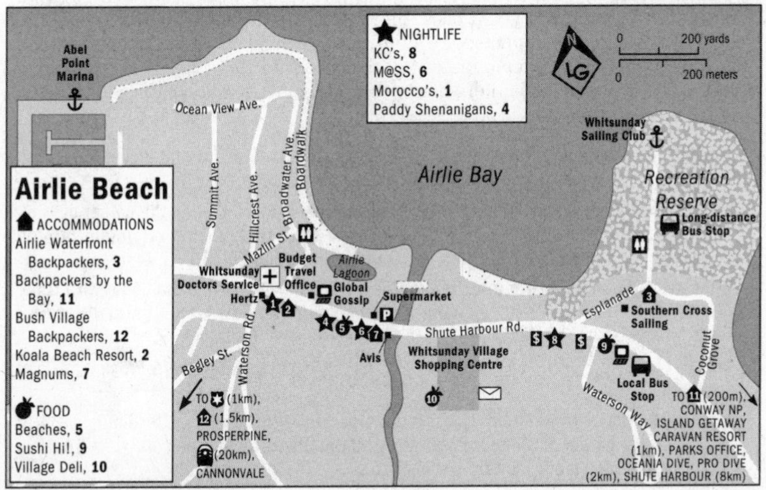

this quaint seaside port. With truckloads of Bowen sand, he put the "Beach" into Airlie. Today, non-stop nightlife, plus the stunning beauty of the nearby Whitsunday Islands and Great Barrier Reef, have made this village the biggest backpacker draw between Brisbane and Cairns.

TRANSPORTATION

Trains: The rail station is in Proserpine, 25km outside of the city. **Whitsunday Transit** (24hr. ☎4946 1800) picks up arriving train passengers and runs down Shute Harbour Rd., stopping in the center of Airlie and at some accommodations ($17); timetables available all over town.

Buses: Travel offices and hostel desks book transport. Prices vary depending on season and weather conditions; the following are approximations. **Greyhound Australia** (☎13 14 99; www.greyhound.com.au) drops off at the end of the Esplanade; accommodations offer courtesy pickup, but most hostels are within walking distance. ISIC/VIP/YHA will save you up to $15 on some tickets. Buses run daily to: **Bowen** (1¼hr., 5 per day, $22); **Brisbane** (18hr., 6 per day, $170); **Bundaberg** (12hr., 3 per day, $124); **Cairns** (10hr., 5 per day, $106); **Hervey Bay** (13hr., 4 per day, $137); **Mackay** (2hr., 6 per day, $30); **Maroochydore** (16hr., 3 per day, $162); **Mission Beach** (8hr., 3 per day, $93); **Noosa** (15hr., 3 per day, $155); **Rockhampton** (7hr., 6 per day, $74); **Townsville** (4hr., 5 per day, $53).

Public Transportation: Whitsunday Transit (☎4946 1800) runs between Cannonvale and Shute Harbour daily at least every 30min. 6am-6:40pm, stopping in front of Global Gossip (257 Shute Harbour Rd.). Unlimited day ticket $6.50. Airlie Beach to Shute Harbour $4.50. Night service Th-Sa 7-11pm.

Taxis: Whitsunday Taxi (☎13 10 08).

Car Rental: There are several companies along Shute Harbour Rd., including **Hertz** (☎13 30 39) next to **Morocco's** (Open M-F 8:30am-5pm, Sa-Su 9:30am-noon).

ORIENTATION AND PRACTICAL INFORMATION

The turn-off for Airlie Beach is at Proserpine, off the Bruce Hwy.; the road passes through Cannonvale and on to Airlie Beach (26km). The main road becomes **Shute Harbour Road,** running parallel to the water as it nears Airlie. Upon entering the town, you'll pass Abel Point Marina; at the opposite end, the road veers left to the **Esplanade** or continues straight toward the commercial Shute Harbour (8km). Picnic tables and BBQs adorn the waterfront area along the Esplanade while sunbathers lie on the newly created beach or on the grass around **Airlie Lagoon.**

Budget Travel: Many travel offices cater to backpackers. Some of the hostel tour booking offices offer free rooms if you book trips with them.

Parks Office: National and Marine Parks Authority (☎4946 7022), on the corner of Mandalay St. and Shute Harbour Rd., 2km outside town toward Shute Harbour. Info on camping and national parks. Open M-F 9am-4:30pm, Sa 9am-1pm.

Currency Exchange: ATMs and banks line Shute Harbour Rd. **Commonwealth Bank** (☎4946 7433), 380 Shute Harbour Rd., charges a flat $10 fee for traveler's checks and foreign exchange. ATM. Open M-Th 9:30am-4pm, F 9:30am-5pm.

Police: (☎4946 6445), on Altman St., off Shute Harbour Rd. toward Proserpine, just outside of town.

Medical Services: Whitsunday Doctors Service (☎4946 6241 or after hours 13 432 584), on the corner of Shute Harbour Rd. and Broadwater Ave. Open M-F 8am-5pm, Sa 11am-1pm. Dive medicals $50.

Internet Access: Most shops offer access, and hostels compete for business with competitive pricing. Try 390 Shute Harbour Rd. (☎4946 6399) $3 per hr. with all the frills: DVD/CD burning, printing, copying, and coffee. Book exchange also. Open daily 8:30am-8:30pm. **Global Gossip,** 257 Shute Harbor Rd. (☎4946 6488) for $3 per hr. for members, more for non-members. Open daily 9am-10pm.

Post Office: (☎4946 6515), in the Whitsunday Village Shopping Center on Shute Harbour Rd. Open M-F 9am-5pm. **Postal Code:** 4802.

ACCOMMODATIONS AND CAMPING

Airlie's cornucopia of budget lodgings barely keeps pace with backpacker demand, so book ahead. Ask about deals when booking tours through hostels; some offer free stays. The nearby Whitsundays have cheap **camping ❶**, but space is limited. Try **Koala Beach Resort** (☎1800 800 421), on Shute Harbour Rd., or **Island Gateway Caravan Resort** (☎4946 6228), 1km past town on Shute Harbour Rd.

Bush Village Backpackers Resort, 2 St. Martins Rd., Cannonvale (☎4946 6177 or 1800 809 256), a 15min. walk from town. The ultimate in cleanliness and hospitality. Cabins with kitchen, TV, and bath flank a palm-lined driveway that leads to the pool, porch, and TV lounge. Relax in picturesque hammocks during the day, watch movies on the gigantic screen over the pool at night, and feed 'roos and wallabies in the backyard sanctuary. Continental breakfast. Free shuttles to town 6:30am-11:30pm. Reception 7am-9pm. Dorms $25-29, members $20; doubles $68-108. AmEx/DC/MC/V. ❷

Airlie Waterfront Backpackers (☎4948 1302; www.airliewaterfront.com), on the Esplanade. Very clean with a quiet atmosphere, kitchens, and large balconies with great views of Airlie Bay. Dorms and doubles are arranged in suites around common rooms; many have spiral staircases up to lofts with awesome views. Internet $4 per hr. Reception 7am-8pm. 10-bed dorms $20; 4-bed $25; doubles $60. AmEx/DC/MC/V. ❷

Backpackers by the Bay, 12 Hermitage Dr. (☎4946 7267 or 1800 646 994; www.backpackersbythebay.com), 650m from town toward Shute Harbour. 4-bed bunk-style rooms, chill atmosphere, and amenities galore. Internet access, BBQ, laundry, pool, game room, free nightly activities, and the best view of the bay in Airlie. Free shuttle to town. Happy hour daily 5:30-6:30pm (beers $3). Reception 7am-7:30pm. Dorms $22; doubles $52; triples $74. VIP. AmEx/DC/MC/V. ❷

Magnums (☎1800 624 634; www.magnums.com.au), on Shute Harbour Rd. Airlie Beach's centrally located party hostel. M foam parties at the attached nightclub, **M@ss** (see **Nightlife**). With over 400 beds hidden in jungle decor and 4 restaurants on-site, this hamlet of hedonism is still somehow endearing—perhaps it's the live music and smashed backpackers at every hour of the day. All rooms clean and ensuite with A/C; for more privacy, request a double. Bring linen. Reception 6am-10pm. Campsites $16 per person; dorms from $16; doubles $49. VIP/YHA. AmEx/DC/MC/V. ❷

FOOD

Cafes and mid-range restaurants line the main drag in Airlie. Several hostels (Beaches, Magnum, and Koala) have affiliated bars and nightclubs that double as restaurants before 9pm. There is a small **supermarket** right in the middle of town, across from Magnums on Shute Harbour Rd. (Open daily 8:30am-8pm.)

Village Deli (☎4946 5745), opposite the post office in Whitsunday Village Shopping Center. A healthy alternative to Airlie's fish 'n' chip joints. Gourmet sandwiches ($9), a variety of pasta and vegetarian entrees, and meat and seafood. Fully licensed bar with extensive wine selection. Open daily 8am-latenight. AmEx/DC/MC/V. ❶

Sushi Hi!, 390 Shute Harbour Rd. (☎4948 0400). The only place for raw fish in town. Massive seafood rolls fill you up without emptying your pocket (½-roll $6.75). Healthy smoothies ($4-6) make the perfect snack. Open daily 10am-9pm. AmEx/DC/MC/V. ❶

Beaches, 356-62 Shute Harbour Rd. (☎4946 6244). A perennially packed backpacker mecca that serves dinner on long picnic tables. Counter meals ($8-15) are surprisingly upscale and include fish and pasta dishes. Get a free drink if you grab a coupon on the street and show up by about 5pm. Party games start daily around 9:30pm and are followed by dancing until midnight. AmEx/DC/MC/V. ❷

NIGHTLIFE

M@ss, 366 Shute Harbour Rd. (☎4946 6266), part of Magnums' metropolis. Nights here get sticky, soapy, noisy, and naughty. Live music outside daily 5pm. Open M-Th and Su until latenight, F-Sa until morning.

Paddy Shenanigan's (☎4946 5055), near Beaches on Shute Harbour Rd. A popular place with Airlie dwellers and a great place to start the night off in style. Try their infamous green shooter teapots for $10. Dance floor and live music. Open daily 5pm-2am.

Morocco's (☎4946 6446), next to Koala on Shute Harbour Rd. Slightly upscale decor with some outdoor tables and a huge TV screen inside. Games and prizes given away daily. Meals for $10-17, but you can usually get a $4 discount on the street or at Koala's for guests. Open daily 7-10am and 3pm-2am.

KC's (☎4946 6320), on Shute Harbour Rd., on the right before the turn-off for the Esplanade. If you're looking for a big piece of steak and some great live music, this is the place. A truly relaxing and intimate pub environment. Open daily 3pm-3am.

ACTIVITIES

While sailing the Whitsunday Islands and diving the Great Barrier Reef are the two most popular reasons for travel to Airlie, affordable alternatives abound.

ON LAND

Conway National Park is a few kilometers east of Airlie Beach. A self-guided walk in the park lasts just over an hour and passes through a variety of Australian habitats. On the way, stop at the QPWS for a detailed leaflet. (☎4746 7022. Open M-F 8am-5pm, Sa 9am-1pm.) Die-hard bush wranglers can try plowing through the bush on a four-wheeler with **Whitsunday Quad Bike.** (☎4946 1020; www.bushadventures.com.au. Departs daily; $115 per 2hr.) If you have a car, go to any local tourist office and ask for some self-drive suggestions, as the area has several other swimming holes and scenic areas. **Whitsunday Crocodile Safaris** cruises the Proserpine River in search of crocs and also offers open-air wagon eco-tours and hikes through the wetlands. (☎4946 5111; www.proserpineecotours.com.au. $89, children $57. Family packages available. Free transfers to and from Airlie.)

IN SEA

Paddle or snorkel alongside sea turtles or camp on deserted island beaches with **Salty Dog Sea Kayaking.** Salty Dog offers half-, full-, 3-, and 6-day tours around the islands. Adventurers can bring their own food, or let the company handle the catering. (☎4946 1388 or 1800 635 334; www.saltydog.com.au. ½-day $58, full-day $115, 3-day $395, 6-day $1190.) **Ocean Rafting** offers daytrips on a raft that can top 65km per hour, making it the fastest way to get to the islands. Trips include a chance to snorkel or dive, tan on the beach, visit Aboriginal caves, or take rainforest walks. (☎4946

6848; www.oceanrafting.com. $97, children $61; lunch $12.) **FantaSea** (p. 398) runs daily catered ferry trips to nearby islands. They also offer trips featuring humpback whales on their run back from Arctic feeding grounds. **CruiseWhitsundays** (p. 398) has adventure packages, cruises, and resort ferries. If you're interested in diving the wreck of the **S.S. Yongala,** considered one of the world's premier dives of its kind, try **Yongala Dive** (p. 405).

Reel it in with **M.V. Jillian;** troll for mackerel, cobia, and tuna, and then enjoy lunch on board. (☎4948 0999; www.airlielocaltours.com.au/mvjillian/mvjillian.htm. Daytrips depart Abel Point 9am and return around 5:30pm. $120.) A more relaxing fishing excursion is aboard the **M.V. Moruya,** a local favorite. (☎4946 7127; www.fishingwhitsunday.com.au. Departs daily at 9:30am from Shute Harbour and returns around 5:30pm. Daytrip $120, concessions $110.) If you're looking to pursue the best game the fishing world has to offer in the outer reef, the beautiful **Marlin Blue** has a very experienced and knowledgeable captain. Come eye-to-eye with sea turtles and glide underneath the shadows of eagles as you explore the islands in a leisurely fashion. (☎4946 5044; www.marlinblue.com.au. 1-day trip $275.)

IN AIR

Cruise 300 ft. above Airlie with **Whitsunday Parasail.** Afterward you can enjoy the resort pool free of charge. (On the jetty near Coral Sea Resort. ☎4948 0000; www.whitsundayparasail.com.au. $55; tandem $88. Jet ski rental $35 per 15min.) **Tandem Skydiving** will drop you from 8000 ft., providing an adrenaline rush and an amazing view of the islands offshore. (At the Whitsunday Airport. ☎4946 9115; www.skydiveoz.com. $249.)

DIVING

The scuba scene is amazing in the Whitsunday area. Dolphins, whales (in the winter months), turtles, manta rays, and even small reef sharks are common inhabitants of these crystal-clear waters. The most popular sites for overnight trips are on the outer reefs that lie just beyond the major island groups, including the **Bait, Hardy,** and **Hook Reefs.** Occasionally, boats will venture to Black Reef or Elizabeth Reef. **Mantaray Bay** is the best spot close by and is also great for snorkeling. All trips incur an extra $5 per day Reef Tax. In addition to the companies listed below, FantaSea Cruises offers trips to the reef for marine-life viewing.

Pro Dive (☎4946 6032 or 1800 075 035; www.prodivewhitsundays.com). 3-day stay aboard with 28 people and all-inclusive PADI course ($575). Also has a 4-day trip for certified divers: 10 dives and unlimited snorkeling ($645).

Oceania Dive, 257 Shute Harbour Rd. (☎4946 6032; www.oceaniadive.com.au). The *Oceania* (max. 30 people) departs Tu and F for 3-days on the Continental Shelf. Advanced courses available. 5-day PADI certification cruise $575. Open daily 7:30am-7pm.

Reef Dive and Sail (☎4946 6508; www.reefdive.com.au). 5-day PADI certification course $580, includes 8 dives and 3-day stay aboard. 2-day cruises on the *Romance* sailboat $295, includes snorkeling and diving. Open daily 7am-7pm.

WHITSUNDAY ISLANDS

Over 90 islands constitute the Whitsunday group, a continental archipelago that was once a coastal mountain range until it was cut off from the mainland by rising sea levels at the end of the last ice age. The thousands of visitors who flock to this majestic area come to sail, enjoy the beaches and coral reefs, or just relax at one of the luxurious resorts. Whitsunday Island, home to the famous Whitehaven Beach, is the largest and most appealing to campers and hikers. Other backpacker favorites include: Hook Island, with its choice snorkeling spots and Aboriginal cave paintings; Daydream Island; Long Island; and the Molle Island Group, of which South Molle is the best. At the posh resorts on Hayman, Hamilton, and Lindeman Islands, many guests arrive by private helicopter or plane, but the islands can make decent daytrips even for those who are strapped for cash.

TRANSPORTATION

Choosing which island to visit can seem overwhelming; one way to experience the group is by taking a multi-day sailing trip, but be aware that you'll be spending most of your time in transit. It is also possible to do island daytrips by ferry. But, if you only have time to visit one place, make it Whitsunday Island (p. 398).

FantaSea, a.k.a. **Blues Ferries** (☎4946 5111; www.fantasea.com.au). Offers direct transfers between the islands and mainland; departs several times daily from Shute Harbour. Schedules are available at almost any booking office or hostel. Multiple ferries leave the harbor daily to: **Long Island** ($24 round-trip); **Hamilton Island Marina** ($37 round-trip); **Daydream Island** ($24 round-trip). Discounts for families and children available. AmEx/MC/V.

CruiseWhitsundays (☎4946 4662 or 1800 426 403; www.cruisewhitsundays.com). Departs Abel Point (Airlie Beach) several times daily to **Daydream Island** ($23, children $16) and **Hamilton Island Airport** ($45/25; with coach transfer from accommodation $52/28). There is also a transfer to **South Molle Island** from Hamilton Island Airport ($61/41). Also offers adventure packages and cruises. AmEx/MC/V.

Island Camping Connections (☎4946 5255) drops campers off at many of the island sites (national park permit required), and has camping, snorkeling, and kayaking equipment for rental. Min. 2 people. $45-150 per person, includes water supply. **Whitehaven Beach** campsite $120 per person; **South Molle** campsite $45 per person. MC/V.

Camping Whitsunday Islands (☎1800 550 751 or 4948 0933; www.campingwhitsundays.com) offers packages to: **Whitehaven Beach** ($270, with Crayfish Bay $330); **Cockatoo Beach** ($190); **Denman Island** ($190); **Dugong Beach** ($238); and many others. Shared accommodations available. AmEx/MC/V.

Air Whitsunday Seaplanes (☎4946 9111; www.airwhitsunday.com.au) fly over the islands. 1hr. scenic flight over reef and Whitehaven $199; 2hr. sightseeing and snorkeling $289. Flight to Hayman $185. AmEx/MC/V.

Aviation Adventures (☎4946 9988; www.av8.com.au). Scenic helicopter flights to the reef and beyond. 10min. $99; 20min. $169; 40min. $299. Other reef and island packages available, including helicopter daytrips from $159. AmEx/MC/V.

ISLANDS

The Whitsundays Island group has a variety of cheap camping options; there are 21 campsites on 17 different islands. Before embarking on your trip, you must get a permit from **QPWS** at the **Marine Parks Authority** (p. 394), on the corner of Shute Harbour Rd. and Mandalay Rd., Airlie Beach. (☎4946 7022. Open M-F 9am-4:30pm, Sa 9am-1pm. Permits $4.50 per night.) Walk-in applications are welcome, but you must book ahead to guarantee your spot. Beware that public transportation to the following islands is limited.

WHITSUNDAY ISLAND. The most renowned destination in the Whitsundays is **Whitehaven Beach,** a 7km slip of white along the western part of the island. Sand swirls like fine snow from one edge of the island to the other; at low tide you can practically walk across the inlet opposite the longer portion of Whitehaven, where most day-tour companies moor and sailing trips stop for sunbathing and swimming. Make sure you get to **Hill Inlet Lookout** farther north on the island at Tongue Bay, an easy 650m walk. Beware: some tour companies will only take you to the portion of the beach that lies across the bay, but Whitehaven might seem a wasted trip unless you see it from above, so ask ahead and make sure the tour includes the lookout. Three tour companies that make daytrips to Whitehaven and Hill Inlet Lookout (with snorkeling and lunch) are **Mantaray** (☎1800 816 365 or 4946 4321; www.mantaraycharters.com; $120), **Reefjet** (☎4946 5366; www.reefjet.com.au; $120), and **Whitehaven Express.** (☎4946 7172; www.whitehavenxpress.com.au; $133.) The **campsite** ❶ at Whitehaven Beach has toilets, picnic tables, and shelter (peak-season limit 60 people, off-peak limit 24). If you plan to camp in the Whitsundays, do it here. On the other side of the island is **Cid Harbour,** a common mooring site for two-night boat trips. The area features three **campgrounds.** The largest is **Dungong Beach** ❶ (limit 36 people), which has toilets, drinking water, sheltered picnic areas, and a walking track (1km, 40min.) that leads to the second campground at **Sawmill Beach** ❶ (limit 24 people). The same amenities are provided there. Bring a water supply if you're camping farther south at **Joe's Beach** ❶ (limit 12 people). All campsites cost $4.50 per night. The beach has excellent **snorkeling;** stingrays and turtles are common.

HOOK ISLAND. The beaches on Hook have beautiful stretches of coral offshore, literally a stone's throw from **Chalkies Beach** and **Blue Pearl Bay.** Blue Pearl Bay is one of the Whitsunday's most popular snorkeling spots, and arguably the best. It's also home to the islands' most popular fish, a gigantic 5 ft. tourist-loving wrasse named Elvis. On the south side of the island lies **Nara Inlet,** a popular spot for overnight boat trips. About 20min. up the grueling path is a cave shelter used by the sea-faring Ngalandji Aborigines, bordered on both sides by middens (piles of shells). The rare paintings inside date back to 1000 BC and may have given rise to the popular Australian myth that a boatload of exiled Egyptians washed ashore ages ago and left hieroglyphic-like traces in various corners of Queensland. Although the story is unsubstantiated, it is true that at least one symbol in the cave is a good match for "king" in Hieroglyphic Luwian, spoken in ancient Troy.

Maureens Cove, on Hook's northern coast, is a popular anchorage and has **camping** ❶ for $4.50 a night (limit 36 people). **Steen's Beach campground** ❶ (limit 12 people), is a good sea-kayaking site. **Hook Island Wilderness Resort** ❷, just east of Matilda Bay, is a bargain with a range of activities from snorkeling (full-day $10) to fish and goanna feeding; there is also a reef 50m offshore. Remember to bring a towel, kitchen utensils, and sleeping bag. Transfers (round-trip $50) are available on the ferry *Voyager* with stops at Whitehaven Beach and Daydream Island. (☎4946 9380. Camping $25 per person, children $15; hut-style dorms $35; beach-front cabins $100; ensuite $140. MC/V.) One of the world's oldest underwater reef observatories is at the end of the jetty; check with the resort for operating hours.

SOUTH MOLLE ISLAND. South Molle, just off the mainland, is a national park that offers some of the best **bushwalking** in Queensland. One of the best tracks is the hike to **Spion Kop** (4.4km, 1½hr. round-trip), a rock precipice on one of the island's many peaks. Adventurous hikers scramble up the rocks for an astounding 360° view of the Whitsundays. Nearby **Sandy Beach** (limit 36 people) has over 15km of hiking trails. Many two-night sailing excursions moor offshore, and guests come ashore to bushwalk or use the pool at the **South Molle Island Resort** ❺, located in Bauer Bay. (☎4946 9433 or 1800 075 080. Packages $125-419. Cheaper standby rates are often available.) Waterskiing ($35), catamarans ($10 per 30min.), jet skiing ($50 per 15min.), and dinghy rental ($25 per 30min.) are all offered at the island's water activities facility. (Open daily 8:30am-4:30pm. AmEx/MC/V.) All-inclusive packages are the cheapest and easiest way to enjoy the resort (includes room, meals, and non-motorized water sports). All island walks are accessible from the resort; reception can give you a map and information.

LONG ISLAND. The closest island to the mainland, Long Island is perfect for snorkeling or hiking, as it has its own reef and 20km of walking trails through 1200 hectares of national park. There is also a **campground** at Sandy Bay (register at QPWS ☎4946 7022) and three resorts.

OTHER ISLANDS. **Hayman Island** is known as one of the world's premier resorts, but unless you have $500 for a night's stay, you're not going to visit for more than a day. **Hamilton Island** is the mini-metropolis of the Whitsundays, featuring the Hamilton Island Resort, high-rise hotels and a main drag with an ATM, general store, and over a dozen restaurants. The budget-friendly **North Molle Island** boasts the mammoth Cockatoo Beach Campground (limit 48 people), fully equipped with facilities and water supply. Other fully equipped campsites include **Gloucester Island's** Bona Bay (limit 36 people), **Henning Island's** Northern Spit (limit 24 people; no water), and the secluded sites at **Thomas Island** and **Armit Island** (limit 12 people). **Shute Harbour** offers basic grounds with bushcamping sites (limit 12 people). **Tancred, Shaw, Saddleback, South Repulse, Olden, Planton,** and **Denman Islands** also have limited campgrounds.

SAILING THE ISLANDS

Traveling to the Whitsundays without sailing the islands is like going to Paris without seeing the Eiffel Tower: a sailing safari is one of the most popular activities in Queensland. Although some hostels may save you money by offering a free night's stay if you book tours with them, it might not get you on the best boat. Make sure you get the full details on every trip before booking. Ask how much time is actually spent on the trip. Many boats offer "three-day, two-night" trips that leave at midday and come back only 48hr. later. Some multiple-day trips only offer an hour on each island; not nearly enough time to enjoy the white sand beaches. Also make sure the company you go with has "WCBIA" certification (Whitsunday Charter Boat Industry Association); some companies will make up their own, unauthorized certification.

There are four classes of boats at play: the uninspiring **motor-powered** variety (boats that have sails but nonetheless motor everywhere); the stately **tallships,** with the rigging of yesteryear and the elegance of age; the **cruising yachts,** which offer more comfort, smaller numbers, and more sailing time; and the proper **racing yachts,** called **maxis,** which are usually well past their racing prime, more expensive, and popular with young crowds and the adventurous. Discounts are greatest during off-peak times (Oct.-Nov. and Feb.-Mar.), and as a result, sailing trips get filled up fast; book ahead.

Southern Cross (☎4946 4999 or 1800 675 790; www.soxsail.com.au). One of Airlie's premier sailing companies; trips have professional crews, spotless boats, gourmet meals, and free transfers. Their fleet includes: the *Southern Cross,* a former America's Cup finalist (max. 14 people); the *Siska,* a spacious 80 ft. maxi that is said to be one of the best (max. 22 people; 3-day, 2-night trip $409); and the *Solway Lass,* a gorgeous 127 ft. tallship built in 1902. (Max. 32 people. 3-day overnight trip 4-bed $429; doubles $449. 6-day overnight trip $839.) AmEx/DC/MC/V.

Prosail (☎4946 5433; www.prosail.com.au). Most 3-day, 2-night trips offer an additional day aboard *On the Edge* for 50% off. Choose between yachts, maxis, or traditional boats. The fleet includes the *Matador,* the largest maxi ever built (3-day, 2-night trip $479). AmEx/DC/MC/V.

Aussie Adventure Sailing (☎1800 359 554 or 4948 2350; www.aussiesailing.com.au). With a wide range of sailboats, from maxis to tallships, they service a diverse group of customers. The maxi *Waltzing Matilda* takes 14 people and departs W and Sa (3-day, 2-night trip $439). AmEx/DC/MC/V.

Queensland Yacht Charters (☎1800 075 013; www.yachtcharters.com.au) rents fully equipped boats for those wishing to go it alone. Yachts from $490 per night; powerboats from $460 per night (excluding the hefty $700-1000 bond and fuel). When divided among a group, this can beat the cost of a cruise. AmEx/DC/MC/V.

NORTH QUEENSLAND

Sandy beaches stretch along some of the world's oldest tropical rainforests as the Queensland coast extends farther north. To the west of the tropics, the earth becomes dry and dirt turns red; much of this land sits on former volcanic shelves with terrain rising high above sea level. Tall green and silver fields, smoking mills, chugging trains, and Bundaberg rum all stand testament to north Queensland's greatest agricultural asset: sugar cane. Just off the coast of tropical Townsville, the region's economic and residential center, sits Magnetic Island, a haven for both koalas and urbanites alike. Between the island and Mission Beach, brilliant waters lap sands sheltered from rough seas by the Great Barrier Reef. Pockets of zealously preserved rainforest (and the inescapable "rainforest boardwalk") grow increasingly common in the tropical north.

BOWEN ☎07

Often dismissed as another bus stop on the coastal service, Bowen is regularly bypassed by travelers in favor of the party atmosphere of Airlie Beach 40min. to the south. Those who do stay are rewarded with gorgeous, secluded beaches on the outskirts of town and the tranquility afforded by its small size. **Fruit-picking and short-term work opportunities** are available April to November; working travelers praise Bowen as Queensland's best stop for short-term employment thanks to an abundance of jobs complemented by the award-winning beaches.

Horseshoe Bay is the town's biggest attraction. To get there, follow Soldiers Rd. out of town, take a right onto Horseshoe Bay Rd., and follow it to the end. Although it can be crowded, the clay, water, and coastal boulders create a picturesque setting in which to take a swim or catch the sunrise. **Murray Bay** is a less frequented but equally beautiful beach. To get there, turn right off Horseshoe Bay Rd. onto unsealed Murray Bay Rd. From the end of the road it's a 10min. walk to the beach. Most of the town borders **Queens Bay,** accessible via Soldiers Rd. Good **fishing** and calm water can be found at **Gray's Bay,** near Horseshoe Bay. **Bowen Bus Service** runs to the beaches from the library on the corner of Herbert and Williams St. (☎4786 4414. Flag down the driver if you want a ride. $2.)

Bowen Backpackers ❷ is a popular, social hostel on the corner of Dalrymple and Herbert St., on the opposite side of town from the bay. If you are looking to make some cash, owners Kate and Andy will set you up with temporary work in the area; buses to farms leave daily from here. The backpackers has a fully equipped kitchen, A/C, and is only minutes from the beach. The hostel is always full during fruit-picking season, so book at least a week ahead. (☎4786 3433; www.users.bigpond.com/bowenbackpackers. Dorms $140 per wk., includes transport to/from work; doubles $150 per wk. Daily rates available. MC/V.) A block down on the corner of Herbert and George St. is the **Central Hotel ❷,** where you can grab a meal in the **Stunned Mullet Bistro ❷,** a beer at the bar, and head upstairs to bed. The rooms are clean and reasonably priced. (☎4786 1812. Rooms from $20.) At the other end of town is **Horseshoe Bay Resort ❷,** a family-friendly place located at the end of Horseshoe Bay Rd. (☎4786 2564. Reception 9am-6pm. Sites for 2 $20, powered $24; cabins from $60. MC/V.)

Greyhound Australia and **Premier** buses make daily stops in Bowen in front of **Bowen Travel,** 40 Williams St. (☎4786 2835. Open M-F 7:15am-5:30pm, Sa 7:15am-noon.) The cafe next door has **Internet** access for $4 per hr.

TOWNSVILLE ☎07

Townsville (pop. 100,000), the largest city in the tropical north, was established long before the backpacking subculture infiltrated the region. The Central Business District (CBD) is surprisingly cosmopolitan and pedestrian-friendly, and it has done an excellent job of expanding to fill tourists' needs. Shopping malls and office buildings mix with hostels and museums in the compact, revitalized CBD. Open-air eateries, night markets, palm-lined promenades, and seemingly endless stretches of uncrowded beach add tropical flavor. Just outside the city (and off the mainland) sits koala-filled Magnetic Island and the world-renowned dive site of the sunken *S.S. Yongala.* Travelers return from treasure-seeking expeditions to sophisticated nightlife dominated by good wine and live music venues. Undervalued by the tourist circuit, Townsville is a lively port city with true Australian flare.

TRANSPORTATION

Flights: The **airport** (☎4727 3211) is west of the city. **Qantas** (☎4753 3311), at the Dimmey's entrance in Flinders Mall, flies direct to: **Brisbane** (1¾hr., 5 per day, $163 one-way); **Cairns** (1hr., 5 per day, $129); **Mackay** (1hr., 2 per day, $125); and **Sydney** (4½hr., 1 per day, $189). An **airport shuttle bus** (☎4775 5544) runs to the city daily 5:30am-9pm. Bookings to the airport must be made 30min. before scheduled pickup time. One-way $7, round-trip $11. To drive from the airport to the city, take John Melton Black Dr., which becomes Bundock St. Bear right onto Warburton St. and again onto Eyre St., then turn left on Denham St.

Trains: Trains depart from the new **train station** (☎4772 8288 or reservations 13 22 32; www.traveltrain.com.au) at the corner of Flinders and Morris St., a 15min. walk from the city. The Inlander train offers concession discounts and departs W and Su 3:30pm for: **Charters Towers** (3hr., $24); **Cloncurry** (16hr., $96); **Hughenden** (8hr., $56); **Mount Isa** (20½hr., $117); **Richmond** (10¾hr., $70). The first-class Tilt Train and economy Sunlander provide coastal service plus **50% discounts to ISIC cardholders.** They depart M, Tu, Th, Sa, Su at 3:55pm southbound for: **Brisbane** (24hr., $169); **Bowen** (5½hr., $43); **Mackay** (7½hr., $67); **Prosperpine** (4½hr., $54); **Rockhampton** (13hr., $112). Northbound trains depart Th and Su at 8:45am for **Cairns** (8hr., $62). Tickets are available at the **Queensland Rail Travel Centre** (☎4772 8358), located in the old train station at the corner of Flinders and Blackwood St. Open M-F 8:30am-5pm. They can also be purchased at the new train station Sa 12:15-4pm and Su 12:15-3:45pm.

Buses: The **Transit Centre** is on the corner of Palmer and Plume St., a 5min. walk from town (Open daily 6am-7:30pm). **Greyhound Australia** (☎13 14 99 or 13 20 30; open daily 5:30am-11pm) runs to: **Airlie Beach** (4hr., 6 per day, $53); **Brisbane** (20hr., 6 per day, $188); **Cairns** (4hr., 6 per day, $66); **Cardwell** (2¼hr., 6 per day, $32); **Charters Towers** (2hr., 2 per day, $35); **Cloncurry** (10hr., 2 per day, $115); **Hughenden** (4hr., 2 per day, $58); **Ingham** (1½hr., 6 per day, $33); **Innisfail** (4¼hr., 6 per day, $54); **Mackay** (5hr., 6 per day, $70); **Mission Beach** (3½hr., 4 per day, $54); **Mt. Isa** (12hr., 2 per day, $126); **Richmond** (5hr., 2 per day, $74); **Rockhampton** (9hr., 6 per day, $104). **Premier** (☎13 34 10) stops in the city twice a day: northbound at 1:35pm, southbound at 1pm.

Public Transportation: Sunbus (☎4725 8482; www.sunbus.com.au) has its main terminal in the center of Flinders Mall. Most tickets $3-4; 24hr. bus passes $10.

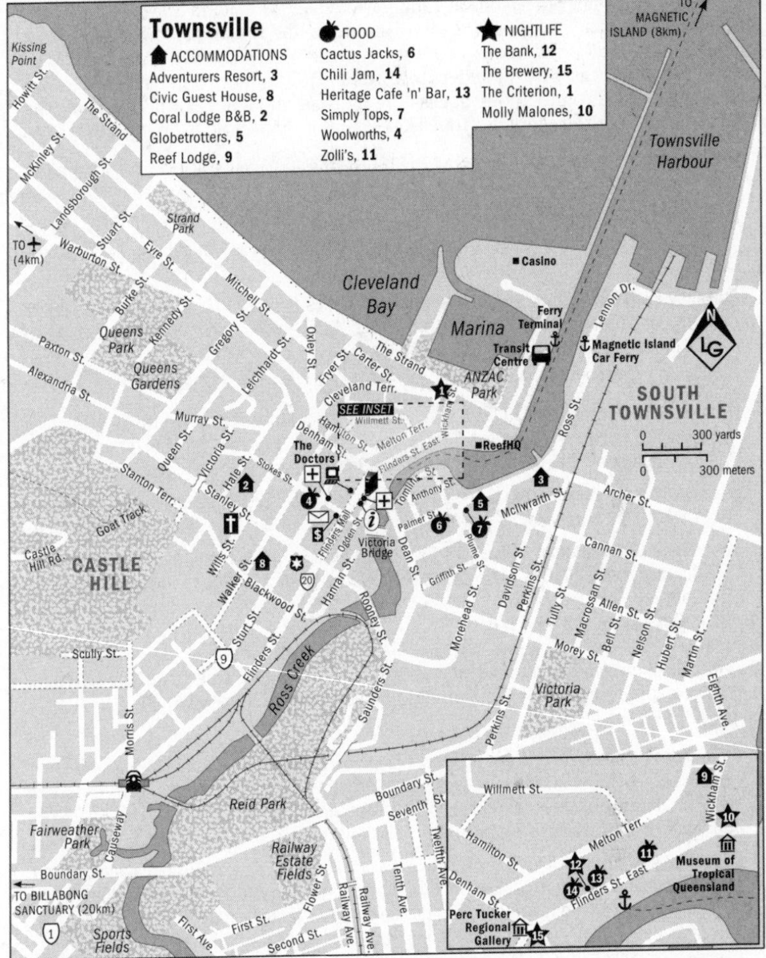

Car Rental: Thrifty (☎13 13 90), at the airport, rents from $55 per day. **Avis** (☎4721 2688, after-hours 4725 6522), is across from the Museum of Tropical Queensland on Flinders St. (open M-Sa 8am-5pm, Su 8am-noon).

Automobile Club: RACQ, 635 Sturt St. (24hr. ☎4721 4888). Open M-F 8am-5pm, Sa 8am-noon.

Taxis: Taxi Townsville (24hr. ☎4772 1555 or 13 10 08).

ORIENTATION AND PRACTICAL INFORMATION

Townsville is a large city with a complex layout, but the CBD area is relatively easy to navigate. Ross Creek separates the mall side of the CBD from the Transit Centre side. Buses stop at the Transit Centre on Palmer St., where you can find several hostels. From Palmer St., it's only a 10min. walk over the **Victoria Bridge** to the open-air **Flinders Mall.** The beach and many restaurants line **The Strand,** a 5-10min. walk from the mall. Most of Flinders's cross streets will take you to The Strand; the easiest way is to walk east down Flinders toward ReefHQ and turn left. **Castle Hill** looms in the city's background and is accessible by road and a steep walking trail (the "Goat Track"); take Gregory St. from The Strand or Stanley St. from the CBD.

Tourist Office: Visitors Centre (☎4721 3660), the big circular kiosk in the center of Flinders Mall. Open M-F 9am-5pm, Sa-Su 9am-1pm.

Reef and National Park Information Centre: (☎4721 2399), located outside of the CBD in Cape Palerando. All the answers regarding marine life. Open M-F 9am-5pm, Sa-Su 10am-4pm.

Currency Exchange: Bank of Queensland, 16 Stokes St. (☎4772 1799), often has the best rates. Commission $8. Open M-Th 9:30am-4pm, F 9:30am-5pm. **ATMs** are common in Flinders Mall and the CBD.

Police: (☎4759 9777), on the corner of Stanley and Sturt St.

Hospital: The Doctors (☎4781 1111) on the corner of Stokes and Sturt St., is open daily 7am-11pm. **Northtown Medical Centre** (☎4720 8100) in Flinders Mall, in front of the Visitors Centre, offers bulk billing. Open daily 8am-5pm.

Internet Access: Internet Den, 265 Flinders Mall (☎4721 4500). $4 per hr. Open daily 9am-8pm. Free at the **library** across the mall; book ahead. Open M-F 9am-5pm, Sa-Su 9am-noon.

Post Office: General Post Office (☎4760 2021), in Post Office Plaza, on Sturt St. between Stanley and Stokes St. Open M-Sa 8:30am-5:30pm, Su 9am-12:30pm. **Postal Code:** 4810.

ACCOMMODATIONS

Townsville is not a backpacker's city, and so is a welcome change from the latenight party atmosphere of some of the other coastal locales. There are quite a few quiet, pleasant places to stay.

Civic Guest House, 262 Walker St. (☎4771 5381 or 1800 646 619; www.backpackersinn.com.au). Small, friendly, family-run service with courtesy bus, F night BBQ, and Internet access. Kitchen, laundry, and TV lounge. Reception 8am-7:30pm. 4- and 6-bed dorms $22; singles $45; doubles $50. Ensuite available. NOMADS. AmEx/MC/V. ❷

Coral Lodge B&B, 32 Hale St. (☎4771 5512 or 1800 614 613; www.corallodge.com.au). From Flinders Mall, follow Stokes St. for 4 blocks, then turn left on Hale St.; it's on the left. Friendly, clean, comfortable B&B; sits on the hillside overlooking the city. Great choice for those on a budget but looking to avoid the hostel scene. All rooms have A/C, TV, and fridge. Singles $60; ensuite $75; twins and doubles $75/90. AmEx/MC/V. ❹

Globetrotters, 45 Palmer St. (☎4771 3242; globetrotters@austarnet.com.au), next to the Transit Centre. Amazing floral displays July-Sept. Laundry, pool, BBQ, TV, tropical garden. Reception 6am-9pm. Dorms $22; twins $55; triples $23. VIP. AmEx/MC/V. ❷

Reef Lodge, 4 Wickham St. (☎4721 1112), off Flinders St. E. Large, clean rooms with cool outdoor TV nooks. Pickup from Transit Centre. Laundry, BBQ, A/C, and kitchen. Reception 8am-10pm. Dorms $20; doubles $50. AmEx/MC/V. ❷

Adventurers Resort, 79 Palmer St. (☎4721 1522 or 1800 211 522). One of the biggest backpackers in the city with over 300 rooms; feels more like an apartment building than a hostel. Enormous, clean bathrooms, a sparsely equipped kitchen, large common areas, secure parking, and a rooftop pool with an excellent view. Courtesy bus to and from Transit Centre. Key deposit $20. Reception 8am-9pm. Dorms $22; singles $35; doubles $50. VIP/YHA/ISIC. AmEx/MC/V. ❷

FOOD

Most of the city's restaurants are located on The Strand, Flinders St. East, or Palmer St. **Woolworths** supermarket, 126-150 Sturt St., is between Stanley and Stoke St. (open M-F 8am-9pm, Sa 8am-5:30pm, Su 9am-6pm).

Simply Tops (☎4772 3078) on the corner of Plume and Palmer St. Fish 'n' chips with flair. Also serves a variety of other seafood. Looks more expensive than it is; main courses $5-12. Open M-Sa 10am-9pm, Su 11:30am-9pm. AmEx/MC/V. ❶

Zolli's, 113 Flinders St. E. (☎4721 2222). Dine on authentic Sicilian cuisine over red wine and Italian music in this cozy cafe. Many seafood and pasta choices like mussel pasta ($9), as well as pizzas ($10-20). Open daily 5pm-latenight. MC/V. ❷

Heritage Cafe 'n' Bar, 137 Flinders St. E. (☎4771 2799). Ultra-trendy scene with a large selection of Australian wines. Modern cuisine includes pasta, seafood, and meat dishes (up to $25). Th bucket of prawns and XXXX beer or glass of wine for $10. F same deal with bucket of oysters. Open M-Sa 5pm-latenight, F 11am-3pm. AmEx/MC/V. ❸

Chili Jam, 207 Flinders St. E. (☎4721 5199). Delicious stir fry $9-14, noodle plates $10. Vegetarian-friendly. Open Tu-F 11:30am-2:30pm and 5:30-10pm, Sa 5-10pm. MC/V. ❷

Cactus Jacks, 21 Palmer St. (☎4721 1478). Sizzling fajitas ($18) and a wide selection of beers from Negro Modelo to Moosehead. Open daily 2pm-latenight. AmEx/MC/V. ❸

DIVING

Townsville is often overlooked as a diving destination—a shame since the coast offers some of the best diving in the tropical north. **Kelso Reef,** Townsville's most exceptional spot on the Great Barrier Reef, is home to schools of tropical fish and over 400 kinds of coral. **John Brewer, Loadstone, the Slashers,** and **Keeper Reefs** are other popular dive sites. Townsville's best dive site, however, isn't on the reef. In 1911 the **S.S. Yongala** sunk off the coast; the still-intact shipwreck is considered one of the world's best wreck sites, but it requires advanced certification or a professional guide. Most Townsville certification programs include a dive to the *Yongala.* **Yongala Dive,** 56 Narrah St., Alva Beach, offers excursions to the wreck, departing from Ayr. (☎1300 766 410; www.yongaladive.com.au. Departs daily and offers Tu transfer from Airlie Beach, 6am, $40. 2 dives with full gear $199.)

Ocean Dive, 252 Walker St. (☎4721 4233; www.oceandive.com.au). The best if you want to learn to dive. 5-day course with 2 days on the reef. VTEC certification course (required by non-recreational divers such as marine biologists) available ($610). Also offers Palm Islands and *Yongala* dives. Times vary; book ahead. AmEx/MC/V.

Adrenalin Dive, 121 Flinders St. (☎4724 0600 or 1300 644 600; www.adrenalin-dive.com.au). A small operation that offers the only daytrip to the *Yongala* wreck. The boat is nothing more than functional, but the company offers some of the best guided dives in north Queensland, including daytrips to the reef. *Yongala* trip with gear $234. Picks up from Townsville and Magnetic Island. AmEx/MC/V.

ProDive, 14 Plume St. (☎4721 1760; www.prodivetownsville.com.au), across from the old Transit Centre, offers a 5-day, open-water course including dives to the *Yongala* ($740) and a 3-day overnight cruise to the *Yongala* aboard the *Pacific Adventure* ($495). Open M-F 9am-5pm, Sa-Su 9am-4pm. AmEx/MC/V.

Sunferries (☎4771 3855 or 1800 447 333; www.sunferries.com.au), at the ferry terminal on Flinders St. Makes daytrips to John Brewer Reef. Departs Tu, W, Sa, and Su at 8:30am; returns 5:20pm. $139, students $125, children $84. Certified dive $70 extra; discover dive $90. AmEx/MC/V.

Tropical Dive (☎4771 6150 or 1800 776 150; www.tropicaldiving.com.au) visits the pristine Wheeler Reef. Departs from Townsville and Magnetic Island. 1st Discover lesson $75, 2nd lesson $40. Daytrips $145, students and backpackers $135, children $79, families $374. 5-day course with 2 days on reef and 4 dives $499. AmEx/MC/V.

SIGHTS

Townsville's sizable population supports a variety of first-rate cultural and historical attractions, gardens, seaside parks, and unspoiled beaches. On the first Friday of the month (May-Dec.), The Strand's **night markets** offer food, crafts, rides, and entertainment (5-9:30pm).

REEFHQ. An extraordinary aquarium and reef education center, ReefHQ is home to a 2.5 million liter aquarium that mimics the reef ecosystem. Tours and shows include shark feeds and a visit to the sea turtle research facility. *(2-68 Flinders St. ☎4750 0800; www.reefhq.com.au. Open daily 9:30am-5pm. $21.50, children $10.50, concessions $16.50, families $54.)*

MUSEUM OF TROPICAL QUEENSLAND. If you can't get to the *Yongala*, visit the next best thing: the relics of the *HMS Pandora*, displayed in this flashy new museum. The museum also showcases Queensland's natural history, from dinosaurs to modern man. Don't miss the great deep sea creatures exhibit, including sculptures of the Loch Ness monster. *(78-102 Flinders St., next to the ReefHQ complex. ☎4726 0606. Open daily 9:30am-5pm. $12, children $7, concessions $8, families $30.)*

BILLABONG SANCTUARY. Daily presentations allow you to take a hot pic with your favorite Aussie animal. *(17km south of Townsville. Coach service available. ☎4778 8344; www.billabongsanctuary.com.au. Open daily 8am-5pm. $26, students and seniors $24, children $15, families $80.)*

ACTIVITIES

Townsville can sometimes feel like nothing more than a stopover en route to the oceanside attractions. If you're not here to dive, however, there are plenty of activities to keep you busy during your stay. Towering **Castle Hill** casts a dominating shadow over the city and offers some challenging **walking paths** that lead to spectacular views of Townsville and Magnetic Island; the best times to go are sunrise and sunset. Bring water and hiking boots; the paths are long, steep, and slippery. There's also a road to the top for the less aerobically inclined. **Coral Sea Skydivers,** 14 Plume St., leads tandem jumps daily, as well as two- and five-day certification courses for solo jumps. (☎4772 4889; www.coralseaskydivers.com.au. Book ahead. Tandem $315-415, depending on altitude.)

NIGHTLIFE

Remedy, a free monthly nightlife publication, will lead you to all the hottest shows and bars in the city. **Molly Malones,** on the corner of Flinders St. E. and Wickham St., has nightly live music and Irish jam sessions on Sundays. They also have a good **restaurant ❷** with main courses around $15 and burgers for $10. The clientele is a combination of locals and backpackers. (☎4771 3428. Open daily noon-2pm and 6-9pm.) The newest hotspot in the city is **The Brewery,** on the corner of Denham and Flinders St. E. Award-winning brewer Brendan Flanagan concocts delicious ales and lagers; the full dinner menu also pleases the crowds. Substantial discounts are available at some hostels. (☎4724 0333. Open daily 11am-latenight.) **The Bank,** 150 Flinders St. E., is one of the most popular clubs in Townsville. Located in an old bank, it is frequented by locals and backpackers alike. (☎4721 1916. Open Tu-Su 8pm-5am.) **The**

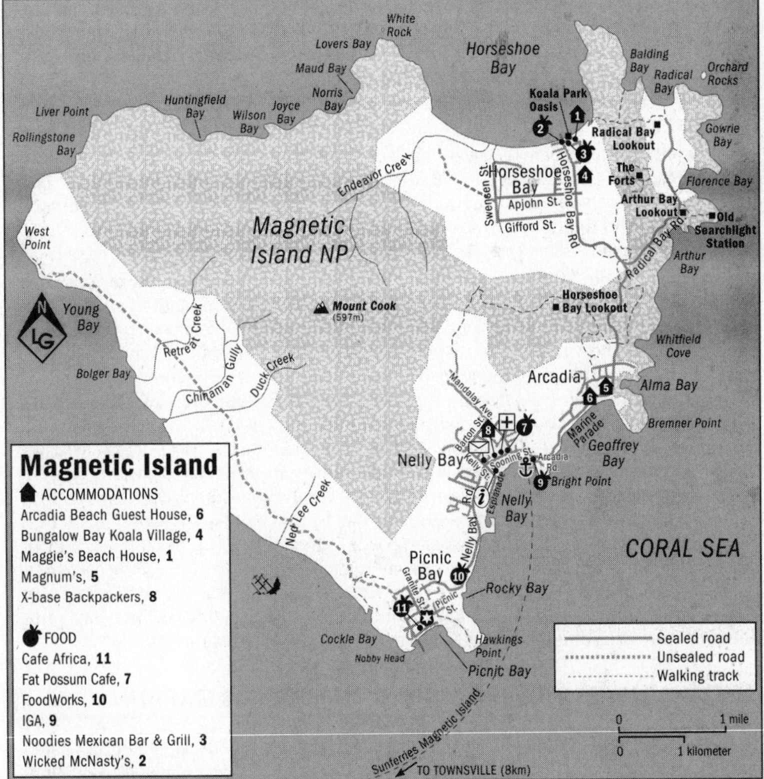

Criterion, on the corner of Wickham St. and The Strand, is a favorite hangout for local youth; it's an old hotel pub that turns into a rowdy club late at night. It's attached beer garden, **The Starter Bar,** has wet t-shirt contests and live music. (☎4721 5777. Open Tu-W 5pm-3am, Th-Sa 5pm-5am, Su 2pm-5am.)

MAGNETIC ISLAND ☎07

Originally named because it interfered with Captain Cook's compass, the description "magnetic" now aptly describes the island's effect on visitors. Seduced by secluded bays, mountains teeming with wildlife, clear waters, and a relaxed atmosphere, many come for a day and stay for a week. Only a short ferry ride from Townsville, the large island is dominated by national parkland and is home to the largest concentration of wild koalas in Australia. The only inhabited area is a mere 20km of eastern coastline; the rest of the island is covered with tracks winding through tranquil wilderness. Averaging 320 sunny days per year, "Maggie Island" is paradise even when the rest of the tropics are wet and dreary.

TRANSPORTATION

The only public transportation to the island is **Sunferries Magnetic Island,** 168-192 Flinders St. East (☎4771 3855; www.sunferries.com.au). Pedestrian **ferries** leave from Townsville's Breakwater terminal (this is also the Greyhound Australia bus station) on Sir Leslie Thiess Dr. by The Strand (25min., 12-15 per day, $25 round-trip) and return from Magnetic Island's Nelly Bay. The only way to get vehicles across is on Capricorn Barge Company's **Magnetic Island Car Ferry,** on Palmer St. Six passengers and a car can travel for $140 round-trip. (☎4772 5422; www.magneticislandferry.com.au. 1hr.; M-F 8 per day, Sa and Su 7 per day. Book ahead.)

There are less than 20km of sealed roads on the island, and the bus system covers all of them. **Magnetic Island Buses** (☎4778 5130) run roughly every 50min. from Picnic Bay to Horseshoe Bay; stops are marked by blue signs. Tickets ($2-5), one-day unlimited passes ($11), and multiple-day passes are sold by drivers. Buses operate daily from 6am-11pm. **Magnetic Island Taxis** (☎13 10 08) charges about $18 to cross the island.

Renting a "moke" (an open-air mini-car) is extremely popular. **Moke Magnetic,** opposite the ferry terminal, rents to ages 21 and over; rentals include 60km plus petrol ($70 per day, 25 and under $80). They also rent 4WD vehicles (from $90 per day) for those who want to make the trek to West Point or Radical Bay. When split between a group, this is an inexpensive way to enjoy some freedom. (☎4778 5377. $300 deposit or credit card imprint required. Open daily 8am-5pm.) **Tropical Topless Car Rentals,** at the Harbour, has small, open-roofed, pink and yellow cars with unlimited kilometers, perfect for indulging Barbie (or Ken) fantasies. (☎4758 1111. $75 per day.) Scooters can also be rented in Horseshoe Bay from **Hooterz Scooterz.** (☎4778 5317. $35 per day, $300 deposit. Open daily 9am-5pm.) But perhaps the best option is to see the island via quiet **electric bikes.** They can be taken off-road (scooters, mokes, and topless cars must remain on sealed roads), they're fast (up to 50 kph), they're eco-friendly, and they're cheap. Rent from Maggie's Beach House (see **Accommodations,** p. 409) or call ☎04 2524 4193 (www.goelectric.com.au. ½-day $15, full-day $25.) **Bicycles** can also be rented at most accommodations for $15 per day—but beware: there are some brutal hills between Nelly and Horseshoe Bay.

ORIENTATION AND PRACTICAL INFORMATION

The island is roughly triangular in shape, with all accommodations, restaurants, and activities along the east coast. The ferry arrives at the brand new **Magnetic Harbour** in **Nelly Bay.** The old ferry port was just to the south in **Picnic Bay,** now a residential neighborhood and upscale resort. From Picnic Bay you can also head west on an unsealed road (no mokes or scooters allowed) to **West Point,** a popular sunset spot. Continuing north from Nelly Bay will take you to **Arcadia,** a 15min. bus ride from the ferry; it boasts great beaches and a couple of nice restaurants. **Horseshoe Bay,** a 30min. bus ride from the ferry, is the island's northernmost populated area and has a water sports center. **Radical** and **Balding Bays,** near Horseshoe Bay, are only accessible by foot or 4WD; the treks are short and rewarding. **Florence** and **Arthur Bays** sit just a bit south and are closer to the main road.

Tourist Office: Information Centre (☎4758 1862), at the Ferry Terminal. Open M-Sa 8am-5pm, Su 8am-3pm.

Banks: The post office is the local agent for **Commonwealth Bank. ATMs** are at the Food-Works in Horseshoe Bay, Arcadia, and Nelly Bay (see **Food,** p. 409), at the Express Food Store in Picnic Bay, at Maggie's Beachhouse in Horseshoe Bay, and at Magnum's in Arcadia.

Police: (24hr. ☎4778 5270), on the corner of Granite and Picnic St., Picnic Bay. Open M 8:30am-noon, W and F 8:30am-2pm.

Medical Services: The **Magnetic Island Medical Centre,** 68 Sooning St., Nelly Bay (emergencies ☎000 or 4778 5107). Diving medical exams $60. Open M-F 9am-5pm, Sa 9am-1pm.

Internet Access: $6 per hr. at most hostels.

Post Office: On Sooning St. in Nelly Bay (☎4778 5118). Open M-F 8:30am-5pm, Sa 9-11am. **Postal Code:** 4819.

ACCOMMODATIONS

Hostels are in Picnic Bay, Arcadia, and Horseshoe Bay. The Magnetic Island Bus Company offers discounted fares to accommodations from the Ferry Terminal.

Bungalow Bay Koala Village, 40 Horseshoe Bay Rd., Horseshoe Bay (☎1800 285 577 or 4778 5577; www.bungalowbay.com.au). Great atmosphere; cabins bordering a eucalyptus forest. Excellent amenities: large kitchen, pool, hammocks, and nightly tropical games like coconut husking and limbo. BBQ and bar with nightly meals (from $12). Visit the attached koala sanctuary and perform the standard hold-and-smile with a croc, koala, or python (presentations at 10am, noon, and 2:30pm; $19, children $10), or have a Bush Tucker Brunch with "koalas on display" ($25, children $12.50). Sites $10 per person, powered $12.50; dorms $22; doubles $57. YHA. ❶

Arcadia Beach Guest House, 27 Marine Pde., Arcadia (☎4778 5668; www.arcadiabeachguesthouse.com.au). Essentially a B&B with a soft spot for backpackers; even claims to be the world's first backpackers, est. 1947). Book far ahead, as there are only 4 single beds available. Excellent view of the Bay from the upper deck. Amenities include spa, kitchen, BBQ, Internet access, and TV. Reception 8am-8pm. Single bed $30 (two per room; can be made into a double); queen-size bed $70; king-size bed $80; suites $110-130. ❷

Maggie's Beach House, 1 Pacific Dr., Horseshoe Bay (☎4778 5144 or 1800 001 544; www.maggiesbeachhouse.com.au), at the end of the beach road. Superb beachfront location; large, clean rooms with A/C; and lively atmosphere. Internet access, cafe, laundry, pool table, TV lounge, electric bike rental, and ATM. Reception 8am-7pm. **Gecko's ❷,** the posh grill, offers good meals at reasonable prices (main courses $8-19) and often has live music. Dorms $21; doubles $59; ensuite $75. VIP. ❷

X-base Backpackers, 1 Nelly Bay Rd. (☎1800 24base) between Nelly and Picnic Bay. Backpacker heaven just a 10min. walk from Picnic Bay. Located on Nelly Bay's long, gorgeous stretch of beach; diving school on-site (Reef Safari; see **Activities**), scooter/motorbike/bicycle/kayak rental. Barefoot DJs host parties almost every night with a sea breeze you won't find in any club. Campsites for 2 $25; dorms $27; doubles $62; cabins $110. ❷

Magnum's, 7 Marine Pde., Arcadia (☎1800 663 660 or 4778 5177; www.magnums.com.au). Located 50m from the beach. New, huge, and chock full of amenities including 2 swimming pools, beach volleyball court, 3 bars, and **restaurant** ❷ (main courses $8.50-17). Lots of tidy, comfortably spaced rooms in a relaxing setting. Reception 10am-10pm. Dorms $18; doubles $55. ❷

FOOD AND NIGHTLIFE

Magnetic Island's few restaurants are innovative but expensive. For cheap food, your best bet is the supermarkets. There are three **FoodWorks:** one at 55 Sooning St., Nelly Bay, 1km past the post office (☎4778 5722; open daily 7am-7pm), one in Arcadia at 5 Bright Ave., off Marine Pde. (☎4778 5387; open daily 7am-7pm), and one in Horseshoe Bay (☎4778 5080; open daily 7am-6:30pm). The **IGA** supermarket at the Harbour is the best-priced and best-stocked (☎4758 1177; open daily 6am-8:30pm). The bar crowd tends to gravitate to Arcadia and Horseshoe Bay; be warned that the island's bus service ends in the early evening.

Noodies Mexican Bar and Grill, 2/6 Pacific Dr., Horseshoe Bay (☎4778 5786). When that nacho craving hits, get your fix here. Tons of Mexican-inspired dishes; try the vegetarian quesadilla ($15). Bar has drink specials; free sombrero with every "Pancho Villa" (pitcher of margarita). Open daily 5:30-9pm, bar open until midnight. ❸

Fat Possum Cafe, 55 Sooning St., Nelly Bay (☎4778 5409). Great sandwiches, burgers, and cakes ($5-10); all-day breakfast ($6-11). M-Th and Su curry nights 5-9pm. ❶

Wicked Mcnasty's, (☎4778 5861) on Pacific Dr., Horseshoe Bay. Far from nasty. Burgers, sandwiches, milkshakes, and salads. Open daily 8am-3pm. ❶

Cafe Africa (☎4758 1119), on the Esplanade, Picnic Bay. Enjoy various types of African cuisine, burgers ($7), or foccacia and salad ($9). Excellent coffee. African arts and crafts on display in attached room. Open daily 9am-5pm. ❶

ACTIVITIES

TOURS. Indulge the rockstar within, and careen around Magnetic Island with **Tropicana Tours,** 2/26 Picnic St. Guests tour the bush in Queensland-style luxury—a 10-seat stretch Jeep Wrangler. Cruise to loud music, feed lorikeets, see gorgeous beaches, and finish with wine at sunset. (☎4758 1800; www.tropicanatours.com.au. 5hr. tour $88; full-day tour with lunch $125.)

OUTDOORS ACTIVITIES. Over 70% of Magnetic Island is comprised of national parklands, with numerous bushwalks and plenty of opportunities to enjoy the natural beauty of the island. The most popular hike is the **Forts Walk** (4km, 1½hr.), which climbs through hills where **koalas** are often spotted to the impressive ruins of a WWII command post and watch station. It's best to go during the evening when the koalas are just waking up from their afternoon nap—walk slowly and listen carefully for the soft sounds of chewing in high treetops. Even if you miss the furry fellows, you can still catch a spectacular sunset at the fort. Another option is to take the **island path** (8km, 3hr.) that leads from Picnic Bay through wetlands and mangroves to **West Point.** From Horseshoe Bay, two great walks lead to secluded **Balding Bay** and **Radical Bay.** Don't miss the **Arthur Bay** lookout, a short walk past the bay on the Radical Bay Rd. At dusk, dozens of rock wallabies come to **Geoffrey Bay,** in Arcadia, for hand-fed snacks. For a list of other walks, go to the tourist office, ask the bus drivers, or grab a map at Maggie's. **Bluey's Horseshoe Ranch,** 38 Gifford St., Horseshoe Bay, will take you riding through the bush and cantering on the beach, then let you ride bareback or go swimming in the bay. The friendly staff matches riders with horses by skill level. (☎4778 5109. 2hr. $80; ½-day $110.)

DIVING. The small, friendly dive shops on Maggie Island offer some of the most inexpensive dive options in Queensland, while the small wrecks and reefs provide opportunities for endless exploration. Open-water courses, daytrips, and overnights are all available. **Pleasure Divers,** 10 Marine Pde., Arcadia, offers good deals on PADI certification classes from the shore (3-day course $300), and also has 4-day courses that include one day on the outer reef ($469). Other options include advanced courses to the *Yongala* wreck ($419) and a PADI open-water advanced *Yongala* package ($699). For those already certified, they offer shore dives (guided or unguided) with equipment for $50. (☎4778 5788 or 1800 797 797; info@pleasure-divers.com.au. Open daily 8:30am-5pm.) **Reefsafari,** located inside **X-base Backpackers** (see **Accommodations,** p. 409), offers a 4-day PADI open-water course ($279), an advanced course with 5 dives including a Yongala wreck dive ($460), single intro dives ($65, repeat dives $50) and certified dives ($50, repeat dives $30). Packages with free nights at X-base are also available. (☎4946 4788; www.reefsafari.com.au.) Note that some of the Townsville dive companies pick up from Magnetic Island.

MORE WATER ACTIVITIES. Magnetic Island Sea Kayaks, 93 Horseshoe Bay Rd., Horseshoe Bay, departs daily at 8:15am and returns around noon. (☎4778 5424; www.seakayak.com.au. Kayak tours including a light tropical breakfast $60.) If you want to forego quiet contemplation, **Adrenalin Jet Ski Tours** allows you to roar around the island. (☎4778 5533; magneticjet@beyond.net.au. 3hr. tours depart Horseshoe Bay at 8:30am and 12:30pm; $145.)

OTHER ACTIVITIES. The Magnetic Island Country Club, Hurst St., Picnic Bay, popular with Townsville and island residents, has a nine-hole golf course plus a licensed bar and restaurant. (☎4788 5188; www.users.bigpond.net.au/migolf. Open daily from 8am. $11, 18 holes $16.) Visit koalas, wombats, emus, and talking cockatoos at the secluded **Koala Park Oasis,** on Pacific Dr., Horseshoe Bay. Follow Gifford St. past Bluey's Horseshoe Ranch for 2km and then make a right, following the signs to the Oasis for another 1.3km, the last 500m of which are unsealed road. (☎4778 5260. Open daily 9am-5pm. $10, children $5.)

INGHAM AND SURROUNDS

Ingham is known as the "Little Italy of the North;" over half the population is of Italian descent. Mediterranean influence is apparent everywhere, from architecture to customs, and it is celebrated annually on the second weekend in May during the Australian-Italian Festival. There is a **visitors center** on Townsville Rd. that provides information about the area's national parks. (☎4776 5211. Open M-F 9am-5pm.) For camping permits, head to the **QPWS,** 49 Cassady St. (☎4776 1700. Open M-F 9am-4:30pm). The **Palm Tree Caravan Park ❶,** just 3km south of town on the Bruce Hwy., offers basic campsites. (☎4776 2403. $17, powered $22.)

The region just west of Ingham has some of the most astounding natural attractions in Queensland. **Lumholtz National Park** (51km west of Ingham with 30km of unsealed road) is one of the world's oldest rainforests and home to **Wallaman Falls,** Australia's largest single-drop waterfall. The forest is also home to several species of endangered plants and animals, as well as the amethystine python, Australia's largest snake. Camping permits are by self-registration ($4.50 per person). Twenty-four kilometers south of Ingham, close to the Bruce Hwy., are the terraced **Jourama Falls.** Freshwater swimming holes, good turtle-spotting, and superb bird watching make this an ideal daytrip destination. Another 20km south, the **Mount Spec** section of **Paluma Range National Park** enchants visitors with crystal-clear streams that snake down the mountain. Camping is permitted only at **Big Crystal Creek;** you'll need a permit and key from the **QPWS** in Townsville (☎4722 5211) or Ingham (☎4777 3112). Campsites can be difficult to access in the Wet.

HINCHINBROOK ISLAND ☎07

Across the Hinchinbrook Channel is Hinchinbrook Island, Australia's largest island national park. It offers unspoiled wilderness with looming granite peaks, mangrove swamps, and a small population of the endangered manatee-like dugong. There are plenty of snorkeling opportunities and some superb bushwalks. The famous **Thorsborne Trail** (32km, 3-7 days) is the most popular hike on the island. Only 40 hikers are permitted on the trail at one time, so it's best to obtain a permit several months in advance; book up to a year ahead if you are planning to hike from April to September. (Permits can be acquired by calling ☎13 13 04 or online at www.qld.gov.au.)

Ferries take visitors to two stops on the island, one at either side of the Thorsborne Trail. **Hinchinbrook Island Ferries,** 131 Bruce Hwy., docks at the north end of the island and offers day-tours, including walks to some of its pristine beaches. One-way tickets are useful if you have a camping permit and want to walk the length of the island. (☎4066 8270 or 1800 777 021; www.hinchinbrookferries.com.au. Transfers available from Cardwell. $66, day-tour or round-trip $90.) **Hinchinbrook Wilderness Safaris** goes to the south end of the island. The small boat leaves from George Point and will bring you back to Lucinda, south of Cardwell. (☎4777 8307. $46, transfer between Cardwell and Lucinda $28.)

Daytrips to the island don't require bookings, but overnight stays (camping or staying in the resort) always do. If you're planning to camp, obtain a permit in advance ($4.50 per night). Facilities at campsites include picnic tables, BBQ, water, and toilets. The folks at the **QPWS,** located at the **Rainforest and Reef Centre,** 14 Victoria St., Cardwell, on the north side of town near the jetty, are eager to help. The center has a free informational walk that details the science behind the rainforest and its inhabitants. (☎4066 8601. Open M-F 8am-4:30pm, Sa-Su 8am-noon.)

MISSION BEACH ☎07

Transformed virtually overnight into a major backpacker destination, this nearly continuous stretch of beach deserves every ounce of the hype surrounding it. The town experiences heavy traffic, but the expansive beach offers enough space for some peace and quiet. The untouched corals and sand cays of the reefs off Mission Beach make it one of the best diving spots on the Great Barrier Reef. In the rainforest, the many cassowaries make for unique nature hikes. Mission Beach flows with adrenaline. It is a major hub of adventure sports, with arguably the best white water rafting in the country on the Tully River, and unbeatable skydiving.

TRANSPORTATION

Greyhound Australia services Mission Beach several times per day to Cairns (2¼hr., 4 per day, $28) and Townsville (3¼hr., 4 per day, $45). **Premier** buses run twice per day. Once you arrive, a hostel courtesy bus will take you to your accommodation. You can also use these buses during your stay, or contact the **Mission Beach Bus Service** (☎4068 7400; www.transnorthbus.com), which runs about once per hr. 9am-6pm ($1.50 per section, day-ticket $10). **Sugarland Car Rentals** is located 50m from the bus-stop on 30 Wongaling Beach Rd. (☎4068 8272). Rentals are available from $55 per day (drop-offs in Cairns are $30 extra).

ORIENTATION AND PRACTICAL INFORMATION

The region known as Mission Beach is actually a group of four communities lining a 14km stretch of waterfront property. From north to south, the towns are: **Bigil Bay, Mission Beach, Wongaling Beach,** and **South Mission Beach.** The main streets are **Porter Promenade,** which runs through Mission Beach proper, and **Cassowary Drive,** which runs through Wongaling. The massive cassowary statue in the center of Wongaling Beach, in front of the bus stop, is a popular landmark. Just off the coast are the **Family Islands,** including popular **Dunk Island.**

You can pick up a map of the area, book tours and accommodations, and surf the net (Internet access $5 per hr.; CD burning available) at the **visitors center** (☎4068 6899; www.missionbeachinfo.com. Open daily 9am-7pm). For information about national parks, try the **Wet Tropics Information Centre,** on Porter Promenade as you leave Mission Beach heading to Bigil Bay. (☎4068 7099. Open daily 9am-5pm.) Local services include: **ATMs** at the **supermarket** in Mission Beach and the Mission Beach Resort; the **police** (☎4068 8422. Open M, W, F 8am-noon; T and Th 8am-11am), 500m past the cassowary statue at the corner of Webb Rd. and Cassowary Dr. in Wongaling Beach; and **Internet** access at **intermission @ the beach** in the Village Green, off Porter Pde. (☎4068 1117). No banks in Mission Beach exchange foreign currency. There is a **pharmacy** behind the bus stop in Wongaling (☎4068 8211. Open M-F 8:30am-5:30pm, Sa 9am-noon). The **post office,** on Porter Pde., exchanges traveler's checks for $8. (Open M-F 9am-5pm.) **Postal Code:** 4852.

ACCOMMODATIONS

All hostels listed book tours, offer free pickup at the bus station, and provide courtesy buses around town. If you're camping or caravanning, try **Mission Beach Camping** ❶ on Porter Pde. (☎4068 7104. Sites from $8 per person.)

Mission Beach Backpacker's Lodge, 28 Wongaling Beach Rd., Wongaling Beach. (☎1800 686 316 or 4068 8317; www.missionbeachbackpacker.com.) Excellent location 70m from the Giant Cassowary and bus station; only 400m from Wongaling Beach. A simple, relaxed place to crash, impeccably clean and with staff that makes the place feel like home. Internet access, pool, laundry, TV room, free BBQ on occasion. Reception 7am-8pm. Dorms $18; doubles $40. VIP/YHA. AmEx/DC/MC/V. ❷

Scotty's Mission Beach House, 167 Reid Rd. (☎4068 8676; scottys@znet.net.au), at the end of Webb St., off Cassowary Dr. The hip staff are friendly and helpful. 24hr. kitchen and mini-market. Every night's a party in **Scotty's Bar** ❶ (meals under $12; backpacker special $6.50), but it's removed enough from rooms to ensure a good sleep. Internet access, laundry, pool, TV room. Reception 7:30am-7pm. 12-bed dorms $21; 4-bed ensuite dorms $26; doubles $50; ensuite $55. AmEx/DC/MC/V. ❷

The Treehouse (☎4068 7137), on Bingil Bay Rd., Bingil Bay. The closest community in Mission Beach is perched high in the rainforest canopy. BBQ, pool, laundry, ping pong, and reading space. Rooms all around a common area where music (guests' choice) plays until 10pm. F night all-you-can-eat BBQ $12. Reception 7:30-11:30am and 3:30-9pm. Sites $12 per person; dorms $23.50; doubles $58.50. YHA. AmEx/DC/MC/V. ❷

The Sanctuary (☎4088 6064 or 1800 777 012; www.sanctuaryatmission.com), on Holt Rd., Bingil Bay. The most remote accommodation in Mission Beach; hit by a cyclone in 2006 and recently rebuilt. Hardwood treehouse nestled in the rainforest, overlooking the ocean; the only thing between you and the cassowaries is the mozzie screen. Surrounded by acres of preserved rainforest with walking tracks. Internet access, yoga classes ($12), massages, kitchen, pool, and 18 hectares of rainforest to explore. No children under 11. Shared hut $32; single huts $60.50; twin and double huts $65; single cabins $145; twin and double cabins $165. AmEx/DC/MC/V. ❸

FOOD

There are several excellent restaurants on the Village Green in Mission Beach proper. Supermarkets include **Foodmarket,** on Porter Promenade, and **Foodstore** (☎4068 8410), in Wongaling Beach, behind the gigantic cassowary. (Both open daily 8am-7pm; both accept major credit cards.)

Piccolo Paradise (☎4068 7008), on David St. in the Village Green. A popular cafe that offers fresh baguette sandwiches, excellent pastas, pizza, and a selection of juices. Meals $10-15. Open Tu-Sa and Su 8:30am-9pm. AmEx/DC/MC/V. ❶

Toba, 37 Porter Promenade (☎4068 7852), next to the Village Green. Serves a variety of Asian cuisine including Indonesian, Vietnamese, and Japanese dishes. Main courses $16-25. Open M and W-Su 6pm-latenight. AmEx/DC/MC/V. ❸

Coconutz (☎4068 7397), next to the Village Green on Porter Pde. One of the few licensed bars in Mission Beach; serves delicious meals, specializing in Asian and Italian food. Lunch $10-16, dinner $16-22. Billiards. Free traveler's check exchange. Open daily in high season 8am-1:30am, in low season 10am-midnight. AmEx/DC/MC/V. ❸

SIGHTS AND ACTIVITIES

DIVING. Mission Beach occupies a unique spot on the reef where coral drop-offs create long walls of underwater gardens. **Calypso Dive,** 100m past Mission Beach Backpackers on Wongaling Beach Rd., offers a range of dive courses and trips to the reef (☎4068 8432; www.calypsodive.com). **Quick Cat** also makes trips to the reef, both directly and via Dunk Island. (☎4068 7289 or 1800 654 242; www.quick-catscuba.com. $110, children $55; 1 intro dive $80, 2 certified dives $95.)

HIKING. Beautiful **walking tracks** crisscross the area. On the back of the Mission Beach street directory (available free around town) you'll find a list of readily accessible parks, forests, and walking tracks. There are several in **Licuala State Forest,** including the **Rainforest Circuit Walk** (1.3km, 30min.), a nice stroll under a canopy of Licuala Fan Palms. Start at the Tully-Mission Beach Rd. carpark. **Licuala Walking Track** (7.8km, 3hr.) stretches north through coastal lowland rainforest to the El Arish-Mission Beach Rd. The **Cutten Brothers Walk** (1.5km, 30min.) snakes through mangroves between Alexander Dr. and Clump Point jetty. The **Bicton Hill Track** (4km; starts 3km past the Wet Tropics Info Centre) and the **Kennedy Track** (7km, 4hr.) are longer walks that feature mangroves, beaches, and rainforest.

OTHER ACTIVITIES. Adventure sports are the most popular activity in Mission Beach. **Jump the Beach** offers tandem **skydiving** with Queensland's only beach landing, complemented by incredible views of the rainforest, beach, reef, and islands. Many consider Mission Beach to be one of Australia's top jumps. (☎1800 638 005; www.jumpthebeach.com.au. 10,000 ft. $219; 14,000 ft. $270.) **Raging Thunder River Rafting** takes groups to the class IV rapids of the Tully River, where the views of the surrounding rainforest are almost as exciting as the roaring white water. (☎4030 7990; www.ragingthunder.com.au. Full-day rafting, lunch, and transfers $145. Also departs from Cairns.)

DAYTRIP FROM MISSION BEACH: DUNK ISLAND

Their proximity makes the **Family Islands** ideal escapes from mainland life. **Dunk Island,** a.k.a. the "father island," is the most frequented, and its proximity makes it the only real daytrip. The island became famous because of E.J. Banfield's *Confessions of a Beachcomber*, an account of his life on the island from 1897 to 1923. Nearby **Bedarra,** a.k.a. "the mother," is uninhabited, save for a swanky resort. The "twins" are slightly farther out and the smaller land masses at the fringe of the group are the "brothers, sisters, and triplets."

The main attractions on Dunk, aside from postcard-perfect beaches, are the **walking tracks.** The local favorite is the walk around the island (10km, 4hr.), which covers diverse landscapes and takes hikers to the island's highest point. An easier option is the coastal hike (1km, 15min.) up to **Muggy Muggy Beach** from the dock. Muggy Muggy is hidden in a pocket of 360 million year-old rocks; find it and treat yourself to excellent **snorkeling.** The hike to the **Mount Kootaloo Lookout** (2hr.), the highest point on the island, provides a good workout and a beautiful view.

The **Dunk Island Resort** ❺ (☎4068 8199) monopolizes all island activities, and the rooms are rather expensive ($139, including breakfast and dinner). Some of the best-equipped **campsites** ❶ in north Queensland are only a short distance away (permits purchased on-site, $4.50). These sites are popular, so book well ahead. **Dunk Island Watersports** (☎4068 8199), near the jetty, issues the **camping permits** and rents a slew of water toys, including paddle skis ($20 per hr.), sailboards ($25 per hr.), snorkel gear ($15 per hr.), dinghies (½-day $65), wakeboarding and waterskiing ($25 per 15min.), and catamarans ($25 per hr.). Daytrippers can purchase the **Resort Experi-**

ence Pass ($40) at the Watersports shed, which entitles visitors to use of the resort facilities and a meal at the Jetty Cafe or at EJ's in the resort. The only place to eat on the island, besides the resort's upscale restaurant, is the **Jetty Cafe ❷,** next door to Dunk Island Watersports, which serves burgers, pizza, grilled fish, and salads. (☎4068 8199. Main courses $9-15. Open daily 11am-7pm.)

Three boats service Dunk Island. Those looking to maximize time there should opt for the **Dunk Island Express Water Taxi,** on Banfield Pde., near Scotty's in Wongaling Beach. (☎4068 8310. 10min., 6 per day, $25 round-trip.) **Quick Cat,** which departs from Clump Point Jetty, 1km north of the village green, also services the island. (☎4068 7289 or 1800 654 242; www.quickcatcruises.com.au. Departs daily 9:30am, returns 4:45pm. $34, children $17.) For those in no rush to get to Dunk, Quick Cat also does a cruising daytrip around the Family Islands ($63, with lunch $75). **Dunk Island Ferry & Cruises** departs from Clump Point or Kurrimine Beach, and offers a daytrip that includes snorkeling, boomnet rides (being dragged behind a boat while sitting on a net), a sail around the islands (including Bedarra), and a BBQ lunch. (☎4068 7211. $72, children $25.) **Coral Sea Kayaking** runs daytrips to Dunk, including small breakfast, lunch, environmental interpretation, and snorkeling gear. (☎4068 9154; www.coralseakayaking.com. ½-day $65, full-day $100.)

NEAR MISSION BEACH

KURRIMINE BEACH

Kurrimine Beach, 10km off the Bruce Hwy. just north of Mission Beach, is a pristine stretch of sand appealing for its quiet remoteness (or even desolation). The north end has a **caravan park ❷**; at the southern end is **Kurrimine Beach Holiday Park ❷,** at the end of Jacob's Rd. (☎4065 6166. Linen $5. Campsites $19, powered $22; ensuite cabins $55. Book ahead.) For a few days in July, the tides are just right to reach King Reef by foot. Ask at the local **Hub Cafe** for a tide chart and advice on the best time to visit. Queenslanders are also drawn to this area for its great fishing.

PARONELLA PARK

Between Cairns and Mission Beach lies the Moorish castle of **Paronella Park** (☎4065 3225; www.paronellapark.com.au). Spaniard José Paronella built the main thoroughfare of the area in the 1930s as a gift for his fiancée. Uninhabited, the buildings degenerated into ruins, a testament to the intense northern Queensland climate. The authenticity of the buildings and encroaching rainforest make this a sight to be seen. Winner of Queensland's highest tourism award, the park was discovered by the entertainment industry and has served as the backdrop for three movies, eight TV shows, a music video, and an international magazine photo shoot. Enthusiastic guides give tours of the grounds, then leave you to explore on your own. The "Darkness Falls Tour" (starting at 6:20pm) is particularly breathtaking as the castle and many ruins are lit up at night. The admission fee ($26, children $13) includes all tours.

Though Paronella Park is inaccessible by public transportation, it is not hard to find a day tour from Cairns or Mission Beach (Dunk Island Cruises, p. 415, offers such services on their transfers between Cairns and Dunk Island). If you are driving, look for signs along the Bruce Hwy. (the South Johnstone exit is the fastest); from the Tablelands, follow the signs to South Johnstone and you'll see the sign for the park. When you've finished gawking at the exquisite architecture, take time to stroll down Kauri Ave., which offers a view of towering Kauri pines. Or feed the fish and eels in the teeming waterfall pool in the ruins of the castle's grand staircase. (Open daily 9am-7:30pm.)

INNISFAIL

North of Mission Beach is the town of Innisfail. Although there are few tourist attractions, the Johnstone River and beautiful beaches make it a pleasant pit stop. There is also a high demand for **fruit-pickers** year-round. Just north of Innisfail, the road to the **Atherton Tablelands** (p. 428) branches inland toward **Millaa Millaa.**

The **bus station** is on Edith St. (which becomes the Bruce Hwy. as it leaves Innisfail) in front of ANZAC Park. **Greyhound Australia** runs daily to Cairns (1¼hr., $21) and Townsville (3½hr., $55). The **railway station** is off the Bruce Hwy. on Station St., west of town heading north toward Cairns (☎13 22 32; www.traveltrain.com.au). The **visitors center,** at the corner of Bruce Hwy. and Eslick St., just before the town center when entering from the south, books tours. (☎4061 7422; www.innisfailtourism.com.au. Open M-F 9am-4pm, Sa-Su 10am-3pm; call Paronella Park after hours until 9:30pm.)

There are four hostels in Innisfail, and all are chiefly intended for backpackers looking for work. Be sure to book ahead for all accommodations. **The Codge Lodge ❸**, 63 Rankin St., off Grace St. (which intersects Edith St.) is the best of them. Amenities include a huge pool, satellite TV, a nice lookout over the Johnstone River, free laundry, Internet access, transport, and certainly the nicest rooms. (☎4061 8055. Reception sometimes unattended, call ahead. Dorms $30, weekly $130; singles $40; twins $60. Cash only.) **Innisfail Backpackers Hostel ❷,** 125 Edith St. across from KFC, is a very social, relaxed hostel full of worn-out fruit-pickers and construction workers. It's got all the necessary extras: kitchens, satellite TV, Internet access, free shuttle to and from work, and laundry. (☎04 0951 8246 or 04 1819 2414. Dorms $20, weekly $130.) The **Walkabout Motel ❷,** on Ernest St. (across from Kmart) as you enter Innisfail on the Bruce Hwy. from the south, also has free buses to and from work, as well as a kitchen, laundry, and satellite TV. (☎4061 2311; motelwalkabout@bigpond.com. Dorms weekly $125.)

BOOK ONLINE. If your hostel can't find you a job, try looking in the Yellow Pages under "construction" or "bananas."

FAR NORTH QUEENSLAND

The northeast corner of the continent is nothing short of heaven for outdoor adventurers. The Great Barrier Reef snakes close to shore, luring divers to its spectacular underwater haven. Vast tropical rainforests press up against the Coral Sea by the green-covered mountains of the Great Dividing Range. The rich variety of wildlife and untouched landscape prove that the Far North's greatest attraction is its natural beauty.

While Cairns caters to travelers seeking urban comforts, the more remote parts of this land remain untamed wilderness. The Captain Cook Hwy. leads modern-day trailblazers north into the rainforest, which becomes increasingly dense around Cape Tribulation. Wilder yet is the Cape York peninsula, which starts beyond Cooktown and stretches to the Torres Strait, separating the Gulf of Carpentaria from the Coral Sea, and Australia from Papua New Guinea. Travelers daring enough to make the journey should anticipate very basic unsealed roads.

CAIRNS ☎07

The last major city at the corner of the great tropical outback, Cairns (pronounced "cans") is both the northern terminus of the backpacker route and the premier gateway to snorkeling and scuba diving on the Great Barrier Reef. The neon signs and

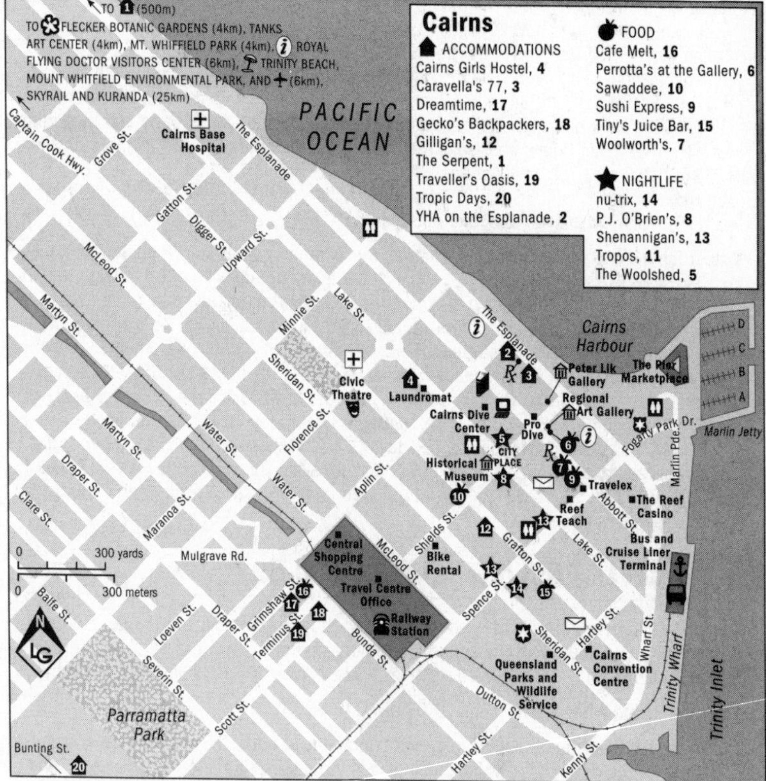

tourist attractions of the Central Business District (CBD) bombard travelers with colors rivaled only by the flamboyant creatures of the underwater world. While tidal mudflats preclude traditional beach activities, bars, nightclubs, and cafes provide plenty of diversions for travelers. The atmosphere is friendly, relaxed, and outrageously touristy. More of a big town than a small city, Cairns is the perfect place for adventure activities of all kinds.

INTERCITY TRANSPORTATION

Flights: The **airport** (☎4052 9744) is 6km north of Cairns on the Captain Cook Hwy. Follow the signs. For the cheapest flights, try **Student Flights** (☎1800 069 063) or major regional carriers. **Virgin Blue** is a great domestic resource; also services New Zealand (☎13 67 89; www.virginblue.com.au). **Qantas** (☎13 13 13; www.qantas.com) has daily flights to: **Adelaide** (5-8hr., 5-7 per day, $425); **Brisbane** (2hr., 11 per day, $189); **Canberra** (5hr., 10-13 per day, $404); **Darwin** (2-5hr., 6 per day, $425); **Hobart** (6-10hr., 6-7 per day, $362); **Melbourne** (5hr., 9 per day, $343); **Perth** (5-10hr., 6-9 per day, $453); **Sydney** (3hr., 7-8 per day, $342). Smaller **Flight West Airlines** (☎13 23 92) has domestic service; also flies to Papua New Guinea. Many hostels run a free airport pickup service; call from the terminal. To get back to the airport, you'll have to book ahead and pay $10 for the **Airport Shuttle** (☎4048 8355). Buses also run to town from the terminal ($5). **Taxis** to town, available 24hr., cost about $15.

Trains: The train station is between Bunda St. and the Cairns Central shopping mall. From the Esplanade, walk inland down Spence St. It's on the right, or straight through to the back of Cairns Central. The **Rail Travel Centre** (☎4036 9341, 24hr. bookings ☎13 22 32), inside the train station, sells tickets. YHA discount 10% for long-distance trips. Open M-Th 7:30am-4:30pm, F 9am-4:30pm, Sa 7:30-10am, Su 7:30-9:30am. The **East Coast Discover Pass** (☎132 232; www.backpackerrailpass.com) offers unlimited travel for up to 6 months and covers rail between Cairns and **Brisbane** ($266.20), **Melbourne** ($465.30), and **Sydney** ($316.20). Trains run to **Brisbane** (31-32hr.; Tu, W, F-Su 8:30am; $187-281) and **Kuranda** (bookings ☎4036 9333. Trains daily 8:30 and 9:30am, Sa 8:30am; $37, $52 round-trip. Student, senior, and family discounts.)

Buses: The bus station, forlorn and a bit run-down, is at Trinity Wharf, on Wharf St. Open daily 6:15am-1am. Luggage storage $7-12 per day. **Sun Palm Coaches** (☎4099 4992) goes to: **Cape Tribulation** (4hr., 2 per day, $90 round-trip); **Cooktown** (Inland route: 5½hr.; W, F, Sa 1 per day; $69, $130 round-trip. Coastal route: 8hr.; June-Oct. Tu, Th, Sa 1 per day; $69, $130 round-trip); and **Port Douglas** (1¼hr., several per day, same day round-trip $45, open round-trip $59). **Greyhound Australia** (☎13 20 30) has 10% ISIC/VIP/YHA discounts and runs to: **Airlie Beach** (11hr., 6 per day, $87); **Brisbane** (28hr., 5 per day, $188); **Cardwell** (3hr., 5 per day, $30); **Ingham** (3½hr., 5 per day, $42); **Innisfail** (1¼hr., 5 per day, $22); **Mackay** (12hr., 5 per day, $120); **Mission Beach** (2¼hr., 2 per day, $22); **Rockhampton** (15hr., 6 per day, $124); **Townsville** (6hr., 5 per day, $49). **Premier** (☎4031 6495 or 13 34 10) has less expensive rates and VIP/YHA discounts, but their buses depart less frequently.

LOCAL TRANSPORTATION

Buses: Sunbus (☎4057 7411; www.sunbus.com.au), on Lake St. in the market in City Place. Buses go south into the suburbs and north to Palm Cove, but not to the airport. ($1-6; unlimited day pass $10.20, families $22.60; central Cairns-only pass $6.30.)

Taxis: Black and White (24hr. ☎13 10 08 or 4048 8333).

Car Rental: The bigger companies in Cairns charge those under 25 a surcharge or significantly raise the deductible, which can increase the daily rental price by up to $50, and even more for 4WD rentals.

A1 Car Rentals, 141 Lake St. (☎1300 301 175), has weekly rates from $39 and a great selection of higher-end vehicles. Some of the lowest prices for 4WD rentals ($135+). Open daily 7am-7pm.

4WD Hire Service (associated with Hertz), 397-399 Sheridan St. (☎4032 3094 or 1800 077 353; www.4wdhire.com.au), specializes in long-distance trips on questionable roads, such as the drive to Cape York. More expensive than **A1 Car Rentals**, but has the toughest trucks available.

National, 135 Abbott St. (☎13 10 45 or 1300 131 407), has weekly rates starting at $45 per day, 4WD $145 per day. Open M-F 7:30am-6pm, Sa-Su 8am-5pm.

Avis, 135 Lake St. (☎4051 5911), rents weekly starting at $49 per day, 4WD $160 per day. Open M-F 7:30am-5:30pm; Sa, Su, and public holidays 8am-4pm.

Leisure Car Rentals, 314 Sheridan St. (☎4051 8988), is a bit far from the CBD but has inexpensive rentals starting at $45 per day. Open daily 7am-5pm.

Travellers AutoBarn, 123-125 Bunda St. (☎4041 3722 or 1800 674 374), rents campervans with unlimited kilometers, local or one-way, from $65 per day. Open M-F 9am-5pm, Sa 9am-1pm.

Road Report: the **Royal Automobile Club of Queensland (RACQ),** 138 McLeod St. (24hr. ☎4051 6543; www.racq.com.au). Open daily 8am-5:15pm.

Bike Rental: Bolwell Scoota 47 Shields St. (☎4031 3444; www.scoota.com.au), between Mcleod and Sheridan St. Rents bicycles for $12 per day, $40 per wk.; scooters (must be 21+ with driver's license) $27 per ½ day, $35 full day, and $130 per wk.

ORIENTATION

Cairns is framed by rainforested hills to the west, a harbor to the east, and mangrove swamps to the north and south. The city's streets are straight and intersect at right angles, making for easy navigation. The **Esplanade,** with its many hostels and eateries, runs along the waterfront. At the street's southern end is **The Pier,** with a man-made lagoon and upscale shopping at the heavily commercial Pier Marketplace. Farther south, the Esplanade becomes **Wharf Street** and runs past **Trinity Wharf** and the **Transit Centre. Shields Street** runs perpendicular to the Esplanade, crossing **Abbott Street** into **City Place,** a pedestrian mall with open-air concert space and coffee shops galore. From this intersection, **Lake Street** runs parallel to the Esplanade. Continuing away from the water, Shields St. also intersects **Grafton Street** and **Sheridan Street** (called Cook Hwy. north of the city). The **Cairns Railway Station** is on **McLeod Street** in front of **Cairns Central,** the city's largest mall.

PRACTICAL INFORMATION

TOURIST AND FINANCIAL SERVICES

Tourist Offices: The **Visitors Info Bureau,** on the Esplanade between Aplin and Florence St., has a 24hr. information line (☎4041 0007) and offers details about local accommodations, tours, and bike rental. **Happy Travels**, 7 Shields St. in City Place (☎4041 0666; cairns@internet-outpost.com) is geared toward backpackers. Free Internet access and meals if you book tours through them. Their "Internet outpost" has CD-burning, scanning, and printing ($.55 per page).

National Parks Office: Queensland Parks and Wildlife Service (QPWS), 5b Sheridan St. (☎4046 6600; fax 4046 6604). Offers the helpful *Australian Guide to National Parks*. Open M-F 8:30am-4:30pm.

Currency Exchange: There are places to change currency and travelers checks throughout the city. The 2nd fl. of Orchid Plaza, 79-87 Abbot St., usually has the best rates for both, but be sure to shop around and ask at your hostel since rates change all the time. **Travelex** charges an $8 minimum for currency and travelers checks, but has negotiable rates for large transactions ($500+). Locations throughout the city: 69 Abbott St. (☎4031 6880. Open daily 9am-9:30pm); Night Markets, Royal Harbour, 71-73 the Esplanade (☎4031 8280. Open daily 5-10pm); 50 Lake St. (☎4051 6255. M-Sa 9am-5pm); 13 Shields St. (M-Sa 9am-5:15pm.)

Ticket Agencies: TicketLink in the **Cairns Civic Theatre** (☎4031 9555; www.ticketlink.com.au), at the corner of Florence and Sheridan St.

EMERGENCY AND COMMUNICATIONS

Police: (☎4030 7000), on Sheridan St., between Spence and Hartley St. Open 24hr. There is also a police station next to the lagoon on the Esplanade. Open 8am-4pm.

Crisis Lines: Alcohol and Drug Information (☎1800 177 833). **Lifeline** (☎13 11 14).

Pharmacy: Chemmart Pharmacy, Shop 10, 85 the Esplanade (☎4051 9011). Open daily 9am-10pm. Gives advice to travelers continuing on to Asia.

Medican Services: Cairns Base Hospital (24hr. ☎4050 6333), on the Esplanade at the end of the Pier. Emergency department. More centrally located **Medical Centre** (24hr. ☎4052 1119), on the corner of Florence and Grafton St.

Internet Access: Internet access is everywhere in Cairns. Many places on the Esplanade and Abbott St. charge $3 per hr. **Global Gossip,** 125 Abbott St., is a little more expensive ($3.90 for first hr., $3 per hr. after that) but has all the frills, including printing ($.45 per page), photocopying ($.35 per page), faxing, digital camera readers, and discount deals on international calls. The **Cairns City Public Library,** 151 Abbott St., charges $3.80 per hr.

Post Office: Cairns General Post Office (GPO), 13 Grafton St. (☎4031 4303), on the corner with Hartley St. Open M-F 8:30am-5pm. Smaller branch located in Orchid Plaza just south of City Place between Abbott and Lake St. **Postal Code:** 4870.

ACCOMMODATIONS

Cairns may not be a big city, but its reputation as the gateway to far north Queensland's ecological wonders has established it as a favorite for backpackers. Most hostels are clustered along the **Esplanade,** though there are others in the CBD and along the **Captain Cook Highway** (Hwy. 1). Prices range from $14-28 for most dorm rooms, though amenities and quality of accommodation vary greatly. Some older hostels sacrifice cleanliness for character, while new hyper-commercial "backpacker resorts" are springing up almost everywhere. Competition is stiff, so most include coin-operated laundry facilities, kitchens, and valuables storage, as well as free airport pickup, a pool, and free or discounted meals at local restaurants. Some also offer free accommodation if you book tours with them. Most dorm beds increase in price by a few dollars ($2-5) during the Dry (May-Oct.) and school holidays (p. 38). Be sure to call ahead, as the best accommodations tend to fill up quickly.

COCKROACH MOTEL. Some hostels are extremely cheap—but also extremely dirty. It's a good idea to check out rooms before booking them (if you're taking a taxi, ask the driver to wait). Make sure you'll be able to handle the grime before committing; this is especially important in the extremely humid tropical north, where mold can be a problem.

CBD

Caravella's 77, 77 the Esplanade (☎4051 2159; www.caravella.com.au), between Aplin and Shields St., 10min. from the bus station. Internet access, movies, and a pool table. About half of the rooms have baths and A/C; request when you book. Key deposit $10. Down the road, sister hostel **Caravella's 149,** 149 the Esplanade (☎4031 5680), has excellent twins/doubles. Flash your *Let's Go* guide and ask about a $5 discount on your first night's stay. Fridge in most rooms, pool, Internet access ($4 per hr). Dorms $20; singles $40; twins and doubles $50. ❷

Cairns Girls Hostel, 147 Lake St. (☎4051 2767), between Florence and Aplin St. This clean, friendly **women-only** hostel has provided a safe haven for over 30yr. No noise after 10pm. 3 kitchens, 3 bathrooms, 2 lounges, laundry, Internet access, and TV. Reception 7:30am-9pm. Dorms $18, $126 per wk.; twins $22, $154 per wk. ❷

Gilligan's, 57-89 Grafton St. (☎4041 6566; www.gilligansbackpackers.com.au). A huge complex rising several stories and stretching half a city block, this place does to hostels what McDonald's did to the burger. A 2000+ capacity bar (see **Nightlife,** p. 426) is attached, with a bed-filled nightclub above—just in case their 540 hostel beds fill up. Restaurant on-site ($8 meals), free gym, pool, laundry, really cheap Internet access ($1 per hr.), free lockers, and several kitchens. Reception 24hr. 4-person dorms $30; 6-person dorms $27; doubles $99. ❸

YHA on the Esplanade, 93 the Esplanade (☎4031 1919; cairnsesplanade@yhaqld.org), near the corner of Aplin St. Extremely close to nightclubs and cheap restaurants. A no-frills place to crash. Laundry, kitchen, TV, storage, and Internet access. Reception 7am-10pm. Dorms $22; doubles $48. ❷

JUST OUTSIDE THE CBD

Tropic Days, 26-28 Bunting St. (☎4041 1521 or 1800 421 521; www.tropicdays.com.au). 20min. walk west from the CBD, behind the Showgrounds north of Scott St. Jungle-themed paintings, a neat tropical garden, and a sparkling pool. Australian BBQ with 'roo, croc, and a M didgeridoo competition ($8.) Free shuttle to the CBD 8 times per day, 7:30am-9:30pm. Internet access ($1 per 15min.) and TV lounge. Reception 7am-noon, 4-8pm. Campsites $11; 3-bed dorms $22; doubles with TV $48. ❷

Traveller's Oasis, 8 Scott St. (☎4052 1377 or 1800 621 353; www.travoasis.com.au). Off Bunda St., near Dreamtime and Gecko's. Renovated and under new ownership, this hostel is a welcome respite from the backpacker factories throughout Cairns. The ever-resourceful and energetic owner, Cathy, is usually around and will get you some of the best deals possible on tours, car rentals, etc. Free shuttle to the CBD several times a day, though it's only a 10min. walk. Internet access ($1 for 15min.), laundry, pool, BBQ every M. TV in doubles. Dorms $22; singles $38; doubles $48. ❷

Dreamtime, 4 Terminus St. (☎4031 6753 or 1800 058 440; www.dreamtime-travel.com.au), just off Bunda St., behind Cairns Central and around the corner from Gecko's. Daily shuttles to the Pier and bus station. 3- or 4-person dorms. Some doubles have fridge. Pool, BBQ, kitchen. Reception 7:30am-noon and 4-8pm. Dorms $22; singles $38; doubles $48. Book ahead. ❷

The Serpent, 341 Lake St. (☎4040 7777 or 1800 737 736; www.serpenthostel.com), a 25min. walk north along the Esplanade from the CBD. A big, brand-new hostel. Relax by the pool and meet new friends over free nightly meals at the bar. The free shuttle bus runs hourly except during early evening. Internet access, laundry, kitchen, beach volleyball, A/C, storage. 10-bed dorms $14; 8-bed dorms $18; 6-bed dorms $10; 4-bed dorms $22; twins and doubles $52, ensuite $62; king deluxe $70. ❷

Gecko's Backpackers, 187 Bunda St. (☎4031 1344 or 1800 011 344), offers clean, bright rooms with comfortable mattresses. Helpful staff make this small backpackers seem like a 2nd home. Internet access $2 per 30min., pool, hammocks, BBQ. Reception 7am-noon and 4-8pm. 3- and 4-bed dorms $21; singles $31; doubles $45. ❷

FOOD

Cairns is overflowing with dining options, from all-night kebab and pizza stalls on the Esplanade to upscale seafood restaurants. **Shields Street** is known by locals as "eat street"—wander around and compare menus. Many restaurants offer discounts of up to 40% if you are seated before a certain time, normally 7pm. Most of the hostels in town hand out meal vouchers for one of the local watering holes, though doing your own cooking is often the most economical dinner option. Diners on a budget love the **Night Markets food court,** 71-75 The Esplanade, for a variety of quick and cheap takeaways. (☎4051 7666. Open 5pm-latenight.) For basic groceries try **Woolworths,** on Abbott St. between Shields and Spence St., or **Bi-Lo and Coles,** in Cairns Central (both open M-F 8am-9pm, Sa 8am-5:30pm, Su 9am-6pm).

SHRIMP ON THE BARBIE. Many restaurants in Cairns offer an interesting option: bring your own food and they'll cook it for you. Besides Coles in Cairns Central and Woolworth's on Abbot St, shops sell fresh and inexpensive seafood down Sheridan St., about 15-20min. (walking) from the CBD.

Cafe Melt, 129 Bunda St. (☎4031 4331). This hip, airy restaurant next door to Dreamtime has one of the best deals in Cairns: huge "nightly revolving feature meals" featuring cuisine from around the world. Vegetarian options available. Wraps and salads $7. Pizzas $7-10. Internet access $4 per hr. Open daily 6:30am-10pm. ❶

Sushi Express, 79-87 Abbott St. (☎4041 4388) in Orchid Plaza. Tasty sushi at an unbelievable price. $2-4 per plate (transported by a sushi locomotive). Most people won't need more than two plates. Open M-Sa 1-3pm and 5-10pm. ❶

Tiny's Juice Bar, 45 Abbott St. (☎4031 4331). Tiny's cheap and popular stop serves some of the healthiest food in Cairns. Try one of the refreshing energy drinks ($3-5), such as the soothing apple, papaya, orange, and watermelon. If you're confident in your creative abilities, order your own blends. The same goes with wraps, salads, and sandwiches made from such ingredients as avocado, feta, cucumber, chicken, and hummus ($7-10). Open for lunch. ❷

Perrotta's at the Gallery (☎4031 5899), at the corner of Abbot and Shields St., next to the Cairns Art Gallery. This modern cafe was named Cairns Restaurant of the Year 2002. Stop in for pre-gallery breakfast ($4-10) or post-painting dinner ($20-25). Open daily 8:30am-10pm. ❹

Sawaddee, 62 Shields St. (☎4031 7993). Traditional Thai cuisine served amid modern decor. Large variety of curries, stir fry, and vegetarian entrees for eat-in or takeaway ($10-18). Open Th-F noon-2pm; dinner daily 6pm-latenight. ❸

SIGHTS

TANKS ART CENTRE. The best local art is on display here, with exhibitions housed in several WWII diesel holding tanks. Each show lasts three weeks. On the last Sunday of every month from June to November, Tanks hosts **Market Day,** a free bazaar with live music and plenty of pottery, crafts, and herbs for sale. *(46 Collins Ave. ☎4032 2349. Accessible by Sunbus #1B. Open daily 11am-4pm. $2.)*

FLECKER BOTANIC GARDENS. Right next to Tanks is this Gondwanan (evolutionary flora track) garden. Take a moment to follow a meandering boardwalk through swampy jungle, and explore fern and orchid houses. *(☎4044 3398. Take Sunbus #1B from City Place or drive north on Sheridan St. and take a left onto Collins Ave. Guided walks M-F 1pm. Open M-F 7:30am-5:30pm, Sa-Su 8:30am-5:30pm. Free.)*

MOUNT WHITFIELD ENVIRONMENTAL PARK. This last bit of rainforest in the Cairns area is home to cassowaries and other jungle creatures. The park's shorter Red Arrow circuit is a steep climb to a breathtaking overlook and only takes 45min., while the more rugged Blue Arrow circuit is a 5hr. round-trip trek up and around Mt. Whitfield. Don't stay after dark—finding a cab or a bus back into Cairns might be difficult. *(Wedged between the Tanks Art Centre and the Botanic Gardens on Collins Ave.)*

CAIRNS CIVIC THEATRE. The Civic Theatre, near the CBD, has nightly performances by magicians, comedians, play companies, and many others. *(At the corner of Florence and Sheridan St. ☎4031 9555; www.ticketlink.com.au.)*

KURANDA. The Skyrail cableway coasts above the rainforest for 7.5km on its way to this popular mountain town. At the highest stop, a boardwalk snakes through the trees; detailed information on the area is given one stop below that one. See p. 428 for more on Kuranda. *(Trains leave regularly from the station. If you are driving, go north on the Cook Hwy. and follow the signs. ☎4038 1555; www.skyrail.com.au. 1¾hr. $37, children $18.50.)*

PETER LIK GALLERY. You've probably already bought his postcards—now see the real thing. Lik's popular prints of Australian panoramas and wildlife are showcased in this modern gallery. *(4 Shields St. ☎4031 8177. Open daily 9am-7pm. Free.)*

 OUTDOOR ACTIVITIES

Cairns owes its tourist town status in large part to its warm winters and proximity to the Great Barrier Reef. At night, travelers stay in town and drink at local pubs, but during the day they're often found outside the city limits enjoying racy thrills, bumps, and spills for reasonable prices. Activities can be booked through hostels or any one of the dozens of tourist centers in Cairns (p. 419). Most companies offer free pickup and drop-off. Booking isn't necessary, however, to enjoy the open-air markets and bountiful outdoor dining in the sunshine of the tropics.

> TIP **AVOID TOUR SCAMS..** Be wary of booking agents who do not provide more than one tour option, as each tour pays a commission to its agents. Some low-quality tours survive by paying high commissions to agents talented at roping in unsuspecting tourists.

CABLE-SKIING. Cable Ski Cairns offers waterskiing, wakeboarding, and kneeboarding sans boat. (Off the Captain Cook Hwy. ☎4038 1304; www.cableskiccairns.com.au. Open daily 10am-6pm; $34 per hr.; children $16 per hr.)

CYCLING. Bandicoot Bicycle Tours offers a day of cycling, wildlife-spotting, swimming, and relaxation in the tablelands above Cairns. Guests enjoy seven rides (3-7km) between trips to waterfalls, giant fig trees, and swimming holes. Lunch and two teas are included; they feature a vegetarian-friendly BBQ and tropical fruit. (☎4055 0155; www.bandicootbicycles.com. Trips depart M-F 8am, return 5:30pm. $109. Cash only.)

BUNGEE JUMPING. You may know it as "bungee" but to **AJ Hackett** it's "bungy"—slang in New Zealand for "elastic strap." This wild Kiwi knows something about the sport—ask him about bungy jumping off the Eiffel Tower (and getting arrested for it), then sign up for one of his (legal) Australian jumps. Night bungy or parabungy (combination of parasailing and bungy jump) on request. (☎4057 7188 or 1800 622 888; www.ajhackett.com. Open daily 9am-5:30pm. $99.)

FISHING. Fishermen can cast their own bait, then tow the line with **Fishing The Tropics,** which runs its 6m boat in the Cairns estuary and Daintree River. (☎4034 1500. Estuary $75, river $140; both include lunch, full bait, and tackle. Book ahead.) **VIP Fishing & Game Boat Services** offers similar packages, along with others featuring fly- and shark-fishing, or black marlin hunting from June-December. (☎4031 4355. ½-day trips around $75, full-day around $140.)

PARASAILING AND SKYDIVING. This is your chance to parasail 300 ft. above Trinity Inlet. **North Queensland WaterSports** (☎4045 2735) offers parasailing and jet skiing ($65, tandem $100). **Skydive Cairns,** 59 Sheridan St. (☎4031 5466 or 1800 444 568), features solo and tandem jumps. (8000 ft. $245; 14,000 ft. $270.)

WHITEWATER RAFTING. Foaming Fury offers a portage-style rafting trip that begins with a hike through dense jungle to the wild rapids of the secluded Russell River. (☎4031 3460. $125, includes lunch.) Other trips in Cairns raft the comparatively tame Barron River, which can become crowded on busy days. **R'n'R Rafting** offers several options, including multi-day and family packages. (☎4051 7777 or 1800 801 540. ½-day $98, full-day $155.) **Raging Thunder Adventures** boasts similar trips, including combination packages that offer activities like ballooning, bungee jumping, skydiving, and reef trips (24hr. reservations ☎4030 7990).

MOTORCYCLING. Cape York Motorcycle Adventures (☎4059 0220; www.capeyork-motorcycles.com.au.) is for the truly adventurous, offering one- to 16-day safaris into Cape York on a dirt bike. Ride through river crossings, beside the ocean, up mountains into the rainforest, even through national parks and ghost towns. (1-day $285; 5-day $2190, camping and meals provided.)

BEACH. Cairns doesn't really have a beach—it has a mud flat. However, there is a new man-made (chlorinated) lagoon and park area that stretch for several hundred meters along the Esplanade. Twenty minutes by bus to the north will take you to **Palm Cove,** a beautiful beach lined with cafes and upscale resorts, offering respite from the burgeoning Cairns nightlife. (Sunbus #1, 1A, 1B, and 2X run to the beaches from the depot in City Place. M-F every 30min., Sa-Su every hr.)

DIVING AND SNORKELING

The most popular way to see Cairns is through goggles, although experienced divers may prefer the less-touristed reefs near Port Douglas. Every day, rain or shine, thousands of tourists and locals suit up with masks, fins, and snorkels to slide beneath the ocean surface and glimpse the Great Barrier Reef. **Reef Teach,** 14 Spence St., offers a great 2hr. lecture by Paddy Colwell, a marine biologist who doubles as a comic. In his passionate and entertaining way, Colwell teaches about the reef's history and biodiversity. Reef Teach will infinitely enhance your reef experience. (☎4031 7794; www.reefteach.com.au. Lectures M-Sa 6:30pm. $13.)

Because it is the main gateway to the reef, Cairns is studded with an overwhelming number of dive shops and snorkeling outfits. Knowing how to choose can be daunting, given the excess of brochures and booking agents by which you'll be bombarded. Think about some questions in advance: for how long do you want to dive? How big do you want your dive group to be? For personal dive instruction and a group atmosphere, smaller boats are usually the way to go. Are you going with other divers or with friends who may prefer other water activities? Unless you're all diving, you won't want a dive trip—maybe instead a cruise with diving options, such as **Noah's Ark Too** or **Passions of Paradise.** Snorkelers are equally welcome aboard these day cruises. **Sailaway-Low Isles** and **Wavelength,** in Port Douglas (p. 432), are the only places in the area that do snorkel-only sails.

To dive in Australia, you need to have open-water certification (a driver's license for the water). The only way to get this certification is to spend around $350 for about four days in scuba school, where you learn about scuba equipment and diving techniques. To enroll in dive classes, you need two passport-sized photos and a medical exam, which can be arranged with a local doctor for about $50.

Introductory dives offer a taste of scuba diving without scuba school. For those not planning to dive more than once, intro dives might be the way to go—you get an idea of what's down there without paying an arm and a leg (provided there aren't any sharks involved). The excursions are led by instructors who give a basic scuba lesson and help first-timers with equipment and techniques. Beware: some companies tack on payments as your day on the reef extends. Ask questions about how long the actual underwater experience will be before signing on. Many companies offer another dive for an additional fee.

DIVING DAYTRIPS

Many divers prefer daytrips to multi-day trips, as they afford different views of the reef each given day. On multi-day trips, it is likely that you will visit only the section of the reef over which your diving company has the right to dive.

Passions of Paradise (☎4050 0676 or 1800 111 346; www.passions.com.au). Offers full-day cruises to Paradise Reef and Upolo Cay. Attracts a young, energetic crowd; spontaneous conga dancing may occur. Face-painting and chocolate cake for the youngsters. High-speed catamaran takes 60-70 passengers. Departs 8am. Base price for snorkeling and lunch $109. Introductory dive $65 extra, certified dive $50.

Ocean Free (☎4053 5888; www.oceanfree.com.au). Sail to the reef in style on this stately tall ship. The tour anchors off Green Island on the Inner Barrier Reef, allowing for both reef and island exploration. Return sunset sail includes complimentary wine and dessert. Lively crew and few passengers means lots of individual attention. Departs 8:15am, returns 6pm. Base price $109 with lunch. Introductory dive $70 (2 dives $105), certified dive $50 (2 dives $70).

Noah's Ark Too (☎4050 0677), located at the Pier, finger E. The motto: "There are no rules." Relax on the boat (max. 28 people), have a laugh, and take the plunge on one of 10 outer reef destinations. Sip a beer on the boat after you dive. A lively tour with a fun-loving crew. Daily 8:45am-5pm. Snorkel-only $70. Introductory dive including a free 10min. lesson underwater $109, additional dive $35. 2 certified dives $109.

MULTI-DAY TRIPS AND SCUBA SCHOOLS

Pro-Dive (☎4031 5255; www.prodivecairns.com), on the corner of Abbott and Shields St. Their most popular trip is the 5-day learn-to-dive course. Although the price tag may seem hefty at $695, it includes all diving equipment, 2 nights accommodation, and 5 dives. They also offer a 3-day, 2-night trip with 11 dives, including 2 night dives for certified divers ($560). Open daily 8:30am-9pm.

Down Under Dive, 287 Draper St. (☎4052 8300 or 1800 079 099; www.downunderdive.com.au). A 2-masted clipper ship with a hot tub runs daytrips ($85). Intro dives $50, certified dives $40. The company also offers diver training; the 4-day courses include 2 days pool training and 2 days on Hastings and Saxon Reefs (from $320). Nitrox diver course $350. Open daily 7am-5pm.

Cairns Dive Centre, 121 Abbott St. (☎4051 0294 or 24hr. 1800 642 591; www.cairnsdive.com.au). Offers a less expensive trip to the outer reef, with a "floating hotel" catamaran as its flagship and a smaller boat for daytrips. Five-day live-aboard, learn-to-dive course $620; 4-day budget course $330. Open daily 7:30am-5pm.

Tusa Dive (☎4031 1028; www.tusadive.com), at Shields St. and the Esplanade. The first 2 days of their 4-day PADI courses ($595) are run in the classroom by ProDive instructors, but the 2 daytrips to the outer reef are on speedy new Tusa boats (max. 28). A diver's dive company, Tusa is more expensive than others but ideal for those who want to get to the outer reef with experts and without the live-aboard experience. Nitrox certification courses available. Open daily 7:30am-9:30pm.

NIGHTLIFE

Cairns nightclubs, the last stop in a backpacker's day, cater to a young, rowdy crowd. Adrenaline-fueled days spent sky- and scuba-diving make for explosive nightlife. Get your hand stamped before 10pm and all venues are free. Hostels usually give out vouchers for the clubs to help draw the crowds. For the trendiest spots, editorials, and listings, pick up a free copy of *Barfly*, found all around town.

Ultimate Party is a Cairns pub crawl held every Saturday night. Pay $35 for entry into five bars and clubs, a drink in each one, two all-you-can eat meals, entertainment, transportation, and a photo. $25 more gets you a t-shirt and a $100 drink card. At the end of the night, pick up a book of vouchers for adventure trips, accommodations, food, and, of course, more alcohol. Sign up at the Tropical Arcade on the corner of Shields and Abbott St., or call ☎4041 0332.

The Woolshed, 24 Shields St. (☎4031 6304 for free shuttle bus until 9:30pm), is a rowdy all-night party and backpacker favorite. Travelers come here to dance on the tables, drink beer, and enter the M night Mr. and Ms. Backpacker contest. Practically every hostel in town offers meal vouchers (free or $4 off; upgrade to T-bone steak $6) for this place. M and W Happy hour 9:30-11:30pm. $6 pitchers. Cover M-Th and Su $5, F $6, Sa free before 10pm. Open nightly 6-9:30pm for meals; club open until 5am. Downstairs is the **Bassment,** playing dance music Th-Sa until 5am. Free until midnight.

P.J. O'Brien's (☎4031 5333), in City Place, at the corner of Shields and Lake St., always finds a reason to celebrate. Tables are made from beer barrels and the pub is decorated with Irish memorabilia; this place looks like an Emerald Isle museum. Pints of Guiness ($5.50) and tasty food (meals $12-18) make P.J.'s a hot spot. Live bands 6 nights per wk. F Happy hour 5-9pm (Guiness $4).

Tropos (☎4031 2530), on the corner of Lake and Spence St. This techno club is everyone's last stop before bed. You can't miss it—the whirling spotlight can be seen across the street. W retro night. Cover $5.50, free before midnight. Open daily until 5am. Neat dress required.

Shenannigan's (☎4051 2490), on the corner of Sheridan and Spence St., boasts the best beer garden in Cairns. Watch the latest sports matches on the 2 large screens, or listen to live music 4 per wk. They also serve huge meals. Open daily 10am-2am.

nu-trix, 53 Spence St. (☎4051 8223), between Grafton and McLeod St. A gay bar and dance club with no dress code. Shows F and Sa nights; cover $5. Open W-Th and Su 9:30pm-latenight, F-Sa 9:30pm-5am.

Gilligan's, 57-89 Grafton St. (☎4041 6566; www.gilligansbackpackers.com.au). A 2000+ nightspot attached to the hostel. Open-air beer hall, a nightclub, and a smaller dance club. Theme nights, such as M Xtreme Bungy and Su Foam Party. Guest DJs. Open M-Th and Su 10am-2am, F-Sa 10am-3am.

Rhino Bar, (☎4031 5305; www.cairnsrhinobar.com) upstairs on the corner of Lake and Spence St. A popular Cairns hotspot. Open daily 4pm-latenight.

DAYTRIPS FROM CAIRNS

TJAPUKAI. Just north of Cairns, off the Cook Hwy. in Smithfield, is Tjapukai, an Aboriginal cultural park. Pronounced "JAB-a-guy," this is one of the most rewarding and balanced presentations of Aboriginal myths, customs, and history in Queensland. Learn how to throw a boomerang, see a cultural dance show, watch a film on Aboriginal history, and more. Set aside at least half a day for the experience. *(☎4042 9999; www.tjapukai.com.au. Open daily 9am-5pm. $31, children $15.50. AmEx/DC/MC/V. Packages and evening events available. Transfers to and from Cairns and the Northern Beaches run $20 round-trip. Kuranda Scenic Rail and Skyrail also have service in the area.)*

CRYSTAL CASCADES. Only 30km from Cairns' center, this freshwater swimming hole provides a refreshing break on hot, lazy days. The best part? It's completely free. Be careful on the slippery rocks in and around the cascades. There is also a short hiking trail through the surrounding area. *(Drive north along Sheridan St., turn left on Aeroglen, head toward Redlynch, and follow the signs. Wheelchair accessible.)*

MOSSMAN GORGE. Mossman Gorge is just a little further north of Crystal Cascades (near Port Douglas, p. 432). It's free, offers a more genuine introduction to the rainforest, and has better swimming holes.

ZOOS

HARTLEY'S CROCODILE ADVENTURES. On the Cook Hwy. 40km north of Cairns, is home to hundreds of crocs, plus an array of kangaroos, koalas, and cassowaries. The impressive grounds are also home to a riverboat that offers lagoon tours. Highlights include daily feeding shows and the heart-stopping "crocodile attack show" daily at 3pm. *(☎4055 3576; www.crocodileadventures.com. Open daily 8:30am-5pm. $28, children $14, families $70.)* Transportation and tours to the park are available from Cairns on Hartley's Express (☎4038 2992) and Down Under Tours (☎4035 5566), as well as from Port Douglas on Wildlife Discovery Tours (☎4099 6612).

THE CAIRNS TROPICAL ZOO. Has a more diverse collection of animals but the enclosures and atmosphere are much less impressive. Situated near Palm Cove on the Cook Hwy., 20min. north of Cairns, the tropical Zoo has a unique, hands-on approach which allows you to hug a koala, feed a kangaroo, or hold a snake. Daily shows and croc feedings add to the excitement. *(☎4055 3669; www.cairnstropicalzoo.com. Open daily 8:30am-5pm. $28, children $14. Accessible by Sun Bus 1X.)*

GREEN ISLAND ☎07

Diminutive Green Island barely pushes above the water's surface; its perimeter can be walked in 15min. Though it is dominated by a huge resort, a boardwalk through the rainforest and a beach path both provide access to natural beauty.

The cheapest and quickest way to the island is by ferry with **Great Adventures,** which offers a day on the island plus a glass-bottom boat tour or snorkeling gear. (☎4044 9944 or 1800 079 080; www.greatadventures.com.au. Departs Cairns daily 8:30, 10:30am, and 1pm; departs Green Island noon, 2:30, and 4:30pm. $60, children $30.) Those looking for a more luxurious experience should skip the high-speed ferry and indulge in a leisurely sailing and snorkeling trip. **Ocean Free** sails to the island daily. On the way, you'll have lunch and stop at the reef for a few hours of snorkeling or diving. After a day on the island, the return sunset sail includes wine, cheese, and desserts. (☎4041 1118. Departs Cairns daily 8:15am. $100, children $65; intro dive $70, certified dive $50.)

The main attraction on the island is **Marineland Melanesia,** a combination oceanic art gallery, aquarium, and croc farm 250m left of the jetty when facing the water. Go at 10:30am or 1:45pm to watch a live feeding of huge crocodiles. If you're lucky (and he's hungry) you might even see Cassius, the world's largest croc in captivity. There are also opportunities to hold yearling crocodiles. If that sounds too daunting, tour the art collection, which includes masks from New Guinea. (☎4051 4032. Open daily 9:30am-4:15pm. $10.50, children $5.) Just off the end of the jetty is the **Marine Observatory,** from which you can observe bits of the coral reef 1.5m below the surface ($5).

FITZROY ISLAND ☎07

Fitzroy Island is larger and less expensive than Green Island. Here, the coral beaches melt into mountainous rainforest, complementing the resort that borders both. For an adventure, try traveling to Fitzroy Island via **sea kayak** with **Raging Thunder Adventures.** A high-speed catamaran takes you most of the way, followed by a half-day on the island, complete with snorkeling and lunch. An overnight package includes bunk accommodations at the Fitzroy Island Resort and a day of kayaking. (☎4030 7990; www.ragingthunder.com.au. Daytrip $125, overnight $145.) You can also get to the island via the **Fitzroy Island Flyer,** which links Cairns to Fitzroy. (☎4030 7907; www.fitzroyisland.com.au. 3 per day. $42, children $21, family $105.) Once there, you can rent kayaks ($15 per hr.), a catamaran ($45 per ½-day), or fishing rods and tackle ($10 per day). **Fitzroy Island Resort** ❸ has a variety of clean bunkhouse accommodations. (Shared bunks $31; private bunks for 1-3 people $116, 4 people $124. Twin cabins $220, family $250.) The resort has a **pool bar** ❷ that serves meals ($5-15) daily 9am-5pm. The **Beach Bar** ❸ serves dinner ($12-22) daily 6-8:30pm. The **Flare Grill** ❷ serves breakfast ($10-12) daily 8-10am.

The resort's **dive shop** offers introductory diving and snorkeling gear. (Open daily 9:30am-4pm. Intro dive $80, certified dive $70; snorkel gear $16. AmEx/DC/MC/V.) Dive trips leave at 10:30am and 1pm; 2:30pm trip by demand.

Fitzroy Island has three main **hikes.** The best is the **Summit Trail,** a steep hike up the mountain (1.3km) with an incredible 360° view of the reef and coastline at the windy peak. You can turn around and head back the way you came (2.5km) or continue on to the lighthouse (an additional 4.2km round-trip, all downhill.) A walk up the **Secret Garden Trail** (1km round-trip) through a canyon is worth it if you haven't seen rainforest before. Another good walk (500m) cuts through the trees to pristine **Nudey Beach,** which offers great views of the surrounding mountain range. It is covered with pieces of coral from the reef offshore, and the snorkeling is great. Landlubbers can marvel at the bay between the beach and the mainland ranges, which was a green valley 6000 years ago.

ATHERTON TABLELANDS

Although much of northern Queensland is picturesque, nothing compares to the Atherton Tablelands. Rolling hills meet unspoiled forests with hidden lakes, pockets of rainforest, and scattered waterfalls—all fringed by roaming herds of cattle and horses. Traveling northeast on the Kennedy Hwy., you'll find the farming village of **Mareeba** and touristy **Kuranda.** The southern route via Gilles Hwy. passes through the township of **Atherton** and charming **Yungaburra.**

The mountainous lakeside roads can be narrow and winding but offer drivers rewarding panoramas. Although having a car provides the best experience, the Tablelands are accessible without a car. **White Car Coaches,** 8 McCowaghie St., Atherton, provides service seven days a week from Cairns to the Tablelands, with stops in Kuranda, Mareeba, Herberton, and Ravenshoe. (☎4091 1855; www.whitecarcoaches.com. $25.) **On The Wallaby Adventure Tours** offers day and overnight guided tours of the Tablelands, including the crater lakes, waterfalls, wildlife spotting, canoeing, and mountain biking. (☎4050 0650; www.onthewallaby.com. Day tours $95. 2-day, all-inclusive tours $165.) The **Skyrail Rainforest Cableway** is a gondola that lifts you up above the rainforest canopy into Kuranda village, with stops at the peak and Barron Falls (7.5km). A 1½hr. round-trip ride originates in Caravonica Lakes, 10min. northwest of Cairns. (☎4041 0007 or 4038 1555; www.skyrail.com.au. Open daily 8:30am-3:45pm. $54, children $27.) The **Kuranda Scenic Railway** runs an antique train ride from downtown Cairns to Kuranda. (☎4031 3636; www.ksr.com.au. From Cairns daily 8:30 and 9:30am; from Kuranda daily 2:00 and 3:30pm. $52, children $26, concession discounts vary.) Special packages allow the indecisive to ride the skyrail one-way and the scenic railway on the way back. (☎4038 1555. $74, children $37.)

KURANDA ☎07

Many travelers get no farther than this mountain town, which serves as the gateway to the Tablelands. River cruises, street performers, and its famous markets draw hordes of tourists from Cairns by day, but when the last train leaves in the afternoon the village returns to its peaceful roots. In the morning, the hustle and bustle begins again when the **original markets** (open W-Su) and **Heritage Markets** (open daily 8:30am-3pm) transform the cozy village into a bazaar of arts, crafts, and clothing. Kuranda's outdoor amphitheater hosts a variety of concerts, including regular performances by local artists.

Kuranda Hotel Motel ❹, on the corner of Coondoo and Arara St. across from the Skyrail, has a garden bar, restaurant, and pool. The tidy rooms with bath, fridge, and TV are perfect for couples. (☎4093 7206. Reception M-Sa 10am-10pm, Su 10am-4pm. Singles $50; doubles $60. Extra adult $15. AmEx/DC/MC/V.) **Kuranda Backpacker's Hostel ❷** (a.k.a. "Mrs. Miller's"), 6 Arara St., is across from the train station on the corner of Arara and Barang St. Stained glass windows and jungle gardens make up for the cast-iron beds and squeaky floors in this historic hostel. Amenities include a kitchen, pool, bike rental, Internet access, laundry, and pickup from Cairns. (☎4093 7355. Reception 9am-noon, 3:30-6:30pm. Dorms $19; singles $46; twins and doubles $49. MC/V.)

Many places in town serve Devonshire tea (tea served with treats such as scones, clotted cream, honey, and jam), but only the **Honey House ❷,** at the entrance to the original Kuranda Markets, makes it all on the premises. A hive of bees in the store produces sweet Kuranda honey, and the accompanying pumpkin scones are made from scratch. (☎4093 7261. Open daily 8am-4pm.) Locals love **Frog's ❷,** 11 Coondoo St., with its spacious jungle porch out back. (☎4093 7405. Open daily 9:30am-4pm. Sandwiches $8; gourmet pizzas from $12. MC/V.)

On the drive up the Kennedy Hwy. from Cairns, the road winds steeply through lush rainforest. Just outside Kuranda, the award-winning **Rainforestation Nature Park** offers everything from Aboriginal tours and walks to boomerang throwing lessons. Hug a koala or ride in an amphibious Army Duck through the rainforest. Shuttles leave for the park daily from Kuranda village. (☎4093 9033. Aboriginal culture tours $20, children $10; wildlife park $12/8.)

Kuranda is also the gateway to the **Barron Gorge National Park,** 2.5km outside of town. By car, follow the signs from the town center. The Kuranda Scenic Railway stops here to allow travelers to hop out for a quick view. A short boardwalk takes those on foot through dense rainforest to a lookout above Barron Falls, one of the largest waterfalls in the Tablelands. Another kilometer down the road is Wright's Lookout, providing a view down the gorge that spills out over the city of Cairns.

MAREEBA AND ATHERTON ☎07

While Mareeba and Atherton may lack the quaint atmosphere of Yungaburra and the scenic views of Kuranda, they offer visitors an authentic example of life in the tropical Tablelands. The towns also claim to have "the best weather in the Tablelands," with over 300 days of sunshine a year. A short stop in Atherton will reveal much about the region's history, while the town of Mareeba has begun to garner attention for its growing industries—90% of Australia's coffee is produced here, as well as the regional specialty, mango wine.

The Coffee Works, 136 Mason St., in Mareeba, lures visitors with its aromatic home brews and tasting tours. (☎4092 4101 or 1800 355 526; www.coffeeworks.com.au. Open daily 9am-4pm. Tours 10am and noon; $9.90, includes free coffee tasting.) Don't miss **The Chocolate Works** inside; be sure to try samples of the lemon myrtle in milk chocolate or coffee in white chocolate. The **Golden Drop Winery,** only a short drive (9km) north on Hwy. 1 toward Mossman, is the world's only mango wine factory and farm. Stop by for a taste of their divine wines and tropical fruit liqueurs. (☎4093 2524. Open daily 9am-10pm. Bottles from $22.)

Atherton, located atop an extinct volcano, is a great base for exploration of Lake Tinaroo and other Tableland destinations. There is a very helpful **visitors center** (☎4091 4222) with friendly staff at the corner of Main and Silo St., across from McDonald's. The **Blue Gum B&B ❺,** 36 Twelfth Ave. (☎4091 5149; www.athertonbluegum.com) is an excellent place to stay; it looks over the green hills of the

Tablelands. (Continental breakfast, poolside BBQ, kitchen, TV in all rooms. Doubles $105-180.) For budget accommodation, try the clean and welcoming **Atherton Travellers Lodge ❷,** 37 Alice St. (☎4091 3552. Dorms $20; singles $35; doubles $50. AmEx/DC/MC/V.) To indulge your sweet tooth, drive down the Gillies Hwy. between Atherton and Yungaburra until you see the sign for **Shaylee's Strawberry Farm** (☎4091 2962), which sells strawberries, homemade ice cream, and fresh jam from $3.50. (Open June-Nov. daily 8am-6pm.)

LAKE TINAROO AND CRATER LAKES NATIONAL PARK

The volcanic soil of the central Tablelands, nourished by crater lakes and waterfalls, sprouts lush forest that lines the shores of **Tinaroo, Barrine,** and **Eacham Lakes.** Unsealed and pristine **Danbulla Forest Drive** circles Lake Tinaroo. The free *Danbulla State Forest Visitor's Guide*, available from **QPWS Forest Management,** 83 Main St., Atherton (☎4091 1844), lists sights along the 40min. loop. If the QPWS office is closed, the Info Center in Atherton (p. 429) usually has copies or can offer you a detailed map of the region.

Lake Tinaroo can be accessed from Atherton or the gateway town of **Tolga,** off Hwy. 1, a barren road that runs through farmland before reaching the forested area of the lake. At the entrance to the lake is the **Lake Tinaroo Holiday Park ❶,** which has a kiosk, petrol, and a game room. (☎4095 8232. Sites $20, powered $23; cabins $60.) The road also passes five QPWS **campsites ❶** with toilets. (Sites $4.50 per person.) The Danbulla Forest Dr. features a few great walks and lies beyond the Tinaroo Dam. There are several basic but excellent campsites along the way. Register in advance, either by calling the QPWS office at ☎07 131 304 (M-F 8am-6pm) or going online at www.qld.gov.au/camping.

The stunning 50m, 500-year-old **Cathedral Fig Tree** is on the east stretch of Dunbulla Forest Dr.; you can stand there gaping, or you can walk straight through it. (Dunbulla Forest Dr. can be accessed from a sealed road via the Gillies Hwy. en route to Cairns.) 2km east down the road from the Cathedral Fig Tree is the turn-off to **Gillies Lookout,** a popular hang-gliding spot. Go four kilometers down an unsealed road, past two cattle-holding gates that must be opened (and closed behind you), and you will find one of the best lookouts in the whole region.

Lake Barrine and **Lake Eacham** were created by volcanic eruptions thousands of years ago. Today, they are popular places to enjoy the beauty of clear waters reflecting rainforest canopy. Lake Barrine is located just off the Gillies Hwy. on the way into Yungaburra from Gordanvale. Tour exotic gardens, dine at the **Lake Edge Teahouse Restaurant ❷** (open daily 9am-5pm), or cruise around the lake on a boat tour (departs daily from Teahouse 10:15, 11:30am, 1:30, 2:30, 3:30pm; $13, children $6.50). The Teahouse also has a Wet Tropics Visitor Centre. Make sure to check out the 1000-year-old twin Kauri pines only 100m from the teahouse. To reach Lake Eacham, continue on Gillies Hwy. from Gordonvale toward Yungaburra and turn left onto Lakes Dr. Lake Eacham is smaller and has no dining or boating options, but it's a better choice for swimming and sunbathing. Camping facilities are available at the **Lake Eacham Tourist Park ❷,** which has showers, laundry, a general store, and a petting zoo. (☎4095 3730. Open M-F 7-11am and 3-7pm, Sa 7am-7pm, Su 8am-6pm. Sites for 2 $15, powered $19; cabins $64. MC/V.) Contact the **QPWS Eacham District Office** (☎4095 3768) at Lake Eacham for info on paths around the picturesque lakes. Muskrat-kangaroos and giant iguanas are often spotted on the paved **Lake Circuit track** (31km) around Lake Eacham.

At Lake Eacham (and several other locations around this area), you will see a sign pointing toward the last of the great cedars, the **Red Cedar Tree.** Eight kilometers past Lake Eacham is the 600m path to the giant. The 500-year-old tree fell during Cyclone Larry in March 2006. The walk from the torn base to the tip takes three to four minutes.

YUNGABURRA ☎07

Tiny Yungaburra (pop. 400) is in the heart of the Tablelands, with Lake Tinaroo and the Danbulla State Forest to the north, Lakes Eacham and Barrine to the southeast, and the volcanic hills of the **Seven Sisters** to the west. The town seems untouched by tourism and is welcoming to visitors. Yungaburra hosts the largest **markets** in the north on the fourth Saturday of each month from 7am-noon, where shoppers can barter for homemade crafts, fresh produce, and even goats. From Cairns, take the Gillies Hwy. 60km west.

THE BASHFUL PLATYPUS. The best place to spot a platypus is at the Atherton Shire Council Pumping Station. From Yungaburra, head past the bridge and down Gillies Hwy. toward Tolga. 4.5km past the Curtain Fig turn-off, take a right onto Picnic Crossing Rd. (the road sign is actually 10m beyond the turn-off). Then take the second right-hand turn. You'll find a concrete picnic table and, with some luck, platypus families, near the bend in the river (you might need to walk left along the bank; head by foot along the path toward the road, then cut back in toward the river). The best time to see them is at dawn or dusk; it is important to be quiet, as they are extremely shy. Another popular platypus-viewing spot is at the bridge 300m before the Curtain Fig turn-off.

To the west of Yungaburra is the **Curtain Fig Tree,** a monstrous strangler fig which forms an eerie curtain in the middle of the rainforest (to the left after the bridge, just outside of town en route to Tolga). About 25km south of nearby Malanda (south on the Gilles Hwy. from Yungaburra), the **waterfall circuit** leads past a series of spectacular swimming holes. From the north, a sign points to the falls. Catch the loop from the south by looking for the "Tourist Drive" sign. **Millaa Millaa Falls** is a picturesque jungle waterfall which thunders into a gorgeous, green pool. **Zillie Falls** starts off as a sedate creek; the best view is from the lip of the falls, as the small stream transforms itself into a large shower of water. A rocky, slippery path through the adjacent rainforest leads to the roaring drop where **Ellinjaa Falls** crashes over a tapestry of rocks. For more information, the **Malanda Falls Visitor Centre** is just past Malanda Falls on the way out of town toward Atherton. (☎4096 6957. Open daily 9:30am-4:30pm.)

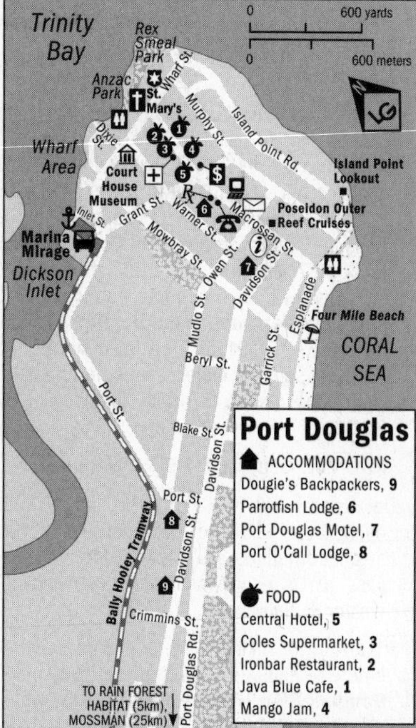

Yungaburra's sole hostel, **On the Wallaby ❶,** is one of the best in Northern Queensland. The common area feels like a mountain lodge with rustic furnishings and a wood-burning stove. The bathrooms are made of stone and wood, and the bunk rooms are clean. Enjoy a BBQ ($10) or breakfast ($4). Guests can also join hostel-run outdoor activities (day and night canoeing, biking, or hikes to swimming holes). Platypus-spotting trips are free. (☎4095 2031; www.onthewallaby.com. Full-day bike rental $15. Cairns transfer $25 one-way. Reception 8am-1pm and 4-8pm. Sites $10 per person; dorms $20; doubles $50. AmEx/DC/MC/V.)

The coffee shop in the **Gem Gallery and Coffee Shop ❶,** 21 Eacham Rd., serves a huge breakfast for $5. The Gem Gallery specializes in inexpensive opals and offers free opal-cutting, and occasional gold-working demonstrations. (☎4095 3455. Open daily 7am-latenight.) Next door is **Flynn's ❷,** which has bigger meals than the Coffee Shop. (☎4095 2235. Open for dinner M-W and F-Su 6pm-latenight. AmEx/DC/MC/V.) **Yungaburra Market,** on Eacham St., serves as the local supermarket. (☎4095 2177. Open daily 7am-7pm. AmEx/DC/MC/V.)

PORT DOUGLAS ☎07

Nestled between tropical rainforest and the Coral Sea, Port Douglas is a friendly outpost bordering two of the world's most unusual environments. The cooler months of the Dry see the departure of the box jellyfish from Port Douglas' pristine four-mile beach and the arrival of wealthy tourists attracted by upscale resorts and ritzy shopping. Easy living in tropical surroundings entices even the most nomadic backpackers to stay longer than planned. Snorkel and scuba trips take travelers to the outer reaches of the Great Barrier Reef, while other adventures head up the coast to the world's oldest rainforest in Daintree National Park.

TRANSPORTATION

Buses: Sun Palm Coaches (Port Douglas: ☎4099 4992, Cairns: ☎4032 4999), at the Marina Mirage, runs door-to-door service daily to the **airport** (1hr., several per day, $25) and **Cairns** (1½hr., same day round-trip $45, open round-trip $59). It also has 6 services per wk. to **Cooktown** (originating in Cairns), 3 via the inland route (M, W, F) and 3 via the bumpy 4WD Coastal Road (T, Th, Sa). The Coastal Road route is a travel pass and allows stopovers in **Cape Tribulation** and Port Douglas itself. A direct shuttle to **Cape Tribulation** costs $90 round-trip and also originates in Cairns. **BTS** (☎4099 5665; www.btstours.com.au) services **Cairns** (1hr.; 6 per day; $23, $40 round-trip) and **Mossman Gorge** (see **Daytrip: Mossman Gorge**). There is also **Port Douglas Bus Service** (☎4099 5351), a local shuttle that runs between the Rainforest Habitat and town, stopping at major resorts and hostels on the way ($3.50, $5 round-trip). **Country Road Coachlines** (☎4045 2794; www.countryroadcoachlines.com.au) also runs to Cooktown (return $125) and Cairns daily.

Taxis: Port Douglas Taxis, 45 Warner St. (24hr. ☎1800 131 008).

Car Rental: Thrifty Car Rental, #2 50 Macrossan St. (☎4099 5555), specializes in **4WD** (from $130 per day). Extra $16 per day for drivers 21-25. Cheaper rates for extended periods. **Holiday Car Hire,** 54 Macrossan St. (☎4099 4999), rents compacts and small 4WDs, as well as beach-buggy "mokes" from $59 per day. **Avis** and **Budget** are on Warner St. between Grant and Wharf St.

Bike Rental: Biking is the best way to get around Port Douglas. Check with the hostels before renting, as some provide bikes or offer discounted rentals. Otherwise, visit **Port Douglas Bike Hire** (☎4099 5799), which has two locations, one on the corner of Wharf and Warner St, and the second on the corner of Davidson and Port St. All types of bikes are available: mountain, racing, child, and tandem. Rental includes lock and helmet. Open daily 9am-5pm. ½-day $14, full-day $18, weekly from $59.

Road Report: The **Royal Automobile Club of Queensland** (☎4033 6711; www.racq.com.au) provides road conditions and closings.

ORIENTATION AND PRACTICAL INFORMATION

Seventy kilometers north of Cairns, Port Douglas Rd. branches right off the **Captain Cook Highway (Hwy. 1)** and turns into **Davidson Street,** which then meets **Macrossan Street,** the town's main drag. Macrossan St. runs across the Port Douglas peninsula, ending at **Four Mile Beach** (on the Esplanade) to the east and **Marina Mirage** (on Wharf St.) to the west. Most shops are open until 5pm.

Tourist Offices: Port Douglas might have more tourist offices than residents. Two of the largest, **Port Douglas Tourist Centre,** 23 Macrossan St. (☎4099 5599), and **BTS Tours,** 49 Macrossan St. (☎4099 5665), have all the necessary tour and activity information and can also book transportation.

Banks: National Australia, Commonwealth, ANZ, and **Westpac** banks are within 200m of each other on Macrossan St. All are open M-Th 9:30am-4pm, F 9:30am-5pm. **ANZ,** 36 Macrossan St. (☎13 13 14), exchanges currency and AmEx Travelers Cheques for a $7 commission per transaction. Some hostels may exchange traveler's checks for free. If heading north, keep in mind that ATMs may be few and far between.

Police: (24hr. ☎4099 5220), Macrossan and Wharf St. office open M-Th 8am-2:30pm.

Medical Services: Port Village Medical Centre, Shop 17 in Port Village Centre on Macrossan St. (24hr. ☎4099 5043). Office open M-F 8am-6pm, Sa-Su 9am-noon. The nearest **hospital** (☎4098 2444) is in Mossman, on Hospital St. Head north on Captain Cook Hwy. (Hwy. 1) into Mossman and follow the signs.

Internet Access: Many hostels and shops on Macrossan St. offer Internet access. Try **Wicked Ice Cream,** 48 Macrossan St. (☎4099 5568). $6 per hr. Open daily 9am-10:30pm.

Post Office: 5 Owen St. (☎4099 5210). On the corner of Macrossan and Owen St., halfway up the hill. Open M-F 8:30am-5:30pm, Sa 9am-2pm. **Postal Code:** 4877.

ACCOMMODATIONS AND CAMPING

There's no shortage of expensive beds in this resort town; luckily, hostels also abound. They tend to be reasonably priced and well equipped; most have a pool, bar, and restaurant, and many offer free transportation between Port Douglas and Cairns. These popular accommodations fill up quickly, so book ahead.

Parrotfish Lodge, 37/39 Warner St. (☎4099 5011 or 1800 995 011; www.parrotfishlodge.com). Close to the action on Macrossan St. Large, modern and equipped with a bar, restaurant, Internet lounge, billiards, a pool, spacious decks, BBQ, and satellite TVs. Carpark underground. All rooms have A/C, require keycard access, and are on the 2nd fl. or above. Reception 7am-9pm. 8-bed dorms $25; doubles $85; ensuite $95. ❷

Port O'Call Lodge (YHA), 7 Craven Close (☎4099 5422 or 1800 892 800). Take a left off Port Douglas Rd. onto Port St. as you enter town. Incredibly comfortable motel-like hostel 15min. from town center has laundry, pool, kitchen, bike rental, and Internet access. Free shuttle bus to and from Cairns M-Sa (departs Port O'Call at 8:30am; picks up from anywhere in Cairns at 10:30am). The popular bistro serves large meals daily 6-9pm (main courses $14-22) and is hopping during Happy hour (5-7pm). Free lockers. Reception 7:30am-7:30pm. Check-out 9:30am. 4-bed dorm with bath $28, YHA $26.50; deluxe motel rooms $69-99. Cheaper during the Wet. ❸

Port Douglas Motel, 9 Davidson St. (☎4099 5248). If you've got a few friends to share the cost, this place is a great find. Only a 2min. walk to the beach. All rooms are impeccably clean and equipped with kitchenettes, bathrooms, TV, and A/C. Covered carpark. Prices $69-77 depending on the number of people. ❺

Dougie's Backpackers, 111 Davidson St. (☎4099 6200 or 1800 996 200; www.dougies.com.au). A jungle-themed retreat with a friendly atmosphere 15min. from town center. Relax in a shady hammock or toss back a few at the lively bar (open 4pm-midnight). Laundry, Internet access, kitchen, pool, BBQ, bike rental ($1 per hr.), and local employment information. Free bus to Cairns M, W, Sa 8:30am; free pickup in Cairns M, W, Sa 10:30am. Campsites $12; tents with mattresses $18; dorms $24; doubles $68. $1 off if you have a picture of your mother or your pet. NOMADS/VIP/YHA. ❶

FOOD AND NIGHTLIFE

With the tourist offices closed and the affairs of sea complete, **Macrossan Street** comes to life at night with flame torches, courtyard restaurants, and live music. Trendy, upscale restaurants crowd the street, offering everything from pizza to sushi, but at a steep price. Mixed into the fray are a few cheaper local eateries, but they're harder to spot. A **Coles** supermarket is located in the Port Village Shopping Centre on Macrossan St. between Wharf and Grant St. (Open M-F 8am-9pm, Sa 8am-5:30pm, Su 9am-6pm.)

Ironbar Restaurant, 5 Macrossan St. (☎4099 4776). With its rusty chandeliers and corrugated iron exterior, it could be an outback bar—except that it's on Macrossan St. The main attraction is the cane toad race run by local entrepreneur Clancy M-F, Su; kids-only 7:30pm, adults 9pm. Choose your own finely dressed amphibian; the winner (human, not toad) gets a prize. Ironbar offers a variety of Queensland delicacies such as kangaroo burgers, skewered croc, and barbecued prawns for $7-30. Open M-F 11am-2am, Sa-Su 8am-2am. ❸

Java Blue Cafe, 2 Macrossan St. (☎4099 5814). Serves tasty sandwiches ($8-11), gourmet breakfasts ($10-15), and huge salads ($7-10). Good coffee. Open daily 7:30am-3:30pm. Cash only. ❷

Central Hotel, 9 Macrossan St. (☎4099 5271). Serves a predominantly local crowd and has area bands Tu-F nights. The bar also hosts a rousing game of "jag the joker," a small local jackpot, every F night. If you work up an appetite during the drinking games, try burgers or fish ($5-15). Lunch special $8. Open daily until midnight. ❶

Mango Jam, 24 Macrossan St. (☎4099 6611), with its lively terrace and good portions, is a good lunch option. Try a mango daiquiri in the trendy cocktail lounge or munch on one of the highly touted pizzas. Meals $11-29. Open daily 7:30am-9:30pm. ❸

SIGHTS AND ACTIVITIES

Most of Port Douglas' historical sites are in the Marina Mirage. **St. Mary's by the Sea,** a small white chapel next to the water, has a beautiful ocean view. Up the wharf, check out the **Courthouse Museum.** Built in 1879, it is the oldest building in town. (☎4099-4635. Open Tu-Sa 10am-1pm.) On Sundays (7am-2pm), there is a **craft market** in Anzac Park near the Courthouse Museum, with stalls selling ice cream, fruit juices, and tropical fruits; try the amazing Mangosteen if it's in season.

The **Rainforest Habitat,** located on Port Douglas Rd. as you enter town, has eight acres, three enclosures, and over 1000 animals without cages or any discernible fear of people. Mingle with cockatoos and parrots, scratch a wallaby behind the ears, or oggle the endangered southern cassowary, a large, flightless bird and keystone species of the Dainsland rainforest. Early risers can enjoy "Breakfast with the Birds" (8-10:30am; $39, children $19.50, families $70; includes admission), a full buffet with champagne in the aviary. Late risers can try "Lunch with the Lorikeets" (noon-2pm) for the same price. (☎4099 3235; www.rainforesthabitat.com.au. Wheelchair accessible. Open daily 8am-5pm; last entry 4pm. $28, children $14, families $70. Student discount 10%.)

WATERFRONT ACTIVITIES

Four Mile Beach, at the east end of Macrossan St., is almost always quiet. This gorgeous stretch of sand attracts an array of locals, backpackers, and swanky resort-types. A netted portion protects swimmers from jellyfish during the Wet, and a lifeguard is on duty (M-Sa 9:30am-5pm).

Extra Action Watersports (☎4099 3175 or 04 1234 6303; extraaction@ledanet.com.au) is just north of Marina Mirage. Steve, the owner and self-described "action man," can set you up with any number of heart-stopping adventures. **Parasailing** experiences last 30min. and offer an astounding bird's eye view of the ocean and the rainforest. $80, tandem $100; inquire about 2hr. family packages.

Wavelength (☎4099 5031) next to Extra Action Watersports, is one of the few snorkeling-only operations. A boat departs daily at 8:30am for 8hr. trips to the outer reef with a marine biologist on board. $165, children $110.

Dan's Mountain Biking (☎4032 0066; www.cairns-aust.com/mtb) offers a burst of adrenaline that will get you sweaty, wet, and dirty. Min. age 12.

CRIKEY, IT'S A CROC. Do not snorkel or swim in the Port Douglas marina area; it has crocs.

SCUBA DIVING

Experienced divers often prefer the untouched reefs near Port Douglas to the heavily touristed spots farther south in Cairns.

Haba Dive (☎4099 5254), in the Marina Mirage. Offers 2 dives on each trip. The smallish group size (max. 40 people) creates a more personal experience than you'll get on some of the larger boats. While some diving trips will surprise you with hidden charges, Haba's prices include everything. Departs daily 8:30am with free pickup and lunch. Snorkeling $130, children $85; scuba $185 including gear.

Poseidon Outer Reef Cruises, 32 Macrossan St. (☎1800 085 674 or 4099 4772; www.poseidon-cruises.com.au). A 1-boat operation offering recreational snorkeling ($155), certified scuba ($175), and introductory scuba ($205). Max. 80 people. Daily 8:30am-4:30pm. Office open daily 8:30am-7:45pm. Offers dive courses in conjunction with **Discover Dive** on Grant St., between Macrossan and Warner St. (☎4099 5544; www.discoverdiveschool.com.au), a five-star PADI dive center specializing in small group training. A 4-day open water course $605. Advanced, Rescue, and Divemaster courses are also available. Day trips are expensive, but service is first rate.

Quicksilver (☎4087 2100; www.quicksilver-cruises.com) in Mirage Marina. One of the most respected operations in the business; immortalized in Peter Lik postcards. Offers a five-star PADI Open Water course with group size limited to 8 per instructor. Packages for divers, non-divers, and snorkelers available. Introductory dives with gear $134, certified dives with gear $92, 2 dives $134; Open Water course with 2 lunches $595.

DAYTRIP: MOSSMAN GORGE

Not all of Port Douglas' natural attractions require a pair of fins and a scuba mask. A few miles outside of town, the rainforest-covered mountains are easily accessible via Mossman Gorge, part of the **Daintree National Park.** The gorge has several hiking paths which originate in the visitors' carpark. Locals and tourists alike often make the easy 0.5km hike to the cool freshwater swimming holes (croc free), while more adventurous hikers tackle the challenging 2.4km circuit track which travels up the river, over a swinging suspension bridge, and into the dark green canopy. Lizards, tropical birds, and bizarrely shaped trees are common sights, as are wet shoes from overflowing creeks during the Wet.

BTS runs to **Mossman** (30min.; $8, round-trip $14). Pickup from hostels at 9:15 and 11:45am, return at 12:30 and 2:30pm. If driving, follow the Captain Cook Hwy. (Hwy. 1) north from the junction with Port Douglas for about 20km. Follow the signs for Mossman Gorge and turn left across from Mossman State High School. Drive about 4km to Kuku Yalanji, and 1km more to the carpark. If you intend to see Cape Tribulation or Daintree by rental car, Mossman Gorge is on the way, so don't bother using BTS.

Aboriginal tours can be arranged with **Kuku-Yalanji Dreamtime Walks,** covering explanations about traditional medicines and "bush tucker" (food found in nature). The Aborigine-owned operation also has a visitors center and shop. (☎4098 2595. Open M-F 9am-4pm. Tours M-F 10am, noon, and 2pm. $20, children $12.50. Book ahead. Mini-bus pickup service for 10am walk from Port Douglas and Mossman $50, children $35.)

DAINTREE ☎07

Kingfishers, kookaburras, and friendly faces abound in this tiny village (pop. 150), a popular bird-watching destination. Most activities revolve around the Daintree River—beautiful but perhaps a bit over-hyped. Daintree Township is about 6km north of the turn-off for the Daintree Ferry on the Cook Hwy. You'll need a car to get there. Beware that this portion of the road can flood; call ☎4033 6711 or one of the local restaurants for road conditions.

The **Daintree General Store** (☎4098 6146) serves as the town watering hole and **post office.** Several boat companies run river excursions which vary in length between 1 and 2½hr. These generally start at $20; children travel for less. The quiet boats of **Daintree Electric Boat Cruises** (☎1800 686 103) make for a peaceful journey on the river. If you want to see the estuarine crocodiles ("salties") that live in the river, check out **Daintree Croc-spot tours.** (☎4098 6125; daintree.store@bigpond.com; wheelchair accessible; 1½hr.; $25, children $12.) Chris Dahlberg also runs excellent morning wildlife and bird-spotting tours from the jetty. (☎4098 7997; www.daintreerivertours.info. 2hr. $45. Book ahead.) You can fish with **Far North River Safaris.** (☎4098 6111; www.daintreefishing.com.au. ½ day $80.) Take your catch to **Ellenor's Place,** part of the General Store, and Ellenor will cook it for about $10. Other entrees $6-25 (Open 7am-7pm).

A TV room, swimming pool, BBQ, and free **Internet** access are just some of the perks that convince many guests to stay an extra day at the wonderful **Red Mill House** ❹ (☎4098 6233; www.redmillhouse.com.au), a bird-watcher's sanctuary 50m up the road from the General Store. Free daily breakfast includes fresh fruit from a tropical garden with homemade yogurt and bread. The older part of the house has a two-bedroom family unit with lounge (4 people $220), and the new section offers ensuite singles ($100) and doubles ($135). One suite is fully wheelchair accessible (including bathroom).

CAPE TRIBULATION ☎07

Cape Tribulation marks the spectacular collision of two World Heritage Parks. The rainforest crashes down onto the ocean surf, and every inch of forest and reef teems with life. About 15km north of the Daintree River, "Cape Trib" is a landmark in the heart of Daintree National Park. When locals talk about Cape Tribulation, they're usually referring to a large general area served by **Cape Tribulation Road,** which runs north past **Cow Bay, Alexandra Bay, Thornton Peak,** and the **Cape.** Travelers continuing up the coast from Daintree will use the **Daintree Ferry,** which shuttles across the river from 6am-midnight. (Walk-on passengers $1; cars $16 round-trip.) Access Cape Tribulation from the south via Cape Tribulation Rd., paved up to the carpark at Cape Tribulation Beach and criss-crossed by causeways and floodways at multiple points. If you are traveling during the Wet, call ahead for road conditions (☎4033 6711). Given the number of river crossings, consider bringing a car with a snorkel, and don't attempt any ill-advised routes.

TRANSPORTATION AND PRACTICAL INFORMATION

The best way to see Cape Trib is by car. Renting a vehicle will cost only slightly more than a tour package, and will allow you the freedom to pick and choose between the many adventures available in and around Cape Trib. If you can't get a car, many of the larger resorts provide shuttles to various sights and offer a number of activities on their premises. **Sun Palm Coaches** provides daily service from Cairns to Cape Trib at 7am ($90 round-trip; stops upon request). It returns to Cairns from Cape Trib Beach House (see **Accommodations**) at 10:30am.

If driving, bear right after the ferry: this sealed road passes the Alexandra Range Lookout on the right. Just a few kilometers farther north is the **Daintree Discovery Centre.** The turn-off for Cow Bay, 30min. farther on Buchanan Creek Rd., brings travelers to Cooper Creek and, finally, Cape Tribulation. A 4WD-only road then continues on to Cooktown (p. 441).

There is no official information center in Cape Tribulation. The **Queensland Parks and Wildlife Service (QPWS) Ranger Station** has public info, but the hours are limited. (☎4098 0052. Open M-F 9:30-11:30am.) Two other sources of info are the Daintree Discovery Centre and the **Bat House** (see **Sights and Activities,** p. 438). The **Rainforest Village,** a few kilometers before Cooper Creek, sells groceries and petrol and has a phone and a post box. (☎4098 9015. Open daily 7am-7pm.)

ACCOMMODATIONS

Hostels here reflect the active beach-going lifestyle and rainforest atmosphere of Cape Trib. Each has a slightly different theme, focusing on the beach, the rainforest, or a combination of the two.

Crocodylus Village (☎4098 9166; crocodylus@austarnet.com.au), on Buchanan Creek Rd., east off Cape Tribulation Rd. If heading north from Daintree Ferry, take a right after the Daintree Discovery Centre. This backpacker oasis offers open-air cabins scattered around a large wooden patio. Tour options include horseback riding, sunrise paddle trek in a hybrid kayak/canoe, overnight kayak adventures, and guided bushwalks. $18-179 depending on duration and type of trip. Organized bus transfers from Cairns or Port Douglas. Laundry, pool, bar, restaurant. Reception 7:30am-11:15pm. Cabin rooms $23, YHA $21; ensuite cabin for two $75, extra person $10, children $5. ❷

Cape Trib Beach House (☎4098 0030), on the right after about 1km on the unsealed portion of Cape Tribulation Rd. Final stop on the Sun Palm bus between Cairns and

Cape Trib. Relax on a pristine, private beach with forest dragons and butterflies. Free yoga on the beach daily 9am. Laundry, bar, restaurant, pool, Internet access, bike rental ($10 per day), lockers ($5 per day). Some beachfront cabins, some 4-person ensuite with fridges. Dorms $25; private cabins $70-135. ❷

PK's Jungle Village (☎4098 0400 or 1800 232 333; www.pksjunglevillage.com). Should be called "PK's Jungle Party." Biggest and baddest hostel on Cape Trib. About 400m past the "Welcome to Cape Tribulation" sign on Cape Tribulation Rd. Free daily activities include pilates and beach volleyball. Bike rental (½ day $15, full day $20). Laundry, kitchen, pool, restaurant, and bar with nightly entertainment. Internet access $6 per hour. Reception 7:30am-8:30pm. Check-out 9:30am. Campsites $10 per person; dorms $22; doubles $65. ❶

CAMPING

Those looking to cut costs can camp at several locations off Cape Tribulation for around $10 per person.

Lync Haven (☎4098 9155; www.lynchaven.com.au), has powered sites bordering the rainforest just past the turn-offs for Daintree Discovery Center and Buchanan Creek Rd.

Rainforest Village (see **Practical Information**), has pristine campgrounds on a hillside near the forest, about 2km further down Cape Tribulation Rd. from Lync Haven.

Noah's Beach Campground (☎07 131 304, www.qld.gov.au/camping), located just after Thornton Beach on the right, 10m from a brilliant stretch of beach. $4, families $16, more for powered sites. Book ahead.

FOOD

Lync Haven ❷ (☎4098 9155), with its wildlife sanctuary full of orphaned 'roos, is the most unusual eating establishment in Cape Trib. Options include huge, tasty burgers ($5-7), sandwiches ($5), and a veggie-friendly menu ($14-16) at dinner. (Open daily 7am-6pm, until 7pm in the Dry.) **Cafe on the Sea** ❷, at Thorton Beach, serves up a hearty breakfast ($14), salads, burgers, and sandwiches. (☎4098 9118. Open daily 7am-5pm.) Most hostels and resorts also have their own bars and restaurants; the most hopping scene is at **PK's Jungle Village** ❶, where the bar is open daily noon-midnight.

SIGHTS AND ACTIVITIES

For a unique taste sensation, visit the **Cape Tribulation Exotic Fruit Farm,** where jungle-expert Digby offers tasting tours of unusual fruits. (☎4098 0057; www.capetrib.com.au. Tour begins daily at 4pm. Book ahead. $15.) **The Daintree Discovery Centre,** just before Cow Bay, off Cape Tribulation Rd., is an informative and popular stop. It has an aerial boardwalk and 23m canopy tower, allowing visitors to view the rainforest from above. You can take a self-guided tour using the info booklet, or rent an audio guide for $5. (☎4098 9171. Open daily 8:30am-5pm. $25, children $7.50, families $45, concessions for those lodging in the area.) A walk around **Jindalba,** just 450m up the road from the center, offers a look into some of the best-preserved, publicly accessible rainforest in Cape Trib. The area has picnic facilities, bathrooms, and a sign-posted walk. The **Bat House,** opposite PK's Jungle Village on the west side of the highway, is a less extensive source of information than the Discovery Centre, but the all-volunteer staff will be happy to take your picture ($2) with their giant flying fox, Rex. (☎4098 0063; www.austrop.org.au.)

Cape Tribulation Wilderness Cruises explores the mangroves of Cooper Creek in search of crocodiles. (☎4033 2052; www.capetribcruises.com. 1-1½hr. Daily departure times vary. $20-25, children under 14 $15. Book ahead.) **Rum Runner** is one of the several Cairns-based tours which runs daily trips to the reef off the Cape, and departs from Cape Trib to explore the Mackay and Undine Reefs. The reefs visited on this tour are more pristine than those in over-touristed Cairns. (☎1300 556 332. Free bus to the beach from all Daintree/Cape Trib resorts, snorkeling equipment included. Snorkeling $120; ages 3-14 $90. Dives available to certified and first-time divers.)

Tropical Sea Kayaks (☎4098 9166) offers a popular two-day, one-night trip to **Snapper Island** ($179; available at Crocodylus Village). The excursion features reef walking, snorkeling, and beach camping, including all equipment and prepared meals. **Wundu Trail Rides,** between Lync Haven and the Rainforest Village, leads horseback tours of the coral coast. (☎4098 9156. 3hr. Departs twice daily. Guided rides $55; 10% discount for groups of 7 or more. Min. age 10.)

ROUTES TO COOKTOWN

There are two routes from Daintree to Cooktown—one inland, one coastal. Both offer stunning views and unique scenery; travelers should try to drive up one and down the other so as to take in the beauty of the far north in its entirety.

The coastal route, called the Bloomfield Track, beats through 150km of bush as it swerves and dips, carving its way through rugged coastal mountains. In bad conditions it is impassable; rainforest creeks often become raging rivers. On a "good" day, however, the road is about as much fun as can be legally had in a 4WD. Thick rainforest canopy melts away to reveal coastal views, while steep inclines and river crossings keep the adrenaline pumping. The trek takes about four hours, with lots of veering, bumping, and swerving to avoid large potholes and fallen trees. Call ahead or check with locals for road conditions. Bring cash, as some places don't take credit. If you'd rather not be the one clutching the steering wheel, **Sun Palm Coaches** (☎4099 4992) departs from Port Douglas and Cairns via the coast road Tu, Th, and Sa.

The inland route to Cooktown doesn't offer the same kind of rugged adventure as the coastal track; most of the road is sealed. That said, the inland path is every bit as visually stunning as it winds through rainforest ravines, over mountain passes, and finally into open savannah. In the late afternoon, drivers should look out for Brahma cattle on the unfenced road.

BLOOMFIELD TRACK

This is a playground for those who desire an intense 4WD experience, and it is generally traveled enough that you will likely not have to wait long for help if you get stuck. From Cape Tribulation, the road turns to dirt and the fun really begins. The first part of the trip is the most intense, as the track follows the coastal mountains up steep inclines and down sharp grades complete with a half-dozen rivers to ford. A little over an hour's drive north brings travelers to **Wujal Wujal,** a tiny Aboriginal community with a **service station** and **general store** that has a **pay phone** and stocks everything from food and meds to camping supplies and clothes. (☎4060 8101. Store open daily 8am-5pm; service station open M-Th 9am-6pm, F 9-11:30am.) Beautiful **Bloomfield Falls** is only five minutes from Wujal Wujal. Take a left after the bridge over Bloomfield River; go in the opposite direction of the Cooktown arrow. Visitors who make the short (2min.) hike from the parking area to the falls are rewarded with a striking view of the 200 ft. torrent of crashing water. It's an excellent place for a picnic after a rough ride—just watch out for feisty crocodiles.

The mountains pull back from the coast between Wujal Wujal and Cooktown, and the wet tropics slowly yield to dry savannah. North of the bridge to Wujal Wujal the road is smoother, even paved at times, and travelers can count on passing the occasional store or small-town hotel. About 10km north of Wujal Wujal is the town of **Ayton,** where the local **IGA Express** has basic groceries, supplies, a **cafe,** a **payphone,** and toilets. (Open M-F 8:30am-5pm, Sa-Su 8:30am-4pm.) **Bloomfield Cabins and Camping** ❶ serves lunch and dinner ($5-15), and offers campsites and cabins. (☎4060 8207; www.bloomfieldcabins.com. Sites $10 per person, rooms for 2 from $65.) The final 1½hr. stretch of road before Cooktown will take you past the popular **Lion's Den Hotel** ❶, where mud-covered trackers stop for grub ($10-13), grog (beer; $3.50), and the chance to etch their names on the wall. (☎4060 3911. Open daily 10am-latenight. Campsites $7 per person. Pay phone in front.)

Four kilometers past the Lion's Den, the coastal road joins the sealed portion of the inland route and a tall, dark shadow appears on the horizon. The source of this silhouette is **Black Mountain National Park,** one of Australia's mysterious and lesser-known natural wonders. The two barren, black peaks (also known as Kalkajakaare, 'Place of the Spears,' in Aboriginal languages) are the subject of many Dreaming tales (p. 49), which are Creation Time stories of the Kuku Yalanji Aboriginal people. Signs at the park lookout explain that these jet-black rock piles are ringed with stinging bushes, house an intricate network of dangerous caves, and provide a habitat for three animal species found nowhere else in the world. Pilots passing over the rocks have reported experiencing turbulence and hearing loud bangs and mournful cries. The dark peaks (black from a film of fungi growing on the exposed rock) and surrounding area inspire many legends of those who have ventured into the mountain, never to return.

INLAND ROUTE

Though the inland route is more developed and well traveled than the coastal road, it is just as scenic. The first stop, **Mount Molloy,** is a 27km drive southwest of Mossman on the Peninsula Developmental Rd. (10min.). The **Mount Molloy National Hotel** ❸ is a grand building built in 1901. The downstairs pub (with outdoor beer garden) has a varied menu, and the hotel offers Old-World style accommodations. (☎4094 1133. Reception at pub 10am-midnight. Meals $7-17. Rooms $30 per person.) Next door, the **Mt. Molloy Cafe** ❶ serves acclaimed burgers ($5.50), calamari, pizza, and homemade meat pies (open daily 10am-midnight). Down the road, there are **public toilets,** a **post office** (☎4094 1135; M-F 9am-5pm), and a petrol station/store. (☎4094 1159. Open M-Sa 7am-7pm, Su 8am-7pm.) The **picnic area** at the junction entering town has toilets, hiking info, and free **camping** (max. stay 48hr.).

Mount Carbine sits 28km north of Mt. Molloy. Once a prosperous tungsten mining town, it now consists of three roadside buildings and an old miners' village which has been converted into a caravan park and residential area. That village, the **Mt. Carbine Caravan Park** ❷, is the best place to stay on the Inland route. It has basketball and tennis courts, a TV lounge, kitchen, and laundry facilities. (☎4094 3160. Reception 7:30am-8:30pm. One-bedroom houses (2 beds) with satellite TV and fully-equipped kitchen $55; 2-bedroom $65; 3-bedroom $75; caravan sites $14, powered $16.) Free caravan parking if you are continuing up Cape York. The **Mount Carbine Roadhouse** ❶, another budget option, has petrol, food ($5-17), and backpacker lodging. (☎4094 3043. Open daily 7am-7pm. Singles $25; doubles $35. Extra person $5.)

As it continues north, the road cuts through the hills, exposing the cores of mountains now bereft of their once-famous gold deposits. The **Palmer River Road-**

house ❶, 110km north of Mt. Molloy, proudly displays artifacts dating back to the goldrush. Friendly service, a ping pong machine, and a pool table make this a good place to regroup while filling up on petrol or diesel. (☎4060 2020. Open daily 7am-10:30pm. Powered caravan sites $15. Permanent tent accommodation $30. MC/V.) Farther north (145km from Mt. Molloy), the tarred road gives way to a snaky gravel descent through the hills with beautiful views. Just before reaching Cooktown the road passes the mysterious **Black Mountain National Park.**

COOKTOWN ☎07

In the winter, the south wind sweeps through Cooktown's dusty streets, bringing with it travelers who have abandoned the monotony of packaged tours and prepaid holidays. Cooktown tends to act as traveler's quicksand, stopping passersby captivated by a place where bars are open until the last patron leaves and shoes are an infrequent addition to the daily wardrobe. The town dates back to 1770, when Captain James Cook of England ran his ship *Endeavour* into the Great Barrier Reef. The 235 years since have witnessed the settlement, abandonment, and resettlement of the area, along with a gold rush and devastating cyclones. Today, Cooktown (pop. 3000) is both a key gateway to the far north and an eccentric community full of small-town charm.

TRANSPORTATION

Buses: Sun Palm Coaches (☎4099 4992) runs between Cooktown and Cairns. One bus departs from each city every day except M, alternating between coastal and inland routes. A round-trip ticket ($135) allows you to get on and off as often as you like, but you will have to wait a day at each stop to catch a bus continuing in the same direction. Buses on the inland route run to: **Cairns** (5hr.; W, F, Su 2:30pm; $69), via **Lakeland** (1¼hr.); **Cape Tribulation** (4¼hr.); **Cow Bay** (4¾hr.); **Kuranda** (4¾hr.); **Mareeba** (4¼hr.); **Mossman** (6hr.); **Mount Carbine** (3¼hr.); **Mount Molloy** (3½hr.); or by the coastal route (7½hr.; Tu, Th, Sa; $69) via **Lion's Den** (30min.).

Taxis: Cooktown Taxis (☎4069 5387). Service from 6:30am to when the pubs close ($6 fare anywhere in the city limits).

Car Rental: A1 Car Rental, 112 Charlotte St. (☎4069 5775, 24hr.) has a small selection. **4WDs** start at $130.

Road Report: Royal Automobile Club of Queensland, Cape York Tyres (☎4069 5233), at the corner of Charlotte and Furneaux St. Open M-F 6am-7pm, Sa-Su 7:30am-6pm.

Service: Caltex Station (☎4069 5354), at the corner of Hope and Howard St., has petrol and groceries. Open 24hr. AmEx/MC/V.

ORIENTATION

The **Cooktown Development Road** becomes **Hope Street** as you enter Cooktown proper and head toward **Grassy Hill,** where Captain Cook first spied the harbor. Take a left off this street and continue two blocks to **Charlotte Street,** which runs parallel to Hope St., the home to the majority of Cooktown's shops and services. It intersects several streets, including Boundary, Howard, Hogg, and Walker St. Head east on Walker St. to visit the Botanic Gardens and Finch Bay. At the northernmost end of town, Charlotte St. runs along the water, curves eastward, and becomes **Webber Esplanade** before coming to a dead end.

QUEENSLAND FROM 14,000 FT.

My first skydiving trip begins with an unglamorous dispute over the cost, though I really have little reason to complain–diving is relatively cheap in Queensland, and considering the spectacular coastal views here, the price tag seems almost a bargain.

I'm jumping tandem; my partner Len is a tall string-bean of a man who tells me he's been jumping for 40 years. We develop a nice rapport.

"Should these be tighter?" I ask.

"Not for Americans," he says.

I'm willing to assume that he means this in the best possible way. I'm willing to assume this because he's going to strap me to him before jumping out of a plane, as only a good Aussie mate would.

When it's my turn, I drop from the door the way I've seen it in the movies: I don't so much jump as get dragged out. Later on video I see my own hesitation, true fear in my face for just an instant. No worries! Well, maybe one.

The cameraman falls with me, so the recorded image is not one of falling but of floating gently, with a fire hose in my face. The minute-long fall seems to last only 10 seconds, and then with a snap the parachute is open. From there it's a three minute drift to the beach, with Len sending us into a swinging, vertiginous spiral, expanding and altering the view. The ocean is revealed not to be

PRACTICAL INFORMATION

Tourist Office: On Charlotte St., across from the Post Office. Also, **The Croc Shop,** 115 Charlotte St. (☎4069 5880), next to Anzac Park, serves as an info center, with a bookings office next door. Visit local legend Linda Rowe, author of *Paradise Found,* for tips on trekking to the Tip of Cape York. Open daily 8:30am-6pm in peak season.

Bank: Westpac (☎4069 6960), on Charlotte St., between Green and Furneaux St., next door to the Post Office. **ATM** but no currency exchange. Open M-F 9am-4:30pm.

Parks Service: Queensland Parks and Wildlife Service (QPWS) (☎4069 5574), at the end of Webber Esplanade. Open M-Th 8am-3:30pm, F 8am-3pm.

Laundromat: (☎4069 6799), under the Parks Office at Webber Esplanade.

Police: (☎4069 5320) across from the wharf on Charlotte St. Staffed M-F 8am-4pm; after hours use the intercom at the office door.

Medical Services: Cooktown Hospital (☎4069 5433), on the corner of Ida St. and the Cooktown Developmental Rd., on the way out of town heading south.

Internet Access: Cooktown Computer Stuff (☎4069 6010), on Charlotte St. $2 per 20min. Open daily 9am-5pm. Also available for $6 per hr. at Pam's Place.

Post Office: (☎4069 5347), on Charlotte St., next to the bank and across from the Sovereign Hotel. Open M-F 9am-5pm. **Postal Code:** 4895.

ACCOMMODATIONS AND FOOD

Groceries can be purchased at the **IGA** supermarket, on the corner of Hogg and Helen St. (☎4069 5633. Open M-W and F-Sa 8am-6pm, Th 8am-7pm, Su 10am-3pm.) There is also a cheap fruit store called **Q-Cumber.** (☎4069 6818) and a butchery behind the IGA (in an outdoor mall on Charlotte St., between Hogg and Walker St.)

Pam's Place (☎4069 5166), at the corner of Charlotte and Boundary St., is Cooktown's backpacker hub. Amenities include large kitchen, laundry, bar, pool table, swimming pool, garden, and morning shuttles to the bus station and airport. Bike rental. Sites $11; dorms $23; singles $40; doubles $49. YHA discount. MC/V, 2% surcharge. ❷

Hillcrest Bed and Breakfast (☎4069 5305; www.hillcrestb-b.com), at the base of Grassy Hill on 130 Hope St., is a friendly B&B with a sunny garden, veranda, pool, laundry, and restaurant. Continental breakfast 7-

9am ($7). Doubles $55, extra person $5-10; motel units with TV, A/C, and bath $70. MC/V. ❺

Alamanda Inn (☎4069 5203), across from the Ampol station on the corner of Hope and Howard St., offers tidy guest house rooms among beds of flowers. All rooms have A/C, fridge, TV, and sink. Singles $40; doubles $55; family units $80. AmEx/MC/V. ❸

Cooktown Caravan Park (☎4069 5536; www.cooktowncaravanpark.com), on Hope St., at the end of Cooktown Developmental Rd. Nestled in the trees at the base of Mt. Sorrow, this is one of the nicest places to camp in Cooktown, with arguably the best camp showers in all of Australia. Sites $16, powered $19. ❷

Nature's Powerhouse Cafe (☎4069 6004), in the Botanical Gardens. This tiny cafe serves the best lunch in Cooktown. Sit on the patio overlooking the garden and enjoy delicacies like smoked salmon quiche or avocado salad ($8-10) made with fresh ingredients. Excellent smoothies ($4.50) and fresh fruit sodas ($3.50). Open 10am-2pm. ❷

SIGHTS

GUURRBI ROCK ART TOURS. The tours present an amazing opportunity to view and experience the ancient rock art of the Nugal-warra tribe. Community Elder and Guide Wilfred Gordon weaves the ancestral story lines together with the lives of his guests, teaching the lessons of Aboriginal culture and history through a very personal and enlightening tour. *(Located in the Aboriginal community of Hope Vale, 45min. outside Cooktown. Take Charlotte St. out of Cooktown and follow the road all the way to Hope Vale (3hr.). ☎4069 6259. Great Emu tour $80, self-drive $55; 5hr. Rainbow Serpent Tour $105, self-drive $70. Book ahead.)*

JAMES COOK HISTORICAL MUSEUM. The crown jewel of a town obsessed with the landing of Captain Cook, this Catholic convent-turned-museum attracted even the Queen of England to its dedication. Since then it has drawn tourists intrigued by an assortment of Cooktown's historical relics, from Cook's anchor to a Chinese shrine to Aboriginal artifacts. *(☎4069 5386. On the corner of Helen St. and Furneaux St. Open daily 9:30am-4pm. $7, discounts for children.)*

COOKTOWN CEMETERY. This cemetery, with its highly segregated plots divided into sections for Christian, Aboriginal, and Jewish residents, is the subject of many legends. The Chinese Shrine sits in the left-hand corner of the cemetery, where 30,000 migrants and their possessions were buried. Fact

solid blue, but extraordinary swirls of aquamarine, sapphire, amethyst, and jade. The spectrum plays out over the depths, from the yellow sand of the shallows to the green mid-depths to blue as solid as stone. On land, gorgeous gold sand rolls into green forested hills, and in the distance the trees fade to beige Australian bush.

On the ground I asked Len about landing, and he said he'd explain it during freefall. I screwed up my face and asked if I'd be able to hear him. "As quiet as a churchyard," he said cheerfully. I failed to appreciate the comparison. But I do indeed hear him as he directs me to pull my legs up to my chest, hook my hands under (ah, fetal comfort), and keep my feet moving so he won't trip over them. As we approach, the detail of distance that revealed the patterns of the river pooling over the sands—depositing the soot, silt and industrial dross it picked up on its way—fades and soon I see only sand and water. Cheering crowds have gathered along the fence by the beach, some to see their loved ones falling, but others just curious. I can't help but wave; the friendliness of the Aussies combined with my pulsing adrenaline and joy at landing inspires a moment of pure love for humanity. I release a scream as we swing down to the ground. Len unhooks me and I scream again and stretch. Check that one off the list.

— Dave Rochelson, Research-Writer
Let's Go Australia 2005

sheets about the cemetery can be found at any local accommodation. (*On McIvor River-Cooktown Rd.)*

OTHER SIGHTS. The lush **Botanic Gardens,** off Walker St., is a great place for picnicking; you may even spot a kangaroo or two. Inside the garden, visit **Nature's Powerhouse,** an interpretive center with excellent croc and snake exhibits and the botanical artwork collection of Vera Scarth-Johnson. Locals swim at **Finch Bay,** reached by following Walker St. to its end. Branching off the path to Finch Bay is a trail to **Cherry Tree Bay.** The trail from Cherry Tree Bay to the lookout is not well marked at the beach and its challenging inclines are unsuitable for small children. However, the lookout and lighthouse on **Grassy Hill** can also be accessed via car or foot from the end of Hope St. The summit provides an astounding 360° view of hundreds of square hectares, including the entirety of Cooktown, the surrounding rainforest, and the Great Barrier Reef. An even better view is at the top of **Mt. Cook** in Mt. Cook National Park. A 4-5hr. trail through rainforest to the mountain's summit starts at the end of Melaleuca St.; ask about it at the Croc Shop. Outside of Cooktown on the Cooktown Development Rd., the **Trevethan Waterfall** is tough to get to (4WD only), but is absolutely stunning and perfect for swimming (there's even a rope-swing). Take Mt. Amos Rd., a few kilometers after the turn-off for Archer Point (leaving Cooktown). It is 13km down the road, but tread lightly as the last 2km are rocky. During the Queen's Birthday weekend in June, the **Cooktown Discovery Festival** features truck-pulling and pie-eating competitions, reenactments of Captain Cook's landing, and other entertainment.

CAPE YORK

Cape York is one of the last great wilderness frontiers in Australia; a forbidding and isolated Outback beckons adventurers to abandon civilization and make the journey of nearly 1000km to **Australia's Tip.** Accessible only via the **Peninsula Developmental Road** (unsealed), the route is peppered with small towns and roadhouses every few hundred kilometers. During the Wet (Dec.-Apr.), most of the roads are impassable; the only way to see the Cape is by flying over it or into one of the small airports on the coast. During the Dry, the trip is arduous but manageable with a 4WD, and the reward is witnessing some of the most beautiful, diverse, and untouched landscape in the world.

If you decide to undertake the journey, check out books specifically about Cape York which offer logistics as well as historical and geographical information. This is particularly important if you're brave and crazy (and insured) enough to drive the **Old Telegraph track** (p. 449). *Cape York: An Adventurer's Guide* by Ron and Viv Moon (www.guidebooks.com.au) is a popular choice to help you on your way.

THE TIP

During the Wet, the unsealed roads are muddy, flooded, and generally impassable. Though they vary in quality the rest of the year, they are mostly drivable (barring major tropical disturbances). According to locals, a 4WD is not essential if you're staying on the Peninsula Developmental Rd., but if you're accustomed to driving on paved roads with well-defined lanes, a 4WD with high ground clearance is strongly recommended. If trekking off the main roads (into the national parks, for example), a 4WD is essential, as river crossings, jagged rocks, and vegetation create plenty of driving hazards. Before tackling any new road, it is important to check with locals for advice.

Aside from renting a 4WD, **tour packages** are often the only other option. Retired bombardiers depart from Cairns to air-drop mail over the Cape on **Cape York Air;** pilots will let passengers accompany them on their daily runs. (☎4035 9399. $236-

472.) **Regional Pacific** (☎07 4040 1400; www.regionalpacific.com.au) and **Aerotropics** (☎1300 656 110; www.aero-tropics.com.au; round-trip to Cairns 2hr., $400) both service Cape York. **John Charlton's Cape York Boat Adventure** has comprehensive tours of Cape York, including an opportunity to fish in the Cape's renowned waters. (☎4069 3302; www.capeyorkadventures.com.au.) **Bart's Bush Adventures** (☎4069 5381; www.bartsbushadventures.com.au) does outback day trips out of Cooktown. **Billy Tea Bush Safaris,** an award-winning company, combines 4WD, flying, and boating in their trips to Cape York from Cairns. (☎4032 3127; www.billytea.com.au. Trips from $2100.)

This journey has long seemed out-of-reach for the budget traveler. Getting to the Tip requires relative self-sufficiency—you need tents and the ability to cook your own food. But if you can get 3 or 4 people together, it can definitely be done, and it is usually a lot cheaper than going by boat, plane, or tour company. To see the national parks (and these can be the best part of the journey), you'll need a 4WD with high ground clearance, such as a Toyota Landcruiser, Hi-lux, or any Land Rover, and a winch to extricate yourself from any creeks or mud-holes. Problems can be avoided if you walk through creeks before driving through them, and if you stay to the packed-down tracks. Again, this is only necessary for national parks; the main roads (Peninsula Development Rd., the **Telegraph Road,** and the **Bamaga Road**) strive to avoid all the river crossings that are the heart of the **Old Telegraph Track.** Camping is generally inexpensive (about $10 per person). The area is also remote enough to allow for free camping: just stay away from the water where crocs may lurk.

There are plenty of supermarkets throughout the Cape, and cheap food is available. Fuel gets increasingly expensive as you head north; Bamaga has the most reasonable prices near the Tip. 4WDs can be rented in Cairns. **Britz** (☎4032 2611; www.britz.com) has a large range of 4WD campervans and 4WDs. **4WDHire** (☎4032 3094 or 1800 077 353; www.4wdhire.com.au) has the toughest fleet of vehicles, but charges high rates with a large excess. They offer a winch for a set price in addition to the rental cost. These companies specialize in 4WDs, but other rental companies in Cairns may have a few available for less, so check around and plan ahead. You might also want to check out the **A1 Car Rental** in Cooktown (p. 441), which has excellent 4WDs.

BASE OF THE CAPE

If you don't have the time, money, or stamina for the full journey up the Cape, you can still have an exciting wilderness experience not too far from Cooktown. For a good two- to three-day trip, try a circuit around **Lakefield National Park** via the **Peninsula Development Road** and the **Battle Camp Track.** 4WD is highly recommended. From Cooktown, the **Cooktown Development Road** runs southwest to Lakeland where it meets the northbound Peninsula Development Rd. This road travels along the edge of Lakefield National Park through the small town of Laura and then on to the outpost of **Musgrave,** the northern gateway to the park. On the Peninsula Development Rd., you can enter the park from either Laura or Musgrave (see **Lakefield National Park,** p. 446). You'll see a variety of wildlife, including kangaroos, wallabies, exotic birds, snakes, and crocodiles. At the southern end of the park, the **Battle Camp Track** returns to Cooktown. Although it is not a long drive, the rough terrain and river crossings (one of which is tidal and avoided by locals) will slow you down a fair bit. Be sure to bring a spare tire, as the Lakefield region roads are known for their numerous sharp rocks.

In **Laura** (pop. 100) you'll find the **Laura Roadhouse ❶,** on the Peninsula Development Rd. just after entering town from the south, which offers fuel, food, an ATM, and campsites. (24hr. emergency service ☎4060 3419.) Limited supplies are also available at the **Laura Store.** (☎4060 3238. Open daily 7:30am-6pm.) The **Ang-gnarra Visitors Centre,** across from the Laura Roadhouse, has a **Caravan Park ❶** with a pool and laundry. (☎4060 3214. $5, powered $6.)

Just 15km. south of Laura is **Split Rock,** on the Peninsula Development Rd., a group of ancient Aboriginal rock art sites. Some of the ancient carvings are over 13,000 years old. The hike is a steep uphill climb with a striking panorama at the top. (15min. self-guided walk $5; 3hr. walk $10.) The **Ang-gnarra Aboriginal Corporation** (☎4060 3200) offers tours of the sites. An hour southwest of Laura (50km, 4WD only), the Aboriginal-run **Jowalbinna Bush Camp** ❶ also offers tours. (☎4060 3236. Sites $11; cabins $69; permanent tents $80. ½-day tour of rock art sites $80, full-day $115; meals included.) Call Jowalbinna or the Cairns office (☎4051 4777) to book. The first pit stop north of Laura on the Peninsula Developmental Rd. is the **Hann River Roadhouse** ❶, 75km away. Pitch your tent under the stars in the open grass fields and fill up on a tasty burger. (☎4060 3242. Sites $8; caravans $12; limited accommodation $30.)

LAKEFIELD NATIONAL PARK REGION

LAKEFIELD NATIONAL PARK AT A GLANCE

AREA: 537,000 hectares.

HIGHLIGHTS: Seasonal billabongs bring an amazing assortment of wildlife; beautiful lily lagoons; historical homestead; bird-watching; excellent barramundi and catfish fishing.

GATEWAYS: Via the Battlecamp Track, from Laura in the south and Musgrave in the north.

CAMPING: Kalpowar, Hann Crossing, and many bush campgrounds.

FEES: Camping $4.50.

Laura is the gateway to the south of the park, while **Musgrave,** 138km north of Laura on the Peninsula Developmental Rd., is the closest point of contact with the northern reaches. The outpost's only building is the **Musgrave Roadhouse** ❶, which has a restaurant, fuel, and friendly staff. (☎4060 3229. Open daily 7:30am-10pm.) Accommodations are also available. (Sites $8; singles $40; doubles $55.)

To reach the heart of the park from Musgrave, travel west toward Cooktown. As the name "Lakefield" suggests, the park and its roads are submerged during the Wet. During the Dry, all but a few billabongs evaporate, attracting the area's wildlife to these critical sources of water. Visitors during these months are treated to an animal extravaganza and world-famous bird watching. Crocodiles, dingoes, wallabies, and feral pigs are commonly spotted in this area. After entering the park, travel east along the clearly marked track past **Lowlake,** a beautiful swamp covered in white lily flowers that is considered sacred to the region's traditional protectors. Farther down this road, **Nilma Plain** seems other-worldly with its endless expanses covered in tall, sharp termite mounds.

Camping ❶ in these areas is by permit only ($4.50); they can be obtained by self-registration at one of the three **ranger stations** in the park. The Lakefield ranger station is in the middle of the park, 112km from Musgrave; register here for the Kalpowar, Seven Mile, Melaleuca, Hanushs, and Midway sites. There are also boards announcing current road conditions. (☎/fax 4060 3271. Open daily 9am-5pm.) Kalpowar is the park's most developed campground, with toilets and cold showers; Hann Crossing is the only other campground with toilets. Camping in the southern section of the park requires a permit from the New Laura Ranger Station, while northern camping requires a permit from the Bizant Ranger Station.

Fishing and canoeing are the most popular activities in the park, with bird watching a close second. Check out **Red Lily Lagoon** for some remarkable bird life alongside the red lilies of the lotus plant. For fishing aficionados: Barramundi and catfish are the most common catches, but you can only keep a limited number, so be sure to consult a ranger or information board while planning your trip. Don't leave fish or fish parts lying about, as they attract crocs.

BEWARE CROCODILES. Most of the swamps, lakes, and rivers in Lakefield NP contain estuarine crocodiles. Never camp within 50m of water or less than 2m above it. Never swim in the park, and exercise caution near the water's edge. (See **Dangerous Animals,** p. 64.)

You can access the Princess Charlotte Bay by boat, but not by car. The Bizant boat ramp, 20km from the Bizant ranger base in the north of the park, provides the best access. Many of the other small lakes are also suitable for small watercraft.

COEN

North of Musgrave, the unexpected shifts in terrain and rapid directional changes of the Peninsula Developmental Rd. will test your reflexes. Fortunately, there aren't many other vehicles to contend with, and the wide road allows for occasional spinouts and extreme maneuvering. After 109km on this "highway" you'll arrive in the tiny town of Coen (pop. 350), a rest stop for weary travelers.

Most services are on **Regent St.** The **Ambrust General Store** has groceries, petrol, a payphone, and a small post office. (☎4060 1134. Open M-F 8am-5pm, Sa 8am-4pm, Su 9am-1pm. MC/V.) You can park your camper here or pitch a tent in the lot next door ($6.60). Across the street is the **BP Fuel Store** (☎4060 1144). Many establishments close or operate with restricted hours in the Wet. **The Queensland Parks and Wildlife Service** (www.epa.qld.gov.au), on the left as you leave town heading north, has info on nearby parks and campgrounds available to travelers 24hr.

The **Homestead Guest House ❸** is filled with goldrush memorabilia. (☎4060 1157. Laundry and kitchen. Reception 7am-9pm. Singles $40; doubles $60; shared rooms $30. Cash only.) The social center of Coen is the **Exchange Hotel ❸.** (☎4060 1133. Reception 10am-midnight. Singles $45; doubles with A/C $62.50.) An Extra-Cash **ATM** can be found at the Exchange Hotel. **Medical services** are available at the **Coen Clinic,** Armbrust St. (☎4060 1166. Open M-F 8am-5pm, 24hr. emergency service.)

NORTH OF COEN

Another 65km north along the Peninsula Developmental Rd., a wet track of red earth and white sand leads to the **Archer River Roadhouse ❸.** A popular spot for those going to and coming from the Tip, this outpost is a welcome reminder that life does exist along these lonely roads. Those returning from the bush should fill their empty stomachs with a famous Archer Burger, stuffed with every topping that has ever been slapped between two buns—and then some. The kitchen also serves beer, sandwiches, and full meals ($6-16). Camping and limited accommodations also available. (☎/fax 4060 3266. Reception 7am-8pm. Doubles $60.)

IRON RANGE NATIONAL PARK

IRON RANGE NATIONAL PARK AT A GLANCE

AREA: 34,600 hectares.

WHERE: On the remote eastern edge of the Cape York Peninsula.

HIGHLIGHTS: Australia's largest lowland rainforest; a diverse assortment of beautiful, endangered animals; picturesque Chili Beach.

GATEWAYS: 100km east of the Peninsula Development Rd.

CAMPING: Two rainforest bush camps; Chili Beach has pit toilets.

FEES: Camping $4.50.

Iron Range National Park, Australia's largest lowland rainforest, is an unparalleled tropical fantasy land of exotic creatures, isolated beaches, and stunning views.

Travelers can access the route to the park 40km north of the Archer River Roadhouse on the Peninsula Developmental Rd. The small dirt track is rough and requires tricky maneuvers over rocky creek beds, through two rivers, and down steep muddy hills—all while dodging wildlife. The road begins in dry eucalyptus savannah and becomes increasingly tropical as you move eastwards. The creek beds fill with water and feed into a river so wide that the road's exit point on the opposite bank is not immediately obvious. It is recommended that you walk through the two rivers and choose the best path before driving through.

From the Peninsula Development Rd., it is a 3½hr., 95km drive to the entrance of Iron Range National Park. As you enter the park via Tozer's Gap, the path leads to a region of expansive scrub land with an impressive view of Mt. Tozer. A short walk to a viewing platform just inside the park provides an excellent panoramic view. From there, the track descends deep into the heart of the rainforest; travelers can expect to negotiate muddy downhill slides and rocky dips leading to small stream crossings. There is another entrance 65km beyond this entrance (from the Telegraph Road) called **Frenchman's Track.** The road has stunning views, but is not driven by many people because of its deep river crossing. It is 52km to the meeting of the track and the main road into the park and 27km to the ranger station.

The Ranger Station is a 30min., 15km drive into the park, and is 110km from the Peninsula Development Rd. entrance. All overnight campers must register here and pick up a permit ($4.50 per person). There are two rainforest campgrounds between the ranger station and the coast, but the most popular site is a 45min. drive past the station at **Chili Beach ❶,** a secluded white sand expanse lined by coconut palms. Don't camp directly under the palms, and look out for falling coconuts. The view from the beach is pretty, but there is some trash around and the wind is fierce. Aside from pit toilets available at the beach, the campgrounds have no amenities and campers must be totally self-sufficient.

Iron Range is a haven for those looking for the most pristine, untouched natural wonders Australia has to offer. The park is so remote that, aside from the Aboriginal Lockheart River community and the occasional safari group, there are no people for hundreds of miles. This kind of remoteness means the park has no substantial walking tracks, but it does offer strolls down pristine Chili Beach without a single footprint to mar the sand.

WEIPA

The Peninsula Development Rd. bears west beyond the Archer River toward the bauxite-mining town of **Weipa** (pop. 2000). It is the only town of substantial size on the Cape York Peninsula, making it a good place to pick up supplies or find a comfortable bed. Bear in mind that a detour to this port on the Gulf of Carpentaria takes 2hr. and 145km, one-way. Unless you're heading there for fishing or a mine tour, you'd be better off continuing on to **Bramwell Junction** for fuel and supplies.

You can camp at **Weipa Camping Ground ❶.** The site also rents small fishing boats and cabins of various sizes, some ensuite and with kitchen. (☎4069 7871. Sites $9; cabins $65-105. ½-day boat rental $70, full-day $110.) Those looking for something more luxurious should check into **Heritage Resort ❺,** behind the shopping center on Commercial Ave. Clean rooms, a bar and restaurant, a pool with rock waterfall, and services including massage, babysitting, and a beauty salon are all welcome comforts after days in the bush. (☎4069 8000. Doubles $120.)

The **police** (☎4069 9119) are across the street from the hospital on Northern Ave. The **hospital** (☎4090 6222) is at the corner of Northern and Central Ave. Supplies can be purchased at the Nanum Shopping Centre on the corner of Commercial Ave. and Keer Point Dr., where you'll find a **pharmacy** (☎4069 7412), a **Woolworths** supermarket (☎4069 7330; open M, W, F 8am-7pm, Th 8am-9pm, Sa 8am-5pm), a bakery and cafe (open M-Th 7am-6:30pm, F 7am-7pm, Sat 7am-noon, Su noon-7pm), a Chinese restaurant, and a **post office** (☎4069 7110. Open M-F 9am-5pm).

THE TELEGRAPH AND BAMAGA/BYPASS ROADS

The Peninsula Development Rd. eventually forks at the junction to Weipa. For more adventures, head right on **Telegraph Road,** which is well marked but rough and narrow at times.

HEAD-ON COLLISIONS. These are the most common type of accident south of the Jardine Ferry. Don't drive too fast, as the road is narrow and there are many blind curves, especially on Bamaga Road.

Dusty, bumpy tracks and river crossings characterize the remaining distance to the Tip. North of the Archer River, the Cape's jungle becomes wilder, the heat hotter, the tracks rougher, and the Wet wetter. **Moreton Telegraph Station** (☎4060 3360) lies 72km past the fork between the Telegraph Rd. and Peninsula Rd. There are campgrounds here (powered and unpowered; power is turned off at 10pm), a pay phone, and some food, but no fuel and few supplies. **Bramwell Junction** (☎4060 3230), another 42km on the Telegraph Rd., has a service station, a garage for limited repairs, powered campsites, and limited accommodations (campsites $8 per person; singles $35; doubles $55).

The road splits at Bramwell Junction, nearly halfway to the Tip from the Archer River. Continuing straight leads to the **Old Telegraph Track,** which is known throughout Australia as the ultimate 4WD experience. For those not willing to risk their necks on this stretch of harrowing road, the **Southern Bypass Road** (or **Bamaga Road**) is an easier alternative.

Before reaching the Tip, travelers must pass the **Heathlands Resource Reserve** and then the **Jardine River National Park.** Campsites are available at **Captain Billy's Landing** on the coast and at the spectacular **Twin Falls,** just off Telegraph Rd. Both sites require pre-registration, which can be obtained at the Heathlands ranger base south of Eliot Falls, 12km off Bamaga Rd. There is a turn-off to **Fruit Bat Falls** and **Eliot/Twin Falls** 110km past Bramwell Junction where the Bamaga Rd. intersects with the Old Telegraph Track again. Fruit Bat Falls, with its spa-like basin, is a great swimming spot—perfect after a dusty, sweaty morning drive—and it's only 2km from Bamaga Rd. It also has toilets. Eliot/Twin Falls are 8km off the road and require some navigation on the Old Telegraph Track, but are well worth it.

Returning to Bamaga Rd. (known as the **Northern Bypass Road** after the second intersection), it is 62km to the expensive **Jardine River Ferry** (☎4069 3252. Vehicles $88 round-trip. Cash only). The fare includes a permit for camping and fishing on the Jardine and Jackey Rivers.

BAMAGA AND SURROUNDS

Before you get to the Tip, take time to observe the diverse communities on the last part of the peninsula; several distinct groups of Aborigines and immigrated Islanders have made this area their home. The biggest community is **Bamaga,** essentially the last town before the Tip. It's on Bamaga Rd. after Injinoo. Alternatively, you can take the gravel road 28km after the ferry.

In Bamaga, there is a very helpful **information center,** with a small museum about the region, adjacent to the highway and next door to the BP fuel station. The center has facts about the entire area, including the Torres Strait Islands (☎4069 3777, after hours 4069 3069; dkyoung@bigpond.com). Down the road is a **police** station (emergency ☎000). Farther along is a T-junction with Adidi St.; you'll find a well-stocked **supermarket** (M-F 8am-7pm, Sa 8am-2pm, Su 9am-1pm; MC/V.), a **post office** (M-F 9am-12:30pm and 1:30-5pm) with a **Commonwealth Bank** inside, the cheap **Bamaga Cafe and Takeaway** (☎4069 3168; open M-F 7am-2pm, Su 7am-8:30pm; cash only), and a **hospital** (24 hr. ☎4069 3166).

There are a few places to stay in **Seisia,** 5km from Bamaga. Follow Adidi St. past the supermarket, away from the T-junction. On your way check out **Loyalty Beach ❷,** which has powered and unpowered campsites, lodge-style accommodations, and a self-contained beach house. Amenities include laundry machines and a public phone. (☎4069 3372; www.loyaltybeach.com. Reception daily 8-10am and 4-6pm. Campsites $9 per person, $2 for power; single lodge $50, double $90; 4-person beach house $165, extra person $20. MC/V.) **Seisia Holiday Park ❷,** 6 Koraba Rd., has a similar beachfront and rents small villas, rooms, and campsites for similar prices. (☎1800 653 243. Singles $66; doubles $106. MC/V.) Seisia also has a **supermarket** and **BP** petrol station (☎4069 3897. Open M-F 6:45am-6pm). If you need to rent a car, look for **Seisia Car Hire** (☎4069 3368). **Cape York Spares and Repairs** (☎4069 4803), across from BP will take care of all your mechanical needs.

Across the street from the **Seisia Supermarket** and in front of the **Fishing Club ❶** is a great beach for watching the sunset or having a picnic. Huge $4 burgers and a live band F 5-10pm draw crowds. Down the road, the tiny, A-frame **St. Francis of Assisi Church,** tucked beside the brilliantly colored sea, is a photographer's dream.

THE TIP

From Bamaga, it's 34km to the absolute Tip. Head toward Adidi St. in the Bamaga town center. After the BP service station, take a right onto the final, unnamed road to put the capstone on your trip to the edge of the continent. The road is potholed gravel for the first 20km; after that, it turns to dirt, deteriorating until it becomes rocky, quite narrow, and full of small stream crossings—a fitting end to a toilsome journey. A 20min. hike gets you right to the Tip.

On the road, 10km from the Tip, is **Lockerbie's** (☎4069 3000), which sells Aboriginal art, dramatic photographs of their own Lockerbie truck fighting (and sometimes floating) across rivers, horse-rides through the rainforest, and a tour of India rubber trees. Lockerbie's also boasts a food stand and the only toilet for kilometers. Across the road from Lockerbie's is the turn-off to **Punsand Bay ❷,** a 10km drive. Punsand has campsites, permanent tents, and cabins with A/C. Amenities include laundry machines, satellite TV, and a **bar/restaurant ❹** with meals starting at $24. (☎4069 1722; punsand1@bigpond.com. Campsites $10 per person, powered $2 extra per site; tents $115 per person; cabins $155 per person.)

If the top of the continent isn't quite enough, you can explore Torres Strait Island culture by catching a **Peddell's Ferry** (☎4069 1551; www.peddelssferry.com.au) from Seisia to the Thursday and Horn Islands (departs M-Sa 8am, returns 3:45pm). The **Punsand Bay Ferry** also services the islands; it departs Punsand Bay M-Sa 7:30am and returns 5pm. Tickets and tours range from $40 one-way (students $30) to several hundred dollar tour packages that make multiple island and reef stops over the course of several days. You can book most of these through the **Bamaga Tourist Office.**

CENTRAL AND WESTERN QUEENSLAND

If you are tired of seeing millions of other backpackers doing the East Coast jaunt, consider heading a few kilometers inland, where you'll be far off the beaten path. The roads across Queensland's interior are long, flat, and straight, crossing immense distances dotted with tiny towns. Central Queensland is filled with coal mines, and the increased trade with Asia has led to a boom in the economy and job market.

Western Queensland, on the other hand, suffers from a harsh, hot environment, which has led to a very slow pace of outback life. The drive offers varied topography, ranging from spectacular gorges and mountains to red dirt and nothingness.

SHARING THE ROAD. Driving through this region is an adventure; some of the highways require battle with roadtrains that demand more road than there is to give. The highways are also graveyards for kangaroos; they line the pavement from collisions with the passing trucks. Don't drive at sunrise, sunset, or in the dark when the marsupials are most active.

CAPRICORN AND LANDSBOROUGH HIGHWAY

The road west from Rockhampton is heavily traveled by large trucks bringing their goods from the interior to the densely-populated coast. The route is known as **Capricorn Highway** until Barcaldine (essentially the beginning of the Outback) where it becomes the **Landsborough Highway,** passing through Longreach and Winton before meeting the Flinders Hwy. 119km east of Mt. Isa.

THE GEMFIELDS

Rather than hoping to win big with the ever-present pokies (slot-machines), thousands of hopeful souls bring their dreams of millions to the gemfields of central Queensland. The area is famous for coughing up precious stones of exceptional value, but good luck finding them; about once a year there is someone who strikes it rich while the rest go home with a photograph and a smile.

EMERALD

The town of Emerald (pop. 14,400), named after a colorful, grassy property north of town, is an affluent community of surprising size; it draws its wealth from the nearby coal mines and high-yielding cotton and wheat fields. In fact, there is so much growth that those looking for work (in the mines or the office) are commonly placed within 24hr. of arrival. The town serves as a jumping-off point for the Gemfields, which are 30min. west. Stop at the **Central Highlands Visitor Information Centre,** in the center of town on Clermont St., before venturing forth. (☎4982 4142. Open M-Sa 9am-5pm, Su 10am-2pm.) Don't miss the world's biggest Van Gogh sunflower painting (25m high) next door in Morton Park. The best budget accommodation in the area is the **Central Inn ❹,** 90 Clermont St., which has rooms with TV and fridge, as well a communal kitchen and lounge area. (☎4982 0800. Shared bath. Breakfast included. Reception M-Th 8am-9:30pm, F-Sa 9am-9pm. Singles $49; doubles $59. Book several days ahead. MC/V.) There's a **Coles** supermarket on the corner of Clermont and Opal St. in Market Plaza. (☎4982 3622. Open M-F 8am-9pm, Sa 8am-5pm.) The **Emerald Public Library,** 44 Borilla St., has free **Internet** access. (☎4982 8347. Open M noon-5:30pm, Tu and Th 10am-5:30pm, W 10am-8pm, F 10am-5pm, Sa 9am-noon.) The best place to eat in town is **Emerald Hotel ❶,** 73 Clermont St., across from Central Inn. It dishes out exceptional specials for only $7.50. (☎4982 1810. Open daily noon-2pm and 6-8:30pm. MC/V.) The open-faced sandwiches ($7-10) at **KT's Coffee Lounge,** 15 Anakie St., are excellent. (☎4982 3384. Open M-F 6:30am-5pm, Sa 8am-3pm, Su 8am-2pm. MC/V.)

ANAKIE

This tiny town forty-three kilometers west of Emerald is the gateway to prime **fossicking** areas. The **Anakie Gemfields Hotel Motel ❺** has spacious, clean ensuite rooms with A/C. The attached **restaurant ❶** has $8.50 dinner specials. (☎4985 4100. Restaurant open noon-2pm and 6-8pm. Singles $60; twins and doubles $70. Reception M-Th 8am-9:30pm, F-Sa 9am-9pm. MC/V.) The **Rubyvale Caravan Park ❶,** on Main St., has a small pool and is close to the action. (☎4985 4118. Reception 8am-6:30pm. Sites $12, powered $16; cabins for 2 $50, extra person $10. Book ahead, especially in winter. Cash only.) This village also has the **last petrol station** for 124km. **The Big Sapphire and Gemfields Information Centre,** 1 Anakie Rd., is a resource for all gemfields activities; you can obtain fossicking licenses ($5.80, families $8.20) and get information on fossicking tours (most run about $40-50 per person). To reach to the heart of the gemfields, most tourists drive 10 or 16km farther north to **Sapphire** or **Rubyvale,** where you can stop along the road to sort through pre-dug buckets of dirt ($7 per bucket). If you find a jewelry-quality stone, most places can facet it for you for around $20-40. **Miners Heritage,** in Rubyvale, offers underground tours of their sapphire mine ($10) and sells buckets of sapphire-bearing dirt. (☎4985 4444. 35min. tours daily 9:15am-4:15pm. AmEx/MC/V.) The timber and stone of the historic **Rubyvale Hotel ❷** give it a mountain-lodge feel. Relax after a long day looking for gems in the refreshing beer garden, and enjoy excellent meals under $15. (☎4985 4754. Open daily noon-2pm and 6-8pm. AmEx/DC/MC/V.)

LONGREACH

The micropolis of Longreach (pop. 4500) is the largest town in the Central West, and a good example of outback life. The town's biggest attractions are on the outskirts of town toward Rockhampton. The **Australian Stockman's Hall of Fame and Outback Heritage Centre,** off the Landsborough Hwy., is a massive multimedia museum that pays tribute to Australia's outback heroes. (☎4658 2166; www.outbackheritage.com.au. Open daily 9am-5pm. $22.50, students $18.50, ages 8-16 $12, under 8 free. AmEx/DC/MC/V.) Across the street, under the giant 747, the **Qantas Founders' Outback Museum** showcases the role airplanes have had on outback life and commemorates the early pioneering days of Australia's largest airline company. (☎4658 3737; www.qfom.com.au. Open daily 9am-5pm. $18, children $9. Tours of Qantas 747, including walking on the wing; $15, children $8. Booking required.) Longreach is also famous for its **Billabong Boat Cruises** along the Thomson River. The 3hr. sunset cruise includes a campfire dinner, Billy tea and damper, and music from local bush minstrels. (☎4658 1776; www.lotc.com.au. Tours run Apr.-Oct. daily; Nov.-Mar. 3 per wk. $44, concessions $40, children $30. Sold-out many nights; book ahead at the **Outback Travel Center,** 115A Eagle St.)

There are a few pubs with budget accommodation upstairs, but most of them you wouldn't even suggest to your worst enemy. The best of the lot is **Commercial Hotel Motel ❸,** at the corner of Eagle and Duck St. across from the post office. It has bright, clean rooms with A/C and a pub with excellent lunch and dinner specials from $5.50. (☎4658 1677. A/C. Restaurant open noon-2pm and 6-8pm. Reception 8am-6pm. Singles $28; twins and doubles $45. AmEx/DC/MC/V.) The **Longreach Caravan Park ❷,** 180 Ibis St., at the street's end, is a small area with a lot of older couples. (☎4658 1770. Reception 7:30am-8pm. Tent sites for 2 $17, powered $20; on-site caravans with A/C for 2 $38; ensuite A/C cabins for 2 $58. Book ahead, especially in winter. MC/V.) For groceries, **IGA** supermarket is on the corner of Eagle and Swan St. (☎4658 1260. Open M-W 8am-6:30pm, Th-F 8am-8pm, Sa 8am-4pm.)

Greyhound Australia buses depart from the **Outback Travel Centre** for Brisbane (daily 3:35pm, $142) and Mt. Isa (daily 10:35am, $105). (☎4658 1776; www.lotc.com.au. Open M-F 9am-5pm, Sa 9am-noon and 3:30-4pm, Su 10-11am and 3:30-4pm.) There is a **visitors center** at Qantas Park on Eagle St. (☎4658 3555; www.longreach.qld.gov.au. Open M-F 9am-4:30pm, Sa-Su 9am-noon.) Free **Internet** access is available at the **library,** 96 Eagle St. (☎4658 4104. Open M 1-5pm, Tu and Th 9:30am-12:30pm and 3-5pm, W and F 12:30-5pm, Sa 9am-noon.) The **post office** is next door (☎13 13 18; open M-F 9am-5pm). **Postal Code:** 4179.

FLINDERS AND BARKLY HIGHWAY

A long, lonely route, Flinders Hwy. is about 800km of straight road from Townsville to Cloncurry (a small town that in 1896 recorded the hottest temperature in Australia's history: 53.7°C or 127.5°F). As you continue west, Barkly Hwy. covers the remaining 119km to Mt. Isa and the Northern Territory. The drive can be hot and exhausting; be sure to carry a lot of water. As you head farther west, the tiny towns get tinier and are often marked by nothing more than a lower speed limit, a general store, and a petrol pump. Most traffic heads straight to Mt. Isa, which serves as a gateway to the Northern Territory.

CHARTERS TOWERS ☎07

Although it is less than 1½hr. from Townsville and the hectic coastline, Charters Towers feels much farther from the backpacker circuit. Once nicknamed "The World" for its cosmopolitan flair, Charters Towers is big on history and character. The 1871 discovery of gold helped the city develop into the 2nd largest in the state. When the gold ran dry in 1916, the town was vacated; now the 10,000 remaining locals live among extravagant architecture and well-celebrated ghosts.

TRANSPORTATION AND PRACTICAL INFORMATION. The **Charters Towers Railway Station** is on Gill St., on the east side of town. **Trains** (☎13 22 32; www.traveltrain.com.au) go to Townsville (3hr., departs Tu and Sa 7:02am, $24.20) and Mt. Isa (18hr., departs Su and Th 3:23pm, $107.80). **Greyhound Australia** departs from the corner of Gill and Church St. and services Townsville (1¾hr., daily 5:15pm, $30) and Mt. Isa (10½hr., daily 8:40am, $124). **Douglas Coaches** also goes to the Transit Centre in Townsville (1¾hr., M-F 8am, $22). Book tickets at **Travel Experience,** 13 Gill St. (☎4787 2622; www.travelexperience.com.au. Open M-Th 7:30am-5:30pm, F 7:30am-5pm, Sa 7:30am-noon.)

The center of Charters Towers is created by the simple T-intersection of Mosman and Gill St., known as the **Historic City Centre. Government offices** and **the Royal Arcade Stock Exchange** are found on Mosman St., while shops, restaurants, and banks line Gill St. The extremely helpful and straightforward **Charters Towers Information Centre,** 74 Mosman St., at the top of Gill St., provides a free "Ghosts of Gold" orientation tour of local historical attractions and an excellent leaflet about local activities. (☎4752 0314; www.charterstowers.qld.gov.au. Open daily 9am-5pm.) There are several **banks** with **ATMs** along Gill St. **Internet** access ($2.50 per 30min.) is available at the **library** in the Old Bank, 34 Gill St. (☎4752 0338. Open M-F 10am-5pm, Sa 9:30am-1pm.) Internet is also available at the information center ($5 per hr.). There is a historical **post office** with a large clocktower on the corner of Gill and Bow St. **Postal Code:** 4127.

ACCOMMODATIONS AND FOOD. If you want to be in the town center, the **Royal Private Hotel ❷,** just up the street from the information center on Mosman St., is perfect, with basic but clean and inexpensive rooms. (☎4787 8688. Shared facilities, A/C, Internet access, laundry, and shared kitchen. Reception 7am-9pm. Singles $25; doubles $35. AmEx/MC/V.) The **York Street Bed and Breakfast ❷,** 58 York St., is situated outside the town center, which gives it a relaxed atmosphere but makes it inconvenient if you don't have a car. Comfortable rooms in the main house are self-contained and include breakfast. Budget accommodations are impressive too, with TV and fridge. (☎4787 1028. 4-bed budget dorms $19; singles $25; doubles $45; main house singles $70; doubles $95. MC/V.) Most of the hostels in town have dirt-cheap lunch specials, but backpacker dinner rates can be found at **Sovereign Tavern ❶,** 180 Gill St., which serves up nightly specials. (☎4787 3077.

Lunch noon-2pm $6.50; dinner 6-8:30pm $9.50. AmEx/DC/MC/V.) The better of the two Chinese restaurants in town is **Gold City Chinese Restaurant ❷,** 118 Gill St., which has freshly cooked meals plus an all-you-can-eat smorgasbord. (☎4787 2414. Smorgasbord Tu-F 11:30am-2pm, $8; dinner smorgasbord W and F-Sa 5-9:30pm, $13.90.) **Woolworths,** on Gill St. at the corner with Deane St., has groceries. (☎4787 3411. Open M-F 8am-9pm, Sa 8am-5pm.)

SIGHTS AND ACTIVITIES. A visit to Charters Towers is really a step into the past, since nearly all the activities are focused on the gold rush era. To understand how the town became so rich, check out the **Venus Gold Battery,** the largest surviving gold battery relic in Australia. (☎4787 4773. 1hr. guided tours every 30min. 9:30am-3:30pm. $12, children $6, concessions $11.) The **lookout** at the top of Towers Hill is spectacular; history buffs can take in the sunset and learn about the old mining town by watching the entertaining **Ghosts After Dark** film. (25min. Nightly 6-7pm; times vary seasonally. Tickets available at Information Centre. $7, children $4, concessions $6.) **Geoff's City and Bush Safari** will keep you laughing and informed as you go "Around 'the world' in 80min." (☎4782 0314. Departs daily 8am and 4pm. Free pickup and drop-off. Tickets available at info center. $20, children $10.) The **Zara Clark Museum,** at the corner of Mosman and Mary St., has a display of Charters Towers memorabilia which reflects the town's golden past. (☎4787 4161. Open daily 10am-3pm. $5, children $2.20.) **Bluff Downs ❷,** a 2hr. drive northwest of Charters Towers, is a working cattle station where sweat, hard work, and play are all part of a day on the farm. Guests are welcomed into the family homestead and can try traditional bush meals. If you're looking for a true outback experience, this is it. (☎4770 4084; www.bluffdowns.com.au. 3-meal special $46 per day. Sites $14 per person, powered $14.50; dorms $27.50. Additional charges for activities. Cash only.)

DINOSAUR COUNTRY

HUGHENDEN

Hughenden (HEW-en-den; pop. 2000) marks the eastern edge of Queensland's marine dinosaur fossil territory. You've probably imagined exactly this kind of landscape—vast, open, and empty—as the habitat for prehistoric creatures. Stop at **Flinders Discovery Centre,** 37 Gray St., to see the Muttaburrasaurus skeleton. The Centre also doubles as the town's visitors center. (☎4741 1021; www.flinders.qld.gov.au. Open daily 9am-5pm. $3.50, children $1.50.) **Porcupine Gorge National Park** (63km north of town) is known as "Australia's Little Grand Canyon" because of its towering sandstone cliffs and deep gorges inside a lush green vine forest. Follow the signs in town, but be warned that the paved road turns to well-kept dirt 29km out. The unsealed tracks are generally 2WD accessible, but check with locals for current conditions. Camping is available at the **Pyramid Lookout Campground ❶**. (☎13 13 04; www.qld.gov.au/camping. Pit toilets and a shelter shed; bring your own water. Self-registration $4.50, pre-registration available.) If you plan to brave the mountains on your own, you are **required to register** at the **QPWS office** in town (☎4741 1113).

To get to the **Great Western Hotel ❷,** 14 Brodie St., from Flinders Discovery Centre, go down the hill and take your first right. The hotel has nice budget beds that will make you glad that you spent the night in this small town. The attached **pub ❶** has cheap specials and Sa night disco. (☎4741 1454. Internet access and A/C. Reception 6am-1am. 2- to 7-bed dorms $25. AmEx/MC/V.) The **Allan Terry Caravan Park ❶,** 2 Resolution St., has a swimming pool, kitchen, laundry, and a BBQ spread out on their large grounds. (☎4741 1190. Reception M-F 7am-9pm. Sites $7 per person, powered $17; singles with A/C $25; doubles $35; triples $45; huge ensuite cabins with A/C $55-65. Extra person $10. Book cabins ahead. Credit card fee $1. MC/V.)

RICHMOND

West of Hughenden along the Flinders Hwy., Richmond packs an impressive prehistoric punch and promotes itself as the fossil capital of Australia. **Kronosaurus Korner,** 93 Goldring St., is home to the regional **visitors center** and the **Marine Fossil Centre,** which houses Australia's best vertebrate fossils, including the complete fossil remains of a pliosaur and an ankylosaur. (☎4741 3429; www.kronosauruskorner.com.au. Open daily 8:30am-4:45pm. $10, students $8, children $5.) After your visit, grab a meal at **Moon Rock Cafe ❷** inside the center, which has a limited but reasonably priced selection. Heading west toward Mt. Isa on the Flinders Hwy., you'll see the **BP Roadhouse,** which has an impressively extensive menu, hot showers ($2), toilets, and **the last petrol station for 146km.** (☎4741 3316. Open daily 6am-9pm.) Free **Internet** access is available at the **library,** 78 Goldring St. (☎4741 3077. Open M-Tu and Th-F noon-4pm, W 9am-1pm); there is also a pay kiosk at the visitors center ($1 per 10min.). The **Lakeview Caravan Park ❷,** on your way into town from Hughenden before the visitors center, is perfectly located on a beautiful swimming lake. It boasts great facilities with A/Ç, shared bathrooms, swimming pool, and a communal kitchen. (☎4741 3772. Key deposit $10. Reception 7am-7pm. Sites $16, powered $20; twin-share bunkhouse with A/C. $16.50 per person; ensuite cabin for 2 $50. Extra person $7. Book cabins ahead. There is a **FoodWorks** supermarket at 78 Goldring St., down the street from the visitors center. (Open M-F 7:30am-5:30pm, Sa 7:30am-12:30pm, Su 7:30am-noon.)

MOUNT ISA ☎07

Mt. Isa (pop. 23,000) is one of the largest cities in the world, covering an area the size of Switzerland and with a main street stretching over 180km. It is also the birthplace of golf legend Greg Norman and tennis champ Patrick Rafter. The town owes its existence to the Mount Isa Mines, one of the world's largest mineral mining operations. Aside from these fun facts, there isn't a whole lot to "the Isa," as it is affectionately referred to by locals, although it's been claimed that you're not a real Aussie until you've been to the Isa. Backpackers commonly use it as a stopover when traveling between the Northern Territory and Queensland. Stock up on supplies, and make sure your car is full of fuel before leaving town.

TRANSPORTATION. The **train station** is on Station St. From the town center, cross the Isa St. bridge and turn right. The Inlander train departs M and F 1:30pm to: Charters Towers (17½hr., $107); Hughenden (13hr., $77); Richmond (10½hr., $64); and Townsville (20¾hr., $117.70). (☎13 22 32; www.traveltrain.com.au. ISIC discount 50%. Open 24hr.) **Harvey World Travel,** 2A Marian St. (☎4743 3399), and **Travel World at the Irish Club,** 1 19th Ave. (☎4749 1267), make bookings as well. **Greyhound Australia** has a small office in the **Outback at Isa complex,** 19 Marian St. (☎13 14 99; www.greyhound.com.au. Open 8:30am-5pm. Concession discount 10%.) Buses heading to the coast (6:50am) and to the interior (7:30pm) leave daily from the complex with service to: Alice Springs (13½hr., $269); Brisbane (26hr., $189); Cairns (30hr., $205); Charters Towers (10½hr., $136); Darwin (22hr., $328); Richmond (5½hr., $75); Rockhampton (23¼hr., $254); and Townsville (12hr., $143). For a 24hr. **taxi,** call **United Cab** (☎13 10 08).

ORIENTATION AND PRACTICAL INFORMATION. The town center is a square grid, bounded by **Grace Street** to the north, **Isa Street** to the south, **Simpson Street** to the east, and **West Street** to the west. The **Barkly Highway** enters from the

Northern Territory and runs parallel to the **Leichhardt River** until the **Grace Street Bridge,** where it turns left over the water into the town center, becoming **Grace Street.** From Cloncurry in the east, the Barkly Hwy. becomes **Marian Street.**

The Outback at Isa complex boasts the town information center, the bus station, Internet access, a cafe, and two of the area's major attractions: the Riversleigh Fossil Centre (p. 456) and underground tours. (☎1300 659 660; www.outbackatisa.com.au. Open daily 8:30am-5pm.) Other services include: **Westpac,** 23-25 Simpson St. across from K-Mart Plaza (☎4743 5344; open M-Th 9:30am-4pm, F 9:30am-5pm); **police,** 7-9 Isa St., at the intersection with Miles St. (☎4744 1111); **Internet** access ($3 per 30min.) at the **library,** 23 West St. (☎4747 3350; open M, Tu, Th 10am-6pm, W and F 10am-5pm, Sa 9am-1pm.); and a **post office** on Simpson St. opposite the K-Mart Plaza (☎13 13 18; open M-F 8:45am-5:15pm, Sa 9am-noon). **Postal Code:** 4825.

ACCOMMODATIONS AND FOOD. Budget options in the Isa are limited. **Travellers Haven ❷,** at Pamela and Spence St., is the only hostel around; it has a kitchen, Internet access, a swimming pool, and a courtesy bus. The rooms and shared facilities in this old building are showing their age, and most of the guests work in the area. (☎4743 0313; www.users.bigpond.net.au/travellershaven. Key deposit $5. Reception 24hr. 3-bed dorms $22; singles $35; doubles $50. MC/V.) **Mount Isa Caravan Park ❷,** 112 Marian St., has nice, clean digs. The atmosphere is unusual for a caravan park as up to 40% of guests are permanent residents. (☎1800 073 456; www.mtisacaravanpark.com.au. Reception M-F 7:30am-6:30pm, Sa-Su 8am-5pm. Sites $17, powered $20; cabins for 2 with shared amenities $55; ensuite villa for 2 with TV, A/C, and kitchen $75, extra adult $7, children $4. MC/V.)

The best places to eat are two casino-like clubs. The **Irish Club ❶,** on 19th Ave. off 4th Ave., has several bars, many food options, and an all-you-can-eat buffet M and Su noon-1am, F-Sa 10am-3am. **Tram Stop ❶,** part of the Irish Club, boasts an enjoyable table atmosphere inside a restored Melbourne Street Tram; menu items are almost all under $10. (☎4743 2577. Open M and Su noon-1am, F-Sa 10am-3pm.) **The Buffs Club ❸,** on the corner of Grace and Simpson St., is a popular place to lounge around and offers a lunch buffet ($13.50) and expensive dinners (from $17.50). (☎4743 2365; www.buffs.com.au. Restaurant open daily noon-2pm and 6-9:30pm, Su until 9pm.) **Coles** supermarket is in K-Mart Plaza, on the corner of Marian and Simpson St. (☎4743 6007. Open M-F 8am-9pm, Sa-Su 8am-5pm.)

SIGHTS. The Outback at Isa complex offers a 2½hr. **Hard Times Mine Tour** where visitors dress in authentic gear before descending into 1.2km of tunnels. There is also an informative 2hr. surface bus tour. The complex is also home to the **Riversleigh Fossil Centre,** which provides insight into the prehistoric inhabitants of the Outback, including life-size models of select beasts. Visitors are also allowed to peer into a working laboratory. (☎1300 659 660; www.outbackatisa.com.au. Underground tour $45, concessions $38, children $26. Surface tour departs June-Nov. $27.50. Fossil Centre Open daily 8:30am-5pm; $10, concessions $6.50. MC/V.) You can take a tour of the eerie **Underground Hospital,** at the end of Joan St. It dates back to 1942, when the local government built the structure in fear of a Japanese air raid. (☎4743 3853. Open Apr.-Sept. 10am-2pm. $10, concessions $8, children $4.) Australia's biggest **rodeo** (☎1800 463 361; www.isarodeo.com.au) comes to Mt. Isa for three days over the 2nd weekend in August. If you plan on attending, book accommodation at least one month ahead. **Lake Moondarra,** just 15min. northwest on the Barkly Hwy., is a nice place for a swim or BBQ, and **Lake Julius,** 30km on Barkly Hwy. toward Cloncurry and another 90km down a dirt track, is a great fishing spot. A 4WD is highly recommended. At night, view the lighted Mt. Isa Mines from the **lookout** off Hillary.

SOUTH AUSTRALIA

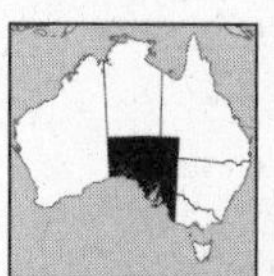

Harsh, vast, and sun-scorched, South Australia's stark interior will either capture your heart or send you running for the next bus to the coast. Those who stick around soon adopt the local mantra of "save water, drink wine," and with good reason—the area's temperate southern valleys are the home of the nation's finest vintages. The Barossa region is particularly renowned, and visitors can enjoy tastings or participate in the wine-making process themselves.

Most of the state's population resides in Adelaide, the port cities of the Murray River, and the fishing towns of the Southern Ocean. The coastline is gorgeous, offering sheltered bays for swimming, excellent surf beaches, abundant wildlife (particularly seals, sea lions, and fairy penguins), and a breezy respite from the inland desert inferno.

As inhospitable as it may seem, South Australia's interior is full of worthwhile sights. The Flinders Ranges are a backpacker's paradise, a gallery of spectacular sculptures created over five billion years. Travelers ready for a more thorough introduction to the region often tackle the Stuart Hwy., which offers over a thousand miles of otherworldly outback landscapes between the coast and Alice Springs. From the infamous Nullarbor to the wildlife of Kangaroo Island, South Australia waits to be explored—just don't get lost.

HIGHLIGHTS OF SOUTH AUSTRALIA

RELAX in **ADELAIDE** and enjoy good food, festivals, culture, and calm in South Australia's capital, the city of churches (p. 458).

GAIN NEW PERSPECTIVE on time and space in the **FLINDERS RANGES,** the ancient, gently folding mountains of the South Australian Outback (p. 500).

SLEEP UNDER THE STARS ON KANGAROO ISLAND in the company of unique native animals, including fur seals, kangaroos, sea lions, and wallabies (p. 480).

SAVOR THE FRUITS of Australia's premier wine region, **BAROSSA VALLEY** (p. 487).

CHILL OUT in **COOBER PEDY** in the underground hostels (p. 512).

TRANSPORTATION

If you don't have a car, the best way to see South Australia is by bus. **Greyhound Australia** (☎13 14 99 or 13 20 30) runs between Adelaide and Melbourne, Sydney, Alice Springs, and Perth, stopping over at a few destinations in between. **Premier Stateliner** (☎8415 5555) services smaller towns throughout South Australia; pick up a copy of their *Bus SA State Guide* for an extensive map of bus routes and timetables. Three major train lines run through South Australia: the **Overland** to Melbourne, the **Indian Pacific** to Perth, and the legendary **Ghan** to Alice Springs. Major **car rental** companies with branches in SA include **Hertz** (☎13 30 39), **Avis** (☎13 63 33), and **Thrifty** (☎1300 367 227). Local outfits often have lower prices. A conventional vehicle is fine for wine and beach country, but 4WD is strongly recommended for forays into the Outback.

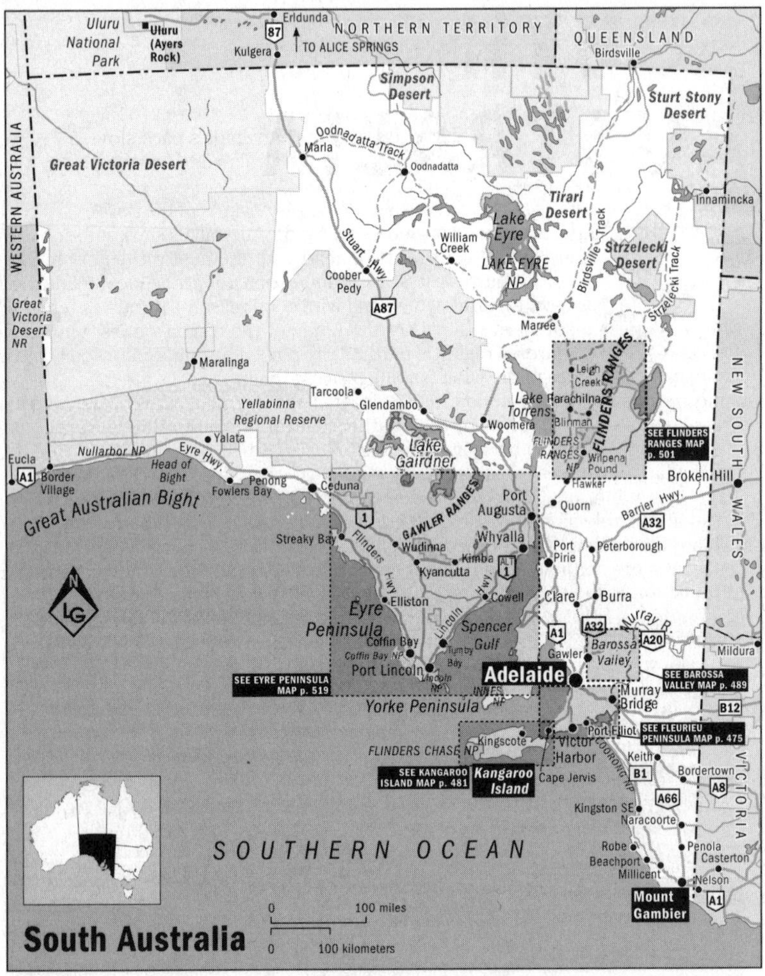

Another good option is to book a **tour.** Many choose jump-on, jump-off backpacker buses like the youthful **Oz Experience** (☎1300 300 028) or the twenty-something favorite **Wayward Bus** (☎8410 8833 or 1300 653 510); plenty of local organizations also run excellent trips, which are listed in the **Practical Information** section of most towns in this chapter.

ADELAIDE ☎08

Spend any time in Australia and you're bound to hear someone describe South Australia's capital as boring. While it's true that Adelaide is short on flashy neon lights and huge skyscrapers, it does have an impressive line-up of festivals, restaurants, and museums. The city is centered around a one-square-mile grid, and vast green parklands separate it from the suburbs, where the majority of the population lives. Goods and services are far less expensive in Adelaide than in its east-coast counterparts. With more restaurants and world-class wines per capita than any other Australian city, Adelaide can satisfy any palate on any budget. The city's cultural attractions include a symphony, experimental theaters, outstanding museums, and Australia's most impressive summer festival season. While travelers coming from the bigger east-coast cities may find Adelaide's pace slow, the city's live music and club scene do kick into gear on the weekends. However, in the end the city proper is not nearly as impressive as its proximity to the extensive coastlines of the Yorke and Fleurieu Peninsulas and the vineyards of the Barossa Valley.

INTERCITY TRANSPORTATION

BY PLANE

The **Adelaide Airport** is 7km west of the city center. Most hostels in the city or Glenelg offer free pickup with advance booking. Failing that, the cheapest way to the city is the **Skylink Airport Shuttle,** which runs to the airport, Keswick Railway Station, and the Central Bus Station on Franklin St., as well as many hotels in town. The shuttle stops at the domestic terminal directly in front of the currency exchange and at international arrivals. (☎8332 0528. Booking 7am-8:30pm. Daily, every ½hr.-1hr. 6am-9:45pm. $7, $13 round-trip.) For two or more, a **taxi** ($12-17) is cheaper and more convenient than the shuttle.

International travelers can get huge discounts on domestic one-way fares. **Regional Express** (**Rex,** ☎13 17 13; www.regionalexpress.com.au) is the biggest local carrier, with flights to 35 South Australian cities, including Coober Pedy, Kangaroo Island, Mt. Gambier, and Port Lincoln. **Virgin Blue** (☎13 67 89; www.virginblue.com.au) and **Qantas** (☎13 13 13; www.qantas.com.au) also offer competitive fares, and local backpacker travel agencies can often get you discounts.

BY TRAIN

All interstate and long-distance country trains use the **Keswick Interstate Rail Passenger Terminal** (☎13 21 47), just off the southwest corner of the central city grid about 1km west of West Terr. (Open M 7:30am-5pm, Tu and Th 6:30am-5pm, W 9am-5pm, F 6:30am-6pm, Sa 7:30-10:30am, Su 7:30am-7pm.) The **Skylink Airport Shuttle** meets every incoming train at Keswick and drops off at the bus station and several points downtown. (☎8332 0528. $4, round-trip $7.) Taxis from the city run about $6. The Keswick terminal has parking. Only suburban commuter trains use the Adelaide Railway Station (☎8218 2277), on North Terr. The **Great Southern Railway Ticket Office,** 422 King William St., sells tickets downtown. (Open M-F 9am-5pm.) The **Overland** runs to **Melbourne** (12-13½hr.; Th-Su 9am; $68, students $49). The **Ghan** runs trains to **Alice Springs** (19hr., M and Th 3pm, $235/150). The **Indian Pacific** runs trains to **Perth** (39hr., Tu and F 6pm, $340/170). The Indian Pacific and Ghan both run to **Sydney** (24-25hr.; W and Su 7:45am, Sa 10am; $245/123).

BY BUS

Adelaide has two central bus stations, both located on Franklin St. **Greyhound Australia** (☎13 14 99) has a station at 101 Franklin St., while **V/Line, Firefly,** and **Premier Stateliner** buses pull in to 111 Franklin St. National bus companies provide regular service to and from Adelaide at fares that generally beat rail and air travel; unfortunately, savings come at the price of comfort. **Greyhound Australia** runs to: **Alice Springs** (19hr., daily 6:30pm, $234); **Brisbane** (29-30hr., daily 11am, $267); **Darwin** (34hr., daily 2:30pm, $496); **Melbourne** (10hr., daily 8pm, $55); **Sydney** (24hr., daily 11am, $156). Prices listed are for booking at the counter; phone booking has an added $6 processing fee, while Internet booking is usually cheaper. Students receive a 10% discount. A new budget-minded carrier, **Firefly Express** (☎1300 730 740) runs directly to Melbourne (10-11hr.; departs daily 7:30am and 8:30pm; $55, concessions $50), where it is possible to transfer and continue on Sydney (Adelaide to Sydney $110). **V/Line** (☎13 61 96 or 8231 7260) runs a daily coach and rail combination to Melbourne via Bendigo (12hr.; M-F 8:25am, Sa-Su 8:50am; $64.90, students and children $32.50) and Sydney via Albury, where you must transfer to an express train (23hr.; once daily; $157.20, concession $104.60). Within South Australia, **Premier Stateliner** (☎8415 5500) is the main carrier, serving over 200 destinations statewide. The free *State Guide*, available at the tourist office and many hostels, is indispensable for area travel.

ORIENTATION

Downtown Adelaide is only one square mile in size, bordered by North, East, South, and West Terr. The city is bisected north-south by **King William Street.** Streets running east-west change names when crossing King William St. **Rundle Street,** home to chic sidewalk cafes, top-notch eateries, and vibrant nightlife, runs from East Terr. west to Pulteney St. in the city's northeast quadrant (known as the **East End**). From there, it becomes the **Rundle Mall,** the city's main shopping area, then it continues west to King William St. before changing names yet again to become Hindley St., a mish-mash strip of everything from adult stores to upscale restaurants. Many hostels are clustered in the western end of the city, while upscale hotels can be found lining North Terr. Gouger St., in the southwest end, has a wide variety of multicultural eateries and the Central Market. On the other side of town, north-south Hutt St. is an up-and-coming dining and nightlife strip. **Victoria Square** lies at the center of the city grid. **Light Square,** in the northwest quadrant, is where most hostels and a host of backpacker pubs are, while **Hindmarsh Square** in the northeast quadrant, is another important landmark.

Keswick, which includes the railway station, is about 2km southwest of the central grid, and the beach suburb of **Glenelg** is 12km southwest of the CBD via the Anzac Hwy. (A5) or the Glenelg Tram. A couple kilometers north of the Central Business District (CBD) and the River Torrens, in the midst of parklands, swank **North Adelaide** makes up a smaller grid centered around the trendy bistros and shopping on upscale **O'Connell Street. Melbourne St.,** southeast of O'Connell, is another boutique strip with hip restaurants and funky shopping. Morphett and King William St. connect North Adelaide to the CBD. Northwest of the CBD, on the Port River, is the suburb of **Port Adelaide,** while **Henley Beach,** 12km west of the CBD, is another popular spot. Just south of the city, **King William St.** in **Hyde Park** has a number of nice cafes and some of Adelaide's best shopping. **The Adelaide Hills,** including Cleland Conservation Park and the scenic Mt. Lofty lookout, are visible just east of the city. Although the city of Adelaide in general is relatively peaceful, *the parklands are unsafe at night,* especially near the **River Torrens** and in the southwest corner of the city. **Hindley Street** also *demands caution at night.*

LOCAL TRANSPORTATION

PUBLIC TRANSPORTATION

Adelaide's **buses** and **trains** make up an integrated public transport system called the **Adelaide Metro** (☎8210 1000; www.adelaidemetro.com.au), which also runs two free bus services around the city: **Beeline** and **City Loop.** These yellow buses are easily identified and wheelchair accessible. Beeline runs in the city center, from the railway station on North Terr. and down King William St. to Victoria Sq. and back. (Every 5-15min. M-Th 7:40am-6:10pm, F 7:40am-9:20pm, Sa 8:30am-5:35pm, Su 10am-5:30pm.) City Loop, true to its name, runs both directions around a loop that covers the north half of the city, with stops at North, East, and West Terr., and most major tourist attractions. Central Market, a very popular locale, is located near the bus station, (every 15-30min. M-Th 8am-5:45pm and F 8am-9:15pm, every 30min. Sa 8:15am-5:45pm, Su 10am-5:15pm.) For those staying in the Adelaide Hills, there's a **Wandering Star** weekend service that runs from the city and drops passengers off at their door. Service runs from 12:30-5am, and the city bus stops are conveniently located in heavily trafficked club areas. (☎8210 1000. $6.)

For those who want to roam farther afield, there are bus and train routes that comprise TransAdelaide's suburban transit system. The **Passenger Transport Information Centre,** at the corner of King William and Currie St., has route schedules and an info line. (☎1800 182 160 or 8210 1000. Open M-F 8am-6pm, Sa 9am-5pm, Su 11am-4pm.) **Single tickets** work on any service for two hours and can be purchased from drivers and vending machines. (Single trip M-F 9am-3pm $2.10, concessions $1.00; all other times $3.50/1.70.) Daytrip tickets ($6.60, concessions $3.30) allow one day of unlimited travel on any service and can be purchased when boarding buses or trams, but must be bought beforehand for trains. Another option is the advanced-purchase **multitrip ticket** (10 trips $22.90, for use M-F 9am-3pm $12.60).

The best way to reach **Glenelg** is by tram ($3.30, M-F 9am-3pm $1.90), which runs every 15-20min. from Victoria Sq. to Moseley Sq. (30min.; M-F 6am-11:50pm, Sa 7:30am-midnight, Su 8:50am-midnight.) For a guided tour of the area, **Adelaide Explorer** does a 3hr. Adelaide-to-Glenelg hop-on, hop-off tour. Catch the small bus anywhere on the route or join at 38 King William St. (☎8231 7172. Pay onboard. Daily 9, 10:30am, noon, 1:30, and 3pm. $30 per day, children $10, families $60.)

BY CAR

All the major rental lines have offices at the airport or in town. Try: **Hertz,** 233 Morphett St. (☎13 30 39 or 8231 2859; open M-F 7:30am-6pm, Sa-Su 8am-2pm); **Budget** (☎13 27 27 or 8223 1400), on the corner of North Terr. and Frome St.; **Avis,** 136 North Terr. (☎8410 5727); or **Thrifty** (airport ☎8234 3029). **Europcar,** 142 North Terr. (☎13 13 90; open M-F 8am-6pm, 8am-4pm, Su 9am-4pm), is typically the cheapest.

Those under 25 can sometimes get better deals from smaller agencies. One of the best outfits for 4WD rentals is **Complete Ute and 4WD Hire,** in the suburb of Findon. They have free pickup and drop-off anywhere in the city, and discounts for longer rentals. (☎8244 5333; www.completeuteandvanhire.com.au.) Friendly **Koala Car Rentals,** on Sir Donald Bradman Dr., has some of the lowest rates in the city and 4WD. (☎1800 882 044 or 8352 7299.) **Smile Rent-a-Car,** 163 Richmond Rd., has friendly service, but no 4WD. (☎8234 0655 or 1800 624 424.) **No Frills Car Rental,** 235 Waymouth St., is another local outfit. (☎8212 8333 or 1800 999 978).

For campervans or motor homes, **Britz,** 376 Sir Donald Bradman Dr. (☎8234 4701 or 1800 331 454), in Brooklyn Park, has two- to six-berth vans and one-way rental with unlimited mileage. Ask about **relocation deals,** where you pay as little as $1 per day plus petrol costs to take a car or camper from Adelaide to another city in a set amount of time (3 days for the 10hr. drive to Melbourne). **Skippy Camper Rentals,** 1505 South Rd., Darlington (☎8296 2999), has regular campervan rentals (min. 5 days, one-way available) as well as some used campervans and 4WDs for sale with buy-back options. Taxis are also an easy way to get around town as there are a number of companies that service the city, including **Suburban Taxis** (☎13 10 08); **Adelaide Independent Taxis** (☎13 22 11) and **Yellow** (☎13 22 27).

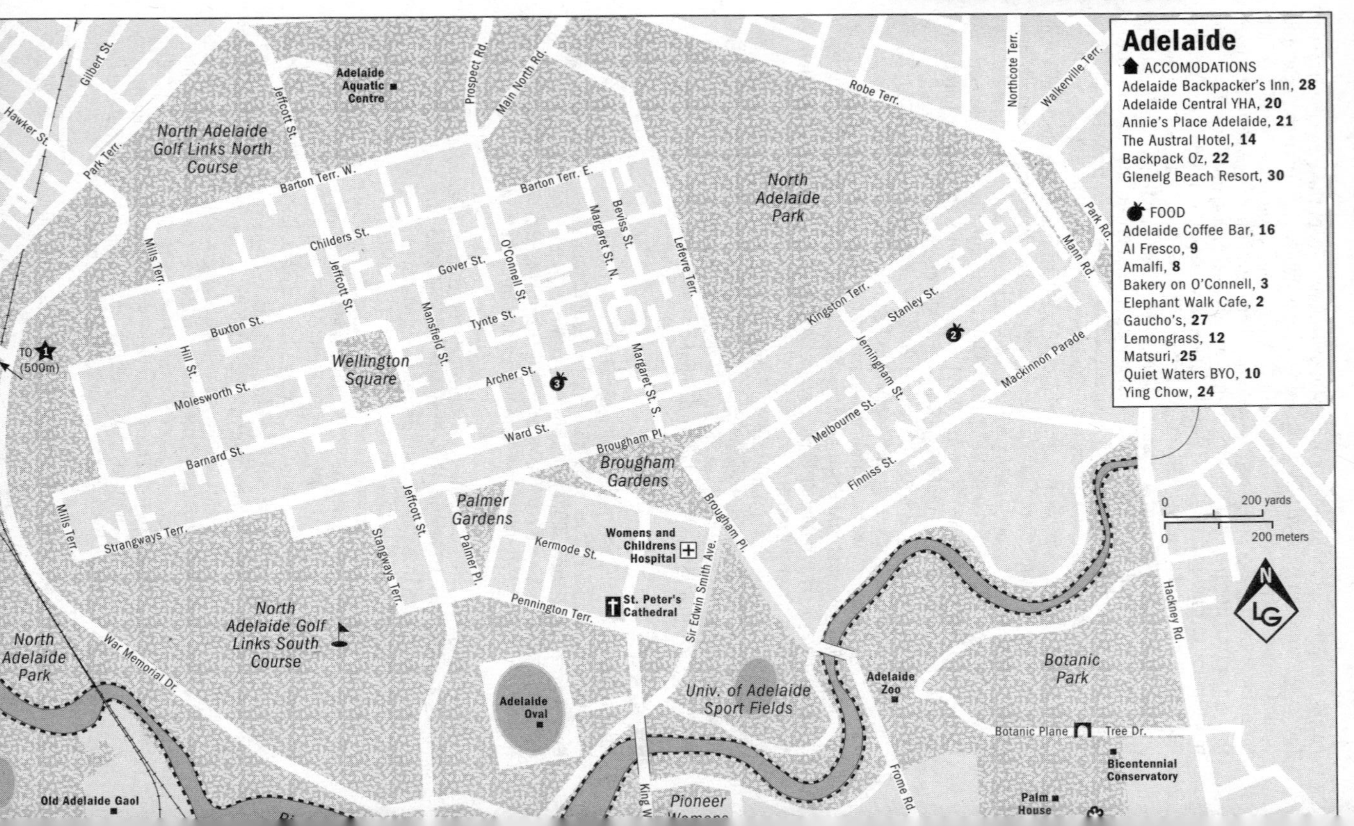
Adelaide
ACCOMODATIONS
Adelaide Backpacker's Inn, 28
Adelaide Central YHA, 20
Annie's Place Adelaide, 21
The Austral Hotel, 14
Backpack Oz, 22
Glenelg Beach Resort, 30
FOOD
Adelaide Coffee Bar, 16
Al Fresco, 9
Amalfi, 8
Bakery on O'Connell, 3
Elephant Walk Cafe, 2
Gaucho's, 27
Lemongrass, 12
Matsuri, 25
Quiet Waters BYO, 10
Ying Chow, 24
0
200 yards
0
200 meters
N
LG
Gilbert St.
Hawker St.
Park Terr.
North Adelaide Golf Links North Course
Jeffcott St.
Adelaide Aquatic Centre
Prospect Rd.
Main North Rd.
Robe Terr.
Northcote Terr.
Walkerville Terr.
Park Rd.
Mann Rd.
North Adelaide Park
Barton Terr. W.
Barton Terr. E.
Margaret St. N.
Beviss St.
Lefevre Terr.
Mills Terr.
Childers St.
Gover St.
O'Connell St.
Jeffcott St.
Kingston Terr.
Stanley St.
Buxton St.
Hill St.
Mansfield St.
Tynte St.
Jerningham St.
Mackinnon Parade
TO 1 (500m)
Wellington Square
Archer St.
Margaret St. S.
Molesworth St.
Melbourne St.
Ward St.
Brougham Pl.
Barnard St.
Brougham Gardens
Finniss St.
Mills Terr.
Jeffcott St.
Palmer Gardens
Brougham Pl.
Strangways Terr.
Stangways Terr.
Kermode St.
Womens and Childrens Hospital
Palmer Pl.
Sir Edwin Smith Ave.
Pennington Terr.
St. Peter's Cathedral
Hackney Rd.
North Adelaide Golf Links South Course
North Adelaide Park
War Memorial Dr.
Botanic Park
Adelaide Zoo
Univ. of Adelaide Sport Fields
Adelaide Oval
Botanic Plane
Tree Dr.
Bicentennial Conservatory
Frome Rd.
King W
Pioneer
Old Adelaide Gaol
Palm House

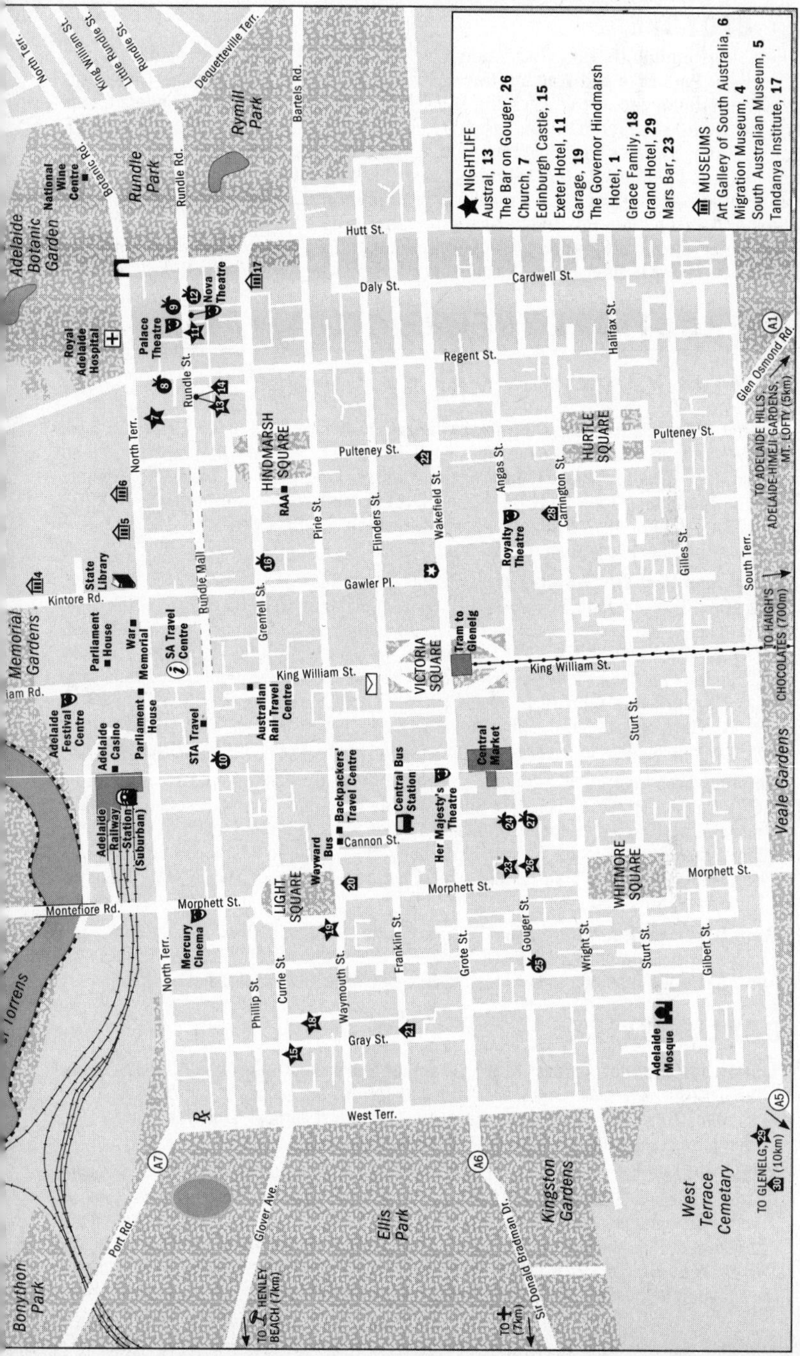

NIGHTLIFE
Austral, 13
The Bar on Gouger, 26
Church, 7
Edinburgh Castle, 15
Exeter Hotel, 11
Garage, 19
The Governor Hindmarsh Hotel, 1
Grace Family, 18
Grand Hotel, 29
Mars Bar, 23

MUSEUMS
Art Gallery of South Australia, 6
Migration Museum, 4
South Australian Museum, 5
Tandanya Institute, 17

BY BICYCLE

Adelaide is eminently bikeable. Many city streets have designated cycling lanes. The **Linear Park Bike and Walking Track** (40km one-way) runs along the River Torrens from the ocean to the Adelaide Hills. Along with most hostels, **Flinders Camping,** 187 Rundle St., rents bikes in the city. (☎8223 1913. Open M-Th 9am-5:30pm, F 9am-7:30pm, Sa 9am-5pm, Su 11am-4pm. $20 per day; maps and helmets included. Lower rates for multiple day rentals.) **Linear Park Mountain Bike Hire,** located in a van behind the Festival Centre on the south bank of the Torrens, has high-quality bikes and extensive knowledge of the terrain. (☎04 0059 6065. Open daily 9am-5pm. Book ahead. $20 per day. Delivery, pickup, and weekly or family rates available.) Keep your helmet on at all times as police are happy to issue tickets.

PRACTICAL INFORMATION

TOURIST AND FINANCIAL SERVICES

Tourist Office: South Australian Travel Centre, 18 King William St. (☎1300 655 276; www.southaustralia.com), is the city's main info center. Open M-F 8:30am-5pm, Sa-Su 9am-2pm. **Glenelg Tourist Information Centre,** Foreshore (by the jetty), Glenelg (☎8294 5833). Open daily 9am-5pm. **Rundle Mall Visitor Information,** (☎8203 7123), at the corner of Rundle Mall and King William St. Open M-Th 10am-5pm, F 10am-8pm, Sa 10am-3pm, and Su 11am-4pm.

Travel Agencies: YHA Travel, 135 Waymouth St. (☎8414 3000) Open M-F 9am-6pm, Sa 10am-1pm. **Cannon St. Travel,** 110 Franklin St. (☎8410 3000 or 1800 069 731), has some of the best air and rail deals in town. Open M-Sa 9am-5:30pm. **STA Travel,** 235 Rundle St. (☎8223 2426), open M-Th 9:30am-5:30pm, F 9:30am-7pm, Sa 10am-3pm; and 38a Hindley St. (☎8223 2426), open M-F 10am-6pm, Sa 10am-3pm. The **Wayward Bus Central Office,** 119 Waymouth St. (☎1300 653 510 or 8410 8833). Open M and F 7am-6pm, Tu and Th 8am-6pm, W 6:45am-6pm, Sa 7am-4pm, Su 10am-4pm. Most travel agencies offer free Internet, usually 2hr., with tour booking.

Currency Exchange: Almost any time, if you're dressed to code and 18+, in the **Adelaide Casino,** (☎8218 8115) at North and Station Rd., in the same building as the train station. ID required for entry to casino. Open M-Th and Su 10am-4am, F-Sa 10am-6am. **Travelex,** 45 Grenfell St. (☎8212 3354). Open M-Th 9am-5pm, F 9am-6pm. **Thomas Cook,** 4 Rundle Mall (☎8231 6977). Open M-Th 9am-5pm, F 9am-7pm, Sa 10am-4pm, Su 10am-2pm.

Work Opportunities: Centrelink, 55 Currie St. (☎13 10 21). Open M-F 8:30am-5pm. They also have an office at 156-158 Jetty Rd., Glenelg, open M-F 8:30am-5pm. *Advertiser* has classifieds W and Sa. Most hostels also have employment notice boards.

LOCAL SERVICES

Library and Internet Access: State Library of South Australia (☎1800 182 013 or 8207 7200; www.slsa.sa.gov.au), on North Terr. at the corner of Kintore Ave. Book ahead for 30min. free Internet access, or wait for a first come, first served 15min. slot. Open M-W 10am-8pm, Th-F 10am-6pm, Sa-Su 10am-5pm.

Ticket Agency: Most cultural and sporting events (especially football matches) are booked through **BASS.** (☎13 12 46; www.bass.net.au. Booking fee varies, usually around $3 per ticket. Open M-Sa 9am-8pm.) Booths are all over the city, including the SA Travel Centre and the Rundle Mall, and the main office is at the Festival Centre (p. 469). **VenueTix** (☎8225 8888; www.venuetix.com.au) also has tickets for major events and is the place to go for cricket and basketball tickets.

RAA: State Headquarters, 55 Hindmarsh Sq. (touring info ☎8202 4600 or 13 11 11). Open M-F 8:30am-5pm, Sa 9am-noon. Maps are free for members of RAA, AAA, or other affiliated organizations.

Swimming Pools: Adelaide Aquatic Centre, on Jeffcott Rd. (☎8344 4411.), in North Adelaide, is a huge indoor complex with a 50m pool, a diving and water polo area, and aqua-aerobics classes. Pools open M-Sa 5am-10pm, Su 7am-8pm. Gym open M-F 6am-10pm, Sa 6am-6pm, Su 9am-5pm. Pool $5.90, children $4.50, under 3 free. Gym $12.00, low season $10.00.

MEDIA AND PUBLICATIONS

Newspapers: *The Advertiser* ($1).

Nightlife: "The Guide" in the Thursday *Advertiser. Rip it Up* and *dB* on the nightlife and alternative club scene (free). For gay nightlife, try *Blaze* or *Gay Times* (free).

Radio: Commercial-free alternative rock, Triple J 105.5 FM; rock, 104.7 FM and 91.9 FM; pop, 107.1 FM and 102.3 FM; news, ABC 831 AM; tourist info, 88.1 FM.

EMERGENCY AND COMMUNICATIONS

Police: Adelaide Police Station, 60 Wakefield St. (☎8463 7400). Another station at 26 Hindley St. (☎8303 0525).

Late-Night Pharmacy: ChemWorld Chemist, 13 West Terr. (☎8231 6333). Open M-Sa 7am-midnight, Su 9am-midnight.

Medical Services: Royal Adelaide Hospital (☎8223 9211), on North Terr.

Post Office: General Post Office, 141 King William St. (☎13 13 18), at the corner of King William and Franklin St. Open M-F 8:30am-5:30pm. *Poste Restante* can be picked up M-F 7am-6pm. **Postal Code:** 5000.

ACCOMMODATIONS

Hostels are scattered all over the city, but are concentrated near **Light Square.** Adelaide hostels are rarely full in winter, but book at least two days in advance during school holidays and in summer, and book a week ahead during festivals. Those looking to escape the city should consider staying in the beach suburb of Glenelg (p. 472) or in the Adelaide Hills (p. 472). Most dorm beds increase in price by $2-5 during high season (Nov.-Feb.) and school holidays.

Adelaide Central YHA, 135 Waymouth St. (☎8414 3010). The most popular with backpackers, this 250-bed complex is clean and modern with ample common area space, A/C, and individual reading lights by all the beds. Friendly and knowledgeable local staff, large kitchen, TV, pool tables, smoking room, and a message board with current movies, lectures, and concerts. Free nightly movie 8pm. Internet access $2 per 30min. Reception 24hr. Bike hire ½-day $10, $20 per day. Dorms $28.50; doubles $66.50, ensuite $77-100; prices lower in low season. $4 discount for YHA members. ❷

Glenelg Beach Resort, 1-7 Moseley St. (☎8376 0007; www.glenelgbeachresort.com.au), take Anzac Hwy. into Glenelg. Turn left at the last roundabout before the ocean and right onto Moseley St. 20min. by tram from Victoria Sq. Clean, bright dorm rooms. Licensed, with a lively bar, and pool tables. Beer garden and BBQ. Internet access $3 per 15min. Dorms $20; singles $25; doubles $50. VIP. ❷

Backpack Oz, 144 Wakefield St. (☎8223 3551 or 1800 633 307; www.backpackoz.com.au), on the corner of Pulteney St., close to Rundle St. Feels like a college dormitory: party by night, post-raging-party by day. Young backpackers chill out with beers on the couches, shoot pool, and check email ($4 per hr.) in the sunny office. The annex across the street has a nicer kitchen and cable TV. Free pickup, employment info, TV and video lounge, and tour bookings. Breakfast and W night BBQ included. Reception 6am-10pm. Dorms $20, $120 per week; singles $45; doubles $55-57. ❷

Annie's Place Adelaide, 239 Franklin St. (☎8212 2668), a few blocks east of the bus station. Like its sister in Alice Springs, Annie's draws a friendly crowd of lively backpackers for ensuite dorm rooms, basic but free breakfast, and an exuberant atmosphere. Various events throughout the wk. $5 dinners include dessert and wine. Dorms $15; doubles $56. ❶

Adelaide Backpacker's Inn, 112 Carrington St. (☎8223 6635 or 1800 247 725; www.adelaidebackpackersinn.net.au), a 10min. walk from Victoria Sq. Free nightly apple pie and ice-cream desserts that are never rationed (4000 pies baked yearly) and complimentary continental breakfast make this a popular stop for malnourished backpackers. Free pickup and drop-off, free parking, and free videos in the lounge. Internet access $1 per 15min. Reception 6am-7:30pm. Dorms $22. ❷

The Austral Hotel, 205 Rundle St. (☎8223 4660). If you want to be the life of the party, stay in the hotel that never sleeps. Fantastic location in the swankiest part of town. Key deposit $10. Singles $35; doubles $55; triples $70; quads $80. ❸

FOOD

For a city its size, Adelaide is a gourmand's dream; it's difficult to go anywhere without tripping over a restaurant. **Gouger Street,** in the city center near Victoria Sq., offers a wide range of inexpensive, multicultural cuisine and houses the **Central Market,** whose stalls overflow with colorful fruits and vegetables, cheeses, and freshly baked breads. (Open Tu 7am-5:30pm, Th 9am-5:30pm, F 7am-9pm, and Sa 7am-3pm.) **Rundle Street,** in the northeast section of the city, caters to the young hipster set with more upscale dining. Clusters of restaurants can also be found on the swanky **Hutt Street** in southeast Adelaide and flashy but cheap **Hindley Street,** across King William St. from **Rundle Street.** For a splurge, the restaurants on **O'Connell** and **Melbourne St.** in North Adelaide offer the best ambience. **Jetty Road,** in the beachside suburb of Glenelg, also bursts with cafes and ice cream shops. Supermarkets dot the city, particularly on Rundle Mall, Hindley St., and Victoria Sq. **Coles,** next to Central Market on Grote St. near Victoria Sq., is almost always open. (Open M-F midnight-9pm, Sa midnight-5pm, Su 11am-5pm.)

GOUGER STREET

Matsuri, 167 Gouger St. (☎8231 3494). Its name meaning "festival" in Japanese, Adelaide's best sushi restaurant features a rock garden. No shoes can be worn inside. Dishes $9-28. M night ½-price sushi. Open M, W-Th, and Sa-Su 5:30-latenight, F noon-2pm and 5:30pm-latenight. Mention *Let's Go* and get a 10% discount. ❷

Gaucho's, 91 Gouger St. (☎8231 2299). Outstanding Argentinian food in a convivial setting. Gaucho's is serious about authenticity. When you order rabbit or fish, you get the whole thing. Main dishes $18-26. Open M-F noon-3pm and 5:30pm-latenight, Sa-Su 5:30pm-latenight. ❹

Ying Chow, 114 Gouger St. (☎8211 7998). Specializing in regional Chinese cuisine, Ying Chow's is packed for lunch and dinner with locals who sing the praises of both the food and the prices. Main courses $7.50-14. Open M-Th and Su 5pm-12:45am, F noon-3pm and 5pm-1am, Sa 5pm-1am. Fully licensed and BYO. ❷

RUNDLE STREET

Amalfi, 29 Frome St. (☎8223 1948), between Rundle St. and North Terr. This popular and packed "Pizzeria Ristorante" sneaks onto upscale gourmet dining lists. The best pizza in

Adelaide is worth every penny and then some. Main courses $14-20. Open M-Th noon-2:30pm and 5:30-11pm, F noon-2:30pm and 5:30pm-midnight, Sa 5:30pm-midnight. ❸

Lemongrass, 289 Rundle St. (☎8223 6627; www.lemongrassbistro.com.au). A popular restaurant with contemporary decor and a creative menu that includes Aussie twists on Thai standards (kangaroo Pad Thai, croc curry, etc.). Lunch specials from $7. Main dishes $12.50-18.50 Open M-F 11:30am-3pm and daily for dinner 5-11pm. ❷

Al Fresco, 260 Rundle St. (☎8223 4589). This people-watching landmark serves a tempting range of Italian cakes, focaccia, and the best *gelato* in the city (small $3). They also have sandwiches ($7), salads, pasta dishes ($6-12), and a full breakfast menu ($5-11). Open daily 6:30am-latenight. ❶

BEST OF THE REST

Elephant Walk Cafe, 76 Melbourne St. (☎8267 2006). Tucked in among the chic bistros of North Adelaide, the Elephant Walk is a coffee lounge whose bizarre decor and menu defy description. Open daily 8pm-latenight.

Quiet Waters BYO, 75 Hindley St., (☎8231 3637). Adelaide's best Lebanese restaurant offers a wide range of vegetarian dishes. Main dishes from $8. Sa night belly dancing. Open M and Sa-Su 5:30pm-latenight; Tu-F noon-2pm and 5:30pm-latenight. ❷

Adelaide Coffee Bar, 73 Grenfell St. (☎8227 2001). Step into this cafe and the 1940s. There's art, jazz on the stereo, and an Italian-style coffee bar. Wine is served by the glass. Food is made fresh daily, including fresh baked bread for the sandwiches ($5.50-6.50) and homemade pastries. Espresso $2.50. Open M-F 7am-5pm. ❶

Bakery on O'Connell, 44 O'Connell St. (☎8361 7377), North Adelaide. There is one reason to visit the bakery: 24hr. pie floaters. Pie floaters ($5.80), a local specialty of steak pie floating in pea soup, are an Aussie must after a night out, and this bakery does them to perfection. Pies and pastries $2.80-3.40. ❶

SIGHTS

ADELAIDE BOTANIC GARDENS. Acres of landscaped grounds surround heritage buildings, a small lake with black swans, and meandering walkways. The peaceful grounds contain the **Australian Arboretum, Yarrabee Art Gallery,** and a beautiful rose garden. The **Bicentennial Conservatory,** the largest glasshouse in the Southern Hemisphere, is the only section of the garden that is not free. In the summer, the gardens host the Moonlight Cinema; for more info, see p. 469. *(On North Terr. General line ☎8222 9311, conservatory 8222 9483; www.botanicgardens.sa.gov.au. Gardens open Dec.-Jan. M-F 7:15am-7pm, Sa-Su 9am-7pm; Oct.-Nov. and Feb.-Mar. M-F 7:15am-6:30pm, Sa-Su 9am-6:30pm; Sept. and Apr. M-F 7:15am-6pm, Sa-Su 9am-6pm; Aug. and May M-F 7:15am-5:30pm, Sa-Su 9am-5:30pm; June-July M-F 7:15am-5pm, Sa-Su 9am-5pm. Conservatory open in summer daily 10am-5pm; in winter 10am-4pm; $4.30, concessions $2.30. Free 1½hr. garden tours leave from restaurant-kiosk daily 10:30am.)*

NATIONAL WINE CENTRE OF AUSTRALIA. Run by the University of Adelaide, the center has five interactive exhibits that cover everything from grape varieties to Australian wine regions and even allow visitors to make virtual wine on a computer. At the end of the exhibits is an extensive cellar with a broad selection of wines. Courses and tastings available. *(Corner of Botanic and Hackney St. on the eastern edge of the Botanic Gardens. ☎8303 3355; www.wineaustralia.com.au. Open daily 10am-5pm. Free; suggested gold coin donation. Guided tours, tastings included, $13. Min. 10 people.)*

ADELAIDE ZOO. Carved out of the Botanic Gardens, the Adelaide Zoo is home to more than 1300 animals, including African wildlife. There are several daily feedings of hippos, pelicans, and big cats. The zoo runs **Monarto Zoological Park,** an open range park 45min. away near Murray Bridge. A shuttle bus can pick up and drop off at the central bus station in Adelaide. Several tours and 30-90min. walks lead visitors through the various habitats. *(**Zoo:** Frome Rd., a 15min. walk from North Terr. through the Botanic Gardens or down Frome Rd. Take bus #272 or 273 from Grenfell St. Popeye boats from the Festival Centre also run to and from the zoo in summer. ☎8267 3255. Open daily 9:30am-5pm. $16, concessions $13, ages 4-14 $10. Guided tours daily 11am and 2pm. **Monarto:** take the Monarto exit off the South Eastern Freeway to the Princes Hwy. and follow the signs. ☎8534 4100; www.monartozp.com.au. Open daily for tours 9:30am-5pm. Tours depart when there are enough people. $18, concessions $15, children $11.)*

HAIGH'S CHOCOLATES VISITORS CENTRE. Australia's oldest chocolate maker, Haigh's has been in business since 1915. At the visitors center and factory, windows open onto areas where workers in white outfits and hairnets inspire comparisons to *Charlie and the Chocolate Factory*. *(154 Greenhill Rd., 1 block south of South Terr. between Pulteney St. and Hutt St. ☎8372 7070; www.haighs.com.au. Open M-F 8:30am-5:30pm, Sa 9am-5pm. Free 20min. guided tours with tastings M-Sa 11am, 1, 2pm. Booking required; tours limited to 20 people. Self tours available when guided tours are not.)*

ADELAIDE GAOL. The Adelaide Gaol was used for 147 years, and 45 inmates were executed and buried within the walls. The creepy prison holds only tourists these days. *(18 Gaol Rd., Thebarton. From the corner of North and West Terr., take Port Rd. and turn right on Gaol Rd. A walk northeast of the city or a 5min. ride to Stop 1 on bus #151, 152, 153, 155, 286, or 287 from North Terr. ☎8231 4062; www.adelaidegaol.org.au. Open M-F 11am-4pm. $7.50, concessions $6, children $5. Open for self-guided tours M-F 11am-3:30pm. Guided tours Su 11am, noon, 1pm. Nightly ghost tours by appointment; scheduled 2hr. ghost tour 1st Th each month 7pm. $15.)*

MUSEUMS

While Adelaide has been termed the city of churches and cathedrals, judging from Northern Terrace it could just as easily be called the city of museums.

SOUTH AUSTRALIAN MUSEUM. This stately building is the brilliant centerpiece of the North Terr. cultural district. It holds huge whale skeletons, native Australian animal displays, rocks and minerals, and an Egyptian mummy. The real highlight of the museum is the **Australian Aboriginal Cultures Gallery,** which has the largest collection of Aboriginal artifacts in the world. *(Next to the State Library, on North Terr. ☎8207 7500, tours 8207 7370; www.samuseum.sa.gov.au. Open daily 10am-5pm. 45min. museum tours M-F 11am; Sa-Su 2 and 3pm. Aboriginal Cultures tours Th-F 10:30am. Wheelchair accessible. $10, concessions $7. Tours free.)*

ART GALLERY OF SOUTH AUSTRALIA. This huge, impressive gallery showcases Australian, Asian, and European prints, paintings, decorative arts, and Southeast Asian ceramics. *(North Terr. near Pulteney St. ☎8207 7000, tours 8207 7075; www.artgallery.sa.gov.au. Open daily 10am-5pm. 1hr. tours daily 11am and 2pm. Wheelchair accessible. Free. Tours free.)*

TANDANYA NATIONAL ABORIGINAL CULTURAL INSTITUTE. The oldest indigenous owned and managed Aboriginal multi-arts complex in Australia hosts rotating indigenous artwork exhibitions from around the country. The institute also has didgeridoo performances M-F at noon, and a Torres Strait Islander Dance Saturday and Sunday at noon. *(253 Grenfell St., at the corner of East Terr. on the City Loop bus route. ☎8224 3200. Open daily 10am-5pm. $5, concessions $4, family $12.)*

MIGRATION MUSEUM. Combining history and oral tradition to explain the patterns of immigration and exclusion that have shaped South Australian society, the museum's harrowing stories and photographs are excellent, if sobering. The exhibits are particularly relevant now, as immigration policy has become one of the nation's most hotly contested political issues. Refreshingly, the museum does not shy away from the historical controversy surrounding Australian policy toward Aborigines during the 20th century. *(82 Kintore Ave., off North Terr., behind the state library. ☎8207 7580. Open M-F 10am-5pm, Sa-Su 1-5pm. Free, $2 donation suggested.)*

ACTIVITIES

Beach bums content to relax the day away can head to the suburb of **Glenelg** for plenty of fun in the sun. Those looking for a bit more action should visit the outdoor goods stores on Rundle St., most of which can point you toward the city's best purveyors of outdoor activities.

BIKING. With hills aplenty and a bike track along the coast, Adelaide is a cyclist's paradise. Rentals are available from Linear Park Mountain Bike Hire (see **By Bicycle**).

EARTH AND SKY. **Rock Solid Adventure** offers abseiling, rock climbing, and a two-night caving trip to Naracoorte Conservation Park. They also run various outdoor trips, including kayaking tours throughout southeastern Australia; check their website for a list of upcoming trips. (☎8270 4244; www.rock-solid-adventure.com. Full day of rock-climbing or abseiling $99.) **SA Skydiving** is pleased to assist in fulfilling your free-fall fantasies. They also offer a full-day solo jump course. (☎8272 7888; www.skydiving.com.au. Tandem from $299, solo from $420, video $85.) **Adelaide Ballooning** offers 1hr. hot air balloon rides with a champagne breakfast for $210-240. Evening flights sometimes available, $150 for 30min. (☎1800 730 330; www.adelaideballooning.com.au.)

SURF, SCUBA, AND SWIM. **Glenelg Scuba Diving** runs a four-day PADI certification class and daily boat dives to Adelaide's wrecks and reefs. (☎8294 7744; www.glenelgscuba.com.au. Dives from $75, $40 for those with equipment. Equipment hire available; PADI class $495.)

ENTERTAINMENT

PERFORMING ARTS. A 2min. walk north on King William Rd. from its intersection with North Terr. at Parliament House leads to the huge **Adelaide Festival Centre** (☎8216 8600), the epicenter of Adelaide's cultural life. You can pick up a calendar of events from inside the complex, access the schedule online at www.southaustralia.com, or call BASS (☎13 12 46). The **State Opera of South Australia** (☎8226 4790; www.saopera.sa.gov.au), the **Adelaide Symphony Orchestra** (☎8233 6233; www.aso.com.au), and the **State Theatre Company of South Australia** (☎8231 5151; www.statetheatre.sa.com.au) all perform at the Festival Centre; it's also the place for big-name traveling musicals and theater performances. The State Opera also performs in the town hall. Student rush tickets for the orchestra are available 30min. before the show at the orchestra office, 91 Hindley St. **Elder Hall,** on North Terr., part of the University of Adelaide, has concerts and some chamber performances by the Adelaide Symphony. (☎8303 5272. Lunch concerts F 1-2pm; $5.)

CINEMAS. Adelaide's two best **alternative cinemas,** the **Palace** and the **Nova, are** across from one another on Rundle St. near East Terr. Between the two they cover most major international and independent films. (☎8232 3434; www.palacenova.com. Tickets $14, concessions $8; Tu tickets $9). **Mercury Cinema,** 13 Morphett St., off Hindley St., has more artsy (read: obscure) showings. (☎8410 1934; www.mercurycinema.org.au. $11, concessions $9; festival ticket prices higher.) Tuesday is usually discount night at Australian theaters. December through February brings outdoor screenings of classics at **Cinema in the Botanic Gardens.** (Tickets at gate from 7pm; ☎1 300 551 908; www.moonlight.com.au, $3 booking fee; or through BASS ☎13 12 46. $14, concessions $12, children $10.)

SPECTATOR SPORTS. Australian Rules Football is played in the suburb of West Lakes (Adelaide Crows) and in Port Adelaide (Port Power). **Cricket** (Oct.-Mar.) is played at the **Adelaide Oval,** north of the city along King William St. There is a 2½hr. tour of the Oval that focuses on "Cricket's Greatest Batsman," the late Sir Donald Bradman. (☎8300 3800. Tours M-F 10am. $10, concessions $5. Museum open M, W, F 10am-12:30pm, Tu and Th 10am-1pm; Su 2-4pm. $2. Tickets and schedules available at BASS ☎13 12 46 or VenueTix ☎8223 7788.)

NIGHTLIFE

The **East End,** which includes Rundle St. east of the mall, Pulteney St., and Pirie St., is the center of Adelaide's "pretty" scene and teems with University students and twenty-something professionals on the weekends. Bouncers here and at most of the city's dance clubs are very mindful of **dress code.** This usually means no sneakers, T-shirts, tank-tops, flip-flops, or hats, but can also be extended to include no jeans. The cafe scene dominates this area, as students and others drink schooners and chat on the sidewalk. Rundle Mall is renamed **Hindley Street** in the **West End,** and is home to many X-rated venues and numerous fly-by-night dance clubs abutting stylish bars and bistros. Rundle Mall itself, next to Hindley St., is quiet at night except for the columns of semi-inebriated partygoers marching from the pubs of Rundle St. to the clubs of Hindley St. and Light Sq. The **Light Square** area is encircled by popular clubs. Beyond the CBD, North Adelaide has swank hotels with pricey cocktails, while the beach suburbs, most notably Glenelg, have a few watering holes right on the ocean. Most bars stay open until "latenight," meaning when the crowd clears out. When the bars shut, usually 1-2am on weekends, the clubs get full.

PUBS

The Governor Hindmarsh Hotel, 59 Port Rd. (☎8340 0744; www.thegov.com.au). North of town on Port Rd., past the entertainment complex, this is the city's best small music venue. From up-and-coming to well-known acts, the Governor grooves to the best live music Adelaide has to offer. Tu $5 pizza. W Open mic. Th and Sa local bands in front bar. F Irish folk. Excellent wood-oven pizza bar ($9.50-11.50) and bar snacks ($5-11). Open M-F 11am-late, Sa 12:30pm-latenight; open Su only for events 2pm-latenight. Cover usually $2-20, more for big-name acts.

Grace Emily, 232 Waymouth St. (☎8231 5500). In the chillest bar in Adelaide, crushed-velvet curtains drape the stage and a pool table and courtyard complete the atmosphere. Modern, relaxing Grace Emily is perfect for lounging. The place to be on M nights for Billy Bob's BBQ Jam. Open daily 4pm-latenight.

Exeter Hotel, 246 Rundle St. (☎8223 2623). Live music club/bar/curry bistro with eclectic crowd. Live music is mostly local and always original. W and Th 6:30-9pm Curry Nights ($13) have a cult following. Open daily 11:30am-as late as 3am.

The Bar on Gouger, 123 Gouger St. (☎8410 0042). The best place to meet up on food-filled Gouger St. with the most comfortable couches in Adelaide and a range of drinks and "talk food." DJs F-Sa make for the busiest nights. Open spaces, small photos on the wall, and deep colors lull happy hour drinkers into a state of bliss. Jagerbombs 2 for $14. Open M-Sa 11am-latenight, Su noon-latenight.

Edinburgh Castle, 233 Currie St. (☎8410 1211). The Ed is the best gay bar in town. The front bar and the courtyard "outback bar" are good places to relax with a friend, while the dance floor is never vacant and the drag queen shows always lively. All meals $11-18. Happy hour pints at schooner prices M-F 5-8pm, Sa-Su after 12:30pm. DJs W-Sa nights. Drag shows F-Sa nights. W night strippers, usually male, but occasionally female. Bar open M-Tu and Su 2pm-latenight, W-Sa 11am-latenight.

Austral, 205 Rundle St. (☎8223 4660). An unmistakable landmark, this old hotel draws a young crowd. F-Sa live bands, beer garden, M-Th and Su DJs. If nothing's happening here, there's probably nothing happening in town. Open daily 11am-3am.

NIGHTCLUBS

Grand Hotel, Moseley Sq. (☎8376 1222), on the beach in Glenelg. Adelaide's most popular waterfront hotel, the grand packs it in W-Su, but the real time to go is Su, when locals flock to partake in that great Aussie institution–the Sunday Sesh. Long wait in summer. Dress neat casual; in other words, no beach gear. W live band. Th Uni Night. F DJ allows members of the crowd to spin for 15min. Open daily 11:30am-latenight.

Mars Bar, 120 Gouger St. (☎8231 9639). Adelaide's best gay club, Mars is mellow enough to make clubbers of any persuasion feel comfortable. In addition to the familiar pulsing lights and beats of the pop tunes coming from the downstairs dance floor, there is a small outdoor beer garden. Floor shows Th-Sa nights, 2 dance floors F-Sa. Open W-Th 10:30pm-3:30am, F-Sa 10:30pm-5am.

Garage, 163 Waymouth St. (☎8212 9577), on Light Sq. With beautiful high ceilings, brick walls, and a trendy adjoining restaurant, Garage is seriously chic. Open M 9:30am-midnight, Tu-W 9:30am-7:30pm, Th 9:30am-2am, F 9:30am-5am, Sa 9pm-5am, Su 11am-10pm. Restaurant open for lunch M-F, dinner M, and brunch Su.

Church, on Synagogue Pl. (☎8223 4233), a little alley just off Rundle St. Church paradoxically occupies a former synagogue. Techno downstairs, hip-hop upstairs. 2-for-1 drinks F 9-11pm and Sa midnight-1am. Cover $8-10, entry free before midnight (look for the spotlight). Open F-Sa 9pm-5am.

DAYTRIPS FROM ADELAIDE

THE COAST

The beaches and coastal spots below are listed from north to south. All can be easily reached via Adelaide's metro system of buses and trains. In addition, a coastal bike path runs south from Henley to Glenelg and the southern coast.

PORT ADELAIDE. Port Adelaide at first glance does not seem a promising coastal destination, but this industrial town and historic port has a lion's share of quirky personalities and eccentric sites. To reach Port Adelaide, take the Outer Harbor line to the Port Adelaide stop or hop on bus #118, 136, 151 or 153. The **visitors center,** on Commercial Rd. at the corner of Vincent St., has information and maps, including maps for an historic pub crawl, and even shipwrecks. They also lead free guided walking tours of the area. (☎1800 629 888 or 8405 6560. Open daily 9am-5pm.)

The Port Adelaide River has 30-40 bottlenose dolphins, and the visitors center has a pamphlet that identifies each of the dolphins by fin shape. Two river cruise companies run from the waterfront in Port Adelaide ($2.50-3). Otherwise, **Blue Water Sea Kayaking** runs 4hr. tours from spring to late autumn; pickup is available from the visitors center and Glenelg. The tour allows visitors to see the dolphins, mangroves, and the graveyards of the many ships that have been put to rest in these waters. (☎8295 8812; www.adventure-kayak.com.au. Booking required. $45, children $25.) The 74-step climb to the top of the **Lighthouse,** on the wharf in front of the market, ends with a great view of the area. (Open M-F 10am-2pm, Su 10am-5pm. $1, or free with a ticket to the Maritime Museum.) **Fisherman's Wharf** (☎8341 2040), Lighthouse Sq., on Commercial Rd., is the place to be Sundays and public holidays 9am-5pm, when vendors sell everything from CDs to seafood to used books.

Port Adelaide might have the world's most bizarre collection of museums. The **National Military Vehicle Museum,** 252 Commercial Rd., holds relics from the past 80 years. (☎8341 3011; www.military-vehicle-museum.org.au. Open daily 10am-4:30pm. $7, concession $5, children $3.) Other transportation-themed museums include the **National Railway Museum** on Lipson St. (☎8341 1690; www.natrailmuseum.org.au. Open daily 10am-5pm. $10, concession $7, children $4.50.) and the **South Australian Aviatian Museum,** also on Lipson St. (☎8240 1230; www.saam.org.au. Open daily 10:30am-4:30pm.) The highlight of the **South Australian Maritime Museum,** 126 Lipson St., one block east of the lighthouse, is the construction of an early immigrant ship; be sure to check out the third-class berth. (☎8207 6255; www.historysa.gov.au. Open daily 10am-5pm. $8.50, concessions $6.50, children $3.50.)

The oldest cafe in the historic district, **Lipson Cafe ❷,** 117a Lipson St., is also the hippest. Within seconds the staff will make you feel like a regular, and the food is as good as the company. Don't leave without getting the legendary pad thai ($14.50). (☎8341 0880. Main dishes $14.50-15.50. Open daily 8am-5pm.)

Finally, the Port wouldn't be the same without its heritage pubs and their tales of resident ghosts. The visitors center has a guide to the pubs, which incidentally maps out South Australia's top pub crawl. The best of the bunch, **Port Dock Brewery Hotel,** 10 Todd St., just off Vincent St., runs tours of its award-winning brewery. (☎8240 0187; www.portdockbreweryhotel.com.au. Open M-W 9am-midnight, Th-Su 9am-late. Tours by arrangement.)

HENLEY. Henley has calm waters, a long stretch of sand, a picturesque jetty, and waterfront restaurants, making it a popular escape for families. For a cheap bite, **Estia Takeaway,** on the foreshore, has amazing yiros for $7. (☎8383 5341. Open Su-Th 11am-8pm, F-Sa 11am-10pm.) To reach Henley, take bus #110, 139, 286, or 287.

GLENELG. The most famous of the beach suburbs, Glenelg has a lengthy strip of restaurants. Jetty St., the main road in town, is chock-full of options, from takeaway fish 'n' chips to classy Italian. The **Oyster Shop,** at Jetty and Moseley St., has fresh seafood and home-grown oysters. (☎8376 7200. ½-dozen oysters $9.90. Fish 'n' chips from $7. Open M-Th 11:30am-8:30pm, F 11am-9pm, Sa 10am-10pm, Su 11am-8:30pm.) For Glenelg accommodations, see p. 465; for nightlife, see p. p. 471.

PORT NOARLUNGA AND THE SOUTHERN BEACHES. Closest to Adelaide, **Christies Beach** has a park and many small shops along Beach Rd. South from Christies, the **Port Noarlunga Aquatic Reserve** has a shallow reef accessible from the end of the jetty and is the best diving and snorkeling spot in the Adelaide area. Farther south, **Seaford** has a walking and biking track along the cliffs. **Moana,** south of Seaford, has the best surf and is suitable for beginners, and **Maslin Beach** draws peeping Toms and free spirits with South Australia's largest nudist colony. To reach the southern beaches, take bus #741 or 742.

THE HILLS

Those who venture from the downtown area are amply rewarded with expanses of native forest, vineyards, and traditional German-style villages. Much of the region is a 15-40min. drive east from the Adelaide city center, along Hwy. A1 (known as Glen Osmond Rd.), departing from the downtown grid's southeast corner. The **Adelaide Hills Visitors Centre,** 41 Main St., Hahndorf, has information and also does booking. (☎ 1800 353 323 or 8388 1185; www.visitadelaidehills.com. **Internet** access $2 per 20min. Open M-F 9am-5pm, Sa-Su 10am-4pm.)

A number of buses run from Adelaide into the hills. Bus #163 and 164 run to Stirling via Crafers. In Crafers, it is possible to catch bus #823 to Cleland Conservation Park and the Mt. Lofty Summit. Bus #850 goes to Strathalbyn via Aldgate, while #164F and 165M go through Stirling and Aldgate before terminating in Bridgewater. Bus #840 goes to Hahndorf via Bridgewater.

MOUNT LOFTY SUMMIT AND CLELAND PARK. Just 15km from the big city, **Cleland Conservation Park** has winding trails through rare eucalyptus forests and parks full of hopping 'roos. Mt. Lofty, part of the Cleland Conservation Park, is one of the most popular and accessible attractions in the Adelaide Hills. To reach the summit, take the Mt. Lofty exit on Princes Hwy. (M1) and follow signs. From the 710m **Mount Lofty Summit,** the city glitters all the way to the coast. On a clear day, the view stretches as far as Kangaroo Island. There is no admission fee for the summit, but parking costs $1 per hr., $2 per day.

From the summit, there are three main hiking trails. One of the trails is a section of the 1200km Heysen Trail which loops from the summit to the Botanic Gardens and back (6.5km, 2hr.). A 4km one-way trail leads from the summit to Waterfall Gully carpark up to Mt. Lofty. Allow 2½hr. for the return trip. A third hike leads to Cleland Wildlife Park (4km, 1.5hr round-trip).

South of the summit, the **Mount Lofty Botanic Gardens** are a great place for a picnic or a leisurely stroll. (☎ 8370 8370. Open M-F 9am-4pm, Sa-Su 10am-5pm. Parking $1 per hr., $2 per day.) In conjunction with the botanic gardens, **Tappa Mai Guided Tours** runs a 40min. Aboriginal tour that examines indigenous plants and their practical uses. (☎ 8341 2777. Call ahead for prices and to book.) The **Mount Lofty YHA ❶,** 20km from Adelaide, is a great choice for groups with a car. Groups of 2-16 can rent out the stone cottage. (Book and pick up keys through Adelaide Central YHA ☎ 8414 3000; M-Th $60, YHA $50; F-Su $80/70. Same conditions apply for two other locations: Mylor and Norton Summit.) The complex at the summit includes a **cafe** and **tourist office** with advice about hikes in the park. They also sell an invaluable map of the hills ($2), which shows the many options clearly connected by main roads. (☎ 8370 1054, cafe ☎ 8339 2600. Tourist office open daily 9am-5pm. Cafe open M-Tu 9am-5pm, W-Su 9am-latenight.)

ALDGATE, STIRLING, AND BRIDGEWATER. The three tiny towns of Aldgate, Stirling, and Bridgewater embody the spirit of the hills with cute cafes and B&Bs tucked into the greenery of the landscape. Their location on bus lines and proximity to area attractions make them a good base for exploring the Hills. The visitor center in Hahndorf does booking for the many B&Bs in the area.

The historic **Bridgewater Mill ❺,** Mt. Barker Rd. in Bridgewater, has everything a classy restaurant and cellar door in the hills needs—tree-shaded al fresco dining, a creative three-course menu, and premium wines from the mill's own vineyards. (☎ 8339 3422; www.bridgewatermill.com.au. 3-course meal $75, 2-course $60. Cellar door open for tastings daily 10am-5pm. Restaurant open M and Th-Su noon-2:30pm.) The **Aldgate Cafe ❶,** 6 Strathalbyn Rd. makes good, inexpensive Italian food and has $8.50 dinner specials M-W. The calzone special is delicious and filling. (☎ 8339 2530. Open M-Tu 3pm-late, W-Su 10am-latenight.) **Bistro 49 ❹,** 49 Mt. Barker Rd. in Stirling, is a good value given the quality of cuisine. Main courses around $11.50-23. (☎ 8339 4416. Open W-Su 11am-2pm and 6-9pm.) **Autumn Gate Cafe ❷,** 120 Mt. Barker Rd. in Stirling, has outdoor seating and everything from pies and pasties to hearty entrees. (☎ 8339 1705. Wraps $8. Main courses $13-15. Open W-Th and Su 9am-5pm, F-Sa 9am-10pm.)

Twenty minutes from Adelaide, at the Stirling exit off the freeway, the **Warrawong Sanctuary** is a conservation park whose five different habitats shelter rare and endangered native species. The dusk walk is your best option for spotting animals, though the dawn walk is more picturesque. (☎8370 9197; www.warrawong.com. Dusk and dawn walks $18, concessions $13. Book ahead for all guided walks, especially the dawn walk. Open for self-guided walks Tu-Su 9am-5pm. Admission $13, concession $8 includes Birds of Prey show at 2pm.) **Smart Car Hire** (☎1300 1300 20, quote VIP #1148) will do a pickup and return from Adelaide ($18; min. 2 person). Public transportation costs about $9.

Visitors with a car should consider driving the **Angas Scenic Drive** on Mt. Barker Rd. from Bridgewater to Strathalbyn. The many cafes are happy to provide picnic fodder for Strathalbyn's scenic riverbank. For an aerial view of the river, **Adelaide Ballooning** (p. 469) flies from Strathalbyn. To reach the towns, take Princes Hwy. (M1) and exit at the Stirling exit. The main road is Mt. Barker Rd., which becomes Strathalbyn Rd. on the way to Strathalbyn. Alternatively, Bridgewater can be reached straight off the Hwy., 5km. past the Stirling/Aldgate exit.

HAHNDORF. Originally settled by Prussian and East German immigrants in 1839, the most touristed village in the Adelaide Hills plays its heritage to the hilt. The avenues are lined with trees and plenty of shops, most of which sell bratwurst; if you were looking for a cheesy impersonation of a german village, congratulations, you've found it. Beyond the German fare are restaurants, galleries, and wineries of all stripes and colors.

A few kilometers from the tourist knick-knack shops of the main strip, Hahndorf has some places worth checking out. One of the most visited sites in Hahndorf, the **Hans Heysen Historic Home and Studio,** at the Cedars, is the homestead where the renowned German-born artist worked and lived with his family in the early 20th century. You can visit the artist's studio and home, still in use by the Heysen family, and see the majestic gum trees on the property that inspired his art. Picnics in the extensive gardens are welcome. To reach the studio, take Ambleside Rd. from Main St., then turn left on Heysen Rd. (☎8388 7277. Open Tu-Su 10am-4pm. Access to the grounds $4. Admission to house and studio by 1hr. guided tour only; Sept.-May 11am, 1, 3pm; June-Aug. 11am and 2pm. $10, concessions $7.50.) The cellar door at the **Hahndorf Hill Winery** is a nice mix of ancient winery and modern cafe. Guests can enjoy coffee, tea, and sweet treats in addition to wine in the cool, white cellar. (☎8388 7512; www.hahndorfhillwinery.com.au. Follow the signs from the main road in Hahndorf. Open daily 10am-5pm.) **Nepenthe Wines,** just outside Hahndorf toward Balhannah, is a hip winery with premium wines. (☎8388 4439; www.nepenthe.com.au. Open daily 10am-4pm.) Most businesses and shops in town are on Main St., including the area's **visitors center,** several **ATMs,** and the **post office,** 73 Main St. **Postal Code:** 5245.

FLEURIEU PENINSULA

The Fleurieu (FLOOR-ee-oh) Peninsula stretches southeast from Adelaide, encompassing the luscious vineyards of McLaren Vale, miles of coastline, and several charming seaside towns. The region's proximity to Adelaide has made it a popular weekend getaway, and affordable accommodations are harder to come by than in other parts of South Australia. Fleurieu's popularity, however, rarely translates into unwelcome crowding. Beautiful country drives weave past quiet pastures and jaw-dropping views. There are myriad water-based activities offered on the Fleurieu, including snorkeling, jet-skiing, and surfing. All tourist offices have a copy of the free and invaluable *Surfing Secrets on the Fleurieu Peninsula*, which provides a map of all the surf spots and detailed information including break descriptions and wind directions.

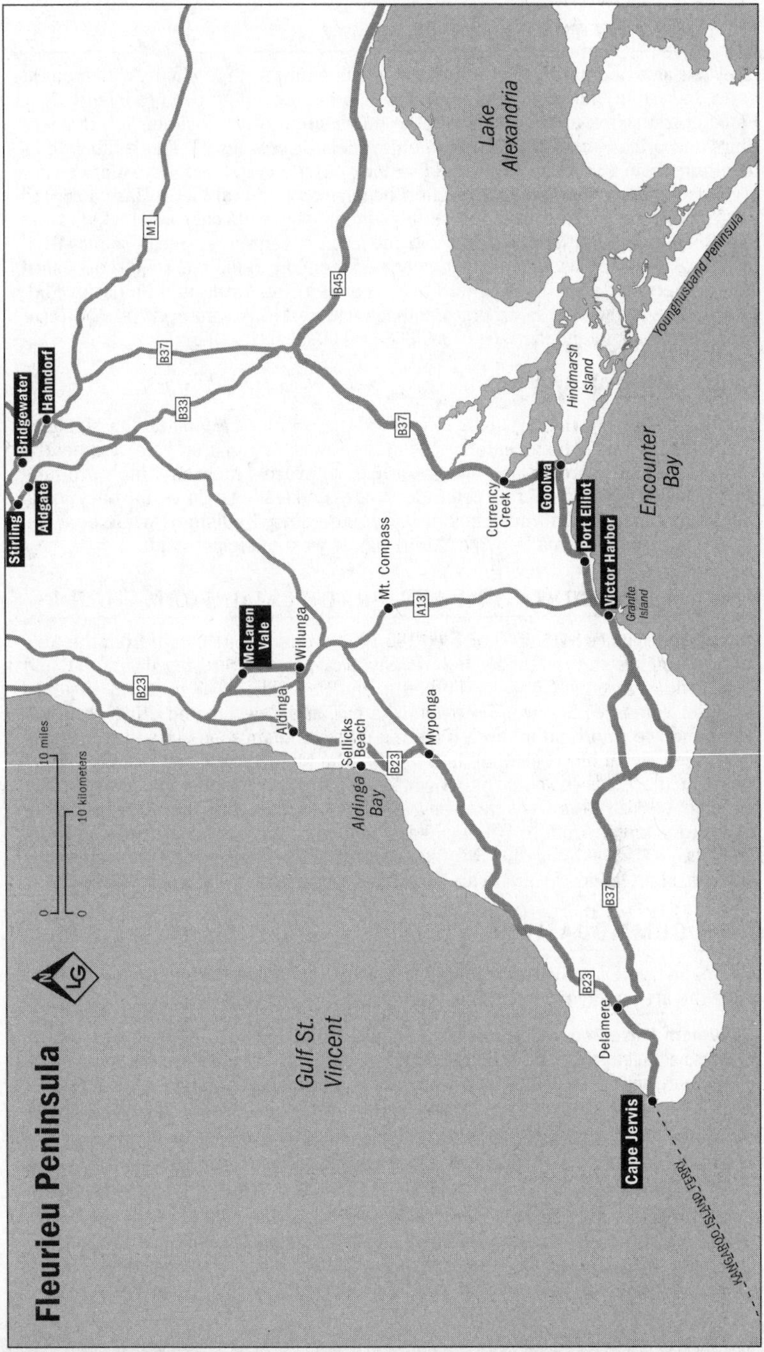

Fleurieu Peninsula

0 10 miles
0 10 kilometers

Gulf St. Vincent
Aldinga Bay
Encounter Bay
Lake Alexandria
Hindmarsh Island
Younghusband Peninsula
Granite Island
Stirling
Aldgate
Bridgewater
Hahndorf
McLaren Vale
Willunga
Aldinga
Sellicks Beach
Myponga
Mt. Compass
Currency Creek
Goolwa
Port Elliot
Victor Harbor
Delamere
Cape Jervis
KANGAROO ISLAND FERRY
M1
B45
B37
B33
B23
A13

TOURS OF THE FLEURIEU

Enjoy Adelaide operates an 8hr. afternoon-evening tour from Adelaide, with stops at two wineries in McLaren Vale, a train ride, and an evening Granite Island Little Penguin tour. Pick up a brochure at the information office for their full range of tours and prices. (☎8332 1401; www.enjoyadelaide.com.au. M, Th, Sa-Su. $65; ½-day tours from $35.) **Blue Sky Camel Charters,** based in Mt. Compass, offers a variety of camelling experiences from short beach excursions at Victor Harbor ($5) to longer 1½hr. forays through a forest. ($35, includes tea and cake and pick up from Mt. Compass bus station.) For $40, you and a camel can share a meal. (☎8556 9109 or 04 1885 6915; www.blueskycamelcharters.com.au. Bookings required.) **Camel Winery Tours,** based at the Camel Farm between Kangarilla and McLaren Flat, offers a one-day winery safari on camelback with up to six winery visits, a bottle of wine, and lunch included. (☎04 0739 9808 or 04 0883 6246. $90.)

MCLAREN VALE ☎08

A quick jaunt from the city, just 45min. (37km) south of Adelaide, the McLaren Vale wine region—which centers around the towns of McLaren Vale, and nearby Willunga and McLaren Flat—has countless vineyards, most of which produce world-class wines and operate cellar-door sales and tastings. Cafes line busy roads that weave among vast stretches of leafy, vine-dotted hillsides, while beaches stretch out from the small town of Aldinga, just west of Mclaren Vale.

TRANSPORTATION AND PRACTICAL INFORMATION

Premier Stateliner (☎8415 5555 or 1800 182 160) comes through town from the Adelaide central **bus station** (1hr.; M-F 3 per day, Sa 2 per day, Su 1 per day; $7.30) and loops around through Goolwa, Middleton, and Port Elliot. The best way to get to McLaren Vale is with a group of friends, a car, and a designated driver; it is not uncommon to find random breath testing units on main roads to and from wine regions (the legal blood-alcohol limit is .05). The **McLaren Vale and Fleurieu Visitors Centre,** on the left as you come into town, has a map of the wineries and handles B&B bookings. (☎8323 9944; www.mclarenvale.info. Open daily 9am-5pm.) The road from the visitors center south to Willunga has wineries at every turn, as does Chalk Hill Rd. **McLaren Flat,** on Kangarilla Rd., 3km east of McLaren Vale is also surrounded by wineries. Main Rd. in McLaren Vale has **ATMs,** a **supermarket,** and a **post office.**

ACCOMMODATIONS

The majority of accommodations are rather expensive B&Bs. Most travelers make the area a daytrip from Adelaide, Port Elliot, or Victor Harbor.

Southern Vales Bed and Breakfast, 13 Chalk Hill Rd. (☎8323 8144; www.southern-vales.net), off the main street after the Visitors Center, has nice ensuite rooms that overlook vineyards, and the owner Allan is an attentive host. The B&B has its own vineyard and the wine produced from these grapes is available to guests. Rooms $130. Weekend package $290. ❺

Willunga Hotel, on High St. (☎8556 2135) in nearby Willunga, down Willunga or Victor Harbor Rd. from McLaren Vale. Their above-average pub-hotel rooms are the only budget rooms available. Generous counter **meals** ❷ ($10-20) and Aussie cider on tap. Rooms under renovations; inquire about prices. ❸

McLaren Vale Lakeside Caravan Park, on Field St. (☎8323 9255), is conveniently located for winery tours and has tennis, volleyball, and a pool. Reception daily 8:30am-6:30pm. Sites $19, powered $23; vans with bath from $50; cabins from $80-100. ❷

FOOD

In McLaren Vale the question isn't what wine goes with the food, but what food with the wine. A host of gourmet restaurants have menus designed to showcase the area wines. While most charge a hefty price, there are a few bargains in the area. Those looking to make their own meal should head to the supermarket, at the corner of Main Rd. and Kangarilla Rd. (Open daily 9am-6pm.)

The Almond & Olive Train, (☎8323 8112, cafe 8333 7689), on Main St. next to Hardy's Tintara is situated in a converted railway car. The area's most affordable and unique eatery. Nut lovers can try olives and almonds of many flavors before lunch at the adjoining cafe, where diner-style booths give an intimate and relaxed feel. Large selection of area wines by the glass. Breakfast all day. Lunch under $12.50; dinner under $20. Sa Loose Caboose live music. Open daily 10am-4:30pm. Cafe open M, W-Th, and Su 10:30am-7pm, F-Sa 10:30am-latenight. ❶

Blessed Cheese, 150 Main St. (☎8323 7958). A trendy little shop that makes a fantastic focaccia ($9-9.50) and holds chocolate-making classes on weekends. Open daily 9am-6pm. Classes 11am-5pm, $90 with lunch and wine tasting. Book ahead. ❶

Limeburner's Restaurant, (☎8323 8599) on the corner of Main St. and Chalk Hill Rd. in the Marienberg Limeburner's Center. Award-winning restaurant with delicious and well-presented meals at reasonable prices (main courses from $24.50). Regional wine suggestions with every meal. Open daily at 10am for lunch; dinner 6pm-9pm. ❸

WINERIES

McLaren Vale is the best-known wine area in South Australia after the Barossa Valley. There are over 45 wineries that offer free cellar-door tastings and sales. The cellars listed below are among the best in the region. Most of the larger vineyards operate cellar doors daily from 10am to 4:30 or 5pm, while smaller, family-run vineyards will open cellar doors only on the weekends. The visitors center has maps and a complete list of hours for all vineyards.

Hugh Hamilton Wines (☎8323 8689; www.hughhamiltonwines.com.au), on McMurtrie Rd. before Wirra Wirra. The beautiful 360° glass tasting area has a view of the Mt. Lofty ranges. "The Mongrel" is a delicious blend of three grapes, and the "Jekyll & Hyde" is their flagship Shiraz/Viognet. Open M-F 10am-5:30pm, Sa-Su 11am-5:30pm.

Kangarilla Road Wines, on Kangarilla Rd. (☎8383 0044; www.kangarillaroad.com.au). A simple cellar door whose wines are some of the best values in the region. The Viognet, a crisp and unique white, is unforgettable. Open M-F 9am-5pm, Sa-Su 11am-5pm.

Hoffmann's (☎8383 0232) in McLaren Flat. Follow signs from Kangarilla Rd. A visit to this small, personal winery feels like sharing a glass in the home of a friend rather than tasting in a commercial venue. Guests are invited to picnic in the charming courtyard enclosed by grape arbors, and the vineyard almost comes through the front door of the tasteful cellar. Open daily 11am-5pm.

Wirra Wirra Vineyards (☎8323 8414; www.wirrawirra.com.au), on McMurtrie Rd.; follow signs from Willunga Rd. Read the labels on the bottles carefully—their humor is as dry as their wine. Their Shiraz is too good to miss. Open M-Sa 10am-5pm, Su 11am-5pm.

Hugo Winery (☎8383 0098), on McLaren Flat. Follow signs from Kangarilla Rd. Modern art adorns the honey-oak walls of this gazebo-style cellar. In the winter, an open wood fireplace makes the atmosphere cozy. Open M-F 9:30am-5pm, Sa noon-5pm, Su 10:30am-5pm.

BEACHES

Just a few kilometers west of McLaren Vale, the beaches near Aldinga are among the finest you'll find on the Fleurieu. A beautiful, popular stretch of beaches line Aldinga Bay, yet no beach in the area has waves bigger than a ripple, so surfers will have to be content with sun-bathing. From the south, the first cluster includes **Sellick's Beach, Silver Sands Beach,** and **Aldinga Beach.** There is car access at each. The road to **Port Willunga** is farther north at the intersection of Commercial and Aldinga Rd. For those who want to live free or those who have forgotten their bathers, **Maslins Beach** has South Australia's oldest nudist colony.

VICTOR HARBOR ☎08

Sheltered from the Southern Ocean by the sands of Encounter Bay, touristy Victor Harbor (pop. 4600) was once used as the summer residence of South Australia's colonial governors. Today, Victor's penguins, parasailing, museums, and whales draw most of the crowds. Despite these attractions—and summer temperatures up to 10°C cooler than Adelaide—many tourists prefer the more peaceful towns of Port Elliot, Middleton, and Goolwa.

TRANSPORTATION. **Premier Stateliner buses** (☎8415 5555) run from Adelaide to Stuart St. in Victor Harbor (1½-2hr.; M-F 5 per day, Sa 2 per day, Su 1 per day; $17) and continue to Goolwa, Middleton, and Port Elliot. Buy tickets at **Travelworld** (☎8552 1200), in the Harbor Mall on Ocean St. To get to Kangaroo Island, book at the **Sealink Bookings Office,** in the same building as the visitors center, for a Sealink bus to Cape Jervis or ferry tickets to the island. (☎1800 088 552 or 8552 7000. Bus daily at 7:25am to Cape Jervis; $16. For ferry prices, see **Cape Jervis,** p. 480. Open daily 9am-5pm.) Other services include: **taxis** (☎13 10 08, 8552 6121, or 8552 2622) and **RAA** (☎13 11 11 or 8552 1033).

ORIENTATION AND PRACTICAL INFORMATION. Victor Harbor is 85km down the Main South Rd. from Adelaide. **Flinders Promenade** runs along the ocean beneath massive fir trees. The main commercial drag, one-way **Ocean Street,** runs parallel one block up, becoming Hindmarsh Rd. The main street on the western side of the city is Victoria St., which leads to the highway toward Cape Jervis. The **visitors center,** near the causeway to Granite Island, is at the foot of Flinders Pde. and has a map of town with shops and services on the back. (☎8552 5738; www.tourismvictorharbor.com.au. Open daily 9am-5pm.) Other services include: **ATMs** on Ocean St.; **police,** 30 Torrens St. (☎8552 2088); **library,** 10 Coral St., just off Ocean St., with free **Internet** access (☎8552 3009; open Tu-Th 10:30am-5:30pm, F 10am-6pm, Sa 10am-1pm); and **post office,** 54 Ocean St. (Open M-F 9am-5pm.) **Postal Code:** 5211.

ACCOMMODATIONS AND FOOD. **The Anchorage ❸,** 21 Flinders Pde., offers waterfront lodging at budget prices, along with a restaurant (lunch specials $7.50-12.50; entrees $12.50-17) and funky, ship-shaped cafe/bar. (☎8552 5970; www.anchorseafronthotel.com. Continental breakfast included. Singles $40; doubles $70-150; 4- to 6-bed family rooms $100-150. Cafe open M-Th and Su 8:30am-8:30pm, F-Sa 8:30am-9pm.) The 100-year-old **Grosvenor Junction Hotel ❷,** 40 Ocean St., has simple rooms and a balcony with a great view. For golfers, the "gulf deal" is quite the bargain: a game of golf, cooked breakfast, and a night's accommodation for $55. (☎8552 1011. TV lounge, fridge. Continental breakfast included. Backpackers $30; singles $35; doubles $70.) **Victor Harbor Beach Front Caravan Park ❷,**

114 Victoria St., has beautiful sea views on the west side of the city. (☎8552 1111. Office open daily 8:30am-7pm. Key deposit $10 during peak season. Book ahead for cabins in summer. Sites for two $26-30; cabins $60-100.)

The **Original Victor Harbor Fish Shop ❷,** 20 Ocean St., is the real deal for fish 'n' chips (up to $13) and cheap burgers. (☎8552 1273. Open M-Th and Su 10:30am-8pm, F-Sa 10:30am-8:30pm.) **Nino's ❷,** 17 Albert Pl., at the end of Ocean St., has excellent pizza and pasta deals. (☎8552 3501. Pasta $10.50-12.50. 9" pizza $8.50-11.50. Open M 8am-9pm, Tu-Th 11am-9pm, F-Sa 11am-10pm, Su 9am-9pm.) A **Woolworths** supermarket is in Victor Central Mall on Torrens St. (Open daily 8am-8pm.)

SIGHTS AND ACTIVITIES. **Granite Island** is the main attraction in Victor Harbor, and the **little penguins** take the center ring. Access to the north shore of the island and the little penguins that live there is limited to those on the **Penguin Interpretive Centre's** guided tour at dusk. (☎8552 7555. $12.50, concessions $11, children $7.50, families $36. Tours begin at dusk, so times vary seasonally. Booking required by phone or through the visitors center. Centre open Sa-Su 11:30am-3:30pm; daily during school holidays. $3, concessions $2, children $1.50, families $7.50.) The island also has the **Kaiki Trail** (45min. loop), a cafe, and a brilliant lookout with views over expansive **Encounter Bay.** The island is accessible via 10min. stroll across the causeway, or on a **horse-drawn tram.** (Tram runs daily every 40min. 10am-4pm; extended hours during holidays. Round-trip $7, children $5.)

Blue Sky Camel Charters offers short camel rides on the Victor Harbor beach every weekend, and daily December through January, weather permitting. The visitors center posts times for camel rides. (☎8556 9109; www.blueskycamelcharters.com.au. $5.) From Victor Harbor, the **Encounter Bikeway** runs to the towns of Port Elliot, Middleton, and Goolwa. Rent a bike at **Victor Harbor Cycle and Skate,** 73 Victoria St. (☎8552 1417. ½-day $14, full-day $20. Open M-F 9am-5:30pm, Sa 9am-noon.) The **Cockle Train** runs along Australia's first steel railway, laid between Goolwa and Victor in 1854. (30min. one-way. Runs Su and school holidays only, check with the visitors center. $17, round-trip $24, concessions $21.)

GOOLWA ☎08

No longer a bustling port of the Murray River, Goolwa has aged gracefully and is undergoing a renaissance with extensive plans for developments on the wharf, including a microbrewery and chocolate factory. The town's main street is the road from Adelaide, which becomes **Cadell Street** in town and leads to the waterfront before making a westward turn and becoming **Victor Harbor Road.** The **Signal Point Interpretive Centre,** at the end of Cadell St. on the waterfront (look for the big information sign), books local tours and excursions, including scenic flights, 4WD tours, and skydiving. The Centre is also a fascinating interactive museum that explains the geological history of the Murray Darling River and highlights its impact on the surrounding landscape. (☎8555 3488. Open daily 9am-5pm. Museum $5.50, concessions $4.40, children $2.75.) The **police** can be reached at ☎8555 2018. **ATMs,** the **post office,** and restaurants can all be found on Cadell St., as can the **library.** (☎8555 7000. Free **Internet** access. Open M-F 9am-5pm, Sa 9am-noon.) The **Foodland** supermarket is on Victor Harbor Rd. in the Goolwa Village Shopping Center. (Open M-Sa 7:30am-8pm, Su 8am-8pm.)

Camping and cabins are available at the **Goolwa Caravan Park ❶,** on Noble Ave. To reach the caravan park, coming into town from the north, turn left at the visitors centre, follow Liverpool St. along the water; from there caravan park signs lead to the park. (☎8555 2737; www.goolwacaravanpark.com.au. Office open daily 8:30am-5pm. Sites $8-10, powered $20-25; cabins for 2 from $65-85.) **Woks 2 Eat ❷,** on the corner of Cadell and Dawson in the center of town, offers fine Asian dining.

(Noodles and curries $14-16. Lunch wraps around $8.) **Aquacaf ❶**, on Victor Harbor Rd. as you head out of town toward Victor Harbor, has food so good they don't need an "e." (☎8555 1235. Baguettes $7.50; focaccia $8.50. Open M and Th-Su 8am-5pm; daily during school holidays.)

The new **bridge** to **Hindmarsh Island,** across the Murray River from Goolwa, enables visitors to drive right out to the Murray's mouth and see the **pelicans** that feed there regularly. The **Encounter Bikeway** is a 37km sealed path along the Murray River that links Goolwa to Victor Harbor. The **Cockle Train** transports passengers back who don't want to complete the whopping round-trip. Boat excursions from Goolwa into the northern reaches of **Coorong National Park** (p. 494) or out to the Murray's mouth are popular options. The free **Wellington Ferry,** east of town at the small hamlet of Wellington, crosses the Murray River, taking about eight cars across on each pass (runs 24hr.).

CAPE JERVIS ☎08

Cape Jervis serves as the jumping-off point for the **Kangaroo Island ferry.** Those who stay the night may be surprised by the quality of the **Cape Jervis Station ❷,** where options range from excellent rooms in the homestead ($100) to the two-person Railway Cottage, a decked-out train car ($80), to the backpacker digs in the Shearers' Quarters. The Sealink bus picks up and drops off at the gate, and guests are entitled to free ferry transfers. (☎8598 0288 or 1800 805 288; www.capejervisstation.com.au. Sites $12, powered $19; dorms $22; cabins $60.) The rest of the town consists of the **pub/gas station/general store** complex between the Station and the Ferry. There is a **Sealink** office at the ferry dock. Book ferries well in advance (☎1800 088 552).

KANGAROO ISLAND ☎08

If ever an island was well-named, it is Kangaroo Island (pop. 4100). With 21 national and local conservation parks on the island, visitors are sure to see koalas and kangaroos, snakes and seals, and everything in between. The hikes through astounding landscapes showcase the wildlife as well as impressive geological formations. In addition, Kangaroo Island's sand dunes and lengthy coastline make for a wide variety of activities, including fishing, surfing, and sand boarding. Budget travelers be forewarned: getting here is an expensive proposition, and there is no public island transportation. While a car is the best way to see the island, many of the 2-3 day tours catch the highlights at reasonable prices.

INTERCITY TRANSPORTATION

BY FERRY AND COACH

Kangaroo Island Sealink ferry has a monopoly on transport to Cape Jervis and Kangaroo Island; consequently, prices are steep and discounts are hard to come by. Sealink has offices in Victor Harbor and at the ferry dock in Cape Jervis, but it is advisable to **book very far in advance,** especially during school holidays, to avoid being turned away. STA travel also handles booking. Ferries take one hour to cross the Backstairs Passage between Cape Jervis and Penneshaw and depart and return five times daily. (☎13 13 01 or 8202 8688; www.sealink.com.au. Booking is mandatory. Daily 7:30am-10pm. Round-trip $70, concessions $56; car costs vary depending on size, round-trip from $116 off-peak, $148 peak.) Sealink offers connecting **coach** service between Adelaide's central bus station, 101 Franklin St., and the Cape Jervis ferry dock (1¾hr.; 6:45am and 3:45pm; round-trip $38, concessions $32; book ahead), as well as service from Goolwa/Victor Harbor to Cape Jervis. (1½hr./1hr.; 6:50am/7:25am; round-trip $28.)

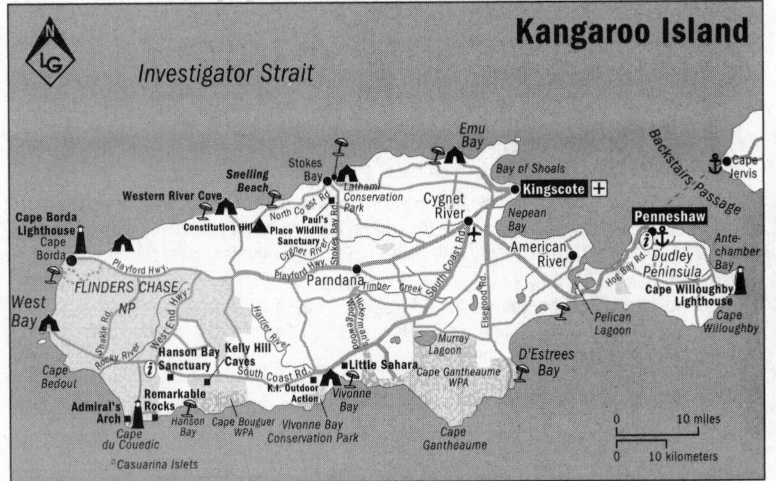

BY PLANE

Two airlines depart 2-4 times per day from Adelaide's airport bound for **Kangaroo Island Airport,** 13km from the town of Kingscote at Cygnet River. **Regional Express (Rex)** occasionally has good deals on airfares during the fall and winter. (☎13 17 13; www.regionalexpress.com.au.) **Emu Airways** (☎1800 182 353 or 8234 3711; www.emuairways.com.au) also flies to Kangaroo Island from Adelaide. The **airport shuttle** service that runs to Kingscote must be pre-booked. (☎8553 2390. $14.)

LOCAL TRANSPORTATION

There is no public transportation or taxi service on the island. The limited **Sealink coach service** runs between Kingscote and the ferry terminal in Penneshaw (1hr., $11), stopping in American River (30min.).

BY CAR

Most of the tourist thoroughfares are paved, and unsealed roads leading to major sights are generally in good condition. However, most rental companies do not insure vehicles on unsealed roads, so check ahead before bringing a car over on the ferry. A 4WD provides maximum flexibility. **Complete Ute and 4WD,** in Adelaide, rents to ages 21+ (p. 461). Wildlife is plentiful, and goats or kangaroos often dart across the road. Avoid driving at dusk and dawn when kangaroos are most active.

Rental companies on the island offer free shuttles to the airport in Kingscote and a ferry pickup option. Be sure to plan carefully when renting on the island, as most companies have limited kilometers and the island is larger than most visitors anticipate. **Budget,** 51a Dauncey St., (☎8553 3133) will arrange pickup anywhere on the island, except American River. Show a copy of *Let's Go: Australia* and receive a 10% discount. They rent to those 21 and over, though there is a surcharge for under 25. Hertz affiliate **Kangaroo Island Rental Cars** (☎8553 2390 or 1800 088 296) is on the corner of Franklin St. and Telegraph Rd., Kingscote; they can do car pickup from the ferry by arrangement. For service, call **RAA** (☎8553 2162).

BY TOUR

Most tours are led by friendly, knowledgeable guides and hit the "must-see" sights. The majority are based out of Adelaide. It's advisable to make arrangements before you leave the mainland. However, the YHA in Penneshaw advertises last-minute or standby-option tours at a discount.

CampWild Adventures (☎1800 444 321; www.campwild.com.au) offers a 3-day 4WD camping trip that hits all the big sights at a relaxed pace. Fun activities include sand-boarding, ATV rides, and sleeping under the stars. Departs daily in summer. $395, ISIC/YHA $360. Price includes pickup in Adelaide, ferry with dolphin watching, meals, accommodations, and park entrance. Max. 13 people.

Adventure Tours Australia (☎1300 654 604; www.adventuretours.com.au) offers a good 2-day tour, along with a 3-day tour that hits more remote areas to the east. 2-day "Slippery Seal" Kangaroo Island tour $365. 3-day Adelaide to Melbourne Safari $345.

Wayward Bus (☎1800 882 823; www.waywardbus.com.au) runs a popular 3½-day tour from Adelaide to Melbourne via the Great Ocean Rd. Departs Adelaide Oct.-Apr. M, W, Sa 8:00am; May-Sept. Tu and Sa 8:00am. $295. Price includes all transport, breakfast, park entry fees, and accommodations.

ORIENTATION

Kangaroo Island is Australia's third-largest island (after Tasmania and Melville Island, Northern Territory). The ferry lands in Penneshaw, on the top of Dudley Peninsula. **Hog Bay Road** heads southwest out of town to the narrow strip of land connecting the peninsula to the mainland before curving northwest toward American River and Kingscote. **Playford Highway** heads west from Kingscote through the middle of the island, passing Parndana before ending at Cape Borda on the island's northwestern tip. The **South Coast Road** diverges from the Playford Hwy. 15km west of Kingscote and swings through most of the attractions on the south coast, leading to the main entrance of Flinders Chase National Park, which spans most of KI's west end. The **West End Highway** runs north through Flinders Chase and connects the South Coast Road to the Playford Hwy. All the main roads are sealed, but access roads to many sights along the way are unsealed. The very scenic but unsealed **North Coast Road** is accessible via the Playford Hwy. and leads to the north coast's tranquil beaches.

PRACTICAL INFORMATION

The Gateway Visitors Information Centre is in Penneshaw, on the road to Kingscote, and has information on everything you could ever want to know about the island. There is also an after-hours board outside the office with maps and information. (☎8553 1185. Open M-F 9am-5pm, Sa-Su 10am-4pm.) Keep in mind that the grocery stores on Kangaroo Island have very limited selections, so consider stocking up beforehand. The Island Parks Pass allows unlimited access to Seal Bay, Kelly Hill Caves, Flinders Chase, and the Cape Borda and Cape Willoughby lighthouse tours, but it's probably only worth it to those staying more than a week. (Pass valid for 1yr. Available at the visitors center and park entrances. $43, concessions $34, family $110.) The island's only hospital (☎8553 4200) is in Kingscote.

EAST END

PENNESHAW AND DUDLEY PENINSULA ☎08

Relaxed Penneshaw (pop. 250) is the arrival point for the ferry from Cape Jervis. A quick jaunt up North Terr. from the jetty leads to the **petrol station,** pub, and a few small restaurants. Tiny Nat Turner St. connects North Terr. to Middle Terr., where the **post office** (open M-F 9am-5pm, Sa 9am-noon) and the **Community Business Center**

(**Internet** access $3 per 30min.) are located. The **IGA Welcome-Mart,** on Middle Terr., sells groceries. (Open daily 8am-8pm.)

Each night after sunset, clans of little **fairy penguins** waddle from the sea to their burrows along the coastline. The **Penguin Interpretive Centre** is just east of the ferry dock, off Middle Terr. The boardwalk is closed to the public after dusk, and visitors must pay at the Penguin Centre to see the penguins. (☎8553 1103 or 8553 1016. Tours daily in summer 8:30 and 9:30pm; in winter 7:30 and 8:30pm. Guided tour $9, concessions $7; self-guided tour $6/5; includes Penguin Centre admission.) **Kingscote** also has penguin tours. The best time to see the penguins is Apr.-Jan. On the road to Kingscote, 32km out of town, **Prospect Hill** has hundreds of stairs leading to a 360° view of the east end of the island. Just next to the hill, **Pennington Bay** is an easily accessible beach with great beginner surf and soft sand. On the eastern tip of the Dudley Peninsula and Kangaroo Island, the dramatic Cape Willoughby sees fewer visitors than the rest of the island. For those with a car and time, a stop at **Dudley Wines,** on Willoughby Rd. at Cape Willoughby, will rank among your most memorable dining experiences. The restaurant looks out over the cape cliffs, and their wine is Kangaroo Island's best. (☎8553 1333. Cellar door open daily 11am-5pm.) Another of the island's wineries, **Sunset Winery,** on Hog Bay Rd., 5km out of Penneshaw, also has cellar door tastings. (☎8553 1378. Open daily 11am-5pm.)

Marty's Place ❷, 43 North Terr., acts as a hostel, pizza joint, and **Internet** cafe. The hostel has a small courtyard and kitchen/lounge. (☎8553 1227. Internet access $2 per 10min. Dorms $20; singles $22; doubles $55. Pizzas from $14. Restaurant open daily 5pm-late.) **Kangaroo Island YHA ❷,** 33 Middle Terr., offers six-bed rooms with stove, refrigerator, and bath. (☎8553 1344. Reception daily 9am-1pm and 5:45-7:45pm. Dorms $26.50, YHA $23; double $63.50/60; ensuite $78.50/75.)

Penneshaw has some amazing eateries at equally amazing prices. The best of them, **Penguin Stop Cafe ❶,** on the corner of Nat Thomas St. and Middle Terr., cooks up innovative food using fresh ingredients and meat from a local farm. Don't leave Kangaroo Island without trying their lamb burger, vegetarians excepted. (☎8553 1211. Baguettes $7.50. Smoothies $5. Small Picker's Platter $14. Hours vary and are posted outside the cafe each week. Closed June-July.) **Fish ❶,** 43 North Terr., next to Marty's Place, serves good, simple seafood. (1pc. Fish from $6. Open daily 4:30-8pm. Cash only.) **Hog Bay Stores Cafe,** on Nat Turner St., does takeaway and sit-down meals in their newly renovated store. (☎8553 1151. Takeaway seafood $4.50-13. Burgers $6-8.50. Meals from $13. Open daily in winter 8am-7pm; longer hours in summer.)

SPERM WHALE BANK

Not many people head to the beach hoping to find whale vomit and strike it rich, but that may soon change. In January 2006, Loralee and Leon Wright, a couple from the Eyre Peninsula, came across what appeared to be a tree stump on the beach. They quickly realized that the substance wasn't of arboreal origin, and despite being involved in the area fishing industry, they were baffled as to what the mystery clump was.

Two weeks later they returned, still eager to know what this thing was. It turned out the unidentified object was a rare substance known as ambergris (sperm whale vomit, in layman's terms) and the Wrights made a cool six-figures with their find. Given the typical Australian's drinking habits, most locals know that vomit is something to be avoided. However, ambergris is vomit that has spent years floating around in the ocean, hardening into a waxy gray substance which produces a sweet, musky scent. Perfume companies will pay a hefty price for it, anywhere from US$20-65 per gram. Since only about 1% of sperm whales are thought to release ambergris, the Wrights' discovery of a 14.75kg sample is incredibly valuable and is expected to sell for at least US $295,000. So for all you beach-goers...it may be time to put the metal detector away and have a sniff around instead.

KINGSCOTE ☎08

Kingscote (pop. 1500), Kangaroo Island's largest town, can be a welcome stop for civilization-starved visitors returning from the western end of the island. Chapman St. runs along the water, while most of the shops and services are on **Dauncey Street,** one block up parallel to Chapman. The **National Park Office,** 37 Dauncey St., sells park passes. (☎8553 2381; www.environment.sa.gov.au/parks/kangaroo_is.html. Open M-F 9am-5pm.) Other services include: **tourist info** at the **Kingscote Gift Shop,** 78 Dauncey St., at the corner of Dauncey and Commercial St. (☎8553 2165. Open M-F 9am-5:30pm, Sa-Su 9am-5pm); an **ATM** at Bank SA, on Dauncey St.; **police** (☎8553 2018), on Drew St., one block from the water; free **Internet** access at the **library,** 41 Dauncey St., opposite Bank SA (☎8553 4516; open M 1-5pm, Tu-W and F 9:30am-5pm, Th 9:30am-7pm); **pharmacy** at Dauncey and Murray St. (☎8553 2153; open M-F 8:30am-3:30pm, Sa 9am-noon, Su 10am-noon); and a **post office** on Dauncey St. (☎8553 2122. Open M-F 9am-5pm.) **Postal Code:** 5223.

Ellson's Seaview ❹, on Chapman Terr. on the south side of town, has rooms in a guest house that share a bathroom and are cheaper than those in the main motel. Ask for a sea view. (☎8553 2030. Reception 8am-8:30pm. Guesthouse singles $65; twins and doubles $75. Extra person $15. Motel singles from $125; doubles from $135.) **Kangaroo Island Central Backpackers ❷,** 19 Murray St., is the cheapest accommodation in Kingscote. (☎8553 2787. Dorms $20; doubles $50.) **Roger's Deli and Cafe ❶,** 76 Dauncey St., has an inexpensive selection of 100 different items, including sandwiches (doorstop $9), burgers, and pies, as well as more formal main courses. (☎8553 2053. Main courses $15-16. Open M-F 8am-6pm, Sa-Su 9am-5pm.) At the **Ozone Hotel ❷,** on the corner of Chapman Terr. and Commercial St., local seafood starts at $14. The hotel also runs free wine-tastings; inquire at the bar for times. (☎8553 2011; www.ozonehotel.com. Open daily noon-2pm and 6-8:30pm; bar open daily 11am-midnight.) A **Foodland** supermarket is on the corner of Commercial and Osmond St. (Open M-W and F 8am-6pm, Th 8am-7:30pm, Sa 8am-5pm, Su 10am-4pm.)

The **KI Marine Centre,** located on the wharf, is home to sea dragons and cuttlefish. Tours of the local **penguin burrows** depart from the center at dusk, and **pelicans** get up close and personal during their 5pm feeding. (☎8553 3112. Aquarium $5. Penguin tours in summer 8:30 and 9:30pm; in winter 7:30 and 8:30pm; building opens 30min. before first tour. $10, concessions $8.50. Pelican feedings daily 5pm; $2.) **Kings Fishing Charters** operates at American River, halfway between Penneshaw and Kingscote. (☎8553 7003. min. 4hr. $300 for up to 5 people.) **Southern Ocean Fishing & Diving Safaris** depart from Kingscote and American River on a wide variety of tours from multi-day fishing and diving excursions to day trips. Diving trips come with a sea dragon sighting guarantee. (☎8242 0352; www.kifishchart.com.au or www.divingsafaris.com.au.)

Every year in mid-February, visitors and locals alike flock to Kingscote for the **West End Draught Kangaroo Island Cup Carnival,** a weekend of horse racing, food, and partying. Book ferries and accommodations far in advance.

SOUTH COAST

Many of KI's most traversed sights line the south coast and are accessible via paved South Coast Rd., which heads to Flinders Chase from Cygnet River. In addition, the south coast has the island's best surfing and opportunities for sandboarding, jet skiing, and kayaking.

SIGHTS

SEAL BAY. One of the most popular stops on the island, Seal Bay would probably draw visitors even without the seals. A long stretch of coast with excellent views, the sand here is covered by Australian sea lions. With a total world population of only 12,000, the majority of these wonderful creatures live off the coast of South Australia. The national park interactive guided tour allows beach access and a chance to learn more about the rare species. From the boardwalk down to the beach, the skeleton of a humpback whale can be seen. *(To reach Seal Bay, take Seal Bay Rd. south from South Coast Rd. for 12km. ☎8559 4207; www.parks.sa.gov.au/sealbay. Guided tour $13, concession $10.50. Self-guided tour (no beach access) $9.50/7.50. Tours daily every 45min. 9am-5pm, last tour 4:15pm; summer holiday 9am-6pm. Pre-sunset tour on school holidays $30/24; book far in advance.)*

LITTLE SAHARA. Just like the name suggests, Little Sahara is a small-scale version of the Sahara. A chain of sand dunes rises seemingly out of nowhere. The dunes are understandably popular with sandboarders, and Kangaroo Island Outdoor Action offers rentals. The poorly marked turnoff for Little Sahara is 7km east of Vivonne Bay on South Coast Rd.

VIVONNE BAY. Vivonne Bay, just west of Seal Bay and Little Sahara on South Coast Rd., hides a stunning stretch of sandy **beach** that is ideal for picnics and surfing. Swimming at Vivonne Bay should only be attempted near the boat jetty or in the mouth of the Harriet River—the rest of the waters have a strong undertow. The jetty is a popular fishing spot, while the beach near the Harriet River mouth has excellent surf for beginners. The surf gets larger the further west you go along the beach break. The beach can be accessed from a trail at the campground carpark. The shallow river separates the beach from the campground, so surfers will have to wade across. **Kangaroo Island Outdoor Action,** just west of the general store on South Coast Rd., can fulfill your every outdoor need. A local KI resident rents surfboards, sandboards, and kayaks (½-day $25, full-day $35; wet suit included in surf rental) as well as running various tours. (☎04 2882 2260 or 8559 4296; kioutdoor@adam.com.au. Must book ahead. 90min. ATV tours $60. Jet ski 2hr. tour $300 for 2-3 people.) The Bay is also a good place on the island to fill up on fuel and supplies at the **general store.** The whiting burger ($10.50) is famous among locals. (☎8559 4285. Open daily 8am-7pm.) **Camping ❶** is available near the beach; a caretaker will collect payment at the campground. From the general store, it is 3km down an unsealed road to the beach. (Camping with toilets and water $4.40.)

KELLY HILL. Arguably Kangaroo Island's finest natural attraction, the **Kelly Hill Caves** are located on South Coast Rd. about halfway between Vivonne Bay and the Flinders Chase visitors center. Formed from a sand dune and soft limestone, the cave is visually stunning. **Adventure caving** tours are a lot of fun; crawling though nooks and crannies is the best way to see the smaller, more delicate formations. There is a picnic area near the carpark, as well as several walking trails through surrounding bushland. (☎8559 7231. 45min. 6-7 tours daily. $11, concessions $8.75, family $28. 1½-2hr. adventure tours daily 2:15pm. $27.50, concessions $22, min. $75. Requires regular tour first.) In addition to the caves, a number of trails start at Kelly Hill, including the moderately difficult Hanson Bay Hike (18km round-trip).

HANSON BAY SANCTUARY. This privately owned wildlife sanctuary, 10km west of Kelly Caves and 4km west of the turn-off for Hanson Bay, is one of the island's best koala-viewing spots. **Nocturnal walks and 4WD tours** are held daily at 8:30pm. In the spring, 2-3hr. **4WD wildflower tours** with tea are available. (☎8559 7344 or 04 2739 7344; www.hansonbay.com. 30min. walks from dawn until dusk $2, concession $1, children free. 90min. Nocturnal walks $15/8; with 4WD $20/13. Wildflower tours $30. Book ahead.)

SURFING. Kangaroo Island provides ample opportunities to hit the **surf,** but watch for rip tides and the Great White sharks that frequent these waters. Visit the Kangaroo Island Gateway Visitor Information Centre in Penneshaw for the *Surfing Guide*, which details the breaks along the South Coast at **Hanson Bay, Vivonne Bay,** and **D'Estrees Bay** as well as **Pennington Bay** (p. 483) on the east end and **Stokes Bay** (p. 487) on the north coast. The most convenient of these are Vivonne and Pennington Bays, both accessible via good roads and suitable for all levels of surfers. Hanson and D'Estrees are for advanced surfers, and Stokes only operates when there's a large swell. The water is cool year-round, so bring your wetsuit.

WEST END

You will find few shops and restaurants on the west end of the island, so bring food along. The serene and secluded **Flinders Chase Farm ❶** is the perfect place to stargaze. On an 800 hectare sheep and cattle farm just 15min. north of the park entrance on the West End Hwy., the friendly owners offer self-contained cabins and spotless dorms with full kitchen, BBQ, and bathrooms. (☎8559 7223 or 04 2772 2778; chillers2@bigpond.net.au. Dorms $20, ensuite $30; cabins for 1 or 2 $60/80.) The **Western KI Caravan Park ❷,** 4km east of the Flinders Chase entrance on the South Coast Rd., has a free koala walk. (☎8559 7201; www.westernki.com.au. Sites $18, powered $22; cabins for 2 $100-130, add $20 for single night booking.) The **KI Wilderness Retreat ❸,** on South Coast Rd. just before the entrance to Flinders Chase, offers luxury suites on a 113 acre property with walking trails to be shared with the local wildlife. (☎8559 7275; www.kiwr.com. Suites $120-330.) The resort also has **petrol** and **Internet** access (for guests only $5 per 30min.)

FLINDERS CHASE NATIONAL PARK

Visitors who bypass western Kangaroo Island are missing out on the best the island has to offer. Wildlife is everywhere, and surreal rock formations dot the coastline. The most popular sights are clustered 15-20km south of Rocky River along a sealed road. Just over 100km from Kingscote, the **visitors center** at Rocky River, along the South Coast Rd., sells day passes and camping permits. (☎8559 7235. Open daily 9am-5pm. Multiple day park entry $7.50 flat rate, concessions $6, families $20.) Numerous short **hikes** and excellent 2- to 7-day coastline treks are available in Flinders Chase. Hikers should pick up the all-inclusive *Bushwalking in Kangaroo Island Parks* brochure from any visitors center.

The **Remarkable Rocks,** precariously perched on a 75m coastal clifftop, are huge hunks of granite sculpted into bizarre shapes by 750 million years of erosion by ice, lichens, water, and wind. The hooked beak of Eagle Rock is a perfect spot to snap a picture to send home, but be careful—it's a long fall to the crashing waves below. West of the rocks, a footpath winds to the edge of Cape du Couedic and then to the cave of **Admiral's Arch.** A few thousand New Zealand **fur seals** live here and can be seen sunning themselves.

Flinders Chase National Park has four main **camping sites ❶,** all non-powered and with toilet facilities. The **Rocky River site,** near the visitors center, offers convenience and the only showers in the park; however, the sites are in a dirt clearing ($19 per vehicle). Nine cheaper sites can be found 13km into the park off the road to Cape du Couedic. **Snake Lagoon** has plentiful wildlife. The campground at **West Bay,** 20km west of Rocky River along an unsealed road, is beautifully remote and just 200m from the beach. The campground at **Harvey's Return** is on the north coast. Permits are available for all sites at Rocky River visitors center. Caravans and campervans are allowed only at Rocky River and Snake Lagoon. All sites, excluding Rocky River, are $8 per car and do not include day fees. Availability is posted outside the visitors center. Rustic **cabins ❷** can be rented at Flinders Chase's three lighthouse stations. (☎8559 7235. Linen $15 per person. Lodges $120 plus $15 per person. Book ahead.)

NORTH COAST

Accessible only by unsealed roads and bypassed by most tours, the north coast remains a tranquil oasis on this heavily touristed island. On the island's northwestern tip, the **Cape Borda Lightstation** is remote and surrounded by rugged beauty. Call ahead to see when Bart, the friendly and knowledgeable lightkeeper, is working, as he gives the best tours. Sunsets are spectacular. (☎8559 3257. $11, concessions $8.75, children $6.50, families $29. Tours daily 11am, 12:30, and 2pm; additional tours during school holidays. Cannon fired 1pm.)

The rustic **Heritage Lightkeepers cottages ❶** have a cozy feel. (☎8559 7235. $125 for 2 people, $16 each additional person.) Cape Borda offers a wide range of more expensive lodging; pick up a pamphlet at any visitors center for a listing. Heading east away from Cape Borda and Scott's Cove is the turn-off for the **Ravine des Casoars Hike.** The 8km, 4hr. round-trip hike winds through the woods before emerging at the mouth of a river, finally emptying onto a beach surrounded by cliffs and coastal caves. Few visitors find the time to do the hike, so you will most likely have the whole beach to yourself.

The drive to **Western River Cove,** at the mouth of the Western River, is alone worth the trip. The road winds down to sea level with views of the secluded north coast before ending up at the cove, where a river runs out to one of the north coast's best beaches. To reach the cove follow signs for the turn-off from Playford Hwy., 8km east of its junction with the West End Hwy. **Campsites ❶** here are $3.85 per night. Buy permits at the information center in Penneshaw (☎8553 1185). **Snelling Beach,** about 15km east of Western River Cove, is a larger beach with a long sweep of empty sand and gentle waves well suited to swimmers. From the west, the descent down Constitution Hill offers stunning views of the beach framed by surrounding cliffs and hills. **Paul's Place,** on Stokes Bay Rd., offers a hands-on wildlife experience including the opportunity to pet a snake and koala. (☎8559 2232. Hours vary seasonally; open school holidays noon-3pm; call ahead. $11, children $7.) **Stokes Bay,** at the end of Stokes Bay Rd. from Playford Hwy., is a popular beach that has big surf swells in the right conditions and camping ($10, book through cafe). **Rockpool Cafe ❷** serves up fine fish 'n' chips ($8-16) looking out on Stokes Bay. They also sell bait for those wishing to wet a line. (☎8559 2277. Open Oct.-Apr. daily 10am-5pm.) Eighteen kilometers northwest of Kingscote, **Emu Bay** is yet another stunning beach with **campsites ❶.** (☎8553 2015. Pay at site, $3.85.)

CENTRAL WINE REGIONS

The center of South Australia's wine universe is 70km northeast of Adelaide in the Barossa Valley. Grapes from the Barossa region produce some of Australia's best wines, particularly Shiraz. The Clare Valley, 45min. north of Barossa, is filled with smaller wineries that specialize in Rieslings and other cool climate whites. For the budget traveler, wine tasting is not only a free buzz, but a cultural endeavor and a chance to take in the scenic rolling valleys of the area.

BAROSSA VALLEY ☎08

Steeped in history and a long tradition of hard-working winemakers, the Barossa Valley is arguably Australia's most well-known wine region. Johann Gramp, a German settler, produced the first crop in 1850 on the banks of Jacob's Creek; in the century and a half since, the Barossa's output has been prolific. Most of Australia's largest wine companies are based here, along with plenty of smaller family operations. Though the vineyards are a fine sight in any season, those visiting during the

SOUTH AUSTRALIA

vintage (from mid-February to late April or early May) will see the vines laden with fruit and taste-test the different types of grapes. Vintage is also the best time to land a **picking job** (see **Short-term Work,** p. 91).

TRANSPORTATION

Renting a car in Adelaide is strongly recommended for those bent on doing a serious wine tour, as many wineries are out of the way. The **Barossa Way loop** from Lyndoch north through Tanunda to Nuriootpa, then west to Angaston and south to Mt. Pleasant, is a breathtaking drive through the region, passing through the main towns and the bulk of the wineries. All of the area visitor centers stock the helpful Barossa Valley pamphlet which has region maps. In addition, Barossa Valley's police are vigilant when it comes to drunk driving, and the legal blood-alcohol limit is .05% (U.S. average is .08% for comparison). In Australia, random breathalyzing is normal, especially in areas where drunk driving is prevalent.

Buses: Barossa Adelaide Coaches (☎8564 3022; www.bvcoaches.com) runs to and from Adelaide (2 each way per day) stopping at: **Angaston** ($15); **Nuriootpa** ($14); and **Tanunda** ($13). Departs from the main bus terminal on Franklin St. in Adelaide.

Taxis: Barossa Valley Taxi, 7 Albert St. in Tanunda, (☎1800 288 294 or 8563 3600). Book early. About $13 from Nuriootpa to Tanunda. 24hr. service.

Automobile Clubs: RAA, in Tanunda (☎8586 6937). For 24hr. service call ☎13 11 11.

Bike Rental: Tanunda Caravan and Tourist Park (☎8563 2784) rents bikes to the general public $10 per hr., $15 per ½-day, $20 per day.

ORIENTATION AND PRACTICAL INFORMATION

The Barossa Valley's main reference points are its three small towns: Tanunda, Nuriootpa, and Angaston. Most of the wineries and tiny hamlets are clustered around them. From Adelaide, take King William St. north to Main North Rd. (A1), and branch off to A20. The **Sturt Highway** (A20) enters the Barossa from the north at Nuriootpa. For a more scenic drive, exit earlier at **Gawler,** where B19, the **Barossa Valley Way,** passes through **Lyndoch** (pop. 1140) and **Rowland Flat** before entering the main town of **Tanunda** (pop. 3500), meaning "water hole," 70km northeast of Adelaide. There, the highway's name changes to **Murray Street** as it continues on to **Nuriootpa** (noor-ee-OOT-pah; pop. 3500), called "Nuri" by the locals. From there, **Nuriootpa Road** leads east to **Angaston** (pop. 2700).

The **Barossa Visitors Centre,** 66-68 Murray St., Tanunda, handles B&B bookings and provides maps. The building also houses the **Barossa Wine Centre,** which has historical exhibits and a short video ($2.50) explaining the development of Barossa as a wine-making valley. (☎1300 852 982 or 8563 0600; www.barossa-region.org. Open M-F 9am-5pm, Sa-Su 10am-4pm.) The banks in the valley all have **ATMs.** The **Nuriootpa Library,** on Murray St. on the south edge of town, has free **Internet** access. (☎8562 1107. Open M-W and F 9am-5pm, Th 9am-7pm, Sa 9am-noon, Su 2-4pm. No Internet on weekends.) The **post office,** on Murray St. in Tanunda, is near the visitors center. (Open M-F 9am-5pm.)

ACCOMMODATIONS

Lodging in Tanunda tends to be more expensive than in Nuriootpa or Angaston as there are more upscale B&Bs to choose from. That said, there are still plenty of affordable places to stay in the area.

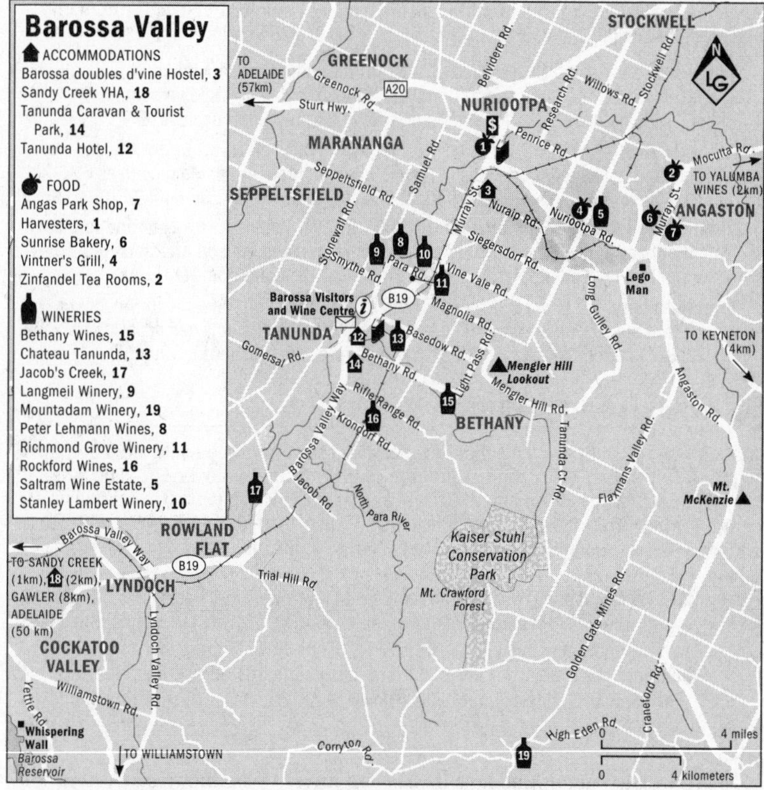

Barossa doubles d'vine Hostel (☎8562 2260), on Nuraip Rd., Nuriootpa. This small hostel is surrounded by a flourishing vineyard and has an outdoor sitting area and garden-enclosed pool. Rooms are clean and high-ceilinged. Wood-burning stove in the lounge area. Free laundry. Jan, the friendly owner, is always up for a chat, and has maps and will offer advice about activities. Bike rentals $15 per day. Doubles $55, multi-night $45. Cottage double with linen $65/55. Extra person $20. Cash only. ❷

Tanunda Hotel, 51 Murray St. (☎8563 2030), Tanunda, within walking distance of many shops and restaurants, has very nice rooms and a bar that's popular with locals on weekends. Singles $50; ensuite $60; doubles $70/80. ❹

Tanunda Caravan and Tourist Park (☎8563 2784), just south of Tanunda on Barossa Valley Way. Convenient location. BBQ, information kiosk, coin laundry, and camp kitchen. Wheelchair accessible. Books tours and rents bikes. Internet access $2 per 20min., wireless $10 per hr. Key deposit $20. Sites $13, Sites for 2 $20, powered sites $25; cabins $59-130; caravans $49. Discount with extended stay. ❶

FOOD

As a wine region, Barossa has a number of cellar doors that also have cafes and bistros; the tourist office provides a list of all such wineries. For those hoping to have a picnic on one of the immaculate lawns, **Angas Park Shop,** 3 Murray St. in

Angaston, sells snack food, including dried fruit, chocolate, and dried fruit in chocolate. (☎8561 0800; www.angaspark.com.au. Open M-Sa 9am-5pm, Su 10am-5pm.)

Harvesters, 29 Murray St. (☎8562 1348), in the main strip in Nuriootpa, is a trendy, friendly bistro on the main street. Candle-lit atmosphere at night. Main courses $17-22. Open Tu-Sa for lunch, F-Sa for dinner; closing times vary with business. ❹

Vintner's Grill (☎8564 2488), on Nuriootpa Rd. between Nuri and Angaston. Very upscale and renowned for its cuisine. Immaculate outdoor patio. Main courses $26-30. Lunches around $15. Open M-Sa noon-2:30pm and 6:30-9pm, Su noon-2:30pm. ❺

Zinfandel Tea Rooms, 58 Murray St. (☎8563 2822), Tanunda, is a cute and laid-back cafe that has sandwiches and German fare as well as morning and afternoon tea. Everything under $14. Full breakfast $13.90. Open daily 8:30am-5pm. ❷

Sunrise Bakery, 28 Murray St. (☎8564 2070), in Angaston, has cheap, freshly baked goods that are a good start to the day or nice for a quick bite between cellar doors. Pies $2.75-3.75. Open M-F 9am-5:30pm, Sa 9am-4pm, Su 10:30am-3:30pm. ❶

SOUTH AUSTRALIA

WINERIES OF BAROSSA VALLEY

A complete tour of the more than 50 wineries that offer free cellar door tastings requires Herculean effort and Olympian ability to hold your liquor. The **vintage** lasts February through April and is the time to find **picking jobs.** (Call the visitors center for information on harvest work or the Australia-wide ☎1800 062 332). Most wineries in Barossa are open daily from 10am to 4 or 5pm.

BE WINE SAVVY. Don't be tempted to buy a wine just because it's won an award. The efficient tourism industry has created so many competitions that virtually every winery has been recognized for some "outstanding" achievement or another. Most cellar door-workers are knowledgeable about their vineyard's wines and love relaying information. However, let your own palate be your guide.

BY FOOT

If you're worried about finding a designated driver, four wineries just north of Tanunda are connected by the bike- and pedestrian-friendly **Para Road Wine Path.** On the left side of Barossa Valley Way as you head north out of Tanunda, you'll find the first, **Stanley Lambert Winery,** which makes a divine chocolate Port. (☎8563 3375; www.stanleylambert.com.au. Open M-F 10am-5pm, Sa-Su 11am-5pm.) Not far away on Para Rd., **Richmond Grove Winery,** in a chateau-style building on the banks of the small Para River, specializes in Rieslings and allows picnics among the gum trees. (☎8563 7303; www.richmondgrovewines.com. Free basket press tours in season 12:30 and 1:15pm. Open daily 10:30am-4:30pm.) Down the Wine Path, **Peter Lehmann Wines** showcases colorful, modern paintings that match the labels on his wines. They also have a cafe, and the $20 platter is a nice complement to the wines. (☎8563 2100; www.peterlehmannlnwines.com. Open M-F 9:30am-5pm, Sa-Su 10:30am-4:30pm.) **Langmeil Winery,** the last winery on the trail, has a good tasting range in a historic cellar door dating from the 1840s. (☎8563 2595; www.langmeil-winery.com.au. Open daily 10:30am-4:30pm.)

BY TOUR

Most Barossa tours are full-day, round-trip outings departing daily from Adelaide in small buses of about 20 people. The visitors center in Tanunda has numerous brochures on tours, including helicopter rides, balloon rides, and forays across the countryside via vintage car. **Groovy Grape Getaways** is the most popular backpackers tour to Barossa, visiting four wineries, the Whispering Wall, and the world's largest rocking horse along the way. (☎1800 661 177 or 8371 4000. BBQ lunch and pickup included. $69.) **Enjoy Adelaide** has been running tours for 16 years. (☎8332 1401 or 04 1215 3443. $64, children $38; ½-day tour $40/20.) If you're staying in Barossa, **Valley Tours** has a full-day winery and sights tour. (☎8563 3587. $47 including lunch, pickup, and return to Barossa Valley accommodations. Full-day without lunch $40, ½-day $29.)

BY CAR

For those not confined to wineries within walking distance, the options seem endless. While you're more likely to see familiar wines at the bigger producers, the small wineries offer a more intimate setting and a better chance to learn about wines from the people who actually make them.

Château Tanunda (☎8563 3888; www.chateautanunda.com), on Basedow Rd. off Murray St. in Tanunda. Largest château in the southern hemisphere, the winery looks like a French château set in an English garden. Wines as beautiful as the grounds. For $24, you can play a game of croquet on their perfectly manicured lawn, enjoying a cheese plate and 2 glasses of wine at the outdoor tables. Basket press tour and barrel tastings available during harvest season. Open daily 10am-5pm.

Yalumba Wines, Eden Valley Rd. (☎8561 3200; www.yalumba.com), in Angaston. A friendly winery with extensive and beautiful grounds. They have a number of labels and a wide selection, usually 30-35, of wines available for tasting, making Yalumba a good introduction to the various types of wine in the region. Open daily 10am-5pm.

Rockford Wines (☎1800 088 818 or 8563 2720), on Krondorf Rd. east of Tanunda. Small winery that strongly emphasizes the winemaking history of the region and the traditional methods of the Barossa Valley. Stone cottages enclose a courtyard where grapes are crushed in traditional basket presses. Emphasis on craftsmanship and quality. Ranked as one of the Top 10 South Australian Cellar Doors of 2002. The 2001 Eden Valley Riesling is superb, as is the 2003 Alicante Bouchet. Tastings of local jams and spreads offered also. Open daily 11am-5pm.

Bethany Wines (☎8563 2099; www.bethany.com.au.), on Bethany Rd. just east of Tanunda. Former quarry high above the rest of the valley, the owners and cellar door staff will make you feel right at home while you sample their acclaimed Shiraz and Riesling. At vintage time, watch as grapes are dumped into the cliff-top, gravity-fed crusher. Open M-Sa 10am-5pm, Su 1-5pm.

Saltram Wine Estate (☎8561 0200; www.saltramwines.com.au.), on Nuriootpa-Angaston Rd., just outside Angaston. Smooth, fruity, and decadent, Saltram's Semillon is the tops. Acclaimed winery has been working on its fantastic reds, whites, and Ports since 1859. The estate recently opened the popular eatery **Salters Bistro ❺.** Open M-F 9am-5pm, Sa-Su 10am-5pm. Bistro open daily 11:30am-3pm, F-Sa for dinner.

Mountadam Winery (☎8564 1900), on High Eden Road, Eden Valley. Past Williamstown, turn left on Wirra Wirra Rd., and then right on Corryton. Though the vineyards are well out of the way, the 7km drive to this family-owned winery is almost as pleasurable as tasting their renowned Eden Valley Reiseling and Shiraz. Open daily 11am-4pm.

SIGHTS AND FESTIVALS

Designated drivers, take heart: not every attraction in Barossa requires drinking. **Mengler Hill Lookout,** on Mengler Hill Rd. east of Tanunda, near Bethany on Tourist Rte. 4, gives a bird's-eye view of all those grapes you've been tasting and also features a sculpture park. Take Tanunda Creek Rd. off Mengler's Hill Rd. to the **Kaiser Stuhl Conservation Park** for a guaranteed kangaroo sighting. An entire colony lives and breeds along the Stringybark Loop Trail (2.4km, 1hr. round-trip) and the longer Wallowa Loop Trail (6.5km, 2hr. round-trip). On the road linking Williamstown and

Sandy Creek, the **Barossa Reservoir** retains over 4500 Olympic-size swimming pools' worth of water. Its most interesting feature is its famous curved **Whispering Wall,** where sweet nothings can be heard 140m away. (☎8204 1437. Open daily 8am-4:30pm.) Festivals abound in Barossa Valley. Foremost among these is the biannual **Barossa Vintage Festival** (☎8563 0600. Late Mar. and early Apr. 2007), a celebration of all things viticultural, including traditional barefoot grape-stomping. Every October, the **Barossa International Music Festival** (☎8564 2511) celebrates the arrival of spring.

CLARE VALLEY ☎08

Between Adelaide and the South Australian Outback, the Clare Valley is the final oasis before the earthy tones of the Flinders Ranges take command of the landscape. The town is small and centered around the wine of the valley with some 30-odd vineyards running north from Auburn along the Main North Rd. The higher altitude offers a respite from some of the lowland heat associated with the Yorke Peninsula, providing the perfect climate for the valley's farmhouse Rieslings.

ORIENTATION AND PRACTICAL INFORMATION. **Main North Road** shoots straight through Clare Valley's small center. **Old North Road,** one block eastward, runs parallel to the Main North Rd. and contains some businesses of interest. At the north end of town, **Farrell Flat Road** heads east through the hills toward Burra. The **Clare Valley Visitor Information Centre** is south of town on the corner of Spring Gully and Main North Rd. (☎8842 2131. Open M-Sa 9am-5pm, Su 10am-4pm.) The banks along Main North Rd. have **ATMs.** Services include free **Internet** access at the **Clare Library,** 33 Old North Rd., one block east of the post office. (☎8842 3817. Open Tu-W and F 10am-6pm, Th 10am-8pm, Sa 10am-noon.) and a **police** station (☎8842 2711) on Main North Rd. The **post office,** 253 Main North Rd., is open M-F 9am-5pm. **Postal Code:** 5453.

ACCOMMODATIONS AND FOOD. Built in 1848, the historic **Clare Hotel ❷,** 244 Main North Rd., has traditional pub rooms. (☎8842 2816. Pub rooms with shared bath $25 per person; ensuite motel singles with TV $50; ensuite doubles $55.) The award-winning **Clare Caravan Park ❶,** 3km south of town on Main North Rd., has a pool, laundry (wash $3), and is located near many winery tours. (☎8842 2724. Reception 8am-7pm. Sites $18, powered $24; cabins for 2 $55-84. Mountain bikes $12 per ½-day, $20 per day.) Clare has two supermarkets: **Woolworths Foodland,** 47 Old North Rd. (Open M-Sa 8am-7pm, Su 9am-5pm) and **IGA,** across from the post office on Main North Rd. (Open daily 8am-8pm.) The **Main Street Bake-house ❷,** 269 Main North Rd., has been churning out pies ($3-3.50), pasties, and sausage rolls for over a century. (☎8842 2473. Open M-F 8am-5pm, Sa 9am-4pm, Su 10am-4pm.) The rustic, stone-covered **Chaff Mill Country Kitchen ❸,** 308 Main North Rd., has daily ciabatta specials ($10), and formal meals from $19. (☎8842 3055. Open Tu-F 11:30am-2:30pm and 5:30pm-latenight, Sa 9:30am-2:30pm and 5:30pm-latenight, Su 9am-2:30pm and 5:30-latenight.) South of Clare near the caravan park, **Coffee and Cork ❷,** 12 Main North Rd., serves modern Australian cuisine (main courses $21-27; entrees $11.50) in a classic setting, perfect for a relaxing afternoon. (☎8842 3477. Outdoor seating available. Open M and F-Sa 11am-latenight, Su 9am-latenight.) In the historic town of **Mintaro,** southeast of Clare, the **Magpie and Stump Hotel,** Burra Rd., is worth a visit. The bar has a real local feel and bakes its breads fresh every day in its impressively large wood oven. (☎8843 9014. Baguettes $7.50. Main courses from $14. Lunch daily noon-2pm. Dinner M-Sa 6pm-latenight.)

WINERIES OF CLARE VALLEY. The granddaddy of Clare wines is the famous **Riesling,** though nearly every other grape and wine variety in the region is starting to catch up. An old railway line, parallel to Main North Rd., has been converted into the 27km scenic **Riesling Trail.** The trail runs between Clare and Auburn, and is suitable for walking and biking. Convenient carparks in Clare, Sevenhill, Watervale, and Auburn allow walkers to take shorter journeys. The trail passes farms and vineyards, as well as a few wineries.

At **Sevenhill Cellars,** 6km south of Clare on College Rd. in Sevenhill, the Jesuit owners have been producing wine since 1851. You can access the winery's underground storage cellar and the small adjoining historical museum. (☎8843 4222; www.sevenhillcellars.com.au. Open daily 9am-5pm.) **Leasingham Wines,** just south of town center on 7 Dominic St., is a perennial medal-winner and venerable institution. The winery is graced with a lovely setting and small wine-making museum. (☎8842 2785; www.brlhardy.com.au. Open M-F 8:30am-5pm, Sa-Su 10am-4pm.)

Every January, Annie's Lane (☎8843 2204) hosts A Day on the Green (www.adayonthegreen.com.au), a concert tour that draws the biggest names in Australian music. The venue, a large outdoor amphitheater, makes for a night of good music and good wine. Tickets available through Ticketmaster (☎13 61 00; www.ticketmaster7.com) and Venuetix (☎8225 8888; www.venuetix.com.au), as well as Annie's Lane.

SOUTH AUSTRALIA

TOURS. Bikes can be rented in Clare from **Clare Valley Cycle Hire,** 32 Victoria Rd., in a private house opposite the primary school (☎8842 2782 or 0418 802 077; ½-day $17, full-day $25; open daily 8am-6pm; pickup and delivery options available), from Sevenhill Cellars, or the caravan park (p. 492). The tourist office also has info on many private tours, including **Clare Valley Experiences** (☎8843 4169; www.visitclarevalley.com.au; $60 per hr. in Mercedes; 3hr. min.) and **Clare Valley Tours.** (☎04 1883 2812; www.cvtours.com.au. $50 per 4hr., $70 with lunch.)

LIMESTONE COAST REGION

This region boasts two national parks, many smaller conservation parks, a number of quiet seaside towns, and a significant amount of—you guessed it—limestone. The coast has also annexed some inland towns and attractions, including the blue lakes of the area's largest city, Mt. Gambier, and the caves at Naracoorte.

Though the region is best seen by car, **Premier Stateliner buses** (☎8415 5500) pass through daily on the Adelaide to Mt. Gambier run. The best place to start any Limestone Coast adventure is at one of the helpful information offices that bookend the region: **The Signal Point Interpretive Centre** in Goolwa in the north (☎8555 3488; open daily 9am-5pm) and the **visitors center** in Millicent in the south (☎8733 0904; open in summer M-F 9am-5pm, Sa-Su 9:30am-4:30pm; in winter M-F 9am-5pm, Sa-Su 10am-4pm). Both offer the *Limestone Coast Secrets* information booklet and *The Tattler*, the essential publication covering the Coorong and other area parks.

SOUTH FROM FLEURIEU PENINSULA: PRINCES HIGHWAY

The road from Tailem Bend south toward Mount Gambier runs along Coorong National Park, providing excellent access to both the wetlands of the coast and the beaches farther south. **Meningie** is the gateway for travelers heading south into the Coorong (p. 494) and is a nice place for a quick swim. The **National Parks and Wildlife Service,** 34 Princes Hwy. (☎8575 1200) has the latest park conditions as well as *The Tattler*, which details hiking trails and camping areas for southeastern coastal parks from Goolwa to the Victoria border. The **Melaleuca Center,** 76 Princes Hwy., has information on the Coorong and camping permits. (☎8575 1259. Open M-F 9am-5pm, Sa-Su 10:30am-2:30pm.) **Kingston SE,** at the other end of the Coorong, is a jumping-off point for travelers approaching the park from the south. What Kingston lacks in population, it makes up for in size with the 17m tall **Larry the Lobster.** The four-ton red-metal crustacean is next door to a **petrol** station, a diner, and an unmanned **information center** with brochures (open daily 6am-8pm).

COORONG NATIONAL PARK

The Coorong is a long, narrow stretch of pure white sand dunes, dry salt lakes, and glittering lagoons that provides temporary refuge for many species of unusual migratory birds. Australia's longest riverway, the **Murray,** passes through the park to the Murray Mouth and empties into the Southern Ocean. The best way to access the park's northern reaches is by **boat** from Goolwa (p. 479), at the mouth of the Murray River on the Fleurieu Peninsula. However, you can visit a remote, northerly section of the park by taking the **road off the Princes Highway to Narrung,** crossing the water on the free 24hr. ferry. The 20km unsealed road is easily accessible with 2WD vehicles. It passes freshwater **Lake Alexandrina** and spectacular, rolling farmlands. A turn-off leads to **Pelican Point,** home to dozens of the large-beaked birds and more graceful swans. The **Signal Point Interpretive Centre** in Goolwa can book tours along the Murray River. **Spirit of the Coorong** offers half- and full-day eco-cruises. (☎1800 442 203; www.coorongcruises.com.au. Pickup from Adelaide available. ½-day cruise year-round M and Th and Oct.-May Tu and Sa. $70, concessions $66, children $52. Full-day cruise Oct.-May W-Su, June-Sept. Su $84/78/57.)

Princes Highway skirts much of Coorong National Park and passes scenic lookouts along the way, as well as a number of campgrounds, historic sites, and walking trails (all described at great length in the essential *Tattler*). About 5km south of where the Loop Rd. rejoins the Princes Hwy., a marked turn-off for the **42 Mile Crossing** leads down an unsealed road past the spectral outlines of several lakes 3km to a campsite, where a 4WD track through the dunes leads to the beach. For those without a 4WD vehicle, this point also represents the most convenient pedestrian access to the beach (20min. one-way).

Campsites ❶ are available at Pranka Point, the 42 Mile Crossing, and along Loop Rd. and Old Coorong Rd. The sites at Pranka Point and the 42 Mile Crossing are among the few in the area that have water and toilets. Permits ($6 per car per night) are required for camping and can be obtained via self-registration or at most gas stations and info centers along the Coorong section of the Princes Hwy. For a budget snack, many people dig into the sand at the ocean's edge to find **cockles.**

ROBE ☎08

Forty-one kilometers farther south and surrounded by water on three sides, Robe is an upscale beach town with more than its fair share of eateries, Victorian buildings, and good surf. Hwy. B101 passes through Robe becoming Main Rd., then Victoria St., and finally Mundy Terr. There is **tourist information** and free **Internet** access at the **Robe Institute and Library,** on Mundy Terr. opposite the foreshore. (☎8768 2465. Open M-F 9am-5pm, Sa-Su 10am-4pm.) **Campbell Cottages ❹,** 26 Smillie St., one block up from the visitors center, rents delightful heritage cottages at fantastic prices. Each cottage has a full kitchen, sitting area with wood fireplace, and outdoor BBQ. (☎8768 2932; campbell@seol.net.au. Doubles $80.) **Lakeside Manor Backpackers ❸,** 22 Main Rd., on the outskirts of town in an old mansion, is reason enough to visit Robe. This new hostel, complete with incredibly helpful owners, a plethora of amenities, and a quiet location, is the perfect place to unwind. (☎8768 1995 or 1800 155 350; www.lakeside-manorbackpackers.com.au. Internet $5 per hr. Free pickup. Dorms $24; doubles $65, ensuite $90.) The YHA-affiliated **Long Beach Caravan Park ❸,** at Long Beach on the Esplanade, has camping as well as backpacker accommodations and is a perfect place for a dip, either at the nearby beach or in the pool. (☎8768 2237; www.robe-longbeach.com. Reception daily 8am-9pm. Sites $26, powered $28; cabins $50-110.)

Camping ❶ areas with toilets, but no other facilities, are available within **Little Dip Conservation Park.** The **Stony Rise campground** ($6.50 on-site registration) has sites 1km down a remote, rocky dirt road that is difficult without a 4WD, though possible with 2WD in good weather. The road past the campground leads to the beach. You can come within 800m of the shore, but beyond the base of the hill where the road forks it becomes 4WD-accessible only. On Robe St., near the **Beacon Hill Lookout,** the **Gums campground** (register on-site; $6) is easier to access.

The **Wild Mulberry Cafe ❸,** at the corner of Robe and Victoria St., serves delicious smoked chicken pizza with goat cheese, spinach, and garlic ($15.50). They also have an array of homemade cakes and desserts. (☎8768 2488. Open daily 8am-5pm; earlier when quiet, later in summer.) Fish 'n' chips can be found at the **Robe Seafood and Takeaway ❶,** 21 Victoria St. Cheap food and long lines characterize this local favorite. (☎8768 2888. Open M-Th 11am-8pm, F-Su 10am-8pm. Cash only.) For unique fare, try the upscale **Gallerie Restaurant ❹,** 2 Victoria St. The "Front Room" section of the restaurant has a cheaper but more basic menu. (☎8768 2256. Entees $18.50-25.50. Open daily 10am-latenight.) The **Foodland** supermarket, on the main road is open daily 7:30am-7:30pm.

With all of the town's available waterfront property, there is certainly no shortage of activities seaside. The beaches in town are good for swimming, diving, and snorkeling, while Stony Rise has heavy surf for experienced surfers. Beginner surfers can rent soft boards from **Steve's Place Surf Shop,** on the main road. The board outside gives the latest surf conditions. (Open in summer daily 9am-5pm; in winter M-F 9am-5pm, Sa 9am-12:30pm, Su 10am-12:30pm.)

SOUTH AUSTRALIA

BEACHPORT ☎08

Forty-eight kilometers south of Robe, Beachport (pop. 440), is a sleepy little town that forces guests to relax. Railway Terr. is the main road through town and connects the jetty to the highway. Premier **buses** stop through Beachport at Jarmos Bus Depot on their way to Mt. Gambier (twice daily) and Adelaide (twice daily). The **Beachport Visitors Centre** is along Millicent Rd. as you enter town. (☎8735 8029. **Internet** access $3 per 30min. Open in summer M-F 9am-5pm, Sa-Su 10am-4pm; in winter M-F 9am-5pm, Sa-Su 11am-2pm.) The friendly **Bompass By the Sea ❷** faces the water near the jetty in a wonderfully restored historic building dating from 1876. Ensuite doubles open onto a wrap-around balcony with views of the jetty. The backpacker rooms don't have the view but are still airy and bright. The cafe/restaurant serves good inexpensive meals from $12. (☎8735 8333; beachportharbourmasters@bigpond.com. Backpackers $25. Ensuite doubles from $55). Bompass also runs Beachport Harbour Masters across the road. (Self-contained units with spa $120-190.) The **Beachport Caravan Park ❶,** the first left off the beach road heading into town, has laundry, BBQ, a playground, and beach views. (☎8735 8128. No linen provided. Unpowered sites $17, powered $19. On-site caravan from $40 in high season, $33 low-season; cabins from $60.) Near the jetty, **The Green Room ❶,** 18 Railway Terr., serves as a video store and sandwich/pizza shop. Their homemade burgers ($6.10) and fish 'n' chips are a good budget option; everything is under $15.50. (Open M-Th 11am-8pm, F-Sa 11am-9pm.)

Wendy's Walk, (30min. round-trip) on McArthur Pl. in the south side of town, is a picturesque ramble among shrubs and hilly sand dunes. The path ends close to its starting point at the caravan park. **Bowman's Scenic Drive** begins just past the walk, winding along the coast with numerous lookout vistas along the way. It passes by the **Pool of Siloam,** a swimming area seven times saltier than the ocean. Beachport's sister city **Southend** (pop. 298) is the gateway to the oft-neglected **Canunda National Park,** which encompasses 23,000 acres of coastal habitat and nearly 50km of coast between Southend and Cape Banks to the south. The park's main attraction in the Southend region is Cape Buffon, where the **Cape Buffon Loop** traverses the cliff tops and provides some outstanding lookouts of the limestone caves and hollows that line the ocean (1hr., 2.5km). The helpful **Visitors Information Centre** in nearby Millicent is convenient for visitors to Southend. (☎8733 0904. Open in summer M-F 9am-5pm, Sa-Su 9:30am-4:30pm; in winter M-F 9am-5pm, Sa-Su 10am-4pm.)

The **Tantanoola Caves Conservation Park,** 15min. southeast of Millicent and 20min. from Mount Gambier on the Princes Highway, is one of the area's best kept secrets. Tantanoola Cave is one of only two Dolomite caves in Australia, and the iron in the mountains tints the stalactites and stalagmites a spectacular honeyed hue. The treasure of the cave is a natural pool which reflects and multiplies the ceiling decorations for an overwhelming visual effect. The ocean-carved cavern is also Australia's first wheelchair-accessible cave. (☎8734 4153; www.environment.sa.gov.au/parks. Seven 25min. tours daily. $8, concessions $6.)

MOUNT GAMBIER ☎08

Mt. Gambier (pop. 21,000) rests on the side of a volcano. Above the city lies the mysterious Blue Lake, a mile-deep lake that sits in the volcano's crater and shimmers with an intense shade of blue through the warmer months before returning to a bland gray hue around March. Mt. Gambier's size also makes it a good base for exploring the nearby wineries of Coonawarra and the caves of Naracoorte.

TRANSPORTATION AND PRACTICAL INFORMATION. **V/Line buses** (☎8725 5037) stop at the **Coles Express** service station, 100 Commercial St., and run to Adelaide daily (6hr., $53) via the coastal towns of Robe, Beachport, and Kingston or via the inland towns of Naracoorte, Tailem Bend, and Murray Bridge; and to Melbourne (7hr.; M-Sa 2 per day, Su 1 per day; $60) via the Victorian cities of Portland, Port Fairy, Warrnambool, and Geelong. Book at Coles Express.

The **Visitors Centre,** in the **Lady Nelson Centre,** has a huge land-locked ship on its front lawn. (☎1800 087 187 and 8724 9750; www.mountgambiertourism.com.au. Open daily 9am-5pm.) The **library,** in the Civic Centre, near the corner of Commercial St. and Bay Rd., has free **Internet** access. (☎8721 2540. Open M-W and F 9am-6pm, Th 9am-7pm, Sa 9:30-12:30pm.) Internet access is also available at the Lady Nelson Discovery and Information Centre. The **police** are on Bay Rd. (☎8735 1020), and the **post office** is at 30 Helen St. (Open M-F 9am-5pm.) **Postal Code:** 5290.

ACCOMMODATIONS. **The Jail ❷,** off Margaret St., promises to scare wayward visitors straight with a short, voluntary prison sentence. This recently converted jail was "decriminalized" in 1995. The bars on the windows remain, but the atmosphere is more hospitable, if somewhat isolating. (☎8723 0032 or 1800 626 844. Continental breakfast included. Dorms $22; singles $33; doubles $52.) **Blue Lake City Holiday Park ❷,** on Bay Rd. just south of the lake, is spotless, and has a pool, tennis and basketball courts, an 18-hole golf course, outdoor cooking facilities, and is a 2km downhill walk to the CBD. (☎8725 9856. Sites in summer $22, off-season $21; powered $27/26; cabins from $67.) The rooms at the **South Australian Hotel ❷,** 78 Commercial Ave. E., are small but clean with large showers. (☎8725 2404. Singles $25; doubles $45.)

FOOD. The Central Business District is packed with chip shops and takeaway joints, supermarkets and greengrocers. For a quality meal that won't break the bank, **Caffe Belgiorno ❷,** on the corner of Percy and Mitchell St., next to the Oatmill complex, is a local favorite. Its wood-fired pizzas (small from $11, large from $15) have been annually voted among Australia's best. (☎8725 4455. Open daily 11am-late-night.) **Plants on Sturt ❶,** 34 Sturt St., a few blocks off Bay Rd., is a nursery and coffee shop. (☎8725 2236. Open daily 10am-4pm.)

SIGHTS. Bay Rd. goes south through town and meets up with John Watson Dr. to encircle **Blue Lake.** The lake itself fills the crater of a volcano that erupted 4000-5000 years ago and holds nine million gallons of water, which are used as the town's supply. You can only get to the lake's surface on a 45min. tour that goes down to the pumping station in a glass lift. (☎8723 1199. Daily tours every hr. Nov.-Jan. 9am-5pm,

Feb.-May 9am-2pm, June-Aug. 9am-noon, Sept.-Oct. 9am-2pm. $6, children $3, family $17.) Just south of the Blue Lake, by the entrance to the Blue Lake City Holiday Park, a road marked "Wildlife Reserve" leads down to a network of walking tracks that access **Mount Gambier,** the **Devil's Punchbowl,** the now-dry **Leg of Mutton Lake,** and **Valley Lake,** fed by a different source than Blue Lake. The 2.3km walk to the top of the mountain is best attempted in the morning.

While the nearby caves at Naracoorte get all the attention, there are a couple interesting holes in the ground right in the town center. The **Cave Gardens,** at Bay Rd. and Watson Terr., surround the town's original water source and are the centerpiece of the picturesque town square park, which is full of roses and trickling waterfalls. (Always open, lit at night. Free.) Another of Mt. Gambier's caves, **Engelbrecht Cave,** on Jubilee Hwy. West, has two chambers available by 45min tour. (Open daily. Tours $6, children $4.) **Umpherston Sinkhole,** on Jubilee Hwy. East, draws visitors at night when the possums come out to feed in the gardens. (Open all day, floodlit until 1am. Free.)

About 20km north of Mt. Gambier, just past Penola on the road to Naracoorte, lies the **Coonawarra wine region,** a small stretch of vineyards. Twenty wineries in the region, the oldest dating from 1890, offer cellar-door sales and tastings, with a complete listing in the *Food and Wine Guide* available at the Lady Nelson Centre.

SOUTH AUSTRALIA

NARACOORTE ☎08

Naracoorte's primary draw is the magnificent network of underground caves that lie 12km south of town. The famed **Naracoorte Caves** have been named a World Heritage site for their extensive deposits of 500,000-year-old megafauna fossils.

ORIENTATION AND PRACTICAL INFORMATION. Almost everything can be found on one of two streets: **Ormerod (Commercial)** and **Smith Street,** both running parallel on either side of the village green. From the south, the Riddoch Hwy. from Mt. Gambier leads into town, becoming **Gordon Street** before hitting the Village Green. **Premier Stateliner buses** pass through town once a day in each direction (on the inland Mt. Gambier to Adelaide route). Tickets can be bought on the corner of Smith and Jones St. at Naracoorte Batteries. (☎8762 2466; 1hr. to Mt. Gambier, 5hr. to Adelaide.) There is a **visitors center** at the Sheepsback Museum, 36 MacDonnell St. 1km out of town (☎8762 1518 or 1800 244 421; open daily 9am-4pm); brochures can also be found at the pub in the **Naracoorte Hotel.** Services include: **ATMs** and banks in CBD; **library** with free **Internet** access, across from the Naracoorte Hotel (open M 10am-5pm, Tu-W and F 9:30am-5pm, Th 10am-8pm, Sa 8:30am-noon); **pharmacy,** on Smith St.; **police,** 66 Smith St. (☎8762 0466, after hours 131 444; open M-F 8:30am-5pm); and **post office,** 23 Ormerod St. (open M-F 9am-5pm). **Postal Code:** 5271.

ACCOMMODATIONS AND FOOD. Naracoorte Backpackers ❷, 4 Jones St., a few blocks up the hill from the Village Green, is a hostel popular with backpackers doing local picking work. The hostel, though comfortable, has common areas that are in need of some renovations. The hostel tends to be in a state of disorder, but the multiple lounge areas give the place a friendly feel. (☎8762 3835 or 04 3982 3835. Internet access $1 per 10min. or $3 per 40min. Dorms $20.) The **Naracoorte Hotel-Motel ❸,** 73 Ormerod St., across from the village green, offers a nice balcony and standard-issue hotel rooms. (☎8762 2400. Hotel singles $35; doubles $55; motel room $75.) Ten kilometers out of town on the way to Mt. Gambier, **Bool Lagoon ❷** provides toilets, but no showers, and permits via on-site self-registration ($16 per car, $8 per motorbike). The **campground ❷** at the caves has toilets, showers, BBQ area, free laundry facilities, and power. Sites are on nice plots of grass, but the area is rather exposed. Follow signs for the Naracoorte Caves. The campground is 300m past the caves at the sign for the Wonambi Fossil Center. (☎8762 2340. $19 on-site registration.)

Maddie's Cafe ❶, on Smith St., is a narrow, understated cafe with tasty, inexpensive sandwiches ($5-6; focaccia $7.50) and large coffees. The apple and almond slice ($3.50) is divine. (☎8762 3953. Open M-F 8:30am-5pm, Sa 9am-2:30pm.) In the Naracoorte Hotel, **Billy Mac's ❸** serves typical pub fare and local wines. The daily special of fish, chicken, or beef is a bargain at $7.50. (Main dishes $10-22. Kitchen open daily noon-2pm and 6-8:30pm, later for drinks.) **Woolworths** supermarket, next to Naracoorte Backpackers, off Jones St., is the place to go to make your own meals while in Naracoorte or to stock up on supplies for camping. (Open M-F 7am-10pm, Sa 9am-9pm, Su 8am-8pm.)

CAVE TOURS. The **Naracoorte Caves National Park** is 12km from the center of town off Rt. 66. The area is well-marked, and the caves are easy to find from the highway and the town. Along with the Riversleigh site 2000km away in northwest Queensland, the caves here are one of only two fossil sites in Australia awarded World Heritage protection. All caves except for the **Wet Cave** are accessible by guided tour. The most famous of the caves, the **Victoria Fossil Cave,** was discovered in 1969, when two cavers wriggled through a tiny passage and emerged in the large chamber where they discovered half-million-year-old fossils. Victoria Fossil is also the only wheelchair accessible cave. (Call ahead to arrange.) The massive **Bat Cave** is home to more than 45,000 bats. Tours inside the cave are not permitted, but you can take a sneak peak at the bat activity from a television. Visit at dusk to watch the colony fly out of the cave for their evening meal. **Alexandra Cave** has three chambers and beautiful decorations.

The **Cathedral Cave** tour is only available on weekends, and focuses more on the geology of the caves. Hard hats are required. ($13, concessions $10.) **Adventure Caving** is an spelunking trip that allows you to squeeze in and out of nooks while taking in the caves. Book in advance. (☎8762 2340. $27.50/20. Buy tickets for the cave tours at the Wonambi Fossil Centre, next to the carpark.) A display re-creates the environment thought to have surrounded the caves 200,000 years ago. (Open daily 9am-5pm. Wet Cave or Fossil Centre $6.50/5. Cave tours daily 9:30, 10:15, 11:30am, 1:30, 2:15, and 3:30pm. 1 cave $11, concessions $8.50, children $6.50; 2 caves $17.50/13.50/10.50; 3 caves $24/18.50/14.50; 4 caves $30.50/23.50/18.50.)

YORKE PENINSULA

On boot-shaped Yorke, sandy flats punctuate rolling farmland, and the sheer cliffs that loom over the hinterland storm into the sea. Sometimes called the "golden plains," the area's extraordinary fertility has made it one of South Australia's leading grain-producing regions. While agriculture may not exactly captivate visitors, the isolated coastline and fishing spots certainly will. Native fauna still claims the bottom of the peninsula in Innes National Park, where rare birds take refuge from the wind and surfers battle some of South Australia's biggest and baddest waves.

COPPER TRIANGLE ☎08

Known as the Copper Triangle, the northern towns of **Kadina, Wallaroo,** and **Moonta** sprang up as a result of discoveries of large copper deposits in the 1860s. Today, the historic towns survive on the seasonal influx of Adelaide weekenders during holidays. Wallaroo (an approximation of the Aboriginal word for "wallaby urine") is on the ocean. Kadina is the largest and has the most services, while Moonta plays its Cornish and mining heritage to the hilt.

ORIENTATION AND PRACTICAL INFORMATION. Kadina, 50km northwest of Port Wakefield, is the farthest inland. Wallaroo is another 9km west of Kadina on the coast. Forming the bottom of the triangle, Moonta is 17km southwest of Kadina and 16km south of Wallaroo. **Premier Stateliner** runs **buses** from Adelaide via Port Wakefield to all three towns. (☎8415 5555; www.premierstateliner.com.au. Buses depart from Adelaide M-F 2 per day, Sa-Su 1 per day. $22, concessions $14.) The **Moonta Station Visitors Centre,** at the end of Blyth St., in the old railway station, stocks a number of handouts about local lore as well as local recipes for the much-touted cornish pasties. (☎8825 1891. Open daily 9am-5pm.) The **Farm Shed Museum and Tourist Centre,** Kadina, has info on the whole Peninsula and a knowledgeable, helpful staff. (☎8821 2333 or 1800 654 991. Books tours for mining expeditions. Free **Internet** access. Open M-F 9am-5pm, Sa-Su 10am-3:30pm.) Kadina and Wallaroo have **ATMs.** There is also free Internet at the **Kadina Community Library,** 1a Doswell Terr., (☎8821 0444. Open Tu-F 9am-5pm.) Kadina has the area **police** station (☎8828 1100). There is a **post office** in each town. (All open M-F 9am-5pm.) **Postal Code:** 5554 (Kadina), 5556 (Wallaroo), 5558 (Moonta).

SOUTH AUSTRALIA

ACCOMMODATIONS. The only backpacker accommodations on the peninsula can be found at the **Iron Horse Junction YHA ❸,** 7 Frances Terr., Kadina. The hostel, decked out in a rail station theme, has the rare amenities of satellite television and a spa tub. Reg, the owner, also runs Harley tours ($80 per hr.) of the Yorke Peninsula coast. (☎8821 3886 or 04 0937 0991. Dorm $30; double $65.) Refuge from pubs can also be found at the beautiful **Sonbern Lodge Motel ❸,** 18 John Terr., Wallaroo; look for the large two-story building near the rail line. (☎8823 2291. Singles $30, ensuite $54; doubles $46/70; deluxe motel singles $74; doubles $90.) In Kadina, the **Wombat Hotel ❷,** 19 Taylor St., has pub rooms and cheap meals from $6.50. (☎8821 1108. Light breakfast included. Singles $30; doubles $40.) Or try the **Kadina Hotel ❹,** 29 Taylor St., which has nice ensuite rooms. (☎8821 1008. Continental breakfast included. Singles $50; doubles $70.) In Moonta, the **Cornwall Hotel ❷,** 20 Ryan St., has cheap counter meals and nice rooms. (☎8825 2304. Singles $30; doubles $50; discount for longer stays. Pub open daily noon-2pm and 6-8pm for meals. Lunch specials $6.50, main dishes $10-16.) There is a caravan park at Moonta Bay and three more along Wallaroo's waterfront, the best of the bunch being the **North Beach Caravan Park ❶.** (☎8223 2531. Office open M-Th 8:30am-6pm, F-Sa 8:30am-7pm, Su 8:30am-5:30pm. Sites $12-14, powered $18-20; cabins for 2 $80-105, with spa $120-120.)

FOOD. The entire Yorke Peninsula is famous for its Cornish cuisine, especially the pasties (about $2.50), but only Moonta is bold enough to claim the moniker "Australia's Little Cornwall." **The Boat Shed Restaurant ❷,** on Jetty Rd., Wallaroo, makes fantastic fish ($11-24) and pizza. (☎8823 3455. 9" pizza $9-13; 12" $11-16. Takeaway counter open daily 11am-9pm; dining room Th-Su 6pm-latenight.) Moonta's impeccably kept **Cornish Kitchen ❶,** 10-12 Ellen St., serves up Little Cornwall's best pasties ($2.30) and other light meals for $3-5. (☎8825 3030. Open M-F 9am-3pm, Sa 9am-2pm.) Next door, casual **La Cantina Cafe ❷,** serves Italian and Argentinian food (pizza $10-18, pasta $10-15, seafood main dishes $18-21) at rough wooden tables. (☎8825 3253. Tu-F all you can eat pizza and pasta $10, children $6. Open daily 3pm-latenight.) For groceries, try the **Woolworths** along Wallaroo Rd. in Kadina. (Open daily 7am-9pm.)

SIGHTS AND ACTIVITIES. The award-winning **Banking and Currency Museum,** 3 Graves St., on the corner of Graves St. and Railway Terr. in Kadina, is the fascinating result of 35 years of collecting all things monetary. The owner Mick takes each visitor on a tour through his massive store of oddities, including used bank pens, piggy-banks, and out-of-print money. (☎8821 2906. Open M-Th and Su 10am-4:30pm; closed June. $5, concessions $4, children $2.) **North Beach** in Wallaroo, just north of the jetty, is the best beach in the area, and the water is always calm and seaweed-free. Both coasts of the peninsula running down to Innes National Park have a number of secluded beaches with excellent fishing and diving. Many are only accessible with 4WD. **Let's Dive** (☎1300 660 370; www.letsdive.com.au) runs dive trips, while **Reef Encounters** handles fishing charters. (☎8349 4271 or 04 0760 9988. Fishing 1-day charter $130 per person, 2-day $250.)

Lovers of Cornish culture and baked goods rush to Moonta every May for Australia's largest Cornish festival, **Kernewek Lowender** (www.kernewek.org). Few know what the festival title means, but that doesn't stop the crowds from enjoying the festivals' week-long lineup of activities.

INNES NATIONAL PARK

Fantastic for surfing and bird-watching, **Innes National Park,** at the toe of the Yorke boot, is the peninsula's most popular attraction. The **Western Whipbird,** which was rediscovered in 1962, is responsible for the area's designation as a national park. There are many other varieties of rare birds within the park; the visitors center has descriptions of them and advice on how to spot them. Buses go no farther south than **Warooka,** making the park inaccessible without a car.

The **National Park Visitors Centre,** at Stenhouse Bay, sells day-passes and camping permits, and has guides for walking, fishing, and surfing in the park. (☎8854 3200; www.parks.sa.gov.au/innes. Open during holidays daily 9am-4:30pm; otherwise M-F 9am-4:30pm, Sa and Su 10:30am-3:00pm. Day-passes $7 per vehicle or $4.50 per motorcycle. Also available from self-registration station near entrance.) The **Innes Park Trading Post,** which includes a **general store** and **petrol station,** is located just inside the park entrance and can refill scuba tanks and give advice on fishing and surfing locations (if the visitors center is closed.) The attached **Rhino Tavern** ❷ has nice views and main dishes from $16. (☎8854 4078. Store open daily 8am-7pm. Tavern serves meals daily noon-2pm and 6-8pm, open for drinks 10am-10pm.)

Innes spreads its several primitive **campsites** ❶ over a few prime locations in the park. There are also three self-registration bays (Gym Beach, outside the general store, and outside the visitors center) for after-hours camping and travel within the park. **Shell Beach** is the only bush camp with water; all bush camping has a fee of $4 per car per night in addition to the park entrance fees. Sites at **Pondalowie Bay** ($8 per car per night) have cold showers, toilets, and water. **Casuarina** ($12 per car per night) is the only campground that can be booked ahead. There is also a **caravan park** ❶ in Marion Bay just before the park entrance. (☎8854 4094. Office open daily 8am-6pm. Sites $17.50, powered $21. On-site vans $67-83.50. Extra person $7.50.) Several **lodges** and **huts** of varying prices are available in the historic ghost village of **Inneston** within the park; contact the visitors center to book. All bookings have a two-night minimum for weekends and school holidays.

There are seven well-marked walking trails in the park ranging from 10min. to 2hr. in duration (pick up the *Innes Walking Trails* brochure at the visitors center). Highlights include the layered limestone cliffs at **The Gap,** views of the Althorpe Islands from **Chinaman's Hat,** and the sunset views from **West Cape,** which overlooks Pondalowie Bay. **Shell Beach** and **Dolphin Beach** are both beautiful and quiet beaches that afford lots of privacy. Snorkelers should head to **Cable Bay. Reef Encounters Fish & Dive Charters** can be hired for one- to two-day fishing trips. (☎8854 4102 or 04 0760 9988. 1-day trip $130 per person; 2-day $250. Insurance surcharge $10 per day per person.)

The visitors center also has a comprehensive list with descriptions of the **surfbreaks** within the park. **Chinaman's** and **Richard's** (also known as **Surfer's**) breaks are the most accessible. **Cutloose Quiksilver Yorke's Classic** (☎04 2779 6845) is an annual surf competition held in late September and early October.

FLINDERS RANGES

The Flinders Ranges may not be the Himalayas or the Andes, but these ancient peaks belong in the pantheon of awe-inspiring ranges. The main road (Hwy. 47) drifts

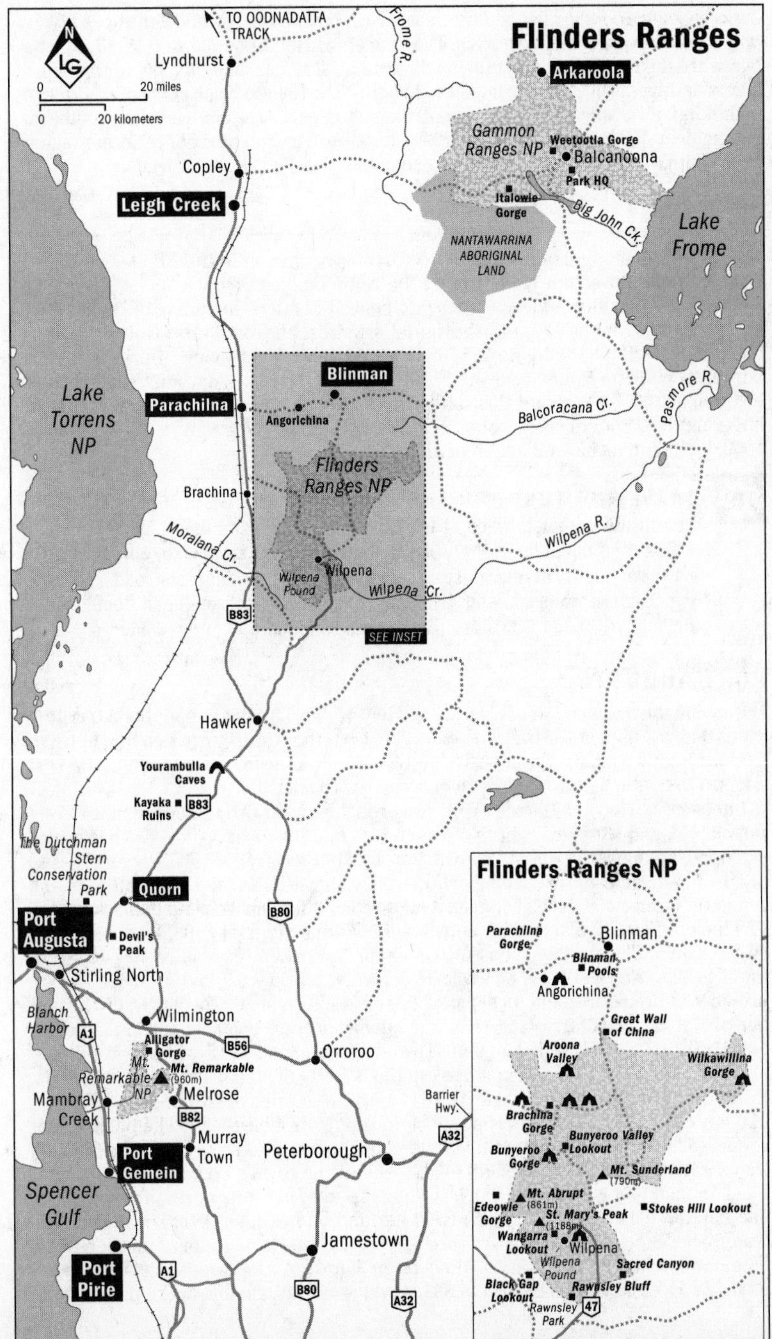
Flinders Ranges
TO OODNADATTA TRACK
Lyndhurst
Frome R.
0 20 miles
0 20 kilometers
Arkaroola
Gammon Ranges NP
Weetootla Gorge
Balcanoona
Park HQ
Italowie Gorge
Big John Ck.
NANTAWARRINA ABORIGINAL LAND
Copley
Leigh Creek
Lake Frome
Lake Torrens NP
Blinman
Parachilna
Angorichina
Balcoracana Cr.
Pasmore R.
Flinders Ranges NP
Brachina
Moralana Cr.
Wilpena R.
Wilpena
Wilpena Pound
Wilpena Cr.
B83
SEE INSET
Hawker
Yourambulla Caves
Kayaka Ruins
The Dutchman Stern Conservation Park
Quorn
Port Augusta
Devil's Peak
Stirling North
B80
Blanch Harbor
Wilmington
A1
Alligator Gorge
B56
Orroroo
Mt. Remarkable NP
Mt. Remarkable (960m)
Melrose
Mambray Creek
B82
Barrier Hwy.
Murray Town
Peterborough
A32
Port Gemein
Spencer Gulf
Jamestown
Port Pirie
Flinders Ranges NP
Parachilna Gorge
Blinman
Blinman Pools
Angorichina
Great Wall of China
Aroona Valley
Wilkawillina Gorge
Brachina Gorge
Bunyeroo Valley Lookout
Bunyeroo Gorge
Mt. Sunderland (790m)
Edeowie Gorge
Mt. Abrupt (861m)
St. Mary's Peak (1188m)
Stokes Hill Lookout
Wangarra Lookout
Wilpena
Wilpena Pound
Sacred Canyon
Black Gap Lookout
Rawnsley Bluff
Rawnsley Park
47
SOUTH AUSTRALIA

between kangaroo-filled flatlands and sagebrush-covered hills, while dirt-tracks (4WD-only) carve through timeless gorges. The Flinders are most popular from April to October, when the nights are chilly and the days sunny. It's hot in summer, but for hardcore hikers or drivers with A/C, it's a worthwhile trip. The Ranges begin at the northern end of the Gulf of St. Vincent and continue 400km into South Australia's northern Outback, ending near Mt. Hopeless. *Let's Go* lists major towns and attractions in the region from south to north, as they would be encountered if driving from Adelaide.

TOURS

Many tours heading from Adelaide to Alice Springs stop in the Flinders Ranges. **Wallaby Tracks Adventure Tours,** run by the Andu Lodge in Quorn, picks up in Port Augusta or Adelaide and leads tours into central Flinders, including bushcamping, and stops at Wilpena Pound, Aboriginal art sites, and Bunyeroo Gorge. (☎8648 6655 or 1800 639 933. 2-3 days $199-299.) **Adelaide Sightseeing** offers two-night jaunts to Wilpena Pound and the Flinders. (☎8231 4144; www.adelaidesightseeing.com.au. $615.) **Wayward Bus,** 119 Waymouth St., Adelaide, runs a six-day tour covering the Flinders and Coober Pedy. (☎8410 8833; www.waywardbus.com.au. $550, including meals and accommodation.)

> **TIP** **TRAVELING THROUGH THE FLINDERS RANGES.** Before setting out on the unsealed roads of the Northern Flinders and the outback tracks, check road conditions. The website **www.transport.sa.gov.au/quicklinks/northern_roads/northern.asp** has up-to-date maps for the region roads, showing closures, warnings, and 4WD only. Alternatively, call the Road Conditions Hotline (1300 361 033). Before hiking, listen to **AM 639** for fire warnings.

PORT AUGUSTA ☎08

Located at the intersection of Hwy. 1 and Hwy. 87, Port Augusta (pop. 14,800) is little more than a stopover for travelers emerging from the Nullarbor or heading north to Coober Pedy and Alice Springs. Those who aren't in need of a rest would be best advised to continue north to Quorn or south to Whyalla.

Intersecting Hwy. 1, Flinders Terr. runs roughly east-west and connects to Commercial Rd. and Maryatt St., both of which lead into the town center. The **bus station** sits opposite the library on Mackay St. **Premier Stateliner** (☎8642 5055) runs buses to and from Adelaide and Whyalla five times daily. **Banks, ATMs,** and a **post office** are all found on **Commercial Road.** The **Tourist Information Office and Wadlata Outback Centre,** 41 Flinders Terr., at Maryatt St., books outback tours. (☎8641 0793, Wadlata ☎8642 4511. Open M-F 9am-5:30pm, Sa-Su 10am-4pm. Centre admission $9, concessions $8, families $20.) **National Parks and Wildlife Service,** 9 Mackay St., 2nd fl. (☎8648 5300), provides information about local parks. (Open M-F 9am-5pm.) The **library,** on the corner of Mackay and Marryatt St., has free **Internet** access, available in 30min. blocks. (☎8641 9151. Open M, W, F 9am-6pm; Tu and Th 9am-8pm; Sa 10am-1pm; Su 2-5pm.)

Port Augusta doesn't have much to offer in the way of unique budget accommodations. The **Flinders Hotel** ❷ (☎8642 2544), on the corner of Commercial Rd. and Mackay St., has standard Aussie pub-style rooms (doubles $70). The backpacker rooms ($22 per person) with only two beds per room are the best bargain, though they lack a kitchen. The Flinders is also one of the town's best bets for a budget meal, though that isn't saying much (burgers from $7). A little north of town, **Shoreline Caravan Park** ❷ (☎8642 2965) can be found on Gardiner Ave. Located on the water, Shoreline provides sites, cabins, and basic hostel-style rooms with access to a common kitchen and toilet area. (Reception 8am-7pm. Unpowered sites $19, powered $22. Hostel bed in 2-bed room $32, 4-bed room $16. Double $55, 4-person suite

$60.) An added bonus for patrons of the caravan park is access to the West Augusta Football Club. Take your drink voucher there for a true taste of Aussie culture—pokies (slot machines), a full bar, and pub meals on Th and F nights ($7.50). Coles **supermarket** is on the corner of Jervis and Maryatt St. (Open daily 6am-10pm.)

The main attraction in Port Augusta, the Wadlata Outback Centre introduces visitors to outback history and culture through hands-on exhibits. The **Arid Lands Botanic Gardens,** north of town off the Stuart Hwy., has bushwalking trails with instructive plant labels. (☎8641 1049. 1hr. guided tours Apr.-Oct. M-F 11am; Nov.-Mar. M-F 9:30am. $6. Gardens open M-F 9am-5pm, Sa-Su 10am-4pm. Free.) **Spinifex Safaris** (☎8642 4442; www.spinifexsafaris.com.au) picks up in Port Augusta and does half- and multiple-day tours of the Flinders (day tour $120, min. 4 people; 2-day $240; 3-day from $250.)

SOUTHERN FLINDERS

PORT PIRIE AND PORT GERMEIN ☎08

On Hwy. 1, heading away from Mount Remarkable National Park, Port Pirie and Port Germein (45km and 22km, respectively, from Mount Remarkable NP) are two noteworthy destinations.

Home to the world's largest lead smelter, Port Pirie is an industrial town with one of the region's best information centers, **Port Pirie Regional Tourism Center and Art Gallery** (☎8633 8000), on Mary Elie St., a left-hand turn off Main Rd. The art gallery exhibits large metal emus as well as regional Aboriginal pieces, while another wing of the center holds a 5.5m shark (admission $2). **Junction Express** ❷, behind the center, is a train restaurant (open daily 10am-2pm) with a mini mock-walk to Broken Hill, a sister mining town to the East. The knowledgeable staff at the tourism center provides maps for the region. (Open M-F 9am-5pm, Sa 9am-4pm, Su 10am-3pm.)

Port Germein is best known for its wooden jetty, the longest in Australia, which boasts tons of popular fishing and crabbing spots. Those looking to fish can get bait and gear from the **Pier Bait Shop & Cafe** (☎8634 5194), on the corner of High St. and the Esplanade. The shop rents nets ($2 per day) and rods ($5 per day) and sells a wide range of baits. For those looking to cast their line beyond the jetty, the shop has boat launching as well ($15, $10 with bait purchase). For those lacking the patience or skill to catch their own, order a plate of fish 'n' chips ($9) at the cafe. (Open M-F 8:30am-4pm, Sa-Su 8:30am-5pm).

MOUNT REMARKABLE NATIONAL PARK

Mount Remarkable National Park, located halfway between **Port Pirie** and **Port Augusta,** is the pride of the southern Flinders. With excellent opportunities to bushwalk, observe wildlife, or just drive the winding scenic roads, Mt. Remarkable serves as a nice introduction to the red, arid peaks of the Flinders Ranges.

The Port Pirie Regional Tourism Center (p. 503) is a good place to stop and pick up maps and area information. Hwy. 1 runs along the west coast of the park and passes through **Mambray Creek,** 55km north of Port Pirie and home to the **park headquarters.** To reach nearby **Melrose,** follow the Port Germein Gorge 27km to Muuray Town; from there it's another 14km on Hwy. B-82 to Melrose. There is a **post office** (☎8666 2014) on Stuart St. in Melrose.

The park headquarters at Mambray Creek has a **self registration kiosk** for day passes and camping permits and provides detailed maps with thorough descriptions of all park trails. (☎8634 7068. Day passes $7 per vehicle. Open Tu and Th-F 9am-4:30pm.) The **campground** ❶ has 54 sites with water, toilets, showers, BBQ, and picnic areas (campers pay the entry fee plus $18 per night, low-season $12). There are also a number of bush camping sites deep within the park ($4). Bush camping is prohibited during the fire ban season (generally Nov.-Apr.). There is a simple **cabin** ❸ for four at Mambray Creek that can be rented through the park service. (☎8634 7068. Linen not included. Book in advance. M-Th and Su $35, F-Sa $40.) Mambray Creek is also the site of numerous trailheads. Visitors on a tight schedule should consider the **Sugar Gum Lookout** (8km, 3hr. roundtrip), an easy trail following Mambray Creek that provides nice views of the surrounds. Those with more time can take a day to hike the ironically well-marked **Hidden Gorge** (18km, 7hr. roundtrip) and see the area red gums as well as some of the best views of Spencer Gulf.

Tiny Melrose, the oldest town in the Flinders, is a good base for hikes in the region. All attractions are well labeled off the main strip. The town's recently renovated **North Star Hotel ❹,** 43 Nott St., has quirky and surprisingly classy chalets built into antique farm trucks. The hotel pool provides welcome relief from dust and heat. (☎8666 2110; www.northstarhotel.com.au. Reception 11am-9:30pm, call in advance to arrange other times. Standard room $90; boutiques $195; truck chalets $130.) The hotel **pub** ❷ has W schnitzel and Th fish nights. (☎8666 2110. Main dishes $10-22. Pub open for meals daily noon-2pm and 6-8pm.) **Bluey Blundstone's Blacksmith Shop ❺,** 30-32 Stuart St., has been in business since 1865, and is now home to a coffee shop (lunch $7-10; open M and W-F 10am-4pm, Sa-Su 10am-5pm) and rustic B&B consisting of a cottage and barn. (☎8666 2173. Continental breakfast included. Cottage $105. Barn $100, $45 each additional person.) The **Melrose Backpackers and Caravan Park ❶,** on Joe's Rd. off Stuart St., also provides tourist info and maps. (☎8666 2060. Linen $5. Sites $6.50 per person, powered $18; dorms $15; cabins from $40.)

Many hikes begin from the **Melrose Caravan Park.** The most well-known is the **summit trail** (12km, 5hr. round-trip), which actually doesn't have much of a summit view, but does provide some nice views on the way up. For a shorter hike with plenty of wildlife, try the **Cathedral Rock trail** (3km, 1hr. round-trip). Mountain bikers should pay a visit to Melrose's **general store,** on Stuart St. The owners are avid mountain bikers who rent bikes and are working to develop over 200km of trails by 2010. (☎8666 2057. Open M-F and Su 8:30am-6pm, Sa 8:30am-7pm. ½-day rental $25, full day $35.)

CENTRAL FLINDERS

The most famous and accessible Flinders attractions, including the vast amphitheater of Wilpena Pound, are located in the ranges' central region. Good roads and well-placed towns allow even the outback novice to marvel at the colorful mountains and plentiful wildlife. To reach Quorn, Rawnsley Park, or Wilpena Pound via public transportation, take **Stateliner** through Port Augusta. (Adelaide ☎8415 5599; Port Augusta ☎8642 5055.) Stateliner services Port Augusta via Hawker, Quorn, and Wilpena Pound (departs Port Augusta W, F, Su; returns Th-F and Su). Connections to Adelaide are available from all three buses. Wilpena Pound marks the end of public transport into the range. If you're without a car, private tours offer the cheapest and most flexible ways to explore the Central Flinders.

BURRA ☎08

Once Australia's largest inland settlement, Burra hosted over 5000 miners and had one of the largest copper mines in the world. Today, Burra revels in its past. The dusty town was declared a State Heritage area in 1993 and its old buildings and historical focus give it a ghostly, albeit friendly, feel.

Burra's tourist favorite is the **Burra Passport,** a key that opens eight locked historical sites and allows visitors as much time as they need to complete the tour. (Basic passport $15, concessions $11; full passport with entrance to all 4 area museums $25, concessions $20.) Most sites are ruins, all are eerily empty, and some of them, including the **Unicorn Brewery Cellars** and the old **Redruth Gaol** (used in the 1979 movie *Breaker Morant*), are downright spooky. Other sights on the tour include the old

Burra Smelting Works, Hampton Village (archaeological remains of an old township), and the old **dugout homes** where the first miners lived.

The large, open cut of the **Burra Mine,** a.k.a. the **Monster Mine,** is indicative of the importance of copper in Burra's history. The mine was one of the world's largest and was last used in the 1970s. **Morphett's Enginehouse Museum,** on the site of Burra Mine, details its mechanical aspects. Be sure to go through the miners' underground tunnel; a mere 5 ft. high, it was just tall enough for the miners to duck through en route to work. (Open daily 11am-2pm. $4.50, concessions $3.50.) Next to the tourist office, **Mongolata Gold Mining Tours,** Market Sq., offers visitors the chance to don boots and a hardhat and be a gold miner for an hour; they also conduct 90min. cemetery tours. (☎8892 2233. Both tours must be booked ahead. Mining tour $15; min. 4 person. Cemetery tours begin at dusk. $10; group discounts available.)

Just out of town, off the main road, **Thorogoods** is a small, privately-owned **winery** that uses an old Italian basket press to make wine out of the apples grown in their orchards. The friendly owner and homey feel ensure you'll have a wonderfully personalized wine-tasting experience. The *Misty Morning* sparkling wine is particularly delicious. (☎8892 2669; www.thorogoods.com.au. Open daily noon-4:30pm.) The first weekend in March brings **Jazz in the Monster Mine,** an annual performance held in the mine crater (☎8892 2154; bvc@capri.net.au). Known as the antique center of the Mid-North, Burra hosts a large **Antique Fair** every year in early May. The **Jailhouse Rock Festival,** held on the last weekend in February, is a celebration full of dancing to the oldies in the Burra Gaol. (☎8892 2154. $25, children $10.) Festival tickets can be booked through the visitors center.

In Burra's early days, many miners lived in mud dugouts along the banks of Burra Creek. In the 1840s, to improve quality of life for miners, the South Australian Mining Association built the **Paxton Square Cottages ❸,** Kingston St., at Bridge Terr., on the east side of town. The 32 restored cottages have stone floors, kitchens, and fireplaces. The cafe at the cottages has lunch deals from $7.80. (☎8892 2622. All rooms ensuite. Doubles $80-100. Extra person $15, children $10.) **Gaslight Collectibles and Old Books,** 20 Market Sq., is a unique cafe where visitors can sip on tea or snack on a homemade scone ($5) amid antiques and old books. (☎8892 3004. Open Tu-Th 10am-5pm.) The 154-year-old **Burra Hotel ❶** has pub meals (yiros for $8 and dinner from $12) and a classier dining section featuring regional produce and local wines. (☎8892 2389. Main courses from $16. Offers basic rooms currently undergoing renovation. Open M-Sa noon-2pm and 6-8pm.)

Burra is 156km (2hr.) north of Adelaide and 42km (30min.) northeast of Clare on Barrier Hwy. (A32), the main route to Sydney via Broken Hill. The highway leads to **Market Square,** at the intersection of Market and Commercial St., before turning left in town. Commercial St. becomes Kingston St. on the other side of the highway. The **Visitors Centre,** 2 Market Sq. (☎8892 2154; www.visitburra.com), is open daily 9am-5pm. The Bank South Australia on Market Square has an **ATM.** There is free **Internet** access at the **library** in the school at the end of Bridge Terr., north of the creek. (Open M-F 8:30am-6pm, 11am-6pm during school holidays; closed for lunch 1-2pm.) The **post office** is on Market Sq., next to the **IGA** supermarket. (Supermarket open M-F 9am-5:30pm, Sa 9-11:30am, Su 10am-1pm.) **Postal Code:** 5417.

QUORN ☎08

An old railway town smack in the middle of the Flinders Ranges, Quorn (pop. 1400) is the outback town of the movies, both figuratively and literally. Its wide streets and hilly backdrop have appeared in at least nine films, including the WWII epic *Gallipoli.* Quorn's country hospitality, best found in the town's pubs, make it an ideal base from which to explore the stunning **Warren Gorge** as well as the **Dutchman's Stern** and **Devil's Peak** bushwalks.

TRANSPORTATION AND PRACTICAL INFORMATION. Quorn is on Hwy. 83 (which later becomes Hwy. 47; the two are used interchangeably on signs), 40km northeast of Port Augusta and Hwy. 1. **Stateliner** (☎8415 5555) runs from Adelaide to Quorn. ($40.90. M-F and Su 5-6 times daily, Sa 2 times daily.) The **Quorn Newsagency** sells bus tickets. (☎8648 6042. Open M-F 8am-5:30pm and Sa-Su 8:30am-2pm, later in peak season.) The historic **Pichi Richi Railway** runs a steam engine train March to October once daily between Port Augusta and Quorn. (☎1800 440 101 or 8648 6598. Tickets $32 one-way, $48 round-trip; concession $42/27; children $16/11.) The **Flinders Ranges Visitors Centre,** on 7th St., between First St. and Railway Terr., has **Internet** access ($3 per 15min.) and area information. (☎8648 6419; www.flindersranges.com. Open daily 9am-5pm.) The only **ATMs** between Port Augusta and Wilpena are in the Transcontinental Hotel and the Austral Hotel, both on Railway Terr. Other services include: **police** (☎8648 6060), 24 Railway Terr.; a small **IGA** supermarket, on 7th St., across from the visitors center (open M-F 8am-6pm, Sa-Su 9am-4:30pm); and free 30min. **Internet** access at the **library,** on West Terr. (☎8648 6101; open during school hours; during holidays Tu and F 1-6pm, W-Th 1-5pm, Sa 10am-noon.) The **post office** is at 21 Railway Terr. **Postal Code:** 5433.

ACCOMMODATIONS. The sprawling **Andu Lodge ❷,** 12 First St., is a family-run hostel that offers clean rooms, an ample kitchen and lounge area, free bike use, wash ($2.40 per load, line dry), and one- to four-day Flinders tours through Wallaby Track Tours. Short-term staff are hired in exchange for free lodging, bike use, breakfasts, and a Flinders trip (see **Beyond Tourism,** p. 81). (☎8648 6070 or 1 300 730 701. Bike hire $10 per day. Dorms $20; singles $30; doubles $50; families $65. Weekly rates available.) The **Quorn Caravan Park ❷,** at the east end of Silo Rd., is an environmentally conscious accommodation with knowledgeable owners and potential work-exchange opportunities. (☎8648 6206. Sites $15-20. Cabins $50-80.) There is **bush camping** with toilets but no water at **Warren Gorge,** a beautiful spot 20km northwest of town off the Arden Vale Rd.; follow signs from West Terr. out of town.

FOOD. The **Quandong Cafe and Bakery ❶,** 31 First St., offers home-cooked meals in a pleasant little dining room adorned with local art. (☎8648 6155. Open Tu 9:30am-3pm, W-Su 9:30am-4pm. Breakfast $9.50, sandwiches and salads from $5. Closed mid-Dec. to mid-Mar.) The cook at the **Buckaringa Better Buy Market ❶,** 40 First St., has tantalizing Thai takeaway for $8-10. (☎8648 6381. Internet access $7.70 per hr. Open M and W-Sa 9am-6pm, Su 10am-6pm; takeaway 11am-6pm. Cash only.) **Pichi Richi Cafe ❶,** next to the newsagency, grills homemade burgers ($4.70, with the lot $6.80) in true Aussie-style. Order the lot to find out exactly what that "style" is. (☎8648 6021. Open M-Th 9am-7:30pm, F-Sa 8:30am-8:30pm, Su 8:30am-7:30pm.)

HIKES. Quorn is a short drive from a number of rewarding hikes. Arguably the area's top hike, **Dutchman's Stern,** a bluff 10km north of Quorn, is the prototypical Australian hike with views of **Spencer Gulf** and the surrounding red-soil hills spotted with kangaroos hopping across the trail. Hikers can choose between two main walks: a ridgetop hike (8.2km, 4hr. round-trip) and a loop walk (10.5km, 5hr.). **Devil's Peak** (2hr. round-trip) affords stunning 360° views of the Flinders region. (Closed summer during fire-ban season.) Another 10km north of Dutchman's, **Warren Gorge** has recently added new hiking trails and is a prime spot to view yellow-footed rock wallabies, recognizable by their striped tails. **Mount Brown Conservation Park,** 16km south of town on Richman Valley Rd., contains (usually dry) **Waukerie Falls** and **Mount Brown.** Allow at least seven hours for the trip to the summit and back. (Closed in summer during fire-ban season. Contact a ranger at Mambray Creek ☎8634 7068 or Port Augusta ☎8648 5300 for hike availability.)

OUTDOOR ACTIVITIES. Located at the base of Devil's Peak, 3km down Devil's Peak Rd., **Pichi Richi Camel Tours** offers short treks through the Flinders on their large, hardy camels. (Bookings required. ☎8648 6640. 30min. tour $20; 1hr. tour $30; sunset tour $55.) The tourist office has a map of many **scenic drives.** The 36km long **Buckaringa Scenic Road** is a charming, narrow dirt road that winds past the Buckaringa private reserve and ends at a lovely lookout on a hill—a perfect spot to watch the sunrise. The driving options off the scenic road offer "soft adventure" (read: less risky, same views) **4WD tracks.** Access to tracks granted through the **Austral Hotel,** 16 Railway Terr. (☎8648 6017).

SIGHTS. The extensive **Kanyaka Homestead Historic Site,** 42km from Quorn on the way to Hawker, are the ruins of an 1850s homestead. *Kanyaka* is an Aboriginal word for "meeting place," and visitors are free to meander through the preserved buildings of the complex. The **Yourambulla Caves,** 12km past the ruins toward Hawker, are a more labor-intensive venture. A steep, rocky trail (45min. round-trip) leads up the side of a mountain to three caves, sites of Aboriginal chalk and ochre drawings.

WILPENA POUND AND FLINDERS RANGES NATIONAL PARK

Wilpena Pound, a valley encircled by the soaring mountains of the Flinders Range, is the de facto gateway to Flinders Ranges National Park. A hilly syncline, or geological upfold, outlined in jagged quartzite and resembling a huge crater, Wilpena Pound is a fitting introduction to the Flinders with its rewarding hikes and scenic drives punctuated by gorges created millions of years ago.

TRANSPORTATION AND PRACTICAL INFORMATION. Most of the tours through the Flinders stop by Wilpena Pound. The **Stateliner bus** (☎8415 5555) also runs to Wilpena Pound from Adelaide (7hr.; W, F, Su 1 per day; $67) or Port Augusta (departs W, F, Su 1 per day; returns Th, F, Su; $17). The helpful **Wilpena Visitor Centre** is the park's headquarters, offering general park and hiking info, passes good for five days or until leaving the park ($7), camping permits ($8 per night), and bookings for scenic flights and 4WD tours. (☎8648 0048. Flights start at $80 per 20min. Open daily 8am-6pm. Day and camping passes can also be obtained from self-registration stations at the park entrances and the Rawnsley Park Station) There's a **general store** just behind the center with a limited selection of food and supplies as well as **petrol,** an **ATM,** and **Internet** access ($6 per 30min; open daily 8am-6pm, hours may vary in summer). Fifty-five kilometers south of Wilpena in **Hawker,** the **Hawker General Store** is a good place to stock up on fresh, decently priced hiking essentials. Try out the delicious pasta salads, thick sandwiches ($5), and a variety of cakes, breads and pastries. (Open M-F 8am-5:30pm, Sa 9am-5pm.)

FOOD AND ACCOMMODATIONS. Camping is available in the park and can be paid for at the visitors center or at self-registration kiosks ($11 per vehicle). A few sites have water and toilet facilities; pick up a park map from the visitors center for a complete list of campgrounds and amenities. For a shower, hit the refurbished **Wilpena Campground ❶,** next to the visitors center. (Permits available at the visitors center. Sites for 2 $16, powered $22. Extra person $4.) The **Wilpena Pound Resort ❷** operates a restaurant, bar, pool, campground, and motel down the road from the visitors center. The resort has nice rooms with A/C and TV. Big meals from the bar run $15-23. The lunch burger ($15.50) is particularly delicious and packed with extras. (☎8648 0004 or 1800 805 802. Restaurant open daily 7:30-10am, noon-2pm, and 6-8:30pm, 6:30-9pm in summer; bar open 4:30pm-latenight. 4-bed dorms $25; doubles from $129.)

HIKING. Walks of varying intensity lead to views of the immense Wilpena Pound. Be sure to pick up the thorough *Bushwalking in the Flinders Ranges National Park* brochure from the visitors center before heading out. All of the walks to the Pound begin at the visitors center and most follow the same flat path for 2-3km, passing **Hill's Homestead,** a cabin equipped with toilet facilities. No cars are allowed inside the park, but a shuttle bus service from the visitors center cuts 2km off the trip each way, leaving you 1.6km (about 1hr. round-trip) from Wangarra lookout (4-6 buses per day; $2.50 one-way, $4 round-trip). In an emergency, contact the **police** (☎8648 4028), the visitors center, or the Wilpena Pound Resort (☎8648 0004; open daily 7am-7:30pm) to be connected to emergency services.

For avid hikers, rangers recommend the high-intensity climb to the summit of **St. Mary's Peak,** which rewards the effort with sprawling views of the Pound. The **St. Mary's outside loop track** (14.6km, 6hr. round-trip) starts up the mountain from the resort and is the fastest way to reach the summit. The **inside loop track** (21.5km, 9hr. round-trip) to the peak is wide, flat, and boring up until Cooinda Camp. Past Cooinda Camp, the remaining 3km (1hr.) becomes wild and overgrown; you will definitely not escape unscratched. The return journey can be slightly confusing; keep a sharp lookout for the short stacks of rocks which serve as path markings when the signposts aren't visible.

The Pound is not the park's only attraction. Seventeen trails branch off throughout the area. A 23.2km, 9hr. round-trip walk leads to **Malloga Falls** (which despite the name is almost always dry) and offers views of **Edeowie Gorge.** Past Stokes Hill lookout, 42km from Wilpena, the road to Arkaroola leads to remote **Wilkawillina Gorge,** home to the rare yellow-footed rock wallaby. You may be able to see one drinking from the water pools along the **Mount Billy Creek Trailhead.** Wilkawillina Gorge is the most isolated part of the park, and the trail is only recommended for serious hikers comfortable with an isolated trail. The ideal way to approach the 11.4km (one-way) trail is with two cars parked at either end of the gorge. If this isn't an option, going only 3.5km will bring you to the heart of the gorge and fantastic views, shortening the 10hr. round-trip excursion to just 2hr. The trail is initially rather confusing; follow the mostly dry creek and look for a signpost leading up and right.

OTHER ACTIVITIES. Those heading north to Parachilna, Leigh Creek, or the Oodnadatta Track should consider exiting the Flinders via the 50km **drive** through the park's gorges. Their sheer, colored walls and geological ramparts are stunning, making every turn something of a surprise. The stretch through **Bunyeroo Gorge** and **Brachina Gorge** is the highlight, and geology buffs will be astounded by the well-labeled and diverse geological trail through Brachina Gorge. The road on the way to the gorges from Wilpena Pound passes the Cazenaux tree, which was made famous when an artist named Cazenaux photographed the tree to national and worldwide acclaim. The turn-off for the gorges is 4km north of the Wilpena junction on the road toward Blinman. **Stokes Hill Lookout,** 17km past the turn-off for the gorges toward Oraparinna and Arkaroola, provides more breathtaking sights and a great spot for a picnic.

Rock climbers should contact the **Edeowie Station** (☎8648 4714), to the west of the park, for information on accessing **Edeowie Gorge,** the area's top rock climbing spot. The gorge is visible from the park, but can only be accessed through the privately owned station.

DAYTRIPS FROM THE FLINDERS RANGES

RAWNSLEY PARK STATION. Rawnsley Park Station (☎8648 0030), south of the Flinders and off the road between Wilpena and Hawker, is an outdoor enthusiast's paradise with well-marked hiking trails, horseback riding (2-person min.; $45 per hr.;

$60 per 2hr.; ½-day $100), scenic flights (2-person min.; 20min. from $80), 4WD tours (½-day $80; full-day $120, includes lunch), mountain bike hire ($10 per hr., ½-day $30, full-day $40), and sheep shearing ($12, children $6, families $30) on school holidays. The station offers a full range of accommodations from **YHA cabins ❷** to basic sites, all with access to a swimming pool and camp kitchen. Sites $17, powered $24; on-site vans for two $48; cabins for two $68, ensuite from $83, ensuite with linen $103.) **Internet** access is available at the **general store.** ($2 per 15 min.) The station also has a licensed restaurant, the **Woolshed ❹.** (☎8648 0126. Meals $18-28.)

PARACHILNA. Parachilna (pop. 7) consists almost entirely of the **Prairie Hotel ❺.** In a fossil-rich region at the crossroads of the Flinders and the Outback, Parachilna is unusual and definitely worth a visit. The best way to get to Parachilna, just north of Flinders, is to drive the 4WD track out the back of the park via Brachina Gorge, joining Hwy. 83 just south of town. The **longest train in the world,** at 2.85km, rolls through town every evening between 6 and 8pm at a rollicking pace. The hotel owners book several tours of the area through **Out 'n' Back Tours.** For travelers without the time to go to the Red Centre, the tours give a taste of the outback in the form of Lake Torrens. (Tours from $150, lunch included. Scenic flights available on request.) Across the street from the hotel, the **Parachilna Overflow ❷** has a pool, kitchen, bar area with **Internet** access ($2 per 10min.), and rooms with A/C. The barren, dusty driveway is also the campground. (☎8648 4814. Sites $10; cabin singles $35; doubles $65. Work exchange available.)

ANGORICHINA AND BLINMAN POOLS. Off the spectacular **Parachilna Gorge Scenic Drive,** halfway between Parachilna and Blinman, **Angorichina ❶** minces no words: the sign at the entrance reads "no yuppies." This basic hostel was created as a refuge for returned soldiers suffering from tuberculosis. Angorichina also has a limited general store with **petrol, Internet** access ($3 per 15min.), bike rental (½-day $25, full-day $40), and tire repair. (☎8648 4842. Store open M-Sa 8:30am-6:30pm, Su 9:30am-6:30pm. Linen $8. Sites $9 per person, powered $10; dorms $22 per person; cabins $65-130.) Angorichina's biggest draw is the walk to **Blinman Pools** (6km round-trip; 3hr.), which is a set of secluded spring-fed pools. The trailhead begins at the carpark. Potential hikers should take note that Blinman is not a maintained trail, so there is no marked trail. Tell someone if you are doing the hike, and take plenty of water.

BLINMAN. At the crossroads of Parachilna and the Flinders Ranges National Park lie several historic, picturesque buildings that comprise lovely Blinman (pop. 25). The **Blinman Hotel ❺** has ensuite rooms with TV and A/C (singles $60; doubles $90, extra person $20), and touts a luxurious, heated indoor pool. Those more interested in roughing it can opt for available campsites or bush camping (powered sites $10). The hotel **restaurant ❸** has reasonable prices and good food; including a pepper leaf 'roo fillet ($18). The hotel also books scenic flights and 4WD tours. (hotel ☎8648 4867, tours ☎8648 4679. Flights from $85 for 2 people.) The recently opened **Wild Lime Cafe** brings a touch of British style to the town, serving Devonshire tea and sandwiches in the old schoolhouse as well as providing **Internet** access. (☎8648 4879; www.wildlimecafe.com.au. Open Mar.-Dec. Tu-Su 9am-5pm; open daily during school holidays.) The town also has **petrol, ATM,** and a **general store.** (Open M-Sa 8:30am-5pm, Su 9am-5pm; fewer hours off-season.) The historic **old mine** site lies just 1km north of town; follow signs from the main road.

NORTHERN FLINDERS

The rare visitors who arrive in Northern Flinders are welcomed by an impressive palate of colors. Sage-green shrubs dot the ground below while orange hills fade to red, blue, and purple mountains in the distance. After a rare rainfall, thousands of yellow flowers blanket the normally dry ground. The vastness of the Outback is apparent here: the mountains are larger, the gorges deeper, and the human company more scarce. To cover the few hundred kilometers between **Flinders Range National Park** and **Gammon Ranges National Park,** drivers can either come up through **Wilpena** (p. 507) and **Blinman** (p. 509) or stick to the highway from Hawker and follow the paved road as far as Copley. The stops described here are along the highway, though the dirt-road route to Gammon will show you what the "back of beyond" is all about.

Travelers looking to head north of Gammon and Arkaroola will require a **Desert Parks Pass.** For info, call the Desert Parks Pass Hotline (☎ 1800 816 078) or talk to the rangers at Balcanoona in Gammon Ranges Park or at the Parks Office in Port Augusta (☎ 8648 5300. Year pass $95, day pass $11, overnight pass $20. Prices may vary.) The pass allows unlimited access to the Simpson Desert, Innamincka, Lake Eyre, and Dalhousie areas, among others. It comes with a packet of brochures and great regional maps.

LEIGH CREEK ☎08

Leigh Creek, 22km south of a coalfield and 110km from the start of the **Oodnadatta track** (p. 515), was planned and built by the **Electricity Trust of South Australia (ETSA),** and it shows. Bizarrely sterile, the town consists of gently curving residential streets lined with gravel "lawns," all clustered around one central shopping center. The **visitors center** is near the supermarket in the central mall. (☎ 8675 2723. Open M-F 9am-5pm, Sa-Su 10am-2pm.) The school also functions as the town **library** and has free **Internet** access. (Open during school term M,W, Th 8:30am-4:30pm; Tu and F 8:30am-4:30pm and 7-9pm; Sa 9am-noon; school holidays Tu and F noon-4:30pm and 7-9pm, W-Th 8:30-11:30am and noon-4:30pm, Sa 9am-noon.) The landscaped downtown area has a **pub** and a well-stocked **supermarket.** (☎ 8675 2009. Open M-F 9am-5:30pm, Sa 9am-12:30pm.) **Leigh Creek South Motors Mobil Station** has **petrol,** tires, showers, and toilets. (☎ 8675 2016. Open M-Th 8am-7pm, F 8am-8pm, Sa-Su 9am-8pm. Showers $3.)

The **Leigh Creek Hotel ❺** in town isn't cheap, but all rooms are ensuite with TV, telephone, and fridge. (☎ 8675 2025. Cabins $80-90. Motel singles $110; doubles $135.) Book through the Mobil Station for the **Caravan Park ❶,** on your right immediately after turning off the highway. (☎ 8675 2016. Sites $6, powered $11, 2 for $18; cabins $60-70.) In a vast desert of sub-par food, the **Quandong Cafe ❷** is an oasis of fresh, homemade goodies. Their specialty is the Quandong pie, a native peach pie ($3.60) that acts as an aphrodisiac and is so good it will make you cry (like love). (☎ 8675 2683. Open Dec.-Mar. daily 9am-4pm.)

Barking Gecko, in the main complex near the visitors center, books three- to seven-day mountain biking tours in the Flinders, most covering some of the Mawson Trail, a mountain biking trail running from Cape Jervis to Penneshaw. (☎ 8675 2366. From $545; includes bike, helmet, accommodation, meals, and guides. Min. 4 people; max. 8.) There's also a 50m **community pool** in town. (☎ 8675 2147. Open daily noon-9pm, closed early in cold weather. $3, children $1.50.) **Postal Code:** 5731.

VULKATHUNHA-GAMMON RANGES NATIONAL PARK

This is where central Australia gets serious. The Gammons are even more craggy, exotic, and remote than the southern Flinders. The local Aboriginals, who co-manage the park with the National Park and Wildlife Service (NPWS), call the area Arrkunha, or "place of red ochre," after the deep colors of the mountains. The park is best explored on unsealed 4WD tracks or on foot. Be sure to bring enough food, water, and supplies to remain self-sufficient.

The **NPWS** headquarters in **Balcanoona** has up-to-date park info and sells the **Desert Parks Pass;** however, it is infrequently staffed. (☎ 8648 4829.) Arkaroola, to the north-east of the park, can provide information when the park office isn't open. Balcanoona has public payphones. All campsites have self-registration booths (free entry, $4 per car camping) and toilets. Most have rainwater tanks, but don't rely on them in summer. For **emergencies,** contact the Leigh Creek Police (☎8675 2004), Hawker Police (☎8648 4028), or the Wilpena Parks Office (☎8648 0049). There are also **cabins** for rent; book through the Parks Office in Hawker (☎8648 4244).

In addition to the campgrounds, the park has a number of unique accommodations, including **Grindell's Hut** ❺ (1-4 people $87.50, 5-8 people $112.50; per week $560) and the old **sheep shearer's quarters** ❸($26 per room; $210 for the whole place, sleeps 18.) The accommodations are excellent with terrific views and access to the park.

Driving the **Wortupa Loop Track** (70km, 4hr.) is the easiest way to see the park. **Italowie Camp** and **Weetootla Gorge** are accessible via 2WD and connect with shorter trails (2km-16km) at the park's fringe. **Lake Frome,** 38km east of Balcanoona (4WD only), is a sprawling lake-bed covered in salt. No access is allowed after 3pm, when the area becomes an Aboriginal hunting ground.

For serious hikers, the park has a number of lengthy and challenging trails. **Italowie Gorge Hike** (15.7km, 8hr. one-way) is considered by many to be the region's best. The trailhead can be found on the park's eastern edge off the main road; a trail map is available from the park headquarters or at the trailhead. There are several one-way options off the track of the **Weetootla Gorge Hike** (18.4km loop, 7hr. round-trip) that traverse uncharted territory. Start the hike from the Weetootla Gorge carpark. Be sure to check with the ranger before starting any hike. The terrain is dangerous if you are unprepared; feral goats aimlessly wear paths into the hills that can lead hikers in circles.

ARKAROOLA

Abutting the northern boundary of Gammon Ranges National Park, 30km from Balcanoona, the private conservation area of Arkaroola showcases stunning terrain. Founders Reg and Griselda Sprigg turned a sheep station into a refuge for native plants and animals. Arkaroola now draws nature lovers with its mountain ridges, perfect for hiking or 4WD forays. The isolation, the beauty, and the variety of activities in Arkaroola will captivate you more than any other town in the South Australian Outback.

The **Arkaroola Resort** ❷ has tourist information, **petrol, Internet** access ($2 per 15min.) and a variety of accommodation options. (☎1800 676 042 or 8648 4848; www.arkaroola.com.au. Reception open daily 7am-5:30pm. Sites $15, powered $20; cabins $40; furnished lodges $95-145.) There is also a general store with an eclectic, if sparse, assortment of goods. The resort also has the only **restaurant** ❷ for many miles. (Lunch $6-12; dinner $14-25. Bar open daily noon-2pm for lunch, dining room open for dinner 6-8pm.)

Arkaroola resort runs a number of tours, including the 4½hr. **ridgetop tour,** wherein a specially constructed open-top 4WD vehicle climbs impossibly steep roads, stopping periodically to take in views of the ancient granite mountains. ($99, under 14 $55; families $85. Runs twice daily. 2-person min.) The resort also runs **scenic flights.** Flights start at $88-165, based on three passengers.

Those hoping to explore on their own can pick up maps at the resort and set out on one of the several **4WD tracks** in the preserve. The **Echo Camp Backtrack** incorporates all the majesty of the region. Make sure you know what you're doing; this roadtrip is a flat tire waiting to happen. Bring spares, know how to change a flat, and tell someone where you're going. The bold can start the 12.5km track from the **Echo Camp Waterhole.** Allow 2hr. round-trip from the village to complete the track. The **Mount Jacob Backtrack** is not as challenging as the Echo Camp track, nor as visually impressive, but it's still fun.

Hikers will also find plenty of options at Arkaroola. It's 7km to the mammoth rocks of **Bararranna Gorge,** which are accessible only via the trailhead off the Echo Camp track (6.8km, 3.5 hr.). Though not a maintained trail, the climb to the top of **Griselda Hill** is nevertheless popular for its amazing sunset views.

SOUTH AUSTRALIA

OUTBACK SOUTH AUSTRALIA

If you've ever wanted to go off the grid, this would be the ideal place to do it. The epitome of "Big Sky Country," Outback South Australia's unsealed roads stretch endlessly across baked earth that your car will promptly transform into a maddening cloud of dust. Intimidating signs read "Next gas: 454km" or "Danger: Extreme Conditions Ahead," and the only living creatures along the way are wandering cattle and soaring eagles. For most, a drive from one end to the other is enough, and the few who call the Outback their home are a rough and rugged crowd as intriguing as the landscape. Prime tourist season in the Outback is April through October; summers are hot, with temperatures reaching 45°C (113°F) in the shade. Swarms of maddening bush flies are a constant presence. The helpful (and difficult to find) *Remote Travel Hints for 4x4 Tourists* offers simple tips for novice drivers tackling the Outback. The two most important things to remember are to bring plenty of water, and to never leave your vehicle should something happen. For more tips and safety information, see **Driving in the Outback** (p. 74).

STUART HIGHWAY: ADELAIDE TO COOBER PEDY

As the Stuart Hwy. winds its way northwest toward Coober Pedy, there is little to see other than the harsh, red, arid terrain. This is pasture land, so beware of free-roaming horses and cattle. Fuel prices will increase the farther you venture north of Port Augusta, so it's a good idea to stop off in Port Augusta or Pimba before continuing on into the sun-baked unknown.

WOOMERA ☎08

Designated a "secret" town by the Australian and British militaries, Woomera (pop. 200) was created in 1947 as the unofficial capital of the **Woomera Prohibited Area,** a long-range weapons testing area that once covered nearly 27 million hectares; the site is still the largest land-locked military test site in the world. The pre-planned village sits at the edge of the area, known affectionately as "the range" by locals. Joint European and Australian forces created the village, the location of which wasn't revealed on maps until the 1960s. From 1970 to 1999, the American military was the primary partner in the Joint Defence Facility-Nurrangar, a satellite and missile tracking center. Reassuringly, the base is currently geared more toward satellite launching than bomb testing.

The **Woomera Heritage Centre,** on Dewrang Ave. in the middle of town, details the nuclear bombs, radio astronomy, and other aspects of Woomera's unusual past. Strangely enough, the center is also home to a ten-pin bowling alley. (☎8673 7768, booking 8673 7704. Museum $4, concessions $3. Open daily 9am-5pm.) Because of the lack of light pollution, Woomera is great for star-gazing. Nightly **astronomy tours** are held at Baker Observatory (book at the visitors center, $5). The **Eldo Hotel ❺** was originally built for rocket scientists (☎8673 7867; www.eldohotel.com.au. Continental breakfast included. Ensuite for single or double occupancy, $89). The town also has a **caravan park ❶, supermarket,** and **petrol** station.

COOBER PEDY ☎08

The "opal capital of the world," Coober Pedy supports 80% of the world's opal industry, but even more colorful than its opals are the people hiding in the dirt. To escape the heat, over half of the town's 3500 residents make their homes underground, and the potential to strike it rich with an opal find has drawn hopeful miners from around the world to this underground town. Locals invariably impress tourists with stories of Latvian crocodile-hunters-turned-opal-miners and Italian playboys blowing hundreds of thousands of dollars earned in the mines in a single year of partying. These characters give Coober Pedy a wild edge, even by outback standards, and a diversity unseen anywhere else in central Australia—over 42 nationalities are represented in the area schools. Between the characters hunting opals and the opals themselves, Coober Pedy is traveler heaven.

DON'T WALK BACKWARD. Outside town boundaries, 1.5 million **abandoned mine shafts** make the danger of carelessly stepping backward and plummeting to your death very real. Mining practices make it unsafe to fill in the holes, so they are left open and uncovered. Signs around town, though co-opted by the tourist industry, are no joke; do not explore opal fields by yourself.

TRANSPORTATION. **Greyhound Australia** (☎13 14 99 or 13 20 30) makes daily runs to Coober Pedy once daily from Adelaide and Alice Springs. The **bus station** is next to the police station on Malliotis Blvd. (☎8673 5151. Open daily 6-9am and 5-8pm.) In addition, virtually every tour between Adelaide and Alice stops off in Coober Pedy. The Stuart Hwy., the main north-south road through Australia's interior, goes straight through town. **Budget** (☎8672 5333) rents 4WDs.

ORIENTATION AND PRACTICAL INFORMATION. Coober Pedy is 685km (6-8hr.) south of Alice Springs, 744km southeast of Uluru, 166km west of William Creek and the Oodnadatta Track, 538km north of Port Augusta, and 846km (8-10hr.) north of Adelaide. The turn-off from the Stuart Hwy. leads into **Hutchison Street,** the main street, where most points of interest are located. The helpful **Visitor Information Centre** (☎8672 5298 or 1800 637 076; open M-F 8:30am-5pm, Sa-Su 10am-1pm), at the south end of Hutchison St. across from the bus depot, has free 30min. **Internet** access. If the visitors center is closed, try the unofficial tourist office, **Underground Books,** on Post Office Hill Rd., left off Hutchison St. (☎8672 5558. Open M-F 8:30am-5:30pm, Sa 10am-4pm.) Other services include: **ATM** at Westpac Bank and at the Opal Inn Hotel; the **police,** on Malliotis Blvd., (☎8672 5056), the first left off Hutchison's from the Hwy.; **RAA** (☎8672 5230), at Desert Traders; a **pharmacy** on Hutchison St. across from the Umoona Mine (☎8672 3333; open M-F 9am-6pm, Sa 9am-2pm); the **Miner's Store,** a supermarket on Hutchison St., on the right after the roundabout (☎8672 5051. Open M-Sa 8:30am-7pm, Su 9am-6pm.); and a **post office** in the Miner's Store. **Postal Code:** 5723.

ACCOMMODATIONS. **Radeka's Backpacker's Inn ❷,** at Hutchison and Oliver St., on the right at the base of the hill after the roundabout, is an underground hostel, with a clean, comfortable maze of underground caves 6.5m below ground. If you're lucky, you can stay in the "dungeon." (☎8672 5223 or 1800 633 891; www.radekadownunder.com.au. Kitchen, pool table, TV room, courtesy bus pickup and drop-off, and the cheapest bar in town only sweeten the deal. Internet access $2 per 15min. Reception daily 8am-9pm. Linen $2, plus $8 deposit. Dorms $22; doubles $55; motel singles and doubles $105.) **Riba's Underground Camping ❶** is on William Creek Rd., outside of town. Coming from Port Augusta, turn off 4km before Hutchison St. (☎8672 5614. Sites $7.50, subterranean sites $11, powered above-ground sites $12, powered subterranean sites $16.) The swankiest spot in town is the **Desert Cave Hotel ❺,** opposite Radeka's on Hutchinson St. Equipped dugout rooms (TV, couch, phone, wine) are accompanied by a swimming pool, gym, and restaurant. (☎1800 088 521 or 8672 5688; www.desertcave.com.au. Reception daily 6:30am-11:30pm. Doubles $192.)

FOOD AND NIGHTLIFE. Run by an immigrant Sicilian family, **John's Pizza Bar ❶,** located in the strip mall on Hutchison St., is a one-of-a-kind restaurant. John's is where Italian tradition meets Coober Pedy quirkiness. It is also the unofficial party spot for those in the know. Every night after closing, backpackers swarm the premises while wine flows, music pumps, and the Italian-Australians party the night away. Pizzas run $7-27. (☎8672 5561. Open daily 10am-10pm.) **Traces ❶**, on the roundabout, is a fully licensed Greek restaurant with a nightly backpacker special for $10. (☎8672 5147. Open daily 4pm-latenight.) Next to Traces, **Breakaways Cafe ❶** serves standard diner food. (☎8672 3177. Breakfast $4-9. Burgers and sandwiches $5-8.50. Open daily 7am-10pm. Like the good outback town it is, Coober Pedy's town pub, the **Opal Inn Hotel,** on the corner of the roundabout, is where all the elements mix. (☎8672 5054. Schooners $3.50. Happy Hour W and F 6-8pm ½-price drinks. Open daily 10am-latenight.)

TOURS. The visitors center books all tours, but you can also contact operators directly. Those that prefer to go at their own pace should note that most destinations can be covered independently by car. The 12hr. **Mail Run** covers a triangular route, stopping at points of interest while delivering mail to cattle stations. (☎1800 069 911; www.mailruntour.com. Book ahead. M and Th 9am. $155, prices rise with petrol costs.) **Radeka's Desert Breakaways Tours** is popular with backpackers and includes Crocodile Harry's, the opal fields, a trip out to the Breakaways (a set of mesas), and a chance to mine for your own opals. (☎8672 5223. Daily at 1pm. 4hr. $50.) The **Desert Cave Hotel's Tour** offers a similar trip for more money as well as scenic flights. (☎1800 088 521. Daily at 8am and 1pm. Min. 4 people. $55 per guest, more for non-guests. 30min. scenic flights $70 per person.) **Riba's Evening Mine Tours** takes guests underground for a 1½hr. mine tour. (☎8672 5614. Daily 7:30pm. $16.) **Martin Smith's Night Sky** tours take advantage of the clear night skies around Coober Pedy for some astronomy lessons and star gazing. (Book at Radeka's, ☎8672 5223, or any accommodation; www.martinsmithsnightsky.com.au. 1½hr. $22, children $11.)

SIGHTS. The **Umoona Opal Mine and Museum** is a landmark on Hutchison St. The complex is an award-winning museum with displays of local Aboriginal culture, town history, and, of course, opals. The underground complex includes a full-sized home which contrasts early and modern dugout styles. Check out the display dedicated to Eric the Plesiosaur, a sea-dwelling dinosaur whose fossilized skeleton (as well as the remains of his last supper) turned to opal. Eric himself is on display at the Australian Museum in Sydney. The mine tours next door allow visitors to go in search of their own opals. (☎8672 5288; www.umoonaopalmine.com.au. Mine and museum open daily 8am-7pm. Tours daily 10am, 2, and 4pm. $10, children $5.) The town's **underground churches** are usually open to visitors. The oldest of these churches is the **Saints Peter and Paul Catholic Church,** next to Radeka's. The underground **Serbian Orthodox Church,** left off Flinders St. (look for the sign), with its gothic design, is unusual and worth a visit. Another sort of underground shrine is **Crocodile Harry's Crocodile's Nest,** the lair of the legendary womanizer, adventurer, and crocodile-slayer who was one of the models for the character Crocodile Dundee. Originally from Latvia, the now 80+ Harry has put his croc-wrasslin' days behind him, but his home, 6km west of town on Seventeen Mile Rd., is covered wall to wall with underwear, graffiti, and photos of a much younger Harry wrestling crocodiles the size of dinosaurs (admission $2). Outside town, 17km north on the Stuart Hwy., the track on **Moon Plain** (70km return; 2hr.), a lunar landscape of glinting rocks and browned pieces of vegetation, is fun to explore. This is also the stretch of road featured in the movie *Priscilla, Queen of the Desert. Mad Max III* was also filmed out here. The famous **Great Dog Fence,** the world's longest fence, is about 15km outside Coober Pedy.

OPAL SHOPPING. Coober Pedy is glinting with opal pushers and their wares, but not all are quality. Decent opals will give off multiple colors as you turn them in the light. The greater the intensity of these secondary colors, the better the opal. **Dreamtime Gems,** on Hutchison St., on the right past John's Pizza Bar, has opals on display, as well as a blue-tongued lizard you can hold and a collection of scorpions and poisonous spiders you cannot. Opal shoppers would do well to stop here for a free demonstration and explanation of opal types and pricing. (☎8672 3888. Open daily 9am-7pm, later depending on business.) Doublets are the cheapest way to buy opal. Triplet stones are doublets with a protective cap of quartz. Solid opal is the priciest and highest quality with different colors varying in price based on how rare they are. Red is the most expensive, and blue the least expensive and most common. Size doesn't necessarily matter, and smaller opals are often of better quality. When buying, choose an opal store that's particularly well-lit; the colors can be seen better in bright light, and dim stores may be hiding flaws.

OFF THE STUART HIGHWAY: OODNADATTA TRACK

The **Oodnadatta Track,** one of the most famous Outback tracks in Australia, runs 619km from Marree, north of Leigh Creek in the Flinders, through William Creek and Oodnadatta to Marla, 235km north of Coober Pedy on the Stuart Hwy. Without a doubt a great way to see the Outback, the track gives visitors a taste of the harsh realities of life in the center. The horizon shimmers like a mirage in the heat, and carcasses of cars that didn't make it join animals that met a similar fate. There is no cellular phone service on the track, and there is no free water anywhere.

After a rare rainfall, the entire track can close, cutting residents off from the rest of civilization. Mostly following the route of the **Old Ghan** train line that used to connect Alice Springs with points south, the Oodnadatta passes the vast salt-beds of **Lake Eyre,** immense stretches of baked red nothing, ruins of ancient farm homes, and the legendary dog fence. The unsealed road can be driven in a 2WD vehicle; drive slower than 40km per hr. Most rental companies do not insure their cars on unsealed roads. It's a good idea to call or check online with the **Northern Road Conditions Hotline** (☎1300 361 033; www.transport.sa.gov.au/quicklinks/northern_roads/northern.asp) for road closures, though signs at each town provide the conditions for the next segment of track. Regardless of your vehicle, the best advice is to **slow down:** the faster you go, the higher the likelihood of flat tires. Be particularly careful around road trains, as they are known to kick up rocks that can shatter windshields.

Pink's Roadhouse puts out a thorough **mudmap** guide to the Oodnadatta Track that includes every detour and detail a traveler could desire. Try to pick it up before you leave Adelaide (p. 464) or the visitors center in Port Augusta (p. 502); otherwise, check the website.

Though larger tours, such as Wayward Bus (p. 458), incorporate the Oodnadatta into some of their itineraries, there are tour groups that operate exclusively in the area. Those who want to take in the vastness of the Outback via air travel should try **Wrightsair** (☎70 79 62; www.wrightsair.com.au), a scenic flight company based in William Creek. For a unique approach to traveling the Outback, the eco-friendly **Camel Safaris** (☎1800 064 244 or 8672 3968; www.austcamel.com.au/explore.htm) runs four-day camel treks along the Oodnadatta track from April to October. See the website for a schedule of tours and prices. (Non-refundable 10% deposit required. Min. 6-person.) Towns are listed below from south to north, as they would be encountered traveling north on the Oodnadatta Track.

MARREE. A mostly unsealed road leads 120km northwest of Leigh Creek to **Marree,** which is the starting point of both the Oodnadatta and **Birdsville Tracks.** The former heads northwest to the Stuart Hwy., while the latter slices through the **Sturt Stony Desert** and parts of the **Strzelecki Desert** to the northeast on the way to western Queensland. The town possesses more than its share of outback charm: locomotives from the Old Ghan dominate the town center, children play on the dusty cricket grounds, and the reconstructed ruins of a mosque uphold the memory of early Muslim cameleers. On the edge of town, the camel sundial made from old railway sleepers records the lumbering hours.

The **Marree Hotel** ❸ is a friendly repository of outback history built in 1883. (☎8675 8344. Dinner from $12. Singles $45; doubles $65; families $90; lower rates off-season.) The **Drover's Rest Tourist Park** ❷, on the south side of town, perfectly fits the stereotype of a dusty outback caravan park. (☎8675 8371. Linen $10. Sites $10 per person, powered $14; budget rooms from $20; on-site vans $40; cabins for 2 from $80.) The old telegraph station next door to the hotel is now the **Oasis Cafe,** providing **Internet** access, tire repair, the cheapest **petrol** in town, and maps of the area. (☎8675 8352. Internet $2.50 per 15min. Open daily 7:30am-7pm.) Oasis Cafe also runs the **Oasis Caravan Park,** just down the road, which lures campers to its outdoor spa for a night view of the outback sky. (Sites $6 per person, powered $9; cabins for 2 $55.) The **Marree General Store** has a **post office.** (☎8675 8360. Store open daily high season 7:30am-7pm, low season 8am-7pm.) **Postal Code:** 5733.

LAKE EYRE. Lake Eyre, 90km northwest of Marree, contains Australia's lowest point at 39 ft. below sea level. Australia's largest salt lake, it acts as the drainage space for an area approximately the size of Western Europe. A normally dry climate makes it especially impressive after a period of heavy rain as the lake swells considerably. The Oodnadatta Track brushes up against the southern edge of **Lake Eyre South,** the smaller of the Lake's two parts, and a brief detour lets you drive right up to its salty edge. The two access roads to the larger **Lake Eyre North** are 4WD only, and depart from Marree (94km from the lake) and from a turn-off on the track 7km south of William Creek (64km from the lake). **Campsites** ❶ are available near the north part of the lake on both access roads; passes are available at the Marree General Store or at the self-registration stations at the Lake Eyre National Park entrances (day-pass $11, overnight pass $20; free with Desert Parks Pass). The **NPWS info line** (☎1800 816 078) provides lake conditions. Take the weather into account before going, as temperatures up to 50°C (122°F) in the summer can make it not only unpleasant to visit, but also unwise.

WILLIAM CREEK. The next watering hole is 204km northwest of Marree at **William Creek,** a hundred-acre freehold in the middle of Anna Creek cattle station (the world's largest at a Belgium-sized 2.4 million hectares). Covered with signs and bedecked with visitors' bras, boxers, driver's licenses, foreign currency, and various other curiosities, **William Creek Pub** ❶ is the idiosyncratic outback pub you've been looking for. (☎8670 7880. Linen $5. Sites $3.50; bunks $15; ensuite singles $50; doubles $70, under 12 half-price. Hotel rooms not available in summer.) The pub also has **petrol** and tire repair. The new **Dingo Cafe and Caravan Park** sits nearby and has a coveted espresso machine. (☎8670 7746. Cafe closed in summer.) Drivers can head east to Coober Pedy directly from William Creek (164km east).

OODNADATTA. Oodnadatta is yet another, slightly larger, outback settlement 203km northwest of William Creek, but it has precious amenities, including **car repair** facilities and the unmistakable **Pink Roadhouse** ❶, which offers valuable info and services, including **petrol,** groceries, and emergency supplies. Longtime owners Adam and Lynnie are happy to help each and every traveler who passes through. Check road and weather conditions with Pink's or with the **police** (☎8670 7805). The roadhouse also has a **post office, Internet** access ($3 per 15min.), and accommodations; they can arrange car repairs and vehicle recovery as well. Essentially, Pink's does everything except arrange marriages, though they make up for that with filling burgers ($6-9). (☎1800 802 074 or 8670 7822; www.pinkroadhouse.com.au. Open daily peak season 8am-6pm; in summer M-F 8am-5:30pm, Sa-Su 9am-5pm. Sites $9.50, powered $15.50; singles $38; hotel-style doubles $48; ensuite cabins for two $80.) From here, you can either continue northwest on the track to its end at Marla (210km) or head southwest to Coober Pedy (195km). Oodna is also a good base for those traveling to the beautiful oasis at **Dalhousie Springs** (190km north) and the expansive **Simpson Desert,** both popular destinations (**Desert Parks Pass** required).

MARLA. Marla, where the Oodnadatta Track rejoins civilization, is an overgrown highway rest area that sits approximately halfway between Adelaide and Alice Springs. The **Traveller's Rest Roadhouse ❸** has **petrol,** a small **supermarket** (both open 24hr.), a bar, a restaurant, **Internet** access ($2 per 15min.), a free community pool ($5 key deposit), showers ($4), and pricey accommodations. (☎8670 7001. Camping $5 per person, power an additional $7; dorms $20-30; budget cabin singles $30; doubles $40; motel singles $75, with TV $85; doubles $80/90) Those heading north toward Uluru and Alice should get fuel here: the next station will be **Kulgera,** 180km north. Those heading south should push on to Cadney Homestead, 153km north of Coober Pedy, rather than staying over in Marla. Cadney's offers one-night camping and use of facilities for $2.

EYRE PENINSULA

Although the landscape may not look promising from the highway, the **Eyre Peninsula** is as spectacular as it is under appreciated. It encompasses the stretch of coastline from Ceduna to the town of Nullarbor, where the Nullarbor Plain begins. Free from the tourist hordes, the tiny towns of the peninsula remain picturesque, authentic fishing villages. Between the towns, dirt tracks turn off the highway for a coastline that has virtually untouched beaches and sparkling water stretching lazily along the coast. While the east coast has gentle rolling dunes and calm waters, the aquamarine waves of the west coast caress rock faces and rough-hewn cliffs.

The abundance of fish on both coasts makes the Eyre Peninsula Australia's premier fishing destination. The free *Seafood and Aquaculture Trail Guide* lists a series of interesting, unusual tours along the peninsula that highlight the importance of the sea in the local economy and culture. The trail includes visits to rock lobster colonies and a seahorse breeding facility in Port Lincoln. The Eyre is also home to several phenomenal national parks, most notably the three clustered at the southern tip of the peninsula: **Lincoln National Park, Coffin Bay,** and **Whaler's Way.** Towns are covered below from east to west, as they would be encountered coming from Adelaide on Hwy. 1 Alt.

TRANSPORTATION

Premier Stateliner (Adelaide ☎8415 5555, Ceduna ☎8625 2279, Port Lincoln ☎8682 1288, Whyalla ☎8645 9911) is the only public **bus** carrier on the Eyre with anything approaching frequent service, though **Greyhound Australia** stops in Ceduna on the way to Perth. Stateliner runs between Adelaide and Whyalla (M-F 5 per day, Sa-Su 3-4 per day; $43). Buses also leave Adelaide bound for Port Lincoln, stopping in towns along the east coast. (M-F 2 per day, Su 1 per day; $75.) Stateliner also runs an overnight bus from Adelaide to Ceduna via Streaky Bay. (Departs Adelaide M-F and Su 1 per day; departs Ceduna daily 1 per day; $87, concessions 50% off.) Traversing the Eyre Peninsula by car means diverging from the Eyre Hwy. (Hwy. 1), which runs 468km across the top of the peninsula from Whyalla to Ceduna. The highlights of the Eyre are on a triangular coastal route via the Lincoln and Flinders Hwy. (Alt. Hwy. 1), which takes 763km to connect the same towns.

WHYALLA ☎08

It's easy to be ambivalent about Whyalla, the largest town on the east end of the Eyre Peninsula. Some brochures say "Whyalla" is from an old Aboriginal word meaning "place of the water," others say it's from a phrase meaning "I don't know." This pretty much sums it up.

Whyalla lacks good budget accommodations, and travelers would do best to head south to Cowell. **Hotel Spencer ❸,** on the corner of Forsyth St. and Darling Terr., has pleasant ensuite rooms with TV, fridge, and A/C. (☎8645 8411. Reception daily 8am-7pm. Singles $35; doubles $50.) The **Whyalla Foreshore Caravan Park ❶,** on Broadbent Terr., is 2km from the post office and close to the beach. (☎8645 7474. Powered sites $24; on-site vans for 2 $40-47; cabins for 2 $61-82.) At the **Cake Shoppe ❶,** 29 Playford Hwy. near the intersection with Nicolson Ave., Charlie, a friendly baker from Jersey (the island off the coast of France), makes delicious, inexpensive pastries and bread for under $3. (☎8645 8037. Open M-F 6am-4pm, Sa-Su 6am-noon. Cash only.)

Tours of the **Whyalla Steelworks** take visitors to the heart of Whyalla, passing the blast furnace, coke ovens, and rolling mill on the way. (Book at the visitors center. 2hr. tours M, W, F at 9:30am. $17, concessions $15.50, children $8.) From May to August hundreds of thousands of the bizarre **giant cuttlefish** spawn near Whyalla. Whyalla has seized upon this unlikely creature, which changes shape, texture, and color to blend with its surroundings, as its mascot (www.cuttlefish-capital.com.au).

The **Whyalla Visitors Centre** is on the east side of the Lincoln Hwy. as you're heading out of the city toward Port Augusta. Look for the big ship that houses the Maritime Museum next door. Pick up a free **map** of the town here. (☎8645 7900 or 1800 088 589; www.whyalla.sa.gov.au. Free **Internet** access. Open M-F 9am-5pm, Sa 9am-4pm, Su 9:30am-4pm.) **ATMs** abound on Forsyth St. in the city center. Monarch ChemMart, in the Westland Shopping Centre on Nicolson Ave., offers **pharmacy** services. (☎8645 5045. Open daily 9am-9pm.) **Hospital:** ☎8648 8300. The **post office** is on Darling Terr. (Open M-F 9am-5pm.) **Postal code:** 5600.

EYRE PENINSULA EAST COAST

As Alt. Hwy. 1 winds along the east coast, the road hosts a few dots of civilization tucked away in seaside breaks from the leisurely rolling plains. Any of these small fishing hamlets is a good place to stop and rest, but **Cowell,** 111km south of Whyalla, has the most to offer visitors. Right on the **Franklin Harbour,** Cowell has a thriving oyster industry, the nation's only commercial jade mining, and a quiet foreshore with excellent fishing. After Cowell, from north to south, **Arno Bay, Port Neill,** and **Tumby Bay** are also good spots to visit. All towns have **petrol stations** and **post offices;** Cowell's post is located at 2 Main St. (Open M-F 9am-noon and 1-5pm). In addition, Cowell's **Town Council Office,** on Main St., has tourist information.

ACCOMMODATIONS. All of the above towns have **caravan parks** and **pub hotels** (singles from around $30; doubles $40). The **Franklin Harbour Hotel ❸,** 1 Main St., in Cowell, has clean rooms and a balcony overlooking the harbor as well as the most character of any of the east coast accommodations; just try the Nigel's Gone Mad Mungo Mungo Juice at the downstairs bar. Mountain bikes and fishing rods are available for guest use. (☎8629 2015 or 1800 303 449. Continental breakfast included. Singles $35; doubles $49.) The **Commercial Hotel ❸,** 24 Main St, in Cowell, has similar accommodations, but lacks the harbor views and personality. (☎8629 2181. Singles $30; doubles $45; family room $50.) Further south, the **Seabreeze**

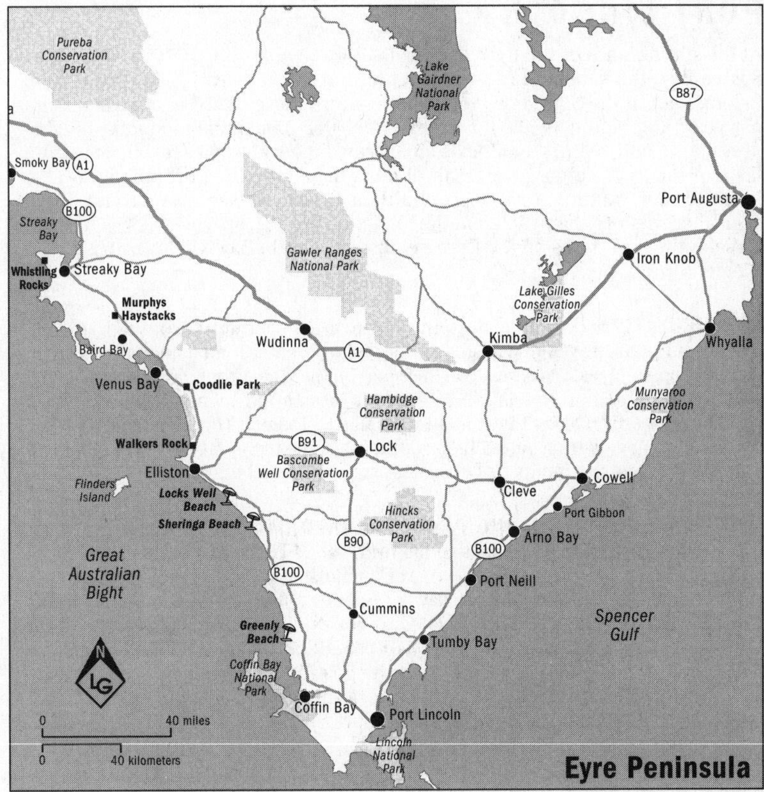

Hotel ❷, 7 Tumby Terr., in Tumby Bay, offers cheap rooms on the waterfront. (☎8688 2362. Singles $20, ensuite $35; doubles $30/65, extra person $5.)

FOOD. Visitors coming from the east can consider Cowell their introduction to Eyre Peninsula's extensive seafood menu. Those who really want the local seafood with local style can try their hands at fishing from any of the town's jetties. Otherwise, **Cowell Seafood Producers,** 72 The Esplanade, follow 3rd St. out of town and then look for signs, sells fresh local seafood, including Cowell's signature oysters. (☎8629 2621. $3.50 per fresh ½-dozen oysters; pickled oysters $7. Open M-F 7:30am-5pm.) **Cowell Bakery,** 25 Main St., bakes pies and pastries ($2.60), but oyster kebabs ($5.50) are the real standout on the menu. (☎8629 2034. Open M-W 8:30am-8pm, Th-F 8:30am-8:30pm, Sa 9am-8:30pm, Su 10am-8:30pm.)

SIGHTS. From Cowell, 3rd St. runs out of town and becomes unsealed (still 2WD accessible) Beach Rd., so named because it provides access to numerous beaches down the coast. The various beaches are well labeled off Beach Rd. On the whole, the east coast beaches have calm waters perfect for swimming and fishing. **Port Gibbons,** 22km south of Cowell, is arguably the best spot on the east coast with massive sand dunes overlooking the ocean.

PORT LINCOLN ☎08

At the southern tip of the Eyre Peninsula, Port Lincoln (pop. 13,000) overlooks **Boston Bay,** the second-largest natural harbor in the world. With the largest fishing fleet in the Southern Hemisphere, worth more than $40 million dollars per year, it should come as no surprise that Port Lincoln is a popular holiday destination and visitors and locals alike crowd the waterfront restaurants for a taste of the local catch. As a result of its fishing industry, Port Lincoln is also home to more millionaires per capita than anywhere else in Australia. However, there's more than yachts in Port Lincoln; the city provides easy access to three of the best parks on the Eyre Peninsula—Coffin Bay NP, Lincoln NP, and Whaler's Way.

ORIENTATION. Port Lincoln sprawls across the southern tip of the Eyre Peninsula, and smart travelers will stop by the visitors center for a map of the town. In general, most places of interest can be found on the waterfront strip near the jetty. Most restaurants and hotels are located on **Tasman Terr.,** which runs east-west along the waterfront. One block inland, parallel to Tasman Terr., **Liverpool St.** is the town's shopping district. About 3km southeast of the town jetty is the ritzy **Lincoln Cove Marina,** where a number of upscale restaurants can be found.

TRANSPORTATION AND PRACTICAL INFORMATION. Premier Stateliner bus services depart from their booking office at 24 Lewis St., a half-block south of Tasman Terr. (☎8682 1288. Open M-F 8am-6:45pm, Sa 8:30-11:30am.) Buses run to Adelaide (M-F and Su 2 per day; Sa 1 per day; $81.70 one-way, concessions $40.85) via Port Augusta ($40.90 one-way, concessions $20.45). Book ahead for buses. If you need a **taxi,** try ☎13 10 08 or 8682 1222. Make the **Visitors Information Centre,** 3 Adelaide Pl., across from the post office, your first stop in town. The visitors center provides information on a variety of area tours, handle bookings, and sell permits for local national parks. (☎8683 3544 or 1300 788 378; www.visitportlincoln.net. **Internet** access $3 per 15min. Open daily 9am-5pm.) The **library,** in the Spencer Institute building, just off Tasman Terr., offers 1hr. blocks of free Internet access. (☎8688 3622. Open M-Tu and Th-F 9am-5pm, W 9am-7pm, Su 1-4:30pm.) The **Port Lincoln Hospital** is on Oxford Terr. (☎8683 2284) and a **pharmacy** can be found at 43 Tasman Terr. (☎8682 2664. Open M-F 9am-5:30pm, Sa 9am-noon, Su 10am-12:30pm and 7-8pm.) Other services include: **banks** and **ATMs** on Tasman Terr. and Liverpool St.; the 24hr. **police station,** 1 Liverpool St. (☎8688 3020); and a **post office** at 68 Tasman Terr. (Open M-F 9am-5pm.) **Postal Code:** 5606.

ACCOMMODATIONS. The **Pier Hotel ❸,** at the center of Tasman Terr., offers adequate rooms, some with bay views, all with cable TV. Night owls will appreciate that the raucous epicenter of Port Lincoln nightlife is just downstairs. (☎8682 1322. Happy hour F 4:30-6pm. Rooms $60-110.) Though not as centrally located, **Hotel Boston ❸,** 19-21 King St. near the silos at the west end of Tasman Terr., has adequate rooms that saw their most distinguished guest in 1954 when Queen Elizabeth II stayed there. (☎8682 1311. Singles $30, ensuite with TV $40; doubles $40/65. Weekly rates available.) **Kirton Point Caravan Park ❶,** at the end of London St., 3km from the town center, has a prime location on the waterfront. To reach the caravan park, take Tasman Terr. east out of town and follow the signs. (☎8682 2537; www.kirtonpointcaravanpark.com.au. Kitchen 8am-9pm. Sites $9 per person, powered $21 for 2 people, $7 each additional person; cabins $47-70.)

FOOD. With a prime waterfront location, **Moorings ❸**, in the Grand Tasman Hotel, 94 Tasman Terr., is the best place to sample local seafood. The dishes are served with minimal seasoning, allowing the quality of the fish to stand out. The sashimi tuna ($23, entree $14) will make you understand why tuna is the backbone of the fishing industry. (☎8682 2133; www.grandtasmanhotel.com.au. Main courses $20-30. Open M-F 7-9am, noon-2:30pm, 6-10pm; Sa-Su 7-9am and 6-10pm.; longer hours sometimes depending on business.) The large fish 'n' chips portions (from $5.50) at **Ocean Delights ❶**, 57 Tasman Terr., are delicious. (☎8682 4993. Open daily 10am-8pm.) Filling sandwiches ($8.90) can be found at **Cafe Chino ❶**, 42 Tasman Terr. (☎8682 5509. Hot food not served after 2:30pm. Open M-F 8am-5pm, Sa 8am-4pm, Su 9am-3pm.) **Coles** is on Liverpool St. (☎8682 2700. Open M-W and F 6am-7pm, Th 6am-9pm, Sa 6am-5pm, Su 11am-5pm.)

SIGHTS AND ACTIVITIES. Fishery Bay, just before Whaler's Way (p. 522), is a long stretch of sand with a consistent surf break and extended shallow waters that make it surfable for all ability levels. Whether for sunbathing or surfing, Fishery is a must for visitors. Be careful of sharks, as great whites do live in nearby waters. **Skin Diving & Surf Center,** 1 King St., just off Tasman Terr., rents dive gear (full kit $50-60 per day). They can also provide information on the best surf and dive spots in the area. (☎8682 4428. Open M-F 9am-5:30pm, Sa 9am-12:30pm.) **Out There Kayaking,** South Quay Blvd., at the Lincoln Cove Marina, rents kayaks and runs tours. (☎8683 5100; www.outtheretours.com.au. Kayak single $15 per hr., doubles $20. Marina sunset tour $30, ½-day $70.)

TOURS. For an insider's look at Port Lincoln's lifeblood, the **Fishing Fleet Tour and Taste** provides an opportunity to view live rock lobsters and explore a working prawn trawler. (Book 90min. tours through the visitors center. $12, concessions $10, children $6.) **Triple Bay Charters** gives visitors a look at the blue-fin tuna farming that, along with prawns, fuels Port Lincoln's economy. Fishing tours are also available. Tours depart from the marina daily, weather permitting. (☎8682 4419 or 04 2982 4119. 2hr. marina tour $40, children $25. Fishing tours ½-day $85, full-day $150. Book tours through the visitors center.) The **Port Lincoln Seahorse Farm,** 5 Mallee Crescent, Australia's only seahorse breeding facility, has a popular tour during which you see thousands of the creatures. (Book through visitors center; www.saseahorse.com. 30min. tours daily 3pm. $10, concessions $8.50.)

GREAT AUSTRALIAN BITE

The waters off the southern tip of the Eyre Peninsula are known for their varied sea creatures, among them the Great White shark. While most visitors tremble at the thought of stepping in shark-infested waters, adrenaline junkies are biting at the chance to get up close and personal with Jaws. Thanks to **Calypso Star Charter,** visitors can step into a shark cage and get as close as they like.

An expensive but thrilling tour with Calypso allows a rare chance to see Great White sharks in their natural environment. Tours depart from Port Lincoln, and when they get into a prime area, the crew drops fish blood and chum in the water to draw the beast close. Then, with the water bloody and the carnivores ready for a feast, divers plunge into the ocean with nothing but a cage to keep the Great White from satisfying its appetite. Most tours are 4 days long, though 2- and 3-day tours are available.

If that description doesn't scare you off, then this is probably a splurge you'll never forget. Calypso offers a once in a lifetime opportunity to see, photograph, and dine with Great Whites—that is if you live to tell the tale.

For departure dates and openings consult the website. (☎8364 4428; www.calypsostarcharter.com.au. Max. 8 people. Book far ahead. $575 per day. 10% non-refundable deposit required.)

FESTIVALS. Port Lincoln showcases its wares in the one-of-a-kind **Tunarama Festival** (☎8682 1300), a four-day extravaganza of fireworks, sand castles, and seafood held annually the week before **Australia Day** in late January. The festival also features live music, a rodeo, a highly competitive tuna-tossing contest, and an Australia Day rodeo (☎1800 629 911). The **Adelaide to Lincoln Yacht Race,** held the last weekend of February, is a chance to see some of the impressive fleet in action. Food, fashion, and general merriment are abundant during the **Port Lincoln Cup Carnival,** a horse-racing event held annually in mid-March (☎8682 3851). The races will be held March 6th and 8th in 2007. The **One World Festival** held annually in mid-April cooks up dishes from around the world in a festival of international cuisine.

LINCOLN NATIONAL PARK AND MEMORY COVE

One of Eyre's best kept secrets, Lincoln NP, just 13km from Port Lincoln, offers outdoor enthusiasts breathtaking scenery, abundant wildlife, and pristine beaches. At the southernmost end of the park, Memory Cove provides the best views and camping in the area.

To reach Lincoln, take Mortlock Terr. out of town, which will eventually become Verran Terr. Turn left after crossing the railroad tracks and follow Proper Bay Rd. toward Tulka and Whaler's Way. **Camping ❶,** with toilets and rainwater facilities, is available at designated park areas along the way. Park passes ($7) are available at self-registration kiosks at the camp entrance. Those looking to camp will have to pay for an additional camping permit ($4 per night). Groups might want to consider renting the five-room **Donington Cottage ❸** at the north tip of the park. (☎8683 3544. Book through Port Lincoln's visitors center (p. 520). Full kitchen. $35 per person, off-season $32.50; children rates available.) In addition to the Port Lincoln Visitor's Center, the **Eyre District Parks Office,** 75 Liverpool St., Port Lincoln (☎8688 3111), has park information.

Most major attractions and campgrounds within the park are 2WD accessible in good weather. The difficult **Sleaford-Wanna Dune** trail is one of the few 4WD tracks in the park, traversing 14km of scorching sand dunes. At the northern tip of the park, **September Beach** is an excellent swimming spot with great camping facilities.

Memory Cove, in the southeast section of the park, is a remote wilderness area accessible by 4WD track. Visitors need a key and permit to access the cove; these are available from the visitors center in Port Lincoln (p. 520). (☎8683 3544. Day pass, including camping $6.50. **Bush camping** is limited to 5 sites and must be booked ahead. $16 per night, 3-night limit. Key deposit $20.) The Memory Cove campsite, 19km (45min.) from the locked gate, rewards visitors who made the effort to visit Memory Cove with a private stretch of beach and the chance to fall asleep to the sounds of the ocean. En route to the campsites, numbered green posts line the road. The numbers correspond to those on the map guide and alert visitors to noteworthy sights.

WHALER'S WAY

Thirty-two kilometers from Port Lincoln, the most spectacular display of the peninsula's untouched, raw beauty is found in Whaler's Way. Access to this privately owned reserve requires a key and an expensive permit, but the experience is worth the extra cost. Purchase permits at the Port Lincoln visitors center. (☎8683 3544. Map with detailed directions to lookout points included. Key deposit $10. $25 per car, includes 1 night of camping, each additional night $5.) The 2002 season of the American hit television show *Survivor* was filmed here in South Australia's harshest, most rugged landscape. The park is 4WD access only. **Bush camping** is allowed at **Redbank** and **Groper Bay;** an additional camping permit must be purchased from the visitors center. Groper Bay has BBQ and toilets, while Redbanks has beach access. Be forewarned that all facilities are very basic. Those without 4WD or unwilling to pay admission to Whaler's Way should visit **Fishery Bay** (p. 521). Just before the turn-off for Whaler's Way, Fishery is a free beach and far more accessible, but still allows for a glimpse of the jagged cliffs and ocean swells that make Whaler's famous.

A 14km dirt road traverses the interior of the park, and numerous, well-marked tracks lead to commanding views of the Southern Ocean. A dip in the reserve's **Swimming Hole,** an isolated pool of ocean water surrounded by limestone cliffs, is sure to rank among your most memorable swimming experiences. **Cape Carnot,** in the southwest, has a blowhole where waves crash against the rocks, often getting as high as the cliffs themselves. Just north of Cape Carnot, **Theakstones** is a narrow crevasse where water rushes in and ricochets off the walls. Throughout the park emus and kangaroos roam the premises year-round and even seals can be found lounging on rocks. To see the park's namesake, visit in September or October when the whales frequent the waters below.

COFFIN BAY NATIONAL PARK ☎08

A mere 47km from Port Lincoln toward Ceduna is the lazy town of Coffin Bay, gateway to the magnificent **Coffin Bay National Park.** Visitors to Coffin Bay will find the camping and accommodation options limited. The **Coffin Bay Caravan Park ❷** is on the Esplanade; turn left on Giles Rd. and follow signs. (☎8685 4170. Sites $8 per person, powered $22-24; on-site vans for two $40-50; cabins for 2 from $55-95; extra person $15.) The **Coffin Bay Hotel/Motel ❺**, on Shepherd Ave., is the sole hotel option and has one of the only **ATMs** in town. (☎8685 4111. Singles $85; doubles $95.) The **Oysterbeds Restaurant ❸**, 61 Esplanade, serves delicious, fresh seafood main dishes ($20.50-28) in an elegant setting. (☎8685 4000. Open Tu-Sa 11am-9pm, Su 11am-2pm. Hours can vary, and booking is recommended.)

Park information pamphlets are available from **Beachcomber Agencies** on the left of the main road as you come into town. The same building also houses the closest thing you'll find to a general store. (☎8685 4057. Open daily 7am-7pm.) The **National Parks and Wildlife Service** (☎8688 3111) in Port Lincoln also provides information on Coffin Bay, as does the Port Lincoln visitors center.

Follow signs from the Esplanade to reach Coffin Bay National Park. This peninsular park is home to beach heaven and a 4WD enthusiast's dream. **Yangie Bay** (15km from the entrance) is the only campground in the park that's 2WD accessible year-round; several bush hikes also originate here. Although **Almonta Beach** (16km from the entrance) and **Point Avoid** (18km from the entrance) are also generally accessible with 2WD, the rest of the park is **4WD only.** Coffin Bay isn't worth visiting unless you can explore it in an off-road vehicle. With 4WD the park is nothing short of amazing; tracks lead to myriad hidden coves and private lookouts. If you are braving the 4WD tracks, be forewarned that they are mostly just markers on sand dunes designed for experienced 4WD drivers. Deflate tires to around 17psi to avoid getting bogged. Tell someone your planned route and have a shovel on hand in case of a bogging.

Camping is allowed at designated sites only, all of which have toilets and a limited rainwater supply (unreliable in summer months). Day passes, camping permits, and maps are available at the park entrance with self-registration. (Entry $7 per car; camping $4 per night.) All of the campgrounds are located in sheltered areas right on the beach. Arguably the most picturesque is **Black Springs,** 28km from the entrance (allow 3hr. round-trip for the drive). A short walk or drive down the road to the left of the campground entrance sign leads to a dead end and cliff area that is one of the most beautiful spots in the park.

Point Sir Isaac, Mullalong Beach, Reef Point Lookout, and **Sensation Beach** all have nice scenery, but the 4WD tracks are the real reason to come this far into the park. The view of **Seven Mile Beach** as you drive along the shore is absolutely dazzling. Before venturing to Seven Mile Beach, be sure to check tides, as it is dangerous at high tide. Visitors shouldn't leave Coffin Bay without venturing south to **Gunyah Beach,** which hides a colorful and varied landscape.

EYRE PENINSULA WEST COAST

The west coast of the Eyre Peninsula runs from Port Lincoln north to the town of Ceduna. With scenery comparable to the Great Ocean Road, these coastal drives see far less traffic, allowing those who take the time to venture off the highway to enjoy secluded coastal views of limestone outcrops, excellent surf and diving, and abundant fishing. With a still-fledgling tourist industry, the west coast lacks the tours and public transport that its scenery deserves, but for those who do make it here, the journey will be half the fun.

ORIENTATION AND PRACTICAL INFORMATION. The Eyre Peninsula booklet has an excellent **map** with beaches and points of interest labeled. In addition, signs on the Eyre Hwy. lead visitors to the prime coastal spots. The two main towns on the coast are Elliston and Streaky Bay, 169km and 294km northwest from Port Lincoln, respectively. The **Elliston Visitors Center,** on the right as you come into town, has **Internet** access ($3 per 30min.) and area information. (☎8687 9200; www.ellistoninfocentre.com.au. Open M-F 9am-5pm, Sa-Su 1-4pm.) Further north, the **Streaky Bay Tourist Centre,** 15 Alfred Terr., has information on the northwest coast. (☎8626 1126; www.streakybay.sa.gov.au. Open daily 6:30am-9pm.) Both Elliston and Streaky Bay have **police, supermarkets, petrol stations, ATMs,** and **post offices** in the town centers.

ACCOMMODATIONS. Most towns on the highway have hotel pub accommodations and caravan parks. By far the best deal on the west coast, **Coodlie Park,** a left off the Hwy. about 40km. north of Elliston, has a wide range of stellar accommodations and the couple that runs it goes out of their way to ensure that each traveler sees the top spots the region has to offer, some of which are on their extensive coastal property. They also run a number of tours in the area, including $5 **wombat tours.** (☎8687 0411; ww.coodliepark.com. Bush camping $9 per night; $35 per week. Shearer's Quarters $15 per person or $25 per room. Self-contained units $65 per night. Linen $15. Work exchange possible; see **Beyond Tourism,** p. 81.) The **Elliston Hotel,** Beach Terrace, left off Memorial Drive, has self-contained rooms. (☎8687 9009. Rooms $60-80. Book ahead in summer.) On Waterloo Bay at the end of Beach Terr., **Waterloo Bay Caravan Park** has a prime location and excellent facilities. (☎8687 9076. Sites for 2 people $17, powered $20; cabins $40-45, ensuite $60-95.) **Venus Bay Caravan Park,** approximately 65km north of Elliston near the jetty in Venus Bay, also has waterfront sites. (☎8625 5073; www.venusbaycpsa.com.au. Sites $15, powered $19; cabins from $40.)

FOOD. While all of the hotel pubs have food, travelers wanting something beyond standard pub fare should stop at Elliston's **Salty Dog Cafe ❸,** 5 Memorial Dr., across from the visitors center. They have local seafood (main courses from $20) as well as lighter fare for under $10. (☎8687 9092. Su night 12" pizza for $16. Open Tu-Th 10am-5:30pm, F-Sa 10am-latenight, Su 10am-8pm.) In Streaky Bay,

Mocean ❹, 30 Alfred Terr., on the waterfront, specializes in local cuisine with top seafood and wine. (☎8626 1775; www.moceancafe.com.au. Msin courses from $25. Open daily 10am-3pm and 5:30pm-latenight.)

BEACHES. With so much relatively untouched coastline, you are practically guaranteed to find a pristine spot anytime you turn off the highway. **Greenly Beach,** a little north of Coulter, is one of the prime west coast surf spots. To get there, turn on to Coles Point Rd. from the Hwy.; the beach is about 12km down, and the drive is quite scenic with turns revealing rocky outcrops over the ocean. Further north, 8km off the highway (turn off just past Sheringa general store), **Sheringa Beach** has great salmon fishing and impressive sand dunes, though the strong waves prevent safe swimming or surfing. (Camping by permit $5.) You'll have to trek down almost 300 stairs to reach **Locks Well Beach,** about 15km north of Sheringa, 3km from the highway, which is renowned throughout Australia for its salmon fishing and is arguably the top fishing beach on the west coast. Just north of Elliston, **Walker's Rocks** has sand dunes and calm waters that are popular with families.

SIGHTS AND TOURS. About 40km north of Elliston, **Talia Caves** affords a chance to go underground. Further north, the odd granite rock formations, **Murphy's Haystacks,** will puzzle visitors. Quite literally in the middle of a field, the large granite structures seem picturesquely out of place. Entry is by donation at the gate. In Baird Bay, 10km off the highway north of Port Kenny, **Baird Bay Ocean Eco Tours** runs tours during which visitors can swim with dolphins and sea lions in their natural habitat. (☎8626 5017; www.bairdbay.com. Dolphin swim $100.)

CEDUNA ☎08

Ceduna (pop. 3800) is the last watering hole before travelers begin the harsh westward trek across the Nullarbor Plain toward Perth. The **ATMs** in town are the last you'll find for the next 1300km west, though **EFTPOS** services are generally available at roadhouses along the way. Ceduna provides basic beds, board, booze, and beaches. Over the last long weekend in October, Ceduna celebrates Oysterfest. The champion speed-oyster-opener goes on to an international competition. **Decres Bay,** 10km east of town in the **Wittelbee Conservation Park,** is a good swimming beach; farther east, **Laura Bay** has more of the same.

Ceduna Gateway Visitors Information Centre, 58 Poynton St., has information on fishing and outback tours. It is also your best source of info on the Nullarbor crossing. Be sure to pick up a copy of *The Nullarbor: Australia's Great Road Journey* and the extremely thorough *Ceduna: from Smoky Bay to the Nullarbor Whales*. The info center also provides **Internet** access and books bus tickets. (☎8625 2780 or 1800 639 413; www.ceduna.net. Internet access $3 per 15min. Open M-F 9am-5:30pm, Sa-Su 9am-5pm.) The town has **police** (☎8626 2020) and a **hospital** (☎8625 2404). **Taxi** service is also available (☎04 2825 3791). **Postal Code:** 5690.

The best of the five area caravan parks, **Shelly Beach Caravan Park ❶,** is 3km east of town on the Decres Bay Rd., on picturesque Shelly Beach. The park offers Internet access, a full kitchen, a game room with a ping-pong table, and beautiful bathrooms. (☎8625 2012. Internet access $3 per 15min. Powered and unpowered sites $22; ensuite cabins for 2 from $68.) Standard motel accommodations can be found at the **Highway One Motel ❺**, on the edge of town along the Eyre Hwy. (☎8625 2208. Singles from $70; doubles from $80.)

On the way out of town, don't miss **Ceduna Oyster Bar** ❸ to the west, where a half-dozen of the freshest, cheapest oysters on the half-shell ($5) will give you the energy to make the long trek across the Nullarbor. (☎8626 9086. Open M-Sa 9:30am-6pm, Su 1-6pm.) **Bill's Chicken Shop** ❶, on Poynton St., serves mouth-watering fish 'n' chips (from $8.50), fried chicken, and delicious local fish. Another stand out is the spectacular lamb yiros ($7). (☎8625 2880. Open daily 9am-9pm.) Across the street, **Cactus Cafe** ❶ has veggie options and makes tasty, unusual sandwiches ($5-7). The Chicken Bandino—a fried chicken roll-up with herb-bacon mayo—is positively addictive. (Open M-F 9am-2pm. Cash only.) The well-stocked **Foodland** is on the corner of Kuhlmann and Poynton St. (☎8625 3212. Open M-W and Sa 8am-6pm, Th 8am-8pm, F 8am-7pm, Su 8am-5pm.)

GAWLER RANGES

For those coming from the Nullarbor, the scrub-covered stretch of Hwy. 1 running from Ceduna to Port Augusta will seem like a gradual re-entry into civilization. There are towns with **petrol** stations (beware 6-8pm closing times) every 100km or so along the way; most have a small general store and basic accommodations as well. From west to east, the towns are as follows: **Wirrulla** (92km from Ceduna), **Poochera** (140km), **Minnipa** (170km), **Wudinna** (209km), and **Kimba** (310km). Wudinna has an **Internet** cafe on the west side of town in the **Wudinna Telecentre,** 44 Eyre Hwy. The Telecentre also has park information and sells park permits. (☎8680 2969. Internet access $5 per 30min. Open M-F 9am-12:30pm and 1:30-5pm.) There is also a food store in town. **Kimba,** the largest of the above, has a caravan park and is home to the **Big Galah,** a huge pink bird that marks the half-way point between one Australian coast and the other.

Kimba, Wudinna, and **Minnipa** act as gateways for the **Gawler Ranges,** which is perhaps South Australia's least appreciated natural park. From Wudinna the **Granite Trail** scenic drive showcases Gawler Ranges' claim to fame—its granite formations. One of the trail's many points of interest is Mt. Wudinna, Australia's second-largest monolith.

For tours in the park, **Gawler Ranges Wilderness Safaris** runs tours of varying lengths, the shortest being one day. (☎1800 243 343; www.gawlerrangersafaris.com). To get an aerial view of the park, try one of Opal Air's **scenic flights.** Flights can be booked from short 20min. stints to full-day tours. (☎8672 3067; www.cooberpedyscenicflights.com.)

CROSSING THE NULLARBOR

Welcome to the Nullarbor—a treeless plain running from the town of Nullarbor west into Western Australia, before ending at Norseman (p. 729). The Nullarbor could fit England, the Netherlands, Belgium, and Switzerland, with 7000 sq. km to spare, and crossing the Nullarbor remains a badge of pride for travelers who are traversing Australia. Commemorative crossing certificates are available for free at tourist offices at either end of the journey.

The main road, Hwy. 1, sees fairly significant traffic compared to the empty stretches up north; accordingly, it's rarely more than 100km between roadhouses, but repair facilities are few and far between. Additionally, this is a road train route (see **Road Hazards,** p. 78), so drivers should brace for turbulence from passing trucks. See **Driving in the Outback,** p. 74, before setting off.

Visitors crossing from Western Australia to South Australia or vice versa must pass through **agricultural roadblocks,** where any organic matter will be confiscated. The roadblocks are located at Border Village (☎9039 3277), for those heading west, and Ceduna, for those heading east (☎8625 2108). Roadhouses and practical information for crossing the Nullarbor are listed below, followed by points of interest. Within each section listings are from east to west.

PRACTICAL INFORMATION AND TRANSPORTATION. Most of the **roadhouses** along the way accept major credit cards. **Police** are located in **Penong** (☎8625 1006) and **Ceduna** (☎8626 2020) For **emergencies** dial ☎000. **Cellular phones do not work anywhere on the Nullarbor;** Ceduna is your last hope for even so-so reception. Keep in mind that there are **quarantine checkpoints** at Norseman for westbound travelers and at Ceduna for eastbound travelers. *The Nullarbor: Australia's Great Road Journey* lists the services provided at each roadhouse along the way. The booklet is free at tourist offices on either end of the road. **Greyhound Australia** (☎12 20 30 or 1800 076 211) buses make the grueling desert haul once a week from Adelaide to Perth (36hr. $284/155) via Ceduna. The highly regarded **Nullarbor Traveller** is a backpacker-oriented camping trip that runs from Perth to Adelaide. Travelers snorkel, whale watch, explore caves, and camp under the stars. For those with the cash and the time, this is the way to cross in style. Tour prices include accommodation, activities, and meals. (☎8687 0455; www.the-traveller.com.au. 9-day Adelaide to Perth tour $995, YHA members $950; 7-day Perth to Adelaide $775/740.)

ACCOMMODATIONS. Roadhouses are relatively frequent on the Eyre Highway and all provide food, fuel, and accommodations. The first roadhouse coming from Ceduna, 78km west of Penong, is **Nundroo Hotel Motel and Caravan Park ❶.** (☎8625 6120. Reception daily 7:30am-11pm. Sites $8 per person, powered $18; backpacker beds $10 per person; on-site vans $30; motel doubles $77, extra person $12.50.) From Nundroo, the next stop is Yalata. From Nullarbor, it's 188km to **Border Village,** where there are cheap accommodations and a chance to pay your respects to the enormous fiberglass kangaroo, Rooey II. Take note that Border Village has its own time zone—1½hr. behind Adelaide and 1hr. ahead of Perth. (☎9039 3474. Sites $12, powered $18; cabins $27; singles $83.50, doubles $93.50; family rooms $91-97.)

PENONG AND CACTUS BEACH. Penong, 75km. west of Ceduna, is the gateway to South Australia's most famous surf—**Cactus Beach.** To reach the beach follow signs for Point Sinclair 21km south down an unsealed, but 2WD-passable road; wood-carved signs stating simply "To Beach" lead to Cactus, where you can watch top-notch surfers on one of the most famous breaks in Australia. The beach has **bush camping** available ($7.50), while back in Penong, the **hotel ❸** has proper rooms. (☎8625 1050. Singles $33; doubles $44; prices may rise with upcoming renovations.)

FOWLER'S BAY. With massive sand dunes, a fishing jetty, and a population of 10, Fowler's Bay is one of the best-kept secrets on the Eyre Hwy. From the Hwy., the turn-off for Fowler's Bay is 33km east of Nundroo. The town's **sand dunes** provide excellent sandboarding and 4WD tracks, and **Back Beach,** on the other side of the dunes, offers great swimming. The town has a **caravan park** (☎8625 6143), and **Fowler's Bay Units** (☎8625 6179; www.fowlersbay.com) rents cozy waterfront units from $75. The town also has a **general store** and a **petrol** station.

YALATA. Yalata Roadhouse ❶, 52km west of Nundroo, is a decent camping spot and contains an Aboriginal museum (open daily in summer 7:30am-9pm, in winter 7am-7pm) with handicrafts for sale. (☎8625 6986. Sites $5, powered $10; caravans from $35; air-conditioned motel rooms $50-60.) A permit is required to

TASMANIA

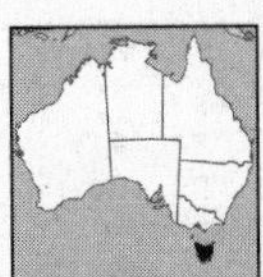

A recent upswing in tourism suggests there may soon come a time when Tasmania is on as many backpacker itineraries as Uluru or the Gold Coast. Until then, Australia's least visited state will continue to offer its many unique treasures to the relative few who are willing to seek them out. Those arriving before the tourist tidal wave hits will be rewarded with a chance to explore one of the last, and certainly one of the best preserved, temperate rainforests on earth in relative isolation.

For all the cosmopolitan bustle of Hobart and Launceston, Tasmania is truly Australia's natural state. A whopping one third of the island is protected by government conservation projects, leaving plenty of space for bushwalkers to stretch their legs. They do so in a famously unique environment; from lovably voracious Tasmanian Devils to slow-growing Huon pines, Tasmania's most famous species are found only within its borders.

The island's rainy and wild west coast gives way to the sunny, tranquil beaches in the east. Tasmania has a ubiquitous physical and cultural legacy as Van Diemen's Land, home to Australia's most feared prison colonies. Tasmania's most defining issue today is the fate of its wild spaces, with conservationists and logging interests fighting a heated battle over the island's future.

HIGHLIGHTS OF TASMANIA

SCORE a bargain and enjoy street performances in **Salamanca Market,** Hobart's eclectic shopping district. (p. 537)

TOUR the ruins of convict-built buildings at the **Tasman Peninsula.** (p. 538)

GET INTO THE BUSH on the world-famous **Overland Track.** (p. 550)

CAMP in total remoteness or scope the other 54 **Furneaux Islands** from the peaks of **Strzelecki National Park** on Flinders Island. (p. 563)

TRANSPORTATION

Tasmania has three principal gateways: the Hobart Airport, the Launceston Airport, and the Devonport Airport. Take a flight, or take the *Spirit of Tasmania* overnight ferry to Devonport or the *Devilcat* ferry to George Town Port in Launceston. Getting around the island on a budget is a bit of a challenge. There is no rail network, and the main **bus** lines—**Redline** and **TWT's Tassielink**—are expensive, limited, and infrequent. Tassielink offers **Explorer Passes,** which are worth the investment when using their buses as a touring service (7 days within any 10-day period $172, 21 days within 30 days $280). On the bright side, many hostel managers offer reasonably priced shuttles and tours on a call-and-request basis. Seek local recommendations and check out hostel information boards.

The most popular way to travel in Tasmania is by **car.** Gateway cities host major national chains and many small companies offering cheaper, older cars, but they are often fully booked during the summer. Visitors unaccustomed to Tassie's narrow, winding roads should drive cautiously. Check with the rental company on their policy regarding unsealed roads; some prohibit driving on them altogether, while others increase the liability excess. 4WD vehicles, necessary for some of Tassie's backroads, come with better insurance policies on unsealed roads. Be aware that hidden speed cameras line roads, and petrol is rare outside towns.

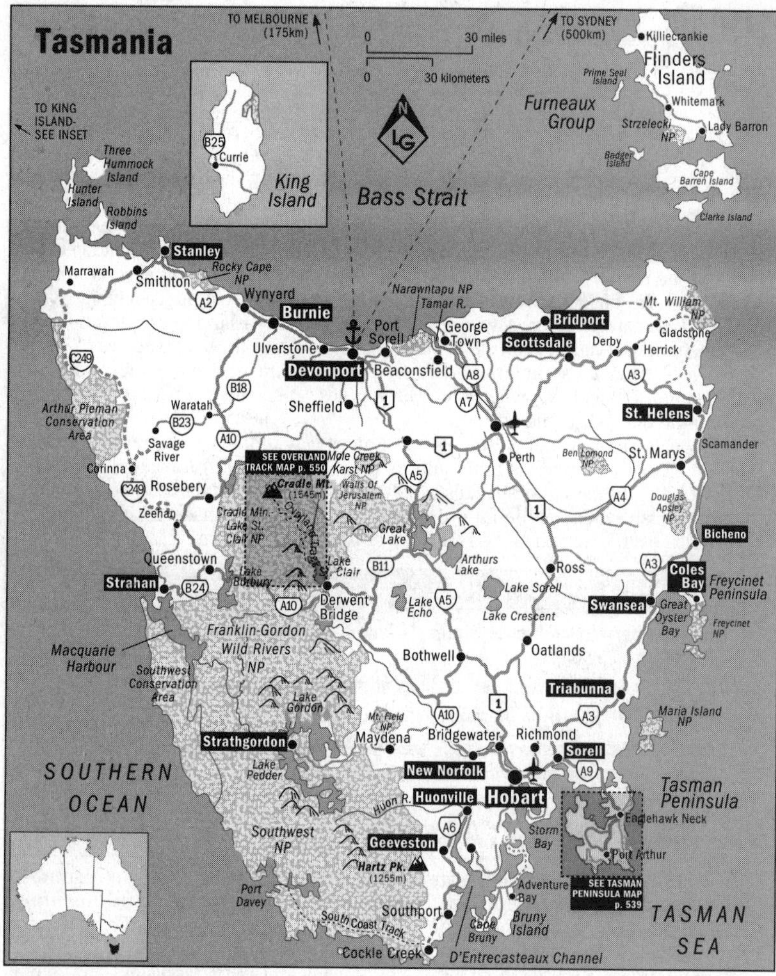

Biking is a satisfying alternative in Tasmania, especially on the more accessible east coast of the island. The guide *Bicycling Tasmania*, by Ian Terry and Rob Beedham, is a helpful resource. The three major gateway cities have bike rental outfits catering to cycle touring, but gear will rarely be found elsewhere. If you're planning on extensive bushwalking on the island, pick up a copy of *100 Walks in Tasmania*, by Tyrone Thomas, which has detailed track descriptions and excellent maps.

Tours also make seeing Tassie easy and enjoyable, allowing travel to places otherwise inaccessible. **Adventure Tours** (☎1300 654 604; www.ozhorizons.com.au/tas/hobart/adventure/tour.htm; 3-day $410, backpackers $369, 7-day $785/707) and **Under Down Under Tours** (☎1800 064 726; www.underdownunder.com.au; 6-day $695 YHA, VIP, and ISIC $669, 3-day east or west $385, YHA, VIP and ISIC $369) offer touring options that include bookings for accommodations and meals, and are geared toward a party crowd. **Escape,** which works closely with Tasmania YHA, runs similar three- and four-day tours, which can be combined into a seven-day tour. (☎1800 133 555. 3-day $399, 4-day $499, 7-day $699.)

PARK IT! All of Tasmania's national parks charge an entrance fee. A **24hr. pass** costs $10 (vehicles $20). There's also a two-month pass available for $30 (vehicles $50) or an annual all-parks pass for vehicles for $60-84 (one park only $30-42). Passes are available at most of the park entrances, or from any of the **Parks and Wildlife Service** offices. Parks and Wildlife prints two helpful pamphlets on the National Parks: *Tasmania: A Visitor's Guide* has a brief summary of every national park in Tasmania, and *Tasmania's Great Short Walks* outlines 30 fantastic walks most under one hour (both free). The service also publishes a handy booklet to reduce your environmental impact called the *Essential Bushwalking Guide & Trip Planner.* For more information, contact the head office in Hobart, 134 Macquarie St. (☎6233 6191), or visit their website at www.parks.tas.gov.au.

HOBART ☎03

Tasmania's capital is a lovely, if not particularly exciting, place to begin or end your Tasmanian travels. Beautifully situated by the mouth of the Derwent River at the foot of Mt. Wellington, Hobart (pop. 192,500) owes its status as Australia's second-driest city to a smattering of islands and breakwaters buffering it from the Great Southern Ocean. A booming mining industry helped establish Hobart economically; today the city is largely defined by remarkably good food and drink as well as remarkably vocal environmental activists.

INTERCITY TRANSPORTATION

Hobart Airport is the most common port of entry into Tasmania—at least for those travelers who are not ferrying their car over to the island. Several well-maintained roads lead into the city center, including Highway 1, connecting Burnie, Devonport, Launceston, and Hobart.

BY PLANE

Hobart Airport is located 17km east of Hobart on Hwy. A3. International flights must make connections to the island on the mainland. **Virgin Blue** (☎13 67 89; www.virginblue.com.au) to Melbourne (4 per day, $65-235). **Qantas** (☎13 13 13; www.qantas.com.au) flies to Melbourne (up to 9 per day, $90-247) and Sydney (2 per day, $156-231). **TasAir** (☎03 6248 5088) charters flights around the island and has two regular flights per day to Burnie ($385). **Redline Airporter Bus** shuttles between the airport and lodgings. (☎1938 2240. $11, round-trip $19.)

BY BUS

Timetables for Redline bus services can be picked up at the **Central Transit Centre,** 199 Collins St. Information for TWT's Tassielink buses can be found at their terminal, 64 Brisbane St.

Tassielink (☎1300 300 520), departing from 64 Brisbane St., buses to the Suncoast: **Swansea** (2¼hr., M-F 2 per day, $24.); **Bicheno** (3hr.; M, W, F, Su 1 per day; $29.50); **St. Helens** (4hr.; F, Su 1 per day; $43); **Dover** (2hr., M-F 2 per day, $18); **Cockle Creek** via **Huonville** (3½hr.; M, W, F 1 per day; $60.70); **Mount Field National Park** (1½hr.; Tu, Th, Sa 1 per day; $27.70); **Port Arthur** (2¼hr., M-F 1 per day, $22.10); and **Strahan**

(9hr.; Tu, Th-Su; $63). In summer, inquire about Overland Track service including Hobart, Lake St. Claire, Cradle Mountain, and return ($110).

Redline Coaches (☎1300 360 000, line open daily 6am-10pm) runs to **Launceston** (2½hr., 2-4 per day, $31.50), and connects from there to **Burnie** (2¼hr., 3 per day, $29.60), **Bicheno** (2¾hr., M-F 1 per day, $28), **Devonport** (1¼hr., 4 per day, $22.10), and **St. Helens** (2hr., M-F and Su 1 per day, $46.90). Student and YHA discount 20%.

Hobart Coaches, 21 Murray St. (☎13 22 01), runs to **Cygnet** (1hr., M-F 1 per day, $10) and **Kettering** (45min., M-F approx. 4 per day, $8.10).

ORIENTATION

Most tourist attractions and services are condensed into the downtown area west of the Sullivan's Cove wharf, which is contained by Macquarie and Bathurst St., and intersected by Elizabeth St., which proceeds uphill to budget-friendly North Hobart. South of the Cove, **Battery Point** is one of the oldest sections of the city and is packed with antique shops and cottages. The northern border of Battery Point is defined by **Salamanca Place,** a row of renovated Georgian warehouses that now house trendy shops and restaurants. Nearby **Franklin Wharf** is the departure point for numerous harbor cruises. Hobart is set amid the **Wellington Range,** with both the imposing **Mount Wellington** on the western skyline and the smaller **Mount Nelson** to the south, which offer fine views of the region. The city proper can be easily navigated on foot, while public buses run to the outer reaches of the suburbs.

Beyond the **Queen's Domain** north of downtown, the **Tasman Bridge** spans the Derwent River. There, the Tasman Hwy. (A3) heads east and connects to A9 and the Tasman Peninsula. **Brooker Avenue** leads north up the Derwent Valley, becoming Hwy. 1 to Launceston and connecting to A10 to the west. **Davey Street** becomes the A6 as it exits downtown, and heads southward to Huon Valley and Bruny Island.

LOCAL TRANSPORTATION

Buses: Metro **city buses** run through Hobart and the suburbs. (☎13 22 01. Buses run daily 6am-10pm. Purchase tickets onboard, $1.70-3.90 depending on the number of sections traveled.) "Day Rover" tickets ($4.40) allow unlimited travel after 9am. **The Metro Shop,** 9 Elizabeth St., in a corner of the post office (open M-F 8:30am-5:15pm), has a complete timetable (free), as does www.metrotas.com.au.

Ferries and Cruises: The best deal around is **Captain Fell's Historic Ferries,** which offers morning, lunch, afternoon, and dinner cruises that depart every day from Franklin Wharf. (☎6223 5893. 2½hr. Dinner cruise departs at 6pm. $33. Lunch cruise $28.) **Derwent River** sails from Hobart's Brooke St. Pier to the Cadbury Chocolate Factory. (☎6223 1914. Daily 10:15, 11:45am, 1:45pm; $17.50.) Departing from Elizabeth St. Pier, the **Lady Nelson** is a replica of an old English ship that once ferried convicts to the continent. (☎6234 3348. 1½hr. In summer Sa-Su 10:30am, 1, 3pm; in winter Sa-Su 11am and 1:30pm. $10.)

Taxis: City Cabs (24hr. ☎13 10 08 or 6234 3633). City to airport $35-40.

Tours: Day tours organized by **Tigerline** (☎1300 300 520) or **Experience Tasmania** (☎6234 3336) are good if you're short on time. Both offer pickup and combo tours highlighting Hobart and southeastern Tassie. Book through the info center (☎6230 8233), at hostels, or direct with the company. Tours $38-145. **Gregory Omnibuses** sends its fleet of bright-red double-deckers on many tours around the city, including ones to Cascade Brewery. (☎6336 9116 or 6224 6169. $20-36. Book at info center.)

Car Rental: Car rental agencies are everywhere in Hobart, but advance bookings required in summer. Low-season rates run as low as $17 per day. Listed companies rent to ages 21-24 with no surcharge. **Autorent Hertz,** 122 Harrington St. (☎6237 1111), $55-85 per day in high season, $40-70 in off-peak season. For a YHA discount, call ☎13 30 39 and quote Discount Program number 317961. **Thrifty,** 11-17 Argyle St. (☎6234 1341), from $59. **Selective Car Rentals,** 47 Bathurst St. (☎6234 3311 or 1800 300 102), from $55 in peak season, $25 in off-peak season. **Range** and **Lo-Cost,** 105 Murray and 122 Harrington St. (☎62 310 300), rent older cars from $35, including minibuses and campervans.

Automobile Club: RACT (☎6232 6300, 24hr. roadside help ☎13 11 11, insurance queries ☎13 27 22), corner of Murray and Patrick St. 1 year coverage $77. Open M-F 8:45am-5pm.

Bikes: Derwent Bike Hire (☎6235 2143), just past the Cenotaph on the cycleway at the Regatta Ground, rents bikes, tandems, and roller blades from $7 per hr., $20 per day, and $100 per wk. Touring hikes $100 per week. Long term and group discounts available. Open daily in summer 9:30am-4pm; in winter W-Su 9:30am-4pm.

PRACTICAL INFORMATION

TASMANIA

TOURIST AND FINANCIAL SERVICES

Tourist Office: Hobart Tasmanian Travel and Information Centre, 20 Davey St. (☎6230 8233), at Elizabeth St., books accommodations and cars for $3, tours for free. Open in summer M-F 8:30am-5:30pm, Sa-Su 9am-4pm; in winter Su 9am-1pm.

Budget Travel Office: YHA's Tasmanian Headquarters, 28 Criterion St., 2nd fl. (☎6234 9617; www.yhatas.org.au). Travel insurance, bus and tour tickets, and travel advice, in addition to YHA memberships and hostel bookings. Open M-F 9am-5pm.

Currency Exchange: Many banks and **ATMs** crowd in and around Elizabeth St. Mall. Most banks charge a $5-10 fee.

Tasmanian Parks and Wildlife Service: Service Tasmania, 134 Macquarie St. (☎6233 6191), in the Service Tasmania Bldg. Open M-F 8:15am-5:30pm. **Forestry Tasmania,** 79 Melville St. (☎6233 8203). Open M-F 8am-5:30pm.

LOCAL SERVICES

Library: 91 Murray St. (☎6233 7511). Free **Internet.** Reference library open M-Th 9:30am-6pm, F 9:30am-8pm, Sa 9:30am-noon.

Market: Salamanca Market at Salamanca Pl. Open Sa 8am-3pm. See **Sights,** p. 536.

Outdoor Equipment: Countless gear stores cluster along Elizabeth St. near Liverpool St. Note that these are the only places to rent gear outside Launceston and Devonport. **Jolly Swagman's Camping World,** 107 Elizabeth St., has a superb supply of gear and rents stoves ($25, $100 bond), packs ($30-100), and sleeping mats ($5-15). Open M-F 9am-6pm, Sa 9am-3:30pm. **Service Tasmania** has a list of all rental gear options.

Fishing Equipment: Get info and fishing tackle (from $25 per day) at **Bridges Bros.,** 142 Elizabeth St. (☎6234 3791). Open M-F 9am-5:30pm, F 9am-6pm, Sa 9am-4pm. *Angling Code for Inland Fisheries,* available at the tourist office, outlines all regulations.

MEDIA AND PUBLICATIONS

Newspapers: *The Mercury.*

Entertainment: *The Mercury* includes *Gig Guide* on Th and *EG* on F.

Radio: Rock, Triple J 92.9FM; News, ABC 747AM

EMERGENCY AND COMMUNICATIONS

Emergency: ☎000.

Police: 37-43 Liverpool St. (☎6230 2111). **Lost and found** (☎6230 2277).

Crisis Lines: Crisis Watchline (24hr. ☎13 11 14). **AIDS Hotline** (☎1800 005 900). Staffed M-F 9am-5pm. **Alcohol and Drugs Hotline** (24hr. ☎1800 811 994).

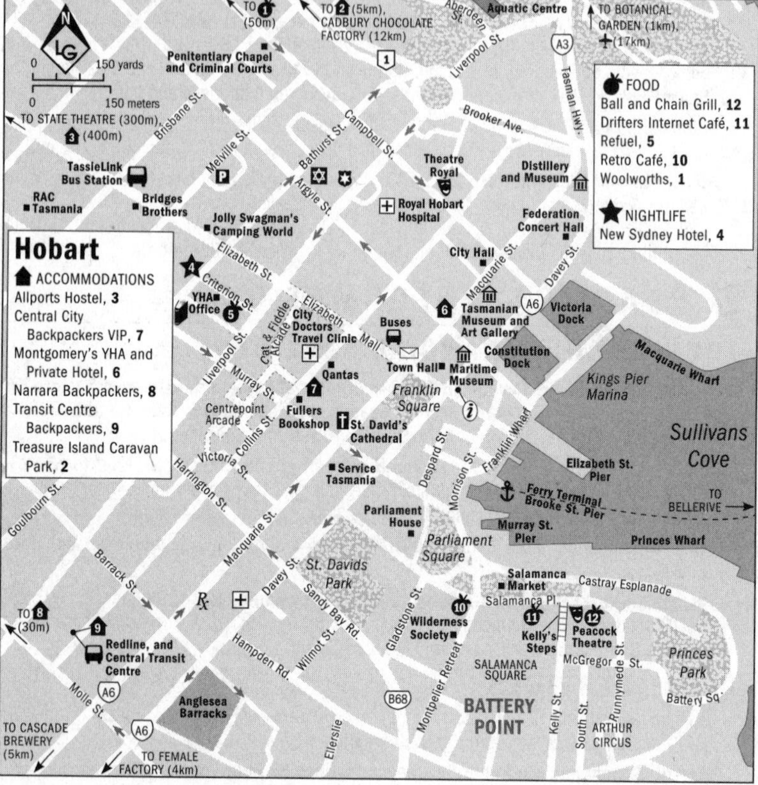

Pharmacy: Macquarie Street Pharmacy, 170 Macquarie St. (☎6223 2339). Open daily 8am-10pm.

Medical Services: Royal Hobart Hospital, 48 Liverpool St. (☎6222 8308). **City Doctors Travel Clinic,** 93 Collins St. (☎6231 3003). Appointment only. Open M-F 9am-5pm.

Internet Access and Library: Service Tasmania, 134 Macquarie St. (☎1300 135 513). Has six **free terminals.** Max. 30min. Open M-F 8:15am-5:30pm. Also try **Drifters Internet Cafe,** 33 Salamanca Pl., which sweetens its Internet deal ($5 per hr.) with soups ($6), coffee, and toasties ($5) and an Errol Flynn-theme decor. Open M-Sa 10am-7pm, Su 11am-7pm. Also available at the library (see above).

Post Office: 9 Elizabeth St. (☎6236 3577), at Macquarie St. From this post office, Roald Amundsen sent a telegram announcing his accomplishment as the first man to reach the South Pole. Open M-F 8:30am-5:30pm. **Postal Code:** 7000.

ACCOMMODATIONS

Allport's Hostel, 432 Elizabeth St., (☎6231 5464). Clean, comfortable, eco-friendly hostel in budget-friendly north Hobart. Hilltop location ideal for travelers with rental cars. Free parking. Coin-op laundry. Dorms $22; doubles $60; triples $75. ❷

Narrara Backpackers, 88 Goulburn St. (☎6231 3191). Turn left off Harrington St. This 3-story house has clean rooms and a comfortable atmosphere. Free Internet access and parking. Bike rental. Reception 8am-10pm. Dorms $21; twins and doubles $53. ❷

Central City Backpackers VIP, 138 Collins St. (☎6224 2404 or 1800 811 507; bookings@centralbackpackers.com.au), on the 2nd fl. through the Imperial Arcade, 3 blocks from the Transit Centre. A large hostel with a kitchen and common areas. Full linens $3. Key deposit $10. Reception 8am-9pm. 8-bed dorms $20; 6-bed $23; 4-bed $24; singles $46; doubles $56. VIP. ❷

Montgomery's YHA and **Montgomery's Private Hotel,** 9 Argyle St. (☎6231 2660). Located downtown. A quiet, well-equipped hostel. Clean kitchen, common room with TV. All rooms have phones; hotel rooms have towels, TV, and refrigerator. Internet access $5 per 30min. Laundry. Luggage storage. Tour bookings. Reception 8am-10pm. Dorms $25, YHA members $22; hotel twins and doubles $69-89. Extra person $20. ❷

Transit Centre Backpackers, 199 Collins St. (☎6231 2400), above the bus terminal. Bright, spacious common area. Friendly proprietors live on-site. Fireplace, heaters, and extra doonas in winter. Also TV, kitchen, laundry, pool table. Free storage. Alcohol discouraged on premises. Reception 8am-10pm. Dorms from $19; double $48. ❷

Treasure Island Caravan Park, 671 Main Rd., Berriedale (☎6249 2379), 12km north of the city center on Hwy. 1. Pleasantly situated on the Derwent River. Clean facilities include showers, laundry, and kitchen. Reception 8am-10pm. Sites for $21, powered $25; on-site caravans $48; cabins $72-80. ❶

TASMANIA

FOOD

Hobart showcases a dizzying array of international cuisine. Restaurants downtown serve meals from every region of Asia, while the pubs and grills of Salamanca Pl. serve lunches and dinners once breakfast ends at the cafes. Elizabeth St. in North Hobart hosts a cluster of restaurants showcasing a variety of cuisines—from Indian to Mexican to Vietnamese. For a taste of traditional local fare, the ultimate Tassie tucker is abalone or salmon with a cold Cascade beer. **Woolworths,** 179 Campbell St., North Hobart, is the only fully stocked supermarket near the city center. (☎6211 6911. Open daily 7am-10pm. Get organic and bulk foods at **Eumarrah Wholefoods,** 45 Goulburn St., at the corner of Barrack St., or 15 Gregory St., Sandy Bay. (☎6234 3229. Open M-W 9am-6pm, Th-F 9am-7pm, Sa 9am-3pm.) The Saturday **Salamanca Market** has several takeaway vendors and deals on produce, sauces, spreads, honey, and cheese, and offers great people-watching on Saturday. (Open Sa 8am-3pm.)

Ball and Chain Grill, 87 Salamanca Pl. (☎6223 2655). Plates of char-grilled meats cover wood tables. Although not cheap (steaks $12.50-38), the meats are specially aged and expertly cooked to order. All main courses come with a fantastic all-you-can-eat salad bar. Open daily noon-3pm and 5:30pm-latenight. ❹

Little Bali, at the corner of Harrington St. and Collins. Follow your nose to this tiny restaurant with a small menu and massive servings of Indonesian curry dishes for eat-in or takeaway. Most expensive dishes ($10.50) comfortably satisfy 2. Open M-F 11:30am-3pm and 5:30-9pm; Sa-Su 5:30-9pm. ❶

Retro Cafe, 31 Salamanca Pl. (☎6223 3073), on the corner of Montpelier Retreat. Regulars enjoy fine food and excellent coffee. It can be hard to get a seat, but their all-day breakfast bagel with smoked salmon ($12) is worth the scramble. Open M-Sa 8am-6pm, Su 8:30am-6pm. Cash only. ❸

Refuel, 30 Criterion St. (☎6231 0890) just up from the YHA office, is one of the best lunch bets in the city center, with daily soup specials ($4.50-6.50), healthful smoothies ($4.50-5.50), and exceptional gourmet toasties ($5.50-7). Open M-F 8am-4:30pm. ❶

SIGHTS

Hobart is brimming with history. The excellent free brochures *Hobart's Historic Places*, *Sullivan's Cove Walk*, and *Women's History Walk*, available from the tourist office, provide interesting background.

DOWNTOWN

TASMANIAN MUSEUM AND ART GALLERY. The Tasmanian Museum explores various aspects of the island, including its early convict history, unique ecology, and artistic heritage. The surrealist and modern art section is excellent, and the megafauna models include a 10 ft. kangaroo. Frequent exhibitions highlight the cultural and artistic history of the region. (40 Macquarie St., near the corner of Argyle St. ☎6211 4177. *(Open daily 10am-5pm. Guided tours leave from the bookstore W-Su 2:30pm. Free.)*

MARITIME MUSEUM. This facility highlights Tassie maritime heritage, with a focus on local shipping and whaling. Accounts of more recent catastrophic shipwrecks make for some riveting reading. *(16 Argyle St., in the Carnegie Building on the corner of Davey St. ☎6234 1427. Open daily 9am-5pm. Adults $6, concessions $5.)*

PENITENTIARY CHAPEL AND CRIMINAL COURTS. One of the oldest, best-preserved buildings in Tasmania. View the courtrooms and gallows built during the grim 1850s, used until 1983. *(6 Brisbane St. Enter on Campbell St. ☎6223 5200. Admission by tour only. Tours daily 10, 11:30am, 1, and 2:30pm. $8, concessions $7. Ghost tours ☎0417 361 392. Daily 8pm. Book ahead. $8.80.)*

THE WATERFRONT. At Sullivan's Cove, the Elizabeth, Brooke, and Murray Street Piers harbor most of Hobart's large vessels. Look for the Antarctic Research Expedition's giant orange icebreaker, *Aurora Australis*, sometimes docked at Macquarie Wharf on the Cove's north side. Constitution and Victoria Docks are teeming with fishmongers and host popular seafood restaurants. Several companies run harbor cruises from this area (see **Ferries and Cruises,** p. 532). Just a few blocks north of the waterfront, in Franklin Square, good, clean, dorky fun can be had with a giant outdoor chess set in the park. *(Free. Pieces available 8:30am-dusk.)*

THE MOUNTAINS

MOUNT WELLINGTON. Several kilometers west of Hobart, Mt. Wellington (1270m) is a must-see. The top is extremely windy, cold, and often snowy. On a clear day, the peaks of the Wellington Range (all clearly marked on signs in the observation shelter) are visible. Although the summit is home to a huge telecommunications tower, which mars the natural beauty, the surrounding walking tracks are spectacular. The road to the top is occasionally closed due to snow and ice. **Fern Tree,** on the lower foothills of the mountain, is a picturesque picnic area with walking tracks up the slope. *(20min. from Hobart on B64 Huon Rd. By bus, take the #48 or 49 Fern Tree bus to stop 27, at the base of the mountain. Mt. Wellington Shuttle Bus Service provides narrated van trips to the top for $25 round-trip. ☎04 1734 1804, min. 2 people. Another van option is Experience Tasmania. ☎6234 3336; tours T, Th, F, Sa. $38, concessions $36. Observation shelter open daily 8am-6pm. For track details, get the Mt. Wellington Walk Map, $4, from the tourist office.)*

MOUNT NELSON. South of Hobart, the mountain offers views of the city and the Derwent estuary. A signal station at the top has a restaurant. *(Take the #57 or 58 Mt. Nelson bus to its terminus. Road to top open daily 9am-9pm. Restaurant open daily 9am-5pm.)*

TASMANIA

SALAMANCA PLACE AND BATTERY POINT

SALAMANCA PLACE. This row of beautiful Georgian warehouses contains trendy galleries, restaurants, and the shops of the much-celebrated Salamanca Market. On Saturdays, a popular outdoor market delights with a wonderful hodgepodge of crafts, produce, food, and performers. *(Open Sa 8am-3pm.)*

BATTERY POINT. Adjacent to Salamanca Place is the historic neighborhood of Battery Point, where many of Hobart's convict-era buildings have been preserved. The point itself, east of Princes park, is popular with local fisherman. Otherwise, are made easy with walking brochures ($2) available from the tourist office.

OUTLYING REGIONS

CASCADE BREWERY. Fed by the clear waters of Mt. Wellington, the magnificent Cascade Brewery was built in 1832 based on designs by a convict in debtors' prison. Tours cover the brewery's process and history, and include a stroll around the surrounding gardens. *(131 Cascade Rd. Take the Claremont bus #43, 44, or 49 to stop 17. If driving, follow Davey St. out of the city, staying in the right lane. When the road connects with A6, turn right, then left on Macquarie St., which becomes Cascade Rd. ☎6221 8300. 2hr. Tours M-F 9:30, 10am, 1, 1:30, and 2pm; more in peak season. Bookings required. Free beer at end. Long pants and flat shoes required. $16, concessions $14, under 18 $7.)*

TASMANIA

CADBURY CHOCOLATE FACTORY. One of Hobart's most popular attractions, the Cadbury factory has exhibits on each stage of the chocolate-making process and offers a tour with free tastings every step of the way. Stock up on chocolate at the bargain shop at the end of the tour. *(In Claremont, north of Hobart and the Derwent River. Take the Claremont service #37, 38, or 39 to the factory. ☎6249 0333 or 1800 627 367. Tours M-F 8am-2pm. Advance booking strongly recommended. Long pants and closed shoes required. $13, concessions $9, children $6.50.)*

BONORONG WILDLIFE PARK. See, hear, pet, and feed the beasts that roam the island's wilderness. Orphaned and injured Tasmanian devils, koalas, quolls, wombats, and birds live in enclosures. Every visitor gets a bag of kangaroo feed; also make sure to catch a devil feeding at 11:30am or 2pm. *(North of Hobart in Brighton. Metro bus X1 from Hobart to Glenorchy Interchange connects with #125 or 126 to Brighton, 1½hr. From Brighton, it's a 30min. walk or a 25min. drive north on Hwy. 1; follow signs in Brighton. ☎6268 1184. Wildlife tours 11:30am and 2pm. Open daily 9am-5pm. $12.50, children $6.)*

ROYAL TASMANIAN BOTANICAL GARDENS. With 13 hectares and 6000 species, the Royal Tasmanian Botanical Gardens are the largest public collection of Tasmanian plants in the world and the largest collection of mature conifers in the Southern Hemisphere. The wildly popular Al Fresco Theatre runs an outdoor play in January and "Shakespeare in the Garden" in February. *(North of the city, near the Tasman Bridge. Take any bus, including the MetroCity Explorer, headed to the eastern shore to stop 4 before the bridge; or take the X3-G express to Bridgewater, which stops at the main gate. Alternatively, walk 25min. from the city to Queen's Domain past Government House. ☎6236 3075. Open daily Oct.-Mar. 8am-6:30pm, Apr. and Sept. 8am-5:30pm, May-Aug. 8am-5pm. Cafe open daily in summer 10am-5pm, in winter 10am-4pm. Gardens free; donations encouraged. Book theater tickets through Centertainment ☎6234 5998. Outdoor theater $22, concessions $11.)*

HISTORIC FEMALE FACTORY. Once the Hobart jail and also a factory worked by women and children in the 1820s, the site is now home to various building ruins and memorial gardens. *(16 Degraves St., South Hobart, near Cascade Brewery. Take bus #43, 44, 46, 47, or 49 from Franklin Sq. to stop 16, cross onto McRobies Rd., and walk right on Degraves St. ☎6223 1559. Shop and gardens open M-F 9am-4:30pm. Tours M-F 9:30am, in* *summer also M-F 2pm and Sa-Su 9:30am. 1¼hr. $10, concessions $8, children $5, families $25. Tours must be booked a day in advance.)*

ENTERTAINMENT AND NIGHTLIFE

Entertainment listings are in the *EG* insert of Friday's *Mercury* newspaper. Tasmania's oldest running and only independent movie theater is the **State Cinema,** 375 Elizabeth St., in North Hobart, with indie films in glamorous facilities. (☎6234 6318; www.statecinema.com.au. $14, concessions $11.50; W $10.) **Showcase Hobart 7 Theatre,** 181 Collins St., is always packed with blockbuster hits. (☎6234 7288. Tu movies $8. Otherwise $14, students $11.50.) The **Theatre Royal,** 29 Campbell St., the oldest theater in Australia, stages plays, musicals, song and dance shows, comedy festivals, and a variety of other crowd-pleasers. (☎6233 2299. Box office open M-F 9am-5pm, Sa 9am-1pm. $25-50.) The experimental **Peacock Theatre,** 77 Salamanca Pl., is in the Salamanca Arts Centre. (☎6234 8414; www.salarts.com. $10-30.) The **Tasmanian Symphony Orchestra,** 1 Davey St., in the Federation Concert Hall at the Grand Chancellor, is over 50 years old and holds performances every few weeks. (☎1800 001 190. Box office open M-F 9am-5pm, Sa concert days 5pm, and all concert nights from 6pm. $35-49, concessions $20.)

Hobart's nightlife only really gets going on Wednesday, Friday, and Saturday nights. Those looking for nocturnal diversions the rest of the week should arrive at pubs early, as most close between 10pm and midnight. **The New Sydney Hotel,** 87 Bathurst St, is an extremely popular Irish pub. (☎6234 4516. Margaritas $10. Tu-Su live music, mainly cover bands. Cover Sa $5. Open M noon-10pm, Tu noon-midnight, W-F 11:30am-midnight, Sa 1pm-midnight, Su 4-9pm. Kitchen open M-Sa noon-2pm and 6-8pm, Su 6-8pm.) Also try the **Telegraph Hotel,** at the corner of Brooke and Morrison, for a laid-back nightspot with snooker, shots, and the best beer selection in town, with 110 imports. (☎6234 6254. Cheap jugs W and Su. W "Toss Your Boss" lets customers flip for a free drink. Sa live music. Open Tu-F noon-latenight, Sa-Su 3pm-latenight.) Non-pub nightlife centers on the waterfront near Salamanca Place. For a bite while out on the town, head to the 24hr. **Salamanca Bakehouse** (☎6224 6300), behind Salamanca Pl. in Salamanca Sq.

THE SOUTH

The South is dotted with picturesque towns. To the east, the Tasman Peninsula and Port Arthur testify to Tassie's colonial history. To the west, the entrance to the vast Southwest National Park welcomes visitors to the Tasmanian Wilderness World Heritage Area. Between the two lie the hop vines of the Derwent Valley and the vast apple orchards of the D'Entrecasteaux Channel region.

TASMAN PENINSULA AND PORT ARTHUR

The narrow **Eaglehawk Neck** isthmus connects the Tasman Peninsula to the rest of Tasmania. One of the island's first attractions, drawing a steady stream of early settlers, was the line of guard dogs stationed at Eaglehawk Neck to alert guards of any attempted escape. Military units once dumped repeat offenders over the peninsula's steep cliffs into shark-infested waters. The ruins of the convict-built sandstone buildings are Tasmania's most popular tourist attraction, drawing 250,000 visitors annually. Less heralded are the walking tracks and gorgeous views afforded by the Tasman Peninsula's unique geography.

TRANSPORTATION. There is no real Port Arthur town, just businesses and government services affiliated with the historical site. **Tassielink** (☎1300 300 520) is the only **bus** company servicing the tourist attraction; buses depart the depot in Hobart (M, W, F 10am and M-F 4pm, summer only). Only 1hr. to the north, **Sorell** is the main stop en route to the Suncoast (via the A3).

PRACTICAL INFORMATION. There is a **tourist office** in the Port Arthur Historic Centre with an expensive cafe and restaurant. (☎6251 2371. Open 8:30am-8pm.) By the Eaglehawk Neck Historic Site on the A9, the **Officers' Mess** has basic groceries and takeaways. (☎6250 3722. Open in summer daily 8am-8pm.) In Sorell, the **Westpac bank,** which as a 24hr. **ATM,** is at 36 Cole St. at the junction of the A3 and the A9. (Open M-Th 9:30am-4pm, F 9:30am-5pm.) Free **Internet** access is available at Service Tasmania, 5 Fitzroy Street, just down the street from the Sorell tourist office. (Open M-F 9am-5pm.) There's a **post office** at 19 Gordon St., Sorell. (☎6265 2579. Open M-F 9am-5pm.) **Postal Code:** 7172.

ACCOMMODATIONS AND CAMPING. The quiet **Roseview YHA Hostel ❷,** on Champ St., the first left past the entrance to the historic site, is only meters from the ruins and is home to a ghost named Alice. (☎6250 2311. Reception 8:30-10am and 5-8pm. Dorms $25, YHA $19; doubles $50/44.) The only other hostel in the area is the tiny but extremely friendly **Eaglehawk Neck Backpackers ❷**, 94 Old Jetty Rd. Look for signs as you pass Officer's Mess. The hostel only has four beds, so be sure to book ahead. (☎6250 3248. Linens $5. Dorms $18. Tent sites $7 per person.) The **Port Arthur Garden Point Caravan Park ❷** is left off the A9, 1km before the historic site. (☎6250 2340. Extremely basic dorms $16; sites for two $18, powered $20.)

SIGHTS AND TOURS. The prison, lunatic asylum, hospital, and church associated with the **Port Arthur Historic Site** are vivid reminders of Australia's convict heritage. From 1830 and 1877, over 12,000 male convicts were transferred to cold, desolate Port Arthur, many sentenced to years of hauling timber and breaking rocks. The museum attempts to bring this turbulent story to life by having each visitor pick a convict and follow his history. The short **walking tours** of the grounds and the free **boat tours** provide further insight into convict life. A 20min. harbor cruise past the **Isle of the Dead,** the colony's cemetery, and **Point Puer,** the convict boys' colony, is included in the price of admission; book at the visitor complex. Cruises that actually land on the Isle of the Dead (6 tours daily) cost an extra $10 (children $6.50). Tours of Point Puer are 2hr., with 3 tours daily, also $10/6.50. The popular **Historic Ghost Tour** (1½hr.) runs nightly, delighting tourists with spooky stories, creepy shadows, and a bit of history. Tickets for all of the above can be purchased from local accommodations or the tourist office. (☎1800 659 101. Open daily 9am-dusk, but most tours end and some buildings close at 5pm, others stay open until 7pm; allow at least 3hr. 2-day admission $25, concessions $20, children $12. Bookings required. $17, children $10.)

TASMANIA

AROUND THE TASMAN PENINSULA

Peter and Shirley Storey's handy *Tasman Tracks*, available at tourist shops on the peninsula, details roughly 50 walks around **Tasman National Park** and has good maps. A great way to view the spectacular cliffs of the park is with **Port Arthur Cruises** on the **Tasman Island Wilderness Cruise.** This 2hr. cruise views the highest sea cliffs in Australia. (☎1300 134 561 or 6231 2655. Book 24hr. in advance. Departs Oct.-May M and Th 8:15am. $65, children $49, concessions $59.)

One of the region's most intriguing sights is the **Tessellated Pavement,** just before Eaglehawk Neck. The grooves and splits across this natural platform of sedimentary rock were etched by salt crystals left behind as sea water evaporated. The crystals dried in the tiny cracks, then expanded, cutting open the rock and giving it the appearance of bathroom tile. The carpark is 500m up Pirates Bay Dr., an easy 15min. round-trip walk to the beach.

Just past Eaglehawk Neck the C338 intersects the A9 and leads to the **Devils Kitchen** and **Tasman Arch** carparks. Both remarkable cliffside sights were etched by centuries of waves, and are easy 10-15min. round-trip walks from both their respective carparks and each other. Continue along the moderate gravel track to **Patersons Arch** (15min.) and **Waterfall Bay** (45min.), where it links up with the steep **Tasman Trail** (1¼hr.) to the falls and **Waterfall Bluff** (1½hr.). Walking from Devils Kitchen to **Fortescue Bay** is a breathtaking 6-8hr. walk. Basic **camping ❶** is available, with drinking water, showers, and toilets ($5.50, park fees apply). The campsite manager (☎6250 2433) has details. To get to Waterfall Bay by car, take the first right off the C338 and follow the road 4km to the cul-de-sac; for Fortescue Bay, follow the sign-posted, unsealed road east off A9, south of the B37 Taranna junction.

From Fortescue Bay, the Tasman Trail leads to the rock formations at **Cape Hauy** (4hr.). Starting with a deep descent from the campground, this difficult trek passes by the spectacular dolorite spires of **The Candlestick, The Needle,** and **The Lanterns,** popular with ambitious rock climbers. The three-day return trip to **Cape Pillar** is something to write home about. **Camping** ❶ is available at **Lime Bay.** (Pit toilets, water. $3.30, children $1.60.) Check with the park office for updates.

The **Tasmanian Devil Conservation Park** in Taranna, houses devils, 'roos, and wallabies, which visitors can feed and touch, with the exception of the devils. They also have the only free flight show in Tasmania. (☎6258 2227. Open daily 9am-5:30pm. $20, children $10. Attached interpretive center and gift shop free. Twice daily Tasmanian devil shows: Devils At Dusk, geared towards families, and Devils at Dark, geared to those 13 and up. Show fees and times vary, call ahead.)

D'ENTRECASTEAUX CHANNEL

The channels, islands, and caves south of Hobart were first charted by Frenchman Bruni d'Entrecasteaux in 1792, more than a decade before the first English settlement in the area. The valley's cool climate and fertile soil, nourished by the Huon River, make the area perfect for growing berries, pears, and apples. The towns of Huonville and Cygnet provide services to the area, and antique shops and vineyards pepper the gorgeous, rolling hills between the river and the D'Entrecasteaux Channel. Bruny Island offers a tranquil escape into the wild, and Geeveston provides a launching point into the southwest.

CYGNET AND THE HUON VALLEY ☎03

Near the mouth of the Nicholls Rivulet on Port Cygnet and 60km southwest of Hobart, the artsy, tourist-friendly community of Cygnet hosts many seasonal fruit pickers. Testaments to the region's booming fruit trade pop up repeatedly along the A6, from Hobart to Huonville. Operating out of the visitors center in Huonville, **Huon Jet** sends visitors hurtling down and back up the gentle rapids of the Huon River on their high-powered jetboat. (☎6264 1838. Pedal boats, aquabikes, and canoes also available for rent. 35min. $58, children $36.) A half hour south of Hobart, **The Huon Apple and Heritage Museum,** in Grove, explores the history of the "apple isle." During harvest (Mar.-June), almost 400 varieties of apples are on display. (☎6266 4345. Open daily 9am-5pm. $5.50, concessions $4.50.)

The Huon Valley is known for its cool-climate wines, and a host of local vineyards offer tastings. **Hartzview Vineyard and Wine Centre,** 10km east of Cygnet near Gardners Bay (via B68 and C626; keep an eye out for the grape sign), offers its own Pinot Noir and fruit wines as well as products from the area's smaller vineyards, affordable coffee, and even desserts. B&B accommodations available on-site. (☎6295 1623. Open daily 10am-5pm. Tastings $2, refunded on purchase. B&B singles $130; doubles $200.) **Home Hill Winery,** 38 Nairn St., Ranelagh, has free wine tasting and local fruit, along with delicious, if expensive, lunches. Home Hill's 2005 Pinot Noir was recently voted best red in Tasmania. (☎6264 1200. Cellar door open daily 10am-5pm, restaurant daily noon-3pm.) **Panorama Vineyard**, 1848 Cygnet Coast Rd., Cradoc, features excellent Cabernet Sauvignon, Pinot Noir, and a unique pear liqueur. (☎6266 3409. Open M and W-Su 10am-5pm.) In town, hardcore history buffs will appreciate the **Cygnet Living History Museum,** at Uniting Church Hall, 37 Mary St. Preserved artifacts, photographs, and histories of the Huon Valley are on exhibit. (☎6295 1394. Open Tu-W 10am-3pm, F-Su 12:30-3pm. Free.) On the second weekend in January, Cygnet comes alive with the **Cygnet Folk Festival** (www.cygnetfolkfestival.org/index.shtml), an open-air celebration of folk music and food. Book lodgings ahead if you plan to visit during the festival.

Hobart Coaches depart from 21 Murray St. in Hobart for the Cygnet carpark. (☎6233 4232. 1hr., M-F 1 per day, $10.) The **Balfes Hill Huon Valley NOMADS Backpackers** ❷, 4 Sandhill Rd., Cradoc, 4.5km north of Cygnet, caters to workers willing to pick berries or prune orchards November to May. The hostel managers will help find employment and provide transportation ($15 per wk.). The sizable compound houses comfortable bunks, clean bathrooms, kitchens, a video lounge, ping-pong, billiards, laundry, **Internet** access ($3 per 30min.), and a pay phone. Call ahead for pickup from the bus stop. (☎6295 1551. Reception 8:30-10am, 1:30-3pm, and 6-8pm. Dorms $20; twins $50, ensuite $60.) Set in an apple orchard, **Talune Host Farm ❺,** a few hundred meters from the intersection of B68 and C627, offers pleasant ensuite cabins with TV and kitchen. (☎6295 1775; wombat@talune.com.au. Cabin doubles $60, additional adult $10.) **Cygnet Caravan Park ❶,** on Mary St. in Cygnet, is tidy and well-managed, with few facilities but centrally located grassy sites. (☎6295 1267. Sites $10, powered $15.) **Red Velvet Lounge ❷,** 87 Mary St., is part art gallery, part whole foods store, and part cafe, serving good coffee and vegetarian-friendly dishes among comfortable couches. (☎6295 0466. Veggie foccaccia with salad $14. Open daily 9am-6pm.) Of the three supermarkets, **Festival IGA,** on Mary St., is open the latest. (Open daily 8am-9pm.)

TASMANIA

BRUNY ISLAND

Home to dramatic coastal scenery, ample opportunities to bushwalk, and only 500 permanent residents, Bruny Island rewards outdoor enthusiasts who make the trip from Hobart. The virtually unpopulated North Bruny is blanketed with thousand-year-old trees, known as "blackboys." South Bruny, accessible via a narrow isthmus, hosts most of the island's inhabitants, walks, and tourist infrastructure.

TRANSPORTATION AND PRACTICAL INFORMATION. Ferries (☎6273 6725) run 10-11 times daily from 6:50am-6:30pm (8 times on Su) from Kettering to north Bruny. (Cars $25, peak hours $30; motorcycles $11/15; bicycles $3; pedestrians free. Cash only.) **Hobart Coaches** leaves 21 Murray St. in Hobart for Kettering and will stop at the ferry terminal upon request. (☎6234 4077. 45min., M-F 4 per day, $8.10.) The island itself has **no public transportation;** and most tourist attractions are more than 30km from the ferry drop-off.

The **Visitors Centre** is across the channel in Kettering, in the ferry-adjacent Mermaid Cafe. (☎6267 4494; www.brunyisland.net. Open daily 9am-5pm.) **The Adventure Bay General Store,** 712 Adventure Bay Rd., has a **post office, petrol,** and **groceries.** (Open daily 7:15am-6:30pm.) Next to the general store, the **Penguin Cafe** has a limited menu, picnic boxes for two ($40-55), and **Internet** access ($3 per 15min.) **The Bruny Island Online Access Centre,** at the Bruny Island District School in Alonnah, has **Internet** access, scanning, and fax service. (☎6293 2036. Open Tu 9-noon and 1-4pm; W 9am-noon, 1-4pm, and 6-8pm, Th 1-40pm, F 1-4pm and 6-9pm, Sa 1-4pm. $5 per 30min.) There are **no banks** or **ATMs** on Bruny. **Postal Code:** 7150.

ACCOMMODATIONS AND FOOD. Bruny Island has no hostels, though free camping is available. **Adventure Bay Holiday Villages ❶,** at the end of the road in Adventure Bay, is decorated with bleached whale bones. (☎6293 1270. After dark, ring bell to the right of door. Coin-op showers. Laundry. Campervan sites $18; cabins for 2 $50.) No longer a YHA, South Bruny's **Lumeah ❺,** on Main Rd. in Adventure Bay, offers spacious doubles, huge common areas, a brick fireplace, laundry, and BBQ. (☎6293 1265; lumeah@tassie.net.au. Closed June-Aug. Doubles $140.) At the start of the Penguin Island and Grass Point tracks, many of the island's protected lands offer **free camping ❶.** Cloudy Bay and Jetty Beach offer camping within the National Park, and both and require national park passes. Those without passes can camp at Neck Beach, on the south end of the connecting isthmus. All offer sites with pit toilets, no water, and no firewood. Contact the ranger for more info (☎6293 1419). Within the Morella Island Retreats is the **Hothouse Cafe ❹,** 46 Adventure Bay Rd., 6km north of Adventure Bay, a sheltered outdoor cafe with fantastic food and a beautiful garden, capped off with a panoramic view of the sea. The cafe's ambience more than makes up for its slightly expensive meals (☎6293 1131. Light meals $7-$15. Open daily in summer 9am-5pm, in winter 10am-4pm. Gardens and Gumtree maze $3.) Across the street, **The Original Tasmanian Fudge Co. ❶,** 53 Adventure Bay Rd., has an assortment of delicious fudges, including orange and mango. (☎6293 1456. Open M-F 10am-4pm.)

SIGHTS AND ACTIVITIES. The **Bligh Museum,** 880 Adventure Bay Rd., contains fascinating old maps, marine photos, and memorabilia relating to Tasmania's early European explorers—including Cook, Bligh, Flinders, and d'Entrecasteaux—and the intrepid settlers who followed. (☎6293 1117. Open daily 10am-3pm. $4, YHA $3.) **Bruny Island Charters** offers popular ecotours of the wild coastlines and adjacent waterways, which showcase spectacular sightings of seals, penguins, and dolphins. (☎6293 1465; www.brunycharters.com.au. Operates Oct.-Apr. 3hr. tour departs from the Adventure Bay Jetty daily at 11am, $95. Full-day tour from Hobart M-F and Su 8am, $145. Book tours ahead.) **Bruny Island Ventures** leads full-day land tours to the island, departing from Hobart daily at 8:30am and returning at 5:30pm. (☎6229 7465. Operates Oct.-Apr. $145.) The **Cape Bruny Lighthouse,** built by convicts between 1836 and 1838, is 30km southwest of Adventure Bay on an unsealed road. (☎6298 3114. Tours by arrangement only $5, children $2.) Near the lighthouse, hike down the hills and through the coastal heath coves of the **Labillardiere Reserve** (round-trip 7hr.; alternate circuit 1½hr.; moderate), but be aware that trails are often poorly marked. From September to February, fairy penguins and mutton birds roost on the neck of the island. The island is also a haven for rare white wallabies, diverse birdlife, and seals. The surrounding waters also host dolphins and migrating southern right whales. **Cloudy Bay** has some of the best surf in Tasmania, while **Jetty Beach** offers more sheltered waters. Some of the best views of the area can be found from the **Fluted Cape Circuit** (3hr.), which starts at the end of the beach on the southeast end of Adventure Bay. The challenging trail scales the tops of some of the highest cliffs in Australia.

TASMANIA

GEEVESTON AND THE FAR SOUTH

Winding 25km south from Huonville along the d'Entrecasteaux Channel is **Geeveston,** a town teetering on the edge of the wilderness. A small town (pop. 800) with limited accommodations, the town serves primarily as a gateway to the Hartz Mountains, Southwest National Park (p. 546), and nearby forest reserves. **Tassielink buses** (☎1300 300 520) run from Hobart to: Cockle Creek (3½hr.; M, W, F 8:30am; $60.70); Dover (2hr., $18.10); and Geeveston (1½hr., M-F, $13.70).

The **tourist office** is the **Forest and Heritage Centre** on Church St. (☎6297 1836. **Internet** access $2 per 15min. Open daily 9am-5pm.) Church St. has an **IGA** supermarket (open daily 7am-7pm), a few **ATMs,** and a **post office.** (☎6297 1102. Open M-F 9am-5pm.) **Postal Code:** 7116.

The **Geeveston Forest House ❷,** on the Arve Rd. at the end of Church St., is a small, quiet, and well-equipped hostel. (☎04 1913 2497. Dorms $20; doubles $40.) The region has many **camping ❶** options, including **Arve River picnic & camping area,** 15km west of Geeveston, **Hastings Forest,** 13km west of Dover, and secluded spots at gorgeous **Cockle Creek,** 25km south of Lune River. All are off unsealed roads and offer pit toilets and drinking water. Cockle Creek also has a phone. For showers and flush toilets, **Dover Beachside Caravan Park,** in Dover, is a good option. (☎6298 1301. 13 sites, all 2-person; powered $25, caravans from $43, cabins from $50.)

The **Arve Road Forest Drive** from Geeveston leads to the Huon River and the Tahune Forest Reserve with its wildly popular **Airwalk.** This walkway, set in the tree canopy 48m (157 ft.) above ground, passes over dazzling patches of temperate eucalyptus rainforest, the Huon and Picton Rivers, and native Huon pines. (☎6297 0068. Open daily 9am-5pm. $17, under 17 $9.) Nearby, the easy **Huon Trail** (20min.) meanders through these ancient pines, which take 500 years to mature and live up to 2500 years. Between Geeveston and the Airwalk are a number of overlooks, picnics, and short walks. The **"Big Tree,"** alleged to be the biggest tree in Australia, is an 87m (285 ft.) swamp gum of enormous girth. An unpaved turnoff from the Arve Rd., 13km from Geeveston, leads into the **Hartz Mountain National Park.** A number of pleasant walks, including the 400m stroll to the jaw-dropping **Waratah lookout,** make the park an attractive, less-crowded alternative to the Airwalk. The challenging 5hr. hike from the carpark at the end of the road leads to the peak of Hartz Mountain, complete with amazing views and a number of scrambles along the way. Regular park fees apply. Twenty-two kilometers south of Geeveston are the **Hastings Caves,** which house impressive dolomite formations, and the relaxing **Hastings Pool,** kept a constant 28°C (82.4°F) by thermal springs. (☎6298 3209. Tours every hr. Jan.-Feb. 10am-5pm, Mar.-Apr. 10am-4pm, May-Aug. 11am-4pm, and Sept.-Dec. 10am-4pm; $19.50, concessions $13.60; includes day-pass to pool. Pool without pass $4.90, open till 6pm.) The carpark past the free camping area in **Cockle Creek** marks the end of Australia's most southerly road. An easy walk (4hr. round-trip) from the camp goes to South Cape Bay, the closest you can get to **Australia's southernmost tip** and neighboring Antarctica. The area west of Cockle Creek is part of the **Southwest National Park** (p. 546). Park passes are available from the tourist office.

DERWENT VALLEY AND THE SOUTHWEST

Largely untouristed, the southwest affords visitors a quiet wilderness experience. The River Derwent divides the agricultural Valley area and the wild southwest. Rocky peaks roll into the south shores of the valley. Stretching toward the Southern Ocean, Southwest National Park includes the hydroelectric Lakes Gordon and Pedder, around which environmental debate rages.

NEW NORFOLK ☎03

A misty valley enfolds the town of New Norfolk, 25km northwest of Hobart on the Derwent. The town deserves notice primarily as the last place to load up on groceries and reasonably priced petrol before heading west, with few attractions that could warrant a longer stay. The climate is perfect for growing hops—regional cultivators harvest up to 45 tons per day. **Oast House,** on the Lyell Hwy. east of town, was once used to process hops; now it's New Norfolk's most popular tourist attraction, with a museum, gallery, and cafe. (☎6261 2067. Open daily 9am-6pm. $5.) A fine stretch of the Derwent River adjoins New Norfolk and makes an attractive spot for rafting, fishing, and swimming. Dating back to 1824, the **Anglican Church of St. Matthew,** on Bathurst St. across from Arthur Sq., is Tasmania's oldest church. The beautiful stained glass windows were donated by a family that lost a young daughter to illness; her likeness appears next to Mary in the right panel.

Tassielink (☎1300 300 520) runs **buses** to: Hobart (40min.; Tu, Th, Sa 6:20pm; F 8:40pm; Su 6:40pm; $5.90); Lake St. Clair (2½hr.; M, W 9:55am; Tu, Th, Sa 7:35am; F 4:50pm; Su 3:10pm; $38.30); and Queenstown (4½hr.; Tu, Th, Sa 7:35am; F 4:50pm; Su 3:10pm; $47.80). **Hobart Coaches** (☎6233 4232) runs from Hobart to Circle St. in New Norfolk (50min.; M-F 8 per day, Sa 3 per day; $6.30). The **Derwent Valley Information Centre** is on Circle St. (☎6261 0700. Open daily 10am-4pm.) The **police station,** 14 Bathurst St., is adjacent to a **Service Tasmania** location, which has free **Internet**

access. (☎6261 4287. Open M-F 9am-5pm.) The **Bush Inn Hotel ❸**, 49-51 Montagu St., north on the Lyell Hwy., is the oldest continuously licensed hotel in Australia. (☎6261 2256. Full breakfast included. Singles $35; twins and doubles $60.) **Wild Planet ❶**, 67a High St., is the best cafe in town, with cheap, filling wraps and breakfast served all day. (☎6261 1766. Open M-Th 9am-4pm, F-Su 9am-late.) The **Woolworths** supermarket is on Charles St. (☎6261 1320. Open daily 8am-9pm.)

MOUNT FIELD NATIONAL PARK

Just a little over an hour away from Hobart, Mt. Field National Park is an astonishingly varied and well-run walker's paradise, spanning a huge spectrum of ecosystems in a relatively small space. Over the course of a few hours, travelers can walk through rainforest, alpine plateau, and everything in between, though the park deserves at least a few days to explore completely. While summer visitors enjoy daywalks and short bushwalks amid waterfalls, winter visitors head for the slopes to downhill and cross-country ski. Bus companies do not service the park or its ski fields during the winter. **Tassielink** (☎1300 300 520) runs **buses** to Hobart (1½hr.; Nov.-Apr. M, W 2 per day; Tu, Th, Sa 1 per day; $27.70). Some tour companies lead trips to Mt. Field from Hobart. Rangers lead free walks, slide shows, and nighttime wildlife-watching trips during the summer. Drive 100m up the road from the highway to the **park shop** (☎6288 1526) for park info, takeaway food, and souvenirs. The **Mount Field Information Line** (☎6288 1319) reports ski and road conditions.

South West Adventure Base ❶, 16 Gourlay St., in Maydena, is a converted home run by one of the area's best authorities on hiking. (☎6288 2280. Dorms $25; doubles $59.) The National Park Office administers three basic six-person **cabins ❶** near Lake Dobson with mattresses, a wood heater, firewood, and cold water. (☎6288 1149. Book ahead. $11 per person, $22 minimum.) The park cafe also runs a self-register **campground ❶** near the park entrance, with showers, bathrooms, BBQ, and laundry. Its grounds fill with adorable pademelons and platypuses. (2-person tent sites $15, powered $25.) Food options are scarce. The terrific **Celtic Dawn ❶**, just west of the park entrance, has phenomenal focaccias ($6-7), a rotating array of homemade desserts, and a variety of coffees and teas ($3). The cafe also offers a double room ($60) and a 2-bed dorm ($25; linen $5.)

The park has walks and lookouts at all altitudes. The lower slopes near the park entrance have picnic and BBQ facilities, a park shop, easy walks to the tallest flowering plant in the world and a trio of water-

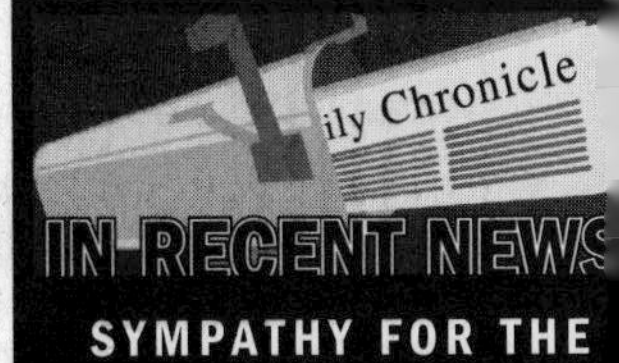

SYMPATHY FOR THE DEVILS

For a state that has come to rely on its unique ecology and related tourism, there could hardly be a more alarming threat than the one currently faced by its most famous inhabitants. The rapacious scamps that define Tasmania in the minds of many travelers are dying en masse.

First noticed in the mid-nineties, Devil Facial Tumor Disease has been seen more and more frequently over the past few years, with outbreaks reported throughout the land. The disease consists of a series of gruesome tumors which eventually make it impossible for devils to feed. The disease is a particularly virulent one—outbreaks can wipe out entire populations of the animals. Estimates place the percent of the total Devil population affected by the disease at somewhere between 20-50%.

While there's not yet serious concern that the epidemic threatens the survival of the species, some worry that the island's devil population won't bounce back from the depletion it's currently experiencing. More troublesome still, there's no known cause, or cure, for the outbreak. Some have suggested that manmade phenomena like pesticides and development have either caused or worsened the problem, which may indicate that this will not be the last ecological challenge in store for the "natural state."

falls. **Russell Falls,** a paved walk (10min.) from the carpark through wet eucalyptus forest, has long been a favorite destination. Continuing onward from Russell Falls will lead to **Horseshoe Falls** and the **Tall Trees Walk** through the tall eucalyptus. The worthwhile drive along the steep gravel road to **Lake Dobson** (16km) leads through eucalyptus, mixed forest, sub-alpine woodland, and alpine mosaic. The upper slopes offer a network of extended bushwalks amid glassy highland lakes, including challenging jaunts up to the peaks of Mt. Field itself. The easy **Pandani Grove Nature Walk** (1hr.) circles Lake Dobson and has unusual vegetation, including pineapple grass, bright red scoparia, endemic conifers, and pencil King Billy pines.

Three kilometers west of the park at 2082 Gordon River Rd., **Something Wild** lets you interact with platypuses, wombats, and baby wallabies. Most of the animals in the park were rescued from Tasmania roadsides. (☎6288 1013. $12, children $6.) Just west of Maydena on the road to Strathgordon, a right turn takes you to the **Giant of the Styx Forest,** currently an environmental hotspot as activists attempt to save the old growth Giant Swamp Gums *(Eucalyptus regnans)* from logging; some of the trees are over 85m tall and among the tallest hardwoods in the world.

SOUTHWEST NATIONAL PARK AND GORDON RIVER DAM

The largest of Tasmania's immense national parks, **Southwest National Park** is mostly inaccessible by car, though Highway B61, better known as **Gordon River Road,** grants easy access to the awesome surrounds of Lakes Gordon and Pedder. From Maydena, B61 traverses 86km of mountainous terrain running through the settlement of **Strathgordon** (pop. 15) 12km before its abrupt end (about 1½hr. down the rd.) at the Gordon River Dam. **Tassielink** (☎1300 300 520) runs summer service between Hobart and Scotts Peak (4hr.; Tu, Th, Sa 1 per day; $68) via Timbs Track (2hr., $64.40), Mt. Anne (2¾hr., $68), and Red Tape Track (3hr., $55). The Gordon River dam, proposed to help create a massive hydroelectric power plant, was an early flashpoint for the environmental activism in Tasmania, and remains one of the movement's most powerful symbols. Though the dam was eventually built despite environmentalists' objections, the creation of Lake Gordon and the great expansion of Lake Pedder ensured that managing the continued impact of the dam would remain a hot topic. Today the Gordon River Power Station is the largest in Tasmania, producing roughly a third of the state's energy.

Carved out of the Tasmanian Wilderness World Heritage Area, the manmade Lakes Gordon and Pedder are captivating. The **Visitor Centre,** on a ledge above the dam, has brochures about the dam's construction and history. To get there, take the 196 steps down to the top of the 140m tall dam. (☎6280 1134. Open daily Nov.-Apr. 10am-5pm, May-Oct. 11am-3pm.) Those looking to get up close and personal with the dam can abseil down it with **Aardvark Adventures,** which runs the world's highest commercial abseil as part of a daytrip from Hobart. (☎0408 127 714. Booking required. $160.) Lake Pedder can be viewed from both the main road and the unsealed Scotts Peak Road. If Mt. Field is relatively untouristed, then the Southwest is completely uncharted; the low ratio of hikers to excellent hikes makes the park one of the best bushwalking spots in the state. The road forks off the Gordon River Rd. 28km into the park at Frodshams Pass, ending 38km later at the Huon Campground. Just 2½km into Scotts Peak Rd. is the short and sweet Creepy Crawly Nature Trail (20min.). Farther down, the Condominium Creek carpark provides access to the strenuous hike up to the **Eliza Plateau** (5-6hr. round-trip) and, 2hr. farther, to **Mt. Anne.** Many hikers climb the plateau, which on a good day affords commanding views of central Tasmania, as part of a three-day circuit including the glacially formed **Lake Judd.**

Rainwater, toilets, and shelter are two hours from Condominium Ck. Lake Judd is also accessible via a tough 8hr. hike from Red Tape Ck., towards the end of

Only attempt hiking in good weather and always bring all-weather gear, as the plateau is completely exposed and weather can change rapidly.

Scotts Peak Rd. Along Gordon River Rd., 13km from the Scotts Peak Rd. junction, is the enjoyable forest **Wedge Nature Walk** (30min.), and the trailhead to **Mount Wedge** (5hr.), whose summit affords outstanding views of the park.

Picnic tables and **free campsites** ❶ at the **Huon Campground** grant easy access to the **Arthur Plains** and **Port Davey** walking tracks. Other sites are at **Edgar Dam,** 8km before the end of Scotts Peak Rd., and **Teds Beach,** east of Strathgordon. (All have pit toilets, tank water, and firewood.) **Scotts Peak** also offers phenomenal bush-camping. Strathgordon's **Lake Pedder Chalet** ❺ is the only other park accommodation, as well as the only food option within 80km of the dam. (☎6280 1166. Continental breakfast included. Twins and doubles $50-110. Restaurant open daily noon-2pm and 6-8pm.) **Trout fishing** is plentiful on Lake Gordon and Lake Pedder from August to April; boat launch sites can be found at Edgar Dam and Scotts Peak Dam, and along the road to Strathgordon (license required). For park info, contact the entrance station (☎6288 1283), or rangers at Mt. Field (☎6288 1149).

WESTERN WILDERNESS

From windy Strahan to the deep glaciers of Lake St. Clair and the slopes of Cradle Mountain, the scenic splendor of Tasmania's western wilderness sits amid stately highland pine forests. One of the world's great temperate zones, it is also one of its last. Most of the land in this region of Tasmania became protected in 1982 by the UNESCO Tasmanian Wilderness World Heritage Area, though logging and mining still threaten the areas just outside the official national park borders. While the region's well-trammeled trails justifiably attract plenty of visitors, most of the west is unspoiled; lush rainforest, forbidding crags, windswept moors, and swirling rivers have been left almost untouched by civilization.

TENSE TIMES FOR THE TENTLESS. Less-touristed areas of Tasmania—including many of the national park areas in the west—are often the most difficult places to find a cheap bed. The budget accommodation options that do exist are usually smaller than their city counterparts, and book up quickly in high season, forcing budget travelers into overpriced alternatives. While tent sites are usually available on short notice (except during holiday weekends), be sure to book ahead whenever possible when traveling tentless into Tasmania's western wilderness.

CRADLE MOUNTAIN ☎03

One of the most popular natural attractions in Tasmania, Cradle Mountain rises majestically above Dove Lake. The surrounding area is a complex, glacially formed fabric of deep creeks and crags that shelter the state's unique jewels: sweet-sapped cider-gum woodlands, rainforests of King Billy and celery-top pine, and lush carpets of cushion plants. Endowed with kilometers and kilometers of well-maintained walking tracks, Cradle Mountain is well worth a multi-day visit.

TRANSPORTATION. The towns of Launceston and Devonport serve as the urban hub for public transportation to Cradle Mountain, though it's also possible to make the long trip from Hobart by connecting in Queenstown. **Tassielink** (☎1300 300 520) runs daily from Launceston (3hr., daily, $49.70) and Devonport (1½hr., daily, $34.20), and on the West Coast from Strahan via Queenstown (3hr.; M, W, F 1pm; Tu, Th, Sa 11:15am; $34.20). A **free shuttle** runs from the Information Centre, across the street from the campground, to the Visitor Centre and Dove Lake. The shuttle operates every 20min., from early morning until late throughout the summer tourist season. In the winter, **Maxwell's Coach and Taxi Service** (☎6492 1431) offers expensive service to the northwest (see **Lake St. Clair,** p. 549; book ahead). For information on transportation for the **Overland Track,** see p. 550.

PRACTICAL INFORMATION. **Cradle Mountain-Lake St. Clair National Park** is the northernmost end of the Tasmanian Wilderness World Heritage Area. It is a 1½hr. drive south from Devonport on B19 and B14, and then west on C132 to the park entrance. From Launceston, it is a 2½hr. drive on A1 to B13, and C156 through Sheffield. From the west, follow A10 for 2hr. to C132 into the park. There is no direct road through the park. Visitors can reach Lake St. Clair most easily via the Belvoir Road (C132) and the Murchison and Lyell Highways (A10). Park fees apply. Before entering the park, the **Information Centre,** in the same building as the Cradle Mountain Cafe, has extensive parking and serves primarily as a jump-off for the free shuttle (see above) into the park proper. The **visitors center,** 3km farther, features displays with helpful layouts of the walking tracks, registry for the Overland Track, and a public telephone. (☎6492 1133. Open daily in summer 8am-5:30pm, in winter 8am-5pm.) A 7.5km sealed road, often one-lane, runs south from the Visitors Center to **Waldheim** and **Dove Lake.**

ACCOMMODATIONS AND FOOD. In high season, accommodations fill up quickly, so book ahead. On the entrance road, opposite the Cradle Mountain Cafe, **Cosy Cabins Cradle Mountain ❶** provides tent sites, Alpine huts, bunk rooms, and self-contained cabins. There's an unequipped cooking shelter with BBQ and sinks, and a kitchen for hostelers. Reception has a limited, expensive supply of groceries. (☎6492 1395; cradle@cosycabins.com. Reception 8am-8pm. Sites $30, powered $35; bunks $30; family room $80; cabins for 2 $125. VIP/YHA.) The visitors center runs **Waldheim Cabins ❺,** 5km inside the park. Heating, basic kitchen, showers, toilets, and power. (☎6492 1110. Bunk cabins $70 for 2, extra adult $25.)

BYOF. Bring your own food—there is no grocer at Cradle Mountain.

The only food option near the park is the overpriced **Cradle Mountain Cafe ❷,** 2km outside the park and across from the campsite. (☎6492 1024. Open daily 8am-8pm.) The **Cradle Mountain Lodge General Store,** right outside the park, sells basic supplies, meals, and petrol at inflated prices. The lodge itself has **Internet** access ($2 per 15min.) and a pay phone. (Open M-F 9am-5pm.)

HIKING. Cradle Valley is the northern trailhead for the **Overland Track** (p. 550), Tasmania's most prominent walk, traversing the length of the Cradle Mountain-Lake St. Clair National Park. The Cradle Mountain area has a web of tracks to accommodate all degrees of fitness and ambition. The free park map is useful only to those hiking the **Dove Lake Circuit** (2hr.), justifiably the most popular walk, consisting of a beautiful, mostly boardwalked lakeside track through old-growth forest. Short tracks around the visitors center and the Cradle Mountain Lodge include **Pencil Pine Falls** (10min.) and a rainforest walk. The map for sale at the visitors center ($4.20) is good for longer dayhikes. The first stage of the **Overland Track** and its side tracks offer more arduous climbs: the hike up to **Marions Lookout** (1223m) begins along the Dove Lake track, continues steeply to the summit, and returning via **Wombat Pool** and **Lake Lilla** (2-3hr.); the ascent of **Cradle Mountain** (1545m) is a difficult hike from Ronny Creek or Dove Lake past Marions Lookout, involving some boulder-climbing toward the summit (6hr.).The lodge organizes bike rental (½-day $20, full-day $30, deposit $100), walking tours (1-3½hr., $10-26), canoe trips (3½hr., $53), and fly fishing (3½hr., $60).

Registration is advised for any walks longer than two hours. It rains 275 days a year, is cloudless on only 32, and can snow at any time—dress accordingly.

LAKE ST. CLAIR ☎03

Half of the headline act of the **Cradle Mountain-Lake St. Clair National Park,** Lake St. Clair is Australia's deepest lake and the source of the River Derwent. The lake anchors the southern end of the famous **Overland Track** (p. 550), with Cradle Mountain at its northern end. One of the most popular activities in Tasmania, a trip to Lake St. Clair and its surrounding forests makes for an excellent excursion.

Tassielink (☎1300 300 520) **buses** run from Hobart (3hr., daily, $43.30), and Strahan via Queenstown (2½hr.; Tu, Th-Su 1 per day; $34.40). From Launceston and Devonport, connect in Queenstown in winter (6hr., M-Sa 1 per day, $63); in summer, take the direct Wilderness shuttle (3hr.; W, Th, and Su 1 per day; $86.10). Overland Track routes include Lake St. Clair and Cradle Mt., with return to Hobart or Launceston available ($80-110; inquire at Tassielink). For group travel, **Maxwell's Coach and Taxi Service** (☎6492 1431) operates a charter service in the Cradle Mountain-Lake St. Clair region to Devonport, Hobart, Launceston and Queenstown. Call ahead for prices, which vary by destination and number of passengers.

The **visitors center** at Cynthia Bay, at the southern end of the lake, is accessible via a 5km access road that leaves the Lyell Hwy. just west of Derwent Bridge. Register for any extended walks, especially the Overland Track. (☎6289 1172. Open daily 8am-5pm.) Next door, **Lakeside St. Clair,** which runs the park's ferries and the nearby campground, is an info center, restaurant, and booking agency. (☎6289 1137. Open daily in summer 8am-8pm, in winter 10am-4pm. Fishing gear $20 per day; canoes $25 per 2hr, full day $45.)

The park has **free camping ❶** sites within the entrance at Fergys Paddock, with pit toilets and walking access (10min. from Cynthia Bay toward Watersmeet) only. Other sites are located at Shadow Lake (no toilet), Echo Point, and Narcissus Bay. **Lakeside St. Clair ❶** has accommodations just outside the park entrance with coin-op showers and a pay phone. (Sites $12 per person, powered for 2 $15; doona $5; heated backpacker bunks $25.) Opposite the Lake St. Clair access road on the Lyell Hwy. is the barn-sized **Derwent Bridge Wilderness Hotel ❷,** which has petrol. Backpacker rooms are in the small modular units detached from the main building. (☎6289 1144. Singles and doubles $25 per person.) The hotel serves meals at reasonable prices. (Open daily noon-2pm and 6-8pm.) A kilometer or so south, in Derwent Bridge, is **The Hungry Wombat Cafe ❷,** which has an extensive breakfast menu ($8-11) and toasted wraps. (☎6289 1125. Open daily 8am-6pm.)

Ferries (Daily in summer 9am, 12:30, 3pm; in winter 10am and 2pm. Echo Point $17, Narcissus Bay $22) run the length of the lake from the Cynthia Bay jetty, on the southern end of the lake by the tourist office; many travelers choose to take a ferry out and then walk back to the visitors center. A return cruise to Narcissus Bay is also available. (Book ahead at the tourist office. 1½hr.; $27, children $22. Minimum $120 in bookings for tour to operate.) All walking tracks branch off from the **Watersmeet Track,** which starts at the carpark a few hundred meters to the west of the visitors center. A little over an hour's walk from the visitors center, at Watersmeet, the **Platypus Bay Trail** (20min.) makes an enjoyable loop through the woods to the water. Longer hikes head west to the sub-alpine forests of **Forgotten**

and Shadow Lakes (4-5hr.) alongside waratah (flowering Nov.-Dec.); over the ridge, you can tackle steep **Mount Rufus** (7hr. round-trip). If you take the ferry out in the morning, the lakeside hike to **Cynthia Bay** from Narcissus Bay amid rainforest and buttongrass takes 5hr.; it's 3hr. from Echo Point.

COLD KILLS. Many people come to Tasmania to hike the untamed wilderness. Make no mistake: it is wild and dangerous. The greatest hazard is the unpredictable weather, which can shift from zephyr to gale in a heartbeat. Even in the warmer months, carry warm and waterproof clothing to prevent hypothermia, which can be fatal (it can snow, even blizzard, in the summer). Dehydration is also a common cause of hypothermia, so stay hydrated. The best way to avoid hypothermia is to plan your trip wisely. Do not attempt bushwalks without the proper equipment and experience. Ask about the expected conditions. Wear wool or fiber pile clothing, including gloves and a hat. Wet cotton, especially denim, is deadly. The Parks and Wildlife Service can advise on gear.

OVERLAND TRACK

The most famous bushwalk in Australia and among the most beautiful in the world, the Overland Track, more so than any other natural attraction, draws adventurers straight to the Tasmanian wilderness. The track, spanning 80km of World Heritage wilderness and taking most travelers five to eight days, has only recently become subject to a permit system, designed to minimize damage to the environment and assure tent sites for all who set out. While these changes are sure to draw more ire from purists who claim the track has become an over-congested tourist highway, the astonishing scenery, such as the state's tallest peak, **Mt. Ossa** (1617m), afforded along the way will continue to make the Overland track a mandatory part of any outdoors lover's Australian itinerary.

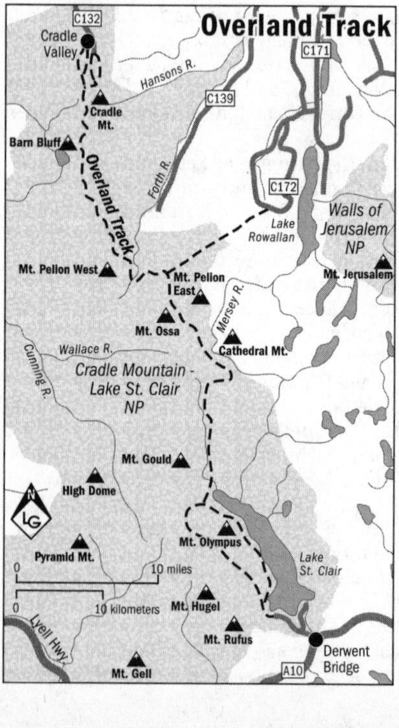

TRANSPORTATION AND PRACTICAL INFORMATION. Rangers advise those with cars to park at Lake St. Clair and take a bus up to Cradle Mountain, as waiting for a bus after a week in the bush is for many travelers an unattractive proposition. Getting to and from the Overland Track by bus requires some advance planning, as shuttle services between the trailheads and the rest of the island are either sporadic or expensive. **Tassielink** (☎03 6272 6611) runs from: Hobart to Cradle Mountain via Queenstown (8hr.; T, Th, Sa 7am; $105, students $94.50); Lake St. Clair to Hobart (2½hr.; M, W 12:30pm; T, Th, Sa 4:15pm; F 6:25pm; Su 4:25pm; $65/58); and Launceston to Cradle Mountain (3hr.; M, W, F, Su 12:30pm; $80/72). Fares and times subject to change.

All walkers starting the Overland Track during the high season (Nov.-Apr.) must purchase a $100 dollar permit from a National Parks office before setting out. Upon purchasing a permit, walkers lock themselves in to a certain start date for their hike, after which point they are free to walk the track at whatever pace they choose. The permit does not guarantee space in any of the huts along the track; therefore, all hikers must bring a tent. The *Essential Bushwalking Guide* is available at kiosks. If you are planning to walk the track, read the walking notes online at www.dpiwe.tas.gov.au and request an info kit from the **Parks and Wildlife Service.** (☎6492 1110. Cradle Mountain Enterprise and Waldheim Huts, P.O. Box 20, Sheffield TAS 7306.) The track can be undertaken from Cradle Mountain (p. 547) or Lake St. Clair (p. 549); starting from Cradle Mountain is most common, as it gives a slight downhill advantage and allows for a ferry trip if necessary.

STRAHAN ☎03

The only sizeable community on the entire west coast, Strahan (STRAWN) is Tasmania's ecotourism capital, populated mostly by families and serving as a gateway to **Franklin-Gordon Wild Rivers National Park** and to all the glories of the southwest wilderness, including the World Heritage Area. Strahan was little more than a sleepy fishing village until the 1980s, when environmental protestors sailed from the town's wharf, situated on Macquarie Harbour, to blockade the construction of dams on the Franklin and lower Gordon Rivers. Since then, environmentalism has been on the rise and tourists flock to experience the history-abundant, scenery-rich Southwest Conservation region. Strahan is now one of the state's most visited cities, as evidenced by the abundance of popular mid-to high-end tourist facilities.

TRANSPORTATION AND PRACTICAL INFORMATION. Tassielink (☎1300 300 520) **buses** run through Queenstown (45min., daily, $8.50) to: Devonport (5½-7hr.; Tu, Th, Sa 1 per day; $53.70); Hobart (5¼-6½hr.; Tu, Th-Su 1 per day; $63) via Lake St. Clair (4hr., $34.40); and Launceston (7hr.; Tu, Th, Sa 1 per day; $68.70) via Cradle Mountain (3½-4½hr., $30). **Strahan and West Coast Taxis** (☎04 1751 6071) provides taxis. The **West Coast Visitor and Information Centre** is on the Esplanade. (☎6471 7622. Open daily Nov.-Apr. 10am-7pm; May-Oct. shorter hours.) The **Parks and Wildlife Office,** in the customs house on the Esplanade, sells passes to national parks. (☎6471 7122. Open M-F 9am-5pm.) **Internet** access is available at the Online Access Centre, adjacent to the **library** in the customs house on Beach St. (Open W 10am-1pm and Th 2-5pm.) The **police** (☎6471 8000) are on Beach St., and the **post office** is at the customs house (open M-F 9am-5:30pm). **Postal Code:** 7468.

ACCOMMODATIONS AND FOOD. Strahan Backpackers (YHA) ❷, 43 Harvey St., provides kitchens, a lounge, a resident platypus, and solid advice on area activities. (☎6471 7255; strahancentral@trump.net.au. Reception 8am-8pm. Dorms $24, members $21; twins $51/44; doubles $57/50. Book ahead.) Depending on whether the yacht *Stormbreaker* is in town, **The Crays ❸** offers bunks on-board for $40. Land-side doubles are $150. (☎6471 7422. Breakfast included. Book at West Coast Yacht Charter, The Esplanade.) **Strahan Central ❶,** on the corner of Harold St. and The Esplanade, is a posh cafe and crafts store with many healthful sandwich options. (☎6471 7612. Meals $6.50-13. Open M-F 9am-5:30pm, Sa-Su 10am-5:30pm.) The hotels also offer good counter meals. Your best bet for groceries is **Festival IGA,** at the junction of Harold St. and B24. (Open daily 7am-7pm.) There is good bush **camping** near Ocean Beach at the end of Macquarie Heads Rd. (C251), 15km southwest of Strahan. ($5 per night, payable to caretaker.)

SIGHTS AND ACTIVITIES. The **Sarah Island Historic Site** was once the penal colony reserved for "the worst description of convicts," subject to unspeakable hardships on this barren rock. Today, it is one of the stops on the Gordon River and World Heritage cruises (see below). Back in town, the local play *The Ship That Never Was* humorously explores the last great escape from Sarah Island's penal settlement. (Shows Jan. daily 5:30 and 8:30pm, Feb.-Dec. 5:30pm. $15, children $9.) Also in the West Coast Visitor and Information Centre is **West Coast Reflections,** an exhibit on Aboriginal and settler life which features artwork and reconstructions of their dwellings. (Open daily 10am-8pm. $2, children $1.) The steam **West Coast Wilderness Railway,** is Australia's only rack-and-pinion railway. The train departs from the station at Regatta Point in the Esplanade for Queenstown, passing pristine rainforest and dozens of restored bridges along the way. (☎6471 1700. 4-5hr.; 2 per day; from $111 round-trip.)

The track to **Hogarth Falls** (40min. round-trip), a few hundred meters from central Strahan, overflows with wildlife. Accessed through **People's Park,** the trail follows **Botanical Creek,** home to the elusive platypus. North of town at the end of Harvey Rd., **Ocean Beach** stretches from Macquarie Head 30km north to Trial Harbour, but the pounding surf of Tasmania's longest beach makes swimming dangerous. In late September, thousands of **mutton birds** descend on the beach to lay a single egg each after flying 15,000km from their Antarctic winter homes. The spectacular **Henty Dunes** rise 30m into the air toward Zeehan. The dunes are sacred to the Aborigines, though 4WD tours explore the area and camping is allowed.

Strahan is at the northern end of the fully protected Macquarie Harbour, one of Australia's largest natural harbors. The tannin-stained waters become choppy only at **Hell's Gates**—the dangerous strait where the harbor meets the Southern Ocean. The Gates compose the smallest harbor strait in the world, and many ships have been wrecked on the surrounding reefs and rocks.

World Heritage Cruises, on the Esplanade, runs the least expensive trips through the harbor and up the Gordon River (south of Sarah Island), and includes passage through Hell's Gates, a 1hr. guided tour of Sarah Island, and 30min. at Heritage Landing, home of a 2000-year-old Huon pine. (☎6471 7174; worldheritagecruises.net.au. Buffet $15. 6hr.; departs daily 9am, in summer also 2pm; $85, children $35, family $220; ½-day 9am-1:30pm in summer $80/32/215. YHA discount 10%.) **Gordon River Cruises** offer similar trips with posher seating and dining arrangements. (☎1800 628 288; $80-175, lunch buffet included.) **West Coast Yacht Charters,** on the Esplanade, offers overnight sailing trips to **Sir John Falls, Heritage Landing,** and other sites; they are the only commercial operator licensed for the stretch of river leading to Sir John Falls. (☎6471 7422. 1 night $290, 2 nights $390.) The **Wild Rivers Jet** gives a faster tour of the King River. (☎6471 7396. 50min. $60, 1¾hr. $78.) **Strahan Seaplanes and Helicopters** (☎6471 7718) tours surrounding heritage areas and Cradle Mountain by plane or helicopter ($110-169). **Wilderness Air** operates a sea-plane flight over the Gordon and Franklin Rivers, with a landing on the former. (☎6471 7280. 1¼hr.; $159.) **Strahan Adventures** (☎6257 0500) offers **kayak tours** to search for platypi on the Henty (3hr., $80) or historic tours around the harbor for $50.

FRANKLIN-GORDON WILD RIVERS NATIONAL PARK

Immense and pristine, Franklin-Gordon Wild Rivers is rightfully part of the Tasmanian Wilderness World Heritage Area. This extraordinary expanse can only be seen on foot or by air; timeless glacial mountains, fast-flowing rivers, deep gorges, and endless rainforest reward the determined traveler. Those just passing through will be able to get a taste of the park's grandeur through a number of short, pleasant walks leading off from the highway.

From Strahan to Hobart, the **Lyell Highway** (A10) runs between Queenstown and the Derwent Bridge through the park, which is otherwise roadless for kilometers. To use any of the Park's facilities, purchase a National Parks Pass, and *Wild Way*, which lists points of interest along the Lyell Hwy.

Three walks in particular stand out. **The Nelson Falls Nature Trail** (10min.), hidden in wet rainforest 25km east of Queenstown, leads to a lovely cataract. **Donaghys Hill Lookout** (40min. round-trip), 50km east of Queenstown, should not be missed. Renowned for sunset views, the track offers incredible views of the Franklin River Valley and **Frenchman's Cap,** its principal peak (1443m, 3- to 5-day round-trip hike to the top). The **Franklin River Nature Trail,** 60km east of Queenstown, is a well-maintained 20min. circuit through rainforest.

Between Queenstown and Nelson Falls, **Lake Burbury** has swimming, boating, trout fishing, and **camping ❶** surrounded by mountains. (No showers or laundry. Sites $5.) Between Nelson Falls and Donaghys Hill, the Collingwood River also has free basic **camping ❶** with fireplaces and picnic facilities. Roadside lookouts at **Surprise Valley** and **King William Saddle** (67km and 70km east of Queenstown, respectively) offer views of the eastern side of the wilderness area. The saddle marks a geographical divide of Tasmania. Dry plains and highlands characterize the east; to the west, an annual rainfall of 2.5m flows into the Franklin-Gordon rivers, through the rainforest, and out to Macquarie Harbour.

THE NORTHWEST

Aside from serving as a gateway to the Overland Track and the rest of the Western Wilderness, the Northwest's major draw is its impressive coastline. While Cradle Mountain is deservedly the first stop for many, the less touristed national parks throughout the North and Northwest are well worth exploring. The region is also an Aboriginal homeland and an important player in Tasmania's mining industry.

DEVONPORT ☎03

Lured by visions of an endless expanse of rainforest, ancient peaks, and wild rivers, travelers arriving in Devonport (pop. 25,000) confront an unpleasant surprise. Its grim waterfront on the Mersey River, dominated by a cluster of huge gray silos, is an unremarkable gateway to Tasmania's wild charms.

DEVOIDPORT. Devonport is perhaps best seen from the rearview mirror of whatever transport you've booked to other parts of the state. If it all possible, minimize the time you'll be spending in Devonport; it's the rarest of travelers who regrets not prolonging his stay in what is unquestionably the least appealing city in the state.

TRANSPORTATION. The **airport** is 8km east of the city center on the Bass Hwy. **Qantas** (☎13 13 13) flies four times a day from Melbourne (1¼hr., $140). **TasAir** (☎6427 9777) flies once a day to King Island (1¼hr., $170) and has on-demand charter flights. A shuttle (☎1300 659 878; $10) transfers passengers between the airport and downtown. **Taxis Combined** is a more expensive but more convenient alternative. (☎6424 1431. One-way to town $18-23.)

Most popular with those transporting a car, the **ferries** *Spirit of Tasmania I* and *II* sail to Melbourne and, new as of 2004, the *Spirit of Tasmania III* sails to Sydney; breakfast, dinner, and accommodation are provided. (☎13 20 10; www.spiritoftasmania.com.au. *Spirit I and II:* 10-11hr.; depart nightly at 8pm from Melbourne and

Devonport; Dec. 17-Jan. 25 also 9am; $86-383. *Spirit III:* 20-22hr.; departs from Sydney T, F, Su at 3pm, and from Devonport M, Th, Sa at 3pm; $180-340. Cars surcharge $59, bikes $6.) The **Mersey River Ferry** *Torquay* transports passengers from east Devonport back to the city center. With your back to the Spirit of Tasmania terminal, turn left at the road and head down the first street to reach the water; the shuttle ferry wharf is straight ahead. (☎04 1835 0142. Runs M-Sa 9am-5pm on demand; $2, children and students $1.20; bike surcharge $0.50.) **MerseyLink** (☎6423 3231; www.merseylink.com.au) also buses around town M-Sa, and links the ferry to local accommodations ($1.70-2.90).

ORIENTATION AND PRACTICAL INFORMATION. The port of Devonport is the mouth of the **Mersey River,** with the ferry terminal on its eastern bank. Devonport is bounded to the west by the **Don River** and to the south by the **Bass Highway** (Hwy. 1), which includes the only bridge across the Mersey. The city center lies on the western bank, with **Formby Street** at the river's edge and the **Rooke Street Mall** one block inland, both intersected by **Best Street** and **Stewart Street;** most essentials lie within a block of these four streets. North of this square, Formby St. leads to **Mersey Bluff** and **Bluff Beach** at the western head of the river. The Bass Hwy. heads west to Burnie (49km) and southeast to Launceston (97km) and Hobart (300km). Hwy. B14 leads through Spreyton and Sheffield to Cradle Mountain.

TASMANIA

Devonport Visitor Centre, 92 Formby Rd., around the corner from McDonald's, books accommodations and transport. (☎6424 4466. Open daily 7:30am-5pm.) **The Backpackers' Barn,** 10-12 Edward St., has all the information and gear you need to engage in environmentally friendly bushwalking throughout Tasmania, including the famed Overland Track. The building also offers a restroom, showers, and announcement board. (☎6424 3628; www.backpackersbarn.com.au. Open M-F 9am-6pm, Sa 8am-3pm. Gear can be sent back by Redline Coaches for a fee. Lockers $1 per day, $5 per wk., with free backpack storage for 1 day. Tents $7 per day, $35 for Overland Track; sleeping bags, packs, cook sets, and stoves $5 each.) **Advantage,** at the corner of King St. and Formby Rd., has the town center's cheapest **Internet** access. (☎6424 9300. $6 per hr. Open M-F 9am-5pm.)

ACCOMMODATIONS. **Mersey Bluff Caravan Park ❶,** a thirty minute walk from town on Mersey Bluff, is situated on a lovely, quiet spot next to the lighthouse with stunning views of the Strait. (☎6424 8655. Laundry. $10 shower key deposit. Sites $7.50 per person; powered for 2 $18; caravan $40; cabin $62.) **Tasman House Backpackers ❶,** 169 Steele St., is a large 102-bed, 11-acre complex with free city center pickup, Internet access, storage, and laundry. (☎6423 2335. Reception 8am-10pm. Dorms $13; twins and doubles $32, ensuite $40. VIP.) **Tasman Bush Tours** (www.tasadventures.com) operates out of the house, with day-trips from $53 and six-day Overland Track trips from $980. **Molly Malone's ❶,** 34 Best St., is the only budget accommodation convenient to the city center. Standard four-bed dorms have sinks and heat. (☎6424 1898. Linen $5. Key deposit $10. 4-night max. stay. Check-in at the pub. Dorms $15; doubles $30, ensuite $50.)

FOOD AND NIGHTLIFE. Good eating is difficult to come by in Devonport, although those looking for fast food have come to the right place. The tastiest vegetarian meals in town can be found at **Rosehip Cafe ❶,** 12 Edward St., next to the Backpackers Barn. A veggie burger ($7) and fresh fruit smoothie make for a delicious and healthful lunch. (☎6424 1917. Open M-Sa 7:30am-5pm.) **Renusha's Curry & Pasta House ❷,** 132 William St., serves up spicy curries. (☎6424 2293. Open M-Th 5:30-9:30pm, F-Sa 5:30-11pm, Su 5:30-8:30pm. $15-19; takeaway $10-14.) **Coles** and **Woolworths** supermarkets share a carpark on Best St., a few blocks up from the waterfront. (Both open daily 7am-10pm.)

Spurs Cantina ❷, 18-22 King St., has country-western theme, video games, and pool tables that attract a young crowd. (☎6424 7851. F-Sa live music. Open W-F 4pm-1:30am, Sa 5pm-1:30am.) After Spurs closes, a stumble next door to **Warehouse** dance club keeps the party alive. (Cover $5-6. Open F-Sa 10pm-3am.)

SIGHTS AND ACTIVITIES. Tiagarra Aboriginal Cultural Centre and Museum, a 30min. walk from the city center to Mersey Bluff, near the lighthouse, explores 40,000 years of Tasmanian Aboriginal history. The Aboriginal Tasmanians are thought to have been the most isolated peoples of the world, having had no outside contact until the 19th century. (☎6424 8250. Open daily 9am-5pm. $3.80, children and students $2.50.) A 15min. walk around the bluffs leads to a series of hard-to-see Aboriginal **rock engravings.** The nearby lighthouse provides a prime view of the shimmering blue Bass Strait. A pleasant bicycling and walking path connects the point to the city and approaches the back beach. The fascinating **Devonport Maritime Museum,** 6 Gloucester Ave., once the harbor master's home, houses a collection of maritime articles, including an extensive photo library. (☎6424 7100. Open Tu-Su 10am-4pm. $4, children $1, families $6.) The **Don River Railway** runs a vintage train along the Don River to Coles Beach, departing on the hour from 10am-4pm for a 30min. round-trip. Ticket includes access to the historic trainyards and retired signal station, as well as complimentary tea and coffee. (☎6424 6335. $10, children $6, families $25.) Farther north off C125, the **Gunns Plains Caves** feature underground wonders as well as a creek with platypuses, crayfish, and lobsters. (☎6429 1388. Tours daily 10am-3:30pm. $10, children $5, families $30.)

TASMANIA

The good eats on the highway between Devonport and Deloraine don't offer much for the lactose intolerant; the rest of us, however, will enjoy the free cheese and chocolate. **Anvers Chocolate Factory,** a few kilometers south of Devonport on the Bass Hwy., allows visitors to watch chocolate being made before sampling the final product. The attached restaurant (open daily noon-5pm) offers expensive meals and even more chocolate. (☎6426 2703. Garden walk by gold coin donation. Open daily 7am-5pm.) **Ashgrove Cheese Factory,** closer to Deloraine, also has viewing windows and plenty of free samples. (Open daily 7:30am-6pm.)

Narawntapu National Park is a small coastal heathland reserve about an hour from Devonport and Launceston. With ample fishing and swimming opportunities at Bakers and Badger Beach, the reserve is also popular for its walking tracks and abundant wildlife, including wombats and Forester kangaroos. The park is accessible by car only via three gravel roads. From Devonport take C740, which heads north from B71 between Devonport and Exeter. Take care driving at dawn and dusk as wallabies abound. Register to camp just past the park entrance at **Springlawn ❶,** with flush toilets, BBQ, tables, water, and a public telephone. (Park office ☎6428 6277. Book ahead in summer. $10, extra person $5.) Two more scenic **camping ❶** areas are 3km farther down the road on the beach near **Bakers Point,** and have pit toilets, fireplaces, tables, water, and wallabies. (Sites $5.50, families $15.) The easy **Springlawn Nature Walk** (45min.) passes through scrub and lagoons, offering another chance to see wallabies and pademelons (their smaller relatives).

DELORAINE AND SURROUNDS ☎03

In the foothills of the Great Western Tiers, huddled in the agricultural Meander Valley between Devonport and Launceston, Deloraine functions as a perfect base for exploring the World Heritage Area to the southwest.

TRANSPORTATION AND PRACTICAL INFORMATION. Redline buses (☎1300 360 000) run out of Cashworks, 29 W Church St., with daily service to: Burnie (2hr., 1-2 per day, $23.60); Devonport (1hr., 1-2 per day, $15); and Launceston (1hr., 3 per day, $11.10). **Deloraine Visitor Information Centre,** 98 Emu Bay Rd., doubles as the folk museum. (☎6362 3471. Open daily 9am-5pm. Museum $7.) Deloraine's services include: **ANZ** with a 24hr. **ATM** on Emu Bay Rd.; **police** on Westbury Pl. (☎6362 4004); a **pharmacy** at 62-64 Emu Bay Rd. (☎6362 2333; open M-F 8:45am-5:30pm, Sa 9am-12:30pm); **Online Access Centre,** 21 West Parade, with **Internet** access (☎6362 3537; open M-F 10am-4pm, Su 1-4pm); **post office** at 10 Emu Bay Rd. (☎6362 2156; open M-F 9am-5pm). **Postal Code:** 7304.

ACCOMMODATIONS AND FOOD. The **Deloraine Highview Lodge YHA ❷,** 8 Blake St., is the best hostel around, with views of Quamby Bluff and the Great Western Tiers, comfy bunks, and proprietors who will arrange tours. Go up Emu Bay Rd., turn right on Beefeater St., then left on Blake St. (☎6362 2996. Reception 8-10am and 5-10pm. Dorms $23.50, YHA $20.) Across the river from the town center on the Bass Hwy., **Bush Inn ❷** has surprisingly nice budget lodging above the pub. (☎6362 2365. Dorms $25.) The **Apex Caravan Park ❶,** on West Pde., parallel to Emu Bay Rd. off the roundabout, has river sites. (☎6362 2345. Sites for two $16, powered $19. Showers for non-guests $4.)

TASMANIA

For lunch, stop in at **Deloraine Deli ❷,** 36 Emu Bay Rd., where you'll find homemade lasagna for $13. (☎6362 2127. Open M-F 9am-5pm, Sa 9am-2:30pm.) One of the few violent-crime themed restaurants in Tasmania, **Gangsters ❷,** across from the Deloraine Deli, serves a wide array of pizzas alongside more expensive main courses. (Open daily 10am-latenight.) About 8km north of town on the Bass Hwy., **Christmas Hills Raspberry Farm Cafe ❷** serves fresh, delicious raspberry desserts ($6-10) and savory sandwiches and burgers for $9-15. (☎6362 2186. Many vegetarian selections. Open daily 7am-5pm.) The **Woolworths** supermarket is a block back from Emu Bay Rd. (Open daily 7am-9pm.)

PARKS. A 1½hr. drive southwest from Deloraine will take you to the arterial walking track to the **Walls of Jerusalem National Park.** Less trafficked than Cradle Mountain, the park contains the same craggy bluffs, vales, and ridges, with lakes and stretches of green moss. The mostly duckboarded track begins from a carpark with a pit toilet off Mersey Forest Rd. (C171) and continues to the dolerite walls in a moderate 3-4hr. one-way trek. The first hour is a steep walk to the park's border and to an old trapper's hut. From there, it's relatively level except for inclines through the gates of the Walls. A compass, a $9.50 park map, and overnight equipment are required, even for dayhikes, due to the highly variable weather and changing elevations. Despite the moderate inclines and boarding, the Walls are not to be taken lightly; rangers recommend it only to experienced hikers, and warn against hiking alone. (☎6363 5133. Call ahead. Park fees apply.)

About 35km west of Deloraine off B12, **Mole Creek Karst National Park** (☎6363 5182), is home to over 300 caves, with two spectacular ones open to the public. The enormous **Marakoopa Cave** features a glowworm chamber, while **King Solomon's Cave** is much smaller and has fewer steps with more colorful formations. Temperatures in the caves can drop to a chilly 9°C (48°F). Park fees do not apply to those visiting the caves, though most area walks require passes. NPWS runs tours hourly from 10am to 4pm ($13, children $7.30, families $33.50). A few pleasant walking tracks traverse the park. One-half kilometer before Marakoopa Cave, **Fern Glade Walk** is a 20min. trail alongside the Marakoopa Creek. **Alum Cliffs,** from a turn-off 1km east of Mole Creek, is a 1hr. hike to a lookout over the cliffs.

About 25km south of Deloraine on the A5 and then the C513 awaits the fantastic **Liffey Forest Reserve.** If your car can handle the steep, pot-holed dirt road, it is well worth the visit as it houses some of the most lush forests in Tasmania and has gone undiscovered by tourism. Hike out to the great **Liffey Falls** (45min. round-trip) on the well-maintained track and viewing blocks. Continuing on to Gulf Road picnic area makes for a longer walk (3hr. round-trip).

NORTHWEST COAST: ALONG THE A2

West of Devonport, Bass Hwy. 1 and the A2 trace the northern coast of Tasmania. Bass Hwy. passes through Ulverstone and Burnie before reaching the junction where A2 continues northwest and A10 branches south toward Zeehan, Strahan, and Queenstown. From Burnie, A2 continues past Wynyard (18km) and Rocky Cape National Park (30km) to Smithton (74km) and nearby Stanley (66km).

BURNIE. The area's major transport hub is Burnie, a relatively large, heavily industrialized paper mill town. **Redline Buses,** 117 Wilson St. (☎1300 360 000), connects Burnie to Stanley (1hr., 1 per day, $17.30) via Boat Harbour (30min., $7.30) and Launceston (2½hr., 2 per day, $29.60) via Devonport (1hr., 2 per day, $23.60) and Deloraine (2½hr., $30). The popular Burnie Rail **Market Train,** by Marine Terrace, chugs to Penguin and Ulverstone and back on the second and fourth Sunday of the month during the summer. The **Tasmanian Travel and Information Centre** is in the Civic Centre complex. (☎6434 6111. Open M-F 8am-5pm, Sa-Su 9am-5pm.) The **Pioneer Village Museum** has an excellent recreation of main street 18th century Burnie. (☎6430 5746. Open M-F 9am-5pm. $6, concession $4.50, children $2.50.) An **ANZ Bank** with a 24hr. **ATM** is on the corner of Wilson and Cattley St. Burnie's **Woolworths,** on Wilmot, is the only large supermarket as you head west until Smithton (☎6431 4688. Open M-F 8am-9pm, Sa-Su 8am-7pm.) Burnie's most savory sight is the **Lactos Cheese Factory,** 145 Old Surrey Rd. (☎6433 9255. Open for free tastings M-F 9am-5pm, Sa-Su 10am-4pm.) **Creative Paper Mill,** which bills itself as Australia's largest handmade paper mill, has tours of the paper-making process and a gallery of local art. (☎6430 7717. East Mill, Old Surrey Rd. Tours at 10am, noon, 2:30pm. $10, children $6, family $28.)

ROCKY CAPE NATIONAL PARK. Rocky Cape National Park (☎6452 4997) features a mountainous coastline, rare flora, and Aboriginal cave sites, which are unfortunately closed to the public. The two ends of the park are accessible by separate access roads. The 9km eastern access road turns off A2 12km west of Wynyard and leads to walking tracks and **Sisters Beach.** The 4km western access road, 18km farther down A2, ends at a lighthouse with great views of Table Cape and the Nut. The Coastal Route track traverses the length of the park along the undeveloped coast (11km, 3hr.) while the Inland Track heads in the same direction with somewhat better views. There is no visitors center, but the shops near both entrances stock park brochures. The small park is geared toward day use; the low-growing vegetation is still recovering from a severe bushfire and offers little protection from the sun during extended walks.

STANLEY. The small town of Stanley had its heyday in the 1840s, and much of the period's Georgian architecture still stands. A pleasant place to visit, the town's main drag offers a number of pleasant cafes and craft shops. The **Nut,** a 152m volcanic plateau rising steeply a block from the town proper, is by far Stanley's main draw and an excellent place to spend a few hours. A steep but short hike (10-15min.) to the top of the Nut becomes a leisurely walk (45min.) on top. Alternatively, a **chairlift** carries visitors up (open in summer daily 9:30am-5:30pm, in winter 10am-4pm; round-trip $9, children $3.) Budget accommodation in town is limited to **Stanley Cabin & Tourist Park (YHA) ❶,** Wharf Rd. which has a terrific seaside location. (☎6458 1256. Laundry, BBQ, kitchen, playground. Dorms $21.50. Sites $22; cabins $80.) There is **bush camping ❶** at Peggs Beach, along the Bass Hwy. 18km east of Stanley. ($2.20 per night, pit toilets, bring water.)

TASMANIA

ARTHUR RIVER ROAD. An alternative route from Strahan to the north coast is the so-called "road to nowhere," the Arthur River Rd. (C249). The road runs from Zeehan through the heart of the Tarkine Wilderness, which stretches from the Pieman River north to the Arthur River along the northwest coast of Tasmania. The road affords stunning views of untamed wilderness, but note that there are no gas stations between Zeehan and Marrawah, a 3hr. trek on a good, but unsealed, road. The **Corinna** punt ferries two cars at a time across the Pieman River. ($20 per car, $25 per caravan. Open daily 9am-7pm; in winter 9am-5pm.) At the north end of the wilderness, **Arthur River Cruises** runs guided trips up the river and into the rainforest with solid commentary along the way. (☎6457 1158. 5hr.; departs 10am; $69. Book ahead in summer.) There is free **camping** ❶ at several points along the route, including Manuka (signposted along Arthur River Rd., 300m north of Arthur River township; no water) and Nelson Bay (on C214, 11km south of Arthur River; no water). For detailed descriptions of the road, pick up the free, informative *Western Explorer Travel Guide* at info centers in Strahan, Zeehan, or Stanley.

THE NORTHEAST

Tasmania's northeast is blessed with a sunny disposition. The pleasant coastline is dotted by quiet fishing and port towns that make for suitable summer holiday spots for families with young children, while the remote Furneaux Islands provide a less cultivated experience for those truly looking to get away from it all.

LAUNCESTON ☎03

Built where the North and South Esk rivers join to form the Tamar, Launceston (LON-seh-ston; pop 90,000) is Tasmania's second-largest city and Australia's third-oldest, founded in 1805. The intense historic rivalry between Hobart and Launceston manifests itself most clearly in beer loyalty: Boag's is the ale of choice in the north, Cascade in the south. Launceston itself is charming, with the vibrancy of a university town set in beautiful Victorian architecture, and the surrounds which include nearby Cataract Gorge, are truly spectacular.

TRANSPORTATION

Flights: Launceston Airport, south of Launceston on Hwy. 1 to B41. **VirginBlue** (☎13 67 89; www.virginblue.com.au) flies four times daily to Melbourne (1hr., $69-269) and once a day to Sydney (2hr., $99-369). **Qantas** (☎13 13 13) also flies to Melbourne (1hr., 5 per day, $150-235) and **Sydney** (1¾hr., 1 per day, $160-330). The reliably low-cost **JetStar** (☎13 15 38) has recently added several daily flights from Melbourne to Launceston ($60-120). An **airport shuttle** connects the airport with city locations. (☎ 0500 512 009. $10, children $5.) A taxi to town will run $25-30.

Buses: Redline Coaches depart from the bus terminal at Cornwall Sq. (☎1300 360 000 daily 6am-9pm; www.tasredline.com). Their buses run to: **Burnie** (2¼hr., 1-2 per day, $29.30); **Devonport** (1¼hr., 3 per day, $22.10); **Bicheno/Swansea** (2¾hr., 1 per day, $30); **St. Helens** (2¼hr., M-F 1 per day, $27); and **Scottsdale/Derby** (2¼hr., M-F 1 per day, $15-21). **Tassielink** buses (☎1300 300 520) run to: **Hobart** (2½hr., 1 per day, $28.20); **Devonport** (1¼hr., 1 per day, $19.20); **Cradle Mountain** (3hr., in summer 3 per day, $49.70); **Strahan** (9hr., M-Sa 3 per day, $68.70) via **Queenstown** (6hr., M-Sa 3 per day, $60.20); and **Bicheno** (2½hr.; F-Su 1 per day, $23.70).

Public Transportation: Metro (☎13 22 01) buses run daily 7am-10pm. Fares $1.70-3.90. All-day ticket $4.40.

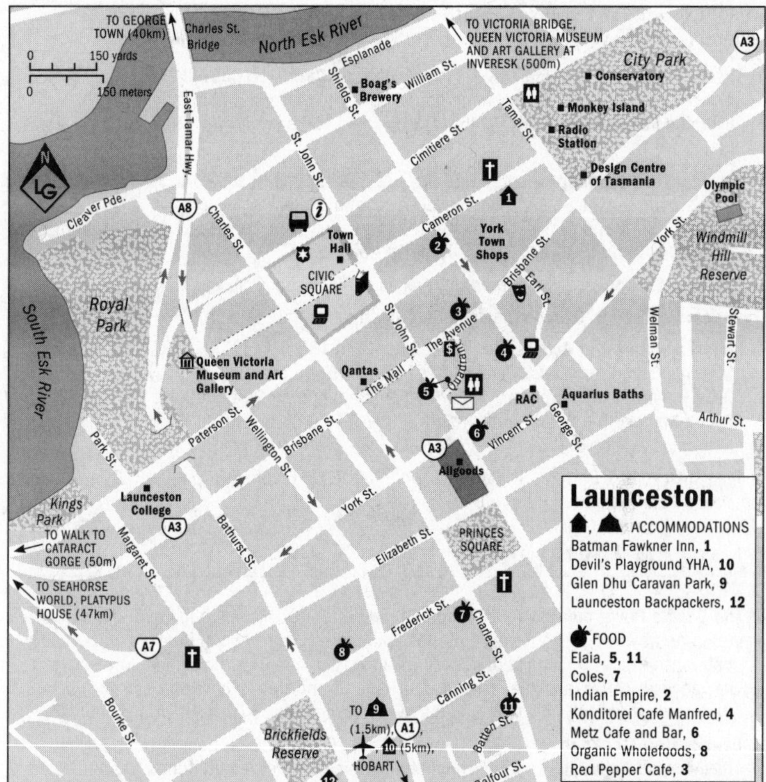

Tours: The bright red, double-decker **City Go Round Bus** (☎6336 3133) hits major tourist stops including the museums, brewery, and gorge. 1½hr. Daily 10am and 1pm. $20.

Taxis: Taxi Combined (☎6331 5555 or 13 10 08).

Car Rental: Budget (☎6391 8566), at the airport, from $31 per day, depending on length of rental. Ages 21-24, $24 surcharge. **Economy,** 27 William St. (☎6334 3299), from $31 per day, 17+.

Automobile Club: RAC Tasmania (☎6335 5633, 24hr. 13 11 11), at the corner of York and George St. Open M-F 8:45am-5pm.

Bike Rental: RentACycle, 4 Pink White St. (☎6334 9779). 1.5km from the town center, follow Brisbane St., which changes its name to Elphin Ln. before becoming Pink White. Daily $14, weekly $130. Discounts available for longer rentals.

ORIENTATION AND PRACTICAL INFORMATION

The town is best explored on foot, since most attractions are within four blocks of the **Brisbane Street Mall,** many of the streets are one-way, and virtually all parking near the city center is metered. **Free parking** is available along the Esplanade. The city center is bounded on the north by the **North Esk River** and on the west by the **South Esk,** which flows through the Cataract Gorge. From here, A8 runs north to

George Town; Hwy. 1 heads south to Hobart through the Midlands and west to Deloraine and Devonport; A3 snakes east to St. Helens and the east coast.

Tourist Office: Launceston Travel and Information Centre (☎6336 3133; www.discoverlaunceston.com), at a new location on the corner of St. John and Citimiere St. 1hr. walking tours from the center M-F 9:45am, $15. Open M-F 9am-5pm, Sa 9am-3pm, Su 9am-noon.

Bushwalking Equipment: Allgoods, 71-79 York St. (☎6331 3644; www.allgoods.com.au), at St. John St. Inexpensive with a great selection that includes army surplus and maps. Basic equipment rental at their **Tent City** annex, 60 Elizabeth St. Open M-F 9am-5:30pm, Sa 9am-4pm, Su 10am-2pm.

Currency Exchange: Commonwealth Bank, is at 97 Brisbane St. The mall has **ATMs.**

Police: (☎6336 3701), on Cimitiere St. Enter through Civic Square.

Library and Internet Access: Service Tasmania (☎1300 366 773), in Henty House, Civic Sq., has 3 free terminals. Open M-F 8:15am-4:45pm. The **library,** 1 Civic Sq. (☎6336 2625) charges $6.50 per hr. Open M-Th 9:30am-6pm, F 9:30am-8pm, Sa 10am-2pm. **Cyber King,** at the corner of York and George St. (☎6334 2802). $4 per 30min. Long term rates available. Open M-F 8:30am-7:30pm, Sa-Su 9:30am-6:30pm.)

Post Office: 111 St. John St. (☎6331 9477). Open M-F 9am-5:30pm, Sa 9:30am-noon. **Postal Code:** 7250.

ACCOMMODATIONS

The Devil's Playground YHA, 10 Morris St. (☎6343 3119), 5km outside of the city center in nearby Foster. Brand-new, purpose-built hostel with several lounges and outdoor patios, as well as a long list of free extras including limited gym facilities, wireless Internet access, coffee and tea. Free shuttle runs to and from city center several times a day; book ahead. Dorms $25; ensuite twins and doubles $70. $3 YHA discount. ❷

Launceston Backpackers, 103 Canning St. (☎6334 2327), across from Brickfields Reserve, off Bathurst St., a 7min. walk from the city center. Clean dorms await travelers in this restored home. Large kitchen, long-term storage, and laundry. Internet access $2 per 30min. Key deposit in summer $10. Female-only dorms on request. Reception 8am-10pm. 4- to 6-bed dorms $18; singles and twins $44; doubles $48. VIP. ❷

Batman Fawkner Inn, 35 Cameron St. (☎6331 7222), only a few blocks from town center. If you don't need cooking facilities, hop on over to the Inn to get a clean bed, duvet, and towel. Complimentary tea and coffee in each room. Singles $35-45; twins and doubles $85, extra bed $15. ❷

Glen Dhu Treasure Island Caravan Park, 94 Glen Dhu St. (☎6344 2600), 2km south of downtown. BBQ, showers, laundry, outdoor campers' kitchen with kettle, hot plate, TV, and toaster-oven. Great tent sites overlooking the city. Reception 8:30am-7pm. Sites for 1 $14, for 2 $21, powered $19/25; caravans $48; cabins $70-78. ❷

FOOD

Coles supermarket is at 198 Charles St. (☎6334 5744. Open daily 7am-10pm.) **Organic Wholefoods** is at 54 Frederick St. (☎6331 7682. Open M-F 10am-6pm.)

The Metz Cafe and Bar, 119 St. John St. (☎6331 7277; www.themetz.com.au), on the corner of York St. Upscale pizza pub and wine bar attract a mixed crowd of young business folk, couples, students, and travelers. Filling, innovative dishes and wood-fired pizzas $15-19. Open daily 8am-midnight. ❸

Konditorei Cafe Manfred, 106 George St. (☎6334 2490). Old-world *pâtisserie* serving excellent baked goods and light meals ($3-5) for a pre-dessert munch. Open M-F 9am-5pm, Sa 8:30am-4pm; open for dinner by prior booking Th-Sa. ❶

Red Pepper Cafe, (☎6334 9449) in Centreway Mall, a quarter-block off Brisbane St. Cheap, healthy light meals served in cramped surroundings by friendly staff. The low-fat breakfast muffins are suspiciously addictive. Open M-Sa 7am-3pm. ❶

Elaia, (☎6331 3307), in the Quadrant Mall. Colorful Mediterranean decor and classy food. Popular pita bread with salmon, chicken, or salami ($11). Outdoor seating available. Main courses $11-20. Open daily 8am-latenight. Second location at 238-240 Charles St., 2 blocks south of Princes Sq. ❸

Indian Empire, 64 George St. (☎6331 2500). Vegetarian, beef, chicken, and seafood Indian-inspired dishes from $10. Eat-in or takeaway. Open M-F by reservation, open daily 5pm-latenight. ❶

SIGHTS AND ACTIVITIES

The most spectacular sight in Launceston is the handiwork of the South Esk River: the awesome sheer cliffs of the **Cataract Gorge Reserve** hold the river flow. The cliffs are a 20min. walk from Paterson St. toward Kings Bridge. Don't expect pristine wilderness; the First Basin of the gorge has been popular since the town's settlement and now hosts peacocks, an exotic tree garden, a restaurant, and a free swimming pool. Walking tracks run on either side of the river from King's Bridge to the First Basin; the one on the north side is easy, while the more difficult **Zig-Zag track** on the south climbs to the gorge's rim for excellent views of the cataracts. A **chairlift** connects the two sides at the First Basin. (Open daily 9am-4:30pm. $9 round-trip, children $6.) The **Band Rotunda,** on the First Basin's north side (cross the Basin on the swinging Alexandra Suspension Bridge), and the **Duck Reach Power Station,** 45min. down from the First Basin, the gorge, provide info about the Gorge's history. Those making the worthwhile walk from the First Basin to Duck Reach should be aware that the track on the south side of the river is much easier and better maintained than the return track on the North side. (Rotunda and power station open daily dawn-dusk.)

The **Queen Victoria Museum and Art Gallery** is split between the exhibits at **Royal Park** and at **Inveresk.** Royal Park, on the corner of Cameron and Wellington St., houses an impressive local and natural history display focusing on Tasmania's wildlife. The upstairs gallery offers a brief but sweet peek at Tasmanian sculpture, paintings, ceramics, and textile art. A highlight is the **Chinese temple** (Joss House) built by immigrant miners in a nearby town in the 19th century. The Planetarium is part of the complex. The **Inveresk Museum** (across the river on Tamar St.) houses a Tasmanian art gallery, which has exhibits on Tasmanian immigration, a railway exhibit, a blacksmith ship, artifacts from the Pacific, and a fantastic display of **Aboriginal shell necklaces.** Be sure to check out the Maireener and rice shells. (☎6323 3777. Open daily 10am-5pm. Both museums $5 suggested donation. Planetarium shows Tu-F 3pm, Sa 2 and 3pm. $5, children $3, families $12. No children under 5.)

A great way to enjoy the city and its fantastic surroundings is on a tour. **Devil's Playground Escape Tours** (☎1800 133 555) offers day tours with excellent guides, lunch, and all entry fees included. Among the most popular tours is Cradle Mountain ($105). For wild adventures, try **Tasmanian Expeditions,** 34 St. Leonard St. (☎6334 3477 or 1800 030 230; www.tas-ex.com. ½-day rock climbing/abseiling $100, full-day $190; 2-day cycling and canoeing $540; 6-day Cradle Mountain and Walls of Jerusalem National Parks $1290.)

For more pampered relaxation, the **Aquarius Roman Baths,** 127-133 George St., have an indoor frigidarium (cold bath), tepidarium (warm bath), and caldarium (hot bath) in the style of ancient Rome. (☎6331 2255; www.romanbath.com.au. $24, 2 trips $40. Open M-F 8:30am-9pm, Sa-Su 9am-6pm.) For an illuminating overview of the beer-brewing process, as well as free samples, take the **Boag's Brewery** tour, 21 Shields St. (☎6332 6300; www.boags.com.au. Tours 1hr., M-F 9am. Adults $18, concessions and children $14.)

The **Tamar Valley Wine Route,** which follows the Tamar River northwest from Launceston, is dotted with small wineries and excellent views, making for a terrific daytrip. Ask at the Lauceston visitors center about one of the many tour companies offering tours of the region. The small town of **Beauty Point,** an hour's drive from Launceston on the West Tamar Hwy, hosts two popular wildlife attractions in the same wharf complex just north of town. Those frustrated in their search of platypuses in the wild should stop by **The Platypus House,** for guided tours of platypus and echidna habitats. (☎6383 4884. Open daily 9:30am-4:30pm. Tours every half hour; all tours include feedings. $16, concessions $13, children $8.) The adjacent **Seahorse World** also has tours of its vast collection of various seahorse species. (☎6383 4111. Tours daily 9:30am-3:30pm. $16, children $9, families $42. Ask about backpacker concessions.)

SCOTTSDALE ☎03

Scottsdale (pop. 7500) lies midway along the A3 between St. Helens and Launceston, thus serving as a good base from which to explore Tassie's northeast, including **Mount William National Park.** Just 8km southeast of town along the A3, **Cuckoo Falls** is a lovely picnic spot. **Redline** (☎1300 360 000) buses run from Launceston to Scottsdale ($12). The **tourist office** is in the building that houses the **Forest EcoCentre,** 46 King St., an exhibit run by Forestry Tasmania. (☎6352 6520. Open daily 9am-5pm, in winter 10am-4pm.) **Postal Code:** 7260. **Northeast Park Campground ❶** (☎6352 2017), along the A3 to Derby, has laundry facilities, a playground, and free sites. Budget hotel rooms with electric blankets are available at the **Lords Hotel ❷,** 2 King St., but guests should expect to share a bathroom. (☎6352 2319. Singles $25; doubles $45.) Twenty-two kilometers west of Scottsdale, just off B81, is the **Bridestowe Estate Lavender Farm,** 296 Gillespies Rd., the largest lavender oil farm in the Southern Hemisphere. Travelers who are in the region in December or January shouldn't miss the chance to enjoy these beautiful lavender fields in bloom. (☎6352 8182. Dec.-Jan. open daily 9am-5pm. $4, children free.)

A3 EAST: LAUNCESTON TO THE SUNCOAST

MOUNT VICTORIA FOREST RESERVE. The reserve is a 45min. drive past Scottsdale. From the A3, follow signs south to Ringarooma and continue 15km on mostly unsealed roads to the carpark. The strikingly thin, single-drop **Ralph Falls,** the tallest in Tassie, is a 10min. walk from the carpark. **Norm's Lookout** provides a fantastic view of the gorge and falls below. The tough hike up Mt. Victoria passes through a variety of ecosystems and provides panoramic views of the Northeast.

NEAR ST. HELENS. Blue Lake is in south Mt. Cameron on the B82 as you approach **Gladstone** and **Mount William National Park.** The lake's gorgeous shade of aquamarine is related to the mineral composition of the soil. **Weldborough Pass Scenic Reserve,** right next to the highway just beyond Weldborough, offers a rainforest walk guided by "Grandma Myrtle." The 15min. circuit weaves beneath huge tree-ferns and myrtle beeches. The **Blue Tier,** accessible via unsealed roads about 15km west of St. Helens on the A3, hosts a number of excellent walking trails, including the easy **Goblin Forest Loop** (20min.).

About 30min. west of St. Helens, in the middle of a pasture in Pyengana just off the A3, **Pub in the Paddock–St. Columba Falls Hotel** ❸ recalls a time before pubs had to be Irish, Western, or have pokies to attract customers. Priscilla, the beer-drinking pig, draws droves of fans. (☎6373 6121. Open daily 11am-late-night. Meals served noon-2pm and 6-8pm. Singles $40; twins $60; doubles $55.) The sole producer of Pyengana Cheddar, the **Pyengana Cheese Factory** ❷, St. Columba Falls Rd., is a great place to stop for a snack. (☎6373 6157. Open daily in summer 9am-6pm; in winter 10am-4pm.) Nearby, the 90m **Saint Columba Falls** unleashes 42,000L of water per minute. Drive 10min. beyond the pub on an unsealed road ending at a carpark, then walk 15min. to the falls. Keep an eye out for the supposedly extinct Tasmanian tiger while in the area; a ranger allegedly spotted one here in 1995.

TASMANIA

MOUNT WILLIAM NATIONAL PARK

More of a hill than a mountain, Mt. William overlooks a quiet stretch of coast in the sunny northeast corner of the park, east of Bridport. Travelers flock to Mt. William to relax and camp near the park's extraordinary beaches—widely considered the best in the state—and to bushwalk among marsupials. Wallabies are everywhere, and echidnas pop up in the daytime. At dusk, Forester kangaroos are common, as well as pademelons, wombats, and chazzwazzers. After dark, flashlight-equipped visitors can spot brushtail possums, spotted-tail quolls, and Tasmanian devils.

Mt. William is a relatively isolated national park with no facilities. Bringing drinking water is essential; food and petrol can be found in Gladstone or St. Helens but not in Anson's Bay. In an emergency, call the ranger (☎6376 1550) at the north entrance. Depending on weather conditions, the road to the park is frequently passable only to 4WD; check ahead before going up. Park entrance fees apply. The park is accessible via the north entrance, at the hamlet of Poole; follow the signposts through the gateway of Gladstone (17km southwest), or from St. Helens to the southern entrance at Ansons Bay via the C843 and C846. From St. Helens, the drive to the southern entrance takes about 1½hr. The gravel access roads are a bumpy ride even at slow speeds. No buses run to the park. Both ends of the park offer ample free coastal **camping** ❶ (only at designated sites), short hikes, and beach walks. The northern access road leads to Forester Kangaroo Dr., past the turn-off for **Stumpy's Bay** and its camping areas (pit toilets), and on to the trailhead for the **Mount William Walk** (1½hr. round-trip; moderate). Starting along the road to campsite 4, a short track passes through coastal heath to the extraordinary coastline at **Cobbler Rocks** (1½hr. round-trip; moderate). At the south end of the park, camp sites are located at **Deep Creek.** Farther south, across the Anson River and outside park boundaries (thus not subject to fees), **Policeman's Point** has delightfully secluded coastal camping, but no toilets or clean water.

FLINDERS ISLAND ☎03

The largest of the Furneaux Island Group (pop. 1000), 60km northeast of Tasmania, is the remote and beautiful Flinders Island. The history of its human inhabitants, however, is quite grim. The original Aboriginal population died off long ago. Later, Tasmanian Aborigines found themselves on Flinders once more—this time as part of an ill-conceived plan by British settlers to "civilize" the community. In this bleak environment, most perished, and the settlement was abandoned.

At 756m, Mt. Strzelecki, in **Strzelecki National Park** (ranger ☎6359 2217), is the highest point on the island and provides a great view of the other 54 Furneaux

Islands. A moderately challenging walk (3km, 5hr.) traverses fern gullies and craggy outcrops. Be sure to bring plenty of water because much of the track is exposed to sun, and wear sturdy shoes, as the track goes over large rocks. At the terminus of the C806 is the peaceful **Trousers Point** beach, great for a picnic and quick dip, or a 2km walk to the point along a striking bit of coastline. Free **camping** (parks fees apply), with pit toilets and tank water, is available just past the beach.

Test your luck by digging for **Topaz diamonds** in Killiecrankie, 40km north of Whitemark. Rent a shovel and sieves ($4) and a treasure map ($4) from the **general store.** (☎6359 8560. Open daily 9am-5pm.) The store also rents cars ($70 per day) and runs seal-watching tours (from $60 per person, depending on group size). **Flinders Island Adventures** provides personalized day tours of the island. (☎6359 4507. Min. 2 people. $156 per person; morning, lunch, and afternoon tea included.) In Emita, 20km north of Whitemark, the excellent **Furneaux Museum** provides an insightful look at the island's history, both human and natural. Nearby, the **Wybalenna Chapel and Cemetery** is all that remains of the settlement where most of the Tasmanian Aborigines were unable to survive.

The island has fantastic **camping** options, mostly along the beaches. Budget options are hard to come by. **Flinders Island Cabin Park ❶,** 1 Bluff Rd., near the airport, has cabin accommodations and rents cars from $65 per day. (☎6359 2188. Sites $10; single cabins from $35; 2-person cabins with outside facilities $50, extra person $15.) **Interstate Hotel ❷,** in Whitemark, has basic rooms and ensuites. (☎6359 2114. Singles $35-60; twins and doubles $70-90.) The hotel also serves good meals Monday to Friday noon-2pm and 6-8pm ($14-18). The island is full of B&Bs and farmstays. **Furneaux Tavern ❶,** in Lady Barron, has standard-issue bar meals. (☎6359 3521. Open daily noon-1:30pm and 6-7:30pm.)

Today, Flinders Island caters to the enterprising and adventurous outdoor enthusiast. Getting to the island can be a challenge. **Airlines of Tasmania** runs flights out of Launceston. (☎6359 2312 or 1800 144 460; flinders@airtasmania.com.au. 40min.; M-F 2 per day, Sa-Su 1 per day; $288 round-trip, $395 round-trip from Melbourne.) **Flinders Island Air Charter Aviation** will take up to seven passengers from Bridport. (☎6359 3641; flindersislandaviation@bigpond.com. $600.) **Southern Shipping** can carry up to 12 passengers on their **cargo freight** from Bridport to Lady Barron. (☎6356 1753. Normally 8hr. M evening; returns Tu, arriving Bridport W. $93 round-trip, children $55. Book 1 month ahead and bring food.) **Flinders Island Car Rentals** (☎6359 2168) provides transportation on the island from $66 per day as do most accommodations as well. The **Marketing & Development Office,** 7 Lagood Rd., in Whitemark, provides tourist information. Pick up a *Critter Spotters Guide*, a *Walking Guide to Flinders Island*, and info on accommodations and rental cars. (☎6359 2380. Open M-F 9am-5pm.) Other services include: **Walkers Supermarket,** 3 Patrick St., which has petrol (☎6359 2010; open M-F 9am-5:30pm, Sa 9am-noon, Su 1-5pm); a Westpac **bank** (open M-Th 11am-2:30pm, F 11am-2:30pm and 4-5pm); **police** (☎6359 2000 or 6359 3506); **Internet** access at **Service Tasmania** (open M-F 10am-4pm); and a **post office** (open M-F 9am-5pm). **Lady Barron Patterson's Store & Fuel** has groceries and petrol (☎6359 3503; open daily 9am-6pm). **Postal Code:** 7255.

THE SUNCOAST

Tasmania's east coast is the island's softer side, where the weather is milder and the people more relaxed. Tasmania's mountainous interior shelters this side of the island from the storms that pound the west, and summer travelers come to fish, swim, and loaf in the sun.

ST. HELENS ☎03

St. Helens, located off the A3 south of Mt. William National Park (p. 563), is the largest and most northern of the coastal fishing and vacation villages on Tasmania's east coast. Peaceful and easygoing, the town is an excellent base from which to visit nearby coastal attractions.

The closest of the outdoor sights are out of town. **Binalong Bay,** gateway to the **Bay of Fires Coastal Reserve,** is 15km northeast of town. Named for the red rocks, Capt. Tobias Furneax mistook for fire, the area has a number of great walks and a number of free, basic campsites. **Humbug Point,** on Binalong Bay Rd., offers great walks and views. As you leave town heading south on A3, signs direct you to **St. Helens Point,** which has free camping with pit toilets, decent fishing, and good surf at **Beerbarrel Beach.** The **Peron Dunes** cover a large expanse of coast, attracting dune buggies and sand boarders.

Redline buses (☎1300 360 000) sell tickets at the newsagency at Quail and Cecilia St. Buses run to: Hobart (4-5hr., M-F 1 per day, $47) and Launceston (2½hr., 1 per day M-F, $27). **Tassielink** (☎1300 300 520) runs to: Hobart (4hr.; F, Su 2pm; $44) via Bicheno (70min., $12), the highway turn-off for Coles Bay (1¼hr., $14), and Swansea (1¾hr., $17). The **St. Helens Travel Centre,** 20 Cecilia St., books for Tassielink. (☎6376 1533. Open M-F 9:30am-4:30pm.) **St. Helens History Room,** 61 Cecilia St., offers history and **tourist information.** (☎6376 1744. Open M-F 9am-5pm, Sa 10am-4pm. History room by donation.) A 24hr. **ATM** is available at **Trust Bank,** 18 Cecilia St. **Service Tasmania,** 23 Quail St., has free **Internet** access. (☎6376 2431. Max. 30min. Open M-F 8:30am-4:30pm.) The **post office** is at 46 Cecilia St. (Open M-F 9am-5pm.) **Postal Code:** 7216.

TASMANIA

The newest, and nicest hostel in town, **St. Helens Backpackers ❷,** 9 Cecilia St., features clean, comfortable rooms and offers transportation and outfitting (prices vary) for backpackers looking to see the Bay of Fires. (☎6376 2017. Linen $2. Dorms $20. Tent rental $25 per night.) Quiet **St. Helens YHA ❷,** 5 Cameron St., off Quail St., has everything a backpacker could desire in a fabulous 70s-esque setting. The hostel owners provide a helpful driving map for nearby attractions. (☎6376 1661. Reception 8-10am and 5-8pm. Dorms $22, YHA $18; doubles $44/40.) The standard but well-situated **St. Helens Caravan Park ❶** is 1.5km from the town center on Penelope St., just off the Tasman Hwy. on the southeast side of the bridge. (☎6376 1290. Sites for 2 from $17.) **Cafe 57,** around the corner from the History Room on Cecila St., is a Mom-and-Pop breakfast joint. Get there early enough to snag a fresh-baked muffin while they're still warm. (☎6376 2700. Big breakfast $11.50. Open M-F 8:30am-2:30pm, Sa 8:30am-3pm.) The Village **IGA** supermarket is at 33 Cecilia St. (☎6376 1177. Open M-W, Su 8am-7pm, Th-Sa 8am-8pm.)

West of St. Helens on the A3, 6.5km from town, the unique **Georges Bay Trading Company** has a remarkable selection of history books, as well as antiques and local woodcrafts. (☎6376 1735. Open daily 9am-5pm.) South of the Scamander Township on the A3, between St. Helen's and Coles Bay, is **Eureka Farm ❷,** 89 Upper Scamander Rd. This is a great place to stop for lunch, as Eureka's fresh fruit and outstanding homemade ice cream are delicious. Their small cafe (located within the farm) also serves superb dishes, like fresh salmon and focaccia, for $8-12. (☎6372 5500. Open Nov.-May M-F 10am-5pm. Cash only.)

BICHENO ☎03

The spectacular 75km drive south from St. Helens along the A3 traces the coastline's sand dunes and granite peaks to the small town of Bicheno (BEE-shen-oh; pop. 750). The community's beautiful, rocky seashore, friendly community, proximity to both Douglas-Apsley and Freycinet National Parks, and a made-for-postcard colony of fairy penguins make Bicheno well worth a visit. The 3km **Foreshore Footway** coastal track begins at the bottom of Weily Ave., left off Burgess St., and leads past a blowhole, a marine reef around Governor Island, and numerous opportunities for swimming, snorkeling, and diving.

Redline buses (☎6376 1182) leave from the main bus stop at **Four-Square Store** on Burgess St. (open M-Sa 8am-6:30pm, Su 8am-6pm) and run to the Coles Bay turn-off (10min., M-F 1 per day, $5.50), and continue to Swansea (35min., $9), with connections to Hobart (5hr., $38) and Launceston (2¾hr., M-F and Su 1 per day, $28). **Tassielink** (☎1300 300 520) runs from the bus stop to the Coles Bay turn-off (5min.; M, W, F, Su 1 per day; $2.50); Hobart (3hr.; M, W, F, Su 1 per day; $26); Launceston (2½hr.; F, Su 1 per day; in summer also M, W 1 per day; $25); St. Helens (1hr.; F, Su 1 per day; $10.10); and Swansea (40min.; M, W, F, Su 1 per day; $5.50). **Bicheno Coach Service** (☎6257 0293) runs to Coles Bay (40min., M-Sa 1-4 per day, $9.50) and **Freycinet National Park** (50min., $8.80), making Redline and Tassielink connections from the Coles Bay turn-off. The **visitors center,** on Burgess near the town center, is a useful source of brochures. (☎6375 1500. Open daily 10am-4pm.) **Internet** access can be found at the **Online Access Centre,** on Burgess St. near the primary school. (☎6375 1892. $5 per 30min. Open W 1-4pm, Th 9am-noon and 1-5pm, F 11am-1pm and 2-4pm, and Sa 10:30am-12:30pm. The **ValuePlus** supermarket (open daily 7:30am-6:30pm) and the **post office** (with limited **banking;** ☎6375 1244; open M-F 9am-12:30pm and 1-5pm), are near the A3 "elbow" in the town center. **Postal Code:** 7215.

Because of its popularity as a holiday destination, Bicheno has no shortage of comfortable accommodations. The above-average **Bicheno Backpackers Hostel ❶,** 11 Morrison St., just off the A3 behind a little white church near the post office, provides guests with comfortable bunks. (☎6375 1651. Kitchen. Free laundry. 10% penguin tour discount available. Dorms $21.) For a fantastic view of the ocean and all the amenities of home, stop at the **Ocean View Retreat ❺,** 18067 Tasman Hwy., about 4km north of town. Each unit has its own washer and dryer, books, and VCR with videos. The view from the balcony of Unit 1 (sleeps 6) can't be beat. (☎6375 1481. Units $150 per night, reduced prices for one night stays. Extra person $20.) Both **pubs** in town have counter meals.

DOUGLAS-APSLEY NATIONAL PARK

Douglas-Apsley lacks the poster appeal of a mountain, rainforest, or windswept beach, but it's the last significant dry eucalyptus forest in Tasmania, and its wide rivers and wildflowers are a pleasant change of pace from surrounding city areas.

There are no roads in the park. From the southern carpark, a short track leads to the **Apsley River Lookout** (15min.). An unusual number of creatures live within the park, such as the endangered Tasmanian bettong and the southern grayling fish. The **Apsley Waterhole** is a deep pool in the middle of the slow Apsley River, 10min. from the southern carpark. The waterhole can be accessed from the carpark and from a shortcut near the lookout. A loop to the **Apsley River Gorge** (3hr.) follows a track from the north side of the waterhole uphill and back down into the gorge, returning on an undefined track downstream along the river.

The return trip from the Apsley River Gorge involves some moderate climbs, tricky scrambling, and river crossings, so only the agile should attempt it, and then only when the river is low and the rocks are dry.

The popular south end of the park (Apsley River and environs) is a 15min. drive from Bicheno. Keep in mind that the park has no telephones or drinking water. The obscure southern access road leaves the A3 5km north of Bicheno, heading west along 7km of gravel road. The northern access road from St. Mary's (mostly along the MG logging road), is even more difficult to find; the turn-off from the A3 is 23km north of Bicheno and 55km south of St. Helens. There is no bus service to the park, but **Bicheno Coach Service** can charter a minibus (☎6257 0293). There are free **campsites** with pit toilets near the carparks; others are 50m from the Apsley waterhole. The nearest **ranger station** (☎6256 7000) is in Bicheno. Park fees apply.

COLES BAY ☎03

The tiny township of Coles Bay (pop. 100) is the service and lodging center for **Freycinet National Park.** Its sunny location in **Great Oyster Bay** makes it popular with summer vacationers, while its remote location (27km south on the C302, off the A3 between Bicheno and Swansea) ensures inflated prices.

Tassielink (☎1300 300 520) runs buses from the Coles Bay turnoff to Hobart (3hr., M-F 1 per day, $29). **Redline** (☎1300 360 000) **buses** run as close as the turn-off for Coles Bay on the A3 south toward Hobart (3-5hr., M-F 1 per day, $28) and north to Launceston (3hr., M-F 1 per day, $34). From the highway turn-off, take Bicheno Coaches (☎6257 0293) to town (20min.; M-F 3 per wk. connect with Tassielink, 5 per wk. with Redline.)The **supermarket,** on Garnet Ave., offers **petrol** and limited **banking,** and houses the **visitors center,** a coffee shop, and the **post office.** (☎6257 0383. Open daily 8am-9pm.) Info on the park can also be found at the **East Coast Interpretation Centre** at the park's entrance.

The **YHA-affiliated Iluka Holiday Centre ❷** is a campground and hostel at the west end of The Esplanade, just a step away from the beach. (☎6257 0115 or 1800 786 512; iluka@trump.net.au. Reception 8am-6pm. Sites $17, powered $20; dorms $22, YHA $19; twins and doubles $75-110; on-site vans for 2 $60.) For a rustic experience, travelers can try the **Coles Bay Youth Hostel (YHA) ❶,** in the national park at Parsons Cove, which has 10 bunks with pit toilets and no running water. Book ahead, especially in summer. (☎6234 9617. Bunks $10; cabins $50.)

Freycinet Sea Cruises (☎6257 0355) offers three excursions on which dolphin, seal, and albatross sightings are common; call ahead to book the Wineglass Bay Cruise (daily 9am-12:30pm; adults $110, children $65), the Explorer Cruise (daily 2-4:30pm; $75/40), or the Beach Bush Cruise and Walk (daily 9am-1pm; $150/75). **Freycinet Air** offers 30min. scenic flights over the national park and Wineglass Bay. (☎6375 1694. From $82.) **Freycinet Adventures** (☎6257 0500; www.freycinetadventures.com) conducts sea kayak ($55-140), abseiling ($125), and four-wheel motorbike ($55-80) tours. They also rent kayaks and mountain bikes. **All4Adventures** (☎04 3850 9022) leads 2hr. 4WD motorbike tours of the park ($105 to operate the vehicle, $65 to ride; book ahead).

FREYCINET NATIONAL PARK

Freycinet (FRAY-sin-nay) National Park is famous for mountains, beaches, and abundant outdoor activities. A 3hr. drive from Hobart or Launceston, the park is home to the striking red-granite Hazards and photogenic Wineglass Bay.

Bicheno Coaches stops in Coles Bay en route to the park's tracks. (☎6257 0293. M-Sa 1 per day; Su and round-trip service by advanced booking only. $8.80, round-trip $16.) They also offer service between Coles Bay, the Coles Bay turn-off (30min., $6.30), and Bicheno (40min., $7.50). At the turn-off, you can connect with Tassielink and Redline services to other destinations (see Coles Bay, p. 567). An hour's walk away, Coles Bay is the service and lodging center for Freycinet, but for information on the park, stop at the **tourist office** near the park entrance. Register and pay at the center; park fees apply. (☎6356 7000. Open daily 8am-5pm.) **Campsites ❶** with water and basic toilets are available at Rich-

TASMANIA

ardson's Beach (sites $5.50, powered $6.60). During summer, all park campsites are only available by ballot system; register after Sept. 30th.

At an outdoor theater past the kiosk, rangers offer free programs, including nocturnal walks and primers on Aboriginal land use. (Dec.-Jan. 3 per day.) Nearly all the short walks in the park are extraordinary. Just past the Freycinet Lodge, there's a turn-off on an unsealed road for Sleepy Bay (1.8km) and the **Cape Tourville Lighthouse** (6.4km). It's an easy 20min. round-trip walk to the Bay, which offers good swimming and snorkeling; the lighthouse provides amazing views of waves. Honeymoon Bay, popular for snorkeling, and Richardson's Beach, popular for swimming, are also on the main road. All major walking tracks begin at the carpark at the end of the road; a moderate 33km hike around the whole peninsula takes two to three days. Be sure to bring water on dayhikes. The **Wineglass Bay Lookout Walk** (1-2hr.) is a very popular hike: the steep, well-maintained trail climbs up through the Hazards and has fabulous views of the bay and the peninsular Freycinet mountains. The 4-5hr. loop by Wineglass Bay and Hazards Beach (11km) is a nice alternative that provides great swimming opportunities, though you should wear insect repellent as the flies are brutal in the summer. The **Mount Amos Track** (3-4hr. round-trip) is difficult, but has spectacular views. The white sands of **Friendly Beach,** can be accessed via the unsealed Friendly Beaches Rd., 18km north of Coles Bay. Free **campsites ❶** with pit toilets are available at **Isaacs Point,** just past Friendly Beach. Bring your own water.

TASMANIA

SWANSEA ☎03

A tourist hotspot on Tassie's increasingly popular Suncoast, Swansea (pop. 500) was settled in the early 1820s by the Welsh. The town is near A3 between Bicheno and Triabunna and is a good base from which to explore Great Oyster Bay.

Swansea Holiday Park ❷, on Shaw St., off the A3 north of town, also has a good seaside location. (☎6257 8177. Sites $22; cabins $90.) Hotel rooms are available at the **Swansea Motor Inn ❺,** 1 Franklin St. (☎6257 8102. Ensuite doubles $66-98.)

The informal **Visitors Information Centre** is located in the **Swansea Bark Mill and Museum,** 96 Tasman Hwy. (☎6257 8382. Open daily 9am-5pm. Museum $10, children $6.) There are a number of **historic buildings** around town—pick up the Swansea Heritage Walk guide for $2 from the visitors center. **Tassielink** (☎1300 300 520) buses run to Hobart daily from the Swansea Corner Store ($25). **Redline** (☎1300 360 000) buses connect to Hobart and Launceston via Campbelltown ($43). There is an **ATM** at the **Swansea Corner Store,** corner of Victoria and Franklin St., which also sells basic supplies. (☎6257 8118. Open daily 7am-7pm.) Other services include the **police** (☎6257 9044) and the **post office** on the corner of Arnol and Franklin St. (Open M-F 9am-5pm.) **Postal Code:** 7190.

TRIABUNNA ☎03

On **Prosser Bay,** 50km southwest of Swansea and 87km northeast of Hobart, Triabunna (try-a-BUN-na; pop. 1200) is a tiny port town where you can stock up on food and spend the night before heading to Maria Island. **Tassielink** (☎1300 300 520) runs to Hobart (2hr., M-F 1 per day, $17) and Swansea (45min., M-F 1 per day, $7). They also connect to the **Maria Island Ferry** in **Triabunna.** The **Tourist Information Centre,** at the Esplanade, has **Internet** access. (☎6257 4772. $2 per 5min. Open daily 10am-4pm.) Managers Don and Fran provide home-baked cookies and warm hospitality at **Udda Backpackers ❷,** 12 Spencer St. Follow Vicary St. toward the fire station, turn left after the bridge onto a gravel road, then left onto Spencer St.; signs point the way. (☎6257 3439. Dorms $20; twins and doubles $45.) **Triabunna Caravan Park ❶,** 6 Vicary St., is also a friendly place to stay. (☎6257

3575. Sites $15, powered $17.) **Value Plus** supermarket is at Charles and Vicary St. (Open daily 8am-6:30pm.) The **post office** is on Vicary St. **Postal Code:** 7190.

MARIA ISLAND NATIONAL PARK

A surprisingly undertouristed gem, Maria (muh-RYE-uh) Island has housed penal colonies, a cement industry, whalers, and farmers. The ruins of a settlement at **Darlington**—along with the area's unique, wildlife and natural beauty—are the island's main attraction. Park brochures are available from the Tourist Information Centre in Triabunna; the ferry has detailed descriptions of walking tracks, and the knowledgeable crew can advise you on the best way to use your time. Walks meander through the **Darlington Township** ruins (30min.), over the textured sandstone of the **Painted Cliffs** (2hr., best at low tide; check schedule at the Tourist Information Centre), and to the rock-scramble up **Bishop and Clerk** (4hr.). The longest walk in the park is to **Mount Maria** (6hr.); the summit affords the best views of the island.

To reach Maria, travelers can take the Maria Island Ferry, which departs from "downtown" Triabunna, 50m from the Tourist Information Centre. (☎6234 9294. 30min. Runs late Dec.-Apr. 9; 10:30am, 1, and 3:30pm. Round-trip $25, children $12; bikes and kayaks $3.) Many travelers bring a bicycle with them on the ferry; it's a great way to traverse the island's 30km of roads. On the island itself, there are no shops or facilities save a **tourist office** and a **ranger station** (☎6257 1420) with a telephone. Pick up the free pamphlet *Historic Darlington* for a good outline of the island's extensive history. The **Old Darlington Prison** ❶ now houses six-bed units, each with a table, chairs, and fireplace. (Book ahead with the ranger station ☎6257 1420. Shared toilets, sinks, and hot showers. Beds $8.80, children $4, families $22.) The island has three **campsites** ❶: **Darlington** (sites $4.40, families $11); **French's Farm,** 11km south down the main gravel road, which has a pit toilet and rainwater tanks; and **Encampment Cove,** 3km down a side road near French's Farm, which has a small bunkhouse and a pit toilet.

TASMANIA

VICTORIA

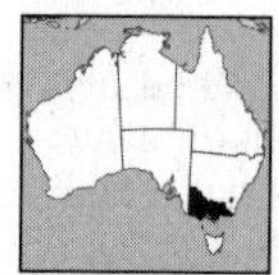

Victoria may be mainland Australia's smallest state, but it's blessed with far more than its fair share of fantastic cultural, natural, and historical attractions. Its landscape varies widely, from the dry and empty western plains of the Mallee to the inviting wineries along the Murray River, from the ski resorts of the Victorian Alps to the forested parks of the Gippsland coast. Nowhere else in Australia is so much ecological diversity only a daytrip away.

Sleek and sophisticated, Melbourne overflows with eclectic ethnic neighborhoods, public art spaces, back-alley bars, verdant gardens, and a vibrant, energetic atmosphere. It's no wonder that many Aussies claim Melbourne as Australia's best-kept secret. West of Melbourne, the Great Ocean Road winds along the roaring ocean and some of Victoria's best parks. Hand-cut between 1919 and 1931 from the limestone cliffs, the road passes surfing beaches, temperate rainforests, and geological wonders like the Twelve Apostles rock formations jutting from the sea below. East of the capital, the coastline unfolds past Phillip Island's penguin colony and the beach resorts on the Mornington Peninsula, before heading into Gippsland. Here crashing waves collide with granite outcroppings to form the sandy beaches at the edge of majestic Wilsons Promontory National Park.

Victoria is remarkable in the richness of its history and in its natural grandeur. The mountainous ranges of the Grampians National Park evoke awe and offer unparalleled opportunity for rock climbing, abseiling, and other adventure sports. North of the Grampians, the river-wrought lands of the Wimmera and the scraggly plains of the Mallee won't knock you off your feet, but is worth checking out if you have some extra time. Victoria's historical heart, meanwhile, beats to the drum of the mid-19th century gold rush, which flooded central Victoria with fortune-seekers. When the ore waned, a host of dusty country towns were left in its wake—the Goldfields and the Murray River towns in north and Central Victoria are defined by a fascinating past of rugged miners and antiquated riverboats. The 20th century brought agricultural and commercial development, including massive hydroelectric public works projects that still impact the state's ecosystems. Still, Victoria's physical beauty remains, tempered by a refined sensibility and cosmopolitan flair.

HIGHLIGHTS OF VICTORIA

HIKE the **Great South West Walk** to the sound of crashing surf and the sight of an endlessly blue horizon on a walk that lives up to its name (p. 633).

ABSEIL 60m down the Ledge in **Grampians National Park** (p. 636).

PAMPER your palate at **Rutherglen Wineries** with tons of free tastings (p. 662).

EXPERIENCE the diversity of terrain at a **UNESCO World Heritage Site** in Sealers Cove dayhike at Wilsons Prom (p. 671).

TRANSPORTATION

Getting around Victoria is a breeze, thanks to the thorough, efficient intrastate train and bus system run by V/Line (☎13 61 96; www.vlinepassenger.com.au). V/Line runs an information center at its main terminal in Melbourne's Spencer Street Station. Greyhound Australia (☎13 14 99 or 13 20 30; www.greyhound.com.au) offers more extensive national service. Renting a car allows more freedom, and Victoria's high-

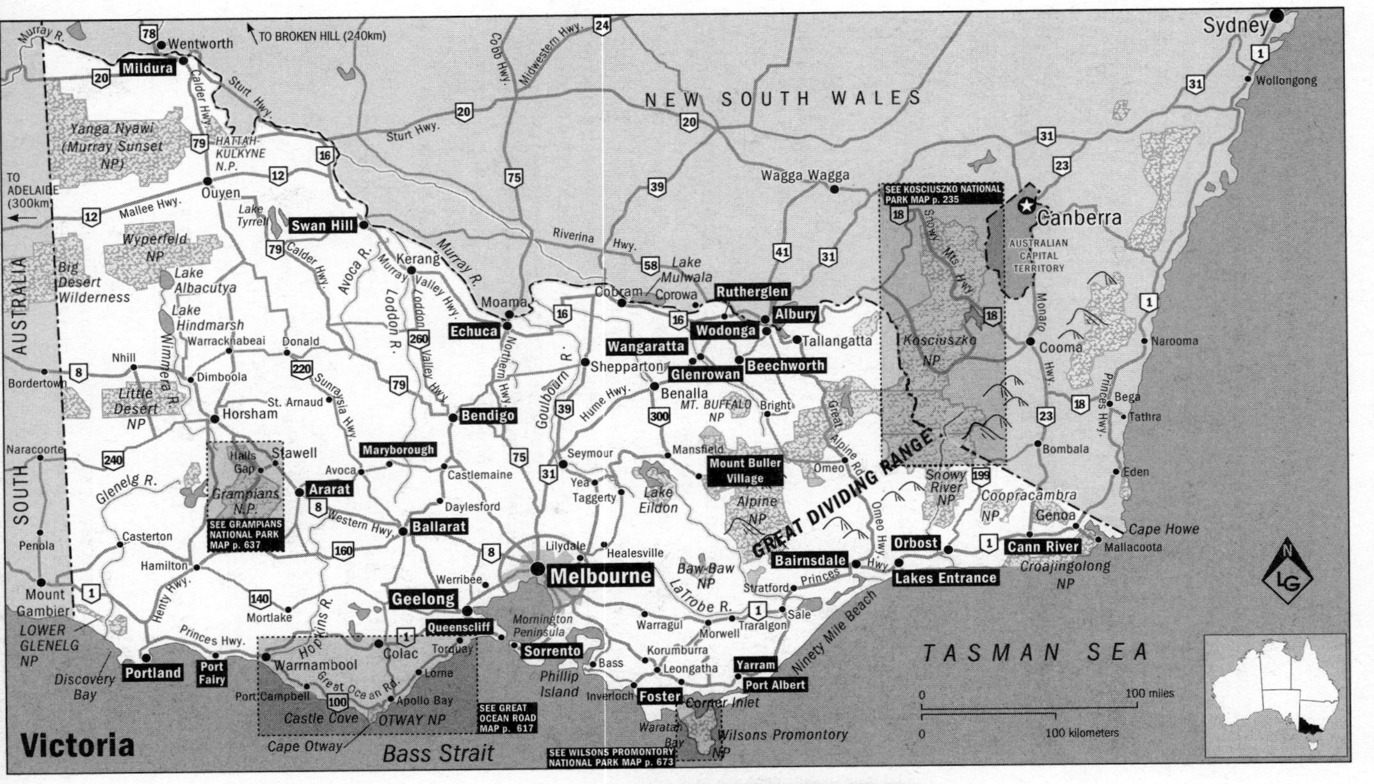
Victoria
NEW SOUTH WALES
SOUTH AUSTRALIA
TASMAN SEA
Bass Strait
TO BROKEN HILL (240km)
TO ADELAIDE (300km)
Murray R.
Wentworth
Mildura
Calder Hwy.
Sturt Hwy.
Yanga Nyawi (Murray Sunset NP)
HATTAH-KULKYNE N.P.
Ouyen
Mallee Hwy.
Lake Tyrrell
Swan Hill
Wyperfeld NP
Big Desert Wilderness
Lake Albacutya
Lake Hindmarsh
Wimmera R.
Warracknabeai
Donald
Nhill
Dimboola
Bordertown
Little Desert NP
Horsham
St. Arnaud
Sunraysia Hwy.
Naracoorte
Halls Gap
Stawell
Grampians N.P.
SEE GRAMPIANS NATIONAL PARK MAP p. 637
Glenelg R.
Avoca
Ararat
Western Hwy.
Maryborough
Castlemaine
Daylesford
Ballarat
Penola
Casterton
Hamilton
Henty Hwy.
Mount Gambier
LOWER GLENELG NP
Discovery Bay
Portland
Port Fairy
Princes Hwy.
Mortlake
Hopkins R.
Warrnambool
Port Campbell
Great Ocean Rd.
Castle Cove
OTWAY NP
Cape Otway
Colac
Lorne
Apollo Bay
Torquay
SEE GREAT OCEAN ROAD MAP p. 617
Geelong
Queenscliff
Werribee
Melbourne
Lilydale
Healesville
Mornington Peninsula
Sorrento
Phillip Island
Bass
Inverloch
Foster
Corner Inlet
Waratah Bay
Wilsons Promontory NP
SEE WILSONS PROMONTORY NATIONAL PARK MAP p. 673
Korumburra
Leongatha
Yarram
Port Albert
Warragul
Morwell
Traralgon
Sale
LaTrobe R.
Baw Baw NP
Stratford
Ninety Mile Beach
Kerang
Avoca R.
Murray Valley Hwy.
Loddon R.
Loddon Valley Hwy.
Murray R.
Moama
Echuca
Northern Hwy.
Bendigo
Goulburn R.
Shepparton
Hume Hwy.
Seymour
Yea
Taggerty
Lake Eildon
Cobb Hwy.
Midwestern Hwy.
Sturt Hwy.
Riverina Hwy.
Wagga Wagga
Lake Mulwala
Cobram
Corowa
Rutherglen
Albury
Wodonga
Tallangatta
Wangaratta
Beechworth
Glenrowan
Benalla
MT. BUFFALO NP
Bright
Mansfield
Mount Buller Village
Alpine NP
Great Alpine Rd.
Omeo
GREAT DIVIDING RANGE
Omeo Hwy.
Bairnsdale
Princes Hwy.
Lakes Entrance
Orbost
Snowy River NP
Coopracambra NP
Genoa
Cann River
Croajingolong NP
Mallacoota
Cape Howe
Eden
Bombala
Monaro Hwy.
Cooma
Kosciuszko NP
SEE KOSCIUSZKO NATIONAL PARK MAP p. 235
Snowy Mts. Hwy.
Canberra
AUSTRALIAN CAPITAL TERRITORY
Princes Hwy.
Bega
Tathra
Narooma
Sydney
Wollongong
0 100 miles
0 100 kilometers
N
LG

VICTORIA

way system is the country's most extensive and navigable. To cut down on occasionally prohibitive rental costs, check hostel ride-share boards. The Royal Automobile Club of Victoria (RACV), 422 Lt. Collins St., Melbourne (☎13 19 55 or 9703 6363; roadside assistance ☎13 11 11; www.racv.com.au), has great maps and sells short-term traveler's insurance. Members of other automobile clubs may already have reciprocal membership. To join, the RACV Roadside Care package (including four free service calls annually and free towing) costs $50, plus a $30 joiner's fee for those 21 and older. For more information see Costs and Insurance, p. 30.

MELBOURNE ☎03

Melbourne (pop. 3.2 million) began rather inauspiciously in 1825 when John Batman sailed a skiff up the Yarra, got stuck on a sandbank, and justified his blunder by claiming he had found the "ideal place for a village." Originally named Batmania, the small town underwent a phenomenal growth spurt at the onset of the Victorian Gold Rush three decades later. "Marvelous Melbourne" celebrated its coming-of-age in 1880 by hosting the World Exhibition, which attracted over a million people. When the Victorian economy crashed after bank failures in the 1890s, Melbourne's infrastructure collapsed and its fetid open sewers earned it the nickname "Marvelous Smellbourne." By the dawn of the 20th century, however, the city had improved enough to challenge Sydney for the honor of being Australia's capital. While the Canberra compromise deprived both of this status, Melbourne was happy to serve as the government's temporary home until the Parliament House in Canberra was completed. The city's 20th-century zenith was the 1956 Olympics, which brought the city's love for sport to an international audience.

Today Australia's second-largest city has blossomed into an impressive cosmopolitan center with an active arts community, a fierce love of sports, and an appetite for gourmet dining and street-side cafes. Recent years have witnessed population growth and an increased international flavor. Melbourne's neighborhoods (called "precincts") invite exploration and are accessible by tram. With its picturesque waterfront, epic sporting events, raging nightlife, and world-class culture, Melbourne offers big city attractions with a refreshing lack of tourist hype.

HIGHLIGHTS OF MELBOURNE

SHOP at the giant **Queen Victoria Market,** which offers everything from fresh produce to souvenirs and bric a brac (p. 589).

EXPERIENCE CAFE CULTURE on Brunswick St., the main drag of youthful, artsy **Fitzroy,** which has a chill cafe vibe and even better shopping (p. 596).

CATCH A GAME of Aussie Rules Football, Melbourne's sports obsession, at the historic **Melbourne Cricket Ground** (p. 590).

SUN YOURSELF outside the city limits in **St. Kilda;** the laid-back, beach-bumming atmosphere is the best place to escape the hectic city (p. 602).

PARTY at the swanky bars hidden in back alleys. Don't leave town without spending a night roving the streets of the **CBD** in search of the poshest digs (p. 586).

INTERCITY TRANSPORTATION

BY PLANE

There are two main airports that service Melbourne. The boomerang-shaped **Tullamarine International Airport,** located 25km northwest of the CBD (25min. by car),

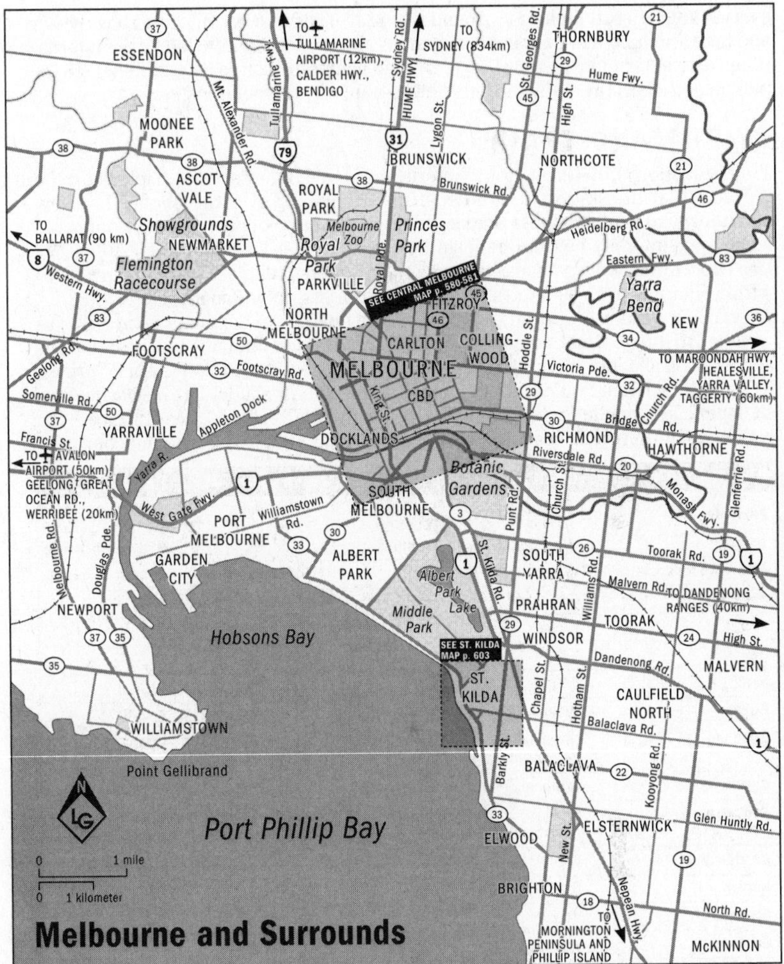

hosts both domestic and international flights. **Qantas International** (☎13 12 11) operates on the first floor. **Travelers Information** (☎9297 1805), near international arrivals, books same-day accommodations and has maps, brochures, and a backpacker bulletin board. **Virgin Blue** (☎13 67 89; www.virginblue.com.au) is in the right domestic terminal and **Qantas** (☎13 13 13; www.qantas.com.au) is in the left. Each airline flies to all state capitals at least once daily. Virgin Blue has last-minute specials that often rival the price of bus tickets. **Avalon Airport** (www.avalonairport.com.au) is the second, newer airport located on the Princes Hwy., 50min. south of the city towards Geelong. Travelers can take **Jetstar** (www.jetstar.com.au) flights from Avalon to anywhere in the country. For more information on airport services, visit www.melair.com.au.

Skybus (☎9335 2811; www.skybus.com.au) provides ground transport to Melbourne's Southern Cross Station in the CBD. (Every 15-25min. in either direction, every 30min.-1hr. at night; $15, round-trip $24.) **Taxis** to the CBD cost roughly $45 and take about 25min. **Car rental** companies are clustered to the left of the international arrival terminal (see **By Car,** p. 29) and generally charge an additional fee for pickup at the airport. Some hostels offer complimentary shuttles.

BY BUS AND TRAIN

Train transportation throughout Victoria is run by V/Line services. Tickets can be purchased at the station before departure, online, or over the phone. The new and improved **Southern Cross Station,** at the intersection of Spencer and Bourke St., is the main intercity bus and train station. (☎9619 2340. Open daily 6am-10pm.) **V/Line** (☎13 61 96; www.vlinepassenger.com.au) offers unlimited travel passes ($75) within Victoria for seven days to overseas tourists only. **Countrylink** (☎13 22 32; www.countrylink.nsw.gov.au) has multiple-day passes to destinations in NSW, as well as Brisbane. **Great Southern** (☎13 21 47; www.gsr.com.au) has destinations across Australia, but if you want to travel from Melbourne to Perth, Alice Springs, or Darwin on Great Southern, you must first travel to Adelaide. The **Melbourne Transit Centre,** 58 Franklin St. (☎9639 0634; open daily 6am-10:30pm), near Elizabeth St., is the hub of **Greyhound Australia** (☎13 14 99 or 13 20 30; www.greyhound.com.au).

DESTINATION	COMPANY	DURATION	FREQUENCY	PRICE
Adelaide	Greyhound V/Line Great Southern	9-10hr. 10½-11hr. 11¼hr.	1 per day 2 per day 3 per wk.	$58 $57-82 $78-167
Albury-Wodonga	V/Line	3½hr.	4-6 per day	$34-49
Alice Springs	Greyhound	28hr.	7 per day	$301-481
Ararat	V/Line	3hr.	3-5 per day	$23-34
Ballarat	V/Line	1½hr.	7-12 per day	$12-17
Bendigo	V/Line	2hr.	5-11per day	$18-26
Bright	V/Line	5hr.	1 per day	$34-49
Brisbane	Greyhound Countrylink	27hr. 35hr.	10 per day 3 per day	$187-335 $121
Cairns	Greyhound	56hr.	3 per day	$416
Canberra	V/Line Greyhound	8½hr. 8hr.	3 per day 1-3 per day	$79 $50-62
Castlemaine	V/Line	1½hr.	5-11 per day	$13-19
Darwin	Greyhound	50hr.	1 per day	$573
Echuca	V/Line	3-3½hr.	2-9 per day	$24-34
Geelong	V/Line	1hr.	11-26 per day	$7.50-11
Mildura	V/Line	7-9½hr.	3-4 per day	$47-68
Sydney	Greyhound Countrylink	11-15hr. 11hr.	3 per day 2 per day	$73 $75
Ayers Rock (Uluru)	Greyhound	25hr.	M-Tu and F-Su 2 per day	$340-386

ORIENTATION

Melbourne lies along the Yarra River just before it meets Port Phillip Bay. The river splits the city into northern and southern regions; the Central Business District (CBD), North Melbourne, Carlton, Fitzroy, along with Collingwood and the Docklands are on the northern bank; South Yarra, Prahran, Southbank, Windsor, St. Kilda, Williamstown, and Brighton are on the southern bank. Each of these precincts has its own well-trodden thoroughfares and unique style. South of the Yarra

VICTORIA

River, several communities enjoy popular beaches and bayside vistas. While the CBD has impressive architecture and most of the museums, the diverse array of attractions in the other precincts is not to be missed.

OUR COVERAGE OF MELBOURNE. Since Melbourne is divided into several precincts, we have grouped together each area's accommodations, food, sights, entertainment, and nightlife listings. General information on these aspects of the city, as well as information about entertainment, sports and recreation, and annual festivals, appears after the practical information. A list of daytrips from Melbourne appears at the end of the section.

LOCAL TRANSPORTATION

PUBLIC TRANSPORTATION

Melbourne's public transportation system, the **Met** (☎131 638 or 1800 652 313; www.metlinkmelbourne.com.au or www.vlinepassenger.com.au) consists of three modes of transportation: light-rail trains, buses, and trams, and is divided into three zones. Most attractions and points of interest are within Zone 1. Tickets within Zone 1 can be used on buses, trams, or trains, and are valid for unlimited travel for a specified period of time. ($3.20 per 2hr., $6.10 per day, $26.70 per wk., $99 per month, $1058 per yr.; 10 2hr. tickets valid only for purchaser $25.70. **The Sunday Saver Metcard** is the best weekly deal, as it allows unlimited Sunday travel through all three zones. ($2.50, under 15 or with valid Australian university ID or pensioner card $1.25.) If you're going to be in town for a while, the long-term passes save time and money; buy them at a station machine or ticket counter. For additional information and route maps, grab Metlink's free *Fares and Travel Guide* from any station. Check the back of the brochure for helplines, including lost property inquiries and translated information.

VICTORIA

BY TRAM

Tram routes crisscross the metropolitan area. Although slow, they are the most useful means of navigating the city and its outskirts. (Trams run M-Sa 5am-midnight, Su 8am-11pm; weekdays every 3-12min., nights and weekend approx. every 20min.) Passengers can purchase tickets at various stations, on trams and buses (coins only), at 7-11 stores, and at the **Met Shop,** 103 Elizabeth St., near Collins St. (Open M-F 8:30am-4:55pm, Sa 9am-1pm.) Passengers who purchase tickets at 7-11 or the Met Shop are required to validate their ticket once they begin traveling. Although it may be possible to ride the trams without a ticket, inspectors do random checks, usually around tram junctions; *Let's Go* recommends always purchasing a ticket as fines can be up to $150. Similar fines apply if you do not validate your ticket once on board. To validate a ticket, place it in one of the green electronic boxes near the bus and tram stops, which will stamp and return it to you.

The burgundy and gold **City Circle Tram** circumnavigates the CBD in both directions, providing running commentary on the city's sights and history. (Every 10min. M-W and Su 10am-6pm, Th-Sa 10am-9:30pm; free.) There are train stops at **Melbourne Central, Flagstaff Gardens, Parliament,** and **Southern Cross Station,** though the main hub is the beautiful golden-colored **Flinders Street Station** at the southern end of Swanston St., identifiable by its big yellow clock.

BY CAR

National car rental chain offices are mostly located in the Melbourne CBD and at the airport, but it's cheaper to rent in the city, as the airport offices generally

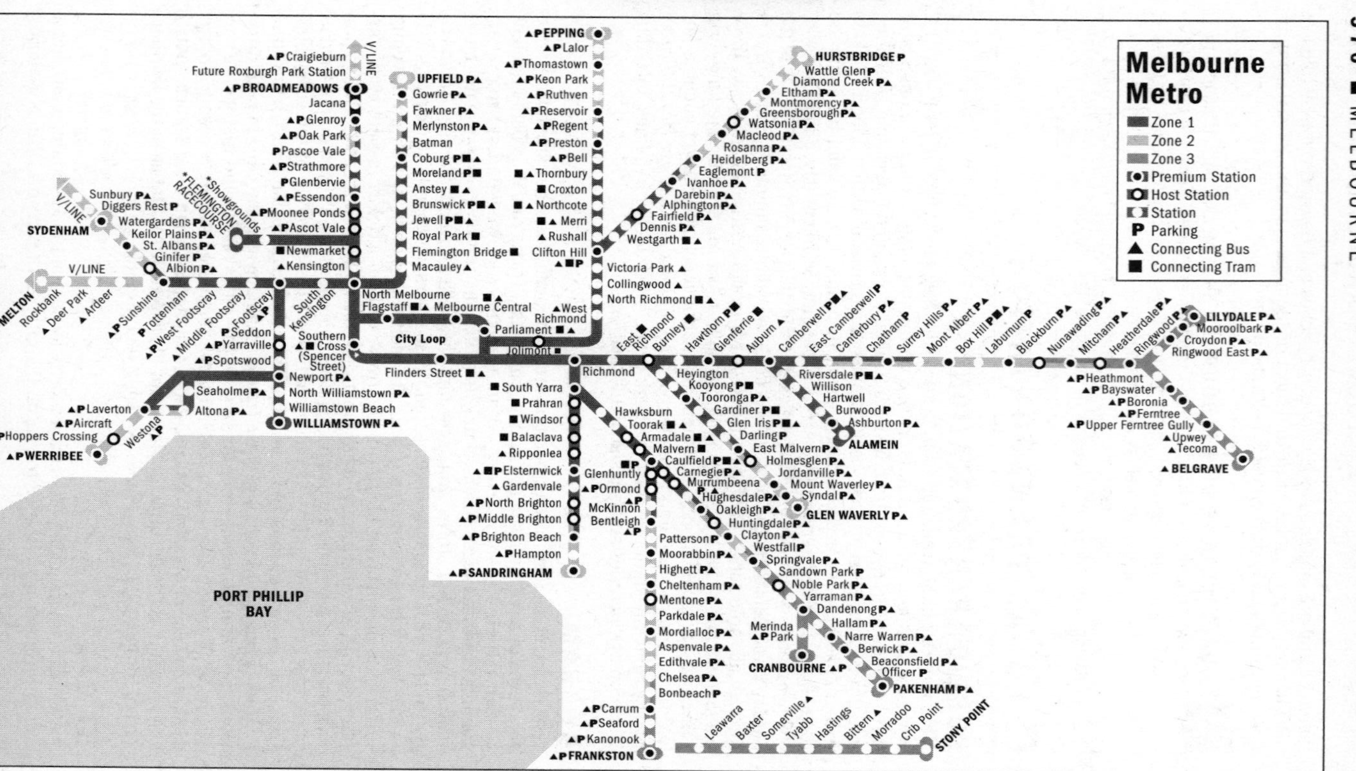
Melbourne Metro
Zone 1
Zone 2
Zone 3
Premium Station
Host Station
Station
P Parking
▲ Connecting Bus
■ Connecting Tram
▲P Craigieburn
Future Roxburgh Park Station
▲P BROADMEADOWS
Jacana
▲P Glenroy
▲P Oak Park
P Pascoe Vale
▲P Strathmore
P Glenbervie
▲P Essendon
▲P Moonee Ponds
▲P Ascot Vale
■ Newmarket
▲ Kensington
V/LINE
*Showgrounds
*FLEMINGTON RACECOURSE
Sunbury P▲
Diggers Rest P
Watergardens P▲
Keilor Plains P▲
St. Albans P▲
Ginifer P
Albion P▲
SYDENHAM
▲P MELTON
Rockbank
▲ Deer Park
▲ Ardeer
▲P Sunshine
P Tottenham
▲P West Footscray
▲ Middle Footscray
Footscray ▲P
P Seddon
▲P Yarraville
▲P Spotswood
South Kensington
Southern ▲■ Cross (Spencer Street)
Newport P▲
North Williamstown P▲
Williamstown Beach
WILLIAMSTOWN P▲
Seaholme P▲
Altona P▲
▲P Laverton
▲P Aircraft
▲P Hoppers Crossing
▲P WERRIBEE
Westona ▲P
UPFIELD P▲
Gowrie P▲
Fawkner P▲
Merlynston P▲
Batman
Coburg P■▲
Moreland P■
Anstey ■▲
Brunswick P■▲
Jewell P■▲
Royal Park ■
Flemington Bridge ■
Macauley ▲
North Melbourne
Flagstaff ■▲
Melbourne Central ■▲
Parliament ■▲
City Loop
Jolimont ■
Flinders Street ■▲
▲P EPPING
▲P Lalor
▲P Thomastown
▲P Keon Park
▲P Ruthven
▲P Reservoir
▲P Regent
▲P Preston
▲P Bell
■▲ Thornbury
■ Croxton
■▲ Northcote
■▲ Merri
▲ Rushall
Clifton Hill ▲■P
Victoria Park ▲
Collingwood ▲
North Richmond ■▲
▲West Richmond
HURSTBRIDGE P
Wattle Glen P
Diamond Creek P▲
Eltham P▲
Montmorency P▲
Greensborough P▲
Watsonia P▲
Macleod P▲
Rosanna P▲
Heidelberg P▲
Eaglemont P
Ivanhoe P▲
Darebin P▲
Alphington P▲
Fairfield P▲
Dennis P▲
Westgarth ■▲
Richmond
East Richmond ■
Burnley ■
Hawthorn P■
Glenferrie ■
Auburn ▲
Camberwell P■▲
East Camberwell P
Canterbury P▲
Chatham P
Surrey Hills P▲
Mont Albert P▲
Box Hill P■▲
Laburnum P
Blackburn P▲
Nunawading P▲
Mitcham P▲
Heatherdale P▲
Ringwood P▲
LILYDALE P▲
Mooroolbark P▲
Croydon P▲
Ringwood East P▲
▲P Heathmont
▲P Bayswater
▲P Boronia
▲P Ferntree
▲P Upper Ferntree Gully
▲ Upwey
▲ Tecoma
▲ BELGRAVE
Riversdale P■▲
Willison
Hartwell
Burwood P
Ashburton P▲
ALAMEIN
Heyington
Kooyong P■
Tooronga P▲
Gardiner P■
Glen Iris P■▲
Darling P
East Malvern P▲
Holmesglen P▲
Jordanville P▲
Mount Waverley P▲
Syndal P▲
GLEN WAVERLY P▲
Hawksburn
Toorak ■▲
Armadale ■▲
Malvern ■
Caulfield P■▲
Carnegie P▲
Murrumbeena P▲
Hughesdale P▲
Oakleigh P▲
Huntingdale P▲
Clayton P▲
Westfall P
Springvale P▲
Sandown Park P
Noble Park P▲
Yarraman P▲
Dandenong P▲
Hallam P▲
Narre Warren P▲
Berwick P▲
Beaconsfield P▲
Officer P
PAKENHAM P▲
Merinda ▲P Park
CRANBOURNE ▲P
■P Glenhuntly
▲P Ormond
▲P McKinnon
Bentleigh ▲P
Patterson P
Moorabbin P▲
Highett P▲
Cheltenham P▲
Mentone P▲
Parkdale P▲
Mordialloc P▲
Aspendale P▲
Edithvale P▲
Chelsea P▲
Bonbeach P
▲P Carrum
▲P Seaford
▲P Kanonook
▲P FRANKSTON
Leawarra
Baxter
Somerville ▲
Tyabb
Hastings
Bittern ▲
Morradoo
Crib Point
STONY POINT
■ South Yarra
■ Prahran
■ Windsor
■ Balaclava
▲ Ripponlea
▲■P Elsternwick
▲ Gardenvale
▲P North Brighton
▲P Middle Brighton
▲P Brighton Beach
▲P Hampton
▲P SANDRINGHAM
PORT PHILLIP BAY

include a nine percent airport tax. Most companies rent only to people over age 25, though some accept renters aged 21-24 with a surcharge. Prices for all vehicles fluctuate seasonally. Be sure to take advantage of special deals. Booking online often saves money. National agencies include those listed below. See **Getting Around Australia,** p. 28 for more information on the car rental process.

The **Royal Automobile Club of Victoria (RACV),** 501 Bourke St. (☎13 13 29 or 13 19 55; www.racv.com.au) is a comprehensive driving resource with good maps for sale. Members receive emergency roadside assistance. A good but out-of-the-way option for **long-term rental** is **Car Connection** near Castlemaine, 120km northwest of Melbourne. Rent a station wagon for up to six months for $1950 plus a $750 insurance charge, complete with camping equipment for 2 for an additional $250. A six month 4WD Toyota runs $4500. They provide free pickup from Melbourne airports or any city hostel as well as free first-night lodging in Castlemaine. (☎5473 4469; www.carconnection.com.au. Book ahead. Open 24hr.)

In addition to the agencies below, there are a few **bargain agencies** that are only half-joking about car quality. **Rent-a-Bomb** (☎13 15 53; www.rentabomb.com.au) has 10 offices in the Melbourne area; the main office is at 149 Clarendon St. Deals can run as cheap as $35-41 for one-day rentals, $23-29 per day for weekly rentals, and $17-23 per day for monthly rentals. Still, it's a good idea to weigh the savings against the potential costs of breaking down in the middle of nowhere. For information on driving in Australia, see **Great Outdoors,** p. 63

Avis, 110 A'Beckett St. (☎9663 6366, airport 9338 1800). From $45-55 per day, surcharge $25. Open M-Th 7:30am-6pm, F 7:30am-7pm, Sa-Su 8am-5pm.

Budget, 398 Elizabeth St. (☎13 27 27, airport 9241 6366). From $39; surcharge $17. Open M-Th 8am-6:30pm, F 8am-7pm, Sa-Su 8am-5pm.

Europcar, 89 Franklin St. (☎13 13 90; www.deltaeuropcar.com.au). From $33-50 per day, surcharge $13. Open M-Th 7:30am-6pm, F 7:30am-6:30pm, Sa-Su 8am-5pm.

Hertz, 97 Franklin St. (☎9663 6244, airport 9338 4044). From $46-53 per day, surcharge $17. Open M-Th 7:30am-6pm, F 7:30am-7pm, Sa 7:30am-5pm, Su 8am-5pm.

Thrifty, 390 Elizabeth St. (☎8661 6000, airport 9241 6111). From $39-68 per day, surcharge $17. Open M-Th 7:30am-6pm, F 7:30am-6:30pm, Sa-Su 8am-5pm.

BY TAXI

After the Met stops running at midnight, taxis are really the only option left. Cabs can be hailed at any time of day on the street. Varying surcharges apply when traveling between midnight-6am, when riding with luggage, or if you book the cab in advance. All companies have a $3 base charge plus $1.41 per km. Try **Silver Top** (☎13 10 08), **Arrow Taxi Service** (☎13 22 11), or **Embassy Taxis** (☎13 17 55). Wheelchair-accessible taxis are available at **13 Cabs** (☎13 27 77).

BY BICYCLE

If you don't fear oncoming traffic, biking is an economical way to get around town; practically every major thoroughfare in the greater Melbourne area has a bike lane. Before finding a rental shop, check with your accommodation; they may have cheap rentals. For recreational riders, an extensive **bike trail** runs along the Yarra River, while others loop through Albert Park and Middle Park, along the Port Phillip beaches, and around North Melbourne's gardens. Southern Melbourne's flat bayside roads are perfect for low-impact, scenic riding. The flat terrain along the shore of Port Phillip Bay is a popular destination for serious bikers who can spend the entire day cycling around the bay. Riders can then take the ferry between Queenscliff and Sorrento, and return to the city on the other side of the bay. **Hire a Bicycle** (☎9639 1803 or 0417 339 203; www.byohouse.com.au/bikehire)

under Princes Bridge, opposite Federation Square, is a great place to "hire" (rent) a bike. (Open daily 10am-5pm. Guided bike tours $50.) **St. Kilda Cycles,** 11 Carlisle St., has good rates. (☎9534 3074. Open M-F 9am-6pm, Sa 9am-5pm, Su 10am-4pm. $15 per ½-day, $22 per full-day, $80 per wk., $200 per month.) **Carlton Borsari Cycles,** 193 Lygon St. can also find you a ride. (☎9347 4100; www.borsaricycles.com.au. Open M-Th 9:30am-6pm, F 9:30am-7:30pm, Sa 9:30am-5pm.)

PRACTICAL INFORMATION

TOURIST AND FINANCIAL SERVICES

Tourist Offices: Melbourne Visitor Centre in Federation Square, across from Flinders St. Station at the corner of Flinders St. and St. Kilda Rd. The sprawling center offers **Internet** access, transport, entertainment ticket sales, the **Best of Victoria** accommodations and tour booking service (☎9650 3663), and the **Melbourne Greeter Service,** which gives free 2-4hr. **tours** of the city tailored to your personal interests. Tours are offered in many languages. Affiliated "roving ambassadors" wearing red jackets canvass nearby streets offering free tourist advice. (☎9658 9658; www.melbourne.vic.gov.au. Visitor Centre open daily 9am-6pm.) Info booth at the **Bourke Street Mall.** Open M-F 9am-6pm, Sa 10am-4pm, Su 11am-4pm.

VICTORIA

Budget Travel: YHA Victoria, 83-85 Hardware Ln. (☎9670 9611; www.yha.com.au). Provides list of YHA hostels and booking service. YHA member international booking surcharge $6, domestic surcharge $5 after 2 free bookings. YHA member domestic booking surcharge $5 after 2 free bookings, international booking surcharge $6. Attached budget travel agency. Internet access $4 per hr. Open M-F 9am-5:30pm, Sa 10am-1pm. **Backpackers Travel Centre,** Shop 1, 250 Flinders St. (☎9654 8477; www.backpackerstravel.com.au). Open M-F 9am-6pm, Sa 10am-4pm. **Branches** at 377 Lt. Bourke St. (☎9642 1811) and 362 Latrobe St. (☎9329 4644). Open M-F 9am-5:30pm, Sa 10am-3pm.

Consulates: Canada (☎9653 9674). **China** (☎9822 0604). **France** (☎9820 0921). **Germany** (☎9828 6888). **Greece** (☎9866 4524). **Italy** (☎9867 5744). **UK,** Level 17, 90 Collins St. (☎9652 1600). Open M-F 9am-4:30pm. **US,** Level 6, 553 St. Kilda Rd. (☎9526 5900). Open M-F 8:30am-noon and 1-4:30pm.

Currency Exchange: Interforex, 109 Collins St. (☎9654 2768). Open daily 8am-7:30pm. All banks exchange money during regular operating hours. Open M-Th 9:30am-4pm, F 9:30am-5pm. **Travelex,** 261 Bourke St. (☎9662 1271), near Swanston St., has a 2% commission on checks and cash. Open M-F 9am-5pm, Sa 10am-5pm, Su 11am-4pm. Several banks have offices at the airport. 24hr. **ATMs** are found throughout the city.

American Express: 233 Collins St. (☎9633 6318). Buys all traveler's checks (no charge); min. $8 or 2% fee on cash exchanges. *Poste Restante* for AmEx card or Travelers Cheques holders. Wire transfers. Open M-F 9am-5pm, Sa 9am-noon.

Work Opportunities: Most accommodations listed in *Let's Go* have employment bulletin boards; some help find temp jobs free of charge or offer work to travelers in exchange for accommodation. **BRC,** in the lobby of Hotel Bakpak (see **Accommodations,** p. 582; ☎9329 7525 or BRC direct 1800 154 664), can help find good jobs. Small finder's fee. Open M-F 7am-5pm, Sa 9am-3pm. Melbourne's biggest daily paper, *The Age,* has classifieds on Sa and can be accessed online at www.theage.com.au or picked up for free at the Melbourne Museum. Try calling **Job Network Employer Hotline** (☎13 17 15) for other opportunities (open M-F 7am-8pm). See **Beyond Tourism,** p. 81 for more work and volunteer opportunities.

MEDIA AND PUBLICATIONS

Newspapers: The main newspapers are *The Age* ($1.10) and *The Herald Sun* ($1) for local coverage, and *The Australian* ($1.10) for national news. *The Melbourne Star* (free) is the gay and lesbian community newspaper.

Nightlife: *Beat* (www.beat.com.au) and *InPress (*free, released W). For gay news and nightlife, check out *MCV* (by subscription, but found in most gay establishments) and *B.News* (free, released every other Th).

Entertainment: *The Age*'s Entertainment Guide and *The Herald Sun*'s Gig Guide (released F).

Radio: Triple M 105.1 FM; 1116AM *News Talk;* Joy 94.9FM *Queer Radio.*

LOCAL SERVICES

Outdoors Information: Information Centre and Bookshop, 8 Nicholson St., at Victoria Pde., East Melbourne (☎9637 8325; www.dse.vic.gov.au). Maps, books, and info on licenses. Open M-F 8:30am-5:30pm. **Parks Victoria** (☎13 19 63; www.parks.vic.gov.au) has state and national park information.

Disabled and Elderly Travelers Information: Travellers Aid, 169 Swanston St., 2nd fl. (☎9654 2600), has a tearoom with great services. Open M-F 8am-5pm. **Branch** at Spencer St. Station (☎9670 2873). Open M-F 7:30am-7:30pm, Sa-Su 7:30am-11:30am. Representatives will meet and assist elderly and disabled travelers on trains and buses M-F 7:30am-7:30pm, Sa-Su 7:30am-11:30am. Arrange ahead.

Library: State Library of Victoria, 328 Swanston St. (☎8664 7000), on the corner of La Trobe St. Open M-Th 10am-9pm, F-Su 10am-6pm. **CAE Library (City Library),** 253 Flinders Ln. (☎9664 0800). Open M-Th 8am-8pm, F 8am-6pm, Sa 10am-1pm.

Gay and Lesbian Resources: The ALSO Foundation, 6 Claremont St., South Yarra (☎9827 4999; www.also.org.au) is a gay and lesbian helpline (☎1800 631 493).

Ticket Agencies: Ticketek (☎13 28 49 or 1800 062 849; www.ticketek.com.au) and **Ticketmaster** (☎13 61 00; www.ticketmaster7.com.au) for sports, performances, and other events. Handling fee for phone booking. Both open daily 9am-9pm. **Halftix,** in Melbourne Town Hall on Swanston St., sells ½-price tickets for shows the day of the performance (Su performances sold Sa), and for bus tours with affiliated companies. Open M and Sa 10am-2pm, Tu-Th 11am-6pm, F 11am-6:30pm. Cash only; no phone orders.

Laundromat: Melbourne City Dry Cleaners, 244 Russell St, CBD (☎9639 3377). Open M-F 7am-6pm, Sa 9am-3pm. 2hr. express service available.

Weather: Forecasts (☎9669 4916

EMERGENCY AND COMMUNICATIONS

Emergency: ☎000.

Fire: ☎000.

Police: 637 Flinders St. (☎9247 6666), at Spencer St.; 226 Flinders Ln. (☎9650 7077), between Swanston and Elizabeth St.; 412 St. Kilda Rd. (☎9865 2111), 200m south of Toorak Rd.; 92 Chapel St. (☎9536 2666), St. Kilda; and 330 Drummond St. (☎9347 1377), Carlton.

Crisis Lines: Victims Referral and Assistance Hotline ☎9603 9797. **Centre Against Sexual Assault** ☎9344 2210. **Lifeline Counseling Service** ☎13 11 14. **Poison Information Service** ☎13 11 26. **Coast Guard Search and Rescue** ☎9598 7003. **Family Drug Helpline** 24hr. ☎1300 660 068. **Substance Abuse Service** 24hr. ☎1800 014 446. **Suicide Helpline** 24hr. ☎1300 651 251.

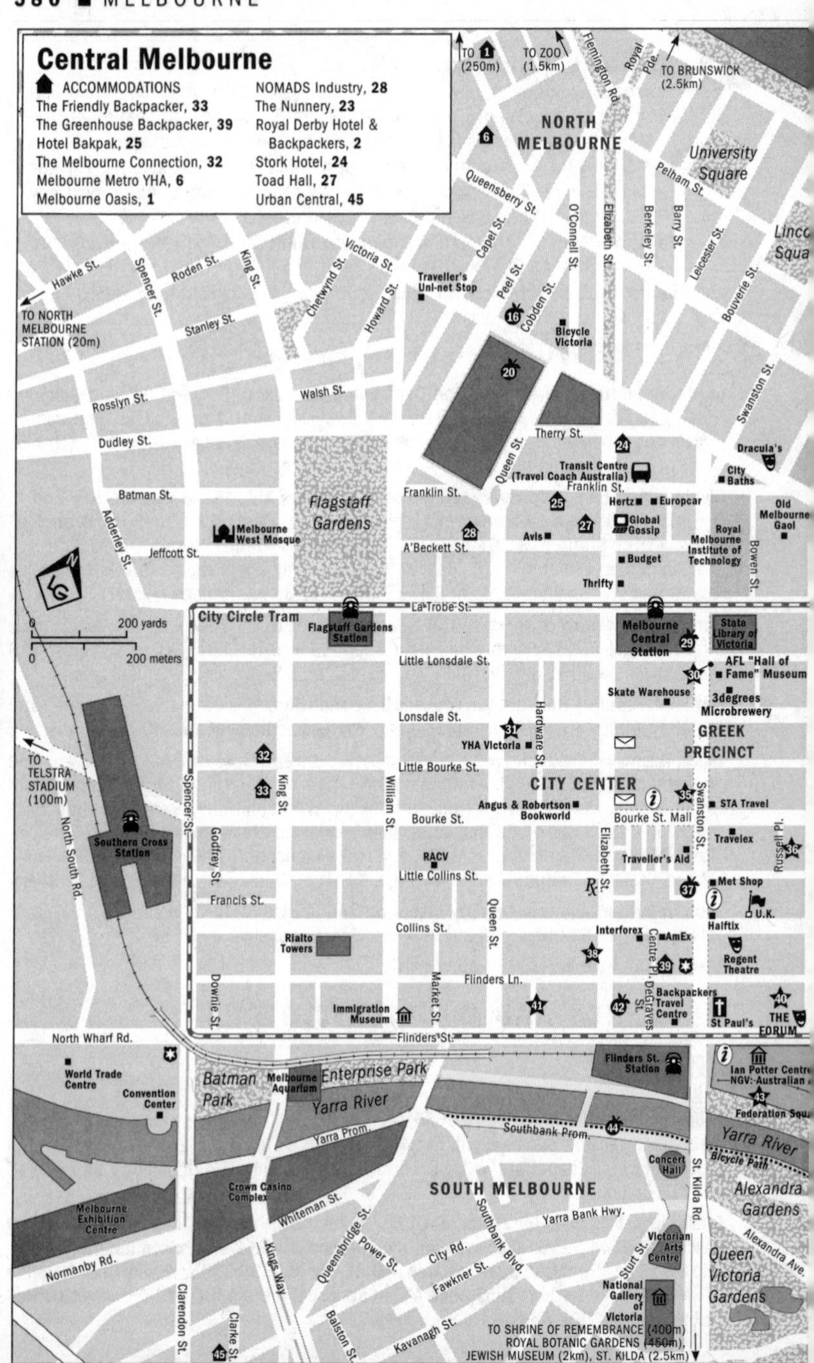
Central Melbourne
ACCOMMODATIONS
The Friendly Backpacker, 33
The Greenhouse Backpacker, 39
Hotel Bakpak, 25
The Melbourne Connection, 32
Melbourne Metro YHA, 6
Melbourne Oasis, 1
NOMADS Industry, 28
The Nunnery, 23
Royal Derby Hotel & Backpackers, 2
Stork Hotel, 24
Toad Hall, 27
Urban Central, 45
TO 1 (250m)
TO ZOO (1.5km)
TO BRUNSWICK (2.5km)
NORTH MELBOURNE
University Square
TO NORTH MELBOURNE STATION (20m)
TO TELSTRA STADIUM (100m)
Flemington Rd.
Royal Pde.
Pelham St.
Queensberry St.
O'Connell St.
Elizabeth St.
Berkeley St.
Barry St.
Leicester St.
Bouverie St.
Swanston St.
Hawke St.
Spencer St.
Roden St.
King St.
Chetwynd St.
Victoria St.
Howard St.
Capel St.
Peel St.
Cobden St.
Stanley St.
Traveller's Uni-net Stop
Bicycle Victoria
Rosslyn St.
Walsh St.
Dudley St.
Therry St.
Queen St.
Dracula's
Transit Centre (Travel Coach Australia)
City Baths
Batman St.
Franklin St.
Flagstaff Gardens
Hertz
Europcar
Old Melbourne Gaol
Adderley St.
Melbourne West Mosque
Global Gossip
Avis
Royal Melbourne Institute of Technology
Jeffcott St.
A'Beckett St.
Budget
Bowen St.
Thrifty
La Trobe St.
City Circle Tram
Flagstaff Gardens Station
Melbourne Central Station
State Library of Victoria
200 yards
200 meters
Little Lonsdale St.
AFL "Hall of Fame" Museum
Skate Warehouse
3degrees Microbrewery
Lonsdale St.
Hardware St.
GREEK PRECINCT
YHA Victoria
Little Bourke St.
CITY CENTER
Southern Cross Station
Spencer St.
William St.
Angus & Robertson Bookworld
Bourke St.
Bourke St. Mall
Swanston St.
STA Travel
North South Rd.
Godfrey St.
Travelex
Russell Pl.
RACV
Traveller's Aid
Little Collins St.
Met Shop
Francis St.
U.K.
Collins St.
Halftix
Interforex
AmEx
Centre Pl.
Rialto Towers
Regent Theatre
Flinders Ln.
Market St.
Downie St.
Backpackers Travel Centre
DeGraves St.
Immigration Museum
St Paul's
THE FORUM
North Wharf Rd.
Flinders St.
World Trade Centre
Flinders St. Station
Ian Potter Centre NGV: Australian
Convention Center
Batman Park
Melbourne Aquarium
Enterprise Park
Yarra River
Federation Squ
Yarra Prom.
Southbank Prom.
Bicycle Path
Concert Hall
Crown Casino Complex
SOUTH MELBOURNE
St. Kilda Rd.
Alexandra Gardens
Melbourne Exhibition Centre
Whiteman St.
Yarra Bank Hwy.
Alexandra Ave.
Victorian Arts Centre
Queen Victoria Gardens
Normanby Rd.
Kings Way
Queensbridge St.
Power St.
City Rd.
Southbank Blvd.
Sturt St.
Fawkner St.
National Gallery of Victoria
Clarendon St.
Clarke St.
Balston St.
Kavanagh St.
TO SHRINE OF REMEMBRANCE (400m)
ROYAL BOTANIC GARDENS (450m),
JEWISH MUSEUM (2km), ST. KILDA (2.5km)

VICTORIA

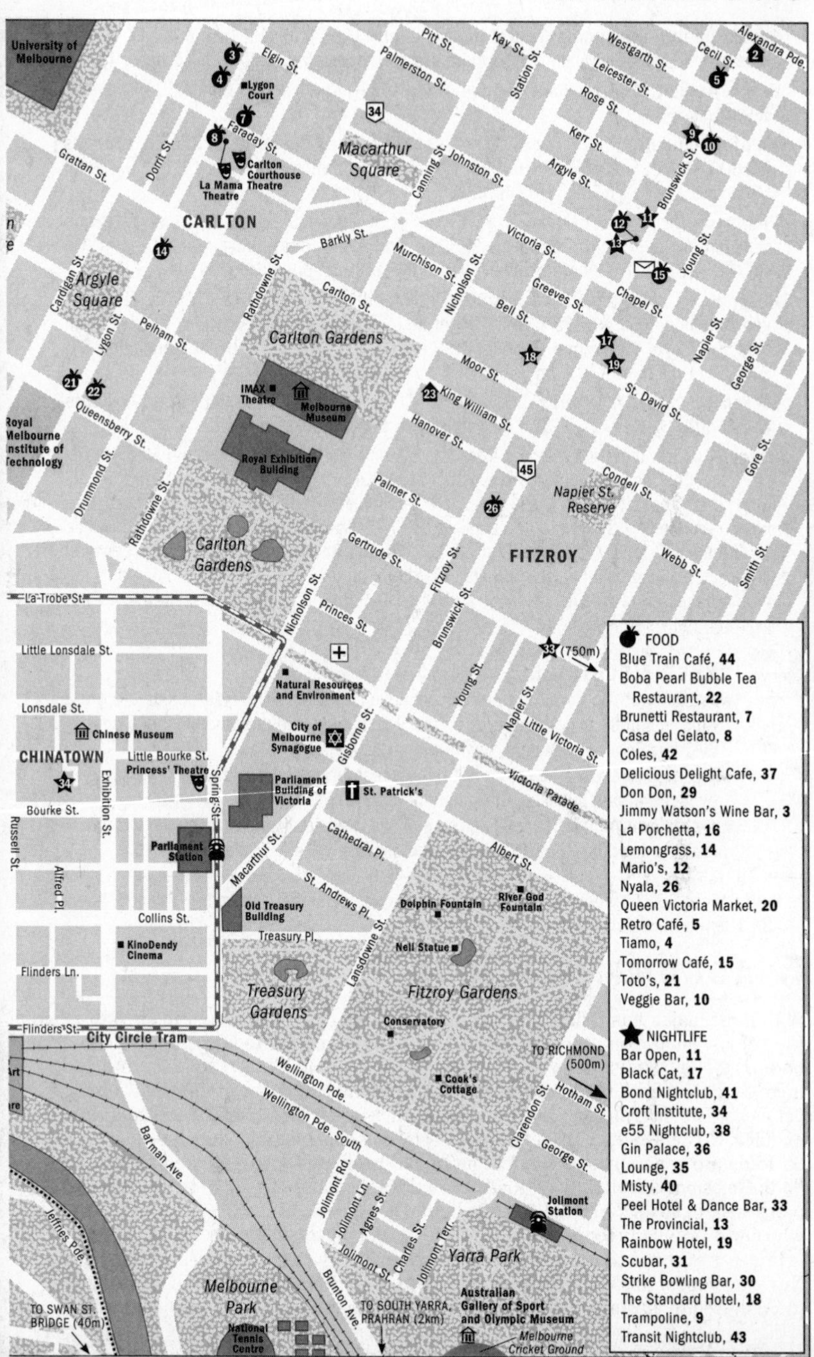
CARLTON
FITZROY
CHINATOWN
Carlton Gardens
Fitzroy Gardens
Treasury Gardens
Yarra Park
Melbourne Park
Macarthur Square
Argyle Square
Napier St. Reserve
University of Melbourne
Royal Melbourne Institute of Technology
Melbourne Museum
Royal Exhibition Building
IMAX Theatre
Parliament Building of Victoria
Parliament Station
Jolimont Station
Old Treasury Building
City of Melbourne Synagogue
St. Patrick's
Natural Resources and Environment
Chinese Museum
Princess' Theatre
KinoDendy Cinema
La Mama Theatre
Carlton Courthouse Theatre
Lygon Court
Dolphin Fountain
River God Fountain
Nell Statue
Conservatory
Cook's Cottage
Australian Gallery of Sport and Olympic Museum
Melbourne Cricket Ground
National Tennis Centre
City Circle Tram
TO RICHMOND (500m)
TO SOUTH YARRA, PRAHRAN (2km)
TO SWAN ST. BRIDGE (40m)
(750m)
FOOD
Blue Train Café, 44
Boba Pearl Bubble Tea Restaurant, 22
Brunetti Restaurant, 7
Casa del Gelato, 8
Coles, 42
Delicious Delight Cafe, 37
Don Don, 29
Jimmy Watson's Wine Bar, 3
La Porchetta, 16
Lemongrass, 14
Mario's, 12
Nyala, 26
Queen Victoria Market, 20
Retro Café, 5
Tiamo, 4
Tomorrow Café, 15
Toto's, 21
Veggie Bar, 10
NIGHTLIFE
Bar Open, 11
Black Cat, 17
Bond Nightclub, 41
Croft Institute, 34
e55 Nightclub, 38
Gin Palace, 36
Lounge, 35
Misty, 40
Peel Hotel & Dance Bar, 33
The Provincial, 13
Rainbow Hotel, 19
Scubar, 31
Strike Bowling Bar, 30
The Standard Hotel, 18
Trampoline, 9
Transit Nightclub, 43

VICTORIA

Sexual Health: Melbourne Sexual Health Centre, (☎1800 032 017 or 9347 0244). Free counselling on sexually transmitted diseases, specialized HIV/AIDS services.

Sexual Assault: Centre Against Sexual Assault, 270 Cardigan St., Carlton. 24hr. hotline ☎9346 1766.

Helpful numbers: Directory assistance ☎12 23, international ☎12 25; collect calls ☎1800 REVERSE or 1800 738 3773; translation and interpretation ☎13 14 50. City of Melbourne Language Link ☎9658 9658.

Pharmacy: Elizabeth Pharmacy, 125 Elizabeth St. (☎9670 3815). Open M-F 7:30am-6:30pm, Sa 9:30am-5:30pm. **Melbourne Boulevard Pharmacy,** 403 St. Kilda Rd. (☎9866 1284). 1hr. photo available. Open M-F 8:30am-6pm, Sa 9am-1pm.

Hospital: St. Vincent's Public Hospital, 41 Victoria Pde., Fitzroy (☎9288 2211, emergencies Princes St. ☎9288 4364). To get there, take any tram east along Bourke St. to stop #9. **Royal Melbourne Hospital** (☎9342 7000), on Grattan St. at Flemington St., Parkville. Take tram #19 from Elizabeth St. to stop 16.

Locksmiths: Stewart Security, 221 King St., CBD (☎13 15 39) Available 24hr. **Absolute Lock Smith** (☎1800 200 222) Available 24hr. Specializes in car locks.

Internet Access: Internet cafes are fairly easy to find; some bars even have hidden terminals. Most budget accommodations offer Internet access, and prices throughout the city tend to be about $4 per hr. There are free terminals at the **State Library** for those who have an Australian student ID or a working visa (see **Essentials,** p. 9); sign up in advance for 30min. sessions. Limit 1 session per day. **Global Gossip,** 440 Elizabeth St. between A'Beckett and Franklin St. (☎9663 0511). Phone cards, CV and resume editing and formatting, mailbox rentals, CD burning, fax machines, scanner, and printers. Internet $4 per hr. Open daily 9am-11pm.).

CYBER MELBOURNE

www.visitvictoria.com. Comprehensive government website with tons of info on food, nightlife, accommodations, and events in Melbourne and all of Victoria. Events searchable by type, town, and date.

www.mdg.com.au. A selection of the best restaurants in Melbourne, searchable by location and cuisine, with online booking.

www.melbournepubs.com. A comprehensive website listing and reviewing hundreds of local bars, pubs, and nightclubs.

Post Office: 250 Elizabeth St., (☎ 13 13 18; www.post.com.au) Open M-F 8am-5:30pm, Sa 10am-5pm. **Postal Code:** 3000.

ACCOMMODATIONS

With most major Australian sporting events taking place in Melbourne, including the recent 2006 Commonwealth Games, budget accommodations have been booming. New, stylish digs are continually popping up all over the city and the increased competition has encouraged a considerable number of impressive budget deals. The largest concentrations of lodgings are within the **CBD** and southern **St. Kilda.** Hostels in the CBD tend to be flashy and commercial, while the cluster in St. Kilda are generally less tidy but more laid-back. The YHA-affiliated hostels in **North Melbourne** are slightly removed from the action and so tend to be quieter and more sedate. **South Yarra** and **Prahran** lie farther afield but are preferred by those who enjoy proximity to these districts' chic shopping and nightlife.

Prices for accommodations change seasonally; during high season (roughly Nov.-Mar.) most hostels raise their prices ($1-6) and availability drops, so be sure to book well in advance. Prices may also fluctuate during long weekends. During summer holiday, you can usually find accommodation at **Melbourne University.** Several residential colleges, including Ormond and University Colleges, offer temporary housing for $65 including linens, breakfast, lunch, and dinner (☎9344 1121).

Most accommodations in Melbourne are wheelchair accessible and accept MasterCard and Visa credit cards. Several hostels will allow guests to work in return for lodging if they plan to stay for an extended period of time. Standard budget lodging in Melbourne usually includes common bathrooms and toilets, common spaces with TV, a guest kitchen, and laundry facilities.

FOOD

Melbourne's diverse population has created a confluence of delicious fare from all over the world. Virtually every type of cuisine is available; local chefs combine distinctive cultural essences to create tantalizing fusion feasts. When strolling through the CBD, it's impossible not to stumble across small Japanese restaurants serving fresh sushi or scrumptious bowls of udon. Slurp up steaming bowls of pasta in Carlton's not-so-Little Italy. Enjoy a frothy latte in Fitzroy or South Yarra and become a part of the burgeoning cafe culture. Look out for markets stocking fresh produce. For travelers on a tight budget, there are numerous grocery stores including **Safeway** in QV Undercroft on the corner of Swanston and Lonsdale St. (☎9650 7355. Open M-W 8:30am-9pm, Th-F 8:30am-10pm, Sa 8:30am-7pm, Su 10am-7pm.) There is also an **IGA Southbank** at 89-91 City Rd. (☎9682 0489. Open M-F 7:30am-9pm, Sa 7:30am-10pm, Su 8am-8pm.)

SIGHTS

Locals would argue that the best sights in Melbourne aren't in museums, but in the myriad cultural and athletic attractions that are mainstays of the city. Recent construction has introduced a variety of architectural gems including the new Southern Cross Station and Federation Square. Sports, a priority for the city that annually hosts the Australian Open and was the site of the 2006 Commonwealth Games, also play a large role in the city's appeal. Don't miss the Telstra Dome and the Melbourne Cricket Ground, even if you're not an Aussie sports fanatic.

ENTERTAINMENT

Melbourne prides itself on its style and cultural savvy, and nowhere are these more evident than in the city's entertainment scene. The range of options can seem overwhelming; the definitive website for performance events is www.melbourne.citysearch.com.au.

PERFORMING ARTS

Book larger shows through Ticketek (☎13 28 49 or 1800 062 849; www.ticketek.com) or Ticketmaster7 (☎1300 136 166; www.ticketmaster7.com), or try Halftix for half-price same-day tickets (p. 579); for smaller productions, call theater companies directly. The hard-to-miss **Victorian Arts Centre,** 100 St. Kilda Rd., sports an Eiffel-like spire right on the Yarra across from Flinders St. Station. It houses five venues: the State Theatre for major dramatic, operatic, and dance performances; the Melbourne Concert Hall, for symphonies; the Playhouse, largely used by the Melbourne Theatre Company; the George Fairfax Studio, similar to the Playhouse but smaller; and the Black Box, for cutting-edge, low-budget shows targeting an under-35 audience. (Victoria Arts Centre switchboard ☎9281 8000, Ticketmaster7 ☎1300 136 166; www.vicartscentre.com.au. Tickets range from free to $180; $2.50 transaction fee when not purchased at the box office. Box office open M-Sa 9am-9pm.)

CINEMA

Melbourne has long been the focal point of Australia's independent film scene, and the city holds dozens of old theaters that screen arthouse and experimental shows, as well as cinema classics. The arthouse crowd logs on to www.urbancinefile.com.au, which features flip reviews of the latest films.

The annual **Melbourne International Film Festival** showcases the year's international indie hits, and the **St. Kilda Film Festival** highlights short films of all shapes and sizes. An especially select crew of home-grown flicks can be viewed in late July at the **Melbourne Underground Film Festival,** an occasionally bizarre showing by local students in Fitzroy. See **Festivals,** p. 585, for more information.

Plenty of cinemas in the CBD show mainstream first-run movies as well. **Cinema Information Line** (☎1902 263 456) has info on showtimes and locations, and tickets can be bought online at www.greaterunion.com.au, www.hoyts.com.au, and www.villagecinemas.com.au. At the theater, try a "choc-top," the chocolate-dipped ice-cream cone ($2-4) that's a staple of Australian movie-going.

Australian Center for the Moving Image, Federation Square (☎8663 2200; www.acmi.net.au), at Swanston and Flinders St. The ACMI screens an eclectic array of film and video works and displays installation pieces and multimedia exhibitions. Also houses the nation's largest public collection of film, video, and DVD titles, as well as the world's largest screen gallery (spanning the entire length of Federation square underground). Open daily 10am-6pm. Free.

Astor Theatre (☎9510 1414; www.astor-theatre.com), on the corner of Chapel St. and Dandenong Rd., St. Kilda. Spectacular Art Deco theater that still has many of its original furnishings and all of its original stately beauty. Mostly repertory and reissues. Seats 1100. Runs much as it did when it opened in 1936, showing mostly double features ($15, concessions $12, children $10, book of 10 tickets $100).

Cinema Nova, 380 Lygon St., Carlton (☎9349 5201; www.cinemanova.com.au), in Lygon Ct. Indie and foreign films. Claims to be the "second-largest art-house megaplex in the world." $14, concessions $9.50. M $5 before 4pm, $7.50 after.

IMAX, Melbourne Museum, Carlton (☎9663 5454; www.imax.com.au), off Rathdowne St. in the Carlton Gardens. Daily screenings of 5 films every hr. M-Th and Su 10am-10pm, F-Sa 10am-11pm. $16, concessions $13, children $11, families $45; 3-D shows $1 extra ($4 for families). YHA and RACV discount 20%, NOMADS 10%.

Moonlight Cinema (☎9428 2203 or 9252 2429; www.moonlight.com.au), in the Royal Botanic Gardens. Special tour-and-movie nights, including a complimentary glass of sparkling wine, a guided tour of the gardens, and a movie screening on the central lawn (mid-Dec. to early Mar.). Tour begins 6pm, films start at sundown, approx. 8:45pm; purchase tickets at the visitor center. $22, concessions $20.

KinoDendy Cinemas, 45 Collins St. (☎9650 2100), downstairs in the Collins Place complex. Independent and foreign films. $15, students $10, special M showing $7.

SPORTS AND RECREATION

Melbournians refer to themselves as "sports mad," but it's a good insanity—one that causes fans of footy (Australian Rules Football), cricket, tennis, and horse racing to skip work or school, get decked out in the colors of their favorite side, and cheer themselves hoarse. Their hallowed haven is the **Melbourne Cricket Ground (MCG),** adjacent to the world-class **Melbourne Park** tennis center (p. 590). A new ward, **Colonial Stadium,** right behind Spencer St. Station, has begun to share footy-hosting responsibilities with the more venerable MCG and also hosts most local rugby action. The lunacy peaks at various yearly events: the **Australian Open,** a Grand Slam tennis tournament in late January; the **Australian Grand Prix** Formula-One car-racing extravaganza in March; the **AFL Grand Final** in late September; the **Melbourne Cup,** the "horse race that stops the nation" in early November; and cricket's **Boxing Day Test Match** on Dec. 26.

Melbourne's passion for sport is not limited to spectator events. City streets and parks are packed with joggers, skaters, and footy players. The tan crushed gravel track encircling the Royal Botanic Gardens is best for **running;** though sports are strictly prohibited in the Gardens proper. Other great routes include the pedestrian paths along the Yarra, the Port Phillip/St. Kilda shore, and the Albert Park Lake. All of these wide, flat spaces make for excellent **in-line skating,** as well; you can rent equipment at sport shops throughout Melbourne.

The **beach** in St. Kilda, accessible by tram #16 and 96, is not Australia's finest, but it'll do for sun and swimming. **Albert Park** has a lake good for sailing but not for swimming. Just inside the park's Clarendon St. entrance, **Jolly Roger** rents boats. (☎9690 5862; www.jollyrogersailing.com.au. Sailboats $45-55 per hr., rowboats $32 per hr., canoes and kayaks $25 per hr., aquabikes $22 per 30min. Open daily 9am-5pm.) The **Melbourne City Baths,** 420 Swanston St., on the corner of Franklin St., offers two pools, sauna, spa, squash courts, and a gym in a restored Victorian building. (☎9663 5888. Open M-Th 6am-10pm, F 6am-8:30pm, Sa-Su 8am-6pm. Pool $4.70, students $3.70, concessions $2.20; 10-ticket pass $42.50/33.70/19.8; gymnasium $18.00/15.80/9.50.)

FESTIVALS

Melbournians create excuses for city-wide street parties year-round. Below are the city's major events. For a complete guide, grab a free copy of *Melbourne Events* at any tourist office, or do an events search at www.visitmelbourne.com. The following festivals are arranged by date.

Midsumma Gay and Lesbian Festival, late Jan. to mid-Feb. (☎9415 9819; www.midsumma.org.au). 3wk. of hijinks all over the city ranging from the erotic (a "Mr. Leather Victoria" contest) to the educational (a Same-Sex Partners Rights workshop), with lots of parades, dance parties, and general pandemonium.

Australian Open, late Jan. (tickets ☎9286 1600 or 1300 888 104; www.ausopen.org). One of the world's elite Grand Slam tennis events, held at Melbourne Park's hard courts. Tickets available online beginning in October.

Yarra Valley Grape Grazing, late Feb. (passes and info ☎5965 2100). 20 wineries in the Yarra Valley region participate in this annual Dionysian festival. Day pass $28, Platinum pass (including Domaine Chandon and Tarrawarra) $129.

Foster's Australian Grand Prix, early Mar. (tickets ☎13 16 41; www.grandprix.com.au). Albert Park, St. Kilda. Formula One racing frenzy holds the city hostage.

Moomba, early Mar. (☎9658 9658; www.melbournemoombafestival.com.au). This 4-day citywide fête with food, performances, and events is a great way to party with the locals.

Melbourne Food and Wine Festival, 2nd and 3rd weekend in Mar. (☎9412 4220; www.melbfoodwinefest.com.au), centering on Collins St. A free and delicious way to celebrate Melbourne as Australia's "culinary capital."

International Comedy Festival, mid-Mar. to mid-Apr. (☎9650 1977; www.comedyfestival.com.au). Huge 3wk. laugh-fest with over 1000 performances.

International Flower and Garden Show, first weekend in Apr. (☎9864 1111). Royal Exhibition Building and Carlton Gardens, Carlton.

St. Kilda Film Festival, late May-early June (☎9209 6777; www.stkildafilmfestival.com.au), Palais Theatre and George Cinemas, St. Kilda. Australia's best short films: documentary, experimental, and comedy.

International Film Festival, late July-early Aug. (☎9417 2011; www.melbournefilmfestival.com.au). The cream of the international cinematic crop, plus top-level local work.

Royal Melbourne Show, mid-Sept. (☎13 28 49; www.royalshow.com.au). At Ascot Vale. Sideshow alleys, rides, entertainment, and animal exhibitions for judging.

Melbourne Fringe Festival, late Sept. to early Oct. (☎8412 8788; www.melbournefringe.com.au). Features local artists. Opens with a parade on Brunswick St., Fitzroy. Performances and parties all across town.

Melbourne Festival, mid-Oct. (☎9662 4242; www.melbournefestival.com.au). A 3wk. celebration of the arts, attracting world-famous actors, writers, and dancers for over 400 performances, workshops, and parties in 30 different venues.

Spring Racing Carnival, Oct.-Nov. (☎1300 139 401; www.springracingcarnival.com.au). Flemington Racecourse. Australia's mad love for horse racing stretches over 50 days.

Melbourne Cup, 1st Tu in Nov. (www.vrc.net.au). Melbournians, along with the rest of Australia, put life on pause to watch, listen, or talk about the most hyped-up and fashionable horse race in the country, if not the world. Ladies, gents, and Australia's elite come dressed to impress for a lovely (and almost always drunken) day at the races.

Melbourne Boxing Day Test Match, Dec. 26-30 (☎9653 1100; www.baggygreen.com.au). More than 100,000 cricket fans pack the MCG to root for the boys in green and gold against top cricketers from around the world.

NIGHTLIFE

Thriving nightlife has developed in Melbourne over the last two decades, and the heart of the party is in the back alleys of the CBD. Rather than rattling off Top-40 hits with a blaring bass, almost all venues prefer live music and guest DJs that spin their own funk recipes. With a spectacularly large number of establishments, both travelers and locals can always find a cool spot on the block to break in dance shoes or chill with friends. Gay nightlife in Melbourne isn't restricted to one portion of the town, but peppered throughout the city. Check out www.melbournepubs.com for a list of hundreds of venues throughout the metropolitan area. Note that in this city, the distinction between bars, pubs, and nightclubs is blurry at best. Many venues belong to all three categories while others swap out the weekday chairs and tables in favor of raucous weekend grind-fests. Some unique venues deserve a category all on their own. Expect a small cover charge on the weekends ($5-10) at venues offering live music or a dance floor.

MELBOURNE BY PRECINCT

CBD

The city center, known as the Central Business District (CBD), is located just north of the Yarra and reaches its northern limit at **Victoria Steet,** just north of the **Queen Victory Market.** Its western border is the recently-gentrified **Docklands** and to the east the ever-popular **Carlton Gardens**. The city is laid out in a neat grid with the center located at the intersection of **Bourke Street** and **Swanston Street.** The CBD is the transit hub for the entire city with numerous tram and railway stations.

ACCOMMODATIONS

The perfect jumping-off point to explore any part of the city, hostels in the CBD are in the heart of the action. A significant cluster of hostels is perched just north of La Trobe street around Elizabeth St. A mere 12min. walk to Federation Square, accommodations in the northern portion of the CBD tend to be slightly cheaper and close to several grocery stores and the Queen Victoria Market.

NOMADS Industry, 196-198 A'Beckett St. (☎9328 4383 or 1800 447 762; www.nomadsindustry.com), just west of Queen St. Party-prone hostel strikes an ideal balance between revelry and relaxation while managing to remain clean. Exceptionally knowledgable staff can assist with any quandary. The quietest rooms are on the higher floors facing the front of the hostel. Free dinner. Hallway bathrooms are separated into individual units for privacy. Wheelchair accessible. Reception 24hr. Internet access $4 per hr. Female-only dorms available. Dorms $19-30. 6- and 8-bed dorms $26; ensuite $28; singles and twins $60; doubles $70; family rooms $30 per person. ❷

The Greenhouse Backpacker, 228 Flinders Ln. (☎9639 6400 or 1800 249 207; www.friendlygroup.com.au), just west of Swanston St. Reception on 6th fl. Continuously garnering tourism awards, this hosteling gem is the most centrally located budget accommodation in the city. Vast common spaces, kitchen, and rooftop garden. **6 Links Bar** on the ground fl. is popular with backpackers and run by the hostel. For a more comfortable stay, request a room with a window. Free Internet access (max. 30min. per day). Coffee, tea, and small breakfast (7-9am) included. Free pasta or BBQ dinner once per wk. Wheelchair accessible. Dorms $25-29; singles $60-65; doubles $70. Weekly dorms $155-175, weekly doubles $455-490. Prices vary. ❸

Toad Hall, 441 Elizabeth St. (☎9600 9010; www.toadhall-hotel.com.au), between A'Beckett and Franklin St. Classy, calm hostel set in an old green mansion. Plenty of private rooms and sparkling bathrooms. Comfy basement den with TV is a plus, as is the quaint garden patio with BBQ. Mostly shared bathrooms, some ensuite; larger dorms have bath. Laundry facilities, kitchen, and secure off-street parking. Heat and fans available in all rooms. Key deposit $20. Reception 7am-10pm. Dorms $25-$30; singles and twins $60-70; doubles $70; family rooms $30 per person. Book ahead. ❸

The Friendly Backpacker, 197 King St. (☎9670 1111 or 1800 671 115; friendly@friendlygroup.com.au), corner of Lt. Bourke and King St. Slightly older and more weathered than the nearby Greenhouse Backpackers. Partitioned dorm rooms provide privacy. Freshly renovated, colorful lobby offers brand new travel help desk. Dark hardwood floors and quaint nooks for watching TV. Heat and A/C. Free Internet access 30min. per day. Free pasta or BBQ dinner once per wk. Coffee, tea, and breakfast included. Key deposit $10. Wheelchair accessible. Oct.-Mar. dorms $29, Apr.-Sept. $26; doubles $80/68; weekly dorms $182/161; weekly doubles $455. Book ahead Oct.-May. ❸

Hotel Bakpak, 167 Franklin St. (☎9329 7525 or 1800 645 200; www.bakpak.com/franklin/index), between Elizabeth and Queen St. This bastion of backpackers sleeps 700 and is a dedicated monument to partying. Industrial-sized bathrooms can be a harrowing trek from far-away rooms, and paper-thin walls may compromise privacy (and sleep). However, few can compete with Bakpak's cornucopia of amenities, which include a budget travel agency, free airport pickup, and an employment service. Basement "Roo Bar" is always bouncing (as are the cafe and small movie theater). Internet access $6 per hr. 16-bed dorms $24, 6- to 8-bed $25-27, 4-bed $27-28; singles $60; doubles $70-80. 7th night free. VIP. ❷

The Melbourne Connection, 205 King St. (☎9642 4464; www.melbourneconnection.com), at the corner of Lt. Bourke and King St. Expect a casual and friendly stay in this small hostel. Request a room on the upper floors as they are fresher than those in the basement. Free pasta dinner once per wk. TV lounge, communal kitchen. Internet access $4.50 per hr. Reception 24hr. Wheelchair accessible. 14-bed dorm $22, weekly $140; 8-bed $23/145; 6-bed $25/150; 4-bed $26/155; doubles and twins $75/460; triples $87/530. AmEx/MC/V. Cash only for weekly rates. ❷

Stork Hotel, 504 Elizabeth St. (☎9663 6237; www.storkhotel.com), at the corner of Therry St., adjacent to the Queen Victoria Market. Low-key family-run lodging above quirky pub.

Each room has a small collection of photographs and paintings. Sunny cafe makes cheap meals with fresh market produce. Towel and soap included. Singles $48; doubles $58; twins $30 per person; quads and triples $25 per person. ❷

FOOD

Every tantalizing taste from around the world can be found in Melbourne's CBD, a veritable culinary UN. Neon **Chinatown** fills the stretch of Lt. Bourke St., hemmed in by red gates between Swanston and Exhibition St. Blink and you'll miss the **Greek Precinct,** on Lonsdale St. between Swanston and Russell St. It consists of only a half-dozen or so expensive Hellenic restaurants and taverns, but each serves transcendent baklava. Experiencing cramped cafe culture is a must; **Degrave Street** and **Centre Street,** between Elizabeth and Swanston St. near Flinders Station, are stuffed to the gills with locals and foreigners alike. The best budget option, by far, is the **Queen Victoria Market** at the north end of the CBD. Venture west to the **Docklands** (p. 606) for slightly more expensive treats at one of the quayside bistros. Above all, the CBD rewards the adventurous gourmet; wander around with only your nose and palate as a guide and you're sure to strike culinary gold.

VICTORIA

Queen Victoria Market, 513 Elizabeth St. (☎9320 5822; www.qvm.com.au), west of Elizabeth St. and south of Victoria St. Glorious, old-fashioned, open-air market that teems with locals and tourists. Venture deep into the bustle for bargain produce, dairy products, fish, and meat, or stop at the food court for dishes under $10. Be sure to bargain with vendors. Don't miss the night market (W) for a rainbow of multicultural eats. Open Tu and Th 6am-2pm, W 6:30-10pm, F 6am-6pm, Sa 6am-3pm, Su 9am-4pm. ❶

QV Food Court, at the corner of Lonsdale St. and Swanston St. (☎9650 7355), 2 blocks west of QVM. A food court offering budget-friendly fare. Sample the gigantic pokari-wrap ($5.50) at the Indian booth, or stop by at closing time and feast on discounted sushi. Ride the elevator underground to the **Safeway** for the cheapest groceries in the CBD. Open M-W 8:30am-9pm, Th-F 8:30am-10pm, Sa 8:30am-7pm, Su 10am-7pm. ❶

Don Don, 229 Swanston St. (☎9662 3577), across the street from the State Library. This cheerful hole-in-the-wall bops to experimental jazz while dishing out tasty bowls of sukiyaki ($5.50). Open M-Sa 11am-8pm, Su 11am-5pm. Cash only. ❶

BBNT, 184 King St. (☎9642 4414), near the intersection of Lonsdale St. Serving burgers, burritos, nachos, and tacos for pennies. One of several locations. The perfect place to cure the munchies. Chow down on your taco ($3) or burger ($6) and read the entertaining writing on the windows. Open M-Th and Su 11am-10pm, F-Sa 11am-3am. ❶

Delicious Delight Cafe, 113 Swanston St. between Collins and Lt. Collins St. in the Capitol Arcade. (☎9662 3347) This hidden gem isn't much to look at, but offers yummy breakfast all day long at record-low prices. Bacon, 2 eggs, tomato and toast for $4.50. Open M-Sa 8:30am-5pm. ❶

La Porchetta, 302-308 Victoria St. (☎9326 9884; www.laporchetta.com.au), corner of Peel St. With over 100 franchises across Australia, "The Pizza Institution" serves satisfying pies (small $6.20, medium $7.80, large $9.40). Try the *quatro gusti,* which crams 4 flavors into 1 pie. Licensed. Open M-Th 11am-midnight, F-Sa 11am-1am. ❶

SIGHTS

FEDERATION SQUARE. The new explosion of post-modern architecture spawned this unique plaza, which is stuffed with museums, bars, and restaurants. It's worth stopping by this amalgam of copper, glass, and metal, if only to look at the design. An exciting public venue, "Fed Square" repositioned the center of the city and acts as the host to all major public spectacles, including fireworks displays and live artistic festivities. A comprehensive tourist information bureau is situated in the basement, and **Transport** and **Transit** nightclubs are along the river. *(Located at the corner of Flinders and Swanston St. which becomes St. Kilda Rd.)*

QUEEN VICTORIA MARKET. (See **Food,** p. 588.) Walking tours explore the market's history and cultural importance and include plenty to eat. From late November to early March, the market is also open for the Wednesday **night market** (6:30-10pm), when the focus turns toward multicultural cuisine and convivial beer drinking. *(On Victoria St. between Queen and Peel St. ☎9320 5822; www.qvm.com.au. Open Tu and Th 6am-2pm, F 6am-6pm, Sa 6am-3pm, Su 9am-4pm.)*

RIALTO TOWERS. The Rialto Towers complex rises 253m above the city. The 55th floor observation deck provides spectacular 360° views of the city and surrounds. The addictive "Zoom City" live-action video cameras allow voyeurs to zoom in and see people crossing the street all the way across town. **Rialtovision Theatre** plays a 20min. film called *Melbourne, the Living City* that highlights tourist spots with unabashedly cheesy music and dramatic, wide-angle shots. *(525 Collins St., 1 block east of Spencer St. Station, between King and William St. ☎9629 8222; www.melbournedeck.com.au. Open M-Th and Su 10am-9pm, F-Sa 10am-11pm. Film every 30min. Film and deck $13, concessions $9.50, children and seniors $7.80, families $38.)*

THE REAL DEAL. At the top of the Rialto Towers, visitors can pay a hefty fee to stroll down the 360° promenade situated high above the skyline. But at the other end of Flinders St., at the Collins Centre, visitors can sneak a bird's-eye peek for free. On the 35th floor of the Sofitel there is a second lobby, with ample common space and glitzy restaurant called Cafe La. The bistro offers views more delicious than the food, and diners pay accordingly. The adjacent bathroom windows, however, are free and offer sweeping panoramas. Grungy backpackers, fear not; the hosts at Cafe La are all too familiar with gawking tourists and politely direct them to the lavatories. - *Brandon Presser*

IMMIGRATION MUSEUM. Chronicling 200 years of Australian immigration, the Immigration Museum combines various and sundry artifacts with moving soundtracks, most of which are triggered by visitors' footsteps in the gallery. A mock ship in the main room recreates typical living quarters aboard ocean-going vessels from the 1840s to the 1950s. The museum space alone is well worth a visit; high ceilings, a grand staircase, and cool marble floors entice casual passersby. The ground-floor resource center contains links to immigrant ship listings as well as a genealogy database. *(400 Flinders St., in the Old Customs House on the corner of William St. A City Circle Tram stop. Wheelchair accessible. ☎9927 2700. Open daily 10am-5pm. $6; concessions, YHA, and children free. Free after 4:35pm.)*

PARLIAMENT OF VICTORIA AND OLD TREASURY. Victoria's Parliament building is a grand, pillared 19th-century edifice every inch as imposing as a seat of government should be. Free tours detail the workings of the Victorian government and the architectural intricacies of the parliament chambers. *(On Spring St. north of Bourke St. A City Circle Tram stop. ☎9651 8568; www.parliament.vic.gov.au. Daily guided tours when Parliament is not in session leave hourly 10am-3pm and 3:45pm. Call ahead.)* Designed in Italian palazzo style by a 19-year-old prodigy, the City Museum at the **Old Treasury Building** chronicles Melbourne's past, with some great stories about the city's first years. The gold vaults in the basement were built to combat a crime wave during the Victorian Gold Rush; they now house a multimedia exhibit detailing daily life and events in Melbourne's gold-rush era. *(On Spring St., at Collins St. ☎9651 2233; www.oldtreasurymuseum.org.au. Open M-F 9am-5pm. $10, concessions $7, families $20.)*

MELBOURNE CRICKET GROUND (MCG). Established in 1853, expanded in 1956 for the Olympics, and again in 1992 to seat 92,000 people, the MCG functions as the *sanctum sanctorum* of Melbourne's robust sports life. It houses Australian Rules Football (AFL) every weekend in winter, including the Grand Final the last Saturday in September. There are, of course, also cricket matches (Oct.-Apr.); particularly popular are the **test matches** between Australia and South Africa, England, New Zealand, Pakistan, and the West Indies. The north side of the MCG contains the **Australian Gallery of Sport and Olympic Museum,** further celebrating Australia's love of sport. The venue houses the **Australian Cricket Hall of Fame** (which requires some understanding of the game to appreciate), an AFL exhibition, a new feature on extreme sports, and the **Olympic Museum,** with a focus on Australian achievements and the 1956 Melbourne games. The best way to see the stadium and gallery is with a guided tour from the northern entrance. Tours offer unique insight into the MCG's history, the **Melbourne Cricket Club Museum,** and even allow you to step inside the players' changing rooms and onto the hallowed turf itself. Entertaining guides make the 1hr. tour worthwhile, even if you don't have the slightest idea what a wicket, over, or googlie is. *(Take the Met to Jolimont. ☎9657 8888 or 9657 8864; www.mcg.org.au. Tours run on all non-event days on the hr., and often every 30min., 10am-3pm. $10, concessions $6, families $25. Admission includes tour and access to galleries with audio.)* **Australian Football League (AFL) games** at the MCG are also an essential aspect of Melbournian culture. To achieve, or at least mimic, authenticity, order a meat pie and beer, choose a favorite team, and blow out your vocal chords along with the passionate crowd. Make sure you stay long enough to hear the winning team's song played after the game. *(The MCG is in Yarra Park, southeast of Fitzroy Gardens across Wellington Pde. Accessible via trams #48, 70, and 75. $15-22, concessions about ½-price; prices vary by entrance gate, so look around for the best price.)*

VICTORIA

AFL HALL OF FAME. A must for sports enthusiasts, the AFL Hall of Fame guides tourists on a "football adventure." Learn the terminology, understand the hype, and practice your virtual moves. Frequent visits by prominent AFL players and an interactive training program only sweetens the deal. A perfect place to blow off some steam or get acquainted with the game before heading to the stadium. *(Located in the QV at 292 Swanston St. ☎8660 5555; www.aflhalloffame.com.au. $17.50, concessions $13.50, children $10.50, families $49.50. Open daily 9am-6pm, last entry 4:30pm).*

MELBOURNE PARK (NATIONAL TENNIS CENTRE). Across the railroad tracks from the MCG and Yarra Park sits ultramodern **Melbourne Park.** The tennis complex, composed of the domed Rod Laver Arena, the sleek Vodafone Arena, and numerous outer courts, hosts the **Australian Open** every January. You can wander around or take a free 40min. guided tour. Though you can't play on center court, the outer courts offer close proximity to greatness for a $25-45 hourly fee. During the Open, a $27 **ground pass** will get you into every court except center; during the first week you're likely to see many of the big names playing. *(Take tram #70 from Flinders St. Australian Open tickets ☎9286 1600 or 1300 888 104. Bookings ☎9286 1244. Courts available M-F 7am-11pm. For upcoming events, check www.mopt.com.au.)*

ST. PAUL'S CATHEDRAL. The Anglican cathedral, completed in 1891, impresses with its immense scale, intricate detail, and glorious stained glass. Keep an eye out for the beautifully stenciled pipes of the 19th-century Lewis organ. They are easy to miss; look up to the right of the altar. Evensong choral services echo through the hallowed hall M-F at 5pm and Su at 6pm. *(Presides over the corner of Flinders and Swanston St., diagonal to Flinders St. Station. Enter on Swanston St. Open daily 8am-6pm. Free.)*

ST. PATRICK'S CATHEDRAL. Guarded by two lonesome gargoyles, this beautiful product of the Gothic revival offers elaborate stained glass, a magnificent altar, and a soft-focus painting of John Paul II. Among the more traditional Catholic relics housed in the cathedral you'll find an Aboriginal message stick and stone inlay, installed as a gesture of welcome to—and reconciliation with—Aboriginal Catholics. The cathedral is most spectacular at night, when its 106m spires are illuminated. *(West of the Fitzroy Gardens' northwest corner on Cathedral Pl. ☎9662 2233. Open daily 7:30am-6pm. Free guided tour M-F 10am-noon. No tourists allowed during mass M-F 7-7:30am and 1-1:20pm, Sa 8-8:30am, Su 8am-12:30pm and 6:30pm.)*

FITZROY GARDENS. These gardens, originally planted in 1848 and laid out in the shape of the Union Jack, bloom year-round. The closest to the CBD of the many public parks in Melbourne, they offer a bucolic break from the city rush without requiring an all-day commitment. On the south end is Cook's Cottage, a small stone home constructed by Captain James Cook's family in England in 1755 and moved to Melbourne in 1934 to celebrate the city's centennial. Next door, the colorfully stocked **Conservatory Greenhouse** overflows with plants and flowers; a few wrought-iron benches nestle amid the blooms. Weekends December to January often bring concerts and other events. *(Gardens bordered by Lansdowne, Albert, Clarendon St., and Wellington Pde. Tram #48 or 75 from Flinders St. www.fitzroygardens.com. Free garden tour W 11am, starting from Sinclair's Cottage. Cook's Cottage ☎9419 4677. $4, concessions $2.50, children $2, families $10. Conservatory ☎9419 4118. Free tour W 12:30pm. Both open daily 9am-5pm.)*

STATE LIBRARY OF VICTORIA. The State Library is worth a visit, if you appreciate elegant interior design; it is also a great space to read, and offers a wide variety of international newspapers. Check out the Cowen Gallery, which presents 150 portraits and busts of famous Victorians. *(At La Trobe and Swanston St. ☎8664 7000; www.slv.vic.gov.au. Free tours M-F 1pm. Open M-Th 10am-9pm, F-Su 10am-6pm.)*

CHINATOWN. The colorful gates at the corner of Swanston and Lt. Bourke St. signal your arrival in Chinatown, a lively two-block stretch of Asian restaurants, grocery stores, and bars first settled by Chinese immigrants in the 1870s. This area is now one of the hippest niches in the CBD. A block and a half east, and left down Cohen Pl., the **Chinese Museum** houses the *Dai Loong* (Great Dragon). The dragon is the **largest imperial dragon in the world**—so large it has to be wound around two entire floors—and a staple of Melbourne's Moomba festival. *(22 Cohen Pl. ☎9662 2888. Open daily 10am-5pm. $7, concessions $5. Wheelchair accessible.)*

MELBOURNE AQUARIUM. Focusing on species of the Southern Ocean, this impressive facility offers a unique look at Australia's lesser-known wildlife. Its three levels include an open-air billabong and an "Oceanarium" with a glass tunnel that allows visitors to walk beneath roaming sharks and rays. Glass-bottom boat tours run daily and offer another perspective on the watery wildlife. *(On the corner of King St. and Queenswarf Rd., across from the Crown Casino. ☎9923 5999; www.melbourneaquarium.com.au. Open daily Jan. 9:30am-9pm; Feb.-Dec. 9:30am-6pm; last entry 1hr. before close. $23, concessions $15, children $13, families $60. Boat tours M-F 11am, noon, 1, and 2:15pm; Sa-Su 11am, 12:30, 1:15, and 2pm. $15, children $7.50. MC/V.)*

TELSTRA DOME. Embark on an informative tour through one of the largest venues in sport-crazy Melbourne. The new Dome hosts an astonishing number of events from Australian Rules Football, boxing, WWE wrestling, rugby, and cricket, to concerts and a regular Catholic mass. *(☎8625 7277; www.telstradome.com.au. 1hr. tours depart from the Customer Service Centre at Gate 2 M-F 11am, 1pm, 3pm.)*

ENTERTAINMENT

Princess' Theatre, 163 Spring St. (☎9299 9850). Home to an annual line-up of big-budget musicals. A 1500-seat venue that has been around since 1885. Tickets $50-100. Book through Ticketek (☎13 28 49).

VICTORIA

Regent Theatre, 191 Collins St. (☎9299 9500), just east of Swanston St. The dazzlingly ornate Regent Theatre, founded in 1929, was once a popular movie house dubbed the "Palace of Dreams." It now hosts big-name touring musicals and international celebrity acts. Tickets $50-100. 2hr. tours of Regent and Forum every Tu. $20, students $15. Book ahead. Box office open M-Tu 10am-5pm, W-Sa 10am-8pm, Su 10am-7pm.

Last Laugh at the Comedy Club, 188 Collins St. (☎9650 1977, booking 9650 6668), boasts dinner and show packages that are "less than the price of a pizza and videos." Hosts local and international acts. Prices vary. Book ahead by phone M-F 9am-5pm, Sa 10am-5pm. You can also book at www.thecomedyclub.com.au; the website also has monthly schedules and information about upcoming acts.

The Forum, 150 Flinders St. (☎9299 9700), looks like a cross between an Arabian palace and a Florentine villa. Big-budget dance and drama ($50-100), as well as periodic concerts (around $25) and occasional movies. Bookings through Regent Theatre.

NIGHTLIFE

The heart of the city and nerve-center of nightlife, the CBD has the best bars in Melbourne, if not the world. The majority of the venues are tucked far away from passersby; with each successive drink, they seem to get harder and harder to find. Fear not: simply ask around for intriguing watering holes, or check out our **Marvelous Melbourne Pub Crawl,** p. 593.

Croft Institute, 21-25 Croft Alley, off Paynes Pl. between Russell and Exhibition St. (☎9671 4399). Croft defines 'laboratory-chic', serving various flavors of ethanol in test tubes and beakers. Check out the 2nd fl., which boasts the department of Alcohology, housing a fully operational vodka distillery and the restrooms (or rather, the "Departments of Male and Female Hygiene"). Beer $5-7. Mixed drinks from $6.50. Open M-Th 5pm-1am, F 5pm-3am, Sa 8pm-3:30am. MC/V.

e fiftyfive, 55 Elizabeth St. (☎9620 3899; www.efiftyfive.com), just north of Flinders Ln. Escape the urban hustle in the velvet sea of shaggy sofas, join the sub-culture of chillout junkies in this sub-level retreat. Lattes $2.70. Beer from $3.50. Open M-Th and Su 10am-1am, F-Sa 10pm-3am. MC/V.

St. Jerome's, 7 Caledonian Ln., off Lonsdale St. (too cool for a phone number). The ultimate cache of hipsters. Tables full of contented regulars overflow from the micro-mecca into the gritty laneways. Delicious beats are regularly spun by weekend DJs in the backalley dance pit. Beer from $4, coffee from $2. Open M-Sa noon-latenight.

Transit, Level 2 Federation Sq. (☎9654 8808; www.transporthotel.com.au) at the corner of Swanston and Flinders St. Warm red lights rescue weary winos from the jungle of tourists below. Enjoy a mixed drink on the balcony perched over the Yarra River and gaze at the urban skyline. (Blended "luxury" martinis $18.) Open daily 5pm-latenight.

Cookie, 252 Swanston St. (☎9663 7660). Previously known as Kookoo, the large upstairs bar has a vaguely Thai-inspired design offset by cravat-wearing barkeeps. Bustling weekends ensure a good time. Beer from $4. Open daily noon-latenight.

Gin Palace, 10 Russell Pl. (☎9654 0533) off Lt Collins. Slightly out of the budget price range but worth the splurge. Many of the mixed drinks are made with fresh fruit, and the martinis ($14.50) are exquisite—all ingredients in the Surrealist Martini, for example, are frozen for two days before serving. Settees strewn on offset floor levels allow for comfort and pleasant disorientation. Large selection of Australian microbrew beers and an extensive collection of bourbon. Open daily 4pm-3am.

Loop, 23 Meyers Pl. (☎9654 0500; looponline.com.au). The only local bar with its own curator, this incredible art space blends booze with a moving image show. Regulars never get tired of this ever-changing venue. Beer from $5. Open M-Sa noon-latenight.

Bond, 24 Bond St. (☎9629 9844). Stylish and vast, patrons soak up the über-sleek futuristic atmosphere with a little more privacy than the clientele of other establishments. Beer from $5. Open M-Sa 5pm-latenight.

Lounge, 243-5 Swanston St. (☎9662 9995), north of Bourke St. Ideally located above Melbourne's main drag, Lounge offers a reliably good time. Upstairs you'll find cheap drinks (pots from $2.80, spirits from $5.50), a thumpin' dance floor, and an indoor party terrace. Downstairs is a more casual bar and eatery with a cool art decor (main courses $14-18, snacks $6-8). W tech house, Th drums 'n' bass, F mixed breaks, Sa electric house. Upstairs cover $5-15. Open daily 10:30am-latenight.

Misty, 3-5 Hosier Ln. (☎9663 9202) off Flinders Ln. between Swanston and Russell St. Another side alley hideout in the former lingerie district, Misty is a small, funky bar bathed in taste that often masquerades as a nightclub. An eclectic brew of theme music nights includes experimental electronica alongside analog synth and bass guitar, soulful 70s-influenced lounge music, and mixed house. Stubbies $4.50, basic spirits $6.50. The house special "Misty Beach" (vodka and campari) is refined but playful. Open M-Th 4pm-1am, F-Sa 4pm-latenight.

Scubar, on the corner of Lonsdale and Queen St. (☎9670 2105). A small basement venue, home to the friendly local broken-beat scene. It looks like a kitsch-bomb exploded, combining a fish tank and vestibule, wicker lanterns, cement ceilings, and soft cushions; all fit comfortably in the bizarre atmosphere. Tu backpacker nights, Th drum 'n' bass, F house, Sa Japanese night and hip-hop 'n' funk. Cover after 10pm Th and Sa $5. Open Tu-F 4pm-5am, Sa 8pm-5am.

3 Degrees, 1 QV Sq. near the intersection of Swanston and La Trobe St. (☎9639 6766; www.3degrees.com.au). Perfect for a Su afternoon beer bender, this 4-story microbrewery is an anomaly in Melbourne. Ample outdoor seating encourage the lively sociable atmosphere. Open daily 11am-latenight.

Strike Bowling Bar, 245 Little Lonsdale St. (☎9656 7171; www.strikebowlingbar.com.au) at the corner of Swanston St. Music videos pulse at the end of each fluorescent lane. Retro glow creates a buzz among competitors. Billiards in the back for the non-bowling types. $12-15 per person per game on the lanes. Open daily 10am-3am.

NORTH MELBOURNE

An older, quiet residential area, North Melbourne has a collection of quaint bungalows with decorative wrought-iron balconies. The action can be

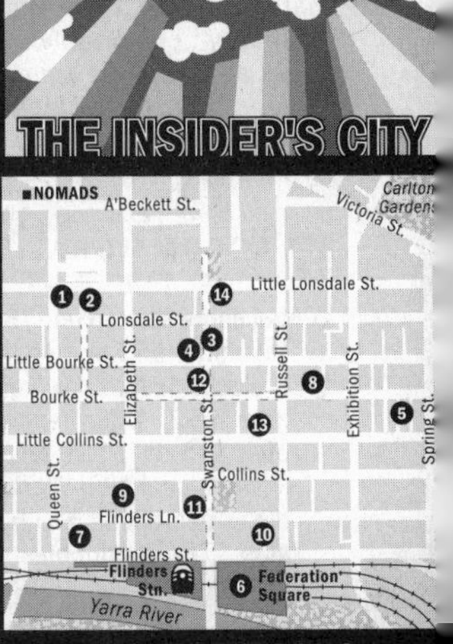

THE MARVELOUS MELBOURNE PUB CRAWL

It would be criminal of us not to give you the guide to an evening out in this happening city. And so, ladies and gentlemen, we at Let's Go are proud to present you with the original Marvelous Melbourne Pub Crawl:

1. **Scubar** (p. 593)
2. **La La Land** (p. 602)
3. **Cookie** (p. 592)
4. **St. Jerome's** (p. 592)
5. **Loop** (p. 592)
6. **Transit** (p. 592)
7. **Bond** (p. 593)
8. **Croft Institute** (p. 592)
9. **e fiftyfive** (p. 592)
10. **Misty** (p. 593)
11. **6 Links** (p. 587)
12. **Lounge** (p. 593)
13. **Gin Palace** (p. 592)
14. **Strike Bowling Bar** (p. 593)

found in the southern portion of the precinct near the bustling **Queen Victoria Market** and near the **University of Melbourne.** As the city's older quarters are gradually becoming fashionable again, **Errol Street** has begun sprouting trendy roots and attracts a small gay population. Take trams #55 or 59 north along Elizabeth St. to the **Melbourne Zoo.** Elizabeth St. eventually becomes Flemington Rd., then Sydney Rd., and ultimately Hume Hwy. which leads all the way to Sydney.

ACCOMMODATIONS

Melbourne Metro YHA, 78 Howard St. (☎9329 8599; queensberryhill@yhavic.org.au). Take tram #55 north from William St. to stop 11 on Queensberry St. From there, walk 2 blocks west to Howard St. Don't miss the impressive roof-top hangout, still sparkling after a $2 million renovation. In addition to clean, same-sex accommodation, they offer $15 daily bike rental, passes to city baths, licensed bistro, travel agency, huge kitchen, pool tables, and free parking. Internet access $6 per hr. Wheelchair accessible. 8-bed dorms $29.50, YHA $26; 4-bed $32.50/29; singles $66/62; ensuite singles $78/74; doubles $79/72; ensuite doubles $94/88; family rooms $87/84; ensuite family rooms $99/94; apartments $125. Book ahead in summer.

Melbourne Oasis YHA, 76 Chapman St. (☎9328 3595; www.yha.com.au). Take tram #57 north to stop 18 and turn right onto Chapman St. This eco-friendly hostel is situated a bit outside the CBD in a quiet neighborhood setting. Worm-fertilized herb garden is available to guests, who are encouraged to recycle and compost virtually all waste. Bathrooms and kitchen are cleaned at least twice per day. Free parking, bike rental, and passes to the City Baths available. Luggage storage $2. Key deposit $5. Reception 24hr. Dorms are all same-sex. No bunk beds. 3- to 5-bed dorms $32.50, YHA discount $30.50; doubles and twins $69/65. 7th night free in winter.

VICTORIA

SIGHTS

OLD MELBOURNE GAOL. This prison opened in 1845 and housed a total of 50,000 prisoners in its 84 years. Today, it offers unparalleled insight into the macabre side of Australian history. The creepiest displays feature the stories and death masks of the most notorious criminals executed here. Kelly, Australia's most infamous bushranger, was hanged in the jail in 1880, and a scruffy wax likeness stands on the original trap door and scaffold. Downstairs is the suit of armor that Kelly, or one of his cohorts, wore in the gang's final shoot-out with police. Wonderfully spooky evening tours led by professional actors provide a chillingly vivid sense of its horrible past. *(On Russell St. just north of La Trobe. ☎9663 7228; click on "properties" at www.nattrust.com.au. Open daily 9:30am-5pm. $13, concessions $9.50, children $7.50, families $34. Night tours Nov.-Feb. W and F-Su 8:30pm, Mar.-Oct. 7:30pm. $20, children $13, families $48. Bookings required; call Ticketmaster ☎13 28 49.)*

MELBOURNE ZOO. Many sections of this world-class, 143-year-old zoo consist of expertly designed habitats that allow visitors to view animals much as they live in the wild. The African Rainforest—with pygmy hippos, arboreal monkeys, and gorillas—is first-rate. From early January until early March the zoo hosts twilight festivals with live bands, on Thursday, Friday, Saturday, and Sunday evenings. *(On Elliott Ave., north of the University of Melbourne. M-Sa take tram #55 from William St. to the Zoo stop; Su take tram #19 or 68 from Elizabeth St. ☎9285 9300; www.zoo.org.au. Free tours 10am-4pm, call ahead to arrange. Open daily 9am-5pm. $20, non-Aussie seniors $17, concessions $15, ages 4-15 $10, families $45.)*

CARLTON

Melbourne's unofficial "Little Italy," Carlton begins at **Nicholson Street** and extends west past the Carlton Gardens (home to the World Heritage **Royal Exhibition Building** and the informative **Melbourne Museum and IMAX**), ultimately reaching the **University of Melbourne.** On **Lygon Street,** its primary thoroughfare, locals are lured by the numerous upmarket Italian bistros. Recently, the precinct has seen a surge in tasty Asian fare that attracts swarms of uni students. While there is a lack of budget accommodation, the food is draw enough. To get to Carlton's Lygon St., either take a tram up Swanston St. (#1, 3, 5, 6, 8, 16, 22, 25, 64, 67, or 72) and then walk east along Queensberry or Faraday St., or take #96 from Bourke St. up Nicholson St. and walk west along Faraday St.

FOOD

Brunetti, 194-204 Faraday St. (☎9347 2801; www.brunetti.com.au) just east of the intersection with Lygon St. A *caffe, paninoteca, pasticceria, gelateria,* and *ristorante* all rolled into one. Although the restaurant is quite pricey, it's worth stopping by for a lunchtime panini (from $8) or the delectable desserts (signature chocolate morsels from $1.20, cannoli $3.20). Open daily 11am-11pm. ❷

Tiamo, 303 Lygon St. (☎9347 5759). Flavorful Italian cuisine at very reasonable prices. Its next-door sequel, **Tiamo2** (☎9347 0911), is a *cucina antica* that is slightly more refined and serves a comparatively sophisticated menu. Tiamo pastas $12.50, Tiamo2 pastas $13.50. Licensed and BYO. Tiamo open M-Sa 7:30am-11pm, Su 9:30am-10pm; Tiamo2 open M-Sa 9:30am-10:30pm. ❷

Lemongrass, 176 Lygon St. (☎9662 2244). A critically acclaimed restaurant serving cuisine deemed "best Thai food in Melbourne." Dine among thickets of bamboo shooting out of the floor. The lunch buffet ($29) is expensive but delectable. Dinner main courses from $15-46. Pad Thai $13.90. Open M-F noon-2:30pm and 5pm-11pm, Sa-Su 5pm-11pm. AmEx/MC/V. ❹

Casa del Gelato, 163 Lygon St. (☎9347 0220), near Argyle Sq. The local favorite, Casa has been around for over 25 years and makes their frozen treats using only fresh produce. Try the popular *bacio* in a cone or medium bowl (both $5). Open daily noon-midnight, closed M in winter. ❶

Boba Pearl Bubble Tea Restaurant, 122 Lygon St. (☎9663 0498). Family-owned and brightly colored, Boba Pearl offers the best bubble-tea beverages in town ($3.50). Try the honeydew milk tea. Also serving dense bowls of noodles starting at $8. Open daily 11am-latenight. ❶

Jimmy Watson's Wine Bar, 333 Lygon St. (☎9347 3985). A Lygon St. institution, Jimmy's is one of the oldest wine bars in Melbourne (est. 1932) serving over 300 types of wine to a generally older crowd. The traditional restaurant serves meals ($20-35). Open M 10:30am-6:30pm, Tu-Sa 10:30am-latenight. ❹

Toto's, 101 Lygon St. (☎9347 1630). Self-proclaimed "first pizzeria in Australia." Cheap pies (small $7.50, large $12.50) and speedy delivery. Licensed and BYO wine. Open M-Th noon-11pm, F-Sa noon-midnight, Su noon-10:30pm. ❷

SIGHTS

CARLTON GARDENS AND MELBOURNE MUSEUM. Spanning three city blocks, the verdant Carlton gardens, crisscrossed with pathways and featuring spectacular fountains, offer peaceful repose. Within the gardens is the grand World Heritage **Royal Exhibition Building,** which was home to Australia's first parliament and now hosts major expositions, temporary exhibits, and blow-out sales. Behind the

Exhibition Building stands the **Melbourne Museum,** a stunning facility with an excellent Aboriginal art and culture center and exhibits on Australian wildlife. There's also an IMAX theater (see **Cinema,** p. 584), a rainforest, a children's museum, and a mind and body gallery. *(Bordered by Victoria, Rathdowne, Carlton, and Nicholson St. Take the city circle tram or tram #96. Museum ☎8341 7777; www.melbourne.museum.vic.gov.au. Open daily 10am-5pm. Public tours of Royal Exhibition Building daily 2pm. Wheelchair accessible. $6, concessions and children free. 3D IMAX showings: $17, concessions $14, seniors $13, children $12, families $49. Tours $4, with museum admission $2.)*

ENTERTAINMENT

La Mama, 205 Faraday St., Carlton (☎9347 6948), about halfway up Lygon St. Head east on Faraday St.; it's near the intersection, hidden down an alleyway and behind a carpark. Esoteric Australian drama in a diminutive, black-box space. M night fiction readings; Sa afternoon poetry and play readings when no performances. Similar cutting-edge work is performed at the affiliated **Carlton Courthouse Theatre,** 349 Drummond St., just around the corner in the old courthouse building across from the police station. Wheelchair accessible. Tickets around $15. Free tea and coffee at performances.

Last Laugh at the Comedy Club, Level 1, 380 Lygon St., Carlton (☎9348 1622), in Lygon Ct. Melbourne's biggest comedy-club, with big-name international performers. Ticket prices vary depending on the act. Show starts 8:30pm and usually ends around 12:30am. Tickets $25-75, depending on whether or not dinner is included.

FITZROY

A mecca for cutting-edge hipsters, Fitzroy does an impressive job of reconciling its grungy roots with the recent influx of a high-end crowd. Tram #11 runs the length of **Brunswick Street,** Fitzroy's main artery. This diverse main drag (drag being the operative word) acts as a thoroughfare just west of Bohemia on the way to Pretention-ville. Generally, the area teems with a healthy mix of "ferals" (Aussie's term for the pierced crowd), families, and everyone in between.Grungy **Smith Street,** which runs parallel to Brunswick Street, has recently become popular and features several gay bars and some unique boutiques. A small Spanish district has popped up along **Johnston Street** with top-notch tapas and flamenco bars.

ACCOMMODATIONS

The Nunnery, 116 Nicholson St. (☎9419 8637 or 1800 032 635; www.bakpak.com/nunnery). Stop 13 on tram #96, at the northeast corner of Carlton Gardens. Housed in the former convent of the Daughters of Mercy, the cordial staff refer to themselves as nuns. Considerably calmer than other digs, the attached guesthouses provide further privacy. Towel and soap included. F wine and cheese night, Su pancakes. Breakfast included. Internet access $2 per 20min. Key deposit passport or $20. Reception M-F 8am-8pm, Sa-Su 5-8pm. 10- to 12-bed dorms $26-28; 6- to 8-bed $28-30; 4-bed $30-32; singles $65; bunk twins $75; doubles $85; triples $95; guesthouse doubles $110; family rooms $30 per person. Discounted weekly rates available. ❸

Royal Derby Hotel and Backpackers, 446 Brunswick St. (☎9417 3231), at Alexandra Pde. The Royal Derby is a lively pub and nightspot that offers accommodations to individuals spending extended amounts of time in Melbourne. Tu pool competition, Th quiz night, Su live acoustic music. Bar open M-Th noon-1am, F-Sa noon-3am, Su noon-11pm. Singles and doubles $25 per person, weekly $120. Additional price reductions given to guests staying longer than 1 month. ❷

FOOD

Food in the self-proclaimed "Bohemian District" of Melbourne is alternative, trendy, and most importantly, tasty. Wander down **Brunswick Street** for an unbeatable breakfast. Try **Johnston Street** for tapas in Melbourne's unofficial Spanish Quarter. **Smith Street** offers an extended sampling of grunge-inspired places.

Nyala, 113 Brunswick St. (☎9419 9128). Mostly Kenyan and Sudanese fare with a dash of Gambian and Moroccan flavor. Try the *kuk na nazi* (Kenyan coconut chicken $17.50), and understand why Nyala is a local fave. Open daily 6-10:30pm. ❸

Veggie Bar, 380 Brunswick St. (☎9417 6935). So tasty that it draws in the general meat-eating populace, Fitzroy's top vegetarian option lives under the wood-beamed roof of a converted textile factory. Main courses from $11.50. Try the popular Mexican Burrito. Loads of vegan and wheat-free options. Open daily 9am-10pm. ❷

Retro Café, 413 Brunswick St. (☎9419 9103; www.retro.net.au), on the corner of Westgarth St. If you think the bright yellow facade on the building is hipster-esque, check out the TV-turned-aquarium inside. Try the "knock your socks off" gourmet pizza ($15), or the 3-course menu ($45), perfect for the big spenders. $3 wine and beer during daily Happy hour 3-6pm. Breakfast served until 6pm. Open daily 7am-latenight. MC/V. ❸

Tomorrow Cafe and Courtyard, 122 Johnston St. (☎9419 7651), just east of Brunswick St. Slightly removed from the usual jaunt, Tomorrow's quaint purple-drenched cafe and courtyard is ideal for slurping home-brewed teas ($3.50) while admiring local art or listening to live music Sa and Su. Breakfast served until 4pm ($6-12), pub grub in the evening ($6-14). Open M-W 10am-5pm, Th-Su 10am-latenight. ❷

Filter, 185 Brunswick St. (☎9416 3752). If the sleek style and succulent smells don't lure you in, the competitive prices definitely will. Eclectic fare ranges from Turkish pide ($10) to savory vegetable risotto ($13.50). Open M-Th 7:30am-6pm, F-Sa 7:30am-latenight, Su 8:30am-6pm. ❷

Trampoline, 381 Brunswick St. (☎9415 8689; www.trampolineHQ.com.au). While the debate continues as to whether or not Trampoline serves ice cream or gelato, one thing is for certain: they have the best dessert in town. A colorful array of flavors including Caramel Pear, Banana, Blood Orange, and "Violet Rumble." Medium $5. Franchised throughout the city. Open daily 11am-11pm. ❶

Bimbo, 229 Victoria St. (☎9328 1090), 2 blocks west of QVM. Bright walls and a garden out back enhance the trendy vibe of this classy, healthy establishment. A variety of wraps run $6.50, while the uniquely blended "aioli cleanser" drink goes for $3.50. Open M-F 7:30am-4:30pm, Sa 8:30am-3:30pm. ❶

Fitz Cafe, 347 Brunswick St. (☎9417 5794). Bright, cheery hotspot with seating that tumbles out onto the street. Stop by for the generously stacked fruit pancakes ($10). BYO wine ($2 corkage per person). Open daily 7am-latenight. AmEx/MC/V. ❷

Mario's, 303 Brunswick St. (☎9417 3343). A small, red neon sign in a cluster of cafe fronts marks one of the best breakfast buys in town. Starting at $6.50, served all day. Those who spurn breakfast can grab one of the pasta dishes starting at $11. Fully licensed. Open daily 7am-midnight. ❷

NIGHTLIFE

Black Cat, 252 Brunswick St. (☎9419 6230). A small cafe-lounge with remarkably discerning musical taste and a gorgeous arboreal sidewalk beer garden. DJs nightly, M-Tu open decks, W hip hop, Th breaks, F-Sa eclectic (jazzy funk, hip-hop, breaks, drum 'n' bass), Su reggae, hip-hop, etc. Light lunch and breakfast until 4pm ($4-7). Open M-F 10am-1am, Sa-Su 11am-1am.

Bar Open, 317 Brunswick St. (☎9415 9601). Portraits of the Queen Mum on thickly painted red walls oversee the youngish mix of uni students and locals in this intimate, experimental environment swathed in purple velvet. W-Sa nights local jazz and funk talent. Beer garden, fireplace, and bohemian camaraderie are the order of the evening. Open daily noon-2am.

The Provincial, 299 Brunswick St. (☎9417 2228), at the corner of Johnston St. The "Prov" is the perfect place to jumpstart a night out in Fitzroy. For over 15 years, it has offered cheap pub grub ($5-10) and a large selection of beers on tap ($3-4). Tu trivia, Th-Sa DJs. Open daily noon-1am.

The Standard Hotel, 239 Fitzroy St. (☎9419 4793), between Bell and Moor St. Hidden just around the corner from busy Brunswick St. The Standard is a homey locale that few travelers ever find. Boasting the biggest, most authentic beer garden in Fitzroy, The Standard serves giant portions of superb pub food (main courses $13-22) and jugs ($12). Open M-Th 3-11pm, F-Sa noon-1am, Su noon-9pm.

The Peel Hotel and Dance Bar, (☎9419 4762), corner of Peel and Wellington St.; turn left up Wellington when coming from Gertrude St. and Fitzroy. An institution in Melbourne's gay nightlife, the Peel is more down-to-earth than its Commercial Rd. counterparts. The club pumps house to an almost exclusively gay male crowd. The attached pub is more laid-back and straight-friendly, with cheap drinks (from $2.50, spirits $4) and relaxed conversation. Cover for special events (from $10). Open W-Su 9pm-dawn.

SOUTHBANK

Set between the bustling beaches of St. Kilda and the urban activity of the CBD, the industrial Southbank is gradually becoming commercialized.

ACCOMMODATIONS AND FOOD

One of the newest lodgings in town, **Urban Central ❸,** 334 City Rd., is a 15min. walk south of the CBD. Guests are shown to their rooms and given a welcome package containing local information and candy. Thick, soundproof walls block out noise from nearby highway traffic. Amenities include tea and coffee, pasta and rice for cooking, electrical outlets within lockable compartments, massive licensed bar on ground level, library, game room, plasma TV room, travel desk, large kitchen, and laundry. (Toll free ☎1800 631 288; www.urbancentral.com.au. Internet $3 per hr. Key deposit $10. 4-bed dorms $28-35. Doubles and family rooms $90-150.) Facing the CBD, across the river on the 2nd floor of the Southbank complex is the **Blue Train Cafe ❶,** 229 Victoria St. The vast, enjoyable menu and freshly baked gourmet desserts are worth the trip across the bridge. Devour the unbeatable eggs benedict ($8.90) while enjoying the view from your riverside table. (☎9328 1090; www.bluetrain.com.au. Open daily 7am-11:30pm. MC/V.)

SIGHTS

KING'S DOMAIN AND ROYAL BOTANIC GARDENS. Over 50,000 plants fill the 36 acres stretching along St. Kilda Rd. east to the Yarra and south to Domain Rd. Stately palms share the soil with oaks, rainforest plants, possums, wallabies, and a rose pavilion. There's also a steamy **rainforest glasshouse** and lake where you can have tea and feed the ducks. (Open daily 10am-4:30pm.) Special events, such as **outdoor film screenings,** take place on summer evenings (see **Cinema,** p. 584). The **Aboriginal Heritage Walk** explores the use of plants by local Aboriginal groups in ceremony, symbol, and food. (Th 11am and alternate Su 10:30am. $16, concessions $11. Book ahead.) Near the entrance closest to the Shrine of Remembrance are the **visitors center** and **observatory.** The visitors center houses an upscale cafe, the Terrace Tearooms, and a garden shop. (Open M-F 7am-5pm, Sa-Su 10am-5:30pm.) The observatory includes an original 1874 telescope accessible by day tours; night tours allow visitors to use the instruments with the help of qualified astronomers. (Tours W 11am, 2pm. Night tour Tu 7:30pm, later in summer. $16, concessions $11, families $38. Tours $2. Book ahead.) **La Trobe Cottage,** by Gate F, was home to Victoria's first lieutenant governor, Charles Joseph La Trobe. (Open M, W, and Sa-Su 11am-4pm.) Tours depart from the cottage to Government House, the Victorian **Governor's residence.** *(4 Parliament Pl. ☎9654 4711; www.rbgmelb.org.au. Wheelchair accessible. Tours $11, concessions $9, children $5.50. Book ahead. Gardens ☎9252 2300. Open daily Nov.-Mar. 7:30am-8:30pm; Apr.-Oct. 7:30am-5:30pm. Free. Garden tours depart the visitors center M-F and Su 11am and 2pm. $4.50.)*

SOUTHBANK. The riverside walk that begins across Clarendon St., Southbank, is known for its shopping and sidewalk-dining scene. It's most crowded on sunny Sundays, when an odd mix of skater kids, athletic health nuts, and the Armani-clad gather here to relax, show off, and conspicuously consume. The area extends along the Yarra for two long city blocks. While a lack of restraint will demolish your bank account in a few hours, you can window-shop, people-watch, and enjoy some unbeatable views of Flinders St. Station and the city skyline. There are also expensive but enjoyable river ferry rides, picturesque fountains, wacky sculptures, and imaginative sidewalk chalk drawings.

NATIONAL GALLERY OF VICTORIA (NGV: INTERNATIONAL). The enormous National Gallery had to adopt the post-phrase "of Victoria" when the Australian National Gallery was built in Canberra. Housing what many consider to be the finest collection in the Southern Hemisphere, the NGV has re-opened as **National Gallery of Victoria: International** after a $136 million renovation. The postmodern facilities of the **Ian Potter Centre,** in the Federation Square building at Swanston and Flinders St., house three levels of Aboriginal, colonial, and contemporary Australian art. This new center, a striking complex of glass and steel prisms, contains the only entirely Australian collection of art anywhere in the world. Recent exhibits prominently feature paintings with rather pointed messages for the Bush and Howard administrations about land sovereignty and the futility of war. *(180 St. Kilda Rd. and Federation Sq. ☎9208 0222; www.ngv.vic.gov.au. Gallery open M-Th 10am-5pm, F 10am-9pm, Sa-Su 10am-6pm. Admission to permanent collection free. Wheelchair accessible. Free guided tours daily 11am, noon, and 2pm.)*

SHRINE OF REMEMBRANCE. A walkway lined with conical Bhutan cypresses leads to this imposing temple with columns and a Ziggurat roof that commemorates fallen soldiers from WWI. Crowning the central space are a stepped skylight and the **stone of remembrance,** which bears the inscription "Greater Love Hath No Man." The skylight is designed so that at 11am on November 11 (the moment of the WWI armistice), a ray of sunlight shines onto the word "Love". Ascend to the balcony for spectacular views of the Melbourne skyline and the neighboring suburbs, or venture into the crypt to view the colorful division flags and memorial statues. Outside, veterans of subsequent wars are honored with a memorial that includes the **perpetual flame,** burning continuously since Queen Elizabeth II lit it in 1954. *(On St. Kilda Rd. www.shrine.org.au. Open daily 10am-5pm. Donations encouraged.)*

VICTORIAN ARTS CENTRE. This enormous complex is the central star of Melbourne's performing arts galaxy. The 162m white-and-gold latticed spire of the **Theatres Building** is a landmark in itself, and inside there's more room for performance than most cities can handle. Home to the **Melbourne Theatre Company, Opera Australia,** and the **Australian Ballet,** this eight-level facility holds three the-

VICTORIA

aters (see **Performing Arts,** p. 583) that combined can seat over 3000. The Theatres Building also serves the visual arts; the space that once belonged to the Performing Arts Museum is now used for free public gallery shows. Next door is the 2600-seat **Melbourne Concert Hall,** which hosts the renowned **Melbourne Symphony** and the **Australian Chamber Orchestra.** Its chic **EQ Cafebar** (☎9645 0644) is a bit pricey but offers award-winning meals and great views of the Yarra. Finally, the third tier of the Victorian Arts conglomerate, the **Sidney Myer Music Bowl** is across St. Kilda Rd. in King's Domain Park. After extensive renovations, the bowl will be the largest capacity outdoor amphitheater in the Southern Hemisphere, sheltering numerous free and not-so-free summer concerts. Its "Carols by Candlelight," in the weeks before Christmas, draws Victorians by the sleighloads. The Centre hosts a free arts and crafts market Su 10am-5pm. *(100 St. Kilda Rd., at the east end of Southbank, just across the river from Flinders St. Station. ☎9281 8000; www.vicartscentre.com.au. Open M-F 7am-latenight, Sa 8:30am-latenight, Su 10am-after the last show. Free admission. Guided tours leave from concierge desk M-Sa noon and 2:30pm, though hours vary. $10, concessions $7.50. Special Su 12:15pm backstage tour $14.)*

SOUTH YARRA AND PRAHRAN

South Yarra, Prahran (per-RAN), and Windsor span the area enclosed by the Yarra to the north, St. Kilda Rd. to the west, Dandenong Rd. to the south, and William St. to the east. Although Melbourne's gay community doesn't have a center per se, **Commercial Road** is home to a significant number of gay-friendly venues. South Yarra sits just north of Prahran, and the two are divided by High Street. The district's main thoroughfare is **Chapel Street;** toward the south, it gradually morphs from a corporate haven into clusters of small privately owned boutiques. St. Kilda is only an 8min. walk from the southernmost end of Chapel Street.

TRANSPORTATION

Trains: From the CBD, take a **Sandringham Line** train from Flinders St. Station to South Yarra, Prahran, or Windsor Stations—each lies only a few blocks west of Chapel St.

Trams: #78 and 79 run along Chapel St. Tram from Flinders St. Station. #8 travels below the Botanic Gardens, then along Toorak Rd. to Chapel St., while #5 and 64 head south along St. Kilda Rd., and then go east along Dandenong Rd. to Chapel.

ACCOMMODATIONS

Clean, charming accommodations, only a few minutes by train from the CBD, are nestled within the vibrant mix of trendy boutiques and cafes.

Claremont Guesthouse, 189 Toorak Rd., South Yarra (☎9826 8000; www.hotelclaremont.com), 1 block east of the South Yarra train station, close to the intersection of Toorak Rd. and Chapel St. A beautifully refurbished 1886 building, it retains much of its Victorian charm while still providing all the modern amenities. Feels much more like a quaint hotel than a budget accommodation. Spotless hallway bathrooms and toilets. Towels and breakfast included. Internet access $6 per hr. Dorms (with skylights instead of windows) $30, singles $68; doubles and twins $78; $20 surcharge during special events, holidays, and festivals. Bookings required. MC/V. ❸

Chapel St. Backpackers, 22 Chapel St., Windsor (☎9533 6855; www.csbackpackers.com.au), just north of Dandenong Rd. across from Windsor train station, on tram routes #78 and 79. A friendly 13-room retreat just minutes from the clubs of Prahran and St. Kilda. Caters to an older clientele. Impeccably maintained. Courtyard with BBQ. Breakfast included. Internet access $4 per hr. Key deposit $20. Check-out 10:30am. Dorms $27, weekly $182; doubles $75/518. MC/V. ❸

Lord's Lodge, 204 Punt Rd., Prahran (☎9510 5658). Take tram #3, 5, 6, 16, 64, or 67 south on St. Kilda Rd. to stop 26, then walk 2 blocks east along Moubray St. Easily accessible on foot from Prahran or St. Kilda. Older mansion with a carefree spirit. All rooms have heater, locker, fan, and fridge. 3 private bungalows have TV and mini-fridge. Request the room with the black-and-white tiled floor. Coffee and tea included. Check-out 9:30am. Free Internet access. Reception M-Sa 8am-noon and 5-6pm, Su 8am-noon. 1 6-bed all-female dorm. 8-bed dorm $22, weekly $132; 6-bed $24/144; 4-bed $26/156. Camping on the premises $10 per person during high season. Prices rise in summer. MC/V. ❷

FOOD

Preened, pricey South Yarra aggressively markets itself as the place to see and be seen in Melbourne, and its chic, mod-Oz bistros with sidewalk seating see their share of black-clad fashion mavens. There are some excellent budget options, however, particularly south of **Commercial Street** in more down-to-earth Prahran. The ubiquitous coffee bars are a wallet-friendly place to sample the scene (cappuccino around $2.50). Check out the **Prahran Market,** on Commercial Rd. at Izett St. (parallel to and west of Chapel St.), for cheap fresh produce, meat, and multicultural food. **Windsor Cellars,** 29 Chapel St., is just north of Dandenong Rd. and has a 24hr. **bottle shop,** one of only two in the city. (☎9501 4050.)

Orange, 124-126 Chapel St. Windsor (☎9529 1644), south of High St. An inviting orange awning and smooth dark hardwood interior provides a chill setting for the hipster clientele. Refreshingly attentive and friendly staff makes dining a pure pleasure. Excellent lattes ($2.80) and foccacia for lunch ($8-9). Open daily noon-latenight. ❷

Borsch Vodka and Tears, 173 Chapel St. (☎9530 2694). Come by for candles bleeding gobs of wax and the eerie glow of antique lamps. Indulge in any of 60 vodkas (drinks $6-8.50) traditionally served in a tall shot glass sunk in a bed of ice. The Spirytus is 160 proof fuel—you bring the rocket (and the tears). Breakfast and lunch until 6pm. Toasties $8.50-9.50. Open M-W 8:30am-1am, Th-Sa 9:30am-3am, Su 9:30-12am. ❷

Gurkha's Brasserie, 190-192 Chapel St. (☎9510 3325; www.gurkhas.com.au). Delicious Nepalese cuisine comes at a reasonable price in a dimly lit, ornate restaurant bedecked with lanterns and permeated by South Asian music. It might take a while to figure out what to order, but a good bet is the *Dal Bhat Masu,* which comes with your choice of meat curry, soup, and rice or bread. Main dishes $10-16. Licensed and BYO wine ($1.50 corkage per person). Check out the other 4 locations, each with unique decor. Open M-Th and Su 5:30pm-1am, F-Sa 5:30pm-3am. ❷

Lamb on Chapel, 394 Chapel Street, South Yarra (☎9826 2442; www.lambonchapel.com), north of Commercial St. This aptly named greasy spoon serves up lamb in a variety of ways. Try the Souvlaki ($8). Open daily M-W and Su 10am-1am, Th 10am-2am, F-Sa 10am-5am. ❶

SIGHTS

CHAPEL STREET. This happening stretch of pavement unfurls through two of the trendiest precincts around: South Yarra and Prahran. With over 1000 storefronts, Chapel St. offers an unbeatable locale for an eclectic assortment of one-of-a-kind trinkets and more standard goods. Following Chapel St. over the Yarra, it becomes Church St. in hip Richmond.

NIGHTLIFE

Revellers, 274 Chapel St. (☎9510 3449). The friendliest spot on Chapel St. Faithful crowd of locals crams in every weekend for all-night romps. Excellent playlists and live music keep the party going until breakfast. Open W and Su 5pm-3am, Th-Sa 5pm-7am.

La La Land, 134 Chapel St. (☎9533 8972). Plush recliners and a hip, low-key atmosphere make this a great pre-game bar. Check out Lala's younger, swankier brother on Lonsdale St. in the CBD. Beers from $6.50, spirits from $7. Open M-Th and Su 5pm-1am, F-Sa 5pm-3am.

Revolver, 1st fl., 229 Chapel St. (☎9521 5985; www.revolverupstairs.com.au). DJs spin every night from 9pm. Lines can get long at night, but once you're in you can literally stay the entire weekend. Thai food available at the in-house restaurant. Beer from $3.50, spirits from $6.50. Live music on weekends. Cover under $12 Th-Sa after 9pm. Open M-Th noon-3am, F noon-Su 3am.

The Social, 116 Chapel St. (☎9521 3979). Sleek lounge/eatery catering to a well-dressed professional crowd (and those drooling on their hemlines). F-Su nights DJ. Brunch daily until 6pm (main courses $10-20). Beer from $5. Mixed drinks from $7. Open M-Th 11:30am-1am, F-Su 11:30am-3am.

Bridie O'Reilly's, 462 Chapel St. (☎9827 7788), with a branch at 62 Lt Collins St. (☎9650 0840), in the CBD. Wooden booths, stag's heads, and Guinness posters: Irish to the bone. Beer from $2.80, spirits from $6.50. Live cover bands. M-Th and Su Traditional Irish, F-Sa Top-40. Open M-Th and Su 11am-latenight, F-Sa 11am-3am.

The Market, 143 Commercial Rd. (☎9826 0933), attracts a mixed crowd–gay, lesbian, and straight. The Market's hard-working dance floor changes faces each night. F is "Grind" night, featuring underground house, while the weekend "straightens" out a bit, with DJs spinning dance house for Sa "Late Night Shopping" and Su "Sunday Market." Cover $5-15. Open Th 9pm-latenight, F 9pm-8am, Sa 11pm-11:30am, Su 9pm-9am.

Frost Bites, 426 Chapel St. (☎9827 7401). Behind the downstairs bar of this popular nightspot are large swirling machines of icy alcoholic concoctions (from $6). A mainly teen Aussie crowd packs in for W and Th live music shows, F retro night, and Su 70s glam. Beer from $3, spirits from $6. Cover $5. Open daily 11am-3am.

ST. KILDA

Officially a part of Port Phillip, St. Kilda is a budget hotspot with cheap accommodations, popular eateries, and relaxed nightlife. Trams #12 and 96 transport people to St. Kilda from Spencer St. Station, while 16 runs from Flinders St. Station. The precinct is focused around the St. Kilda Beach, with the **Esplanade** following the curvature of the coastline. About a block inland is the infamous **Acland Street** with loads of tasty pastry joints and scrumptious restaurants. **Fitzroy Road** to the north offers an abundance of shopping opportunities. Running between Fitzroy and Barkly St., **Grey Street** hosts many of St. Kilda's budget accommodations.

ACCOMMODATIONS

A hub for hostels, St. Kilda offers budget travelers the cheapest deals in the area. Beware that the accommodations tend to be older and unkempt in comparison to the lodgings across the Yarra River; they mirror the precinct's fun-loving, gritty flavor. Although St. Kilda is removed from the CBD, the area is easily accessible by tram (stop 131-134 on lines #16 and 96) and functions as a thriving self-sustained community all on its own. If you're coming in March, book way ahead to avoid the hassle of the Grand Prix crowd.

Olembia, 96 Barkly St. (☎9537 1412; www.olembia.com.au), tucked behind a canopy near the intersection with Grey St. Nestled in the residential community of St. Kilda, this sanctuary provides comfortable quarters in a beautiful mansion. Well-informed, friendly staff will point you to all the best spots in town. Free car and bicycle parking. Bike rental $10. Key deposit $10. Reception 7am-1pm and 5-8pm. Max. stay 1wk. Book ahead in summer. 3-bed dorms $25-27; singles $50; twins and doubles $75-80. MC/V. ❷

Base Backpackers, 17 Carlisle St. (☎1800 24 BASE; www.basebackpackers.com), follow Carlisle St. east away from the tram stop at the intersection of Carlisle and Acland St., on the right. Shiny red facade attracts weary travelers from afar. The uber-sleek interior has an aquarium built into the ground floor. Request a room on the higher floors as the thumping bar bass encourages carousing until the wee hours. All rooms are ensuite with heat and A/C. 10-bed dorms $26; 6- and 8-bed $30; 4-bed $34; doubles from $95. Private all-female dorms available for $2 extra. MC/V. ❷

Pint on Punt, 42 Punt Rd. (☎9510 4273; stkilda@pintonpunt.com.au), just north of St. Kilda Junction, on the corner of Peel St. Take tram #3, 5, 16, 64, or 67 from Flinders St. Station. A 10min. stroll to the fashionable Prahran or chilled-out St. Kilda beach. Despite being above a bar, the hostel is well groomed and calm. Gigantic breakfast included. W pub grub dinner $6. Discount on pub meals 10%. Pub events include trivia and Tu $10 steak nights. Live music Su 5-8pm. Internet access $1 per 15min. Key deposit $10.

Check-in at reception 7am-noon or at the bar until 1am. Bar open M-Sa noon-1am, Su noon-11pm. All dorms $20; singles $50; twins and doubles $50. 7th night free. ❷

Tolarno Boutique Hotel, 42 Fitzroy St. (☎9537 0200 or 1800 620 363; www.hoteltolarno.com.au). Sassy boutique hotel decked out in eccentric modern art. Built in 1884 by the mayor of St. Kilda, the building underwent additions and renovations in the 1930s and 60s, emerging as an amalgam of styles from Deco to Retro. All with TV, heat, queen-sized bed, and coffee maker; balconies, kitchenettes, and Japanese baths available. Suites $120-320. ❺

Jackson's Manor, 53 Jackson St. (☎9534 1877; www.jacksonsmanor.com.au). The yellow Edwardian manse is well worn but charming nonetheless. Sweeping common areas are accented with plants and stained glass. Amenities include a kitchen, ping-pong table, foosball, and job and travel assistance. Small breakfast included. Internet access $3 per hr. Free parking. 8- and 10-bed dorms $22, weekly $130; 4-bed $24/145; doubles $60/360. ❷

The Ritz for Backpackers, 169 Fitzroy St. (☎9525 3501 or 1800 670 364). Tram #16 lets off at stop 132 out front. A smaller hostel with sparse rooms. The 10-bed apartment suite upstairs has a couch, kitchen, and windows with a view of Albert Park. TV room. Free pancake breakfast, nightly dinner deals. Internet access. Reception 24hr. 8-bed dorms $22; 6-bed $24; 3-bed $26; twins and doubles $60. VIP. MC/V. ❷

Oslo Hotel, 38 Grey Street (☎9525 4498 or 1800 501 752; www.oslohotel.com.au). Take tram #16 or 96 to stop 133 on Fitzroy St. Big and beachy, ample outdoor lounge areas are perfect for a summer stay. Rooms and bathrooms vary in quality and size, but all are cheap. Inner courtyard with BBQ (midnight noise curfew), kitchen with industrial fridges, TV room with DVD, board games, and billiard table. Internet access $5 per 80min. M-F morning pickup from CBD. 12-bed apartment has private lounge, kitchen and bathroom. Dorms $20-25; twins and doubles $70; apartment $160-250 per wk. ❷

Coffee Palace Backpackers Hotel, 24 Grey St. (☎9534 5283 or 1800 654 098; info@coffeepalace.com.au), 1 block off Fitzroy St. The popular house of cards is under new management and is being slowly renovated. Organized pub crawls are perfect for the partiers. Morning pancakes included. Internet access $5 per hr. Key deposit $10. Pickup available. Prices vary by season. 8- and 10-bed dorms $17-23; 6- and 4-bed $19-27; small ensuite dorms $23-29, twins and doubles $50-70. VIP. ❷

FOOD

As hip as South Yarra and Chapel St., cheaper and less pretentious St. Kilda offers a diverse selection of affordable eateries interspersed with many decidedly non-budget options. The result is a great mix of value and vogue. You can't go wrong with the fancy bistros on Fitzroy St. The Barkly St. end of Acland St., legendary among locals for its divine cake shops, also has wonderful multicultural choices. **Coles** 24hr. supermarket is in the Acland Court shopping center near Barkly St.

Soul Mama, 10-18 Jacka Blvd., at the St. Kilda Seabaths, on the 2nd fl. (☎9525 3338; www.soulmama.com.au). The mama-lode of incredible vegetarian options. Love the earth and your meal while looking out over the ocean. Salad/soup bowl $8, medium plate $14.50, large plate $16.50. Open daily noon-latenight. AmEx/MC/V. ❷

Monarch Cake Shop, 103 Acland St. (☎9534 2972). The oldest cake shop on Acland St.'s cake-shop row (est. 1934 in Carlton, moved to St. Kilda late 1930s) and still the best. Their famous plum cake is the most popular seller ($3 per slice), but the chocolate *kugelhopf* is near bliss ($14-15). Open daily 7am-10pm. ❶

Spud Bar, 51 Blessington St. (☎9534 8888), near the intersection with Acland St. A simple and brilliant concept: design your own potato. Choose from 30 toppings to smother your spud. Takeaway $7.50, eat in $8. Open daily noon-10pm. ❶

Blue Corn, 205 Barkly St. (☎9534 5996). Blue Corn features fresh gourmet Mexican fare at moderate prices. Try the array of dips with blue corn bread (guacamole, sesame rojo, pumpkin, rocket coriander, and chipotle olive; $12.50). Don't miss the spicy fajitas ($17). Items can be prepared without dairy and gluten. Open daily 6am-10pm. MC/V with 2% credit surcharge. ❸

Cicciolina, 130 Acland St. (☎9525 3333). Named for an Italian-Hungarian porn star who joined the Italian government in 1979. Tasty Italian fare that gives Lygon St. a run for its money. Delicious main courses ($13.50-34) and affable service keep patrons coming back for more. Chill out in a dimly lit bar behind the restaurant while waiting for a table. Open M-Sa noon-11pm, Su noon-10pm, bar open until 1am every night. ❸

SIGHTS

St. Kilda has recently undergone a shift away from its image as a den of drugs and prostitution. There aren't a lot of tourist sights per se, but the offbeat shops, gorgeous sandy shoreline, and comfortably mixed population are indeed a sight to behold. St. Kilda Beach is easily accessed by any number of trams (see **Orientation,** p. 574), and swarms with swimmers and sun bathers during the summer. The **Esplanade,** along the length of the strand, is a great place for in-line skating, biking, and jogging. On Sundays, the Esplanade craft market sells art, toys, housewares, and more, all handmade.

LUNA PARK. The entrance gate of this St. Kilda icon is a grotesque clown mouth that devours visitors. Venture through to find classic carnival rides, all permanently protected by the historical commission. Built in 1912 by a trio of American entrepreneurs hoping to capitalize on the fame of Coney Island's successful Luna Park, Melbourne's Luna has the largest wooden rollercoaster in the world. *(On the Lower Esplanade. ☎9525 5033; www.lunapark.com.au. Open F 7-11pm, Sa 11am-11pm, Su 11am-6pm; public and school holidays M-Th 11am-5pm, F-Sa 11am-11pm, Su 11am-6pm. Unlimited ride tickets $34, ages 4-12 $24; family pass $100.)*

JEWISH MUSEUM OF AUSTRALIA. The Jewish Museum outlines the history of the Jewish people as a whole and the 200-year history of Australia's 90,000 Jews from the time of the First Fleet. A captivating hallway display draws a timeline of Jewish history, complete with fascinating multimedia displays and gorgeously illustrated texts from the Roman era and the Middle Ages. The Belief and Ritual Gallery provides a thorough overview of Judaism's basic tenets, including an excruciatingly detailed French woodcut of a circumcision ceremony. There are also rotating displays of art and Judaica, and an extensive reference library and archive, available for use upon request. *(26 Alma Rd., east of St. Kilda Rd. by stop 32 on tram #3 or 67. ☎9534 0083; www.jewishmuseum.com.au. Museum open Tu-Th 10am-4pm, Su 11am-5pm. Wheelchair accessible. $7, students and children $4, families $16. Present a print-out of the front page of the website and get a 50% discount on admission. 30-40min. tours of the adjacent synagogue Tu-Th 12:30pm, Su 12:30 and 3pm. Free with admission. Open services F 6pm at the Reform synagogue on Alma Rd. Inquire for details.)*

ENTERTAINMENT

National Theatre (☎9534 0221 or 9534 0213; www.nationaltheatre.org.au), on the corner of Barkly and Carlisle St., St. Kilda. Offbeat, cosmopolitan shows like modern dance, drama, opera, and world music. Ticket prices $10-75, depending on show.

Palais Theatre (☎9534 0651), on the Esplanade, St. Kilda. Holds the largest chandelier in the Southern Hemisphere. Seats 3000. Tickets around $50.

NIGHTLIFE

Esplanade Hotel, 11 Upper Esplanade (☎9534 0211; www.espy.com.au). Multifaceted seaside hotel known as the "Espy." Down-to-earth Lounge Bar with gorgeous sea views offers live music acts daily, while the ornate Gershwin Room has bigger-name live music acts Th-Sa (usually rock 'n' roll; cover under $10). Beneath is the gritty Public Bar which has Happy hour 5 days per wk. (pots $1.50 5-7pm). Public Bar open daily 11am-1am. Lounge Bar and Gershwin Room open M-Th and Su noon-1am, F-Sa noon-3am.

The Vineyard, 71a Acland St. (☎9534 1942; www.thevineyard.com.au), near Luna Park. Home away from home for an extremely varied clientele. Warm and friendly, a great place for a post-beach beer ($5). Main courses $15-25. Open daily 7:30am-3am.

The George Public Bar, 127 Fitzroy St. (☎9534 8822). Not to be confused with the George Melbourne Wine Room next door, which carries over 500 wines ($18-500). The subterranean style of the George Public Bar's old-fashioned fittings and room-length bar pack the place on weekend nights. Try their "world-famous" chili mayo chips ($5 for a big basket.) Beer from $3.20, spirits from $5.80. Live music Sa 4-7pm and Su 6-9pm; trivia night M 7:30pm. Open M-Th and Su noon-1am, F-Sa noon-3am.

OTHER PRECINCTS

BRIGHTON. For the serious beach bum, Brighton is far removed, located south of St. Kilda, but offers calmer waters and less commercial hoo-ha. A nice mix of technicolor beach boxes and unbeatable views of the distant city. Take the train south from Flinders Station along the Sandringham Line and get off at Brighton Beach and walk west towards the water.

DOCKLANDS. Long ago the area was a dank and marshy port. In anticipation of the 2006 Commonwealth Games, the warehouses of the once-industrial area were transformed into sparkling commercial venues. The NewQuay development promises smooth architecture and gourmet restaurants. Take the free city tram to the eastern edge of the Docklands near Southern Cross Station.

RICHMOND. East of the CBD, sedate Richmond has recently been dubbed "Little Saigon" for its numerous Vietnamese establishments along **Church Street.** Further south, **Bridge Street** is the place to be with a large shopping district and significant cafe culture. Take the light-rail one or two stops east from Flinders Station to reach Richmond Station or East Richmond Station.

SOUTH MELBOURNE. South Melbourne, west of St. Kilda Rd. and stretching south from the West Gate Freeway to **Albert Park,** is more working-class than either the northern suburbs or its neighbors to the southeast, but offers some quality restaurants and nightspots along its main thoroughfare, **Cecil Street.** Directly across from the CBD is the Southgate commercial development, which is full of cafes with views of the city skyline. From Southgate, it's a quick tram ride to the **Royal Botanic Gardens** (p. 598), the CBD, or the **beach** at Port Phillip Bay. Take tram #96 or 12 from Spencer St.

STATION PIER AND ALBERT PARK. West of South Melbourne along Port Phillip Bay are three of Melbourne's quietest, poshest suburbs. Station Pier marks the division between **Port Melbourne,** the more commercial side of the area, and **Albert Park,** the urbane residential neighborhood with stately seaside bungalows. Ferries to **Tasmania** depart from Station Pier at the terminus of tram #109.

WILLIAMSTOWN. Intended to be the main port of Port Phillip Bay, the beautiful peninsular precinct is one of Melbourne's quieter districts. It boasts gorgeous beaches, manicured gardens, and picture perfect photo-ops of the bay and skyline. Although mostly residential, Williamstown is extremely tourist-friendly and offers delicious dining and modestly priced accommodations ideal for a weekend away from city life. From the CBD, head west on the Melton or Sydenham line and switch at Footscray station to the Williamstown line. Alternatively, catch the ferry from Southgate which departs for Williamstown every 30min.

DAYTRIPS FROM MELBOURNE

There are a variety of opportunities to escape the city and head out on exciting expeditions just a stone's throw away. Popular trips include visits to **Rutherglen** (p. 661), the **Yarra Valley** (see below), and **Phillip Island** (p. 609). George Josevski, Melbourne's unofficial backpacking king, regularly sets tourists up with an array of daily trips including the popular Ramsey St., home of the hit TV show "Neighbours." Call George at ☎9534 4755. Stop by the **Melbourne Visitor Centre** in Federation Sq., across from Flinders St. Station at the corner of Flinders St. and St. Kilda Rd. (☎9658 9658; open daily 9am-6pm) to receive additional information about daytrips. Several tour companies also offer round-trip daily service to seemingly distant destinations. Don't be put off by perceived travel time; many travelers who are strapped for time have enjoyed day-long journeys through the picturesque **Great Ocean Road** (p. 616) or panned for gold at Sovereign Hill in **Ballarat** (p. 642). Stop by Federation Sq.'s tourist center for a bevy of brochures and helpful agents who can provide additional information about daytrips. Also check out www.backpackerking.com.au, a website that specializes in trips and activities for the budget traveler.

VICTORIA

YARRA VALLEY WINERIES

The Yarra Valley produces top-grade wines and attracts a large crowd from the Melbourne area. The unending supply of booze is a definite plus, but it's the scenery that keeps the crowds coming. Located about 60km from Melbourne, the Yarra's first vineyards were started in 1835 with 600 vine cuttings procured from the Hunter Valley. After a depression in the 1890s decimated wine demand, the Yarra essentially shut down. Vineyards were replanted in the 1960s, and today the valley has more than tripled in size. The cool climate is ideal for growing Chardonnay, Pinot Noir, and Cabernet Sauvignon grapes; virtually all of the more than 30 wineries produce these varieties. Quality sparkling wines abound, as Chardonnay and Pinot Noir are two of the principal grapes used for the bubbly.

For accommodation information in the area, call the **Yarra Tourist Association** in Healesville (☎5962 2600). There are several tour options from Melbourne, though the best and most affordable is **Backpacker Winery Tours** (☎9419 4444; www.backpackerwinerytours.com.au), recipients of the 2004 Victoria Tourism Award for being the best daily tour operators. The $95 tour runs daily and offers pickup and drop-off near major hostels in the CBD and St. Kilda, free tastings at four wineries, and a gourmet lunch overlooking the valley, not to mention knowledgeable commentary and lessons on wine quality and tasting from entertaining guides who have worked in the industry themselves. Tours usually last from 9:15am until 4:45pm, depending on where you get picked up.

Public transportation to the wineries is limited. Lilydale, 10-20km outside the Yarra, is on the Met train line, but after that there's no way to get to the wineries without renting a car; remember Let's Go does not recommend drinking and driving, and perhaps more importantly, neither do the police. Pick up a free copy of

Wineries of the Yarra Valley or *Wine Regions of Victoria* at the Melbourne tourist office, or check out www.yarravalleywineries.asn.au.

You can't go wrong with any of the selections offered here, especially at an average price of $2 for a taste of their whole selection (tasting fee usually refundable upon purchase). Call ahead to arrange a walkthrough with the winemaker.

Domaine Chandon (☎9739 1110; www.chandon.com.au), "Green Point" on Maroondah Hwy. Founded in 1986 by Moët & Chandon, this lavishly landscaped vineyard produces the company's signature sparkling wine, as well as Green Point stills. Owned and operated under the Louis Vuitton corporate umbrella, the most polished vineyard in the Yarra offers an in-depth exhibit on wine production and breathtaking views from its restaurant. No free tastings. $5.50 flutes with a free bread, cheese, and chutney plate, or $18-40 bottles to go. Free tours 11am, 1pm, 3pm. Open daily 10:30am-4:30pm.

Rochford Wines (☎5962 2119; www.rochfordwines.com), on Maroondah Hwy. and Hill Rd. in Coldstream. A gorgeous winery with a bar and excellent gourmet **restaurant ❹.** Small art gallery up a spiral staircase displays local painting, jewelry, and crafts. Restaurant open daily 10am-3pm, winery 10am-5pm.

Yering Station, 38 Melba Hwy. (☎9730 1107; www.yering.com), 1hr. east of the city. On the site of Yarra's 1st vineyard (founded in 1838), Yering's tasting area has a delightful art gallery, and the multi-million dollar complex next door has a top-notch restaurant with a huge glass wall overlooking the valley. Bottles $15.50-58. Open M-F 10am-5pm, Sa-Su 10am-6pm. Restaurant open M-F noon-3pm, Sa-Su noon-4pm.

St. Huberts (☎9739 1118), on St. Huberts Rd. Founded in 1863. Small winery offering a very popular Cabernet, and one of only 4 Australian wineries to produce Rhone River Valley Roussane, a unique flavor. The vineyard hosts regular musical events Nov.-Apr.; call for details. All its wines are sold only in Australia. Bottles $19-30. Open M-F 9:30am-5pm, Sa-Su 10:30am-5:30pm.

OTHER DAYTRIPS

HEALESVILLE SANCTUARY. An open-air zoo that has won numerous awards for ecotourism, the Healesville Sanctuary lies in the Yarra Valley, 65km from Melbourne, a place better known for its wineries than its wildlife. The sanctuary's daily "Meet the Keeper" presentations allow visitors to interact with and ask questions about native animals. Keeper talks start at 11am and occur roughly every 30min. The popular "Birds of Prey" presentation has been revamped to include additional birds, with double the seating capacity. The sanctuary also has programs on Warundjeri Aborigines and Aboriginal culture. *(On Badger Creek Rd. By car, take the Maroondah Hwy. and follow signs. By public transport, take the Met's light rail to Lilydale, then take McKenzie's tourist service bus #685 for about 35min. Buses leave directly from the station weekdays at 9:40 and 11:30am. McKenzie's ☎9853 6264. Sanctuary ☎5957 2800; www.zoo.org.au. Open daily 9am-5pm. $22, concessions $16.50, ages 4-15 $11, families $51-69. Free guided tours 10:30am-3:30pm. Bookings required.)*

WERRIBEE PARK AND OPEN RANGE ZOO. The mansion at **Werribee Park** is a great, relaxing daytrip from Melbourne, with serene sculptured gardens, an imposing billiards room, and an expansive nursery. From October to May, the bloom of 5000 roses colors the garden. *(On K Rd. 30min. west of Melbourne along the Princes Hwy., or take the Werribee line to Weribee, then bus #439. ☎9741 2444 or 13 19 63. Open Nov.-Apr. daily 10am-5pm; in May-Oct. M-F 10am-4pm, Sa-Su 10am-5pm. Wheelchair accessible. $12, concessions $7.50, ages 3-15 $6, families $29.50.)* Animals from the grasslands of Australia, Africa, and Asia give the **Open Range Zoo** the feel of a safari. The zoo also runs an overnight "camping" program from September to April that includes dinner, craft workshops, night spotting, accommodations, and breakfast. To explore on your own, take the two 45min. **walking trails;** a tour of the 200 hectare park takes about three hours. *(By the mansion on K Rd. ☎9731 9600; www.zoo.org.au. Open daily 9am-5pm, last entry 3:30pm, last tour 3:40pm. 50min. safaris daily 10:30am-3:40pm; Jan-Feb. safaris Sa-Su also 10:30am-7:70pm. Wheelchair accessible. Zoo entrance $17, with mansion admission $26, concessions $12/18, ages 3-15 $7.80/13, families $43/65.)*

ORGAN PIPES NATIONAL PARK. Although the six-meter metamorphic landmarks look more like french fries than organ pipes, they're still a good daytrip or stop en route to the central Goldfields. Look for the **Rosette Rock,** which resembles a flowing stone frozen in time (400m past the Organ Pipes). The park is also a laboratory for environmental restoration and has been largely repopulated with native plants and trees since the early 1970s, when weeds concealed the pipes. The park has picnic facilities and charges no entrance fee. *(Just off the Calder Hwy. (Hwy. 79), 20km northwest of Melbourne. Public transport from Melbourne is slightly tricky: M-Sa take tram #59 from Elizabeth St. to Essendon Station, then switch to bus #483 to Sunbury (doesn't run Su). ☎9390 1082. Open daily for cars 8am-4:30pm, open anytime for visitors on foot; on weekends and public holidays during Daylight Saving Time 8am-6pm. Wheelchair accessible.)*

HANGING ROCK RESERVE. The unique rock formations on this bit of crown land are technically part of a mamelon—a small, steep-sided volcano—and were featured in the famous 1975 film (first a novel by Joan Lindsay) *Picnic at Hanging Rock*, in which young schoolgirls disappear during the course of a school outing in 1900. *(Calder Hwy., past Organ Pipes National Park to the Woodend exit; follow signs and enter at the south gate on South Rock Rd. Or, take V/Line from Spencer St. Station to Wood End and walk or take a cab 7km from the station. Park ☎1800 244 711; Picnic Cafe ☎5427 0295. Open daily 8am-6pm. $8 per car.)*

PUFFING BILLY STEAM RAILWAY. The train is a relaxing way to see the interior of northeast Victoria's **Dandenong Ranges,** as it travels through a verdant netherworld of lush rainforest terrain. Note: you will be sharing this train with many small children. *(40km east of Melbourne on the Burwood Hwy. to Belgrave. Or, take a 70min. Connex Hillside Train (☎13 16 38) from Flinders St. Station. ☎9754 6800; www.puffingbilly.com.au. Train from Belgrave to Lakeside: 1hr.; 2-6 per day; high season $20, low season $18.50, round-trip $34/31.50; concessions $15.50/15, round-trip $26.50/25.50; children 4-16 $10/9.50, round-trip $17/16. From Belgrave to Gembrook: 1¾hr.; 1-2 per day; $29.50/28, round-trip $46/43.50; concessions $24/22, round-trip $36/34; children $14.50/14, round-trip $23/21.*

VICTORIA

PORT PHILLIP AND WESTERNPORT BAYS

Two strips of land, the Bellarine Peninsula to the west and the Mornington Peninsula to the east, curve south from Melbourne around Port Phillip and Westernport Bays. Travelers short on time should head straight to Phillip Island's plentiful wildlife attractions and excellent surf beaches, while Mornington Peninsula offers tranquil picnics, water activities, and scenery.

PHILLIP ISLAND ☎03

A whopping 3.5 million visitors gather on Phillip Island every year to witness the smallest species of penguin scamper back to their burrows nightly in a "Penguin Parade" on one corner of the island. The island's other features draw surfers, koala-cuddlers, history buffs, and bikers.

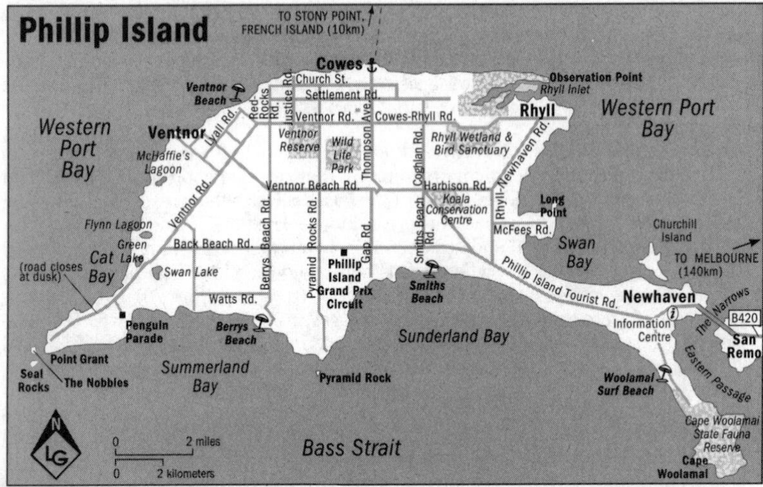

TRANSPORTATION. Phillip Island lies across a narrow strait from **San Remo.** Numerous backpacker tours take groups to the island. **Duck Truck Tours,** run by the folks at Amaroo Park Hostel, offers a trip that includes Melbourne transfers, up to three nights at the hostel, a tour of the island, meals, and a half-day of bike use. (☎5952 2548. $145. Day tours of the island, Wilson's Prom, and Great Ocean Road from $75.) Phillip Island is 2hr. from Melbourne; take the South Eastern Arterial (M1) to the Cranbourne exit to the South Gippsland Hwy. (M420), then turn onto the Bass Hwy. (A420) and onto Phillip Island Tourist Rd. (B420). This road becomes Thompson Ave. when it reaches **Cowes,** the island's biggest township. **V/Line buses** serve Cowes from Melbourne (3hr.; M-F 3 per day, Sa-Su 2 per day; $17.30). Buy tickets at **Going Places Travel,** 130 Thompson Ave. (☎5952 3700. Open M-F 9am-5:30pm.) **Inter Island Ferries** offers service between Stony Point and Cowes. (☎9585 5730; www.interislandferries.com.au; 30min., 2-4 per day; $9.)

PRACTICAL INFORMATION. Once on Phillip Island, you'll see the **Phillip Island Information Centre** on the left after the bridge. (☎5956 7447; www.penguins.org.au. Open daily 9am-5pm.) Buy tickets for the Penguin Parade here to avoid long lines. Other services include: **ATMs** on Thompson Ave.; **police** (☎5952 2037); **hospital** (☎5952 2345); and **Internet** access at **Waterfront Computers,** 130 Thompson Ave. (☎5952 3312; www.waterfront.net.au; $1.50 per 15min. Open M-F 9am-8pm, Sa 10am-1pm.) The **post office** is at 73 Thompson Ave. (Open M-F 9am-5pm.) **Postal Code:** 3922.

ACCOMMODATIONS AND FOOD. A hostel and several caravan parks on the island meet the needs of most campers and backpackers; try the **Amaroo Park Hostel (YHA)** ❷, 97 Church St., Cowes. Head down Thompson Ave. and hang a left on Church St.; the entrance is on Douglas Rd., a left turn off Church St. Combining a trailer park with backpacker lodgings, the Amaroo has a pool table, a pub with cheap drinks, **Internet** access ($2 for 20min.), and a swimming pool. The friendly staff runs Duck Truck Tours and serves $10 dinners. (☎5952 2548; www.amaroopark.com. Free breakfast. Call to inquire about pickup in Melbourne. Book ahead. Sites from $15; dorms $25, YHA $22; singles $39/33; doubles $30/25; cabins from $135.) **Cowes Caravan Park** ❸, 164-188 Church St., boasts access to a stretch of adjacent beach. (☎5952 2211. Laundry, showers, camp kitchen. Sites $38, low-season $25; cabins $90.) If you're looking to splurge, it doesn't get much better than

Holmwood Guesthouse ❺, on Chapel St. at the corner of Steele St. Accommodation options include a traditional guesthouse, cottages (with kitchenette and wood fire), and townhouses (with full kitchen, laundry, and 2 bedrooms) for groups or families. Relax in the guest lounge with an open fire or on the sunny veranda overlooking the garden. All rates include home-cooked breakfast. (☎5952 3082; www.holmwood-guesthouse.com.au. Guest rooms for 2 people $175; self-contained cottages $215; townhouses for 4-6 people $215.)

Virtually all food options in Cowes are clustered along the two blocks of Thompson Ave. approaching the northern beach. For delicious baked goods and deli fare (around $7), steer to **MadCowes ❷**, 17 the Esplanade. They also arrange picnic baskets and takeaway meals. (☎5952 2560. Open daily 8am-5pm.) For more upmarket eats, **Café Terrazzo ❷**, 5 Thompson Ave., specializes in gourmet wood-fired pizza in a whimsical bistro. (☎5952 3773. Open daily noon-latenight.) A **Coles** supermarket is at the corner of Thompson and Chapel St. (☎5952 2244. Open daily 7am-10pm.)

ACTIVITIES AND WILDLIFE. Phillip Island's tourist magnet is the **Little Penguin Parade,** at the Phillip Island Nature Park. Each night, up to 1000 little "fairy" penguins return to their burrows after lengthy fishing expeditions to rest or tend to their hungry chicks. These dark-blue, wobbly little creatures are the world's smallest variety of penguin. People await the penguins from a large grandstand along the boardwalk at sunset (get there early for a good position and bring a coat, as you may have to wait a while); eventually, the penguins emerge and their "parade" lasts nearly an hour. The Penguin Information Centre provides extensive information about the penguins, including interactive exhibits. (☎5951 2800; www.penguins.org.au. Wheelchair accessible. Open daily 10am-10:30pm. $17, children $8.50, families $42.50. Book ahead.)

Although the penguins are the main draw, Australia's largest colony of **Australian fur seals** lives offshore from the **Nobbies** volcanic rock formation. These are the largest fur seals in the world (the male seals can exceed 350kg). A boardwalk approaches the Nobbies, enabling you to take in the beautiful eroded hills and crashing sea. Bring powerful binoculars or a $2 coin for the boardwalk telescopes if you want to sealwatch. (Open daily 7:30am-dusk.) The **Koala Conservation Centre,** south of Cowes on Phillip Island Rd., is a sanctuary housing 23 koalas in eucalyptus canopies. The marsupials are most active at feeding time, 1½hr. before dusk. (☎5952 1307. Open daily 10am-6pm. $9, children $4.50, families $22.50.) Farther towards Cowes, **Phillip Island Wild Life Park** has a few koalas of its own, as well as a wide cross section of other Aussie wildlife favorites. Visitors will have little choice but to hand-feed wallabies, wombats, kangaroos, and emus—the animals come to you. (☎5952 2038. Open daily in summer 10am-6pm; in winter 10am-5pm. Bag of animal feed included with admission. $11, children $5.50, families $30.) Originally home to the Aborigines, **Churchill Island** became one of the first European settlements in Victoria. The pleasant grounds include a number of walking tracks and a working farm. (☎5956 7214. $9, children $4.50, families $22.50. Open daily 10am-4:30pm.) The info center offers a **Rediscover Nature Ticket,** which covers the Parade, the Koala Centre, and Churchill Island. ($30, children $15, families $75.)

Throughout the year, and especially in summer, Phillip Island offers great outdoor recreation. Surfers swarm to the island's southern coast, particularly Woolamai and Smith's Beaches. **Island Surfboards,** 147 Thompson Ave. and 65 Smith's Beach Rd., can set you up with a board and excellent instruction. (☎5952 2578 and 5952 3443, respectively. 2hr. lesson $45.) View the area by boat on **Wildlife Coast Cruises,** departing from Cowes pier. (☎5952 3501; www.bayconnections.com.au. $55, students $50, children $40, families $155; 5hr. French Island tour $60/56/39/190.) **Cape Woolamai,** on the southeast corner, has the island's highest point, numerous walking trails, and a patrolled beach. Bushwalking trails cover the island, ranging from casual to difficult. Host to the late-October Motorcycle Grand Prix and several other fuel-injected frenzies, the **Phillip Island Grand Prix Circuit,** Back Beach Rd., Cowes, also hosts a year-round visitors center, with racing displays and circuit tours. (☎5952 9400; www.phillipislandcircuit.com.au. 10min. Go-Kart ride $25. Tours daily 11am and 2pm. Open daily 10am-5pm.)

SORRENTO ☎03

Near the very tip of the Mornington Peninsula, Sorrento (pop. 1500) is a relaxing weekend getaway that draws flocks of summer visitors to its history-rich parklands, rocky cliffs, and popular beaches.

The bay is popular for swimming and sailing in summer, but exercise caution: the riptides here change rapidly. Just across the peninsula on the ocean side, **Back Beach** has decent surfing. For an unforgettable experience, swim with dolphins and seals with **Polperro Dolphin Swims.** (☎5988 8437; www.polperro.com.au. Oct.-Apr. 8:30am and 1:30pm. Booking required. 3-4hr. $99, observers $44, children observers $28.) The **Collins Settlement Historic Site,** just east of Sorrento on Pt. Nepean Rd., is the location of the 1st European settlement in Victoria. Founded in 1803, the site was abandoned after eight months for lack of fresh water. Farther along Point Nepean Rd., just past Portsea, lies Point Nepean, the very tip of the peninsula, and the **Point Nepean National Park.** A walk (3.5km, 1½hr.) departs from Gunners carpark and leads to Fort Nepean, built in 1882, as well as to a memorial for Prime Minister Harold Holt, who disappeared from nearby Cheviot Beach in 1967. ($7.50. Irregular bus transport to Gunner's carpark $7.50. 3hr. bike rental $16, helmet included. Park open daily in summer 9am-6pm; in winter 9am-5pm.)

Ideally located 1min. away from town and 5min. from Back Beach, **Sorrento Beach House YHA ❸,** 3 Miranda St., is the only budget accommodation in town, and features an outdoor patio with BBQ. The hostel operators can secure discounts on various activities. From the roundabout at Melbourne and Ocean Beach Rd., follow the YHA signs up Ossett St.; Miranda St. is the first right. (☎5984 4323; sorrentoyha@iprimus.com.au. Book ahead in summer. Dorms $30, YHA $25.)

Ocean Beach Rd. is lined with upscale eateries. **Sunny Side Up Cafe ❶,** across from the ferry terminal as you go into town, has cheap meals, **Internet** access ($2.50 per 20min.) and plenty of sun. (☎5984 4255. Open daily 8am-latenight.) For Danish hot dogs ($6.20-7.20) and great ice cream, head to **The Little Mermaid ❶,** 70 Ocean Beach Rd. (☎5984 0202. Open in summer daily 11am-10:30pm.)

From Melbourne, take a **train** to Frankston (1hr., $12.50 all-day pass), then a **train** (80min., M-F every 15min., $12.50 or included from last leg). If you're coming from the Great Ocean Road, you can reach Sorrento via **ferry** from Queenscliff, on the Bellarine Peninsula. (☎5258 3244; www.searoad.com.au. 1hr.; every hr. 7am-6pm; $9, concessions $8, cars from $47.) Along **Ocean Beach Road,** Sorrento's main street and traffic nightmare, you'll find numerous **ATMs.** There is a **post office** at 16 Ocean Beach Rd. (Open M-F 9am-5pm.) **Postal Code:** 3943.

MORNINGTON PENINSULA NATIONAL PARK

Mornington Peninsula National Park is divided into regions of coastline and bush country spanning over 40km in length. The western tip of the peninsula is **Point Nepean.** The scenic drive along the peninsula is dotted with **vineyards** and picnic stops. The **Dromana Estate Vineyards,** on Old Moordooch Rd. in Tuerong, is open for free tastings. (☎5974 4400. Open daily 11am-4pm.) Pick-your-own fruit farms also abound; check out **Sunny Ridge,** on the corner of Mornington-Flinders and Shands Rd. (☎5989 6273. Open Nov.-Apr. daily 9am-5pm; May-Oct. Sa-Su 9am-5pm. Strawberries $10 per kg.) At the very southern end of the park are **Cape Schank** and its **lighthouse.** Several walking tracks depart from here, including a short boardwalk to the spectacular coast, and the **Bushrangers**

Bay Walk, a 45min. walk by basalt cliffs with breathtaking vistas. The lighthouse, functioning since 1859, has a visitors center that runs tours. (☎5988 6184. Open daily in summer 9am-5pm; in winter 11am-4pm. Tours and admission $12, children $10.)

QUEENSCLIFF

☎03

Tiny Queenscliff retains its Victorian elegance, enticing many, mostly older, visitors who seek a relaxing holiday vacation to its rambling, rocky shores. One hundred and twenty kilometers southwest of Melbourne, Queenscliff overlooks the Rip, renowned among sailors for its strong current and perilous shoreline. The main thoroughfare is dotted with shops whose colorful, old-fashioned signs advertise hand-cut meats and *gelato*. The grand old architecture and leisurely ambience, well-suited for beach-sitting and twilight strolls, inspire some to start their journey on the **Great Ocean Road** (p. 616) in Queenscliff.

Take the **V/Line train** from Melbourne to Geelong (1hr., daily every hr., $10.20) and then **McHarry's Buslines** (☎5223 2111; www.mcharrys.com.au; 1hr.; M-F 9 per day, Sa 7 per day, Su 4 per day; $11.70 round-trip, $6.90 one-way) to Queenscliff. **Ferries** run from the Sorrento Pier, just across the bay. (☎5258 3244; www.searoad.com.au. 40min.; daily every hr. on the hr. 7am-6pm; $9 for passengers. Cars $47, low-season $40, plus additional $6 per person.) The **Visitor Information Centre** at 55 Hesse St. has **Internet** access for $3 per 30min. (☎5258 4843 or 1 300 884 842; www.queenscliff.org. Open daily in summer 9am-6pm, otherwise 9am-5pm.) The **library,** in the same building as the information center, has two free Internet terminals: 1hr. with advanced booking, or a 15min. fly-by. (Open M-Tu 2-5pm, Th-F 10am-1pm and 2-5pm, Sa 9:30am-noon.) The ANZ **bank** is at 71 Hesse St. (24hr. **ATM**), and the **post office,** 47 Hesse St., is right nearby (☎5258 4219. Open M-F 9am-5pm, Sa 9am-noon.) **Postal Code:** 3225.

Inexpensive lodging is scarce in Queenscliff. Book well in advance in the summer. If you can't get a room, contact the information center for assistance with finding accommodations in Point Lonsdale, 6km west of Queenscliff. It's a 1hr. walk west along the coast, but public buses also cover the distance.

Located in a 1906 Edwardian building, the YHA-affiliated **Queenscliff Inn B&B ❷,** 59 Hesse St., has a drawing room with an open fire, outdoor BBQ, and kitchen facilities. Breakfast ranges from continental ($7) to fully cooked meals ($14). Private rooms are as lovely as they are expensive. Hostel accommodations are nice as well, though the service is quite slack. (☎5258 4600. Towels $1.50. Dorms $27, YHA $22; twin-shares $27-35 per person; singles $50; doubles $54. Book ahead.) The **Queenscliff Dive Centre ❸,** 37 Learmonth St., has bright and comfortable backpacker accommodations, with high ceilings, a huge kitchen, a dartboard, and a TV with DVD. (☎5258 1188. Continental breakfast included. $30, weekends $35.)

Queenscliff Fish and Chips ❶, 77 Hesse St., is probably the best restaurant in Victoria. The fish is as fresh as they boast, unbeatably tasty, and perfectly priced at $4-8. (☎5258 1312. Open daily 11am-8:30pm.) For a cheerful outdoor dining experience, the **Acoustic Garden Cafe ❷,** 2 Hobson St., has an array of tasty and trendy foods with vegetarian options. Having one of their excellent desserts on the back patio is a true indulgence. (☎5258 4945. Lunch $5.50-13. Breakfast served 9-11:30am. Open daily 9am-5pm.) **Beaches Cafe ❶,** 1/84 Hesse St., serves the best smoothies ($4-5.50) for miles as well as a reasonably priced and very filling breakfast for $10. (☎5258 4470. Open daily 8am-5pm, closes early in off-season.) There's a **supermarket** at 73 Hesse St. (☎5258 1727. Open M-Sa 8am-7pm, Su 9am-6pm.)

The Dive Centre (see above) runs scuba certification classes and a dive charter service, as well as a **snorkel tour** among playful fur seals and dolphins. Rentals available. (☎5258 1188. Book ahead. 3hr. tour $65. Snorkel equipment $30 per day, wetsuits $20 per day.) **Sea All Dolphin Swim** also runs 3½hr. swim and snorkel tours with the dolphins. (☎5258 3889; www.dolphinswims.com.au. $110, on boat without snorkeling $55.) **Gamerec.com Fishing Charters** has sport and shark fishing trips as well as non-fishing sunset cruises on a small boat. (☎5258 2802; www.gamerec.com. 5hr. sport fishing $95. 8hr. shark fishing $140. Sunset cruise, BYO $30.) Visit Queenscliff's imposing **Fort** for a glimpse of the city's military history. (☎5258 1488. Entry only by 1hr. guided tour. Meet at the fort gates. M-F 1pm, Sa-Su 1pm and 3pm. $8.) The immensely popular **Blues Train** jives selected Sa; contact the visitors center for a schedule or book through Ticketek and local outlets. (☎5258 4343; www.thebluestrain.com.au. $72, concessions $65, includes lunch or dinner. Book well in advance.)

GEELONG ☎03

The second largest city in Victoria, Geelong (pop. 200,000) is an hour southwest of Melbourne on the Princes Hwy. (Hwy. 1). Historically a hub for the wool trade, today the city seeks to reinvent itself as an up-and-coming tourist destination and has achieved marginal success. Most travelers on a tour of the **Great Ocean Road** still bypass the town, but those that don't will find an industrial town with some hidden gems—the famous boardwalk bollards, nearby wineries, and some excellent drinking and eating establishments in the downtown area.

TRANSPORTATION. At the **V/Line Station** (☎13 61 96) on the western edge of the downtown area, **trains** run to Melbourne (1hr., daily every hr., round-trip $21.40) and Warrnambool (2¼hr., 3 per day, one-way $30). V/Line **buses** depart for the Great Ocean Road, making numerous stops before arriving in Apollo Bay (2½ hr.; M-F 5 per day, Sa-Su 2 per day; $22). Buses also head to Ballarat (1½hr.; M-Sa 3 per day, Su 2 per day; $12). In summer, a **free shuttle bus** circles town. Route maps and schedules are available at visitors centers and the train station.

ORIENTATION AND PRACTICAL INFORMATION. Geelong is situated on the northern side of the Bellarine Peninsula, and Corio Bay forms the northern border of the city. Princes Hwy. (Latrobe Terr.) runs north-south along the western edge of town. **Moorabool Street** heads south from the waterfront, and its intersections with **Malop** and **Little Malop Street** host most of the town's action. Detailed maps of the city are available at the visitors center. The Market Square mall lies at the intersection of Moorabool and Malop St. and contains the **visitors center.** (☎5222 6126; www.visitgeelong.org. Open daily 9am-5pm.) There is another excellent visitors center located in the Wool Museum. (☎5229 9000. Open daily 9am-5pm.) **Banks** with **ATMs** line Moorabool St., and free **Internet** access is available at the city **library,** 49 Little Malop St., on the south side of Johnston Park. (☎5222 1212. Open M-F 10am-8pm, Sa 9:30am-noon, Su 2-5pm; book at reception desk.) **Geelong Hospital** (☎5226 7111) is on Ryrie St. between Bellarine and Swanston. The **post office,** 99 Moorabool St., is located in the Market Square Mall (open M-F 9am-5:30pm, Sa 9am-1pm.) **Postal Code:** 3220.

ACCOMMODATIONS. Though far from the waterfront, **Irish Murphy's ❷,** 30 Aberdeen St., has welcoming rooms and is easy on the wallet. From the train station, take a right on Fenwick St., keeping Johnston Park to your left, then make a right on Ryrie St. and follow it for two blocks as it becomes Aberdeen St. Amenities include laundry, kitchen, and a comfortable TV lounge. The pub below features beautiful wood finishing and great Guinness. (☎5221 4335. Pub open M-W 11am-midnight, Th-Sa 11am-1am, Su 11am-11pm. Live music Th-Su nights. Bunks $25.) The **National Hotel ❷,** 191 Moorabool St., accommodates backpackers with basic dorm rooms. Downstairs is an inexpensive noodle bar and a rollicking, raucous pub that showcases most of the town's headline gigs. (☎5229 1211; www.nationalhotel.com.au. Pub open Tu-Su nights. Bunks $22.) The **Carlton Hotel ❸**, on Malop St. near the park between Gheringhap and Moorabool St., offers clean, decent private rooms with shared baths above a pub, as well as kitchen and laundry facilities. (☎5229 1955. Singles $49; doubles $69.)

FOOD AND ENTERTAINMENT. Noodle bars cluster together on Malop St., while Little Malop St. features slightly more upscale cafes and restaurants. A variety of eating options line Moorabool St. as it approaches the bay. Boasting 12 types of homemade cakes and pastries, the dessert case at the **Black Sheep Cafe ❸**, 26 Moorabol St., abutting the wool museum at Brougham St., lures visitors inside. Large pasta, meat, and seafood lunch dishes ($11-17) serve as a perfect precursor to dessert. (☎5223 2536. Dinner $16-28. Open daily 9am-9pm.) **Lamby's,** underneath the cafe, has in-house bands F 5pm-3am, Sa-Su 8pm-3am. (☎5223 2392. Wine-tastings on F. Admission $5, free before 10pm; more on holiday weekends.) The colorfully decorated **Wayans,** 82A Little Malop St., in city center, has authentic Balinese food in a small and lively setting. (☎5222 5422. Noodles and rice main dishes $10-14. Open M-Sa 11:30am-latenight.) Gourmet beer lovers pack the chill **Scottish Chief's Tavern Brewery ❸**, 99 Corio St., where even the fish is battered in amber ale. Enjoy the bright, conservatory-like setting or attached beer garden, down Malop St, pass Bay City Plaza on the left, and turn left on Yarra St. (☎5223 1736. Lunch $7-10; dinner $10-18. Open M-Sa 11am-1am, later on weekends. No dinner M-Tu. Live bands F-Sa.) The **Wharf Shed Cafe ❸**, 15 East Beach Rd., to the right of the carousel when facing the water, has ocean views and plentiful dining options, from wood-fired pizza ($14-22) to kangaroo fillets ($22). Monstrous desserts are $7. (☎5221 6645; www.wharfshedcafe.com.au. Live music F 7:30pm. Open M-F 10am-latenight, Sa-Su 9am-latenight. No cover.) **Le Parisien ❺**, upstairs in the same building, is about double the cost, but boasts over 350 wines. (☎5229 3110; www.leparisien.com.au. Open M-Sa noon-3pm and 6-10:30pm, Su noon-10:30pm.)

SIGHTS. The **Wool Museum,** 26 Moorabol St., displays the history of Geelong's passionate love affair with wool in an abundance of revealing exhibits, including a stuffed descendant of Oz's first flock. Don't miss the knitted tea party on the top floor, complete with woolen cookies. Every visitor is escorted through the museum by a knowledgeable guide. (☎5227 0701. Open daily 9:30am-5pm. $7.30, concessions $5.90, children $3.65. Allow 1hr.; taxidermy enthusiasts and wool aficionados may require longer.)

Geelong's **waterfront,** centered around **Cunningham Pier,** which juts out into the Bay, may not be in the same league as the Great Ocean Road, but what Geelong lacks in natural beauty it makes up for in quirky attractions. The most famous attractions along the waterfront are 104 painted wooden sculptures called the **Baywalk Bollards.** Created by artist Jan Mitchell from old timber and pilings, the tall bollards illustrate figures from Geelong's history. Inquire at the visitors center about guided tours as well as a new gallery dedicated to her work that is due to open soon. Also on the pier is a glass-enclosed 1892 **carousel.** (☎5224 1547. Open M-F 10:30am-5pm, Sa-Su 10:30am-6pm. $3.50, children $3.)

A 10min. walk away from the pier will bring you to **Eastern Beach.** The wraparound swimming enclosure in the bay has a boardwalk along the top and kiddie pool with a fountain. The beautifully designed **Botanic Gardens,** past Eastern Beach away from the city center, repres.ent Australia's diverse climate with a wide array of foliage. Follow signs from the waterfront. (☎5227 0387. Gardens open daily 7:30am-7pm. Free. Tea house on the premises open daily 11am-4pm. Guided tours W 10:30am and Su 2:30pm.)

GREAT OCEAN ROAD

The **Great Ocean Road** is one of the world's greatest driving experiences and one of Australia's proudest tourism showpieces. The 175km road snakes around celebrated surf beaches, through forests clinging to the edge of cliff-tops, across windswept coastal plains, all the while passing through idyllic hamlets, vibrant beach communities, and national parks teeming with plants and animals. Beside the road, the turbulent waves of the Southern Ocean—tossed up by winds that blow unimpeded all the way from Antarctica—have sculpted the coast's impressive stone formations. Full of natural wonders, the Great Ocean Road is what great roadtrips are made of.

Though the road itself runs from Torquay to Warrnambool, the Great Ocean Road region encompasses the entire serene and spectacular southwestern coast of Victoria, from Geelong to Nelson. Heading west from Melbourne, the first part of the Road is called the **Surf Coast.** Stretching from Torquay to Lorne, this area hosts some of the country's best surfing on seemingly endless beaches. The **Great Otway National Park,** on the 73km stretch from Anglesea to Apollo Bay, has a cool, rainy climate that nurtures tree ferns, large pines, breathtaking waterfalls, and a range of fauna. Rejoining the shoreline on the other side of the park, the Great Ocean Road follows the Shipwreck Coast. Aptly named, **Shipwreck Coast** is home to the unrelenting winds and unpredictable offshore swells that made the region a graveyard for 19th-century vessels and shaped the famous **Twelve Apostles** rock formations. Moving west, drivers can discover whales off **Warrnambool,** mutton birds in **Port Fairy,** seal colonies at **Cape Bridgewater,** towering sand dunes in **Discovery Bay Coastal Park,** and estuary fishing in **Lower Glenelg National Park.** Though visitors have been known to complete the entire Road in just a day or two, it is worth as much time as you've got; a week on the Great Ocean Rd. is a week well spent.

Peak season for the Great Ocean Road is December and January when Australians are on school holidays. To avoid the crowds, but still catch the best of Victoria's moody weather, try to plan a trip in late-November or February-March. In winter, the crowds are gone, but so is the sun. Most travelers drive the road from Melbourne heading west toward Adelaide, and *Let's Go* generally lists towns and attractions as they would be encountered by someone driving west.

PUBLIC TRANSPORT

The most popular way to see the Great Ocean Road is by **car.** Public transport along the road is infrequent and doesn't serve the national parks and other more remote, scenic areas. **V/Line trains** (☎13 61 96) from Melbourne will get you as far as Geelong, or Warrnambool on the other end. **Buses** run both ways along the Great Ocean Rd. between Geelong and Apollo Bay, passing through Torquay, Anglesea, Lorne, and other towns along the way (M-F 5 per day each way, Sa-Su 2 per day each way). On Fridays year-round and also on Mondays from December to January, one special **"coast link" V/Line bus** runs between Apollo Bay and Warrnambool, making stops in Port Campbell and other towns, with brief forays into lookout points along the Shipwreck Coast; otherwise, it is difficult to progress farther west than Apollo Bay via public buses, which often run only once a week.

Breathtaking in both senses of the word, **bicycling** along the highway is increasingly popular. For those with the time and the motivation, it may well be the best way to get off-the-beaten path on one of the most trafficked roads in Australia. Cyclists should be well prepared, as the narrow, winding road (with no protective shoulder in most places) and the steep hilly topography of some sections of the route make for difficult riding conditions.

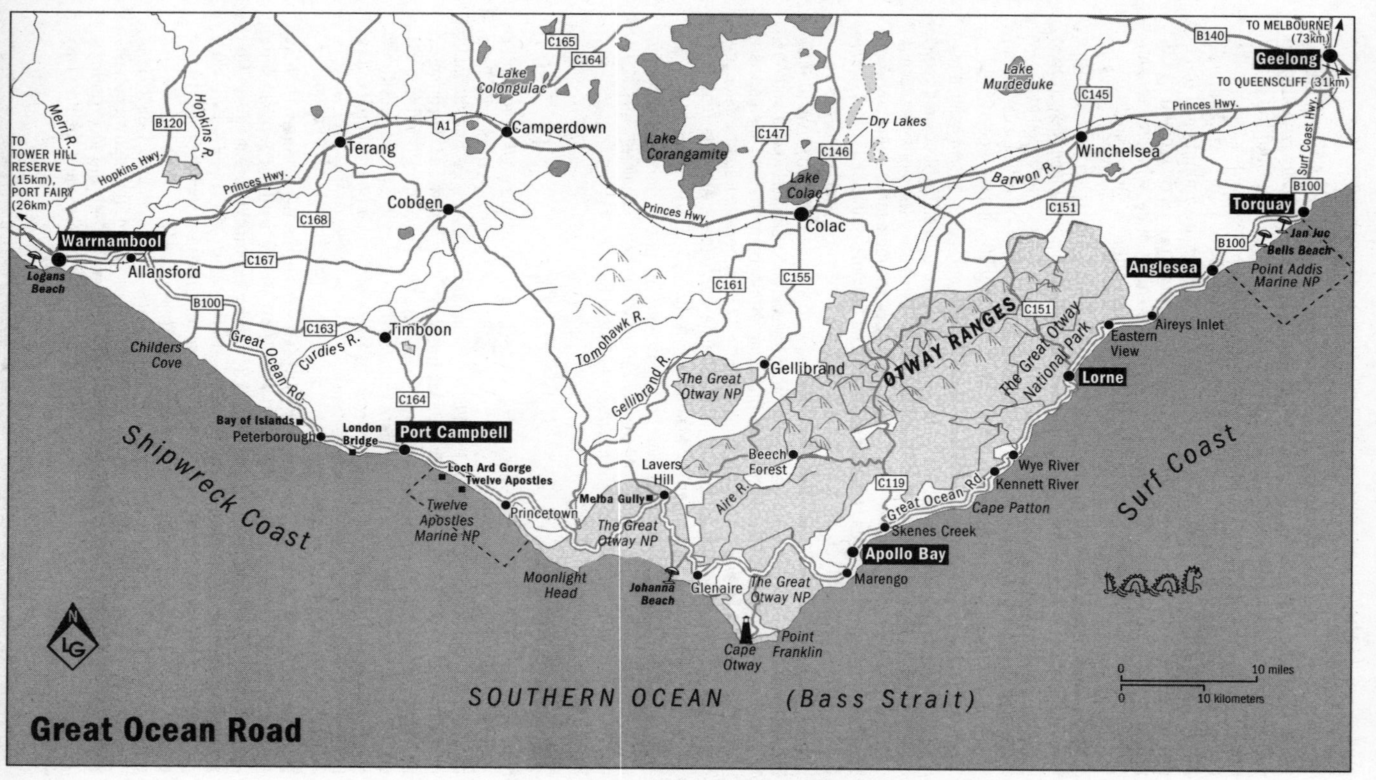
Great Ocean Road
TO MELBOURNE (73km)
Geelong
TO QUEENSCLIFF (31km)
B140
Lake Murdeduke
C145
Princes Hwy.
Surf Coast Hwy.
Winchelsea
Barwon R.
B100
Torquay
Jan Juc
Bells Beach
Point Addis Marine NP
Anglesea
Aireys Inlet
Eastern View
Lorne
The Great Otway National Park
OTWAY RANGES
C151
Wye River
Kennett River
Cape Patton
Great Ocean Rd.
Skenes Creek
Apollo Bay
Marengo
Surf Coast
C119
The Great Otway NP
Point Franklin
Cape Otway
Glenaire
Johanna Beach
Aire R.
Beech Forest
Lavers Hill
Melba Gully
Moonlight Head
Princetown
Gellibrand
Gellibrand R.
Tomahawk R.
C161
C155
Colac
Lake Colac
C146
C147
Dry Lakes
Lake Corangamite
Princes Hwy.
C165
C164
Lake Colongulac
Camperdown
A1
Terang
Cobden
C168
Timboon
Curdies R.
C163
Twelve Apostles
Loch Ard Gorge
Twelve Apostles Marine NP
Port Campbell
London Bridge
Peterborough
Bay of Islands
Shipwreck Coast
Childers Cove
B100
Allansford
C167
Warrnambool
Logans Beach
Hopkins Hwy.
Hopkins R.
B120
Merri R.
TO TOWER HILL RESERVE (15km), PORT FAIRY (26km)
SOUTHERN OCEAN (Bass Strait)
0
10 miles
0
10 kilometers

VICTORIA

BUS TOURS

Those without a car should consider one of the **bus tours** along the Great Ocean Road. They offer more flexibility than public transport, and generally come in two varieties: those that make a loop starting and ending in Melbourne and those that run between Melbourne and Adelaide. The loop option is less scenic, leaving the Great Ocean Road for the relatively nondescript Princes Hwy. at Port Campbell. For those heading west from Melbourne to Adelaide, there are a number of three-day tours connecting the cities via the Great Ocean Rd. at prices rivaling air or rail travel. Those short on time can choose to do the trip all at once, while some companies allow those with more time to get on and off as often as they want.

Otway Discovery (☎9654 5432; www.otwaydiscovery.primetap.com) is the most affordable and flexible of the loop tours. The friendly drivers run along the Road from Melbourne to Port Campbell and then back to Melbourne via the inland route, with the option to hop on and off. There is no time limit for those paying for the hop-on, hop-off option, but you only get to do the loop once. Hostel pickup daily 7-8am. Day tour $85, hop-on, hop-off $95.

Wildlife Tours (☎1300 661 730; www.wildlifetours.com.au) runs a 1-day highlight tour of the Great Ocean Road (Melbourne to Port Campbell), as well as structured 3-day round-trip tours that include the Grampians and 2- or 3-day Melbourne-to-Adelaide trips. Stopovers may be allowed, provided the next bus has room for you. One-day Great Ocean Road tour $75; 2-day Great Ocean Road and Grampians tour $135; Melbourne-Adelaide from $185; $10 off with ISIC/NOMADS/VIP/YHA.

Groovy Grape Getaways (☎1800 661 177; www.groovygrape.com.au) runs a backpacker-oriented all-inclusive 3-day trip in either direction between Melbourne and Adelaide, hitting all the main sights and providing all accommodation, meals, park entrance fees, and even a knowledgeable guide. $325 per person. Departs Melbourne year-round Tu and F 7am, additional tour in summer Su; departs Adelaide Tu and Sa 7am, additional tour in summer Th. No hop-on/hop-off.

Goin' South (☎1800 009 858; www.goinsouth.com.au) does a tour similar to the Groovy Grape with 3-day trips whose costs cover everything except lunches. From $295. Departs Adelaide M and Th; departs Melbourne Th and Su.

VICTORIA

TORQUAY ☎03

Torquay (tor-KEY) is a lively mecca for Victoria's surfers during the summer months, and boarders from all over the world make the pilgrimage to nearby **Bells Beach** every Easter for the Rip Curl Pro Classic. Ubiquitous gear shops line the main boulevard, appropriately named **Surf Coast Highway** (also known as Torquay or Geelong Rd.). The first city along the Surf Coast stretch, Torquay, a town infused with surf culture, lures as many tourists to its surf shops as it does surfers to its shores. Whether shopping or surfing, Torquay is the spot to rip it up or whip it out (a credit card, that is) on the Great Ocean Road.

TRANSPORTATION. **V/Line buses** (☎13 61 96) leave from the Torquay Holiday Resort by Bells Beach Lodge on the Surf Coast Hwy. Buses head north to Geelong (25min.; M-F 4 per day, Sa-Su 2 per day; $5.30) and west on the Great Ocean Rd., making numerous stops, before arriving in Apollo Bay (2hr.; M-F 4 per day, Sa-Su 2 per day; $18). **Bellarine Transit** (☎5223 2111) provides buses to Geelong (M-F 14 per day, Sa 6 per day, and Su 3 per day; $5.30) and to Apollo Bay (M-F 4 per day, Sa-Su 2 per day; $18). Most commercial activity takes place along the Surf Coast Hwy. (Geelong Rd.), a continuation of the Great Ocean Rd., or just off the highway on Gilbert St., where there is a well-marked shopping district with **ATMs** and food options. The **Visitors Centre,** 120 Surf Coast Hwy., is in the Surfworld Museum in the Surf City

Plaza retail center. (☎5261 4219. Open daily 9am-5pm. **Internet** access $7 per hr.) The **Torquay Pharmacy** is on Gilbert St. (☎5261 2270. Open M-Sa 9am-6pm, Su 10am-5pm.) The **post office** is located at 23 Pearl St. **Postal Code:** 3228.

ACCOMMODATIONS AND FOOD. Book ahead in summer and for the Easter surfing competition. **Bells Beach Lodge ❷**, 51-53 Surf Coast Hwy., is a brightly painted, bungalow-style bunkhouse with surfing posters, magazines, and nearly constant screenings of surf documentaries. Bells Beach has clean bathrooms, lockers, bike and surf equipment rentals, Internet access ($5 per hr.), and good vibrations. There's a free courtesy bus to town and nearby beaches three times daily. (☎5261 7070; www.bellsbeachlodge.com.au. Key and linen deposit $10. Dorms $20-25; doubles $50-60.) **Torquay Holiday Resort ❸**, 55 Surfcoast Hwy., next to Bells Beach Lodge, has a pool, spa, and tennis court and is a great family park with a host of activities for kids. (☎5261 2493. Check-in 2-8pm. Powered sites $25-54; cabins $55-87, deluxe $127-219.)

Hordes of surfers with the munchies provide a large market for the takeaway joints that dominate Torquay's food scene, centered on Gilbert and Bell St. near the beach. There are also a few notable options on Surf Coast Hwy. **Soul Fuel ❷**, 1/57 Surfcoast Hwy., is a hip eatery with a welcoming atmosphere and eclectic fare. (☎5261 4999. Open daily 7:30am-4:30pm, or until the crowd leaves. Large wraps up to $7.50. Cash or EFTPOS only.) Next door, **Spooner's ❶**, 2/57 Surfcoast Hwy., is a cheap and friendly coffeehouse with big wraps and sandwiches for $7-9.50. (☎5261 3887. Open daily 7am-5pm.) **Sandbah Cafe ❷**, 21 Gilbert St., is a chill cafe with award-winning coffee. Always original and usually local live music acts play every Su. (☎5261 6414. Lattes $3. Focaccias and wraps $12-15. Open daily 7am-6pm; Dec.-Mar. F-Sa longer hours for dinner.) There's a **Safeway** supermarket with a LiquorWorks attached on Gilbert St. (open daily 7am-midnight) and a local **market** at the end of Gilbert St. all day Su, featuring food, artwork, and bands. Pick up a schedule at the visitors center.

SURFING. Peak **surfing** season is March to September. The **Torquay Surf Beach,** off Bell St., a 10min. walk from Bells Beach Lodge, is the first in a string of surfable beaches that stretch down the coast. The king of them all is **Bells Beach,** the first surfing reserve in the world, where the reef breaks attract top professional surfers for the Easter **Rip Curl Pro Classic**. Beware, Bells is for advanced surfers only. It's a 10min. drive from town, though the most scenic way to reach it is via the **Surf Coast Walk,** a trail that begins at the beach in Torquay. The pedestrian trail, also great for mountain biking, follows the coast for nearly 35km, passing **Jan Juc,** comprised of reef and beach breaks, the second-best surfing site after Bells. The trail continues to Bells, then Point Addis, Anglesea, and Airey's Inlet. For closer swimming beaches, cross the highway from Bells Beach Lodge and continue 10min. down Zeally St. to Zeally Bay, where **Cozy Corner, Torquay Front Beach,** and **Fisherman's Beach** await.

Surf lessons are available from **Go Ride a Wave** (see **Anglesea,** below) and **Eco-Adventure Sports,** 55b Surfcoast Hwy. Eco-adventure rents surfboards and offers surf classes. (lessons ☎5261 9170, general ☎5261 2170; www.southernexposure.com.au.) The **Torquay Surfworld Museum,** 120 Surf Coast Hwy., located in the Surf City Plaza retail center, has a higher concentration of boards than most of the area shops. The museum pays tribute to surfing history and culture, providing interactive video tours, explanations of surfable waves, and info on the evolution of the surfboard. (☎5261 4219. Open daily 9am-5pm. Adults $8.50, concessions $6.)

FROM TORQUAY TO LORNE

POINT ADDIS. The turn-off for **Point Addis** appears abruptly about 8km west of Torquay on the Great Ocean Rd. The point offers outstanding views of Victoria's western coast, broken up by silty clay and gray cliffs. A trail to the left, 200m before

VICTORIA

the carpark, will take you to the **Pixie Caves,** a small cove beach on the east side of the point with small caves carved out of the sandstone. Between Point Addis and the highway is the beginning of the **Koorie Cultural Walk** (2km, 1hr. round-trip) which leads through the **Ironbark Basin Reserve.** Displays along the way narrate the history of the Aborigines who once inhabited the area.

ANGLESEA. Anglesea has two main attractions: an excellent **swimming beach** just off the Great Ocean Rd. and a **golf course** whose trees provide shade to reclining kangaroos (off Noble St., follow the sign). You can photograph the kangaroos from afar, but tramping around on the fairways is treacherous as there's danger of being attacked by irritated kangaroos (and flying golf balls). Anglesea sees considerably fewer overnighters than neighboring Lorne and Torquay, and those looking for a break from the crowds should consider **Anglesea Backpackers ❸,** 40 Noble St., a hostel with relaxed common areas and breezy rooms. (☎5263 2664; www.home.iprimus.com.au/angleseabackpacker. Dorms $23-25; double ensuite $70-80, extra person $23-25. Prices vary.) Surf lessons, including board and wetsuit rentals, can be found with **Go Ride A Wave,** 143B Great Ocean Rd. They also have sea kayaking expeditions through www.gopaddling.com.au. (☎1300 132 441; www.gorideawave.com. Standard 2hr. surf lesson, $50. Booking required.) **Eco-Adventure Sports,** see p. 619, also operates in Anglesea, Torquay, and Lorne.

LORNE ☎03

If you had to choose only one town to visit along the Great Ocean Rd., Lorne would be it. Visitors stream into the town to experience the impressive peaks of the **Otways** (for info on the **Great Otway National Park,** see p. 623), the beautiful and expansive beaches, backpackers in the shadow of million-dollar vacation homes, and the multitude of trendy shops, bistros, and surf shacks.

The Great Ocean Rd. morphs into **Mountjoy Parade** as it passes through town. **V/Line buses** depart four times daily during the week and twice daily on weekends from the Commonwealth Bank at 68 Mountjoy Pde. to: Apollo Bay (1hr., $5.80), Geelong (1½hr., $13.30), and Melbourne (2½hr., $26.20). In January there is free shuttle bus service along Mountjoy Pde. from the supermarket to the Lorne pier. (Every half hour, daily 10am-6pm.) The **visitors center,** 15 Mountjoy Pde., has excellent maps and information on activities, hiking, and camping in the area as well as **Internet** access. (☎5289 1152; www.visitsurfcoast.com or www.greatoceanroad.org. Internet $6 per hr. Open daily 9am-5pm.) Behind the visitors center, there is a good **book exchange** (Open daily 11am-4pm).

Great Ocean Backpackers (YHA) ❷, 15 Erskine Ave., is a colony of wooden cabins set amid the trees on the hillside behind the supermarket, just before the bridge. Free amenities include a communal kitchen, laundry, BBQ, boogie board loan, and birdseed to feed the native birds, as well as maps for the Great Otway National Park. (☎5289 1809. Book months in advance for school holidays. Dorms $23.50, $20 with YHA; private rooms $50-70; family rooms $75-90.) The **Erskine River Backpackers ❷,** 4 Mountjoy Pde., on the right just over the bridge as you enter town from Geelong, sports airy facilities and a large, tidy kitchen. A balcony with hammocks and picnic tables overlooks a leafy courtyard on one side and the town on the other. (☎5289 1446. Pool table, TV, and table tennis. Dorms $25; doubles $60. Weekly rates available. Cash only.)

Free **camping ❶** without amenities is available inside the Great Otway National Park (☎5289 1732, see p. 623). Complete camping facilities are available 7km west of town at the beautiful **Cumberland River Camping Reserve ❶.** Several short walks lead from the area and there is a little swimming beach across the road. (☎5289 1790; cumberland@netconnect.com.au. Sites from $15; cabins $60.) The visitors center has info on the numerous **B&Bs ❺** in the area and will help with booking.

Trendy **Q-dos ❸**, off Alenvale Rd., makes up for its distance from town with a wealth of offerings, including outdoor seating in a forest overlooking a pond. Follow signs from Mountjoy Parade; take Otway St. from Mountjoy Pde., then Alenvale Rd. at the rotary. The atmosphere is chic but relaxed. If the meal prices ($18-29) aren't in your budget, have a glass of wine at the bar and tour the spacious modern-art gallery. Local bands play frequently. They have also recently added modern Asian-style accommodations (from $180, includes full breakfast) to the compound. (☎5289 1989; www.qdosarts.com. Open Jan. daily 9am-5pm, dinner 6-9:30pm; off-peak daily 9am-5pm, dinner W-M 6-9:30pm.) **Grandma Shields Bakery ❶**, on Mountjoy Parade across from the beach, has award-winning pies ($3.70) that are the best budget meal in town. (Open daily 7am-6pm, later in summer. Cash only.) **Reifs Restaurant and Bar ❷**, 84 Mountjoy Pde., next to the movie theater, is cool, casual, and loaded with beer on tap. (☎5289 2366. Gourmet sandwiches $10-16. Open daily 8:30am-latenight. Hours reduced in winter.) Underneath Erskine River Backpackers, **Lorne Greens** sells somewhat expensive but high-quality produce and delicious breads and cheeses. (☎5289 1383. Open daily in summer 8am-7pm; in winter 9am-6pm. Cash and debit only.) **FoodWorks** supermarket, 1 Great Ocean Rd., is just before the bridge as you enter town from Geelong. (Open daily 7am-9pm.) The **Lorne Hotel,** 176 Mountjoy Pde., is the place to be on Friday and Saturday nights. Lorne's entire 20-something population turns out to dance the night away at this hip locale with floor-to-ceiling picture windows. (☎5289 1409; www.lornehotel.com.au. Ages 18 and older. Cover up to $10, more for special events. Open 10am-late, usually 1-3am.)

Lorne has good **surf** right in town, (both beach and reef breaks) although the area is not as famous for surfing as Torquay or Apollo Bay. Prime spots with parking are available all along the Great Ocean Rd. toward Apollo Bay. Beginners who want to rent a board should head to **Lorne Surf Shop,** 130 Mountjoy Pde. The shop rents foam boards for new surfers as well as wetsuits and boogie boards. (☎5289 1673. Boards $25 per ½-day, $40 per day. Wetsuit $15/20. Boogie boards $15/20. Open daily 9:30am-5:30pm.) You can also take a **reef, gamefishing,** or **scenic tour** with **Lorne Fishing Charters.** (☎0412 840 755 or 0407 891 049. 4-person min., 10-person max.) Sleepy koalas lounge in trees on Grey River Rd., in Kennet River, halfway between Lorne and Apollo Bay on the Great Ocean Rd. To get a glimpse of these quintessential Australian creatures, head west along the road, turn right directly after the bridge and the Kennet River sign, just before the caravan park.

APOLLO BAY ☎03

In an idyllic cove at the base of the rolling Otway mountains, Apollo Bay is a sleepy beach hamlet that has seen a boom in tourism in recent years. As increasing numbers of sun-lovers gather at beachfront cafes, waves lap at the shore, and glow-worms light up the quiet nights. Apollo Bay remains a placid setting with ample accommodations, making it a good choice for a few days' rest on the Great Ocean Road. The town also boasts one of Australia's largest summer music festivals.

TRANSPORTATION AND PRACTICAL INFORMATION. The Great Ocean Rd. is the main street through town, with side streets running north. **Buses** leave from the front of the visitors center (M-F 3 per day; Sa-Su 2 per day) going to: Geelong (2½hr., $22); Lorne (1hr., $5.80); and Melbourne (3½hr., $33). Buses also run occasionally to Warrnambool (3½hr., $25) and other points west along the Great Ocean Rd. (Feb.-Nov. F only, Dec.-Jan. M and F. Concession tickets are half price.) Helpful volunteers will book accommodations and tours and advise on road closures and campsite availability in the Otways at the **Tourist Information Centre,** 100 Great Ocean Rd. (☎5237 6529. Open daily 9am-5pm.) The stretch of highway through town also has two 24hr. **ATMs. Internet** access is available at **Nautigals Cafe,** 58 Great Ocean Rd. (Open daily 8:30am-9pm. $5 per 30min.)

ACCOMMODATIONS. Apollo Bay has some of the best hostels on the Great Ocean Road. The newest of the bunch, **Eco Beach YHA ❸,** 5 Pascoe St., is a large modern beach house with tons of space to relax and enjoy top facilities. They also rent equipment and organize everything from local tours to surf lessons. (☎5237 7899, rentals ☎04 0549 5909. Dorms $33, YHA $28. Singles $65/60; doubles $80/70; family room $100/90. Surf board rentals $50 per day; body board, snorkel, or wet suit $11 per day; mountain bike $35 per day. Surf lesson $45.) **Surfside Backpackers ❶,** on the corner of the Great Ocean Rd. and Gambier St., provides guesthouse comfort at backpacker prices with two kitchens and lounge areas, a record player and TV, and great ocean views. Robyn, the owner, is one of the friendliest, most helpful people you're likely to meet. (☎5237 7263, 04 1932 2595, or 1800 357 263. Wheelchair accessible. Internet access $2 per 15min. Book ahead in summer. Reception 8am-10pm. Sites $10 per person; dorms from $20; doubles from $50, ensuite from $65.) Billing itself as "the chilled out cottage by the sea," the relaxed **Apollo Bay Backpackers ❷,** 47 Montrose Ave., is on a quiet residential street, 10min. walk from the Great Ocean Rd. For surfing enthusiasts, owner provides lessons and free transport to the ocean. (☎1800 113 045, 5237 7360, or 04 1934 0362; abbp@icisp.net.au or www.apollobaybackpackers.com.au. Free breakfast and surfboard loan. Internet access $5 per hr. Dorms $20; singles and doubles in neighboring cottage $50. Cash only.)

FOOD. Beautiful beach views come free with the meals at **La Bimba ❷,** 125 Great Ocean Rd. The upstairs cafe creates unique meals, albeit at a hefty price. Good salad and breakfast options are more reasonable. (☎5237 7411. Main courses $23-31. Open daily 8am-10pm.) The cosmic center of Apollo Bay's hippie culture is **The Sandy Feet Cafe & Health Foods ❶,** 139 Great Ocean Rd., where you can get your very own astrological calendar for $10, along with a veggie burger or salad. Award-winning pies are $4.50. (☎5237 6995. Open daily 8:30am-4:30pm. Cash only.) **The Bay Leaf Cafe ❶,** 131 Great Ocean Rd., has cheap toasted sandwiches like feta, pesto, olive, and tomato for $5.50. (☎5237 6470. Open Oct.-Mar. Su-M 8am-3:30pm, Tu-Sa 8am-latenight; Apr.-Sept. daily 8am-3:30pm.) There are two supermarkets on the Great Ocean Rd. in town. (**FoodWorks** open daily 8am-6:30pm, later in summer. **IGA** open daily 8am-8pm.)

SIGHTS AND ACTIVITIES. While the Otways get all the attention, there are plenty of things to see right around town, starting with the gently curving bay itself, best viewed from the **Marriner's Lookout.** From the carpark on Marriner's Lookout Rd., about 1.5km from Apollo Bay toward Lorne, a short, steep trail leads to the lookout. The **Apollo Bay Shell Museum,** on Noel St., with shells from all over the world, is the quirkiest museum you're likely to find on the Great Ocean Rd. (☎5237 6395. Open daily 9:30am-8pm. $3.) Apollo Bay's most illuminating feature is its **glowworms. Sunroad Tours,** 71 Costin St., picks tourgoers up just after dark for a 1½hr. daily tour (☎5237 6080 or 0429 002 296. $30, under 12 free.) Each year in March, the town grooves to the folksy sounds of the **Apollo Bay Music Festival,** which attracts acts from all over the world and a crowd that books every available bed and campsite in town. (☎5237 6761; www.apollobaymusicfestival.com. All-weekend tickets $120, concessions $100.) On Saturday mornings the **Apollo Bay Market** sets up on the foreshore and sells local handicrafts.

Hodgy's Surf Center, 143 Great Ocean Rd., rents boards and wetsuits. (Surf board $20 per 2hr.; wetsuit $10 per 2hr.; $15 per 2hr.) The best surf beach in the area for advanced surfers is **Johanna Beach,** 30min. of Apollo Bay west along the Great Ocean Rd. Johanna Red is a sealed road leading to the beach, while Johanna Blue is unsealed. For non-surfers, the beach is an excellent, and often underestimated, scenic stop amid rolling green hills. There is also surf for all levels at **Marengo** within walking distance from town and **Skenes Creek** east of town; catch the bus to Geelong to reach Skenes Creek. **Cape Otway Aviation** does round-trip scenic flights (45min.) from Apollo Bay to Port Campbell and the Twelve Apostles. (☎0407 306 065; www.capeotwayaviation.com.au. $145 for 2. Group discounts available. Book in advance.) Recreational **fishing** is a popular activity in Apollo Bay, both from the beach and with **Apollo Bay Fishing & Adventure Tours.** (4hr. tours $80, children $70.) They also organize scenic tours ($30, children $20) and shark fishing. (☎5237 7888 or 0418 121 784; www.apollobayfishing.com.au. Booking required.) For chartered fishing boats, book at the visitors center. (4hr. tours $60. Required fishing permit $5.) Those looking for a bit of exercise might want to try a **mountain biking** tour with **Otway Expeditions.** (☎5237 6341 or 0419 007 586; 2-3hr. tour for 6 or more from $55.) **Apollo Bay Sea Kayak Tours** does 2hr. kayak tours ($50) in the area. (☎04 0549 5909; www.apollobaysurfkayak.com.au.) For an airborne adventure **Wingsports** has hangliding and parasailing, and on a sunny day a flight off Mariner's Lookout can't be beat. (☎04 1937 8616; www.wingsports.com.au. Tandem paragliding from $150; tandem hangliding $250.)

VICTORIA

GREAT OTWAY NATIONAL PARK

Starting at Cape Otway, 60km west of Apollo Bay, and continuing east as far as Anglesea, the Great Otway National Park encompasses a wide variety of terrain from waterfalls to the rugged coastal walks of the Great South West Walk. Before heading off on any adventures, stop at the Apollo Bay (p. 621) or Lorne (p. 620) **visitors center,** which have the latest information on trail and campsite closures and conditions. If you arrive after visitors center hours, the YHA hostel in Lorne has maps for their guests. There is also a permanent map posted outside the Lorne visitors center beside a list of hotel vacancies that is updated nightly.

HIKES AND SIGHTS. A number of highlights can be seen by making a counterclockwise loop from **Apollo Bay** toward **Melba Gully.** From Apollo Bay, start your tour by heading east along the Great Ocean Rd. and turn left onto **Skenes Creek Road,** which offers stunning views of the surrounding mountains. Follow the sign for the **Sabine Picnic Ground,** starting point for the trail down to **Sabine Falls,** an easy to moderate walk through the rainforest. The unspectacular falls at the hike's conclusion are overshadowed by the exotic foliage and bubbling brooks along the way (1hr. round-trip). Another 10min. back down the same road will bring you to the turn-off for **Beech Forest,** C159. This is the start of **Turton's Track,** (30min.) a 12km stretch of gravel switchbacks that twist their way through the heart of the rainforest—driving down this one-lane, two-way road is a not-to-be-missed experience. Signs lead to two more waterfalls at the end of Turton's: **Hopeturn Falls,** whose roaring waters are visible from the carpark and the valley below, and **Beauchamp Falls** (30min. round-trip). The three-tiered **Triplet Falls** are nearby, just off Beech Forest Rd., on Phillip's Rd. heading west.

Along Beech Forest Rd., signs lead to the brand new steel structure, **The Otway Fly Tree Top Walk,** which is the longest (600m) and highest (25m) forest canopy walk in the world. A ranger is always on hand to answer any questions. Allow 45min. for the walk. (☎1800 300 477 or 5235 9200; www.otwayfly.com. Open daily 9am-5pm. Last ticket 6pm in summer. Adults $17, children $9.) **Madsen's Track,** 5km past Lavers Hill, 40min. from Apollo Bay, in **Melba Gully** is a short walk (30min. round-trip) through a spectacular section of rainforest that contains the grand and imposing "Big Tree," a 200-year-old Otway Messmate. Glowworms are prolific along this track at night. The **Mait's Rest trail** (30min. loop), one of the best-known rainforest walks in Victoria, is 17km west of Apollo Bay, halfway to the cape. Check out the Myrtle beech, whose roots sprang from three trees and grew together. Shortly after Johanna's Beach, heading east toward Apollo Bay, is the turn-off for the **Cape Otway Lightstation.** (☎5237 9240. Open daily 9am-5pm. $11.50, concessions $9.50. Guided tours included with admission.)

The northeastern section of the park, which used to be Angahook-Lorne State park, has more than 64km of walking trails that meander through temperate rainforests, cool fern gullies, and past striking waterfalls. It is helpful to have a car to access most of the trailheads, though several walks do start from Lorne. **Erskine Falls** (7.5km, 4hr. one-way) begins at the bridge over the Erskine River in Lorne and follows the river through the rainforests of the park and past **Splitter** and **Straw Falls** before arriving at the 38m Erskine Falls, the most famous in the area. The falls are also accessible by car; follow signs from town. Those without a ride can get a taxi from Lorne (approximately $20; inquire at the Lorne visitors center). A much shorter walk from town will bring you to **Teddy's Lookout,** a high point at the southern edge of town that presents sweeping views of forested mountains abutting wide-open ocean. (30min. walk; go up Bay St. from the Great Ocean Rd. in Lorne and make a left on George St.) The **Allenvale Mill Site,** a 30min. walk or 10min. drive from town along Allenvale Rd., is a good jumping-off point for a beautiful trail that leads to **Phantom Falls, the Canyon, Henderson,** and **Won Wondah Falls** before winding up at the Sheoak Carpark. From there, walk back along the road to Allenvale carpark (9km, 4hr. round-trip).

VICTORIA

The other main trailheads in the area, the **Blanket Leaf Picnic Area** and the **Sheoak Picnic Area,** are best reached by car, though you can also walk to them from Lorne. Various easy tracks begin at the Sheoak Picnic Area, a 1hr. walk up Allenvale Rd. from Lorne. The walk to **Sheoak Falls** follows a gentle track by the creek and eventually reaches the ocean (1½hr.), while the **Lower Kalimna Falls Walk** (1hr.) leads beneath a waterfall. From there you can continue on to the **Upper Kalimna Falls Walk** (additional 30min.). A little farther, **Phantom Falls** (1½hr. one-way) is one of the most stunning hikes in the park, providing a sense of the majesty and isolation of the rainforest. The trail is for more experienced hikers and not advisable after a heavy rain as it involves a lot of rock-hopping and can be dangerously slippery. The trail ends at Allenvale Rd., close to the Allenvale Mill Site.

CAMPING. For camping, check into the vast Bimbi Park, or use one of the five **camping ❶** areas in Otway National Park. Get information at the tourist office in Apollo Bay, or call Parks Victoria (☎13 19 63. Open daily 9am-5pm.) All camping facilities in the Otways are free, except during peak times when fees may apply. Camping in picnic areas or carparks results in a fine. There are powered sites at caravan parks but none at the campgrounds. **Blanket Bay** has nice, remote sites. Follow Lighthouse Rd., then watch signs for a left turn. The area is safe for swimming. The **Aire River** camping areas can be reached from the Great Ocean Rd., another 5km west by way of the Horden Vale turn-off. The Aire River is suitable for swimming and canoeing, and three walks diverge from the grounds. **Johanna Beach** also has basic campsites (p. 622).

Lorne Foreshore Committee of Management, Inc. runs paid camping facilities, powered and unpowered, in town. (☎5289 1382; www.lorneforeshore.asn.au. Open M-Th and Su 8am-8pm, F-Sa 8am-9pm.) **Allenvale Mill,** a 200m walk from the carpark, is among the park's nicest spots and has pit toilets. Take Otway St. from Lorne center; at the rotary, follow Allenvale Rd. The carpark is past Q-dos cafe on the left. The largest free facility is on **Hammonds Road,** in Airey's Inlet, a 30min. drive east of Lorne. Take Banbra Rd. from the Inlet.

PORT CAMPBELL

☎03

The Great Ocean Rd. makes a turn in town and becomes Lord St., the home of the Central Business District (CBD). **V/Line Buses** leave once or twice per week (Feb.-Nov. F; Dec.-Jan. M and F) from Ocean House Backpackers and head to **Melbourne** ($25) and **Warrnambool** ($13), stopping at most towns along the way. If you have no other transportation, you can call a **taxi** (☎5598 3777) to visit the Twelve Apostles. The **visitors center,** on the corner of Morris and Tregea St., one block south of Lord St., has a wealth of data on the Great Ocean Rd. (☎5598 6089. Open daily 9am-5pm.) Wireless **Internet** access ($5 per 30min) is available at Loch Ard Motor Inn, on Lord St. The **post office** is in the **Port Campbell General Store,** Lord St., which also has basic **groceries.** (☎5598 6379. Open daily 8am-7pm.) **Postal Code:** 3269.

The **Port Campbell National Park Cabin and Camping Park ❷,** Morris St., next to the visitors center, has BBQ, showers, and laundry. (☎5598 6492; www.portcampbell.nu/camping. Reception 8:30am-9pm; closed earlier in winter. Powered sites for two $24; unpowered sites $21.50; ensuite cabins from $95, extra adult $12, extra child $6.) The caravan park also runs the best hostel in town, the **Ocean House Backpackers ❷,** facing the beach on Cairns St., has a log-cabin feel and ocean views. The common area has board games and a fireplace. Check in at the camping park (see below) if the owner is out. (☎5598 6223; www.portcampbell.nu/oceanhouse. $25.) The **Port Campbell Hostel ❷,** 18 Tregea St., one block south of Lord St., around the corner from the beach, has a huge kitchen and great location, but has a vacant feel as the staff is often out. Laundry facilities and a BBQ area with picnic tables are available. Weary travelers are also offered free tea, coffee, and soup. (☎/fax 5598 6305. Key deposit $5. Towels $1. **Internet** access $2 per 15min. Reception 8-10am and 5-10pm. Dorms $24; doubles $55; cabins $70. The annex has dorms for $21 and camping facilities for $10 per person, $15 for two.)

The throngs of tourists passing through Port Campbell have created a demand for all kinds of restaurants, from beachfront takeaways to expensive balcony restaurants. Closing hours fluctuate depending on the crowds. The best place to grab a quick meal is **12 Rocks Cafe ❶,** on Lord St. The smoothies ($5) are the perfect refreshment after a day on the beach, while their cheap breakfasts ($4-6.50) are an excellent start to the day. (☎5598 6123. Focaccias and wraps $7. Open daily 7:30am-3pm.) Nearly everything at **Nico's Pizza and Pasta ❸,** 25 Lord St., is delicious. The large pizza ($16-20.50) will satiate a standard lunch appetite. Mediums are much smaller. (☎5598 6131. Open daily 6pm-late.) The touristy **Bombora Beach Bar ❷,** 19 Lord St., has upscale meals with an ocean view worth the price. (☎5598 6166. Day meals $14.50-17.50; dinner from $19.50. Open M and Th-Su 11am-late-night, Tu-W 11am-5pm.)

The gentle Port Campbell **Discovery Walk** (3.9km) begins at the cliff base at the western end of the beach or at the carpark west of the bay. There are several reef breaks for more advanced surfers along the rocky coast, while the small beach along Cairns St. is good for swimming and has lifeguards on duty Sa-Su during school holidays. **Port Campbell Boat Charters,** headquartered at the service station on Lord St., offers crafts for diving, fishing, or sightseeing. (☎5598 6411. $50-150 per person, 4-person min.)

THE SHIPWRECK COAST

Stretching from Port Fairy in the west to the rock formations just east of Port Campbell, the Shipwreck Coast has panoramic views that attract thousands of visitors each year. From the Twelve Apostles to Tower Hill, tourists pull out their cameras to get a snapshot of the picturesque coastline. Though most of the big sights can be covered in a day of driving, slowing down to get to the lesser-known sights or hikes will afford a chance to encounter this stretch of coastline without the crowds. The sights below are listed from east to west.

CHILDERS COVE. Halfway between Port Campbell and Warrnambool, **Childers Cove** is off the Great Ocean Rd. at the end of a narrow, 7km dead-end road. It is comprised of three private inlets with access to pristine, deserted beaches. Paths from the carpark meander along the craggy coast leading to stunning views, each more spectacular than the last, of limestone cliffs and aqua-blue waters. The last cove, **Marnane's Bay,** has bathroom facilities, but there is no camping.

TWELVE APOSTLES AND LOCH ARD GORGE. The **Twelve Apostles,** 12km east of Port Campbell on the Great Ocean Rd., are the most famous of the rock formations in the area, and with good reason. At sunset, the stones blaze red before fading slowly to shadows in the waning light, and the spectacular vista will be enough to make you forget the hordes of tourists jostling for a view. Black flies abound in the summer; take bug spray with you. The **Interpretive Centre** has displays that give more information about the rocks, and from the center a walkway goes under the highway to the Twelve Apostle boardwalk. (Center open daily 9am-5pm.) For information about the Apostles and surroundings visit www.12apostlesnatpark.org. **The Gibson Steps,** 2km east of the Twelve Apostles, provide a view of one of the Apostles from sea level, where you can better appreciate its enormous scale.

A number of aerial tours of the Twelve Apostles are available. **12 Apostles Helicopters,** 9400 Great Ocean Rd., flies over the rocks from just outside of Port Campbell. (☎5598 6161 or 04 1852 3561; www.12ah.com. Open daily 9am-5pm.) **Great Ocean Road Helicopters** takes off from behind the Centre, providing breathtaking views at heartbreaking prices. (☎5598 8266; www.greatoceanroadhelicopters.com. Open daily 9am-dusk. 10min. flight over the Apostles $90. 15min. flights to London Bridge and back $120. 25min. flights all the way up to the Bay of Martyrs $195 per person for 2 people, $170 per person for 3.)

Another worthwhile stop-off, 3km west of the Twelve Apostles toward Port Campbell, is **Loch Ard Gorge,** named for the clipper *Loch Ard* that wrecked there in 1878, killing 52 people. The park around the gorge offers lookout points and walks to sights like **Thunder Cave, Island Archway, Mutton Bird Island,** and the **Blowhole,** a churning, spitting seawater lake a few hundred meters inland, connected to the ocean by an underground tunnel. You can visit the **Historic Glenample Homestead,** 1km east of the Apostles, which provided refuge to two shipwreck survivors. The small museum inside tells the history of the wreck and contains authentic artifacts from the original homestead. (☎5598 8004; www.glenamplehomestead.com.au. Open daily 10am-5:30pm. Free.) Theater companies occasionally stage apt productions in the Gorge, including Shakespeare's *The Tempest.* The homestead also offers parking ($5) for those doing the Great South West Walk.

BAY OF ISLANDS AND BAY OF MARTYRS. To the west of Port Campbell, the **Bay of Islands Coastal Park** begins at little Peterborough and stretches 33km west along the coast. A number of scenic stopovers allow views of other limestone oddities, from pillars to islands to arches, all shaped by the Southern Ocean and the unrelenting Antarctic winds from 3000km away. Notable features include **The Arch, The Grotto,** and **London Bridge.** The **Bay of Martyrs** and **Bay of Islands** (both turn-offs clearly labeled on the Great Ocean Rd.) offer stunning views and walks among smaller limestone formations on the beach; in general the crowds are thinner than at Twelve Apostles. **Worm Bay,** a poorly-marked turn-off directly before the Bay of Martyrs, is perhaps the best viewpoint along this stretch. Turn where the sign reads "Carpark not suitable for trailers."

TIMBOON FARMHOUSE CHEESE. The **Mousetrap** shop, on a rustic farm 15min. west of Port Campbell and 13km off the Great Ocean Rd., offers free samples of its homemade organic cheeses. All of the cheeses are for sale, as well as other local products such as ice cream and cheesecake. There is an outdoor seating area in a garden where you can enjoy a cheese platter ($12-34) and local wines for $5 per glass. (☎5598 3387. Open Oct.-Apr. daily 10:30am-4pm; May-Sept. W-Su 10:30am-4pm. Follow the well-marked signs from Port Campbell or the Great Ocean Rd.)

TOWER HILL. Tower Hill, 15km west of Warrnambool on the Princes Hwy., is a game reserve encapsulated in a dormant volcano. Kangaroos, emus, and koalas run about the grounds and carpark. Be extra careful when driving around corners. There are toilets and picnic areas but no camping inside the park. The entrance to the park leads past lava cliffs and numerous 4WD tracks which only park rangers can use. Wandering off on the tracks is not forbidden, but not encouraged as they are unmarked and it is easy to lose your way. Public access is by foot only.

There are four short guided walks in the park that provide a good overview of the reserve. All leave from the main carpark at the **information center** (open M-F 9am-5pm, Sa-Su 10am-4pm.) The **Peak Climb** is a steep, paved walkway up to the top of Tower Hill and affords a view of the lake within the park grounds (20min. round-trip). **Wagon Bay** and **Lava Tongue Boardwalk** are both scenic, easy loops through the woods (each 30min. round-trip). The **Journey to the Last Volcano** is an easy, longer walk that stretches farther into the park (1hr. round-trip). As you exit the park, it is possible to drive around the outer rim of the volcano for a spectacular view of the reserve.

VICTORIA

WARRNAMBOOL ☎03

The largest city on the Great Ocean Rd., Warrnambool (pop. 30,000) is just developed enough to support dance-until-3am nightlife and a host of amenities not found elsewhere along the coast. While its natural attractions lag behind some of the other stops on the Great Ocean Road, it does have beautiful beaches and southern right whales off the coast Jun.-Sept. The variety of entertaining activities like bowling, miniature golf, whale watching, beaches, and parks makes Warrnambool a popular holiday destination for families.

TRANSPORTATION. The **V/Line Railway Station** (☎5561 4277) is on the south end of town, just north of Lake Pertobe on Merri St. **V/Line trains** run to Melbourne (3hr. 10min., 3 per day; $43.20, off-peak $30.20) and Geelong (2hr. 10min., 3 per day; $30.90, off-peak $21.70). **V/Line buses** run to: Apollo Bay (3hr.; F only, $26.20); Ballarat (2½hr.; M-F 1 per day; $22.70); Mount Gambier (2½hr.; 1 per day; $34); Port Fairy (30min.; M-Sa 2 per day, Su 1 per day; $5.10); and Portland (1½hr.; M-Sa 2 per day, Su 1 per day; $15.30). Student tickets are half price. In town, **Transit Southwest** runs seven bus routes across the city, with stops at each location roughly on the hour; pick up a timetable from the visitors center or buy one at a newsstand for $0.20. (☎5562 1866. $1.20, concessions $0.80. Tickets good for 2hr. of unlimited rides.) For a **taxi,** call ☎13 10 08.

ORIENTATION AND PRACTICAL INFORMATION. The Princes Hwy., which becomes **Raglan Parade** in town, runs along the top edge of the downtown area. The town's main streets run south toward the sea from Raglan Pde., with Banyan St., on the east side of downtown, turning into **Pertobe Road** to round the lake (before heading down to the bay, the beach, and the breakwater). **Liebig Street,** the town's main drag, heads south from Raglan Pde. at the McDonald's, crossing Lava St., Koroit St., and Timor St. before winding up at Merri St. on the southern edge of downtown. It is lined with restaurants, pubs, **banks,** and **ATMs.** The **visitors center,** in the Maritime Museum at Flagstaff Hill on Merri St. near Ban-

THE TIM TAM INDEX

Tim Tams, the famous Australian cookies, are as elusive to foreigners as they are delicious. Available at every Aussie grocery store, these rectangles of chocolatey heaven are one of the best reasons to go Down Undah.

When traveling through Australia, I use the omnipresent desserts to gauge my whereabouts. Like any good budget traveler, my first stop in any town is the grocery store, where I saunter through the cookie aisle and consider the prices. In metropolitan areas such as Melbourne, Tim Tams can be purchased for as little as $1.98; in remote locations, like convenience stores deep within the Snowy Mountains, they are sold for as much as $4.60. The sharp increase in price is directly proportional to how far I have trekked into the "Never Never"—thus, the Tim Tam becomes a numerical representation of exactly how deep in the middle of nowhere I am.

I call this phenomenon the "Tim Tam Index." With an average price of $2.72, the cookie acts as an unofficial currency.

Ironically, you'll find that your desire to consume Tim Tams grows with their increasing scarcity and price. So when in Australia's most distant reaches, offer your fellow travelers a nibble of the chocolate peace-pipe; take it from me, it's the best way to make new friends.

—Brandon Presser

yan, provides free maps of the area and has a message board with current events. (☎5559 4620 or 1800 637 725; www.warrnamboolinfo.com.au. Open daily 9am-5pm.) Other services include: **police,** 214 Koroit St. (☎5560 1333); **library,** in the city council building at the south end of Liebig St. near the intersection with Timor St., with free **Internet** access (☎5562 2258; open M-Th 9:30am-5pm, F 9:30am-8pm, Sa 10am-noon); and two **post offices,** one on Koroit St. and the other on Timor St., both between Kepler and Liebig. (Open M-F 9am-5pm.) **Postal Code:** 3280.

ACCOMMODATIONS. Book well ahead in summer for the **Warrnambool Beach Backpackers ❷,** 17 Stanley St., as their colorful rooms close to the beach are undoubtedly the best in town. The friendly owners provide everything a backpacker could want, including Internet access ($6 per hr.), a licensed bar with a tiki theme, big screen TV with DVD, a pool table, a full kitchen, free use of mountain bikes, coin laundry, and coke and snack machines. The back bunkrooms are quiet and the mattresses are thick. (☎5562 4874; www.beachbackpackers.com.au. Key deposit $10. Reception till 11pm, Tu and F until 10pm. Dorms $23; ensuite doubles $65, extra person $20.) **Cooee ❷,** 4 Liebig St., right by Smith Ave., has basic accommodations at low rates. (☎5562 1455. Internet access $1.50 per 15min. Dorms $20; singles $25; doubles $45-55. Also has multi-night deals.) **Hotel Warrnambool ❸,** 185 Koroit St., on the corner with Kepler, is an old-fashioned hotel with a nice pub downstairs. (☎5562 2377; ozonel@hotkey.net.au. Rooms $40, includes cooked breakfast. Pub open daily 11am-latenight.) If all the other beds in town are booked up, the **Stuffed Backpacker ❷,** 52 Kepler St., next to the cinema, has rooms in an old building. Check in at the candy shop below the hostel. The sign out front reads "Backpackers." (☎5562 2459. Internet access $2-3 per 15min; price depends on time of day. Key deposit $10. Reception 9am-10pm. Dorms $20; singles $30; doubles $45; $2 off with VIP, NOMADS, and YHA.)

FOOD. The bottom half of Liebig St. has a cluster of great restaurants and bars. It's worth coming to Warrnambool just to eat the food at **Bojangles ❷,** 61 Liebig St. Simon's award-winning, gourmet wood-fired pizzas are teeming with delicious, creative toppings, providing a frenzy of delight for the taste buds. The *Back of Bourke* pizza, which features kangaroo prosciutto with rocket leaves, slow roasted bush-spiced tomatoes, and seeded mustard aioli, is a masterpiece. (Restaurant ☎5562 8751, takeaway 5562 0666; www.bojangles.com.au. Open daily 5pm-latenight.) Right up the street from Bojangles, **Figseller's Cafe ❷,** 89 Liebig St., has a nice feel and a variety of food options ($7-14). Breakfast ($7-12) is served all day. (☎5562 7699; www.figsellers.com. Open M-F 7am-5:30pm, Sa-Su 8am-5:30pm.) A block down, hip **Fishtales ❶,** 63 Liebig St., cooks up a varied menu of fish, vegetarian pasta, and Asian food for under $12. (☎5561 2957. Open daily 7:45am-latenight.) **Coles** supermarket is on Lava St. between Liebig and Kepler St. (Open daily 7am-10pm.)

NIGHTLIFE. Warrnambool has the best nightlife on the Great Ocean Road. The neighborhood around the bottom of Liebig St. is where everybody in town hits the pubs. The **Seanchai Irish Pub,** 62 Liebig St., is popular with university students and backpackers. Even on slow nights, the casual atmosphere makes for a good time, as do drinks that are as cheap as they are strong (Red Bull iced tea $12). It's the only place in town with live music during the week and has 10 different beers on tap. Show *Let's Go: Australia* to Danny to get a free drink of his choice. (☎5561 7900. Open M-Tu 4pm-latenight, W-Su 2pm-latenight. Internet access $1 per 10min.). Across the street, the **Whaler's Inn** has a contemporary style for the discerning drinker, while the attached dance club, **C59,** has three dance floors with Top 40, techno, and house music. (Pints $6, cocktails from $7.50. Bar open M-Sa 11:30am-late; club open W and F-Sa 10pm-late.) The diehard latenighters hit **The Gallery Nightclub,** on the corner of Kepler and Timor St., and dance to funk and soul downstairs, or acid and trance upstairs. (Open until 3am. Cover Sa $5.)

SIGHTS AND ACTIVITIES. Whale watching is the thing to do in Warrnambool from June to October; the info center has booklets on **southern right whales.** Every winter in late May or June, a population of whales stops just off **Logans Beach,** to the east of the Bay, to give birth to their calves. They stay until September when the calves are strong enough to swim south to Antarctica. To watch these beautiful beasts roll, blow, and breach, tourists gather on viewing platforms built above the beach's delicate dune vegetation. Guests at Warrnambool Beach Backpackers can borrow bikes and ride along the Promenade to the beach. **Southern Right Charters and Diving** is Warrnambool's catch-all tour company and leads whale watches as well as fishing or diving tours. (☎5562 5044 or 0419 349 058; www.southernrightcharters.com.au. Whale watching from $35. 3½hr. fishing tour $60, includes equipment. 4-day dive course $385.)

If your visit doesn't coincide with that of the whales, don't despair; the **Flagstaff Hill Maritime Museum,** overlooking Lady Bay on Merri St., is fascinating even for those not usually intrigued by nautical history. The huge museum is an outdoor re-creation of a late 19th-century coastal village. *Shipwrecked,* the museum's spectacular light show, uses special effects to tell the story of Tom Pearce and Eva Carmichael, the ship's only survivors. (☎5564 7841. Museum open daily 9am-5pm; last entrance 4pm. 2 day pass $14, concessions $11. *Shipwrecked* shows daily at sundown, $20. Book ahead. Package deals available for museum and *Shipwrecked* with dinner option in adjoining restaurant.)

Boasting ample beach-space and parks, Warrnambool is a great spot for outdoor recreation. The 5.7km **Promenade** lining Warrnambool Bay is popular with cyclists, in-line skaters, and evening strollers. West of the bay, the lookout at **Thunder Point** has trails along the coast and inland along the Merri River. Step off the path to explore the rocks and find a secluded spot to watch the sun meet the sea. At low tide it is possible to cross the breakwater over to **Middle Island,** where a colony of fairy penguins returns at dusk to roost. (Guests at nearby Warrnambool Beach Backpackers can borrow flashlights from the front desk.) Be careful wading to the island as tides change, making the walk dangerous. Families will enjoy **Adventure Playground,** adjacent to Lake Pertobe. The park, built over 35 hectares of former swampland, features a maze, giant slides, BBQ, picnic area, and leisure walks. The protected bay has a beautiful, curved **beach,** great for swimming. **Easyrider Surf School** offers surf lessons at good prices. (☎5521 7646; www.easyridersurfschool.com.au. Daily 90min. group lessons $35, 2hr. $40; private lessons $69; 3 lessons for $99; boards, wetsuits, and sunscreen provided. Book ahead.) **Cheeseworld,** 13km east of Warrnambool in Allansford, has lots of free samples of tasty cheeses and a small farm museum. (☎5563 2130; www.cheeseworld.com.au. Open M-Sa 8:30am-5pm, Su 10am-5pm.)

PORT FAIRY

☎03

There's not much to do in Port Fairy—which is exactly its appeal. Most of the action in this sleepy town occurs on Banks St. and Sackville St., which intersect a few blocks from the water. Historical details and tour maps are available from the **Tourist Information Centre,** on Bank St. (☎5568 2682; www.port-fairy.com. Open daily 9am-5pm.) **Buses** leave from the bus depot next to the tourist center on Banks St. (☎5568 1355; office open M-F 9:10am-3pm) and head to **Hamilton** (M-Th 4:05pm, F 12:20pm) via **Warrnambool** (M-F 6 per day, Sa 4 per day, Su 1 per day; $5.40). The **library,** Sackville St. (☎5568 2248), has free **Internet** access. (Open M 10am-1pm, W and F 10am-4pm, Sa 10am-noon.) The **post office,** 25 Sackville St., also has Internet access. (Open M-F 9am-5pm. $5 per hr.) **Postal Code:** 3284.

VICTORIA

Budget travelers are welcomed by the hospitable couple at the **Emoh YHA Hostel ❷,** 8 Cox St. Located in a lovely old house built by Port Fairy's first official settler, William Rutledge, the Emoh has satellite TV, a pool table, BBQ, laundry, and Internet access ($2 per 20min.). There is a roomy kitchen, and the owners sometimes leave fresh herbs and tomatoes from their garden for guests. Free use of bikes, boogie boards, and fishing rods. (☎5568 2468; akzehir@austarnet.com.au. Book ahead Dec.-April. Dorms $23.50, YHA $20; singles $40.50/37; doubles $59/52.) **Eumarella Backpackers ❷,** on High St. in Yambuk, 17km west of Port Fairy, is the perfect spot to relax. The remote hostel is a converted 19th-century schoolhouse, run by the Peek Whurrong people of the Framlingham Aboriginal Trust. The log-cabin-like sitting area has an open wood fireplace. Amenities include a kitchen, free laundry, and canoe rental. Showers and toilets are available outside. (☎5567 1003. Dorms and doubles $17 per person.) Although the rooms at the five-star **Victoria Hotel ❺,** 42 Bank St. are decidedly non-budget, the gorgeous cottages can make great bargains for groups. Each has a huge sitting area, wood burning stove, gorgeous kitchen, full laundry facilities, and outdoor patio with BBQ. (☎5568 2891; www.vichotel.com. Cottages $165-295.)

With a creative menu, reasonable prices, and large windows overlooking the ocean, **Time and Tide Cafe,** 21 Thistle Place, down a dirt road just out of town toward Portland, is without a doubt the best place to eat on the Great Ocean Road. (☎5568 2134. Filling sandwiches from $8. Open M and Th-Su 10am-5pm.) One of the most popular breakfast spots in town, **Rebecca's Cafe ❶,** 70-72 Sackville St., sells homemade ice cream and slices of delicious apricot-plum torte ($7) along with sandwiches and soup. (☎5568 2533. Breakfast $6.50-15. Open daily 7am-6pm. Cash only.) **Jules Wine Bar,** 55 Banks St., is an upscale wine bar with a friendly feel and well-priced gourmet meals. (☎5568 3000. Lunch $12-16. Dinner $17-24. Open 10am-latenight.) Down the road, the newly opened **Ramella's Cafe Restaurant,** 19 Banks St., is one of the top lunch spots in town with a Mediterranean influenced menu. (☎5568 3322. Lunch sandwiches $9-11; risotto $13. Dinner main courses $17-24. Open daily 9:30am-latenight.) The **IGA Everyday** on Sackville St. is both grocery store and bottle shop. (Open daily 8am-8pm.)

Activities in Port Fairy are lowkey and center around the waterfront. The **beach** is excellent for swimming (lifeguards on duty daily in Jan and Sa-Su in Dec. and Feb.), and the **wharf** is a great place to watch the ships coming in while enjoying fresh seafood. **Lady Julia Percy Island,** 19km out into the Bass Strait, is home to seals, fairy penguins, and peregrine falcons. Visits can be arranged at the wharf. **Port Fairy Boat Charter,** stationed at the harbor, goes to Lady Julia for $55. The **Port Fairy Surf Shop,** 33 Bank St., is well-equipped for outdoor activities of all sorts. They rent wetsuits, body boards, water skis, and snorkel gear, and also sell new and used boards. (☎5568 2800; www.daktarisport.com.au. Open daily in summer 9am-5:30pm; otherwise 11am-5:30pm. Board rental $5 per hr. 2hr. surf lesson $30; book ahead by email or phone.) The **Kitehouse,** 27 Cox St., sells all kinds of kites, wind socks, and other high-flying toys. Free kite-flying workshop during school holidays at George Dodd's Reserve daily 3-5pm. (☎04 0831 2422 or 5568 2782. Open daily Jan. 9am-6pm; Feb.-Dec. 10am-5pm.)

Port Fairy has made a name for itself as the unlikely host for some of the world's best music. Almost every bed on the Shipwreck Coast is booked during the **Port Fairy Folk Festival,** held during Australia's Labor Day weekend in March. The festival attracts folk, blues, and country music acts from all over the world. During the weekend, the population of the town jumps from 2600 to over 30,000. (☎5568 2227; www.portfairyfolkfestival.com. Order tickets months in advance. Tickets in 2006 were $150.) From Dec. 24-Jan. 26 the town is transformed by the **Moyneyana Festival,** while mid-October brings the **Spring Music Festival.**

MOUNT ECCLES NATIONAL PARK

Mt. Eccles National Park is 50km northwest of Port Fairy toward MacArthur and 45km south of Hamilton. The 8375 hectare park was formed from the cooled lava of ancient volcanic eruptions. Now a lush landscape covers the basalt, and Lake Surprise lies nestled in the craters. All of Mt. Eccles' trails begin from the carpark and are exposed, offering no protection from the elements; so plan accordingly.

The **Summit Walk** is a 15min. round-trip walk along a grass path that leads to a lookout over Lake Surprise. If you only have time for one hike, the **Crater Rim Walk** (1½hr. round-trip) offers the best overview of the park. It also has the most difficult and varied topography. There are several photography points along the path, and koalas are a common sight in the surrounding trees. At one point the trail leads over uneven lava-encrusted terrain, which makes for slow, difficult going. The path leads past the **Natural Cave** and comes out at the access road to the park before finishing at the summit of Mt. Eccles. Another excellent hike is the **Lava Canal Walk** (1hr. round-trip); 10min. along the trail will bring you to the **Lava Cave.** The stone steps leading into the cave are slippery and a flashlight is recommended for exploring the interior. The **Lake Surprise Walk** (45min.) is a flat, easy path that circles the lake, which is also safe for swimming.

There are beautiful **camping facilities ❶** in a wooded area of the park with lots of privacy for each site. Amenities include toilets, BBQ, and running water, but no power. If the ranger is not available, registration can be done at the information office (Dec.-Feb. $14.50 per site. Low-season $10.50).

PORTLAND ☎03

Portland was the first town settled in Victoria, and its weary industrial feel betrays its age. This area was once a base for whalers, sealers, and escaped convicts, before the Henty brothers and their sheep enterprise permanently settled the area in 1834. Its harbor is still active, and maritime history buffs may take pleasure in its storied past; however, most travelers use the town as a jumping off point for the Great South West Walk or Discovery Bay and Lower Glenelg National Parks.

TRANSPORTATION AND PRACTICAL INFORMATION. V/Line buses (☎1800 800 120 or 136 196; www.metlinkmelbourne.com.au) depart from the north side of Henty St., just west of Percy St. One heads east through Port Fairy (1hr., 2 per day, $10.50) to Warrnambool (1½hr., 2 per day, $15.30), where connections can be made to Melbourne. On Friday, a bus runs to Port Campbell (2½hr., $27.60). Buses head west to Mount Gambier (1½hr., 1 per day, $14). Tickets can be purchased at **Harvey World Travel,** 53 Julia St., near the corner with Percy. (☎5521 7895; www.harveyworld.com.au. Open M-F 9am-5:30pm and Sa 9am-noon.)

The two main north-south streets in town are the waterfront **Bentinck Street,** with cafes, takeaway joints, and pubs, and **Percy Street,** one block up, which has the majority of the town's commercial activity. Percy is the continuation of the Henty Hwy., which enters the city from the north. Percy and Bentinck St. are connected in the center of town by (from north to south) Henty, Julia, and Gawler St. At the town's southern end, Bentinck St. becomes Cape Nelson Rd. and heads southwest to Cape Nelson State Park. The **Portland Visitors Centre** is on Lee Breakwater St., down the hill by the bay. (☎5523 2671 or 1800 035 567. Open daily 9am-5pm.) If there's a crowd at the visitors center, you can also obtain brochures and maps on the Lower Glenelg and Discovery Bay from the **Parks Victoria** office, 8-12 Julia St. (☎13 19 63. Open M-F 9am-4:30pm.) **Internet** access is available at the **library,** 40 Bentinck St., just south of Gawler St. (☎5522 2265. Open M-Th 10am-5:30pm, F 10am-6pm, Sa 10am-1pm. $3 per 30min.) The **post office** is at 108 Percy St. (open M-F 9am-5pm). **Postal Code:** 3305.

ACCOMMODATIONS. Close to the waterfront in town, the **Gordon Hotel ❸,** 63 Bentinck St., provides pub accommodations with great harbor views. (☎5523 1121. Continental breakfast included. Backpackers $20 per person. Singles from $35; doubles from $50.) The restaurant downstairs has Schnitzel Night every Wednesday from 6-8:30pm ($9.50). For those willing to venture farther afield, the opportunity to wake up to the sounds of breaking waves awaits at **Bellevue Backpackers ❷,** Sheoke Rd., on the way to Cape Nelson. Keep a lookout for the white sign on the left just before Yellow Rock. Accommodation consists of uniquely decorated trailers complete with dining area, TV, kitchen, and bunk and double beds. (☎5523 4038. Camp sites $10. Trailer $25 per person. Cash only.) The classiest downtown hotel is **Mac's Hotel Bentinck ❹,** 41 Bentinck St., on the corner of Gawler and Bentinck St., where the Victorian ensuite rooms will cost a pretty penny; motel rooms in back are a better bargain. (☎5523 2188; www.richmondhenty.com.au/macs. Motel doubles $65; hotel doubles $182-205.)

VICTORIA

FOOD. **Kokopelli's Kafe and Ice Bar ❸,** 79 Bentinck St., is decorated with images of the flute-playing Kokopelli. This trendy lounge has a layer of ice lining the top of the bar to keep drinks cold. There are tapas as well as pasta and risotto main courses for around $20. (☎5521 1200. Live music Th. Open daily 8:30am-latenight.) **Sully's Cafe and Wine Bar ❶,** 55 Bentinck St., emphasizes healthy, tasty, and affordable meals. Salads, sandwiches, and focaccias range $4.50-10. There's a fully stocked bar in the back. (☎5523 5355. Open daily 9am-latenight.) **Juicy Bitz ❶,** at 57 Bentinck St. next door, has smoothies, sandwiches, and gourmet pies. (☎5521 1777. Open M and W-Su 10am-4pm. Cash only). A **Safeway** supermarket is on Percy St., across from the post office (Open daily 7am-10pm).

SIGHTS. Though this stretch of waters is safer today, in the past many ships in the Portland harbor area became intimately acquainted with the ocean floor. The **Maritime Discovery Centre,** in the same building as the visitors center, memorializes some of those ships and celebrates the city's fishing and whaling history. The prized display is the reconstructed skeleton of a sperm whale beached in 1987, complete with a bench built under the rib cage (☎5523 2671. Open daily 9am-5pm. $5, concessions $4, children free.) Behind the Maritime Centre, a restored 1885 **cable tram** will take you on a waterfront ride to several of Portland's tourist attractions. (Runs daily 10am-4pm. Buy tickets on board or at the visitors center. $12, concessions $10, children $6.) The **Powerhouse Motor and Car Museum,** at the corner of Glenelg and Percy St., has a beautiful collection of privately owned antique cars and a restored tram. (Open holidays daily 10am-4pm; off-peak M-F 1-4pm, Sa-Su 10am-4pm. $5, concessions $4, children $1.)

OUTDOOR ACTIVITIES. The waters off Portland are popular among both divers and fishermen. Exploring the wreckage of the many ships moored in the waters here ranks among Australia's best dive adventures. For the experienced **diver,** equipment rental and charters are available at **The Dive Shop,** 14 Townsend St., off Percy St. on the north end of town. (☎5523 6392. Open M-F 9am-5:30pm, Sa-Su 10am-2pm. Gear rental from $55; 3-week diving classes from $430.) **Fishing** charters and **harbor cruises** are available from **Southwest Charters.** (☎5523 3202 or 04 1830 6714; www.geocities.com/swcharters. Call ahead as prices vary.) **Bikes** can be rented from the visitors center for coastal rides (half-day $12; full-day $20). **Glenelg Adventure Services,** 67 Bentinck St., rents mountain bikes and surfboards and offers a series of tours including coastal walks, canoeing, and sea expeditions. (☎5521 7646 or 04 1957 8545. Open M-Tu noon-4pm, W-Th and Sa 10am-5pm, F 10am-7pm, Su 10:30am-3:30pm. YHA discounts.)

Starting and ending at Portland's information center, the looping, 250km **Great South West Walk** rambles along the coast through the Discovery Bay Coastal Park, then doubles back through the Lower Glenelg National Park. The walk traverses a variety of terrains and provides a grand introduction to the wildlands of southwest Victoria. There are four main sections of the walk: the Three Capes and Bays, Discovery Bay Beach and Mt. Richmond, the Glenelg River and Gorge, and the Cobbboboonee Forest. Campsites are provided all along the trail for walkers, and detailed maps are available at the Portland visitors center (p. 632). The trail is clearly marked, occasionally with a black emu badge but more often with red metal arrows and signs pointing you in the right direction. Daytrip access sections range 8-20km in length, although shorter sections, the most accessible of which are in **Cape Nelson State Park** (p. 633), can be walked as well. Most of those choosing to walk it in its entirety can do so in about 12 days. If you want to walk a section and need pickup or drop-off services, call the **Friends of the Great South West Walk.** (☎5523 4248; kandgpage@eftel.net.au or www.greatsouthwestwalk.com. Prices for this service vary depending on distances and time of year.) Register with the tourist info center in Portland or Nelson before beginning your hike.

CAPE NELSON STATE PARK

Cape Nelson State Park, a 243 hectare reserve, lies just 11km southwest of Portland and has some beautiful bushwalks, impressive coastal cliffs, a prime surf beach, and a **lighthouse.** The view from the lighthouse alone is worth the trip. Currently, the lighthouse is unstaffed, so the grounds are always open and free. The park service is currently looking to staff the lighthouse, so before planning a visit contact the park center or visitor center in Portland (p. 632) for updated prices and times. The best approach to the park is to head south out of Portland on Bentinck St., which becomes Cape Nelson Rd., and then make a left on Sheoke Rd., heading east. As Sheoke Rd. swings south, it becomes the Scenic Rd. Almost immediately you'll see the carpark for **Yellow Rock,** the area's top surf spot, where a boardwalk leads down from the clifftops and provides several spots to take in the view of the yellow monolith, for which the beach is named. For more info, consult *Surfs Up in Portland*, available at the Maritime Centre.

The **Great South West Walk** intersects the park, affording the opportunity to walk short sections of it; one of the best is the **Enchanted Forest** walk (3km round-trip), which winds through groves of short trees twisted into strange shapes by strong winds. The carpark is just off Sheoke Rd., about halfway to the lighthouse. The **Sea Cliff Nature Walk** (a 3km loop) begins at the Sea Cliff carpark, at the intersection of the Scenic Rd. and Cape Nelson Rd., and includes numbered markers and a self-guide pamphlet that explains some of the rare plants and animals protected in the park. At the end of the loop, hikers can opt to do a part of the Great South West Walk and take in more of the astounding coastal views before heading back out on the loop. The **Lighthouse Walk** (6km, marked with blue arrows), which can be started from either the Sea Cliff carpark or the lighthouse, wanders through inland areas and also joins with the Great South West Walk east of the lighthouse for clifftop views of the ocean.

There's no camping in the park itself, but the visitor area has toilets, water, and BBQ. The nearest budget accommodation to the park is the small **Bellevue Backpackers** (p. 632), which sits on the northern edge of the park near Yellow Rock.

CAPE BRIDGEWATER AND DISCOVERY BAY COASTAL PARK

Discovery Bay Coastal Park stretches 65km from Portland to the South Australia border. Most points of interest are clustered around **Cape Bridgewater,** at the park's southern end, 18km west of Portland via Bridgewater Rd. (from town, take Otway St. west until it becomes Bridgewater Rd.), including a resident **seal colony,** an excellent surfing and swimming beach, and three of the park's most well-known attractions: **Blowholes,** the **Petrified Forest,** and the **Springs.**

Cape Bridgewater has a long crescent of sand and gentle surf. The kiosk on the beach has limited **tourist info.** The **Bridgewater Bay Cafe,** 1661 Bridgewater Rd., overlooks the beach and has cheap sandwiches, burgers ($7-10), and of course, fish 'n' chips. (☎5526 7155. Open M-Th and Sa 9am-6pm, F and Su 9am-5pm.) Just up the hill from the beach is the carpark for the **seal walk.** The winding cliff trail (1½hr. round-trip) is fairly steep, but worth it. At the end is a **viewing platform** high above a rock-shelf on which Australian fur seals sun themselves. A less strenuous, longer hike (9km, 3hr.) to the seals runs in the opposite direction, following the Great South West Walk from the blowholes carpark to the seal walk carpark, but requires that you find a way back to your car. To avoid the hard work altogether, **Seals By Sea** runs 45min. tours from Cape Bridgewater, allowing you to get up close and personal with the seals. (☎5526 7247 or 1800 267 247. $28, concessions $23. Book ahead.) The **Cape Bridgewater Holiday Camp** ❶, up the hill from the beach, offers great views of the bay and beach as well as a range of accommodation options from camping to more upscale rooms in the town's first church, dating from 1870. (☎5526 7267; www.capebridgewatercamp.com. Campsite $10 per person, powered $15. Doubles from $40, more in peak season, extra person $15. Cash only.)

At the end of Bridgewater Rd. is a carpark with access to the Springs, the Blowholes, and the Petrified Forest. Straight up from the carpark, waves crash into the **Blowholes** at the foot of the sea cliffs. To the left is the **Petrified Forest,** eerie rock formations in cavities left when trees rotted away centuries ago. Virtually indistinguishable from tidal pools, the **Springs** (45min. round-trip) are in fact freshwater springs formed as rainwater seeps through limestone farther inland. From Cape Bridgewater, the Bridgewater Lakes Rd. will lead you back to the Nelson-Portland Rd., passing by the Amos Rd. turn-off, which heads to a nice surf break at **White's Beach** on the northern side of the Cape. The freshwater **Bridgewater Lakes,** a popular swimming, boating, and picnicking area, are on the way to the beach.

Shortly after Bridgewater Lakes Rd. rejoins the main road is the turn-off for **Mount Richmond National Park,** where an 8km sealed road runs to the summit of Mt. Richmond, with views of the towering dunes of Discovery Bay. Short, clearly marked, but not very exciting hikes branch off from the picnic area at the summit. **Noel's Walk** (45min.) is steep toward the end and returns along the road for 15min. to the carpark. The **Ocean View Walk** (a 30min. loop) leads to a lookout deck over the ocean, but there are better views at Discovery Bay. The park has abundant bird life, kangaroos and echidnas, and a wide variety of wildflowers. To get there, take the Portland-Nelson Rd. (Hwy. C192) 18km west of Portland.

VICTORIA

LOWER GLENELG NATIONAL PARK

Lower Glenelg National Park protects a patch of dense forest surrounding the Glenelg River, the best bream fishing river in Victoria. The 22km unsealed **Glenelg Drive,** which is accessible by 2WD, provides access to the park, but the best way to see the interior is via canoe or cruise boat. The Glenelg River meanders through virtually the entire length of the park and passes a succession of campgrounds, many accessible only to boaters and canoeists. The **Nelson Visitors Centre and Parks Victoria Office,** on Leake St. in Nelson, sells permits (peak season $14.50, off-peak $10.50) for the numerous **campsites** ❶ (all unpowered and without showers) and can answer questions about river conditions and canoe rental. (☎08 8738 4051; www.parkweb.vic.gov.au. Open daily 9am-5pm.)

Five days of paddling from Dartmoor will bring the water-borne to the mouth of the river at Nelson. The paddle from Dartmoor to Pines Landing is low and snaggy, and many paddlers opt to skip this section. **Nelson Boat and Canoe Hire,** on Leake St. in Nelson, has a variety of canoes, kayaks, and motorboats. They run daytrips with pickup or drop-off options (additional fees apply, prices vary depending on location). They can arrange multi-night trips and also rent camper boats from $440 (peak season, $365 off-peak) for two nights. (☎08 8738 4048; 2-person canoes from $38.50 per day, singles $33.50; motorboats $31 per hr. Open M-W and F-Su 9am-5pm, high season daily 8:30am-6pm. No boat license required.) Across the dock, **Glenelg River Cruises** offers a 2hr. scenic cruise along the river to Princess Margaret Rose Cave. (☎08 8738 4191; www.glenelgrivercruises.com.au. $25, concession $22.50. Call ahead or check website for tour availability; high season tour daily 1pm.) To access the park from the east, turn right onto the Nelson-Winnap Rd. shortly after passing the Lake Monibeong turn-off, and then make a left onto Glenelg Dr. about 4km after that. From the west, take the North Nelson Rd. out of Nelson. Glenelg Dr. will appear on your right.

Limestone dominates the topography, and percolating rainwater and underground watercourses have formed many caves. The only one open to the public is the spectacular **Princess Margaret Rose Cave,** 2km east of the South Australia border and 15km south of the Princes Hwy. The cave is noted for its abundance of helectites—rock formations which continue to puzzle geologists by defying gravity and growing sideways out from the cave wall, and the tour explains the history and geological components of the cave. (☎08 8738 4171. Several 1hr. tours daily 10am-4:30pm. $11, concessions $8.50, children $6.) The area attracts more than 68 types of birds, which experienced bird watchers will find easy to spot. There are two easy walks by the cave: the short **River View Walk,** and **Laslett's Trail,** a 4.5km loop that runs along the Glenelg River. The **campsites** on the premises almost rival the cave's beauty. Each site has its own BBQ and birdbath on a manicured plot of grass, and the surrounding trees offer a surprising amount of privacy. Hot shower facilities are available. Camping arrangements must be made by 5pm with the ranger at the **Cave Information Centre,** in the same building as the cave. (All sites unpowered. Sites $14; 4-bunk cabins $50 per person.) Signs off main roads in the vicinity of Mt. Gambier direct visitors to the cave. From Nelson, you can paddle the river (3km) or take Donovan's Rd.

THE WIMMERA AND MALLEE

The Wimmera and Mallee regions fill the remote northwestern part of Victoria. Mountains, lakes, swamps, wildlife reserves, rich farmland, and rugged bushland can all be found in this area. West of the Goldfields, inland Victoria rises with the rugged peaks of Grampians National Park before gradually settling into an immense plain that stretches west into South Australia and north into New South Wales. The Wimmera region draws its name from the river that begins in the Grampians and wanders north past the Little Desert National Park. North of Little Desert and west of the Sunraysia Hwy., all the way up to Mildura, is the semi-arid expanse of the Mallee, named for the mallee eucalyptus, a hardy water-hoarding tree that thrives in the rugged plains.

For those with ample time and an adventurous spirit, the remote national and state parks of the Wimmera and Mallee regions offer some of the only untouched, semi-arid land left in the world. Distant **Murray Sunset National Park** has numerous walking and driving trails through captivating vistas filled with packs of red kangaroos. **Mt. Arapiles-Tooan State Park,** close to the Grampians, boasts some of the best amateur rock climbing sites in the country. The oddly-named **Little Desert National Park** is in fact not a desert at all, but rather a valley of bright flowers.

GRAMPIANS (GARIWERD) NATIONAL PARK

In 1836, Major Mitchell, in command of a British expedition, was hiking through seemingly endless plains, when he suddenly spotted a range of majestic hills. He named them the Grampians, after a range in his home country of Scotland. Ensuing hordes of settlers steadily pushed the Koori Aborigines out of their ancestral home of Gariwerd. A park visit can offer travelers insight into Aboriginal cultural history (80% of the Aboriginal rock art sites in Victoria can be found here, including five major sites open to the public), as well as access to breathtaking ranges, peerless rock climbing and hiking, abundant wildlife, rare birds, and a springtime carpet of technicolor wildflowers. In early 2006, a devastating fire tore through the park, scorching much of the landscape. The path of the blaze created dazzling patterns through the range. Though the ecosystem is slowly regenerating, complete recovery will take many years.

VICTORIA

GRAMPIANS NATIONAL PARK AT A GLANCE

AREA: 167,000 hectares.

FEATURES: Lookouts, waterfalls, hiking, rockclimbing, and lakes.

HIGHLIGHTS: Koori rock paintings, 160km of hiking tracks, the lookouts in the Wonderland, extensive rock climbing opportunities.

GATEWAYS: Halls Gap (east); Horsham (north); Dunkeld (south).

CAMPING: 13 campgrounds, each with dozens of sites. Camping $11 for up to 6 people and 1 car. $5 per additional car.

TRANSPORTATION AND ORIENTATION

The northern approach passes through **Horsham,** at the junction of **Western** and **Henty Hwy.,** roughly 18km north of the park. From the south, the town of **Dunkeld,** on the **Glenelg Hwy.,** provides access via **Mt. Abrupt Rd.** From the east, the town of **Stawell** is 26km away. The most convenient **point of entry** is on the eastern edge of the park at **Halls Gap,** a tiny settlement nestled in a crevasse between two mountains which is the park's only town. Nonetheless it has basic amenities and is within walking distance of many of the park's points of interest. When reading about the town's offerings, remember that almost everything is clustered together in a small strip on **Grampians Road,** also called Dunkeld Rd., Stawell Rd., and sometimes even Main Rd., which runs from Halls Gap to Dunkeld.

One **V/Line** bus per day leaves from opposite the newsagency in Halls Gap bound for: Stawell (30min.; $9.30, off peak $6.60); Ararat (1hr.; $14/9.80); Ballarat (2½hr.; $30.90/21.70); and Melbourne (4½hr. $49.20/34.40). Many V/Line routes may include stopovers along the way, some up to several hours long.

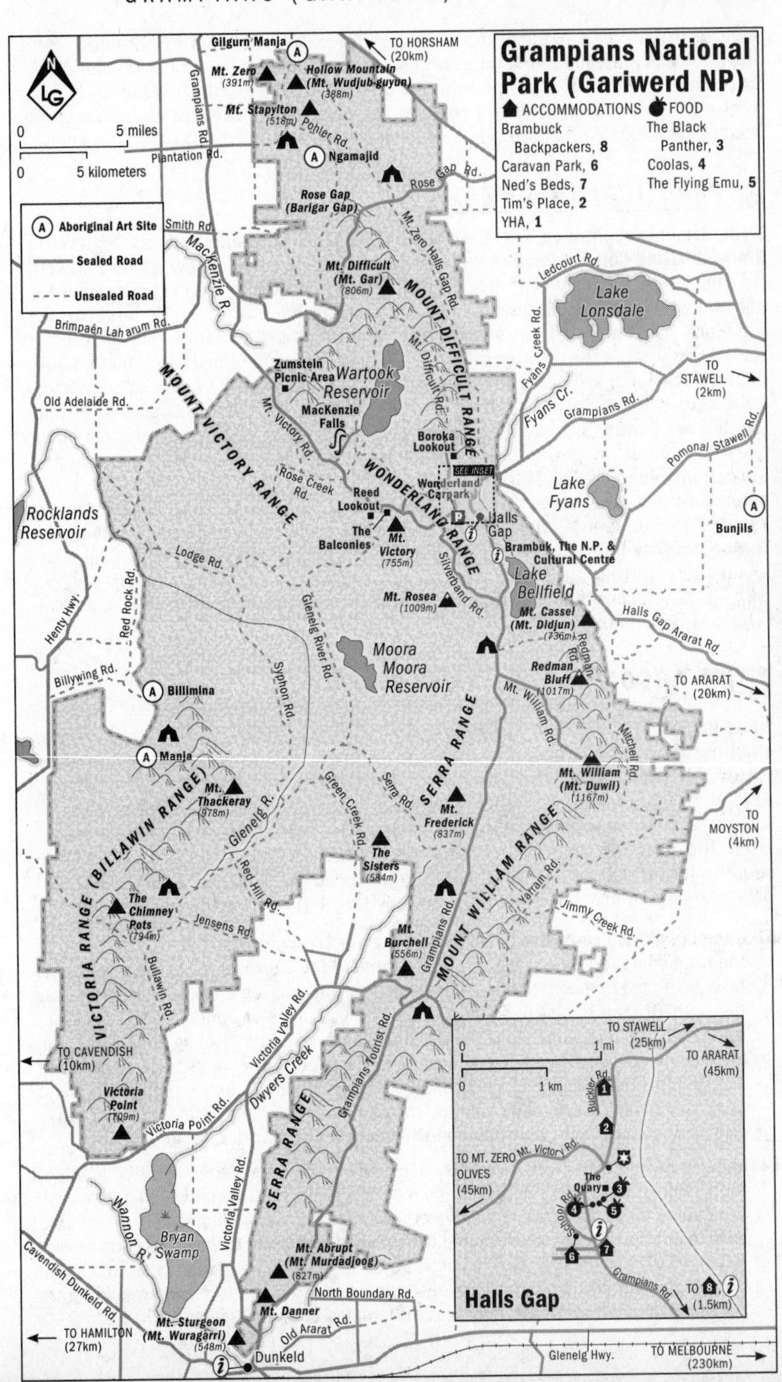
Grampians National Park (Gariwerd NP)
ACCOMMODATIONS
FOOD
Brambuck Backpackers, 8
Caravan Park, 6
Ned's Beds, 7
Tim's Place, 2
YHA, 1
The Black Panther, 3
Coolas, 4
The Flying Emu, 5
Aboriginal Art Site
Sealed Road
Unsealed Road
0 5 miles
0 5 kilometers
TO HORSHAM (20km)
TO STAWELL (2km)
TO ARARAT (20km)
TO MOYSTON (4km)
TO CAVENDISH (10km)
TO HAMILTON (27km)
TO MELBOURNE (230km)
Gilgurn Manja
Mt. Zero (391m)
Hollow Mountain (Mt. Wudjub-guyun) (388m)
Mt. Stapylton (518m)
Ngamajid
Rose Gap (Barigar Gap)
Mt. Difficult (Mt. Gar) (806m)
MOUNT DIFFICULT RANGE
MOUNT VICTORY RANGE
WONDERLAND RANGE
Zumstein Picnic Area
Wartook Reservoir
MacKenzie Falls
Boroka Lookout
Reed Lookout
The Balconies
Mt. Victory (755m)
Wonderland Carpark
SEE INSET
Halls Gap
Lake Lonsdale
Lake Fyans
Bunjils
Brambuk, The N.P. & Cultural Centre
Lake Bellfield
Mt. Rosea (1009m)
Mt. Cassel (Mt. Didjun) (736m)
Redman Bluff (1017m)
Rocklands Reservoir
Moora Moora Reservoir
Billimina
Manja
SERRA RANGE
Mt. Thackeray (978m)
VICTORIA RANGE (BILLAWIN RANGE)
Mt. Frederick (837m)
The Sisters (584m)
Mt. William (Mt. Duwil) (1167m)
MOUNT WILLIAM RANGE
The Chimney Pots (794m)
Mt. Burchell (556m)
Victoria Point (709m)
Bryan Swamp
Mt. Abrupt (Mt. Murdadjoog) (827m)
Mt. Danner
Mt. Sturgeon (Mt. Wuragarri) (548m)
Dunkeld
Grampians Rd.
Pohler Rd.
Plantation Rd.
Rose Gap Rd.
Smith Rd.
MacKenzie R.
Mt. Zero Halls Gap Rd.
Ledcourt Rd.
Brimpaen Laharum Rd.
Mt. Difficult Rd.
Fyans Creek Rd.
Fyans Cr.
Old Adelaide Rd.
Mt. Victory Rd.
Grampians Rd.
Pomonal Stawell Rd.
Rose Creek Rd.
Lodge Rd.
Silverband Rd.
Red Rock Rd.
Henty Hwy.
Glenelg River Rd.
Halls Gap Ararat Rd.
Billywing Rd.
Syphon Rd.
Redman Rd.
Mt. William Rd.
Mitchell Rd.
Green Creek Rd.
Serra Rd.
Glenelg R.
Red Hill Rd.
Yarram Rd.
Jimmy Creek Rd.
Jensens Rd.
Bullawin Rd.
Victoria Valley Rd.
Grampians Rd.
Grampians Tourist Rd.
Dwyers Creek
Victoria Point Rd.
Wannon R.
Cavendish Dunkeld Rd.
North Boundary Rd.
Old Ararat Rd.
Glenelg Hwy.
Halls Gap
TO STAWELL (25km)
TO ARARAT (45km)
0 1 mi
0 1 km
Buckler Rd.
Mt. Victory Rd.
TO MT. ZERO OLIVES (45km)
The Quary
School Rd.
Grampians Rd.
TO 8 (1.5km)
VICTORIA

Several private companies also run tours from Melbourne and Adelaide. One option is **Eco Platypus Tours,** which runs a round-trip bus from Melbourne Tu, F, Sa (☎1800 819 091. $85 per person; group discounts available). From late Feb. to early Nov. you can hitch a ride on the **schoolbus** between Halls Gap and Stawell (☎5356 9342; 20min., M-F 3 per day, Sa-Su 1 per day, $8).

PRACTICAL INFORMATION

The Brambuk Centre (a.k.a., **Brambuk the National Park and Cultural Centre** and **Brambuk Living Cultural Centre**), 2.5km south of Halls Gap town center on Dunkeld Rd., has been recently renovated, and the new facility is the best resource for nature lovers and those interested in the local Aboriginal culture. For handicapped travelers, the Brambuk Centre has a handy pamphlet listing wheelchair-accessible routes throughout the park. (☎5356 4381. Open daily 9am-5pm. Hiking maps $3.30, detailed park maps $6; donations appreciated.) From outside Halls Gap, **Parks Victoria** (☎13 19 63; www.parkweb.vic.gov.au) is also an excellent resource. The **Halls Gap Visitors Centre** in the town center next to the Mobil Station can answer many questions about the park as well, though it is geared toward accommodation and dining options. (☎5356 4616 or 1800 065 599. Open daily 9am-5pm.) The Mobil **petrol** station has basic provisions and an **ATM.** (☎5356 4206. Open daily in summer 7am-9:45pm, in winter 7am-7:45pm.) If your car breaks down, **Stawell & Grampians Towing** (☎5358 4000) is open 24hr. The Halls Gap **police station** (☎5356 4411) is located just north of the town center, at the intersection of Grampians and Mt. Victory Rd. The **post office** is rather small and located just beside the **general store.** (Open M-F 9am-5pm.) **Postal Code:** 3381.

VICTORIA

ACCOMMODATIONS AND CAMPING

In addition to the excellent hostels in and around Halls Gap, there are 14 major **camping** ❶ areas in the park, all with toilets and fireplaces and most with water. All sites operate on a first come, first served basis; campers must pay $11 (up to 6 people and 1 vehicle) for permits available at the Brambuk Centre. Rangers advise stopping at the park center first for a map of the park's campsites and new information. Bush camping is free but prohibited in certain regions including the Wonderland Range, the Lake Wartook watershed, and other areas demarcated on maps; check with the park center before camping.

Grampians YHA Eco-Hostel (☎5356 4544; grampians@yhavic.org.au), 700m north of the town center on Grampians Rd., at the corner of tiny Buckler St. Friendly managers take great care of the immaculate complex. Highlights include a sparkling kitchen, cozy den with TV, and quaint bedrooms, each with balconies or doors into the backyard brush. A florid herb garden, chicken coop, compost, and solar-heating are just some of the eco-friendly amenities. Internet access $2 per 20min. Key deposit $10. Wheelchair accessible. Reception 8-11am and 3-10pm. Book ahead, as its reputation alone attracts a steady stream of visitors year-round. 3- to 4-bed dorms with lockers $24; singles $54; doubles $60. Dec.-Apr. non-YHA add $5, May-Nov. $3.50. ❷

Tim's Place (☎5356 4288; www.timsplace.com.au), on Grampians Rd., 500m north of town center. Stay at Tim's cozy digs and meet the owner, who is committed to providing a paradise for budget travelers. Several new units, including immaculate 2-bedroom ensuite apartments with kitchens and dining areas. Tim helps travelers organize rounds of golf ($10, including clubs), tennis ($10 all-day), *petanque,* badminton, mountain biking, discounted dinners at local restaurants, and tickets to the Brambuk Centre Dreaming theater. Dorms $25; doubles $60; triples $80, apartments $100-120. ❷

Brambuk Backpackers (☎5356 4609; www.brambuk.com.au), is a modest facility located directly across the street from the Brambuk Centre. Basic amenities include ensuite bathrooms, kitchen, and lounge with TV. Laundry $2. Internet $6 per hr. Dorms $24-27; singles $65; family $92. ❷

Ned's Beds (Grampians Backpackers), 2 Heath St., just south of the Halls Gap Information Centre. (☎5356 4296.) Ned's collection of quaint cabins offers casual lodging and extras including TV/DVD player, kitchen, game room, laundry, and BBQ. Internet access $6 per hr. If you can't find the manager, walk over to the public pool across the street from the Mobil station and ask for Blanche. Dorms $23-24; doubles $55. ❷

Halls Gap Caravan Park (☎5356 4251; www.hallsgapcaravanpark.com.au), in the center of Halls Gap across from the Mobil station. Many walking trails start just behind the campground. Reception 8:30am-7:30pm. BYO linens. Key deposit $20. Sites for 2 $23, low-season $19; powered $26/22. Extra person $10. On-site caravans for 2 $53/47. 7th night free during low season. ❷

FOOD

Budget-savvy travelers purchase food at a supermarket before arriving in the Grampians. There is a large **Safeway** in Stawell in the town centre at 26-32 Scallon St. (Open M-Sa 9am-10pm, Su 10am-10pm.) Groceries can also be purchased at the **Halls Gap General Store,** although high prices drive the locals elsewhere. For those on the go, the Brambuk Centre (p. 638) offers authentic bush tucker for lunch ($10-15).

Mt. Zero Olives & Millstone Cafe, (☎5383 8280; www.mountzeroolives.com), close to Mt. Zero. Great local eats prepared with home-grown, biodynamic products. Foodies will be sated twice over with a savory olive and tapanade tasting. Swathed in modern art; notice the menu written on the large chalkboard left over from the building's past as a classroom. Open daily 10am-5pm, cafe open M and Sa-Su 10am-4:30pm; hours vary, sometimes open Th-F. Call ahead. ❸

Coolas Ice Cream, Stoney Creek Stores (☎5356 4466). The 1st shop in the complex; bakes fresh waffle cones and offers an assortment of ice cream flavors. Try the popular Honeycomb or Bailey's with scorched almonds. Cheap hotdogs and spuds available as side dishes. (Waffle cone with 1 scoop $3, 2 scoops $4, 3 scoops $5; sundaes $6. Open daily 9am-6pm or later.) ❶

The Flying Emu, Stoney Creek Stores (☎5356 4400), has a respectable selection of vegetarian and gluten-free options for $8-13, with lighter fare starting at $4. (Open daily 9am-4pm, sometimes later. 10% YHA discount.) ❷

Black Panther Cafe, Shop 6, Stoney Creek Stores, is a licensed bar which offers a wide selection of pizzas ($12-20), pastas ($13-17), focaccia with salad ($8.50, served until 5pm), and a range of main courses ($15-19). (☎5356 4511. Open M-F 4pm-9:30pm and Sa-Su 8:30pm-latenight.) ❸

Quarry Restaurant (☎5356 4858) at the back of the Stoney Creek Stores, serves up some of the tastiest dishes in Halls Gap. Open daily noon-2pm and 6pm-9pm. Lunch $6-15, dinner $17-30. Book ahead for dinner. ❸

SIGHTS AND LOOKOUTS

Before heading into the park, visit the **Brambuk Aboriginal Culture Centre,** part of the Brambuk Centre, located 2.5km south of Halls Gap. The invaluable information available at the center includes displays about the cultural history of the **Koori,** the local Aboriginal people and traditional inhabitants of Gariwerd. The **Dreaming Theatre's** 30min. light-and-sound show tells a traditional Koori story and offers a geographic perspective of the national park. The Brambuk Centre also offers a **guided**

rock-art tour. (☎5356 4452. Open daily 9am-5pm. Entry free. Theater $4.40, concessions $2.80, children $2.20, families $16.40. 2hr. tours F 10am-noon. Book ahead. $15, concessions $11, children $8.)

Unfortunately, most sights are a good distance from Halls Gap and so require a car. This does not deter some tourists, who hitch rides throughout the park; however Let's Go does not recommend hitchhiking. The best lookouts in the park are at the ends of arduous treks; however there are some spectacular vistas available in the Wonderland region, easily accessible with a vehicle. The **Balconies** (Jaws of Death), the Grampians' predominant icon, lie about 1km up from the Reed Lookout carpark off Mt. Victory Rd. The mostly flat approach (20min.) ends in sweeping panoramas. The Balconies themselves, a pair of parallel slabs of sandstone, jut out over the steep sides of Mt. Victory and are a superb spot to watch the sunset. The **Boroka lookout,** also on Mt. Victory Rd., near the balconies, offers an excellent view of the eastern side of the range and is at its best in the early hours of the morning. Those who brave the steep, downhill path to **MacKenzie Falls,** which begins at the car park just off Lake Wartook Rd., are rewarded with one of Victoria's most spectacular waterfalls—an 25m wall of crashing water. Just be sure to save energy for the walk. There is a wheelchair-accessible approach to the top of the falls, but none to the base. **Zumstein picnic area,** west of Lake Wartook on Mt. Victory Rd., is popular because it's hopping with kangaroos, but you can see herds of 'roos just about everywhere in the park, especially at sunset. There are over 100 **Aboriginal rock art sites** scattered through the brush of Grampians, five of the most impressive sites are open to the public.

HIKING

Indescribably beautiful and rugged, the Grampians' sights can be reached via relatively easy walking trails, without the need to drive to a trailhead or camp overnight in the bush. The park is thus a favorite among families and weekend nature lovers. At the same time, the park caters to more experienced hikers and rock-climbers with difficult tracks in the northern and southern regions (most of which are hard to reach without a car.)

WALKING THROUGH A GRAMPIAN WONDERLAND. The **Wonderland Range** adjacent to Halls Gap in the park's eastern end holds a number of the main attractions; **Mount Victory Road** is particularly beautiful. The indispensable *Northern Walks, Southern Walks,* and *Wonderland Walks* maps (each $3.30 in the Brambuk Centre) give details on hiking, art sites, and driving.

Some Wonderland walks lead to serene waterfalls and rock formations. To the south, **Victoria Valley** is carpeted with red gum woodlands and is home to emus and kangaroos. **Manja** and **Billimina,** at the park's western edge, contain some of the Grampians' best **Aboriginal art sites.** Experienced hikers might want to tackle some of the steep trails on the range's highest peak, **Mount William** (1168m), at the park's extreme eastern end; the "trail" to the summit is fully paved and well traveled. The Wonderland hikes vary by difficulty and duration (from 30min. to 6hr. to several days). The trails below start near Halls Gap; all distances are round-trip, although budget extra time if you want to ponder the meaning of life at the summit.

Wonderland Loop (9.6km, 5hr.). The loop trail starts behind the town center carpark; walk past the swimming pool and rear asphalt road and turn left before the Botanical Gardens. Moderately difficult, this hike traverses many of the most touristed sites; slightly more strenuous detours abound. The ½-day loop along well-formed tracks leads first to the **Venus Baths,** a series of rock pools popular for swimming in summer (when water levels are high enough), then to **Splitters Falls.** The trail continues through the lush forest along a creek to the Wonderland carpark, then up the spectacular **Grand Canyon** and eventually to the narrow rock tunnel **Silent Street.** At the awe-inspiring **Pinnacle,** sweeping views of the valley reward breathless hikers. The quick descent through stringy-bark forests offers completely unobstructed ridge-line views of Halls Gap and the surrounding countryside. The trail is well marked (and well traveled). To reach the Pinnacle, follow the orange arrows that point up into the rock.

Mount Rosea Loop (12km, 4-5hr.). A more difficult hike that should be attempted only with a copy of the *Wonderland Walks* map ($3.30), sold at the Brambuk Centre. Starts at the Rosea Campground, located on Silverband Rd. off Mt. Victory Rd. The hike ascends through forest to a sandstone plateau. The orange markers are somewhat difficult to follow in this area; be careful not to lose the trail. After a bit of scrambling over rocky ledges, turn left at the sign for Mt. Rosea and continue to a summit with one of the most spectacular vistas in the Grampians. Follow the trail back to the intersection and head left, away from the Rosea campground, through a forest, then onto a 4WD track, which leads to the Burma Track. Keep left around the outlying portions of the Sierra Range. At Silverband Rd., turn right and walk for 200m to the Dellys Dell Track, then uphill for about 700m to the Rosea Campground.

Boronia Peak Trail (6.6km, 2-3hr.). Starts past the kangaroo fields next to the Brambuk Centre or, alternatively, from the narrow path by the bridge just north of Tim's Place (add roughly 2km to the latter route). This trail is more difficult than the Wonderland Loop, but shorter. For the first half of the hike, the dense forest provides plentiful opportunities to observe birds and other wildlife. The moderate terrain ends in a short, unmarked scramble to the peak. With a lake to the south, flat bush country to the east, and the jagged Wonderland range to the west, the view is worth the haul to the top.

Chatauqua Peak Loop (5.6km, 2-3hr.). Starts from behind the Recreation Oval on Mt. Victory Rd., 150m from the intersection with Grampians Rd. The hike opens with an up-close view of the tranquil **Clematis Falls,** best seen after rain. The final 400m boulder climb to the peak is long and strenuous, but the views of Halls Gap and the valley are perfect. The less nimble can skip the boulder hop; the main trail continues on through to **Bullaces Glen,** a green fern gully, and ends in the botanical gardens in Halls Gap.

Mount Stapylton Summit (4.6km, 2-3hr.) A challenging hike that requires a bit of scrambling over elevated ledges, as well as some basic navigation skills. Starts at the Mount Zero picnic area in the northern Grampians; before setting off, purchase the *Northern Walks* map ($3.30) from the Brambuk Centre, and also ask them for a (free) photocopy of a topographical map of the area. The hike begins with a long uphill walk over unshaded **Flat Rock,** then passes through a wooded area to the base of Mt. Stapylton. The hike to the summit is extremely strenuous; **beware of crevasses and stay close to the trail markers.** The view from the top includes many of the surrounding mountain ranges and plains. On the way back down, you have the option of returning to the Mt. Zero Picnic area directly or turning the outing into a ½-day hike by tackling the entire **Mount Stapylton Loop** (12.2km, 5-7hr.) Follow the signs for the trail to the Stapylton Campground (4.4km), which passes through dense scrub. From the campground, signs mark the trail back to the Mt. Zero Picnic Area. The loop and summit can also be attempted by starting from, and returning to, the Stapylton Campground.

VICTORIA

OTHER ADVENTURES

The Grampians offer thousands of routes to some of the best rock climbing in the entire world, and there are plenty of companies in the area to hook you up with your next adrenaline rush. Nearby Mt. Arapiles is the best bet for diehard climbers; most routes are accessible from a central location. Those who prefers the crags of the

Grampians will need a car to get from site to site. Several small adventure companies operate in the region and offer guided climbs at all skill-levels in the northern section of the park at crags such as "Asses Ears," "Wall of Fools," "Manic Depressive," "Golden Shower," and "Group Sex." **Grampians Mountain Adventure Company** (☎0427 747 047; www.grampiansadventure.com.au) is run by an adventurous Aussie named Troy who strikes an excellent balance between good times and safety. Prices start at $60 for a half-day climb and abseil. The **Grampian Adventure Services** (☎5356 4540 or 04 0882 8432; www.adventurecompany.com.au) hasn't been quite the same since the brush fires, but enthusiastic guides still offer adventures of every type. Their selection of adventures includes canoe trips, climbs, mountain biking, abseiling, and bushwalking. (Climbs start at $65 per ½-day. Groups tend to be larger here than at Grampians Mountain Adventure Company.) **Hangin' Out** (☎5356 4535; www.hanginout.com.au) is another one-man company which offers half-day or full-day single-pitch and multi-pitch climbing tutorials for individuals or small groups (½-day $125 for 1 person; $75 per person for 2 or 3 people; includes pickup anywhere in Halls Gap). The above activities can be booked directly or through the **Grampians Central Booking Office,** in the Halls Gap newsagency. (☎5356 4654; www.grampianstours.com. Open daily 9am-5pm, but desk may be unattended during tours.)

GOLDFIELDS

In 1851, the first year of Victorian statehood (and just two years after the California gold rush in the United States), a group of miners unearthed one of the largest gold nuggets ever to be discovered. A year later, the *London Times* reported that over 50,000 diggers had converged upon Victoria's goldfields. As paupers prospered, the Australian government began taxing the *nouveau-riche* and the soon-to-be-*riche*, igniting the brief and bloody Eureka Rebellion of 1854.

The chaotic hustle of the Goldrush has dissipated in recent times and today visitors enjoy a relaxed stay amid picturesque historical townships. The biggest attraction in the entire region is Sovereign Hill, a large living museum in Ballarat which offers an accurate portrayal of life in the 1850s. Looking beyond the rich regional history, tourists have come to savor the region's picturesque vistas and soothing spa region. Although most of the gold has been harvested, towns like Ballarat and Bendigo remain prominent centers in Victoria.

BALLARAT ☎03

Ballarat is the self-appointed capital of the Goldfields and, as the site of the Eureka Rebellion, the birthplace of Australian democratic idealism. Although the gold is long gone, much of the 19th-century architecture has been preserved, and the city's golden past has been channeled into a bustling tourist trade that centers on the critically acclaimed **Sovereign Hill,** a large theme park dedicated to transporting visitors back in time to the gold rush era. Most of the gold in the region came from the deep alluvial deposits in town, and at the height of the gold rush, over 60,000 miners camped out around town hoping to strike it rich.

TRANSPORTATION

Trains and Buses: V/Line (☎13 61 96) runs buses and trains, depending on destination, from **Ballarat Station,** 202 Lydiard St. N., reached from Curtis St. by bus #2. To: **Ararat** (1¼hr., 6 per day, $15); **Bendigo** (2¼hr., 2 per day, $25); **Castlemaine** (1½hr., 1 per day, $15); **Daylesford** (40min., 1 per day, $12); **Geelong** (1¾hr., 3 per day, $15); **Mary-**

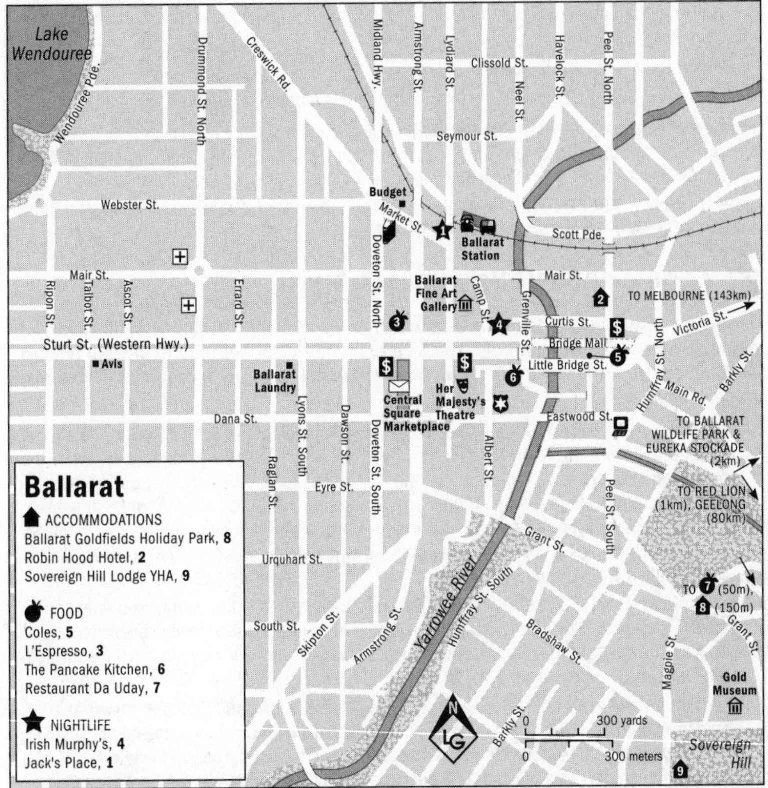

borough (1hr., 1 per day, $10); and **Melbourne** (1½hr., 12 per day, $20). Frequency varies Sa-Su. **Firefly** operates a bus service to Adelaide ($50).

Public Transportation: (☎5331 7777). Most **bus** routes depart from behind Bridge Mall, on Curtis St. $1.70 ticket valid for 2hr. of unlimited use. Purchase from driver. Pick up a helpful transit guide ($0.50) from the tourist office or a bus driver. Services typically run every 35min. M-F 7am-6pm; Sa limited schedule. **Ballarat Taxis** (☎131 008 or 5331 4367) line up in the city center and run personal tours of Ballarat and nearby wineries. Wheelchair accessible.

Car Rental: Avis, 1113 Sturt St. (☎5332 8310), between Talbort St. and Ascot St. **Budget,** 106 Market St. (☎5331 7788).

ORIENTATION AND PRACTICAL INFORMATION

The name Ballarat comes from a local Aboriginal word meaning "resting place" and was originally spelled "Ballaarat." Recently, the city has begun to revert back to the original spelling; several signs and maps have added the double 'a'. The town straddles the Western Hwy., called **Sturt Street** as it runs through town east to west. The **train station** is a few blocks north of Sturt on **Lydiard Street.** At its eastern end, Sturt becomes the pedestrian **Bridge Mall,** which has shops, restaurants, and supermarkets.

Tourist Office: Eureka Centre, on the corner of Eureka and Rodier St. (☎1800 44 66 33; www.visitballarat.com.au). The new, well-stocked facility is located 2km east of the city center along Eureka St. The large Southern Cross flag makes it very hard to miss. Open daily 9am-5pm.

Banks: Banks and **ATMs** line Sturt St.

Police: (☎5337 7222), on the corner of Dana and Albert St., behind the tourist center.

Internet Access: Free at the **library,** 178 Doveton St. (☎5331 1211). Open M 1-6pm, Tu-Th 9:30am-6pm, F 9:30am-7pm, Sa 10am-1pm, Su 1:15-4pm. Book ahead. **Chariot NetConnect,** 33 Peel St. S. (☎5332 2140). $5 per 30min. Open M-F 9am-5:30pm.

Post Office: (☎5336 5736), in the Central Sq. Marketplace. **Fax** services. Open M-F 9am-5pm, Sa 9am-noon. **Postal Code:** 3350.

ACCOMMODATIONS AND CAMPING

There are only two kinds of accommodations in Ballarat: dreary budget digs and expensive B&Bs or chain hotels. The former are plentiful but unexciting and tend to be attached to pubs. The latter options tend to exceed the price range of the average budget traveler.

Sovereign Hill Lodge YHA (☎5333 3409; www.sovereignhill.com.au), on Magpie St. a block uphill from the main carpark for Sovereign Hill. Located over 3km away from the train station. Elegant Victorian bungalows that are by far the best budget option in town. The YHA portion offers 4 small rooms positioned around a cozy kitchen and sitting area. Courteous staff issues discounted tickets for Sovereign Hill events. Reception M and Su 7am-10:30pm, Tu-Sa 24hr. Book well in advance. Limited wheelchair access. Dorms $20; singles $30; doubles $25; add $4 for non-YHA members. ❷

Robin Hood Hotel, 33 Peel St. N (☎5331 3348). Fairly basic pub accommodation conveniently located 1 block from Bridge Mall. Billiards bar and bistro downstairs (bistro open daily noon-2pm and 6-8:30pm). Reception 24hr. Book several days in advance for holidays and weekends. Bunks $30. ❸

Goldfields Holiday Park, 108 Clayton St. (☎5332 7888 or 1800 632 237; www.ballarat-goldfields.com.au). One of the finest holiday park sites in all of Victoria, located only 300m from Sovereign Hill. Modern, clean kitchens, recreation rooms, playground, heated pool, and heated communal bathrooms. 4- to 6-person ensuite cabins with A/C, kitchenette, and color TV. Reception 8am-8pm. Book cabins in advance. Sites for 2 $20-30; cabins from $70. ❶

FOOD

Sturt St., which defines the CBD, offers a variety of small cafes and cheap asian fare. A few other good deals are sprinkled about town. **Coles** 24hr. supermarket, a produce shop, and a bakery are at the far eastern end of Sturt St., behind the Bridge Mall at Peel St. Several inexpensive eateries sit just east of Sovereign Hill.

L'Espresso, 417 Sturt St. (☎5333 1789). The cafe is hard to miss with its dark black decor and giant wall covered with CDs. Patrons can request music from the lengthy playlist. Lunch $8-16. Open daily 7:30am-6pm, F open later. ❷

Red Lion, 217-229 Main Rd. (☎5331 3393; www.redlionhotel.biz). Located en route from the town center to Sovereign Hill on the east side of the road. The Red Lion is part of a larger conference center that includes a bar and casino. The restaurant is modern and polished, outfitted with big-screen TVs and bop-worthy music. The diverse and delicious menu offers everything from club sandwiches ($6.90) to lamb mignon ($25). Open M, T-Th, and Su 9am-1am; F-Sa 9am-3am. ❸

Restaurant Da Uday, 7 Wainwright St. (☎5331 6655), at the corner of Grant and Wainwright St., just a stone's throw from the Sovereign Hill guest carpark. Set in a colorful bungalow covered with iron-wrought frills, the budget-friendly joint serves a smorgasbord of nearly 200 dishes of Indian, Thai, or Italian origin ($7.20-20). Open daily noon-2pm and 5:30-10:30pm. Reservations required F-Su. ❸

The Pancake Kitchen, 2 Grenville St. South (☎5331 6555). Savor pancakes and crepes with assorted fruit and meat ($6.40-13.80) in this restored 1870s building. Offers a wonderfully dated atmosphere enhanced by the decor. Daily specials. Open M-Th 9am-10pm, F-Sa 7:30am-11pm, Su 7:30am-10pm. ❷

SIGHTS

Inquire at the visitors center about tours of Ballarat's historic areas. The **Ballarat Begonia Festival** (Mar. 8-12, 2007) is an open-air arts and crafts fair. **Royal South Street** music, debate, and performance competitions attract top talent (late Aug. to mid-Oct.). The tree-lined pathways of **Victoria Park,** south of Lake Wendouree, make for a good view of the city, and a hike up to the **lookout** on Black Hill is a peaceful nighttime stroll.

SOVEREIGN HILL. Voted the best tourist attraction in Australia by the Australian tourism board in 2006, Sovereign Hill is a living museum that gives visitors a taste of what life was like during the region's gold rush in the 1850s. Sovereign Hill staff, dressed in period attire, roam about town pretending to be miners and townfolk. Demonstrations and exhibits include smelting, musket-firing, and the pouring of over $70,000 worth of gold. A 40min. tour of the mine reveals the often brutal conditions in which miners worked. Pan for gold or ride a horse-drawn carriage through the streets. In the evening, tourists can enjoy the 90 minute **Blood on the Southern Cross** interactive light show which reenacts the events leading up to the infamous Eureka Rebellion. *(☎5337 1100. Open daily 10am-5pm. Day pass combined with Gold Museum admission $32.50, concessions $24.50, children $15.50, families $83. Blood on the Southern Cross $39, children $21, families $105, advanced booking required.)*

VICTORIA

GOLD MUSEUM. The Gold museum, housed in an unusual modern structure directly across the street from Sovereign Hill, has extensive exhibits detailing man's fascination with the glittering substance. Check out replicas of the two largest gold nuggets ever found. Culture-vultures and trivia connoisseurs will enjoy the history of gold movie, narrated by George Plimpton. The museum also houses some interesting but unrelated exhibits, including one on the Chinese in Australia and an another on Aboriginal boomerangs. *(☎5331 1944. Open daily 9:30am-5:20pm. $7.30, concessions $4.90, children $3.50.)*

BALLARAT WILDLIFE PARK. The park's open bush habitats are home to some of Australia's most diverse fauna including fearsome saltwater crocodiles, Tasmanian devils, and the less imposing emus, goannas, wombats, koalas, and free-roaming 'roos. Be sure not to miss the recently acquired group of Tiger Quolls, an endangered carnivorous marsupial. Weekend animal feedings are also a special thrill. *(On Fussel St. From the Eureka Centre, continue away from Sovereign Hill and turn right on Fussel St. ☎5333 5933. Tours 11am. Open daily 9am-5:30pm. $19.50, students $17.50, children $12.50, families $59.)*

EUREKA STOCKADE. From afar the museum looks like a giant sailing ship which has run aground. On the inside, this informative space carefully documents the events of the Eureka Rebellion through a multi-million dollar exhibit. The 1hr. self-guided tour ambles through larger-than-life exhibition spaces and a solemn reflective pool. Ballarat's main information center is located at the entrance. *(Eureka St. at Rodier St. Drive 2km out of town on Main Rd. and turn right at the Eureka St. roundabout; it's 1km up the road. Or, take bus #8. ☎5333 1854; www.eurekaballarat.com. Open daily 9am-5pm. Last entry 4pm. $8, concessions $6, children $4, families $22.)*

NIGHTLIFE AND ENTERTAINMENT

On weekends, the **Bridge Mall** at the east end of Sturt St. fills with pedestrians and street musicians. Numerous hotels and pubs serve as venues for live bands. **Jack's Place,** 121 Lydiard St., across from the train station, is a local haunt with cheap budget accommodation upstairs. (☎5332 1660. Open daily 1pm-latenight. Schooners $5. Dorm bed $25.) **Irish Murphy's,** 36 Sturt St. (☎5331 4091), is a popular Aussie pub chain with live music Th-Su nights. A casual dress code is enforced after 7pm. (Open daily noon-latenight. F-Sa after 10pm cover $4-5.) The historic **Her Majesty's Theatre,** 13 Lydiard St. (☎5333 5888; www.hermaj.com), presents live drama. (Box office open 9:15am-5pm. Tickets $20-50.)

FROM BALLARAT TO BENDIGO

The stretch of curvaceous Midland Highway between Ballarat and Bendigo is dotted with scenic provincial towns; Daylesford and Castlemaine are the largest. **Buses** run between the towns and depart every 25-45min. from the main roundabout in the center of Daylesford.

DAYLESFORD AND HEPBURN SPRINGS. Daylesford is 107km northwest of Melbourne and 46km northeast of Ballarat. Visitors come here to soak in the waters of the nearby Hepburn Springs, the largest concentration of **curative mineral springs** in Australia. Lake Daylesford boasts a significant number of natural mineral deposits freely accessible to the public, although most visitors prefer to be pampered in a spa. The main spa complex offers elaborate aromatherapy sessions and pricey dips in homemade curative concoctions. Maps are available at the **Daylesford Visitors Centre,** 98 Vincent St. (☎5321 6123. Open daily 9am-5pm.) The **Hepburn Spa Resort,** in Hepburn Springs, is a self-proclaimed "wellness retreat" and provides the works. Services range from the relaxation pool and spa (M-F $15, Sa-Su $20, $5 concessions) to massages (30min., $55-60) to body wraps ($95-105). Use of spring waters is free. (☎5348 8888; www.hepburnspa.com.au. Open M-F and Su 10am-6pm, Sa 9am-7pm.)

Although overpriced accommodations surround the spa facilities, a few budget options do exist. The **Daylesford YHA ❷,** 42 Main Rd. in Hepburn Springs, is located in a small country home aptly called **Wildwood.** It's hidden in a thicket and has an interesting, Gaudí-inspired BBQ pit in the backyard. (☎5348 4435. Dorms from $20; singles $32; doubles $48; non-YHA members add $5. Book ahead.) **Continental House ❷,** 9 Lone Pine Ave., is hidden behind wild hedges and stands in striking contrast to the tidy B&Bs next door. (☎5348 2005. Linens $3. Dorms from $20. Prices vary depending on length of stay.)

BENDIGO ☎03

Like almost all Victorian Goldfields towns, "the Go" (pop. 100,000) sprang into existence in the 1850s when the region was flooded by miners lured by tales of striking it rich. While many of its neighbors fell from prosperity to obscurity in the boom-and-bust cycle, Bendigo continued to prosper into the 20th century thanks to a seemingly endless supply of gold-rich alluvial quartz; today it's a lovely commercial center with a plethora of street-side sculptures and private galleries. The grand main street and pedestrian-only shopping arcades make it a pleasant stopover for travelers headed elsewhere.

TRANSPORTATION

Trains and Buses: Bendigo Station is behind the Discovery Centre at the south end of Mitchell St. **V/Line** (☎13 61 96) has **trains** and **buses,** depending on destination, to: **Adelaide**

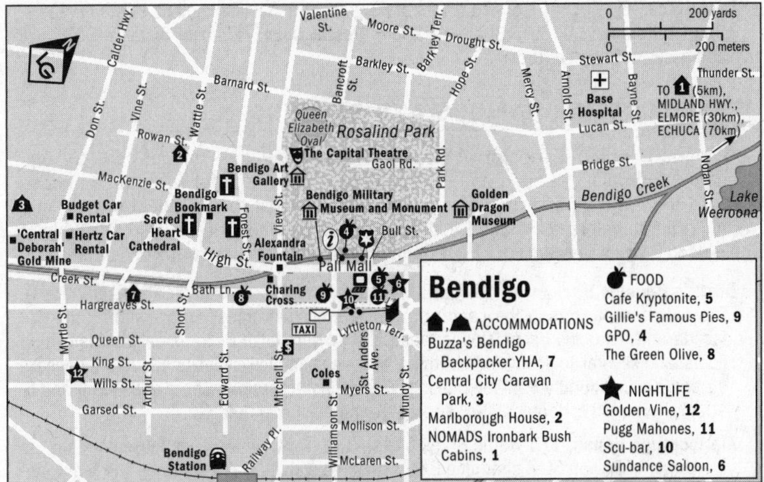

(8½hr., 1 per day, $65); **Ballarat** (2hr., 1 per day, $25); **Daylesford** (1¼hr., 1 per day, $12); **Geelong** (3¾hr., 1 per day, $38); **Maldon** (2hr., 2 per day, $8) via **Castlemaine** (22min., 11 per day, $6); **Melbourne** (2hr., 11 per day, $25); **Mildura** (5hr., 4 per day, $60).

Public Transportation: Bendigo Airport Bus (☎5447 9006) transports visitors to and from the airport.

Taxis: Bendigo Taxis (☎131 008).

Car Rental: A small group of car rental centers are located around the Central Deborah Mine and Tram Depot. **Hertz,** 235 High St. (☎5443 5088), at Thistle St. Open M-F 8:30am-5:30pm, Sa 8:30am-12:30pm, Su 9-11am. **Budget,** 150-152 High St. (☎5442 2766). Open M-F 8:30am-5:30pm, Sa 8am-4pm, Su 8am-noon. There is free 3hr. **parking** on the roof of the Coles supermarket on the corner of Myers St. and Williamson St.

ORIENTATION AND PRACTICAL INFORMATION

In Bendigo, neatly planned streets intersect with winding gullies packed down by diggers' feet. Most points of interest are near the city center, bounded on the south and east by railroad tracks and on the north by Rosalind Park. The **Calder Highway (Hwy. 79)** from Melbourne runs into the city center, becoming High St., then Pall Mall (at Charing Cross), then McCrae St., and finally **Midland Highway,** which leads to Elmore and Echuca. The popular pedestrian **Hargreaves Mall** runs one block along Hargreaves between **Mitchell St.** and **Williamson St.**

Tourist Office: 51-67 Pall Mall St., at Williamson (☎5444 4445 or 1800 233 422), in the ornate post office building. A mini-museum details Bendigo's history. Extensive information about nearby towns also available. Open daily 9am-5pm.

Currency Exchange: ANZ (☎5443 9399), on the corner of Queen and Mitchell St. 24hr. **ATM.** Open M-Th 9:30am-4pm, F 9:30am-5pm.

Police: (☎5440 2510), on Bull St. behind the law courts.

Internet Access: Renaissance Computers, 70 Pall Mall St. (☎5442 5856). Brand-new computers and fast connections. $1 per 10min. Open M-F 9am-5:30pm, Sa 9am-1:30pm. Remains open for those wishing to spend ample time online. **Public Library,** 259 Hargreaves St. (☎5449 2700). $5 per hr. Open M-F 10am-7pm, Sa 10am-1pm.

Post Office: (☎ 13 13 18), on the corner of Hargreaves and Williamson St. *Poste Restante*. Open M-F 9am-5pm, Sa 9:30am-12:30pm. **Postal Code:** for *poste restante* 3552; for addresses in Bendigo 3550.

ACCOMMODATIONS AND CAMPING

Lodging in Bendigo is a colorful array of B&Bs, backpackers, and beds for big-spenders. Although the majority of digs will break the bank for those on a budget, visitors content to spend the extra money will find that the excellent service and rooms offer travelers real bang for their buck. Accommodation is also available at the **Golden Dragon Museum** (p. 649), which is perfect for small groups or families.

Buzza's Bendigo Backpacker YHA, 33 Creek St. (☎ 5443 7680; buzza@bendigo.net.au). The only backpackers in the center of town warmly welcomes visitors with its colorful facade and domestic decor. Comfortable reading den, large dining area with hardwood floors, and several self-contained bathrooms. Linens and towels included. Internet access $2 per 30min. Laundry $2. Free parking. Wheelchair accessible. Check-in 8-10am and 5-10pm. Dorms $21; doubles $54, add $4 per non-YHA member. ❷

Marlborough House, 115 Wattle St. (☎ 5441 4142; www.marlboroughhouse.com.au), on the corner of Rowan St. A charming B&B with large stained-glass windows. The family-run lodging offers calm common spaces and dainty private rooms with sparkling ensuites. The 135-year-old house overlooks the city and sits just a block from the Sacred Heart Cathedral. The adjoining restaurant offers gourmet French fare. Breakfast included. Singles from $99; doubles and twins from $165. ❺

NOMADS Ironbark Bush Cabins (☎ 5448 3344; www.bwc.com.au/ironbark), on Watson St. Located 5km from the city center on a large plot of wooded land. By car, follow the Midland Hwy. out of town toward Echuca and turn left on Holdsworth Rd. Make a right on John St. which curves into Crane Rd., and then make a right onto Watson St. Open-air bar (beer $3). Fire pit. Private cabins available. Basic backpacker accommodations with separate bathroom hut. Try the monstrous green 75m **waterslide,** go horseback riding or gold panning, or enjoy the "Great Australian Pub Ride" ($85). **The Bendigo Goldfields Experience** (p. 650) runs on the premises. Laser warfare games (www.locs.com.au) also available on-site. Dorms $20, cabins $55. ❷

Central City Caravan Park, 362 High St. (☎ 5443 6937), at the corner with Beech St. Take bus #1 from Hargreaves Mall. The conveniently located park has BBQ facilities and a playground. Wheelchair accessible. Reception M-F 8:30am-6pm, Sa-Su 9am-5pm. Sites for 2 from $20. ❶

FOOD

Although small in size, Bendigo has a considerable cafe culture; just look around the tourist office, particularly on Pall Mall and Hargreaves St. Several pubs around town offer cheap eats as well. The **Hargreaves Mall** has a food court that bustles during lunch hours. **Coles** supermarket (☎ 5443 6311; open 24hr.) is on the corner of Myers and Williamson St.

GPO, 60-64 Pall Mall (☎ 5443 4343; www.gpobendigo.com.au). The hippest place in town proves that trendy can be cheap. Smooth beats and sleek decor lure locals and visitors alike. Most come for the striking assortment of delicious flat bread pizzas ($15 including beer). Open daily noon-1am. ❷

Gillie's Famous Pies (☎ 5443 4965), on the corner of Hargreaves Mall and Williamson St. The tastiest way to clog an artery. Locals love the assortment of meat pies and fried food starting at $2.50. Open daily 10am-7pm; closing hours may vary. ❶

Cafe Kryptonite, 92 Pall Mall (☎5443 9777). Features funky main courses ($8.50-18.50) served in a trendy atmosphere with outdoor seating. Open daily 8am-5pm. ❸

The Green Olive, 11 Bath Ln. (☎5442 2676). A good choice for those seeking hearty breakfasts. Generous platters of eggs, bacon, tomatoes, and toast for $10. Breakfast and lunch prices range from $8-20. Open M-F 7am-5:30pm, Sa 7am-3:30pm. ❷

SIGHTS

The budget-savvy way to see Bendigo is to purchase the "Welcome Stranger" pass, available at tourist centers such as the Central Deborah Mine or Bendigo Tram office. It includes entry into the mine, the Discovery Centre, the Golden Dragon museum, the Bendigo pottery museum, the local aviary and the butterfly garden, and two days on the tram. ($51, concessions $43, children $31, families $145.)

CENTRAL DEBORAH MINE. Ninety-minute tours take visitors 61m down the last mine to operate commercially in Bendigo. Explanations of mining history and techniques are interactive; volunteer and you may even get to show off your skill with the drill. The **Underground Adventure Tour** allows participants to don miner's garb and go down one extra level to use real mine equipment for 2½hr. The headquarters of the historic **Bendigo Trams** are located just next door to the mine, and trams operate every hour through town. Discount combo tickets are available at the mine, tram office or the tourist information office. *(76 Violet St. ☎5443 8322, group bookings 5443 8255; www.central-deborah.com.au. Open daily 9:30am-5pm. Regular tours run 1 per hr. on the ½ hr. Admission $18.90, concessions $15.90, children $9.90; combined package with tram tour $28.50/24.50/15.50.)*

LANDMARKS. Tours with recorded commentary cover the town in the restored, turn-of-the-century Bendigo Trams. Trams run hourly, picking up tourists from the elaborate **Alexandra Fountain** near the tourist office or from the Central Deborah Mine. *(1hr.; $12.90, concessions $11.50, children $7.50, families $37.)* The late-Victorian feel of Bendigo's architecture is most pronounced along Pall Mall. Most impressive are the **old post office building** (which now houses the visitors center) and the adjacent Bendigo Law Courts, both with ornate facades on all four sides. The **Shamrock Hotel,** at the corner of Williamson St. and Pall Mall, began as a roaring entertainment hall in the golden 1850s. **Rosalind Park,** on the site of the old 1850s police barracks north of Alexandra Fountain, is a vast expanse of greenery scattered with winding pathways, trees, and statues—including a fairly unflattering likeness of Queen Victoria. If you brave the long climb up its observation tower you'll be rewarded with a view of Bendigo and surrounding gold country. The stunning **Sacred Heart Cathedral,** on High St. between Wattle and Short St., sends its spires soaring toward heaven from atop a hill overlooking town. Details about prominent landmarks are available at the information center.

GOLDEN DRAGON MUSEUM. This collection provides an overview of both Chinese culture in Australia and the culture's particular impact on Bendigo. Displays offer a look at the Chinese-Australian experience in the place dubbed *Dai Gum San* (Big Gold Mountain), but remain notably silent on the racism that Chinese-Australians often faced. The collection's highlight is the fantastically ornate *Sun Loong,* the longest imperial (five-clawed) dragon in the world at just over 100m. The adjacent gardens are a recreation of the imperial water garden in China. The **tea room** ❷ serves light meals and snacks for $6-12, and **accommodation** ❺ is available adjacent to the museum. *(5-9 Bridge St. ☎5441 5044; www.goldendragonmusem.org. Open daily 9:30am-5pm. $8, concessions $6, children $5, families $20. Tea room open during museum hours. Accommodations: singles $55; twins $66; small group $88.)*

BENDIGO GOLDFIELDS EXPERIENCE. Located on the Ironbark property (see **Accommodations**), the Goldfields Experience is pricey. If you're lucky, your findings could pay for the entire trip. *(On Watson St., 5km outside of town. ☎5448 4140; www.bendigogold.com.au. Metal detector rental $35-75 per day depending on quality of detector. Gold panning including 15min. lesson, $10 per hr. Full-day guided tour $220 per person, ½-day $130 per person. Open M-Sa 8:30am-5pm, Su 8:30am-2pm.)*

DISCOVERY SCIENCE & TECHNOLOGY CENTRE. With over 100 hands-on exhibits, the colorful museum is a haven for curious children. Attractions include Australia's largest vertical slide, a planetarium with regular showings, and a dazzling water vortex. Tickets can be purchased along with the Central Deborah Mine and Bendigo Tram tour. *(7 Railway Place ☎5444 4400; www.discovery.asn.au. Open daily 10am-4pm. $9.50, concessions $8, children $6.95, families $30.)*

ENTERTAINMENT AND NIGHTLIFE

Pubs are everywhere in Bendigo. Most are tame local hangouts that close around midnight, but weekends can be rowdier as tourists funnel into the small watering holes and live music pubs. "Uni" nights are also popular, and pubs lower their prices to lure the local students. The main late-night entertainment options are on Pall Mall and Hargreaves St. between Williamson and Mundy St.

Scu-bar, 238 Hargreaves St. (☎5441 6888). Formerly "The Old Crown"; caters to the trendy by employing a dress code: "No effort, no entry." Beer flows freely from behind the chic stainless steel bar, as a late-night crowd lounges on foamy blue chairs. Occasional live music on weekends. Open Th and Sa 8pm-3am, F 5pm-3am.

Pugg Mahones, on the corner of Bull and Hargreaves St. Offers a selection of Irish beers on tap and live music (W-Sa 10pm), in a dark green and hardwood interior. Locals love the hearty pub grub, such as chicken parm ($11). Open daily until 1 or 2am.

Sundance Saloon, on Pall Mall and Mundy St. There's live music behind the fluorescent pink-and-blue facade. W open mic, Th DJ Dru and student discounts, F "crush" night, Sa radio puppets, and Su acoustic night with free pool until 9pm. Happy hour daily 7pm-9pm, beers $4. Cover $5 after 2am. Open M-W and Su 7pm-3am, Th-Sa 7pm-5am.

The Golden Vine Hotel, 135 King St. (☎5443 6063). A bit more out of the way; attracts a young local crowd with chill music. Jam sessions Tu, live bands F-Sa. Weekly comedy club shows $5-15. Open M-Sa 11am-1am, Su noon-11pm.

MURRAY RIVER AREA

Surging through the land is Australia's longest river, the Murray, which defines the border between New South Wales and Victoria and completes its 2600km journey when it empties out into the salty ocean near Adelaide. The ashen eucalyptus trees that haunt the banks of the muddy waters have been a hallowed home to Aboriginals for years. The river was an essential artery in the late 19th century, its waters traveled by giant freight-toting paddle steamers, but extensive rail and road networks rendered these boats obsolete by the end of the 1930s.

BUGGAH. The crops in the Murray area are guarded by a fruit-fly exclusion zone, which means that no fresh fruits or vegetables can enter the region. Several postings along major roads will remind travelers; those who are caught can face fines from $250 to $2000.

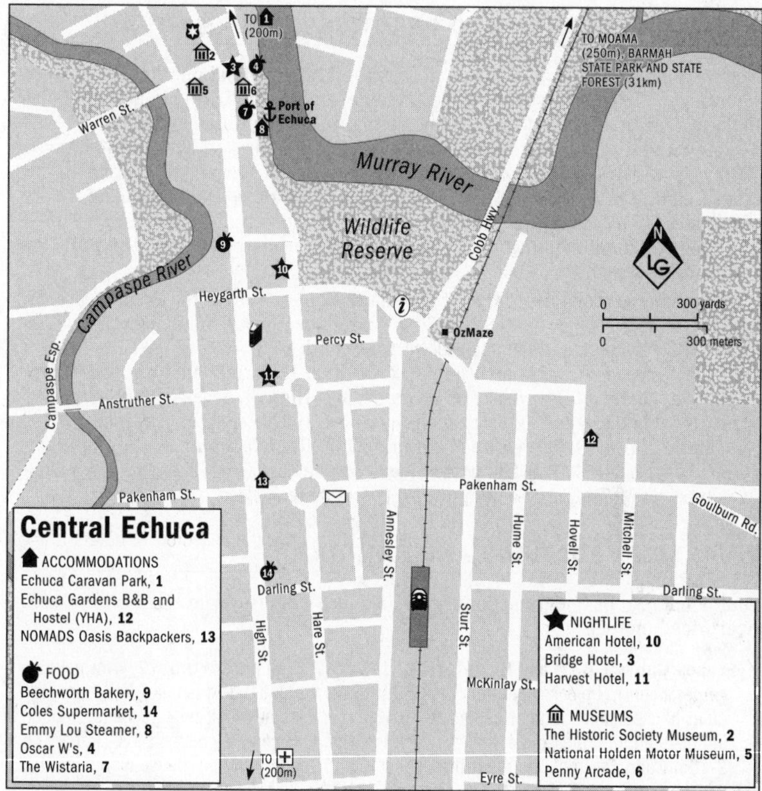

ECHUCA

☎03

The self-declared "Paddle Steamer Capital of Australia," colorful Echuca was founded at the site where the Campaspe and Goulbourn Rivers meet the gushing Murray (Echuca is the Aboriginal word for "meeting of the waters"). Founded by an ex-con in 1853, Echuca quickly became the biggest inland port in all of Australia, transporting supplies halfway across the nation. In its prime the port precinct stretched over a 1km distance and boasted a whopping 79 pubs. However, due to excessive drunkenness and general stoogery, a drinking ban was enacted which greatly decreased such activity. Although the ban has long been lifted, Echuca remains quiet, despite the plethora of informative sights and gourmet dining. Immerse yourself in the Murray riverboat culture by boarding one of the numerous cruises or taking a stroll along the authentic riverside walks.

TRANSPORTATION

V/Line buses run from the visitors center or the Ampol Road House on the Northern Hwy. to: Albury-Wodonga (3-4hr., 1-3 per day, $25-50); Bendigo (1¼hr., 1-3 per day, $8); Melbourne (3½-4hr., 4-6 per day, $34); Mildura (5½hr.; 1 per day M, W, Th, Sa; $42); Swan Hill (2hr., 1-2 per day, $25).

ORIENTATION AND PRACTICAL INFORMATION

Echuca, and the adjacent Moama across the Murray, lie about 200km north of Melbourne. Two highways intersect in the region as well—the **Murray Valley Highway** and **Northern Highway.** Echuca's main thoroughfares are **Hare** and **High Street,** parallel roads that run north-south from the Murray River to the Murray Valley Hwy. From the visitors center, take the bridge across the Murray to the **Cobb Highway** to **Moama** in New South Wales—notable predominantly for its diverse array of gambling clubs. Beware: the layout of Echuca can be rather confusing as most establishments are scattered around town and the port district is quite small.

The **visitors center,** 2 Heygarth St., is on the Echuca side of the Echuca-Moama bridge. (☎5480 7555 or 1800 804 446; www.echucamoama.com. Open daily 9am-5pm.) **ANZ, National,** and **Commonwealth banks** with 24hr. **ATMs** are side-by-side on Hare St., just south of Anstruther St. (All open M-Th 9:30am-4pm, F 9:30am-5pm.) The **library,** at the corner of Heygarth and High St. across the intersection from McDonald's, offers **Internet** access. (☎5482 1997. Research free, email $2.60 per 30min. Book ahead. Open M-Tu and Th-F 10am-5:30pm, W noon-8pm, Sa 10am-1pm, Su 2-4:30pm.) The **post office** is on the corner of Hare and Pakenham St. (Open M-F 9am-5pm, Sa 9am-noon.) **Postal Code:** 3564.

ACCOMMODATIONS AND CAMPING

Only a handful of budget accommodations lurk among several dainty B&B and overpriced motels.

Echuca Gardens B&B and Hostel (YHA), 103 Mitchell St. (☎5480 6522; www.echucagardens.com), 8 blocks east from the CBD. Built in the 2nd oldest building in Echuca, the quiet backpackers' cottage behind the B&B emits a homey feel; only 10 beds, antique upholstered furniture, and a shaggy watchdog named Baron. Key deposit $10. Reception 8-10am and 5-10pm. Cottage: high season $45, children $20; low season $25/10. B&B: high season $130-160, low season $100-140. YHA discount. ❷

NOMADS Oasis Backpackers, 410-422 High St. (☎5480 7866; www.backpackersechuca.com), on the corner of Pakenham St. Set inside an imposing brick structure, the guesthouse is surprisingly comfortable and caters mostly to fruit pickers. Request the suite with its own kitchen and bathroom; avoid the room across from the front desk. Kitchen, TV lounge, outdoor courtyard, and Internet access ($5 per hr.). Ask the manager about discounts for guests at local restaurants. Alcohol is strictly prohibited inside the building. Transportation to work sites $5.50 per day. Reception 24hr. 4- to 12-bed dorms $23; doubles $46. Weekly $132/276. NOMADS members get a $3 discount per night. ❷

Emmy Lou Steamer, Murray River, boarding at 57 Murray Esplanade (☎5480 2237; www.emmylou.com.au). For a real (expensive) treat, enjoy your slumber aboard 1 of the perennial paddleboats of Echuca. Available for 1-night stays Sa, 2-night stays W-Th. All meals included. Overnight cruise: twin shared lower deck $190 per person, upper deck $205; double cabin $220. 2-night cruise: twin shared lower deck $395, upper deck $415; double cabin $435. ❺

Echuca Caravan Park, 57 Crofton St. (☎5482 2157; www.echucacaravanpark.com.au). A massive plot of land heavily peppered with campervans, especially during the holiday seasons. Idyllic location on the Murray River next to a new tennis court. Pricing depends on season. Linens $10. Tent sites $24-30; powered sites $25-36; cabins $90-130. Extra adult $14-17, child $8-12. Book ahead. ❷

FOOD

Don't miss **Oscar W's Wharfside ❷**, 101 Murray Esplanade, which promises an unforgettable dining experience with amazing views of the Murray. All of the scrumptious servings are created on a red gum grill. Each culinary creation is a clever fusion of traditional gourmet dishes and the local palate. The twice-cooked boned duck ($33) is their signature dish, although diners won't go wrong with any of the options on the diverse menu. The deck bar, hovering over the river, offers cheaper fare ($7.50-16.50) and guests can sit in old kegs which have been refitted into surprisingly comfortable seats. (☎5482 5133; www.oscarws.com.au. Open daily 11am-11pm, lunch served from noon and dinner from 6pm.) Take a trip back in time and indulge in the turn-of-the-century atmosphere at **The Wistaria ❷**, 51 Murray Esplanade, featuring waitstaff in 19th-century black aprons. Enjoy a tasty breakfast ($12.50) in the color garden. (☎5482 4210. Open daily 8am-4:30pm.) The **Beechworth Bakery ❶**, 513 High St., has also set up shop in Echuca. Try the fabulous snickerdoodles ($3) or the beestings ($3.50). They offer focaccia ($7.30) for those seeking lunch. (☎5480 6999. Open daily 6am-7pm.) A **Coles** supermarket is on the corner of High and Darling St. (Open daily 6am-midnight.)

NIGHTLIFE

Numerous pubs on High and Hare St. are filled with friendly locals. The sleek bar at the **Harvest Hotel,** 193 Hare St., keeps the booze flowing with $2.50 beer and spirits. (☎5482 1266. Happy hour F-Sa 10-11pm and midnight-1am. Open M-Th 11am-1am, F-Sa 11am-4am, Su 3-11pm.) The **Bridge Hotel,** at Hopwood Pl. right by the port, is set inside an elegant brick manse. (☎5482 2247. Open M-Sa 7:30am-1am, Su 7:30am-11:30pm.) Younger locals and backpackers head to the **American Hotel,** at Hare and Heygarth St. for pots ($3) and schooners ($4). (☎5482 5044. $2.50 spirits. Happy hour Th-Sa 10-11:30pm. Open M-Sa 11am-1am, Su 11am-11pm.)

SIGHTS

HISTORIC PORT. The main attraction in Echuca is its port, consisting of the wharf and several historic buildings. The 1865 red gum wharf has three levels to accommodate changing river conditions. Blacksmith and woodturning shops sell handmade wares, and a steam display explains the workings of the portentous invention that brought on the Industrial Revolution. *(Historic Port Area, entrance at 52 Murray Esplanade. ☎5482 4248; www.portofechuca.org.au. Open daily 9am-5pm. $11.50, concessions $10, children $7.50, families $35.)*

PORT PRECINCT. The most interesting stop along the promenade is **Sharp's Magic Movie House and Penny Arcade,** which has the ultimate collection of sundry artifacts. Antique enthusiasts will have a field day traipsing through the largest functioning penny arcade in the Southern Hemisphere. Have your fortune read or watch one of the many silent movies screened daily. Before calling it a day, taste-test over 30 different fudge flavors created in-house. *(☎5482 2361; nsharp@mcmedia.com.au. Open daily 9am-5pm. $15, concessions $12, children $10.)* The **Star Hotel** (☎5480 1181), on the Port Precinct, is one of the only surviving bars in town. During the prohibition, patrons would gather in the secret underground tunnel during police raids (assorted wines $5.50 per glass). The **Bridge Hotel** has a carefully preserved suite and gallery upstairs. At the other end of the precinct is the old **Customs House,** which exacted tariffs from passing watercraft during Echuca's days as the commercial hub of the Murray. Today, the Customs House building is home to the **Murray Esplanade Cellars,** which allows visitors to sample its excellent wines and spirits. *(2 Leslie St. ☎5482 6058. Open daily 9:30am-5:30pm.)* An even tastier stop is **Iron House Coopers,** in the old Freeman's Foundry at 13-17 Murray Esplanade, where you can sample myriad intriguing Port wines, including Jack Daniels and Jim Beam varieties. *(☎5480 6955. Open M-Sa 9am-5pm, Su 10am-5pm.)*

PADDLESTEAMERS. Several paddlesteamers still ply the waters off the old port and are now open to the public for leisurely cruises. The Port Authority runs 1hr. cruises on *P.S. Pevensey*, *P.S. Alexander Arbuthnot*, and the *P.S. Adelaide*, the oldest wooden paddlesteamer in Australia. *(The Historic Port building, 52 Murray Esplanade. ☎5482 4248. 5 per day. $20, concessions $15, children $9, families $42. Joint port and cruise: $23/19/13/57.)* Just across the street are the paddlesteamers *Pride of the Murray* and *Emmylou;* the *Emmylou* is worth the slightly higher price, and so are its overnight accommodations, if you really want to splurge. *(Tickets at the Customs House or at 57 Murray Esplanade. ☎5480 2237 or 5482 5244. Pride of the Murray: 1hr.; 6 per day; $15, seniors $13, children $7, families $42. Emmylou: 1hr.; 5 per day; $18.50, children $9; 1½hr. $22.50/10.50.)* The same company also runs 1hr. cruises on the steamer *P.S. Canberra. ($17.50, seniors $14.50, children $8, families $45.)*

VICTORIA

NATIONAL HOLDEN MOTOR MUSEUM. For car-lovers or those with an old-fashioned need for speed, the Holden Motor Museum is a must-see. It showcases over 50 years of "Australia's Own" automobile, with over 40 lovingly restored Holden models and rare prototypes. The amusing video retrospective spotlights not only the car, but also Australia's love for Holden ads. *(7-11 Warren St. ☎5480 2033. Open daily 9am-5pm. $6, concessions $4.50, children $3, families $14.)*

ECHUCA HISTORICAL SOCIETY MUSEUM. Located in the old police station, the building now holds artifacts from the founding years of the town. The society is run by elderly locals who are not shy about recounting tales of life in town 60 years ago. A truly interesting place to visit simply to catch an insider's point of view about the town that locals are proud to call home. *(At the corner of Warren and Dickson St. Open daily 11am-3pm. $3.50, children $1.)*

DAYTRIP FROM ECHUCA

BARMAH. Thirty kilometers east of Echuca, the gnarled trees and dappled branches of Barmah form the largest red gum eucalyptus forest in the world. The **Dharnya Centre** is on the edge of the haunting forest, offering visitors information about the park. *(☎5869 3249. Open daily 10:30am-4pm. Free.)* Be sure to check out the museum dedicated to the native Yorta Yorta people. There are several intriguing walking trails in the park; they give tourists the chance to view wildlife and to get better acquainted with the environs. The **Lakes Loop Track** (4km) begins at the Dharnya Centre and leads deep into the red gum forest, passing numerous indigenous oven mounds before reaching the Murray River and Broken Creek. The **Yamyabuc Discovery Trail** (1.5km) is an exceptionally easy introduction to the unique terrain and history. Visitors who wish to stay the night may camp anywhere within the park, though beware that red gum branches can snap off.

SWAN HILL ☎03

This small town on the Murray River between Echuca and Mildura was named by Major Mitchell, a famous explorer of southeastern Australia who sought refuge in the area. The legend claims that he could never get a full night's sleep due to the incessant cooing of the nearby swans. Today, Swan Hill is best known for its fishing spots and fields for reaping. To tourists, the town is remarkable for having the oldest outdoor museum in the entire country. The **Pioneer Settlement Museum,** on Horseshoe Bend, details a full century (1830-1930) of frontier life through the display of original buildings and antique equipment. Free rides in horse-drawn carriages are available to guests. Actors dressed in turn-of-the-century clothing get tourists in the mood by performing slapstick street theater. Guests who stay into the evenings can watch the rather cheesy, although family-friendly, **Sound and Light Tour** at dusk. (☎5036 2410. Open Tu-Su 10am-5pm. Entry to the village $20, concessions $15, children $11, family $50. Pyap Cruise or the Sound and Light Tour $16/13/9/38 each. All events package $40/30/20/90.) Swan Hill's pride in its fishing industry is manifest in the **Giant Murray Cod,** located by the north end of the rail station. Dwarfing its living brethren at an enormous 6m by 11m, the cod was originally built as a prop for the movie *Eight Ball,* and has since taken its place in Australia "Big" lore. Stop by the new **visitors center** on the corner of Curlewis and McCrae St. (☎5032 3033; www.swanhillonline.com.au; open 9am-5pm) for additional information about the area's attractions. They'll fill you in on the best **fishing** spots like Pental Island Floodway on the Murray River, 21km south of Swan Hill.

The majority of budget accommodations in the Swan Hill area are dedicated to fruit pickers and are located quite far outside of town. The two main clusters of backpacker digs are at Lake Boga (14km south) and Nyah (24km north). The **Commercial Hotel ❷,** at Lake Boga on Marraboor St., off Station St. from the highway, has a small number of tidy rooms. (☎5037 2140. Continental breakfast included. Singles $25; twins and doubles $30.) The **Nyah West Grand Hotel ❷** on Station St. is a bit larger. (☎5030 2403. Singles $25; twins and doubles $30; families $75.) The **Riverside Caravan Park ❷,** 1 Monash Dr., by the Pioneer Settlement, has a pool, BBQ, and kitchen. (☎5032 1494; cammpark@swanhill.net.au. Reception 8am-8pm. 2-person sites $24-32; cabins $60-150.) Try the **Swan Hill Club ❶,** 5-17 McCallum St. on the corner of Curlewis St., for big cheap meals. All visitors must present a valid ID at the door. (☎5032 2060. Weekday 2-course lunch $9.50. Open M-Th noon-2pm and 6-8pm, F-Sa noon-2pm and 6-9pm, and Su noon-2pm.) **Java Spice ❷** is popular among locals and offers succulent southeast Asian fare. (☎5033 0511. Open daily for lunch and dinner. Daily $11 takeaway lunch available.)

V/Line trains leave daily for Melbourne, passing through Bendigo (5hr., $55) from the station on Curlewis St., between McCrae and Rutherford St. Daily **bus** service is available to Echuca (1½hr., $23); and Mildura (2½hr., $37). **ATMs** are on Campbell St. The **post office is** on 164 Campbell St. (Open M-F 9am-5pm.) **Postal Code:** 3585.

MILDURA ☎03

A palm-lined oasis in dry Mallee country, Mildura can hit record-breaking temperatures during the summer. The town is mostly working-class and is a haven for hungry backpackers as there are 11 months of reaping and planting each year.

TRANSPORTATION

For those seeking transportation to farming jobs, note that your hostel can assist you with finding suitable means. The train and bus station is on 7th St., across from the northern end of Langtree Ave. **V/Line** runs to: Albury-Wodonga (10hr.; 1 per day Tu, W, F, Su; $67); Echuca (5hr.; 1 per day Tu, W, F, Su; $42); Melbourne (7-9hr., 2-3 per day, $67) via Bendigo (5-7hr., $58); Swan Hill (3-4hr., $37). Countrylink runs to Sydney (15hr., daily 4am, $120). Tom Evans coaches (☎5027 4309) services Broken Hill (3½hr.; M, W, F 9am; $52). For car rentals, **Avis** (☎5022 1818),

Budget (☎5021 4442), **Hertz** (☎5022 1411), and **Thrifty** (☎5023 2989) are in the airport, 8km out of town on the Sturt Hwy., with rentals from $55-70 per day. Avis also has a branch at 7th and Madden St. (☎5023 1263).

ORIENTATION AND PRACTICAL INFORMATION

The commercial center of Mildura is the strip of **Langtree Avenue** from 7th to 10th St., which includes a **pedestrian mall** chock full of retail and dining options. **The Mildura Visitor Information and Booking Centre,** on the corner of Deakin Ave. and 12th St. can assist with any queries. (☎5018 8380; www.mildura.vic.gov.au/tourism. Open M-F 9am-5:30pm, Sa-Su 9am-5pm.) The attached **library** offers free **Internet** access ($2 for 30min.) for research. (☎5018 8350. Book ahead. Open Tu-F 10am-7pm, Sa 10am-2pm, Su 1-5pm.) For **work opportunities,** ask for the free Working Holiday and Backpacker Information Sheet from the visitors center, or contact **MADEC Jobs Australia,** 95 Lime Ave., off 10th St. (☎5021 3359. Open M-F 8am-7pm.) Work can often be found in the Sunraysia Daily's employment section. There are also over a dozen hostels in town which help guests locate farming work. The **police** are on Madden Ave. between 8th and 9th St. (☎5023 9555) and the **post office** is on the corner of 8th St. and Orange Ave. (Open M-F 9am-5pm.) **Postal Code:** 3500.

VICTORIA

ACCOMMODATIONS

Hostels in Mildura serve the constant influx of travelers searching for fruit-picking jobs; there are more than a dozen basic budget options scattered around town, as well as in nearby Red Cliffs and Wentworth. These self-proclaimed "working hostels" offer shelter and help find work. **Oasis Backpackers ❷,** 230-232 Deakin Ave., is located past the visitors center when heading up Deakin Ave. from the train station and Murray River. This sparkling hostel is an oasis for weary fruit pickers; they are invited to laze in the pool or chill out in front of a plasma TV. (☎04 1738 0744 or 04 1723 0571; www.milduraoasis.com.au. On-site licensed bar. Transport to work $5 per day. Internet $4 per hr. F free dinner. 4-bed ensuite dorms $20, weekly $140.) **Mildura City Backpackers ❷,** at 50 Lemon Ave., has tidy bungalows with smooth hardwood floors; just try to avoid the bedroom with a skylight instead of a window. (☎5022 7922 or 04 0750 2120; www.milduracitybackpackers.com.au. Lockers $2 per day. Key deposit $10. Transport to work $6 per day. F free dinner. Dorms $22, weekly $130; twins $25, weekly $150; doubles $55, weekly $330.) **Riverboat Bungalow and Zippy Koala ❷** is located at 157 7th St. and 206 8th St., almost at the intersection with Chaffey St. This is the original working hostel in Mildura. The Riverboat portion consists of three neighboring bungalows, and the Zippy Koala cabins are currently being refurbished; call ahead for details. (☎5021 5315; transport to work $3 per day; dorms $22, weekly $120. VIP discount $1.)

FOOD AND NIGHTLIFE

The best option for a night out is the **Langtree Avenue Mall,** one block west of Deakin Ave. between 7th and 9th St. **Pizza Cafe at the Grand ❶**, 18 Langtree Ave., dishes out gooey slices of wood-oven pies. (☎5022 2223. Open daily.) **Fasta Pasta ❷,** 30 Langtree Ave., serves decent and (as the name suggests) quickly prepared pastas ($8-13) and pizzas ($11-16) at reasonable prices. (☎5022 0622. Open M-Sa 11:30am-3pm and 5-10pm, Su 11:30am-3pm and 5-9:30pm.) There is a 24hr. **Coles** supermarket at 8th St. and Lime Ave.

The bars of downtown Mildura owe their prosperity to the constant string of fruit pickers who need to unwind with a frothy beer after a grueling day in the field. Generally all of the pubs around town have varied happy hours and the weary workers soporifically hop from one establishment to the next imbibing the cheapest beer possible. **Setts Cafe Bar,** 110-114 8th St., on the corner of Orange Ave., has a sprawling bar with high ceilings. (☎5023 0474. F trivia night. Open M-W and Su 10am-midnight, Th-Sa 10am-2am.) **Sandbar** has a great outdoor beer garden, perfect for cool nights. (☎5021 2181. Happy hour Tu-Sa 5-8pm; W-Sa live bands 10:30pm. Cover $5 F-Sa after 10pm. Open Tu noon-midnight, W-Sa noon-3am.) There are also a few nightclubs at 8th St. and Langtree Ave.

SIGHTS

Mildura is the base camp for nearby national parks and other outback sights. The visitors center (p. 656) books all commercial tours. For nearly 30 years, **Junction Tours'** Tom Evans has been running tours in the Mildura area, offering up his encyclopedic knowledge of Mungo National Park. (☎5027 4309. Tours Su $70; local hotspots Tu, Th, Sa $46-57; Broken Hill M, W, F $120.) **Harry Nanya Tours** runs full-day trips to Mungo and Wentworth focusing on Aboriginal history and the Dreaming. (☎5027 2076 or 1800 630 864; www.harrynanyatours.com.au. $75-300.) **Jumbunna** runs trips to Mungo as well as a Mildura nature walk. These tours are led by an Aboriginal guide and focus on tribal culture. They also offer trips to Thegoa Lagoon and to the surrounding vineyards. (☎04 1258 1699. Day-tour $75, seniors $70, children $40, families $200.) As is often the case for the towns along the **Murray River,** the main summertime attraction is the local swimming hole. **Apex Park,** a sandbar in the Murray, is perfect on hot days, as it's shaded by ash trees and red gum trees. From town, take 7th St. past the train station and turn right across the tracks on Chaffey Ave., which winds its way to the park. The 1881 paddlewheeler *Rothbury* cruises to **Trentham Estate Winery.** (☎5023 2200. 5hr.; Th 10:30am; $48, ages 5-14 $22.) Of the 10 local wineries in the immediate area, the most internationally famous is **Lindemans,** on Edey Rd. in Karadoc. To get there, you'll need a car; drive from Mildura down 15th St. (the Calder Hwy.) through Red Cliffs, then look for the signs. (☎5051 3285. Open daily 10am-4:30pm.)

HUME CORRIDOR

The Hume Hwy. links Melbourne and Sydney via 872km of relatively unspectacular scenery; intrepid travelers who venture off the Hume, however, are amply rewarded. Quaint mining towns and ski resorts are sprinkled throughout the sunburnt hills. Farther west along the Murray Valley Hwy. are the billabongs of Yarrawonga and Cobram, perfect for fishing, swimming, and snoozing.

MANSFIELD ☎03

Mansfield's *raison d'être* is its proximity to Mt. Buller, allowing tourists to stop and rent skis and chains before making the 45km ascent to Victoria's most popular ski resort. The **Mansfield Passenger Terminal** is at 137 High St. **V/Line buses** (☎13 61 96) serve Melbourne (3hr., 1-2 per day, $34) and Mt. Buller (1hr., 7 per day, $72) during ski season. Law requires all vehicles heading to Mt. Buller to carry **snow chains** from June until the end of ski season. You can leave them in the trunk, but there are spot checks and hefty fines ($135) for not carrying them at all. Drivers heading to the top of the mountain should be careful to fill their cars with petrol in Mansfield, as it is not widely available at the summit.

The **Mansfield Visitors Centre** is just outside town at 167 Maroondah Hwy. (☎5775 7000, bookings 1800 039 049; reservations@mansfield-mtbuller.com.au. Open daily 9am-5pm.) Heading east into town on **High Street,** the town's main drag, you'll find ski rental stores and a few **ATMs.** The **library,** at the corner of High and Collopy St., has **Internet** access; you must fill out a form, even for one-time use. (☎5775 2176. $2 per 30min. Open Tu 2-6pm, W 9:30am-1pm, Th 9:30am-5:30pm, F 9:30am-6pm, Sa 9:30am-noon.) The **police** station is at 92-94 High St. (☎5775 2555). The **post office** is next door at 90 High St. (☎5775 2248. Open M-F 9am-5pm.) **Postal Code:** 3722. **Ski Centre Mansfield,** 131 High St. (☎5775 2859 or 1800 647 754), and its nearby affiliate, **PJ's Ski Hire,** 149 High St. (☎5775 1624), rent **chains** (full-day $15) and a range of ski equipment and clothing. (Open June-Oct. M-Th, Sa, and Su 6am-7pm, F 6am-midnight.) There are similar ski rental shops all along High St., all offering comparable deals (full-day skis, boots, and poles $25-30; snowboard and boots $45-50).

The best budget beds in town are at the **Mansfield Backpackers Inn ❷,** 116 High St., part of the brick bungalows at the Travellers Lodge Motel. The friendly owners keep the place clean and comfortable, and provide a large common area for backpackers that includes a tidy kitchen, lockers, library, and TV. (☎5775 1800; www.mansfieldtravellodge.com. Only the motel portion has A/C. Book ahead in winter. Reception 24hr. Dorms $25; singles $75; doubles $80-95; family rooms $135-145.) The **Delatite Hotel ❸,** on the corner of High and Highett St., offers simple accommodation above a smoky bar. (☎5775 2004. Shared bath and toilet. Towels, soap, and continental breakfast included. Singles $35; doubles $70. Bar open daily 10am-1am.) For a satisfying bite, try the **Ski Inn Cafe ❶,** 61 High St., which offers chicken breast burgers ($5), a range of fish 'n' chips options, and pastries ($2-8). (☎5775 2175. Open daily 6am-9pm.) There are two supermarkets: **FoodWorks,** 12 Highett St. (☎5775 2255), and **IGA,** 47-51 High St. (☎5775 2014. Both deliver to Mt. Buller. Both open daily 8am-8pm.)

VICTORIA

MOUNT BULLER ☎03

Victoria's largest and most accessible ski resort, Mt. Buller is a 3hr. drive from Melbourne and has arguably the best terrain in Victoria. While it may not compare to popular skiing destinations in Europe or the US (despite the local moniker "Aussie Alps"), it's a mecca for skiers and snowboarders between mid-June and early October. Though generally quiet in the low season, several weekends during summer attract large groups of tourists; look for the luxury car races at the end of January or the annual Easter weekend art show.

TRANSPORTATION AND PRACTICAL INFORMATION. Along with **V/Line** (see **Mansfield,** p. 657), **Mansfield-Mount Buller Bus Lines** operates coach service to Mt. Buller from Mansfield. (☎5775 6070; www.mmbl.com.au. 1hr., 6-8 per day, $40.) **V/Line** (☎13 61 96) offers round-trip service from Melbourne to Mt. Buller. ($115, including ski fees.) **Snowcaper Tours** departs from Melbourne and offers packages that include round-trip transport, entrance fees, and a full-day lift ticket. Participants leave Melbourne at 4am and return by 9:30pm. (☎5775 2367, reservations 1800 033 023. Mid-week $115, Sa-Su $130.) Only Mansfield-Mt. Buller and V/Line buses pull into the **Cow Camp Plaza,** in the center of Mt. Buller village; all others stop at the base of the mountain, making a cab ride to the top necessary. If going by car, bring snow chains (cars without chains will be fined $135 and given 3 demerit points) and take Buller Rd. (Hwy. 164) east to Mt. Buller. (Car admission $35 per day; overnight fee $8 per night.) There is free parking at the bottom of the mountain. To get to the village from the carpark, visitors without luggage can take a free shuttle; those with bags must take a taxi ($12). Beware: all these daily charges add up fast. Consider taking the bus, especially if you're staying on the mountain for a while.

The village is the hub of accommodations, food, and ski services. The **Cow Camp Plaza** houses lockers, **ATMs,** and **Cow Camp Alpine Ski Rentals.** (☎5777 6082. Skis, boots, and poles $32-70; snowboard and boots $45-70.) The **information center,** located in the nearby post office in summer and opposite the plaza in winter, has maps of the resort and slopes, as well as info on work and long-term accommodations options. (☎5777 7800, reservations 1800 039 049; reservations@mansfield-mtbuller.com.au. Open daily 8:30am-5pm.) The **lift ticket office** sits across the village center from the info tower. (☎5777 7800 or 5777 7877. Day pass $85, children and high school students with valid ID $46. University students with valid ID receive 50% discount Tu, 20% M and W-Su.) For the latest **snow conditions,** call the official Victorian Snow Report (☎1902 240 523; www.vicsnowreport.com.au. $0.55 per min.) or tune into 93.7FM. The Resort Management Building in the village center has a **post office.** (☎5777 6013. Open daily 8:30am-5pm.) **Postal Code:** 3723.

ACCOMMODATIONS. In the winter, **Mount Buller YHA Lodge ❹** is the least expensive lodging on the mountain, and you can ski to its front door. (☎5777 6181; mountbuller@yhavic.org.au. 2-night min. stay on weekends. Book at least 3wk. ahead July-Aug. Ski lockers available. Reception 8-10am and 5-10pm. Dorms $43-68 depending on season, YHA discount $5.) Next door, the **Kooroora Hotel ❺** has more intimate four-person dorms with showers. There is a 15% guest discount for on-site ski rental. (☎5777 6050; kooroora@bigpond.com. Open only during ski season. 18+. Reservations require a 50% deposit. Dorms M-Th $85, and F-Su $100.)

FOOD AND NIGHTLIFE. A polar bear guards the doorway at **ABOM ❷,** on Summit St., a convivial lodge offering affordable bistro fare and an ideal refuge from the cold. (☎5777 7899; www.mtbuller.com/abom. Lower-end lunch fare of sandwiches and soups are around $10.) The campy Cow Camp Plaza houses **Uncle Pat's ❷,** with second floor decks overlooking the valley and the only budget dining option in the village open all year. (☎5777 6949. Focaccias $8. Pizzas $7-16.) Though only open during ski season, **Kooroora's Pub** is hands-down the place to go for nightlife. Besides their great atmosphere, it's the only place on the mountain regularly open past midnight. (Sa live music, M-F and Su DJs. Open until 3am; kitchen open until 10pm.)

SKIING. Nearly half of Mt. Buller's terrain is classified as "intermediate," but several expert trails traverse the southern slopes, including **Fanny's Finish,** which separates the skiers from the snow-bunnies. First-time skiers have plenty of long runs (beginner terrain 25%) to choose from, as well as numerous lesson packages. Twenty-five lifts service the mountain, and lift lines are usually short. Those who prefer the flatlands will find 75km of cross-country skiing trails (approx. half of which are groomed) and an entire mountain, **Mount Stirling,** set aside for their use. (Resort management ☎0419 514 65, ticket office 5777 5624. Open June-Sept. dawn-dusk. No overnight accommodations on Mt. Stirling except camping, which is free.) The **information center** (next to the carparks) contains a public shelter with fireplace, ski and toboggan rental, and food. (Car entry $23; trail $10; cross-country ski rental $35; telemark $47.)

HIKING AND MOUNTAIN BIKING. After many of its trails were destroyed by bushfire damage, Mt. Buller is slowly regaining its status as a prime mountain biking and hiking destination. The Horsehill chairlift near the carpark operates intermittently in January and the end of December (subject to bushfires), transporting bikers and hikers to higher-altitude trails. The **Summit Walk** (1½hr. round-trip; easy), beginning and ending at the Arlberg Hotel at the western edge of town, has informative plaques on local flora and fauna and rewards hikers with views of blue-green mountains and cattle country rolling to the horizon. The summit can also be reached by driving to the end of Summit Rd. and following a marked unsealed road to the base of the final leg of the summit hike (200m). Popular with mountain bikers, a longer hike to **Mount Stirling** via **Corn Hill** and **Howqua Gap** (5-7hr. round-trip; moderate) offers a grand view of Mt. Buller. The shortest of the hikes, the **Blind Creek Falls** walk (40min. round-trip; moderate), is accessible from Boggy Corner, 3.5km below the village. The path leads down a switchback to the Chalet Creek and then to the falls.

WANGARATTA ☎03

Referred to endearingly as "Wang" by locals, Wangaratta (pronounced WANG-uh-RET-ta) was erected at the junction of the Hume Hwy. and the Great Alpine Rd. Don't believe what you hear about Wang—its reputation as a sleepy, ho-hum town is quite the fallacy. Wangaratta, an Aboriginal word meaning "resting place of the cormorant," is a great base from which to bush-wrangle in Kelly Country, fruitpick among fertile plains, or explore picturesque vistas in the nearby High Country.

TRANSPORTATION AND PRACTICAL INFORMATION. Schedules and prices vary; contact the train station (☎5721 3641) for up-to-date info. **V/Line** (☎13 61 96) runs from the station at 51 Norton St. to: Albury station (1hr., 1 per day, $13); Beechworth (30min., 1 per day, $7); Bright (1½hr., 1 per day, $13); Melbourne (2½hr., 3 per day, $40); Rutherglen (30min., 1 per day, $6); Wodonga station (50min., 1 per day, $10). **Countrylink** runs to Sydney (9hr., 2 per day, $100).

Visit the **Worktrainers Employment Services** on the corner of Ovens and Faithful St. for assistance with finding available farmhand work. (☎1800 062 332; www.worktrainers.com.au. Open M-F 9am-5pm.) The **visitors center** at 100 Murphy St. in the CBD has a useful, free map of town and significant information about fruit-picking opportunities and nearby activities. An Internet terminal has recently been installed in the center. (☎5721 5711 or 1800 801 065. Open daily 9am-5pm.) Additional **Internet** access can be found at the **library,** 62 Ovens St. (☎5721 2366. Book ahead. Open M-Tu and Th-F 9:30am-6pm, W 9:30am-8pm, Sa 9am-noon. $2 per 30min., 1hr. max.) Also check out **Your Computer Zone,** down the street from the visitors center at 64A Murphy St., near the corner of Reid St. (☎1800 636 553. $2 per 10min. Open M-F 9am-6pm, Sa 9am-1pm.) The **post office** is by the intersection of Murphy and Ely St. (Open M-F 9am-5pm.) **Postal Code:** 3677.

ACCOMMODATIONS AND FOOD. The best budget digs in town is the **Billabong Motel ❸,** 12 Chisholm St., at the end of Reid St. The diligent manager ensures that the rooms are always prim and proper. (☎5721 2353. Singles $30; ensuite $45; doubles from $55.) Just around the corner is the **Hotel Pinsent ❸,** 20 Reid St., known by locals as the "Pino." With an expansive bar and restaurant, the Pino has inexpensive, simple ensuite rooms with TVs. Towels, soap, tea, coffee, and a small continental breakfast are included. (☎5721 2183. Singles $35-45; doubles from $60; triples $70; quads $80.) Across the Ovens River on Pinkerton Cr., just north of Faithful St., is **Painters Island Caravan Park ❶,** with a swimming pool and a playground. (☎5721 3380; paintersisland.cpark@bigpond.com. Reception 8am-8pm. Powered sites $22-25; cabins from $55.) If none of these lodgings is available, the visitors center has color-coded handouts with additional options.

For travelers on a tight budget, the "shopper docket" is of note. Available at any local supermarket with purchase of groceries, the coupon entitles users to receive a meal for $3 at the Hotel Pinsent with the purchase of an additional meal. **Scribbler's Cafe ❶,** 66 Reid St., is so named because patrons are given bits of paper and encouraged to leave their prophetic words behind. Scribbler's serves breakfast ($6-16) and dessert all day, and also offers lunch and early dinners. (☎5721 3945. Open daily 9am-2:30pm, Tu-Sa 8am-5:45pm. Kitchen closes around 5pm. BYO.)

Casual **Hollywood's Pizza Cafe ❷**, 1 Murphy St., is as classy as Wang gets. Vast outdoor seating, fresh coffee, and tasty pizzas (from $9) keep the locals coming back for seconds. (☎5721 9877; www.hollywoods.com.au. Open Tu-Th and Su 9am-11pm, F-Sa 9am-latenight.) The **Wangaratta Club ❷** and the **Wangaratta R.S.L. ❷** are located across the street from one another on Victoria Pde. and offer discount dining. (☎5721 3711 and 5721 2501 respectively. Both open M-Th and Su noon-2pm and 6-8pm, F-Sa noon-2pm and 6-8pm. Meals $8-20.) Groceries are available at **Safeway,** on Ovens St. between Reid and Ford St. (open daily 7am-midnight) and **Coles,** on Tone Rd., south of the CBD (open 24hr.).

SIGHTS AND WINERIES. Although there is a lack of major sights within the city of Wangaratta itself, it is a good base for regional exploration. Take the opportunity to explore **Milawa Gourmet Region,** a sleepy village that produces its own wines and cheeses, and has a smattering of B&Bs. Take Oxley Flats Rd. from town all the way to tiny Milawa and stop at the **Milawa Cheese Factory** on Factory Rd., which has generous free samples of over 20 sinfully delicious gourmet cheeses, handmade from the milk of local goats and cows. If the samples don't sate your appetite, there is a snazzy new **restaurant ❸** (main courses from $20) and a first-rate bakery that has a 13-year-old sourdough culture named George. (☎5727 3589. Bakery open daily 9am-5pm. Lunch daily noon-3pm. Dinner Th-Sa starting at 6:30pm. Book ahead for dinner.) About 1km down the road, the classy **Brown Brothers Vineyard** could satisfy a small nation with its five tasting bars, though the experience doesn't come cheap. Every course at its **Epicurean Centre Restaurant ❸** includes an accompanying glass of wine; the attached lounge serves lighter fare. (☎5720 5500. Vineyard open daily 9am-5pm. Restaurant open daily 11am-3pm. Lounge open daily 9am-4pm.)

Visitors can bike, hike, or ride horses on the **Murray to the Mountains Rail Trail.** (☎1800 801 065; www.railtrail.com.au.) The 94km paved trail follows historical railway lines and passes through **Bowser, Beechworth,** and **Myrtleford** all the way to **Bright.** For the musically inclined, Wangaratta's renowned **Jazz Festival** (☎5722 1666 or 1800 803 944; www.wangaratta-jazz.org.au), on the weekend prior to the Melbourne Cup (late Oct. or early Nov.), ranks among Australia's best; accommodations are often booked full by June.

VICTORIA

GLENROWAN ☎03

Blink and you might miss this tiny town along the Hume Hwy. near Wangaratta. Home to more cattle than people, the village would be an unlikely pitstop for tourists if it weren't for Ned Kelly, the infamous bushranger and bank robber. In 1880, Kelly's bloody highjinks finally came to an end here in Glenrowan when he and his "merry men" were ambushed, captured, and eventually hanged in Melbourne. The prime attraction is **Ned Kelly's Last Stand** with kitschy, "rip snorting" animatronic shows. (☎5766 2376. Shows daily every 30min. 9:30am-4:30pm. $18, families $50.) Keep an eye out for "Big Ned Kelly" clad in his makeshift armor (it's virtually impossible to miss him). Visit the **Ned Kelly Memorial Museum and Homestead** and find out why this callous criminal is also a revered folk hero. (At the corner of Kate and Gladstone St. ☎5766 2448. Open daily 9am-5:30pm. $4.50, children $1.)

RUTHERGLEN ☎02

"Sydney may have a beautiful harbor, but Rutherglen has an excellent Port," says a billboard in the center of the sleepy town. Known for some of the world's best fortified wines, the Rutherglen area offers the finest varieties of Muscats and Tokays. Stop at the informative visitors center and dine at one of the numerous restaurants before making your way into the vineyards. In Rutherglen, the Murray Valley Hwy.

(Hwy. 16) is called Main St. and runs from Yarrawonga (45km west) through the town to Albury-Wodonga (50km east). Several private wine tours run from Rutherglen and Albury-Wodonga; call the visitors center (p. 662) before arrival for further details. **Wine de Tour** operates from Albury-Wodonga ($50), Yarrawonga ($50), Rutherglen ($30), and Melbourne ($130) and offers daily tours of the region's best wineries (☎1300 3685 22; www.winedetour.com.au).

The **Star Hotel ❸,** 105 Main St., is the best option for budget digs in town offering large, private ensuite motel units with TV, A/C, and continental breakfast. (☎6032 9625. Singles $35; doubles $60; quads $100.) The hotel **restaurant ❶** serves cheap Chinese fare. If the Star is full, try the **Victoria Hotel ❸,** 90 Main St., where you'll find cozy, older rooms. The attached **bistro ❺** serves meals on a gorgeous balcony. (☎6032 8610. Breakfast included. Singles M-Th and Su $40, F-Sa $45; twins and doubles $50/55; ensuite $65/70.) For a truly original lodging experience, try the **Still House at Terravinia Vineyards ❺,** 987 Gooramadda Rd. The self-contained stay has been constructed inside an old winery's pine distillery, leaving the structure perfectly intact while furnishing the interior with simple country-style decor. BBQ, A/C and heat, laundry, and parking are included. (☎6026 5353; couples or small groups $130-150.)

VICTORIA

For **free camping,** or just a quick swim, drive north toward Yarrawonga for 5km and turn right on Moodamere Rd. It becomes an unsealed road after 2km and eventually leads through a cattle gate down into **Stantons Bend,** a low-lying riverbed area. Drive slowly, especially in a 2WD vehicle. From the cattle gate, veer left at every turn toward **Moodamere Lake,** which is more of a wide eddy in the Murray River than a proper lake. Locals inhabit caravans near the lake and practice wakeboarding; short-term camping is free. Be aware that the current is strong; **don't swim into the middle of the river.** Moodamere is occasionally closed due to slow blue algae growth; check with the visitors center before heading out.

Before heading out to the wineries, stop for lunch at **Parker Pies ❶,** 86-88 Main St. This famous meat pie shop has garnered nationwide awards including "Best Game Pie" in 2003 (for a savory buffalo pie) and 2005 (for an emu pie). The *pièce de résistance* is the less-exotic but amazingly delicious chicken pie with mustard, avocado, and ham—winner of "Best Chicken Pie in Australia" in 2000. The ultra-friendly staff deserves national recognition as well. (☎6032 9605. Pies $3.50-6.50.) The **Poachers Paradise Hotel ❶,** 120 Main St., serves pub lunches from $10.50. (☎6032 9502. Open M-F 8am-10pm, Sa-Su 8am-midnight.) The **IGA** supermarket, 95 Main St., caters to all your budget dining needs. (☎6032 9232. Open M-W and Sa 7:30am-7pm, Th-F 7:30am-7:30pm, Su 8:30am-6pm.)

V/Line buses leave Rutherglen's BP service station for Melbourne via Wangaratta (3½hr.; M, W, F 6:35am; $40). Purchase tickets from the news agency on Main St. **Webster** buses shuttle to Albury-Wodonga at 9:30am on weekdays from the BP station west of the city center (☎6033 2459. $7). The **visitors center** (officially called the **Rutherglen Wine Experience**) is located on the town's central roundabout at 55 Main St., and is the place to go for wine literature and bike rental. It also stocks the *Official Visitor's Guide*, an indispensable map of the region's vineyards. (☎6032 9009 or 1800 622 871. Open daily 9am-5pm. ½-day bike rental $20, full-day including helmet, pump, and bottled water $30.) The **post office** is at 83 Main St. (Open M-F 8am-5pm.) **Postal Code:** 3685.

WINERIES NEAR RUTHERGLEN

Rutherglen's temperate climate allows vineyards to keep grapes on their vines longer, favoring full-bodied red wines and fortified varieties of Tokay and Muscat. Choosing from among the excellent local wineries can be quite difficult, especially since they all offer free tastings. For those traveling by car, the *Official Visitor's*

Guide, available at the **Rutherglen Wine Experience** (see above) and most wineries, is a must-have. Also check out the *Touring Rutherglen* map, which makes finding the wineries significantly easier (both brochures are free). If traveling by bike, pick up the free *Muscat Trail Map* as well.

The Rutherglen vineyards sponsor several festivals throughout the year. The most popular is the carnival-like **Rutherglen Winery Walkabout** (on the Queen's Birthday weekend in June), featuring food and entertainment at the estates and a street fair downtown. True connoisseurs would probably prefer to skip the big production and instead sample the impressive food and wine combinations during **Tastes of Rutherglen,** held the second weekend in March. Remember, the local specialty is fortified wine, which indicates an alcohol content far greater than that of wine from other parts of Australia. If you are driving, be responsible when tasting.

St. Leonards Vineyards (☎6033 1004; wwww.stleonardswines.com) on St. Leonards Rd. just off All Saints Rd. Combines an idyllic setting with delicious, unique flavors. Enjoy the signature Orange Muscat (crisp, light, and dry) while lounging near a placid billabong fed by the Murray River. Dine at the **St. Leonards Cafe,** which offers warm BBQ meals that go perfectly with the fruity fortifieds. The vineyard also features twilight movies in the vines once a month ($10). Live music 1st and 3rd Su of the month. Frequent art expositions. Cellar open for tastings M-Sa 9am-5pm, Su 10am-5pm.

All Saints Estate (☎6035 2222; www.allsaintswine.com.au). Same owners as St. Leonards. The tree-lined entrance to the estate is irrefutably majestic, as is the red-brick castle which hosts the tasting room. The brand-new **Indigo Cheese Company** is located on the premises and offers homemade cow and goat cheeses. (☎6035 2250; www.indigocheese.com. Open daily 10am-5pm.) A self-guided tour takes you past picture-perfect gardens and huge display casks; pick up a map from the cellar door. Peek into the Chinese Dormitory and Gardens for a sense of early laborers' living conditions, and be sure to check out the hall's plaques detailing the histories of other regional vineyards listed here. Winery open M-Sa 9am-5:30pm, Su 10am-5:30pm. Restaurant open M-F and Su 10am-5:30pm, Sa 10am-11pm. Book ahead on weekends.

Morris Wines (☎6026 7303), off Mia Mia Rd. from the Murray Valley Hwy. This small, family-run vineyard boasts the best Muscat in the entire world (and has won the award for the last 5 years). It also took second-place in 2005 for a Tokay. The award-winning fortifieds come at a whopping price, although the 3-year-old Port-style wine is available for a very reasonable $11. Open M-Sa 9am-5pm, Su 10am-5pm.

Pfeifer Wines (☎6033 2805), on Distillery Rd. A small, unpretentious family-run winery that has recently been collecting nationwide awards for vintage Port-style wines. Taste the sumptuous table wines, the 2002 Merlot and the 2006 Riesling. Open M-Sa 9am-5pm, Su 10am-5pm.

Cofield Wines (☎6033 3798; mellissa@cofieldwines.com.au), northwest of Rutherglen on Distillery Rd., just off Corowa Rd. Cofield Wines is quite small relative to nearby vineyards, and completely family-run. The winery's signature press is a fantastic sparkling Shiraz. The superb 2002 Quartz Vein Shiraz, rich with a touch of cherry, a floral nose, and a round-bottomed finish, is also popular. The **Pickled Sisters Cafe,** located next door, is enormously popular as well. Cellar open M-Sa 9am-5pm, Su 10am-5pm. Cafe open M and W-Su 10am-4pm.

Chambers Rosewood Winery (☎6032 8641; info@chambersrosewood.com.au). An easy-to-miss building on Barkley St., 1km from the tourist office. The unpretentious tasting area gives no hint of the international praise lavished on its rare Tokays and Muscats. Let 6th-generation owner Steven or his father, semi-retired wine panel judge Bill Chambers, lead you through a proper tasting. Open M-Sa 9am-5pm, Su 10am-5pm.

WHAT'S IN A NAME?

How 'Strine has influenced the pop-culture you thought you knew.

The Never-Never: Although Never Never Land was introduced to a global audience by J.M. Barrie's *Peter Pan,* and has since become associated with a dreamworld of child-like innocence, the term was originally coined to describe the remote regions of the Australian Outback. To this day, parts of Queensland and the Northern Territory are known by the moniker, and Aussie claims to the Never-Never have been immortalized in song and literature.

Tasmanian Devil: You may know it as a mischevious Looney Tunes character hidden in an omnipresent tornado of dust, but the real Devil is known less for its drooling destructive tendencies, instead earning its name through disturbing grunt-like bellows, rumored ill temper, dark color, strong odor emitted when under stress, and ferocious appearance. Interestingly, the carnivorous Devils are actually part of the marsupial family, along with the kangaroo and the koala.

Van Diemen's Land: Although popularly recalled in English and Irish folk songs—including a famous ballad written and recorded by U2's the Edge—this was the name that Abel Tasman bestowed upon Tasmania in 1642 to honor Anthony Van Diemen, the Governor-General of the Dutch East Indies.

Gehrig Estate (☎6026 7296), 22km east of town on the Murray Valley Hwy. Victoria's oldest winery, established in 1858. Produces a wide range including excellent Shiraz and Durif, as well as a fresh, zesty Cherin Blanc. Vintage Port and Muscat are also specialties. Open M-Sa 9am-5pm, Su 10am-5pm.

HIGH COUNTRY

Tucked between the Murray River and Gippsland's thick coastal forest is a lush contrast to iconic ocean vistas and the scorched red rocks of the Outback. Mere hills compared to the skyscraping mountains of other continents, Victoria's high country is nonetheless a favored destination for Australian winter sports enthusiasts. The region is also spectacular in the summer, with challenging terrain for hikers, climbers, and mountain bikers. Competition is fierce among the villages in the mountains, encouraging the spread of high-end hotspots.

BEECHWORTH ☎03

Beechworth, Victoria's best-preserved gold town, lies off Owens Hwy. in the northeast. Traces of gold were discovered here in February 1852, and by 1866, over 128 tons had been found. Today, the town has become a haven for weekend getaways at endearing B&Bs. Some visit to immerse themselves in the history of Australia's most famous crook, Ned Kelly, who stood trial in the mining town for theft and murder. And some make the trek just to sample the delicious treats at the noteworthy Beechworth Bakery.

TRANSPORTATION AND PRACTICAL INFORMATION. The bus stop is on Camp St., just west of Ford St. **V/Line buses** (☎13 61 96) run to: Bright (1hr., 1-2 per day, $6.10); Melbourne (3½hr., 1-4 per day, $58); Wangaratta (35min., 1-6 per day, $5.30); Wodonga (1hr., 1-4 per day, $21). **Wangaratta Coachlines** (☎5722 1843) run M-F between Beechworth and Albury-Wodonga (1hr., 2 per day, $7.20), making stops in Yackandandah (15min., 2 per day, $3.60), Baranduda (30min., 2 per day, $7.20), and Wodonga (45min., 2 per day, $7.20). There are also **taxis** (☎5728 1485). **Beechworth Cycles and Saws,** 17 Camp St., rents bicycles. (☎5728 1402. Open Sept.-Apr. daily 9am-5pm; May-Aug. M-F 9am-5pm, Sa 9am-noon. About $20 per afternoon.) The **Visitors Information Centre** is in Shire Hall on **Ford Street,** Beechworth's main north-south thoroughfare, and offers a plethora of information about the town. Pick up the official *Beechworth's Visitors Guide* for a handy map and a list of attractions. (☎5728 8064 or 1300 366 321; www.beechworth.com. 2-day museum pass $10, students and concessions $6, ages 5-16 $4. Ned Kelly tour departs daily 10:30am; 1-1½hr. Goldfields tour departs noon.) The **police** office (☎5728 1032) is located on Williams St., around the corner from the visitors center.

ACCOMMODATIONS AND FOOD. Centrally located **Tanswell's Commercial Hotel ❹**, 30 Ford St., offers freshly refurbished rooms with wrought-iron balconies. (☎5728 1480. Shared bath and toilet. Singles $45; doubles $65.) Simple bedrooms are available above the **Empire Hotel ❸**, on the corner of Camp and High St. Check out the mounted, nicotine-stained Tasmanian Trumpeter on the wall, proof that this pub loves its fishing. (☎5728 1030. Singles $30; doubles $50.) The sprawling **Old Priory ❹** is a B&B built in an old stone-and-brick Brigidine convent. Vast common spaces and quaint private cottages create a charming atmosphere. (☎5728 1024; www.oldpriory.com.au. Dorms for groups $40 per person; singles $50; doubles and twins $80; ensuite cottages $105. Call ahead.) **Lake Sambell Caravan Park ❷** is 1.5km outside of town. Take Ford St. north, veer right on Junction St., and follow the blue signs which guide visitors toward the left at the fork in the road. (☎5728 1421. Reception 8am-8pm. Laundry, BBQ, and minigolf. Sites $20, powered $25, $22 per night if staying for longer than 1 night; 4-person caravans $40; 4-person cabins from $60.)

It is worth going to Beechworth simply to try the divine desserts at the acclaimed **Beechworth Bakery ❶**, 27 Camp St. Don't miss the popular almond and custard beestings ($3.50) or the raspberry snickerdoodles ($3). Have a streetside focaccia lunch ($7.30) or dine in the quieter upper level. (☎5728 1132. Open daily 6am-7pm.) For a memorable splurge, try the elegant **Bank Restaurant ❹**, 86 Ford St. Situated in the old Bank of Australasia building and attached to a luxurious B&B, the dining rooms have 18 ft. ceilings and beautiful period decor. Dishes are served on sparkling china atop silky tablecloths. Although dinner portions start at $27 and extend far beyond the budget traveler's wallet, weekend brunches (starting at $12.50) are worth the price (☎5728 2223. Open M-F 6:30-9:30pm, Sa-Su 9am-noon.)

SIGHTS. Inquire at the visitors center about 1½hr. Ned Kelly and Goldfields **walking tours** in historic Beechworth. Behind the visitors center, on Loch St., the **Burke Museum** displays gold-rush era artifacts, a comprehensive collection of Victorian Aboriginal weapons, and animal and bird specimens, including the Thylacine, a now-extinct Tasmanian marsupial. (Open daily 9am-5pm. $5, concessions $3, families $10.) Inside the **Beechworth Historic Court House,** 94 Ford St., the courtroom has been preserved in its 19th-century condition, right down to the dock where bushranger Ned Kelly stood during his trials and the cells in which he and his mother were (at separate times) detained. A surround-sound system recreates the trial as you walk through. (☎5728 8066. Open daily 9am-5pm. $5, concessions $3, families $10.) At the Beechworth **cemetery,** north of the town center on Cemetery Rd., you'll find the **Chinese Burning Towers** and rows of headstones with epitaphs in Chinese characters—reminders of the Chinese presence in gold-rush Beechworth. Chinese miners once outnumbered whites five to one. After growing resentment of their perceived success exploded in the violent Buckland riots of 1857, many moved to Beechworth's relatively peaceful Chinese community.

YACKANDANDAH ☎03

The road less-traveled leads to "Yak," as most travelers opt for a pitstop in the larger Beechworth. It's a goldminer's haven where visitors can try their hand at panning for precious metals, and where modern businesses operate from behind carefully preserved facades. **Wangaratta Coachlines** (☎5722 1843) makes stops in

Yackandandah on weekdays, and travels from Albury-Wodonga to Beechworth three times per day (prices vary). Stop off in the **Yackandandah Visitor Information Centre,** located in the Athanaeum at 27 High St. (☎6027 1988. Open daily 9am-5pm.) The center can suggest a variety of walks through the area. The Historic Gorge Walk is a local favorite, treating visitors to a jaunt through a hand-chipped tunnel, created during the gold rush of the 1850s.

The town's finer points can be enjoyed in an afternoon, but if you want to savor the small-town flavor, try either the **Yackandandah Holiday Park** ❷ on Taymac Rd. (☎6027 1380 or 0427 105 115; www.yhp.com.au; reception 8:30-10:30am and 4:30-6:30pm; powered sites for 2 $18; cabins $75-85), or the **Yackandandah Hotel** ❸ at 1 High St. (☎6027 1210; singles $30; doubles $50), which regularly offers discount dinner nights, including steak, fries, and salad for $10. If you get hungry, stop in the back garden of **Sticky Tarts** ❶, 26 High St. across from the visitors center. (☎6027 1853. Focaccias and salads $7.50-12. Baked goods from $4. Open W-Su 10am-4:30pm.) Nearby **Yackandandah Bakery** ❶ offers pastries and heavier meals, including a delicious sausage sandwich for $5.50. (☎6027 1549. Open daily 7am-5:30pm.)

MOUNT BUFFALO NATIONAL PARK

Driving down the Great Alpine Rd., Mt. Buffalo dominates the landscape, signaling the site of a rich sub-alpine ecosystem with plenty of outdoor adventure opportunities year-round, including some of the most challenging rock-climbing in Australia. Check out *Discovering Mount Buffalo*, a small book published by the Victorian National Parks Association, for a detailed guide to walks and camping areas within the vast park. Founded in 1898, Mt. Buffalo is one of Australia's oldest national parks, and though its craggy walls may intimidate from afar, the wide plateau at the top provides gentle, family-oriented ski slopes. In addition to rock-climbing, the summer months offer numerous easy-to-moderate hikes, leading to a cool lake, winding falls, and mesmerizing outlooks over Buckland Valley. The **park entrance gate** (☎5756 2328) serves as the primary information source on site, while the actual **Parks Victoria Office** is 20km beyond the entry. (☎5755 1466, 24hr. 13 19 63. Open daily 8:30am-4:30pm.) The entrance, 5km north of Bright (p. 667), is just off the Great Alpine Rd. roundabout by Porepunkah. (Entrance fee $15, off-season $10; free for those staying at mountaintop lodging.)

Mount Buffalo Lodge ❺, 7km along the main road from the **visitors center,** is the mountain's main source of accommodations, food, and services. Guests have access to laundry, game room, and a TV lounge. Groups should look into the family unit with 16 beds, a kitchen, and shared facilities. (☎5755 1988 or 1800 037 038. Twin with shared bath $150; family unit $800. Closed in summer.) The main lounge and **bistro** ❶ overlook the slopes (main courses around $10). The lodge ski shop serves cross-country and downhill skiers, as well as snowboarders. Rates are comparable to those in Bright (downhill package from $33). The **Mount Buffalo Chalet** is owned by the same company and is available year-round for cheaper lodging. Great **campsites** ❶ exist throughout the park, including one beside **Lake Catani,** 2km beyond the park office, with toilets, water, hot showers, and a laundry basin. (Peak season $19 per night for 4 people; extra person $4, extra vehicles $5. Off-peak $14/4/5; in winter $6 per site. Peak season is Dec.-Feb., Easter, Melbourne Cup weekend, Apr. school holidays and Labour Day weekend. Open year-round.)

Lift passes are available for the **Cresta Valley site** adjacent to the Mt. Buffalo Lodge. ($53; 2-day $99; ages 8-15 $36 per day. Lift ticket and lesson package $74, under 16 $57.) In the park, 11km of groomed (and 2km ungroomed) cross-country ski trails lie across the road from the Lodge carpark. Cross-country skiing is free; an information sheet is available at the entrance gate. (On-site rental of cross-country skis and boots $20 per day.)

Mt. Buffalo is also an excellent choice for hikers. Within the park are numerous walking tracks with some spectacular lookouts which are described at length in *Discovering Mount Buffalo*. The most challenging hike is **The Big Walk** (11.3km, 4-5hr. from park entrance to the Gorge Day Visitor Area). It ascends over 1km in only 9km of trail as it climbs the plateau. The **Eurobin Falls** track (1.5km, 45min. round-trip), starts approximately 2km past the park entrance. Beginning with an amble and ending in a steep clamber, the walk features spectacular views of the falls as they careen down bare rock. Several trailheads are by the Mt. Buffalo Chalet, where **Bent's Lookout** dazzles with a panoramic sweep across the Buckland Valley. On clear days, **Mount Kosciuszko** is visible. The terminus of **View Point Nature Walk** (4km, 1½hr. round-trip) offers a similar, but grander and more solitary view from a boulder seemingly balanced on a point the size of a pancake. Driving past the park office toward the Mt. Buffalo Lodge, you'll see numerous marked walking trails. The steep but relatively short **Monolith Track** (1.8km, 1hr. round-trip), with a trailhead across from the park office, leads to a precariously balanced granite monolith and is definitely worth the effort. Information and descriptions of the walks are available at the park entrance and the visitors center.

Mt. Buffalo supports a wealth of activities for the adventurous traveler. Abseilers go over the edge near Bent's Lookout year-round, and rock climbers come from far and wide to test themselves against sheer granite walls. The climbing on the north wall of the gorge is world-renowned. **Adventure Guides Australia** (☎5728 1804; www.adventureguidesaustralia.com.au) in association with the **Mount Buffalo Chalet Activities Centre** (☎5755 1500; www.mtbuffalochalet.com.au) runs rock climbing, abseiling, caving, and rugged mountaineering expeditions. The site of several World Championships, Mt. Buffalo has superb hang gliding and paragliding. Lake Catani is a small manmade lake perfect for swimming, fishing, and canoeing; its surroundings also provide good bushwalking.

BRIGHT ☎03

An ideal jumping-off point for any adrenaline junkie, full of skiers in the winter and paragliders in the summer, Bright is an apt name for this town of radiant natural beauty. Most streets are lined with majestic European oaks that change colors with the seasons. Bright has the best collection of discount digs and cheap eats in high country, making it ideal for those on tight budgets.

ORIENTATION AND PRACTICAL INFORMATION. Bright is located 79km southeast of Wangaratta on the **Great Alpine Road** (called **Gavan Street** and then **Delaney Avenue** within town limits). The town center lies along Ireland St., just off the highway behind a roundabout with an Art Deco clock tower. Public transportation in and out of Bright is limited. However, **V/Line** (☎13 61 96) serves Melbourne (4½hr., 1-2 per day, $47.40) and Wangaratta (1½hr., 1-2 per day, $12). The **Bright Visitors Centre** is at 119 Gavan St. (☎5755 2275 or 1800 500 117; bright@dragnet.com.au. Open daily 8:30am-5pm.) and has **Internet** access ($4 per 30min). The **post office** is at the bottom of Ireland St., near the roundabout at Cobden St. (Open M-F 9am-5pm, Sa 10am-noon.) **Postal Code:** 3741.

ACCOMMODATIONS AND FOOD. Bright's centrally located backpacker accommodation is the **Bright Hikers Backpackers Hostel ❷**, 4 Ireland St., two doors down from the town library. Guests of the hostel are welcome to borrow a limited selection of snow chains and skiing gear. Although the rooms are small, spacious common areas plus a kitchen, wooden veranda, and sparkling bathrooms will be sure to please. (☎5750 1244; www.brighthikers.com.au. Linens $3. Complimentary tea and coffee. Sleeping bags not allowed. Non-suspension mountain bikes $18 per ½ day. Internet access $4 per hr. Reception 9am-10pm. Dorms $21; doubles $44; weekly from $180/264.) If you're booking with a small group, try the **Star Hotel ❺**, 91 Gavan Rd. (☎5755 1277), located in the town center. There is a flat rate of $65 for a room which can sleep between one and five guests. Recently refurbished ensuite rooms (including heat, A/C, fridge, towels, soaps, and tea) stand in contrast to the motel's bleak facade. The **Bright and Alpine Backpackers ❷**, 106 Coronation Ave., is 5min. outside town; follow the Great Alpine Rd. east past the visitors center, turn right sharply onto Hawthorne St., then left onto Coronation Ave. The Backpackers is on the right, just before the small bridge. Though slightly far afield, it boasts an unbeatable price. Accommodations in corrugated metal and wood plank cabins lure extreme sports fanatics and nostalgic summer camp enthusiasts. (☎/fax 5755 1154 or 0418 528 631; www.brightbackpackers.com.au. Free pickup from town if arriving by public transportation. Continental breakfast $3. Linens $5. Kitchen, laundry. Reception 24hr. Sites $10; singles $20; doubles with fridge $40.) Bright is peppered with enticing little cafes and restaurants, but very few of them fall under a budget heading. Throwing something together with ingredients from the supermarket is probably your best bet: the **Bright Licensed** supermarket is at 16 Ireland St. (☎5755 1666. Open daily 8am-9pm.)

SKIING. At the center of town, a handful of ski-rental establishments will outfit you with a full range of skiing and snowboarding equipment, snow chains, and clothing. **Adina Ski Hire,** 15 Ireland St., offers both new and used budget skis for rent. (www.adina.com.au. Open M-Th and Sa-Su 7am-7pm, F 7am-latenight. Downhill skis, boots, and poles $46 per day, $135 per wk.; budget $34/97; snowboard and boots $46/132. Deposit required. 20% YHA discount.) **Bright Ski Centre,** 22 Ireland St. (☎5755 1093), and **JD's for Skis** (☎5755 1557), on the corner of Burke and Anderson St., offer similar services and hours.

OTHER OUTDOOR ACTIVITIES. Thermal air currents make the valleys surrounding Bright ideal for hang gliding and paragliding—the area was host to the 1986 World Hang Gliding Championships and every year gliding buffs return to hone their skills. **Alpine Paragliding,** across from the visitors center, offers intro flights as well as advanced options and licensing courses. (☎5755 1753. 25min. tandem $150, 2-day licensing course $370.) **Bright Microlights** (☎5750 1555), out at Porepunkah airfield, offers a 20min. "Mt. Buffalo Flight" ($125) that takes you over the gorge before gliding back to earth. The local ranges are perfect for mountain biking. **CyclePath Adventures,** 74 Gavan St., has customized and fully supported one- to five-day high-country and singletrack bike tours. They also offer rentals. (☎5750 1442 or 0427 501 442; www.cyclepath.com.au. ½-day $18, full-day $24. Credit card required for security deposit.) **Adventure Guides Australia** (☎5728 1804 or 0419 280 614; www.adventureguidesaustralia.com.au) conducts full-day abseiling (from $155), full- and half-day caving trips ($155/90), full-day rock climbing (from $155), and bushwalking and camping excursions. All except rock climbing are year-round, subject to weather.

MOUNT HOTHAM ☎03

With Victoria's highest average snowfall, 13 lifts, and a partnership with nearby Falls Creek (p. 670), Mt. Hotham is Victoria's intermediate and advanced skiing and snowboarding headquarters. The mountain is considered the hottest place in Victoria for all varieties of thrill-seekers but is held in especially high regard by **snowboarders.** The slopes are more challenging than in the rest of Australia, with short but steep double-black diamonds cutting through the trees in the **Extreme Ski-**

ing Zone. Beginner skiing is limited, though lessons are available. With a constant stream of university groups filling club lodges in the ski season, the mountain is a little younger and hipper than nearby Falls Creek, though *après-ski* offerings are more or less on par with those of its rival. In the summer, Hotham is relatively quiet, with nature trails and a few shops and lodgings open for visitors.

Mt. Hotham is accessible by a sealed road from the north. Entrance from Omeo in the south is safer and more reliable, but is inconvenient for those coming from Melbourne or Sydney. **Buses** to Mt. Hotham depart from Melbourne's Spencer St. Station (6¼hr.; 1 per day; $80, $130 round-trip) and Bright's Alpine Hotel (1½hr., 2 per day, $30). Book with **Trekset Tours** (☎9370 9055 or 1300 656 546; www.mthothambus.com.au). There is also **shuttle** service between Mt. Hotham and Dinner Plain (☎5156 7320; 8 per day from 7:40am-5:20pm). Tickets for round-trip **helicopter rides** to Falls Creek are $140 or $90 with a valid lift ticket. Trips must be booked in person on the day of travel.

From the Queen's Birthday in June to mid-October, resort entrance requires a fee, payable at the tollbooth 1½hr. from Bright on the Great Alpine Rd.; the fee is waived if you're just driving through without stopping. ($10 per person; season pass $95. Cars 3hr. $20; 24hr. $28; season pass $250-290. Lift tickets not included.) Drivers coming from Bright can rent mandatory **snow chains** from **Hoy's A-Frame Ski Centre,** on the right just after the school bridge in Harrietville. (☎5759 2658. $30 per day, 2 days $40. Deposit $50. Chain-fitting service free.) These can be returned to the BP **petrol station** in Omeo, on the south side of Mt. Hotham. Omeo does not have chain service.

The resort is constructed around the Great Alpine Rd., which scales the mountain. The lodges are clustered to the south, with ski lifts and services farther north. Village buses transport folks for free around the resort. The **visitors center** (☎5759 3550; www.mthotham.com.au) is on the first floor of the resort management building, just above the Corral carpark. Directly across the street, Hotham Central houses the **Snowsports Centre** (☎5759 4444), ski rental shops (skis/boots/poles or snowboards/boots $58, children $40), a small **grocery store,** and a **lift ticket** office, which sells passes valid both here and at Falls Creek. (Full-day ticket $87, students $74, children $45, family $251; lift and lesson packages from $131, students $96, children $95.) The Big D lift hosts night skiing. (Open W and Sa 6:30-9:30pm. With lift ticket $6, without $11.)

Lodging on Mt. Hotham is pricey; the excellent hostels in Bright and Dinner Plain offer an inexpensive alternative. The cheapest accommodation on the hill is the **Shepard and Alpine Club ❺.** (☎5759 3597. Shared rooms M-F $75 during peak season.) Call **Hotham Holidays** for accommodation booking (☎1800 354 555). There are four supermarkets atop Hotham: the **Alberg** and **Jack Frost** general stores are in Hotham Central, and there is one at Davenport Village. The **Summit Bar ❶,** in the Snowbird Inn, features outstanding views, live bands (Th and Sa), and happening crowds. (☎5759 3503. Open daily during peak season 3:30pm-2am.)

DINNER PLAIN ☎03

A mere snow-bunny hop from Hotham's hills lies the only village in prime snowfields that isn't corporately run. When describing Dinner Plain (www.visitdinnerplain.com), visitors often allude to the Hansel-and-Gretel-like cottages of the resort. Although the chalets are not made of candy and there is a noticeable dearth of witches, this bewitching little haven exudes a fairy-tale essence. It is an excellent base for cross-country skiing and offers more to do during the summer than nearby Hotham. The most affordable accommodation in Dinner Plain and Hotham is the **Currawong Lodge ❺** on Big Muster Dr. Guests enjoy a huge kitchen, billiard room, and large spa. (☎5159 6452; www.currawonglodge.com.au. Peak season

June 29-Aug. 30 4- to 6-person rooms $130 per 2 nights, $405 per wk.; off-peak season $40 per night.)

FALLS CREEK

☎03

An hour's drive from Bright along tangled, serpentine roads, **Falls Creek Ski Resort** peaks at 1842m. **Lift ticket** prices are comparable to other resorts (☎1800 232 557; www.fallscreek.com.au. Tickets from $86 per day, students $73, children $45; lifts with lessons start at $127/96/87.) Falls's ambience is more quaint and family-oriented than nearby Mt. Hotham's (p. 668), though their partnership gives multi-day skiers the chance to try both (all lift tickets allow access to both resorts). The ample snowfall, both natural and manmade, is a selling point at Falls, and the spread of trails means that bad weather conditions from one direction leave good skiing elsewhere on the mountain. Few trails are very long and most are intermediate level–advanced skiers can expect to spend more time on the chairlifts than on the slopes. However, with over 92 alpine trails, few visitors complain. Just over 23% of Falls Creek is advanced terrain, and the black diamond trails are clustered in an area known as **The Maze;** a snowboarding terrain park with Australia's only **superpipe** opens when snowfall permits. A Kat service transports skiers in heated Kassbohrers up the back-country slopes of **Mount McKay** for black and double-black diamond bowl runs. In the summer, a comparatively quiet Falls Creek offers bushwalking, tennis, fly-fishing, hiking, and extensive high-altitude cross-training trails open from October to June (many of Australia's Olympians come to the region to train). Scenic walks include the **Home and Away Circuit** (6.5km round-trip), which is quite narrow and steep, and the **Mountain and Castle Adventure Trail** (11km round-trip), which follows the cliffs during an ascent to Mt. McKay. (**Police** ☎5758 3424; **Ski Patrol** ☎5758 3502.)

VICTORIA

While traveling from Bright to Falls Creek, visitors pass Mt. Beauty, a winter haven with no prospects for budget travelers. However, the **Alpine Discovery Centre,** at 31 Bogong High Plains Rd., is worth a visit or phone call on the way to the Falls. The large center has a museum about the local ecology and offers comprehensive information and booking services for accommodations and activities in High Country. (☎1800 808 277; www.visitmtbeauty.com. Open daily 9am-5pm, hospitality specialists work M-F.) The best option for accommodations is the **Alpha Lodge ❸,** at the back left corner of the resort on 5 Parallel St. Open year-round, this comfortable lodge has luxurious facilities, including large balconies extended from odd-numbered dorms. Also available is a huge kitchen, spacious common area with TV and video games, laundry, drying room, miniature beer garden, and cedar-paneled sauna. (☎5758 3488; manager@alphaskilodge.com.au. 4-bed dorms $27-97; 2- to 3-bed ensuite dorms $34-112.) Inquire within the Alpine Discovery Centre for other moderately priced lodges throughout the village. **The Man ❷,** 20 Slalom St., a mainstay on the mountain, has several bar areas, billiards, and foosball, and offers the cheapest options in town for dining out. (☎5758 3362. Delicious personal pizzas $13. Open daily in winter noon-latenight; in summer 5pm-latenight.) The **Frying Pan Inn ❹,** 4 Village Bowl Cir., at the base of the Summit and Eagle chairlifts, is the place to be on winter weekends, when there are live bands, dance parties, and drink specials to fuel the debauchery. (☎5758 3390. Pub open daily 5pm-latenight. Happy hour 5-6pm. Bistro open daily 8am-8pm.)

Driving to the slopes from June to October requires carrying **snow chains** (24hr. rental in Tawonga and Mt. Beauty $20-25) and paying a hefty entrance fee ($25 per day). Note that there is nowhere to get fuel on the mountain, so fill up in Mt. Beauty. It is more practical to stay in Bright and use public transport to reach the resort for the day. **Pyle's Falls Creek Coach Services** (☎5754 4024) runs a ski-season service from Melbourne (6hr., 1-2 per day, $135 round-trip), Albury-Wodonga

(3½hr., 1-2 per day, $69 round-trip), and Mt. Beauty (50min.; 5-8 per day; $45 round-trip, children $30). All prices include entrance fee.

GIPPSLAND

Southeast of Melbourne, the Princes Highway snakes toward the border of New South Wales, loosely following the contours of the Victoria coast through verdant wilderness interspersed with small towns and extensive lake systems.

FOSTER ☎03

While gold-hungry miners used to flock to Foster (pop. 1000) in search of supplies and a warm bed, most of today's visitors are headed to the Prom. Foster is just 30km north of the entrance to **Wilson's Promontory National Park.** To drive from Melbourne (170km), take the South Eastern Arterial (M1) to the South Gippsland Hwy. (M420), following signs to Phillip Island, then to Korumburra (where the road becomes A440), and finally to Foster. **V/Line** (☎13 61 96) **buses** run from Melbourne (2¾hr.; M-F 4:30pm, Sa 6:45pm; returns M-Sa 7:50am, Su 3:25pm; $28). **Tourist information,** including a phone for booking accommodations, can be found inside the Stockyard Gallery building on Main St. **Parks Victoria** has an office in the same building. (☎5683 9000. Open M-F 8am-4:30pm.)

With a national park just next door, **Prom Coast Backpackers ❶,** 50 Station Rd., is a brand-new, bright purple, and altogether livable place for budget travelers to hang their hats. (☎5682 2171. Unlimited Internet access $5. Book ahead. Dorms $23, YHA members $21. Doubles $60/57.) For a quick meal, **Dezzy & Nics ❶,** 10 Station St., makes a good hamburger "with the lot" ($5.50) as well as pizzas and sandwiches. (☎5682 2625. Internet access $2 for 15min. Open M 10:30am-7:30pm, Tu 10:30am-5pm, W-Sa 10:30am-8pm, Su 11am-7:30pm.) **FoodWorks,** on the corner of Main St. and Station Rd., sells groceries. (Open M-Sa 8am-7pm, Su 9am-5:30pm.)

WILSONS PROMONTORY NATIONAL PARK

The southernmost tip of the Australian continent, Wilsons Promontory National Park is wildly popular (attracting 400,000 visitors a year) and virtually unspoiled, thanks to a history of local enthusiasm for conservation.

THE PROM AT A GLANCE	
AREA: 490 sq. km of parkland; 83 sq. km of marine parks. **FEATURES:** A UNESCO World Biosphere; home to Mt. Oberon and Sealers Cove. **HIGHLIGHTS:** Easy to challenging hikes and walks, from day to overnight routes.	**GATEWAYS:** Foster and Yanakie. **CAMPING:** Must register with the ranger. Fees vary through the park. **FEES:** $9.70 per vehicle. Fishing permits are required; all payments and inquiries at Tidal River.

TRANSPORTATION AND PRACTICAL INFORMATION

From Foster, turn left at the end of Main St. onto the **Foster Promontory Road,** which snakes 30km to the park entrance. ($9.70 per car, 2-day pass $15.30). Some touring companies offer trips into the park; **Duck Truck Tours** has two-day tours leaving from Phillip Island. (☎5952 2548. Summer only.)

From the entrance station, the park's only sealed road, **Wilsons Promontory Road,** winds 30km along the Prom's western extremity, providing glimpses of breathtaking coastal vistas and numerous opportunities to turn off for picnics and hikes. The grassy airfield between Cotter's Lake and Darby River is the best place in the park to spot wildlife, particularly around dawn and dusk. The road ends at **Tidal River,** a township with basic facilities, camping, and lodging. During its busiest periods (Christmas, January school holidays, and weekends through to Easter), the park runs a **free shuttle bus** between the Norman Bay carpark, at the far end of Tidal River, and the Mt. Oberon carpark.

Visitors who wish to stay overnight, obtain a fishing license, or get weather updates should go to the **Tidal River Information Centre** at the end of the main road. (☎5680 9555. Open daily 8:30am-4:30pm.) A 24hr. **Blue Box phone** for contacting a ranger is outside the info center. Tidal River offers free storage for superfluous gear, along with the only toilets, pay phones, and food available in the park. During the summer and Easter holiday period, Tidal River's amenities include an **open-air cinema** with nightly screenings of recent releases. For more **information** on Wilsons Promontory, contact Parks Victoria (☎13 19 63; www.parkweb.vic.gov.au).

ACCOMMODATIONS AND CAMPING

While **campsites** ❶ at Tidal River function on a first come, first served basis most of the year, booking is recommended for holidays and Melbourne Cup weekend (Nov. 4-5 in 2007). Booking for the Christmas and January school holiday period are subject to a ballot, with applications accepted only in June.

Formal lodging is considerably more difficult to come by and always requires booking in advance. Options in Tidal River range from basic **cold-water huts** ❶ to ensuite **cabins** ❺ with microwaves. Try to reserve three to six months in advance, and even earlier for summer weekends. Bookings here also operate under a ballot system for the Christmas holiday and January (1 wk. min., 3 wk. max.), and ballots are accepted only in May. Cabins have bath, kitchen, and living room, and include towels and linen. (☎5680 9555. Sites Nov.-Apr. $21 for up to 3 people, additional adult $4.50, May-Oct. $17/4.50; cabins Sept.-Apr. $151, additional adult $20, May-Aug. $137/20; 4-bed huts Sept.-Apr. $57, May-Aug. $55; 6-bed huts Sept.-Apr. $87, May-Aug. $83.) For **camping** ❶ outside the Tidal River camping area ("outstation camping") there's no need to book ahead, but you must obtain a permit and pay nightly fees ($6.60, children $3.30). All sites have a two-night maximum stay, except southern sites November through April, which have a one-night maximum stay. Toilets in outstation sites have no toilet paper, and no sites are powered.

HIKING

To best experience the Prom, tackle a few bushwalking areas or take a dip in the crystal-clear water. Although some visitors sample the Prom in a day, consider allowing at least three to five days to take in the entire park. A terrific assortment of tracks enables walkers of all abilities to explore the diverse landscape. The info center's *Discovering the Prom* ($15) details over 100km of trails in the park, and *Down Under at the Prom* ($20) lists dive sites for scuba diving and snorkeling. One of the most popular swimming beaches is at **Norman Bay,** past the Tidal River.

SHORT HIKES

Past the entrance to the park, the first left leads to the **Five Mile Road Carpark.** Originating at the carpark, the **Millers Landing Nature Walk** (4km, 3hr. round-trip, easy) leads to mangroves at Corner Inlet. Several short walks depart from Tidal River, including **Pillar Point** (3.6km, 1¼hr. round-trip, easy to moderate), a loop track winding gradually uphill through tea-trees, banksias, and sheoaks to a

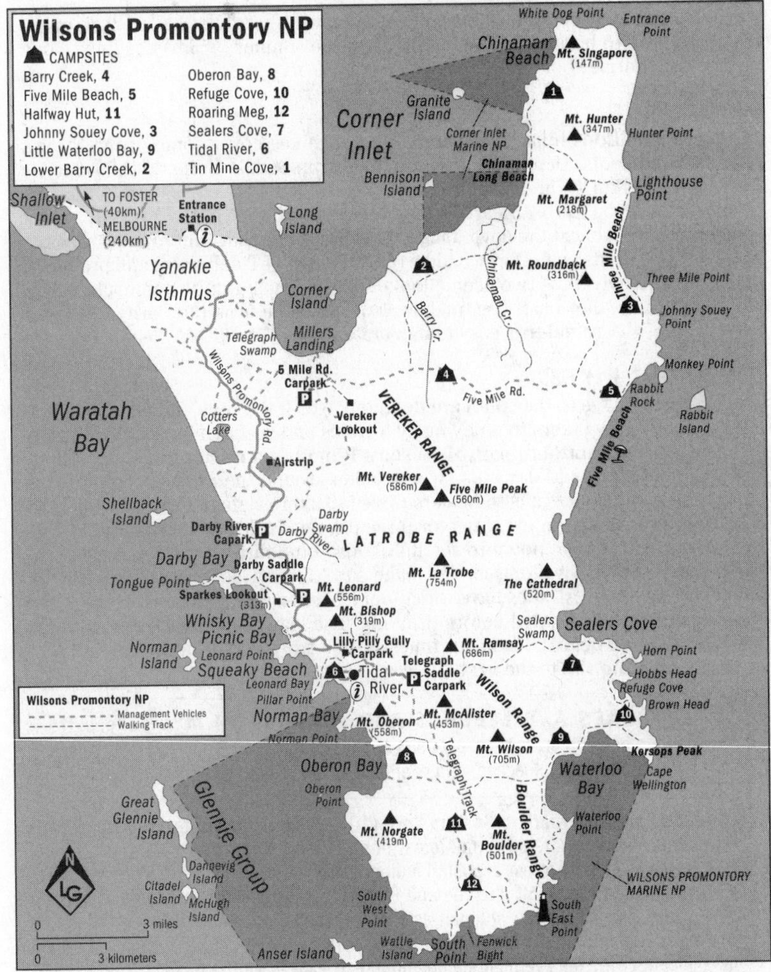

granite outcrop with delightful views of Norman and Squeaky Beaches, and **Loo-Errn Track** (2km, 1hr. round-trip, easy), a wheelchair accessible boardwalk leading through swamp paperbark and fishing stations. For a longer walk with decent views, try **Squeaky Beach Nature Walk** (4.2km, 1¾hr. round-trip, moderate), which passes through dunes, coastal scrub, and granite outcroppings before descending to the beach. Look for wombats in the scrub, and once on the beach, slide your feet to hear the white-grained quartz sand squeak. **Lilly Pilly Gully Nature Walk** (5.2km, 2hr. round-trip, easy), starting from the Lilly Pilly carpark 2km up the road from Tidal River, follows a slight incline through coastal woodlands of paperback thickets and eucalyptus into the rainforest. This walk can be extended by leaving from Tidal River (7.2km, 2¾hr. round-trip, easy); the section between Tidal River and Lilly Pilly Gully is wheelchair accessible. About 5km on the main road from Tidal River is a turn-off for the Telegraph Saddle carpark, where the **Mount Oberon Summit Walk** begins. The walk (6.8km, 2hr. round-trip, moderate to hard) climbs steadily up to the summit (558m), leading to one of the best sunrise spots in the park.

DAYHIKES

For more ambitious hikers, two incredible dayhikes cover some of the Prom's most beloved spots. Departing from the Telegraph Saddle Carpark, the **Sealers Cove Track** (20.4km, 6-7hr. round-trip, moderate to hard) traverses most of the peninsula, taking you across nearly every ecosystem found in the Prom (p. 671). Camping is available at the cove. **Tongue Point Track** (11.2km, 5hr. round-trip, moderate to hard) starts from Darby Saddle (6.7km north of Tidal River) and proceeds, sometimes steeply, past two scenic lookouts to a small granite peninsula with a stunning view of the coast. The track is also accessible from the Darby River carpark (7.6km, 4hr. round-trip, easy to moderate).

OVERNIGHT HIKES

The overnight hikes in the south are definitely worth the time and extra preparation, as they allow hikers to enjoy many terrains and spectacular secluded spots. The less-traveled northern part of Wilson's Prom has a circuit but lacks toilets. The most popular multi-day hike sweeps 36km around the eastern coastal areas along well-maintained trails to Sealers Cove (10.2km), Refuge Cove (6.4km), and Waterloo Bay (7km). An extra two or three days will allow access to the Prom's full beauty with a hike down to the lighthouse on South East Point. Overnight camp areas are near walking tracks; make sure to carry a stove, as fires are not allowed at any time. All sites have water, but it's taken directly from the creek and should be boiled or treated before drinking. The legs of the southern overnight hike are outlined below; distances, times (round-trip), and difficulty levels listed are from one campsite to the next.

CUTGRASS AND LEECHES AND SNAKES, OH MY! Take extra caution to avoid the less-savory parts of nature on these routes. Watch for raised roots, sharp rocks, leeches, and overhanging snakes, among other dangers.

Telegraph Saddle Carpark to Sealers Cove (10.2km, 3hr., moderate). This track leads through a burnt-out stretch of rainforest filled with brown stringy bark and banksia, then into a Messmate forest of austral mulberry and musk daisy-bush before arriving at Windy Saddle, between Mt. Latrobe and Wilson. It's all downhill from there. The forest gets darker and the terrain muddier as the trail heads into Sealers Swamp. Keep an eye out for colorful fungi. The track switches to a boardwalk before opening out to the magnificent cove. The overnight campground is 0.7km down the beach.

Sealers Cove to Refuge Cove (6.4km, 2hr., easy-moderate). This track offers beautiful views, and the coast eventually merges with the lush forest. Climbing a few large granite rocks rewards you with a stunning view. The track is poorly marked at this point, so stay on the high side of the first rock; directly ahead, at the top of another large rock, is the pebble track. A short detour along the coast heads inland again into stringy bark, then a fern-filled rainforest. A short decline leads you to the beach before heading briefly back into forest, taking you to a campground with water and a flush toilet.

Refuge Cove to Waterloo Bay (7km, 2½hr., moderate to difficult). The track ascends steeply through stringy bark woodland, dipping briefly into a gully before heading up again to reach the Kersops Peak lookout. Leave your pack at the signpost to catch a glimpse of the bay (look for humpback whales) via the detour (600m, 10min. round-trip). The track then heads steeply down to the beach and traces the coast on an extremely narrow path with raised roots and large rocks. After a quick bend around the coast, the track inclines before heading briefly back into the forest. The beach, directly in front of the Little Waterloo Campground, is available for a quick dip. From here, you can follow the lower part of the circuit, which joins up with Telegraph Track (5.8km, 2hr.), taking you north to return to the carpark (6.1km, 2hr.), or south to Roaring Meg camp (6km, 2hr.), or farther west to Oberon Bay (3.4km, 1hr.). The fit and ambitious can continue directly to the lighthouse from Little Waterloo camp.

Waterloo Bay to Lighthouse (10.9km, 3½hr., difficult). This long uphill stretch is exposed to the sun, has sword-grass, and is rocky. Heading inland, the track opens onto a large-faced rock with an amazing view, then passes through a eucalyptus forest into rainforest. The track then rolls through fern forests to the turn-off for the lighthouse.

The Lighthouse to Roaring Meg (7.2km, 2hr., moderate to difficult). This portion of the track is a rollercoaster of ups and downs. The track mostly winds its way through moist rainforest, so be wary of leeches. Turn right where the track empties onto the Telegraph Track and follow the road 700m until the walking track to Roaring Meg splits off on your left. Deceptively flat at the beginning, the track later presents hikers with extreme uphill climbs followed directly by steep downhill descents, ending at the bridge over the creek.

Roaring Meg to Halfway Hut and Oberon Bay (3.3km, 1¼hr., easy-moderate). Though the road is shorter, the walking track has better views. After a short, steep incline, the track is relatively flat before opening into a short growth forest. A left at Telegraph Track will go downhill to the Halfway Hut. This campground has a compost toilet, water, and a stone hut. The flat track leading to Oberon Beach crosses shaggy forest. Walk along the beach and cross over a small tidal pool to find the track to Tidal River.

VICTORIA

YARRAM ☎03

Yarram (pop. 2000) is a small rural service town; most of its out-of-state visitors are on their way to the **Tarra-Bulga National Park.** A 15km turn-off in Toora, will lead you to **Agnes Falls,** the highest single-span waterfall in Victoria, dropping 59m into the Agnes River. In the other direction, about 30km east of Yarram, you can access the southern portion of **Ninety Mile Beach,** an unusually long and quite exceptional stretch of white-sanded coastline extending north past Lakes Entrance. To reach **Woodside Beach,** popular for **swimming** and **surfing,** follow the S. Gippsland Hwy. to Woodside and turn right onto Woodside Beach Rd.

Yarram has a few motels and caravan parks within budget range. The **Ship Inn Motel ❹,** on Commercial Rd. just before town, has a pool and spacious rooms with TV and minibar. (☎5182 5588. Singles from $56; doubles from $66.) Not far down the road, the **Tarra Yarram-Motel ❺,** 387 Commercial Rd., is a family-run establishment with nice amenities. (☎5182 5444. Singles from $65; doubles from $75.)

For food, the **Federal Coffee Palace ❸,** 305 Commercial Rd., housed in Yarram's oldest building, is the hippest place in town, with cushioned chairs, books, and board games. (☎5182 6464. Open M-Tu and Su 9am-5pm, W-Sa 9am-late.) The walls of the **Bush Nook Cafe ❶,** 206 Commercial Rd., are lined with paintings for sale. Though significantly cheaper than the artwork, the roast chicken and avocado focaccia ($7.50) are no less delectable. (☎5182 5254. Open M-Sa 9am-8pm.) **FoodWorks** supermarket, 263 Commercial Rd., has groceries. (☎5182 5033. Open M-F 8am-6pm, Sa 8:30am-4pm, Su 9am-4pm.)

Yarram is 50km east of Foster on the S. Gippsland Hwy. (A440), which becomes Commercial Rd. in town. The **Tourist Information Centre,** in the old Courthouse at Commercial Rd. and Rodgers St., has helpful info. (☎5182 6553. Open M-Tu and Th-Su 10am-4pm.) The **library,** 156 Grant St., has free **Internet** access. (☎5182 5135. Open M and Th-F 10am-6pm, Tu-W 2-6pm, Sa 10am-noon.) **Banks, ATMs, pharmacies,** and a **post office** (open M-F 9am-5pm) line Commercial Rd. **Postal Code:** 3971.

PORT ALBERT

☎03

In the 1850s, gold and agricultural products from the interior were shipped from Port Albert, once the premier coastal gateway to Gippsland, to every corner of the globe. At one point export quantities rivaled even those of Melbourne. Today, Port Albert (pop. 300) is a tiny fishing village 15km south of Yarram that offers travelers lovely ocean views, fantastic fishing, and an award-winning seafood restaurant.

The **Gippsland Regional Maritime Museum,** on the corner of Tarraville Rd. and Bay St., is not to be missed; the displays on local history, including grisly tales of nearby shipwrecks, are superb. It also serves as the town **visitors center.** (☎5183 2520. Open daily in summer 10:30am-4pm, on weekends and by appointment in winter. $5, students $1.) Accommodation in town is limited: the **Port Albert Caravan Park ❷,** 9 Bay St., is right on the water. (☎5183 2600. Sites $18, powered $20.) For fantastic seafood, follow Wharf St. all the way to **Wharf Fish & Chips ❶** and its delicious takeaway menu, including flake (read: shark, for all you non-Aussies) for $5; it also has fishing supplies. (☎5183 2432. Open daily 10am-7:30pm.)

BAIRNSDALE

☎03

Bairnsdale (pop. 11,000) is a useful place to refuel before exploring **Mitchell River National Park,** the **Australian Alps,** and **Gippsland Lakes.**

The town's main attraction is the magnificent **St. Mary's Church,** next to the visitors center. Completed in 1937, the church showcases spectacular murals by Italian artist Frank Floreani. (Open daily 9am-5pm.) The **Krowathunkoolong Keeping Place,** 37-53 Dalmahoy Rd., is an Aboriginal cultural museum run by the Gippsland and East Gippsland Aboriginal Co-operative. The museum houses an excellent collection of local Aboriginal artifacts. Coming from the visitors center, take the first right on Service St. then the second right onto Dalmahoy Rd. (☎5152 1891. Open M-F 9am-5pm. $3.50, children $2.50.) Bairnsdale is the starting point of the **Great Alpine Road,** a 300km drive through the **Australian Alps** to **Wangaratta. Walhalla** (approximately 50km from Bairnsdale) is the start of the epic **Australian Alps Walking Track,** which ends in **Mount Tennent** (655km), outside Canberra. This monster bushwalk, which traverses many of the area's highest mountains, can be completed in 10 weeks. For more info, contact **Parks Victoria** (☎13 19 63).

Just south of Bairnsdale, near Paynesville, **Eagle Point** is best known for its gigantic **mud silts,** second in size only to those of the Mississippi River in the US. The silt jetties are lined with fishing spots and stretch out for kilometers, with the Rivermouth Road traveling their length. A **bluff lookout** provides the best views of the surprisingly impressive jetties. Ten kilometers farther, on the Paynesville waterfront, you'll find the ferry to **Raymond Island,** a great daytrip destination for wildlife watching. (☎04 1851 7959. 2min. Ferry runs M-Th 7am-10:30pm, F-Sa 7am-midnight, Su 8am-10:30pm. Cars $7, pedestrians and bicyclists free.) The tiny island boasts a huge population of **wild koalas,** which are most easily spotted off Centre Rd. and the walking tracks that branch off of it toward the south.

The **Bairnsdale Holiday Park ❷,** 139 Princes Hwy., is outside of town, just past the turn-off to Omeo. The sprawling park has campsites and cabins, as well as a swimming pool, minigolf, tennis courts, and trampolines. (☎5152 4066; www.bairnsdaleholidaypark.com. Sites $20, high-season $22, powered $23/28; cabins $50/68, ensuite $65/95.) For motel-style lodging, try the **Bairnsdale Main Motel ❹,** 544 Main St., just west of town, with BBQ, and free laundry. (☎5152 5000. Expansive singles $62; doubles $72; triples $85.) For slightly more out-of-town accommodation, fifty kilometers west of Bairnsdale on Princes Hwy. is the spotlessly clean Stratford Top Tourist Park ❷. (☎5145 6588 or 1800 787 275. Dorms $20; sites for 2 $16, high-season $18, powered $18/20; vans $40/45; ensuite cabins $65/70.) **Mitchell Gardens ❷,** a few blocks past the supermarket on Main St., has pleasant campsites on the banks of the river. (☎5152 4654; www.mitchellgardens.com.au. Linen $6. Sites for 2 $18, powered $21; cabins $46, extra person $6.)

Cheap takeaways clutter Main St., broken up by the occasional panini vendor. For quick food, grab a $5 sandwich at **Bairnsdale Gourmet Deli ❶**, 144 Main St. (☎5152 1544. Open M-F 9am-5pm, Sa 9am-noon.) A **Coles** is on Nicholson St. (☎5152 2743. Open daily 6am-midnight.)

About 275km east of Melbourne and 35km west of Lakes Entrance, Bairnsdale is accessible by the Princes Hwy. (A1), called **Main Street** in town. **V/Line trains** go to Lakes Entrance (30min.; M-F 3 per day, Sa-Su 1 per day; $9.30) and to Melbourne (4hr.; M-F 2 per day, Sa-Su 2 per day; $43.20). **Bairnsdale Visitors Centre,** 240 Main St., has a knowledgeable staff. (☎5152 3444. Open daily 9am-5pm.) The **library,** 22 Service St., around the next block, has free **Internet** access available by prior booking. (☎5152 4225. Open M 10am-5pm, Tu 10am-1pm, W and F 9am-6pm, Th 9am-7pm, Sa 9:30am-noon.) Other services include: a **hospital** on Day St. (☎5150 3333); **police,** 155 Nicholson St. (☎5152 0500); and a **post office,** 16-18 Nicholson St. (Open M-F 9am-5pm.) **Postal Code:** 3875.

MITCHELL RIVER NATIONAL PARK

Flowing from the alpine high country down to the Gippsland Lakes, the Mitchell River bisects 12,200 hectares of warm temperate rainforest and rugged gorge land. Canoeing, rafting, and hiking through the **Mitchell River Gorge** are the best ways to see the park's splendors. To reach the park from Bairnsdale (45km), turn right about 3km west of town onto Lindenow Rd., which becomes Dargo Rd., and follow the many signs to the park. Most roads through Mitchell River are unsealed and are navigated most safely in a 4WD, although three major attractions—the Den of Nargun, Billy Goat Bend, and Angusvale—are accesible via extremely narrow 2WD roads; drive slowly and look out for debris.

The **Den of Nargun** and its walk are the park's biggest draws. Gunnai/Kurnai legend describes Nargun as a terrifying giant stone female, said to abduct children who stray from camp and to kill attackers by reflecting their spears. The **Den of Nargun Circuit** (5km, 1½hr. round-trip) loops around **Bluff Lookout**, sweeping down to the **Mitchell River** and the Den of Nargun before heading back up to the carpark. Much of the walk is through chilly rainforest and the many rock steps are slippery when wet. At the Den, you can sit by the water's edge to absorb this site's mystical energy, but the Gunnai/Kurnai people ask that visitors respect the place and not enter the actual cave. More ambitious hikers can tackle the two-day **Mitchell River Walking Track** (18km one-way), which traces the river from Angusvale past Billy Goat Bend to the Den, taking in awesome scenery along the way.

There are two free campsites, one accessible by 2WD. **Angusvale ❶** can be reached by turning right off Dargo Rd. onto the unsealed Mitchell Dam Rd. (Pit toilets. No camping within 50m of the water.) **Billy Goat Bend ❶** is accessible only by foot: turn right off Dargo Rd. onto Billy Goat Bend Rd., continue 1km past the picnic area. A natural amphitheater at the Bend yields spectacular views of the Mitchell River Gorge. **Bairnsdale Parks Victoria** (☎5152 0600) has more info.

LAKES ENTRANCE ☎03

In good weather, Lakes Entrance and its array of outdoor activities border on paradise, although when the weather turns sour you'll be looking for the first bus out of town. With inviting beaches, excellent fishing, and numerous boating opportunities, it's no surprise that Lakes Entrance is heavily touristed in the summer.

TRANSPORTATION AND PRACTICAL INFORMATION. V/Line buses leave near the post office to Melbourne (5hr.; M-F 3 per day, Sa-Su 1 per day; $52.10) via Bairnsdale (30min., $9.30). For reservations, call **Esplanade Travel,** 317 The Esplanade. (☎5155 2404. Open M-F 9am-5pm.) The Princes Hwy. becomes **The Esplanade** in town, a waterfront strip lined with shops, eateries, and motels. The **Lakes Entrance Visitors Centre,** on the corner of Marine Parade and The Esplanade, has a wealth of regional and local information. (☎5155 1966. Open daily 9am-5pm.) **Banks** and **ATMs** can be found all along The Esplanade and opposite the footbridge on Myer St. The **library,** 18 Mechanics St., in the Mechanics Institute building, offers free **Internet** access. (☎5153 9500. Open M-F 8:30am-5pm.) The **post office** is at 287 The Esplanade. (☎5155 1809. Open M-F 9am-5pm.) **Postal Code:** 3909.

ACCOMMODATIONS. Tempting as it may be, beach camping is illegal and the area is frequently patrolled; luckily, reasonably priced alternatives abound. Though slightly institutional in feel, **Riviera Backpackers (YHA) ❷,** 669 The Esplanade, has clean facilities, a large lounge with TV, a solar-heated pool, billiards, Internet access ($2 per 15min.), bike rental ($15 per day), laundry, and a kitchen. (☎5155 2444; lakesentrance@yhavic.org.au. Dorms $22; doubles $47, ensuite $57. $3.50 discount for YHA members. Book weeks ahead Dec.-Jan.) **Echo Beach Tourist Park ❹,** 33 Roadknight St., is a four-star park with kitchen, BBQ, laundry, pool, playground, TV, and billiards. The three-bedroom flat sleeps up to six people. (☎5155 2238; www.echobeachpark.com. Powered sites $24, high season $40; self-contained 1-bedroom flats $70/150; 3-bedroom with spa bath $120/240.)

VICTORIA

FOOD. The Esplanade brims with takeaways, and the hotels in town tend to have good bistros in the mid-price range. Deals can be found by walking along the Esplanade looking for advertised lunch specials. **Pinocchio Inn Restaurant ❷,** 569 The Esplanade, has frequent specials and a full menu of Italian fare. (☎5155 2565. Open M-Th and Su 5-9:30pm, F-Sa 5-9pm.) The **Lakes Entrance Bakery ❶,** 537 The Esplanade, rises above the average meat pie vendor. (☎5155 2864. Open daily 7am-4pm.) **Riviera Ice Cream Parlour ❶,** opposite the footbridge on The Esplanade, sells huge portions of homemade ice cream. (☎5155 2972. Open daily 9am-5pm; in summer 9am-11pm.) The pub at the **Kalimna Hotel ❷,** a few hundred meters from the lookout west of town, has the best view and a $7.50 lunch special. (☎5155 1202. Su Roast Lunch $9. Open daily noon-2pm and 6-8pm. Pub open noon-latenight.) Get groceries at **FoodWorks,** 30-34 Myer St. (☎5155 1354. Open daily 8am-9pm.)

SIGHTS AND ACTIVITIES. On a good day Lakes Entrance has dozens of affordable activities: your best bet is to check with the visitors center for deals. **Ninety Mile Beach,** a long, thin stretch of sand that encloses the region's lakes and swampland, is the town's biggest attraction, accessible via the footbridge by Myer St. From the snack bar, a 1hr. walking track follows the coast to the boat entrance to the deep, blue waters of the Bass Strait. You can paddle out from the far end of the footbridge by renting a canoe ($10 per 20min.), paddle boat ($15), aquabike ($15), or catamaran ($40 per hr.) at **Lakes Entrance Paddleboats** (☎04 1955 2753). **Barrier Landing** is the western strip of land created by the entrance. Only accessible by boat, the landing has great fishing, a lake beach, and a **surf beach.** Contact **Mulloway,** on the Marine Pde., for a 3hr. all-inclusive **fishing trip.** (☎5155 3304. Trips 9am-noon and 1-4pm. $40.) A **scenic lookout** at Kalimna Hill, about 2km west of town, affords an excellent view of the patchwork Gippsland Lakes.

BUCHAN ☎03

Large numbers of visitors pass through the tiny town of Buchan (BUCK-in; pop. 200), 58km north of Lakes Entrance, on the Snowy River scenic drive. Surrounded by rolling hills, Buchan is also a great base for exploring the spectacular limestone Buchan Caves and beautifully austere Snowy River National Park.

No public transport serves Buchan; visitors drive or arrive on **touring buses** from Melbourne or Sydney. From Lakes Entrance, take the Princes Hwy. 23km east to

Nowa Nowa, turn left onto C620, right onto C608, and follow signs to Buchan. From Orbost, turn left off Princes Hwy., veer under the overpass and turn right at the T, then take the next right onto Buchan Rd. The **Buchan General Store,** on Main St. in the town center, has **tourist brochures** alongside basic **groceries.** It also serves as the town's **post office.** (☎5155 9202. Open M-F 8:30am-5:30pm, Sa 8:30am-noon.) The **Parks Victoria office,** right before the caves, has the most info on camping and the national parks, as well as tickets for the caves and reservations for the 100 closely-packed **campsites ❶** in the area. (☎5155 9264. Sites $12.50, powered $21; cabins $56.50, high-season $16.50/21/69.) Drive over the bridge to Orbost Rd. then right onto Davidson St. to find the **Buchan Outreach Resource Centre,** which has **Internet** access. (☎5155 9294. $4 per hr. Open daily 9am-4:30pm.) **Postal Code:** 3885.

Buchan Lodge ❷, left after the bridge on Saleyard Rd. just north of the town center, provides a genuinely welcoming environment in a beautifully constructed wooden building. The grand main room houses a lounge, dining area, wheelchair facilities, and a well-stocked kitchen. The lodge is a short 5min. walk to town or 15min. walk to the caves. (☎5155 9421; www.buchanlodge.com. Breakfast included. Dorms $20.) Freshly baked scones and "cobs" of bread are the standouts at **The Two Fat Ladies Cafe ❷,** across the highway from the general store. (☎5155 9387. Devonshire tea $8.50. Open daily 9am-approx. 8pm.)

Over the past 25 million years, underground rivers have formed over 300 caves in the Buchan Caves Reserve. Rain falling down the surface has left behind trace deposits of calcite, adding an impressive array of stalactites, stalagmites, curtains, and flowstone to the caves. **Fairy Cave** and **Royal Cave** are open for guided tours. Though the caves are similar in size and ornamentation, Fairy has more narrow passages. (1hr. Oct.-Mar. 10, 11:15am, 1, 2:15, 3:30pm; Apr.-Sept. 11am, 1, 3pm. $12.50, children $6.50, families $31.50.) The Buchan Caves Reserve has a few pleasant bushwalks, none longer than 2½hr. The **Spring Creek Walk** (3km, 1½hr. round-trip) travels the tea-tree track past limestone, old volcanic rock, and fern-filled forest to Spring Creek Falls. Watch for lyrebirds on the creekside portion of the walk. The Parks Office has information on other short walks.

SNOWY RIVER NATIONAL PARK

With some of the starkest and most unspoiled wilderness in Australia, Snowy River National Park surrounds the river with jagged hills dressed in alpine ash and pine. The landscape's beauty inspired Banjo Paterson to pen his bush ballad "The Man From Snowy River," which glorifies those who take on the harsh bush life.

The park is perhaps best seen in a two-day driving tour from Buchan to Orbost, which allows plenty of time for bushwalking and sightseeing. If driving from Buchan, take the **Buchan-Jindabyne Road** (C608) north through Gelantipy and veer right onto the **Gelantipy-Bonang Road** which leads into the park. The park road is mostly unsealed, becoming increasingly windy and narrow as it heads east. Its suitability for 2WD vehicles depends on weather, road conditions, and your skill as a driver. Check in with **Parks Victoria** in Orbost (☎5161 1222) Buchan (☎5155 9264), or their central info center (☎13 19 63) for up-to-date driving reports.

Karoonda Park ❷, 1½hr. from the Princes Hwy. and 40km north of Buchan in Gelantipy on the corner of Gelantipy and Glenmore Rd., is a functioning sheep and cattle farm with a pool, bar, ping-pong, billiards, tennis, darts, and Internet access. Evening meals are available for $22 and camp lunches for $10. Guests often stay on as farm workers in exchange for room and board. On-site, **Snowy River Expeditions** has many adventure options including white-water rafting trips (from $135) and full-day horseback trail rides (from $130). **Oz Experience** stops here; call ahead for pickup from Lake's Entrance. (☎5155 0220; www.karoondapark.com. Wheelchair accessible. Dorms $26; motel singles $45; doubles $70; cabins $105.)

Those driving from Buchan often stop and camp at **MacKillop Bridge ❶.** Farther into the park are **Raymond Falls** and **Hicks Campsite,** which can be reached off

Yalmy Rd. on dirt tracks suitable for 2WD. All have pit toilets. Bush camping is also permitted. The area around MacKillop Bridge, the only portion of the river accessible by conventional vehicles, is the starting point for many of the park's most popular activities. A canoe launch sets rivergoers downstream to explore rocky gorges; the most popular part of the Snowy River for canoeing and kayaking is the three-to-four-day stretch between MacKillop Bridge and the Buchan River junction; those considering going downriver should check in with a local **Parks Victoria** office beforehand. Several dayhikes start from MacKillop Bridge, as well as the 18km **Silver Mine Trail.** Just upstream, river beaches invite swimming. West of MacKillop Bridge, a turn-off from Bonang Rd. leads to the 400m track to look out over Victoria's deepest gorge, **Little River Gorge.**

ORBOST ☎03

Orbost, a logging and service town 60km northeast of Lakes Entrance, serves locals as a commercial hub and visitors mostly as a pit stop on the way to nearby beaches and national parks. The town is the start and finish of the Snowy River National Park Scenic Drive. To the north, **Errinundra National Park** is home to Victoria's largest stretch of rainforest. To the south, **Cape Conran** offers beautiful beaches away from the tourist hubbub.

VICTORIA

Snowy River Orbost Camp Park ❶, 2-6 Lochie St. at Nicholson, has basic facilities. A trail along the Snowy River starts nearby. (☎5154 1097. Sites $14.50, high-season $17, powered $19/21.50; caravans $35/55; cabins for two $45/65.) The **Orbost Club Hotel ❷,** 63 Nicholson St., has unremarkable budget rooms and a restaurant that serves Australian-Chinese cuisine. (☎5154 1003. Singles $30; doubles $40; twins $45.) The **FoodWorks** is opposite the Club Hotel. (Open daily 8am-8pm.)

Orbost is just off the Princes Hwy. via Lochiel or Salisbury St.; both exits intersect Nicholson St. **V/Line buses** between Melbourne and Canberra run to Orbost from Bairnsdale (1½hr., 1 per day, $22) and Melbourne (5½hr., 1 per day, $57). Buy tickets at **Orbost Travel Centre,** 86 Nicholson St. (☎5154 1481. Open M-F 9am-5:30pm, Sa 9am-noon.) The **visitors center,** 152 Nicholson St., has info on East Gippsland's national parks. (☎5154 2424. Open daily 9am-5pm.) The **Parks Victoria** office, just down the street, is your best bet for weather conditions and park info. (☎5161 1222. Open M-F 8am-5pm.) In town, find **ATMs;** a **library,** just off Nicholson on Ruskin St., with free **Internet** access (☎5153 9500; open M-F 8:30am-5pm); and a **post office,** 84 Nicholson St. (Open M-F 9am-5pm.) **Postal Code:** 3888.

ERRINUNDRA NATIONAL PARK

Normally, cool rainforests like the Errinundra are dominated by ancient myrtle beeches, as in the Otway Ranges of southwestern Victoria. Here, however, black olive berry and cinnamon-scented sassafras cover the forest floor, while a tall, wet eucalyptus overstory extends through much of the Errinundra Plateau. Less popular than nearby Snowy River, Errinundra is primarily a daytrip destination for nature walks and forest drives, although camping is available nearby.

The forest can be reached by the winding **Bonang Road** from the north or via **Princes Highway** from the south. About 11km south of Bonang and 54km east of Orbost, these roads meet Errinundra Rd., which leads into the park. The signs and markers within the park are notably inconsistent—be sure to get a map beforehand. Most of the roads in the park are unsealed but navigable in a 2WD on good days; in the winter, some roads may become impassable due to rain or snow. Call the **Parks Victoria** office in Orbost for current closings. (☎5161 1222. Open M-F 8am-5pm.)

To tackle the park on your own, get a map and the *Guide to Walks and Tours* (available at the info center in Orbost) and ask which tracks are in good condition. Most visitors make their first stop at **Errinundra Saddle,** where scenic Errinundra

Rd. passes through the plateau. Here, a 1km **nature walk** along a raised boardwalk leads visitors through spectacular rainforest. Perhaps the park's best views come at the end of a steep scramble to the top of **Mt. Ellery** (2.5km round-trip), which is usually only accessible by 4WD vehicle. To get there, take Errinundra Rd. to Big River Rd. at the Mt. Morris picnic area, and follow signs to Mt. Ellery. Errinundra is the rainiest area in eastern Gippsland; most visitors flee to permanent shelter at nightfall. The only campground in the park, **Frosty Hollow ❶**, is only accessible by 4WD. There are two camping options just outside of the park, **Delegate River ❶** to the north, accessible by taking Bonang Rd. to Gap Rd., and **Ada River ❶**, just south of the park on Errinundra Rd. Check with Parks Victoria for camping regulations.

CAPE CONRAN ☎03

Just 35km southeast of Orbost, Cape Conran Coastal Park offers sandy beaches, a network of walks, and many opportunities for water sports. The cape's geography is a mix of dunes, heath, wetlands, swamps, and woods.

To reach the park from Orbost, go south on Nicholson St. which becomes the Marlo-Cape Conran Rd. From farther east, turn left off Princes Hwy. onto Cabbage Tree Rd., 30km east of Orbost, and avoid the right fork to Marlo. The road ends at Marlo-Cape Conran Rd. The road offers serene spots just past **Marlo.** One of the best is **French's Narrows,** where the Snowy River meets the sea, 5km east of Marlo. Two thin strips of land divide the river's end from its shallow estuary and the breaks of the Bass Strait. Farther down the road is **Point Ricardo,** a popular fishing beach. A short jaunt from the park's accommodations is the main **East Cape Beach.** The primary walking options both begin at the beach carpark, where there is a **map.** The **Dock Inlet Walk** (14km) along the coast is for the fit and ambitious. The track leads to the Dock Inlet, a body of fresh water separated from the sea by dune barriers, and continues to **Pearl Point** (11km farther), known for its rock formations and surf fishing. The **Cape Conran Nature Trail** goes inland (2.5km) and there's a map and info sheet for markings along the way. Check with rangers (☎5154 8438) before leaving. The trail connects with the **East Cape Boardwalk,** also accessible from East Cape Beach, which leads around the East Cape to Cowrie Bay. The trail continues past the West Cape as far as Salmon Rocks. The **Yeerung River** is good for fishing and **swimming.** The best places to swim in the area are **Sailors Grave** (East Cape Beach) and **Salmon Rocks** (near West Cape Beach).

Parks Victoria operates **cabins** and **campsites** at Banksia Bluff, near East Cape Beach. Turn left off Cape Conran Rd. onto Yeerung River Rd., just before East Cape Beach. The eight wooden self-contained cabins, one of which is wheelchair accessible, are right next to the beach, and feature toilets, hot showers, laundry, and outdoor BBQs. Bring sleeping gear, towels, and food. (☎5154 8438; www.conran.net.au. Book ahead. Sites for up to 4 $20.50; cabins for 4 $128.) Food supplies, as well as standard accommodation options, are available in **Marlo.**

CROAJINGOLONG NATIONAL PARK

Temperate rainforest opens to a wild coastline stretching from the New South Wales border to Sydenham Inlet in the phenomenal Croajingolong (crow-a-JING-a-long) National Park. Recognized as a UNESCO World Biosphere Reserve, it covers 87,500 hectares, encompassing a remarkable diversity of landscapes.

ORIENTATION. Croajingolong is located 450km east of Melbourne and 500km south of Sydney. **Cann River** and **Mallacoota** serve as the park's gateway towns. The Princes Hwy. passes through Cann River and Genoa before crossing the border into New South Wales. At Cann River, the highway connects with Tamboon Rd., leading south into the park. The 45km drive down unsealed roads leads to the

Thurra and **Mueller Inlet,** ending at a trail to the Point Hicks Lighthouse. The turnoff for the unsealed West Wingan Rd., which leads to Wingan Inlet, is about 30km east of Cann River on Princes Hwy. At Genoa, farther east along the Princes Hwy., the Mallacoota-Genoa Rd. forks south toward Mallacoota.

TRANSPORTATION AND PRACTICAL INFORMATION. Cann River and Mallacoota both provide services to the park. **V/Line buses** stop at the intersection of Cox St. and Princes Hwy. in Cann River (6½hr., 1 per day, $62.70); no public transportation makes the turn-off to Mallacoota. The **Parks Victoria Information Centre,** on Princes Hwy. in the east end of Cann River, has info on the park's road and trail conditions, and area accommodations. (☎5158 6351. Open M-F 10am-4pm depending on ranger availability.) In an emergency, call **police** at ☎5158 6202. Services include a **Parks Victoria Office** on the corner of Buckland and Allan Dr. with info on local walks (☎5158 0219; open M-F 9:30am-noon and 1-3:30pm), and a **FoodWorks** at the top of Maurice Avenue (open daily 8:30am-6:30pm).

ACCOMMODATIONS. There are five main **camping ❶** areas within the park, as well as several in the immediate surrounds. The campgrounds at **Thurra River** (46 sites) and **Mueller Inlet** (8 sites) are run by Point Hicks Lighthouse (☎5158 4268). Both have fire pits, river water, and pit toilets. Thurra is more popular because of its private sites, caravan access, overnight parking, and proximity to trailheads. Between Cann River and Genoa is a turn-off for the park's best sites at **Wingan Inlet,** with popular bushwalking as well as fire pits, a water source, and pit toilets. The park's two other campsites at **Peachtree Creek** (12 sites) and **Shipwreck Creek** (5 sites) also have fire pits, a water source, and pit toilets. (Contact the Cann River Parks Victoria office at ☎5158 6351 for permits.) For more outdoor comforts, head to **Mallacoota Shady Gully Caravan Park,** on Genoa Rd. in Mallacoota, which has a pool and laundry. (☎5158 0362; www.mallacootacaravanpark.com. Sites $18, high-season $22, powered $20/28; cabins from $40, ensuite $50-60.)

HIKING. The **Heathland Walk** (2km, 30min. round-trip), leaving from the Shipwreck Creek Day Visitor Area, affords gorgeous views of Little Rame Head to the east and the Howe Range to the west. **Wingan Inlet Nature Trail** (3km, 45min. round-trip) leaves from the Wingan Day Visitor Area and leads past a tidal estuary populated by flocks of waterfowl, ending with a sweeping view of the coast. Starting near campsite 14 in Thurra River, the **Dunes Walk** (4km, 2hr. round-trip) leads through tea-tree forest to 150m-high dunes. Take adequate water and protective clothing and avoid wearing contact lenses—during the summer temperatures can exceed 40°C (104°F) in the dunes and strong winds can create sandstorms. There are no track markers in the dunes. The **Elusive Lake Walk** (6km, 3hr. round-trip) leaves from a carpark on W. Wingan Rd., 3km from the campground, and leads to the lake through fields of wildflowers. The still, deep lake (22m deep in some places) has no above-ground feeds; its fresh water reserves are fed by underground seepage and rainfall. The **Wilderness Coast Walk** is a 100km multi-day trek that takes you along a beautiful, sandy shoreline punctuated by grassy outcroppings and massive algae-coated boulders at the water's edge. The walk stretches from Sydenham Inlet in Croajingolong National Park all the way to the Nadgee Nature Reserve in New South Wales. There are 10 **campsites** along the walk, starting with Shipwreck Creek and ending at Bemm River. Trekkers can access the trail at several points, though Thurra River is the most popular and convenient. All overnight hikers must receive a permit from the Parks Victoria office in Cann River or Mallacoota before hitting the trail.

WESTERN AUSTRALIA

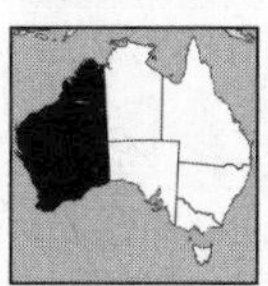

Western Australia's genial attitude toward life means that despite its emergence as an economic center with a rapidly growing mining industry, Westralians maintain a stress-free lifestyle unique to their slice of the world. The state was the first to be seen by European eyes and covers about a third of the continent; visitors soon realize that simply getting from place to place is often an adventure, and tiny pieces of the map translate into full days on empty roads. The upside of the region's immensity is an unparalleled collection of outdoor activities and natural wonders. Surfers flock to gorgeous beaches at Prevelly, while divers descend on Albany and Exmouth to swim amid brightly colored sponges and enormous whale sharks. Hikers head north to the awe-inspiring gorges of Karijini National Park or southwest to hauntingly beautiful forests rising from mist-shrouded roots.

While some may argue that these activities could be enjoyed at more easily accessible locations, the very remoteness of Western Australia is what makes it so appealing. With few adventurers traveling out to Fitzgerald River National Park to watch the setting sun turn the beaches a fiery red, those who do make the journey are able to enjoy the magnificent sight in blissful tranquility. Sunbathers at Cape Le Grand National Park never have to jostle for space on crowded sand, and drivers on the Great Northern Highway quickly forget the meaning of the phrase "traffic jam." Of the state's 1.9 million people, 1.4 million live in the Perth area, which has allowed sights to remain pristine and unspoiled. To top it all off, prices in the growing tourist industry are still very reasonable. Western Australia's charms may be one of the best-kept secrets in the budget travel universe, but don't wait to discover them—it won't be long before the rest of the world does.

HIGHLIGHTS OF WESTERN AUSTRALIA

SWIM with whale sharks at NIngaloo Reef along 250km of coral (p. 739).

ENJOY white sand beaches at **Cape Le Grand NP,** a deserted paradise of unrivaled natural beauty (p. 725).

HANG with quokkas in **Rottnest Island,** one of the few places on Earth that these little wallabies are found (p. 701).

SINK your toes in the pearly white sand of **Cable Beach,** Western Australia's most famous stretch of sand (p. 747).

STUMBLE through the **Gibb River Road** and find a tropical gorge and other surreal wonders along this untouched desert track (p. 753).

TRANSPORTATION

Because of the vast distances between attractions and the dearth of long-haul transportation, many travelers—even those on a budget—**buy a car** for long visits (see **Buying and Selling Used Cars,** p. 32). A thriving market exists for used cars, 4WDs, and campervans, fueled by message boards and *The West Australian* classifieds. **Used car dealerships** line Beaufort St. in and around Mt. Lawley, north of

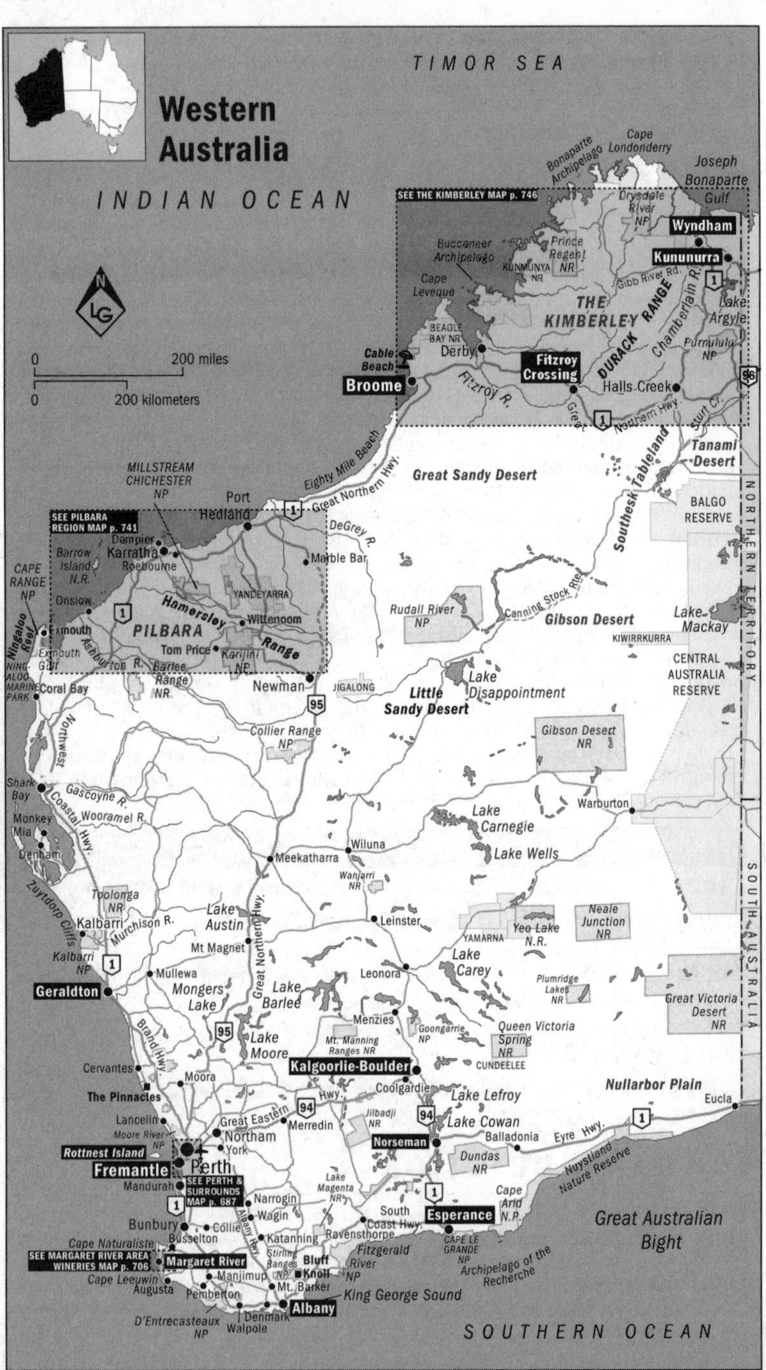

Western Australia
TIMOR SEA
INDIAN OCEAN
SOUTHERN OCEAN
Great Australian Bight
SEE THE KIMBERLEY MAP p. 746
SEE PILBARA REGION MAP p. 741
SEE PERTH & SURROUNDS MAP p. 687
SEE MARGARET RIVER AREA WINERIES MAP p. 706
0 200 miles
0 200 kilometers
Broome
Wyndham
Kununurra
Fitzroy Crossing
Derby
Halls Creek
Cable Beach
THE KIMBERLEY
DURACK RANGE
Port Hedland
Karratha
Marble Bar
Exmouth
Onslow
Tom Price
Wittenoom
Newman
PILBARA
Hamersley Range
Great Sandy Desert
Gibson Desert
Little Sandy Desert
Tanami Desert
Lake Disappointment
Lake Mackay
Lake Carnegie
Lake Wells
Warburton
Wiluna
Meekatharra
Leinster
Leonora
Menzies
Kalgoorlie-Boulder
Coolgardie
Norseman
Balladonia
Eucla
Nullarbor Plain
Esperance
Geraldton
Kalbarri
Shark Bay
Monkey Mia
Denham
Coral Bay
Mullewa
Mt Magnet
Cervantes
The Pinnacles
Lancelin
Moora
Northam
York
Merredin
Rottnest Island
Fremantle
Perth
Mandurah
Bunbury
Collie
Busselton
Margaret River
Augusta
Cape Leeuwin
Manjimup
Pemberton
Walpole
Denmark
Albany
Mt. Barker
Katanning
Narrogin
Wagin
Ravensthorpe
King George Sound
NORTHERN TERRITORY
SOUTH AUSTRALIA

Northbridge. Before paying, have the car checked by a mechanic; some car dealers prey on backpackers. The **Royal Automobile Club (RAC),** 832 Wellington St., offers inspections for members and provides roadside assistance. (☎13 17 03, roadside assistance 13 11 11. 1yr. roadside assistance $105, includes $36 joining fee.) For more info on cars and driving, see **On the Road,** p. 76.

If backpacking, the most popular and reasonably priced way to get around Western Australia is on **Easyrider bus tours,** which offers "jump on, jump off" service to nearly all towns worth visiting. Drivers are usually young and act as de facto tour guides; they work with local hostels to arrange convenient pickup and drop-off times, and have deals with some restaurants to offer cheaper food for Easyrider clients. Passenger **rail** service is virtually nonexistent with the exception of the Kalgoorlie-Perth route, serviced by the **Indian Pacific** and **Transwa Prospector** trains, and a commuter train from Perth to Bunbury. **South West Coach Lines** operates **bus** services southwest of Perth. Transwa buses operates in the southwest as well as north to Kalbarri, while **Integrity Buslines** runs to Port Hedland. **Greyhound Australia** offers flexible travel options and runs buses to Adelaide, Darwin, and Exmouth, with stops at major cities along the way. For more info, see **By Bus,** p. 29.

Portions of Western Australia can be toured by **bicycle,** but you should carry significant amounts of water. In northern reaches of the state, it's not advisable to bike in the hot, wet months (Nov.-Apr.). Advise regional police of your itinerary. The **Department of Sport and Recreation** (☎9492 9700; www.dsr.wa.gov.au) has more information on traveling by bicycle.

WESTERN AUSTRALIA NATIONAL PARKS. Access to national parks in Western Australia requires a pass, available from CALM (Conservation and Land Management) offices and most visitors centers. **Individual Parks:** Day Pass $9 per vehicle; annual $18. **All Parks in WA:** Holiday Pass (4wk.) $23 per vehicle; annual pass $51.

PERTH ☎08

Perth (pop. 1.4 million) is blessed with beautiful weather and a prime location on the Swan River, giving it a far more laid-back atmosphere than comparable cities. Asian immigration and an increasing role as a tourist gateway have given the city a cosmopolitan character; it's easy to forget that Perth is the world's most isolated capital city. Yet, a short trip outside the city will make this fact abundantly clear; 90% of the enormous state lives within the Perth region. Most of the city's attractions—from the surf beaches of Scarborough, to the raging nightlife of Northbridge, to the museums of the Cultural Centre—are easily accessible by public transportation or on foot, making Perth an ideal destination for those without a car. Moreover, the many tours that depart from Perth make the city a convenient base from which to explore the Wild West.

INTERCITY TRANSPORTATION

BY PLANE

Flights arrive at and depart from Perth Airport, east of the city. The international terminal is 8km away from all domestic terminals; keep this in mind if you're planning a connection. If you are flying with Qantas, they offer a free shuttle between terminals. **Qantas,** 55 William St. (☎13 13 13; www.qantas.com.au; open

M-F 9am-5pm), flies daily to: Adelaide (2¾hr.), Brisbane (4¼hr.), Darwin (3½hr.), Melbourne (3¼hr.), and Sydney (4hr.). **Virgin Blue** (☎13 67 89; www.virginblue.com.au) connects Perth with the eastern states, as well as Alice Springs, Broome, and Darwin. For trips within the state, try regional **SkyWest** (☎1300 660 088; www.skywest.com.au). Most major towns in the region are serviced by one or all of these airlines. There are a few transport options between the city and airport. **TransPerth** bus #37 runs between the domestic terminal and the city, leaving from the north side of St. Georges Terr., stop 39 (40min., every 30min., $3.20). An **Airport-City Shuttle** (☎9277 7958) runs between most city accommodations and the domestic ($12) and international ($15) terminals. A **taxi** to the CBD costs around $25 from the domestic terminals (20min.) and $25-30 from the international terminal (30min.).

BY TRAIN

All eastbound inter- and intrastate trains depart from the **East Perth Terminal,** on Summer St. off Lord St., a 30min. walk northeast of the CBD. **TransPerth** trains run between the station and the CBD every 15min. on weekdays and every 30min. on weekends. **Transwa** (☎1300 6622 05; www.transwa.wa.gov.au) serves Bunbury (2½hr.) on the Australind line and Kalgoorlie (6½hr.) on the Prospector line. The **Indian Pacific** runs east on Wednesday and Saturday to: Adelaide (59hr.; $340, students $170, children 4-15 and pensioners $153); Melbourne (53hr., $408/219/192; change trains to the Overland in Adelaide); and Sydney (66hr., $560/280/252).

BY BUS

Easyrider offers flexible budget tours to the major sights and towns throughout the state, and will pick you up at your hostel. The office at 224 William St. also has **Internet** access for $3 per hr. (☎9227 0824, outside WA 1300 308 477; www.easyridertours.com.au). **Transwa** (☎1300 662 205; www.transwa.wa.gov.au) runs buses from the East Perth Terminal, as does the more expensive **Greyhound Australia** (☎13 14 99 or 13 20 30; www.greyhound.com.au). **Integrity Buslines** (☎1800 226 339; www.integritycoachlines.com.au) departs from Perth Station in the CBD and goes through the interior to Port Hedland. **Southwest Coach Lines** (☎9324 2333) leaves from the Perth City Bus Port, 3 Mounts Bay Rd., next to the convention center. For more destinations, see the table on p. 688.

BY CAR

There are over 100 rental companies in greater Perth. Some quote dirt-cheap daily rates, but read the fine print: many have 100km driving limits, voiding your insurance if you drive over a certain distance. All companies listed rent 2WDs to drivers over 21. Though there are exceptions, **4WD** vehicles are generally the only way to explore unsealed areas; 4WDs start at $100 per day, often with extra charges for unlimited kilometers. For insurance reasons, it is extremely rare for companies to rent 4WDs to drivers under 25. **Backpackers World Travel,** 236 William St. (☎9328 1477 or 1800 67 67 63; www.backpackersworld.com), helps with rentals and insurance. **The Royal Automobile Club (RAC)** offers roadside assistance to members and those of several associated overseas associations, including AAA.

Bayswater, 160 Adelaide Terr. (☎9325 1000), allows drivers to travel within a 500km radius with no extra fees, and as far north as Exmouth for an additional $100. Under 25 surcharge $6 per day.

Europcar, 3-5 Gordon St. (☎9226 0026), allows its cars to go farther north than many companies for no extra charge, so long as you inform them beforehand.

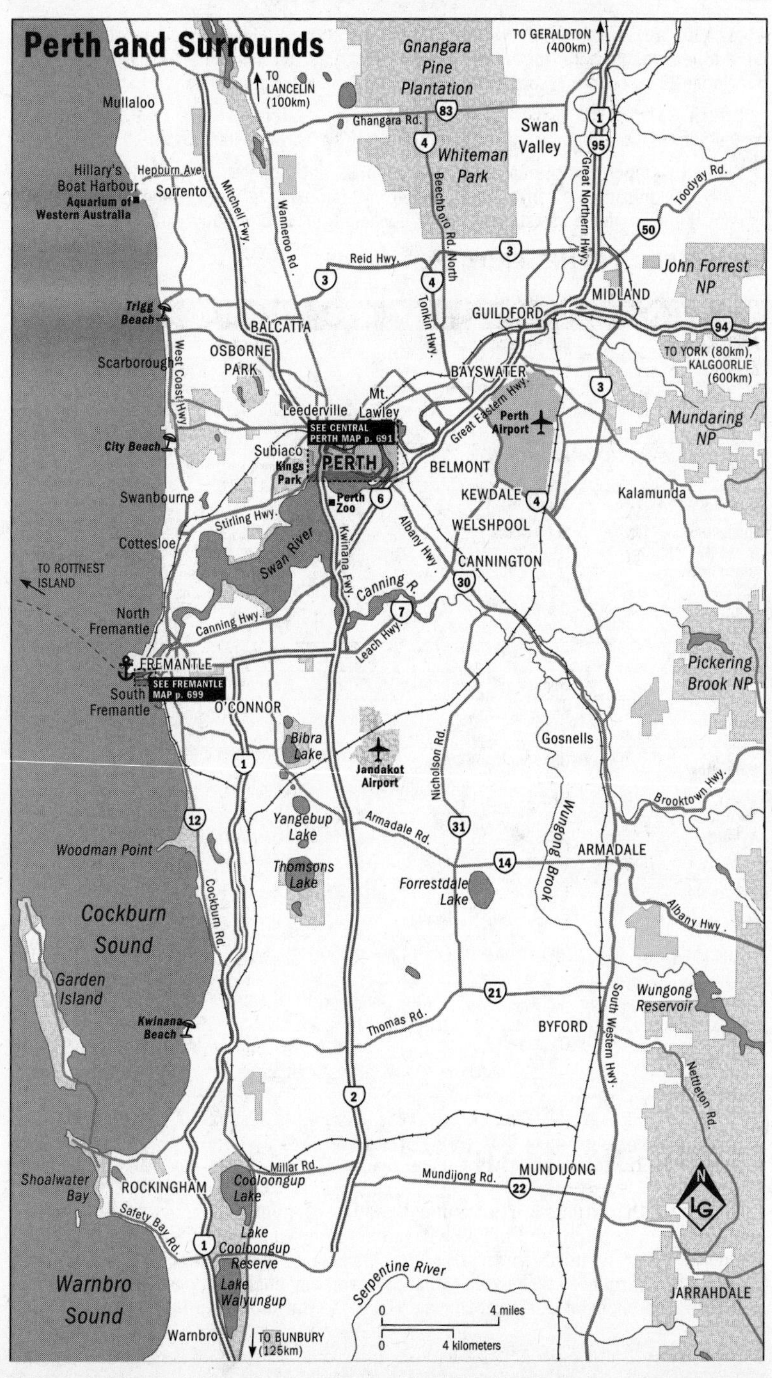

WESTERN AUSTRALIA

M2000, 166 Adelaide Terr. (☎9325 4110), guarantees that it will beat any other quote, and lets you go north for an extra $100 as long as you head to a tourist destination. Under 25 surcharge $6 per day.

South Perth 4WD Rentals, 80 Canning Hwy., Victoria Park (☎9362 5444; enquire@sp4wd.com.au), rents a wide range of 4WDs. No rentals to drivers under 25.

Wicked Campers, at the corner of Aberdeen St. and Shenton St. (☎1800 2468 69; www.wickedcampers.com), rents campers with cooking facilities, unlimited mileage, and 24hr. roadside assistance to backpackers from $60 per day.

BUSES AND TRAINS FROM PERTH TO:

DESTINATION	COMPANY	DURATION	FREQUENCY	PRICE
Adelaide	Indian Pacific	59hr.	2 per wk. (W, Su)	$340
Albany (via Bunbury)	Transwa	6-8hr.	1 per day	$60.85
Albany (via Mt. Barker)	Transwa	6hr.	1-2 per day	$41.70
Augusta	Southwest	5-5½hr.	1 per day (Sa, Su 2)	$39.65
Broome	Greyhound Australia	34hr.	1 per day	$366
Bunbury	Southwest	2¾hr.	3 per day	$23
Busselton	Southwest	3¾hr.	3 per day	$27
Carnarvon	Greyhound Australia	12hr.	1 per day	$145
Darwin	Greyhound Australia	56hr.	1 per day	$719
Dunsborough	Southwest	4¾hr.	1 per day	$29
Esperance	Transwa	10hr.	2 per day (W, F, Su)	$71.65
Exmouth	Greyhound Australia	16½hr.	1 per day	$219
Geraldton	Greyhound Australia/ Transwa	6hr./ 6-8hr.	1 per day/ 1-2 per day	$56/ $50.05
Kalbarri	Greyhound Australia/ Transwa	8hr./ 8hr.	3 per wk. (M, W, F)/ 1-2 per day	$112/ $62.45
Kalgoorlie	Transwa	6½hr.	1 per day (M, F 2)	$71.80
Margaret River	Southwest	5hr.	1 per day (Sa, Su 2)	$31
Monkey Mia	Greyhound Australia	12-14hr.	3 per wk. (M, W, F)	$156
Pemberton (via Bunbury)	Transwa	5½hr.	1-2 per day M-Th and Su	$41.60
Port Hedland	Greyhound Australia/ Integrity	24hr./ 21½hr.	1 per day/ 1 per day	$278/ $215
York	Transwa	1½hr.	1-2 per day M-F and Su	$13.20

WESTERN AUSTRALIA

ORIENTATION

Although Perth's streets are not quite aligned north-south or east-west, it helps to think of them as such, and locals will understand what you mean if you refer to them that way. The north-south streets run parallel to **William Street.** The east-west avenues run parallel to **Wellington Street.** The railway cuts east-west through town, separating the Central Business District (CBD) to the south from the cultural, culinary, and backpacker center of **Northbridge.** Near the center of the city, east-west streets **Hay** and **Murray Street** become pedestrian malls between William and Barrack St. Shopping arcades and overhead walkways connect the malls to each other and to the Perth Railway Station. The **Wellington Street Bus Station** is a block west of the railway station, across William St. Central Perth is relatively safe, but poorly lit; it empties after dark, so *avoid walking alone at night.*

In Northbridge, a multitude of restaurants, nightclubs, travel agencies, and budget accommodations cluster in the square bounded by Newcastle St. to the north, James St. to the south, Beaufort St. to the east, and Russel Sq. to the west. Upmarket **Subiaco,** west of Northbridge, is a hotspot for chic cafes and cuisine, and has weekend market stalls on either side of the Subiaco train stop on the Fremantle line. It is also the home of the Subiaco Oval, and both the Fremantle Dockers and West Coast Eagles of the Australian Football League. A few blocks north of Northbridge on Beaufort St., the up-and-coming **Mount Lawley** neighborhood offers wonderful restaurants and more sophisticated nightlife. In the northwest, **Leederville,** one stop north of Perth on the Currambine line, is a pleasant place to spend the day, with plenty of pubs, cafes, and funky shops centered on Oxford St. The green expanse of **Kings Park** rises just southwest of downtown, overlooking the city and the Swan River. The train to nearby **Fremantle** (30min., p. 697) passes through the lively beach suburbs of **Swanbourne** and **Cottesloe.**

LOCAL TRANSPORTATION

The CBD and Northbridge are compact and easy to navigate on foot. Free **CAT buses** whisk passengers around central Perth and Fremantle. The **blue CAT** runs a north-south loop from the Swan River to Northbridge; the **red CAT** runs east-west; and the **yellow CAT** travels down Wellington St. to Hale St. before curling back up to Claisebrook Station in East Perth. If you're in a rush, you can take any bus as long as you stay within the free-fare downtown zone. (☎13 62 13. Blue CAT: every 7min. M-F 6:50am-6:20pm; every 15min. F 6:20pm-1am, Sa 8:30am-1am, Su 10am-5pm. Red CAT: every 5min. M-F 6:50am-6:20pm; every 25min. Sa-Su 10am-6:15pm. Yellow CAT: every 10min. M-F 6:50am-6:20pm; every 30min. Sa-Su 10am-6:15pm.)

The **TransPerth** network of **buses, trains,** and **ferries** is divided into eight **fare zones** connecting to outlying areas; a 2-zone ride costs $3.20 and will get you from the CBD to the airport, Fremantle, or the beach. Save your **ticket stub;** it allows transfer between bus, train, and ferry services. Tickets are valid for 2hr. or more depending on how far you are traveling. **All-day passes** ($7.60) and **multi-ride cards** are available at TransPerth InfoCentre machines and newsagents. It may be tempting to ride without paying, but $50 penalties await freeloaders who get caught, and there's no shortage of ticket-checking officers on trains. Maps, timetables, and additional information are available by phone (☎13 62 13; www.transperth.wa.gov.au) or at the four TransPerth InfoCentres: Plaza Arcade, Wellington St. Bus Station, City Busport, and the train station.

It's also easy to get around by **taxi;** a ride between the international airport terminal and Northbridge costs $25-30. **Swan Taxi** on Harvey St. (☎13 13 30), or **Black and White Taxi** (☎13 10 08) can be hailed around the city, especially along Wellington or William St. Fares start at $2.90 on weekdays and $4.20 on weeknights/weekends, plus $1.17 per km. The visitors center has maps of **bike** routes. The **Bicycle Transportation Alliance,** 2 Delhi St. (☎9420 7210; www.btawa.org.au), has information, maps, and advice on bike routes. (Open W and F 8:30am-4pm.) Bikes can be rented through **About Bike Hire** (☎9221 2665), at the corner of Plain St. and Riverside Dr., for $6 per hr. and $30 per day.

PRACTICAL INFORMATION

TOURIST AND FINANCIAL SERVICES

Tourist Office: Perth Visitors Centre (☎1300 361 351), on the corner of Wellington St. and Forrest Pl. Books tours and sells maps of WA. Open Aug.-Apr. M-F 8:30am-6pm, Sa 9:30am-4:30pm, Su noon-4:30pm; May-July M-F 8:30am-5:30pm, Sa 9:30am-4:30pm, Su noon-4:30pm.

Outdoors Information: CALM, 17 Dick Perry Ave. (☎9334 0333; www.naturebase.net), near the corner of Hayman Rd. and Kent St., Kensington. Take bus #33 east to stop 19. Has info on WA parks and sells park passes. Open M-F 8am-5pm.

Budget Travel: YHA Western Australia, 300 Wellington St. (☎9427 5100; travel@yhawa.com.au), next to the train station. Arranges YHA discounted travel and sells memberships. Open M-F 9am-5pm. **STA Travel,** 100 James St., Northbridge (☎9227 7569). Open M-F 9am-5pm, Sa 10am-3pm.

Consulates: Canada, 267 St. Georges Terr. (☎9322 7930); **Germany,** 16 St. Georges Terr. (☎9325 8851); **Ireland,** 10 Lilika Rd., City Beach 6015 (☎9385 8247); **United Kingdom,** 77 St. Georges Terr. (☎9224 4700); **United States,** 16 St. Georges Terr. (☎9231 9400).

Currency Exchange and Banks: Travelex (☎9481 7900), at the Piccadilly Arcade on Hay St. Open M-F 8:45am-4:45pm, Sa 10am-2pm. **American Express,** 645 Hay St. Mall (☎9221 0777), London Court. Foreign exchange open M-F 9am-5pm, Sa 9am-noon. **ATMs** and **banks** are everywhere, especially on William St. in Northbridge and on Hay St. in the mall area between Barrack and William St.

WESTERN AUSTRALIA

Work Opportunities: WA is full of high-paying work opportunities, thanks to its booming natural resources industry. Most hostels maintain notice boards with job openings.

Workstay, 9th fl. of Carillion City Office Tower in Murray St. Mall. (☎9226 0510; www.workstay.com.au. Open M-F noon-5pm.) Great resource for work in the WA countryside. Arranges live-in work situations at country pubs, roadhouses, and cattle stations. Min. time 4-12wk. depending on location. Participants must start from Perth or Broome. Seasonal fruit picking opportunities abound; check www.jobsearch.gov.au/harvesttrail or call ☎1800 062 332. Note: Employment agencies are generally uninterested in backpackers staying less than a couple of months.

Hays Personnel Services, 172 St. Georges Terr. (☎9322 5198), on the 8th fl. of the State One Bldg. A bit more traveler-friendly than employment agencies. Caters to traveling office workers.

LOCAL SERVICES

Public Markets: Head to Subiaco to find shops and an international food court at the Pavilion at Rokeby and Roberts Rd. Open Th-F 10am-9pm, Sa-Su 10am-5pm. Produce and plants can be found at the Station St. market. Open weekends 9am-5:30pm.

Library: The **Alexander Library Building** (☎9427 3111), at the north end of Perth Cultural Centre (p. 695). Internet for research only. Contains a used book store with great deals (hardbacks $2-4). Open M-Th 9am-8pm, F 9am-5:30pm, Sa-Su 10am-5:30pm.

Ticket Agencies: For sporting events, try **Ticketmaster,** located in the newsagency at 863 Hay St. (☎13 61 00; www.ticketmaster7.com. Open M-F 9am-5:30pm, Sa 9am-5pm.) For theatrical and musical events, contact **BOCS Tickets,** Perth Concert Hall, 5 St. Georges Terr. (☎9484 1133; www.bocsticketing.com.au. Open M-F 8:30am-5pm.)

EMERGENCY AND COMMUNICATIONS

Emergency: ☎000.

Police: ☎13 14 44.

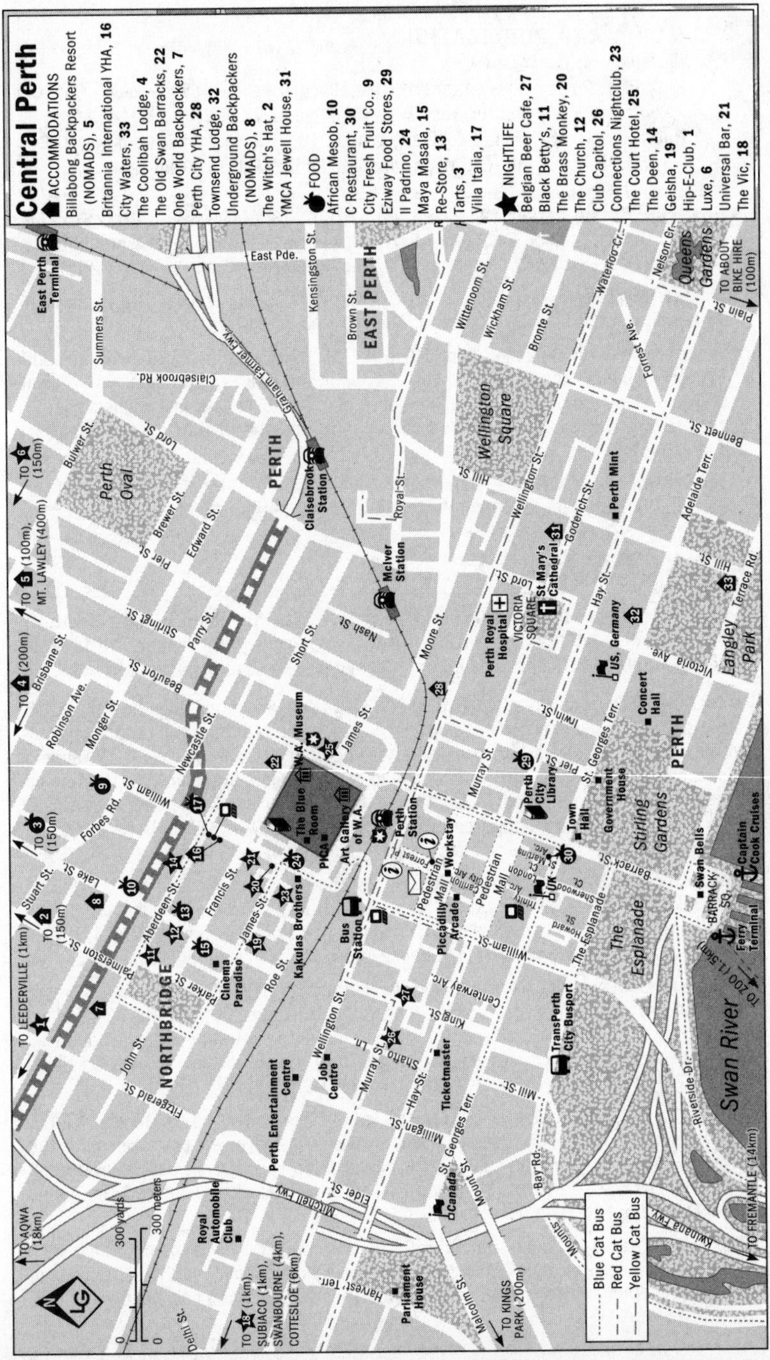

Central Perth

ACCOMMODATIONS
Billabong Backpackers Resort (NOMADS), **5**
Britannia International YHA, **16**
City Waters, **33**
The Coolibah Lodge, **4**
The Old Swan Barracks, **22**
One World Backpackers, **7**
Perth City YHA, **28**
Townsend Lodge, **32**
Underground Backpackers (NOMADS), **8**
The Witch's Hat, **2**
YMCA Jewell House, **31**

FOOD
African Mesob, **10**
C Restaurant, **30**
City Fresh Fruit Co., **9**
Eziway Food Stores, **29**
Il Padrino, **24**
Maya Masala, **15**
Re-Store, **13**
Tarts, **3**
Villa Italia, **17**

NIGHTLIFE
Belgian Beer Cafe, **27**
Black Betty's, **11**
The Brass Monkey, **20**
The Church, **12**
Club Capitol, **26**
Connections Nightclub, **23**
The Court Hotel, **25**
The Deen, **14**
Geisha, **19**
Hip-E-Club, **1**
Luxe, **6**
Universal Bar, **21**
The Vic, **18**

Blue Cat Bus
Red Cat Bus
Yellow Cat Bus

0 300 yards
0 300 meters

TO AQWA (18km)
TO LEEDERVILLE (1km)
TO 2 (150m)
TO 3 (150m)
TO 4 (200m)
TO 5 (100m), MT. LAWLEY (400m)
TO 6 (150m)
TO 18 (1km), SUBIACO (1km), SWANBOURNE (4km), COTTESLOE (6km)
TO KINGS PARK (200m)
TO FREMANTLE (14km)
TO ZOO (1.5km)
TO ABOUT BIKE HIRE (100m)

NORTHBRIDGE
PERTH
EAST PERTH
Perth Oval
Wellington Square
The Esplanade
Stirling Gardens
Langley Park
Queens Gardens
Swan River
VICTORIA SQUARE
BARRACK SQ.

East Perth Terminal
Claisebrook Station
McIver Station
Perth Station
Bus Station
TransPerth City Busport
Ferry Terminal
Captain Cook Cruises
Royal Automobile Club
Perth Entertainment Centre
Job Centre
Cinema Paradiso
Kakulas Brothers
The Blue Room
PICA
W.A. Museum
Art Gallery of W.A.
Parliament House
Ticketmaster
Piccadilly Arcade
Workstay
Pedestrian Mall
Perth City Library
Town Hall
Government House
Concert Hall
Perth Royal Hospital
St Mary's Cathedral
Perth Mint
Swan Bells
Canada
UK
US, Germany

Delhi St., Fitzgerald St., John St., Palmerston St., Stuart St., Lake St., Parker St., Aberdeen St., Francis St., James St., Roe St., Forbes Rd., William St., Robinson Ave., Brisbane St., Monger St., Newcastle St., Beaufort St., Stirling St., Parry St., Pier St., Brewer St., Edward St., Lord St., Bulwer St., Summers St., Claisebrook Rd., Graham Farmer Fwy., East Pde., Kensington St., Brown St., Short St., Nash St., Royal St., Moore St., Wellington St., Murray St., Hay St., Mitchell Fwy., Elder St., Harvest Terr., Milligan St., Shafto Ln., King St., Centerway Arc., Forrest Pl., Carillon City Arc., Trinity Arc., London Ct., St. Martins Arc., Howard St., Sherwood Ct., Barrack St., Irwin St., Hill St., Goderich St., Wittenoom St., Wickham St., Bronte St., Waterloo Cr., Forrest Ave., Nelson Cr., Plain St., Bennett St., Adelaide Terr., Terrace Rd., Victoria Ave., St. Georges Terr., The Esplanade, Riverside Dr., Kwinana Fwy., Mounts Bay Rd., Mill St., Mount St., Malcolm St.

WESTERN AUSTRALIA

MEDIA AND PUBLICATIONS

Newspapers: *The West Australian* ($1.10).

Nightlife: *XPress* comes out weekly (free). For gay nightlife, try the weekly *Out in Perth* (free). *Women Out West* is a lesbian monthly ($4.95).

Radio: Rock, 96FM and 92.9FM; hip-hop 101.7FM; mix 94.5FM; news, ABC 1080AM; tourist Info, 88FM; gay and lesbian 92.1FM (Th 11pm-1am).

Crisis Lines: Sexual Assault (24hr. ☎9340 1828 or 1800 199 888). **AIDS/STD Line** (☎9429 9944). **Suicide Emergency Service** (24hr. ☎9223 1111). **Poisons Information Centre** (☎13 11 26). **Gay Counseling Services of WA** (24hr. ☎9420 7201).

Hospital: Royal Perth Hospital (☎9224 2244), on Wellington St. near Lord St. **Fremantle Hospital** (☎9431 3333), corner of Alma St. and South Terr.

Internet Access: Backpackers World Travel, 236 William St. (☎9328 1477 or 1800 676 763; www.backpackersworld.com). $3 per hr. The **Internet Station** at 131 William St. (open 9am-10pm) and 271 William St. (open 9am-6am) has fast connections. $3 per hr., YHA/VIP $2.40. **The Grind** coffee shop, located in Trinity arcade near St. Georges Terr., offers wireless.

Post Office: 3 Forrest Pl. (☎9237 5460). *Poste Restante* M-F before 5pm. Open M-F 8am-5:30pm, Sa 9am-12:30pm. **Postal Code:** 6000 (Perth); 6003 (Northbridge).

ACCOMMODATIONS

Hostels in Northbridge tend to be large and loud. Converted houses north of Northbridge and hostels in the CBD offer more privacy and space. All hostels listed arrange tours; most offer pickup, luggage storage, laundry, and kitchens.

Underground Backpackers (NOMADS), 268 Newcastle St., Northbridge (☎9228 3755 or 1800 003 089; www.nomadsworld.com). Enough beds and amenities to accommodate an army. Licensed bar, pool, and basement lounge with big-screen TV. Superb location close enough central Northbridge to be convenient, but removed enough to be quiet. Internet access $4 per hr. Continental breakfast included. Free beer upon check-in. 8- to 10-bed dorms $20; 6-bed $22; 4-bed $24; doubles $60, with TV, DVD, and fridge $65. Prices decrease with stays of 3 nights or more. MC/V. ❷

Perth City YHA, 300 Wellington St. (☎9287 3300; www.yha.com.au). Brand new facility is mecca of YHA hostels. Renovated firehouse located next to the train station. Boasts sparkling rooms, friendly staff, and Internet access ($3 per hr.). Dorms $21-24; singles $50, ensuite $62; doubles $62/75; family rooms $95. 7th night free. AmEx/MC/V. ❷

One World Backpackers, 162 Aberdeen St., Northbridge (☎9228 8206; www.oneworldbackpackers.com.au). An oasis on the fringe of Northbridge, this family-run hostel offers a relaxed environment. Eco-friendly; uses solar power to heat water. Continental breakfast included. Cheap Internet access ($5 per 2hr.). 6-bed dorms $22; 8-bed $24; 4-bed $25; doubles $58. YHA/VIP $1 discount. MC/V. ❷

Townsend Lodge, 240 Adelaide Terr., East Perth (☎9325 4143; www.townsend.wa.edu.au). A great deal for singles in a convenient central location. The rooms are popular with students, so book ahead. Internet access $5 per hr. Key deposit $50. Singles $35, 2-6 nights $30, over 7 nights or students $26; doubles $48; ensuite studio (kitchenette, bathroom, double, single) $62. MC/V. ❸

The Witch's Hat, 148 Palmerston St. (☎9228 4228; www.witchs-hat.com), 10min. walk from Northbridge center. Beautiful place with bay windows; built in 1837 by architect of Horseshoe Bridge. Clean rooms with hardwood floors, grand front hall, courtyard. Small lockers. Most dorms 4- to 6-bed. Internet access $5 per 2½hr. Dorms $23; singles (available Apr. 1-Nov. 30) $50; twins $54; doubles $64. VIP $1 discount. MC/V. ❷

The Old Swan Barracks, 6 Francis St. (☎9428 0000; www.theoldswanbarracks.com), next to cultural center. A castle next to the Western Australian Museum, dominated by the arched ceiling. Clean rooms, friendly staff, and close to nightlife and restaurants. Internet $5 per 100min. 6-, 8-, 10-bed dorms $21; 4-bed $22; singles $54; doubles $59, executive $65; triples $76; family $89. VIP $1 discount. AmEx/MC/V. ❷

Billabong Backpackers Resort (NOMADS), 381 Beaufort St. (☎9328 7720; www.billabongresort.com.au). Old uni dormitory renovated into state-of-the-art, 180-bed hostel with exercise room, game room, library, and pool. All rooms ensuite with balconies. Breakfast included. Internet access $4 per hr. Guests who stay min. 1 month can work 12hr. per wk. cleaning or doing laundry in exchange for accommodation. 4-bed dorms $23, $138 weekly; 6-bed $22/132; 8-bed $20/120; singles and doubles $65/390. NOMADS $1 discount. MC/V. ❷

City Waters, 118 Terrace Rd. (☎9325 1566 or 1800 999 030; www.citywaters.com.au). Apartment-style accommodation across Langley Park from the Swan River. Large units. Good deal for groups. Kitchen, bathroom, and bedroom with lounge and TV. Parking available. Singles $85, winter $82; doubles $90/87; triples $105/102; 2-bedroom units $140/135. AmEx/MC/V. ❺

The Coolibah Lodge, 194 Brisbane St., Northbridge (☎9328 9958 or 1800 280 000; www.coolibahlodge.com.au). Remodeled colonial home with inconvenient set-up (you have to walk through the kitchen to get to the showers) and friendly atmosphere. Helps guests find work. Free pickup. Internet access $1.50 per 30min.; wireless available. Dorms $20-21; singles $38; doubles $54; triples $57. VIP. AmEx/MC/V. ❷

Britannia International YHA, 253 William St., Northbridge (☎9427 5122; britannia@yhawa.com.au). 5min. from train station. Right in Northbridge's social scene. Decent option if you don't plan to spend too much time hanging around your hostel. Internet access $3 per hr. Continental breakfast included. Reception 24hr. 6- to 8-bed dorms $15-17; 4-bed $19; singles $32; doubles $50; triples $63. MC/V. ❷

YMCA Jewell House, 180 Goderich St. (☎9325 8488; www.ymcajewellhouse.com). Option for those who need budget accommodation with some privacy. Small TV room and kitchen on every fl. Maid service daily. Tennis courts. Single-sex fl. Towels provided. Singles $36, students $26, with TV and fridge $40; doubles $46, with TV and fridge $51; family rooms $80. MC/V. ❸

FOOD

Perth has received many accolades for its multicultural cuisine. Northbridge has many Italian restaurants and noodle houses, while several Asian restaurants line **William Street** starting at the Aberdeen St. intersection. Hungry travelers also find food in **Mount Lawley.**

Grab meats and produce at **City Fresh Fruit Company,** 375 William St. (☎9237 5659; open M-Sa 7am-8pm, Su 7am-7pm), or hike to the better stocked **Eziway Food Stores,** 556 Hay St. (☎9325 9544. Open M-F 7:30am-8pm, Sa 7:30am-7pm, Su 10:30am-7pm. MC/V.) For cheap pasta, cereals, and deli foods, elbow through the crowds at **Kakulas Brothers Wholesale Importers,** 185 William St. (Open M-F 8am-5:30pm, Sa 8am-5pm. Cash only.)

Il Padrino, 198 William St. (☎9227 9065). Perth's best pizza ($16-25) even complimented by the Pope. ½-price pizza and pasta ($12.50) at lunch Tu-F and dinner Tu. Open Tu-F 11am-3pm and 5pm-latenight, Sa 5pm-latenight. AmEx/MC/V. ❶

African Mesob, 100 Lake St. (☎9228 1544). Sample diverse African cuisine in this new restaurant in Northbridge. Specializes in Ethiopian dishes and hearty vegetarian

WORK IT. With so much fine dining available around the corner of Lake St. and James St., it can be hard to choose. Go on a slow night (Mondays for example) and let the hostesses fight for your business. At the very least you can expect to be offered a free beer or glass of wine.

options; promotes African culture and employment opportunities. Open Tu-Su noon-2pm and 6pm-latenight. MC/V. ❸

Tarts, 212 Lake St. (☎9328 6607). A fantastic neighborhood cafe that buzzes during lunch hour. The panini ($9.90) are pricier than at basic cafes, but worth every penny for their quality and originality—pumpkin, onion marmalade, feta, and capsicum. Open daily 7am-6pm. AmEx/MC/V. ❶

C Restaurant, Level 33, St. Martins Tower, 44 St. Georges Terr. (☎9220 8333). Eat on top of it all, with a gorgeous 360° view of Perth. Open for lunch M-F and Su 11am-latenight; high tea ($30) 2pm; dinner daily 6pm-latenight. AmEx/MC/V. ❺

Re-Store, 72 Lake Rd. (☎9328 1032), a fine foods market with extensive deli in the back with gourmet design-your-own sandwiches ($3-7). Outdoor seating available. Open M-F 8am-5:30pm, Sa 8am-12:30pm. ❶

Chef Han's Cafe, 245 William St. or 546 Hay St. (☎9328 8122). Chef Han is the emperor of local budget cuisine. Speedy and delicious heaps of vegetarian-friendly noodles and stir-fry ($7-9). Open daily 11am-10pm. AmEx/MC/V. ❶

Villa Italia, 279 William St. (☎9227 9030). In a city addicted to caffeine, the espresso ($3) here stands out. M-Th pasta $12, otherwise $14-19; M-Th after 5pm pizza $12, otherwise $13-18. Open M-F 7am-latenight, Sa 8am-latenight. AmEx/MC/V. ❷

Maya Masala (☎9328 5655), at the corner of Francis and Lake St. Styles itself as an "Indian brasserie," dishing up curry plates ($14-18) and *thalis* ($14-17). Reduced prices for takeaway. Open daily 11:30am-2:30pm and 5:30pm-latenight. ❷

SIGHTS

SWAN BELLS. Perth's most recognizable landmark is a glass bell tower designed to recall the city's ship-building past. Perched like a swan on the shores of the river, with Perth's skyline as a backdrop, the tower houses 12 bells originally cast in 14th-cent. England and given to Perth on Australia's bicentenary in 1988. The bells are rung Mondays, Tuesdays, Thursdays, and on weekends noon-1pm. Bell demonstrations are given Wednesday and Friday at 11:30am and 12:30pm. *(Barrack Sq., at the river end of Barrack St. Take the blue CAT to stop 19. ☎9218 8183; www.swanbells.com.au. Open daily 10am-4:30pm. $6; under 15, seniors, and students $4.)*

AQUARIUM OF WESTERN AUSTRALIA. Leafy sea dragons, saltwater crocodiles, and four kinds of sharks live at AQWA, which displays sea life from all along the state's incredibly diverse coastline. Visitors walk through an underwater tunnel surrounded by fish, and watch divers feed the sharks by hand (daily 1pm and 3pm). Guests can also touch squid and stingrays in the discovery pools. Those 18 and older can book ahead to dive with the sharks, turtles, and stingrays off the coast or go whale watching ($90 per person). *(North of Perth along the West Coast Hwy. at Hillary's Harbour, off the Hepburn Ave. exit. Take the Joondalup train to Warwick, then bus #423 to Hillary's. ☎9447 7500; www.aqwa.com.au. Open daily 10am-5pm. $24, concessions $17.50, ages 4-15 $13, families $65, under 4 free.)*

PERTH ZOO. If you won't be seeing Australian wildlife in its natural habitat during your visit to Oz, the zoo is an essential stop. The highlight is an Australian bush-walk, which leads you past koalas, echidnas, and has nothing but a "stay on the path" sign separating you from the kangaroos. The reptile exhibit lets you safely see some of the region's most dangerous natives, and the new orangutan treetop walk places you right next to these gentle giants. *(20 Labouchere Rd. in South Perth. Take the blue CAT to the jetty and then ferry across the river for $1.20, or take bus #30 or 31 from the City Bus Port. 24hr. infoline ☎9474 3551; www.perthzoo.wa.gov.au. Free walking tour daily 11am. Open daily 9am-5pm. $16, children $8, under 4 free.)*

PERTH MINT. Several million dollars worth of gold is just beyond your fingertips at this historic mint, built in 1899 to turn the burgeoning gold rush into an economic boom for the state. The world's largest display of gold bars moved here from Singapore in 2004. Marvel at the brilliance of molten gold, and then relax outside over traditional tea ($20) in the new Tea Garden. *(310 Hay St., East Perth. Take the red CAT to stop 3 or 11. ☎9421 7223. Open M-F 9am-5pm, Sa-Su 9am-1pm. Gold pour 10am-4pm, guided heritage walk 9:30am-3:30pm; both on the hr. $9.90, concessions $8.80, children $4.40, families $24. Tea Garden: ☎9421 7205. Open M-F 10am-4pm.)*

KINGS PARK. Perched atop Mt. Eliza just west of the city, Kings Park offers a spectacular view of Perth and the Swan River. The enormous area (larger than New York's Central Park) contains a **War Memorial, Botanic Gardens** featuring 1700 plant species, and the **DNA tower,** with views of Rottnest Island. Free guided walks depart from the karri log opposite the War Memorial daily at 10am and 2pm. A secluded path begins at the riverside edge of the park, next to the old brewery. *(20min. walk west from the CBD up St. Georges Terr., or take the #37 bus free to Fraser Ave., #39 on weekends. Free parking. Info center ☎9480 3600. Gardens open daily 9am-4pm.)*

BEACHES. The Perth beach experience is calm and carefree, complemented by numerous clusters of shops and cafes. Families flock to **Cottesloe Beach** (on the Fremantle line) for swimming and mild surf, while **Swanbourne Beach** is a favorite spot for nude sunbathers. *(Bus #71, 72, or 75, or a 2km walk from the Swanbourne stop on the Fremantle train.)* **City Beach** is a great swimming spot. *(Bus #81, 84, or 85 from the stop in front of Hobnobs on Wellington St.)* **Scarborough** has bigger surfing waves and crowds of twenty-somethings. *(Bus #400 from Wellington St. Station.)* The best surfing is through the tubes at **Trigg Beach,** just north of Scarborough; the waves here can get a bit rough. *(Joondalup train to Warwick, then bus #423.)*

CULTURAL CENTRE. The Perth Cultural Centre packs several good museums, performance centers, and the state library into one block. **The Art Gallery of**

THE LOCAL STORY

FOOTY NATION

Two teams of men, clad in shor shorts and sleeveless shirts, ru madly across a cricket pitch an battle for a leather ball. There ar few rules, little padding, and stadium full of waving flags an fans clad in team-colored scarve and jerseys.

The game is Aussie Rules Foot ball or "Footy," as it is commonl known. It is the quintessentia Australian sport: physicall demanding, high scoring, an injury inflicting. Head to Perth' Subiaco Oval to watch the Wes Coast Eagles—difficult to get tic ets for—or the upstart Freo Doc ers. If you make it to a game, gra a beer and a meat pie and tak note of these next few guidelines.

A game consists of four quar ters with almost no break in th action. If a player has the ball, h can run with it as long as h bounces it once every 15 steps or he can pass it by kicking o punching it toward a teammate. I a player catches the ball withi 50m of the goal, he has a fre kick. Scoring occurs when a ba is kicked between the goalpost 6 points for the central posts or for the outer posts.

The only way to appreciate th sport is to see it live. Tickets a the Subiaco Oval, located in Eas Subiaco on Wellington Rd., sta at $11 if purchased at the gate.

Tickets also available throug Ticketmaster (☎13 61 00 www.ticketmaster7.com).

Western Australia has collections of modern and classical Australian art, including Aboriginal carvings and paintings, and hosts international exhibits. *(☎9492 6600; www.artgallery.wa.gov.au. Open daily 10am-5pm. Guided tours available. Free, except for special exhibitions.)* **The Perth Institute of the Contemporary Arts (PICA)** has many art displays and hosts evening performances. Pick up a booklet of events or call for schedules. *(☎9227 6144. Open Tu-Su 11am-6pm. Gallery free, performance prices vary.)* The **Western Australian Museum** showcases the state's natural history. Don't miss the "diamonds to dinosaurs" and the Aboriginal exhibits. *(☎9427 2700; www.museum.wa.gov.au. Open daily 9:30am-5pm. Suggested donation $2.)* **The Blue Room** provides a great venue for local theater. Productions range from classics to experimental pieces by local playwrights. *(☎9227 7005; www.blueroom.net.au. $10-20.)*

EARTH, SEA, AND SKY. Captain Cook Cruises, Pier 3 Barrack Sq., runs a variety of tours, including a wine cruise ($125), a Fremantle explorer cruise with tea and a wine tasting ($36), and the "Zoocrooz" to Perth Zoo ($42). (☎9325 3341; www.captaincookcruises.com.au.) **Malibu City Dive** has diving tours to Rottnest Island (p. 701), noted for its unique coral and fish, and also offers a four-day scuba certification class. (126 Barrack St. ☎9225 7555; www.rottnestdiving.com.au. Rottnest trips including equipment start at $150, without equipment $105; scuba certification class $395.) **Planet Perth** has several tour options, including wine tours and trips to Broome, Exmouth, Monkey Mia, and Swan Valley. (☎9225 6622; www.planettours.com.au. Tours from $55.) For Pinnacles tours (see **Nambung NP,** p. 731), popular options are **Go West Tours** (☎9226 3348; www.gowesttours.com.au; daytrip to Pinnacles $115, YHA $95) and **Western Travel Bug** eco-tours (☎9204 4600; www.travelbug.com.au; daytrip to Pinnacles $115). **W.A. Skydiving Academy** offers tandem jumps. (199 William St., Northbridge. ☎1300 13 78 55; www.waskydiving.com.au. From $230 for a 6000 ft. jump to $390 for a 14,000 ft. jump.)

NIGHTLIFE

Perth's laid-back attitude means there's never a shortage of good pubs, clubs, and cafes. The scene in Northbridge starts around 10pm and rages late into weekend nights. Mt. Lawley and Subiaco have more upscale, subdued nightlife. Pick up the free weekly *XPress* at hostels, news agencies, or record stores to find out what's going on. Cover charges and formal dress codes are rare, but jeans may get the occasional scowl and most places require closed-toed shoes.

A number of pubs and clubs cater specifically to the backpacker set, enlivening the crowds with free or cheap meals and drink specials. The determined can find free food almost every night, usually in the form of BBQs—vegetarians beware! Monday is a good day to check out **The Deen,** 84 Aberdeen St. (☎9227 9361). The **Hip-E-Club** (☎9227 8899), on Newcastle and Oxford St., is popular on Tuesday and Thursday, and **Black Betty's** (☎9228 0077; www.blackbettys.com.au), on Aberdeen and Parker St., has good Wednesday events. Head out to Subiaco on the weekends and catch the post-footy game crowd at **The Vic** (☎6380 8222) at 236 Hay St.

Perth is reasonably **gay- and lesbian-friendly.** The **Cinema Paradiso,** 164 James St., posts a variety of local events, including gay/lesbian highlights and up-to-date information on the arts scene. (☎9227 1771. Open daily 10:30am-11pm.)

The Brass Monkey, 209 William St., Northbridge (☎9227 9596; www.thebrassmonkey.com.au). Fantastic ex-hotel serving local microbrews. Billiards, indoor courtyard, leather sofas, and veranda. Connects to **Grapeskins,** a suave wine bar and brasserie. Open M-Tu 11am-midnight, W-Th 11am-1am, F-Sa 11am-2am, Su noon-10pm.

The Belgian Beer Cafe, 347 Murray St. (☎9321 4094). Leave it to the Belgians to put together the best combination of beer and food in the city. Run by the same company as Stella Artois, the cafe is the perfect place to unwind after a day wandering around the CBD. Open M-F 11am-midnight, Sa 11am-1am, Su 11am-10pm.

Luxe, 446 Beaufort St., Mt. Lawley (☎9228 9680). Trendy bar with plush seating and modern fixtures. Serves up drinks with touch of class. Open W-Su 7pm-latenight.

The Church, 69 Lake St. (☎9328 1065). Former church turned club with trance and Sa disco mixes. Bring your own glow sticks; scene picks up at 1am. Open F-Sa 9pm-6am.

Universal Bar, 221 William St., Northbridge (☎9227 9596). Frequent live bands and a slightly older, sophisticated crowd. No jeans; closed-toed shoes required. Open Tu 5pm-midnight, W-Th 5pm-1am, F-Sa 5pm-2am, Su 6pm-midnight.

Connections Nightclub, 81 James St., Northbridge (☎9328 1870; www.connectionsnightclub.com). Popular gay-friendly club with DJ-spun beats. Theme nights like "Lesbian Mud Wrestling." Free entry and Happy hour the first hr. daily, except during special events. Open W, F (cover $10), and Sa ($12) 10pm-6am; Su ($5) 9pm-latenight.

Hip-E Club (☎9227 8899), on the corner of Newcastle and Oxford St., Leederville. Groovy 60s and 70s club, with Su 80s and W "Old Skool". Free entry until 10 or 11pm. Tu and Th backpacker nights with free BBQ. Open 8pm-1am.

Geisha, 135a James St., Central Perth (☎9328 9808). Pulsates with various genres of dance music, sometimes from celebrity guest DJs. (Heath Ledger and Toni Collette have spun here.) Sign at the door tells male patrons to "turn off your engines" as it is a female-friendly establishment. Open F-Sa 11pm-6am, Su 9:30pm-latenight.

The Court Hotel, 50 Beaufort St., Northbridge (☎9328 5292), on the corner of James St. The scene at this gay-friendly bar varies from drag queens and theme nights to standard dance pub. In the summer, live bands play outside in the beer garden. Open M-W 11am-midnight, Th-Sa 11am-latenight, Su 3pm-latenight.

FREMANTLE ☎08

Although it is connected to Perth by a string of suburbs, Fremantle is a wonderful destination in its own right, and many travelers prefer it to the big city because of its unique character. "Freo" has successfully blended an unrivaled collection of Victorian architecture with a vibrant cafe culture, most visible on the famous "cappuccino strip" on South

DIDGERI-DO-IT-YOURSELF

Australia owes much of its musi cal fame to the resonant drone o its native instrument, the didgeri doo. Emitting a low, intermitten sound, it may very well be the old est instrument in the world, dating back approximately 40,000 years. The 'doo was traditionall found only in northern Australia but has since become popula throughout the country. The bes part is, even a tourist can learn how to play this versatile instru ment...for free!

At **Didgeridoo Breath,** in downtown Fremantle, visitors are encouraged to try their hand a playing the didgeridoo. While extensive lessons for the serious musician are offered, the tips pro vided during the free introduction will give the curious passerby enough know-how to earn brag ging rights back home.

The easiest Didgeridoos to play have a wider mouth, since you create sound by "blubbering your lips. 'Doos can vary in size from the small bamboo variety (a great bargain at $20) to eucalyp tus instruments the size of a child Typically, a didgeridoo of abou 120cm produces the best range.

Spend enough time here, and you just might be ready to start a didgeri' band.

Didgeridoo Breath, 6 Market St. Fremantle. (☎9430 6009 www.didgeridoobreath.com. Open daily 10am-5:30pm.)

Terr. Fremantle, traditionally a popular port, gained international attention with the arrival of the America's Cup race in the 1980s, launching the city into a new era of upscale improvements to the waterfront area and the shopping district. The newly renovated waterfront boasts state-of-the-art museums, while Italian, the language of many of Fremantle's original fishermen, is still spoken in many restaurants and cafes.

TRANSPORTATION AND PRACTICAL INFORMATION

The most common way to get to Freo is via **TransPerth trains** that frequently connect the city with Perth (30min.; approx. every 15min. 6am-midnight, then every 30min. until 2:30am; $3.20). The **Fremantle Airport Shuttle** goes to both terminals of the Perth Airport, departing from the Fremantle Railway Station regularly until midnight; pickup at Fremantle accommodations is available 24hr. when booked ahead. (☎9335 1614; www.fremantleairportshuttle.com.au. $25 for the first person, $5 per additional passenger.) Although downtown Freo is easily walkable, the free **Fremantle CAT** buses trace a loop along the harbor. (☎13 62 13. Every 10min. M-F 7:30am-6:30pm, Sa-Su 10am-6:30pm.) **Car rentals** are widely available in this region; **Bayswater,** 13 Queen Victoria St. (☎9430 5300), allows drivers to travel within a 500km radius with no extra fees. Free parking is available on Ode St., off of High St. roughly 1km from town center.

Tourist Office: Fremantle Tourist Bureau (☎9431 7878; www.fremantlewa.com.au), corner of High and William St., Kings Sq., is privately owned and offers free accommodation and tour bookings. Open M-F 9am-5pm, Sa 10am-3pm, Su 11:30am-2:30pm.

Budget Travel: STA Travel, 53 Market St. (☎9430 5553). Open M-F 9am-5pm, Sa 10am-3pm.

Police: (☎9430 1222), corner of Queen St. and Henderson St.

Hospital: Fremantle Hospital (☎9431 3333), corner of Alma St. and South Terr.

Internet Access: Access in Fremantle typically $4 per hr. Try the **Travel Lounge,** 16 Market St. (☎9335 4822). Open daily 7am-11pm.

Post Office: Fremantle GPO (☎9335 1611), corner of Market St. and Short St. Open M-F 8:30am-5pm. **Postal Code:** 6160.

ACCOMMODATIONS

The tourist office books apartment rentals that offer comfortable accommodations for two at a budget rate. For $70 you can have an apartment with a kitchen, TV, and laundry facilities, but you may have to stay a minimum of 2 nights. **805 in the Heart,** 23 Adelaide St., offers great views of the city.

Sundancer Backpackers Resort, 80 High St. (☎1800 061 144; www.sundancerbackpackers.com). This centrally located, social hostel is a restored turn-of-the-century resort, and has one of the most interesting, elegant lobbies around. Futuristic artwork, well-kept rooms, a heated spa, and an in-house bar. Dorms $17-20, NOMADS $16-19; doubles $50; ensuite $65/60, NOMADS $45. MC/V. ❷

Old Firestation Backpackers, 18 Phillimore St. (☎9430 5454; www.old-firestation.net), at Henry St. Short walk from cafes and nightlife, this hostel more than makes up for its location with Internet access, videos, digital jukebox, and Playstation. Separate women's wing with kitchen and lounge. Curries available from the attached Indian restaurant ($4-7). Dorms $19-20; doubles $50. 7th night free. MC/V. ❷

Pirates Backpackers, 11 Essex St. (☎9335 6635; www.piratesbackpackers.com). Close to "cappuccino strip" toward the Esplanade. Low-key, social hostel with best loca-

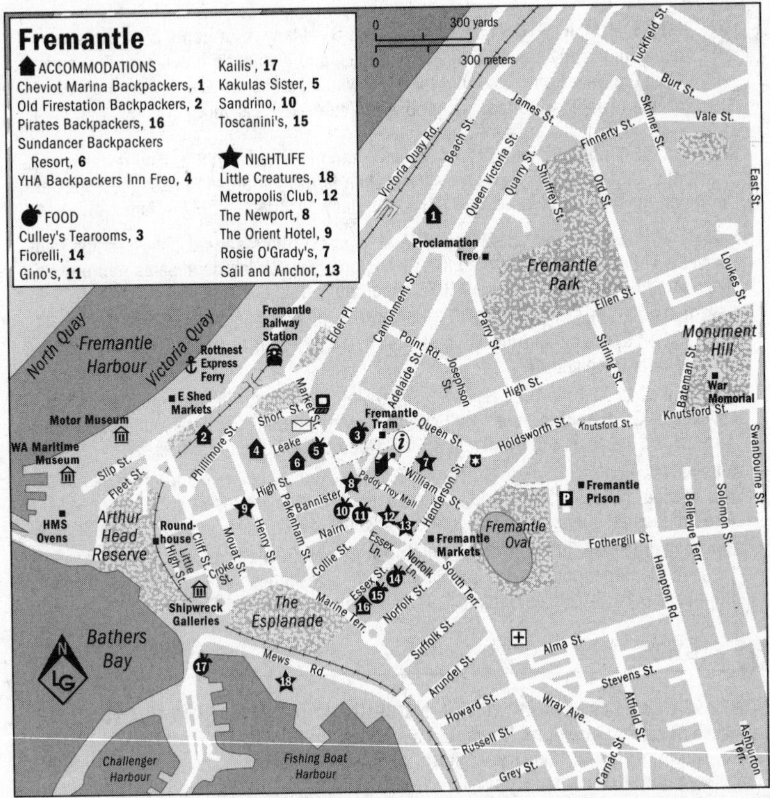

tion in town. Offers BBQ, helpful staff, and free parking. Check-in 24hr. Internet $4 per hr., first 30min. free. Dorms $21; doubles and twins $65. NOMADS/VIP/YHA. MC/V. ❷

YHA Backpackers Inn Freo, 11 Pakenham St. (☎9431 7065). From train station, turn right on Phillimore St., then left on Pakenham. Attractive, renovated warehouse space. Relaxed and quiet. Free videos. Reception 7am-11:30pm; Check-in 24hr. Bike rental $10 per day. Dorms $15-18; singles $30; doubles $40. NOMADS/VIP/YHA. MC/V. ❷

Cheviot Marina Backpackers, 4 Beach St. (☎9344 2055). Turn left down Elder St. from train station (becomes Beach St.) or take the Freo CAT to stop 8. A big, sunny hostel with friendly lounge upstairs and discounted drinks at the bar next door. Internet access $1 per 20min. 6-bed dorm $18, YHA $16; 4-bed $20/18; singles $35/30; twins $44/40. Weekly rates available. MC/V. ❷

FOOD

The scent of garlic and rosemary is everywhere in this city of Italian immigrants, and Italian restaurants are outnumbered only by the cafes at the heart of Freo's cappuccino culture. For fresh produce at rock-bottom prices, head to the Fremantle Markets on the weekend (p. 701), or try **Kakulas Sister** (☎9430 4445), a quaint Italian grocery store at 29-31 Market St.

HONE YOUR PICNICKING SKILLS. Many restaurants offer the same meals for slightly cheaper takeaway prices, and Fremantle has a beautiful park along the waterfront. Take your food with you for a chance to enjoy the Freo doctor, the oceanic wind that is supposed to cure what ails you.

Sandrino, 95 Market St. (☎9335 4487; www.sandrino.com.au). Stands out with a popular patio, and a unique take on classic italian fare. Their artisan pizzas are especially tempting; try the pumpkin pizza ($18). Open daily 11:30am-latenight. AmEx/MC/V. ❸

Kailis', 46 Mews Rd. (☎9335 7755). A step above the standard fish 'n' chips joint. Serves a variety of lightly-battered fish as customers watch the pearl ships return to harbor. Bar and cafe. Fish 'n' chips $8.70. Open daily 8am-8:30pm. ❶

Fiorelli, 19C Essex St. (☎9430 6119). Friendly staff, hip clientele, and satisfying Italian food ($12-16). Large and delicious pizzas ($10-12). Open M and W-Su 11:30am-3pm and 5:30pm-latenight. ❷

Toscanini's, 1/17 Essex St., (☎9431 7709), on the way to the waterfront from downtown Freo. Great spot for lunch with good vegetarian options. Frittata with salad $7.50. Focaccias $9. Lassis $5. Breakfast $5-12. Open daily 7:30am-4pm. ❶

Culley's Tearooms, 116 High St. (☎9335 1286). Serves full meals from crepes to salads to meat pies ($9-13) in addition to bakery fare (two scones with tea or coffee $5). Shelf of ½-price items. Open M-F 8:30am-4:30pm, Sa 8:30am-5pm, Su 10am-5pm. ❶

Gino's, at the corner of South Terr. and Market St. (☎9336 1464). The place to see and be seen on the "cappuccino strip," with a few families interspersed among the hipsters. Cappuccino $3.50. Mixed drinks $7-9. Open daily 8am-10pm. ❶

SIGHTS

WESTERN AUSTRALIA MARITIME MUSEUM AND SUBMARINE OVENS. Fremantle's maritime museum, housed in a striking building at the mouth of the Swan River, tells the unique history of sailboat racing, warships, and fishing practices from Aboriginal times to today. The real highlight is the tour, sometimes led by former captains of the Oberon-class submarine *Ovens*, which were in active service until 1997. A path marked by anchors leads from the museum to the other must-see: the Shipwreck Galleries on Cliff St. Exhibits are continuously updated as new wrecks are excavated off the WA coast. *('A' Shed Victoria Quay. ☎9431 8444; www.mm.wa.gov.au. Open daily 9:30am-5pm. Sub tours every 30min. 10am-3:30pm; sign up early before tours fill. Museum only: $10, concessions $5, children $3, families $22. Sub only: $8/5/3/5/22. Museum and sub $15/8/5/8/35. Shipwreck Galleries: $2 suggested donation.)*

FREMANTLE PRISON. Get a thorough look at a maximum-security prison without committing a felony. The prison, which opened in the 1850s, closed in 1991, three years after a riot. Excellent guides recall daring tales of escape as well as the horrors of incarceration, while works of art left on the walls by convicts reveal a different side of life behind bars. The Torchlight Tour is especially thrilling with spooky surprises along the way. A limited portion of the prison is wheelchair accessible. *(1 The Terrace. ☎9336 9200. 75min. tours depart every 30min.; last tour 5pm. Torchlight tours W and F; book ahead. Open daily 10am-6pm. Day tour $15, concessions $12, children 4-15 $7.50, families $40; candlelight tour $19/15/10/45.)*

FREMANTLE MOTOR MUSEUM. Home to one of six pre-WWI Rolls Royce limos in the world today, and also the car from the film "Crocodile Dundee." The massive collection of vintage luxury automobiles, race cars, and motorbikes will make you yearn for the open road. *('B' Shed Victoria Quay. ☎9336 5222; www.fremantlemotor-*

museum.net. Open daily 9:30am-5pm. $9.50, seniors $8, children $5, families $23.)

FREMANTLE MARKETS. The place to be on a weekend afternoon in Freo. One can find just about anything here, from massages to marsupials. Fresh veggies abound; produce prices hit rock bottom Sunday around closing time. *(On the corner of South Terr. and Henderson St. ☎9335 2515. Open F 9am-9pm, Sa 9am-5pm, Su 10am-5pm.)*

NIGHTLIFE

Freo's strip quickly changes from cafe to club as the sun sets, making it one of the most attractive late-night scenes in the entire Perth region. Look for old hotels; they have been converted into bars under the Aussie law that traditionally lets hotels sell alcohol.

Little Creatures, 40 Mews Rd. (☎9430 5555). This microbrewery offers the best beer in town, great views of the harbor, and the trendiest set of Freo locals. Once a crocodile farm, the building now lends itself to late evening conversation. Open M-F 10am-midnight, Sa 9am-midnight, Su 9am-10pm.

Sail and Anchor, 64 South Terr. (☎9335 8433). Another microbrewery; locals here greatly outnumber backpackers. Home of Redback beer, making this the perfect place to hoist one. Open M-Th 11am-midnight, F-Sa 11am-1am, Su 11am-10pm.

The Orient Hotel, 49 High St. (☎9336 2455). A relaxed venue that offers live music 6 nights per wk. Captures the artsy vibe at the heart of Freo's lifestyle. Open M-Th 10am-midnight, F-Sa 10am-1am, Su 10am-10pm.

Rosie O'Grady's, 23 William St. (☎9335 1645). Irish pub in town center, with live music on weekends. Open M-Th 11am-midnight, F-Sa 11am-1am, Su 11am-10pm.

The Newport, 2 South Terr. (☎9335 2428). A converted hotel with billiards, outdoor space, and a large dance fl. at the heart of Freo's latenight sector. Good place to see local bands. Cover varies. Open M-Th 11am-midnight, F-Sa 11am-1am, Su noon-10pm.

Metropolis Club, 58 South Terr. (☎9228 0500). Glitzy, multi-level dance club where the elite abound. Cover F and Sa $10 after 10pm. Open Th and Sa 9pm-6am, F 9pm-5am.

ROTTNEST ISLAND ☎08

Dubbed a "rat's nest" by Dutch explorers who mistook the island's quokkas (small wallabies) for giant rodents, Rottnest Island is anything but. Just 30min. from Fremantle and 90min. from Perth, the island is a spectacular haven for wildlife and visitors; peacocks

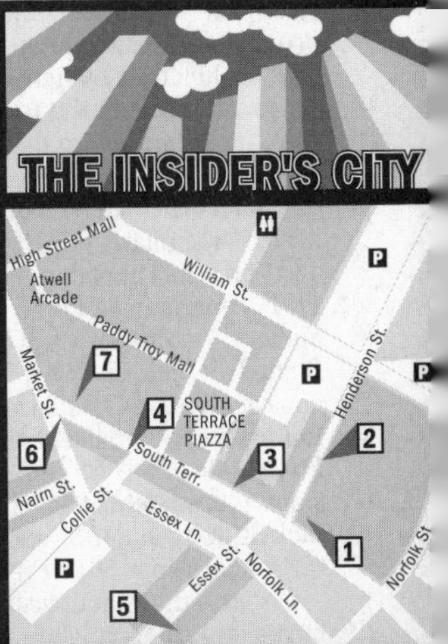

VERY FREO

Fremantle's famous "Cappuccino Strip" offers a cosmopolitan oasis where you can sip lattes or dig through literary treasure chests.

1. Browse the famous **Fremantle Markets** (☎9335 2515) and add to your boomerang collection while you grab groceries.
2. Find that out-of-print gem at musty **Magpie Books** (☎9335 1131).
3. Grab a pastry and coffee at **The Mill Bakehouse** (☎9430 4252).
4. Look sophisticated while sitting at a sidewalk table with your latte at **Dome** (☎9336 3040).
5. Indulge your cultural side by catching an artsy independent flick at the **Luna on SX** theater (☎9430 5999).
6. Stop for cake or a cocktail at **Gino's** (☎9336 1464).
7. Peruse the extensive selection of used books at **Elizabeth's Bookshop** (☎9433 1310).

roam freely and vacationers cycle, swim, snorkel, surf, and kayak. The coastline provides a beautiful setting for water sports: white beaches meet rolling green hills broken only by lighthouses or stony outcroppings. Remnants of a darker past, however, linger in the form of buildings constructed by Aboriginal prisoners who were incarcerated on the island in the 19th century.

TRANSPORTATION AND PRACTICAL INFORMATION. Several companies offer similarly priced **ferry** service to Rottnest from Fremantle, Hillary's Harbour, and Perth; call ahead to make sure that all boats are running. **Oceanic Cruises** (☎9325 1191) departs from Pier 5 of the Barrack St. Jetty, Perth (daily 8:45, 10am; F-Su also noon; $63, concessions $58, students $44, children $23) and from the East St. Jetty or B Shed on Victoria Quay, Fremantle (daily 8, 8:30, 10, 11:30am; F-Su also 2pm; same-day round-trip $49, children $19, concessions $44; extended stay $54/49/21). **Rottnest Express** (☎9335 6406) has several daily departures from Victoria Quay, C Shed, Frem.antle (7:30, 9:30, 11:30am, 3:30pm; F 5:30pm; same-day round-trip $51, concessions $46, students $41, children $21; extended-stay $56/50/44/23) and from the Barrack St. Jetty in Perth (daily 8:45, 9:45am, 2pm; round trip $66, students $52, children $28, concessions $61). Free pickup is available from Perth and Fremantle hotels.

Once on the island, visitors can explore by bus, bike, or foot. **Free transfer shuttle buses** depart from the main bus stop near the museum every 30min. 8:15am-5:15pm, with additional buses at 6 and 7pm, and head to the airport, Geordie Bay, and Kingstown. The **Bayseeker Bus** offers a quick overview of the island (45min.; day-ticket $7.50, students $5.40, children $3.80). The best way to see Rottnest is by **biking**—the island is only 11km long and 4.5km wide, although the terrain is slightly hilly. **Rottnest Island Bike Hire,** 300m left of the jetty, has a wide selection and is a better option than renting before you arrive. (☎9292 5105. Open daily in high season 8:30am-5pm; in low season 8:30am-4pm. Fixed-gear $17 per day, 18-speed $23; deposit $25. Locks and helmets included. AmEx/MC/V.)

WESTERN AUSTRALIA

The **Visitors Centre** is at the end of the jetty at Thomson Bay and provides useful maps and accommodation booking. (☎9372 9752. Open M-Th and Sa-Su 7:30am-5pm, F 7:30am-7pm.) Free **tours** of Rottnest depart frequently from the Salt Store to the left of the visitors center. To the right of the jetty is a pedestrian mall with an **ATM,** bakery (open M-F 8am-3:30pm, Sa-Su 7:30am-4pm), and grocery store (open daily 8am-6pm). A half kilometer north of the mall is a **nursing post.** (☎9292 5030. Open daily 8:30am-4:30pm.) The **police station** (☎9292 5029) is across the street. The **post office** is located inside the Rottnest Island Gift Shop at Thomson Bay (open M-F 9am-1pm and 1:30-4pm). **Postal Code:** 6161.

ACCOMMODATIONS AND FOOD. Before heading to Kingstown, you must check in at the visitors center at the base of the jetty where the ferries arrive. The **YHA Kingstown Barracks Youth Hostel ❷** is in Kingstown, a 20min. walk from the visitors center or short shuttle ride via the transfer bus (see above). Though there are meals available in the barracks complex ($7), travelers who do not want to relive the noise and chaos of their primary school cafeterias may prefer to cook in the hostel's kitchen. (☎9372 9780. Linen $5. Internet access $1 per 10min. Lockers $2-5. Dorms $24, YHA $21; units in high season from $60, low $38; bungalows from $45/29. Book ahead in summer.) In the Thomson Bay settlement, fish 'n' chips ($8.50), milkshakes ($4.50), or a midday drink at the bar can be found at **Rottnest Tearooms and Cafe ❶.** Next door, **Dôme Cafe ❶** serves up Anzac biscuits or biscotti ($2-2.60), gourmet coffee ($3.60), and soups and salads ($8.50-15) to satisfy the hungry traveler. (☎9292 5026.) Both afford splendid views of Thomson Bay.

ACTIVITIES. Rottnest Island's beaches get emptier as you head away from settled areas—go far enough and you may have a cove to yourself. **Narrow Neck** and

Salmon Bay offer good **fishing** as does the **jetty. The Basin, Pinky Beach,** and **Parakeet** are nice swimming spots near the settlement. **Little Salmon Bay** and **Parker Point** are ideal for snorkeling, while **Strickland Bay** boasts Rottnest's best surfing. Whales and dolphins are often seen from the windy cliffs at **West End,** where 10 ft. high waves crash upon the limestone, ending their long journey across the Indian Ocean. **Rottnest Malibu Dive,** located below Dôme Cafe, is the only dive shop on the island. (☎9292 5111; www.rottnestdiving.com.au. Dive $70, 2 dives $130; snorkel gear $16.50; fishing rod $12.50 per day.) The Catholic Church provides an interesting break from sun and surf; visitors can ring the bells every day from 3-4:30pm.

SOUTHWEST

Tourism in the Southwest is booming and it's not hard to see why—Mother Nature has been kind to the region. The adventurous can hike in the Stirling and Porongurup ranges or dive with dolphins and surf in the warm coastal waters. Connoisseurs can sample award-winning vintages, peruse local art studios, or drive through majestic forests. In the low season, the crowds depart and rates go down, but many activities, including surfing, whale-watching, cave exploration, and wine tasting, are still available.

TRANSPORTATION

The easiest way to see the Southwest is by car; many sights are well off the bus routes, and public transportation is often inadequate or nonexistent. Once completely out of Perth, the 3hr. drive south toward Margaret River takes you past shoreline, forests, farms, cattle stations, and the occasional limestone quarry. Options do exist for those without cars. The **Easy Rider Backpackers** bus offers a three-month pass that covers service between most regional hostels as far as Albany. (Nov.-Apr. 3 per wk., May-June and Sept.-Oct. 2 per wk., July-Aug. 1 per wk. 24hr. notice required for pickup. $219 with YHA card.) **Transwa's** (☎1300 662 205) handy 28-day **Southern Discovery Pass** allows for travel in a one-way loop to most destinations in the region, including Albany, Esperance, and Kalgoorlie.

PERTH TO BUNBURY

The drive southward from Perth to Bunbury offers the opportunity to experience pristine Westralian flora and fauna without venturing too far from "civilization." There are also about 20 wineries, some of which offer tours and wine tastings, along the 100km of Hwy. 1 between Perth and **Yalgorup National Park.** Yalgorup is the Noongar word meaning "place of lakes" and the park's 10 lakes are indeed its centerpiece. It also features nature reserves, miles of dunes, thrombolites, and a forest of tuart and jarrah trees with peppermint undergrowth. Drive carefully; kangaroos, emus, and wallabies are frequently in the road. Park and Peel Region information is available at the **Mandurah Visitor Centre,** on the quaint waterfront at 75 Mandurrah Terr. (☎9550 3999. Open M-F 9am-4:30pm, Sa-Su 9:30am-4pm).

Clifton, one of the two largest lakes, offers travelers a rare chance to see thrombolites, a variety of microbialite that was one of earth's earliest life forms. To view the thrombolites from an observation deck, turn off Hwy. 1 at the sign for the viewing platform onto Lakeside Pkwy. Take a right on Mt. John Rd., continue 3km to the carpark, and then follow the short footpath. Farther south, the area around **Preston Beach** is one of the most beautiful sections of the park (turn left on Preston Beach Rd., marked by the Yalgorup National Park sign, just south of the turn-offs for Pinjarra and Warnoona).

There is camping in the woods at **Martin's Tank** ❶, 7km from the turn-off and 5km down an unsealed road. (Pit toilets, no running water. $5, children $2.) From there, take one of several trails to the beautiful, clear lakes. Powerboats are allowed on some, while on others only sailboards and canoes are permitted—information boards at each site indicate which specific vessels can be used. Those in search of an ocean view should check *The West Australian* newspaper weekend travel section for rental home listings. Those heading on to Bunbury may want to take the 26km scenic detour along the beach through **Australind,** ending in the Bunbury CBD. In Australind, the 500m long boardwalked outcropping into the estuary at the southern end of the Leshenault Inlet provides an excellent opportunity for bird watching.

BUNBURY ☎08

Dolphins are the main attraction in Bunbury (pop. 55,000), 2hr. south of Perth, where over 100 bottlenose have made their home. Though there is no shortage of dolphin-admirers, Bunbury has escaped the tourist deluge that plagues Monkey Mia. This may be due to Bunbury's one-act show: many visitors feel that they have seen all the town has to offer after visiting the Dolphin Discovery Centre.

TRANSPORTATION. Downtown Bunbury is located 3km from the Wollaston train station on the southern end of Western Australia's **train** network. Trains depart for Perth daily (2½hr., 6am and 2:45pm, $23.90). There is a free shuttle between the station and the visitors center. **South West Coachlines** is in the Old Railway Station at Carmody Pl. and Haley St. (☎9791 1955. Open M-F 8am-6pm, Sa-Su 8am-2pm and 3:30-6pm.) Buses run to Perth (2½hr.; 8:45am, 2, 6:45pm; $23, YHA $20.70) and Augusta via Busselton and Margaret River (2½hr.; M-F 11:35am and 4:20pm, Sa-Su 8:45am and 4:05pm; $17, seniors $9.60, YHA/VIP discount 10%). **Transwa** also offers service to Perth (3hr.; M, W, F 11:40am, Tu, Th, Sa 11:15am, and M-F and Su 5:40pm; $23.90, YHA/VIP discount 10%) and Augusta (3hr.; M-Th and Su 3:45pm, M-F and Su 12:05pm, F also 8:35pm; $20, YHA/VIP $18). Local **buses** circle the city (M-F 7am-9pm, Sa 8am-5pm. $2.10, outlying areas $3.20, all destinations for students, children, and seniors $0.90.)

PRACTICAL INFORMATION. The Old Railway station off Blair St. houses the **Bunbury Visitors Centre** (☎9721 7922; open M-F 9am-5pm, Sa 9:30am-4:30pm, Su 10am-2pm), the bus station, and the **Bunbury Internet Cafe** (☎9791 1254; $5 per hr.; open M-Sa 8am-4:30pm). Other services include: **banks** along Victoria St.; **police** (☎121 444), on the corner of Wittenoom St. and Stephen St.; and a **hospital** (☎9722 1000), located south of town at Bussell Hwy. and Robertson Dr. There is a **post office** on the corner of Victoria and Stirling St. (☎13 13 18. Open M-F 8:30am-5pm). **Postal Code:** 6230.

ACCOMMODATIONS. The **Dolphin Retreat YHA** ❷, 14 Wellington St., is a friendly new hostel with free bikes and boogie boards, billiards, a ping-pong table, and Internet access for $4 per hr. (☎9792 4690. Dorms $19; singles $29; doubles $48; family rooms $80. Non-YHA $3.50 extra. MC/V.) The **Wander Inn YHA** ❷, 16 Clifton St., near Wittenoom St., also has ping-pong, billiards, and BBQ. They rent snorkel gear, bikes, and body boards, and can book various tours. (☎9721 3242. Internet access $4 per hr., first 10min. free. Coin laundry. Dorms $23, VIP/YHA $19; singles $36/33; doubles $54-56/50-52.) **Koombana Bay Holiday Resort** ❷, just across Koombana Dr. from the Dolphin Discovery Centre, features impeccably maintained grounds and extensive facilities including laundry, tennis courts, video rental, a cafe, and a convenience store. (☎9791 3900. High season sites for 2 $14, powered $32; ensuite $37; cabins for 2 $85. Low season $13/28/32/80. MC/V.) For a change of pace, the **Paradise Found Bed and Breakfast** ❹, 3 Thomas Ct., 15min. north of town, is tucked away into the woods around the estuary. Take Old Coast Rd. in Australind to Cathedral Ave., then right on Australind Dr. to Knapp Dr., and right on Thomas Ct. (☎9725 9739. Breakfast included. Singles $65; doubles $90.)

FOOD. The stretch of Victoria St. between Wellington and Clifton St. has a collection of restaurants that locals refer to as "the cappuccino strip"; after dark this street boasts Bunbury's up-and-coming nightlife. The acclaimed **Aristos Waterfront ❶**, at 15 Bonnefoi Blvd., on the harbour off Casuarina Dr., offers fish 'n' chips ($8.90) made by Aristos, a popular Aussie television chef. (☎9791 6477. Open daily 11:30am-9pm.) Customers sip smooth cappuccinos ($3.30) while sitting on plush leather couches at **Benesse ❶**, 83 Victoria St. (☎9791 4030. Open daily 7am-5pm. MC/V min. $10.) **Buck's Diner ❶**, at the corner of Symmons and Victoria St., serves up hearty meals to a local crowd. A chicken breast fillet, salad, fries and coffee costs just $9.50. (Open M-W 7:30am-8pm, Th-Sa 7:30am-9pm, Su 8am-3pm. Cash only.) The more frugal should try **Orka Kebabs and Turkish Bakery ❶**, 57-59 Victoria St. (☎9791 2440. Kebab combo with tabouleh and soda $9.30. Open daily morning-latenight.) **Coles** is in the Centrepoint Shopping Center behind the visitors center. (☎9795 1800. Open M-W and F 8am-6pm, Th 8am-9pm, Sa 8am-5pm.)

SIGHTS. The **Dolphin Discovery Centre,** on Koombana Dr., is the best way to learn about the local dolphins; it is run by a friendly volunteer staff. (☎9791 3088; www.dolphindiscovery.com.au. Open daily Nov.-Apr. 8am-4pm, May and Oct. 8am-3pm, June-Sept. 9am-3pm. $4, children and concessions $2, families $9.) **Naturaliste Charters,** located on the adjacent jetty, runs dolphin-watching and swimming tours. (☎9755 2276. 1½hr. tours daily 11am and 2pm. Sighting tour $37, students $28, children $24; 3hr. swim tour Nov.-Apr. $125.) Across the street from the discovery center, the **Mangrove Boardwalk** weaves through the southernmost mangrove ecosystem in Western Australia. The **Big Swamp Wetlands** on Prince Philip Dr., just south of the CBD, is home to over 70 species of birds. The **Big Swamp Wildlife Park,** also on Prince Philip Dr., lets you interact with white kangaroos, tawny frogmouths, and exotic birds. From Ocean Dr., turn onto Hayward St. and look for the sign at the next roundabout. (☎9721 8380. Open daily 10am-5pm. $5.50, seniors $4.50, ages 2-12 $3.50.) The **Marlston Hill Lookout,** near the oceanside end of Koombana Dr., provides panoramic views of the area. There are also beautiful beaches along Ocean Dr., including the popular **Back Beach.**

MARGARET RIVER AREA ☎08

Margaret River's famous vineyards, gourmet food, and stunning scenery make it a popular year-round destination for vacationing Perthites. Dramatic rock and coral formations rise from the pounding surf, vast cave systems weave through subterranean depths, celebrated vineyards cover the countryside, and artisans of every medium draw inspiration from it all. Perhaps even more remarkable than the wide variety of landscapes and activities in the region is that it is all contained within a fairly small area—the drive from Dunsborough, near the peninsula's northernmost point, to Augusta, at the southern tip, takes only an hour.

TRANSPORTATION

The size of the region and lack of centralized attractions means transportation is often a hassle. The best way to get around is by car. Rental is most easily arranged in Perth or Bunbury before arriving in Margaret River. In Busselton, **Avis** (☎9754 1175) operates out of the Toyota dealership at the west end of Peel Terr. In Margaret River, **Margaret River Car Hire** (☎04 1794 4485) is your best option with small cars and 4WDs from $55 per day. **South West Coachlines** departs Margaret River from Charles West St., two blocks from the Bussell Hwy., and goes to Perth (4½hr.; 2 per day; $31, YHA $27.90). **Transwa** (☎1300 662 205) uses **Margaret River Travel,** 109 Bussell Hwy., as its area agent. (☎9757 2171. Open M-F 9am-5pm, Sa 9am-noon.) You can also rent **bikes** at various places in town.

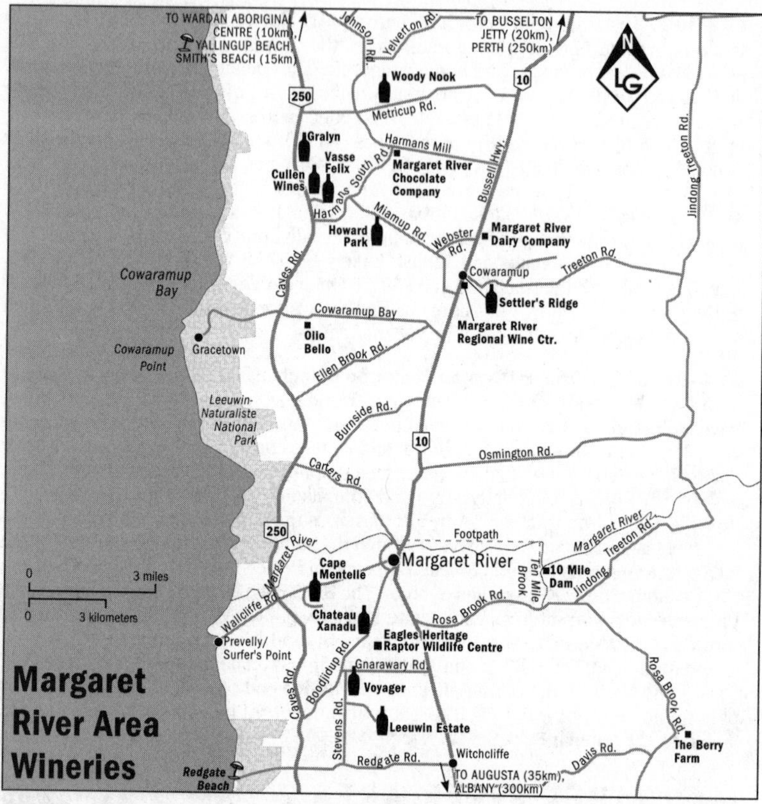

ORIENTATION AND PRACTICAL INFORMATION

Margaret River lies 100km south of Bunbury on the **Bussell Highway** (Hwy. 10). The scenic **Caves Road** branches off the Bussell Hwy. at **Busselton,** 52km from Bunbury, and winds its way by Margaret River through wineries, beaches, and the towns of **Yallingup** and **Dunsborough.** About 45km south of Margaret River, the **Blackwood River** meets the ocean at **Augusta.**

Tourist Offices: Augusta Visitor Centre (☎9758 0166), on the corner of Bussell Hwy. and Ellis St. Free accommodation booking. Open daily 9am-5pm.

Busselton Tourist Bureau, 38 Peel Terr. (☎9752 1288). Open M-F 9am-5pm, Sa 9am-4pm, Su high season 10am-4pm, low 10am-2pm.

CALM, 14 Queen St., Busselton (☎9752 5555). National park hiking and camping info, and maps. Open M-F 8am-5pm.

Dunsborough Visitor Centre (☎9755 3299), in the shopping center on Seymour Blvd., Dunsborough. Books tours and accommodations, and has information for **Yallingup**. Open M-F 9am-5pm, Sa 9am-4pm, Su 10am-2pm.

Margaret River Visitor Centre (☎9757 2911; www.margaretriver.com), on the corner of Bussell Hwy. and Tunnbridge St. Maps, brochures, and a wine showroom. Open daily 9am-5pm.

Work Opportunity: Labour Solutions, 157 Bussell Hwy. (☎9758 8136). An employment agency for people seeking short-term work. Jobs are easier to find in winter; in summer the area is flooded by eager candidates. Open M-F 8:30am-5pm.

Police: 42 Willmott Ave., Margaret River (☎9757 2222).

Internet Access: Cybercorner Cafe, Shop #2, 72 Willmott Ave., Margaret River (☎9757 9388). $6 per hr. Open in summer daily 8am-8pm; in winter M-F 8am-8pm, Sa-Su 9am-5pm.

Post Office: 53 Townview Terr., Margaret River (☎9757 2250), 1 block up Willmott Ave. from Bussell Hwy. Open M-F 9am-5pm. **Postal Code:** 6285.

ACCOMMODATIONS AND CAMPING

Visitors to the Margaret River area can choose to stay in a wide range of settings, from vineyards to beaches to tuart forests. Those looking to splurge can contact the Margaret River Visitor Centre (☎9757 2911) to book a room in one of the many wonderful B&Bs. Rooms fill up quickly from October to March; be sure to book ahead for summer weekends. From June to August, more bargain options are available. Contact **CALM** (☎9752 5555) if you want to camp in Leeuwin-Naturaliste National Park.

MARGARET RIVER

Surfpoint Resort (☎1800 071 777; www.surfpoint.com.au), on Riedle Dr. south of Prevelley, about 500m from Gnarabup Beach. Clean, simple rooms around a small courtyard; a beautiful beach escape. Internet access $6 per hr. Bike and boogie board rental. BBQ. Dorms high season $24, low season $22; doubles $79/67; ensuite $99/85. Book ahead in summer. ❷

Margaret River Lodge YHA, 220 Railway Terr. (☎9757 9532), 1.5km southwest of the Bussell Hwy. off Wallcliffe Rd. Standard hostel rooms in a relaxed atmosphere within walking distance of Cape Mentelle and Xanadu wineries. Pool and organic vegetable garden. Internet access $5 per hr. Free pickup from bus station. Bike rental $10. Dorms $21-24; singles $53; doubles $63. Non-YHA $3.50 extra. ❷

Inne Town Backpackers, 93 Bussell Hwy. (☎9757 3698 or 1800 244 115; www.innetown.com). Great location on the main drag in Margaret River keeps it hopping even in low season. Internet access $5 per hr. Laundry. Dorms high season $25, low season $23; singles $55; doubles $65; family room (5 beds) $100. Cash only. ❷

Prevelly Park Beach Resort (☎9757 2374), turn right on Mitchell Rd. off Wallcliffe Rd. west out of Margaret River. Close to great surfing. Check in at the adjoining general store. Linen $4.50-6.50. Sites high season $17, low $11; basic on-site vans $90/50; 5-person cedar cabins with cooking facilities $110/60. ❶

WESTERN AUSTRALIA

BUSSELTON, DUNSBOROUGH, AND YALLINGUP

Dunsborough Beach House YHA, 201-205 Geographe Bay Rd., Dunsborough (☎9755 3107). Excellent location on beach gives this social hostel a laid-back vibe. Manager Andy is knowledgeable and amiable. Internet access $4 per hr. Bike rental $10 per 4hr., $15 per day. Dorms $23, YHA $22; singles $36/34; doubles $54/52. MC/V. ❷

Hideaway Holiday Homes, 24 Elsegood Ave., Yallingup (☎9755 2145). Big simple cabins just a 10min. walk from the beach. Bathrooms, laundry, TV, and kitchen. No linen. Doubles from $60, weekly $295; quads from $70/400. ❸

Busselton Backpackers, 14 Peel Terr., Busselton (☎9754 2763). Small hostel (sleeps 20) with basic rooms. Laundry. Dorms $20, $100 per wk.; singles $35; doubles $45. Cash only. ❷

Yallingup Beach Holiday Park, 1 Valley Rd. (☎1800 220 002), as you drive down to Yallingup Beach. Great location across the street from the area's biggest surf. High season sites for 2 $50, low season $25; cabins for 2 $175-255/70-110. ❷

AUGUSTA

Baywatch Manor Resort YHA, 88 Blackwood Ave. (☎9758 1290). Cozy atmosphere, superb facilities, spacious, and well maintained. Native jarrah wood dining tables. Owners arrange whale-watching trips at 10% discount. Internet access $4 per hr. Bikes ½-day $8, full-day $12. Free lockers. Dorms $23, YHA $21; doubles and twins $58/55; ensuite doubles $75. ❷

Flinders Bay Caravan Park (☎9758 1380), 2.5km south of the Visitor Centre. Basic camping about 10m from the ocean. Sites for 2 Dec.-Jan. $20-22, powered $25; Feb.-Nov. $18/20. ❶

FOOD AND NIGHTLIFE

Margaret River's restaurants are concentrated along the Bussell Hwy. Many are BYO (customers are allowed to bring their own wine; a small corkage fee may be charged). **River Fresh IGA** supermarket is next to the visitors center on the Bussell Hwy. in Margaret River (open daily 7:30am-8pm). Margaret River also hosts a market every Sunday (10am-1pm) on Bussell Hwy. across from the pharmacy. In Augusta, there is a **fruit market** and **grocery store** on Blackwood Ave., about 500m north of the visitors center. Small restaurants line **Dunn Bay Road,** which runs through Dunsborough. Many area wineries also have restaurants. Margaret River's laid-back nightlife begins in the evenings at **Knights Inn** on Wallcliffe Rd. or **Corner Bar** in town on the corner of Bussell Hwy. and Willmott St.

WESTERN AUSTRALIA

MARGARET RIVER

Wino's, 85 Bussell Hwy. (☎9758 7155). This trendy wine bar is the quintessential end to a Margaret River day. Serves light tapas appropriately named "bar grits" ($4-7), gourmet pizzas ($12.50), and more expensive main courses. Open M-F 3pm-latenight, Sa-Su noon-latenight. MC/V. ❷

Goodfellas Cafe Woodfire Pizza, 97 Bussell Hwy. (☎9757 3184). Exotic pizzas and ample bowls of pasta ($14-18) in a nice setting. Open daily 5:30-9pm. AmEx/MC/V. ❷

The Green Room, 113b Bussell Hwy. (☎9757 3644). Locals rave about the meat and veggie burgers ($6.50-8.50). Open Th-Su 4:30pm-latenight. ❶

Sails Cafe, 2/117 Bussell Hwy. (☎9757 3573). The terrace has great views for people-watching over Margaret River's busiest street. Scrumptious BLTs ($9) and design-your-own sandwiches ($6.50). Breakfast available all day (pancakes with maple syrup $9). Open daily 7am-4:30pm. Cash only. ❶

Settler's Tavern, 114 Bussell Hwy. (☎9757 2398). At the end of the night, all roads lead to Settler's. Live bands 4 nights per wk. Billiards and big screen TV. Healthy, innovative dishes like spicy baja tacos ($12) until 8:30pm (YHA discount 10%). Cover varies. Open M-Th 11am-midnight, F 11am-1am, Sa 10am-1am, Su noon-10pm. ❷

BUSSELTON, DUNSBOROUGH, AND YALLINGUP

Dunsborough Bakery (☎9755 3137), in the Centrepoint Shopping Center on Dunn Bay Rd., Dunsborough, has achieved legendary status among local surfers for its meat pies, especially the phenomenal pepper-steak variety ($4). Open daily 6am-5pm. ❶

Evviva (☎9755 3811), on the corner of Cyrillean Way and Naturaliste Terr., Dunsborough. Take a break from tired breakfasts and indulge in muesli with yogurt and stewed fruit ($9). Open daily 7am-2:30pm. ❶

The Food Farmacy, Shop 9 in Dunsborough Park Shopping Centre, Dunn Bay Rd., Dunsborough (☎9759 1877). With menu titles like $C_6H_{12}0_6$ (glucose), and gourmet items that change daily, it's a modern gourmet joint with a sense of humor. Breakfast and lunch ($6-20), pricier dinner ($15-30). Open M-Tu and Th-Su 8am-latenight. ❸

AUGUSTA

Augusta Bakery and Cafe, 121 Blackwood Ave (☎9758 1664). A bakery with superb pastries and meat pies ($2-4). Gigantic, topping-laden pizzas F nights ($7.50-10 for a small). Open M-Th and Sa-Su 7am-3pm, F 7am-8:30pm. ❶

Colourpatch Cafe (☎9758 1295), on Albany Terr., just south of town. Specializes in fish 'n' chips ($9-10.40). The patio boasts a great view of the Blackwood River flowing into Flinders Bay. Open daily 8am-8pm. ❶

SIGHTS

BUSSELTON JETTY. At 2km, this is the longest wooden jetty in the Southern Hemisphere. An underwater observatory at the end of the jetty allows visitors to view sea life deep below the water's surface without getting wet. *(At the end of Queen St. in Busselton. ☎9754 3689; www.busseltonjetty.com.au. Observatory open daily weather permitting 10:30am-3:30pm. Wheelchair accessible. Jetty access $2.50, under 15 free. Includes trolley ride to the end; $20, children $11.50.)*

WARDAN ABORIGINAL CENTRE. The Wardan Aboriginal Centre, run by the native Wardandi People, is the only facility of its kind in Western Australia. Cultural custodians lead bush story trail walks and demonstrate spear and boomerang throwing. *(Head 6km south on Caves Rd. from Yallingup, turn right on Wyadup Rd. and then left on Injidup Springs Rd. ☎9756 6566. Open daily 10am-4pm. Entry with one activity $12, each additional activity $10.)*

EAGLES HERITAGE RAPTOR WILDLIFE CENTRE. Located on Boodjidup Rd. 5km southwest of Margaret River, the Centre houses Australia's largest collection of birds of prey. It is dedicated to the rehabilitation of injured birds, breeding projects, and public education. Be sure to catch a flight display, where you may get to handle an eagle. *(☎9757 2960. Open daily 10am-5pm. Flight displays daily 11am and 1:30pm. Wheelchair accessible. $10, seniors $8, children $4.50, families $25.)*

OTHER SIGHTS. The 15km **Ludlow Tuart Forest Drive** between Bunbury and Busselton runs through picturesque groves of tuart trees, broken only by the occasional picnic site. Visitors can explore the early days of European settlement in Australia at **Wonnerup House,** a meticulously preserved homestead first settled in 1834 and now maintained by the National Trust. *(Turn off Bussell Hwy. onto Tuart Dr. 5km east of Busselton and follow the signs. ☎9752 2039. Open W-Su 10am-4pm. $5, children and concessions $3, families $12.)* The Margaret River area boasts numerous farms which offer food tastings, demonstrations, and farmstays. There are also dozens of regional art galleries around the wine country. In Dunsborough, these are localized near the town center, while in Busselton they're housed in the unique ArtGeo Center in the old Court House complex on Queen St.

WINERIES AND WINE TOURS

WINERIES

The Margaret River area boasts over 80 wineries, most of which are clustered in the region bordered by caves and Johnson Rd. between Yallingup and Margaret River. Older, relatively large vintners include **Vasse Felix,** which welcomes visitors to its cellars with modern sculpture (☎9756 5000; www.vassefelix.com.au; open daily 10am-5pm), and **Cullen** (☎9755 5277; www.cullenwines.com.au), which hosts a chardonnay tasting every October, attracting vintners from France, California, New Zealand, and other areas of Australia. Smaller wineries generally offer a more personal tasting experience. **Settler's Ridge,** at 54b Bussell Hwy. in Cowaramup, has reasonably priced, award-winning organic wines. (☎9755 5883; www.settlersridge.com.au. Open daily 10am-5pm.) Gralyn, one of the region's first vineyards, specializes in fine ports. Today it remains a friendly family-run operation in a beautiful modern facility. (☎9755 6245; www.gralyn.com.au. Open daily 10am-5pm.) **Woody Nook** is a relaxed option with several award-winning wines including its flagship Gallagher's Choice Cabernet Sauvignon, or the more playful Nooky Delight tawny port. (☎9755 7547. Metricup Rd., north of Cowaramup. Open daily 10am-4:30pm.) **Howard Park** on Miamup Rd., purveyor of the excellent Mad Fish line, has an award-winning, futuristic tasting center set in a grove of jarrah trees. (☎9756 5200; www.howardparkwines.com.au. Open daily 10am-5pm.)

WINING AND DRIVING. Although wineries are a major attraction in the Margaret River area, visitors should be wary of driving between tastings. Australia's legal **blood alcohol limit** for driving is a very low 0.05. Walking, going on a wine tour, or riding with a designated driver (called "the skipper" in Oz) are all good ways to avoid run-ins with the law, and trees.

Those walking from Margaret River can reach at least two wineries on foot. **Chateau Xanadu** features superb Chardonnay, a welcoming setup, and a label that makes an effort to appeal to a younger crowd with a variety of trendy wines. (☎9757 2581; www.xanaduwines.com. Walkers and bikers may take Railway Terr. 3km south to Terry St. and the gravel service road. Drivers should take the smoother entrance off Boodijup Rd. Open daily 10am-5pm; restaurant noon-4pm.) **Cape Mentelle** is a relaxed, friendly winery, and one of only a few to grow zinfandel grapes. (☎9757 0888. Just off Wallcliffe Rd. west of town. Open daily 10am-4:30pm.) A long walk or a short bike ride takes you to the beautiful gardens and award-winning vineyards of **Voyager.** The fine wines here are matched by one of the most beautiful estates in the entire region. (☎9757 6354. Open daily 10am-5pm; restaurant noon-3pm.) Around the corner sits the **Leeuwin Estate Winery** production facilities, which boast sweeping, picnic-perfect grounds. The estate hosts a wildly popular concert in February or March every year. (☎9759 0000; www.leeuwinestate.com.au. Off Gnarawy Rd. Open daily 10am-4:30pm. 1hr. tours at 11am, noon, and 3pm. $9.90, children $4.40.)

WINE TOURS AND WINE EDUCATION

While renting a car makes area wineries more accessible, drinking and driving don't mix. Wine tours are a popular alternative; they generally cost about $55 for a half-day and $90 for a full-day. The tours listed below offer pickup and drop-off at most locations in Margaret River.

The mission of **Wine for Dudes**—making the culture of wine accessible to everyone—attracts an enthusiastic younger crowd. Don't be fooled by the laid-back attitude as knowledgeable owner and guide, Cathy, has years of experience in Europe and Australia. (☎9758 8699; www.winefordudes.com. Tour includes 4-5 wineries, contemporary vineyard lunch, and unique wine blending session. $60.) The widely acclaimed **Bushtucker Great Wineries Tour** packs 40 wine tastings, a gourmet lunch, and stops at chocolate and cheese factories into one day. (☎9757 9084. 5hr. tour daily 11am. $65.) A more economical option is the wine mini-tour run by **Margaret River Vintage Wine Tours,** which visits Voyager, Leeuwin, Redgate, and Xanadu. (☎9757 1008; winetours@swisp.net.au. Tours daily 2:30pm. $35.) **Milesaway Tours** offers a full-day scenic tour that explores some of the non-alcoholic delicacies in the region, like local soaps, beers, and wildlife, along with the wineries and a traditional sausage sizzle. (☎9754 2929 or 1800 818 102; www.miles-away.com.au. Tours Th 9am.)

ACTIVITIES

Although Australian wine can stand on its own, many fine food artisans exist around Margaret River, providing samples of their own to accompany any vintage. No trip would be complete without a visit to **The Berry Farm,** southeast of town off Rosa Glen Rd. They offer samples of jams and fruit wines, and have a reasonably priced cafe with a mouth-watering menu. (☎9757 5054; www.berryfarm.com.au. Open daily 10am-4:30pm.) **The Margaret River Chocolate Company** will entice you with free tastings and viewings of the chocolate-making process; it is a great place to find discount chocolates and fudges. (☎9755 6555; www.chocolatefactory.com.au. Corner of Harman's Mill Rd. and Harman's South Rd. Open daily 9am-5pm.) Find the perfect cheese to complement your wine at **The Margaret River Dairy Company,** which has free tastings daily at their store just north of Cowaramup on Bussell Hwy. (☎9755 7588. Open daily 10am-5pm.) Finish your behind-the-scenes culinary quest at **Olio Bello,** which produces several types of olive oil, including four organic varieties and a delicious lime-infused variation. (☎9755 9771 or 1800 982 170; www.oliobello.com. Off Cowaramup Bay Rd. on Armstrong Rd. Open daily 10am-4:30pm.)

The beaches and surf along the coast are stunning, and **Caves Road** south of Margaret is one of the area's most spectacular drives. It runs through karri forests, beside verdant pastures, and past hundreds of hidden caves, six of which are open to the public. Biking is a good way to get around, and there are many rewarding trails. One of the best hiking and biking trails is the 15km round-trip walk east to **10 Mile Brook Dam** along the Margaret River. (Trailhead less than 1km north of Margaret River on Bussell Hwy. at the Rotary Park.) **Margaret River Cycles,** located at 31 Station Rd. off Wallcliffe Rd., rents and services bikes (☎04 2145 0677. Open M-F 9am-5pm, Sa 9am-1pm. $20 per 24hr.) There are also a number of **walking tracks** and **canoeing** options in the region.

LEEUWIN-NATURALISTE NATIONAL PARK

Spanning much of the coast from Cape Naturaliste to Cape Leeuwin, Leeuwin-Naturaliste National Park encompasses beaches with jagged rock formations rising from the water, imposing forests, caves with fossils of extinct megafauna, and excellent whale-watching spots. The CALM offices in Busselton

WEEKEND WARRIORS BEWARE

Busselton (pop. 20,000), a smal[l] town nearly 220km southwest o[f] Perth, is normally associated wit[h] the lush vineyards and luxuriou[s] cellars of the Margaret River Area[.] Yet every year in early December[,] visitors flock to this grape-infuse[d] tourist haven for an entirely differ-ent reason. Elite athletes from al[l] over the world travel to Busselto[n] to test themselves in the ultimat[e] endurance event: the Ironma[n] Western Australia triathlon.

This grueling race pits competitors against an elite field of athletes, a seemingly endles[s] course, and the indomitable elements of the Outback. Racer[s] swim 3.8km (2.4 mi) i[n] Geographe Bay, bike 3-loo[p] 180km (112 mi) course, and finish with a 42.2km (26.2 mi) ma[r]athon run along the shore[.] Participants take anywhere fro[m] 8-17hr. to complete the course[,] battling exhaustion, dehydration[,] intense heat, and high wind[s] along the way.

Like its counterpart, Ironma[n] Australia in Port Macquarie, th[e] Busselton race is garnerin[g] increased attention. With ove[r] 10,000 competitors already regis-tered for this year's race, Busse[l]ton can expect a temporary boos[t] in population (and to its win[e] sales) come December.

2005 Winners: Mitchell Anderso[n] (8:27:36) and Angela Miln[e] (9:31:32)

(☎9752 5555) and Margaret River (☎9780 5500) service the park, and there are several places to stay. **Conto's Spring** ❶ is a basic campsite where thundering waves crash on enormous boulders rising from the sea. From the site, you can walk north along ocean cliffs or south through the majestic Boranup forest. (At the Lake Cave turn-off from Caves Rd. south of Margaret River. Pit toilets. Sites $6, children $2.) **Boranup Campground** ❶ provides secluded sites ($6, children $2; payable to ranger) at the southern end of the **Boranup Forest scenic drive.** The 45min. drive is an attraction in itself. Those who get out of their cars can stand next to a towering karri tree and listen to the sounds of the forest. Three kilometers from the drive's southern entrance, the **Boranup Lookout** peaks over treetops to see the nearby rocky coast.

SIGHTS. Whales can be seen north of Margaret River at **Cape Naturaliste, Gracetown, Canal Rocks,** and **Injidup Beach** in the spring, and in **Flinder's Bay** near Augusta in late fall and winter. Beware when standing on the rocks near breaking surf—locals warn about "King Waves" that come in unexpectedly from the Indian Ocean and wash sightseers and rock fishermen to a watery grave. There are also many bushwalks along the coast and near Margaret River. Cape Naturaliste's walks wind past the lighthouse to cliff lookouts. The best hiking in the region is the **Cape to Cape Walk** from Cape Leeuwin in the south to Cape Naturaliste in the north. The 130km trail includes everything from soaring forests to towering cliffs and isolated beaches, and takes five to seven days. For a short glimpse at one of the more spectacular segments of the walk, go to **Prevelly Beach** and hike north along the Cape Walk, following it across the Margaret River mouth for 3km. The **Cape Leeuwin Lighthouse** is at the southwesternmost point of the park (and Australia), and has a great view of Indian Ocean. (☎9758 1920. Drive south on Hwy. 10 through Augusta; continue to follow it after it changes to Leeuwin Rd. Tour $10, children $6; free to walk grounds. Open daily 9am-5pm; last entry 4:20pm.)

WESTERN AUSTRALIA

CAVES. A network of caves runs through the Margaret River region, containing fossils of extinct species and evidence of Aboriginal occupation dating back some 32,000 years. Six caves are open to visitors, displaying the amazing underground world at a comfortable temperature year-round. They are all located along Caves Rd. **Jewel Cave,** the largest, most magnificent tourist cave in Australia, is near Augusta. Closer to Margaret River, **Lake Cave, Mammoth Cave,** and **Calgardup Cave** offer unique sights. Lake Cave is the only permanent underground lake and boasts the modern CaveWorks eco-center. Mammoth Cave offers a wheelchair-accessible MP3-player guided tour. For a little more excitement, Calgardup Cave provides a dark underground plunge. (Jewel, Mammoth, and Lake ☎9757 7411. Jewel and Lake tours daily every hr. on the ½hr. 9:30am-4:30pm. Mammoth open daily 9am-5pm. Each cave $16.50, children $8.50; all 3 $42.50/20. Calgardup open daily 9am-4:15pm; $10/5.) Near Yallingup, **Ngilgi Cave** (☎9755 2152), named after an Aboriginal spirit believed to inhabit the cave, offers guided, lighted tours (daily every 30min. 9:30am-3:30pm; $15.50, children $6.50), and guided flashlight "adventure" tours. (By request. Max. 6 people. 3hr. $90; 1½hr. short adventure $30. 16+.)

SURFING. Packs of grommets (young surfers) learn the ropes at Rivermouth and Redgate near Margaret River; more experienced surfers delight in the breaks off Surfer's Point, or head farther north to Gracetown (a good surfing beach protected from southern winds) and Injidup Point. There are tons of other surf spots nearby; stop at Beach Life Surf Shop, 117 Bussell Hwy., near the visitors center, to get information and advice, or to book a surfing lesson. (☎9757 2888. Group lessons $40 per person.) Surf reports are posted at surf shops or at www.srosurf.com/thereport.html. Farther north, **Yallingup Beach** was one of the first breaks surfed in Western Australia in the 1950s. October through April is the best time for surfing, though it gets very crowded, especially in December and January. Just to the south, **Smith's Beach** is another great spot. In Dunsborough, surfboards can be rented from **Yahoo Surfboards,** at the corner of Clark St. and Naturaliste Terr. (☎9756 8336. M-Sa 9am-5pm. ½-day $20, full-day $30, 2 or more days $20 per day.)

DIVING AND SNORKELING. Eagle and Meelup Bays in Dunsborough both have great beaches for snorkeling and surfing; turn-offs are well marked on Cape Naturaliste Rd., north of town. **Cape Dive,** 222 Naturaliste Terr., Dunsborough, runs diving trips to the wreck of the *HMS Swan* off Cape Naturaliste. (☎9756 8778 or 04 1892 3802; www.capedive.com. Open Nov.-Apr. daily 9am-5pm. Double dive to wreck with gear $135; intro dive $150; PADI course $425.) **Hamelin Bay,** near Augusta, may be beautiful to the point of distraction—the area has seen some 11 shipwrecks since 1882. You can scuba dive or go snorkeling at the four visible wrecks, but you have to swim from shore to get there. Check with someone before diving; the wrecks are old and shift around a bit. Swimming here is sheltered, and fishing in the area is superb. Stingrays often feed below the boat ramp. **Augusta X-treme Outdoor Sports,** at the corner of Ellis St. and Blackwood Ave., has info and gear for diving and fishing. (☎9758 0606. Open M-F 9am-5pm, Sa 8:30am-4pm.)

OUTDOOR TOURS. Several companies organize half- or full-day adventure tours of the area, most of which can be booked through tourist bureaus. **Naturaliste Charters** runs **whale-watching** tours that bring sightseers to the humpback whales off Augusta in the winter (June-Aug.) and Dunsborough in the spring (Sept.-Dec.). In addition to humpbacks, southern right whales frequent the area in August, while December brings blue whales. (☎9755 2276; www.whalesaustralia.com. Departs daily at 10am from the boat ramp on Geographe Bay Rd. in Dunsborough or Davies Rd. in Augusta. 3hr. $60, students 13-17 $44, seniors $55, children $33, under 4 free. YHA 10% discount.) **Augusta Eco Cruises** (☎9758 4003) has deep sea fishing expeditions, seal and dolphin observation trips, and river cruises; they leave from Fishermans Jetty off Ellis St. **Bushtucker River Tours** gives guided canoe trips up the Margaret River to historical sights, with native flora, fauna, and bush medicine recipes identified along the way. (☎9757 1084. Departs from the Margaret River mouth off Wallcliffe Rd. in Prevelly Beach. Tour 10am-2pm, lunch included. $70, children $30.) **Dirty Detours** (☎04 1799 8816; www.dirtydetours.com) organizes biking tours ($55) of the Boranup karri forest.

WESTERN AUSTRALIA

PEMBERTON ☎08

Pemberton, the capital of the self-proclaimed "kingdom of the karri," has learned to embrace the trees that once fed its mills. This sleepy hamlet makes a good base for hiking and fishing in the nearby national parks, and is home to a curious number of towering trees to climb. Even a simple drive among the local farms and forests is well worth the views of rolling countryside.

TRANSPORTATION AND PRACTICAL INFORMATION. **Transwa buses** (☎1300 6622 05; www.transwa.wa.gov.au) run once per day (twice on F) to Albany (3¾hr., $28.90) and Bunbury (3hr., $22.20). The **Pemberton Visitors Centre,** on Brockman St., the town's main artery, provides a comprehensive guide to the town and surrounding region. It also contains a small **Pioneer Museum** and informative **Karri Forest Discovery** ($1 suggested donation). The center sells passes to the local national parks and books tours and accommodations. (☎9776 1133; www.pembertontourist.com. Open daily 9am-5pm.) The **CALM office,** on Kennedy St., also sells passes and has info on nearby national parks. (☎9776 1207. Open M-F 8am-5pm.)

The **Telecentre,** 29 Brockman St., offers **Internet** access. (☎9776 1745. $6 per hr. Open M and F 9am-6pm, Tu-Th 9am-6:30pm, Sa 9am-noon.) The **police** (☎9776 1202) are at the corner of Ellis St. and Jamieson St. **Public restrooms** and a **post office** are located on Brockman St. (☎9776 1034. Open daily 8am-5pm.) **Postal Code:** 6260.

ACCOMMODATIONS AND FOOD. **Pemberton Backpackers YHA ❷,** 7 Brockman St., provides basic rooms on Pemberton's main street, within a 10min. walk of the town center. It has Internet access ($5 per hr.), bike rental ($10 per day), laundry, and a kitchen. (☎9776 1105. Dorms $22, YHA $18; singles $36/32; twins $25/22; cottage with queen $55/52. MC/V.) **Pemberton Caravan Park ❷,** 1 Pump Hill Rd., is perfectly situated in a lovely forest within walking distance of all the local services. (☎9776 1300; park@karriweb.com.au. Sites $22, low season $20; budget cabins with kitchen $70/60; ensuite cabins $89/79. MC/V.) Toward the Gloucester Tree, the **Gloucester Motel ❹** on Ellis St. offers luxury and budget options, and has a fantastic restaurant attached. (☎9483 1111. Budget singles $70, singles $80; doubles $77/88; triples $85/95. MC/V.) The historic **Pemberton Hotel ❺,** 66 Brockman St., offers ensuite rooms. (☎9776 1017. Singles $84; doubles $99. MC/V.)

Trout and marron are the most popular local freshwater fare, and at **King Restaurant & Marron Farm ❶,** on the corner of Northcliffe Rd. and Old Vasse Rd. (en route to the Bicentennial Tree), guests can fish for both ($5 rod rental), and then have the kitchen cook their catch ($3.50). (☎9776 1352. Main courses $12-25. Open daily 9:30am-5pm; closed Th in winter. MC/V.) The **Cafe Mazz ❷,** in the Pemberton Hotel, serves hearty dinners ($7-19), including the Timberman's Cheese Platter ($15). Its adjacent bar provides nightlife for the quiet town. (☎9776 1017. Open M-Th 11am-11pm, F 11am-midnight, Sa 10am-11pm, Su 2-9pm. MC/V.) **Jan's Diner ❶,** on Brockman St., has hearty "farmer" and "hiker" breakfasts ($9-10) along with lunch offerings. (☎9776 0011. Open daily 8am-3pm.) **The Coffee Connection ❶,** on Dickinson St., 1km southeast of Brockman St., delights with a shaded patio overlooking a garden. (☎9776 1159. Open daily 9am-5pm.) On the same grounds, the **Fine Woodcraft Gallery** has an astonishing array of furniture, bowls, and sculptures made of local karri, marri, and jarrah wood. (☎9776 1399. Open daily 9am-5pm.)

ACTIVITIES. Three national parks lie within a 10km radius of Pemberton, and the number of opportunities they offer for fishing, swimming, hiking, or gazing at the magnificent karri trees can be overwhelming. The 86km **Karri Forest Explorer** self-guided driving tour is a convenient way to hit all the highlights of the area's natural wonders; maps are available at the visitors center and CALM. Travelers can listen to 100FM to learn about the history of the area and its forests while they complete the drive. All of the following sites are included in the tour, and most offer BBQs, picnic tables, and toilets.

Gloucester Tree boasts an unparalleled view of the surrounding forests from a former fire-lookout platform 61m in the air. The climb up is not for the faint of heart; you must carefully navigate the pegs which wind around the tree, and there is no safety net. (Located 3km southeast of town; take Ellis St. off Brockman until it turns left into Kennedy St., then follow the signs. Park entry fees apply.) Another dizzying climb is up the **Bicentennial Tree.** This 60m lookout tree takes its name from the 200th anniversary of European settlement in Australia, celebrated in 1988, and has a platform halfway up that may be a good goal for new climbers. It is also the origin of several short walking trails (200m, 1km, and 2.4km) that meander through the 3000 hectares of virgin karri forest in **Warren National Park.**
Stately karris tower over the tranquil reservoir at **Big Brook Dam,** which has a 4km paved, wheelchair-accessible walk along its banks. (Take Golf Links Rd. off Vasse Hwy., just north of town.) **Beedelup National Park,** 18km west of town on Vasse Hwy., features a cable bridge walk over the clear, rushing waters of **Beedelup Falls.**

A DIFFERENT POINT OF VIEW. In the 1930s and 40s the pegged karri lookouts were constructed as a means of spotting fires in the expansive forest. Today, adventurous tourists are the only ones gazing from the rickety platforms atop the Gloucester, Bicentennial, and Diamond Trees. It is well worth the dizzying climb, but climbers should take their time, especially when headed down.

The Pemberton region has a growing number of excellent **wineries;** the **Woodsmoke Estate** off Golf Links Rd. north of town has a beautiful boutique cafe and also brews **Jarrah Jacks** beer. (☎9776 1333 or 9776 0225; www.woodsmoke-estate.com.au. 6 beer sampler $10.) **Pemberton Tramway Co.** has tram tours to Warren River Bridge on an old logging rail line, which passes over trestle bridges with magnificent views of the forest. Stops are made at a picnic area on the banks of Lefroy Brook. Steam trains to Eastbrook and Lyall are also available from Easter to November. (☎9776 1322. 1¾hr.; departs daily at 10:45am and 2pm from Pemberton Station; $18, children $9.) **Pemberton Discovery Tours** offers a half-day 4WD trek to D'Entrecasteaux and Warren National Parks. (☎9776 0484; www.pembertondiscoverytours.com.au. 4hr. tour includes tea; $75, children $50.)

Southwest of Pemberton sprawls the mammoth **D'Entrecasteaux National Park.** Most of it is inaccessible without a 4WD, except for the paved Windy Harbour Rd., heading south out of Northcliffe to the aptly named **Windy Harbour.** Fifteen kilometers south of Northcliffe on this road, **Mount Chudalup,** a 188m high granite rock, rears up above the surrounding bush, allowing views of up to 30km on a clear day. Visitors can access these views by attempting the steep 1.5km hike from the carpark. If you're heading on to Denmark and wish to see more of the park, turn off Windy Harbour Rd. onto Chesapeake Rd. 5km south of Northcliffe. The gravel track winds through the heart of the park and is usually 2WD accessible, though be sure to check on road conditions in Northcliffe.

A TEMPERAMENTAL MISTRESS. Little has changed in the years since D'Entrecasteaux charted the coast that now bears his name, and adventurers who head to the southwest shores should be aware that these tides are rough. There is a reason for all those shipwrecks; swimmers and seafarers beware.

GREAT SOUTHERN

The beautiful, diverse region known as the Great Southern earns its title from the sprawling karri and tingle forests on the rugged mountain ranges in the west, to the vast nothingness of the Nullarbor Plain in the east. The South Western Hwy. links most of the region's attractions, and Albany functions as an urban hub for the less populated southern coast. While the Great Southern has been growing popular with Australians, offering gourmet food and many boutique wineries, the region's wonders remain under appreciated by the world at large, allowing visitors to enjoy its natural beauty in relative peace.

WALPOLE-NORNALUP NATIONAL PARK ☎08

Tiny, congenial Walpole lies along the northern shore of the Nornalup Inlet and makes a great base for exploring Mt. Frankland, Shannon, and Walpole-Nornalup. **Walpole-Nornalup National Park** boasts inlets from the ocean, sand dunes, beaches, and the Franklin River, but the highlight is the forest of giant tingle trees.

Walpole Lodge ❷, on the corner of Pier St. and Park Ave., has lovely rooms around a spacious common area. The owners will drive visitors within a 20km radius. (☎9840 1244; walpolebackpackers@bigpond.com. Internet access $4 per hr. Dorms $20, YHA or VIP $17; singles $35; twins and doubles $55; ensuite $65. MC/V.) **Tingle All Over YHA** ❷, 60 Nockolds St., has a BBQ, kitchen, laundry, and a beautiful outdoor chess set with 2 ft. pieces made from red gum and jarrah woods. (☎9840 1041; tinglealloverr2000@yahoo.com.au. Dorms $20, summer $22; singles $40; twins and doubles $52. MC/V $1 charge per person.) The **Rest Point Holiday Village** ❷ is right on the water west of town, next to the country club, at the end of Rest Point Rd. (☎9840 1302; www.restpoint.com.au. Sites for 2 $24, low season $22, extra adult $10, extra child $5.50; ensuite cabins for 2 $110/95, extra adult $28, extra child $11.) Nockolds St. has several cafes and restaurants. The **Top Deck Cafe** ❶, 25 Nockolds St., serves breakfast (2 croissants and jam $4.80) and lunch (BLT $7.80) in a sun-filled room with a stove in winter, and on a sheltered patio in summer. (☎9840 1344. Open daily 8:30am-3pm.) Next door is an **IGA** grocery store. (☎9840 1031. Open M-F 7:30am-5:30pm, Sa 7:30am-5pm, Su 8am-4:30pm.)

The park's claim to fame is undoubtedly the **Tree Top Walk,** 13km east of town. A 600m state-of-the-art metal catwalk lets visitors scale dizzying heights through the canopy of tingle trees. The views are incredible, but those scared of heights be forewarned—the swaying walkways reach heights of 40m. (☎9840 8263. Open daily 9am-5pm; school holidays 8am-6pm; last entry 45min. before close. $6, children $2.50, families $14.) The **Ancient Empire** boardwalk departs from the Tree Top Walk info center and passes through a grove of red tingle trees, some of which are hollowed out, allowing visitors to stand inside or pass through. Another way to visit these giants is on **Hilltop Road,** which passes the Giant Tingle Tree. There are many scenic drives; the **Valley of the Giants Road** through towering forests and the **Knoll Drive,** through dunes with dramatic views of the inlets, are two of the best. The **Nuyts Wilderness Peninsula** portion of the park is accessible by way of the superb **Wow Wilderness Cruises,** which offers a 2½hr. cruise through the double inlets, punctuated by an 800m hike across the peninsula and a traditional tea. Gary, the captain and guide, is an energetic encyclopedia of local lore. (☎9840 1036; www.wowwilderness.com.au. Departs daily at 10am from the Jones St. Jetty in Walpole. Book at tourist bureau in Walpole. $35, ages 6-14 $14, under 5 free.)

Transwa buses (☎1300 6622 05; www.transwa.wa.gov.au) run daily to Albany (1¾hr., $17) and Bunbury (4½hr., $36). The volunteer-staffed **Walpole-Nornalup Visitors Centre,** in an old pioneer's cabin off the highway, is a great source of information about the many nearby natural wonders, and can also book tours. (☎9840 1111. Open M-F 9am-5pm, Sa-Su 9am-4pm.) The **Telecentre** on Latham St. offers **Internet** access. (☎9840 1395. $4 per 30min. Open M-F 9am-5pm, Sa-Su 10am-noon.) Around the corner on Vista St. is the **police** station (☎9840 1618). Nockolds St., a service road adjacent to the South Coast Hwy., which serves as the town's main street, has a **post office.** (☎9840 1048. Open M-F 9am-5pm.) **Postal Code:** 6398.

STIRLING RANGE AND PORONGURUP

These two national parks, separated by just 40km, differ dramatically in their geological history. The Porongurups date back over a billion years, making them one of the oldest mountain ranges on the planet. By comparison, the Stirlings are relative newcomers, emerging no more than 100 million years ago. Giant eucalyptus trees and the occasional karri fill the sides of the Porongurups, while in the higher Stirling Range hardier scrub predominates. In spring, over 1200 species of wildflowers electrify the hills. **Mount Barker** acts as a gateway to both parks.

TRANSPORTATION AND PRACTICAL INFORMATION. From Albany, the Porongurups are 40km north on the **Chester Pass Road.** The Stirling Range is another 40km along the road. **Porongurup Road** is a sealed road running west through its namesake to Mt. Barker, 20km away. **Stirling Range Drive** is a pretty but corrugated road running west through the Stirlings from Chester Pass. **Transwa buses** (☎1300 6622 05; www.transwa.wa.gov.au) run to Mt. Barker from Albany (40min., $7.45) or Perth (6¼hr., $41.60) once per day. The best way to see the parks, however, is by car. **Rental** is easily arranged in Albany (p. 718). There are **ranger stations** in Stirling Range National Park at Moingup Spring (☎9827 9320) and Bluff Knoll (☎9827 9278), and a ranger is assigned to Porongurup National Park (☎9853 1095). The helpful **Mount Barker Tourist Bureau,** in a renovated train station on Albany Hwy., has information about the town and parks, including trail maps. (☎9851 1163. Open M-Sa 9am-3pm, Su 10am-3pm.) The **police** are located in Mt. Barker at the corner of Mt. Barker and Montern St. **Public restrooms** are available at the Tourist Bureau and in Wilson Park, at the corner of Lowood Rd. and Muirs Hwy. (Open M-F 8am-5pm, Sa 8am-noon.)

ACCOMMODATIONS AND FOOD. The **Porongurup Shop and Tearooms ❷,** on Porongurup Rd. nestled among the trees at the main entrance to Porongurup National Park, is an ideal mountain getaway. Along with budget accommodations, they offer good meals ($12-15) incorporating vegetables fresh from the garden, and a delicious sticky date pudding ($6.50). The owners can arrange pickup from Mt. Barker or Albany upon request, making a stay here the best option for those without a vehicle. (☎9853 1110; www.porongurupinn.com. Restaurant open daily 8am-5:30pm. Dorms $25; self-contained flat for 2 $60; ensuite cabin with kitchen, lounge area, and bedroom for 2 $80. Extra person $10. MC/V.) There are several options near the Stirling Range National Park. On the north border, the **Stirling Range Retreat ❶** is on Chester Pass Rd. less than 500m beyond the turn-off for Bluff Knoll and offers scenic camping at the base of the mountains. (☎9827 9229. Sites $10, powered for 2 $24; dorms $20; single and double rooms $50; triples $60; cabins for 2 $59-120.) **Glenelg Quarters ❷,** Sandalwood Rd., offers basic accommodations on an operating farm at the base of Mt. Ellen. (☎9827 9274; glenelg@wn.com.au. Turn off Chester Pass Rd. onto Sandalwood Rd. at the Amelup station 12km north of the Bluff Knoll turn-off. Glenelg is 15km down the road on the right. Call before arrival. Linen $5. Singles, doubles, and dorms $20 per person.) In Mt. Barker, the **Mount Barker Caravan and Cabin Accommodation ❷** offers cozy rooms in town. Owners Steve and Shirley Smith are friendly and helpful. (☎9851 1691; mtbarkercaravanpark@bigpond.com. Sites $10, powered $22, ensuite powered $27; dorms $22; cabins $60, ensuite $70. Extra adult $6. MC/V.)

Ten kilometers north of the Bluff Knoll turn-off sits an unexpected sight: an enormous traditional Dutch windmill which signals that you have arrived at **The Lily ❸.** With an affordable and delicious lunch menu ($9-20) and a three-course meal by candlelight several times per week ($39; book ahead), this is a must-see if you are in the southwest. (☎9827 9205; www.thelily.com.au. Open Tu-Su 10am-5pm, dinner until latenight. MC/V.) In Mt. Barker, **The Sail-Inn Cafe ❶,** 39 Lowood Rd., has gourmet options like chicken camembert ($23), but also offers basic sandwiches ($4) and pizza ($9) in a laid-back atmosphere. (☎9851 1477. Open daily 9am-9pm.) **Wing Hing Chinese Restaurant ❷,** 26 Albany Hwy., has takeaway lunch specials for $8 and dinners for $11-18. (☎9851 1168. Open Tu-Sa 5-9:30pm, W-F also noon-2pm, Su 5-9pm.) **Supa IGA,** the local grocery store, is on Lowood Rd. (☎9851 3333. Open M-W and F 8:30am-5:30pm, Th 8:30am-6:30pm, Sa 8am-4pm.)

HIKING. Visitors to both the Porongurups and the Stirlings must display **national park passes** (day pass $9, 4wk. "holiday" pass $22.50), which can be purchased at park entry points, CALM offices, or www.naturebase.net. All of the trails listed here, save Hassell and Talyuberlup, are accessible by smooth gravel roads shorter than 10km. The others require longer drives along the corrugated Stirling Range Dr.

The ancient Porongurups can be traversed on one of three thrilling hikes. The challenging **Castle Rock trail** (3km, 1½hr. round-trip) is a jaunt to the top of a massive granite boulder perched on the mountaintop. The last 30m include a scramble through a crevasse, a short ladder, and a catwalk which affords tremendous views. Just before this last section is the mind-boggling **Balancing Rock,** an enormous boulder that looks like it will tumble at any second. The Castle Rock trail has been updated with a new carpark and ample picnic areas. There are also plans to build a boardwalk in the future. The **Tree in the Rock circuit** (approx. elevation 625m; 6km, 3hr.) originates at a picnic area at the end of Bolganup Rd., clearly marked off Porongurup Rd. After passing the namesake karri tree sprouting from a crack in a boulder, the track continues to Hayward Peak for panoramic views of the countryside. A side trail (2hr. round-trip from picnic area) off the Tree in the Rock circuit winds up the slippery rock of the Devil's Slide to a summit of stark rock faces and towering granite.

The Stirlings are more rugged than the Porongurups and feature a variety of walks. The most popular is **Bluff Knoll** (1094m), which is best described by its Aboriginal name *Bullah Meual*, which means "Great Many-Faced Hill." The trail that climbs its sides (6.2km, 3-4hr. round-trip) is well maintained and has stairs, but is a steep climb and windy at points on the southwestern face. The views of the surrounding formations are exhilarating, and the contrast with the flat, vast surrounding farmlands is impressive. Bluff Knoll is accessible by sealed road. The most challenging option in the Stirlings is the **Stirling Ridge Walk,** linking Bluff Knoll to **Mount Ellen.** This 20km hike promises three days of narrow ledges, jagged rocks, and steep climbs. Those planning on tackling this trek should register with the CALM ranger beforehand (☎9827 9278). The hike up **Toolbrunup Peak** (1052m), the second highest in the park, is a challenging 3hr. round-trip climb over rocks of varying sizes. Toolbrunup is less crowded than Bluff Knoll, even though it offers unobstructed 360° views from the top. **Mount Trio** (856m) is a shorter hike (3km, 2hr. round-trip).

ALBANY ☎08

Albany (pop. 32,000) was the first colonial settlement in Western Australia, founded in 1826 to protect the western half of the continent, then called New Holland, from the possibility of French annexation. The evolution of environmental sensibility in Australia can also be traced back here. While much of the city's early income came from whaling, visitors today will find an abundance of eco-tours, national parks, and nature reserves. Many Perthites flock to Albany as a summer retreat, and the city has responded with trendy new restaurants, outdoor activities, and a wide range of accommodations that make it the perfect getaway.

TRANSPORTATION

Transwa buses (☎1300 662 205; www.transwa.wa.gov.au) depart from the visitors center to: Bunbury (6hr.; M and Th 8:35am, Tu-W and F-Su 8am; $45.60) via Augusta, Margaret River, Pemberton, and Walpole; Esperance (6½hr., M and Th 11:45am, $53.50); and Perth (6hr.; M-Sa 9am and Su 3pm, extra buses F 5:30pm and Sa 11am; $47.80). The two hostels in town have a steady stream of travelers sharing rides; hitchhikers usually wait by the "Big Roundabout" on the Albany Hwy., 2km west of the north end of York St. Despite the convenient option, *Let's Go does not recommend hitchhiking.* **Love's Bus Service** provides city transport for $2-3 per trip; schedules are available at the tourist bureau. (☎9841 1211. Open M-Sa.) **Amity Taxis** (☎9844 4444) service the Albany area. **Car rental** is easily arranged in Albany: try **King Sound Vehicle Hire,** 6 Sanford Rd. (☎9841 8466; www.kingsoundcars.com); **Budget,** 360 Albany Hwy. (☎9841 7799; the office is behind the Toyota dealership); **Avis,** 557 Albany Hwy. (☎9842 2833); or **Albany Car Rentals,** 386 Albany Hwy. (☎9841 7077). Prices range $45-55 per day.

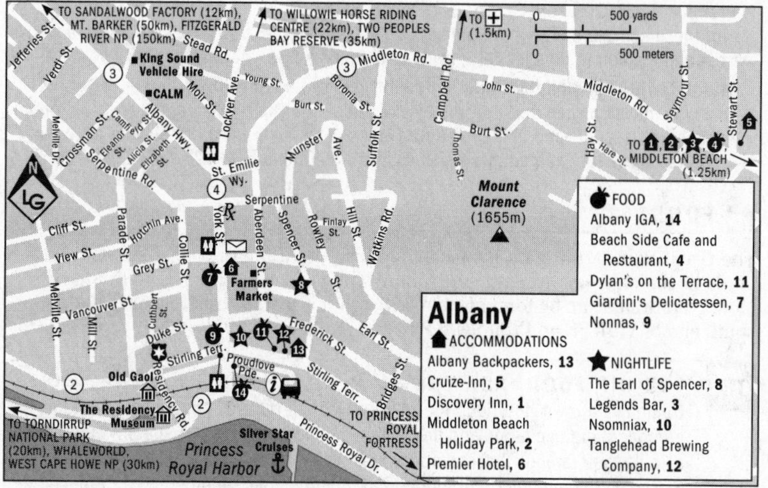

ORIENTATION AND PRACTICAL INFORMATION

York Street is the main strip and runs north-south through the center of town. The **visitors center** is in the Old Railway Station, just east of the southern end of York St. near Stirling Terr. (☎1800 644 088. Open daily 9am-5pm.) York St. also has several **ATMs.** The **police** (☎9841 0555) are located on Stirling Terr. west of York St., while the **Albany Regional Hospital** (☎9892 2222) is northeast of town in Spencer Park on Warden Ave. off Collingwood Rd. There are plenty of **Internet** cafes along York St.; the going rate is $6 per hr. Albany Backpackers offers Internet access to the public for $6 per hr. and to guests for $4 per hr. The **post office** is on the corner of York St. and Grey St. (Open M-F 8:30am-5pm.) **Postal Code:** 6330.

WESTERN AUSTRALIA

ACCOMMODATIONS

Albany has excellent budget accommodations. They are split between two centers: the old town of Albany, with historic buildings and ample amenities, and the laid-back Middleton Beach, a waterside escape away from major attractions.

Cruize-Inn, 122 Middleton Rd., Middleton Beach (☎9842 9599; www.cruizeinn.com). A step up from your average hostel with beautiful, homestyle accommodations. Kitchen, TV lounge, and a superb stereo system. Perfect for a group getaway. Singles $42; twins $62; doubles $69; ensuite $75; entire house from $210. MC/V. ❹

Discovery Inn, 9 Middleton Rd., Middleton Beach (☎9842 5535; www.discovery-inn.com.au), 100m from the water. Comfortable, well-furnished rooms situated around an atrium. Internet access $5 per hr. Continental breakfast included. Dorms $25, in winter $20; singles $40/30; doubles $60/50. MC/V. ❷

Albany Backpackers (☎9841 8848; www.albanybackpackers.com.au), corner of Stirling Terr. and Spencer St. Lively hostel with common spaces and free coffee and cake each evening at 6:30pm. Cheap home-cooked meals ($5) every night at 7pm. Internet access $4 per hr., first 10min. free. Bike rental ½-day $10, full-day $15. Continental breakfast included. Dorms $23-25, with discount $21-23; singles $40/36; twins $56/52; doubles $78/72. ISIC/NOMADS/VIP/YHA. MC/V $1 surcharge. ❷

Premier Hotel, 208 York St. (☎9841 1544; premier@omninet.net.au). The best option for those seeking a little more privacy right in the heart of town. Located above a lively bar and restaurant. Singles $25; twins and doubles $35; motel units $60. MC/V. ❷

Middleton Beach Holiday Park, Middleton Beach (☎9841 3593 or 1800 644 674; www.holidayalbany.com.au), at the end of Middleton Rd. Hydrospa, theater, rec room, beachfront access, and golf course next door. Sites for 3 $44, low season for 2 $27, powered $45/28. Extra adult $10/9, child $8/7. Cabins $83-125. MC/V. ❷

FOOD

The Great Southern region is blessed with some of the best pastures and farmlands in the entire continent, and Albany showcases the bounty of the harvest. Most restaurants can be found near York St.; for a market try the **Albany IGA** at the south end of York St. on Proudlove Pde. (Open daily 7am-9pm.)

FOR HIP FOOD, ASK THE HIPPIES. A short hop west of Albany lies Denmark, a town notorious for its sizeable "alternative" population and large number of organic farms and fine wineries. If you cannot make the 35km trip to sample their famous Riesling and Shiraz, go by the **Albany Farmers Market** on Saturday 8am-noon for fruit, meat, and other gourmet produce.

Dylan's on the Terrace, 82-84 Stirling Terr. (☎9841 8720; www.dylans.com.au). Top-notch food and atmosphere. Serves salads, sandwiches, burgers ($9-11), and breakfast ($5-15). Discount takeaway menu. Open daily 7am-latenight. AmEx/MC/V. ❷

Nonna's, 135 York St. (☎9841 4626). Lively Italian restaurant with a certain Aussie flare. Famous for its "15 for 15" deal: main course and drink for $15. Be sure to go by for Fish Fridays, a local favorite. Open M-F 11am-latenight, Sa 5pm-latenight. MC/V. ❷

Giardini's Delicatessen, 189 York St. (☎9841 2532). This gourmet grocer has aisles of high-quality cheeses, meats, and rolls. Makes a mouth-watering deli sandwich ($4) using all local ingredients. Open daily 7am-8pm. MC/V. ❶

Beach Side Cafe and Restaurant, 2 Flinders Pde., Middleton Beach (☎9841 7733). Perfect place to satisfy your appetite during a day at the beach. The restaurant is a bit pricey; the alfresco cafe has cheaper daytime options. Cafe open daily 8:30am-4pm. Restaurant open 5:30pm-latenight. MC/V. ❶

SIGHTS

Thanks to its early founding and strategic location, Albany boasts many historic sites; the visitors center provides a free map with a walking tour. At the end of Apex Dr., there is a lookout with stunning views of Princess Royal and Oyster Harbours. Located near the lookout, an inspirational monument to the ANZAC (Australia New Zealand Army Corps) troops who died in WWI shouldn't be missed. Because Albany was the staging point for convoys heading to Gallipoli, **Mount Clarence** was, for many soldiers, the last glimpse of home soil. On Mt. Adelaide to the east is the **Princess Royal Fortress.** It was built in 1893 as a coastal defense, and later used by the American Navy as a base in WWII. The site today includes the Military Heritage Centre and Australian War Memorial Gallery, both of which complement the monument at Mt. Clarence. (☎9841 9333. Open daily 9am-5pm. $4, seniors $3, children $2, families $9.)

Albany's most impressive natural formations are in **Torndirrup National Park,** 20km south of town on Frenchman Bay Rd. The **Natural Bridge** is a rock formation that spans 24m above crashing waves. The gigantic waves of the **Gap** pound into a 30m inlet. The rock formations here align with some in Antarctica, showing the shared past of the two continents. During rough weather at the **blowholes,** spray from the ocean shoots up 10m through the rocks. Do not go beyond the blowholes; people have died trying to get a photo. **King George Sound** boasts a recent shipwreck. The intentionally submerged *HMAS Perth,* a decommissioned navy vessel, now serves as an artificial diving reef. The **Middleton Bay Scenic Path** runs from **Middleton Beach** to Emu Point. **West Cape Howe National Park** (about 30km west of Albany) has a treacherous 4WD track through secluded bush and beach. Those in a 2WD can head to **Shelley** and **Cosy Corner** beaches or go 35km east of town to **Two Peoples Bay Reserve,** where the Noisy Scrub-bird and Gilbert's Potoroo, once thought to be extinct, have been rediscovered.

NIGHTLIFE

This popular destination for Perth vacationers has an entertaining latenight scene.

The Earl of Spencer (☎9841 1322; www.earlofspencer.com.au), on the corner of Earl and Spencer St. Historic pub with cozy English feel and great foreign beer selections. The hearty "Earl's Famous Pie and Pint" ($18) shares the menu with lighter fare including soups and salads. Open M-Sa noon-midnight, Su 2-9pm. AmEx/MC/V.

Tanglehead Brewing Company, 72 Stirling Terr. (☎9841 1733; www.tanglehead.com.au). Demure storefront contrasts with trendy modern microbrewery inside. Serves ales and cheap deli boards ($3). Open M-Sa 11am-midnight, Su 11am-10pm.

Legends Bar, Esplanade Hotel on Adelaide Cres., Middleton Beach (☎9842 1711). Upscale bar is perfect spot to relax in style. Open daily 11am-latenight.

Nsomniax Lounge (☎9841 7688), corner of York St. and Stirling Terr. For those hoping to shake it. Open late on weekends and keeps the party going when the pubs have closed. Cover $8 when busy (roughly after 11:30pm). Open F-Sa 11pm-3:30am.

ACTIVITIES

The **Sandalwood Factory** offers the weary traveler a gong relaxation session three times a day; lose yourself in the scent of sandalwood oil and the rhythmic melody of the gong. (On Down Rd., off Albany Hwy. just past the airport. ☎9841 7788; www.mtromance.com.au. Gong session $15.) Albany has the distinction of being home to the world's largest whaling museum, **Whaleworld,** on Frenchman Bay Rd. past the Gap and Blowholes. It may be the only place in

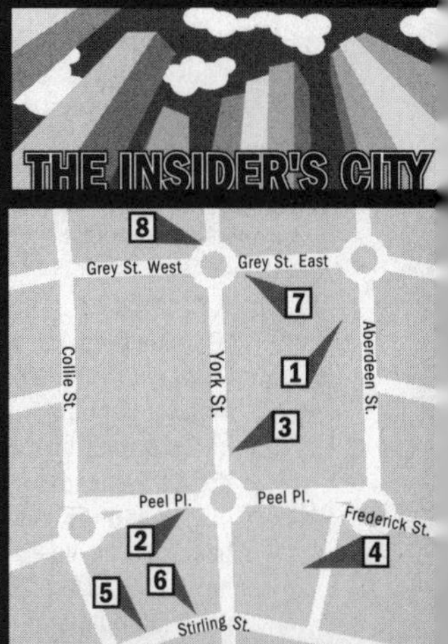

AL-YOU-WANT-BANY

In Albany, you need only know one road: York St. Find all the local flavors that give Albany its charm.

1. Head to the **Albany Farmers Market** (☎9841 4312) to stock up on fine regional foods. (Open Sa 8am-noon.)
2. Warm up with tea ($2.60) at **Cosis Cafe** (☎9841 7899).
3. Find a new read at **Gemini Book Sales and Exchange** (☎9841 7711).
4. Buy that feng shui frog you've had your eye on in the **Fredrickstown Markets** warehouse. (Open daily 9am-4pm.)
5. Sip cappuccino ($3.30) over a classic from **Stirling Terrace BookCafe** (☎9841 4611).
6. Purchase African arts and crafts at **Peddler of Dreams** (☎2779 3694).
7. People-watch over cake ($6) at the **CBD** (☎9842 9551).
8. Applaud a performance at the Albany Town Hall Theatre (Box Office ☎9841 1661).

the world where you can watch a 3D video in a blubber vat. Also features a whaling ship you can enter, three oil vat theaters, and an interesting tour of the facilities. The descriptions and photos of dead whales being processed are not for those with weak stomachs. (☎9844 4021; www.whaleworld.org. Open daily 9am-5pm. 30min.-tours every hr. 10am-4pm. $18, concessions $16.20, families $45.) Live whales are frequently seen near the shore, but for a closer look try **Silver Star Cruises.** (☎04 2893 6711. Departs Town Jetty June-Oct. 9:30am and 1pm. $65, concessions $45, ages 5-17 $25.)

EPIC HIKE. The popular **Bibbulmun Track** runs 964km from Kalamunda, (Outside Perth) to Albany, passing through North Bannister, Dwellingup, Collie, Ballingup, Bridgetown, Manjimup, Pemberton, Northcliffe, Walpole, and Denmark. It is named after the Bibbulmun people, an Aboriginal group that inhabited the area before European settlement and had a tradition of walking long distances to ceremonial events. The trail passes campsites, shelters with bunks, and towns with hostels and B&Bs that pick up hikers from the trails. The track can be easily divided into sections or used for short day hikes. Contact any local CALM office (www.calm.wa.gov.au) or The Friends of Bibbulmun Track (www.bibbulmuntrack.org.au) for details.

To learn more about Albany's history and geological past, check out the **WA Residency Museum** off Stirling Terr., west of York St., next to the replica of the Brig Amity. (☎9841 4844; albany@museum.wa.gov.au. Open daily 10am-5pm. $5 suggested donation.) **Albany Air Charter** offers scenic flights over Albany and the coastline. (☎04 2720 6210. Departs Albany airport. 30min. flight for 5 people $240.) Deep-sea fishing is offered by **Spinners Charters.** (☎9841 7151. Departs Emu Point at 7am. Full-day including lunch $132.) Horseback riding along a 4km scenic trail is available at **Willowie Horse Riding Centre,** 20km east of Albany. (☎9846 4365. By appointment. Scenic ride $30, 4 or more people $27.50.) At **Albany Motorcycle Touring Co.** (☎9841 8034), Rob takes visitors on a variety of "joy rides": $10 gets you around town while $65 covers a ride to the Gap and Natural Bridge. Deep-water diving to *HMAS Perth* and the whaling ship *Cheynes III* is available through **Albany Dive Company,** at the corner of York St. and Stirling Terr. Highlights of the local sea life include Australian sea lions, western blue devils, and sponges in an array of colors. (☎9842 6886; www.albanydive.com. Departs every 2hr. 6:30am-2:30pm and at 6:30pm. Dive with full gear rental $120. Snorkeling with full gear rental $75.)

FITZGERALD RIVER NATIONAL PARK

Halfway between Albany and Esperance lies the enormous **Fitzgerald River National Park.** UNESCO has designated the park as one of only a handful of World Biosphere Reserves. Rare creatures like the chuditch (a carnivorous marsupial) and the dibbler (once thought to be extinct) live in the park, while **whales** can be seen from the tower at Point Ann, near the reserve's western edge. The park is home to over 2000 species of plants including wildflowers from September to November.

Two main roads cut through each end of the park. **Pabelup Drive,** which runs through the west side, offers access to Point Ann via Point Ann Rd. It can be reached by turning east onto Devils Creek Rd. 140km east of Albany. **Hamersley Drive,** in the park's eastern half, is more scenic, with views of the Whoogarup Range and stunning beaches; the interior road away from the coast is not as pretty unless the wildflowers are in bloom. To reach Hamersley Dr., turn directly from Hopetoun Rd., 48km south of Ravensthorpe, or turn southeast on West River Rd., 64km east of Jerramungup. Both Pabelup and Hamersley Dr. are unsealed but can be managed by 2WD. Watch out for kangaroos and emus crossing the road, and leave plenty of time because they can be slow going. Caravans are not permitted in the park. All visitors must display a **national park pass,** available from CALM offices in Albany (☎9842 4500) or Esperance (☎9071 3733). Day passes ($9) are also available at the park entrance.

The area features good diving and hiking for all skill levels. The **East Mount Barren Walk** (3hr.), starting about 15km down Hamersley Dr. from the Hopetoun Rd. turn-off, is of medium difficulty and offers great views of the beach. The **Horrie and Dorri Walk** (4km, 2hr.) winds through mallee-heath to the top of the **Horrie Mesa** (120m), from which hikers can survey the rest of the park. Contact a ranger for maps of the three- to five-day walk along the coast from Bremer Bay to Hopetoun.

The well-maintained **Four Mile Beach** (just west of Hopetoun) and **Saint Mary Inlet** (at Point Ann) are the easiest **campsites ❶** to access by car. Showers and pit toilets are available, but bring your own water. (Sites for 2 $12.50. Extra person $5.50, extra child $4.) Fires are not allowed in the park, but free gas BBQs are available at Mylies, Point Ann, and Fitzgerald Inlet areas, many campsites, and **Quoin Head campground.** An alternative is the **Quaalup Homestead ❶,** off Devils Creek Rd. as you enter the park from the west, which offers rooms in a solar-powered retreat. (☎9837 4124; www.whalesandwildflowers.com.au. Campsite $7, powered $8; on-site van for 2 $30; shared rooms $21; units for 2 $70; 3-bedroom chalet $75.)

There is no reliable clean water in the park, so be sure to bring enough for the duration of your stay. **Mount Madden, Mount Short,** and **Mount Desmond** are not in the park itself but are all near Ravensthorpe and offer excellent views of the area. There are **ranger stations** in the park at East Mt. Barren (☎9838 3060), Murray Rd. (☎9837 1022) toward Bremer Bay, and the Quiss Rd. turn-off (☎9835 5043).

ESPERANCE ☎08

Esperance (pop. 14,500) is one of Western Australia's best-kept secrets, nestled among magnificent surroundings with some of the premier beaches and diving in the country. The town's coastline is unsurpassed, and nearby Cape Le Grand National Park is one of the southwest's jewels. Summer tourists flock to the area to swim, dive, and explore nearby parks.

TRANSPORTATION. **Transwa buses** (☎1300 662 205; www.transwa.wa.gov.au) stop on Dempster St. at the **Love of the Earth Photo Gallery** between the visitors center (where tickets are sold) and the Municipal Museum. Buses offer a YHA/VIP 10% discount and run to: Albany (7hr.; Tu, W, F, Sa 8am; $54); Kalgoorlie (5hr.; W and F 8:30am, Su 2pm; $46); and Perth (10hr., M-Sa 8am, $72). **Skywest** (☎1300 660 088; www.skywest.com.au) flies between Esperance and Perth daily. Two major **car rental** companies operate in Esperance and both offer airport pickup: **Budget,** at the airport (☎9071 2775; esperance@budgetwa.com.au), and **Avis,** 63 the Esplanade (☎9071 3998; avisesperance@wn.com.au).

ORIENTATION AND PRACTICAL INFORMATION. The **South Coast Highway** (Monjingup Rd.) intersects **Harbour Road,** which circles the primary commercial area. **Dempster Street,** the main road through downtown, runs parallel to the **Esplanade,** which follows the bay. The **visitors center** is downtown, on the corner of Dempster and Kemp St. (☎9071 2330; www.visitesperance.com. Open Sept.-Apr. M-F 9am-5pm, Sa 9am-4pm, Su 9am-2pm; May-Aug. M-F 9am-5pm, Sa 9am-2pm, Su 9am-noon.) **Internet** access is available at **Computer Alley,** 69c Dempster St. (☎9072 1293. $5.50 per hr. Open M-F 9am-5pm, Sa 9am-4pm.) The **police** (☎9071 1900) are located at 100 Dempster St., while the **hospital** (☎9071 9222) is two blocks west of the visitors center on Hicks St. The **post office** is on the corner of Andrew St. and Dempster St. (Open M-F 9am-5pm.) **Postal Code**: 6450.

WESTERN AUSTRALIA

ACCOMMODATIONS. Esperance Backpackers ❷, 14 Emily St., a 5min. walk from the town center, is convenient and busy. The family-run hostel runs reasonably priced half-day 4WD fishing tours to Cape Le Grande for $50. (☎9071 4724; esperancebackpackers@westnet.com.au. Internet access $5 per hr. Free pickup from the bus stop. Dorms $22, NOMADS/VIP/YHA $20; singles $40; twins and doubles $50. Discounts for extended stays. MC/V.) The **Blue Waters Lodge YHA ❷,** 299 Goldfields Rd., near the intersection of Dempster and Norseman St., sits right on the bay. A former Australian Army Corps building in Kalgoorlie, it was transported to Esperance, reassembled, and spruced up. The hostel is a 15min. walk from the town center along the harbor bike path. Perks include Internet access ($5 per hr.), a pool table, ping pong, and bike rental for $10 per day. (☎9071 1040; yhaesperance@hotmail.com. Free bus station pickup and drop-off. Dorms $21, YHA $20; singles $31/30; twins and doubles $50.) The **Esperance Seafront Caravan Park ❷** is next to the YHA at the base of Goldfields Rd. (☎9071 1251; www.esperancesseafront.com. Sites for 2 $22, powered $25, extra person $5; standard cabin for 2 $60, extra person $10; ensuite 2-bedroom cabin for 2 $90, extra person $10. MC/V.)

FOOD. Great dining is easily found in this cozy ocean town, but be aware that many restaurants have reduced hours in the winter. Patrons enjoy good meals and spectacular views of Esperance Bay at **Taylor Street Tearooms ❷,** at the Taylor St. jetty, just off the Esplanade. Here visitors enjoy dishes such as "nachos by the fire" ($12.50), in beautiful, traditional surroundings. (☎9071 4317. Breakfast $4-10, lunch $8-16, dinner $10-30. Open daily 7am-10pm.) **Ocean Blues Cafe ❶,** 19 the Esplanade, affords unparalleled beach access and is a good place to grab a bite after fun in the sun. Tasty fish 'n' chips ($10) is another great catch. (☎9071 7107. Meals $6-15. Open Tu-F 9:30am-8:30pm, Sa-Su 8am-8:30pm; hours vary in winter. MC/V.) **Ollie's ❷** offers cafe fare for breakfast ($3-17), lunch ($3-11), and dinner ($8-19) at the corner of the Esplanade and Andrew St. (☎9071 5268. Open Tu-F 10am-9pm, Sa-Su 8am-8:30pm. MC/V.) Several **pubs** can be found on Andrew St. and Dempster St.; the **Pier** on the corner of Andrew St. and the Esplanade is a local favorite. **IGA** supermarket is on Dempster St. between William and Andrew St. (Open M-W and F 8am-6pm, Th 8am-8pm, Sa 8am-5pm.)

WESTERN AUSTRALIA

SIGHTS AND OUTDOOR ACTIVITIES. The 38km loop on the **Great Ocean Drive** snakes along the coast before circling inward and past the **Pink Lake.** The coastal part of the loop is narrow, with steep drop-offs into the bays and spectacular views, while the inland portion is flat and boring until Pink Lake. The visitors center has maps and the road is clearly marked. The drive begins at the southern end of Dempster St. and turns right onto Twilight Beach Rd., passing **Twilight Beach,** the most popular beach in Western Australia in 2006, and **Free Beach,** which offers nude bathing, at the nine mile beach turn-off. The **Rotary Lookout,** off Orr St. at the beginning of the scenic drive on Wireless Hill, is a great place to watch the sunset. A 30min. round-trip walk down from the lookout leads to a gazebo with a picnic table overlooking the bay.

Esperance justly styles itself as the "Bay of Isles," and with more than 500 islands just off its coast, diving opportunities are available for all ability levels. The *Sanko Harvest*, the second-largest **wreck dive** in the world, is popular among experienced divers. **Esperance Diving and Fishing,** 72 the Esplanade, guides dives and charters fishing trips. (☎9071 5111; www.esperancedivingandfishing.com.au. Single dive with equipment $100; double dive including lunch and tea $195. Full-day fishing charter with lunch and tea $195.) **Mackenzie's Island Cruises,** 71 the Esplanade, runs daily 3½hr. cruises to **Woody Island** in the Recherche Archipelago. (☎9071 5757. Departs 9am, weather permitting, from Taylor St. Jetty. $65, ages 5-16 $24.) Woody Island offers posh **camping** administered by Mackenzie's Island Cruises. (☎9071

5757. Sites $12; single tents with foam mattresses $25; doubles $45; elevated safari huts with queen bed and private deck $85, with linen $97.)

The islands near Esperance are known for having some of the most difficult surfing in the world, including Cyclops, the "most hyped, least surfed wave in the world." Many 4WD opportunities on the beach and among the sand dunes north of town are incredible, but beware of quicksand. Esperance Backpackers runs a popular tour of Cape Le Grand (p. 725), as does **Esperance Eco-Discovery Tours,** whose 4WD trips travel to Cape Le Grand and Cape Arid; packages include meals and park fees. It's also possible to tag along with your own 4WD. (☎04 0773 7261; www.esperancetours.com.au. ½-day $71.50, under 16 $55; full-day $137.50/110.)

PRETTY IN PINK. Why are many lakes in Western Australia pink? The *Dunaliella salina* algae and a bacteria called *Halobacterium cutirubrum* thrive along the salt crusts at the bottom of lakes. They are capable of living in water with salinity (saltiness) as high as 35% sodium chloride–over ten times the salinity of seawater. When high levels of salt are combined with warm temperatures and sunlight, the beta carotene produced by the bacteria for protection gives the water a pink hue. The algae is even farmed in some places to make food coloring and dietary supplements.

CAPE LE GRAND NATIONAL PARK

Nature has outdone herself at **Cape Le Grand National Park.** Hiking trails of all lengths and difficulties give visitors access to cavernous granite formations, breathtaking views of the coast, and a varied collection of stunning and unusual plants. The highlight of the park is its pristine, secluded beaches, where pure blue water laps onto the white sands in sheltered bays. Despite their beauty, the beaches are often deserted—locals complain that a beach is "crowded" if there are more than ten people enjoying it. To reach Cape Le Grand, take Goldfields Rd. north to Fisheries Rd., turn right on Merivale Rd., and right again on Cape Le Grand Rd.; signs point the way. Without a car, the best way to get to the park is with a tour from Esperance Backpackers or Esperance Eco-Discovery Tours (p. 725). Most roads in the park are sealed; the handful of unsealed roads can be easily managed by careful 2WD drivers.

A 15km coastal trail connects the park's five beaches: Le Grand Beach, Hellfire Bay, Thistle Cove, Lucky Bay, and Rossiter Bay, from west to east. The best are the middle three, which are characterized by smaller retreats with impressive rock formations enshrouding the beautiful blue waters. Despite the name, **Hellfire Bay** is particularly pleasant and offers fishing off the rocks on its east side. The stretch from **Le Grand Beach to Hellfire** (3hr.) is classified as a "hard walk" due to its steep, rocky areas. The path runs through sandy coastal plains and along the slopes of the lichen-encrusted **Mount Le Grand.** The challenging **Hellfire to Thistle** track (2½hr.) weaves through low scrub and snowy banksia flowers. The track from **Thistle to Lucky** (1hr.) is the easiest of the four legs, with heart-stopping views of caves, waves, and granite formations. The moderate hike from **Lucky to Rossiter** (2hr.) features more granite outcrops and windswept dunes. Those attempting the entire walk should register with the ranger at the entrance to the park (☎9075 9072), or with the CALM office, 92 Dempster St., in Esperance (☎9071 3733; open M-F 8:30am-4:30pm), which offers a brochure about the trail. Another steep track (2hr. round-trip) ascends **Frenchman Peak** to magnificent views of coast and sea. In summer, there is good snorkeling, but beware of rips. **Hellfire Gallery,** on Tyrrell Rd., off Merivale Rd., 30km east of Esperance, displays local art inside and in its beautifully landscaped garden. There is a lovely **cafe** ❶ attached that serves fabulous coffee, tea, scones, and cakes ($3-6). A variety of musicians perform on the grounds during spring and summer. (☎9075 9042; www.wn.com.au/hellfiregallery. Open M and Th-Su 10am-5pm. MC/V.)

At the eastern end of the park, **Wharton** caters to those willing to make the 83km trek from Esperance to the virtually unpopulated beaches of **Duke of Orleans Bay,** a popular fishing spot. With on-site petrol, a convenience store, tennis courts, a playground, and a kitchen, **Orleans Bay Caravan Park ❶** has everything but linen. (☎9075 0033; orleansbay@wn.com.au. Take Fisheries Rd. east and turn south on Orleans Bay Rd. at Condingup. Sites for 2 $19, powered $20; park homes for 2 $40; ensuite chalets for 2 $70. Extra person $6.) There is **camping ❶** with full facilities at Cape Le Grand National Park's Le Grand Beach and Lucky Bay, 56km east of town ($9 park pass; sites for 2 $12.50. Extra adult $5.50, extra child $2), and on **Woody Island** from Sept. 23-Apr. 30. **Duke Charters & Scenic Tours,** based in the caravan park, offers whale and dolphin sight-seeing cruises and fishing charters for tuna, snapper, and harlequin. (☎9076 6223. Rates vary with group size.)

On Fisheries Rd., 120km east of Esperance, lies the remote **Cape Arid National Park,** where more surf-pounded granite headlands and white sand beaches can be enjoyed along one of the most isolated coastlines on the Southern Ocean. Entrance fees apply, but camping is free; there are BBQ facilities and pit toilets, but you should bring your own water as none is available in the park.

GOLDFIELDS

Hundreds of kilometers east of Perth, a handful of towns produce a surprising amount of wealth in Western Australia's harsh interior. In 1893, a group of Irish prospectors stumbled onto an area known as the Golden Mile, the most gold-rich square mile in the world, and the city of Kalgoorlie was born. The continuing promise of mineral exploration keeps the area bustling with miners hoping to strike it big, while Kal's colorful nightlife and wild west atmosphere lure visitors from the coast. Kal offers a drastic change from the rest of the beach-mad southwest, but it's a long trip there and a long trip back with nothing in between but 'roos and road trains. Unless you're particularly interested in gold mining, when heading west to Perth from Eyre you should consider taking the South Coast Hwy., which provides a much more relaxed and varied trip.

GREAT EASTERN HIGHWAY

At 600km, the drive from Perth to Kalgoorlie will build your endurance for a Nullarbor crossing, or at least your appreciation for the proximity of towns on the southwest coast. The traffic in Perth's eastern suburbs can be frustrating and slow, but the tension melts away as you drive through the verdant fields and wildflower-filled forests of the Darling Range. By the time you reach the towns of **Merredin** and **Southern Cross,** the only traffic is swaggering road trains bearing farm equipment or livestock. Roadhouses are spaced no more than 150km apart.

MERREDIN. Merredin (pop. 3700), proud home to the world's longest road train (over 600m), is the largest town on the Great Eastern Hwy. between Coolgardie and Perth. The **visitors center, bank, supermarket,** and **post office** are all within one block of each other on Barrack St., which is just one block north of the highway. There are several hotels in town, including **Commercial Hotel ❸,** on Barrack St. (☎9041 1052; www.commercialhotel.net.au. Singles $27.50, with heat and A/C $35; doubles $50. MC/V.) The **Merredin Caravan Park ❷,** 2 Oats St., has sites and backpacker rooms. (☎9041 1535. Sites for 2 $17, powered $22; singles $25; doubles $35; cabins $75.) The comfortable **Hay Loft Coffee Lounge ❶,** tucked away off Bates St.

one block north of the visitors center, is one of several nice eateries in town, with cakes ($4.50) and meals ($5-8).

COOLGARDIE. Coolgardie is a dusty frontier town and residential satellite for families of Kalgoorlie miners. The main street, Hwy. 94 (Bayley St. in town), houses a **visitors center.** (☎9026 6090. Open M-F 9am-4pm, Sa-Su 10am-4pm.) The Caltex Roadhouse on the way into town has an **ATM,** and the **post office** does banking. The **Denver City Hotel ❸,** across from the visitors center, has a nice pub downstairs. (☎9026 6031. Singles $25; doubles $40; family rooms $45.)

KALGOORLIE-BOULDER ☎08

There is a certain electricity in the air in Kalgoorlie-Boulder (kal-GOO-lee; pop. 32,000), a direct result of the money made from its valuable mineral resources. Kalgoorlie was historically the economic center, while Boulder was home to the miners, closer to the pits on the "golden mile"; today the two blend together in round-the-clock activity. The Victorian hotels lining the streets of downtown Kal lend the town a wild west atmosphere, but for those coming in from the Nullarbor, the town is a taste of modernity. Visitors will find that Kal's mood reflects the luck of the mines: when the gold flows generously, so does the drink.

WORKING IN KAL. The main reason people come to Kal is to work, but finding a mining job is not as easy as one might expect. Many companies will only hire employees who have previous experience and pass a drug test. They also require safety training and certification, which takes time (expect to commit at least a year) and costs money. Females beware: mining work is a traditionally male profession in Kalgoorlie. As an alternative, the service industry offers a fairly good number of jobs, though openings in this sector reportedly come and go. **Gold Dust Backpackers** (p. 728) is a good place to start your search.

TRANSPORTATION

The **airport** is south of the city off Gatacre St. **Qantaslink** and **Skywest** offer daily flights to Perth (1-3 per day). The **bus stop** is between the visitors center and the post office on Hannan St. The **Goldfields Express** runs to Perth. (☎1800 620 440. 7hr.; M 11am, Tu-F and Su 2:45pm, also F 11pm; $65, students $40.) **Prospector trains** (☎13 10 53) depart from the station, on the corner of Forrest and Wilson St., for Perth (6hr.; M-Sa 7:05am, also M and F 3pm, Su 2:05pm; $71.80, YHA $64.65).

ORIENTATION AND PRACTICAL INFORMATION

The **Great Eastern Highway** (Hwy. 94 from Coolgardie) becomes **Hannan Street,** the main drag running northeast through town. One block northwest is **Hay Street,** where the town's hostels sit alongside Kal's famous brothels. **Lionel Street, Wilson Street,** and **Boulder Road** are all major roads running perpendicular to Hannan and Hay St. To reach Boulder from downtown Kalgoorlie, turn right on Boulder Rd. at the north end of Hannan St. and follow it to **Federal Road.**

The **visitors center,** in the Town Hall at the corner of Hannan and Wilson St., books accommodations and tours. (☎9021 1966. Open M-F 8:30am-5pm, Sa-Su 9am-5pm.) **Internet** access is available at the **library** on Roberts St., near the Arts Center off Boulder Rd. (☎9091 1693. $3 per 30min. Open M-F 9:30am-8pm, Sa 9am-noon, Su 2-5pm.) Or try **NetZone,** in St. Barbaras Sq. on Hannan St. (☎9022 8342. $10 per hr. Open M-F 10am-7pm, Sa-Su 10am-5pm.) The Kalgoorlie Regional **Hospi-**

tal (☎9080 5888) is northwest of Hannan St. on Piccadilly St. The **post office** is on Hannan St. (☎9024 1093. Open M-F 9am-5pm.) **Postal Code:** 6430.

The **police** (☎9021 9777), on Bookman St. behind the post office, maintain that no areas of Kalgoorlie-Boulder are particularly unsafe, although they do warn visitors to be careful of deep mining holes when bushwalking. In recent years, burglaries have become common; locals are careful to keep their personal belongings under lock and key, and banks require two forms of ID to exchange money. Watch your wallet, use lockers, and don't leave valuables in your car. There are three brothels on Hay St. between Lionel and Lane St. Women should not walk alone in this area after dark. Twin City Cabs provides **taxi** service (☎13 10 08).

ACCOMMODATIONS

At the turn of the century Kal boasted 93 hotels, more than any other town its size in the world. Some still offer reasonably priced accommodations behind their historic facades. Those who are uncomfortable with the idea of prostitution should note that both hostels are close to the discreet-but-working brothels on Hay St. The **caravan parks** on the way out of town toward Coolgardie or the Hannan St. hotels are a good alternative. The area hosts a week of famous horse races in September, as well as a popular mining expo in October; book ahead for these times.

Kalgoorlie Backpackers YHA, 166 Hay St. (☎9091 1482), near the intersection with Lionel St. The best bet for backpackers. Functional exterior masks a cozy interior. Shared kitchen, laundry, lounge, A/C, and swimming pool. Notice board for work opportunities. Dorms $20, with discount $19; singles $40/35; doubles and twins $55/50. Weekly rates available. ISIC/NOMADS/VIP. ❷

Gold Dust Backpackers, 192 Hay St. (☎9091 3737). Spacious common areas and kitchen. Many staying here work in Kalgoorlie. Internet access $6 per hr. A/C. Free pickup. Dorms $24, with discount $20; singles $35/30; twins and doubles $55/50. 7th night free. ISIC/NOMADS/VIP/YHA. ❷

The Palace Hotel (☎9021 2788; admin@palacehotel.com.au), on the corner of Hannan and Maritana St. Nice rooms and an in-house movie channel set within a historic building. The mirror in the foyer, along with a poem, was given to a barmaid by the young Herbert Hoover. Backpacker singles $35; doubles $45; twins $65 (men only); doubles $80, small $75; singles $60/55; family room $110. AmEx/MC/V. ❸

Caledonia House, 122 Piesse St. (☎9093 1413; caledoniahouse@optusnet.com.au). Offers cozy rooms and a reprieve from the hustle of Kalgoorlie nightlife. Singles $25; doubles $40; weekly rates from $85. Book ahead. ❷

Prospector Holiday Park (☎9021 2524; prospector@acclaimparks.com.au), on the corner of the Great Eastern Hwy. and Ochiltree St., has Internet access ($1 per 5min.) and a swimming pool. Sites $24, powered $26; cabins $80; ensuite $94. MC/V. ❷

FOOD AND NIGHTLIFE

With miners working around the clock, Kalgoorlie's services cater to any schedule. **Cafes** line Hannan St.; many open early and close late. Set apart from the pub grub is the chic **Saltimbocca ❸,** 90 Egan St. (☎9022 8028), one block southeast of Hannan St. Travelers can order fine Italian food served in a trendy atmosphere, with a tantalizing rosemary-laced thin crust pizza ($9.50). **Monty's ❸** (☎9022 8288), at the corner of Hannan and Porter St., is open 24hr. and has $10 pasta on Tuesdays and main courses ($17-25) in an elegant setting complete with comfy leather chairs. **Goldfields Bread Shop ❶,** on Wilson St. between Brookman and Hannan St., bakes delicious meat pies ($2.20) and mouthwatering pastries for early risers. (☎9091 9113. Open daily 5am-5pm.) **Peter Pan Milk Bar ❶,** 312 Hannan St., is known for its hearty $6-8 breakfast. (☎9021 2330. Open M-Sa 7am-3pm.) A **Coles** supermarket is located at the corner of Wilson and Brookman St. (☎9021 8466. Open M-W and F 8am-6pm, Th 8am-9pm, Sa 8am-5pm.)

Kal boasts nearly 30 **pubs,** many of which are clustered at the corner of Hannan and Maritana St. Some bars are attended by "skimpies," or scantily clad women; such establishments are clearly labeled outside. **Paddy's Ale House,** at the **Exchange Hotel** on the corner of Hannan and Maritana St., is a popular, laid-back spot where many locals spend their Friday nights. (☎9021 2888. Open daily 11am-latenight.) The historic **Cornwall Hotel** (☎9093 2510), at the corner of Hopkins St. and Goldfields Hwy. in Boulder, has a lively upscale bar with Little Creatures beer on tap and jazz nights on Sunday in the outdoor beer garden. (Open Th-Sa 6:30pm-latenight, Su 12:30pm-latenight.) Located 38km north of Kal on Kalgoorlie-Meekatharra Rd., **Broad Arrow Tavern** is a local legend, especially for its Broadie burgers, topped with bacon, cheese, and a fried egg ($9). Patrons of this pub can inscribe their names on the wall, ceiling, or doors. (The tavern turn-off is clearly marked with signs. ☎9024 2058. Kitchen open daily 11am-9pm.)

SIGHTS

The best place to learn about the local industry is the extensive **Mining Hall of Fame,** located at **Hannans North Historic Mining Reserve,** a right turn off Goldfields Hwy., 2km north of Hannan St. It features new Chinese gardens, demonstrations of gold pouring and panning, and a tour of an underground mine. (☎9026 2700; www.mininghall.com. Open daily 9am-4:30pm. $24, without underground tour $17; concessions $18/14, children $14/9, families $60/45.) The **Super Pit,** an immense working mine, is one of the largest holes in the world. Miners usually set off explosions once a day; check with the visitors center for the time of the blast. The lookout is just outside town; head toward Boulder on Goldfields Hwy., then turn left at the sign for the pit. (Open daily 6am-7pm. Free.) The **WA Museum of Kalgoorlie-Boulder,** 17 Hannan St., features a traditional local home that has been reconstructed on-site. It features exquisitely rebuilt mining board rooms paneled in Jarra wood and British Arms, and is the Southern Hemisphere's narrowest hotel. (☎9021 8533. Open daily 10am-4:30pm. Suggested donation $5.) The visitors center at the **Royal Flying Doctor Service,** located at the airport on Hart Kerspien Dr., gives tours explaining the organization's impressive medical service to isolated outback communities. Guests can check out the state-of-the-art plane used to transport patients and staff—provided it isn't out on a mission. (☎9093 7595. Open M-F 10am-3pm. Tours on the hr. Admission by donation.) Take a glimpse of Kalgoorlie's kinky side on a working brothel tour at **Langtree's Club 181,** 181 Hay St. (☎9026 2111. 18+. Tours daily 1, 3, and 6pm; $35, randy seniors $25. Coffee, tea, and cake available 10am-6pm.) If you find yourself awake on a Sunday morning, head to Burt St. for the **Boulder Town Market,** where merchants peddle their wares on the street from 9am-1pm.

NORSEMAN ☎08

About 100 years ago, "Hardy Norseman" was tethered here overnight as his rider slept. The restless horse pawed at the dusty ground, uncovering a chunk of gold. At the news of his discovery, prospectors rushed to the area, and the town of Norseman was born. Today, most visitors are on their way elsewhere, and there's little to keep them in this one-horse town. For those heading north from Esperance, Norseman is the first encounter with the Goldfields. For those heading east across the Nullarbor Plain, it is the last taste of civilization for over 1000km.

The family-run **Lodge 101** ❷ on Prinsep St. offers convenient, homey accommodations. Backpackers can use a small kitchen and an outdoor sheltered lounge area. Free local bus pickup is also available. (☎9039 1541. Dorms $22; singles $35; doubles $55.) Another option is the **Gateway Caravan Park ❷**, on the corner of the highway and McIvor St. (☎9039 1500. Sites for 2 $18, powered $23.50; cabins $69; ensuite $82-87.) There aren't many options for dining out in Norseman. **Dromedary Cafe ❶**, in the general store on the corner of Ramsay St. and Prinsep St., is one of few places that serves lunch. All meals are under $12. (Open daily 6am-8:30pm; closed Su in winter.) The **BP 24-hour Travelstop**, north of town at the exit for the Eyre Hwy., has a diner, convenience store, ATM, and **petrol**. The **SupaValu**, 89 Robert St., is your best bet for groceries. (Open M-F 8:30am-6pm, Sa 8:30am-5pm, Su 9:30am-1pm.)

The **visitors center**, on Robert St., one block east on the highway between Sinclair and Richardson St., has information about driving the Eyre Hwy. They also offer free showers, a dream come true for Nullarbor survivors. (☎9039 1071. Open daily 9am-5pm.) An **ATM** is also on Roberts St., and the **Telecentre**, which offers **Internet** access, is on Prinsep St. (the Coolgardie-Esperance Hwy.) next to the town hall. (☎9039 0538. Open Tu, W, F 9:30am-5pm.)

CROSSING THE NULLARBOR

The **Eyre Highway**, running between Norseman and Adelaide across the **Nullarbor Plain**, is a grueling desert haul with little to entertain you on your way. **Ninety Mile Straight**, the longest completely straight stretch of highway in the world, is just west of Cocklebiddy. The Plain can be crossed by car or by the Indian Pacific train out of Perth (see **Intercity Transportation**, p. 686). For information on crossing the border into South Australia, call the **agriculture department**. Fruit and vegetables are not permitted across, and those trying to sneak by get slapped with a hefty $2500 fine. (☎9039 3227 in WA or 8625 2108 in SA; www.agric.wa.gov.au.) The **visitors center** in Norseman has helpful info and handles train bookings. When you reach **Ceduna** at the eastern corner of SA's **Eyre Peninsula**, pick up a Nullarbor certificate of completion at the visitors center; or, if you're headed the other direction, get your certificate at the Norseman visitors center. See **Crossing the Nullarbor**, p. 526, in the South Australia chapter, for more information.

BATAVIA COAST AND MIDLANDS

The region just northeast of Perth represents different things to different people. For windsurfers, Lancelin and Geraldton offer world-class gusts; for fishermen, Batavia's treacherous coast promises a bountiful harvest; and for the Dutch mariners of the vessel Batavia, which wrecked upon its reefs in the 17th century, it was the first European glimpse of the land down under. Those who take the time to explore will be treated to a beautiful coastal road, thrilling water sports, a glorious wildflower season (June-Nov.), and pristine coastal dunes.

LANCELIN ☎08

Lancelin (pop. 800), 126km north of Perth, is considered by many to be the windsurfing capital of Australia, with thrillseekers flocking here October to March. The famed four-day **Ledge Point Sailboard Classic** is held during the second week of January, but even in the low-season there's almost always a good breeze. The Aborigines called the area Wangaree, meaning "Good Fishing Place," and this small village thrives on the ocean's bounty; the season runs from September to June.

Windsurfing lessons and equipment are available October through March at **Werner's Hotspot** on the South End beach (☎9655 1553). Another Lancelin attraction is its sand dunes, accessible by car, which extend for miles northeast of town. The dunes are a 4WD playground as well as a practice area for the Australian military; check with the info center before going, as practice bombings may close some portions of the beach and national park to the north. **Desert Storm Adventures** sends you sandboarding down the dunes, brought in by a schoolbus with monster truck tires and an equally monster stereo. (☎9655 2550; www.desertstorm.com.au. $40, concessions $35, children $25. YHA 10% discount.) **Lancelin Off Road Motor Bike Hire** lets you jump on a dirt bike and explore on your own. (☎04 1791 9550; www.dirtbike-hire.com.au. $45 per 30min., $80 per hr.) **Lancelin Beach Surf School** offers 3hr. lessons daily at 9am. (☎04 1790 5789. $40, boards and wetsuits included. Call between 4pm and 8pm. Booking required.) **Lancelin Surfsports,** 127 Gingin Rd., rents sandboarding and surfing gear. (☎9655 1441. Sandboards $10 per 2hr., surfboards $15 per 3hr. Open daily 9am-4pm, later in summer.)

The visitors center and hostel provide maps of coastal **nature walks** in the area. Lancelin's coral reefs are unusually close to shore, which makes for convenient snorkeling and diving. The protected lagoon on the far side of the **Lancelin Island** bird sanctuary is one of the best spots. Experienced divers enjoy the **Key Biscayne Dive** around a sunken oil rig, 19km northwest of Ledge Point. Other nearby dive sites include the **Grace Darling,** a 1914 wooden schooner wrecked off the coast, and the **Gilt Dragon,** a Dutch East India vessel shipwrecked in 1656 off Ledge Point.

The sparkling, well-run **Lancelin Lodge YHA ❷**, 10 Hopkins St., has two comfy lounges, free bikes, boogie boards, fishing rods, a lovely kitchen, wonderful showers, beach volleyball, and a new pool. The sound of crashing waves is a happy reminder that Lancelin's beautiful beach is only a short walk away. (☎9655 2020; www.lancelinlodge.com.au. Internet access $5 per hr. Dorms $23; doubles $55; family rooms $70. YHA $2 discount. MC/V.) **Lancelin Caravan Park ❶** is just down the street from the YHA. (☎9655 1056. Sites $9, powered $11; on-site 4-person van $75. MC/V.) The well-appointed **Windsurfer Beach Chalets ❺,** at the corner of Cunliff and Hopkins St., are across the street from the beach. Each of the five chalets has a queen-size bed, a pull-out double, and two bunks. (☎9655 1454; www.automated.com.au/LAS. 2 people $120. Extra person $25. MC/V.) Food options are limited. Several fish 'n' chips joints are located on Lancelin's self-proclaimed "cappuccino strip" in the shopping center. **Endeavor Tavern ❷,** on the corner of Cray St. and Gingin Rd., offers pub fare for $9-14. (Open M-F noon-2pm and 6-8pm, Sa-Su noon-2:30pm and 6-9pm. MC/V.) A **supermarket** is located at the shopping center on Gingin Rd. (☎9655 1172. Open daily summer 7am-8pm, winter 7am-7pm.)

There is no public transportation to Lancelin, but the YHA offers pickups from Perth for $30; if you are staying elsewhere you can call the day before to see if they have spots on their van. The easiest way to reach Lancelin is by car; from Perth, take Bulwer St. to Charles St., which becomes Hwy. 60 (Wanneroo Rd.) before hitting Lancelin. The **visitors center** is at 102 Gingin Rd. (☎9655 1100. Open daily 9am-6pm.) There are **ATMs** in the adjacent general store (open daily 7am-7pm), and at the Gull petrol station (open daily 7am-7pm), and in the Endeavour Tavern. The **police** (☎131 444) are down Hammersly Rd., and the **hospital** (☎1800 022 222) is north on Gingin Rd. **Internet** access is available at the telecenter off Vins St. for $5 per 30min. (Open M-F 10am-4pm, Sa 10am-2pm.) The **post office** is located in the main shopping center (M-F 7am-5pm, Sa 7am-4pm.) **Postal Code:** 6044.

NAMBUNG NATIONAL PARK: THE PINNACLES

Between Lancelin and Geraldton, the **Pinnacles Desert,** in **Nambung National Park,** is a popular destination for daytrips from Perth. The barren, jagged landscape isn't really a desert at all, but an expanse of sand dunes with thousands of wind-eroded limestone pillars up to 4m tall. When not crowded, the park has the feel of a ghost town, and the forms of the worn rocks are intriguing. Climb the **Pinnacles Lookout** at the northernmost edge of the vehicle loop for gorgeous views of the contrasting

Red Desert to the east and the White Desert to the west. Try to visit at dawn or sunset when the hordes of daytrippers from Perth are gone, the heat is bearable, and the sand and pillars glow in the changing light.

The park is a good 250km north of Perth, near the small town of **Cervantes. Greyhound Australia** (☎13 14 99 or 13 20 30) drops off right in town (3½hr.; daily 3:30pm; $46, concessions $42). Those driving to Nambung must have a **national park pass,** sold at the Pinnacles Visitor Centre and the entrance to the Pinnacles Desert loop. (Day pass $9 per vehicle; 4wk. holiday pass for all national parks $23; annual all-parks pass $51.) The brand-new **Pinnacles Visitors Centre,** on Cadiz St. in Cervantes, books accommodations and tours. (☎9652 7700. Open M-F 9am-5pm, Sa 9:30am-5pm, Su 10am-4pm.) There aren't many advantages to a guided tour over a self-guided walk around the Pinnacles—the track is easy and no 4WD is necessary. Renting a car is the cheapest way to see the park and allows the most flexibility. Travel 1hr. west from Brand Hwy.; turn left into the park just before Cervantes. Once inside the park, the **Kangaroo Point** and **Hangover Bay** turn-offs provide beach access. **Lake Thetis,** between the park turn-off and Cervantes, is home to ancient stromatolites. Day-tours from Perth range in price from $95-150. **Go West** departs from the Wellington St. Bus Station in Perth and includes sand boarding and a swim. (☎9226 3348; www.gowesttours.com.au. $115, concessions $95.)

Cervantes Lodge and Pinnacles Beach Backpackers ❷, 91 Seville St., offers clean and cozy accommodations; the dorms in the new lodge are nicer than the ones in the older building. (☎9652 7377; www.cervanteslodge.com.au. Internet access $4 per hr. Wheelchair accessible. Dorms $23; twins $65; ensuite $75; deluxe room with TV, fridge, and coffee/tea facilities $95. Extra person $10. MC/V.) The **Cervantes Pinnacles Caravan Park ❷,** 35 Aragon St., is another option. (☎9652 7060; cervpinncpark@westnet.com.au. Sites $20; powered $22; cabin $50. All prices for 2 people. Extra adult $7, extra child $4. MC/V.)

GERALDTON ☎08

Geraldton (pop. 33,000) is the gateway to the beautiful **Abrolhos Islands,** where the scuba diving is superb. Windsurfers eager to test their skill in the strong southerly winds flock to the area in the summer.

TRANSPORTATION AND PRACTICAL INFORMATION. From the Brand Hwy., head straight through the rotary and up Cathedral Ave. to get to the town center. The town's main drag, **Chapman Road,** and the shop-lined **Marine Terrace** both run parallel to the coast and intersect Cathedral Ave. **Greyhound Australia** (☎13 14 99 or 13 20 30; www.greyhound.com.au) runs buses to Broome ($295/266), Exmouth ($156/143), and Perth (6hr.; 12:30pm; $54, concessions $49). **Transwa** (☎1300 662 205; www.transwa.wa.gov.au) goes to Perth (6hr., 1 per day, $50/45) and Kalbarri (2hr., 1 per day, $29/25). There is also a local bus that serves the greater Geraldton area ($2-3.10, concessions $0.80-1.30). The **visitors center** is inside the Bill Sewall Complex at the corner of Bayly St. and Chapman Rd., about 1km north of Cathedral Ave. (☎9921 3999; www.geraldtontourist.com.au. Open M-F 9am-5pm, Sa-Su 10am-4pm.) **Internet** is available at many locations for $6 per hr.; Suncity Books (49 Marine Terr.) offers wireless. The **police** station (☎9923 4555) is also in the downtown area, while the **hospital** (☎9956 2222) is off Cathedral St. on Shenton St. The **post office** is located off Chapman St. behind the art gallery. (Open M-F 8:30am-5pm.) **Postal code:** 6530.

ACCOMMODATIONS AND FOOD. Geraldton YHA Foreshore Backpackers ❷, 172 Marine Terr., a block southwest of Cathedral Ave., is in an older building right on the water in the center of town. The clean dorms have 3 to 4 beds each, and some have patios overlooking the ocean. (☎9921 3275; foreshorebp@hotmail.com. Free pickup and drop-off. Internet access $5 per hr. Dorms $22; singles $30; twins and doubles $50. ISIC/NOMADS/VIP/YHA. MC/V.) A lively pub and an ideal location make the **Freemasons Hotel ❸**, on the north end of Marine Terr., another great option. (☎9964 3457; www.freemasonshotel.com.au. Singles $30, with queen $40; suite for 2 $80. AmEx/MC/V.) **Batavia Backpackers ❷**, next to the visitors center, has basic rooms. Dorms are single-sex. (☎9964 3001. Internet access $6 per hr. Dorms $20; singles $25; doubles and twins $40; family rooms $60. ISIC/NOMADS/VIP/YHA $1 discount. MC/V.) The **Belair Caravan Park ❷**, near the lighthouse on Willcock Dr. in the West End, has a pool, tennis court, and playground. (☎9921 1997 or 1800 240 938. Sites $16, powered $20; chalets from $70.) Restaurants line the streets downtown; the visitors center has a helpful guide to Geraldton's cuisine. One standout is **Planet Bean ❶**, in the Marine Terr. mall, with good, inexpensive breakfasts and lunches for $7-14. (☎9965 2233. Open M-F 6:30am-2:30pm, Sa 6:30am-noon.) **Tanti's Restaurant ❸** excels in exquisite Thai meals for $15-20. (☎9964 2311. Open M-Sa 5:30-9:30pm, W-F 11am-2pm. MC/V.) **Woolworths,** on Sanford and Durlacher St., has cheap groceries. (☎9921 4088. Open M-W and F 8am-6pm, Th 8am-9pm, Sa 8am-5pm.)

ACTIVITIES. Most people come to Geraldton for one reason: **windsurfing.** The best conditions are Oct.-Nov. and Mar.-Apr., though it is a great activity year-round in this area. Equipment can be rented from **Sailwest,** at the Point Moore Lighthouse on Willcock Rd. west of town. (☎9964 1722. Windsurfing gear $95 per day, $50 per ½ day. Open M 9am-5pm in summer, Tu-F 9am-5pm, Sa 9am-12pm; closed when windy.) The best windsurfing in the area is at **Point Moore,** the gnarliest spot around. Locals travel 30km north of town to **Coronation Beach,** where you can camp for $5 per night. Surfers prefer **Greys Beach, Sunset Beach,** and **Back Beach.** The **Abrolhos Islands,** an archipelago comprising over 120 islands about 60km off the coast of Geraldton, were the site (and cause) of the Batavia wreck (p. 730). The islands are rich with marine life, making for incredible diving. **Abrolhos Odyssey Charters** (☎04 2838 2505; abrolhosodyssey@westnet.com.au) runs daytrips and extended tours to the islands for $250 per person per day, but be sure to book ahead. Geraldton's waterfront is also home to one of the impressive **Western Australia museums,** which offers displays on the storied past of the Batavia Coast, including a thrilling shipwreck exhibit. (☎9921 5158; www.museum.wa.gov.au. Open daily 10am-4pm. Entry by donation.)

KALBARRI NATIONAL PARK

Kalbarri National Park (kal-BERRY) encompasses miles of sculpted coastline and spectacular gorges, carved over millions of years. The diverse landscape is further enhanced in the late winter and early spring by stretches of wildflowers.

ORIENTATION AND PRACTICAL INFORMATION. The township of **Kalbarri,** with its grassy riverfront and picturesque view of the mouth of the **Murchison River,** is the primary starting point for exploring this natural wonderland. Most services lie on or near **Grey Street,** which follows the river and turns into the southbound **Red Bluff Road** and northeastbound **Ajana-Kalbarri Road** at either end of town. The former leads to Geraldton via newly sealed road, making for a great coastal drive; the latter goes to the North West Coastal Hwy. The **visitors center** is on Grey St. between Woods St. and Porter St.; be aware that they might try to sell you a tour you don't necessarily want. (☎9937 1104; www.kalbarriwa.info. Open daily 9am-5pm.) The **CALM** office (☎9937 1140) is on the Ajana-Kalbarri Rd., 1km east of town. Transportation in town or to the coastal cliffs and inland gorges is available through **Kalbarri Taxi** (☎9937 1888). In the shopping center off Porter St. there is a **pharmacy,** as well as a **book exchange** that offers **Internet** access for $6 per hr. (☎9937 2676. Open M-F 9am-5pm and Sa 9am-12:30pm.) The **police** station (☎9937

1006) is located adjacent to the pharmacy. West of the pharmacy on Kaiber St. is the **Medical Center** (☎9937 1000). The **post office** is located next to the marina jetty, north on Grey St. past Ajana Kalbarri Rd. (☎9937 2212. Open M-F 8am-5pm and Sa 8am-noon.) **Postal code:** 6536.

ACCOMMODATIONS AND FOOD. From the visitors center, turn right on Grey St., then right on Woods St. to reach **Kalbarri Backpackers** ❷ at 52 Mortimer St. The hostel offers a pool, cozy lounges, BBQ, bike rental ($10 per day), 4WD rental ($59 per hr., $99 per 2hr., $130 per 3hr.; ages 18+), and free use of snorkel gear and boogie boards. Consider staying in a private room if you are concerned about sharing a bathroom with half the hostel. (☎9937 1430. Dorms $25, YHA $22; twins $60/55; doubles $85, low season $75; ensuite motel room $115/95; 2 bedroom chalet $120/99. Extra adult $10, extra child $5. MC/V.) **Kalbarri Anchorage Caravan Park** ❷, across from the jetty at the north end of Grey St., is on a grassy knoll offering great views, and has an enclosed kitchen, a pool, and a playground. (☎9937 1181; anchor@wn.com.au. Sites for 2 $21, powered $24. Cabins $50, ensuite $70. Extra adult $7, extra child $5. MC/V.) **Finlay's Fresh Fish BBQ** ❷ serves up huge portions of delicious seafood with a folksy flare ($10-25). To get there from Grey St., turn left at Porter St., right on Walker St., then right onto Magee Cres. (☎9937 1260. Open Tu-Su 5:30-8:30pm. BYOB.) **Kalbarri supermarket,** in the shopping center, is family-owned and has a large produce section. (Open daily 6:30am-6:30pm. MC/V.)

SIGHTS AND HIKING. The park has two main sections: the coastal cliffs and the river gorges. Access to the river gorges area costs $9 per vehicle. Bring exact change in case no one is on duty. The park's unsealed roads are generally in good 2WD condition, but the 25km to the Loop and Z Bend can be corrugated at times and caravans should be left behind. It's always a good idea to check with **CALM** (☎9937 1140) to obtain current reports. The river gorges were carved by the waters of the Murchison River, and offer spectacular views and jagged hikes. **Nature's Window** is a red rock arch that frames a river landscape behind it. It is found near the beginning of the **Loop trail** (8km, 4hr.), a challenging but rewarding climb that runs along clifftops, down to the river bed, and then along the river-level ledges before climbing up again to the top of the gorge. Keep the river on your right and stay close to water level, even if it seems like you're not on the trail. One unique outdoor opportunity is the intensive 38km **hike** from the **Ross Graham Lookout** to the Loop trail, running alongside the river. Allow four days and hike in groups (CALM requires parties of 5 or more). For any overnight hiking, alert CALM beforehand, and bring a satellite phone and 5 liters of water per person per day. Along the 10km of the coastal road just south of Kalbarri, numerous sideroads lead to dramatic cliffs dropping into the Indian Ocean. The **Natural Bridge** was created by waves that eroded part of a cliff, leaving a rock slab atop a gap filled with crashing whitecaps. Nearby, **Island Rock** rises 20m from the surf. Other must-see formations include **Red Bluff Lookout, Rainbow Valley,** and **Pot Alley Gorge,** which has great fishing. The eye-popping **cliffside hike** (10km, 4hr. one-way) takes in the whole series of cliffs, running from **Eagle Gorge** to the Natural Bridge. Kalbarri Coach Tours provides mini charters that can take you to the Red Bluff for $8.80 each way (☎9937 1161; call for service.) Just beyond the cliffs, on the way back to town, the **Kalbarri Rainbow Jungle** parrot sanctuary is both exhilarating and educational. Visit the aviary during a feeding to see over 100 bird species. (☎9937 1248. Open M-Sa 9am-5pm, Su 10am-5pm; no entry after 4pm. $11.50, children $4.50.)

Visitors to the nearby **Hutt River Province,** which has been an independent principality since it seceded from Australia in 1970, can go on a tour given by the ruler, Prince Leonard, purchase official currency and stamps, and get their passport stamped. (www.hutt-river-province.com. 30km south of Kalbarri, then another 40km on Ogilvie Rd. West. Open daily 9am-4pm.)

OUTBACK COAST AND GASCOYNE

The Outback Coast is an unfathomable expanse of bushland, broken only by termite mounds and the occasional befuddled emu crossing the road. Although the distances between towns are daunting, the desolate landscape holds its own sense of wonder. The dazzling ocean that abuts this semi-desert counters its sparseness with an impressive abundance of marine life, from the dolphins and dugongs of Shark Bay to the whale sharks and coral of the Ningaloo Marine Park. Winter is high season, when Perthites park themselves along the sunny coast.

SHARK BAY

Shark Bay, Western Australia's popular World Heritage area, was the site of the earliest recorded European landing in Australia. Today, Shark Bay is known for the dolphins at Monkey Mia, the tranquil Shell Beach, and the "living fossils" (stromatolites) at Hamelin Pool. The pool is 34km from the North West Coastal Hwy., while Monkey Mia lies beyond Denham towards the end of the peninsula. The best way to see the area is by car or on a tour as buses are infrequent.

MONKEY MIA. At Monkey Mia (pronounced my-UH), the Indian bottlenose dolphins of Shark Bay swim right up to the shore to be fed by herds of tourists. Another way to get close to the dolphins is to volunteer; forms are available at the visitors center and the minimum time commitment is four days. The dolphins have been visiting Monkey Mia since it was nothing but a sheep-farming area, but in the past ten years the playful creatures have become an international sensation. Some think Monkey Mia provides an unparalleled opportunity to interact with intelligent, sociable animals; others find it a contrived and exploitative show. Access to the site costs $6 per person or $12 per family. Generally there are three feedings daily between 8am and 1pm; it's best to get there early in the morning. The **Monkey Mia Visitors Center** has displays, videos, and talks. (☎9948 1366. Open daily 8am-4pm.) If you've just missed a dolphin-feeding, there is an easy **walking trail** (2km, 1½hr. round-trip) that starts from the carpark and proceeds along the coast and up a ridge. **Camel rides** can also be found in the mornings ($14 per 10min.) After dark, don't miss the hot tub at the Francois Peron National Park homestead. It is filled with a natural hot spring; sitting under the stars, you can admire the Milky Way.

The backpackers lodging at **YHA Monkey Mia Dolphin Resort ❶**, right next to the dolphin interaction site, is really a resort, with a beachside location and many amenities, including a tennis court, hot tub, and pool. The rooms are simple, with little more than beds and lockers, but everything is fresh and new. Guests at the resort must still pay park entrance fees, so if you will be staying longer than two days, get a week pass ($9) to save paying the $6 daily fee every time you come and go. (☎9948 1320 or 1800 653 611; www.monkeymia.com.au. Sites $10.15; dorms $22; vans from $26.90. AmEx/MC/V.) The only reasonably priced meals ($10) are at the **Monkey Bar ❶**. The road to Monkey Mia from Denham is well marked and departs from the western tip of Knight Terr. Those without a car can take Denham YHA's **shuttle.** ($5; guests free. Departs daily 7:45am, returns 4:30pm.)

DENHAM. The westernmost town in Australia is a good base for exploring Shark Bay. The main street, Knight Terr., runs parallel to the beach. Sticking out on the boardwalk is the sleek new **Shark Bay Interpretive Centre,** an interactive museum that showcases the history and future of the world heritage site. It also displays monthly art exhibits. (☎9948 1590; sbic@sharkbay.wa.gov.au. Open daily 9am-6pm. $10, concessions $8, children $6.)

The **YHA Denham Bay Lodge ❷**, 95 Knight Terr., has shared ensuite dorms with kitchens. The managers will help arrange transportation, and the lodge has kayaks and occasional evening tours for free. (☎9948 1278 or 1800 812 780. Free bus to Monkey Mia daily 7:45am, returns 4:30pm. Dorms $25, YHA/VIP $22; twins and doubles $60/55. MC/V.) A quaint building made of shell bricks houses the **Old Pearler ❸**, which serves the best fresh seafood on the coast. (☎9948 1373; oldpearler@westnet.com.au. Open daily for lunch and dinner.) **Shark Bay Supermarket** is at the BP Station, 1 Knight Terr. (Open daily 7am-7pm.)

The area is best visited with a car, which can be rented at **Shark Bay Car Hire** (☎9948 1247; located in the beauty shop). Next to the Caltex gas station, the **CALM** office provides information and sells national park passes. (☎9948 1208. Open M-F 8am-5pm.) There is an **ATM** at the Heritage Resort Hotel on Knight Terr. The **Telecenter,** on Knight Terr., has expensive but fast **Internet** access. ($10 per hr. Open M and F 9:30am-2:30pm, Tu-W 9am-4:30pm, Th 9am-3:30pm.) Also nearby are the **police** (☎9948 1201), and the **health clinic** is one block north on Hughes St. (☎9948 1213). The local **post office** is also centrally located downtown (open M-F 9am-5pm). **Postal Code:** 6537.

CARNARVON ☎08

Carnarvon (pop. 7000) is a good place to catch your breath between destinations on the coast. Most backpackers come here looking for work at one of the local fruit plantations, or to see the 30m high blowholes north of town.

TRANSPORTATION AND PRACTICAL INFORMATION. Greyhound Australia (☎13 14 99 or 13 20 30) runs daily to: Broome (20hr.; $232, children $188, backpackers $210), Coral Bay (2½hr., $57/48/53), Exmouth (9hr., $104/86/95), and Perth (14hr., $153/125/139). A **big yellow banana** welcomes visitors as they head into town along Robinson St. from the North West Coastal Hwy. The main road through Carnarvon is **Robinson Street,** while major sights are also on **Babbage Island Road** and **Olivia Terrace,** which run along the water. The **visitors center** is in the Carnarvon Civic Centre on Robinson St., and has a guide to the town's history and services. (☎9941 1146. Open M-F 9am-5pm, Sa 9am-1pm, Su 10am-1pm.) Also located downtown are the **police** (☎9941 1444), **fire station** (☎9941 1222), and an **ATM**. The **hospital** is located one block south on Johnston St. (☎9941 0555). **Internet** access is available in the **library** on Stuart St. ($1 per 10min.) The **post office** (open M-F 9am-5pm), is also located in the town center. **Postal Code:** 6701.

TIP **WORKING IN CARNARVON.** There are only two consistently successful ways to find work in Carnarvon. Those with their own mode of transport can visit the **plantations** that line the north and south sides of the Gascoyne River and inquire about work. Those without transportation are dependent on the **The Port Hotel,** which finds work for guests (the process generally takes 3-5 days) and provides transportation to work sites. They keep a list of guests looking for work and pass out available jobs to those who have waited the longest.

ACCOMMODATIONS AND FOOD. The Port Hotel ❷ on Robinson St. is a recently renovated family-run enterprise with clean rooms, a lively recreation area, and an outdoor BBQ area. The owners will help travelers find work, and many of their guests work in the nearby plantations. (☎9941 1704; www.theporthotel.com.au. Dorms $22; singles $35; motel-style singles $66; double $77. Extra person $11. MC/V.) The **Coral Coast Tourist Park ❷,** the caravan park nearest the town center, is located on Robinson St. (☎9941 1438; coralcoastpk@westnet.com.au. Sites for 2 $18.50, powered

$21.50, extra adult $7, extra child $3; cabins with TV and A/C for 2 in low season $55, in high season $65.) **River Gums Cafe ❶** is a popular local hangout with main courses from $4-7 and delicious mango smoothies for $4; turn at the big banana on Boundary Rd. and follow the signs. (☎9941 8281. Open W-Su 10am-3pm.) For a taste of the fresh seafood in Carnarvon, head over to the Snapper Jetty to **Hacienda Crab ❶** for a steamed crab ($4) or some prawns. (☎9941 4078. Open daily 10am-6pm). Get messy eating these on the beach as you watch the sunset, and then walk next door to the **Harbourside Cafe ❶** for savory main courses like fish 'n' chips ($7) or prawns seasoned with a variety of sauces for $14-23. (☎9942 4111. Open 10am-8:30pm.) The **Dragon Pearl ❶,** corner of Johnston and Francis St., serves up Chinese fare for $6-11. (☎9941 1941. Open W-Su 6-9pm.) **Woolworths** supermarket, in the shopping center on Robinson St., has cheap groceries. (☎9941 2477. Open M-W and F-Su 8am-8pm, Th 8am-9pm.)

SIGHTS AND ACTIVITIES. **The Blowholes** are natural wave-driven water jets that spurt 30m high as water slams against the rocky shore. Attacking the porous coastline, they make a wondrous sight that shouldn't be missed. Time your visit so you arrive between tides for the largest jets. A lovely beach is located just 1km south. (Take the North West Coastal Hwy. 24km north of North River Rd. and turn left onto Blowholes Rd., taking it 49km to the blowholes. The road is sealed to the blowholes, but not beyond.) Babbage Island Rd. tracks the coast from Carnarvon to **Pelican Point,** allowing for pleasant bike rides among mangroves. Along the way, the mile-long jetty has good **fishing** and crabbing, but be careful about swimming—it is called Shark Bay for a reason. A drive or bike ride east of town on the **"Fruit Loop"** of North and South River Rd. north of the North West Coastal Hwy., passes **banana** and **mango plantations.** Fresh fruit and veggies are plentiful and cheap. Every Saturday from May to November local plantations sell their goods at a **produce market** (8am-noon) at the Civic Centre. **Stockman Safaris** visits the plantations as well as the prawn factory, boat harbor, salt mine, blowholes, jetty, and the OTC—an out-of-use NASA communications center on the town's outskirts. (☎9941 1146. Town tour $35, children $17.50; salt mine and blowholes $70/40.) Carnarvon is a popular base for trips to **Mount Augustus,** the largest rock in Australia, twice the size of Uluru (p. 307), with a summit at 1105m. The trip is 430km from Carnarvon via Gascoyne Junction on an unsealed road; check road conditions at the visitors center before leaving.

CORAL BAY ☎08

Coral Bay is one of two gateways (Exmouth is the other) to the splendid Ningaloo Marine Park. The Ningaloo Reef, over 250km long, starts south of Coral Bay and stretches north around the Northwest Cape and back into Exmouth Gulf. For many Aussies, Coral Bay is the only way to see the Ningaloo, a tranquil beach town with fantastic swimming and snorkeling at your doorstep.

Divers flock to Ningaloo in droves, and while they'll find more options in Exmouth, Coral Bay provides a relaxing alternative. **Ningaloo Reef Dive Centre** (☎9942 5824; www.ningalooreefdive.com; MC/V) offers the only scuba diving in town. Located in the shopping arcade, it offers two-dive trips from $145 (with equipment) and a four- or five-day PADI certification course for $495 (starts Sa). If you stay at the Ningaloo Club, you can get the course and accommodations for $585. Some of the best **snorkeling** in Australia is just a few feet off the beach. The cheapest gear is at Bayview for $10 per day; walk down the beach to the south. Enter the water in the shallows and swim out until you hit the reef. Watch out for the occasional boat and let the northerly current carry you back into the bay. In general, the farther from shore, the more spectacular the reef. Between March and July, whale shark snorkeling trips are offered to spot the sharks as they migrate up the Ningaloo towards Exmouth. **Coral Bay Charter** offers the cheapest opportunity to swim with giant manta rays. Their office is at the Bayview, but you can get a discount if you book through the Ningaloo Club. (☎9942 5932; bayview.coralbay@bigpond.com. Open 9:15am-1:30pm. $110, children $55, backpackers $99. MC/V.) **Coastal Adventure Tours** offers exciting 4x4 treks along the dunes that offer snorkeling options just off the shore. (Located in the shopping arcade. ☎9948 5190; www.coralbaytours.com.au. 3hr. snorkel trek $85; 2½hr. sunset snorkel trek $80. MC/V.) Those who prefer to stay dry should stick with **Coral Bay Adventures;** their 1hr. cruise allows you to spy the reef's 2m-long cod through underwater windows. (☎9942 5955; www.coralbayadventures.com.au. $30. MC/V.) For those looking for a bit of eco-tourism, CALM hosts a bimonthly Coral Bay Clean Up, where you can pick up trash on the beaches and then enjoy some free beers at sunset. Contact CALM (www.calm.wa.gov.au) for upcoming events.

The palatial **Ningaloo Club ❷,** has an amazing pool, spotless kitchens, free movie nights, BBQ, **Internet** access ($6 per hr.), stonework patio, and brightly lit rooms. Even though it's huge, it fills up fast, so book well in advance. Travelers on a budget can work 2hr. per day to pay for their room. (☎9948 5100; www.ningalooclub.com. 10-bed dorms $22; 6-bed $24; 4-bed $25; twins and doubles $70 for 2; ensuite $90. MC/V.) Across the street is the **Bayview Coral Bay Holiday Village ❷,** an extensive caravan park with grassy sites. (☎9385 6655. Apr.-Oct. sites for 2 $25, Nov.-Mar. $22; powered $28/25; 4-person cabins (min. 4 nights) with kitchen and A/C $80. MC/V.) **Reef Cafe ❷,** at Bayview Coral Bay Holiday Village, serves salads, pizzas, and seafood for $10-25. (☎9942 5882. Open daily 6pm-latenight. MC/V.) There is a small **supermarket** in the shopping center. Items can be pricey, so bring food if you plan on staying long. (Open daily 7:30am-7pm. MC/V.)

Greyhound Australia (☎13 14 99 or 13 20 30; www.greyhound.com.au) runs to Exmouth (1½hr.; daily 12:55am; $71, YHA/VIP/ISIC $65) and Perth (15hr., daily 2:30am, $171/155). Coral Bay has no official **visitors center;** however, every accommodation and most stores in the shopping arcade provide visitor information and book tours. Coral Bay News and Gifts, in the arcade, serves as the local **post office.** (☎9942 5995. Open M-Sa 9am-5pm, Su 9am-12:30pm. MC/V.) **Postal Code:** 6701.

WESTERN AUSTRALIA

EXMOUTH ☎08

The scuba diving epicenter of the west coast, Exmouth (pop. 3500) is the place to swim with enormous whale sharks and majestic manta rays. The famed Ningaloo Reef is complemented on land by beautiful Cape Range National Park. The main township area is inland and not much to look at, conveniently leaving you with the real attractions: diving and fishing around the Cape.

TRANSPORTATION. Most action takes place around **Maidstone Crescent,** where the shopping center is located. **Greyhound Australia** (☎13 20 30) **buses** run to Broome (18hr., $219) and Perth (18hr., $213); both leave from the Exmouth Visitors Centre at 12:30am. **Allen's,** at the Autopro on Nimitz St., provides **car rental.** (☎9949 2403. 1 day from $55, 2-6 days from $50 per day, 7+ from $45 per day. 2WD only. Requires credit card and license. MC/V.) **What Scooters,** south of town on the corner of Pellew St. and Murat Rd., rents scooters that come with snorkel gear. (☎9949 4748. $20 per hr., $53 per day, YHA $45.) They also rent 4WD vehicles through **Avis.** ($100 per day standby, $145 per day reserved, 7+ days $132 per day.) **Bikes** can be rented from the Exmouth minigolf on Murat Rd. (☎9949 4644. $4 per 4hr., $20 per day. Open 9am-latenight.)

PRACTICAL INFORMATION. The **Exmouth Visitors Centre,** on Murat Rd., has info on Cape Range National Park as well as helpful sheets that summarize available accommodations, tours, and transportation services. (☎9949 1176; www.exmouthwa.com.au. Open daily 9am-5pm, holidays 9am-1pm.) The shopping center just off Maidstone has a **pharmacy.** (Open M-F 9am-5:30pm, Sa 9am-

12:30pm.) Two blocks west, on Lyon St. off Fyfe St., is a **hospital,** the only medical facility until Carnarvon. (☎9949 3666. Dive medicals $100; call ahead.) **Westpak,** on Learmouth St. next to the shopping center, has an **ATM. Internet** access is available at most hotels and at **Blue's Internet Cafe,** at the corner of Kennedy and Thew St. (☎9949 1119. $3 per 30min. Open daily 9am-5:30pm.) Across the street is the **police station** (☎9949 2444) and the **post office.** (Open M-F 9am-5pm.) **Postal Code:** 6707.

ACCOMMODATIONS. Most of the backpacker joints in Exmouth are part of sprawling tourist villages that also contain campsites, cabins, varied amenities, and sometimes hotel rooms. Few dorms provide blankets, so come prepared during the winter months. **Camping ❶** is permitted only in designated sites within Cape Range National Park ($5; $9 vehicle entry fee not included), and rangers patrol the area. Fires are prohibited and there is no drinkable water in the park. **Excape Backpackers ❷,** within the Potshot Resort on Murat Rd., is a 5min. walk from the town center. This social hostel boasts lively pubs, ensuite dorms, and the best location in town. (☎9949 1200. Internet access $4 per hr. Key deposit $20. Dorms $24, with YHA/VIP $22; twins/doubles $59. MC/V.) **Exmouth Cape Tourist Village ❶,** immediately on the right upon entering town, has backpacker beds in small cabins with A/C and a mini-kitchen, as well as campsites. A free bus service runs to Bundegi Beach from the tourist village. (☎1800 621 101 or 9949 1101; exmouth@aspenparks.com.au. Nov.-Mar.: sites for 2 $18, powered $21; dorms $24; singles $37; doubles $56. Apr.-Oct.: sites for 2 $22, powered $29; dorms $28; singles $37; doubles $68. Extra adult $10, extra child $5. YHA/VIP discount 12.5%. MC/V.) The cheapest accommodations can be found at **Winstons Backpackers ❷,** part of the Ningaloo Caravan and Holiday Resort. This complex is conveniently right across from the visitors center on Murat Rd., and contains restaurants and dive shops. (☎9949 2377; www.exmouthresort.com. Sites Nov.-Mar. $19, Apr.-June $22, July-Oct. $23, powered $22/26/28; dorms $20, weekly $120; doubles $60/360. AmEx/MC/V.)

FOOD AND NIGHTLIFE. Exmouth offers an impressive selection of quality dining at reasonable prices. On Kennedy St., behind the shopping center, **Whaler's Restaurant ❸** serves delicious gourmet food ($10-25) in an upscale setting. They also offer small plates that let you savor the food while saving your wallet. (☎9949 2416. Open daily 8am-4pm and 6pm-latenight.) Right next door, a treat for both your taste-buds and your health can be found with the tempting menu at **Ningaloo Health Foods ❶.** The panini ($8.50) are especially tantalizing. (☎9949 1400. Open M-F 8am-5pm. MC/V.) The shopping center off Maidstone has two supermarkets, **Farmer Jacks** (open daily 6:30am-7:30pm) and **IGA** (open M-W and Sa-Su 7am-7pm, Th-F 7am-7:30pm.) **Grace's Tavern,** at 829 Murat Rd. across from the Exmouth Tourist Village, is a pleasant hangout with an outdoor area and excellent takeaway pizza. (☎9949 1000. Open M-Sa 10am-midnight, Su 4pm-10pm.) The **Potshot Resort,** on Murat Rd., has a complex of nightspots including an elegant main bar, the Bamboo Room, and the more crowded Vance's Bar. Friday is the big night; beer flows until the wee hours. (☎9949 1200. Open M-Th 10am-midnight, F 10am-1:30am, Sa 9:30am-1:30am, Su 10am-10pm.)

NINGALOO MARINE PARK

Most people come to Exmouth to see the impressive **Ningaloo Reef,** and the town is full of dive shops catering to all experience levels. Introductory PADI courses run about $450-500; they take four or five days and include four ocean dives. Arrange a diving medical check-up in advance, or pay $100 in cash at the local hospital. Shop around before choosing a dive shop; all have certified instructors and good equipment, but class size and quality of instruction vary. For veteran divers, there are many great dives in the area, including **Lighthouse Bay, Navy Pier,** the **Muiron Islands,** and the **Hole-in-the-Wall,** on the outside of the reef near the North Mandu campsite.

SNORKEL FOR LESS. If you plan on snorkeling on the Ningaloo, purchase a mask, snorkel, and flippers before you come. Rentals can add up, and purchasing even the most basic set in one of the beach stores can cost you upward of $60.

The cheapest PADI course in town is run by **Ningaloo Reef Dreaming,** located in the shopping center. They will let you do all of your diving off the Muiron Islands for an additional $50. (☎9949 4777; www.ningaloodreaming.com. 3 Murion Island dives including equipment $175; 3 Ningaloo Reef dives including equipment $150; PADI $450.) **Exmouth Dive Centre** (☎9949 1201; www.exmouthdiving.com.au) offers the most professional instruction but is more expensive. PADI runs $495 and lasts five days, with a maximum of eight people. They also run advanced dive trips from $99. **Village Dive** goes to the Ningaloo Reef ($185, including equipment) and the Murion Islands ($220, including equipment) and offers well-organized PADI classes ($495 for 4-5 days, max. 8 people.) One of the biggest draws of the Ningaloo Reef, **whale shark snorkeling,** is expensive ($310-335) but offers a unique chance to swim with the world's largest fish. Whale sharks appear most frequently April to July. A number of eco tour companies in town, as well as the dive shops listed above, do whale shark tours. If you already have your dive certification, during high season you may be able to encounter a whale shark while on a cheaper single dive. The best surfing is found at **Surfers Beach** at Vlamingh Head, at the northern end of the cape. Surf lessons are available through **Surf Ningaloo,** starting at $60 for a three hour lesson. (☎04 2920 2523; www.yallingupsurfschool.com. Booking available through the Exmouth Visitors Centre.)

CAPE RANGE NATIONAL PARK

West of Exmouth, the rugged limestone cliffs and long stretches of sandy white beach of **Cape Range National Park** provide a haven for bungarras, emus, and Stuart's desert peas. The solar- and wind-powered **Milyering Visitors Centre,** 52km from Exmouth, hands out maps and info on the parks and has some interesting displays on local geography. (☎9949 2808. Open daily 9am-3:45pm.) The visitors center offers free 45min. guided walks during holidays and high traffic seasons; call ahead or check with the Exmouth visitors center for dates and times. The center only has limited water; bore water is available at Ned's and Mesa Campgrounds, but bring your own drinking water. The main road into the park is sealed and leads north from Exmouth to the tip of the cape, and then south along the west coast of the cape to Yardie Creek, a relatively long trip. Keep a sharp eye for kangaroos, echidnas, and perenties (large lizards) on the road, especially at night. Shothole Canyon and Charles Knife Rd. (both unsealed) enter the eastern section of the park before you reach Exmouth. It can be rough going; check with **CALM** (☎9949 1676) before heading into the park this way. If you don't have a car, you can use the Cape's shuttle service, **Ningaloo Reef Bus,** which stops at the lighthouse, Yardie Creek, Turquoise Bay, Reef Retreat, the Milyering Visitor Centre, and Tantabiddi Reef. (☎1800 999 941. $20 to Turquoise Bay, children $10; includes park entry.)

The highlight of the park is its beautiful coastline. **Swimming** and **snorkeling** are very popular along the tropical coast. However, the **riptides** caused by the nearby stretch of coral reef, can make swimming very dangerous outside of the area's sheltered coves. The coves of **Turquoise Bay, Sandy Bar,** and **Mesa Bay** are the best swimming spots, and many amateur divers practice their skills along the nearby reefs. Snorkelers should be careful, especially in Turquoise Bay as the current can drag you out. Snorkeling gear is available for $10 at the visitors center.

For the hydrophobic visitor, the park has many short walking trails that reveal ocean views and the jagged sandstone characteristic of the area. Accessible from Yardie Creek Rd., the best of the walking trails is the **Mandu Mandu Gorge Walk** (3km, 2½hr. round-trip), which treks along the gorge ridge to a nice lookout, then descends through the gorge. Further south, the shorter **Yardie Creek Walk** (1.5km, 1hr.) lets visitors explore a limestone ledge overlooking a creek.

PILBARA REGION

The beauty of the Pilbara is rugged and dramatic. The land can be harsh to those who travel unprepared: hundreds of kilometers of arid bush separate the region's small industrial towns, and summer temperatures are searing. In the late winter and early spring, however, the heat becomes bearable, and the landscape explodes into fields of pale yellow spinifex dotted with red Stuart peas and purple mulla-mullas, interrupted only by stunning red gorges and mesas slicing the horizon. The Pilbara has recently seen a large increase in mining activity, resulting in some of the most lucrative seasonal work opportunities in Australia.

KARRATHA ☎08

Karratha is the Pilbara coast region's administrative center and is a good re-supply point for travelers heading to the Karijini and Millstream-Chichester National Parks. Budget accommodations in Karratha are not abundant, and many backpackers choose to continue on to Port Hedland, or to camp in the nearby national parks. **Karratha Backpackers ❷**, 110 Wellard Way, off Searipple Rd., is run by an entertaining cast of Karratha characters. The cinderblock building is less than picturesque, and the dorms lack lockers. There is free pickup and drop-off from the bus station, and Garth will take you on an entertaining 3hr. tour of the Dampier Archipelago for $25. Short-term housing is available for those working in the area. (☎9144 4904. Dorms $20; doubles and twins $55.) **Pilbara Holiday Park ❷** has pleasant, shaded sites and the most inexpensive motel-style accommodations in town. To get there, take Dampier Rd. west out of the city and turn right on Rosemary Rd.

WESTERN AUSTRALIA

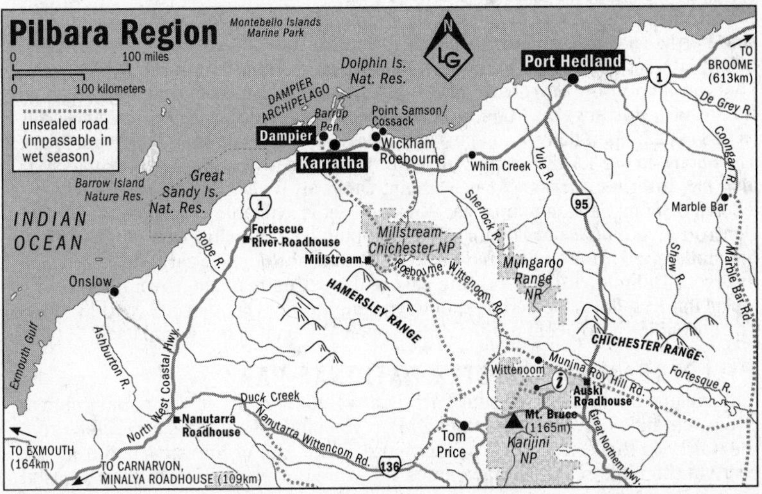

(☎9185 1855 or 1800 451 855; www.aspenparks.com.au. Campsites for 2 $28; camper sites for 2 $30, powered $31, extra adult $10, extra child $7; motel unit for 2 $120; studio unit for 2 $135; Holiday unit for 2 $157. MC/V.)

Karratha has many restaurants that cater to the latenight crowd. On the corner of Balmoral Rd. and Morse Ct. is the busy **Karratha Pizza Bar ❷,** which has hearty pizzas for delivery or takeaway for $8-18. (☎9185 2780. Open M and W-Su 5pm-latenight.) **Al's Burgers and Kebabs ❷,** across the street, serves up a great kebab as late as 4am. (☎9144 1419. Open M 11am-9pm, Tu-Th 11am-10pm, F 11am-4am, Sa 11:30am-4am, Su 11:30am-9pm. Cash only.) For a cold escape from the Pilbara sun, **Elephant Juice ❶** in the Centro Karratha offers *gelato* for $4. (☎9144 4914. Open M-W and F 9am-5:30pm, Th 9am-9pm, Sa 8:30am-5pm, Su 10am-2pm.)

An easy daytrip from Karratha is **Point Samson,** whose beaches grace the peninsula on the east side of the Pilbara coast. Point Samson is well known for its fishing, and **Moby's Kitchen ❷** at the end of Samson Rd. on Miller Ct. serves up some of the best seafood on the northwest coast. (☎9187 1435. Open M-F 11am-2pm and 5-8:30pm, holidays and weekends 11am-8:30 or 9pm. MC/V.) A community bus runs between Dampier, Karratha, and Point Samson several times a day during the weekends ($2-7.60, concessions $0.80-3.10).

Dampier is 16km northwest of Karratha, along Dampier Rd. Primarily a fishing town and a port, it serves as a harbor for seafarers. The **Dampier Archipelago,** a string of 42 untouched granite and basalt islands, most of which are now nature reserves, can be reached by tours as well as private boats. **Blue Destiny Charters** runs a daytrip (10am-4:30pm) out of Karratha to the Archipelago for snorkeling, swimming, and sightseeing on Wednesday and Sunday. Book at the tourist bureau. (☎04 1893 7610. $125, including lunch, afternoon tea, and snorkel gear.) The **Dampier Seafarers Centre** provides information about the area and is located on the Esplanade in Dampier. (☎9183 1424; seafarers@kisser.net.au. Open M-F 9am-5pm.) A trip up the **Burrup Peninsula,** immediately to the east of town, reveals some of the secrets of the Pilbara coast. Turn off toward Hearson's Cove for a secluded seashell beach. About 1.2km down there is a dirt road which leads to nearly 10,000 Aboriginal rock engravings. The **Dampier Chinese Restaurant ❸,** in the Dampier Shopping Centre, lends a bit of variety to an otherwise fish 'n' chips town. (☎9183 1555. Lunch $9. Open M-Th 11:30am-1:30pm and 5-9pm, F 11:30am-1:30pm and 5-10pm, Sa 5-10pm, Su 5-9pm. DC/MC/V min. $20.)

Karratha is also home to the largest shopping center in Western Australia outside Perth. The **Tourist Bureau** is on Karratha Rd. 1km before you enter town and offers **Internet** access. (☎9144 4600. $5 per 30min. Open Dec.-Mar. M-F 8:30am-5pm, Sa 9am-noon; Apr.-Nov. M-F 8:30am-5pm, Sa-Su 9am-4pm.) The Centro Karratha holds several **ATMs,** a **pharmacy,** and two supermarkets: **Woolworths** (☎9185 2322; open daily 7am-9pm) and **Coles** (☎9185 4633; open daily 6am-9pm). The **library,** in the TAFE campus, located west of the town center off Dampier Rd., also has Internet access. ($4 per 30min. Open M, W, F 8:30am-5pm; Tu and Th 8:30am-8:30pm; Sa 9am-noon.) Wireless internet is available at **Jamaica Blue** in the Centro Karratha ($2 per 30min.). The shopping center, **police** (☎9144 2233), and **fire station** (☎000) are clustered between Balmoral Rd. and Searipple Rd., which intersect Dampier Rd. at both the east and west ends of the town center. The **Nickol Bay Hospital** is located west of town center off of Dampier Rd. (☎9143 2333.) The **post office** is adjacent to the Centro (open M-F 9am-5pm). **Postal Code:** 6714.

MILLSTREAM-CHICHESTER NATIONAL PARK

Millstream-Chichester National Park is a welcome oasis of fan palms, plunge pools, and hills between Karratha and Port Hedland. The park is accessible from the north via the Wittenoom-Roebourne Rd. 70km east of Karratha, and from the east via the Millstream-Pannawonnica Rd. which meets the North West Coastal

Hwy. 118km north of the Nanutarra Roadhouse. It is also accessible from the north or south on the Tom Price Railway Rd. (also referred to as the Hammersley Iron Rd.). However, the railway route is by far the roughest access road and can only be traversed with a permit, obtainable from the Karratha or Tom Price visitor centers after watching a 10min. safety video. Recently, the Tom Price Railway Rd. has been undergoing construction; it may not be open while it is being sealed. All these roads are gravel, but are usually accessible during the Dry to the careful 2WD driver; check with **CALM** (☎9143 1488) in Karratha for road conditions.

Millstream Homestead, built in the 1920s, now houses the **visitors center** (☎9184 5144) and is the starting point for a 750m walk with informational signposts about early settlers and native flora and fauna. The walk passes a lookout over **Crossing Pool,** offering views of playful blue martens, before ending at **Chinderwarriner Pool.** Respite can be found in the park's two **campsites ❶**, located at **Snake Creek,** 2km beyond Python Pool on Wittenoom Roebourne Rd., and **Deep Reach Pool,** 1km along the road that leads from Millstream Yarrloola Rd. to the visitors center. (Pit toilets at both sites, BBQs only at Deep Reach. Sites for 2 $10 for the 1st night, $5 each additional night. Extra person $5.50.)

The park's other major sites are located 20km north of Millstream on the Roebourne-Wittenoom Rd. Travelers can take a refreshing dip in **Python Pool,** a deep freshwater plunge pool characteristic of the Pilbara region. It can be surprisingly cool in winter, despite the heat of the open country. The summit of **Mount Herbert** can be reached by a short 300m walk, offering fabulous views for minimal effort.

KARIJINI NATIONAL PARK

Karijini is a rugged and magnificent wonderland in the heart of the Pilbara. The park is home to the Banjima, Yinhawangka, and Kurrama peoples, and Aboriginal legend has it that the gorges were formed by *Thurru,* giant serpents that snaked through the rocks and now reside in the glistening waters of Karijini. While the short, easy walks in the park draw bus loads of tourists, the park's true glory is found deep within the gorges and remains guarded from crowds by challenging, sometimes dangerous, passageways.

KARIJINI NATIONAL PARK AT A GLANCE	
AREA: 100,000 sq. km. **FEATURES:** Junction Pool, Dales Gorge, Kalmina Gorge, the Hancock and Weano Gorges, Fortescue Falls, and Mt. Bruce. **HIGHLIGHTS:** Hiking the expansive gorges and swimming in the rock pools.	**GATEWAY:** Tom Price. **CAMPING:** At Dales Gorge $5 per adult and $2 per child; at Savannah Campground $10 per adult and $5 per child; max. $25 per family. **FEES:** $9 vehicle entry fee.

ORIENTATION AND TRANSPORTATION

Karijini's northern entrances through Yampire Gorge and Wittenoom are **closed.** Both are contaminated by cancer-causing asbestos. The sealed **Karijini Drive** cuts across the park from the Great Northern Hwy. to Marandoo Rd., which leads to **Tom Price.** Most attractions are accessed by **Banjima Drive,** which meets Karijini Dr. at two points: 30km west of Great Northern Hwy. and 5km east of Marandoo Rd. Banjima Dr. is unsealed and at times corrugated, but navigable with care in a 2WD during the the Dry. Check **road conditions** before heading to the park by calling the visitors center (☎9189 8121). A 4WD is safer; rentals from Karratha run $110-125 per day and are available through **Thrifty** (☎9143 1711) on Bayly Ave., **Budget** (☎9144 2136) at the airport terminal, or **Avis** (☎9144 4122) on Warambie Rd.

There are several tour groups that go into Karijini that offer a ride and a meal for tourists without a car. Out of Tom Price, **Lestok Tours** runs daytrips to the major gorges and provides lunch. (☎9188 2032; www.lestoktours.com.au. $130, $120 with 3-day advance booking; 14 and under $65.) **Pilbara Gorge Tours** offers a similar trip with a focus on ecotourism. (☎9188 1534; www.pilbaragorgetours.com.au. Full tour adults $120, children 6-14 $60, under 6 free. Part tour $90/45/free.)

PRACTICAL INFORMATION

Karijini is a big place with limited infrastructure, so come prepared. Untreated **water** is available in the park at the fork between Dale's Gorge area and the new visitors center, as well as on Banjima Dr. near the turn-off for Weano gorge and the Savannah campground; it's best to bring plenty with you. **Petrol** and supplies are available west of the park in **Tom Price** and at the **Auski Roadhouse** (see below) to the northeast. Maps, updates on road conditions, and weather forecasts, as well as **Internet** access ($3 for 15min., $5 per 30min.) can be found at the **Tom Price Tourist Bureau.** (☎9188 1112. Oct.-Mar. M-F 9:30am-3:30pm, Sa 9am-noon; Open Apr.-Sept. M-F 8:30am-5:30pm, Sa-Su 9am-noon.) Karijini's **visitors center,** on the sealed part of Banjima Dr., is an impressive multi-million-dollar structure with exhibits on local flora and fauna, geology, and history, as well as trail maps for the few marked trails in the park. It also has a public phone, ice, and hot showers. The visitors center also sells various park passes, which is helpful if you plan on visiting more than one park during your time in Western Australia. (☎9189 8121. Showers $2. Open daily 9am-4pm.) For practical info, ask attendants at park entrances and campsites, or contact the **CALM ranger station** (☎9189 8147 or 9189 8157, after-hours emergency 9189 8101, 9189 8102, or 9189 8103). There is an **emergency radio** in the Weano Gorge day-use area. Also in Tom Price are the nearest **Police** and **Fire Department** stations; both can be reached by the emergency number ☎000. The **hospital** (☎9159 5222) is a left turn off Mine Rd., immediately before Tom Price.

ACCOMMODATIONS AND FOOD

Camping ❶, with gas BBQs, pit toilets, and power, is permitted in the rocky, designated areas at **Dale's Gorge** ($5, children $2) and **Savannah Campground.** ($10, children $5, families $25.) For more comfortable quarters, head to the **Tom Price Tourist Park ❷**, 3km outside of town, which has showers, camp kitchen, playground, small pool, and spacious dorms with mini-fridge and A/C. (☎9189 1515; tompricetouristpark@westnet.com.au. Tent sites $10 per person; caravans powered $25 per site, $20 without power; 4-bed dorms $25; cabins for 2 $102-105; chalets $127. AmEx/MC/V.) If you have had enough of the outdoors, the **Windiwarri Lodge ❺** is a luxurious retreat. Located on the corner of Stadium St., the Lodge offers an excellent buffet for breakfast, lunch, and dinner. (☎9189 1110; karijinilodge@spotless.com.au. Breakfast included. Singles $152.25; doubles $168. AmEx/MC/V.)

On Central St., the **Millstream Cafe ❶** serves tasty breakfasts for $11-20. (☎9189 1271. Open daily 8am-8pm.) The **Moon Palace Chinese Restaurant ❷** offers a change of pace from the standard fare of the Outback. Located in the town square off Stadium Rd., the lunch special ($9) is one of the best deals around. (☎9189 1331. Open for lunch M-F 11:30am-2:30pm, for dinner M-Th and Su 5-9pm, F-Sa 5-10pm.) The Tom Price Hotel's **Bistro ❸** has main courses for $14-26 and pizzas for $10-16. (Open M-Sa noon-1:30pm and 6-8:30pm, Su 6-8pm.) There is a large **Coles** supermarket in Tom Price, on Central St. (Open M-W and F-Sa 8am-6pm, Th 8am-9pm, Su 10am-6pm.)

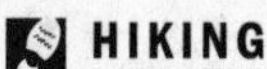

HIKING

DALE'S GORGE. One of the more verdant gorges, Dale's is 20km into the park from the east, accessible by sealed roads. A great picnic area has gas BBQ and plenty of shade; camping is within walking distance, offering amazing sunrise hikes. The various hiking paths are labeled according to their level of difficulty. A short trek leads to **Fortescue Falls** (800m; 30min. round-trip), a spring-fed watercourse that runs year-round that cascades into a deep turquoise pool, the ideal spot to take a dip. Follow the stream as it gurgles over roots and stones down the gorge for a moderately difficult 1.5km (2hr. round-trip) hike until reaching **Circular Pool,** a small amphitheater where emerald moss trails down the rock walls. Hike back up a stairway to the **Rim Trail,** following it past stunning views of the gorge.

KALAMINA FALLS. This little gorge, 25km west of the visitors center, is a good introduction to the park. A walk through the lush valley of the gorge (3km, 2hr. round-trip) leads past a small waterfall and along a creek to Rock Arch Pool, which sits beneath a natural archway. The sure-footed traveler can climb up the gorge wall through a doorway aided by a tree that clings miraculously to the rock.

JOFFRE FALLS AND KNOX GORGE. Another 10km west on Banjima Dr., turn right to discover the tallest waterfall in the park. Though the flow is often fairly weak, the falls are picturesque as they cascade downward. The walk (2km, 2hr. round-trip) down to the pool at the base of the falls is a steep descent and may require you to climb along the rock walls for the last stretch. Farther up the road, Knox Gorge is one of the deeper gorges in the park, and a trek (2km, 2hr. round-trip) to its base reveals its true magnitude.

WEANO GORGE. This gorge is the deepest in the park, plunging into shadowy depths reached by the sweltering Australian sun only at high noon. The magnificent views overlook the area where Weano, Joffre, Red, and Hancock gorges meet. A walk (1.5km, 2hr. round-trip) runs to the base of Hancock, and a longer, more difficult trail takes you to Kermit's Pool.

MOUNT BRUCE. The turn-off to Mt. Bruce, the second tallest peak in WA, is 3km east of the western entrance to the park. The walk (9km, 5hr. round-trip) to the summit (1235m) should be started in the morning, but there are several excellent vantage points along the way if you haven't the time nor the energy for the full ascent. That said, the views from the top are breathtaking and worth the effort.

PORT HEDLAND ☎08

Located about 200km from Karratha and over 600km from Broome, Port Hedland has two major attractions: a booming mining industry and Karijini National Park. Travelers looking for seasonal employment will be pleased by the abundance of work opportunities, which are advertised in the town center and at recruitment offices. Around the corner, the well-kept and family-run **Harbour Backpackers ❷,** at 11 Edgar St., has a **sushi bar ❶.** (☎9173 4455; www.harbourlodge.com.au. Free bus pickup. Dorms $20, $120 per wk.; doubles $45.) Also nearby, **Frogs Backpackers ❷,** 20 Richardson St., is equally cozy with a comfortable patio looking out on the ocean. (☎9173 3282; www.frogbackpackers.com.au. Dorms $22, YHA $20; singles $50/45; twins $27/25 per person; doubles $55/50.) For dinner, **Bruno's Pizza Bar ❷,** 7 Richardson St., is the local favorite. Try the "bloody hot" pizza ($11) and wait for a late night brawl when the other pubs in town close. (☎9173 2047. Open 5:30pm-latenight.) The shopping center at the south edge of town, on the corner of Wilson St. and McGregor St., has a **Woolworths.** (Open M-W and F 8am-7pm, Th 8am-9pm, Sa-Su 8am-5pm.) If

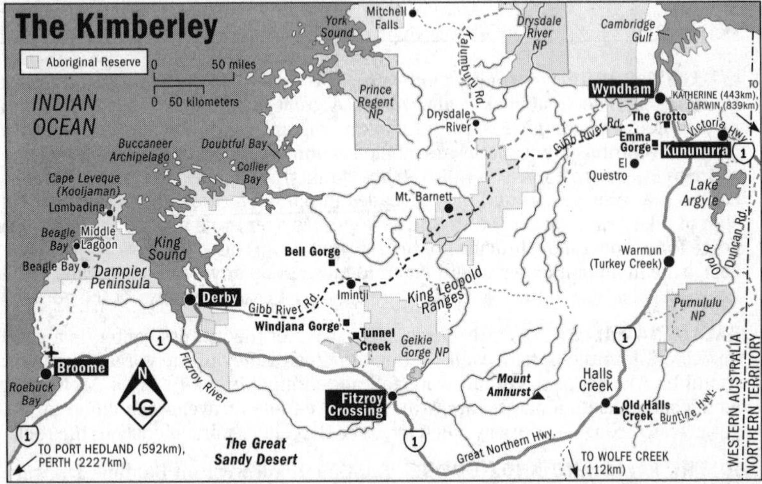

you are looking for the Hedland nightlife, head to the Esplanade at the end of town for the pubs at the Pier Hotel and the Esplanade Hotel. The **Cooke Point Holiday Park** ❷, on the other end of the peninsula at the corner of Athol and Taylor St., has a pool, rec room, kitchen, and beach access. (☎9173 1271; www.aspenparks.com.au. Tent sites for 2 $30; caravan site $31, extra adult $10, extra child $5. Bunkhouse singles $45; doubles $70; motel-style doubles $97.)

From Port Hedland, the boring Great Northern Hwy. winds 621km along the coast to **Broome.** Roadhouses can be up to 300km apart, so fuel up whenever you get the chance. Although humans are scarce, kangaroos, cows, sheep, and wild camels populate the scrubland, so take your time. At the western edge of the peninsula, Wedge St. is stocked with the **Port Hedland Visitors Centre** (☎9173 1711; **Internet** access $7.50 per hr.; open May-Oct. M-F 8:30am-4:30pm, Sa 9am-4pm, Su 10am-2pm; Nov.-Apr. M-F 9am-4pm, Sa 9am-1pm), several 24hr. **ATMs,** and the **post office** (open M-F 9am-5pm). **Postal Code:** 6721.

THE KIMBERLEY

Entire swaths of the vast, open Kimberley remained uncharted and untouched until recent decades. The highway splits east of Broome into the two major routes running through the Kimberley. The quick but dull Great Northern Highway runs through tiny Fitzroy Crossing and Halls Creek on the way to Kununurra and finally Wyndham, while the Gibb River Road connects Derby to Kununurra along a rough 4WD-only track that provides access to the Kimberley's remote gorges and stunning waterfalls. Traveling the Gibb requires planning, as only a few roadhouses dot the long stretches of road, but the gateway to the splendors of the Kimberley is well worth the effort. Rainfall levels change drastically between the Kimberley's two seasons. Flooded rivers engulf roads during the the Wet (Nov.-Mar.), while during the the Dry (Apr.-Oct.) the parched land bakes under cloudless skies.

BROOME ☎08

Sprawling between the ocean and the mangroves, beachy Broome (pop. 17,500) has an immaculate shoreline and a carefree aura, in stark contrast to the harsh territory stretching in every direction around it. This seaside mecca's fame grew as a result of a thriving pearl industry that flourished in the 1880s and continues to be a prominent industry in town. Today, Broome attracts vacationers yearning to sink their toes into the cool sands of its gorgeous white beaches. Many visitors to Broome quickly plan longer stays in the area in order to avoid the harsher realities of the seemingly endless Outback outside the city.

TRANSPORTATION

Airport: Broome International Airport (☎9193 5455). A 10min. walk from downtown. Follow the signs from Coghlan St. in the city center to McPherson St. **Qantas** flies to Melbourne (4hr.) and Sydney (4hr.); **Virgin Blue** flies to Adelaide (3.5 hr.); **Skywest** has flights to Darwin (2hr.) with connections to other cities. Number of flights depends on season. Hostels run free shuttles to airport based on demand and availability.

Intercity Buses: Bus station next to tourist bureau. **Greyhound Australia** (☎9192 1561) has service to **Perth** (32½hr., daily 8:30am, $384) and **Darwin** (27hr., daily 7:15pm, $336), via **Kununurra** (14hr., $202).

Public Transportation: Town Bus (☎9193 6585; www.broomebus.com.au) connects **Chinatown, Cable Beach,** and several hotels. 1st bus of the day departs town at 7:10am and reaches **Gantheaume Point** with no round-trip service. $3, ages 6-16 and concessions $1.30, under 6 free. After 6:30pm, take the **Nightrider** (☎9192 8987) with music and surfing videos on the TV screens inside. (1 per hr. 6:30pm-12:30am. One-way $3.50, children and concessions $2.50; all night pass $6/3.)

Taxis: Broome Taxis (☎9192 1133); **Roebuck Taxis** (☎1800 880 330); **Chinatown Taxis** (☎1800 811 772); **Pearl Town Taxi** (☎1800 622 433). A trip from town center to Cable Beach runs approximately $15.

Car Rental: Avis, Britz, Budget, Europcar, Hertz, and Thrifty all have offices at the airport carpark. **Budget** (☎9193 5355 or 1800 649 800); **Hertz** (☎9192 1428 or 1800 655 972); and **Broome Broome** (☎9192 2210), corner of Hamersley and Frederick St., each offer 1-way rental options from $450. Broome Broome caters to backpackers with 3-door hatches for $63 per day (insurance included). **Britz** (☎9192 2647; www.britz.com) on Livingston St. has campervans starting at $80 per day. All listed companies have 4WDs and all, with the exception of Hertz, will rent to drivers age 21-24 for an additional fee. Book ahead in high season (Apr.-Oct.) **Note:** Car rentals vary drastically in price and availability due to weather concerns, especially during the Wet.

ORIENTATION

In true Aussie spirit, Broome occupies part of a kangaroo-shaped peninsula and is centered around two clusters of activity: one in the town and business center **(Chinatown)** and the other a few kilometers north around **Cable Beach.** From the east, the **Great Northern (Broome) Highway** runs into Chinatown, becoming **Hamersley Street** as it crosses **Napier Terrace.** Most shops and restaurants in town cluster along **Carnarvon Street.** A block south of Napier Terr., **Frederick Street** heads west. To get to Cable Beach from Frederick, take a right on Cable Beach Rd. E., then a right onto Gubinge Rd. followed by a left on Cable Beach Rd. W., which runs along the beach to the carpark and snack bar area.

PRACTICAL INFORMATION

Tourist Office: Broome Visitor Center (☎9192 2222; www.broomevisitorcenter.com.au). On Broome Hwy. at the corner of Short St. Offers same maps and sightseeing info provided by hostels. Open Oct.-Mar. M-F 9am-5pm, Sa-Su 9am-1pm; Apr.-Sept. M-F 8am-5pm, Sa-Su 9am-4pm, public holidays 9am-4pm.

Budget Travel: Harvey World Travel (☎9193 5599), Paspaley Shopping Centre in Chinatown. Serves as a broker for Qantas and other carriers. Open M-F 8:30am-5pm, Sa 9am-12pm. **Travelworld,** 9 Johnny Chi Ln. (☎9193 7233), off Carnarvon St. across from the movie theater. Open M-F 9am-5pm, Sa 9am-noon.

Currency Exchange: ANZ Bank, 16 Carnarvon St. (☎13 13 14). Open M-Th 9:30am-4pm, F 9:30am-5pm. **Commonwealth Bank** (☎9192 1103), on Hamersley and Barker St. Open M-Th 9:30am-4pm, F 9:30am-5pm. **Bankwest** (☎13 17 18) on the corner of Napier and Carnarvon St. Open M, W, Th 9am-4pm, Tu 10am-4pm, and F 9am-5pm. All have a $7-8 charge for currency exchange and **ATMs** outside. In Cable Beach, ATMs can be found in both Divers Tavern and the store next door (open daily 9am-6pm).

Work Opportunities: There is typically plenty of temporary food-service work in the Dry; check message boards at hostels for postings and requests.

Police: (☎9194 0200), on Frederick St. between Hamersley and Carnarvon St.

Internet Access: At institutions from souvenir shops to travel agencies along Carnarvon St., and at hostels. Going rate is $6 per hr.

Post Office: (☎9192 1020), in Paspaley Shopping Centre on Carnarvon St. *Poste Restante.* Open M-F 9am-5pm. **Postal Code:** 6725.

ACCOMMODATIONS AND CAMPING

During the Dry (Apr.-Oct.), book ahead for all accommodations. Cheaper rates are often available during the Wet. Most hostels have their own bars; alcohol purchased elsewhere is strictly prohibited. All hostels have a tropical resort feel; the decision when choosing a place is whether you want to be close to Cable Beach, where camping is popular, or near the shops and nightlife of Chinatown.

Cable Beach Backpackers, 12 Sanctuary Rd. (☎9193 5511 or 1800 655 022; www.cablebeachbackpackers.com). An ideal location for beach lovers, just 5min. from the shore. Isolation from town is eased by free shuttles to Chinatown, the Greyhound depot, and the airport. Intimate and lively, with friendly staff, Internet access, pool, kitchen, bar with fabulous Happy hour, laundry, billiards, and scooter rentals. Bike rental $12 per day, surfboard $20, bodyboard $8. Deposits: key $5; blanket, sheet, and pillow $15; plate set $10. Reception 6:30am-1pm and 4:30pm-10pm. 7-bed dorms $20; 4-bed $25; singles $50; doubles $65. Book several days in advance. VIP/YHA. ❷

Kimberley Klub (☎9192 3233; www.kimberleyklub.com), on Frederick St. between Robinson and Herbert St., a 5min. walk from Chinatown. Free pickup from Greyhound depot. Larger and less personal than other hostels, but luxurious by backpackers' standards. Enormous lagoon-shaped pool, full bar, snack counter, ping pong, billiards, TV lounge, and volleyball court. Kitchen, laundry, and tour booking desk. Internet access $6 per hr. Cutlery and linen deposit $10. Reception 6:30am-8pm. Dorms $24; 6-bed $26; twins and doubles $80. Book 2 days in advance. YHA $3 discount. ❷

Broome's Last Resort, 2 Bagot St. (☎9193 5000 or 1800 801 918; www.broomeslastresort.com.au). The feel of a beach lodge with the conveniences of the town center. Fast Internet access ($4 per hr.), pool tables, and a popular bar open daily until 11pm. Breakfast included. Key deposit $10. 3-4 bed dorms $23; 6-8 bed $20-22. ❷

Broome Motel, 34 Frederick St. (☎9192 7775; www.broomemotel.com.au), near Robinson St. Just outside of Chinatown, total convenience with none of the late night ruckus. Spacious ensuite rooms with A/C. Free parking. Pool, BBQ, and laundry facili-

ties. Wheelchair accessible. Reception 7am-8pm. Motel $115, self-contained $145. Discounts for multi-night stays and during the Wet. ❺

Cable Beach Caravan Park (☎9192 2066), on Millington Rd. 12min. from the beach. Good location and solid facilities compensate for seemingly endless crowds. Wheelchair accessible. Sites for 2 in Dry $30.50, in Wet $24.50; powered sites from $20. ❷

Tarangau Caravan Park, 16 Millington Rd. (☎9193 5084), on the corner of Millington Rd. and Lullfitz Dr. Quieter and much less crowded, but a good 20min. walk from the beach. Sites $10 per person, powered for 2 $28. Extra person $7. ❶

FOOD

Food offerings in Chinatown are varied and enticing, though ironically non-Chinese and often expensive. The cheapest sandwiches can be found at **Coles** supermarket after 6:30pm, when prices for baked goods and sandwiches are slashed. (☎9192 6299; in the Paspaley Shopping Centre. Open daily 6am-midnight.)

Shady Lane Cafe (☎9192 2060), on Johnny Chi Ln. off Carnarvon St. Hidden away in a pedestrian alley, this cafe serves great pancakes ($9), toasted focaccia ($11), and smoothies ($5). Open daily 7am-3pm. ❶

Zoo Cafe (☎9193 6200), Cable Beach at the intersection of Sanctuary, Koolama, and Challenor St. Built in the original feeding house of the Pearl Coast Zoological Gardens (park set up by Lord Alistar McAlistair McAlpine upon discovering Broome). Lush greenery serves as a reminder that you have survived the Outback. Try the popular Kimberley Taste Plate, a combo of pearl meat, barramundi, croc, kangaroo, and camel (serves 2, $29). Entrees $17-30. Opens 7am for breakfast and lunch, 6pm for dinner. ❹

Blooms Cafe and Restaurant, 31 Carnarvon St. (☎9193 6366). Choose from huge portions of pasta, pizza, and Thai curry ($12-25). Lots of vegetarian options. BYO. Great lunch options until 5pm $6-9. Open daily 7am-9:30pm. ❷

Fong Sam's Cafe (☎9192 1030), on Carnarvon St. across from the cinema. Delicious, chocolatey baked goods, large portions, and reasonable prices. Pastries from $1.50. Fresh quiche $4.50. Open M-F 6:30am-5pm, Sa-Su 6:30am-4pm. ❶

Cable Beach Sandbar and Grill (☎9193 5090), on Cable Beach Rd. W., adjacent to pedestrian access to the beach. Prices are steep but the location can't be beat. A snack stand sells ice cream ($2.80), hot dogs ($4.50), and other junk food while the restaurant serves meals ($15-35) and frozen drinks ($6-15). Outside, wave to Mom on the webcam pointed toward the beach (www.broomecam.com). Open daily 7am-9pm. ❷

BEACHES AND ACTIVITIES

CABLE BEACH. At this small slice of paradise, 22km of clear Indian Ocean lap against glowing, pearly-white sand. Take a camel ($40), sailing ($50-100), or hovercraft tour, or just chill at the clothing-optional portion of beach past the rocks to the north. Other options include surfing (board rental $8 per hr.), parasailing, jet skiing, and tubing. Whatever you do, don't miss the sunset.

TOWN BEACH. Town Beach is farther south than Cable Beach on the Roebuck Bay shore, at the end of Robinson St. Though you can't swim here, the mix of blue hues in the water behind red and black rocks and lush greenery is spectacular. For three days each month from March to October (check tourist bureau for exact dates), Broome's 10m tide is so low that the exposed mudflats stretch for kilometers, reflecting the light of the full moon in a staircase pattern. The city celebrates with the **Staircase to the Moon Market** at Town Beach. At the lowest tides, the waters off the beach recede to uncover skeletons of sunken WWII boats.

REPTILES. Get up close and personal with the aggressive 5m saltwater crocodiles that populate this part of Australia at **Malcolm Douglas Broome Crocodile Park.** (200m from the beach access on Cable Beach Rd. next to Divers Tavern. ☎9192 1489. In the Dry: guided feeding tours M-F 11am and daily 3pm. Open M-F 10am-5pm, Sa-Su 2-5pm. In the Wet, call for times. Adults $20, students and concessions $16, children $12, families $50.) **Gantheaume Point** is home to a set of **dinosaur footprints** preserved in the rocks. On the far western tip of the Broome Peninsula, located 5km from Cable Beach, the 120 million-year-old prints surface only during very low ocean tides. Also here is **Anastasia's Pool,** a small circular pool that fills at high tide. It was cut into the rock by a former lighthouse keeper for his arthritic wife so she could take a dip without walking to the bottom of the rocks. Take a left onto Gubinge Rd., where Cable Beach Rd. veers right to the pool.

PEARLS. You can't come to Broome without encountering the pearl industry. Pearl shops line the streets of Chinatown. Restaurants serve pearl meat, and tours run daily during the the Dry. To get your fill of pearl history try a tour at **Pearl Luggers** (☎9192 2059) on Dampier Terr. and get a free taste of pearl shell meat (daily tours 1¼hr., call for times. Adults $18.50, concessions $16.50, ages 10-18 $9), or take a tour to the Willie Creek Pearl Farm to see how pearls are produced. (☎9193 6000; www.williecreekpearls.com.au. Tours from $32; call for booking.) After your history lesson head over to the **Japanese Cemetery** to see the burial sites of all the Japenese divers who lost their lives during pearl harvests.

TOURS. Sunset **sailing cruises** are offered by several companies and range in price from $50-100 for 2-4hr. The 100 ft. MC Oceanic departs on a 2hr. cruise beginning at 4pm and sports a full bar. Book through **Broome Eco Adventures** at 12 Carnarvon St. (☎9193 7997; www.kimberleyadventure.com). If the oasis of Broome leaves you yearning for the desert, try a camel ride on the beach and thread through the dunes to reach the hilltop at twilight. **Ships of the Desert** has morning, sunset, and twilight camel tours. (☎9192 6383. $40 per hr., full-day $175). Without a 4WD, **land tours** may be your only way to see the Kimberley or the northern shoreline. **Aussie Off Road Tours** and **Kimberley Getaway Safaris** offer trips to Cape Leveque (daytrips from $219). **Kimberley Wild Expeditions** runs longer trips down the Gibb River Rd.

ENTERTAINMENT AND FESTIVALS

For information on local events, pick up a copy of the weekly *Broome Happenings* from any hostel or the visitors center. No visit to Broome is complete without catching a feature at the world's oldest operating outdoor movie theater: **Sun Pictures Outdoor Cinema**, on Carnarvon St., spun its first reel in 1916. (☎9192 1077. Shows nightly at 6:30 and 8:15pm. $14, concessions $11.50, children $9.) The **Easter Dragon Boat Regatta** is held on Easter Saturday at the Town Beach. Horse racing is big throughout July when the town starts hopping for the **Broome Cup.** The **Shinju Matsuri Pearl Festival** runs for 10 days in early September. The **Mango Festival** (last weekend in Nov.) marks the harvest with a Mardi Gras celebration and the popular **Great Chefs of Broome Mango Cook Off.**

NIGHTLIFE

Compared to the Kimberley and towns to the south, Broome nightlife is thumping. The venue changes nightly, and each night there is a migration from the bars that close between midnight and 2am to clubs that close at 4am. All bars take major credit cards. The **Roebuck Bay Hotel,** or "Roey," on Carnarvon St., has a consistently up-beat scene with several bars: sing your favorite hits while locals dance and clap during karaoke on Monday nights at the sports bar, or kick back and watch a rugby game in the classier Pearlers Bar. (☎9192 1221. Sports and Pearlers bar open M-W 10am-midnight, Th-Sa 10am-1am.) Tuesdays and Fridays bring live music to **Murphy's,** an Irish Bar in the Mercure Inn Hotel on Weld St. If you have ever dreamed of being a rock-star, you can sign up to play a hit for the packed crowd on one of the band member's guitars. Get there early to grab a place in line. (☎9192 1002. Open noon-midnight.) On Thursdays, the crowd heads to **Divers Tavern** on Cable Beach Rd. for $8 beer jugs. (☎9193 6066. W jam night. Su live bands. Beers from $2.20. Open M-Sa 10am-midnight, Su 10am-10pm, later for sporting events.) For clubbing, your best option is the **Nippon Inn** on Dampier Terr. near Short St., which has a small dance floor and outdoor patio. (☎9192 1941. Cover $5 after midnight. Open 11pm-4am.)

CAPE LEVEQUE

Secluded, pristine beaches lie a few hundred kilometers north of Broome, accessible by private 4WD or day tours. The red cliffs and spectacular beach at **Cape Leveque (Kooljaman) ❷,** 180km north (3hr. on a 4WD-only track) are magical, but if you plan to spend the night, booking is required. Note that a day pass (often included in the camp site payment) is required and no petrol is sold in Cape Leveque. (☎9192 4970; www.kooljaman.com.au. Sites $30 per person; cabins $60-105 per person, min. 2-night stay.) En route to the Cape is unspoiled **Middle Lagoon ❶,** 33km off the main road. The circular lagoon has clear, gentle waters and a white, sandy beach. Camping here is a good option if Cape Leveque is booked. (☎9192 4002; www.users.bigpond.com/pindan. Sites $13 per person, powered $16 per person; 4-person cabins $125. MC/V.) Petrol and other supplies are available at **Beagle Bay,** 117km from Broome. **Tours** to Cape Leveque run approximately $220 for a 1-day tour.

GREAT NORTHERN HIGHWAY

There's no use pretending: this road is flat, repetitive, and long, and connects Perth to the eastern end of The Kimberley. Two of the towns along the way in this region, Fitzroy Crossing and Halls Creek, are little more than pit stops. The closest sight to Fitzroy Crossing is **Geikie Gorge,** 18km north (park open 6:30am-6:30pm). In town, there is a **supermarket** on Forrest Rd. (☎9191 5004. Open M-F 8:30am-5:30pm, Sa-Su 8am-1pm.) Another 287km down the highway is **Halls Creek.** The remains of **Old Halls Creek,** 16km down the unsealed Duncan Hwy., mark the site of the original gold rush in Western Australia. The **Eziway** grocery store (☎9168 6186; open M-W and F-Su 8am-6pm, Th 8am-8pm) and the **Shell Station** (☎9168 6060; open daily 6am-9pm) are the only other diversions. From Halls Creek it's 107km to the Purnululu turn-off and another 235km to Kununurra.

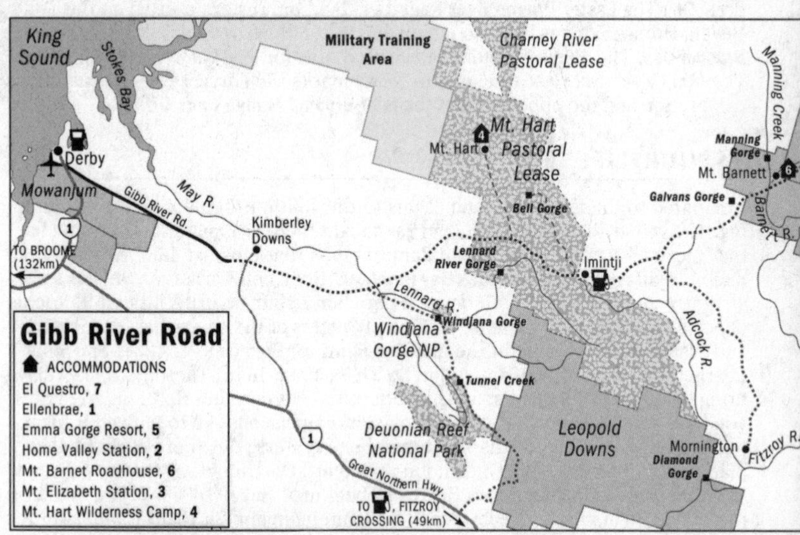

DERBY

☎08

A west-to-east voyage along the Gibb River Rd. starts at tiny Derby (pop. 4000). Stop by the **Prison Boab Tree** (7km outside of town) on your way in and then check in at the **visitors center** at the end of Clarendon St. for information on the latest road conditions. (☎9191 1426 or 1800 621 426; www.derbytourism.com.au. Open Oct.-Mar. M-F 8:30am-4:30pm, Sa-Su 9am-4pm; Apr.-Sept. M-F 8:30am-4:30pm, Sa-Su 9am-1pm.) The **West Kimberley Lodge ❺**, at the corner of Sutherland and Stanwell St., has quiet rooms with A/C and fridge. (☎9191 1031. Twins $65; doubles $78; 3- to 4-person rooms $130.) The **Kimberley Entrance Caravan Park ❶**, on Rowan St., around the curve from the visitors center, overlooks mudflats. (☎9193 1055. Sites $9, powered $24.) Get petrol at the **BP station** on Loch St. (☎9191 1256. Open M-Sa 5:30am-7pm, Su 6am-6pm.) Across the road is a **Woolworths**. (Open M-W and F 8am-6pm, Th 8am-8pm, Sa 8am-5pm, Su 9am-5pm.)

GIBB RIVER ROAD

The Gibb River Road is one of Australia's last frontiers. Created over a century ago for transport between the cattle stations of Wyndham and Broome, the road can be challenging and corrugated, with multiple stream crossings. It offers unparalleled access to the famed beauty of the region's towering rock faces and waterfall-carved pools. From popular sign-posted tracks to chasms and gorges, the twists and turns of the Kimberley landscape afford endless opportunities for exploration.

GIBB RIVER ROAD AT A GLANCE	
LENGTH: 647km. **FEATURES:** Windjana Gorge, Tunnel Creek NP, King Leopold Range. **HIGHLIGHTS:** Dips into pristine, massive gorges, unpopulated walks, and wicked cliff-jumping for the foolhardy.	**GATEWAYS:** Derby (p. 753) and Kununurra (p. 757). **DURATION:** In good conditions the road can take as few as 2 days, but it takes 4-5 days to enjoy the primary gorges and the more remote turn-offs.

WESTERN AUSTRALIA

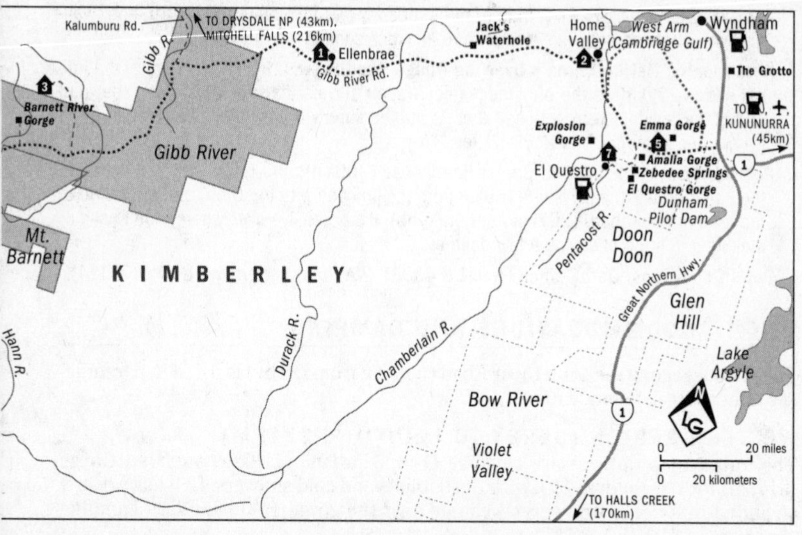

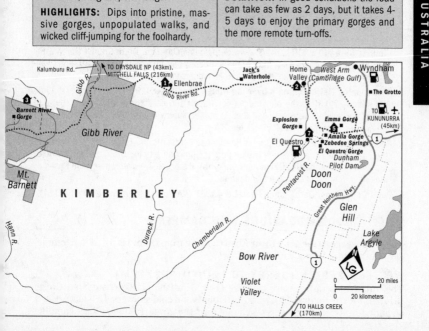

ORIENTATION AND PRACTICAL INFORMATION

The Gibb River Road begins 6km south of **Derby** off the **Derby Highway** and ends at the **Great Northern Highway,** halfway between **Wyndham** (48km from end) and **Kununurra** (45km from end). The most commonly visited gorges are concentrated anywhere from 120 to 220km east of Derby, as well as in the privately-run **El Questro,** 35-45km from the road's eastern end. Gorges along the 400km between the two regions are harder to get to; if you have limited time, you may want to drive straight through. Those with extra time might consider a detour on the **Kalumburu Road,** which intersects the Gibb 406km east of Derby and continues northward to **Drysdale National Park** and **Mitchell Falls.**

Services along the way are limited. Roadhouses and stations with accommodations may have some groceries and camping supplies, but you should pack everything you'll need, including cash. The Broome, Derby, and Kununurra **visitors centers** are good places to pick up advice before heading out. Camping supplies are available in Kununurra and Broome.

REGISTER YOUR TRIP. The Gibb is a long, tough road, and cell phones don't work in the Kimberley; be sure to register with the Derby police (☎9191 1444), on Loch St. near the Old Derby Gaol, before starting on the road.

Tours: Many people do the Gibb River Rd. via small private group tours, which can be cheaper than renting a 4WD and going it alone. **Kimberley Adventure Tours** (☎1800 805 101; www.kimberleyadventure.com) offers a 6-day Gibb trek ($3295) and a 13-day tour that runs round-trip from Broome ($4895). **Wilderness 4WD Adventures** (☎1300 666 100; www.wildernessadventures.com.au) offers a good 9-day, personalized tour called the Kimberley Challenge ($1410).

Guides: Visitors centers in Kununurra, Derby, and Fitzroy Crossing sell the *Traveller's Guide to the Gibb River and Kalumburu Roads,* with limited information on distances and services along the roads. The *Guide* ($4) can also be purchased from the **Derby Tourist Bureau** (☎9191 1426; www.derbytourism.com.au. Derby Tourist Bureau, PO Box 48, Derby WA 6728). A map of the Kimberley ($8.50), put out by HEMA and available at visitors centers, is essential and includes summaries of all major sites.

Auto repairs: Neville Heron's Over the Range Repairs (☎9191 7887), next to the Imintji store (222km) is the only mechanical repair service that operates along the road and is the only place to get used tires. A limited supply of new tires is available in Mt. Barnet and sometimes in Home Valley.

Petrol: Diesel at Iminitji, Mt. Barnet Roadhouse (306km), and El Questro (614km). On the Kalumburu Rd. at Drysdale (59km from the junction with the Gibb) and at the top of the road at Kalumburu (267km from the Gibb). It's expensive everywhere; don't risk not making it in hope of saving a few dollars.

Road Conditions: Derby office (☎9158 4333). WA Road Report (☎1800 013 314).

ACCOMMODATIONS AND CAMPING

The distance along the Gibb River Road (coming from Derby) is listed in parentheses after each accommodation.

WESTERN REGION (DERBY TO IMINTJI: 0-221KM)

The only cheap options are **camping** ❶ at Windjana (119km) and Bell Gorge (214km) for $9 (children $2), with flush toilets and cold showers. Bell has private, secluded first-come first-served camps near the gorge, with standard camping available when these are full. The **Mount Hart Wilderness Lodge** ❺ (184km, down a 50km access road) is an upscale lodge with gardens and a pool. (☎9191 4645; www.mthart.com.au. $150, children $75. Book ahead.)

CENTRAL REGION (IMINTJI TO HOME VALLEY: 221-581KM)

Camping ❶ is available at a few free no-frills sites along the way. An especially nice one is on the **Barnet River** (329km). Camping with facilities is available at Manning Gorge, behind the **Mount Barnet Roadhouse** ❶ (306km). The area right next to the river can be crowded; more tranquility can often be found down the road to the right. Warm showers and flush toilets are available from 5:30am-5:30pm. (☎9191 7007. Showers for non-guests $2.20. Sites included with park entrance fee.) Quite possibly the best place to stay on the Gibb, **Ellenbrae** ❷ (476km) is composed of canvas- and rammed-earth cabins clustered around an open-air homestead—this is as close to sleeping outdoors as you can get without the accompanying inconveniences. (☎9691 4325. Sites for 2 $10; doubles $80.) The **Mount Elizabeth Station** ❺ (338km, down a 30km access road) has sites and rooms. (☎9191 4644. Powered sites $12 adult, $2 child; tent-style rooms $160, children $88. Booking required.)

EASTERN REGION (HOME VALLEY TO GREAT NORTHERN HIGHWAY: 581-647KM)

The **Home Valley Station** ❸ (581km) is a friendly place to stay; it has very basic hut-style rooms. (☎9161 4322. Sites $10, children $5; bed and breakfast homestead room $80, children $60.) Lodge accommodations and **private campsites** overlooking the river are available at **El Questro** ❺ (614km, down a 16km access road that passes Zebedee Springs and El Questro Gorge) in El Questro Wilderness Park. (☎9169 1777; www.voyages.com.au. Sites $15 per person, children free; bungalows with A/C for 1-4 people $240.)

SIGHTS AND GORGES

The distance along the Gibb River Road (coming from Derby) is listed in parentheses after the description of each sight below.

> **TIP** **ON THE WATER.** Drive through creek crossings in first or second gear to give yourself more control, and never stop in the middle of the crossing.

WESTERN REGION (DERBY TO IMINTJI: 0-221KM)

WINDJANA GORGE. Some 360 million years ago, when the area to the northwest was underwater, Windjana was the coast; a huge coral reef thrived here. Erosion of surrounding areas has unearthed the hard coral skeletons. Purple and tan, they now loom hundreds of meters above the Lennard River and its sandy banks. Hundreds of resident white cockatoos only add to the magical aura. A 7km round-trip hike through the gorge offers the best readily accessible opportunities to observe freshwater crocodiles in the Kimberley. *(119km. Off a 21km access road.)*

TUNNEL CREEK. Tunnel Creek is exhilarating and beautiful, though somewhat over-touristed. The walk through this 850m cave is in total darkness, with carnivorous ghost bats flapping overhead as you wade through knee-deep water inhabited by freshwater crocodiles, no less. A good flashlight and closed-toe shoes are essential for navigating the rocky floor. *(119km. Drive 55km down the Windjana Gorge access road. Toilets are available at the carpark.)*

BELL GORGE. Down a flat 1km walking path, Bell Gorge condenses into one spot much of what the Gibb gorges offer in total: beautiful waterfalls, cliff-jumping into

WESTERN AUSTRALIA

swimming holes, endless exploration of the river above the falls, and scrambles over rocky outcroppings. Go early to avoid the mobs of tourists. *(213km.)*

CENTRAL REGION (IMINTJI TO HOME VALLEY: 221-581KM)

GALVANS GORGE. A wonderful, hidden refuge just beyond a desolate stretch of road, the gorge is worth the detour. An 800m walk passes lily-ponds to a beautiful waterfall plunging into a blue lagoon. Daredevils undertake the "widowmaker" jump, a 10m plunge from the cliffside through two large tree branches and into the pool below, while the more sane adventurers stick to swinging in on the vine. *(286km. The entrance is in an unmarked carpark. From the east, it's on the right across from a scenic photo-op sign. From the west, it's at the foot of a steep decline following a scenic lookout.)*

MANNING GORGE. The best sights at Manning Gorge are located down a trail from the campsite that leads to the first waterfall. The large plunge pool allows you to swim behind the falls and climb to various levels of the falls to jump back in. You can place your belongings in one of the white esquis and swim across the water to the trail head (cuts off 20min.) or take the longer walk, wading back and forth through the knee-deep creek waters. *(306km. The road to the falls begins from behind the Mt. Barnet Roadhouse.)*

EASTERN REGION (HOME VALLEY TO GREAT NORTHERN HIGHWAY: 581-647KM)

All listings are part of the million-acre **El Questro Wilderness Park** (☎9169 1777, www.voyages.com.au), down a side road 33km from the east end of the Gibb River Rd. (614km from Derby). Admission costs $15 per person for a week at the park or $7.50 per person for a day at Emma Gorge only, accessed by a separate entrance 10km east of the main entrance. Detailed maps are available at the Emma Gorge Resort and at the Station Township. Organized tours are available, but a tremendous amount of El Questro is accessible with your own 4WD.

WESTERN AUSTRALIA

AMALIA GORGE. This rewarding walk requires careful foot placement to negotiate the boulders and rock slabs along the way. The waterfall-fed pool at the end is a relaxing finish to the trek. Amalia gets more sunlight and is hotter than most gorges, so early mornings and late afternoons are the best times to hike it. *(7km along the main El Questro road.)*

EL QUESTRO GORGE. A 3.6km round-trip path leads over fairly easy terrain to to Middle Pool, a pleasant swimming spot. Beyond this, the trail rapidly gets more challenging. After wading through water that rises as high as your neck, a climb over a field of large boulders leads to a narrow gorge with a small but pristine waterfall. The full walk is 7.4km, 3-5hr. round-trip. *(11km along the main El Questro road then down a 1km side road.)*

EXPLOSION GORGE. 4WD fanatics will enjoy this rough track which runs to three overlook points on the rim of Explosion Gorge. It bumps along for 10km beside the attractive Elgee Cliffs, passing a turn-off for Branco's Lookout, which offers a view of the area. *(Past El Questro Station Township. Follow the signs.)*

EMMA GORGE. Winding through the gorge amid lush greenery, the shady track leads to a chilly swimming hole and then along a short path modestly labeled "Waterfall" to the real highlight. Overhanging cliffs carpeted with ferns surround a round pool fed at several points along its circumference by trickling waterfalls. *(A 1.6km trail leaves from the Emma Gorge Resort carpark.)*

WYNDHAM ☎08

A 20m crocodile statue welcomes you to Wyndham (pop. 900), the northernmost point on the Great Northern Hwy. and gateway to the Bungle Bungle and Cockburn Ranges. Wyndham is neatly divided into two clusters: the northern one is residential, while most shops and services (and the big crocs) are found in the southern section (vaguely referred to as "town"). This includes the **visitors center** in the Mobil station (☎9161 1281; open daily 6am-6pm) and **Internet** access at **Telecentre** on Koojarra St. (Open M-F 8am-4pm). The staff at the **Wyndham Caravan Park ❶**, near the Mobil station, will show you the town's most impressive sight, the 2000-year-old boab tree at the back of the park. (☎9161 1064. Sites $10 per person, powered $13; budget doubles $45.) **Gulf Breeze Guest House ❸** is cozy and relaxed. Book rooms at the Caravan Park. (☎9161 1401. Singles $35; twins $45; doubles $55; family rooms $65.)

Follow the signs east from the highway for the **Five River Lookout,** which is a popular lunch spot 7km up a steep road with beautiful sunset views of mudflats and the Ord, Forrest, King, Durack, and Pentecost Rivers emptying into the gulf. At **Wyndham Zoological Gardens and Crocodile Park,** just north of the wharf, a series of enthusiastic placards applaud the mating successes of males in the captive breeding program. (☎9161 1124. Open in the Dry daily 8:30am-4pm; feedings at 11am. Call ahead in the Wet. $15.) Thirty kilometers along the road to Kununurra, a 1km gravel road leads to **The Grotto,** where nearly 200 stone steps descend to a pool and waterfall. Tarzan impersonators often swing into the pool from a rope hanging high overhead. The scene is more impressive and less crowded in the Wet.

KUNUNURRA ☎08

Five hundred kilometers west of Katherine, a small pocket of civilization known as Kununurra (kuh-nah-NUR-ah; pop. 6000) sleeps beneath the sandstone formations of the eastern Kimberley. Travelers use it as a base from which to explore the dramatic natural attractions of the Kimberley region, including Purnululu (Bungle Bungle) National Park, Lake Argyle, and the Gibb River Rd.

TRANSPORTATION. The **airport** is 5km down the Victoria Hwy. toward Wyndham. **Air North** (☎1800 627 474) flies daily to Broome (from $180) and Darwin (from $170). **Buses** arrive at the tourist bureau at the corner of Coolibah Dr. and White Gum St. **Greyhound Australia** (☎13 20 30) departs for Broome (13½hr., daily 5:50pm, $202); Katherine (5½hr., daily 9:45am, $110); and Darwin (13hr., daily 9:45am, $178). There are several car rental companies in town: **Budget,** 9 Poincettia Way (☎9168 2033), and at the airport; **Avis** (☎9169 1258), on Bandicoot Dr., at the airport; **Thrifty Territory Rent-a-Car,** 596 Bandicoot Dr. (☎9169 1911), and at the BP service station; and **Hertz** (☎9169 1424), on Coolibah Dr. **Gibb River Camping Hire** (☎9169 1616) rents 4WDs, trailers, and camping equipment. Two **taxi** companies operate in town: **Spuds Taxis** (☎9168 2553 or 04 0893 8888) and **Alex Taxi** (☎13 10 08).

ORIENTATION AND PRACTICAL INFORMATION. Messmate Way turns off the Victoria Hwy. at a petrol station and heads into town, where it crosses **Konkerberry Drive** and ends at **Coolibah Drive.** The **Kununurra Visitor Center** is on Coolibah Dr. near the windmill. (☎9168 1177. Open in the Dry M-F 8am-5pm, Sa-Su 9am-4pm; call for times in the Wet.) The **Commonwealth Bank,** on the corner of Coolibah Dr. and Cotton Tree Ave. near the tourism office, has a 24hr. **ATM** (☎13 22 21; open M-Th 9:30am-4pm, F 9:30am-5pm), as does **National Bank** on Ebony St. (☎9169 1622. Open M-Th 9:30am-4pm, F 9:30am-5pm.) **Police** are located at the corner of Coolibah

Dr. and Banksia St. (24hr. ☎9166 4530.) **Internet** access is available at Kimberly Croc Backpackers (see below) for $6 per hr. **Telecentre,** in the same building as the visitors center, has Internet access for $1.15 per 10min. (☎9169 1868. Open M-F 9:30am-5pm, Sa 1:30-4pm.) The **post office** is across from the police station. (☎9168 1072. Open M-F 9am-5pm.) **Postal Code:** 6743.

ACCOMMODATIONS AND FOOD. All accommodations in town fill up quickly during the Dry; book ahead. **Kununurra Backpackers Adventure Centre ❷,** 24 Nutwood Cres., is a 10min. walk from the visitors center; follow Konkerberry Dr. away from the highway, then turn right on Nutwood. With new stoves, a bubbling fountain, pool, and small VCR-equipped theater, the Adventure Centre has great facilities. They also provide free pickup and drop-off. (☎9169 1998. Key deposit $10. Dorms $21; twins and doubles $54. VIP $2 discount.) **Desert Inn Kimberley Croc Backpackers ❷,** two blocks from the shopping center on Tristania St. near Konkerberry St., has a pool, patio, lounge areas, spacious kitchen, laundry, and offers free pickup and drop-off. (☎9168 2702. Internet access $6 per hr. Key deposit $10. 8-bed dorms $22, 6-bed $23, 4-bed $25; twins and doubles $60. $2 YHA discount.) **Ivanhoe Village Caravan Resort ❷,** on Coolibah Dr., has laundry, pool, spa, and kitchen. (☎9168 1995. Sites for 2 $24.) Food options in Kununurra are limited. The main pub in town is **Gulliver's Tavern ❷,** on Konkerberry Dr. at Cotton Tree Ave., with great fish 'n' chips ($15.50). (☎9168 1666. Open daily noon-10pm. MC/V.) **Coles** in the shopping center has groceries. (☎9168 2711. Open daily 5am-midnight.)

SIGHTS. Kelly's Knob overlooks the stunning terrain of Kununurra. Take Konkerberry Dr. to its end; turn left on Ironwood, right on Speargrass, and right again at the large stone tablet. **Mirima (Hidden Valley) National Park,** 2km east of town, looks like a miniature Purnululu range, without the 6hr. drive. Three paths wind past the 350-million-year-old formations. The **Derdebe-Gerring Banan Lookout Trail** (400m) ascends a steep hill for a view of the Ord Valley and nearby sandstone ranges. The **Demboong Banan Gap Trail** (250m) heads through a gap in the range, then through a small valley, to a lookout over Kununurra. Ranger-led walks meet at the carpark at the end of Hidden Valley Rd. and at the secluded retreat of Lily Pool in Hidden Valley. Female travelers should avoid Lily Pool, along with the area that extends away from it down Lily Creek; they are sacred men's places for the Miriwoong people. **Wild Adventure Tours** (☎0945 6643; www.gowild.com.au) offers travelers a more interactive and ecologically friendly take on the Kununurra area, with abseiling tours and lessons at local sites, including **Kelly's Knob** ($60) and the **Grotto** ($110).

LAKE ARGYLE

Nestled between ancient orange sandstone hills and dotted with 90 islands, Lake Argyle is the largest freshwater lake in the Southern Hemisphere during the the Wet. The lake was created in 1971 as part of the ambitious Ord River Irrigation Project, which flooded the Miriwoong people's land and submerged their sacred sights. To reach Lake Argyle, drive 35km south of Kununurra on the Victoria Hwy. and turn onto the access road. Another 35km on the open road leads to the **Lake Argyle Tourist Village.**

Cruises are a popular way to see a small fraction of the lake. **Lake Argyle Cruises** has a booking office at the Lake Argyle Tourist Village. (☎9168 7687; www.lakeargylecruises.com. Tours May-Sept. daily, Oct.-Apr. by demand. 2hr. morning wildlife cruise $50; 2½hr. sunset cruise $85; 6hr. best of Lake Argyle cruise $130. Children 40-50% off. Pickup in Kununurra $15.) **Kimberley Eco-noeing** offers a 3-day self-guided tour. (☎1300 663 369. $145, includes pickup, drop-off, canoe and camping gear; min. 2 people.) The **Lake Argyle Tourist Village** has accommodations, including a **caravan park** ❶ with showers and laundry. (☎9167 1050. Sites $9 per person, powered $13.)

PURNULULU (BUNGLE BUNGLE) NATIONAL PARK

Purnululu, a national park since 1986 and a region unknown to the outside world before 1983, is famous for its towering orange-and-black eroded dome structures of layered rock, which is often compared to beehives. While an oft-repeated sentiment holds that the domes' grandeur can only be appreciated from the air, the views from the bottom are equally impressive. The awkward name "Bungle Bungle" is thought to be either a corruption of the Kija word *purnululu*, meaning "sandstone," or a misspelling of a common grass in the area, Bundle Bundle.

PURNULULU AT A GLANCE

AREA: 209,000 hectares.

FEATURES: Bungle Bungle Range, Ord River, the Western Hikes.

HIGHLIGHTS: Scenic helicopter flights, walks through gorges, and the unique sandstone domes.

GATEWAYS: Kununurra (p. 757), Halls Creek, Warmun (p. 752).

CAMPING: At Walardi and Kurrajong campsites, or registered overnight bush camping ($10 per person).

FEES: Entry $10 per vehicle.

TRANSPORTATION AND PRACTICAL INFORMATION

There are two ways into Purnululu: by road or by air. The grueling drive into the park offers wonderful scenery and the independence of having a car while traveling. Alternatively, a scenic flight offers spectacular aerial views, but it doesn't come cheap. Book with **Alligator Airways** at the Kununurra Airport. (☎1800 632 533 or 9168 1333; www.alligatorairways.com.au. 2½hr. scenic flight $245. Departs daily. Book in advance.) To drive to Purnululu, you need a high-clearance 4WD. The **Spring Creek Track** leaves the Great Northern Hwy. 250km south of Kununurra and 109km north of Halls Creek. For 53km, the track rumbles and grinds its way to the visitors center. Allow 5hr. driving time from Kununurra (or 4hr. from Halls Creek) to reach the park; the Spring Creek Track alone takes 1½-3hr. depending on conditions and traffic. The vehicle **entry fee** is $10; fees are payable 24hr. at the **visitors center** (open daily 9am-noon and 1-4pm) near the entrance to the park.

CAMPING

The only two legal campsites available within the park have untreated water, toilets, and firewood. A left at the T-intersection after the visitors center leads 7km to **Kurrajong campsite** ❶, in the region of the park near Echidna Chasm and Froghole Gorge. After a right at the T, it's 13km to the quieter **Walardi campsite** ❶, closer to the domes. (Sites $10 per person.)

HIKING

BUNGLE BUNGLE RANGE

This range is composed of fragile sandstone. In order to protect this natural wonder, people are not allowed to climb to the top, although fantastic walking trails wind around and through the formations. They can occasionally be difficult to find, but nearly all follow dry stream beds—when wandering away from the stream bed, stay on marked and well worn trails, as moving off the trail can damage plant life. Bring plenty of water. Three walks depart from Piccanninny Gorge carpark, 25km south of the visitors center.

Piccanninny Creek and Gorge Trail (30km round-trip). The longest walk; hiking the entire length requires overnight camping (register with the ranger station or the visitor center) at the park entrance before departing). The first 7km is a smooth trail over bedrock and makes a nice day hike. From there, the trail turns into a rocky, much more difficult track. A **lookout point** that provides a great view of the domes is located at the end of a 600m walk from the start of the trail (branches off the main trail to the right).

Domes Walk (1km). The only trail to actually feature the famous domes, the relaxed circuit links up with the Cathedral Gorge Walk.

Cathedral Gorge Walk (3km; 1½hr. round-trip). This easy trail follows a river bed up the gorge to the immense waterfall at the end. The hollowed-out pool and surrounding amphitheater are of a humbling scale and beauty. The Domes Walk loops into the Cathedral Gorge Walk; both hikes are best done together.

WESTERN HIKES

The western section of the park features an imposing escarpment. Though none of the famous domes are to be found here, the walks through the gorges are just as awe-inspiring as their eastern counterparts.

Echidna Chasm (2km round-trip). A flat gravel path threads the improbably narrow crevasse cut in the towering red rock by millions of Wet-season downpours. The passage squeezes past a pair of boulders fallen from the rock walls and leads up a short steel ladder to a modest chamber at the end of the crack. At mid-day, the spectacle is heightened by the sun's rays probing the tops of the walls along the path.

Mini Palms Gorge (5km round-trip). A difficult day trail follows rocky river beds to a steep and boulder-strewn final ascent up to an observation platform. The view from atop is less captivating, looking as much back over the trail as forward into an area of palms.

APPENDIX

AUSSIE BEVERAGE GUIDE

TERMS OF ENBEERMENT

Nothing's more Australian than **beer,** and accordingly, the language used for it has an Aussie twist too. Because of the hot climate, Australian pubs generally eschew the British pint in favor of smaller portions, which stay cold until you're done. Thus, size is a major variable in the argot of ale. If you're too drunk to think of the proper terms, ordering by size, in ounces, usually works. On the mainland, try a "5," "7," "10," or "15." In Tasmania, order a "6," "8," "10," or "20." Don't forget to **shout** your mates a round—that is, buy them all a drink.

REGION	BRING ME A...	STATE BEER
New South Wales	**Pony** 140mL (5 oz.), **Beer/Glass** 200mL (7 oz.), **Middy** 285mL (10 oz.), **Schooner** 425mL (15 oz.)	Tooheys, Victoria Bitter
Northern Territory	**Handle** 285mL (10 oz.), **Darwin Stubbie** 1.25L (40 oz.) bottle	(None)
Queensland	**Beer/Glass** 200mL (7 oz.), **Pot** 285mL (10 oz.), **Schooner** 425mL (15 oz.), **Jug** 1125mL (40 oz.),	XXXX
South Australia	**Butcher** 200mL (7 oz.), **Middy/Schooner** 285mL (10 oz.), **Pint** 425mL (15 oz., smaller than the British or American pint), **Real Pint** 560mL (20 oz.)	Coopers, Lion Nathan's West End Brand
Tasmania	**Small Beer** 115mL (5 oz.), **Real Pint** 560mL (20 oz.)	Boag's, Cascade
Victoria	**Small Glass** 170mL (6 oz.), **Beer/Glass** 200mL (7 oz.), **Pot** 285mL (10 oz.), **Pint** 568mL (20 oz.)	Victoria Bitter, Canton Draught
Western Australia	**Shetland** 115 mL (4 oz.), **Bobbie/Beer** 200mL (7 oz.), **Middy** 285mL (10 oz.), **Pot** 425mL (15 oz.)	Emu Bitter, Swan
Australia	**Handle** 285mL (10 oz.) glass with handle, **Stubbie** 375mL (12 oz.) bottle, **Tinny** 375mL (12 oz.) can, **Long Neck** 750mL (25 oz.) bottle, **Slab** case of 24 beers	

COOL BEANS

Australians love **coffee** (so much that Melbourne boasts the Coffee Academy at the William Angliss Institute of Technical and Further Education) and have plenty of ways to prepare it. Drinks can be made weak, medium, or strong. Coffee drinks are all made with espresso, as opposed to automatic-drip machines, so black coffee is generally a bit stronger in Australia. Whole milk is always used unless you specify low-fat ("skim"). The American milk variety of "cream" is not used.

WHAT TO ORDER...	...AND WHAT YOU'LL GET
short black	60mL of espresso
long black	120-200mL of espresso
flat white	espresso with cold milk
cafe latte	espresso, hot milk, and froth
cappuccino	espresso, hot milk, and heaps of froth
macchiato	espresso with a bit of froth
vienna coffee	espresso, whipped cream, and powdered chocolate

GLOSSARY OF 'STRINE

'Strine is 'stralian for "Australian." The main thing to remember when speaking Australian slang is to abbreviate everything: **Oz** for Australia, **brekkie** for breakfast, **cuppa** for cup of tea, **uni** for university. Australian **pronunciation** is harder to learn than the lingo—with Aboriginal words especially, but even with English-derived proper nouns, it's difficult to pin down any definite "rules." One quirk to note: when Australians spell out a word or pronounce a number, they always use the expression "double," as in "double-seven" (77).

ablution block: shower/toilet block at a campground
abseil: rappel
ace: awesome
aggro: aggravated
ANZAC biscuits: honey-oat cookies
arvo: afternoon
Aussie: Australian (pronounced "Ozzie"—thus, "Australia" is "Oz")
backpackers: hostel
bagged: criticized
barbie: barbecue (BBQ)
bathers: bathing suit, "cossie," "swimmers"
beaut: positive exclamation, as in "You beaut!"
beetroot: beet, a common hamburger filling
belt bag: known to Americans as a "fanny pack" (don't say "fanny" in Oz: it's a crude word for a female body part)
billabong: a water hole
biro: pen
biscuit: cookie
bitumen: a rough black asphalt used to pave roads
bloke: guy, man (familiar), "chap"
bludger: malingerer
bluey: someone with red hair (seriously)
bonnet: hood of a car
boofhead: fool
to book: to make reservations
boot: trunk of a car
bottle shop: liquor store
brekkie: breakfast
Brizzy: Brisbane, QLD
bugger: damn
Bundy: Bundaberg, QLD, as in the rum
bush: scrubby countryside
bush tucker: traditional Aboriginal wild foods
bushwalking: hiking
busk: to play music on the street for money
BYO: bring your own (booze)
campervan: mobile home, RV
capsicum: bell peppers
caravan: a trailer; term for any sort of cabless campervan
carpark: parking lot
Central Business District (CBD): a city's commercial center, "downtown" (US)
chap: guy, man, "bloke"
chemist: pharmacy
chips: thick french fries, often served with vinegar and salt
chock-a-block: crowded
chook: chicken
chunder: vomit
coldie: a cold beer
concession: discount; usually applies to students, seniors, or children, sometimes only to Australian students and pensioners
cordial: concentrated fruit juice
cossie: swimsuit, "bathers," "swimmers"
crook: sick
crow eater: South Australian (a tad disparaging)
D&M: deep and meaningful conversation
dag: often used in familial context as an affectionate version of "daggy" (see below)
daggy: unfashionable, goofy
damper: a term for traditionally unleavened bread
dear: expensive
dill: silly person (affectionate)
dobber: tattle-tale
dodgy: sketchy
doona, duvet: comforter, feather blanket
dramas: problems. "no dramas" means "no worries"
drink driving: driving under the influence of alcohol
drongo: idiot
dunny: toilet, often outdoors
ensuite: with bath
entree: appetizer ("main" is a main dish)
esky: cooler
excess: deductible (as in car insurance)
fair dinkum: genuine
fair go: equal opportunity
fairy floss: cotton candy
to fancy: to like; as in "would you fancy...?"
feral: wild, punky, grungy
flash: fancy, snazzy
free call: toll-free call
full on: intense
full stop: period (punctuation)

furphy: tall tale, exaggerated rumor (as in, "tell a furphy")
g'day: hello
to give it a go: to try
good onya: good for you
glasshouse: greenhouse
grommet: young surfer
ground floor: American first floor ("first floor" is second floor, etc.)
grog: booze
to hire: to rent
hitching: hitchhiking
hoon: loud-mouth, show-off
icy-pole: popsicle (any sweet frozen treat on a stick)
jackaroo: stationhand-in-training
jersey: sweater, sweatshirt
jillaroo: female jackaroo
journo: journalist
jumper: see "jersey"
keen: enthusiastic ("a keen surfer")
Kiwi: New Zealander
knackered: very tired
lad: guy, man, "chap"
licensed: serves alcohol
like hen's teeth: rare
lollies: candies
magic: really wonderful, special
mate: friend, buddy (used broadly)
milk bar: convenience store
Milo: chocolate product in bar and drink varieties
mobile: cell phone
moke: an open-air, golf cart-esque vehicle
mozzie: mosquito
nappy: diaper
narky: annoyed
newsagent: newsstand/convenience store
nibblies: snacks
no worries: sure, fine, or "you're welcome"
ocker: hick, *Crocodile Dundee*-type
ordinary: bad; an "ordinary" road is full of potholes.
Owyergoin'?: How are you?
Oz: Australia
pavlova: a creamy meringue dessert garnished with fruit
pensioner: senior citizen
perve: a pervert; also used as a verb, "to perve"
petrol: gasoline
piss: beer (usually)
pissed: drunk (usually)
pokies: gambling machines
polly: politician
Pohm: person from England
powerpoint: power outlet
prawn: jumbo shrimp
raging: partying
ratbag: corrupt, unethical person
rego: car registration papers
return: round-trip
'roo: as in kanga-
roobar: bumper protecting your car from 'roo damage
roundabout: traffic rotary
rubber: eraser
sauce: usually tomato sauce; closest equivalent to ketchup
serviette: napkin
sheila: (slang) woman
shout: buy a drink or round of drinks for others; also a noun, as in an evening's worth of everyone buying rounds for each other
side: team
singlet: tank top or undershirt
skivvie: turtleneck sweater
sook: crybaby
spider: ice cream float or nasty arachnid (use context clues here)
squiz: a look, as in, "to take a squiz at something"
sticky beak: nosy person
'strine: Aussie dialect (from Australian)
'straya: Australia
swimmers: swimsuit, "cossie," "bathers"
sunnies: sunglasses
to suss: figure out, sort out
ta: short for thank you—usually said softly
TAB: shop to place bets, sometimes in pubs
takeaway: food to go, takeout
Tassie: Tasmania (TAZ-zie)
tea: evening meal
thongs: flip-flops
throw a wobbly: get angry
Tim Tams: chocolate-covered cookie
torch: flashlight
touch wood: knock on wood
trackies: sweatpants
track suit: sweat suit, jogging suit
uni: university (YOU-nee)
unsealed: unpaved roads, usually gravel, sometimes dirt
ute (yute): utility vehicle, pickup truck
upmarket: upscale, expensive
Vegemite: yeast-extract spread for toast and sandwiches
veggo: vegetarian
wanker: jerk (rude term)
winge: to whine or complain
yakka: hard work
yobbo: slobby, unthinking person
zed: Z (American "zee")

TEMPERATURES

CELSIUS–FARENHEIT CONVERSION

To convert from °C to °F, multiply by 1.8 and add 32. For a rough approximation, double the Celsius and add 30. To convert from °F to °C, subtract 32 and multiply by 0.55. For a rough approximation, subtract 30 and divide by two.

°CELSIUS	-5	0	5	10	15	20	25	30	35	40
°FAHRENHEIT	23	32	41	50	59	68	77	86	95	104

AVERAGE TEMPERATURES

LO/HI *PRECIPITATION*	JANUARY			APRIL			JULY			OCTOBER		
	°C	°F	*mm*	°C	°F	*mm*	°C	°F	*mm*	°C	°F	*mm*
Adelaide, SA	16/28	61/82	*19*	12/22	54/72	*43*	7/15	45/59	*65*	10/21	50/70	*43*
Alice Springs, NT	21/36	70/97	*40*	13/28	55/82	*17*	4/19	39/66	*12*	15/31	59/88	*20*
Brisbane, QLD	21/29	70/84	*161*	17/26	63/79	*89*	10/20	50/68	*57*	16/26	61/79	*77*
Cairns, QLD	24/31	75/88	*407*	22/29	72/84	*200*	17/26	63/79	*27*	20/29	68/84	*38*
Canberra, ACT	13/28	55/82	58	7/20	45/68	53	0/11	32/52	*40*	6/19	43/66	67
Darwin, NT	25/32	77/90	*393*	24/33	75/91	*103*	20/31	68/88	*1*	25/34	77/93	52
Hobart, TAS	12/22	54/72	*48*	9/17	48/63	52	4/12	39/54	54	8/17	46/63	64
Melbourne, VIC	14/26	57/79	*48*	11/20	52/68	*58*	6/13	43/55	*49*	9/20	48/68	68
Perth, WA	18/30	64/86	9	14/25	57/77	*46*	9/18	48/64	*173*	12/22	54/72	*55*
Sydney, NSW	18/26	64/79	*98*	14/23	59/72	*129*	8/16	46/61	*100*	13/22	55/72	*79*

AUSTRALIAN GOVERNMENT

The Commonwealth of Australia is a Federation, a Constitutional Monarchy, and a Parliamentary Democracy. There are three branches of government: executive, legislative, and judicial. Although Australia has several political parties, the system is dominated by the Liberal Party (also known as The Coalition when joined with the Nationals and the Country Liberal Party) and the Australian Labor Party.

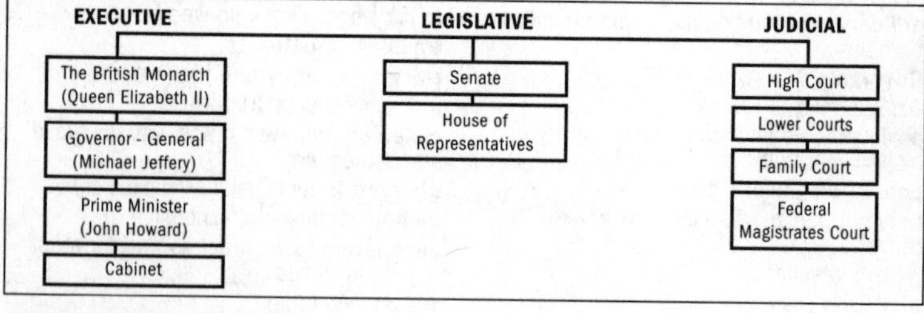

CURRENT OFFICIALS

Monarch: Queen Elizabeth II
Governor-General: Major-General Michael Jeffery
Prime Minister: John Howard (Liberal Party)
Deputy Prime Minister and Minister for Trade: Mark Vaile

HOLIDAYS AND FESTIVALS

Banks, museums, and other public buildings are often closed or operate with reduced hours during holidays and festivals. Tourism generally peaks during school holidays. Although dates differ between regions, **summer holidays** typically run from mid-December through January, and **winter holidays** run from late June through early July. Virtually every Australian town boasts a festival of some sort during the year; listed below are only a few of the major ones. More specific festival info can be found in the **Festivals** sections throughout this book.

2007 DATE	HOLIDAY	DESCRIPTION
Jan. 1	New Year's Day	National public holiday
Jan. 19-28	Telstra Country Music Festival (Tamworth, NSW)	Over 2500 performances and golden guitars galore in Australia's country music capital (www.tamworth.nsw.gov.au)
Jan. 26	Australia Day	National day to commemorate the arrival of the First Fleet in 1788, with festivities centered in Sydney (www.australiaday.com.au)
Feb. 10-Mar. 3	Sydney Gay and Lesbian Mardi Gras	Famous display of pride that culminates in a spectacular street parade (www.mardigras.org.au)
Late Feb. to early Mar.	Adelaide Fringe Festival	The largest independent alternative festival in Australia; held biannually (note: not in 2007) to showcase cutting edge artists (www.adelaidefringe.com.au)
Mar. 20-25	Australian Surf Life Saving Championships	Grueling ironman and ironwoman contests, as well as the world's biggest surf party (www.slsa.asn.au)
Apr. 6	Good Friday	National public holiday
Apr. 9	Easter Monday	National public holiday
Apr. 25	ANZAC Day	National commemoration that marks the anniversary of WWI ANZAC troops in Gallipoli (www.anzacday.org.au)
June 11	Queen's Birthday	National public holiday
Mid July to early Aug.	Melbourne International Film Festival	Once a year, buffs, stars, and critics flock to this exhibition of world film (www.melbournefilmfestival.com.au)
Nov. 6	Melbourne Cup	The horse race that entrances the nation (www.melbournecup.com)
Dec. 25-27	Christmas Day and Boxing Day	National public holiday

EXCHANGE RATES

AUSTRALIAN DOLLARS		
	US$1 = AUS$1.31	AUS$1= US$0.76
	CDN$1 = AUS$1.17	AUS$1= CDN$0.85
	UK£1 = AUS$2.48	AUS$1= UK£0.40
	NZ$1 = AUS$0.84	AUS$1= NZ$1.19
	EUR€ = AUS$1.69	AUS$1= EUR€0.59

The currency chart above is based on August 2006 exchange rates between local currency and Canadian dollars (CDN$), European Union euros (EUR€), New Zealand dollars (NZ$), British pounds (UK£), and US dollars (US$). Find current exchange rates in large daily newspapers, or on websites like www.xe.com or www.bloomberg.com.

INDEX

A

INDEX

H

I

J

K

L

N

O

P

Q

R

S

INDEX

T

INDEX

Y

Z

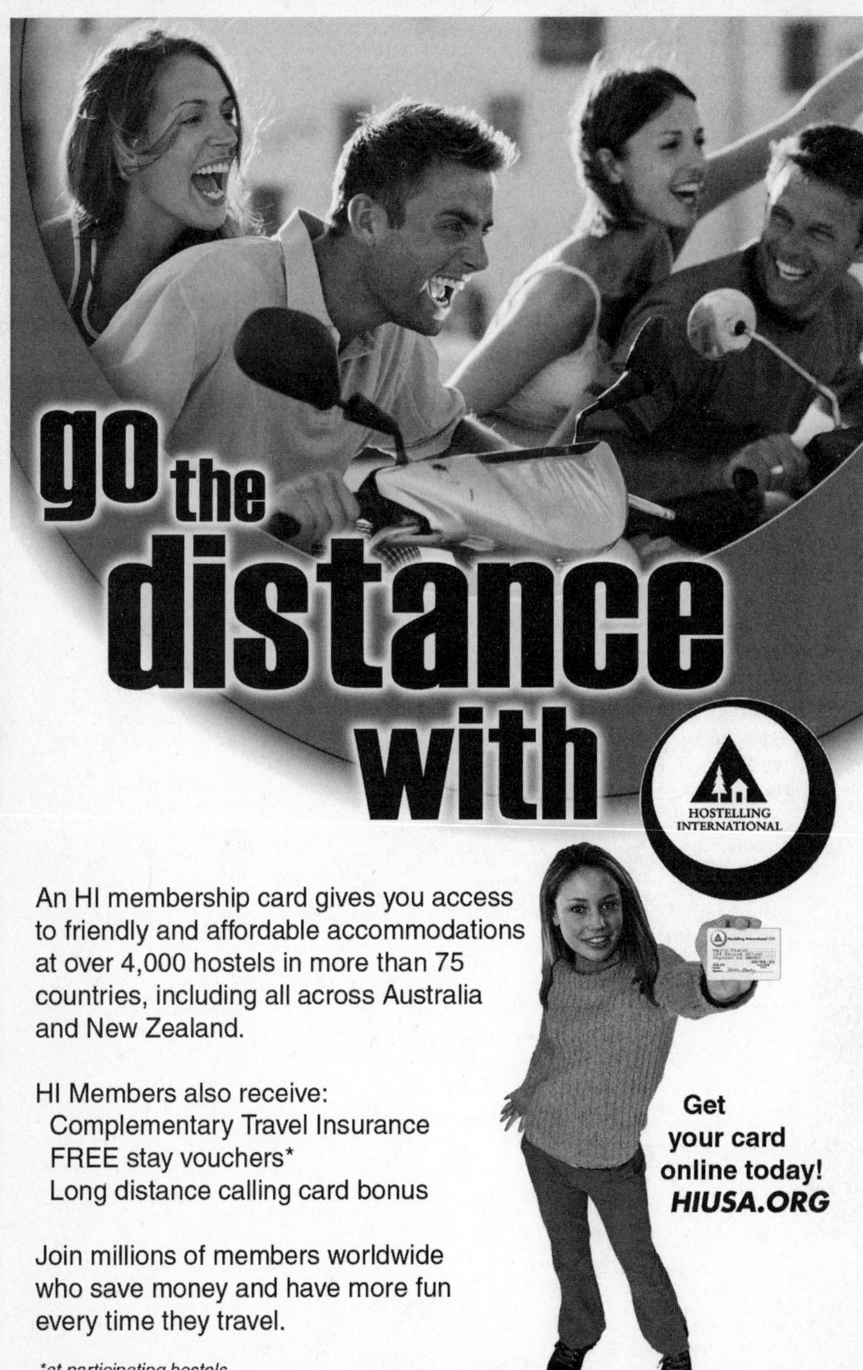

go the
distance
with
HOSTELLING
INTERNATIONAL

MAP INDEX

MAP LEGEND

Point of Interest	Church	Pharmacy	Beach
Accommodations	Consulate	Police	Park
Camping	Ferry Landing	Post Office	Building
Food	Garden	Ranger Station	Water
Nightlife	Golf Course	Restrooms	4WD Road
Shopping	Hospital	Shipwreck	Ferry Line
Winery	Internet Café	Synagogue	Pedestrian Zone
Airport	Library	Telephone Office	Railroad
Bank	Lighthouse	Theater	State Boundary
Beach	Mosque	Tourist Office	Unsealed Road
Bus Station	Mountain	Train Station	Walking Trail
Cave	Museum	Waterfall	

The Let's Go compass always points NORTH.